ELEMENTS OF COMMON LAW MURDER

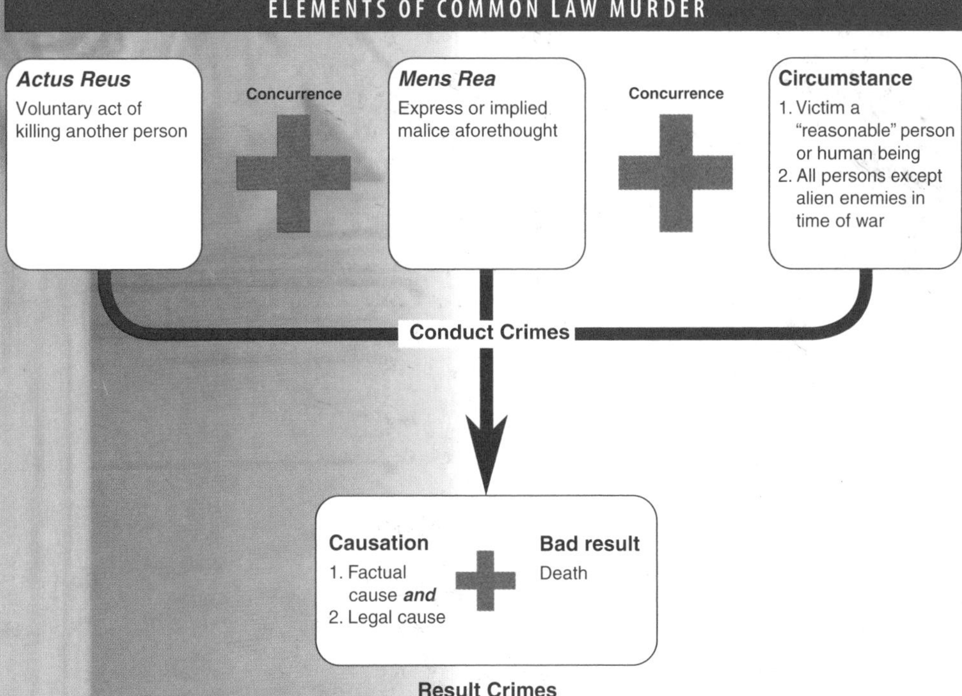

ELEMENTS OF MATERIAL SUPPORT TO TERRORIST ORGANIZATIONS

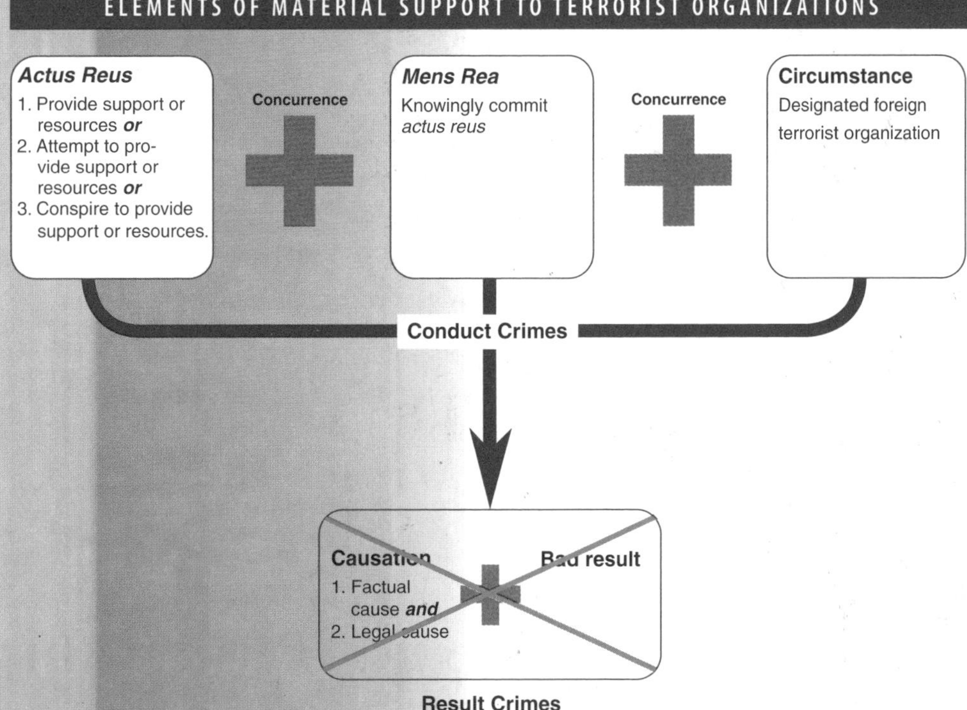

CRIMINAL LAW

11th EDITION

Joel Samaha

Horace T. Morse Distinguished Teaching Professor
University of Minnesota

Australia • Brazil • Japan • Korea • Mexico • Singapore • Spain • United Kingdom • United States

***Criminal Law*, Eleventh Edition**
Joel Samaha

Editor-in-Chief: Linda Ganster

Senior Acquisitions Editor: Carolyn Henderson Meier

Assistant Editor: Virginette Acacio

Editorial Assistant: Casey Lozier

Media Editor: Ting Jian Yap

Senior Marketing Manager: Michelle Williams

Senior Marketing Communications Manager: Heather Baxley

Senior Content Project Manager: Christy A. Frame and Rita Jaramillo

Senior Art Director: Maria Epes

Senior Manufacturing Planner: Judy Inouye

Rights Acquisitions Specialist: Roberta Broyer

Production Service: Ruth Cottrell

Photo Researcher: Sarah Evertson

Text Researcher: PMG

Copy Editor: Lura Harrison

Text Designer: Marsha Cohen

Cover Designer: Bartay Studio

Cover Image: Getty Images / Sylvester Adams

Compositor: Integra Software Services Pvt Ltd, Pondicherry

Library of Congress Control Number: 2012947172

ISBN-13: 978-1-285-06191-7

ISBN-10: 1-285-06191-8

Wadsworth
20 Davis Drive
Belmont, CA 94002-3098
USA

Cengage Learning is a leading provider of customized learning solutions with office locations around the globe, including Singapore, the United Kingdom, Australia, Mexico, Brazil, and Japan. Locate your local office at **www.cengage.com/global.**

Cengage Learning products are represented in Canada by Nelson Education, Ltd.

To learn more about Wadsworth, visit **www.cengage.com/wadsworth**

Purchase any of our products at your local college store or at our preferred online store **www.CengageBrain.com.**

Printed in the United States of America
1 2 3 4 5 6 7 16 15 14 13 12

For My Students

About the Author

Professor Joel Samaha teaches Criminal Law, Criminal Procedure, and Introduction to Criminal Justice at the University of Minnesota. He is both a lawyer and a historian whose primary interest is crime control in a constitutional democracy. He received his BA, JD, and PhD from Northwestern University. Professor Samaha also studied under the late Sir Geoffrey Elton at Cambridge University, England. He was named the College of Liberal Arts Distinguished Teacher in 1974. In 2007, he was awarded the title of University of Minnesota Distinguished Teaching Professor and inducted into the Academy of Distinguished Teachers.

Professor Samaha was admitted to the Illinois Bar in 1962, where he practiced law briefly in Chicago. He taught at UCLA before going to the University of Minnesota in 1971. He has taught both television and radio courses in criminal justice and co-taught a National Endowment for the Humanities seminar in legal and constitutional history. At the University of Minnesota, he served as chair of the Department of Criminal Justice Studies from 1974 to 1978.

In addition to *Law and Order in Historical Perspective* (1974), an analysis of law enforcement in pre-industrial English society, Professor Samaha has transcribed and written a scholarly introduction to a set of local criminal justice records from the reign of Elizabeth I. He has also written several articles on the history of criminal justice, published in the *Historical Journal, American Journal of Legal History, Minnesota Law Review, William Mitchell Law Review,* and *Journal of Social History*. In addition to *Criminal Law,* he has written two other textbooks, *Criminal Procedure*, now in its eighth edition, and *Criminal Justice,* now in its seventh edition. He continues to teach and write full time.

BRIEF CONTENTS

CONTENTS

PREFACE

Criminal Law was my favorite class as a first-year law student at Northwestern University Law School in 1958. I've loved it ever since, a love that has only grown from teaching it at least once a year at the University of Minnesota since 1971. I hope my love of the subject comes through in *Criminal Law*, which I've just finished for the eleventh time. It's a great source of satisfaction that my modest innovation to the study of criminal law—the text-casebook—has endured and flourished. *Criminal Law*, the text-casebook, brings together the description, analysis, and critique of general principles with excerpts of cases edited for nonlawyers.

Like its predecessors, *Criminal Law,* Eleventh Edition, stresses both the general principles that apply to all of criminal law and the specific elements of particular crimes that prosecutors have to prove beyond a reasonable doubt. Learning the principles of criminal law isn't just a good mental exercise, although it does stimulate students to use their minds. Understanding the general principles is an indispensable prerequisite for understanding the elements of specific crimes. The general principles have lasted for centuries. The definitions of the elements of specific crimes, on the other hand, differ from state to state and over time because they have to meet the varied and changing needs of new times and different places.

That the principles have stood the test of time testifies to their strength as a framework for explaining the elements of crimes defined in the fifty states and in the U.S. criminal code. But there's more to their importance than durability; it's also practical to know and understand them. The general principles are the bases both of the elements that prosecutors have to prove beyond a reasonable doubt to convict defendants and of the defenses that justify or excuse defendants' criminal conduct.

So *Criminal Law*, Eleventh Edition rests on a solid foundation. But it can't stand still, any more than the subject of criminal law can remain frozen in time. The more I teach and write about criminal law, the more I learn and rethink what I've already learned; the more "good" cases I find that I didn't know were there; and the more I'm able to include cases that weren't decided and reported when the previous edition went to press.

Of course, it's my obligation to incorporate into the eleventh edition these now-decided and reported cases, and this new learning, rethinking, and discovery. But obligation doesn't describe the pleasure that preparing now eleven editions of *Criminal Law* brings me. It's thrilling to find cases that illustrate a principle in terms students can understand and that stimulate them to think critically about subjects worth thinking about. It's that thrill that drives me to make each edition better than the last. I hope it will make my students—and you—more intelligent consumers of the law and social reality of criminal law in the U.S. constitutional democracy.

ORGANIZATION/APPROACH

The chapters in the text organize the criminal law into a traditional scheme that is widely accepted and can embrace, with minor adjustments, the criminal law of any state and/or the federal government. The logic of the arrangement is first to cover the general part of the criminal law—namely, principles and doctrines common to all or most crimes—and then the special part of criminal law—namely, the application of the general principles to the elements of specific crimes.

Chapters 1 through 8 cover the general part of criminal law: the sources and purposes of criminal law and criminal punishment; the constitutional limits on the criminal law; the general principles of criminal liability; the defenses of justification and excuse; parties to crime; and incomplete crimes.

Chapters 9 through 13 cover the special part of the criminal law: the major crimes against persons; crimes against homes and property; crimes against public order and morals; and crimes against the state.

Criminal Law has always followed the three-step analysis of criminal liability (criminal conduct, justification, and excuse). *Criminal Law* brings this analysis into sharp focus in two ways. First, the chapter sequence: Chapters 3 and 4 cover the general principles of criminal conduct (criminal act, criminal intent, concurrence, and causation). Chapter 5 covers the defenses of justification, the second step in the analysis of criminal liability. Chapter 6 covers the defenses of excuse, the third step. So the chapter sequence mirrors precisely the three-step analysis of criminal liability.

Criminal Law also sharpens the focus on the three-step analysis by means of the *Elements of Crime* art. The design of the boxes is consistent throughout the book. All three of the analytic steps are included in each Elements of Crime graphic, but elements that aren't required—like crimes that don't require a "bad" result—have a gray "X" through the elements. The figures go right to the core of the three-step analysis of criminal liability, making it easier for students to master the essence of criminal law: applying general principles to specific individual crimes.

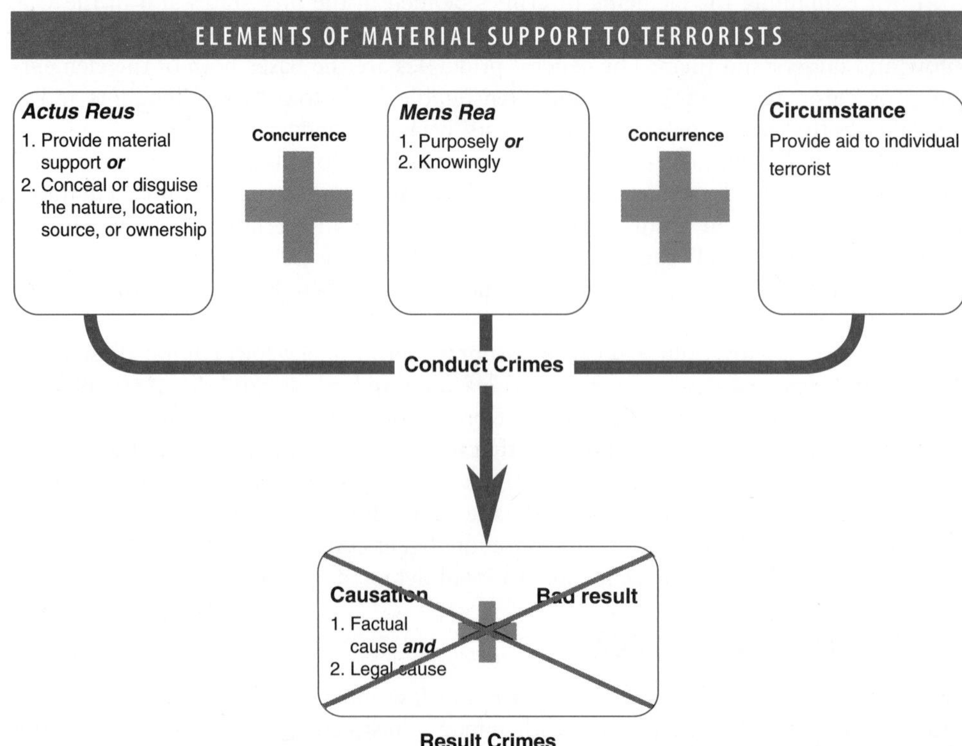

CHANGES TO THE ELEVENTH EDITION

Criminal Law, Eleventh Edition includes new case excerpts; an increased selection of relevant legal and social science research; a rich collection of examples to illustrate main points; all new chapter-opening vignettes to enhance student relevancy; and numerous new "Ethical Dilemmas" to give students an opportunity to prepare for on-the-job challenges.

For the first time, we have also included a running glossary to define terms as each chapter progresses—a tool we think students will find invaluable. Additionally, the Eleventh Edition includes entirely new sections, including some on such high-profile topics as the ban on carrying concealed guns in churches, mandatory life without parole for juveniles, the duty to intervene (as exemplified in the Penn State child sex assault case), physician-assisted suicide, "homegrown" (U.S. born and/or longtime resident non–U.S. born) terrorists, and more.

There are also new charts and tables, and all retained graphics are updated to reflect the most recent information available. Finally, I've included a few *sample documents* that criminal justice professionals encounter in their daily work—a police report (Chapter 1), a probation report (Chapter 2), a grand jury presentment (Chapter 3), and a forfeiture order (Chapter 11). Here are the highlights of the changes in each chapter.

Chapter 1, Criminal Law and Criminal Punishment: An Overview

NEW

- **Case Excerpt** *State v. Chaney* (1970) "Did the punishment devalue the victim?" Did the sentence of one year in prison with early parole send the message that the suffering he caused the woman he raped twice and then robbed was worthless?
- **Figure** "Elements of Criminal Liability"
- **Table** "Crimes and Torts: Similarities and Differences"
- **Ethical Dilemma** "Are the private paparazzi informants doing ethical work?"
- **Sample Document** Sample police report

REVISED Explanation of the distinction between *mala in se* and *mala prohibita* with examples

- **Figure** Updated "World Imprisonment Rates, 2009"
- **Table** Updated "Estimated Number of Arrests, 2010"

Chapter 2, Constitutional Limits on Criminal Law

NEW

- **Section** "Life without Parole for Juveniles"
- **Case Excerpts:**
  - *GeorgiaCarry.Org, Inc. v. Georgia* (2011) "Did he have a right to carry a gun in church?" Tests a "hot button" issue—the constitutionality of a Georgia ban on carrying guns in churches
  - *Lawrence v. Texas* (2003) "Do consenting adults have a right to privacy in their private sexual conduct?" Tests whether there's a constitutional right to privacy, involving adult consensual homosexual sex
  - *State v. Ninham* (2011) "Is it cruel and unusual punishment to sentence Omer Ninham to "death in prison"? Tests the constitutionality of a sentence of life in prison without parole for a fourteen-year-old convicted of murder
- **Table** "The U.S. Supreme Court and the Right to Privacy," with leading cases on the issue from *Griswold* to *Lawrence*
- **Sample Document** Probation form

REVISED

- "The 'Right to Bear Arms'" Major revision reflects extension of *D.C. v. Heller* (2008) to states in *McDonald v. Chicago* (2010)
- Expansion of the Ethical Dilemma, "Is Shaming 'Right'?"

Chapter 3, The Criminal Act: The First Principle of Criminal Liability

NEW

- **Vignette** "Was His Sleep Sex a Voluntary Act?"
- **Section** "Epileptic Seizures" New information from the Epilepsy Therapy Project on the effects of failing to take medication, auras, and warning signs of imminent seizures
- **Case Excerpts**
  - *State v. Burrell* (1992) "Did he fire the gun voluntarily?" Tests whether Burrell's last act before firing the gun that killed his friend had to be voluntary
  - *People v. Decina* (1956) "Was killing while driving during an epileptic seizure voluntary?" Leading epileptic seizure case tests the culpability of Emil Decina who, during an epileptic seizure as he drove his vehicle, hit six schoolgirls, killing four
  - *Miller v. State* (1999) "Did he possess illegal drugs?" Tests whether Miller legally "possessed" the drugs in the car in which he was a passenger
- **Exploring Further**
  - Voluntary acts—"Is sleep sex a voluntary act?" Did he commit rape in his sleep?
  - Possession—"Did she possess alcohol?" Did the minor "possess" the alcohol in the car in the DWI case?
- **Ethical Dilemma** "Did Assistant Coach Michael McQueary (of Penn State) have a moral duty to intervene in the alleged sexual assault he witnessed?"
- **Sample Document** Excerpt of grand jury indictment in the Penn State case

Chapter 4, The General Principles of Criminal Liability: *Mens Rea*, Concurrence, Causation, Ignorance, and Mistake

NEW

- **Vignette** "Did He Intend to Give Them AIDS?"

REVISED

- **Section** "Ignorance and Mistake" section to clarify the "failure of proof" theory

Chapter 5, Defenses to Criminal Liability: Justifications

NEW

- **Vignette** "When Seconds Count, the Police Are Only Minutes Away"
- **Section** "Proving Defenses" Revised and expanded "Affirmative Defenses and Proving Them" from *Criminal Law* 10
- **Case Excerpts**
  - *U.S. v. Haynes* (1998) "Can a sneak attack be self-defense?"
  - *Toops v. State* (1994) "Was driving drunk a lesser evil than a car out of control?" Choice of evils and drunk driving
- **Table** Hot-button issue—"Summary of Florida Castle Law Changes"

REVISED

- **Section** "Self-Defense" Expanded, adding new material on inevitable and imminent attack and sneak attacks and self-defense
- **Figure** "Castle Doctrine Map" Updated to reflect state statutes in 2009

Chapter 6, Defenses to Criminal Liability: Excuses

NEW

- **Vignette** "Did He Know It Was 'Wrong' to Kill His Father?"
- **Major Sections**
  - — "The History of Insanity Defense" Explores the history of the insanity defense from Plato (350 B.C.) to modern times, with emphasis on historical cases, especially from eighteenth-century England to the right-wrong test created in the famous *McNaughtan* case and its development up to the present. I've stressed the major legal and historical evidence regarding the myth that the insanity defense is a way to escape punishment.
  - — "The Insanity Defense: Myths and Reality" Explores the enormous gap between the public *perception* of how the insanity defense works and how it actually works. The myth is that the defense allows many dangerous people to escape punishment for the crime; the reality is that few do escape.
- **Subsection** "The Product of Mental Illness Test (*Durham* Rule)"
- **Case Excerpts**
  - — *U.S. v. Hinckley* (2009) "Should his furlough releases be expanded?" Latest decision in the series of opinions expanding John Hinckley's furlough privileges since he attempted to kill President Reagan in 1981
  - — *State v. Odell* (2004) "Did he know 'the nature and wrongfulness' of his acts?" Insanity case tests whether Darren Odell knew it was wrong to kill his father
- **Table** "Juveniles Tried as Adults" Briefly summarizes cases
- **Figure** "Duress Statutes" Highlights examples of defense of duress statutes from three states

REVISED Sections

- "The Right-Wrong Test" Expanded to explain the controversy between lawyers and mental health experts on the definition of insanity, especially on reason (cognition) and will (volition)
- "The Substantial Capacity Test (Model Penal Code)" Expanded to include criticisms of this test of insanity

Chapter 7, Parties to Crime and Vicarious Liability

NEW

- **Vignette** "Was He an Accessory?
- **Figure** Examples of "Accomplice *Mens Rea*"

REVISED Section "Parties to Crime" Expanded explanation and discussion of the two theories of liability for someone else's crime—"agency" and "forfeited personal identity"

Chapter 8, Inchoate Crimes

NEW

- **Vignette** "Did He Attempt to Rape?"
- **Major Section** "The Racketeer and Corrupt Organizations Act (RICO)" describes the history of RICO; **Four New Subsections** "Prosecuting Organized Crime," "Prosecuting White-Collar Crimes," "Prosecuting Government Corruption," and Punishing RICO Offenders"
- **Section** Added "Defenses to Attempt Liability" to clarify and simplify two concepts, which are now two **New Subsections** under defenses: "Legal Impossibility" and "Voluntary Abandonment"

- **Case Excerpts**
  - — *Mims v. U.S.* (1967) "Did he attempt to rob the bank?" (application of the Model Penal Code "substantial steps")
  - — *Alexander v. U.S.* (1993) "Was the forfeiture an excessive fine?"
  - — *State v. Schleifer* (1923) "Did he solicit his audience to destroy their employers' homes and businesses?"

REVISED Sections

- "Attempt *Actus Reus*" Revised to clarify and simplify the tests of the criminal act in attempt law, adding **New Subsections** for each test—all but the last act test; dangerous proximity to success test; indispensable element test; unequivocality test; probable desistance test; and the substantial steps (Model Penal Code) test
- Expanded "Solicitation *Actus Reus*"

Chapter 9, Crimes against Persons I: Murder and Manslaughter

NEW

- **Vignette** "Is Doctor-Assisted Suicide Murder?
- **Section** "The Deadly Weapon Doctrine" History and modern application of the doctrine, explaining how prosecutors can prove the element of intent to kill by proving the defendant attacked the victim with a deadly weapon
- **Subsection** "Provocation by Nonviolent Homosexual Advance (NHA)" Debate over whether "gay panic" killings are murder or voluntary manslaughter
- **Case Excerpts**
  - — *State v. Snowden* (1957) "Did he premeditatedly and deliberately murder?"
  - — *People v. Phillips* (1966) "Is 'grand theft' an underlying felony for felony murder?"
  - — *Commonwealth v. Carr* (1990) "Did seeing the lesbian lovemaking cause a 'gay panic'?"
- **Table** "Stage of Fetal Development in Feticide Statutes"
- **Figures**
  - — "The FBI's Index of Serious Crimes in the United States (2010)"
  - — "Inherently Dangerous to Life in the Abstract Felonies" Cases illustrating the range and variety of felonies that qualify for the felony murder rule
  - — "Model Penal Code Homicide Sections"
- **Sample Document** Sample jury instruction on provocation

REVISED Sections

- "When Does Life Begin?" More emphasis on fetal death, especially feticide statutes
- "Felony Murder" Includes the history, the debate over, and the modern trend toward restricting, and even abolishing, the ancient rule
- "Manslaughter" Expanded by adding an introduction providing more background and history of manslaughter
- "Adequate Provocation" Expanded to clarify and elaborate on the complex definition and application of the concept, including a new list of the definition of legally accepted provocations

Chapter 10, Crimes against Persons II: Sex Offenses, Bodily Injury, and Personal Restraint

NEW

- **Vignette** "Did He Seduce or Rape Her?"
- **Case** *People v. Evans* (1975) "Was it rape or seduction?"

- **Figures**
  - "Relationship of Rape Victim to Rapist"
  - "Michigan Criminal Sexual Conduct Statute"

Chapter 11, Crimes against Property

NEW

- **Vignette** "Did He Commit Credit Card Fraud?"
- **Sections**
  - "Ponzi Schemes" History and impact of the 2007 "Great Recession" on Ponzi crimes
  - "White-Collar Crime" History and application to federal mail fraud
- **Case Excerpts**
  - *People v. Gasparik* (1981) "Did he 'steal' the leather jacket?" Description and analysis of adapting the ancient offense of larceny to fit the modern crime of shoplifting
  - *U.S. v. Maze (1974)* "Did he commit federal mail fraud?" Maze stole his roommate's credit card to pay for his road trip from Kentucky to California

REVISED Section "Cybercrimes" Added history, showing that "digital people" weren't the first "victims" of data collection and mining, giving an example of how GM used it in the 1920s to "steal" Ford's customers by "target marketing"

Chapter 12, Crimes against Public Order and Morals

NEW

- **Vignette** "Violent Video Games"
- **Sections**
  - "Violent Video Games" Do they cause violent behavior like the killings at Columbine and other schools?
  - "Prostitution" Focuses on the inequality issue captured in this opener to the section: "The law's desire to punish bad girls has often been moderated by its wish to save nice boys from harm, inconvenience or embarrassment" **Subsections** include:
    - The History of Prostitution Laws
    - The Double Standard Today
    - Court Remedies for the Double Standard
    - Local Government Programs Targeting Johns (car forfeiture, driver's license revocation, and publishing the names of arrested johns in local newspapers and online)
- **Case Excerpts**
  - *Interactive Digital Software Association v. St. Louis County* (2002) "Can counties ban juveniles from playing violent video games in arcades?"
  - *Commonwealth v. An Unnamed Defendant* (1986) "Is it constitutional to arrest only prostitutes and not johns?"
- **Figure** "Male–Female Prostitution Arrests, 2010"

UPDATED Table "Estimated Number of Arrests, 2010"

Chapter 13, Crimes against the State

MAJOR CHAPTER REVISION In response to reviewers' excellent suggestions, and to developments in the law, as well as my own interests in the history of espionage and its application to present law, this is almost a 75 percent rewrite of the old chapter. The result: a chapter that engages more deeply the issues of the substantive criminal law and crimes against the state.

NEW

- **Vignette** "Did He Provide Material Support to a Terrorist Organization?" *Holder v. Humanitarian Law Project* (2010); U.S. Supreme Court case
- **Ethical Dilemma** "Which of the following actions is it ethical to ban as 'material support and resources' to terrorists?"
- **Table** Statute "Attempted Intentional Damage to Protected Computer"

REVISED Sections

- "Espionage" Major rewrite includes:
    - — **New Subsection** "The History of the Espionage Act" Discussion of leading cases of the WWI era
    - — **New Subsection** "The Espionage Act Today" Includes analysis of major cases
        - Bradley Manning and WikiLeaks
        - Thomas Drake, former executive in the NSA, whistleblower charged with transferring top secret national defense documents
        - Jeffrey Sterling, former CIA agent who disclosed secret national defense information to the *New York Times* reporter James Risen, which later appeared in Risen's *Secret History of the CIA* book
        - John Kiriaku, former CIA officer and member of the team that captured and "waterboarded" the top Al Qaeda hierarchy, who disclosed the identity of a CIA analyst that interrogated Zubaydah
- "Antiterrorist Crimes" Major rewrite includes:
    - — **New Subsections** All new text for "The Top Terrorist Plot Cases," which discusses cases since 9/11, and "'Homegrown' Terrorists"
    - — **Table** "Statutes Charged in Top 50 Terrorist Plots, 2001–2010"
    - — **Figures** "Top 50 Plot Prosecutions, 2001–2010" and "Homegrown Terrorist Defendants Born in the United States, 2001–2010"
- "Material Support to Terrorists and Terrorist Organizations" Major rewrite places special emphasis on constitutional challenges on First Amendment speech and assembly rights
- "Sabotage" Expanded explanation of its use and added an extended analysis of the case of Douglas James Duchak, a computer analyst responsible for updating the TSA "No Fly List" who tried to destroy it because he was laid off
- **NEW U.S. Supreme Court Case** *Holder v. Humanitarian Law Project* (2010), upholding "material support" provisions of the USA Patriot Act

Supplements

RESOURCES FOR INSTRUCTORS

- **Instructor's Resource Manual with Test Bank** The manual, which has been updated and revised by Valerie Bell of Loras College, includes learning objectives, key terms, a detailed chapter outline, a chapter summary, discussion topics, student activities, media tools, and a newly expanded test bank. The learning objectives are correlated with the discussion topics, student activities, and media tools. Each chapter's test bank contains questions in multiple-choice, true–false, completion, and essay formats, with a full answer key. The test bank is coded to the learning objectives that appear in the main text and includes the page numbers in the main text where the answers can be found. Finally, each question in the test bank has been carefully reviewed by experienced criminal justice instructors for quality, accuracy, and content coverage. Our Instructor Approved seal, which appears on the front cover, is our assurance that you are working with an assessment and grading resource of the highest caliber. The manual is available for download on the password-protected website and can also be obtained by e-mailing your local Cengage Learning representative.

- **ExamView® Computerized Testing** The comprehensive Instructor's Manual is backed up by ExamView, a computerized test bank available for PC and Macintosh computers. With ExamView, you can create, deliver, and customize tests and study guides (both print and online) in minutes. You can easily edit and import your own questions and graphics, change test layouts, and reorganize questions. And using ExamView's complete word-processing capabilities, you can enter an unlimited number of new questions or edit existing questions.
- **PowerPoint Lecture Slides** Helping you make your lectures more engaging while effectively reaching your visually oriented students, these handy Microsoft PowerPoint® slides outline the chapters of the main text in a classroom-ready presentation. The PowerPoint® slides are updated to reflect the content and organization of the new edition of the text and feature some additional examples and real-world cases for application and discussion. Available for download on the password-protected instructor book companion website, the presentations can also be obtained by e-mailing your local Cengage Learning representative. The PowerPoint® slides were updated for the current edition by Mark Brown of the University of South Carolina.
- **Lesson Plans** The Lesson Plans, which were updated by Valerie Bell of Loras College, bring accessible, masterful suggestions to every lesson. This supplement includes a sample syllabus, learning objectives, lecture notes, discussion topics and in-class activities, a detailed lecture outline, assignments, media tools, and "What if…" scenarios. The learning objectives are integrated throughout the Lesson Plans, and current events and real-life examples in the form of articles, websites, and video links are incorporated into the class discussion topics, activities, and assignments. The lecture outlines are correlated with PowerPoint slides for ease of classroom use. Lesson Plans are available on the instructor website.
- **Real-World Resources: Tools to Enhance Relevancy** The media tools from across all the supplements are gathered into one location and organized by chapter and learning objective. Each item has a description of the resource and a directed learning activity. Available on the instructor website, WebTutor and CourseMate, these can be used as resources for additional learning or as assignments.
- **Wadsworth Criminal Justice Video Library** So many exciting new videos—so many great ways to enrich your lectures and spark discussion of the material in this text. Your Cengage Learning representative will be happy to provide details on our video policy by adoption size. The library includes these selections and many others.
  - **ABC® Videos.** ABC videos feature short, high-interest clips from current news events as well as historic raw footage going back forty years. Perfect for discussion starters or to enrich your lectures and spark interest in the material in the text, these brief videos provide students with a new lens through which to view the past and present, one that will greatly enhance their knowledge and

understanding of significant events and open up to them new dimensions in learning. Clips are drawn from such programs as *World News Tonight*, *Good Morning America*, *This Week*, *PrimeTime Live*, *20/20*, and *Nightline*, as well as numerous ABC News specials and material from the Associated Press Television News and British Movietone News collections.

— **Introduction to Criminal Justice Video Series.** This Cengage Learning video series features videos supplied by the BBC Motion Gallery. These short, high-interest clips from CBS and BBC news programs—everything from nightly news broadcasts and specials to *CBS News Special Reports, CBS Sunday Morning, 60 Minutes*, and more—are perfect classroom discussion starters. They are designed to enrich your lectures and spark interest in the material in the text. Clips are drawn from the BBC Motion Gallery.

- **Criminal Justice Media Library** Cengage Learning's Criminal Justice Media Library includes nearly three hundred media assets on the topics you cover in your courses. Available to stream from any web-enabled computer, the Criminal Justice Media Library's assets include such valuable resources as Career Profile Videos, featuring interviews with criminal justice professionals from a range of roles and locations; simulations that allow students to step into various roles and practice their decision-making skills; video clips on current topics from ABC® and other sources; animations that illustrate key concepts; interactive learning modules that help students check their knowledge of important topics; and Reality Check exercises that compare expectations and preconceived notions against the real-life thoughts and experiences of criminal justice professionals. The Criminal Justice Media Library can be uploaded and used within many popular Learning Management Systems, and all video assets include assessment questions that can be delivered straight to the grade book in your LMS. You can also customize it with your own course material. Please contact your Cengage Learning representative for ordering and pricing information.
- **WebTutor™ on Blackboard® and WebCT®** Jump-start your course with customizable, rich, text-specific content within your Course Management System. Whether you want to web-enable your class or put an entire course online, WebTutor delivers. WebTutor offers a wide array of resources, including media assets, test banks, practice quizzes linked to chapter learning objectives, and additional study aids. Visit http://www.cengage.com/webtutor to learn more.

RESOURCES FOR STUDENTS

- **Study Guide** An extensive student guide has been developed for this edition by Mark Brown of the University of South Carolina. Because students learn in different ways, the guide includes a variety of pedagogical aids to help them. Each chapter is outlined and summarized, major terms and figures are defined, plus media tools for directed learning and self-tests are provided.
- **CourseMate** Cengage Learning's Criminal Justice CourseMate brings course concepts to life with interactive learning, study, and exam preparation tools that support the printed textbook. CourseMate includes an integrated e-book, quizzes mapped to chapter learning objectives that have been updated for the current edition by Roreita Joy Walker of Bauder College, flashcards, videos, and more, and EngagementTracker, a first-of-its-kind tool that monitors student engagement in the course. The accompanying instructor website offers access to password-protected resources, such as an electronic version of the instructor's manual and PowerPoint® slides.

- **Careers in Criminal Justice Website** (Can be bundled with this text at no additional charge) Featuring plenty of self-exploration and profiling activities, the interactive Careers in Criminal Justice website helps students investigate and focus on the criminal justice career choices that are right for them. Includes interest assessment, video testimonials from career professionals, resume and interview tips, links for reference, and a wealth of information on "soft skills," such as health and fitness, stress management, and effective communication.
- **CLeBook** Cengage Learning's Criminal Justice e-books allow students to access our textbooks in an easy-to-use online format. Highlight, take notes, bookmark, search your text, and, for most texts, link directly into multimedia. In short, CLeBooks combine the best features of paper books and e-books in one package.
- **Current Perspectives: Readings from Infotrac® College Edition** These readers, designed to give students a closer look at special topics in criminal justice, include free access to InfoTrac College Edition. The timely articles are selected by experts in each topic from within InfoTrac College Edition. They are available free when bundled with the text and include the following titles:
  - — Introduction to Criminal Justice
  - — Community Corrections
  - — Cyber Crime
  - — Victimology
  - — Juvenile Justice
  - — Racial Profiling
  - — White-Collar Crime
  - — Terrorism and Homeland Security
  - — Public Policy and Criminal Justice
  - — Technology and Criminal Justice
  - — Ethics in Criminal Justice
  - — Forensics
  - — Corrections
  - — Law and Courts
  - — Policy in Criminal Justice

Acknowledgements

Criminal Law, Eleventh Edition (like the other ten), didn't get to you by my efforts alone; I had a lot of help. I'm grateful for all those who have provided feedback over the years. Many thanks also to Criminal Justice Editor Carolyn Henderson Meier who has helped me at every stage of the book. Thanks, too, to my indefatigable, sharp, careful copy editor Lura Harrison, whose work definitely improved the final manuscript throughout the book but most of all on the new and expanded sections. And Ruth Cottrell's calm efficiency, warm kindness, meticulous editing, and infinite patience really is a gift that keeps on giving.

But there are still more to thank. Professor Ann Bunch provided major assistance on refining the learning objectives and chapter summaries as well as to creating the new marginal glossary. I'm confident that you'll benefit from Ann's efforts. My student Charlotte Culbertson came through for me when I needed help "right now," particularly on identity theft statistics and tracking down valuable sources on the new section on the World War I espionage cases. From the three semesters that she was my student and one in which she was my teaching assistant, I've learned that when Charlotte sets out to do something, she doesn't let go until she succeeds.

Additionally, I would like to thank the following reviewers of the Tenth Edition for providing invaluable feedback and direction for this revision:

- Ann Bunch, *State University of New York–Brockport*
- Robert A. Del Sordo, *Camden County College*
- Jason Hale, *County College of Morris*
- Jean Gabriel Jolivet, *Southwestern College*
- Kenneth Mentor, *University of North Carolina at Pembroke*
- Jo Ann M. Scott, *Ohio Northern University*
- David L. Weiden, *Indiana University–Purdue University Indianapolis*
- James L. Wright, *Chattanooga State Community College*

What would I do without Doug and Steve? Doug takes me there and gets me here and everywhere, day in and day out, days that now have stretched into years. And my old and dearest friend Steve, who from the days when he watched over our Irish Wolfhounds in the 1970s, to now decades later when he keeps "Frankie" the Standard Poodle, "Kitty Cat," the Siamese, me, and a lot more around here in order. And they do it all while putting up with what my beloved mentor at Cambridge, the late Sir Geoffrey Elton, called "Joel's mercurial temperament." Only those who really know me can understand how I can try the patience of Job! Friends and associates like these have given *Criminal Law*, Eleventh Edition whatever success it enjoys. As for its faults, I own them all.

Joel Samaha
Minneapolis

CRIMINAL LAW

LEARNING OBJECTIVES

1. To define and understand what behavior deserves criminal punishment.
2. To understand and appreciate the relationship between the general and special parts of criminal law.
3. To identify, describe, and understand the main sources of criminal law.
4. To define criminal punishment, to know the difference between criminal and noncriminal sanctions, and to understand the purposes of each.
5. To define and appreciate the significance of the presumption of innocence and the burden of proof as they relate to criminal liability.
6. To understand the role of informal discretion and appreciate its relationship to formal criminal law.
7. To understand the text-case method and how to apply it to the study of criminal law.

Evelyn Nesbit Thaw (1884–1967) was a celebrity teen-age model. She was also the object of two powerful rivals for her affections—millionaire Harry Thaw and famous architect Stanford White. Here she is on February 7, 1907, testifying during the first murder trial of her husband, Harry Thaw. Thaw, in a jealous rage, shot and killed White in front of a crowd in Madison Square Garden, which White had designed.

1 CRIMINAL LAW AND CRIMINAL PUNISHMENT

An Overview

CHAPTER OUTLINE

Two Years in Prison for the Unlawful Sale of Liquor?

Joseph Pete sold a bottle of Gilbey's vodka and a bottle of Seagram's Seven Crown whiskey to Edward N. Sigvayugak. The prosecuting witness, Edward N. Sigvayugak, had been engaged by a state police officer to buy liquor from Pete with money provided by the officer, and was paid for his services by the officer.

(*State v. Pete* 1966)

"Every known organized society has, and probably must have, some system by which it punishes those who violate its most important prohibitions" (Robinson 2008, 1). This book explores, and invites you to think critically about, the answers to the two questions implied in Professor Robinson's quote:

1. What behavior deserves criminal punishment?
2. What's the appropriate punishment for criminal behavior?

Criminal law, and most of what you'll read about it in this book, boils down to varying answers to these questions. To introduce you to the possible answers, read the brief summaries presented from real cases that we'll examine deeper in the remaining chapters. After you read each summary, assign the case to one of the five following categories. Don't worry about whether you know enough about criminal law to decide which category it belongs in. In fact, try to ignore what you already know; just choose the category you believe best describes the case.

1. **CRIME.** If you put the case into this category, then grade it as very serious, serious, or minor. The idea here is to stamp it with both the amount of disgrace (stigma) you believe a convicted "criminal" should suffer and roughly the kind and amount of punishment you believe the person deserves.
2. **NONCRIMINAL WRONG.** This is a legal wrong that justifies suing someone and getting money, usually for some personal injury. In other words, name a price that the wrongdoer has to pay to another individual, but don't stamp it "criminal" (Coffee 1992, 1876–77).
3. **REGULATION.** Use government action—for example, a heavy cigarette tax to discourage smoking—to discourage the behavior (Harcourt 2005, 11–12). In other words, make the price high, but don't stamp it with the stigma of "crime."
4. **LICENSE.** Charge a price for it—for example, a driver's license fee for the privilege to drive—but don't try to encourage or discourage it. Make the price affordable, and attach no stigma to it.
5. **LAWFUL.** Let individual conscience and/or social disapproval condemn it, but create no legal consequences.

HERE ARE THE CASES

1. A young man beat a stranger on the street with a baseball bat for "kicks." The victim died. (*Commonwealth v. Golston* 1977, "Atrocious Murder" in Chapter 9, p. 318)
2. A husband begged his wife, who had cheated on him for months, not to leave him. She replied, "No, I'm going to court, and you're going to have to give me all the furniture. You're going to have to get the hell out of here; you won't have nothing." Then, pointing to her crotch, she added, "You'll never touch this again, because I've got something bigger and better for it."

   Breaking into tears, he begged some more, "Why don't you try to save the marriage? I have nothing more to live for."

   "Never," she replied. "I'm never coming back to you."

   He "cracked," ran into the next room, got a gun, and shot her to death. (Commonwealth v. Schnopps 1983, Chapter 9, "Voluntary Manslaughter," p. 335)
3. Two robbers met a drunk man in a bar, displaying a wad of money. When the man asked them for a ride, they agreed, drove him out into the country, robbed him, forced him out of the car without his glasses, and drove off. A college student, driving at a reasonable speed, didn't see the man standing in the middle of the road waving him down, couldn't stop, and struck and killed him. (*People v. Kibbe* 1974, Chapter 4, "Proximate Cause," p. 147)
4. During the Korean War, a mother dreamed that an enemy soldier was on top of her daughter. In her sleep, she got up, walked to a shed, got an ax, went to her daughter's room, and plunged the ax into her, believing she was killing the enemy soldier. The daughter died instantly; the mother was beside herself with grief. (*King v. Cogdon* 1951, Chapter 3, "Voluntary Act," p. 100)
5. A neighbor told an eight-year-old boy and his friend to come out from behind a building, and not to play there, because it was dangerous. The boy answered belligerently, "In a minute."

Losing patience, the neighbor said, "No, not in a minute; get out of there now!"

A few days later, he broke into her house, pulled a goldfish out of its bowl, chopped it into little pieces with a steak knife, and smeared it all over the counter. Then, he went into the bathroom, plugged in a curling iron, and clamped it onto a towel. (*State v. K.R.L.* 1992, Chapter 6, "The Excuse of Age," p. 212)

6. A young man lived in a ground-level apartment with a large window opening onto the building parking lot. At eight o'clock one morning, he stood naked in front of the window eating his cereal in full view of those getting in and out of their cars. (*State v. Metzger* 1982, Chapter 2, "Defining Vagueness," p. 46)
7. A man knew he was HIV positive. Despite doctors' instructions about safe sex and the need to tell his partners before having sex with them, he had sex numerous times with three different women without telling them. Most of the time, he used no protection, but, on a few occasions, he withdrew before ejaculating. He gave one of the women an anti-AIDS drug, "to slow down the AIDS." None of the women contracted the HIV virus. (*State v. Stark* 1992, Chapter 4, "MPC Mental Attitudes: Purpose," p. 132)
8. A woman met a very drunk man in a bar. He got into her car, and she drove him to her house. He asked her for a spoon, which she knew he wanted to use to take drugs. She got it for him and waited in the living room while he went into the bathroom to "shoot up." He came back into the living room and collapsed; she went back to the bar. The next morning she found him "purple, with flies flying around him." Thinking he was dead, she told her daughter to call the police and left for work. He was dead. (*People v. Oliver* 1989, Chapter 3, "Omissions as Acts," p. 109)

WHAT BEHAVIOR DESERVES CRIMINAL PUNISHMENT?

LO 1

"Welcome to Bloomington, you're under arrest!" This is what a Bloomington, Minnesota, police officer, who was a student in my criminal justice class, told me that billboards at the city limits of this Minneapolis suburb should read.

"Why," I asked?

"Because everything in Bloomington is a crime," he replied, laughing.

Although his comments were exaggerated, the officer spoke the truth. Murders, rapes, robberies, and other "street crimes" have always filled the news and stoked our fears. "White-collar crimes" have also received attention in these early years of the twenty-first century. And, of course, since 9/11, crimes committed by terrorists have also attracted considerable attention. These types of crimes will also receive most of our attention in this book—at least until Chapter 12, when we turn to the "crimes against public order and morals." In numbers, crimes against public order and morals dwarf all the others combined (see Table 1.1). But from now until Chapter 12, you'll read about the 600,000 violent and 2.5 million property crimes in Table 1.1, not the 17.7 million minor offenses.

Let's look briefly at the American Law Institute's (ALI) Model Penal Code (MPC) definition of behavior that deserves punishment. It's the framework we'll use to guide our analysis of criminal liability, "conduct that unjustifiably and inexcusably inflicts or threatens substantial harm to individual or public interests" (ALI 1985, § 1.02(1)(a)).

criminal liability, conduct that unjustifiably and inexcusably inflicts or threatens substantial harm to individual or public interests

Here's a breakdown of the words and phrases in the definition:

1. Conduct that
2. Unjustifiably and inexcusably
3. Inflicts or threatens substantial harm
4. To individual or public interests

ELEMENTS OF CRIMINAL LIABILITY:
ELEMENTS OF MATERIAL SUPPORT TO TERRORISTS

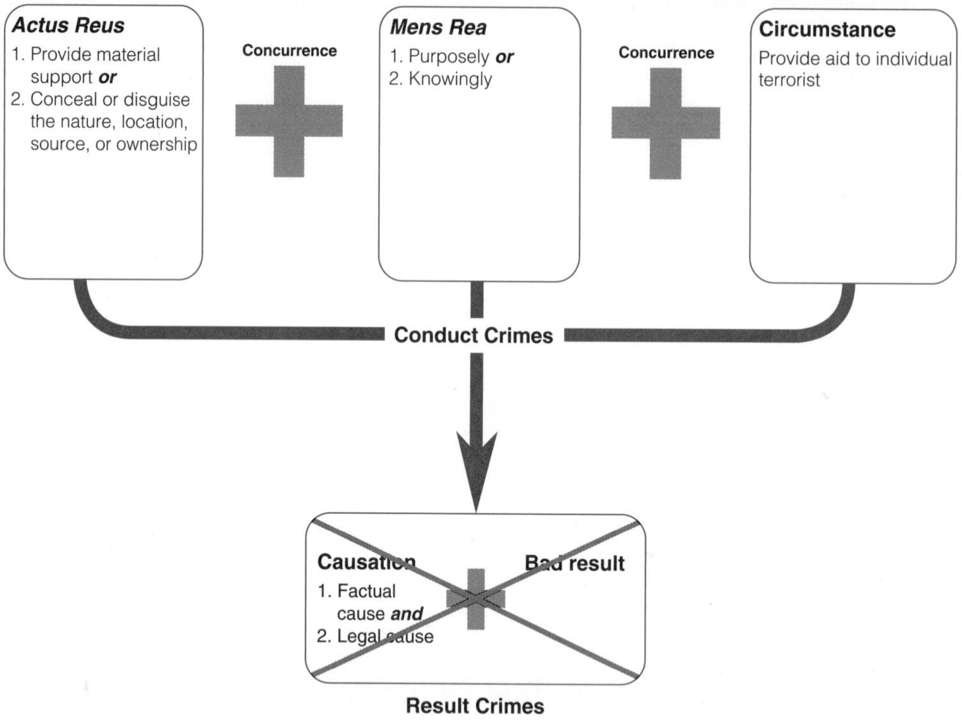

Actus Reus
1. Provide material support ***or***
2. Conceal or disguise the nature, location, source, or ownership

Concurrence

Mens Rea
1. Purposely ***or***
2. Knowingly

Concurrence

Circumstance
Provide aid to individual terrorist

Conduct Crimes

Causation
1. Factual cause ***and***
2. Legal cause

Bad result

Result Crimes

The Elements of Criminal Liability figure illustrates these elements as they apply to the crime of providing support to terrorists (which we'll discuss in Chapter 13).

These few words and phrases are the building blocks of our whole system of criminal law and punishment. We'll spend the rest of the book exploring and applying them to a wide range of human behavior in an equally wide range of circumstances. But, first, let's examine some propositions that will help prepare you to follow and understand the later chapters. Let's begin by looking at the difference between criminal wrongs and other legal wrongs that aren't criminal.

LO 4

CRIMES AND NONCRIMINAL WRONGS

The opening case summaries demonstrate that criminal law is only one kind of social control, one form of responsibility for deviating from social norms. So in criminal law, the basic question boils down to "Who's criminally responsible for what crime?" We won't often discuss the noncriminal kinds of responsibility in this book. But you should keep them in mind anyway, because in the real world, criminal liability is the exceptional form of social control. The norm is the other four categories mentioned in the beginning of the chapter (p. 4). And they should be, because criminal liability is the harshest and most expensive form of social control.

torts, private wrongs for which you can sue the party who wronged you and recover money

In this section, we'll concentrate on the noncriminal wrongs called **torts**, private wrongs for which you can sue the party who wronged you and recover money.

Crimes and torts represent two different ways our legal system responds to social and individual harm (Table 1.2). Before we look at their differences, let's look at how they're similar. First, both are sets of rules telling us what we can't do ("Don't steal") and what we must do ("Pay your taxes"). Second, the rules apply to everybody in the

TABLE 1.1

Estimated Number of Arrests, United States, 2010

CRIME	ARRESTS*
Murder and nonnegligent manslaughter	11,201
Forcible rape	20,088
Robbery	112,300
Aggravated assault	408,488
Burglary	289,769
Larceny-theft	1,271,410
Motor vehicle theft	71,487
Arson	11,296
Violent crime†	552,077
Property crime†	1,643,962
Other assaults	1,292,449
Forgery and counterfeiting	78,101
Fraud	187,887
Embezzlement	16,616
Stolen property; buying, receiving, possessing	94,802
Vandalism	252,753
Weapons; carrying, possessing, etc.	159,020
Prostitution and commercialized vice	62,668
Sex offenses (except forcible rape and prostitution)	72,628
Drug abuse violations	1,638,846
Gambling	9,941
Offenses against the family and children	111,062
Driving under the influence	1,412,223
Liquor laws	512,790
Drunkenness	560,718
Disorderly conduct	615,172
Vagrancy	32,033
All other offenses	3,720,402
Suspicion	1,166
Curfew and loitering law violations	94,797

*Total 13,120,947. Does not include suspicion.

†Violent crimes are offenses of murder and nonnegligent manslaughter, forcible rape, robbery, and aggravated assault. Property crimes are offenses of burglary, larceny-theft, motor vehicle theft, and arson.

Source: FBI Uniform Crime Report 2011 (Sept.), Table 29.

ETHICAL DILEMMA

Are the private paparazzi informants doing ethical work?

With his dapper red scarf and orange-tinted hair, Kim Rae-in is a card-carrying member of the "paparazzi" posse, cruising Seoul on his beat-up motorcycle on the lookout for the next "gotcha" moment. He's not stalking starlets or pop singers. He's after moneymaking snapshots: the salary man lighting up in a no-smoking area, the homeowner illegally dumping trash, the merchant selling stale candy to kids. Kim, 34, a former gas-station attendant, isn't choosy. Even small crime pays big time—more than $3,000 in January alone. "It's good money," he says. "I'll never go back to pumping gas. I feel free now."

Kim is among a new breed across South Korea—referred to as "paparazzi," although their subjects are not the rich and famous but low-grade lawbreakers whose actions caught on film are peddled as evidence to government officials. In recent years, officials have enacted more than 60 civilian "reporting" programs that offer rewards ranging from 50,000 won, or about $36, for the smallest infractions to 2 billion won, or $1.4 million, for a large-scale corruption case involving government officials. (That one has yet to be made.) The paparazzi trend even has inspired its own lexicon. There are "seon-parazzi," who pursue election-law violators; "ssu-parazzi," who target illegal acts of dumping garbage, and "seong-parazzi," who target prostitution, which is illegal.

Amid the nation's worsening economic crisis, officials say there are fewer government investigators to maintain public order. So they increasingly rely on a bounty-hunter style of justice. Many paparazzi are out-of-work salary men, bored homemakers, and college students who consider themselves deputized agents of the government.

To meet a growing demand, scores of paparazzi schools have sprung up, charging students $250 for three-day courses on how to edit film, tail suspected wrongdoers, and operate button-sized cameras. Schools estimate 500 professional paparazzi now work in South Korea. Few officials question the ethics of arming a citizenry against itself with zoom video and long-range lenses. "They don't violate any laws, so there's no reason to restrict them," said a National Tax Service official, who declined to give his name.

Some paparazzi students say they hate ratting out their neighbors, but the money is too good to resist. "It's shameful work—I'm really not proud of it," said one student who declined to give her name. Said another, who also asked to remain anonymous, "Let's put it this way: I don't want to be called a paparazzi; I'm a public servant" (Glionna 2009).

Others disagree.

Bang Jae-won, 56, an eight-year veteran of the trade, said he felt proud of the times he caught people dumping garbage at a camping site or exposed marketing frauds, one of which once bankrupted him. "I regret the early, desperate days when I reported the misdemeanors of people as poor as I was," said Mr. Bang, who turned to this work after he was told he was too old by prospective employers. "I don't tell my neighbors what I do because it might arouse unnecessary suspicions," he said. "But, in general, I am not ashamed of my work. To those who call us snitches, I say, 'Why don't you obey the law?'"

Critics, however, say the reward program has undermined social trust. "The idea itself is good, but when people make a full-time job of this, it . . . raises ethical questions," said Lee Yoon-ho, a professor of police administration at Dongguk University in Seoul (Sang-Hun 2011).

Instructions

1. List all the crimes the paparazzi report.
2. Which, if any, do you consider it ethical to report?
3. Which, if any, do you consider it unethical to report?
4. Would you recommend that your state adopt a reporting reward policy? Why would it be ethical (or unethical)?

Sources: Glionna, John. 2009. "South Korean Cameras Zero in on Crime." *Los Angeles Times*, February 17. Accessed October 13, 2011. http://seattletimes.nwsource.com/html/nationworld/2008751061_korea17.html.

Sang-Hun, Choe. 2011. "Help Wanted: Busybodies with Cameras." *New York Times*, September 28. Accessed October 13, 2011. http://www.nytimes.com/2011/09/29/world/asia/in-south-korea-where-digital-tattling-is-a-growth-industry.html?_r=1&scp=1&sq=Bang%20Jae-won&st=cse.

TABLE 1.2

Crimes and Torts: Similarities and Differences

CRIMES	TORTS (PRIVATE WRONGS)
Crimes originate from a list of "can'ts" and "musts."	Torts originate from a list of "can'ts" and "musts."
The list applies to everybody.	The list applies to everybody.
Crimes injure another individual and the whole community.	Torts injure another individual and the whole community.
Criminal prosecutions are brought by the state against individuals.	Private parties bring tort actions against other parties.
Convicted offenders pay money to the state or serve time in the custody of the state.	Defendants who lose in tort cases pay money to the plaintiff who sued.
Criminal conviction is the condemnation by the whole community, the expression of its "hatred, fear, or contempt for the convict."	The tort award compensates the plaintiff who brought the suit.
The state has to prove all elements of the crime by "proof beyond a reasonable doubt."	The burden on the plaintiff is to prove responsibility by a preponderance of the evidence.

community, and they speak on behalf of everybody, with the power and prestige of the whole community behind them. Third, the power of the law backs up the enforcement of the rules (Hart 1958, 403).

How are they different? Some believe that crimes injure the whole community, whereas torts harm only individuals. But that's not really true. Almost every crime is also a tort. Many crimes and torts even have the same name (there's a crime and a tort called "assault"). Other crimes are torts even though they don't have the same names; for example, the crime of murder is also the tort of wrongful death. In fact, the same killing sometimes is tried as murder and later as a civil wrongful death suit.

One famous example is in the legal actions against the great football player O. J. Simpson. He was acquitted in the murder of his ex-wife and her friend in a criminal case but then lost in a tort case for their wrongful deaths. Also, torts don't just harm other individuals; they can also harm the whole community. For example, breaches of contract don't just hurt the parties to the contract. Much of what keeps daily life running depends on people keeping their word when they agree to buy, sell, perform services, and so on.

Are crimes just torts with different names? No. One difference is that criminal prosecutions are brought by the government against individuals; that's why criminal cases always have titles like "*U.S. v. Rasul*," "*People v. Menendez*," "*State v. Erickson*," or "*Commonwealth v. Wong*." (The first name in the case title is what that government entity calls itself, and the second name, the defendant's, is the individual being prosecuted.) Nongovernment parties bring tort actions against other parties who may or may not be governments.

A second difference is that injured plaintiffs (those who sue for wrongs in tort cases) get money (called *damages*) from defendants for the injuries they suffer. In criminal actions, defendants pay fines to the state and/or serve time doing community service, in jail, or in prison.

The most important difference between torts and crimes is the conviction itself. It's "the expression of the community's hatred, fear, or contempt for the convict . . ." (Hart 1958). Professor Henry M. Hart sums up the difference this way:

> [Crime] . . . is not simply anything which a legislature chooses to call a "crime." It is not simply antisocial conduct which public officers are given a responsibility to

suppress. It is not simply any conduct to which the legislature chooses to attach a criminal penalty. It is conduct which . . . will incur a formal and solemn pronouncement of the moral condemnation of the community. (405)

But you should understand that words of condemnation *by themselves* don't make crimes different from torts. Not at all. When the legislature defines a crime, it's issuing a threat—"Don't steal, *or else* . . ." "File your taxes, *or else* . . ." What's the "or else"? The threat of punishment, a threat that society will carry out against anyone who commits a crime.

In fact, so intimately connected are condemnation and criminal punishment that some of the most distinguished criminal law scholars say that punishment has two indispensable components, condemnation and "hard treatment." According to Andrew von Hirsch, honorary professor of Penal Theory and Penal Law at the University of Cambridge, England, a prolific writer on the subject, and his distinguished colleague, Andrew Ashworth, the Vinerian Professor of Law at Oxford University, "Punishment conveys censure, but it does not consist solely of it. The censure in punishment is expressed through the imposition of a deprivation ('hard treatment') on the offender" (Von Hirsch and Ashworth 2005, 21).

If the threat isn't carried out when a crime is committed, condemnation is meaningless, or worse—it sends a message that the victim's suffering is worthless. Punishment has to back up the condemnation. According to another respected authority on this point, Professor Dan Kahan (1996), "When society deliberately forgoes answering the wrongdoer through punishment, it risks being perceived as endorsing his valuations; hence the complaint that unduly lenient punishment reveals that the victim is worthless in the eyes of the law" (598).

You're about to encounter your first case excerpt, in which the Alaska Supreme Court examined the importance of condemnation and hard treatment. (Unless your instructor recommends otherwise, I strongly recommend that before you read the excerpt, you take the time to study "The Text-Case Method," later in the chapter, p. 33.])

CASE

State v. Chaney (*1970*) *explores the idea that the trial court's "light treatment" of sentencing U.S. Army soldier Donald Scott Chaney to one year in prison with early parole would send the message that the suffering he caused the woman he raped twice and then robbed was worthless.*

Did the punishment devalue the victim?

State v. Chaney

477 P.2d 441 (Alaska 1970)

HISTORY

A jury convicted Donald Scott Chaney on two counts of forcible rape and one count of robbery and the trial court sentenced him to concurrent one-year terms of imprisonment with provision for parole in the discretion of the Parole Board. The state appealed. The Supreme Court was of the opinion that the sentence was too lenient and was not well-calculated to achieve the objective of reformation of the defendant, condemnation of the community, and reaffirmation of societal norms for the purpose of maintaining respect for the norms themselves. The Supreme Court disapproved the sentence.

RABINOWITZ, J., JOINED BY BONEY, CJ., AND DIMOND, CONNOR, AND ERWIN, JJ.

FACTS

At the time Donald Chaney committed the crimes of forcible rape and robbery, he was an unmarried member of the United States Armed Forces stationed at Fort Richardson, near Anchorage, Alaska. His commanding officer stated, prior to sentencing, that

Chaney "was an excellent soldier, takes orders well, and was on the promotion list before his crimes." He was born in 1948, the youngest of eight children. His youth was spent on the family's dairy farm in Washington County, Maryland. He played basketball on the Boonsboro High School team, was a member of Future Farmers of America and the Boy Scouts. Chaney did not complete high school, having dropped out one month prior to graduation. He asserts he was forced to take this action because his father needed his help on the family dairy farm. After a series of varying types of employment, he was drafted into the United States Army in 1968. At sentencing, it was disclosed that he did not have any prior criminal record, was not a user of drugs, and was only a social drinker.

. . . It appears that Chaney and a companion picked up the prosecutrix [victim] at a downtown location in Anchorage. After driving the victim around in their car, Chaney and his companion beat her and forcibly raped her four times. She was also forced to perform an act of fellatio with Chaney's companion. During this same period of time, the victim's money was removed from her purse. Upon completion of these events, the victim was permitted to leave the vehicle to the accompaniment of dire threats of reprisals if she attempted to report the incident to the police.

The presentence report which was furnished to the trial court prior to sentencing contains Chaney's version of the rapes. According to Chaney, he felt "that it wasn't rape as forcible and against her will on my part." As to his conviction of robbery, Chaney states: "I found the money on the floor of the car afterwards and was planning on giving it back, but didn't get to see the girl." At the time of sentencing, Chaney told the court that he "didn't direct any violence against the girl."

The State of Alaska has appealed from the judgment and commitment which was entered by the trial court.

OPINION

[According to the Alaska Sentence Appeal Act of 1969,]

(a) A sentence of imprisonment lawfully imposed by the superior court for a term or for aggregate terms exceeding one year may be appealed to the supreme court by the defendant on the ground that the sentence is excessive. . . .

(b) A sentence of imprisonment lawfully imposed by the superior court may be appealed to the supreme court by the state on the ground that the sentence is too lenient; however, when a sentence is appealed by the state and the defendant has not appealed the sentence, the court is not authorized to increase the sentence but may express its approval or disapproval of the sentence and its reasons in a written opinion.

Sentencing is a discretionary judicial function. When a sentence is appealed, we will make our own examination of the record and will modify the sentence if we are convinced that the sentencing court was clearly mistaken in imposing the sanction it did. Under Alaska's Constitution, the principles of reformation and the necessity of protecting the public constitute the touchstones of penal administration.

Multiple goals are encompassed within these broad constitutional standards. Within the ambit of this constitutional phraseology are found the objectives of (1) rehabilitation of the offender into a noncriminal member of society, (2) isolation of the offender from society to prevent criminal conduct during the period of confinement, (3) deterrence of the offender himself after his release from confinement or other penological treatment, as well as (4) deterrence of other members of the community who might possess tendencies toward criminal conduct similar to that of the offender, and (5) community condemnation of the individual offender, or in other words, reaffirmation of societal norms for the purpose of maintaining respect for the norms themselves.

The determination of the exact period of time that a convicted defendant should serve is basically a sociological problem to be resolved by a careful weighing of the principle of reformation and the need for protecting the public. The Division of Corrections, in its presentence report, recommended Chaney be incarcerated and parole be denied. The assistant district attorney who appeared for the state at the time of sentencing recommended that he receive concurrent seven-year sentences with two years suspended on the two rape convictions, and he be sentenced to a consecutive five-year term of imprisonment on the robbery conviction, and that this sentence be suspended and he be placed on probation during this period of time.

(continues)

(continued)

At the time of sentencing, a representative of the Division of Corrections recommended that Chaney serve two years on each of the rape convictions and be sentenced to two years suspended with probation on the robbery conviction. In his opinion, there was "an excellent possibility of early parole." Counsel for Chaney concurred in the Division of Corrections' recommendation.

The trial court imposed concurrent one-year terms of imprisonment and provided for parole at the discretion of the parole board. These were minimum sentences under the applicable statutes. Rape carries a potential range of imprisonment from 1 to 20 years while a conviction of robbery can result in imprisonment from 1 to 15 years. The trial judge further recommended that appellee be placed in a minimum security facility.

In imposing this sentence, the trial judge remarked that he was sorry that the (military) regulations would not permit keeping (Chaney) in the service if he wanted to stay because it seems to me that is a better setup for everybody concerned than putting him in the penitentiary. Collateral consequences flowing from an accused's conviction may be considered by the trial judge in arriving at an appropriate sentence. In addition to giving weight to the fact that military regulations prohibited Chaney's retention in the service, the trial judge also took into consideration that Chaney's conviction would result in an undesirable discharge from the military service.

At a later point in his remarks, the trial judge said:

> Now as a matter of fact, I have sentenced you to a minimum on all 3 counts here but there will be no problem as far as I'm concerned for you to be paroled at the first day, the Parole Board says that you're eligible for parole. If the Parole Board should decide 10 days from now that you're eligible for parole and parole you, it's entirely satisfactory with the court.

Supreme Ct.R. 21(f) requires that: "At the time of imposition of sentence the judge shall make a statement on the record explaining his reasons for imposition of the sentence." The basic reasons for this requirement are that a statement of the reasons by the sentencing judge should greatly increase the rationality of sentences, such a statement can be of therapeutic value to the defendant, and the statement can be of significance to an appellate court faced with the prospect of reviewing the sentence.

Exercising the appellate jurisdiction vested in this court, we express our disapproval of the sentence which was imposed by the trial court in the case at bar. In our opinion, the sentence was too lenient considering the circumstances surrounding the commission of these crimes. It further appears that several significant goals of our system of penal justice were accorded little or no weight by the sentencing court.

Forcible rape and robbery rank among the most serious crimes. In the case at bar, the record reflects that the trial judge explicitly stated, on several occasions, that he disbelieved Chaney and believed the prosecutrix's version of what happened after she entered the vehicle which was occupied by Chaney and his companion. Considering both the jury's and the trial judge's resolution of this issue of credibility, and the violent circumstances surrounding the commission of these dangerous crimes, we have difficulty in understanding why one-year concurrent sentences were thought appropriate.

Review of the sentencing proceedings leads to the impression that the trial judge was apologetic in regard to his decision to impose a sanction of incarceration. Much was made of Chaney's fine military record and his potential eligibility for early parole. A military spokesman represented to the sentencing court that: "An occurrence such as the one concerned is very common and happens many times each night in Anchorage. Needless to say, Donald Chaney was the unlucky 'G.I.' that picked a young lady who told."

On the one hand, the record is devoid of any trace of remorse on Chaney's part. Seemingly all but forgotten in the sentencing proceedings is the victim of Chaney's rapes and robbery. On the other hand, the record discloses that the trial judge properly considered the mitigating circumstance that the victim, who at the time did not know either Chaney or his companion, voluntarily entered Chaney's car. But the crux of our disapproval of the sentence stems from what we consider to be the trial judge's de-emphasis of several important goals of criminal justice.

In view of the circumstances of this record, we think the sentence imposed is not well calculated to achieve the objective of reformation of the accused. Considering the apologetic tone of the sentencing proceedings, the court's endorsement of an extremely early parole, and the concurrent minimum sentences which were imposed for these three serious felonies, we fail to discern how the objective of reformation was effectuated. At most, Chaney was told that he was only technically guilty and minimally blameworthy, all of which minimized the possibility of appellee's comprehending the wrongfulness of his conduct.

We also think that the sentence imposed falls short of effectuating the goal of community condemnation, or the reaffirmation of societal norms for the purpose of maintaining respect for the norms themselves. In short, knowledge of the calculated circumstances involved in the commission of these felonies and the sentence imposed could lead to the conclusion that forcible rape and robbery are not reflective of serious antisocial conduct. Thus, respect for society's condemnation of forcible rape and robbery is eroded and reaffirmation of these societal norms negated. We also doubt whether the sentence in the case at bar mitigates the persistent problem of disparity in sentences. What is sought is reasonable differentiation among sentences.

We believe that a concurrent sentence calling for a substantially longer period of incarceration on each count was appropriate in light of the particular facts of this record and the goals of penal administration. A sentence of imprisonment for a substantially longer period of imprisonment than the one-year sentence which was imposed would unequivocally bring home to appellee the seriousness of his dangerously unlawful conduct, would reaffirm society's condemnation of forcible rape and robbery, and would provide the Division of Corrections of the State of Alaska with the opportunity of determining whether appellee required any special treatment prior to his return to society. Operation of our system of penal administration in Alaska is dependent upon a properly staffed and functioning Division of Corrections which has, in addition to probation and parole functions, the responsibility for treatment, rehabilitation, and custody of incarcerated offenders.

QUESTIONS

1. Summarize the trial judge's arguments for Donald Chaney's sentence.
2. Summarize the reasons the Alaska Supreme Court unanimously disapproved the sentence.
3. What sentence in your opinion would best further the purpose of retribution? Of rehabilitation? Back up your answer with information from the text and the court's opinion.
4. Does the trial court judge's sentence fit the two components of retribution—condemnation and hard treatment? Defend your answer with information in the text and in the court's opinion.

EXPLORING FURTHER

Punishment

Did the appeals court have the power to reduce the trial court's sentence?

State v. Pete, 420 P.2d 338 (Alaska 1966)

FACTS

Joseph Pete was found guilty by a jury of two counts involving the unlawful sale of intoxicating liquor. One count involved the sale of a 4/5 bottle of Gilbey's vodka to Edward N. Sigvayugak, and the other, the sale of a 4/5 bottle of Seagram's Seven Crown whiskey to the same person on the same day. The prosecuting witness, Edward N. Sigvayugak, had been engaged by a state police officer to buy liquor from Pete with money provided by the officer, and was paid for his services by the officer. The trial court convicted Pete on both counts, and sentenced him to two one-year sentences, to be served consecutively. Pete appealed, arguing that the sentence was unduly harsh. Did the appellate court have the power to reduce the sentence?

DECISION

Yes, answered the Alaska Supreme Court. The court held that consecutive sentences of one year each on two counts involving the unlawful sale of intoxicating liquor was excessive where the two offenses were part of one general transaction. Under the circumstances, the sentence would be modified to the term of imprisonment that Pete already served, approximately seventeen and one-half months. "In light of the fact that the two offenses were really part of one general transaction involving the unlawful sale of liquor, we believe the judgment of conviction should be modified so as to limit appellee's sentences to the term of imprisonment that he has now served" (338).

We'll come back to the subject of punishment later in this chapter, where we'll discuss its purposes more fully, and again in Chapter 2, where we'll discuss the constitutional ban on "cruel and unusual punishment." But here it's important to emphasize the intimate connection (often overlooked) between punishment and the meaning of crime itself.

Even on this important point of expression of condemnation backed up by punishment, the line between torts and crime can get blurred. In tort cases involving violence and other especially "wicked" circumstances, plaintiffs can recover not only compensatory damages for their actual injuries but also substantial punitive damages to make an example of defendants and to "punish" them for their "evil behavior" (Black 1983, 204).

Now that you've got some idea of what criminal wrongs are and how they differ from private wrongs, let's go inside criminal law to see how the law classifies crimes so we can make sense of the enormous range of behavior it covers.

LO 2

CLASSIFYING CRIMES

There are various ways to classify crimes, most of them with ancient roots. One scheme divides crimes into two categories: *mala in se* crimes and *mala prohibita* offenses.

mala in se **(inherently evil) crimes,** offenses that require some level of criminal intent

Mala in se **(inherently evil) crimes** require some level of criminal intent (discussed in Chapter 4). We don't need a law to tell us murder, rape, robbery, and stealing are crimes because they're inherently evil.

mala prohibita **offenses,** are crimes only because a specific statute or ordinance prohibits them

Mala prohibita **offenses** are crimes only because a specific statute or ordinance prohibits them. They include minor offenses, such as parking illegally, drinking in public, and the countless other minor offenses that don't require criminal intent, only a voluntary act (Chapter 3). Professor Wayne Logan (2001, 1409) calls them "the shadow criminal law of municipal governance." For a selection from Professor Logan's (1426–28) list, see the "Municipal Ordinances" section (p. 20).

felonies, crimes punishable by death or confinement in the state's prison for one year to life without parole

misdemeanors, offenses punishable by fine and/or confinement in the local jail for up to one year

The most widely used scheme for classifying crimes is according to the kind and quantity of punishment. **Felonies** are crimes punishable by death or confinement in the state's prison for one year to life without parole; **misdemeanors** are punishable by fine and/or confinement in the local jail for up to one year.

Notice the word "punishable"; the classification depends on the possible punishment, not the actual punishment. For example, Viki Rhodes pled guilty to "Driving under the Influence of Intoxicants, fourth offense," a felony. The trial court sentenced her to 120 days of home confinement. When she later argued she was a misdemeanant because of the home confinement sentence, the appeals court ruled that "a person whose felony sentence is reduced does not become a misdemeanant by virtue of the reduction but remains a felon" (*Commonwealth v. Rhodes* 1996, 532).

Why should the label "felony" or "misdemeanor" matter? One reason is the difference between procedure for felonies and misdemeanors. For example, felony defendants have to be in court for their trials; misdemeanor defendants don't. Also, prior felony convictions make offenders eligible for longer sentences. Another reason is that the legal consequences of felony convictions last after punishment. In many states, former felons can't vote, can't serve in public office, and can't be attorneys. Felony conviction also can be a ground for divorce. This isn't true of misdemeanor offenders.

Now, let's turn from the classifications of crimes to the two divisions of criminal law: the general and special parts.

THE GENERAL AND SPECIAL PARTS OF CRIMINAL LAW

LO 2

Criminal law consists of a general part and a special part. The general part of criminal law consists of principles that apply to more than one crime. Most state criminal codes today include a general part.

general part of criminal law, principles that apply to more than one crime

The special part of criminal law defines specific crimes and arranges them into groups according to subject matter. All states include the definitions of at least some specific crimes, and most group them according to subject matter.

special part of criminal law, defines specific crimes and arranges them into groups according to subject matter

The special part of criminal law is more than a classification scheme; it's part of the larger organizational structure of the whole criminal law and the one followed in this book. So we'll discuss the classification scheme in the context of the general and special parts of the criminal law.

THE GENERAL PART OF CRIMINAL LAW

The general principles of criminal law are broad propositions that apply to more than one crime. Some general principles (Chapters 3–8) apply to all crimes (for example, all crimes have to include a voluntary act); other principles apply to all felonies (for example, criminal intent).

In addition to the general principles in the general part of criminal law, there are two kinds of what we call "offenses of general applicability" (Dubber 2002, 142). The first is complicity, crimes that make one person criminally liable for someone else's conduct. There's no general crime of complicity; instead, there are the specific crimes of accomplice to murder; accomplice to robbery; or accomplice to any other crime for that matter (Chapter 7).

complicity, crimes that make one person criminally liable for someone else's conduct

Other crimes of general applicability are the crimes of attempt, conspiracy, and solicitation. There are no general crimes of attempt, conspiracy, or solicitation. Instead, there the specific crimes of attempting, conspiring, or solicitation to commit specific crimes, such as attempting to rape, conspiring to murder, or solicitation to sell illegal drugs.

Finally, the general part of criminal law includes the principles of justification (Chapter 5, self-defense) and excuse (Chapter 6, insanity), the principles that govern most defenses to criminal liability.

THE SPECIAL PART OF CRIMINAL LAW

The special part of criminal law (Chapters 9–13) defines specific crimes, according to the principles set out in the general part. The definitions of crimes are divided into four groups:

1. Crimes against persons (such as murder and rape, discussed in Chapters 9–10)
2. Crimes against property (stealing and trespass, discussed in Chapter 11)
3. Crimes against public order and morals (illegal immigration, gang crimes, aggressive panhandling, and prostitution, discussed in Chapter 12)
4. Crimes against the state (domestic and foreign terror, discussed in Chapter 13)

The definitions of specific crimes consist of the elements prosecutors have to prove beyond a reasonable doubt to convict defendants. From the standpoint of understanding how the general principles relate to specific crimes, every definition of a specific crime is an application of one or more general principles.

To show you how this works, let's look at an example from the Alabama criminal code. One section of the general part of the code reads, "A person is criminally liable for an offense [only] if it is committed by his own behavior" (Alabama Criminal Code 1975, ß 13A-2-20). This general principle of *criminal liability* (liability is the technical legal term for responsibility) is required in the definition of all crimes in Alabama.

In the special part of the Alabama Criminal Code, Chapter 7, "Offenses Involving Damage to and Intrusion upon Property," defines the crime of first-degree criminal trespass as, "A person is guilty of criminal trespass in the first degree if he . . . enters or remains unlawfully in a dwelling" (ß 13A-7-4). So the general principle of requiring behavior is satisfied by the acts of either entering or remaining.

Now, let's turn from the subject of classifying crimes to the sources of criminal law and where you're most likely to find them.

LO 3

THE SOURCES OF CRIMINAL LAW

Most criminal law is found in state criminal codes created by elected representatives in state legislatures and municipal codes created by city and town councils elected by the people. There's also a substantial body of criminal law in the U.S. criminal code created by Congress.

Sometimes, these elected bodies invite administrative agencies, whose members aren't elected by the people, to participate in creating criminal law. Legislatures weren't always the main source of criminal lawmaking. Judges' court opinions, not statutes or constitutions, were the original source of law. This judge-made law was called the **common law**.

common law, judge-made law, the original source of law, in which judge's court opinions formed the law

Let's look first at the crimes created by judges' opinions and then at the legislated criminal codes, including state and municipal codes and the Model Penal Code (MPC). Then, we'll look briefly at criminal lawmaking by administrative agencies.

COMMON LAW CRIMES

Criminal codes didn't spring full-grown from legislatures. They evolved from a long history of ancient offenses called **common law crimes.** These crimes were created before legislatures existed and when social order depended on obedience to unwritten rules (the *lex non scripta*) based on community customs and traditions. These traditions were passed on from generation to generation and modified from time to time to meet changed conditions. Eventually, they were incorporated into court decisions.

common law crimes, crimes created before legislatures existed and when social order depended on obedience to unwritten rules (the *lex non scripta*) based on community customs and traditions that over the centuries became incorporated into court decisions

The common law felonies still have familiar names and have maintained similar meanings (murder, manslaughter, burglary, arson, robbery, stealing, rape, and sodomy). The common law misdemeanors have familiar names too (assault, battery, false imprisonment, libel, perjury, corrupting morals, and disturbing the peace) (LaFave 2003a, 75).

Exactly how the common law began is a mystery, but like the traditions it incorporated, it grew and changed to meet new conditions. At first, its growth depended mainly on judicial decisions (Chapter 2). As legislatures became more established, they added crimes to the common law. They did so for a number of reasons: to clarify existing common law; to fill in blanks left by the common law; and to adjust the common law to new conditions. Judicial decisions interpreting the statutes became part of the growing body of precedent making up the common law. Let's look further at common law crimes at both the state and federal levels.

State Common Law Crimes

The English colonists brought this common law with them to the New World and incorporated the common law crimes into their legal systems. Following the American Revolution, the thirteen original states adopted the common law. Almost every state created after that enacted "reception statutes" that adopted the English common law.

For example, the Florida reception statute reads: "The Common Law of England in relation to crimes shall be of full force in this state where there is no existing provision by statute on the subject" (West's Florida Statutes Annotated 2005, Title XLVI, § 775.01).

Most states have abolished the common law crimes. But it isn't that easy to kill the common law. Several states still recognize the common law of crimes. Even in *code states* (states that have abolished the common law), the codes frequently use the names of the common law crimes without defining them. So to decide cases, the courts have to go to the common law definitions and interpretations of the crimes against persons, property, and public order and morals (Chapters 9–12); the common law of parties to crime (Chapter 7) and attempt, conspiracy, and solicitation (Chapter 8); and the common law defenses, such as self-defense and insanity (Chapters 5–6).

Take California for a good example. It's a code jurisdiction that includes all of the common law felonies in its criminal code (West's California Penal Code 1988, § 187(a)). The California Supreme Court relied on the common law to determine the meaning of its murder statute in *Keeler v. Superior Court* (1970; see Chapter 9, "When Does Life Begin?" section). Robert Keeler's wife Teresa was pregnant with another man's child. Robert kicked the pregnant Teresa in the stomach, causing her to abort the fetus. The California court had to decide whether fetuses were included in the murder statute. To do this, the court turned to the sixteenth-century common law, which defined a human being as "born alive." This excluded Teresa's fetus from the reach of the murder statute.

Federal Common Law Crimes

In *U.S. v. Hudson and Goodwin* (1812), the U.S. Supreme Court said there are no federal common law crimes. During the War of 1812, Hudson and Goodwin published the lie that President Madison and Congress had secretly voted to give $2 million to Napoleon. They were indicted for criminal libel. But there was a catch; there was no federal criminal libel statute. The Court ruled that without a statute, libel can't be a federal crime. Why? According to the Court:

> The courts of [the U.S.] are [not] vested with jurisdiction over any particular act done by an individual in supposed violation of the peace and dignity of the sovereign power. The legislative authority of the Union must first make an act a crime, affix a punishment to it, and declare the Court that shall have jurisdiction of the offence. Certain implied powers must necessarily result to our courts of justice from the nature of their institution. But jurisdiction of crimes against the state is not among those powers. (34)

The rule of *U.S. v. Hudson and Goodwin* seems perfectly clear: there's no federal criminal common law. But, like many other rules you'll learn in your study of criminal law, the reality is more complicated. It's more like:

> There is no federal criminal common law. But there is. . . . The shibboleth that there is no federal criminal common law—that Congress, not the courts, creates crimes—is simply wrong. There are federal common law crimes. (Rosenberg 2002, 202)

Here's what Associate U.S. Supreme Court Justice Stevens had to say about federal criminal common lawmaking:

> Statutes like the Sherman Act, the civil rights legislation, and the mail fraud statute were written in broad general language on the understanding that the courts would have wide latitude in construing them to achieve the remedial purposes that Congress had identified. The wide open spaces in statutes such as these are most appropriately interpreted as implicit delegations of authority to the courts to fill in the gaps in the common law tradition of case-by-case adjudication. (*McNally v. U.S.* 1987)

According to Professor Dan Kahan (1994), Congress has accepted the prominent role Justice Stevens ascribes to the federal courts in developing a "federal common law" in noncriminal subjects. Moreover, Kahan contends that Congress actually prefers "law-making collaboration" to a "lawmaking monopoly" (369). Judicial common criminal lawmaking can be a good thing when it punishes conduct "located not on the border but deep within the interior of what is socially undesirable" (400).

STATE CRIMINAL CODES

From time to time in U.S. history, reformers have called for the abolition of the common law crimes and their replacement with criminal codes created and defined by elected legislatures. The first criminal codes appeared in 1648, the work of the New England Puritans. The Laws and Liberties of Massachusetts **codified** (put into writing) the colony's criminal law, defining crimes and spelling out punishments.

codified, written definitions of crimes and punishment enacted by legislatures and published

John Winthrop, the author of the code, stated the case for a code this way: "So soon as God had set up political government among his people Israel he gave them a body of laws for judgment in civil and criminal causes. . . . For a commonwealth without laws is like a ship without rigging and steerage" (Farrand 1929, A2).

Some of the codified offenses sound odd today (witchcraft, cursing parents, blasphemy, and idolatry), but others—for example, rape—don't: "If any man shall ravish any maid or single woman, committing carnal copulation with her by force, against her own will, that is above ten years of age he shall be punished either with death or some other grievous punishment" (5).

Another familiar codified offense was murder: "If any man shall commit any willful murder, which is manslaughter, committed upon premeditated malice, hatred, or cruelty not in a man's necessary and just defense, nor by mere casualty against his will, he shall be put to death" (6).

Hostility to English institutions after the American Revolution spawned another call by reformers for written legislative codes to replace the English common law. The eighteenth-century Enlightenment, with its emphasis on reason and natural law, inspired reformers to put aside the piecemeal "irrational" common law scattered throughout judicial decisions and to replace it with criminal codes based on a natural law of crimes. Despite anti-British feelings, reformers still embraced Blackstone's *Commentaries* (1769) and hoped to transform his complete and orderly outline of criminal law into criminal codes.

Reformers contended judge-made law was not just disorderly and incomplete; it was antidemocratic. They believed legislatures representing the popular will should make laws, not aloof judges out of touch with public opinion. Thomas Jefferson proposed such a penal code for Virginia (Bond 1950). The proposed code never passed the Virginia legislature, not because it codified the law but because it recommended too many drastic reductions in criminal punishments (Preyer 1983, 53–85).

There was also a strong codification movement during the nineteenth century. Of the many nineteenth-century codes, two codes stand out. The first, the most ambitious, and least successful, was Edward Livingston's draft code for Louisiana, completed in 1826. Livingston's goal was to rationalize into one integrated system criminal law, criminal procedure, criminal evidence, and punishment. Livingston's draft never became law.

The second, David Dudley Field's code, was less ambitious but more successful. Field was a successful New York lawyer who wanted to make criminal law more accessible, particularly to lawyers. According to Professors Paul Robinson and Markus Dubber (2004):

> Field's codes were designed to simplify legal practice by sparing attorneys the tedium of having to sift through an ever rising mountain of common law. As a result, Field was more concerned with streamlining than he was with systematizing or even reforming New York penal law. (3)

Field's New York Penal Code was adopted in 1881 and remained in effect until 1967, when New York adopted most of the Model Penal Code (described next in "The Model Penal Code (MPC)" section).

The codification movement gathered renewed strength after the American Law Institute (ALI) decided to "tackle criminal law and procedure" (Dubber 2002, 8). ALI was founded by a group of distinguished jurists "to promote the clarification and simplification of the law and its better adaptation to social needs, to secure the better administration of justice, and to encourage and carry on scholarly and scientific legal work" (8). After its first look at criminal law and procedure in the United States, the prestigious group "was so appalled by what it saw that it decided that . . . what was needed was a fresh start in the form of model codes (8).

THE MODEL PENAL CODE (MPC)

The Great Depression and World War II stalled the development of a model penal code. But after the war, led by reform-minded judges, lawyers, and professors, ALI was committed to replacing the common law. From the earliest of thirteen drafts written during the 1950s to the final version in 1962, in the Model Penal Code (MPC), ALI (1985) made good on its commitment to draft a code that abolished common law crimes.

Model Penal Code (MPC), proposed criminal code drafted by the American Law Institute and used to reform criminal codes

Section 1.05, the first of its core provisions, provides: "No conduct constitutes an offense unless it is a crime or violation under this Code or another statute of this State" ([1], § 1.01 to 2.13).

After its adoption in 1962, more than forty states changed their criminal codes. None adopted the MPC completely; but criminal law in all states, not just states that rewrote their codes, felt its influence (Dubber 2002, 6). More than two thousand opinions from every state, the District of Columbia, and the federal courts have cited the MPC (7). Many of the case excerpts are from those two thousand. Moreover, this book follows the general structure and analysis of the MPC, because if you understand the MPC's structure and analysis, you'll understand criminal law itself. Although you'll encounter many variations of the MPC throughout the book, "If there is such a thing as a common denominator in American criminal law, it's the Model Penal Code" (Dubber 2002, 5). So let's look at an analysis of the MPC.

The structure of the MPC follows closely the description of "The General and Special Parts of Criminal Law" section, so we won't repeat it here. Here, we'll focus on the MPC's analysis of criminal liability—namely:

MPC's analysis of criminal liability, analysis of statutes and cases to determine what behavior deserves criminal punishment and its definition of criminal liability: "conduct that unjustifiably and inexcusably inflicts or threatens substantial harm to individual or public interests"

- How it analyzes statutes and cases to answer the question posed at the beginning of the chapter, "What behavior deserves criminal punishment?"
- The MPC's definition of criminal liability: "conduct that unjustifiably and inexcusably inflicts or threatens substantial harm to individual or public interests." (ALI 1985, MPC § 1.02(1)(a))

There you have, in a nutshell, the elements of criminal liability in the states and the federal government that we'll elaborate on and apply to the definitions of individual crimes throughout the book. Let's turn next to another source of criminal law: municipal ordinances.

MUNICIPAL ORDINANCES

City, town, and village governments enjoy broad powers to create criminal laws, a power local governments are enthusiastically using in today's atmosphere of "zero tolerance" for drugs, violence, public disorder, and other "quality of life" offenses that violate community standards of good manners in public (Chapter 12). Municipalities have a "chorus of advocates" among criminal law reformers who've helped cities write a "new generation" of their old vagrancy and loitering ordinances that "cleanse" them of prior objections that they're unconstitutional and discriminatory (Logan 2001, 1418).

Municipal criminal lawmaking isn't new; neither is the enthusiasm for it. In his provocative book *The People's Welfare*, historian William Novak (1996) convincingly documents the "powerful government tradition devoted in theory and practice to the vision of a well-regulated society" from 1787 to 1877:

> At the heart of the well-regulated society was a plethora of bylaws, ordinances, statutes, and common law restrictions regulating nearly every aspect of early American economy and society.... These laws—the work of mayors, common councils, state legislators, town and county officers, and powerful state and local judges ... taken together ... demonstrate the pervasiveness of regulation in early American versions of the good society: regulations for public safety and security; ... the policing of public space ... ; all-important restraints on public morals (establishing the social and cultural conditions of public order). (1–2)

Here's a sample from current ordinances collected by Professor Wayne Logan (2001):

> Pick-pocketing; disturbing the peace; shoplifting; urinating in public; disorderly conduct; disorderly assembly; unlawful restraint; obstruction of public space; harassment over the telephone; resisting arrest; obscenity; nude dancing; lewdness, public indecency, and indecent exposure; prostitution, pimping, or the operation of "bawdy" houses; gambling; graffiti and the materials associated with its inscription; littering; aggressive begging and panhandling; vandalism; trespass; automobile "cruising"; animal control nuisances; excessive noise; sale or possession of drug paraphernalia; simple drug possession; possession of weapons other than firearms; possession of basic firearms and assault-style firearms; discharge of firearms; sleeping, lying, or camping in public places; driving under the influence of drugs or alcohol; carrying an open container of alcohol; underage drinking; and public drinking and intoxication; vagrancy and loitering; curfews for minors; criminal assault and battery. (1426–28)

Municipal ordinances often duplicate and overlap state criminal code provisions. When they conflict, state criminal code provisions are supposed to trump municipal ordinances. A number of technical rules control whether they're in conflict, and we don't need to get into the details of these rules, but their gist is that unless state criminal codes make clear that they're preempting local ordinances, local ordinances remain in effect (*Chicago v. Roman* 1998).

In *Chicago v. Roman*, Edwin Roman attacked 60-year-old Anthony Pupius. He was convicted of the Chicago municipal offense of assault against the elderly and was sentenced to ten days of community service and one year of probation. However, the ordinance contained a mandatory minimum sentence of at least ninety days of incarceration. The city appealed, claiming that the sentence violated the mandatory minimum required by the ordinance. The Illinois Supreme Court overruled the trial court's decision. According to the court, the Illinois legislature can restrict Chicago's power to create crimes, but it has to pass a law specifically spelling out the limit. Because the legislature hadn't passed a law preempting the penalty for assaulting the elderly, Chicago's mandatory minimum had to stand.

The long list of ordinances Professor Logan found illustrates the broad power of municipalities to create local crimes. But, as the example of *Chicago v. Roman* indicates, the power of municipalities goes further than creating crimes; it includes the power to determine the punishment, too. They also have the power to enact forfeiture laws.

Under New York City's alcohol and other drug-impaired driver's law, thousands of impaired drivers have forfeited their vehicles (Fries 2001, B2). Another example: an Oakland, California, ordinance authorizes forfeiture of vehicles involved in "solicitation of prostitution or acquisition of controlled substances." The ordinance was passed after residents complained about individuals driving through their neighborhoods looking to buy drugs or hire prostitutes (*Horton v. City of Oakland* 2000, 372).

Don't get the idea from what you've just read that municipalities have unlimited powers to create crimes and prescribe punishments. They don't. We've already noted two limits—constitutional limits (which we'll discuss further in Chapters 2 and 12) and the power of states to preempt municipal criminal lawmaking and punishment. Municipalities also can't create felonies, and they can't prescribe punishments greater than one year in jail.

ADMINISTRATIVE AGENCY CRIMES

Both federal and state legislatures frequently grant administrative agencies the authority to make rules. One example is familiar to anyone who has to file a tax return. The U.S. Internal Revenue Service income tax regulations are based on the rule-making authority that Congress delegates to the IRS. Another example, this one from the state level: state legislatures commonly authorize the state highway patrol agencies to make rules regarding vehicle safety inspections. We call violations of these federal and state agency rules administrative crimes; they're a controversial but rapidly growing source of criminal law.

administrative crimes, violations of federal and state agency rules that make up a controversial but rapidly growing and source of criminal law

CRIMINAL LAW IN THE U.S. FEDERAL SYSTEM

Until now, we've referred to criminal law in the singular. That's inaccurate, and you'll see this inaccuracy repeated often in the rest of the book because it's convenient. But let's clear up the inaccuracy. In our federal system, there are fifty-two criminal codes, one for each of the fifty states, one for the District of Columbia, and one for the U.S. criminal code.

federal system, fifty-two criminal codes, one for each of the fifty states, one for the District of Columbia, and one for the U.S. criminal code

The U.S. government's power is limited to crimes specifically related to national interests, such as crimes committed on military bases and other national property; crimes against federal officers; and crimes that are difficult for one state to prosecute—for example, drug, weapons, organized and corporate crime, and crimes involving domestic and international terrorism (Chapter 13). The rest of criminal law, which is most of it, is left to the state codes. These are the crimes against persons, property, and public order and morals in the special part of the criminal law (Chapters 9–12).

So we have fifty-two criminal codes, each defining specific crimes and establishing general principles for the territory and people within it. And they don't, in practice, define specific crimes the same. For example, in some states, to commit a burglary, you have to actually break into and then enter a building. In other states, it's enough that you enter a building unlawfully, as in opening an unlocked door to a house the owners forgot to lock, intending to steal their new 3D TV inside. In still other states, all you have to do is stay inside a building you've entered lawfully—for example, hiding until after closing time in your college bookstore restroom during business hours, so you can steal your criminal law textbook and sneak out after the store closes (Chapter 11).

The defenses to crime also vary across state lines. In some states, insanity requires proof both that defendants didn't know what they were doing and that they didn't know it was wrong to do it. In other states, it's enough to prove either that defendants didn't know what they were doing or that they didn't know that it was wrong (Chapter 6). Some states permit individuals to use deadly force to protect their homes from intruders; others require proof that the occupants in the home were in danger of serious bodily harm or death before they can shoot intruders (Chapter 5).

Punishments also differ widely among the states. Several states prescribe death for some convicted murderers; others prescribe life imprisonment. Capital punishment states differ in how they execute murderers: by electrocution, lethal injection, the gas chamber, hanging, or even the firing squad. The death penalty is only the most dramatic example of different punishments. Less-dramatic examples affect far more people. For example, some states lock up individuals who possess small quantities of marijuana for private use; in other states, it's not a crime at all.

This diversity among the criminal codes makes it clear there's no single U.S. criminal code. But this diversity shouldn't obscure the broad outline that's common to all criminal laws in the United States. They're all based on the general principles of liability that we touched on earlier in this chapter and that you'll learn more in depth about in Chapters 3 through 6. They also include the defenses of justification and excuse, which you'll learn about in Chapters 5 and 6.

The definitions of the crimes you'll learn about in Chapters 9 through 12 differ more, so there we'll take account of the major differences. But even these definitions resemble one another more than they differ. For example, "murder" means killing someone on purpose; criminal sexual assault includes sexual penetration by force; "robbery" means taking someone's property by force or threat of force; "theft" means taking, and intending to keep permanently, someone else's property. And the crimes against the state (Chapter 13) and other crimes in the U.S. criminal code don't recognize state lines; they apply everywhere in the country.

Now, let's turn to the other big question in the big picture of American criminal law, the law of punishment.

LO 4

WHAT'S THE APPROPRIATE PUNISHMENT FOR CRIMINAL BEHAVIOR?

The United States has less than 5 percent of the world's population. But it has almost a quarter of the world's prisoners. Indeed, the United States leads the world in producing prisoners, a reflection of a relatively recent and now distinctive American approach to crime and punishment. Americans are locked up for crimes—from writing bad checks to using drugs—that would rarely produce prison sentences in other countries. And in particular they're kept locked up far longer than prisoners in other countries (Liptak 2008).

rates of imprisonment, measured by the numbers of prisoners per 100,000 people in the general population

Most telling are the rates of **imprisonment**, measured by the numbers of prisoners per 100,000 people in the general population. Here, too, the United States clearly leads the world (see Figure 1.1).

It's not just the numbers of prisoners and rates of imprisonment that stand out. Gender, age, race, and ethnicity aren't equally represented in the prisoner population. Black men are imprisoned at the highest rate, 6.5 times higher than White men, and 2.5 times higher than Hispanic men. Similarly, the imprisonment rate for Black women is nearly double the imprisonment rates for Hispanic women and three times the rate for White women (West and Sabol 2009, 4). With all the attention imprisonment deservedly receives, you should keep in mind that there are millions more Americans on probation and parole and other forms of "community corrections" than are locked up in prisons and jails. Also, a few convicted offenders are executed (Chapter 2).

FIGURE 1.1

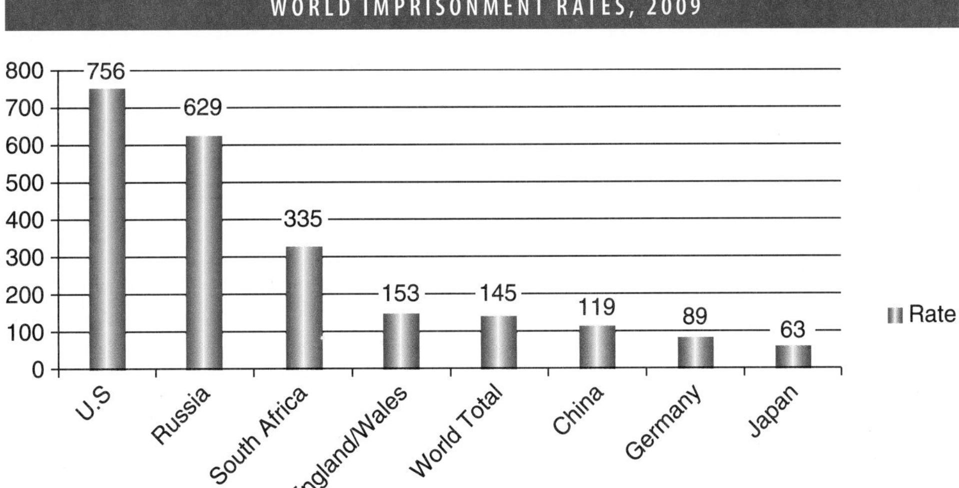

Source: Walmsley 2009.

These numbers tell us the quantity of punishment, which we should surely acknowledge and accept—that for good or ill—it's probably not going to change any time soon. But the quantity of punishment doesn't tell us anything about other essential aspects of punishment:

- It doesn't define "punishment" as we use it in criminal law.
- It doesn't explain the purposes of (also called justifications for) criminal punishment.
- It doesn't tell us what the limits of criminal punishment are. (You'll learn about the limits of punishment in Chapter 2 in the sections on the U.S. Constitution's Eighth Amendment ban on "cruel and unusual punishments," the Sixth Amendment's "right to trial by jury," and the due process requirement of proof beyond a reasonable doubt.)
- It doesn't tell us about the social and cultural reality of punishment, such as the geography (rural, urban, and suburban), demography (class, race, ethnicity, age, gender, and education), and culture of punishment.

Let's turn now to the definition of, and the justifications for, "punishment."

THE DEFINITION OF "CRIMINAL PUNISHMENT"

In everyday life, **punishment** means intentionally inflicting pain or other unpleasant consequences on another person. Punishment takes many forms in everyday life. A parent grounds a teenager; a club expels a member; a church excommunicates a parishioner; a friend rejects a companion; a school expels a student for cheating—all these are punishments in the sense that they intentionally inflict pain or other unpleasant consequences ("hard treatment") on the recipient.

punishment, intentionally inflicting pain or other unpleasant consequences on another person

However, none of these is criminal punishment. To qualify as **criminal punishment,** penalties have to meet four criteria:

criminal punishment, penalties that meet four criteria: (1) inflict pain or other unpleasant consequences; (2) prescribe a punishment in the same law that defines the crime; (3) administered intentionally; (4) administered by the state

1. They have to inflict pain or other unpleasant consequences.
2. They have to prescribe a punishment in the same law that defines the crime.
3. They have to be administered intentionally.
4. The state has to administer them.

The last three criteria don't need explanation; the first does. "Pain or other unpleasant consequences" is broad and vague. It doesn't tell us what kind of, or how much, pain. A violent mental patient confined indefinitely to a padded cell in a state security hospital suffers more pain than a person incarcerated for five days in the county jail for disorderly conduct. Nevertheless, only the jail sentence is criminal punishment. The difference lies in the purpose of the confinement. Hospitalization aims to treat and cure the mental patient; the pain is a necessary but unwanted side effect, not the reason for the confinement. On the other hand, the pain of confinement in the jail is inflicted intentionally to punish the inmate's disorderly conduct.

This distinction between criminal punishment and treatment is rarely clear-cut. For example, the government may sentence certain convicted criminals to confinement in maximum-security hospitals; it may sentence others to prison for "treatment" and "cure." Furthermore, pain and pleasure don't always distinguish punishment from treatment. Shock treatment and padded cells inflict more pain than confinement in some minimum-security federal prisons with their "country club" atmospheres. When measured by pain, those who receive it may well prefer punishment to treatment. Some critics maintain that the major shortcoming of treatment is that "helping" a patient can lead to excessive measures, as it sometimes has, in such examples as massive surgery, castration, and lobotomy (Hart 1958, 403–5).

LO 4

THE PURPOSES OF CRIMINAL PUNISHMENT

Thinking about the purposes of criminal punishment has divided roughly into two schools that have battled for five centuries, maybe even for millennia. Those on the **retribution** side of the divide, retributionists, insist that offenders can only pay for their crimes by experiencing the actual physical and psychological pain ("hard treatment") of having punishment inflicted on them. In other words, punishment justifies itself. Those on the **prevention** side of the divide, utilitarians, insist with equal passion that the pain of punishment can—and should—be only a means to a greater good, usually the prevention or at least the reduction of future crime. Let's look at each of these schools.

retribution, inflicting on offenders physical and psychological pain ("hard treatment") so that they can pay for their crimes

prevention, punishment is only a means to a greater good, usually the prevention or at least the reduction of future crime

Retribution

Striking out to hurt what hurts us is a basic human impulse. It's what makes us kick the table leg we stub our toe on. This impulse captures the idea of retribution, which appears in the texts of many religions. Here's the Old Testament version:

> Now a man, when he strikes down any human life, he is put to death, yes death! And a man, when he renders a defect in his fellow, as he has done, thus is to be done to him—break in place of break, eye in place of eye, tooth in place of tooth. (Fox 1995, translating Leviticus 24:17, 19–20)

Of course, we don't practice this extreme form of payback in the United States, except for murder—and, even for murder, the death penalty is rarely imposed (Chapter 2). In other cases, the Old Testament version of retribution is unacceptable to most retributionists; it's also highly unrealistic: raping a rapist? robbing a robber? burning down an arsonist's house?

Retribution looks back to past crimes and punishes individuals for committing them, because it's right to hurt them. According to the great Victorian English judge and historian of the criminal law Sir James F. Stephen (1883), the wicked deserve to suffer for their evil deeds:

> The infliction of punishment by law gives definite expression and a solemn ratification and justification to the hatred, which is excited by the commission of the offense. The

> criminal law thus proceeds upon the principle that it is morally right to hate criminals, and it confirms and justifies that sentiment by inflicting on criminals punishments, which express it. I think it highly desirable that criminals should be hated, that the punishments inflicted upon them should be so contrived as to give expression to that hatred. . . . The forms in which deliberate anger and righteous disapprobation are expressed, and the execution of criminal justice is the most emphatic of such forms. . . . (81–82)

Retributionists contend that punishment benefits not only society, as Stephen emphasized, but also criminals. Just as society feels satisfied by "paying back" criminals, giving criminals their "just deserts," offenders benefit by putting right their evil. Society pays back criminals by retaliation; criminals pay back society by accepting responsibility through punishment. Both paybacks are at the heart of retribution.

But retribution is right only if offenders choose between committing and not committing crimes. In other words, we can blame criminals only if they had these choices and made the wrong choice. So in the popular "Do the crime, do the time," what we really mean is, "You chose to do the crime, so you have to do the time." Their wrong choice makes them blameworthy. And their blameworthiness (the criminal law calls it their "culpability") makes them responsible (the criminal law calls it "liable"). So as culpable, responsible individuals, they have to suffer the consequences of their irresponsible behavior.

Retribution has several appealing qualities. It assumes free will, thereby enhancing individual autonomy. Individuals who have the power to determine their own destinies aren't at the mercy of forces they can't control. Retribution also seems to accord with human nature. Hating and hurting wrongdoers—especially murderers, rapists, robbers, and other violent criminals—appear to be natural impulses (Gaylin 1982; Wilson and Herrnstein 1985, ch. 19).

Retribution's ancient pedigree also has its appeal. From the Old Testament's philosophy of taking an eye for an eye, to the nineteenth-century Englishman's claim that it's right to hate and hurt criminals, to today's "three strikes and you're out" and "do the crime, do the time" sentences (Chapter 2), the desire for retribution has run strong and deep in both religion and criminal justice. Its sheer tenacity seems to validate retribution.

Retributionists, however, claim that retribution rests not simply on long use but also on two firm philosophical foundations, namely, culpability and justice. According to its proponents, retribution requires **culpability**. Only someone who intends to harm her victim deserves punishment; accidents don't qualify. So people who load, aim, and fire guns into their enemies' chests deserve punishment; hunters who fire at what they think is a deer and hit their companions who they should know are in the line of fire, don't. Civil law can deal with careless people; the criminal law ought to punish only people who harm their victims "on purpose."

culpability, only someone who intends to harm her victim deserves punishment; accidents don't qualify

Retributionists also claim that **justice** is the only proper measure of punishment. Justice is a philosophical concept whose application depends on culpability. Culpability depends on blame; we can punish only those whom we can blame; we can blame only those who freely choose, and intend, to harm their victims. Therefore, only those who deserve punishment can justly receive it; if they don't deserve it, it's unjust. Similarly, justice is the only criterion by which to determine the quality and quantity of punishment (see "Disproportionate Punishments," in Chapter 2).

justice, depends on culpability; only those who deserve punishment can justly receive it

Opponents find much to criticize in retribution. First, it's difficult to translate abstract justice into concrete penalties. What are a rapist's just deserts? Is castration for a convicted rapist justice? How many years in prison is a robbery worth? How much offender suffering will repay the pain of a maimed aggravated assault victim? Of course, it's impossible to match exactly the pain of punishment and the suffering caused by the crime.

Another criticism is that the urge to retaliate isn't part of human nature in a civilized society; it's the last remnant of barbarism. Retributionists can only *assume* that human nature cries out for vengeance; they can't *prove* it. So it's time for the law to reject retribution as a purpose for punishment.

Determinists, which include many criminologists, reject the free-will assumption underlying retribution (Mayer and Wheeler 1982; Wilson and Herrnstein 1985). They maintain that forces beyond human control determine individual behavior. Social scientists have shown the relationship between social conditions and crime. Psychiatrists point to subconscious forces beyond the conscious will's control that determine criminal conduct. A few biologists have linked violent crime to biological and biochemical abnormalities. Determinism undermines the theory of retribution because it rejects blame, and punishment without blame is unjust.

general deterrence, aims, by the threat of punishment, to prevent the general population who haven't committed crimes from doing so

special deterrence, aims, by punishing already convicted offenders, to prevent them from committing any more crimes in the future

incapacitation, prevents convicted criminals from committing future crimes by locking them up, or more rarely, by altering them surgically or executing them

rehabilitation, aims to prevent future crimes by changing individual offenders so they'll want to play by the rules and won't commit any more crimes in the future

Probably the strongest argument against retribution is the vast number of crimes that don't require culpability to qualify for criminal punishment (Diamond 1996, 34). This includes almost all the crimes against public order and morals (mentioned earlier and discussed in Chapter 12). It includes some serious crimes, too—for example, statutory rape—where neither the consent of the victim nor an honest and reasonable mistake about the victim's age relieves statutory rapists from criminal liability (discussed in Chapter 10)—and several kinds of unintentional homicides (discussed in Chapters 4 and 9).

Prevention

Prevention looks forward and inflicts pain, not for its own sake, but to prevent (or at least reduce) future crimes. There are four kinds of prevention:

1. **General deterrence** aims, by the threat of punishment, to prevent the general population who haven't committed crimes from doing so.
2. **Special deterrence** aims, by punishing already convicted offenders, to prevent them from committing any more crimes in the future.
3. **Incapacitation** prevents convicted criminals from committing future crimes by locking them up, or more rarely, by altering them surgically or executing them.
4. **Rehabilitation** aims to prevent future crimes by changing individual offenders so they'll want to play by the rules and won't commit any more crimes in the future.

hedonism, the natural law that human beings seek pleasure and avoid pain

rationalism, the natural law that individuals can act to maximize pleasure and minimize pain, permitting human beings to apply natural laws *mechanistically* (according to rules) instead of having to rely on the discretionary judgment of individual decision makers

deterrence theory, rational human beings won't commit crimes if they know that the pain of punishment outweighs the pleasure gained from committing crimes

As you can see, all four forms of prevention inflict pain, not for its own sake, but to secure the higher good of preventing future crimes. Let's look at each of these forms of prevention.

DETERRENCE Jeremy Bentham, an eighteenth-century English law reformer, promoted deterrence. Bentham was part of the intellectual movement called "the Enlightenment." At the Enlightment's core was the notion that natural laws govern the physical universe and, by analogy, human society. One of these "laws," **hedonism**, is that human beings seek pleasure and avoid pain.

A related law, **rationalism**, states that individuals can, and ordinarily do, act to maximize pleasure and minimize pain. Rationalism permits human beings to apply natural laws *mechanistically* (according to rules) instead of having to rely on the discretionary judgment of individual decision makers.

These ideas, oversimplified here, led Bentham to formulate classical **deterrence theory**. According to the theory, rational human beings won't commit crimes if they know that the pain of punishment outweighs the pleasure gained from committing crimes.

Prospective criminals weigh the pleasure they hope to get from committing a crime now against the threat of pain they believe they'll get from future punishment. According to the natural law of hedonism, if prospective criminals fear future punishment more than they derive pleasure from present crime, they won't commit crimes. In short, they're deterred.

Supporters of deterrence argue that the principle of utility—permitting only the minimum amount of pain necessary to prevent the crime—limits criminal punishment more than retribution does.

principle of utility, permits only the minimum amount of pain necessary to prevent the crime

English playwright George Bernard Shaw, a strong deterrence supporter, put it this way: "Vengeance is mine saith the Lord; which means it is not the Lord Chief Justice's" (Morris 1974). According to this argument, only God, the angels, or some other divine being can measure just deserts. Social scientists, on the other hand, can determine how much pain, or threat of pain, deters crime. With this knowledge, the state can scientifically inflict the minimum pain needed to produce the maximum crime reduction.

Deterrence supporters concede that there are impediments to putting deterrence into operation. The emotionalism surrounding punishment impairs objectivity, and often, prescribed penalties rest more on faith than evidence. For example, the economist Isaac Ehrlich's (1975) sophisticated econometric study showed that every execution under capital punishment laws may have saved seven or eight lives by deterring potential murderers. His finding sparked a controversy having little to do with the study's empirical validity. Instead, the arguments turned to ethics—whether killing anyone is right, no matter what social benefits it produces. During the controversy over the study, one thoughtful state legislator told me that he didn't "believe" the findings, but if they were true, then "we'll just have to deep-six the study."

Critics find several faults with deterrence theory and its application to criminal punishment. According to the critics, the rational, free-will individual that deterrence supporters assumes exists is as far from reality as the eighteenth-century world that spawned the idea. Complex forces within the human organism and in the external environment, both of which are beyond individual control, strongly influence behavior (Wilson and Herrnstein 1985).

Furthermore, critics maintain that individuals and their behavior are too unpredictable to reduce to a mechanistic formula. For some people, the existence of criminal law is enough to deter them from committing crimes; others require more. Who these others are and what the "more" consists of hasn't been sufficiently determined to base punishment on deterrence. Besides, severity isn't the only influence on the effectiveness of punishment. Certainty and speed may have greater deterrent effects than severity (Andenæs 1983, 2:593).

Also, threats don't affect all crimes or potential criminals equally. Crimes of passion, such as murder and rape, are probably little affected by threats; speeding, drunk driving, and corporate crime are probably greatly affected by threats. The leading deterrence theorist, Johannes Andenæs (1983), sums up the state of our knowledge about deterrence this way:

> There is a long way to go before research can provide quantitative forecasts. The long-term moral effects (both good and evil) of the criminal law and law enforcement are especially hard to isolate and quantify. Some categories of crime are so intimately related to specific social situations that generalizations of a quantitative kind are impossible. An inescapable fact is that research will always lag behind actual developments. When new forms of crime come into existence, such as hijacking of aircraft or terrorist acts against officers of the law, there cannot possibly be a body of research ready as a basis for the decisions that have to be taken. Common sense and trial by error have to give the answers. (2:596)

Finally, critics maintain that even if we could obtain empirical support for criminal punishment, deterrence is unjust because it punishes for example's sake. Supreme Court Justice Oliver Wendell Holmes (Howe 1953) offered this analogy: If I were having a philosophical talk with a man I was going to have hanged (or electrocuted) I should say, "I don't doubt that your act was inevitable for you but to make it more avoidable by others we propose to sacrifice you to the common good. You may regard yourself as a soldier dying for your country if you like. But the law must keep its promises" (806).

Punishment shouldn't be a sacrifice to the common good; it's only just if it's administered for the redemption of particular individuals, say the retributionists. Punishment is personal and individual, not general and societal. Deterrence proponents respond that as long as offenders are in fact guilty, punishing them is personal; hence, it is just to use individual punishment for society's benefit.

INCAPACITATION *Incapacitation* restrains convicted offenders from committing further crimes. At the extreme, incapacitation includes mutilation—castration, amputation, and lobotomy—or even death in capital punishment. Incapacitation in most cases means imprisonment. Incapacitation works: dead people can't commit crimes, and prisoners don't commit them—at least not outside prison walls. Incapacitation, then, has a lot to offer a society determined to repress crime. According to criminologist James Q. Wilson (1975):

> The chances of a persistent robber or burglar living out his life, or even going a year with no arrest, are quite small. Yet a large proportion of repeat offenders suffer little or no loss of freedom. Whether or not one believes that such penalties, if inflicted, would act as a deterrent, it is obvious that they could serve to incapacitate these offenders and, thus, for the period of the incapacitation, prevent them from committing additional crimes. (209)

Like deterrence and retribution, incapacitation has its share of critics. They argue that incapacitation merely shifts criminality from outside prisons to inside prisons. Sex offenders and other violent criminals can and do still find victims among other prisoners; property offenders trade contraband and other smuggled items. As you might imagine, this criticism finds little sympathy (at least among many of my students, who often answer this criticism with an emphatic, "Better them than me"). Of course, because almost all prisoners "come home," their incapacitation is always temporary.

REHABILITATION In his widely and rightly acclaimed book *The Limits of the Criminal Sanction*, Herbert Packer (1968) succinctly summarized the aims of rehabilitation: "The most immediately appealing justification for punishment is the claim that it may be used to prevent crimes by so changing the personality of the offender that he will conform to the dictates of law; in a word, by reforming him" (50).

medical model of criminal law, crime is a "disease," and criminals are "sick" in need of "treatment" and "cure

Rehabilitation borrows from the "**medical model" of criminal law**. In this model, crime is a "disease," and criminals are "sick" in need of "treatment" and "cure." According to rehabilitationists, the purpose of punishment is to "cure" criminal patients by "treatment." The length of imprisonment depends on how long it takes to cure the patient. Supporters contend that treating offenders is more humane than punishing them.

determinism, forces beyond offenders' control cause them to commit crimes

Two assumptions underlie rehabilitation theory. The first is **determinism**; that is, forces beyond offenders' control cause them to commit crimes. Because offenders don't choose to commit crimes, we can't blame them for committing them.

Second, therapy by experts can change offenders (not just their behavior) so that they won't want to commit any more crimes. After rehabilitation, former criminals will control their own destinies. To this extent, rehabilitationists adopt the idea of free will and its consequences: criminals can choose to change their life habits; so society can blame and punish them.

The view that criminals are sick has profoundly affected criminal law—and generated acrimonious debate. The reason isn't because reform and rehabilitation are new ideas; quite the contrary is true. Victorian Sir Francis Palgrave summed up a seven-hundred-year-old attitude when he stated the medieval church's position on punishment: it was not to be "thundered in vengeance for the satisfaction of the state, but imposed for the good of the offender; in order to afford the means of amendment and to lead the transgressor to repentance, and to mercy." Sixteenth-century Elizabethan pardon statutes were laced with the language of repentance and reform; the queen hoped to achieve a reduction in crime by mercy rather than by vengeance. Even Jeremy Bentham, most closely associated with deterrence, claimed that punishment would "contribute to the reformation of the offender, not only through fear of being punished again, but by a change in his character and habits" (Samaha 1978, 763).

Despite this long history, rehabilitation has suffered serious attacks. First, and most fundamental, critics maintain that rehabilitation is based on false, or at least unproven, assumptions. The causes of crime are so complex, and the wellsprings of human behavior as yet so undetermined, that sound policy can't depend on treatment. Second, it makes no sense to brand everyone who violates the criminal law as sick and needing treatment (Schwartz 1983, 1364–73).

Third, critics call rehabilitation inhumane because the cure justifies administering large doses of pain. British literary critic C. S. Lewis (1953) argued:

> My contention is that good men (not bad men) consistently acting upon that position would act as cruelly and unjustly as the greatest tyrants. They might in some respects act even worse. Of all tyrannies a tyranny sincerely exercised for the good of its victims may be the most oppressive. It may be better to live under robber barons than under omnipotent moral busybodies.
>
> The robber baron's cruelty may sometimes sleep, his cupidity may at some point be satiated; but those who torment us for our own good, will torment us without end for they do so with the approval of their own conscience. They may be more likely to go to Heaven yet at the same time likelier to make a Hell of earth.
>
> Their very kindness stings with intolerable insult. To be "cured" against one's will and cured of states which we may not regard as disease is to be put on a level with those who have not yet reached the age of reason or those who never will; to be classed with infants, imbeciles, and domestic animals. But to be punished, however severely, because we have deserved it, because we "ought to have known better," is to be treated as a human person made in God's image. (224)

TRENDS IN PUNISHMENT

Historically, societies have justified punishment on the grounds of retribution, deterrence, incapacitation, and rehabilitation. But the weight given to each has shifted over the centuries. Retribution and rehabilitation, for example, run deep in English criminal law from at least the year 1200. The church's emphasis on atoning for sins and rehabilitating sinners affected criminal law variously. Sometimes, the aims of punishment and reformation conflict in practice.

In Elizabethan England, for example, the letter of the law was retributive: the penalty for all major crimes was death. Estimates show that in practice, however, most accused persons never suffered this extreme penalty. Although some escaped death because they were innocent, many were set free because of their chances for rehabilitation. The law's technicalities, for example, made death a virtually impossible penalty for first-time property offenders. In addition, the queen's general pardon, issued almost annually, gave blanket clemency in the hope that criminals, by this act of mercy, would reform their erring ways (Samaha 1974, 1978).

Gradually, retribution came to dominate penal policy, until the eighteenth century, when deterrence and incapacitation were introduced to replace what contemporary humanitarian reformers considered ineffective, brutal, and barbaric punishment in the name of retribution. By 1900, humanitarian reformers had concluded that deterrence was neither effective nor humane. Rehabilitation replaced deterrence as the aim of criminal sanctions and remained the dominant form of criminal punishment until the 1960s. Most states enacted indeterminate sentencing laws that made prison release dependent on the rehabilitation of individual prisoners.

indeterminate sentencing laws, prison release depends on the rehabilitation of individual prisoners

Most prisons created treatment programs intended to reform criminals so they could become law-abiding citizens. Nevertheless, considerable evidence indicates that rehabilitation never really won the hearts of most criminal justice professionals, despite their strong public rhetoric to the contrary (Rothman 1980).

In the early 1970s, there was little convincing evidence to show that rehabilitation programs reformed offenders. The "nothing works" theme dominated reform discussions, prompted by a highly touted, widely publicized, and largely negative study evaluating the effectiveness of treatment programs (Martinson 1974). At the same time that academics and policy makers were becoming disillusioned with rehabilitation, public opinion was hardening into demands for severe penalties in the face of steeply rising crime rates. The time was clearly ripe for retribution to return to the fore as a dominant aim of punishment.

In 1976, California, a rehabilitation pioneer in the early 1900s, reflected this shift in attitude. In its Uniform Determinate Sentencing Law, the California legislature abolished the indeterminate sentence, stating boldly that "the purpose of imprisonment is punishment," not treatment or rehabilitation. Called "just deserts," retribution was touted as "right" by conservatives who believed in punishment's morality and as "humane" by liberals convinced that rehabilitation was cruel and excessive. Public opinion supported it, largely on the grounds that criminals deserve to be punished (Feeley 1983, 139). The new philosophy (actually the return to an old philosophy) replaced the indeterminate sentence with fixed (determinate) sentences, in which the sentence depends on the criminal harm suffered by the victim, not the rehabilitation of the offender.

fixed (determinate) sentences, sentence depends on the criminal harm suffered by the victim, not the rehabilitation of the offender

Since the mid-1980s, reformers have championed retribution and incapacitation as the primary purpose of criminal punishments. The Model Penal Code (p. 19) clung to prevention, namely, in the form of rehabilitation from its first version in 1961, when rehabilitation dominated penal policy. After thoroughly reviewing current research and debate, its reporters decided to retain rehabilitation but to replace it as the primary form of punishment with incapacitation and deterrence (ALI 2007). According to the new provisions, the purpose of sentencing is retribution—namely, to impose sentences "within a range of severity proportionate to the gravity of offenses, the harms done to crime victims, and the blameworthiness of offenders. . . ."

presumption of innocence, which means that the prosecution has the burden of proof when it comes to proving the criminal act and intent

burden of proof, to have to prove beyond a reasonable doubt "every fact necessary to constitute the crime charged"

And only "when reasonably feasible, to achieve offender rehabilitation, general deterrence, incapacitation of dangerous offenders, restoration of crime victims and communities, and reintegration of offenders into the law-abiding community, provided these goals are pursued within the boundaries of proportionality" . . . (1).

Before the government can punish criminal behavior—however it's defined and classified and whatever source it's derived from—the government has to prove that the defendant committed the crime. Let's turn now to some of the basics of proving defendants are guilty.

LO 5

THE PRESUMPTION OF INNOCENCE AND PROVING CRIMINAL LIABILITY

Under our legal system, criminal defendants enjoy the presumption of innocence, which means that the prosecution has the burden of proof when it comes to proving the criminal act and intent. The burden of proof means the government has to prove beyond a reasonable doubt, "every fact necessary to constitute the crime charged" (*In re Winship* 1970, 363).

Criminal conduct is defined as voluntary criminal acts triggered by criminal intent. As you learned earlier in the chapter (p. 5), proving criminal conduct is *necessary* to impose criminal liability and punishment. But it's not enough. The criminal conduct must be without justification or excuse. Here, the burden of proof can shift from the prosecution to the defense. Let's look at the burden of proof of criminal conduct and the burden of proof in justification and excuse defenses.

criminal conduct, voluntary criminal acts triggered by criminal intent

THE BURDEN OF PROOF OF CRIMINAL CONDUCT

LO 5

According to the U.S. Supreme Court (*In re Winship* 1970), the government has the burden of proof of criminal conduct. Proof beyond a reasonable doubt is the highest standard of proof known to the law. Notice that highest doesn't mean beyond all doubt or to the level of absolute certainty. "A reasonable doubt is an actual and substantial doubt, [not] a doubt arising from mere possibility, from bare imagination, or from fanciful conjecture" (*Victor v. Nebraska* 1994, 20).

The great Victorian Massachusetts judge Lemuel Shaw (1850) wrote this about trying to define reasonable doubt:

> Reasonable doubt is a term often used, probably pretty well understood, but not easily defined. It is not a mere possible doubt; because every thing relating to human affairs . . . is open to some possible or imaginary doubt. It is that state of the case, which after all the comparison and consideration of the evidence, leaves the minds of the jury in that condition that they cannot say they feel an abiding conviction, to a moral certainty, of the truth of the charge. (320)

Judge Shaw refers to proving guilt to juries, whom we usually associate with trials. But not all trials are jury trials. In bench trials, the accused give up their right to a jury trial and are tried by judges who decide whether prosecutors have proved their guilt.

We need to clear up an often-misunderstood and wrongly used term related to the proof of criminal behavior: corpus delicti (Latin for "body of the crime"). The misunderstanding arises from associating the term only with the body of the victim in homicides. However, it also properly applies to the elements of criminal conduct (for example, stealing someone's property in theft; Chapters 3 and 4) and bad result crimes (for example, criminal homicide; Chapters 9–13).

proof beyond a reasonable doubt, evidence that removes an actual and substantial doubt about the defendant's guilt

reasonable doubt, a real and substantial uncertainty about guilt, an uncertainty that would cause a reasonable person to hesitate before acting on an important matter

bench trials, cases where the accused give up their right to a jury trial and are tried by judges who decide whether prosecutors have proved their guilt

corpus delicti, Latin for "body of the crime," it refers to the body of the victim in homicides and to the elements of the crime in other offenses

PROVING THE DEFENSES OF JUSTIFICATION AND EXCUSE

The defenses of justification (Chapter 5) and of excuse (Chapter 6) are called affirmative defenses because defendants have to present evidence. Affirmative defenses operate like this: Defendants have to "start matters off by putting in some evidence in support" of their justification or excuse (LaFave and Scott 1986).

We call this the burden of production. Why put this burden on defendants? Because "We can assume that those who commit crimes are sane, sober, conscious, and acting freely. It makes sense, therefore, to make defendants responsible for injecting these extraordinary circumstances into the proceedings" (52).

The amount of evidence required "is not great; some credible evidence" is enough. In some jurisdictions, if defendants meet the burden of production, they also have the burden of persuasion (see p. 32), meaning they have to prove their defenses by a preponderance of the evidence (see p. 32), defined as more than 50 percent. In other jurisdictions, once defendants meet the burden of production, the burden shifts to the government to prove defendants weren't justified or excused (Loewy 1987, 192–204).

affirmative defenses, defendants have to "start matters off by putting in some evidence in support" of their defenses of justification and excuse

burden of production, to make defendants responsible for presenting evidence in their own justification or excuse defense

FIGURE 1.2 A LAW ENFORCEMENT REPORT FORM

Plymouth Police Department
3400 Plymouth Blvd. • Plumouth, MN 55447
(763) 509-5160
fax: (763) 509-5167

PLYMOUTH POLICE MINNESOTA

Type	MOC

No.

	Date			
Reported	call	asn	arr	clr
Location				
Occurred	date	time	SAA	
Badge no.	report	assist		

Person 1 ☐ Complainant ☐ Victim ☐ Witness ☐ Mentioned

Name (last, first, middle)		DOB	☐ M ☐ F Sex
Address	home phone	work phone	
City, state, zip	school	misc/insurance	
Driver's license	☐ White ☐ African Am ☐ Am Indian ☐ Hispanic ☐ Asian race ☐ Other		
misc/parents/work			

Person 2 ☐ Complainant ☐ Victim ☐ Witness ☐ Mentioned

Name (last, first, middle)		DOB	☐ M ☐ F Sex
address	home phone	work phone	
city, state, zip	school	misc/insurance	
driver's license	☐ White ☐ African Am ☐ Am Indian ☐ Hispanic ☐ Asian race ☐ Other		
misc/parents/work			

☐ **Additional names/vehicle supplement attached**

Patrol Investigation ☐ video tape ☐ audio tape (statement or evidence)
☐ solvability factors ☐ photos taken ☐ forced entry ☐ domestic/vic info **victim will prosecute** **SFD**
☐ written statement ☐ prints lifted ☐ attached garage ☐ none ☐ yes ☐ no ☐

Narrative

☐ Continued

Disposition ☐ pending ☐ clear arrest Patrol supervisor Inv Supervisor Inv assigned Entry
☐ assist and advised ☐ clear exceptionally
☐ unfounded

Source: Hess, Kären M. and Orthmann, Christine Hess. "Police Report." In *Criminal Investigation,* 9th edition, 76–77. Delmar: Cengage Learning, 2010.

burden of persuasion, defendants have to prove their justification or excuse defenses by a preponderance of the evidence

preponderance of the evidence, more than 50 percent of the evidence proves justification or excuse

All that you've learned up to now, valuable as it is, neglects an entire dimension to criminal law and punishment—informal discretionary decision making hidden from view. Let's look briefly at this enormously important dimension.

DISCRETIONARY DECISION MAKING

LO 6

Most of what you'll learn in this book focuses on decisions made according to formal law—namely, rules written and published in the Constitution, laws, judicial opinions, and other written sources. But you can't really understand what's happening in your journey through criminal law and punishment without understanding something about decision making that's not visible in the written sources. This invisible informal discretionary decision making—consisting of judgments made by professionals, based on unwritten rules, their training, and their experience—is how the process works on a day-to-day basis.

informal discretionary decision making, the invisible day-to-day process, in which law enforcement professionals make judgments based on unwritten rules, their training, and their experience

Think of each step in the criminal process as a decision point. Each step presents a criminal justice professional with the opportunity to decide whether or not to start, continue, or end the criminal process. The police can investigate suspects, or not, and arrest them, or not—initiating the formal criminal process, or stopping it. Prosecutors can charge suspects and continue the criminal process, divert suspects to some social service agency, or take no further action—effectively terminating the criminal process. Defendants can plead guilty (usually on their lawyers' advice) and avoid trial. Judges can suspend sentences or sentence convicted offenders to the maximum allowable penalty—hence, either minimizing or maximizing the punishment the criminal law prescribes.

Justice, fairness, and predictability all require the certainty and the protection against abuses provided by written rules. These same goals also require discretion to soften the rigidity of written rules. The tension between formal law and informal discretion—a recurring theme in criminal procedure—is as old as law; arguments raged over it in Western civilization as early as the Middle Ages.

One example of the need for discretionary decision making comes up when laws are applied to behavior that "technically" violates a criminal statute that the legislature never really meant to be enforced. This happens because it's impossible for legislators to predict all the ramifications of the statutes they enact. For example, it's a misdemeanor to drink in public parks in many cities, including Minneapolis. Yet, when a gourmet group had a brunch in a city park, because they thought the park had just the right ambience in which to enjoy their salmon mousse and imported French white wine, not only did the police not arrest the group for drinking in the park, but the city's leading newspaper wrote it up as a perfectly respectable social event (see Figure 1.2 on p. 32).

A young public defender wasn't pleased with the nonarrest. He pointed out that the police had arrested, and the prosecutor was at that moment prepared to prosecute, a Native American caught washing down a tuna fish sandwich with cheap red wine in another Minneapolis park. The public defender—a bit of a wag—noted that both the gourmet club and the Native American were consuming items from the same food groups.

This incident displays both the strengths and weaknesses of discretion. The legislature obviously didn't intend the statute to cover drinking of the type the gourmet club engaged in; arresting them would have been foolish. On the other hand, arresting and prosecuting the Native American might well have been discriminatory, a wholly unintended and unacceptable result of law enforcement that is discretionary and selective.

THE TEXT-CASE METHOD

LO 7

Now that you've got the big picture of criminal liability and punishment, the overarching principles that apply to all of criminal law, the sources of criminal law in a federal system, proving criminal conduct and the justifications and excuses to criminal liability, and the importance of discretionary decision making, it's time to take a closer look at the method this book uses to help you learn, understand, and think critically about criminal law.

It's called the "text-case method," and *Criminal Law 11* is called a "text-case book," meaning that it's part text and part excerpts from criminal law cases specially edited for nonlawyers like you. The text part of the book explains the general principles of criminal law and the definitions of specific crimes. The case excerpts involve real-life crimes that apply the general information in the text to real-life situations.

The application of principles and definitions of crimes to the facts of specific cases serves two important purposes. First, it helps you understand the principles and the elements of specific crimes. Second, it stimulates you to think critically about the principles and their applications. I believe the combination of text and case excerpts is the best way to test whether you understand and can think about general concepts rather than just memorizing and writing them by rote. So, although you can learn a lot from the text without reading the case excerpts, you won't get the full benefit of what you've learned without applying and thinking about it by reading the case excerpts.

For most of my students (and from emails that you and professors send me), reading and discussing the case excerpts are their favorite parts of the book. That's good. Cases bring criminal law to life by applying the abstract general principles, doctrines, and rules described in the text to real events in the lives of real people. But keep in mind that judges write the reports of the cases the excerpts are taken from. So don't be surprised to learn that they don't all write with college students or other nonlawyers in mind. Reading the excerpts may take some getting used to. This section is designed to help you get the most out of the cases.

The cases in this book are all excerpts, edited versions of the complete reports of the cases. In almost all the case excerpts, you'll read reports of the appeals of guilty verdicts, not transcripts of the criminal trial. A jury or trial court judge has already found a defendant guilty, or, more likely, the defendant has pleaded guilty in a trial court; the trial judge has entered a judgment of conviction; and the defendant has appealed the conviction.

"not guilty" verdict, doesn't mean "innocent"; it means that the government didn't prove its case beyond a reasonable doubt

"guilty" verdict, *legally*, not necessarily *factually*, guilty; it means the government proved its case beyond a reasonable doubt

trial courts, where the cases for the state and the defense are presented; their witnesses and the physical evidence are introduced; and the fact finders (juries in jury trials or judges in nonjury bench trials) decide what the "true" story is and whether the evidence all adds up to proof of guilt beyond a reasonable doubt

Incidentally, you'll never read the appeal of an acquittal. Why not? In the criminal law of the United States, a "not guilty" verdict is final and not subject to review. (There's an exception, sort of, to this rule, but we'll take it up in the first of the few case excerpts where the exception applies.)

Let's look at a few technical, but essential, points about the verdicts "not guilty" and "guilty." A **"not guilty" verdict** doesn't mean innocent; it means the government didn't prove its case beyond a reasonable doubt. Think of "not guilty" as "not legally guilty." A **"guilty" verdict** doesn't mean not innocent; it means the government proved its case beyond a reasonable doubt. Think of "guilty" as "legally guilty."

These differences are not just technicalities. As you read the cases, remember that some of the legally guilty defendants you're reading about are factually innocent. The flip side is also true; some acquitted defendants are factually guilty. The number of factually guilty people who "got off" is probably less than many people believe ("Symposium: Wrongful Convictions and Systemic Reform" 2005).

Criminal cases start in **trial courts**. It's in the trial courts that the cases for the state and the defense are presented; where their witnesses and the physical evidence are introduced; and where the fact finders (juries in jury trials or judges in nonjury bench trials) decide what the "true" story is and whether the evidence all adds up to proof of guilt beyond a reasonable doubt. If there's reasonable doubt, the jury renders its "not guilty" verdict; the judge enters a judgment of acquittal; and, the case is over—for good. There's no appeal to an acquittal; the fact finders' not guilty verdict is always final.

If there's proof beyond a reasonable doubt, the fact finders render their "guilty" verdict; the judge enters a judgment of guilty—and the case might be over. Rarely (contrary to popular perception), defendants appeal judgments of guilt. These appeals go to **appellate courts**. (The case excerpts are drawn from the official reports of these courts' decisions.)

appellate courts, in most states and the federal government, the two levels of appeals courts: an intermediate court of appeals and a supreme court

Most states and the federal government have two levels of appeals courts (see Figure 1.3): an intermediate court of appeals and a supreme court. The usual procedure is to appeal first to the intermediate court of appeals and then to the state supreme court. In a tiny number of cases involving issues about the U.S. Constitution, the case may go to the U.S. Supreme Court.

We enter the picture in these appellate court case excerpts. Let's look at the parts of the appellate cases you'll be reading excerpts from.

THE PARTS OF THE CASE EXCERPTS

Don't worry if reading cases intimidates you at first. Like students before you, you'll get the hang of it before long. To help you get the most out of the case excerpts, I've outlined the main parts of each case: the (1) title, (2) citation, (3) procedural history, (4) judge, (5) facts, (6) judgment, and (7) opinion.

1. **TITLE.** The case title consists of the names of the parties, either appellants (the party appealing the case) and appellees (party appealed against) or petitioners (parties bringing a case in habeas corpus or certiorari) and respondents (parties petitioned against in habeas corpus and certiorari).
2. **CITATION.** The citation is like the footnote or endnote in any text; it tells you where to find the case. (See "Finding Cases" section, p. 37.)
3. **PROCEDURAL HISTORY.** The case history is a brief description of the steps and judgments (decisions) made by each court that has heard the case.
4. **JUDGE.** The name of the judge who wrote the opinion and issued the court's judgment in the case.
5. **FACTS.** The facts of the case are the critical starting point in reading and analyzing cases. If you don't know the facts, you can't understand the principle the case is teaching. One of my best law professors, Professor Hill, frequently reminded us: "Cases are stories with a point. You can't get the point if you don't know the story."

FIGURE 1.3

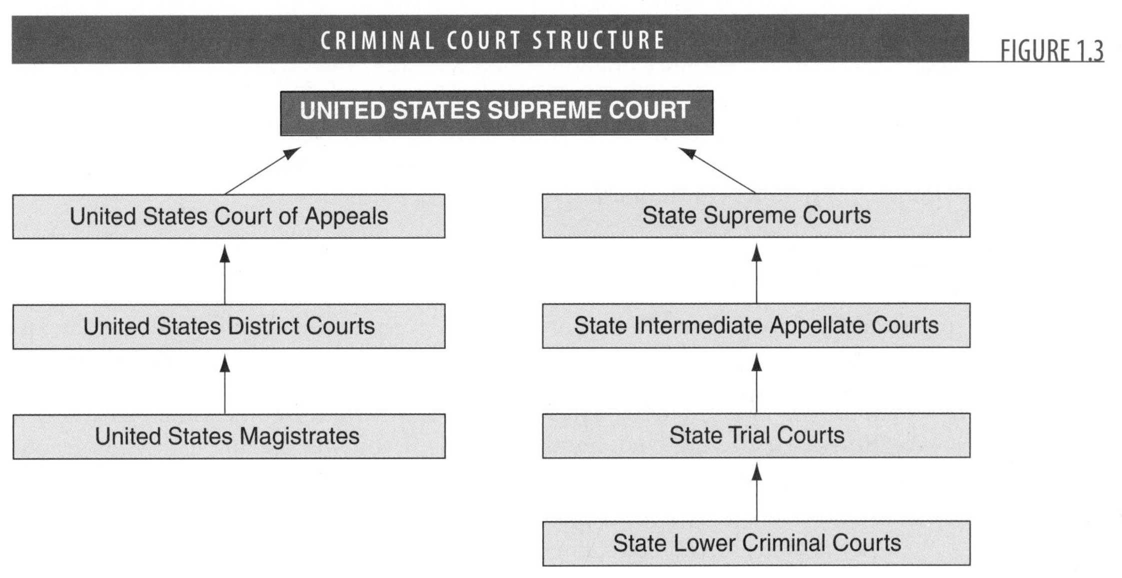

He also gave us some helpful advice: "Forget you're lawyers. Tell me the story as if you were telling it to your grandmother who doesn't know anything about the law."

6. **JUDGMENT** (DECISION). The court's **judgment** (sometimes called the court's "decision") is how the court disposes of the case. In the trial court, the judgments are almost always guilty or not guilty. In appeals courts, the judgments are affirmed, reversed, or reversed and remanded (sent back to the trial court). This is the most important legal action of the court, because it's what decides what happens to the defendant and the government.

judgment, the court's judgment (sometimes called the court's "decision") is how the court disposes of the case

7. **OPINION.** For students wanting to learn criminal law, the court's **opinion** is more important than the judgment: it's "the point of the story." In the opinion, the court backs up its judgment by explaining how and why it applied the law (general principles and the elements of crimes) to the facts of the case.

opinion, "the point of the story"; the court backs up its judgment by explaining how and why it applied the law (general principles and the elements of crimes) to the facts of the case

The law in the case excerpts includes the constitutional principles in Chapter 2; the principles of criminal liability in Chapters 3 and 4; the defenses in Chapters 5 and 6; the law of parties to crime and incomplete offenses in Chapters 7 and 8; and the law of crimes against persons, property, public order, and the state in Chapters 9 through 13.

The opinion contains two essential ingredients:

1. **COURT'S HOLDING.** The legal rule the court has decided to apply to the facts of the cases.
2. **COURT'S REASONING.** The reasons the court gives to support its holding. In some cases, the justices write majority and dissenting opinions.

court's holding, the legal rule the court has decided to apply to the facts of the cases

court's reasoning, the reasons the court gives to support its holding

A **majority opinion**, as its name indicates, is the opinion of the majority of the justices on the court who participated in the case. The majority opinion lays out the law of the case.

majority opinion, the law of the case; the opinion of the majority of the justices on the court who participated in the case

Although the majority opinion represents the established law of the case, dissenting opinions present a plausible alternative to the majority opinion. Dissents sometimes become the law in future decisions. For example, dissents in U.S. Supreme Court opinions of the 1930s became the law in the 1960s, and many of the dissents of the 1960s became law by the 1990s and remain the law as you're reading this.

Mostly in U.S. Supreme Court cases, you'll also see a **concurring opinion**. In concurring opinions, justices agree with the conclusions of either the majority or the dissenting opinion, but they have different reasons for reaching the conclusion.

concurring opinion, agrees with the conclusions of either the majority or the dissenting opinion but provides different reasons for reaching the conclusion

Sometimes, enough justices agree with the result in the case to make up a majority decision, but not enough agree on the reasoning to make up a majority opinion. In these cases, there's a **plurality opinion**, an opinion that represents the reasoning of the greatest number (but less than a majority) of justices.

plurality opinion, an opinion that represents the reasoning of the greatest number (but less than a majority) of justices

All of the differing perspectives in the opinions will stimulate you to think about all the topics in criminal law. They also clearly demonstrate that there's more than one reasonable way to look at important questions.

BRIEFING THE CASE EXCERPTS

To get the most from your reading of the case excerpts, you should write out the answers to the following questions about each. This is what we call "briefing" a case.

1. *What are the facts?* State the facts in simple narrative form in chronological order. As Professor Hill said, "Tell me the story as if you were telling it to your grandmother." Then, select, sort, and arrange the facts into the following categories:
   a. *Actions of the defendant* List what the defendant did in chronological order. (Remember, there's no criminal case without a criminal act by the defendant.)

   b. *Intent of the defendant required, if any* If none is required, say "none."
   c. *Circumstances required by the statute defining the crime (such as age in statutory rape), if any* If none is required, answer "none."
   d. *Causing a harmful result, if one is required* If none is required, say "none."
   e. *Justification and excuse (defense), if any* If none, answer "none."

2. *What's the legal issue in the case?* State the principle and/or element of a specific crime raised by the facts of the case.
3. *What are the arguments in the court's opinion?* List the reasons the court gives for its decision. The court's opinion consists of how and why the court applies the principle, doctrine, and/or rule to the facts of the case.
4. *State the court's judgment (decision).* The most common judgments are
   a. *Affirmed* Upheld the judgment (decision) of the lower court
   b. *Reversed* Overturned the judgment (decision) of the lower court
   c. *Reversed and remanded* Overturned the judgment (decision) of the lower court and sent the case back for further proceedings in accord with the appellate court's decision

You can't answer all these questions in every case. First, the answers depend on the knowledge you'll accumulate as the text and your instructor introduce more principles, doctrines, and rules. Second, courts don't necessarily follow the same procedure in reviewing an appeal as the one outlined here. Third, not all of the questions come up in every case—except for one: What did the defendant do? That's because there's no criminal case without some action by the defendant (Chapter 3).

Developing the skills needed to sort out the elements of the case excerpts requires practice, but it's worth the effort. Answering the questions can challenge you to think not only about the basic principles, doctrines, and rules of criminal law but also about your own fundamental values regarding life, property, privacy, and morals.

FINDING CASES

Knowing how to read and brief cases is important. So is knowing how to find cases. You may want to look up cases on your own, either in the library or in the rapidly expanding quantity of cases published on the Internet. These might include cases your instructor talks about in class, those discussed in the text, or the full versions of the case excerpts and the note cases following the excerpts. You may even want to look up a case you read or hear about outside of class.

The case citation consists of the numbers, letters, and punctuation that follow the title of a case in the excerpts or in the bibliography at the end of the book. These letters and numbers tell you where to locate the full case report. For example, in *State v. Metzger,* just after the title of the case, "*State v. Metzger,*" you read "319 N.W.2d 459 (Neb. 1982)." Here's how to interpret this citation:

case citation, the numbers, letters, and punctuation that tell you where to locate the full case report; they follow the title of a case in the excerpts or in the bibliography at the end of the book

1. 319 = Volume 319
2. N.W.2d = *North Western Reporter, Second Series*
3. 459 = page 459
4. (Neb. 1982) = Nebraska Supreme Court in the year 1982

So if you're looking for the full version of *State v. Metzger,* you'll find it in Volume 319 of the *North Western Reporter, Second Series,* page 459. The *North Western Reporter, Second Series,* is the second series of a multivolume set of law books that publishes reports of cases decided by the supreme courts and intermediate appellate courts in Nebraska and several other states in the region. There are comparable reporters for other regions, including the Northeast (N.E.), Southern (So.), Southwest (S.W.), and Pacific (P.).

Case citations always follow the same order. The volume number always comes before the title of a reporter and the page always comes immediately after the title. The abbreviation of the name of the court and the year the case was decided follow the page number in parentheses. You can tell if the court was the highest or an intermediate appellate court by the abbreviation. For example, in *Metzger,* the court is the Nebraska Supreme Court. (If the Nebraska intermediate appeals court had decided the case, you'd see "Neb. App.")

SUMMARY

LO 1, LO 4

Define what behavior deserves criminal punishment. Crimes are acts deserving of the strongest sanction and stigma of a society. Criminal punishment is the least common and most drastic reaction to unwanted behavior.

LO 2

Describe the relationship between the general and special parts of criminal law. General principles of criminal law apply to many or all crimes. General principles include the standard of voluntary action, criminal intent, complicity (crimes that make one person responsible for another's behavior), attempt, conspiracy, and solicitation. Specific crimes include crimes against persons, property, and public order (or morals), and crimes against the state. The prosecution of crime involves application of one or more general and/or specific principles.

LO 3

Identify and describe the main sources of criminal law. Criminal law is established by elected representatives (state legislatures, city and town councils, U.S. Congress), administrative agencies (IRS tax regulations, vehicle safety standards of the state highway patrol), and judges (common law).

LO 4

Define "criminal punishment," "criminal and noncriminal sanctions," and the purposes of each. Criminal punishment is a special form of pain or other unpleasant consequence that goes beyond noncriminal sanctions (deserving of monetary award in a civil lawsuit), regulated behavior (laws formally discourage), licensed behavior (a price is charged), and lawful behavior (subject to individual conscience and social disapproval).

LO 5

Define "presumption of innocence" and "burden of proof" as they relate to criminal liability. The most common and well-known burden of proof in prosecuting criminal conduct is proof beyond a reasonable doubt. Another standard, used for affirmative defenses such as justification and excuse, places the burden of production (evidence exists) or of persuasion (most of the evidence) on the defendant.

LO 6

Describe the role of informal discretion and its relationship to formal criminal law. Discretionary decision making is decision making that's hidden from view. It includes the police decision to investigate or not, the prosecutor's decision to charge, judges suspending sentences, and more.

LO 7

Describe the text-case method and how to apply it to the study of criminal law. The text part of the book describes principles of criminal law, while the case excerpts involve real-life crimes that apply them to real-life situations. This book is one example.

KEY TERMS

criminal liability, p. 5
torts, p. 6
mala in se (inherently evil) crimes, p. 14
mala prohibita offenses, p. 14
felonies, p. 14
misdemeanors, p. 14
general part of criminal law, p. 15
special part of criminal law, p. 15
complicity, p. 15
common law, p. 16
common law crimes, p. 16
codified (criminal law), p. 18
Model Penal Code (MPC), p. 19
MPC's analysis of criminal liability, p. 19
administrative crimes, p. 21
federal system, p. 21
rates of imprisonment, p. 22
punishment, p. 23
criminal punishment, p. 23
retribution (and criminal punishment), p. 24
prevention (and criminal punishment), p. 24
culpability, p. 25
justice, p. 25
general deterrence (and criminal punishment), p. 26
special deterrence (and criminal punishment), p. 26
incapacitation (and criminal punishment), p. 26
rehabilitation (and criminal punishment), p. 26
hedonism (and criminal punishment), p. 26
rationalism (and criminal punishment), p. 26
deterrence theory, p. 26
principle of utility, p. 27
"medical model" of criminal law, p. 28
determinism (and criminal punishment), p. 28
indeterminate sentencing laws, p. 30
fixed (determinate) sentences, p. 30
presumption of innocence, p. 30
burden of proof, p. 30
criminal conduct, p. 31
proof beyond a reasonable doubt, p. 31
reasonable doubt, p. 31
bench trial, p. 31
corpus delicti, p. 31
affirmative defenses, p. 31
burden of production, p. 31
burden of persuasion, p. 31
preponderance of the evidence, p. 31
informal discretionary decision making, p. 33
not guilty verdict, p. 34
guilty verdict, p. 34
trial courts, p. 34
appellate courts, p. 35
judgment (in criminal cases), p. 36
opinion (in criminal cases), p. 36
court's holding, p. 36
court's reasoning, p. 36
majority opinion, p. 36
concurring opinion (in criminal cases), p. 36
plurality opinion (in criminal cases), p. 36
case citation, p. 37

LEARNING OBJECTIVES

1. To understand and appreciate the reasons for the limits on criminal law and criminal punishment in the U.S. constitutional democracy.
2. To understand the principle of legality and the importance of its relationship to the limits of criminal law and punishment.
3. To appreciate the nature and importance of retroactive criminal lawmaking.
4. To know the criteria for identifying vague laws and to understand and appreciate their constitutional significance and consequences.
5. To know, understand, and appreciate the limits placed on the criminal law and criminal punishment by the specific provisions in the Bill of Rights.
6. To understand and appreciate the constitutional significance and consequences of the principle of proportionality in criminal punishment.
7. To understand the importance of the right to trial by jury in the process of sentencing convicted offenders.

Christian Albright, 11, and his dad, Chip Albright of Spanaway, Washington, join about 200 other gun rights supporters for the Second Amendment Rally on the capitol campus in Olympia, Washington, on Saturday, April 24, 2010.

AP Images/The Olympian, Tony Overman

CONSTITUTIONAL LIMITS ON CRIMINAL LAW 2

CHAPTER OUTLINE

The Death Penalty for Child Rape?

She could have been anyone's eight-year-old daughter. The image of the Harvey, Illinois, youngster sorting Girl Scout cookies in the family garage when two men grabbed her and dragged her to a vacant lot where she was raped was recounted repeatedly by the girl and her stepfather. Then the story fell apart. The stepfather was charged with the crime and then convicted by a Jefferson Parish jury that also decided he should pay the ultimate price for the crime: his life. The two-and-a-half-week-long trial reached a historic climax when the 38-year-old Harvey man became the first person in the nation in more than 25 years to be sentenced to death for rape.

(Darby 2003, 1)

The authors of the U.S. Constitution were suspicious of power, especially power in the hands of government officials. They were also devoted to the right of individuals to control their own destinies without government interference. But they were realists who knew that freedom depends on order, and order depends on social control. So they created a Constitution that balanced the power of government and the liberty of individuals. No one has expressed the kind of government the Constitution created better than James Madison (1787, 1961), one of its primary authors:

> If men were angels, no government would be necessary. If angels were to govern men, neither external nor internal controls on government would be necessary. In framing a government

which is to be administered by men over men, the great difficulty is this: You must first enable the government to control the governed; and in the next place, oblige it to control itself. (349)

constitutional democracy, the majority can't make a crime out of conduct protected by the fundamental rights in the U.S. Constitution

James Madison was describing the U.S. democracy—a ***constitutional democracy***—not a pure democracy. In a pure democracy, the majority can have whatever it wants. In a **constitutional democracy**, the majority can't make a crime out of what the Constitution protects as a fundamental right. Even if 90 percent of the people want to make it a crime to say, "The president is a socialist," they can't. Why? Because the First Amendment to the U.S. Constitution guarantees the fundamental right of free speech.

LO 1

A central feature of criminal law in a constitutional democracy is the limits it places on the government's power to create crimes and punish offenders. In this chapter, we focus on the limits imposed by the U.S. and state constitutions. But the idea of limited government power in criminal law and punishment is older than the U.S. Constitution; it has deep roots in English and American colonies' history. It begins more than two thousand years ago with the ancient Greek philosopher Aristotle, who wrote in 350 BC:

> He who bids the law rule may be deemed to bid God and Reason alone rule, but he who bids man rule adds an element of the beast; for desire is a wild beast, and passion perverts the minds of rulers, even when they are the best of men. The law is reason unaffected by desire. (quoted in Allen 1993, 3)

rule of law, the idea that government power should be defined and limited by laws

Almost nine hundred years later, in 1215, in the Magna Carta, King John promised his barons the **rule of law**, when he agreed not to proceed with force against any free man, "except by the lawful judgment of his equals or by the law of the land." And in 1240, the great English jurist Bracton (1968) wrote that even the king ruled "under God and the law," and "it is a saying worthy of the majesty of a ruler that the prince acknowledges himself bound by the laws" (2:305–6).

LO 2, LO 3

THE PRINCIPLE OF LEGALITY

principle of legality, no one can be convicted of, or punished for, a crime unless the law defined the crime and prescribed the punishment before the person engaged in the behavior that was defined as a crime

In criminal law, and in criminal punishment, there's an ancient proposition based on the **principle of legality**: "No crime without law; no punishment without law." This means that no one can be convicted of, or punished for, a crime unless the law defined the crime and prescribed the punishment before a person engaged in the behavior that was defined as a crime. It's called "the first principle of criminal law" (Packer 1968, 79); all other principles you'll learn about in this book are subordinate to it. And it applies even when following it allows morally blameworthy, dangerous people to go free without punishment (Dressler 2001, 39).

For example, in *Hughes v. State* (1994), an appeals court reversed a fetal homicide conviction because the state's homicide statute didn't give the defendant fair warning that it included the death of the unborn (731). According to the appeals court, "The retroactive application of criminal law . . . is so abhorrent that we must occasionally endure some frustration in order to preserve and protect the foundation of our system of law" (736).

Why is a retroactive criminal law so "abhorrent"? Because retroactive criminal laws undermine the "central values" of free societies (Allen 1993, 15). First, knowing what the law commands provides individuals with the opportunity to obey the law and avoid punishment. Second, providing individuals with this opportunity promotes the value of human autonomy and dignity. Third, the ban on retroactive criminal lawmaking also prevents officials from punishing conduct they think is wrong but which no existing criminal law prohibits. To allow this would threaten the rule of law itself; it would become a rule of officials instead (Kahan 1997, 96).

THE BAN ON EX POST FACTO LAWS

LO 3

So fundamental did the authors of the Constitution consider a ban on retroactive criminal lawmaking, or ex post facto laws, that they raised it to constitutional status in Article I of the U.S. Constitution. Article I, Section 9, bans the U.S. Congress from enacting such laws; Article 1, Section 10, bans state legislatures from passing them. And most state constitutions include their own ban on retroactive statutes (LaFave 2003b, 1:153).

ex post facto law, a retroactive law that does one of three things: (1) criminalizes an act that wasn't a crime when it was committed, (2) increases the punishment for a crime after the crime was committed, or (3) takes away a defense that was available to a defendant when the crime was committed

An ex post facto law does one of three things:

1. It criminalizes an act that wasn't a crime when it was committed.
2. It increases the punishment for a crime after the crime was committed. (The ban doesn't apply to reductions in punishment. So, for example, there's no ban on reducing the punishment for possessing marijuana from one year in prison to a fine.)
3. It takes away a defense that was available to a defendant when the crime was committed. (*Beazell v. Ohio* 1925, 169)

Statutes that criminalize acts after they're committed are the clearest example of ex post facto laws. They're also the rarest, because in modern times, legislatures never try to make them crimes. Equally clear, and equally rare, are statutes that change an element of a crime after it's committed—for example, raising the age of the victim in statutory rape from 16 to 21 or removing the "nighttime entry" in a burglary statute. Statutes that increase punishment occur more often (LaFave 2003a, 110–11).

The ex post facto ban has two major purposes. One is to protect private individuals by ensuring that legislatures give them fair warning about what's criminal and that they can rely on that requirement. The second purpose is directed at preventing legislators from passing arbitrary and vindictive laws. ("Arbitrary" means legislation is based on random choice or personal whim, not on reason and standards.)

THE VOID-FOR-VAGUENESS DOCTRINE

LO 4

A law is void for vagueness if it forbids conduct and prescribes punishments in terms so uncertain that ordinary people can't intelligently choose in advance a lawful course to pursue (*State v. Metzger* 1982, 461).

void-for-vagueness, doctrine, the principle that statutes violate due process if they don't define a crime and its punishment clearly enough for ordinary people to know what is lawful (*Lanzetta v. New Jersey* 1939, 453)

The U.S. Supreme Court has ruled that vague laws violate the guarantees of two provisions in the U.S. Constitution. The Fifth Amendment to the U.S. Constitution guarantees that the *federal* government shall not deny any individual life, liberty, or property without due process of law. The Fourteenth Amendment provides that no *state* government shall deny any person life, liberty, or property without due process of law.

How do vague laws violate the due process guarantees? The reasoning behind the void-for-vagueness doctrine goes like this:

1. The Fifth and Fourteenth Amendments to the U.S. Constitution ban both federal and state governments from taking any person's "life, liberty, or property without due process of law."
2. Criminal punishment deprives individuals of life (capital punishment), liberty (imprisonment), or property (fines).
3. Failure to warn private persons of what the law forbids and/or allowing officials the chance to define arbitrarily what the law forbids denies individuals their life, liberty, and/or property without due process of law.

LO 4

THE AIMS OF THE VOID-FOR-VAGUENESS DOCTRINE

The void-for-vagueness doctrine takes aim at two evils similar to those of the ban on ex post facto. First, void laws fail to give fair warning to private individuals as to what the law prohibits. Second, they allow arbitrary and discriminatory law enforcement. A famous case from the 1930s gangster days, *Lanzetta v. New Jersey* (1939), still widely cited and relied on today, is an excellent example of both the application of the doctrine and its purposes. The story begins with a challenge to this New Jersey statute:

> Any person not engaged in any lawful occupation, known to be a member of any gang consisting of two or more persons, who has been convicted at least three times of being a disorderly person, or who has been convicted of any crime, in this or in any other State, is declared to be a gangster. . . . Every violation is punishable by fine not exceeding $10,000 or imprisonment not exceeding 20 years, or both. (452)

The challengers attacking the statute for vagueness were Ignatius Lanzetta, Michael Falcone, and Louie Del Rossi. On June 12, 16, 19, and 24, 1936, the four challengers, "not being engaged in any lawful occupation"; "known to be members of a gang, consisting of two or more persons"; and "having been convicted of a crime in the State of Pennsylvania" were "declared to be gangsters."

The trial court threw out their challenge that the law was void for vagueness; they were tried, convicted, and sentenced to prison for "not more than ten years and not less than five years, at hard labor." The New Jersey intermediate appellate court and the New Jersey Supreme Court also threw out their challenges. But they finally prevailed when a unanimous U.S. Supreme Court ruled that the New Jersey statute was void for vagueness. Why?

> No one may be required at peril of life, liberty or property to speculate as to the meaning of penal statutes. All are entitled to be informed as to what the State commands or forbids; and a statute which either forbids or requires the doing of an act in terms so vague that men of common intelligence must necessarily guess at its meaning and differ as to its application violates the first essential of due process of law. (453)
>
> The phrase "consisting of two or more persons" is all that purports to define "gang." The meanings of that word indicated in dictionaries and in historical and sociological writings are numerous and varied. Nor is the meaning derivable from the common law, for neither in that field nor anywhere in the language of the law is there definition of the word. Our attention has not been called to, and we are unable to find, any other statute attempting to make it criminal to be a member of a "gang." (454–55)

fair notice, in ex post facto laws, it isn't whether the defendant knows there's a law against the act but whether an ordinary, reasonable person would know that the act is a crime

Notice that the answer to the question, "What's **fair notice**?" in ex post laws isn't subjective; that is, it's not what a particular defendant actually knows about the law. For example, the Court didn't ask what Lanzetta and his cohorts knew about the gangster ordinance: Were they aware it existed? Did they get advice about what it meant? Did their life experiences inform them that their behavior was criminal (Batey 1997, 4)?

That's because, according to the courts, the proper question, "What's fair notice in ex post facto law" is objective; namely, "Would an ordinary, reasonable person know that what he was doing was criminal?" Perhaps the best definition of objective fair warning is U.S. Supreme Court Justice Byron White's blunt: "If any fool would know that a particular category of conduct would be within the reach of the statute, if there is an unmistakable core that a reasonable person would know is forbidden by the law, the enactment is not unconstitutional . . . " (*Kolender v. Lawson* 1983, 370–71).

Despite the importance of giving fair notice to individuals, in 1983, the Supreme Court decided that providing "minimal guidelines to govern law enforcement" trumps notice to private individuals as the primary aim of the void-for-vagueness doctrine (*Kolender v. Lawson* 1983, 357). According to the Court:

> Where the legislature fails to provide such minimal guidelines, a criminal statute may permit a standardless sweep [that] allows policemen, prosecutors, and juries to pursue their personal predilections. (358)

And, quoting from an old case (*U.S. v. Reese* 1875), the Court in *Lawson* elaborated further on the choice to give priority to controlling arbitrary and discriminatory enforcement:

> It would certainly be dangerous if the legislature could set a net large enough to catch all possible offenders, and leave it to the courts to step inside and say who could be rightfully detained, and who should be set at large. This would, to some extent, substitute the judicial for the legislative department of government. (221)

Giving priority to controlling law enforcement is more realistic than giving fair notice to hypothetical reasonable, ordinary people. Police officers and prosecutors are more likely to read what's in the criminal statutes and know about the cases that interpret them. So it makes sense for courts to ask whether statutes clearly indicate to ordinary police officers and prosecutors what the law prohibits. Inquiries that seem "wrongheaded" when they're directed at guaranteeing fair notice to ordinary noncriminal justice experts become reasonable when they're examined to decide whether they're clear enough to limit arbitrary and discriminatory enforcement (Batey 1997, 6–7).

DEFINING VAGUENESS

LO 4

Whether the emphasis is on notice to individuals or control of officials, the void-for-vagueness doctrine can never cure the uncertainty in all laws. After all, laws are written in words, not numbers. U.S. Supreme Court Justice Thurgood Marshall expressed this opinion when he wrote, "Condemned to the use of words, we can never expect mathematical certainty from our language" (*Grayned v. City of Rockford* 1972, 110). It's not just the natural uncertainty of words that creates problems. It's also because the variety of human behavior and the limits of human imagination make it impossible to predict all the variations that might arise under the statutes. So courts allow considerable leeway in the degree of certainty required to pass the two prongs of fair warning and avoidance of arbitrary law enforcement.

Furthermore, challengers face a strong presumption that statutes are constitutional. The Ohio Supreme Court summarized the heavy burden of proof challengers have to carry:

> The challenger must show that upon examining the statute, an individual of ordinary intelligence would not understand what he is required to do under the law. Thus, to escape responsibility . . . [the challenger] must prove that he could not reasonably understand that . . . [the statute] prohibited the acts in which he engaged. . . . The party alleging that a statute is unconstitutional must prove this assertion beyond a reasonable doubt. (*State v. Anderson* 1991, 1226–27)

CASE

In* State v. Metzger *(1982), *the Nebraska Supreme Court held that a Lincoln, Nebraska, city ordinance that made it a crime to "commit any indecent, immodest, or filthy act" was void for vagueness.*

Was his act "indecent, immodest, or filthy"?

State v. Metzger

319 N.W.2d 459 (Neb. 1982)

HISTORY

Douglas E. Metzger was convicted in the municipal court of the city of Lincoln, Nebraska, of violating § 9.52.100 of the Lincoln Municipal Code. The District Court, Lancaster County, affirmed the District Court judgment. Metzger appealed to the Nebraska Supreme Court. The Supreme Court reversed and dismissed the District Court's judgment.

KRIVOSHA, CJ.

FACTS

Metzger lived in a garden-level apartment located in Lincoln, Nebraska. A large window in the apartment faces a parking lot that is situated on the north side of the apartment building. At about 7:45 A.M. on April 30, 1981, another resident of the apartment, while parking his automobile in a space directly in front of Metzger's apartment window, observed Metzger standing naked with his arms at his sides in his apartment window for a period of five seconds. The resident testified that he saw Metzger's body from his thighs on up.

The resident called the police department and two officers arrived at the apartment at about 8:00 A.M. The officers testified that they observed Metzger standing in front of the window eating a bowl of cereal. They testified that Metzger was standing within a foot of the window, and his nude body, from the mid-thigh on up, was visible.

The pertinent portion of § 9.52.100 of the Lincoln Municipal Code, under which Metzger was charged, provides as follows: "It shall be unlawful for any person within the City of Lincoln . . . to commit any indecent, immodest or filthy act in the presence of any person, or in such a situation that persons passing might ordinarily see the same."

OPINION

The . . . issue presented to us by this appeal is whether the ordinance, as drafted, is so vague as to be unconstitutional. We believe that it is. Since the ordinance is criminal in nature, it is a fundamental requirement of due process of law that such criminal ordinance be reasonably clear and definite.

In the case of *Papachristou v. City of Jacksonville*, 405 U.S. 156 (1972), the U.S. Supreme Court declared a vagrancy statute of the city of Jacksonville, Florida, invalid for vagueness, saying "It would certainly be dangerous if the legislature could set a net large enough to catch all possible offenders, and leave it to the courts to step inside and say who could be rightfully detained, and who should be set at large."

The ordinance in question makes it unlawful for anyone to commit any "indecent, immodest or filthy act." We know of no way in which the standards required of a criminal act can be met in those broad, general terms. There may be those few who believe persons of opposite sex holding hands in public are immodest, and certainly more who might believe that kissing in public is immodest. Such acts cannot constitute a crime. Certainly one could find many who would conclude that today's swimming attire found on many beaches or beside many pools is immodest. Yet, the fact that it is immodest does not thereby make it illegal, absent some requirement related to the health, safety, or welfare of the community. The dividing line between what is lawful and what is unlawful in terms of "indecent," "immodest," or "filthy" is simply too broad to satisfy the constitutional requirements of due process. Both lawful and unlawful acts can be embraced within such broad definitions. That cannot be permitted. One is not able to determine in advance what is lawful and what is unlawful. We therefore believe that § 9.52.100 of the Lincoln Municipal Code must be declared invalid. Because the ordinance is therefore declared invalid, the conviction cannot stand.

We do not attempt, in this opinion, to determine whether Metzger's actions in a particular case might not be made unlawful, nor do we intend to encourage such behavior. Indeed, it may be possible that a governmental subdivision using sufficiently definite language could make such an act as committed by Metzger unlawful.

Reversed and dismissed.

DISSENT

BOSLAUGH, J., JOINED BY CLINTON AND HASTINGS, JJ.

The ordinance in question prohibits indecent acts, immodest acts, or filthy acts in the presence of any person. Although the ordinance may be too broad in some respects . . . the exhibition of his genitals under the circumstances of this case was, clearly, an indecent act. Statutes and ordinances prohibiting indecent exposure generally have been held valid. I do not subscribe to the view that it is only "possible" that such conduct may be prohibited by statute or ordinance.

QUESTIONS

1. State the exact wording of the offense Douglas Metzger was convicted of.
2. List all of Metzger's acts and any other facts relevant to deciding whether he violated the ordinance.
3. State the test the court used to decide whether the ordinance was void for vagueness.
4. According to the majority, why was the ordinance vague?
5. According to the dissent, why was the ordinance clear enough to pass the void-for-vagueness test?
6. In your opinion, was the statute clear to a reasonable person? Back up your answer with the facts and arguments in the excerpt and information from the void-for-vagueness discussion in the text.

EQUAL PROTECTION OF THE LAWS

In addition to the due process guarantee, the Fourteenth Amendment to the U.S. Constitution commands that "no state shall deny to any person within its jurisdiction the equal protection of the laws." **Equal protection of the law** is a constitutional command that criminal laws can treat groups of people and types of conduct differently only if the different treatment is reasonable. Equal protection is far more frequently an issue in criminal procedure than it is in criminal law. Let's, therefore, note briefly here the limits it puts on criminal lawmaking and punishment.

equal protection of the law, a constitutional command that criminal laws can treat groups of people and types of conduct differently only if the different treatment is reasonable

First, equal protection of the law doesn't require the government to treat everybody exactly alike. Statutes can, and often do, classify particular groups of people and types of conduct for special treatment. For example, almost every state ranks premeditated killings as more serious than negligent homicides. Several states punish habitual criminals more harshly than first-time offenders. Neither of these classifications violates the equal protection clause. Why? Because they make sense. Or, as the courts put it, there's a "rational basis" for the different treatment (*Buck v. Bell* 1927, 208).

Classifications in criminal codes based on *race* are another matter. The U.S. Supreme Court subjects all racial classifications to "strict scrutiny." In practice, strict scrutiny means race-based classifications are never justified. According to the U.S. Supreme Court, any statute that "invidiously classifies similarly situated people on the basis of the immutable characteristics with which they were born . . . *always* [emphasis added] violates the Constitution, for the simple reason that, as far as the Constitution is concerned, people of different races are always similarly situated. Gender classifications stand somewhere between the strict scrutiny applied to race and the rational basis applied to most other classifications.

The U.S. Supreme Court has had difficulty deciding exactly how carefully to scrutinize gender classifications in criminal statutes. The plurality, but not a majority, of the justices in *Michael M. v. Superior Court of Sonoma County* (1981, 477) agreed that gender classifications deserve heightened scrutiny, meaning there has to be a "fair and substantial relationship" between classifications based on gender and "legitimate state ends."

Michael M., a 17-year-old male, challenged California's statutory rape law, which defines unlawful sexual intercourse as "an act of sexual intercourse accomplished with a female not the wife of the perpetrator, where the female is under the age of 18 years." The U.S. Supreme Court denied the equal protection challenge. "The question boils down to whether a State may attack the problem of sexual intercourse and teenage pregnancy directly by prohibiting a male from having sexual intercourse with a minor female. We hold that such a statute is sufficiently related to the State's objectives to pass constitutional muster" (473).

LO 5

THE BILL OF RIGHTS AND THE CRIMINAL LAW

The ban on ex post facto laws, denial of due process, and equal protection of the laws are broad constitutional limits that cover all of criminal law. The Bill of Rights bans defining certain kinds of behavior as criminal. One is the ban on making a crime out of the First Amendment rights to speech, religion, and associations; another is the Second Amendment right to bear arms; and the third is the right to privacy, a right created by the U.S. Supreme Court, from an amalgam of parts of the Bill of Rights. Let's look at these three rights.

LO 5

FREE SPEECH

"Congress shall make no law abridging the freedom of speech," the First Amendment commands. The U.S. Supreme Court has expanded the ban beyond this already sweeping scope. First, the Court has expanded the meaning of "speech" by holding that the protection of the amendment "does not end with the spoken or written word" (*Texas v. Johnson* 1989, 404). It also includes expressive conduct, meaning actions that communicate ideas and feelings. So free speech includes wearing black armbands to protest war; "sitting in" to protest racial segregation; and picketing to support all kinds of causes from abortion to animal rights. It even includes giving money to political candidates.

expressive conduct, nonverbal actions that communicate ideas and feelings

Second, although the amendment itself directs its prohibition only at the U.S. Congress, the U.S. Supreme Court has applied the prohibition to the states since 1925 (*Gitlow v. New York*). Third, the Court has ruled that free speech is a fundamental right, one that enjoys preferred status. This means that the government has to provide more than a rational basis for restricting speech and other forms of expression. It has the much higher burden of proving that a compelling government interest justifies the restrictions.

Despite these broad prohibitions and the heavy burden the government faces in justifying them, the First Amendment doesn't mean you can express yourself anywhere, anytime, on any subject, in any manner. According to the U.S. Supreme Court, there are five categories of expression not protected by the First Amendment:

1. *Obscenity* Material whose predominant appeal is to nudity, sexual activity, or excretion
2. *Profanity* Irreverence toward sacred things, particularly the name of God
3. *Libel and slander* Libels are damages to reputation expressed in print, writing, pictures, or signs; slander damages reputation by spoken words
4. *Fighting words* Words that are likely to provoke the average person to retaliation and cause a "breach of the peace"

5. *Clear and present danger* Expression that creates a clear and present danger of an evil, which legislatures have the power to prohibit (*Chaplinsky v. New Hampshire* 1942, 574)

Why doesn't the First Amendment protect these forms of expression? Because they're not an "essential element of any exposition of ideas, and are of such slight value as a step to truth that any benefit that may be derived from them is clearly outweighed by the social interest in order and morality" (*Gitlow v. New York* 1925, 572).

These exceptions create the opportunity for the government to make these kinds of expression a crime, depending on the manner, time, and place of expression. For example, under the clear and present danger doctrine, the government can punish words that "produce a clear and present danger of a serious substantive evil that rises far above public inconvenience, annoyance, or unrest." So the First Amendment didn't save Walter Chaplinsky from conviction under a New Hampshire statute that made it a crime to call anyone an "offensive or derisive name" in public. Chaplinsky had called the marshal of the city of Rochester, New Hampshire, "a God-damned racketeer."

In perhaps the most famous reference to the doctrine, U.S. Supreme Court Justice Oliver Wendell Holmes wrote, "The most stringent protection of free speech would not protect a man in falsely shouting fire in a theatre and causing a panic" (*Schenck v. U.S.* 1919, 52).

The most difficult problem in making a crime out of speech and expressive conduct is when laws reach so far they include not just expression the Constitution bans but also expression it protects.

The **void-for-overbreadth doctrine** protects speech guaranteed by the First Amendment by invalidating laws written so broadly that the fear of prosecution creates a "chilling effect" that discourages people from exercising that freedom. This "chilling effect" on the exercise of the fundamental right to freedom of expression violates the right to liberty guaranteed by the due process clauses of the Fifth and Fourteenth Amendments to the U.S. Constitution.

void-for-overbreadth doctrine, protects speech guaranteed by the First Amendment by invalidating laws written so broadly that the fear of prosecution creates a "chilling effect" that discourages people from exercising that freedom

The U.S. Supreme Court dealt with the chilling effect of a St. Paul, Minnesota, hate crime ordinance in *R.A.V. v. City of St. Paul* (1992). In this case, R.A.V., a juvenile, was alleged to have burned a crudely constructed wooden cross on a Black family's lawn. He was charged with violating St. Paul's Bias-Motivated Crime Ordinance. The ordinance provided that anyone who places a burning cross, Nazi swastika, or other symbol on private or public property knowing that the symbol would arouse "anger, alarm or resentment in others on the basis of race, color, creed, religion or gender commits disorderly conduct and shall be guilty of a misdemeanor."

The Minnesota Supreme Court ruled that the ordinance was constitutional because it could be construed to ban only "fighting words," which aren't protected by the First Amendment (380). The U.S. Supreme Court, on the other hand, ruled that, even when a statute addresses speech that's not protected (in this case "fighting words"), states still can't discriminate on the basis of the content of the expression. The Court concluded that the St. Paul ordinance violated the First Amendment because it would allow the proponents of racial tolerance and equality to use fighting words to argue in favor of tolerance and equality but would prohibit similar use by those opposed to racial tolerance and equality.

According to Justice Scalia, "One could hold up a sign saying that all 'anti-Catholic bigots' are misbegotten, but not that all 'papists' are, for that would insult and provoke violence 'on the basis of religion.' St. Paul has no such authority to license one side of a debate to fight freestyle, while requiring the other to follow Marquis of Queensberry rules" (391–92).

CASE

In **People v. Rokicki** *(1999), the Illinois Appellate Court ruled that Illinois' hate crime statute doesn't run afoul of the First Amendment, at least when a prosecution is based on "disorderly conduct."*

Does the hate crime statute violate free speech?

People v. Rokicki

718 N.E.2d 333 (Ill.App. 1999)

HISTORY

Kenneth Rokicki was charged with a hate crime based on the predicate (underlying) offense of disorderly conduct. Before trial, Rokicki moved to dismiss the charges, alleging that the hate crime statute was unconstitutional. The trial court denied his motion. Rokicki waived his right to a jury, and the matter proceeded to a **bench trial** [trial by a judge without a jury].

Rokicki was convicted, sentenced to two years' probation, and ordered to perform 100 hours of community service and to attend anger management counseling. He appealed, contending that the hate crime statute is unconstitutionally overly broad and chills expression protected by the First Amendment to the U.S. Constitution. Conviction and sentence affirmed.

HUTCHINSON, J.

FACTS

Donald Delaney, store manager of a Pizza Hut in South Elgin, testified that Rokicki entered the restaurant at approximately 1:30 P.M. The victim was a server there and took Rokicki's order. The victim requested payment, and Rokicki refused to tender payment to him. Donald Delaney, the store manager, who was nearby, stepped in and completed the sale. Rokicki told Delaney not to let "that faggot" touch his food. When Rokicki's pizza came out of the oven, Delaney was on the telephone, and the victim began to slice the pizza. Delaney saw Rokicki approaching the counter with an irritated expression and hung up the telephone. Before Delaney could intervene, Rokicki leaned over the counter and began yelling at the victim and pounding his fist on the counter. Rokicki directed a series of epithets at the victim including "Mary," "faggot," and "Molly Homemaker." Rokicki continued yelling for ten minutes and, when not pounding his fist, shook his finger at the victim. Delaney asked Rokicki to leave several times and threatened to call the police. However, Delaney did not call the police because he was standing between the victim and Rokicki and feared that Rokicki would physically attack the victim if Delaney moved. Eventually, Delaney returned Rokicki's money and Rokicki left the establishment.

The victim testified that he was working at the South Elgin Pizza Hut on October 20, 1995. Rokicki entered the restaurant and ordered a pizza. When Rokicki's pizza came out of the oven, the victim began to slice it. Rokicki then began yelling at the victim and pounding his fist on the counter. Rokicki appeared very angry and seemed very serious. The victim, who is much smaller than Rokicki, testified that he was terrified by Rokicki's outburst and remained frightened for several days thereafter. Eventually, the manager gave Rokicki a refund and Rokicki left the restaurant. The victim followed Rokicki into the parking lot, recorded the license number of his car, and called the police.

Christopher Merritt, a sergeant with the South Elgin Police Department, testified that, at 2:20 P.M. on October 20, 1995, Rokicki entered the police station and said he wished to report an incident at the Pizza Hut. Rokicki told Merritt that he was upset because a homosexual was working at the restaurant and he wanted someone "normal" to prepare his food. Rokicki stated that he became angry when the victim touched his food. He called the victim a "Mary," pounded on the counter, and was subsequently kicked out of the restaurant. Merritt asked Rokicki what he meant by a "Mary," and Rokicki responded that a "Mary" was a homosexual. Merritt conducted only a brief interview of Rokicki because shortly after Rokicki arrived at the police station Merritt was dispatched to the Pizza Hut.

Deborah Hagedorn, an employee at the Pizza Hut in St. Charles, testified that in 1995 Rokicki came into the restaurant and asked for the address of the district manager for Pizza Hut. When asked why he wanted the address, Rokicki complained that he had been arrested at the South Elgin restaurant because he did not want a "f___g faggot" touching his food.

Rokicki testified that he was upset because the victim had placed his fingers in his mouth and had not washed his hands before cutting the pizza. Rokicki admitted calling the victim "Mary" but denied that he intended to suggest the victim was a homosexual. Rokicki stated that he used the term "Mary" because the victim would not stop talking and "it was like arguing with a woman." Rokicki denied yelling and denied directing other derogatory terms toward the victim. Rokicki admitted giving a statement to Merritt but denied telling him that he pounded his fist on the counter or used homosexual slurs. Rokicki testified that he went to the St. Charles Pizza Hut but that Hagedorn was not present during his conversation with the manager. Rokicki testified that he complained about the victim's hygiene but did not use any homosexual slurs.

The trial court found Rokicki guilty of a hate crime. In a post trial motion, Rokicki argued that the hate crime statute was unconstitutional. The trial court denied Rokicki's motion and sentenced him to two years' probation. As part of the probation, the trial court ordered Rokicki not to enter Pizza Hut restaurants, not to contact the victim, to perform 100 hours' community service, and to attend anger management counseling. Rokicki appealed.

OPINION

On appeal, Rokicki does not challenge the sufficiency of the evidence against him. Rokicki contends only that the hate crime statute is unconstitutional when the predicate offense is disturbing the peace. Rokicki argues that the statute is overly broad and impermissibly chills free speech.

The Illinois Hate Crime Statute reads in part as follows:

> A person commits a hate crime when, by reason of the actual or perceived race, color, creed, religion, ancestry, gender, sexual orientation, physical or mental disability, or national origin of another individual or group of individuals, [she or] he commits assault, battery, aggravated assault, misdemeanor theft, criminal trespass to residence, misdemeanor criminal damage to property, criminal trespass to vehicle, criminal trespass to real property, mob action or disorderly conduct. . . .

1. Infringement on Free Speech Rights

Rokicki's conviction was based on the predicate [underlying] offense of disorderly conduct. A person commits disorderly conduct when she or he knowingly "does any act in such an unreasonable manner as to alarm or disturb another and to provoke a breach of the peace." Disorderly conduct is punishable as a Class C misdemeanor. However, hate crime is punishable as a Class 4 felony for a first offense and a Class 2 felony for a second or subsequent offense. . . .

The overbreadth doctrine protects the freedom of speech guaranteed by the first amendment by invalidating laws so broadly written that the fear of prosecution would discourage people from exercising that freedom. Rokicki is not being punished merely because he holds an unpopular view on homosexuality or because he expressed those views loudly or in a passionate manner. Rokicki was charged with a hate crime because he allowed those beliefs to motivate unreasonable conduct. Rokicki remains free to believe what he will regarding people who are homosexual, but he may not force his opinions on others by shouting, pounding on a counter, and disrupting a lawful business. Rokicki's conduct exceeded the bounds of spirited debate, and the first amendment does not give him the right to harass or terrorize anyone. Therefore, because the hate crime statute requires conduct beyond mere expression . . . , the Illinois Hate Crime Statute constitutionally regulates conduct without infringing upon free speech.

2. Content Discrimination

Rokicki cites *R.A.V. v. City of St. Paul* and argues that the hate crime statute is constitutionally impermissible because it discriminates based on the content of an offender's beliefs. Rokicki argues that the statute enhances disorderly conduct to hate crime when the conduct is motivated by an offender's views on race or sexual orientation but that it treats identical conduct differently if motivated by an offender's beliefs regarding abortion or animal rights. . . .

(continues)

(continued)

However, in *R.A.V.*, the Court recognized several limitations to its content discrimination analysis, including statutes directed at conduct rather than speech. . . . One year later, in *Wisconsin v. Mitchell*, the Court held that the State could act to redress the harm it perceived as associated with bias-motivated crimes by punishing bias-motivated offenses more severely. . . . We too decide that the legislature was free to determine as a matter of sound public policy that bias-motivated crimes create greater harm than identical conduct not motivated by bias and should be punished more harshly. Consequently, we reject defendant's content discrimination argument.

3. Chilling Effect

Rokicki also argues that the hate crime statute chills free expression because individuals will be deterred from expressing unpopular views out of fear that such expression will later be used to justify a hate crime charge. We disagree. The overbreadth doctrine should be used sparingly and only when the constitutional infirmity is both real and substantial. We find Rokicki's argument speculative, and we cannot conclude that individuals will refrain from expressing controversial beliefs simply because they fear that their statements might be used as evidence of motive if they later commit an offense identified in the hate crime statute.

CONCLUSION

We hold that the hate crime statute is not unconstitutional when the predicate offense is disorderly conduct because (1) the statute reaches only conduct and does not punish speech itself; (2) the statute does not impermissibly discriminate based on content; and (3) the statute does not chill the exercise of first amendment rights.

Accordingly, we affirm defendant's conviction.

The judgment of the circuit court of Kane County is affirmed.

QUESTIONS

1. State the elements of the Illinois Hate Crime Statute.
2. List all of the facts relevant to deciding whether Kenneth Rokicki violated the hate crime statute.
3. According to the court, why doesn't the Illinois Hate Crime Statute violate Rokicki's right to free speech?
4. In your opinion, does the statute punish speech or nonexpressive conduct?
5. Do you think the purpose of this statute is to prevent disorderly conduct or expression?
6. Does Rokicki have a point when he argues that the statute prohibits only some kinds of hatred—race, ethnic, and sexual orientation—but not other kinds, for example, hatred for animal rights and abortion? Defend your answer.

EXPLORING FURTHER

Free Speech

1. Is "nude dancing" expressive speech?

Barnes v. Glen Theatre, Inc. et al., 501 U.S. 560 (1991)

FACTS

An Indiana statute prohibits nude dancing in public. Glen Theatre, a bar that featured nude dancing, sought an injunction against enforcing the law, arguing it violated the First Amendment. The law permitted erotic dancing, as long as the dancers wore "G-strings" and "pasties." It prohibited only totally nude dancing. The law argued that dancers can express themselves erotically without total nudity. Did the ordinance unduly restrict expressive conduct protected by the right to free speech?

DECISION

No, said the U.S. Supreme Court. Chief Justice Rehnquist, writing for a plurality, admitted that nude dancing is expressive conduct, but he concluded that the public indecency statute is justified because it "furthers a substantial government interest in protecting order and morality." So the ban on public nudity was not related to the erotic message the dancers wanted to send.

2. Is flag burning expressive conduct?

Texas v. Johnson, 491 U.S. 397 (1989)

FACTS

During the 1984 Republican National Convention in Dallas, Gregory Lee Johnson participated in a political demonstration called the "Republican War Chest Tour." The purpose of this event was to protest the policies of the Reagan administration and of certain Dallas-based corporations. The demonstrators marched through the Dallas streets, chanting political slogans and stopping at several corporate locations to stage "die-ins" intended to dramatize the consequences of nuclear war. On several occasions, they spray-painted the walls of buildings and overturned potted plants, but Johnson himself took no part in such activities. He did, however, accept an American flag handed to him by a fellow protestor who had taken it from a flagpole outside one of the targeted buildings.

The demonstration ended in front of Dallas City Hall, where Johnson unfurled the American flag, doused it with kerosene, and set it on fire. While the flag burned, the protestors chanted, "America, the red, white, and blue, we spit on you." After the demonstrators dispersed, a witness to the flag burning collected the flag's remains and buried them in his backyard. No one was physically injured or threatened with injury, though several witnesses testified that they had been seriously offended by the flag burning.

Johnson was charged and convicted under Texas's "desecration of a venerated object" statute, sentenced to one year in prison, and fined $2,000. Did the flag-burning statute violate Johnson's right to free speech?

DECISION

Yes, said a divided U.S. Supreme Court:

> If there is a bedrock principle underlying the First Amendment, it is that the Government may not prohibit the expression of an idea simply because society finds the idea itself offensive or disagreeable. We have not recognized an exception to this principle even where our flag has been involved. Justice Jackson described one of our society's defining principles in words deserving of their frequent repetition: "If there is any fixed star in our constitutional constellation, it is that no official, high or petty, can prescribe what shall be orthodox in politics, nationalism, religion, or other matters of opinion or force citizens to confess by word or act their faith therein."

Although Justice Kennedy concurred, the flag burning obviously disturbed him. He wrote:

> The hard fact is that sometimes we must make decisions we do not like. We make them because they are right, right in the sense that the law and the Constitution, as we see them, compel the result. And so great is our commitment to the process that, except in the rare case, we do not pause to express distaste for the result, perhaps for fear of undermining a valued principle that dictates the decision. This is one of those rare cases. The case here today forces recognition of the costs to which [our] . . . beliefs commit us. It is poignant but fundamental that the flag protects those who hold it in contempt. . . . So I agree with the court that he must go free.

Four justices dissented. Perhaps none of the justices felt more strongly than the World War II naval officer Justice Stevens, who wrote:

> The ideas of liberty and equality have been an irresistible force in motivating leaders like Patrick Henry, Susan B. Anthony, and Abraham Lincoln, schoolteachers like Nathan Hale and Booker T. Washington, the Philippine Scouts who fought at Bataan, and the soldiers who scaled the bluff at Omaha Beach. If those ideas are worth fighting for—and our history demonstrates that they are—it cannot be true that the flag that uniquely symbolizes their power is not itself worthy of protection from unnecessary desecration.
>
> I respectfully dissent.

LO 5

THE "RIGHT TO BEAR ARMS"

> A well regulated Militia, being necessary to the security of a free State, the right of the people to keep and bear Arms, shall not be infringed. (U.S. Constitution, Amendment II)

> For most of our country's history, the Second Amendment was absent from the Supreme Court's agenda. When arguments based on the amendment reached the Court, they were ineffectual. (Cook, Ludwig, and Samaha 2009, 16)

Outside the Court, however, there was a lot of excitement, generated by heated debate between gun rights and gun control activists, and by a booming Second Amendment scholarship produced by a growing number of constitutional law professors and historians. It caught legislators' attention, too. There were even "rumblings" among judges (Cook, Ludwig, and Samaha 2009, 16–17).

Then, in 2008, the U.S. Supreme Court case *District of Columbia v. Heller* became the "first successful Second Amendment challenge in the Court's history—a full 207 years after the Amendment was ratified" (Cook, Ludwig, and Samaha 2009, 17–18). Dick Heller, a D.C. special police officer, is authorized to carry a handgun while he's on duty at the Federal Judicial Center in Washington, D.C. He applied to the D.C. government for a registration certificate for a handgun that he wished to keep at home, to have it operable, and to "carry it about his home in that condition only when necessary for self-defense" (17–18).

The District of Columbia, not friendly to gun rights, as part of its gun control regime had two laws that stood in the way of Heller's application. One banned private citizens from possessing handguns (D.C. Gun Laws 2009, § 7–2502.01). The second provides that

> Except for law enforcement personnel . . . each registrant shall keep any firearm in his possession unloaded and disassembled or bound by a trigger lock or similar device unless such firearm is kept at his place of business, or while being used for lawful recreational purposes within the District of Columbia. (§ 7–2507.02)

The D.C. government denied Heller's application. Heller filed suit in the U.S. District Court for the District of Columbia seeking, on Second Amendment grounds, an order to stop the D.C. government from:

> (1) enforcing the ban on registering handguns;
> (2) the licensing requirement insofar as it prohibits the carrying of a firearm in the home without a license; and
> (3) the trigger-lock requirement insofar as it prohibits the use of "functional firearms within the home." (*District of Columbia v. Heller* 2008, 2)

The U.S. District Court dismissed Heller's complaint. The Court of Appeals for the D.C. Circuit reversed. The District of Columbia appealed, and the U.S. Supreme Court granted certiorari (2). The Court (5–4) struck down both the D.C. code provision banning the possession of handguns and the one requiring that firearms in the home be kept nonfunctional even when necessary for self-defense. According to the majority, the core of the **Second Amendment** is "the right of law-abiding, responsible citizens to use arms in defense of hearth and home" (63). And the two D.C. gun control provisions stand in the way of exercising this right.

Second Amendment, "the right of law-abiding, responsible citizens to use arms in defense of hearth and home"

> The American people have considered the handgun to be the quintessential self-defense weapon. There are many reasons that a citizen may prefer a handgun for home defense: It is easier to store in a location that is readily accessible in an emergency; it cannot easily be redirected or wrestled away by an attacker; it is easier to use

> for those without the upper-body strength to lift and aim a long gun; it can be pointed at a burglar with one hand while the other hand dials the police. Whatever the reason, handguns are the most popular weapon chosen by Americans for self-defense in the home, and a complete prohibition of their use is invalid.
>
> We must also address the District's requirement that firearms in the home be rendered and kept inoperable at all times. This makes it impossible for citizens to use them for the core lawful purpose of self-defense and is hence unconstitutional. (57–58)

After the decision, there was lots of ballyhooing about the triumph of the individual right to carry handguns. But the decision applied only to the District of Columbia, not to state and local governments. Although the Court, in *McDonald v. City of Chicago* (2010), made clear that the right recognized in *Heller* fully applied to state and local governments, it reiterated that it's decision in *McDonald* did no more than apply it's *Heller* holding to the state and municipalities. The Court struck down the Chicago ordinance because, like the D.C. ordinance, it banned possession by:

1. Law-abiding citizens
2. With a functional *handgun*
3. In their own homes
4. For the purpose of self-defense

According to the majority, "Like most rights, the right secured by the Second Amendment is not unlimited. . . . The right [is] not a right to keep and carry any weapon whatsoever in any manner whatsoever and for whatever purpose" (2816–17). It then provided a list of examples, which it made clear was not "exhaustive," such as bans on

1. Carrying concealed weapons
2. Felons possessing firearms
3. Mentally ill persons possessing firearms
4. Carrying firearms in sensitive places such as schools and government buildings
5. Laws imposing conditions and qualifications on the commercial sale of arms

Despite all the talk about limits, *Heller* is an important decision for at least three reasons. First, it renders the first clause in the Second Amendment irrelevant: "A well regulated Militia, being necessary to the security of a free State . . ." Second, it doesn't rule out expanding the right beyond the narrow boundaries of *Heller* and *McDonald*. Third, and extremely important, it's a "litigation magnet" (Cook, Ludwig, and Samaha 2009, 22), largely because, "unfortunately, the [U.S. Supreme] Court declined to 'undertake an exhaustive historical analysis' . . . of the full scope of the Second Amendment" (*GeorgiaCarry.Org, Inc.* 2011, 1313).

So far, therefore, it's left up to lower federal courts and state courts to determine how far protection extends beyond the "only conduct the Court clearly located within the Second Amendment right, [namely] the possession and carrying of a handgun by an otherwise qualified person within his home for self-defense" (*GeorgiaCarry.Org, Inc. v. Georgia*, 1313).

According to the Legal Community Against Violence (2011), as of September 2011, it had examined over three hundred federal and state cases discussing the Second Amendment in preparing its *Post-Heller Litigation Summary* update. You can find a sample of these cases in Figure 2.1. One of these cases is our next case excerpt, *GeorgiaCarry.Org, Inc. v. Georgia*.

LOWER COURT DECISIONS APPLYING THE SECOND AMENDMENT AFTER *HELLER*

Mishaga v. Monken, Director of Illinois State Police

753 F.Supp.2d 750 (C.D. Ill. 2010)

Ellen Mishaga, an Ohio resident, frequently travels to Illinois. While in Illinois, she stays with friends. She wants to possess a working firearm for personal protection while she's in her friends' home. The Illinois Firearm Owners Identification Card Act (430 ILCS 65/0.01 and following) requires individuals to have an Illinois Firearm Owner's Identification Card (FOID) to possess a weapon in Illinois. Mishaga has applied for a FOID twice, but the Illinois State Police (ISP), which issues the cards, rejected her application both times because she doesn't have an Illinois driver's license.

Mishaga contends that the ISP's refusal to issue her a FOID card violates her Second Amendment right to bear arms. The Second Amendment guarantees an individual the "right to possess a weapon within one's own home that may be used for personal protection." The act prohibits a person from possessing a weapon without a FOID. So the act "interferes with Mishaga's right to have a weapon at her temporary residency in Illinois that she may use for her personal protection.

Mishaga alleges that she has regularly resided in Illinois as a guest of her friends and that she intends to reside in Illinois in the future. The Second Amendment guarantees Mishaga the right to possess a weapon at her residence that she may use for personal protection in case of a confrontation.

Williams v. State

10 A.3d 1167 (Md. 2011)

As Officer Molake of Prince George's County Police Department was driving, he saw Charles Francis Williams Jr. going through a backpack near a wooded area. When Officer Molake turned his cruiser around, he saw Williams turn and place something in the brush. Molake approached Williams and asked what he was doing. Williams told him he was going through the backpack to see what was in it. Then, Molake asked Williams what he had hidden in the bushes. Williams hesitated, then said, "My gun." Officer recovered an Austrian-made black Glock handgun with 15 rounds in the magazine.

After receiving the *Miranda* warnings, Williams gave a written statement, admitting that he possessed the gun and that he put it in the bushes. Williams had bought the gun for self-defense after completing the application and affidavit to buy a regulated firearm and receiving the certificate of completion. In a bench trial, Judge Wallace found Williams guilty of wearing, carrying, or transporting a handgun in violation of Maryland law and sentenced him to three years' incarceration, two years suspended. The Court of Special Appeals affirmed.

State v. Robinson

2011 N.J. Super. Unpub. (App.Div. Aug. 23, 2011)

On August 23, the Superior Court of New Jersey rejected Robinson's Second Amendment challenge to his conviction for possessing a handgun without a permit. Robinson, a long-distance truck driver who lived in his truck for days at a time, argued that his truck was a second home that deserved Second Amendment protection under *Heller* and *McDonald*. Although the court resolved the case without deciding whether a truck could qualify as a home, it emphasized that *Heller* and *McDonald* "dealt exclusively with guns in the home," and that to consider a truck as a second home "requires acceptance of an expansive definition of the word "home."

DiGiacinto v. Rector and Visitors of George Mason University

704 S.E.2d 365 (Va. 2011)

Rudolph DiGiacinto (DG) sought an injunction against the Rector and visitors of George Mason University (GMU) to enjoin GMU from enforcing the university regulation against him. The regulation provides as follows:

> [P]ossession or carrying of any weapon by any person, except the police officer, is prohibited on University property in academic buildings, administrative office buildings, student residence buildings, dining facilities, or while attending sporting, entertainment or educational events. Entry upon the aforementioned University property in violation of this prohibition is expressly forbidden.

DG is not a student or employee of GMU, but he visits and utilizes the university's resources, including its libraries. He desires to exercise his right to carry a firearm not only onto the GMU campus but also into the buildings and at the events enumerated in the regulation. He argues in his complaint that the regulation violates his constitutional right to carry a firearm.

In this case, George Mason University is a public educational institution and an agency of the Commonwealth. It was stipulated at trial that George Mason University has 30,000 students enrolled, ranging from age 16 to senior citizens and that over 350 members of the incoming freshmen class would be under the age of 18. Also, approximately 50,000 elementary and high school students attend summer camps at George Mason University and approximately 130 children attend the Child Study Center preschool there. All of these individuals use GMU buildings and attend events on campus. The fact that GMU is a school and that its buildings are owned by the government indicates that GMU is a sensitive place.

(continues)

FIGURE 2.1

Further, the statutory structure established indicates that it is a sensitive place, and it is also consistent with the traditional understanding of the University. Unlike a public street or park, the University traditionally has not been open to the general public, "but instead is an institute of higher learning that is devoted to its mission of public education." Moreover, parents who send their children to the University have a reasonable expectation that the University will maintain a campus free of foreseeable harm.

The regulation does not impose a total ban of weapons on campus. Rather, the regulation is tailored, restricting weapons only in those places where people congregate and are the most vulnerable–inside campus buildings and at campus events. Individuals may still carry or possess weapons on the open grounds, and in other places on campus not enumerated in the regulation. We hold that George Mason University is a sensitive place and that the regulation is constitutional and doesn't violate the Constitution of Virginia or the Second Amendment of the federal Constitution.

Accordingly, for the reason stated we will affirm the circuit court's judgment.

Affirmed.

FIGURE 2.1 *(Continued)*

CASE

In* GeorgiaCarry.Org. Inc. v. Georgia *(2011), *GeorgiaCarry.Org. Inc., a nonprofit corporation whose mission is to "foster the rights of its members to keep and bear arms," the Baptist Tabernacle [church] of Thomaston Georgia; Edward Stone, a Georgia Carry member; and Jonathan Wilkins challenged a Georgia statute ban on "carrying a weapon . . . in a place of worship."*

Did he have a right to carry a gun in the church?

GeorgiaCarry.Org, Inc. v. Georgia

764 F.Supp.2d 1306 (M.D.Ga. 2011)

HISTORY

Plaintiffs GeorgiaCarry.Org, Inc. ("GCO"), The Baptist Tabernacle of Thomaston, Georgia, Inc. ("Tabernacle"), Edward Stone, and Jonathan Wilkins seek a ruling on the constitutionality of a provision of Georgia's firearm laws regulating the possession of weapons in a place of worship. The court determined that the plaintiffs failed to state a claim for relief, and granted defendants, the state of Georgia, Gov. Sonny Perdue, and other Georgia officials' motion to dismiss.

ROYAL, J.

FACTS

On June 4, 2010, Governor Sonny Perdue signed into law Senate Bill 308, which contained various amendments to Georgia's firearms laws. In particular, the bill amended O.C.G.A. § 16–11–127, which at that time prohibited the carrying of firearms at a "public gathering." In pertinent part, O.C.G.A. § 16–11–127 now provides that:

A person shall be guilty of carrying a weapon or long gun in an unauthorized location and punished as for a misdemeanor when he or she carries a weapon or long gun while:

(1) In a government building;

(2) In a courthouse;

(3) In a jail or prison;

(4) In a place of worship;

(5) In a state mental health facility as defined in Code Section 37–1–1 which admits individuals on an involuntary basis for treatment of mental illness, developmental disability, or addictive disease . . . ;

(6) In a bar, unless the owner of the bar permits the carrying of weapons or long guns by license holders;

(7) On the premises of a nuclear power facility . . . ;

(8) Within 150 feet of any polling place. . . .

O.C.G.A. § 16–11–127(b). A weapon, for purposes of section 16–11–127, is defined as a knife or handgun.

- Plaintiff GeorgiaCarry.Org, Inc., is a non-profit corporation organized under the laws of the state of Georgia. Its primary mission is to foster the rights of its members to keep and bear arms. Most of GCO's members possess valid Georgia Weapons Licenses issued pursuant to O.C.G.A. § 16–11–129.
- Plaintiff Edward Stone is the former President of GCO and a current member of its board of

(continues)

(continued)

directors. Stone has a valid Georgia Weapons License. Stone regularly attends worship services. While attending services, he would like to carry a firearm to defend himself and his family, but he alleges that he fears arrest and prosecution under O.C.G.A. § 16–11–127 for doing so.

- Plaintiff Baptist Tabernacle of Thomaston, Georgia, Inc., is a non-profit corporation organized under the laws of the state of Georgia. The Tabernacle is a religious institution and owns real property in Thomaston, Georgia, where it conducts religious worship services. The Tabernacle would like to allow certain members with valid Georgia Weapons Licenses to carry firearms on Tabernacle property, but alleges that it fears its members will be arrested and prosecuted for doing so.
- Plaintiff Jonathan Wilkins is the CEO and pastor of the Tabernacle. He is also a member of GCO and has a valid Georgia Weapons License. He regularly conducts worship services on Tabernacle property and would like to carry a weapon to defend himself, his family, and his congregation while doing so. He also has an office in the Tabernacle building and is frequently the only occupant of the building. He would like to keep a firearm in his office for self-defense, but he alleges that he fears being prosecuted for carrying a firearm while conducting services or keeping one in his office.

Plaintiffs filed this action against the following Defendants: the State of Georgia; Upson County, Georgia; Governor Sonny Perdue, in his official capacity as Governor of Georgia; and Kyle Hood, in his official capacity as County Manager for Upson County.

In this action, Plaintiffs allege that O.C.G.A. § 16–11–127(b)(4) violates . . . their Second Amendment right to keep and bear arms. The Plaintiffs seek declaratory relief in the form of a ruling that the statute is unconstitutional both on its face and as applied to them and an injunction prohibiting enforcement of the statute.

OPINION

Second Amendment

Plaintiffs . . . contend that the statute impermissibly burdens their right to keep and bear arms secured by the Second Amendment. . . . In determining whether the statute impermissibly burdens their right, the decision in *District of Columbia v. Heller* (2008) is the appropriate starting point. . . . In *Heller*, the Supreme Court . . . identified the Second Amendment as guaranteeing an "individual right to possess and carry weapons in case of confrontation." The Court went on to describe "the inherent right of self-defense" as "central to the Second Amendment right." . . . Although an "individual right to possess and carry weapons in case of confrontation" in support of "the inherent right of self-defense" seems quite broad, . . . unfortunately, the Court declined to "undertake an exhaustive historical analysis" . . . of the full scope of the Second Amendment." . . .

With those principles in mind, the Court turns to whether this state law passes constitutional muster. Unfortunately, *Heller* does not explicitly answer the question. The Supreme Court recognized that the Second Amendment protects a right to possess and carry weapons for self defense; however, given the "severe" nature of the law in that case, the only conduct that the Court clearly located within the Second Amendment right was the possession and carrying of a handgun by an otherwise qualified person within his home for self-defense.

. . . Defendants argue, based on the *Heller* list of presumptively lawful regulatory measures, that the conduct lies beyond the Second Amendment. That list includes laws prohibiting carrying a firearm in "sensitive places such as schools and government buildings." . . . Given . . . that the Supreme Court did not indicate why a certain place might be considered "sensitive" for purposes of prohibiting firearms, the Court is hesitant to accept that whatever "sensitive" might mean, it must include places of worship. . . . Schools and government buildings do not immediately suggest any unifying theme or greater purpose that would go unserved if places of worship were not included, nor have Defendants suggested one.

Given the indeterminacy of what the Supreme Court intended to capture with the term "sensitive places," the Court finds that the better analytical approach is to lay aside the *Heller* list for the moment, to assume that Georgia's law burdens conduct within the scope of the Second Amendment, and to test whether the State can make the necessary showing to demonstrate that categorically prohibiting the possession of firearms in places of worship is permissible.

. . . Defendants suggest that a place might be considered sensitive for any number of reasons. Certainly true. A place, such as a school, might be considered sensitive because of the people found there. Other places, such as government buildings, might be considered sensitive because of the activities that take place there. A reasonable argument can be made that places of worship are also sensitive places because of the activities that occur there. In the absence of clearer guidance as to what the Supreme Court meant to capture within the net of "sensitive places," however, the Court concludes that the safer approach for now is the one taken—assuming that possession at a place of worship is within the Second Amendment guarantee and applying intermediate scrutiny. [The law is constitutional law as long as it is *substantially* related to an important government interest, such as protecting the First Amendment right to the free exercise of religion.] Prohibiting the carrying of firearms in a place of worship bears a substantial relationship to that important goal by protecting attendees from the fear or threat of intimidation or armed attack. [Therefore, the Court found that the statute] passes intermediate scrutiny. . . .

[The Court then considered] Pastor Wilkins' contention that the statute is unconstitutional because it prevents him from keeping a firearm in his office at the Tabernacle. . . . Although the statute generally prohibits persons with valid Georgia Weapons Licenses from carrying a firearm in a place of worship, the statute also provides that the prohibition on carrying in the unauthorized locations listed in subsection (b) does not apply to . . . "a license holder who approaches security or management personnel upon arrival . . . and notifies such security or management personnel of the presence of the weapon . . . and explicitly follows the security of management personnel's direction for removing, securing, storing, or temporarily surrendering such weapon."

As a result, the statute would allow Wilkins to keep a firearm in his office if he obtained permission from security or management personnel of the Tabernacle and kept it secured or stored as directed. If management or security personnel at the Tabernacle, which presumably includes Wilkins as CEO, did not grant him permission to secure or store a firearm in his office, then that would be at their discretion. Plaintiffs do not argue, however, that they possess a constitutional right to carry a firearm onto private property against the wishes of the owner or controller of the property.

For the foregoing reasons, the Court concludes that even accepting the Plaintiffs' well-pleaded allegations as true, they have failed to state a claim for relief under the Second Amendment.

QUESTIONS

1. Summarize the provisions in the Georgia statute that the plaintiffs contend violate their Second Amendment right to bear arms.
2. Summarize the Court's reasons for concluding that the statute doesn't violate plaintiffs' right to bear arms.
3. Do you agree with the District Court that the U.S. Supreme Court's decisions in *Heller* and *McDonald* don't provide much help in guiding the lower courts in deciding how far beyond the "right to bear arms" the Second Amendment goes than the right of law-abiding individuals to possess an operable handgun in their homes for self-defense?
4. Do you agree that it doesn't go as far as allowing these plaintiffs to carry their handguns in the church? Defend your answer.

THE RIGHT TO PRIVACY

LO1

Unlike the rights to free speech and to bear arms, which are spelled out clearly in the First and Second Amendments, you won't find the word "privacy" anywhere in the U.S. Constitution. Nevertheless, the U.S. Supreme Court has decided there is a constitutional right to privacy, a right that bans "all governmental invasions of the sanctity of a man's home and the privacies of life" (*Griswold v. Connecticut* 1965, 484).

constitutional right to privacy, a right that bans "all governmental invasions of the sanctity of a man's home and the privacies of life"

Not only is privacy a constitutional right, it's a *fundamental* right that requires the government to prove that a compelling interest justifies invading it. According to the

fundamental right to privacy, a right that requires the government to prove that a compelling interest justifies invading it

Court (*Griswold v. Connecticut* 1965), the **fundamental right to privacy** originates in six amendments to the U.S. Constitution:

- The First Amendment rights of free speech, religion, and association
- The Third Amendment ban on the quartering of soldiers in private homes
- The Fourth Amendment right to be secure in one's "person, house, papers, and effects" from "unreasonable searches"
- The Ninth Amendment provision that "the enumeration in the Constitution, of certain rights, shall not be construed to deny or disparage others retained by the people"
- The Fifth and Fourteenth Amendments' due process right to liberty

This cluster of amendments sends the implied but strong message that we have the right to be let alone by the government. In the First Amendment, it's our beliefs and expression of them and our associations with other people that are protected from government interference. In the Third and Fourth Amendments, our homes are the object of protection. And, in the Fourth Amendment, it's not only our homes but our bodies, our private papers, and even our "stuff" that fall under its protection. The Ninth, or catchall, Amendment acknowledges we have rights not named in the Constitution. In other words, "specific guarantees in the Bill of Rights have penumbras, formed by emanations from those guarantees that help give them life and substance" (484).

According to the Court, privacy is one of these rights "not named in the Constitution." Based on this right, the Court struck down two Connecticut contraception statutes. The first statute provided:

> Any person who uses any drug, medicinal article or instrument for the purpose of preventing conception shall be fined not less than fifty dollars or imprisoned not less than sixty days nor more than one year or be both fined and imprisoned. (quoted in *Griswold*, 480)

The second provided:

> Any person who assists, abets, counsels, causes, hires or commands another to commit any offense may be prosecuted and punished as if he were the principal offender.

In several cases after *Griswold*, the Court decided several controversial cases based on the right to privacy (Table 2.1).

TABLE 2.1 The U.S. Supreme Court and the Right to Privacy from *Griswold* to *Lawrence*

CASE	DECISION
Griswold v. Connecticut, 381 U.S. 479 (1965)	Struck down laws (1) making it a crime for married couples to use contraceptives and (2) to counsel couples on birth control
Stanley v. Georgia, 394 U.S. 557 (1969)	Struck down a state law making it a crime for adults to possess pornography in the privacy of their homes
Eisenstadt v. Baird, 405 U.S. 438 (1972)	Invalidated a law banning distribution of contraceptives to unmarried persons
Roe v. Wade, 410 U.S. (1973)	Struck down a law banning abortions
Carey v. Population Services International, 431 U.S. 678 (1977)	Struck down a law banning the use or sale of contraceptive devices to persons under sixteen
Planned Parenthood v. Casey, 505 U.S. 833 (1991)	Struck down a law requiring a pregnant wife to notify her husband of her intention to abort the fetus

CASE

In **Lawrence v. Texas** ***(2003),*** *the U.S. Supreme Court struck down a Texas statute that made homosexual sodomy a crime.*

Do consenting adults have a right to privacy in their private sexual conduct?

Lawrence v. Texas

539 U.S. 558 (2003)

HISTORY

Defendants John Geddes Lawrence and Tyrone Garner were convicted in the County Criminal Court at Law No. 10, Harris County, Texas, of engaging in homosexual conduct. They appealed. On rehearing en banc, the Texas Court of Appeals affirmed. Certiorari was granted. The Supreme Court overruled its prior decision in *Bowers v. Hardwick* and held that the Texas statute making it a crime for two persons of the same sex to engage in certain intimate sexual conduct was unconstitutional, as applied to adult males who had engaged in a consensual act of sodomy in the privacy of their home.

KENNEDY, J., JOINED BY STEVENS, SOUTER, GINSBURG, AND BREYER, JJ.
JUSTICE KENNEDY DELIVERED THE OPINION OF THE COURT.

FACTS

In Houston, Texas, officers of the Harris County Police Department were dispatched to a private residence in response to a reported weapons disturbance. They entered an apartment where one of the petitioners, John Geddes Lawrence, resided. The right of the police to enter does not seem to have been questioned. The officers observed Lawrence and another man, Tyron Garner, engaging in a sexual act. The two petitioners were arrested, held in custody overnight, and charged and convicted before a Justice of the Peace.

The complaints described their crime as "deviate sexual intercourse, namely anal sex, with a member of the same sex (man)." The applicable state law is Tex. Penal Code Ann. § 21.06(a) (2003). It provides: "A person commits an offense if he engages in deviate sexual intercourse with another individual of the same sex." The statute defines "deviate sexual intercourse" as follows:

"(A) any contact between any part of the genitals of one person and the mouth or anus of another person; or

"(B) the penetration of the genitals or the anus of another person with an object." § 21.01(1).

The petitioners were adults at the time of the alleged offense. Their conduct was in private and consensual.

OPINION

[The opinion is an excerpt taken from the Syllabus of the Court.]

Resolution of this case depends on whether petitioners were free as adults to engage in private conduct in the exercise of their liberty under the Due Process Clause. . . . Although the laws involved . . . here purport to do no more than prohibit a particular sexual act, their penalties and purposes have more far-reaching consequences, touching upon the most private human conduct, sexual behavior, and in the most private of places, the home. They seek to control a personal relationship that, whether or not entitled to formal recognition in the law, is within the liberty of persons to choose without being punished as criminals. The liberty protected by the Constitution allows homosexual persons the right to choose to enter upon relationships in the confines of their homes and their own private lives and still retain their dignity as free persons.

. . .

The stigma the Texas criminal statute imposes, moreover, is not trivial. Although the offense is but a minor misdemeanor, it remains a criminal offense with all that imports for the dignity of the persons charged, including notation of convictions on their records and on job application forms, and registration as sex offenders under state law. Where a case's foundations have sustained serious erosion, criticism from other sources is of greater significance. In the United States, criticism of *Bowers* has been substantial and continuing, disapproving of its reasoning in all respects, not just as to its historical assumptions.

. . .

This case does not involve minors, persons who might be injured or coerced, those who might not easily refuse consent, or public conduct or prostitution. It does involve two adults who, with full and mutual

(continues)

(continued)

consent, engaged in sexual practices common to a homosexual lifestyle. Petitioners' right to liberty under the Due Process Clause gives them the full right to engage in private conduct without government intervention. The Texas statute furthers no legitimate state interest which can justify its intrusion into the individual's personal and private life.

The judgment of the Court of Appeals for the Texas Fourteenth District is reversed, and the case is remanded for further proceedings not inconsistent with this opinion.

It is so ordered.

CONCURRING OPINION

O'CONNOR, J.

. . . Rather than relying on the substantive component of the Fourteenth Amendment's Due Process Clause, as the Court does, I base my conclusion on the Fourteenth Amendment's Equal Protection Clause. The Equal Protection Clause of the Fourteenth Amendment "is essentially a direction that all persons similarly situated should be treated alike." . . .

This case raises . . . [the] issue . . . whether, under the Equal Protection Clause, moral disapproval is a legitimate state interest to justify . . . a statute that bans homosexual sodomy, but not heterosexual sodomy. It is not. . . . We have never held that moral disapproval, without any other asserted state interest, is a sufficient rationale under the Equal Protection Clause to justify a law that discriminates among groups of persons.

Texas argues, however, that the sodomy law does not discriminate against homosexual persons. Instead, the State maintains that the law discriminates only against homosexual conduct. While it is true that the law applies only to conduct, the conduct targeted by this law is conduct that is closely correlated with being homosexual. Under such circumstances, Texas' sodomy law is targeted at more than conduct. It is instead directed toward gay persons as a class. "After all, there can hardly be more palpable discrimination against a class than making the conduct that defines the class criminal." . . .

DISSENT

SCALIA, J., JOINED BY REHNQUIST, CJ. AND THOMAS, J.

. . . Today's opinion is the product of a Court, which is the product of a law-profession culture, that has largely signed on to the so-called homosexual agenda, by which I mean the agenda promoted by some homosexual activists directed at eliminating the moral opprobrium that has traditionally attached to homosexual conduct. . . . It is clear from this that the Court has taken sides in the culture war, departing from its role of assuring, as neutral observer, that the democratic rules of engagement are observed.

Many Americans do not want persons who openly engage in homosexual conduct as partners in their business, as scoutmasters for their children, as teachers in their children's schools, or as boarders in their home. They view this as protecting themselves and their families from a lifestyle that they believe to be immoral and destructive. The Court views it as "discrimination" which it is the function of our judgments to deter. So imbued is the Court with the law profession's anti-anti-homosexual culture, that it is seemingly unaware that the attitudes of that culture are not obviously "mainstream"; that in most States what the Court calls "discrimination" against those who engage in homosexual acts is perfectly legal; that proposals to ban such "discrimination" under Title VII have repeatedly been rejected by Congress.

Let me be clear that I have nothing against homosexuals, or any other group, promoting their agenda through normal democratic means. Social perceptions of sexual and other morality change over time, and every group has the right to persuade its fellow citizens that its view of such matters is the best. That homosexuals have achieved some success in that enterprise is attested to by the fact that Texas is one of the few remaining States that criminalize private, consensual homosexual acts.

But persuading one's fellow citizens is one thing, and imposing one's views in absence of democratic majority will is something else. I would no more *require* a State to criminalize homosexual acts—or, for that matter, display *any* moral disapprobation of them—than I would *forbid* it to do so. What Texas has chosen to do is well within the range of traditional democratic action, and its hand should not be stayed through the invention of a brand-new "constitutional right" by a Court that is impatient of democratic change. It is indeed true that "later generations can see that laws once thought necessary and proper in fact serve only to oppress," and when that happens, later generations can repeal those laws. But it is the premise of our system that those judgments are to be made by the people, and not imposed by a governing caste that knows best.

. . .

I dissent.

JUSTICE THOMAS, DISSENTING.

I join Justice SCALIA's dissenting opinion. I write separately to note that the law before the Court today "is . . . uncommonly silly." If I were a member of the Texas Legislature, I would vote to repeal it. Punishing someone for expressing his sexual preference through noncommercial consensual conduct with another adult does not appear to be a worthy way to expend valuable law enforcement resources.

Notwithstanding this, I recognize that as a Member of this Court I am not empowered to help petitioners and others similarly situated. My duty, rather, is to decide cases agreeably to the Constitution and laws of the United States. And, I "can find neither in the Bill of Rights nor any other part of the Constitution a general right of privacy," or as the Court terms it today, the "liberty of the person both in its spatial and more transcendent dimensions."

QUESTIONS

1. State exactly what the Court decided regarding homosexual sodomy.
2. Summarize the majority opinion's argument supporting its decision.
3. Summarize Justice O'Connor's arguments in her concurring opinion.
4. Summarize Justice Scalia's arguments in his dissent.
5. Summarize Justice Thomas's arguments in his dissent.
6. Whose opinion do you support? Defend your answer.

EXPLORING FURTHER

The Right to Privacy

Does the right to privacy protect pornography?

Stanley v. Georgia, 394 U.S. 557 (1969)

FACTS

Federal and state law enforcement agents, armed with a search warrant, searched Eli Stanley's home for evidence of his alleged bookmaking activities. They didn't find evidence of bookmaking, but while they were searching his bedroom, they found three pornographic films. Stanley was charged, indicted, and convicted under a Georgia statute that made it a crime to "knowingly have(ing) possession of . . . obscene matter. . . ." The Georgia Supreme Court affirmed the conviction. The U.S. Supreme Court reversed.

DECISION

According to the Court:

Georgia contends that since obscenity is not within the area of constitutionally protected speech or press, the States are free, subject to the limits of other provisions of the Constitution, to deal with it any way deemed necessary, just as they may deal with possession of other things thought to be detrimental to the welfare of their citizens. If the State can protect the body of a citizen, may it not, argues Georgia, protect his mind? . . .

In the context of this case—a prosecution for mere possession of printed or filmed matter in the privacy of a person's own home—is the . . . fundamental . . . right to be free . . . from unwanted governmental intrusions into one's privacy.

The makers of our Constitution undertook to secure conditions favorable to the pursuit of happiness. They recognized the significance of man's spiritual nature, of his feelings and of his intellect. They knew that only a part of the pain, pleasure and satisfactions of life are to be found in material things. They sought to protect Americans in their beliefs, their thoughts, their emotions and their sensations. They conferred, as against the government, the right to be let alone—the most comprehensive of rights and the right most valued by civilized man. (quoting *Olmstead v. U.S.* [1928] and citing *Griswold v. Connecticut* [1965])

LO 5, LO 6

THE CONSTITUTION AND CRIMINAL SENTENCING

cruel and unusual punishments, "barbaric" punishments and punishments that are disproportionate to the crime committed

The Eighth Amendment to the U.S. Constitution commands that "cruel and unusual punishments" shall not be "inflicted." According to the U.S. Supreme Court, there are two kinds of **cruel and unusual punishments**: "barbaric" punishments and punishments that are disproportionate to the crime committed (*Solem v. Helm* 1983, 284). Let's look at each.

Is shaming "right"?

Shawn Gementera pilfered letters from several mailboxes along San Francisco's Fulton Street on May 21, 2001. A police officer who observed the episode immediately detained Gementera and his partner in crime, Andrew Choi, who had been stuffing the stolen letters into his jacket as Gementera anxiously kept watch. After indictment, Gementera entered a plea agreement pursuant to which he pled guilty to mail theft, and the government dismissed a second count of receiving a stolen U.S. Treasury check.

The offense was not Gementera's first encounter with the law. Though only twenty-four years old at the time, Gementera's criminal history was lengthy for a man of his relative youth, and it was growing steadily more serious. At age nineteen, he was convicted of misdemeanor criminal mischief. He was twice convicted at age twenty of driving with a suspended license. At age twenty-two, a domestic dispute led to convictions for driving with a suspended license and for failing to provide proof of financial responsibility. By age twenty-four, there was a conviction for misdemeanor battery. Other arrests and citations included possession of drug paraphernalia, additional driving offenses (most of which involved driving on a license suspended for his failure to take chemical tests), and, soon after his twenty-fifth birthday, taking a vehicle without the owner's consent.

On February 25, 2003, Judge Vaughn Walker of the United States District Court for the Northern District of California sentenced Gementera. The U.S. Sentencing Guidelines range was two to eight months' incarceration; Judge Walker sentenced Gementera to the lower bound of the range, imposing two months' incarceration and three years' supervised release. The court explained that, while it would have been strongly inclined to impose home confinement had Gementera's criminal history been better, the court felt that "given the unpromising road that the defendant has been following, that he needs to have a taste of federal custody, to be sure a brief one, but he needs to understand that if he continues on the course that he has set for himself at his age he's going to be facing a lot more serious charges in the future."

He also imposed conditions of supervised release. One such condition required Gementera to "perform 100 hours of community service," to consist of "standing in front of a postal facility in the city and county of San Francisco with a sandwich board which in large letters declares: 'I stole mail. This is my punishment.'"

"Gementera later filed a motion to correct the sentence by removing the sandwich board condition. Judge Walker modified the sentence after inviting both parties to present "an alternative form or forms of public service that would better comport with the aims of the court." In lieu of the 100-hour signboard requirement, the district court imposed a four-part special condition. Three new terms, proposed jointly by counsel, mandated that the defendant observe postal patrons visiting the "lost or missing mail" window, write letters of apology to any identifiable victims of his crime, and deliver several lectures at a local school. It also included a scaled-down version of the signboard requirement:

> The defendant shall perform 1 day of 8 total hours of community service during which time he shall either (i) wear a two-sided sandwich board-style sign or (ii) carry a large two-sided sign stating, "I stole mail; this is my punishment," in front of a San Francisco postal facility identified by the probation officer. For the safety of defendant and general public, the postal facility

designated shall be one that employs one or more security guards. Upon showing by defendant that this condition would likely impose upon defendant psychological harm or effect or result in unwarranted risk of harm to defendant, the public or postal employees, the probation officer may withdraw or modify this condition or apply to the court to withdraw or modify this condition.

Gementera was ordered to surrender on March 31, 2003. On March 12, 2003, prior to his surrender, Gementera was arrested for possession of stolen mail.

Instructions

1. Assume you're an advisor to the Criminal Law Committee in the California state legislature, which is considering legislation banning "shaming" punishments for selected crimes. You're asked to write a memorandum for the committee that answers the following questions and then recommends what, if any, legislation the committee should draft:
   a. Do shaming punishments violate the Eighth Amendment ban on "cruel and unusual punishments"?
   b. Assuming they don't, are they wise public policy? According to the dissent in *U.S. v. Gementera* (2004), "A fair measure of a civilized society is how its institutions behave in the space between what it may have the power to do and what it should do."
   c. Recommend what, if any, legislation the committee should enact.
2. To prepare the memorandum, read the following:
   a. *U.S. v. Gementera* (2004) (http://law.justia.com/cases/federal/appellate-courts/F3/379/596/475040/)
   b. "Shame on You: Enough with Humiliating Punishments" by Jonathan Turley (http://www.washingtonpost.com/wp-dyn/content/article/2005/09/17/AR2005091700064.html)
   c. "Can Shaming Punishments Educate?" by Stephen Garvey (http://www.google.com/url?sa=t&rct=j&q=&esrc=s&source=web&cd=3&ved=0CGUQFjAC&url=http%3A%2F%2Fscholarship.law.cornell.edu%2Fcgi%2Fviewcontent.cgi%3Farticle%3D1345%26context%3Dfacpub&ei=CoypT5yLDojliAK5soDpAg&usg=AFQjCNFlFgbzYRSLF6oy2rDu_9rFmCRiHw&sig2=rHquhh7RBMzuHm1L6W_Zlw)

Sources: *U.S. v. Gementera*, 379 F.3d 596 (2004); Turley 2005; Garvey 1998.

BARBARIC PUNISHMENTS

barbaric punishments, punishments considered no longer acceptable to civilized society

Barbaric punishments are punishments that are considered no longer acceptable to civilized society. At the time the Eighth Amendment was adopted, these included burning at the stake, crucifixion, breaking on the wheel, torturing or lingering death (*In re Kemmler* 1890, 446); drawing and quartering, the rack and screw (*Chambers v. Florida* 1940, 227); and extreme forms of solitary confinement (*In re Medley* 1890, 160).

For more than a hundred years after the adoption of the Bill of Rights, no "cruel and unusual" punishment cases reached the U.S. Supreme Court because these medieval forms of execution weren't used in the United States. But, in 1885, the governor of the state of New York, in his annual message to the legislature, questioned the use of hanging as a method of execution:

> The present mode of executing criminals by hanging has come down to us from the dark ages, and it may well be questioned whether the science of the present day cannot provide a means for taking . . . life . . . in a less barbarous manner. (*In re Kemmler* 1890, 444)

The legislature appointed a commission to study the matter. The commission reported that electrocution was "the most humane and practical method [of execution] known to modern science (*In re Kemmler* 1890, 444)." In 1888, the legislature replaced the hangman's noose with the electric chair.

Shortly thereafter, William Kemmler, convicted of murdering his wife and sentenced to die in the electric chair, argued that electrocution was "cruel and unusual punishment." The U.S. Supreme Court disagreed. The Court said that electrocution was certainly unusual but not cruel. For the first time, the Court defined what "cruel" means in the Eighth Amendment. According to the Court, punishment by death isn't cruel as long as it isn't "something more than the mere extinguishment of life."

The Court spelled out what it meant by this phrase: First, death has to be both instantaneous and painless. Second, it can't involve unnecessary mutilation of the body. So, according to the Court, beheading is cruel because it mutilates the body. Crucifixion is doubly cruel because it inflicts a "lingering" death and mutilates the body (*In re Kemmler* 1890, 446–47).

LO 6

DISPROPORTIONATE PUNISHMENTS

principle of proportionality, the punishment has to fit the crime

The **principle of proportionality**—namely, that the punishment should fit the crime—has an ancient history (Chapter 1). The U.S. Supreme Court first applied proportionality as a principle required by the Eighth Amendment in *Weems v. U.S.* (1910). Paul Weems was convicted of falsifying a public document. The trial court first sentenced him to fifteen years in prison at hard labor in chains and then took away all of his civil rights for the rest of his life. The Court ruled that the punishment was "cruel and unusual" because it was disproportionate to his crime. *Weems* banned disproportionate punishments in federal criminal justice.

In extending the cruel and unusual punishment ban to state criminal justice in the 1960s, the Court in *Robinson v. California* (1962) reaffirmed its commitment to the proportionality principle. The Court majority ruled that a ninety-day sentence for drug addiction was disproportionate because addiction is an illness, and it's cruel and unusual to punish persons for being sick. "Even one day in prison would be a cruel and unusual punishment for the 'crime' of having a common cold," wrote Justice Marshall for the Court majority (Chapter 3).

Let's look at the issues surrounding whether many modern forms of punishment are proportional punishments.

The Death Penalty: "Death Is Different"

A majority of the U.S. Supreme Court has consistently agreed that the proportionality principle applies to death penalty cases; as the Court puts it, "death is different." There are numerous capital crimes where no one is killed; they include treason, espionage, kidnapping, aircraft hijacking, large-scale drug trafficking, train wrecking, and perjury that leads to someone's execution (Liptak 2003).

In practice, no one is actually sentenced to death for them, so it's difficult to tell whether the Court would rule that death is disproportionate to a crime where no one gets killed. With one exception—rape. In 1977, the Court heard *Coker v. Georgia;* it decided that death was disproportionate punishment for raping an adult woman.

In fact, it looked as if a majority of the Court was committed to the proposition that death is always disproportionate, except in some aggravated murders. That proposition held, but barely, in a bitterly contested case that reached the Court in 2008. In that case, our next case excerpt, the Court decided (5–4) that executing Patrick Kennedy was "cruel and unusual punishment" because it was disproportionate to his rape of his eight-year-old stepdaughter.

CASE

In* Kennedy v. Louisiana *(2008)*, *the Court decided that executing Patrick Kennedy was "cruel and unusual punishment" because it was disproportionate to his rape of his eight-year-old stepdaughter.

Is the death penalty for child rape cruel and unusual?

Kennedy v. Louisiana

554 U.S. 407 (2008)

HISTORY

Patrick Kennedy was convicted of the aggravated rape of his eight-year-old stepdaughter under a Louisiana statute that authorized capital punishment for the rape of a child under twelve years of age and was sentenced to death. On his appeal, the Supreme Court of Louisiana affirmed. Kennedy petitioned for certiorari, which was granted. The U.S. Supreme Court reversed and remanded.

KENNEDY. J., JOINED BY STEVENS, SOUTER, GINSBURG, AND BREYER, JJ.

FACTS

At 9:18 A.M. on March 2, 1998, Patrick Kennedy called 911 to report that his stepdaughter, L. H., had been raped. When police arrived at Kennedy's home between 9:20 and 9:30 A.M., they found L. H. on her bed, wearing a T-shirt and wrapped in a bloody blanket. She was bleeding profusely from the vaginal area. Kennedy told police he had carried her from the yard to the bathtub and then to the bed. Once in the bedroom, Kennedy had used a basin of water and a cloth to wipe blood from the victim.

L. H. was transported to the Children's Hospital. An expert in pediatric forensic medicine testified that L. H.'s injuries were the most severe he had seen from a sexual assault in his four years of practice. A laceration to the left wall of the vagina had separated her cervix from the back of her vagina, causing her rectum to protrude into the vaginal structure. Her entire perineum was torn from the posterior fourchette to the anus. The injuries required emergency surgery.

At the scene of the crime, at the hospital, and in the first weeks that followed, both L. H. and Kennedy maintained in their accounts to investigators that L. H. had been raped by two neighborhood boys. L. H. was interviewed several days after the rape by a psychologist. She told the psychologist that she had been playing in the garage when a boy came over and asked her about Girl Scout cookies she was selling; then that the boy "pulled her by the legs to the backyard," where he placed his hand over her mouth, "pulled down her shorts," and raped her.

Eight days after the crime, and despite L. H.'s insistence that Kennedy was not the offender, Kennedy was arrested for the rape. The state's investigation had drawn the accuracy of Kennedy and L. H.'s story into question. Police found that Kennedy made two telephone calls on the morning of the rape. Sometime before 6:15 A.M., Kennedy called his employer and left a message that he was unavailable to work that day. Kennedy called back between 6:30 and 7:30 A.M. to ask a colleague how to get blood out of a white carpet because his daughter had "just become a young lady." At 7:37 A.M., Kennedy called B & B Carpet Cleaning and requested urgent assistance in removing bloodstains from a carpet. Kennedy did not call 911 until about an hour and a half later.

About a month after Kennedy's arrest, L. H. was removed from the custody of her mother, who had maintained until that point that Kennedy was not involved in the rape. On June 22, 1998, L. H. was returned home and told her mother for the first time that Kennedy had raped her. And on December 16, 1999, about 21 months after the rape, L. H. recorded her accusation in a videotaped interview with the Child Advocacy Center.

The state charged Kennedy with aggravated rape of a child under La. Stat. Ann. § 14:42 (West 1997 and Supp. 1998) and sought the death penalty. According to the statute, "aggravated" applies to anal or vaginal rape without the consent of the victim—when it's committed under any of 10 aggravating circumstances, one of which is when the victim was under 12 years of age at the time of the rape. The penalty for aggravated rape is life in prison at hard labor without parole, probation, or suspension of sentence. But, if the victim is under 12, the prosecutor asks for the death penalty: "The offender shall be punished by death or life imprisonment at hard labor without benefit of parole, probation, or suspension of sentence, in accordance with the determination of the jury."

(continues)

(continued)

The trial began in August 2003. L. H. was then 13 years old. She testified that she "woke up one morning and Patrick was on top of her." She remembered Kennedy bringing her "a cup of orange juice and pills chopped up in it" after the rape and overhearing him on the telephone saying she had become a "young lady." L. H. acknowledged that she had accused two neighborhood boys but testified Kennedy told her to say this and that it was untrue.

After the jury found Kennedy guilty of aggravated rape, the penalty phase ensued. The jury unanimously determined that Kennedy should be sentenced to death. The Louisiana Supreme Court affirmed. We granted certiorari.

OPINION

The Eighth Amendment's protection against excessive or cruel and unusual punishments flows from the basic precept of justice that punishment for a crime should be graduated and proportioned to the offense. Whether this requirement has been fulfilled is determined not by the standards that prevailed when the Eighth Amendment was adopted in 1791 but by the norms that currently prevail. The Amendment draws its meaning from the evolving standards of decency that mark the progress of a maturing society.

Capital punishment must be limited to those offenders who commit a narrow category of the most serious crimes and whose extreme culpability makes them the most deserving of execution. In these cases the Court has been guided by objective indicia of society's standards, as expressed in legislative enactments and state practice with respect to executions. Whether the death penalty is disproportionate to the crime committed depends as well upon the standards elaborated by controlling precedents and by the Court's own understanding and interpretation of the Eighth Amendment's text, history, meaning, and purpose.

The evidence of a national consensus with respect to the death penalty for child rapists, as with respect to juveniles, mentally retarded offenders, and vicarious felony murderers, shows divided opinion but, on balance, an opinion against it. Thirty-seven jurisdictions—36 States plus the Federal Government—have the death penalty. Only six of those jurisdictions authorize the death penalty for rape of a child. Though our review of national consensus is not confined to tallying the number of States with applicable death penalty legislation, it is of significance that, in 45 jurisdictions, Kennedy could not be executed for child rape of any kind.

There are measures of consensus other than legislation. Statistics about the number of executions may inform the consideration whether capital punishment for the crime of child rape is regarded as unacceptable in our society. These statistics confirm our determination from our review of state statutes that there is a social consensus against the death penalty for the crime of child rape. Louisiana is the only State since 1964 that has sentenced an individual to death for the crime of child rape; and Kennedy and Richard Davis, who was convicted and sentenced to death for the aggravated rape of a 5-year-old child by a Louisiana jury in December 2007, are the only two individuals now on death row in the United States for a nonhomicide offense. After reviewing the authorities informed by contemporary norms, including the history of the death penalty for this and other nonhomicide crimes, current state statutes and new enactments, and the number of executions since 1964, we conclude there is a national consensus against capital punishment for the crime of child rape.

Objective evidence of contemporary values as it relates to punishment for child rape is entitled to great weight, but it does not end our inquiry. It is for us ultimately to judge whether the Eighth Amendment permits imposition of the death penalty. We turn, then, to the resolution of the question before us, which is informed by our precedents and our own understanding of the Constitution and the rights it secures.

It must be acknowledged that there are moral grounds to question a rule barring capital punishment for a crime against an individual that did not result in death. These facts illustrate the point. Here the victim's fright, the sense of betrayal, and the nature of her injuries caused more prolonged physical and mental suffering than, say, a sudden killing by an unseen assassin. The attack was not just on her but on her childhood. Rape has a permanent psychological, emotional, and sometimes physical impact on the child. We cannot dismiss the years of long anguish that must be endured by the victim of child rape.

It does not follow, though, that capital punishment is a proportionate penalty for the crime. The constitutional prohibition against excessive or cruel and unusual punishments mandates that the State's power to punish be exercised within the limits of civilized standards. Evolving standards of decency that mark the progress of a maturing society counsel us to be most hesitant before interpreting the Eighth Amendment to allow the extension of the death penalty, a hesitation that has special force where no life was taken in the commission of the crime.

It is an established principle that decency, in its essence, presumes respect for the individual and thus moderation or restraint in the application of capital punishment. We do not discount the seriousness of rape as a crime. It is highly reprehensible, both in a moral sense and in its almost total contempt for the personal integrity and autonomy of the female victim. Short of homicide, it is the ultimate violation of self. But the murderer kills; the rapist, if no more than that, does not. We have the abiding conviction that the death penalty, which is unique in its severity and irrevocability, is an excessive penalty for the rapist who, as such, does not take human life.

Consistent with evolving standards of decency and the teachings of our precedents we conclude that, in determining whether the death penalty is excessive, there is a distinction between intentional first-degree murder on the one hand and nonhomicide crimes against individual persons, even including child rape, on the other. The latter crimes may be devastating in their harm, as here, but in terms of moral depravity and of the injury to the person and to the public, they cannot be compared to murder in their severity and irrevocability.

The judgment of the Supreme Court of Louisiana upholding the capital sentence is reversed. This case is remanded for further proceedings not inconsistent with this opinion.

It is so ordered.

DISSENT

ALITO, J., JOINED BY ROBERTS, CJ., SCALIA AND THOMAS JJ.

The Court today holds that the Eighth Amendment categorically prohibits the imposition of the death penalty for the crime of raping a child. This is so, according to the Court, no matter how young the child, no matter how many times the child is raped, no matter how many children the perpetrator rapes, no matter how sadistic the crime, no matter how much physical or psychological trauma is inflicted, and no matter how heinous the perpetrator's prior criminal record may be. The Court provides two reasons for this sweeping conclusion: First, the Court claims to have identified "a national consensus" that the death penalty is never acceptable for the rape of a child; second, the Court concludes, based on its "independent judgment," that imposing the death penalty for child rape is inconsistent with "the evolving standards of decency that mark the progress of a maturing society." Because neither of these justifications is sound, I respectfully dissent.

I turn first to the Court's claim that there is "a national consensus" that it is never acceptable to impose the death penalty for the rape of a child. I believe that the "objective indicia" of our society's "evolving standards of decency" can be fairly summarized as follows. Neither Congress nor juries have done anything that can plausibly be interpreted as evidencing the "national consensus" that the Court perceives. State legislatures, for more than 30 years, have operated under the ominous shadow of the *Coker* dicta [cruel and unusual punishment to execute a man for raping an adult woman] and thus have not been free to express their own understanding of our society's standards of decency. And in the months following our grant of certiorari in this case, state legislatures have had an additional reason to pause. Yet despite the inhibiting legal atmosphere that has prevailed since 1977, six States have recently enacted new, targeted child-rape laws.

The Court is willing to block the potential emergence of a national consensus in favor of permitting the death penalty for child rape because, in the end, what matters is the Court's "own judgment" regarding "the acceptability of the death penalty." The Court's final—and, it appears, principal—justification for its holding is that murder, the only crime for which defendants have been executed since this Court's 1976 death penalty decisions, is unique in its moral depravity and in the severity of the injury that it inflicts on the victim and the public. Is it really true that every person who is convicted of capital murder and sentenced to death is more morally depraved than every child rapist? Consider the following two cases. In the first, a defendant robs a convenience store and watches as his accomplice shoots the store owner. The defendant acts recklessly, but was not the triggerman and did not intend the killing. In the second case, a previously convicted child rapist kidnaps,

(continues)

(continued)

repeatedly rapes, and tortures multiple child victims. Is it clear that the first defendant is more morally depraved than the second?

I have little doubt that, in the eyes of ordinary Americans, the very worst child rapists—predators who seek out and inflict serious physical and emotional injury on defenseless young children—are the epitome of moral depravity.

With respect to the question of the harm caused by the rape of child in relation to the harm caused by murder, it is certainly true that the loss of human life represents a unique harm, but that does not explain why other grievous harms are insufficient to permit a death sentence. The rape of any victim inflicts great injury, and some victims are so grievously injured physically or psychologically that life is beyond repair. The immaturity and vulnerability of a child, both physically and psychologically, adds a devastating dimension to rape that is not present when an adult is raped. Long-term studies show that sexual abuse is grossly intrusive in the lives of children and is harmful to their normal psychological, emotional and sexual development in ways which no just or humane society can tolerate.

The harm that is caused to the victims and to society at large by the worst child rapists is grave. It is the judgment of the Louisiana lawmakers and those in an increasing number of other States that these harms justify the death penalty. The Court provides no cogent explanation why this legislative judgment should be overridden. Conclusory references to "decency," "moderation," "restraint," "full progress," and "moral judgment" are not enough.

The party attacking the constitutionality of a state statute bears the "heavy burden" of establishing that the law is unconstitutional. That burden has not been discharged here, and I would therefore affirm the decision of the Louisiana Supreme Court.

QUESTIONS

1. According to the Court, why is death a disproportionate penalty for child rape? Do you agree? Explain your reasons.
2. Who should make the decision as to what is the appropriate penalty for crimes? Courts? Legislatures? Juries? Defend your answer.
3. In deciding whether the death penalty for child rape is cruel and unusual, is it relevant that Louisiana is the only state that punishes child rape with death?
4. According to the Court, some crimes are worse than death. Do you agree? Is child rape one of them? Why? Why not?

The death penalty is disproportionate even for some murders. Let's look at two kinds: mentally retarded persons and juveniles who murder.

The Death Penalty for Mentally Retarded Murderers

Thirty-five mentally retarded persons were executed between 1976 when the death penalty was reinstated and 2001 (Human Rights Watch 2002). The American Association on Mental Retardation (AAMR) includes three elements in its definition of mental retardation:

1. The person has substantial intellectual impairment.
2. That impairment impacts the everyday life of the mentally retarded individual.
3. Retardation is present at birth or during childhood. (*Atkins v. Virginia* 2002, 308)

In *Atkins v. Virginia* (2002), the U.S. Supreme Court ruled that executing anyone who proved the three elements in the AAMR definition applied to them violated the ban on cruel and unusual punishment. The decision grew out of a grisly case. On August 16, 1996, Daryl Atkins and William Jones were drinking alcohol and smoking "pot." At about midnight, they drove to a convenience store to rob a customer. They picked Eric Nesbitt, an airman from Langley Air Force Base, abducted him, took him in their pickup truck to an ATM machine, and forced him to withdraw $200. Then, they drove him to a deserted area. Ignoring his pleas not to hurt him, they ordered Nesbitt to get out of the car. Nesbitt took only a few steps when (according to Jones, who made a deal with prosecutors to testify against Atkins in exchange for a life instead of a death sentence), Atkins fired eight shots into Nesbitt's thorax, chest, abdomen, arms, and legs (338).

The jury convicted Atkins of capital murder. At the penalty phase of Atkins' trial, the jury heard evidence about his sixteen prior felony convictions, including robbery, attempted robbery, abduction, use of a firearm, and maiming. He hit one victim over the head with a beer bottle; "slapped a gun across another victim's face, clubbed her in the head with it, knocked her to the ground, and then helped her up, only to shoot her in the stomach" (339).

The jury also heard evidence about Atkins' mental retardation. After interviewing people who knew Atkins, reviewing school and court records, and administering a standard intelligence test, which revealed Atkins had an IQ of 59, Dr. Evan Nelson, a forensic psychologist concluded that Atkins was "mildly mentally retarded." According to Nelson, mental retardation is rare (about 1 percent of the population); it would automatically qualify Atkins for Social Security disability income; and that "of the over 40 capital defendants that he had evaluated, Atkins was only the second" who "met the criteria for mental retardation." Nelson also testified that "in his opinion, Atkins' limited intellect had been a consistent feature throughout his life, and that his IQ score of 59 is not an 'aberration, malingered result, or invalid test score'" (309).

In reversing the death sentence, the U.S. Supreme Court based its decision on a change in public opinion since its 1989 decision that it's not cruel and unusual punishment to execute retarded offenders (*Penry v. Lynaugh* 1989). How did the Court measure this change in public opinion? First, since 1989, nineteen states and the federal government had passed statutes banning the execution of mentally retarded offenders (*Atkins v. Virginia* 2002, 314). Second, it wasn't just the number of bans that was significant, it was "the consistency of the direction of the change":

> Given the well-known fact that anticrime legislation is far more popular than legislation providing protections for persons guilty of violent crime, the large number of States prohibiting the execution of mentally retarded persons (and the complete absence of States passing legislation reinstating the power to conduct such executions) provides powerful evidence that today our society views mentally retarded offenders as categorically less culpable than the average criminal.
>
> The evidence carries even greater force when it is noted that the legislatures that have addressed the issue have voted overwhelmingly in favor of the prohibition.
>
> Moreover, even in those States that allow the execution of mentally retarded offenders, the practice is uncommon. Some states, for example New Hampshire and New Jersey, continue to authorize executions, but none have been carried out in decades. Thus there is little need to pursue legislation barring the execution of the mentally retarded in those States.
>
> And it appears that even among those States that regularly execute offenders and that have no prohibition with regard to the mentally retarded, only five have executed offenders possessing a known IQ less than 70 since we decided *Penry*. The practice, therefore, has become truly unusual, and it is fair to say that a national consensus has developed against it. (315–16)

Third, executing retarded offenders doesn't serve the main purposes for having death sentences: retribution and deterrence. Mentally retarded offenders aren't as blameworthy or as subject to deterrence as people with normal intelligence because of their "diminished capacity to understand and process information, to learn from experience, to engage in logical reasoning, or to control their impulses" (319–20).

The Death Penalty for Juvenile Murderers

The execution of juveniles began in 1642, when Plymouth Colony hanged sixteen-year-old Thomas Graunger for bestiality with a cow and a horse (Rimer and Bonner 2000). It continued at a rate of about one a year until Oklahoma executed Scott Hain on April 3, 2003, after the U.S. Supreme Court refused to hear his appeal.

Hain and a twenty-one-year-old acquaintance killed two people in the course of a carjacking and robbery. He was a "deeply troubled" seventeen-year-old kid who dropped out of the seventh grade after repeating the sixth grade three times. As a teenager, Scott's father got him a job in a warehouse so he could steal stuff and give it to his father, who sold it. At the time of the carjacking murders, Scott was living on the street in Tulsa, drinking, and using other drugs daily, but he'd never committed a violent crime (Greenhouse 2003, A18).

Just a few months before the U.S. Supreme Court refused to hear Scott Hain's case, four Supreme Court justices (John Paul Stevens, David Souter, Ruth Bader Ginsburg, and Stephen Breyer) had called the death penalty for juveniles a "shameful practice," adding that "the practice of executing such offenders is a relic of the past and is inconsistent with the evolving standards of decency in a civilized society" (Greenhouse 2003, A18).

In *Trop v. Dulles* (1958), the Court first adopted the "evolving standards" test to decide whether sentences run afoul of the Eighth Amendment ban on "cruel and unusual punishments." In 1944, U.S. Army private Albert Trop escaped from a military stockade at Casablanca, Morocco, following his confinement for a disciplinary violation. The next day, Trop surrendered willingly. A general court martial convicted Trop of desertion and sentenced him to three years at hard labor, loss of all pay and allowances, and a dishonorable discharge. In 1952, Trop applied for a passport. His application was rejected on the ground that he had lost his citizenship due to his conviction and dishonorable discharge for wartime desertion. The Court decided the punishment was "cruel and unusual." Why? Because "the words of the Amendment are not precise, and their scope is not static. The Amendment must draw its meaning from the evolving standards of decency that mark the progress of a maturing society" (100–101).

The Court applied the "evolving standards of decency" approach in *Thompson v. Oklahoma* (1988) to ban the execution of juveniles under sixteen. But the next year, in *Stanford v. Kentucky* (1989), the Court ruled that executing juveniles between sixteen and eighteen didn't offend "evolving standards of decency." (After serving fourteen years on death row, Stanford was granted clemency in 2003 and is now serving a life sentence.)

In 2005, the Court decided whether standards of decency had evolved enough since 1989 to be offended by executing Christopher Simmons for a carjacking murder he committed when he was seventeen (*Roper v. Simmons* 2005). By a vote of 5–4, the U.S. Supreme Court held that the Eighth and Fourteenth Amendments forbid the execution of offenders who were under the age of eighteen when they committed their crimes. According to Justice Kennedy:

> When a juvenile offender commits a heinous crime, the State can exact forfeiture of some of the most basic liberties, but the State cannot extinguish his life and his potential to attain a mature understanding of his own humanity. (554)

The Court relied on "the evolving standards of decency that mark the progress of a maturing society" (561) to determine which punishments are so disproportionate as to be cruel and unusual. The Court argued that the majority of states' rejection of the death penalty for juveniles; its infrequent use in the states that retain the penalty; and the trend toward its abolition show that there's a national consensus against it. The Court determined that today our society views juveniles as categorically less culpable than the average criminal.

Justice Stevens, joined by Justice Ginsburg, wrote in a concurring opinion, that "if the meaning of . . . [the Eighth] Amendment had been frozen when it was originally drafted, it would impose no impediment to the execution of 7-year-old children today" (587).

Justice Scalia, joined by Justice Thomas and Chief Justice Rehnquist, dissented. Justice Scalia maintained that the Court improperly substituted its own judgment for the state legislature's. He criticized the majority for counting non–death penalty states toward a national consensus against juvenile executions. Scalia also objected to the Court's use of international law to support its opinion, claiming that "Acknowledgement of foreign approval has no place in the legal opinion of this Court . . ." (628).

Life without Parole for Juveniles

Does the proportionality principle extend to sentencing juveniles to life without parole for juveniles who don't kill? Over a strong dissent, the U.S. Supreme Court said yes (6–3) in *Graham v. Texas* (2010). Terrence Graham's parents were crack addicts when he was born. Terrence began drinking and smoking tobacco at nine and was smoking marijuana at thirteen. At sixteen, he and three other teenagers attempted to rob a barbecue restaurant. One, who worked in the restaurant, left the back door unlocked just before closing time. Graham and the other teenager, wearing masks, came through the unlocked door. The other masked accomplice hit the restaurant manager twice in the back of the head with a steel bar. When the manager started to yell at them, they fled in one of the accomplice's car. The manager had to get stitches for his head injury. No money was taken.

Graham was arrested for "armed burglary" and "attempted armed robbery" and was charged as an adult. Graham pleaded guilty to both charges. He wrote a letter to the trial court. In it, he said "this is my first and last time getting in trouble. I've decided to turn my life around. I made a promise to God and myself that if I get a second chance, I'm going to do whatever it takes to get to the NFL" (2). The judge sentenced Graham to a year in jail, followed by three years of probation.

Less than six months later, Graham participated in a home invasion robbery. Graham and two twenty-year-old accomplices knocked on Carlos Rodriguez's door, forcibly entered, and held a pistol to his chest. For thirty minutes, while they held Rodriguez and his friend at gunpoint, they ransacked his house looking for money. They barricaded Rodriguez and his friend in a closet and left (3).

Later that same evening, the three attempted a second robbery. Bailey, one of the twenty-year-olds, got shot during the attempt. Graham drove Bailey to the hospital in Graham's father's car, leaving him there with the other twenty-year-old. As he drove away, a police officer signaled him to stop. Graham speeded up and drove away, crashing into a telephone pole. He tried to run away on foot but was caught. Three handguns were found in the car. The night he was arrested Graham was thirty-four days short of his eighteenth birthday (3).

Under Florida law, Graham could be sentenced to five years to life imprisonment. At his sentencing, the trial judge explained the sentence he was about to pronounce:

> Mr. Graham, as I look back on your case, yours is a really sad situation. You had a lot of people who wanted to try and help you get your life turned around including the court system, and you had a judge who took the step to try and give you direction. I don't know why you threw your life away. . . . But you did. . . . We can't do anything

> to deter you. So, if I can't do anything to get you back on the right path, then I have to start focusing on the community and trying to protect the community from your actions. . . . Given your escalating pattern of criminal conduct, . . . the only thing I can do now is try and to protect the community from your actions. (4–5)

The judge sentenced Graham to life imprisonment. In effect, this is a sentence to life without parole because Florida has abolished its parole system (of course, the governor might grant him clemency) (6).

Graham appealed. The U.S. Supreme Court reversed, holding that it's cruel and unusual punishment to sentence a juvenile offender to life without parole for a nonhomicide offense (1). Headed for the U.S. Supreme Court is a Wisconsin life without parole ("death in prison") case, *State v. Ninham* (2011), for an intentional murder committed by a juvenile when he was fourteen.

CASE

In* State v. Ninham *(2011), the Wisconsin Supreme Court upheld Omer Ninham's "death in prison" sentence for the horrific intentional murder of thirteen-year-old Zong Vang. Ninham committed the murder when he was fourteen.

Is it cruel and unusual punishment to sentence Omer Ninham to "death in prison"?

State v. Ninham

797 N.W.2d 451 (Wis. 2011)

HISTORY

Omer Ninham (Defendant) was convicted of first-degree intentional homicide and was sentenced to life in prison without possibility of parole. Ninham filed a motion for relief from his life sentence, seeking to allow for the possibility of parole. The Circuit Court denied the motion. Ninham appealed. The Supreme Court affirmed.

ZIEGLER, J.

FACTS

On September 24, 1998, around dusk, 13-year-old Vang was bicycling home along Webster Avenue in Green Bay, Wisconsin. Vang's older brother had sent Vang to the grocery store for tomatoes. Vang was returning home on his bicycle, carrying a plastic grocery bag filled with tomatoes, when he was approached by five juveniles: 14-year-old Ninham, 13-year-old Richard Crapeau (Crapeau), 13-year-old Jeffrey P., 14-year-old Amanda G., and 14-year-old Christin J.

Ninham and the other four juveniles did not know or recognize Vang. Moreover, by all accounts, Vang never said or did anything to provoke the five juveniles. Rather, at the time, Crapeau was upset with his mother and "wanted to fight or see a fight." Consequently, Crapeau said to Ninham, "Let's mess with this kid," and Ninham responded, "'I got your back,' meaning he would back [Crapeau] up in a fight." Ninham and Crapeau began by verbally taunting Vang, while the other three juveniles "egg[ed]" them on. Ninham and Crapeau's assaults escalated into physical attacks. Crapeau bumped into Vang's shoulder and yanked his bicycle away from him. Crapeau also grabbed Vang's grocery bag out of his hands and threw it in the direction of St. Vincent's Hospital, located along the same street. When Vang asked for his bicycle back, Ninham punched Vang, knocking him down.

Vang got up and started running towards the nearby St. Vincent's Hospital parking ramp. All five juveniles chased after Vang, eventually catching up to him on the top, or fifth floor, of the parking ramp. When they caught up to him, Crapeau punched Vang in the face. Vang repeatedly asked why they were trying to hurt him and pleaded with them to leave him alone. Instead, Ninham and Crapeau began pushing Vang back and forth between them, in a game Jeffrey P. referred to as "chicken." Ninham punched Vang in the chest as he pushed him back and forth. Ninham then pinned Vang by his wrists against the parking ramp's concrete wall. While Vang squirmed to get out of Ninham's grasp, Crapeau again punched Vang in the face. According to Crapeau, Vang was crying and screaming, "Let me go."

With Ninham still holding Vang by his wrists, Crapeau grabbed Vang's ankles. Ninham and Crapeau then began swinging Vang back and forth out over the parking ramp's concrete wall—a drop that measured nearly 45 feet to the ground. Vang was crying and screaming, begging Ninham and Crapeau not to drop him. While swinging Vang out over the wall, Crapeau let go of Vang's feet and told Ninham to "drop him." Ninham let go of Vang's wrists, and in Crapeau's words, Vang "just sailed out over the wall."

Vang landed on his back on the parking ramp's paved exit lane, 12 feet from the base of the ramp. Rescue personnel, dispatched at 8:03 P.M., detected a faint pulse from Vang. Vang was transported to St. Vincent's Hospital where physicians were unable to revive him. An autopsy revealed that Vang suffered a blunt impact to his head and trunk and died from craniocerebral trauma due to a fall from height.

Ninham and the other four juveniles never checked on Vang's condition and instead ran from the scene. Still, the Green Bay Police Department was able to focus its investigation on the five juveniles after some of them, in particular, Jeffrey P. and Amanda G., indicated to relatives and police that they knew who was responsible for Vang's death. In his statement to police, Jeffrey P. described how Ninham stood for several seconds looking over the edge of the wall at Vang below. Ninham then looked at Jeffrey P. and said, "Don't say nothing. Better not say shit."

The pre-sentence investigation (PSI) revealed that "Ninham emanates from an extremely dysfunctional family structure," in which both of his parents and several of his siblings engage in severe substance abuse and domestic violence. The PSI described Ninham as a "serious substance abuser" who snorted cocaine on a weekly basis and, since grade school, drank alcohol every day, often alone, and usually to the point of unconsciousness. The PSI also revealed that Ninham, a member of the Menominee Indian Tribe, claimed to have a newfound interest in Native American spirituality.

In addition, the PSI described the Vang family as devastated by the loss of their son and brother. Vang's parents indicated that they fled Laos and Thailand because they believed that the United States would be a safer and more prosperous country to raise their children; however, according to the Vangs, they fled evil only to discover it in a different place. Vang's parents further expressed that they had lost faith in the basic goodness of people and that their remaining children are fearful of leaving the safety of their home.

Relevant to this case, at the sentencing hearing, Vang's brother, Seng Say Vang (Seng Say), gave a statement on behalf of Vang's family and friends. Seng Say asked the circuit court to impose on Ninham the maximum sentence of life imprisonment without parole.... Seng Say then articulated to the circuit court a belief held by his family's Hmong culture:

> In our Hmong culture we believe that the spirit of a murdered person cannot be set free to go in peace until the perpetrators be brought to justice. Therefore, we ask the Court, who is the only one to have the power to set free the spirit of our beloved son, brother, and friend, Zong, to go in peace by bringing Omer Ninham and his accomplices to justice.

Ninham also spoke at sentencing. He told the circuit court that he was sorry about Vang's death, but "there wasn't nothing I could do. I wasn't there. I'm going to keep saying that until the day I die. I was not there, and that's the honest truth."

In imposing Ninham's sentence, the circuit court considered three primary factors: the gravity of the offense, the character of the offender, and the need to protect the public. First, the circuit court regarded the gravity of the offense as "beyond description" and indisputably "horrific." The circuit court noted that the offense has had an indescribable impact on Vang's family and friends and on the Green Bay community. Second, concerning the character of the offender, the circuit court "conceded for the sake of discussion that Omer Ninham is a child" but nevertheless described Ninham as "a frightening young man." The circuit court acknowledged that Ninham derives from a dysfunctional family but refused to let that excuse Ninham's conduct, explaining that Ninham is "a child of the street who knew what he was doing. . . ." Third, the circuit court reasoned that the community needs to be protected from Ninham: "Society needs to know, and especially this community needs to know, that you can send your child to the grocery store and expect to see him again."

OPINION

First, we hold that sentencing a 14-year-old to life imprisonment without the possibility of parole for committing intentional homicide is not categorically

(continues)

(continued)

unconstitutional. We arrive at our holding by applying the two-step approach employed by the United States Supreme Court, most recently in *Graham,* 130 S.Ct. 2011. First, we conclude that Ninham has failed to demonstrate that there is a national consensus against sentencing a 14-year-old to life imprisonment without parole when the crime is intentional homicide. Second, we conclude in the exercise of our own independent judgment that the punishment is not categorically unconstitutional.

In regard to Ninham's second argument, we conclude that his sentence of life imprisonment without the possibility of parole is not unduly harsh and excessive. Under the circumstances of this case, Ninham's punishment is severe, but it is not disproportionately so.

Third, we conclude that Ninham has not demonstrated by clear and convincing evidence that the scientific research on adolescent brain development to which he refers constitutes a "new factor." While the studies themselves may not have been in existence at the time of Ninham's sentencing, the conclusions they reached were widely reported.

Fourth, we conclude that Ninham has not demonstrated by clear and convincing evidence that the circuit court actually relied upon the religious beliefs of Vang's family when imposing Ninham's sentence.

The decision of the court of appeals is affirmed.

DISSENT

ABRAHAMSON, CJ.

The Eighth Amendment cruel and unusual punishment issue before this court is easy to state and difficult to decide. The question before the court is the constitutionality of imposing a death-in-prison sentence on a 14-year-old juvenile boy who committed an intentional, brutal, senseless, grotesque, reprehensible murder of a 13-year-old innocent stranger.

In Wisconsin, both the adult offender and the juvenile offender (10 years old or older) who have committed first-degree intentional homicide are treated the same: the maximum penalty is a death-in-prison sentence, that is, life in prison without the possibility of parole. The circuit court need not impose this maximum sentence. It did in the present case.

A death-in-prison sentence is the most severe penalty authorized in Wisconsin. This penalty means that "whatever the future might hold in store for the mind and spirit of the young juvenile, he will remain in prison for the rest of his days. A death-in-prison sentence is an especially severe punishment, made harsher for a young juvenile 14 years old or younger because of the increased time and proportion of life that the juvenile will serve in prison.

I conclude, as has the United States Supreme Court (*Roper v. Simmons,* 543 U.S. 551 [2005]), that the differences between juveniles and adults mean that juvenile offenders "cannot with reliability be classified among the worst offenders." The three general differences are: (1) juveniles have a lack of maturity and an underdeveloped sense of responsibility resulting in impetuous and ill-considered actions and decisions; (2) juveniles are more susceptible to negative influences and outside pressures; and (3) the character of a juvenile is not as well formed as that of an adult. Retribution is a legitimate penological goal, but retribution "must be directly related to the personal culpability of the criminal offender." The case for retribution is not as strong with a minor as with an adult." Accordingly, I conclude, that a juvenile cannot be sentenced to life without parole for a homicide committed when 14 years old or younger.

QUESTIONS

1. Summarize the majority's four reasons for deciding that Omer Ninham's sentence to life in prison without possibility of parole is not cruel and unusual punishment.
2. Summarize the dissent's reason for arguing that "death in prison" for a juvenile is cruel and unusual punishment.
3. The U.S. Supreme Court (SCOTUS) has agreed to hear the case in 2012. In your opinion, how should SCOTUS rule? Defend your answer.

SENTENCES OF IMPRISONMENT

The consensus that the ban on cruel and unusual punishment includes a proportionality requirement in capital punishment doesn't extend to prison sentences. The important case of *Solem v. Helm* (1983) revealed that the U.S. Supreme Court was deeply divided over whether the principle of proportionality applied to sentences of imprisonment. The case involved Jerry Helm, whom South Dakota had convicted of six nonviolent felonies by 1975. The crimes included three third-degree burglaries, one in 1964, one in 1966, and one in 1969; obtaining money under false pretenses in 1972; committing grand larceny in 1973; and "third-offense driving while intoxicated" in 1975. A bare majority of five in the U.S. Supreme Court held that "a criminal sentence must be proportionate to the crime for which the defendant has been convicted" (290).

The split over the constitutional status of proportionality in prison sentences was revealed again when the constitutionality of three-strikes-and-you're-out laws reached the Court in 2003. Before we look at the Court's division, let's put three-strikes laws in some perspective. **Three-strikes laws** are supposed to make sure that offenders who are convicted of a third felony get locked up for a very long time (sometimes for life).

three-strikes laws, intended to make sure that offenders who are convicted of a third felony get locked up for a very long time (sometimes for life)

The laws are controversial, and they generate passions on both sides. Supporters claim that the laws "help restore the credibility of the criminal justice system and will deter crime." Opponents believe the harsh penalties won't have much effect on crime, and they'll cost states more than they can afford to pay (Turner et al. 1995, 75).

Despite controversy, three-strikes laws are popular and widespread. Twenty-four states have passed three-strikes laws (Shepherd 2002). California's law, the toughest in the nation, includes a twenty-five-year-to-life sentence if you're "out" on a third strike. The law passed in 1994, after the kidnapping, brutal sexual assault, and murder of twelve-year-old Polly Klaas in 1993 (Ainsworth 2004, 1; Shepherd 2002, 161). A bearded stranger broke into Polly Klaas's home in Petaluma, California, and kidnapped her. He left behind two other girls bound and gagged. Polly's mother was asleep in the next room. Nine weeks later, after a fruitless search by hundreds of police officers and volunteers, a repeat offender, Richard Allen Davis, was arrested, and, in 1996, convicted and sentenced to death.

Liberals and conservatives, Democrats and Republicans, and the public all jumped on the three-strikes bandwagon, taking it for granted these laws were a good idea. Why were they popular? Here are three reasons:

1. They addressed the public's dissatisfaction with the criminal justice system.
2. They promised a simple solution to a complex problem—the "panacea phenomenon."
3. The use of the catchy phrase "three strikes and you're out" was appealing; it put old habitual offender statute ideas into the language of modern baseball. (Benekos and Merlo 1995, 3; Turner et al. 1995)

What effects have three-strikes laws had? Everybody agrees that they incapacitate second- and third-strikers while they're locked up. But incapacitate them from doing what? Some critics argue that most strikers are already past the age of high offending. Most of the debate centers on deterrence: Do the laws prevent criminals from committing further crimes? The conclusions, based on empirical research, are decidedly mixed: three-strikes laws deter crime; three-strikes laws have no effect on crime; three-strikes laws increase crime.

Whatever the effectiveness of three-strikes laws may be, the U.S. Supreme Court has ruled they're constitutional, even if the justices can't agree on the reasons. This is clear from the Court's 5–4 decision in *Ewing v. California* (2003), upholding the constitutionality of California's three-strikes law.

CASE

In* Ewing v. California *(2003), the Court upheld the constitutionality of California's three-strikes law.

Is 25 years to life in prison disproportionate to grand theft?

Ewing v. California

538 U.S. 11 (2003)

HISTORY

Gary Ewing was convicted in a California trial court of felony grand theft and sentenced to 25 years to life under that state's three-strikes law. The California Court of Appeal, Second Appellate District, affirmed the sentence, and the State Supreme Court denied review. Certiorari was granted. The Supreme Court held that the sentence did not violate the Eighth Amendment's prohibition against cruel and unusual punishment.

O'CONNOR, J., JOINED BY REHNQUIST, CJ., AND SCALIA, KENNEDY, AND THOMAS, JJ.

FACTS

On parole from a 9-year prison term, petitioner Gary Ewing walked into the pro shop of the El Segundo Golf Course, in Los Angeles County, on March 12, 2000. He walked out with three golf clubs, priced at $399 apiece, concealed in his pants leg. A shop employee, whose suspicions were aroused when he observed Ewing limp out of the pro shop, telephoned the police. The police apprehended Ewing in the parking lot.

Ewing is no stranger to the criminal justice system. In 1984, at the age of 22, he pleaded guilty to theft. The court sentenced him to six months in jail (suspended), three years' probation, and a $300 fine. In 1988, he was convicted of felony grand theft auto and sentenced to one year in jail and three years' probation. After Ewing completed probation, however, the sentencing court reduced the crime to a misdemeanor, permitted Ewing to withdraw his guilty plea, and dismissed the case.

In 1990, he was convicted of petty theft with a prior and sentenced to 60 days in the county jail and three years' probation. In 1992, Ewing was convicted of battery and sentenced to 30 days in the county jail and two years' summary probation. One month later, he was convicted of theft and sentenced to 10 days in the county jail and 12 months' probation. In January 1993, Ewing was convicted of burglary and sentenced to 60 days in the county jail and one year's summary probation. In February 1993, he was convicted of possessing drug paraphernalia and sentenced to six months in the county jail and three years' probation. In July 1993, he was convicted of appropriating lost property and sentenced to 10 days in the county jail and two years' summary probation. In September 1993, he was convicted of unlawfully possessing a firearm and trespassing and sentenced to 30 days in the county jail and one year's probation.

In October and November 1993, Ewing committed three burglaries and one robbery at a Long Beach, California, apartment complex over a 5-week period. He awakened one of his victims, asleep on her living room sofa, as he tried to disconnect her video cassette recorder from the television in that room. When she screamed, Ewing ran out the front door. On another occasion, Ewing accosted a victim in the mailroom of the apartment complex. Ewing claimed to have a gun and ordered the victim to hand over his wallet. When the victim resisted, Ewing produced a knife and forced the victim back to the apartment itself. While Ewing rifled through the bedroom, the victim fled the apartment screaming for help. Ewing absconded with the victim's money and credit cards.

On December 9, 1993, Ewing was arrested on the premises of the apartment complex for trespassing and lying to a police officer. The knife used in the robbery and a glass cocaine pipe were later found in the back seat of the patrol car used to transport Ewing to the police station. A jury convicted Ewing of first-degree robbery and three counts of residential burglary. Sentenced to nine years and eight months in prison, Ewing was paroled in 1999.

Only 10 months later, Ewing stole the golf clubs at issue in this case. He was charged with, and ultimately convicted of, one count of felony grand theft of personal property in excess of $400. As required by the three-strikes law, the prosecutor formally alleged, and the trial court later found, that Ewing had been convicted previously of four serious or violent felonies for the three burglaries and the robbery in the Long Beach apartment complex.

As a newly convicted felon with two or more "serious" or "violent" felony convictions in his past, Ewing was sentenced under the three-strikes law to 25 years to life.

OPINION

When the California Legislature enacted the three-strikes law, it made a judgment that protecting the public safety requires incapacitating criminals who have already been convicted of at least one serious or violent crime. Nothing in the Eighth Amendment prohibits California from making that choice. To be sure, California's three-strikes law has sparked controversy. Critics have doubted the law's wisdom, cost-efficiency, and effectiveness in reaching its goals.

This criticism is appropriately directed at the legislature, which has primary responsibility for making the difficult policy choices that underlie any criminal sentencing scheme. We do not sit as a "superlegislature" to second-guess these policy choices. It is enough that the State of California has a reasonable basis for believing that dramatically enhanced sentences for habitual felons advances the goals of its criminal justice system in any substantial way.

Against this backdrop, we consider Ewing's claim that his three strikes sentence of 25 years to life is unconstitutionally disproportionate to his offense of shoplifting three golf clubs. Ewing's sentence is justified by the State's public-safety interest in incapacitating and deterring recidivist felons, and amply supported by his own long, serious criminal record. To be sure, Ewing's sentence is a long one. But it reflects a rational legislative judgment, entitled to deference, that offenders who have committed serious or violent felonies and who continue to commit felonies must be incapacitated. The State of California was entitled to place upon Ewing the onus of one who is simply unable to bring his conduct within the social norms prescribed by the criminal law of the State.

We hold that Ewing's sentence of 25 years to life in prison, imposed for the offense of felony grand theft under the three-strikes law, is not grossly disproportionate and therefore does not violate the Eighth Amendment's prohibition on cruel and unusual punishments. The judgment of the California Court of Appeal is affirmed.

It is so ordered.

CONCURRING OPINION

SCALIA, J. CONCURRING IN THE JUDGMENT.

The Eighth Amendment's prohibition of cruel and unusual punishments was aimed at excluding only certain modes of punishment, and was not a guarantee against disproportionate sentences. Because I agree that petitioner's sentence does not violate the Eighth Amendment's prohibition against cruel and unusual punishments, I concur in the judgment.

CONCURRING OPINION

THOMAS, J. CONCURRING IN THE JUDGMENT. In my view, the Cruel and Unusual Punishments Clause of the Eighth Amendment contains no proportionality principle. Because the plurality concludes that petitioner's sentence does not violate the Eighth Amendment's prohibition on cruel and unusual punishments, I concur in the judgment.

DISSENT

BREYER, J., JOINED BY STEVENS, SOUTER, AND GINSBURG, JJ.

A comparison of Ewing's sentence with other sentences requires answers to two questions. First, how would other jurisdictions (or California at other times, i.e., without the three-strikes penalty) punish the same offense conduct? Second, upon what other conduct would other jurisdictions (or California) impose the same prison term? Moreover, since hypothetical punishment is beside the point, the relevant prison time, for comparative purposes, is real prison time, i.e., the time that an offender must actually serve. Sentencing statutes often shed little light upon real prison time. That is because sentencing laws normally set maximum sentences, giving the sentencing judge discretion to choose an actual sentence within a broad range, and because many States provide good-time credits and parole, often permitting release after, say, one-third of the sentence has been served. Nonetheless, Ewing's sentence, comparatively speaking, is extreme.

As to California itself, we know the following: First, between the end of World War II and 1994 (when California enacted the three-strikes law), no one like Ewing could have served more than 10 years in prison. We know that for certain because the maximum sentence for Ewing's crime of conviction, grand theft, was for most of that period 10 years. From 1976 to 1994 (and currently, absent application of the three-strikes penalty), a Ewing-type offender would have received a maximum sentence of 4 years. And we know that California's "habitual offender" laws did not apply to grand theft. We also know that the time that any offender actually served was likely

(continues)

(continued)

far less than 10 years. This is because statistical data show that the median time actually served for grand theft (other than auto theft) was about two years, and 90 percent of all those convicted of that crime served less than three or four years.

Second, statistics suggest that recidivists of all sorts convicted during that same time period in California served a small fraction of Ewing's real-time sentence. On average, recidivists served three to four additional (recidivist-related) years in prison, with 90 percent serving less than an additional real seven to eight years.

Third, we know that California has reserved, and still reserves, Ewing-type prison time, i.e., at least 25 real years in prison, for criminals convicted of crimes far worse than was Ewing's. Statistics for the years 1945 to 1981, for example, indicate that typical (nonrecidivist) male first-degree murderers served between 10 and 15 real years in prison, with 90 percent of all such murderers serving less than 20 real years. Moreover, California, which has moved toward a real-time sentencing system (where the statutory punishment approximates the time served), still punishes far less harshly those who have engaged in far more serious conduct. It imposes, for example, upon nonrecidivists guilty of arson causing great bodily injury a maximum sentence of 9 years in prison; it imposes upon those guilty of voluntary manslaughter a maximum sentence of 11 years. It reserves the sentence that it here imposes upon (former-burglar-now-golf-club-thief) Ewing for nonrecidivist, first-degree murderers.

As to other jurisdictions, we know the following: The United States, bound by the federal Sentencing Guidelines, would impose upon a recidivist, such as Ewing, a sentence that, in any ordinary case, would not exceed 18 months in prison. The Guidelines reserve a Ewing-type sentence for Ewing-type recidivists who currently commit murder, robbery (involving the discharge of a firearm, serious bodily injury, and about $1 million), drug offenses involving more than, for example, 20 pounds of heroin, aggravated theft of more than $100 million, and other similar offenses. The Guidelines reserve 10 years of real prison time (with good time)—less than 40 percent of Ewing's sentence—for Ewing-type recidivists who go on to commit, for instance, voluntary manslaughter, aggravated assault with a firearm (causing serious bodily injury and motivated by money), kidnapping, residential burglary involving more than $5 million, drug offenses involving at least one pound of cocaine, and other similar offenses. Ewing also would not have been subject to the federal three-strikes law, for which grand theft is not a triggering offense.

Justice SCALIA and Justice THOMAS argue that we should not review for gross disproportionality a sentence to a term of years. Otherwise, we make it too difficult for legislators and sentencing judges to determine just when their sentencing laws and practices pass constitutional muster. I concede that a bright-line rule would give legislators and sentencing judges more guidance. But application of the Eighth Amendment to a sentence of a term of years requires a case-by-case approach. And, in my view, like that of the plurality, meaningful enforcement of the Eighth Amendment demands that application—even if only at sentencing's outer bounds.

A case-by-case approach can nonetheless offer guidance through example. Ewing's sentence is, at a minimum, two to three times the length of sentences that other jurisdictions would impose in similar circumstances. That sentence itself is sufficiently long to require a typical offender to spend virtually all the remainder of his active life in prison. These and the other factors that I have discussed, along with the questions that I have asked along the way, should help to identify "gross disproportionality" in a fairly objective way—at the outer bounds of sentencing.

In sum, even if I accept for present purposes the plurality's analytical framework, Ewing's sentence (life imprisonment with a minimum term of 25 years) is grossly disproportionate to the triggering offense conduct—stealing three golf clubs—Ewing's recidivism notwithstanding.

For these reasons, I dissent.

QUESTIONS

1. List Gary Ewing's crimes, and match them to the three-strikes law.
2. Define "proportionality" as the plurality opinion defines it. Summarize how the majority applies proportionality to Ewing's sentence. How does Justice Scalia define "proportionality," and how does his application of it to the facts differ from the majority's? Summarize how the dissent applies the principle of proportionality to the facts of the case.
3. In your opinion, was Ewing's punishment proportional to the crime? Back up your answer with the facts of the case and the arguments in the opinions.
4. If Justice Thomas is right that the Eighth Amendment contains no proportionality principle, what is cruel and unusual punishment?

Three-strikes laws are an example of one kind of sentencing scheme in the United States—mandatory minimum sentences. **Mandatory minimum sentencing laws** require judges to impose a nondiscretionary minimum amount of prison time that all offenders have to serve.

mandatory minimum sentencing laws, statutes that require judges to impose a nondiscretionary minimum amount of prison time that all offenders have to serve

Mandatory minimum sentences promise offenders that "If you do the crime, you will do the time." Mandatory minimum sentences are old, and the list of them is long (the U.S. Code includes at least one hundred). By 1991, forty-six states and the federal government had enacted mandatory minimum sentences. But the main targets are drug offenses, violent crimes, and crimes committed with weapons (Wallace 1993).

Mandatory minimum sentences are the more rigid form of the broad scheme of **fixed (determinate) sentences** (Chapter 1). This scheme, which fixes or determines sentence length according to the seriousness of the crime, places sentencing authority in legislatures.

fixed (determinate) sentences, a legislative sentencing scheme that "fixes" or determines sentence length according to the seriousness of the crime

The less extreme form of fixed sentencing is sentencing guidelines. In **sentencing guidelines**, a commission establishes a narrow range of penalties, and judges are supposed to choose a specific sentence within that range. The guideline sentence depends on a combination of the seriousness of the crime and the prior criminal record of the offender. If the judge sentences above or below the range, she has to back up her reasons (from a list prescribed in the guidelines) for the "departure" in writing.

sentencing guidelines, a commission establishes a narrow range of penalties, and judges choose a specific sentence within that range. The guideline sentence depends on a combination of the seriousness of the crime and the prior criminal record of the offender

THE RIGHT TO TRIAL BY JURY AND CRIMINAL SENTENCING

LO 6, LO 7

Until 2000, the guidelines and mandatory forms of fixed sentencing created only possible cruel and unusual punishment problems. Beyond that, the U.S. Supreme Court took a hands-off approach to sentencing procedures, leaving it up to state legislatures and judges to share sentencing authority and administration without interference from the Court. Then came *Apprendi v. New Jersey* (2000), called by two authorities (Dressler and Michaels 2006) "the first in a series of constitutional explosions that have rocked the world of criminal sentencing and caused fundamental alterations" in federal and state sentencing systems (366). (See Table 2.2 for some of the leading cases.)

Charles C. Apprendi Jr. fired several .22-caliber bullets into a Black family's home; the family had recently moved into a previously all-White neighborhood in Vineland, New Jersey. Apprendi was promptly arrested and admitted that he was the shooter. Later, he made a statement—which he soon after retracted—that "even though he did not know the occupants of the house personally, 'because they are black in color he does not want them in the neighborhood' " (469).

Apprendi was convicted of possessing a firearm with an unlawful purpose, a felony in New Jersey, punishable by five to ten years in prison. New Jersey also has a hate crime statute providing for an extended punishment of ten to twenty years if the judge finds by a preponderance of the evidence that the defendant committed the crime with a "purpose to intimidate an individual or group of individuals because of race, color, gender, handicap, religion, sexual orientation or ethnicity" (469).

Apprendi argued that "racial purpose" was an element of the crime that the state had to prove beyond a reasonable doubt. New Jersey argued that the legislature had chosen to make "racial purpose" a sentencing factor. The U.S. Supreme Court (5–4) brought the Sixth Amendment right to trial by jury into the heart of criminal sentencing procedures with a sweeping rule (the ***Apprendi* rule**):

> Other than the fact of prior conviction, any fact that *increases* the penalty for a crime beyond the prescribed statutory maximum must be submitted to a jury, and proved beyond a reasonable doubt. (490, emphasis added)

***Apprendi* rule,** other than the fact of prior conviction, any fact that *increases* the penalty for a crime beyond the prescribed statutory maximum must be submitted to a jury and proved beyond a reasonable doubt

TABLE 2.2 Major U.S. Supreme Court Trial by Jury Rights Cases

CASE	COURT DECISION
Apprendi v. New Jersey (2000) 5–4	Struck down New Jersey statute authorizing judges to increase maximum sentence based on facts judge found to be true by a preponderance of the evidence but not proof beyond a reasonable doubt Affirmed judge's authority to increase maximum based on prior convictions, or crimes defendants confess to, without jury finding there were prior convictions or defendants, or prior crimes defendants confessed to
Blakely v. Washington (2004) 5–4	Struck down Washington State statute that authorized judge to increase the length of prison time beyond the "standard range" in the Washington sentencing guidelines based on facts not proved beyond a reasonable doubt
U.S. v. Booker (2005) 5–4	Struck down provisions in the U.S. sentencing guidelines that allowed judges to increase individual sentences beyond the "standard range" based on facts not proved beyond a reasonable doubt to the jury Guidelines are advisory only but enjoy "a presumption of reasonableness"
Gall v. U.S. (2007) 7–2	Upheld a sentence of thirty-six months' probation imposed on a man who pleaded guilty to conspiracy to distribute ecstasy in the face of a recommended sentence of thirty to thirty-seven months in prison Federal appeals courts may not presume that a sentence falling outside the range recommended by the Federal Sentencing Guidelines is unreasonable

Between 2000 and 2005, the Supreme Court extended the *Apprendi* rule. In a series of 5–4 decisions made up of shifting member majority and dissenting justices, the Court stirred up uncertainty and anxiety about the effect of the rule on state and federal proceedings, particularly on the by now firmly established U.S. and state sentencing guidelines. In *Blakely v. Washington* (2004) 5–4, the Court struck down a Washington State statute that allowed judges to increase the length of prison time beyond the "standard range" prescribed in the Washington sentencing guidelines based on facts not proven to a jury beyond a reasonable doubt. (Figure 2.2 suggests some of these facts.)

In that case, after Ralph Blakely's wife Yolanda filed for divorce, he abducted her from their orchard home, bound her with duct tape, and forced her at knifepoint into a wooden box in the bed of his pickup truck (300). When the couple's thirteen-year-old son Ralphy returned home from school, Blakely ordered him to follow in another car, threatening to harm Yolanda with a shotgun if Ralphy didn't do it. Ralphy escaped and sought help when they stopped at a gas station; Blakely continued on with Yolanda to a friend's house in Montana. He was finally arrested after the friend called the police (300).

The state charged Blakely with first-degree kidnapping. Then, in a plea agreement, the state reduced the charge to second-degree kidnapping involving domestic violence and use of a firearm. Blakely pleaded guilty, admitting the elements of second-degree kidnapping and the domestic violence and firearm allegations but no other relevant facts.

In Washington State, second-degree kidnapping is punishable by up to ten years in prison. Washington's sentencing guidelines specify a "standard range" of forty-nine to fifty-three months for second-degree kidnapping with a firearm. A judge may impose a sentence above the standard range if she finds "substantial and compelling reasons justifying an exceptional sentence." In a plea agreement, the state recommended

A SENTENCING GUIDELINES PROBATION WORKSHEET

FIGURE 2.2

☐ Modified EWS Data Entry Form Page _____ of _____

1. OFFENDER ENTRY

Last Name		
First Name	Middle Name	Suffix
Date of Birth	State ID #	

Gender:	Race:		Ethnicity:
☐ Male	☐White	☐Asian	☐Hispanic
☐ Female	☐Black	☐Other	☐Non-Hispanic
	☐Am. Indian	☐Unknown	☐Unknown

2. AGENCY ENTRY

Agency	
Agent Name (Last, First)	Expected Sent. Date

3. COURT CASE ENTRY/GROUP INFORMATION

County	Dist. Court Case #	Conv./Plea Date

☐ Revoked EJJ?

Case Sentenced:
☐ Alone (No other offense in group)
☐ Other offenses (same Case #)
☐ Other offenses (different Case #)

4. OFFENSE ENTRY

Sent. Order#	Count #	Offense Date	Sev. Level

Offense Title (property value / drug type / drug amount)

Conviction Statute	Penalty Statute

Additional Statute(s)

Conditional Release:
☐ 5 Years
☐10 Years
☐ Life

Weapon:
☐Firearm Used
☐Firearm Possessed
☐Other Wpn Used

☐ Sub. Weapon

Custody Status:
☐Probation
☐Parole/Sup. Release
☐Confined
☐Released Pending Sentence
☐Escape
☐EJJ Status
☐W/In Orig. Probation Term
☐Conditional Release

☐ Additional Custody Status Point for Specified Sex Offense

Modifiers:
☐Attempt 609.17 Cited
☐Subsequent Sex Offense
☐Solict Minor
☐Benefit of a Gang – Vic. 18 or >
☐Benefit of a Gang – Vic. <18
☐Terrorism
☐Revoked EJJ
☐Sub. Felony DWI
☐Conspiracy 609.175 Cited
☐Sub. Drug Offense
☐Solict Mentally Impaired
☐Aiding Offender – Responsible for Crim. Acts
☐Crim. Sex. Predatory
☐Sub. Crim. Sex. Predatory

5. CRIMINAL HISTORY

	Prior Juvenile Adjudications	Disp. Date
1		
2		
3		
4		

	Prior Misd. /Gross Misdemeanor Sentences	Units	
1			
2			
3			
4			
5			
6			
7			
8			

	Prior Felony Sentences and Stays, and prior EJJ	Weight	
1			
2			
3			
4			
5			
6			
7			
8			

6. TOTAL CRIMINAL HISTORY / PRESUMPTIVE SENTENCE

Presumptive Guidelines Sentence

Disposition: ☐ **Stay** ☐ **Commit to Commissioner**

Recommended Duration: *Length of Presumptive Sentence (Mos.)*

Ranges: Lower *Upper* ☐ **Life**

Durations include 3 month Custody Status Enhancement ☐

Presumptive Consecutive ☐

IT IS THE RESPONSIBILITY OF THE PROBATION AGENT TO HAVE THIS WORKSHEET ENTERED ONTO THE ELECTRONIC WORKSHEET PORTION OF THE STATEWIDE SUPERVISION SYSTEM.

Source: "Probation report," Minnesota Sentencing Guidelines Commission, accessed July 12, 2012, http://www.msgc.state.mn.us/msgc5/reports.htm#special_guidelines_reports, click on "EWS Data Entry Form"

a sentence within the standard range of forty-nine to fifty-three months. After hearing Yolanda's description of the kidnapping, the judge rejected the state's recommendation and imposed an exceptional sentence of ninety months—thirty-seven months beyond the standard maximum. He justified the sentence on the ground that the petitioner had acted with "deliberate cruelty."

Faced with an unexpected increase of more than three years in his sentence, Blakely objected. The judge accordingly conducted a three-day bench hearing featuring testimony from Yolanda, Ralphy, a police officer, and medical experts. He concluded that

> Blakely used stealth and surprise, and took advantage of the victim's isolation. He immediately employed physical violence, restrained the victim with tape, and threatened her with injury and death to herself and others. He immediately coerced the victim into providing information by the threatening application of a knife. He violated a subsisting restraining order. (301)

The judge adhered to his initial determination of deliberate cruelty. Blakely appealed, arguing that this sentencing procedure deprived him of his federal constitutional right to have a jury determine beyond a reasonable doubt all facts legally essential to his sentence.

In *U.S. v. Booker* (2005), the Court applied the *Apprendi* rule to the U.S. sentencing guidelines. In Justice Stevens' words, writing for the five-member majority, "there is no distinction of constitutional significance" between the federal sentencing guidelines and the Washington sentencing guidelines in *Blakely*. Therefore, the Court held, judges can't increase defendants' sentence without proving beyond a reasonable doubt to a jury facts justifying the increase.

That raised a second question: What should be done instead? Four of the five justice majority would have continued sentencing according to the guidelines, except for cases that increased sentence lengths. In those cases, the government would have to "prove any fact that is required to increase a defendant's sentence under the Guidelines beyond a reasonable doubt" (284–85). But that's not what happened.

Justice Ginsburg, one of the five-member majority, broke with the majority on the remedy to join with the dissent to give them the majority on the remedy. What remedy? It had two parts:

1. Sentencing guidelines would operate as they did before, but they're now advisory, not mandatory as they were before *Booker.* In the remedy majority's words, the new rule "requires judges to consider the Guidelines" but they don't have to follow them (259).
2. Sentences are still subject to review by the U.S. Courts of Appeal. When they do, they have to consider whether the sentence is "unreasonable" in light of the guidelines and the general purposes of sentencing under federal law (261).

There was—and still is—much hand-wringing over where the Court is headed in its decisions on the right to trial by jury and sentencing and what implications it has for sentencing guidelines under state and federal law. But it's important not to exaggerate the impact of the *Apprendi* rule and its impact after *Blakely* and *Booker*. Remember, the rule applies only to cases in which judges increase sentences. According to a U.S. Sentencing Commission (2006) special report on the impact of *Booker*:

> The majority of federal cases continue to be sentenced in conformance with the sentencing guidelines. National data show that when within-range sentences and government-sponsored, below-range sentences are combined, the rate of sentencing in conformance with the sentencing guidelines is 85.9 percent. This conformance rate remained stable throughout the year that followed *Booker*. (vi)

Nevertheless, there's still great concern and uncertainty about what "advisory" and "unreasonable" mean in the remedy elements of *Booker*. The Court didn't seem to clear up very much in our next case excerpt, *Gall v. U.S.* (2007), the first case to apply the *Booker* rule.

CASE

In* Gall v. U.S. *(2007), *the five-member majority upheld the trial judge's sentence of Brian Michael Gall to thirty-six months of probation instead of a mandatory prison term.*

Did the probation sentence abuse the trial judge's discretion?

Gall v. U.S.

552 U.S. 38 (2007)

HISTORY

Brian Michael Gall (hereafter "Petitioner") was convicted, on his guilty plea, in the U.S. District Court for the Southern District of Iowa, of conspiracy to distribute ecstasy and was sentenced to 36 months of probation. The government appealed, challenging the sentence. The Eighth Circuit Court of Appeals remanded for resentencing. Certiorari was granted.

STEVENS, J., JOINED BY ROBERTS, CJ., AND SCALIA, KENNEDY, SOUTER, GINSBURG, AND BREYER, JJ.

FACTS

In February or March 2000, petitioner Brian Gall, a second-year college student at the University of Iowa, was invited by Luke Rinderknecht to join an ongoing enterprise distributing a controlled substance popularly known as "ecstasy." (Ecstasy is sometimes called "MDMA" because its scientific name is "methylenedioxymethamphetamine.") Gall—who was then a user of ecstasy, cocaine, and marijuana—accepted the invitation. During the ensuing seven months, Gall delivered ecstasy pills, which he received from Rinderknecht, to other conspirators, who then sold them to consumers. He netted more than $30,000.

A month or two after joining the conspiracy, Gall stopped using ecstasy. A few months after that, in September 2000, he advised Rinderknecht and other co-conspirators that he was withdrawing from the conspiracy. He has not sold illegal drugs of any kind since. He has, in the words of the District Court, "self-rehabilitated." He graduated from the University of Iowa in 2002, and moved first to Arizona, where he obtained a job in the construction industry, and later to Colorado, where he earned $18 per hour as a master carpenter. He has not used any illegal drugs since graduating from college.

After Gall moved to Arizona, he was approached by federal law enforcement agents who questioned him about his involvement in the ecstasy distribution conspiracy. Gall admitted his limited participation in the distribution of ecstasy, and the agents took no further action at that time. On April 28, 2004—approximately a year and a half after this initial interview, and three and a half years after Gall withdrew from the conspiracy—an indictment was returned in the Southern District of Iowa charging him and seven other defendants with participating in a conspiracy to distribute ecstasy, cocaine, and marijuana that began in or about May 1996 and continued through October 30, 2002.

The government has never questioned the truthfulness of any of Gall's earlier statements or contended that he played any role in, or had any knowledge of, other aspects of the conspiracy described in the indictment. When he received notice of the indictment, Gall moved back to Iowa and surrendered to the authorities. While free on his own recognizance, Gall started his own business in the construction industry, primarily engaged in subcontracting for the installation of windows and doors. In his first year, his profits were more than $2,000 per month.

Gall entered into a plea agreement with the government, stipulating that he was "responsible for, but did not necessarily distribute himself, at least 2,500 grams of [ecstasy], or the equivalent of at least 87.5 kilograms of marijuana." In the agreement, the government acknowledged that by "on or about September of 2000," Gall had communicated his intent to stop distributing ecstasy to Rinderknecht and other members of the conspiracy. The agreement further provided that recent changes in the guidelines that enhanced the recommended punishment for distributing ecstasy were not applicable to Gall because he had withdrawn from the conspiracy prior to the effective date of those changes.

In her presentence report, the probation officer concluded that Gall had no significant criminal history; that he was not an organizer, leader, or manager; and that his offense did not involve the use of any weapons. The report stated that Gall had truthfully provided the government with all of the evidence he had concerning the alleged offenses, but that his evidence was not useful because he provided

(continues)

(continued)

no new information to the agents. The report also described Gall's substantial use of drugs prior to his offense and the absence of any such use in recent years. The report recommended a sentencing range of 30 to 37 months of imprisonment.

The record of the sentencing hearing held on May 27, 2005, includes a "small flood" of letters from Gall's parents and other relatives, his fiancé, neighbors, and representatives of firms doing business with him, all uniformly praising his character and work ethic. The transcript includes the testimony of several witnesses and the District judge's colloquy with the Assistant U.S. Attorney (AUSA) and with Gall. The AUSA did not contest any of the evidence concerning Gall's law-abiding life during the preceding five years but urged that "the Guidelines are appropriate and should be followed," and requested that the court impose a prison sentence within the guidelines range. He mentioned that two of Gall's co-conspirators had been sentenced to 30 and 35 months, respectively, but upon further questioning by the District Court, he acknowledged that neither of them had voluntarily withdrawn from the conspiracy.

The District judge sentenced Gall to probation for a term of 36 months. In addition to making a lengthy statement on the record, the judge filed a detailed sentencing memorandum explaining his decision, and provided the following statement of reasons in his written judgment:

> The Court determined that, considering all the factors under 18 U.S.C. 3553(a), the Defendant's explicit withdrawal from the conspiracy almost four years before the filing of the Indictment, the Defendant's post-offense conduct, especially obtaining a college degree and the start of his own successful business, the support of family and friends, lack of criminal history, and his age at the time of the offense conduct, all warrant the sentence imposed, which was sufficient, but not greater than necessary to serve the purposes of sentencing.

At the end of both the sentencing hearing and the sentencing memorandum, the District judge reminded Gall that probation, rather than "an act of leniency," is a "substantial restriction of freedom." In the memorandum, he emphasized:

> [Gall] will have to comply with strict reporting conditions along with a three-year regime of alcohol and drug testing. He will not be able to change or make decisions about significant circumstances in his life, such as where to live or work, which are prized liberty interests, without first seeking authorization from his Probation Officer or, perhaps, even the Court. Of course, the Defendant always faces the harsh consequences that await if he violates the conditions of his probationary term.

Finally, the District judge explained why he had concluded that the sentence of probation reflected the seriousness of Gall's offense and that no term of imprisonment was necessary:

> Any term of imprisonment in this case would be counter effective by depriving society of the contributions of the Defendant who, the Court has found, understands the consequences of his criminal conduct and is doing everything in his power to forge a new life. The Defendant's post-offense conduct indicates neither that he will return to criminal behavior nor that the Defendant is a danger to society. In fact, the Defendant's post-offense conduct was not motivated by a desire to please the Court or any other governmental agency, but was the pre-Indictment product of the Defendant's own desire to lead a better life.

The Court of Appeals reversed and remanded for resentencing. It held that a sentence outside of the guidelines range must be supported by a justification that "is proportional to the extent of the difference between the advisory range and the sentence imposed." Characterizing the difference between a sentence of probation and the bottom of Gall's advisory guidelines range of 30 months as "extraordinary" because it amounted to "a 100% downward variance," the Court of Appeals held that such a variance must be—and here was not—supported by extraordinary circumstances.

Rather than making an attempt to quantify the value of the justifications provided by the District judge, the Court of Appeals identified what it regarded as five separate errors in the District judge's reasoning: (1) He gave "too much weight to Gall's withdrawal from the conspiracy"; (2) given that Gall was 21 at the time of his offense, the District judge erroneously gave "significant weight" to studies showing impetuous behavior by persons under the age of 18; (3) he did not "properly weigh" the seriousness of Gall's offense; (4) he failed to consider whether a sentence of probation would result in "unwarranted" disparities; and (5) he placed "too much emphasis" on Gall's post-offense rehabilitation.

As we shall explain, we are not persuaded that these factors, whether viewed separately or in the aggregate, are sufficient to support the conclusion that the District judge abused his discretion. As a preface to our discussion of these particulars, however, we shall explain why the Court of Appeals' rule requiring "proportional" justifications for departures from the guidelines range is not consistent with our remedial opinion in *United States v. Booker*, 543 U.S. 220 (2005).

OPINION

While the extent of the difference between a particular sentence and the recommended Guidelines range is relevant, courts of appeals must review all sentences—whether inside, just outside, or significantly outside the Guidelines range—under a deferential **abuse-of-discretion standard** "failure to exercise sound, reasonable, and legal decision-making; an appellate court's standard for reviewing a decision that is asserted to be grossly unsound, unreasonable, illegal, or unsupported by the evidence" (Garner 2004, 11).

Because the Guidelines are now advisory, appellate review of sentencing decisions is limited to determining whether they are "reasonable" (*United States v. Booker*, 543 U.S. 220 [2005]), and an abuse-of-discretion standard applies to appellate review of sentencing decisions. A district judge must consider the extent of any departure from the Guidelines and must explain the appropriateness of an unusually lenient or harsh sentence with sufficient justifications.

An appellate court may take the degree of variance into account and consider the extent of a deviation from the Guidelines, but it may not require "extraordinary" circumstances or employ a rigid mathematical formula using a departure's percentage as the standard for determining the strength of the justification required for a specific sentence. Such approaches come too close to creating an impermissible unreasonableness presumption for sentences outside the Guidelines range.

The mathematical approach also suffers from infirmities of application. And both approaches reflect a practice of applying a heightened standard of review to sentences outside the Guidelines range, which is inconsistent with the rule that the abuse-of-discretion standard applies to appellate review of all sentencing decisions—whether inside or outside that range.

A district court should begin by correctly calculating the applicable Guidelines range. The Guidelines are the starting point and initial benchmark but are not the only consideration. After permitting both parties to argue for a particular sentence, the judge should consider all of 18 U.S.C. § 3553(a)'s factors to determine whether they support either party's proposal. The factors include

(a) The court, in determining the particular sentence to be imposed, shall consider—
  - (1) the nature and circumstances of the offense and the history and characteristics of the defendant;
  - (2) the need for the sentence imposed—
    - (A) to reflect the seriousness of the offense, to promote respect for the law, and to provide just punishment for the offense;
    - (B) to afford adequate deterrence to criminal conduct;
    - (C) to protect the public from further crimes of the defendant; and
    - (D) to provide the defendant with needed educational or vocational training, medical care, or other correctional treatment in the most effective manner;
  - (3) the kinds of sentences available;
  - (4) the kinds of sentence and the sentencing range established for—
    - (A) the applicable category of offense committed by the applicable category of defendant as set forth in the guidelines—
      - (i) issued by the Sentencing Commission pursuant to section 994 (a)(1) of title 28, United States Code, subject to any amendments made to such guidelines by act of Congress (regardless of whether such amendments have yet to be incorporated by the Sentencing Commission into amendments issued under section 994 (p) of title 28); and

(continues)

(continued)

(ii) that, except as provided in section 3742 (g), are in effect on the date the defendant is sentenced; or

(B) in the case of a violation of probation or supervised release, the applicable guidelines or policy statements issued by the Sentencing Commission

(5) any pertinent policy statement issued by the Sentencing

(6) the need to avoid unwarranted sentence disparities among defendants with similar records who have been found guilty of similar conduct; and

(7) the need to provide restitution to any victims of the offense.

He may not presume that the Guidelines range is reasonable but must make an individualized assessment based on the facts presented. If he decides on an outside-the-Guidelines sentence, he must consider the extent of the deviation and ensure that the justification is sufficiently compelling to support the degree of variation. He must adequately explain the chosen sentence to allow for meaningful appellate review and to promote the perception of fair sentencing. In reviewing the sentence, the appellate court must first ensure that the district court made no significant procedural errors and then consider the sentence's substantive reasonableness under an abuse-of-discretion standard, taking into account the totality of the circumstances, including the extent of a variance from the Guidelines range, but must give due deference to the district court's decision that the § 3553(a) factors justify the variance. That the appellate court might have reasonably reached a different conclusion does not justify reversal.

On abuse-of-discretion review, the Eighth Circuit gave virtually no deference to the district court's decision that the variance was justified. The Circuit clearly disagreed with the district court's decision, but it was not for the Circuit to decide *de novo* ("a court's nondiscretionary review of a lower court's factual or legal findings," Garner 2004, 865) whether the justification for a variance is sufficient or the sentence reasonable. On abuse-of-discretion review, the Court of Appeals should have given due deference to the district court's reasoned and reasonable decision that the § 3553(a) factors, on the whole, justified the sentence. Accordingly, the judgment of the Court of Appeals is reversed.

It is so ordered.

CONCURRING OPINIONS

SCALIA, J.

I join the opinion of the Court. The highly deferential standard adopted by the Court today will result in far fewer unconstitutional sentences than the proportionality standard employed by the Eighth Circuit. The door therefore remains open for a defendant to demonstrate that his sentence, whether inside or outside the advisory Guidelines range, would not have been upheld but for the existence of a fact found by the sentencing judge and not by the jury.

SOUTER, J.

After *Booker*'s remedial holding, I continue to think that the best resolution of the tension between substantial consistency throughout the system and the right of jury trial would be a new Act of Congress: reestablishing a statutory system of mandatory sentencing guidelines, but providing for jury findings of all facts necessary to set the upper range of sentencing discretion.

DISSENT

THOMAS, J.

I would affirm the judgment of the Court of Appeals because the District Court committed statutory error when it departed below the applicable Guidelines range.

ALITO, J.

In reading the *Booker* opinion, we should not forget the decision's constitutional underpinnings. *Booker* and its antecedents are based on the Sixth Amendment right to trial by jury. The Court has held that (at least under a mandatory guidelines system) a defendant has the right to have a jury, not a judge, find facts that increase the defendant's authorized sentence (*Blakely v. Washington,* 542 U.S. 296 [2004]). It is telling that the rules set out in the Court's opinion in the present case have nothing to do with juries or fact-finding and, indeed, that not one of the facts that bears on petitioner's sentence is disputed. What is at issue, instead, is the allocation of the authority to decide issues of substantive sentencing policy, an issue on which the Sixth Amendment says absolutely nothing. The yawning gap between the Sixth Amendment and the Court's opinion should be enough to show that the *Blakely-Booker* line of cases has gone astray.

A sentencing system that gives trial judges the discretion to sentence within a specified range not only permits judicial fact-finding that may increase a sentence, such a system also gives individual judges discretion to implement their own sentencing policies. This latter feature, whether wise or unwise, has nothing to do with the concerns of the Sixth Amendment, and a principal objective of the Sentencing Reform Act was to take this power out of the hands of individual district judges.

The *Booker* remedy, however, undid this congressional choice. In curing the Sentencing Reform Act's perceived defect regarding judicial fact-finding, *Booker* restored to the district courts at least a measure of the policymaking authority that the Sentencing Reform Act had taken away. (How much of this authority was given back is, of course, the issue here.)

I recognize that the Court is committed to the *Blakely-Booker* line of cases, but we are not required to continue along a path that will take us further and further off course. Because the *Booker* remedial opinion may be read to require sentencing judges to give weight to the Guidelines, I would adopt that interpretation and thus minimize the gap between what the Sixth Amendment requires and what our cases have held.

Read fairly, the opinion of the Court of Appeals holds that the District Court did not properly exercise its sentencing discretion because it did not give sufficient weight to the policy decisions reflected in the Guidelines. Petitioner was convicted of a serious crime, conspiracy to distribute "ecstasy." He distributed thousands of pills and made between $30,000 and $40,000 in profit. Although he eventually left the conspiracy, he did so because he was worried about apprehension. The Sentencing Guidelines called for a term of imprisonment of 30 to 37 months, but the District Court imposed a term of probation.

If the question before us was whether a reasonable jurist could conclude that a sentence of probation was sufficient in this case to serve the purposes of punishment set out in 18 U.S.C. § 3553(a)(2), the District Court's decision could not be disturbed. But because I believe that sentencing judges must still give some significant weight to the Guidelines sentencing range, the Commission's policy statements, and the need to avoid unwarranted sentencing disparities, I agree with the Eighth Circuit that the District Court did not properly exercise its discretion.

The court listed five considerations as justification for a sentence of probation: (1) petitioner's "voluntary and explicit withdrawal from the conspiracy," (2) his "exemplary behavior while on bond," (3) "the support manifested by family and friends," (4) "the lack of criminal history, especially a complete lack of any violent criminal history," (5) and his age at the time of the offense.

Two of the considerations that the District Court cited—the support manifested by family and friends and his age—amounted to a direct rejection of the Sentencing Commission's authority to decide the most basic issues of sentencing policy. In response to Congress's direction to establish uniform national sentencing policies regarding these common sentencing factors, the Sentencing Commission issued policy statements concluding that "age," "family ties," and "community ties" are relevant to sentencing only in unusual cases. The District Court in this case did not claim that there was anything particularly unusual about petitioner's family or community ties or his age, but the Court cited these factors as justifications for a sentence of probation. Although the District Court was obligated to take into account the Commission's policy statements and the need to avoid sentencing disparities, the District Court rejected Commission policy statements that are critical to the effort to reduce such disparities.

The District Court relied on petitioner's lack of criminal history, but criminal history (or the lack thereof) is a central factor in the calculation of the Guidelines range. Petitioner was given credit for his lack of criminal history in the calculation of his Guidelines sentence. Consequently, giving petitioner additional credit for this factor was nothing more than an expression of disagreement with the policy determination reflected in the Guidelines range.

The District Court mentioned petitioner's "exemplary behavior while on bond," but this surely cannot be regarded as a weighty factor.

Finally, the District Court was plainly impressed by petitioner's "voluntary and explicit withdrawal from the conspiracy." As the Government argues, the legitimate strength of this factor is diminished by petitioner's motivation in withdrawing. He did not leave the conspiracy for reasons of conscience, and he made no effort to stop the others in the ring. He withdrew because he had become afraid of apprehension.

Because I believe that the Eighth Circuit correctly interpreted and applied the standards set out in the *Booker* remedial opinion, I must respectfully dissent.

(continues)

(continued)

QUESTIONS

1. Summarize the facts of the case.
2. Summarize the arguments of the majority opinion, applying the Sixth Amendment right to trial by jury.
3. Summarize the arguments of the concurring and dissenting opinions, applying the Sixth Amendment right to trial by jury.
4. Should the right to trial by jury apply to sentencing? Back up your answer with details from the facts and opinions of the Court.
5. In your opinion, what is the "fair" punishment Gall deserves? Back up your answer with details from the facts and opinions of the Court.

SUMMARY

LO 1 The constitution balances the power of government with the liberty of individuals. The rule of law ensures criminality is not subject to the passions of rulers, democratic or otherwise.

LO 2 The principle of legality establishes: "No crime without law, no punishment without law."

LO 3 Because of the principle of legality and its sanction against retroactive criminal lawmaking, no one can be punished for a law that didn't exist at the time of the behavior.

LO 4 Vague laws fail to give fair warning to individuals and to law enforcement. The First Amendment ensures people aren't criminally punished for expressive behavior.

LO 5 The Second Amendment protects against the government's ability to restrict the individual right to use handguns to protect ourselves in our homes.

LO 6 Collectively, the Bill of Rights implies a right to privacy, and this right has been confirmed by the Supreme Court.

LO 7 The Eighth Amendment ensures people aren't subject to excessive punishment and codifies the principle that "punishment should fit the crime." Many special considerations of proportionality are made when the penalty is death.

LO 8 The U.S. Supreme Court has ruled that the right to a jury trial guarantees that no increase in sentencing can occur without the finding of all relevant facts by a jury.

KEY TERMS

constitutional democracy, p. 42
rule of law, p. 42
principle of legality, p. 42
ex post facto law, p. 43
void-for-vagueness doctrine, p. 43
fair notice (in void-for-vagueness doctrine), p. 44
equal protection of the laws, p. 47
expressive conduct (in First Amendment), p. 48
void-for-overbreadth doctrine, p. 49
bench trial, p. 50
Second Amendment, p. 54
intermediate scrutiny, p. 59
constitutional right to privacy, p. 59
fundamental right to privacy, p. 60
cruel and unusual punishment, p. 64
barbaric punishments, p. 65
principle of proportionality, p. 66
three-strikes laws, p. 77
mandatory minimum sentencing laws, p. 81
fixed (determinate) sentences, p. 81
sentencing guidelines, p. 81
Apprendi rule, p. 81
abuse-of-discretion standard, p. 87

LEARNING OBJECTIVES

1. To be able to identify the elements of criminal liability and to explain why the voluntary act is the first principle of criminal liability.
2. To be able to differentiate conduct crimes from bad result crimes.
3. To be able to distinguish between criminal conduct and criminal liability and, therefore, punishment.
4. To understand and appreciate the importance of requiring a voluntary act before there can be a crime.
5. To understand the legal definition of a voluntary act.
6. To identify the circumstances when, and to be able to explain why, status is treated, sometimes, as an affirmative act.
7. To be able to understand how the general principle of *actus reus* includes a voluntary act and how it's viewed by the Constitution.
8. To understand and identify the circumstances when, and to be able to explain why, omissions are treated as acts.
9. To understand and identify the circumstances when, and to be able to explain why, possession can be treated as an act.
10. To know the different types of possession recognized by the law.

Jonathan McGraw, left, wore a shirt with a botanical motif in the Sitka courtroom April 27, 2011 as he awaited a verdict following his week-long trial on felony marijuana possession charges. His attorney, David Graham, is at the right. The jury found McGraw guilty. The Sitka man said he was not the owner of the marijuana seized at his residence. "I took the rap for someone else's weed," he said after the trial.

AP Images/Daily Sitka Sentinel, James Poulson

THE CRIMINAL ACT 3

The First Principle of Criminal Liability

CHAPTER OUTLINE

Was His "Sleep Sex" a Voluntary Act?

Jan Luedecke, a 30-year-old landscaper, got drunk during a party in 2003 at a Toronto house and fell asleep on a couch. Some time later, he approached a woman who was sleeping on an adjacent couch, put on a condom, and began sexual intercourse with her. The woman awoke to discover that her underwear had been removed and a glassy-eyed Luedecke was trying to rape her. She pushed him off, ran to the washroom, and returned to find him standing there bewildered.

(Bering 2011)

No one should be punished except for something she does. She shouldn't be punished for what wasn't done at all; she shouldn't be punished for what someone else does; she shouldn't be punished for being the sort of person she is, unless it is up to her whether or not she is a person of that sort. She shouldn't be punished for being blond or short, for example, because it isn't up to her whether she is blond or short. Our conduct is what justifies punishing us. One way of expressing this point is to say that there is a voluntary act requirement in the criminal law (Corrado 1994, 1529).

The voluntary act requirement is called the "first principle of criminal liability." You'll learn why in this chapter. But, before we get to that, you need to be sure how the voluntary act requirement fits into the analytic framework of criminal liability introduced in Chapter 1. Recall the definition of **criminal liability**: "conduct that unjustifiably and inexcusably inflicts or threatens substantial harm to individual or public interests" (ALI 1985, MPC § 1.02(1)(a), Chapter 1, p. 6). The three elements of criminal liability consist of:

criminal liability, "conduct that unjustifiably and inexcusably inflicts or threatens substantial harm to individual or public interests"

- Conduct that is
- Without justification and
- Without excuse

Criminal liability falls only upon cases that progress through all the following analytic steps. We express them here as questions:

1. *Is there criminal conduct?* If there's no criminal conduct, there's no criminal liability. If there is, there might be criminal liability. To determine if there is, we proceed to the second question. (See this chapter on criminal acts; Chapter 4 on criminal intent and causation.)
2. *Is the conduct justified?* If it is, then there's no criminal liability. If it isn't justified, there still might not be criminal liability. To determine if there is, we proceed to the third question. (See Chapter 5 on the defenses of justification.)
3. *Is the conduct excused?* If it is, then there's no criminal liability. (See Chapter 6 on the defenses of excuse.)

elements of a crime, to convict, the prosecution must prove beyond a reasonable doubt (1) a criminal act (in all crimes) (2) criminal intent (in some crimes), (3) concurrence (in all crimes), (4) attendant circumstances (in some crimes), and (5) that criminal conduct caused a criminal harm (in bad result crimes only)

This scheme applies to almost everything you'll learn, not just in the rest of this chapter and Chapters 4 through 6. It also applies to the crimes covered in Chapters 7 through 13. Furthermore, the scheme applies whether you're learning about criminal liability under the federal government or the government of the state, city, or town where you live or attend school. It applies whether it's the common law, a criminal code, or the MPC being analyzed. (The "Elements of Crime" boxes that you'll find throughout the book illustrate the scheme.)

THE ELEMENTS OF CRIMINAL LIABILITY

actus reus, the requirement that all crimes have to include a voluntary criminal act, which is the physical element and the first principle of criminal liability

***mens rea*,** criminal intent, the mental element in crime

The drafters of criminal codes have five building blocks at their disposal when they write the definitions of the thousands of individual crimes and defenses. These building blocks are the **elements of a crime** that the prosecution has to prove beyond a reasonable doubt to convict individual defendants:

1. Criminal act (*actus reus*)
2. Criminal intent (*mens rea*)
3. Concurrence
4. Attendant circumstances
5. Bad result (causing a criminal harm)

These are illustrated in the Elements of Criminal Conduct Crimes box.

LO 1

All crimes have to include a voluntary criminal act (*actus reus* or "evil act"; the *physical element* in crime). That's why it's called the first principle of criminal liability. The vast majority of minor crimes against public order and morals (the subject of Chapter 12) don't include either a mental element—namely, criminal intent (*mens rea*)—the element of causation, or conduct that causes a bad result (Chapter 4).

LO 2

Serious crimes, such as murder (Chapter 9), sexual assault (Chapter 10), robbery (Chapter 11), and burglary (Chapter 11), include both a criminal act and a second element, the mental attitudes included in *mens rea* ("evil mind"). You'll learn more about *mens rea* in Chapter 4 and apply it to specific crimes in Chapters 8 through 13.)

conduct crimes, requiring a criminal act triggered by criminal intent

We call crimes requiring a criminal act triggered by criminal intent **conduct crimes**. Let's look at burglary as an example of a criminal conduct crime. It consists of the act of breaking and entering a house, triggered by the *mens rea* of, say, intending to steal

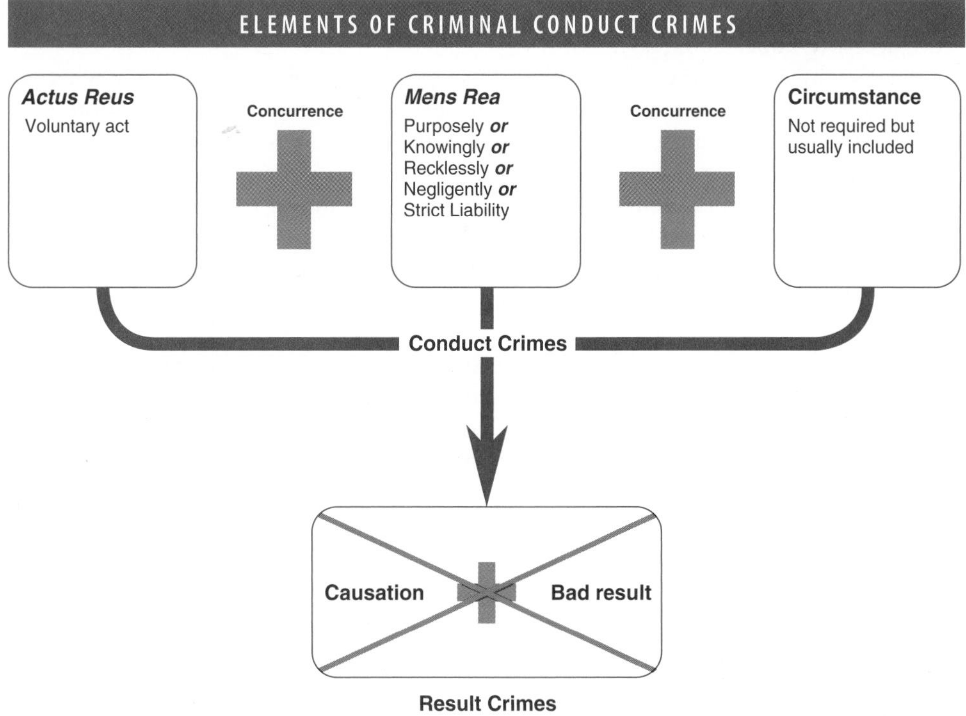

an iPad once inside the house. The crime of burglary is complete whether or not the burglar actually steals the iPad. So the crime of burglary is criminal conduct whether or not it causes any harm beyond the conduct itself.

LO 3

Don't confuse *criminal acts* with *criminal conduct* as we use these terms. **Criminal acts** are voluntary bodily movements (Holmes 1963, 45–47); criminal conduct is the criminal act triggered by *mens rea*. *Criminal liability* takes this one step further; it's criminal conduct that qualifies for punishment. Table 3.1 summarizes the differences among these important concepts.

criminal acts, voluntary bodily movements

Crimes consisting of a criminal act and a *mens rea* include a third element, **concurrence**, which means that a criminal intent has to trigger the criminal act. Although concurrence is a necessary element that you have to know exists, you won't read much about it because it's practically never a problem to prove it in real cases.

concurrence, the principle of criminal liability that requires that a criminal intent has to trigger the criminal act

It's a rare crime that includes only a criminal act. This is partly because without something more than an act, a criminal statute would almost certainly fail to pass the test of constitutionality (Chapter 2). For example, a criminal statute that made the simple act of "driving a car" a crime surely would be void for vagueness or for

TABLE 3.1

Criminal Acts, Criminal Conduct, and Criminal Liability	
Criminal act (also called *actus reus*)	The physical element of a crime; a bodily movement, muscular contraction
Criminal conduct	Criminal act + criminal intent (also called *mens rea*)
Criminal liability	Criminal conduct that qualifies for criminal punishment—namely, it's both unjustified and not excused

overbreadth; a ban on "driving while intoxicated" just as surely would pass the constitutional test (Dubber 2002, 44).

attendant circumstances element, a "circumstance" connected to an act, an intent, and/or a bad result

That's why most of the offenses that don't require a *mens rea* do include what we call an **attendant circumstances element**. This element isn't an act, an intention, or a result; rather, it's a "circumstance" connected to an act, an intent, and/or a result. In our driving example, "while intoxicated" is the circumstance element.

LO 2

Some serious crimes include all five elements. In addition to (1) a voluntary act, (2) the mental element, and (3) circumstantial elements, they include (4) causation and (5) criminal harm. We call these crimes *bad result crimes* (we'll usually refer to them simply as **result crimes**). The Elements of Bad Result Crimes box illustrates these elements.

result crimes, crimes that include five elements: (1) a voluntary act, (2) the mental element, (3) circumstantial elements, (4) causation, and (5) criminal harm

There are several result crimes (LaFave 2003b, 1:464-65), but the most prominent, and the one discussed in this and other criminal law books most often, is criminal homicide—conduct that causes another person's death (Chapter 9). For example, murder consists of (1) a criminal act (it can be any act—shooting, stabbing, running down with a car, beating with a baseball bat), (2) triggered by (3) the intent to kill, (4) which causes (5) someone's death.

This is a good time to review also what you learned in Chapter 1 about proving criminal behavior, especially proving the commonly misunderstood and misused *corpus delicti* (Latin "body of the crime"). The misunderstanding arises from applying "body of the crime" only to the body of the victim in homicides. This is where the term *corpus delicti* most often appears. However, it also, more broadly, applies to the elements of conduct crimes (such as stealing someone's *property* in theft) and result crimes (such as burning a *house* in arson). You'll encounter these concepts again in Chapters 4 and 9 through 13.

Now, at last, it's time to turn to the main topic of the chapter: the requirement of a criminal act (*actus reus*).

ELEMENTS OF BAD RESULT CRIMES

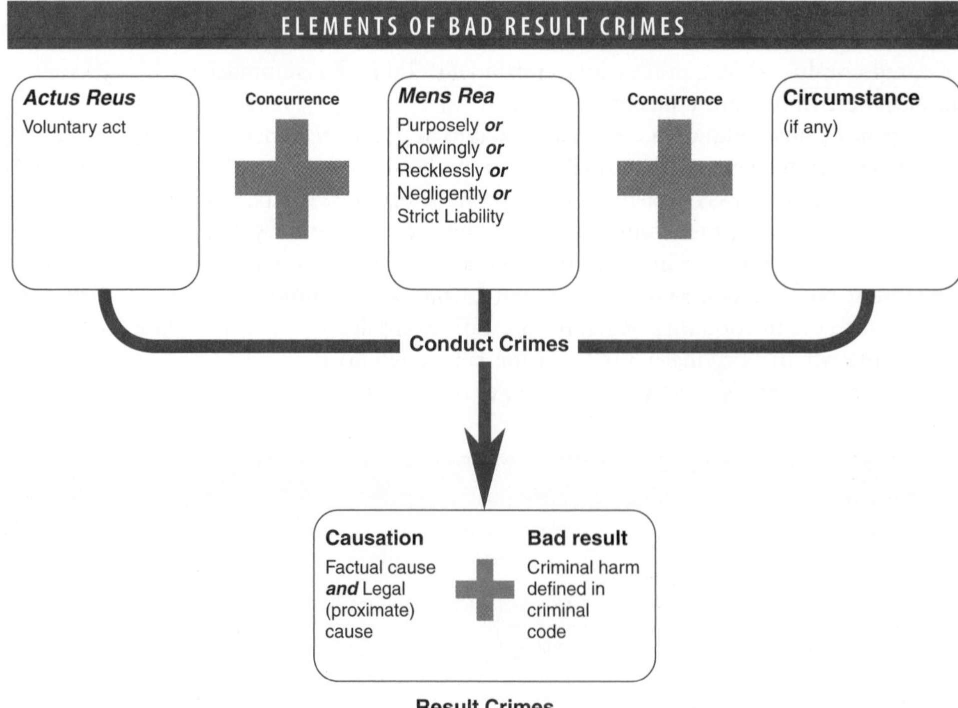

THE CRIMINAL ACT (*ACTUS REUS*): THE FIRST PRINCIPLE OF LIABILITY

We punish people for what they *do*, not for who they *are*. You'll see this idea phrased variously, such as "we punish acts not status" or "we punish actions not intentions." However expressed, the phrase has to capture the idea of the first principle of criminal liability. So it's not a crime to wish your cheating boyfriend would die; to fantasize about nonconsensual sex with the person sitting next to you in your criminal law class; or to think about taking your roommate's wallet when he's not looking. "Thoughts are free," a medieval English judge, borrowing from Cicero, famously remarked.

Imagine a statute that makes it a crime merely to intend to kill another person. Why does such a statute strike us as absurd? Here are three reasons: First, it's impossible to prove a mental attitude by itself. In the words of a medieval judge, "The thought of man is not triable, for the devil himself knoweth not the thought of man." Second, a mental attitude by itself doesn't hurt anybody. Although the moral law may condemn you if you think about committing crimes, and some branches of Christianity may call thoughts "sins" ("I have sinned exceedingly in thought, word, and deed"), the criminal law demands *conduct*—a mental attitude that turns into action. So punishing the mere intent to kill (even if we could prove it) misses the harm of the statute's target—another's death (Morris 1976, ch. 1).

A third problem with punishing a state of mind is that it's terribly hard to separate daydreaming and fantasy from intent. The angry thought "I'm gonna kill you for that!" rarely turns into actual killing (or for that matter even an attempt to kill, discussed in Chapter 8), because it's almost always just a spur of the moment way of saying, "I'm really angry." Punishment has to wait for enough action to prove the speaker really intends to commit a crime (Chapter 8).

Punishing thoughts stretches the reach of the criminal law too far when it brings within its grasp a "mental state that the accused might be too irresolute even to begin to translate into action." The bottom line: we don't punish thoughts because it's impractical, inequitable, and unjust (Williams 1961, 1–2). Now you know why the first principle of criminal liability is the requirement of an act. This requirement is as old as our law. Long before there was a legal principle of *mens rea*, there was the requirement of a criminal act.

The requirement that attitudes have to turn into deeds is called **manifest criminality**. It leaves no doubt about the criminal nature of the act. The modern phrase "caught red-handed" comes from the ancient idea of manifest criminality. Then, it meant catching murderers with the blood still on their hands; now, it means catching someone in the act of wrongdoing. For example, if several people are seen, by bank customers, entering the bank, drawing guns, threatening to shoot if the tellers don't hand over money, taking the money the tellers give them, and leaving the bank with the money, their criminality—the *actus reus* and the *mens rea* of robbery—is manifest (Fletcher 1978, 115–16).

manifest criminality, the requirement that mental attitudes have to turn into deeds for a "crime" to be committed

The *actus reus* requirement serves several purposes. First, acts help to prove intent. We can't see states of mind; we can only infer them from actions. Second, it reserves the harsh sanction of the criminal law for cases of actual danger. Third, it protects the privacy of individuals. The law doesn't have to pry into the thoughts of individuals unless the thinker crosses "the threshold of manifest criminality."

Although simple to state as a general rule, much in the principle of *actus reus* complicates its apparent simplicity (Fletcher 1978, 117). We'll examine four of these complications: the requirement that the act be voluntary; status or condition; criminal omissions; and criminal possession.

THE "VOLUNTARY" ACT REQUIREMENT

LO 4

Only voluntary acts qualify as *actus reus*. In the words of the great justice and legal philosopher Oliver Wendell Holmes, "An act is a muscular contraction, and something more. The contraction of muscles must be willed" (Holmes 1963, 46–47). Why do only voluntary acts qualify as criminal acts? The rationale consists of four logical steps:

1. Criminal law punishes people.
2. We can only punish people we can blame.
3. We can only blame people who are responsible for their acts.
4. People are responsible only for their voluntary acts.

The American Law Institute's (ALI) Model Penal Code's (MPC) widely adopted definition of "criminal act" provides: "A person is not guilty of an offense unless his liability is based on conduct that *includes* a voluntary act . . ." (emphasis added) (ALI 1985, § 2.01). (We'll call the MPC definition the **one-voluntary-act-is-enough rule.**) Notice that according to the MPC, even though a voluntary act is "an absolute requirement for criminal liability," it's not necessary that "every act up to the moment" the crime is completed be voluntary (LaFave 2003, 307).

one-voluntary-act-is-enough rule, conduct that includes a voluntary act satisfies the voluntary act requirement

Take the example in our next case excerpt. Marc Burrell, voluntarily, pulled his gun, raised it, pointed it at Joey Baglione, and then the gun fired when Baglione bumped Burrell, causing the gun to fire involuntarily. Burrell was held accountable for the firing because of his voluntary acts *before* the involuntary firing. Most statutes adopt the MPC's one-voluntary-act-is-enough rule.

CASE

In* State v. Burrell *(1992)*, *the New Hampshire Supreme Court had to decide whether Marc Burrell's last act before the shooting death had to be voluntary.

Did he fire the gun voluntarily?

State v. Burrell

609 A.2d 751 (N.H. 1992)

HISTORY

Marc Burrell, the defendant, was convicted of manslaughter after a jury trial in the Superior Court. Burrell appealed, arguing that the trial court committed an error in its jury instruction concerning the requirement under a New Hampshire statute that provides that conduct creating criminal liability must include a voluntary act. The New Hampshire Supreme Court affirmed the Superior Court.

THAYER, J.

FACTS

Douglas Saari and Joey Baglione made plans to have a few drinks at Baglione's house. Before going there, Saari, a minor, stopped at Burrell's house and asked Burrell to purchase beer. Burrell agreed and decided to accompany Saari to Baglione's. When they arrived, Baglione answered the door holding a .357 revolver. Inside the house were an AR-15 rifle, possibly a shotgun, a .44 revolver, and a .38 snub-nose revolver. The .357 and .44 revolvers were loaded.

During the afternoon the three drank beer and watched an X-rated movie. Baglione and Burrell played a form of Russian roulette with the .357 revolver. One bullet was placed in the chamber, the chamber was spun, one player placed the gun to his head with his finger on the trigger, and then the gun was examined to see whether the bullet would have been discharged if the trigger had been pulled. At some point in the afternoon, all three went out on Baglione's back porch and fired one or two rounds with the .44 revolver.

At trial, Saari testified that while Baglione was out of the room, Saari told Burrell that he was going to steal the .38 and placed it in the lining of his leather jacket. Burrell agreed to go along with Saari, and stated that he was going to steal the AR-15, the .44, and the .357. When Baglione returned, Burrell announced his intention to steal the weapons. Baglione said, "You're not going to steal those guns, so I'll stop you." Baglione ran out of the room, and returned with a shotgun. By then, Burrell had put down the AR-15, but kept the .44 in his belt and the .357 in his hand.

Saari testified that Baglione "came running out of the basement . . . and told [Burrell], . . . 'You're not going to steal those guns because I'll blow your f_______ head off.'" Saari added that Baglione was not "serious . . . [and] he pumped the shotgun more than once, so I know it wasn't loaded." Saari then "looked at Burrell to see what his response was. And before I had time to do anything, he had shot in Baglione's direction" and hit him. Burrell dropped the gun, tried to call an ambulance, but panicked and went outside. At that time, Baglione's brother-in-law, Greg Eastman, arrived and called the ambulance. After the ambulance arrived, Eastman, Saari and Burrell went to the hospital.

At trial, Burrell testified that the fatal shooting did not occur when Baglione threatened him, but later in the afternoon while he and Baglione were preparing to take some of the guns back to a closet in Baglione's father's bedroom. Before storing the guns, Baglione told Burrell that his father always kept the .357 loaded.

Burrell testified that, after loading the .357 revolver, he was seated on the forward edge of the loveseat with his feet outstretched. Baglione passed in front of him from right to left. While Baglione was to his left, he sighted the gun on the hearth and put his finger on the trigger. He heard a noise and saw Baglione move from left to right in front of him. Thinking that they were going to collide, he jerked back and the gun went off. Burrell admitted on cross-examination that because of a lazy left eye, a problem he was aware of on the day of the shooting, he had great difficulty seeing anything to his left.

OPINION

In New Hampshire, "a person is not guilty of an offense unless his criminal liability is based on conduct that includes a voluntary act or the voluntary omission to perform an act of which he is physically capable." RSA 626:1, I. Burrell does not dispute either the statutory requirement or the fundamental principle that criminal liability must be predicated upon conduct that includes a voluntary act. Burrell, however, contends that the court erred in failing to instruct the jury that it must find that Burrell's act of pulling the trigger was voluntary.

The trial court gave the jury the following instruction on the voluntary act requirement:

> A person is not guilty of an offense unless his criminal liability is based upon conduct that includes a voluntary act. A voluntary act is defined as conduct which is performed consciously as a result of effort or determination. To find Burrell guilty of an offense, any offense, you must find that the criminal liability is based upon conduct that includes a voluntary act. And although a voluntary act is an absolute requirement for criminal liability, you do not have to find that every single act in the circumstances presented to you was voluntary. It is sufficient to satisfy the requirement of a voluntary act if you find that Burrell's conduct causing the death of Joseph Baglione, Jr. included a voluntary act.

Burrell requested this instruction:

> A person is not guilty of an offense unless his criminal liability is based on conduct that includes a voluntary act. If you find Burrell's act of pulling the trigger of the handgun in this case not to have been a voluntary act, then you must find Burrell not guilty.

Burrell essentially asks this court to require the State to prove that Burrell's last act was voluntary in order to establish criminal liability. There is no support for this proposition in either the statute or in our case law. The statute only requires that Burrell's conduct that gives rise to criminal liability include a voluntary act. Although a voluntary act is absolutely necessary for criminal liability, there is no requirement that every act preceding the actual commission of the offense be voluntary. We hold that the trial court's refusal to instruct the jury that Burrell's act of pulling the trigger must have been a voluntary act was not error. Affirmed.

QUESTIONS

1. State the facts relevant to deciding whether Marc Burrell "voluntarily" shot Joey Baglione.
2. State the court's definition of "voluntary act."
3. Summarize the court's reasons for holding that the trial judge wasn't required to give the jury instruction that Burrell asked for.
4. In your opinion, which is the better rule for determining whether an act is voluntary: (a) the last act has to be voluntary or (b) that conduct has to include a voluntary act? Defend your answer.

automatism, unconscious bodily movements

The MPC—and many state criminal codes—defines "voluntary," not by telling us what a voluntary act is, but by listing acts that aren't voluntary. The list usually includes movements during various forms of **automatism** (bodily movements while unconscious). The MPC adds a fourth catchall to these: "a bodily movement that otherwise is not a product of the effort or determination of the actor, either conscious or habitual" (ALI 1985, § 2.01(2)).

LO 5

fault-based defenses, defenses based on creating a reasonable doubt about the prosecution's proof of a voluntary act

affirmative defenses of excuse, defenses of excuse for criminal liability, which take place after the prosecution has proved the defendant's criminal conduct

Let's look at two examples: conduct during sleepwalking and during epileptic seizures. Before we do, we need to make clear that there are two kinds of defenses that these examples of involuntary acts can bring about. The first are **fault-based defenses,** defenses based on creating a reasonable doubt about the prosecution's proof of a voluntary act. Fault-based defenses occur during the first step in our analytic framework of criminal liability (conduct that results from a voluntary act). The second kind of defenses are the **affirmative defenses of excuse**—insanity and diminished capacity. They take place after the prosecution has proved that the defendant's conduct caused the harm to the victim. (We'll discuss the affirmative defenses of excuse in Chapter 6.)

Sleepwalking

Look first at the sleepwalking episode in our next case excerpt. While she was asleep, Mrs. Cogdon brutally killed her daughter Pattie and was charged with murder. The court decided that Mrs. Cogdon wasn't insane and, therefore, not entitled to the excuse of insanity. But the court acquitted her because she killed Pattie involuntarily.

CASE

In* King v. Cogdon *(1951), the court had to decide whether Mrs. Cogdon's killing her daughter while she was sleepwalking was voluntary.

Did she kill Pattie voluntarily?

King v. Cogdon

(Morris 1951)

HISTORY

Mrs. Cogdon was charged with the murder of her only child, a daughter called Pat, aged nineteen. To the charge of murdering Pat, Mrs. Cogdon pleaded not guilty. Her story, though somewhat bizarre, was not seriously challenged by the Crown, and led to her acquittal.

FACTS

Mrs. Cogdon told how, on the night before her daughter's death, she had dreamt that their house was full of spiders and that these spiders were crawling all over Pat. In her sleep, Mrs. Cogdon left the bed she shared with her husband, went into Pat's room, and awakened to find herself violently brushing at Pat's face, presumably to remove the spiders. This woke Pat. Mrs. Cogdon told her she was just tucking her in. At the trial, she testified that she still believed, as she had been told, that the occupants of a nearby house bred spiders as a hobby, preparing nests for them behind the pictures on their walls. It was these spiders which in her dreams had invaded their home and attacked Pat.

There had also been a previous dream in which ghosts had sat at the end of Mrs. Cogdon's bed and she had said to them, "Well, you have come to take Pattie." It does not seem fanciful to accept the psychological explanation of these spiders and ghosts as the projections of Mrs. Cogdon's subconscious hostility towards her daughter; a hostility which was itself rooted in Mrs. Cogdon's own early life and marital relationship.

The morning after the spider dream she told her doctor of it. He gave her a sedative and, because of the dream and certain previous difficulties she had reported, discussed the possibility of psychiatric treatment. That evening Mrs. Cogdon suggested to her husband that he attend his lodge meeting, and asked Pat to come with her to the cinema.

After he had gone Pat looked through the paper, not unusually found no tolerable program, and said that as she was going out the next evening she thought she would rather go to bed early. Later, while Pat was having a bath preparatory to retiring, Mrs. Cogdon went into her room, put a hot water bottle in the bed, turned back the bedclothes, and placed a glass of hot milk beside the bed ready for Pat. She then went to bed herself.

There was some desultory conversation between them about the war in Korea, and just before she put out her light Pat called out to her mother, "Mum, don't be so silly worrying there about the war, it's not on our front door step yet."

Mrs. Cogdon went to sleep. She dreamt that "the war was all around the house," that soldiers were in Pat's room, and that one soldier was on the bed attacking Pat. This was all of the dream she could later recapture. Her first "waking" memory was of running from Pat's room, out of the house to the home of her sister who lived next door. When her sister opened the front door Mrs. Cogdon fell into her arms, crying, "I think I've hurt Pattie." In fact Mrs. Cogdon had, in her somnambulistic state, left her bed, fetched an axe from the woodheap, entered Pat's room, and struck her two accurate forceful blows on the head with the blade of the axe, thus killing her.

Pat had for some time been receiving psychiatric treatment for a relatively minor neurotic condition of which, in her psychiatrist's opinion, she was now cured. Despite this, Mrs. Cogdon continued to worry unduly about her. Describing the relationship between Pat and her mother, Mr. Cogdon testified: "I don't think a mother could have thought any more of her daughter. I think she absolutely adored her."

OPINION

On the conscious level, at least, there was no reason to doubt Mrs. Cogdon's deep attachment to her daughter. Mrs. Cogdon's story was supported by the evidence of her physician, a psychiatrist, and a psychologist. The burden of the evidence of all three, which was not contested by the prosecution, was that Mrs. Cogdon was suffering from a form of hysteria with an overlay of depression, and that she was of a personality in which such dissociated states as fugues, amnesias, and somnambulistic acts are to be expected. They agreed that she was not psychotic, and that if she had been awake at the time of the killing no defense could have been spelt out under the M'Naghten Rules [Chapter 6].

The jury believed Mrs. Cogdon's story, and regarded the presumption that the natural consequences of her acts were intended as being completely rebutted by her account of her mental state at the time of the killing, and by the unanimous support given to it by the medical and psychological evidence. She was acquitted. Insanity was not pleaded as a defense—she was acquitted because the act of killing itself was not, in law, regarded as her act at all.

QUESTIONS

1. State the facts relevant to deciding whether Mrs. Cogdon "voluntarily" killed her daughter Pattie.
2. How did the court define "voluntary act"?
3. Summarize the court's reasons for holding that Mrs. Cogdon didn't murder Pattie.
4. In your opinion, did Mrs. Cogdon's conduct "include a voluntary act"? Defend your answer.

EXPLORING FURTHER

Voluntary Acts: "Sleep Sex"

Is "sleep sex" a voluntary act?

(Bering 2011)

FACTS

Jan Luedecke, a 30-year-old landscaper, got drunk during a party in 2003 at a Toronto house and fell asleep on a couch. Some time later, he approached a woman who was sleeping on an adjacent couch, put on a condom, and began sexual intercourse with her. The woman awoke to discover that her underwear had been removed and a glassy-eyed Luedecke was trying to rape her. She pushed him off, ran to the washroom, and returned to find him standing there bewildered.

DECISION

At his trial in 2005, Luedecke was acquitted of sexual assault after University of Toronto psychiatry professor testified for the defense that Luedecke wasn't conscious of his actions. According to Dr. Shapiro, Luedecke was experiencing "sexsomnia" and was, therefore, not "consciously aware of his actions" during the assault. In February 2008, a Canadian provincial appellate court upheld Luedecke's acquittal.

Epileptic Seizures

Experts agree that epileptic seizures and acts committed during the seizures are involuntary. But can epileptics be criminally liable because of voluntary acts before their seizures (Kadish, Schulhofer, and Steiker 2007, 189)? Voluntary acts that might create liability include choosing not to follow the laws of individual states.

The laws vary, but all fifty states restrict driver's licenses for persons who don't control their seizures with medication. Common restrictions include proof of being six months' free of active seizures and a physician's statement confirming that the seizures are controlled and that, if the person has a driver's license, he or she "will not present an unreasonable risk to public safety." According to the Epilepsy Therapy Project (2011a), being seizure free for twelve months "greatly reduces" the risk of traffic accidents of persons with epilepsy. Driving also "may be safe for some people with epilepsy after a shorter seizure-free period, depending on individual circumstances."

Circumstances that could make a person with epilepsy unsafe include missing even one dose of antiepileptic medication. Taking the medication at the wrong time is another of these circumstances. So is failing to heed the warning signs of oncoming seizures (auras). Auras vary significantly among individuals; they may occur right before a seizure, or several minutes, or even hours, before. Common warning signs that occur right before seizures include "changes in bodily sensations; changes in your ability to interact with things happening outside you; and changes in how familiar the outside world seems to you." Auras occurring hours before seizures include "depression, irritability, sleep disruption, nausea, and headache" (Epilepsy Therapy Project 2011b).

Probably the most widely cited case of a crime occurring during an epileptic seizure is our next case excerpt. *People v. Decina* (1956) was decided more than a half-century ago. On a bright and sunny day in 1956, Emil Decina, during an epileptic seizure as he drove his vehicle, hit six schoolgirls from behind, ages six to twelve, as they were walking on the sidewalk. Three were pronounced dead on arrival at the hospital; a fourth died in the hospital two days later. Decina was tried and convicted of involuntary manslaughter.

CASE

In* People v. Decina *(1956)*, *the court found that the deaths of four children resulted from a voluntary act by Emil Decina, who had suffered an epileptic seizure while driving.

Was killing while driving during an epileptic seizure voluntary?

People v. Decina

138 N.E.2d 799 (1956)

HISTORY

Emil Decina was charged with criminal negligence in the operation of a vehicle resulting in death. He was convicted in the trial court and appealed. The intermediate appellate court reversed and granted a new trial. The highest court reversed (4–3).

FROESSEL, J.

FACTS

At about 3:30 P.M. on March 14, 1955, a bright, sunny day, Emil Decina (defendant) was driving alone in his car, going north on Delaware Avenue. Decina's car swerved to the left, across the center line in the street, so that it was completely in the south lane, traveling 35 to 40 miles per hour. It then veered sharply to the right, crossing Delaware Avenue and mounting the east curb, and continued at about 50 or 60 miles per hour, or more.

A group of six schoolgirls were walking north on the east sidewalk of Delaware Avenue, two in front and four slightly in the rear, when Decina's car struck them from behind. One of the girls escaped injury by jumping against a wall. The bodies of the girls were propelled onto the street and the lawn in front of a coal company. Three of the girls, 6 to 12 years old, were found dead on arrival by the medical examiner, and a fourth, 7 years old, died in a hospital two days later as a result of injuries sustained in the accident.

After striking the girls, Decina continued on the east sidewalk, and then swerved back onto Delaware Avenue. His car continued north, passing under a viaduct before it again veered to the right and remounted the east curb, striking and breaking a metal lamp post. With its horn blowing steadily apparently because Decina was "stooped over" the steering wheel, the car proceeded on the sidewalk until it finally crashed through the 7¼-inch brick wall of a grocery store, injuring at least one customer and causing considerable property damage.

A number of bystanders pulled Decina out of the car, and laid him on the sidewalk. When the police arrived, Decina attempted to get up, staggered and appeared dazed and unsteady. When informed that he was under arrest, and would have to accompany the police to the station house, he resisted and, when he tried to get away, was handcuffed.

OPINION

Decina knew he was subject to epileptic attacks and seizures that might strike at any time. [He had a seizure a few weeks before the present incident.] He also knew that a moving motor vehicle uncontrolled on a public highway is a highly dangerous instrumentality capable of unrestrained destruction. With this knowledge, and without anyone accompanying him, he deliberately took a chance by making a conscious choice of a course of action, in disregard of the consequences which he knew might follow from his conscious act, and which in this case did ensue.

To hold otherwise would be to say that a man may freely indulge himself in liquor in the same hope that it will not affect his driving, and if it later develops that ensuing intoxication causes dangerous and reckless driving resulting in death, his unconsciousness or involuntariness at that time would relieve him from prosecution.

DISSENT

DESMOND, J.

Until this case, no attempt was ever made to penalize the wrong done by one whose foreseeable blackout while driving had consequences fatal to another person. Just what is the court holding here? No less than this: that a driver whose brief blackout lets his car run amuck and kill another has killed that other by reckless driving. Thus, it must be that such a blackout-prone driver is guilty of reckless driving, whenever and as soon as he steps into the driver's seat of a vehicle. Every time he drives, accident or no accident, he is subject to criminal prosecution for reckless driving or to revocation of his operator's license. And how many of this State's 5,000,000 licensed operators are subject to such penalties for merely driving the cars they are licensed to drive? No one knows how many citizens or how many or what kind of physical conditions will be gathered in under this practically limitless coverage. . . . It is no answer that prosecutors and juries will be reasonable or compassionate.

QUESTIONS

1. List Emil Decina's voluntary acts *before* his seizure.
2. Which of his voluntary acts do the majority and dissent rely on to argue that he was, or was not, criminally liable for his involuntary acts during the seizure?
3. In your opinion, should Decina be criminally liable for killing the girls? Back up your answer with specific details from the case excerpt and the excerpts from the Epilepsy Therapy Project's "Driving and the Law," and "Auras" (summarized in the text before the excerpt).

EXPLORING FURTHER

Voluntary Acts Prior to Involuntary Acts

Were his acts following exposure to Agent Orange voluntary?

State v. Jerrett, 307 S.E.2d 339 (1983)

FACTS

Bruce Jerrett terrorized Dallas and Edith Parsons—he robbed them, killed Dallas, and kidnapped Edith. At trial, Jerrett testified that he could remember nothing of what happened until he was arrested and that he had suffered

(continues)

(continued)

previous blackouts following exposure to Agent Orange during military service in Vietnam. The trial judge refused to instruct the jury on the defense of automatism.

Did he act voluntarily? It's up to the jury said the appeals court.

DECISION

The North Carolina Supreme Court reversed and ordered a new trial:

> Where a person commits an act without being conscious thereof, the act is not a criminal act even though it would be a crime if it had been committed by a person who was conscious. In this case, there was corroborating evidence tending to support the defense of unconsciousness. Defendant's very peculiar actions in permitting the kidnapped victim to repeatedly ignore his commands and finally lead him docilely into the presence and custody of a police officer lends credence to his defense of unconsciousness. We therefore hold that the trial judge should have instructed the jury on the defense of unconsciousness.

STATUS, *ACTUS REUS*, AND THE CONSTITUTION

LO 6

status, the character or condition of a person or thing

"Action" refers to what we *do*; **status** (or condition) denotes who we *are*. Most statuses or conditions don't qualify as *actus reus*. Status can arise in two ways. Sometimes, it results from prior voluntary acts—methamphetamine addicts voluntarily used methamphetamine the first time, and alcoholics voluntarily took their first drink. Other conditions result from no act at all, and individuals have no control over them. The most obvious examples are the characteristics we're born with: sex, age, sexual orientation, race, and ethnicity.

LO 7

Is the voluntary act requirement a constitutional command? It's clear that, according to the general principle of *actus reus*, every crime has to include at least one voluntary act, but is the principle of *actus reus* a constitutional command? Twice during the 1960s, the U.S. Supreme Court considered this question.

In the first case, *Robinson v. California* (1962), Lawrence Robinson was convicted and sentenced to a mandatory ninety days in jail for violating a California statute making it a misdemeanor "to be addicted to" narcotics. Five justices agreed that punishing Robinson solely for his addiction to heroin was cruel and unusual punishment (Chapter 2). The Court expressed the ban on status crimes in various ways: The California statute created a crime of personal condition, punishing Robinson for who he was (heroin addict), not for what he did. The statute punished the sickness of heroin addiction—"even one day in prison would be a cruel and unusual punishment for the 'crime' of having a common cold"; the statute punished a condition that may be "contracted innocently and involuntarily" (667).

The decision that legislatures can't make status or personal condition by itself a crime brought into question the constitutionality of many old status crimes, such as being a prostitute, a drunkard, or a disorderly person. But what if these statutes include the requirement of some act in addition to the condition? That's where *Powell v. Texas* (1968) comes in. On December 19, 1966, Leroy Powell was arrested and charged under a Texas statute, which provided:

> Whoever shall get drunk or be found in a state of intoxication in any public place, or at any private house except his own, shall be fined not exceeding one hundred dollars. (517)

Powell was tried, found guilty, and fined $50. Powell appealed to the U.S. Supreme Court. Powell's argument to Court was that "the disease of chronic alcoholism" destroyed "his will power to resist drinking and appearing drunk in public." In other words, there was no voluntary act. So the statute, which "criminally punishes an ill person for conduct" he can't control, violates the ban on cruel and unusual punishment (*Powell v. Texas* 1968, Brief for Appellant, 6).

In its argument to the Court, Texas relied on Powell's own witness, a nationally recognized psychiatrist, author, and lecturer on alcoholism, to make its own case that Powell's being drunk in public was a voluntary act. From this and other expert testimony, Texas argued that although it's very tough, chronic alcoholics can become "chronic abstainers, although perhaps not moderate drinkers." In other words, with a lot of effort, they can stop themselves from taking the first, but not the second, drink of a "drinking bout." You might want to think about it this way: "barely" voluntary is good enough (*Powell v. Texas* 1968, Brief for Appellee, 8).

The U.S. Supreme Court's opinions reflected contrasting views on the critical question of how far the U.S. Constitution goes into the principle of *actus reus*. A plurality of four justices answered firmly: not one bit further than *Robinson v. California* took the principle. After making clear that the Constitution bans only pure status as a basis for criminal liability, the plurality concluded:

> *Robinson* brings this Court but a very small way into the substantive criminal law. And unless *Robinson* is so viewed, it is difficult to see any limiting principle that would serve to prevent this Court from becoming, under the aegis of the Cruel and Unusual Punishment Clause, the ultimate arbiter of the standards of criminal responsibility, in diverse areas of the criminal law, throughout the country. (533)

Finally, the plurality invoked federalism to support its hands-off position regarding the principles of criminal liability:

> *Actus reus, mens rea*, insanity, mistake, justification, and duress have historically provided the tools for a constantly shifting adjustment of the tension between the evolving aims of the criminal law and changing religious, moral, philosophical, and medical views of the nature of man. This process of adjustment has always been thought to be the province of the States. (535–36)

Justice White wrote a separate opinion concurring in the plurality's judgment, because "Powell showed nothing more than that he was to some degree compelled to drink and that he was drunk at the time of his arrest. He made no showing that he was unable to stay off the streets on the night in question" (553–54).

Four dissenting justices were eager to bring the Court, by means of the U.S. Constitution, fully into the business of supervising the general principles of criminal liability. Writing for the dissent, Justice Fortas wrote:

> Powell is charged with a crime composed of two elements—being intoxicated and being found in a public place while in that condition. Powell was powerless to avoid drinking; that having taken his first drink, he had "an uncontrollable compulsion to drink" to the point of intoxication; and that, once intoxicated, he could not prevent himself from appearing in public places. (567–68)

Most criminal law books, and I'm sure most criminal law classes, spend lots of time and space on the Constitution and the general principles of criminal liability. At the time the cases were decided, there was great hope, and great fear (depending on your point of view), that an "activist" Supreme Court would use the "cruel and unusual punishment" ban and other provisions in the U.S. Constitution to write a constitutional doctrine of criminal liability and responsibility. It never happened. Real cases in real courts since *Powell* haven't tried to bring the Constitution further into the principles of criminal liability than *Robinson* brought it in 1962. It's left in the hands of legislatures to adopt general principles of liability and elements of specific crimes in criminal codes. It's left in the hands of courts to interpret and apply the code's provisions in decisions involving individual defendants.

OMISSIONS AS CRIMINAL ACTS

LO 8

We support punishment for people who rape, murder, and rob because their actions caused harm. But what about people who stand by and do nothing while bad things are happening around them? As Professor George Fletcher (1978) describes these people, "They get caught in a situation in which they falter. Someone needs help and they cannot bring themselves to render it" (633). Can these failures to act satisfy the *actus reus* requirement? Yes, **criminal omissions** satisfy the voluntary act requirement, but only when there's a legal duty to the person in danger of harm.

criminal omission, the failure to act when there's a legal duty to act

There are two kinds of criminal omission. One is the simple failure to act, usually the **failure to report** something you're required by law to report, such as reporting an accident; reporting child abuse; filing an income tax return; registering a firearm; or notifying sexual partners of positive HIV status. The other type of omission is the **failure to intervene**—that is, not actively preventing or interrupting injuries and death to persons or damage and destruction of property. Both omissions—failure to report and failure to intervene—are criminal omissions only if defendants had a **legal duty** (a duty enforced by law), not just a moral duty, to act.

failure to report, not reporting something the law requires you to report

failure to intervene, not actively preventing or interrupting injuries and death to persons or damage and destruction of property

A legal duty is an attendant circumstance element that the prosecution has to prove beyond a reasonable doubt. Legal duties are created in three ways:

legal duty, a duty created by a statute, contract, or special relationship, and enforceable by law

1. Statutes
2. Contracts
3. Special relationships

Statutes are the basis for legal duties to report—for example, the duty to file income tax returns, report accidents and child abuse, and register firearms. Individuals can also contract to perform duties; for example, law enforcement officers agree to "protect and serve." Failure to perform those duties can create criminal liability. The main special relationships are the parent-child relationship, the doctor-patient relationship, the employer-employee relationship, the carrier-passenger relationship, and, in some states, the husband-wife relationship.

Failure to perform moral duties (enforced by conscience, religion, and social norms) doesn't qualify as a criminal omission. According to Professor Wayne LaFave (2003a):

> Generally one has no legal duty to aid another person in peril, even when that aid can be rendered without danger or inconvenience to himself. He need not shout a warning to a blind man headed for a precipice or to an absent-minded one walking into a gunpowder room with a lighted candle in hand. He need not pull a neighbor's baby out of a pool of water or rescue an unconscious person stretched across the railroad tracks, though the baby is drowning or the whistle of the approaching train is heard in the distance. A doctor is not legally bound to answer a desperate call from the frantic parents of a sick child, at least if it is not one of his regular patients. A moral duty to take affirmative action is not enough to impose a legal duty to do so. But there are situations which do give rise to legal duties. (311)

"Good Samaritan" doctrine, imposes a legal duty to help or call for help for imperiled strangers

There are two approaches to defining a legal duty to rescue strangers or call for help. One is the **"Good Samaritan" doctrine,** which imposes a legal duty to help or call for help for imperiled strangers. Only a few jurisdictions follow the Good Samaritan approach. Nearly all follow the approach of the **American bystander rule** (*State v. Kuntz* 2000, 951). According to the bystander rule, there's no legal duty to rescue or summon help for someone who's in danger, even if the bystander risks nothing by helping. So, although it might be a revolting breach of the moral law for an Olympic swimmer to stand by and watch a child drown, without so much as even placing a 911 call on her cell phone, the criminal law demands nothing from her.

American bystander rule, there's no legal duty to rescue or summon help for someone who's in danger, even if the bystander risks nothing by helping

Restricting criminal omissions to the failure to perform legal duties is based on three assumptions: First, individual conscience, peer pressure, and other informal mechanisms condemn and prevent behavior more effectively than criminal prosecution. Second, prosecuting omissions puts too heavy of a burden on an already overburdened criminal justice system. Third, criminal law can't force "Good Samaritans" to help people in need. In our next case excerpt, the Pennsylvania Superior Court upheld a conviction for failure to act in *Commonwealth v. Pestinikas* (1992).

CASE

In **Commonwealth v. Pestinikas** *(1992), the Pennsylvania Superior Court upheld a conviction for failure to act based on a legal duty to act.*

Did the Pestinikases owe Joseph Kly a legal duty?

Commonwealth v. Pestinikas

617 A.2d 1339 (Pa.Sup. 1992)

HISTORY

Walter and Helen Pestinikas were convicted of third-degree murder in the Court of Common Pleas, Criminal Division, Lackawanna County. Each was sentenced to serve not less than five years or more than ten years in prison. Defendants appealed. The Superior Court, Nos. 375 and 395 Philadelphia 1989, affirmed.

WIEAND, J.

FACTS

Joseph Kly met Walter and Helen Pestinikas in the latter part of 1981 when Kly consulted them about prearranging his funeral. In March 1982, Kly, who had been living with a stepson, was hospitalized and diagnosed as suffering from Zenker's diverticulum, a weakness in the walls of the esophagus, which caused him to have trouble swallowing food. In the hospital, Kly was given food, which he was able to swallow and, as a result, regained some of the weight that he had lost. When he was about to be discharged, he expressed a desire not to return to his stepson's home and sent word to the Pestinikases that he wanted to speak with them. As a consequence, arrangements were made for the Pestinikases to care for Kly in their home on Main Street in Scranton, Lackawanna County.

Kly was discharged from the hospital on April 12, 1982. When the Pestinikases came for him on that day they were instructed by medical personnel regarding the care that was required for Kly and were given a prescription to have filled for him. Arrangements were also made for a visiting nurse to come to the Pestinikases' home to administer vitamin B-12 supplements to Kly. The Pestinikases agreed orally to follow the medical instructions and to supply Kly with food, shelter, care, and the medicine he required.

The prescription was never filled, and the Pestinikases told the visiting nurse that Kly did not want the vitamin supplement shots and that her services, therefore, were not required. Instead of giving Kly a room in their home, the Pestinikases removed him to a rural part of Lackawanna County, where they placed him in the enclosed porch of a building, which they owned, known as the Stage Coach Inn. This porch was approximately 9 feet by 30 feet, with no insulation, no refrigeration, no bathroom, no sink, and no telephone. The walls contained cracks that exposed the room to outside weather conditions.

Kly's predicament was compounded by the Pestinikases' affirmative efforts to conceal his whereabouts. Thus, they gave misleading information in response to inquiries, telling members of Kly's family that they did not know where he had gone and others that he was living in their home.

(continues)

(continued)

After Kly was discharged from the hospital, the Pestinikases took Kly to the bank and had their names added to his savings account. Later, Kly's money was transferred into an account in the names of Kly or Helen Pestinikas, pursuant to which moneys could be withdrawn without Kly's signature. Bank records reveal that from May 1982, to July 1983, the Pestinikases withdrew amounts roughly consistent with the $300 per month Kly had agreed to pay for his care.

Beginning in August 1983, and continuing until Kly's death in November 1984, however, the Pestinikases withdrew much larger sums so that when Kly died, a balance of only $55 remained. In the interim, the Pestinikases had withdrawn in excess of $30,000.

On the afternoon of November 15, 1984, when police and an ambulance crew arrived in response to a call by the Pestinikases, Kly's dead body appeared emaciated, with his ribs and sternum greatly pronounced. Mrs. Pestinikas told police that she and her husband had taken care of Kly for $300 per month and that she had given him cookies and orange juice at 11:30 A.M. on the morning of his death. A subsequent autopsy, however, revealed that Kly had been dead at that time and may have been dead for as many as 39 hours before his body was found. The cause of death was determined to be starvation and dehydration. Expert testimony opined that Kly would have experienced pain and suffering over a long period of time before he died.

At trial, the Commonwealth contended that after contracting orally to provide food, shelter, care, and necessary medicine for Kly, the Pestinikases engaged in a course of conduct calculated to deprive Kly of those things necessary to maintain life and thereby cause his death.

The trial court instructed the jury that the Pestinikases could not be found guilty of a malicious killing for failing to provide food, shelter, and necessary medicines to Kly unless a duty to do so had been imposed upon them by contract. The Court instructed the jury as follows:

> In order for you to convict the defendants on any of the homicide charges or the criminal conspiracy or recklessly endangering charges, you must first find beyond a reasonable doubt that the defendants had a legal duty of care to Joseph Kly.
>
> There are but two situations in which Pennsylvania law imposes criminal liability for the failure to perform an act. One of these is where the express language of the law defining the offense provides for criminal [liability] based upon such a failure. The other is where the law otherwise imposes a duty to act.
>
> Unless you find beyond a reasonable doubt that an oral contract imposed a duty to act upon Walter and Helen Pestinikas, you must acquit the defendants.

OPINION

The Pestinikases contend that this instruction was error. The applicable law appears at 18 Pa.C.S. § 301(a) and (b) as follows:

(a) *General rule.* A person is not guilty of an offense unless his liability is based on conduct which includes a voluntary act or the omission to perform an act of which he is physically capable.

(b) *Omission as basis of liability.* Liability for the commission of an offense may not be based on an omission unaccompanied by action unless:

(1) the omission is expressly made sufficient by the law defining the offense; or

(2) a duty to perform the omitted act is otherwise imposed by law.

Unless the omission is expressly made sufficient by the law defining the offense, a duty to perform the omitted act must have been otherwise imposed by law for the omission to have the same standing as a voluntary act for purposes of liability. It should, of course, suffice, as the courts now hold, that the duty arises under some branch of the civil law. If it does, this minimal requirement is satisfied, though whether the omission constitutes an offense depends as well on many other factors.

Consistent with this legal thinking, we hold that when the statute provides that an omission to do an act can be the basis for criminal liability if a duty to perform the omitted act has been imposed by law, the legislature intended to distinguish between a legal duty to act and merely a moral duty to act.

A duty to act imposed by contract is legally enforceable and, therefore, creates a legal duty. It follows that a failure to perform a duty imposed by contract may be the basis for a charge of criminal homicide if such failure causes the death of another person and all other elements of the offense are present. Because there was evidence in the instant case that Kly's death had been caused by the Pestinikases' failure to provide the food and medical care which they had agreed by oral contract to provide for him, their omission to act was sufficient to support a conviction for criminal homicide.

The Pestinikases argue that, in any event, the Commonwealth failed to prove an enforceable contract requiring them to provide Kly with food and medical attention. It is their position that their contract with Kly required them to provide only a place for Kly to live and a funeral upon his death. This obligation, they contend, was fulfilled. Although we have not been provided with a full and complete record of the trial, it seems readily apparent from the partial record before us that the evidence was sufficient to create an issue of fact for the jury to resolve. The issue was submitted to the jury on careful instructions by the learned trial judge and does not present a basis entitling the Pestinikases to post-trial relief.

AFFIRMED.

DISSENT

McEWEN, J.

The theory of the Commonwealth at trial was that the failure of the Pestinikases to fulfill the alleged civil contract to provide food, shelter, personal, and medical care to Mr. Kly was alone sufficient to support a finding of first and/or third degree murder. Section 301(b)(2) of the Crimes Code provides, in relevant part:

> Liability for the commission of any offense may not be based on an *omission unaccompanied by action* unless a duty to perform the omitted act is *otherwise imposed by law.* (emphasis added by the dissent; 18 Pa.C.S. § 301(b)(2))

The precise issue thus becomes whether the legislature intended that a "contractual duty" constitutes a "duty imposed by law" for purposes of ascertaining whether conduct is criminal. While I share the desire of the prosecutor and the jury that the Pestinikases must not escape responsibility for their horribly inhuman and criminally culpable conduct, I cling to the view that an appellate court is not free to reshape the intention or revise the language of the Crimes Code. Rather, our constitutional obligation is to implement the intent and comply with the direction of the legislature.

It is true that this Court has upheld convictions for endangering the welfare of children. However, all of the cases where liability is based upon a failure to act involved the parent-child relationship and the statutory imposition of duties upon the parents of minors. In the instant case, where there was no "status of relationship between the parties" except landlord-tenant, a failure to perform a civil contract cannot alone sustain a conviction for third degree murder. Thus, it is that I dissent.

QUESTIONS

1. List all the facts relevant to deciding whether the Pestinikases had a legal duty to Joseph Kly.
2. List all of the failures to act and voluntary acts that are relevant to deciding whether the Pestinikases failed to perform a legal duty to Mr. Kly.
3. Summarize the arguments regarding criminal omission of both the majority and dissenting opinions.
4. In your opinion, did the Pestinikases have a legal duty to Joseph Kly? Assuming they did have a legal duty, did they reasonably perform their duty? Back up your answer with facts and arguments in the case excerpt.

EXPLORING FURTHER

Omissions

1. Did she have a special relationship with the man in her house?

People v. Oliver, 258 Cal.Rptr. 138 (1989)

FACTS

Carol Ann Oliver met Carlos Cornejo in the afternoon when she was with her boyfriend at a bar. She and her boyfriend purchased jewelry from Cornejo. In the late afternoon, when Oliver was leaving the bar to return home, Cornejo got into the car with her, and she drove him home with her. At the time, he appeared to be extremely drunk. At her house, he asked her for a spoon and went into the bathroom. She went to the kitchen, got a spoon, and brought it to him. She knew he wanted the spoon to take drugs. She remained in the living room while Cornejo "shot

(continues)

(continued)

up" in the bathroom. He then came out and collapsed onto the floor in the living room. She tried but was unable to rouse him. Oliver then called the bartender at the bar where she had met Cornejo. The bartender advised her to leave him and come back to the bar, which Oliver did.

Oliver's daughter returned home at about 5:00 P.M. that day with two girlfriends. They found Cornejo unconscious on the living room floor. When the girls were unable to wake him, they searched his pockets and found $8. They did not find any wallet or identification.

The daughter then called Oliver on the telephone. Oliver told her to drag Cornejo outside in case he woke up and became violent. The girls dragged Cornejo outside and put him behind a shed so that he would not be in the view of the neighbors. He was snoring when the girls left him there. About a half hour later, Oliver returned home with her boyfriend. She, the boyfriend, and the girls went outside to look at Cornejo. Oliver told the girls that she had watched him "shoot up" with drugs and then pass out.

The girls went out to eat and then returned to check on Cornejo later that evening. He had a pulse and was snoring. In the morning, one of the girls heard Oliver tell her daughter that Cornejo might be dead. Cornejo was purple and had flies around him. Oliver called the bartender at about 6:00 A.M. and told her she thought Cornejo had died in her backyard. Oliver then told the girls to call the police and she left for work. The police were called.

Oliver was convicted of involuntary manslaughter and appealed.

Did Oliver have a "special relationship" with Cornejo that created a legal duty? "Yes," said the appeals court.

DECISION

We conclude that the evidence of the combination of events which occurred between the time appellant left the bar with Cornejo through the time he fell to the floor unconscious established as a matter of law a relationship which imposed upon appellant a duty to seek medical aid. At the time appellant left the bar with Cornejo, she observed that he was extremely drunk, and drove him to her home. In so doing, she took him from a public place where others might have taken care to prevent him from injuring himself, to a private place—her home—where she alone could provide care.

2. Did he have a legal duty to his girlfriend's baby?

State v. Miranda, 715 A.2d 680 (1998)

FACTS

Santos Miranda started living with his girlfriend and her two children in an apartment in September 1992. On January 27, 1993, Miranda was twenty-one years old, his girlfriend was sixteen, her son was two, and her daughter, the victim in this case, born on September 21, 1992, was four months old. Although he was not the biological father of either child, Miranda took care of them and considered himself to be their stepfather.

He represented himself as such to the people at Meriden Veteran's Memorial Hospital where, on January 27, 1993, the victim was taken for treatment of her injuries following a 911 call by Miranda that the child was choking on milk. Upon examination at the hospital, it was determined that the victim had multiple rib fractures that were approximately two to three weeks old, two skull fractures that were approximately seven to ten days old, a brachial plexus injury to her left arm, a rectal tear that was actively "oozing blood," and nasal hemorrhages.

The court determined that anyone who saw the child would have had to notice these injuries, the consequent deformities, and her reactions. Indeed, the trial court found that Miranda had been aware of the various bruises on her right cheek and the nasal hemorrhages, as well as the swelling of the child's head; that he knew she had suffered a rectal tear, as well as rib fractures posteriorly on the left and right sides; and that he was aware that there existed a substantial and unjustifiable risk that the child was exposed to conduct that created a risk of death.

The trial court concluded that despite this knowledge, the defendant "failed to act to help or aid the child by promptly notifying authorities of her injuries, taking her for medical care, removing her from her circumstances and guarding her from future abuses. As a result of his failure to help her, the child was exposed to conduct which created a risk of death to her, and the child suffered subsequent serious physical injuries."

Did Santos Miranda have a legal duty to "protect health and well-being" of the baby?

Yes, said the Connecticut Supreme Court.

DECISION

We conclude that, based upon the trial court's findings that the defendant had established a familial relationship with the victim's mother and her two children, had assumed responsibility for the welfare of the children, and had taken care of them as though he were their father, the defendant had a legal duty to protect the victim from abuse.

ETHICAL DILEMMA

*Did Assistant Coach Michael McQueary have a moral duty to intervene in the alleged sexual assault he witnessed?**

Introduction

We, the members of the Thirty-Third Statewide Investigating Grand Jury, having received and reviewed evidence regarding violations of the Crimes Code occurring in Centre County, Pennsylvania, and elsewhere pursuant to Notice of Submission of Investigation No. 1, do hereby make the following findings of fact and recommendation of charges.

Findings of fact

The Grand Jury conducted an investigation into reported sexual assaults of minor male children by Gerald A. Sandusky ("Sandusky") over a period of years, both while Sandusky was a football coach for the Pennsylvania State University ("Penn State") football team and after he retired from coaching. Widely known as Jerry Sandusky, the subject of this investigation founded The Second Mile, a charity initially devoted to helping troubled young boys. It was within The Second Mile program that Sandusky found his victims.

Sandusky was employed by Penn State for 23 years as the defensive coordinator of its Division I collegiate football program. Sandusky played football for four years at Penn State and coached a total of 32 years. While coaching, Sandusky started "The Second Mile" in State College, Pennsylvania, in 1977. It began as a group foster home dedicated to helping troubled boys. It grew into a charity dedicated to helping children with absent or dysfunctional families. It is now a statewide, three region charity and Sandusky has been its primary fundraiser.[1] The Second Mile raises millions of dollars through fundraising appeals and special events. The mission of the program is to "help children who need additional support and would benefit from positive human interaction." Through The Second Mile, Sandusky had access to hundreds of boys, many of whom were vulnerable due to their social situations.

Victim 1

The Grand Jury conducted an investigation into the reported sexual assault of a minor child, Victim 1, by Sandusky, when Victim l, a Second Mile participant, was a houseguest at Sandusky's residence

[1] Sandusky retired from The Second Mile in September 2010.

*Source: Factora-Borchers, Lisa. 2011. "Penn State Sexual Abuse Scandal: How Not to Walk Like Mike McQueary." Accessed November 23, 2011. http://www.myecdysis.com/2011/11/penn-state-sexual-abuse-scandal-how-not-to-walk-like-mike-mcqueary/

in College Township, Centre County, Pennsylvania. During the course of the multi-year investigation, the Grand Jury heard evidence that Sandusky indecently fondled Victim 1 on a number of occasions, performed oral sex on Victim 1 on a number of occasions and had Victim l perform oral sex on him on at least one occasion. . . .

Another youth, F.A., age fifteen, testified that Sandusky had taken him and Victim l to a Philadelphia Eagles football game and that Sandusky had driven. He witnessed Sandusky place his right hand on Victim 1's knee; Sandusky had also done this to F.A. on more than one occasion when they were in Sandusky's car. F.A. was uncomfortable when Sandusky did this and moved his leg to try to avoid the contact. Sandusky would keep his hand on F.A.'s knee even after F.A. tried to move it. F.A. also testified that Sandusky would reach over, while driving, and lift his shirt and tickle his bare stomach. F.A. did not like this contact. F.A. also witnessed Sandusky tickling Victim 1 in similar fashion. Sandusky invited F.A. to stay over at his house but F.A. only stayed one time when he knew Victim 1 was also staying over, after returning from the Philadelphia Eagles game. F.A. confirmed that Victim l slept in Sandusky's basement room when F.A. stayed there. F.A. testified that he stayed away from Sandusky because he felt he didn't want to be alone with him for a long period of time, based on the tickling, knee touching and other physical contact. Victim 1 confirmed that Sandusky would drive with his hand on Victim 1's leg.

Victim 2

On March 1, 2002, a Penn State graduate assistant ("graduate assistant") who was then 28 years old, entered the locker room at the Lasch Football Building on the University Park Campus on a Friday night before the beginning of Spring Break. The graduate assistant, who was familiar with Sandusky, was going to put some newly purchased sneakers in his locker and get some recruiting tapes to watch. It was about 9:30 p.m. As the graduate assistant entered the locker room doors, he was surprised to find the lights and showers on. He then heard rhythmic, slapping sounds. He believed the sounds to be those of sexual activity. As the graduate assistant put the sneakers in his locker, he looked into the shower. He saw a naked boy, Victim 2, whose age he estimated to be ten years old, with his hands up against the wall, being subjected to anal intercourse by a naked Sandusky. The graduate assistant was shocked but noticed that both Victim 2 and Sandusky saw him. The graduate assistant left immediately, distraught.

The graduate assistant went to his office and called his father, reporting to him what he had seen. His father told the graduate assistant to leave the building and come to his home. The graduate assistant and his father decided that the graduate assistant had to promptly report what he had seen to Coach Joe Paterno ("Paterno"), head football coach of Penn State. The next morning, a Saturday, the graduate assistant telephoned Paterno and went to Paterno's home, where he reported what he had seen.

Joseph V. Paterno testified to receiving the graduate assistant's report at his home on a Saturday morning. Paterno testified that the graduate assistant was very upset. Paterno called Tim Curley ("Curley"), Penn State Athletic Director and Paterno's immediate superior, to his home the very next day, a Sunday, and reported to him that the graduate assistant had seen Jerry Sandusky in the Lasch Building showers fondling or doing something of a sexual nature to a young boy.

Approximately one and a half weeks later, the graduate assistant was called to a meeting with Penn State Athletic Director Curley and Senior Vice President for Finance and Business Gary Schultz ("Schultz"). The graduate assistant reported to Curley and Schultz that he had witnessed what he believed to be Sandusky having anal sex with a boy in the Lasch Building showers. Curley and Schultz assured the graduate assistant that they would look into it and determine what further action they would take. Paterno was not present for this meeting.

The graduate assistant heard back from Curley a couple of weeks later. He was told that Sandusky's keys to the locker room were taken away and that the incident had been reported to The Second Mile. The graduate assistant was never questioned by University Police and no other entity conducted an investigation until he testified in Grand Jury in December, 2010. The Grand Jury finds the graduate assistant's testimony to be extremely credible. . . .

The Grand Jury concludes that the sexual assault of a minor male in 2002 should have been reported to the Pennsylvania Department of Public Welfare and/or a law enforcement agency such as the University Police or the Pennsylvania State Police. The University, by its senior staff, Gary Schultz, Senior Vice President for Finance and Business and Tim Curley, Athletic Director, was notified by two different Penn State employees of the alleged sexual exploitation of that youth. Pennsylvania's mandatory reporting statute for suspected child abuse is located at 23 Pa.C.S. §63ll (Child Protective Services Law) and provides that when a staff member reports abuse, pursuant to statute, the person in charge of the school or institution has the responsibility and legal obligation to report or cause such a report to be made by telephone and in writing within 48 hours to the Department of Public Welfare of the Commonwealth of Pennsylvania. An oral report should have been made to Centre County Children and Youth Services but none was made. Nor was there any attempt to investigate, to identify Victim 2 or to protect that child or any others from similar conduct, except as related to preventing its re-occurrence on University property. The failure to report is a violation of the law which was graded a summary offense in 2002, pursuant to 23 Pa.C.S. §63l9.2[2]

The Grand Jury finds that Tim Curley made a materially false statement under oath in an official proceeding on January 12, 2011, when he testified before the 30th Statewide Investigating Grand Jury, relating to the 2002 incident, that he was not told by the graduate assistant that Sandusky was engaged in sexual conduct or anal sex with a boy in the Lasch Building showers.

Furthermore, the Grand jury finds that Gary Schultz made a materially false statement under oath in an official proceeding on January l2, 2011, when he testified before the 30th Statewide Investigating Grand Jury, relating to the 2002 incident that the allegations made by the graduate assistant were "not that serious" and that he and Curley "had no indication that a crime had occurred."

Victim 3

Victim 3, now age 24, met Sandusky through The Second Mile in the summer of 2000, when he was between seventh and eighth grade. The boy met Sandusky during his second year in the program. Sandusky began to invite Victim 3 to go places with him. Victim 3 was invited to Sandusky's home for dinner, to hang out, walk the family dogs and to go to Penn State football games and to Holuba Hall and the gym. When Victim 3 went to the gym with Sandusky, they would exercise and then shower. He recalls feeling uncomfortable and choosing a shower at a distance from Sandusky. Sandusky then made him feel bad about showering at a distance from him, so Victim 3 moved closer. Sandusky initiated physical contact in the shower with Victim 3 by patting him, rubbing his shoulders, washing his hair and giving him bear hugs. These hugs would be both face to face and with Sandusky's chest to Victim 3's back. Victim 3 said that on at least one occasion, Sandusky had an erection when he bear hugged Victim 3 from behind. He also recalled that when he slept over at Sandusky's residence, he slept in the basement bedroom.

He testified that Sandusky would come into the bedroom where he was lying down. He sometimes said he was going to give Victim 3 a shoulder rub; sometimes he would blow on Victim 3's stomach; other times he tickled Victim 3. Sandusky would rub the inside of Victim 3's thigh when he tickled him. On two occasions Victim 3 recalls that Sandusky touched Victim 3's genitals through the athletic shorts Victim 3 wore to bed. Victim 3 would roll over on his stomach to prevent Sandusky from touching his genitals.

Victim 3 knew Victim 4 to spend a great deal of time with Sandusky.

---

[2]The grading of the failure to report offense was upgraded from a summary offense to a misdemeanor of the third degree in 2006, effective May 29, 2007.

I spent a lot of time on Twitter, reading the latest updates [on the Penn State sexual abuse scandal], minute by minute. The bold op-ed on an entire front page of a Pennsylvania newspaper calling for Penn State President Spanier and head coach Joe Paterno's resignation. The two officials who stepped down because they'll likely be charged with perjury. And, of course, Jerry Sandusky, the rapist himself. As of just now, I read about 12 more people have come forward saying they were sexually abused in some way. That brings the number to 20 survivors.

There are so many angles to approach this clusterf*ck. The entire thing is a train wreck of biblical proportion. The grotesque nature of the crimes. The people who KNEW. What was at stake. The choices that were made. Sports culture. An ivy league name. College football's most winningest [*sic*] coach.

It seems like everyone's got a detail they just can't get over, and I'm not excluded.

My hang up isn't on JoePa, Sandusky, Spanier, or any of those fools who would actually call themselves men and/or fathers who cared about NOTHING but the potential scandal and fallout and decided to sweep it under the rug. My hang-up is on the 28 year old graduate assistant who walked away from a 10 year old boy being raped by a grown man. He walked away, also saying that he believed both Sandusky and the boy saw him. I do not even want to imagine what that 10 year old kid was thinking as McQueary walked away and called his father.

"He was distraught."

"He saw something horrifying."

"He didn't know what to do."

I wonder if his reaction would be different if, say, he looked up and saw Sandusky beating this same kid with a bat. I would bet that he would've screamed bloody hell and tried to wrestle him to the ground. But because of the vile, sexual, and evil nature of what was taking place, he was stunned. But not stunned enough to not call his own father to figure out what he should do. May I offer his age again: he was 28 at the time.

If I sound judgmental, it's because I am. Even if you're stunned to paralysis, after about 10 minutes, once you realize you just witnessed a child rape, how do you NOT call the police? Or have some kind of thought resembling, "God, I hope that kid's alright."

I think my favorite response on Twitter was something like, "As a 104 lb grandmother, there's no way I wouldn't have done everything to get that kid safe." But a former football player, someone who had been bred to fearlessly throw himself in the path of other beastly men with brute strength to get a first down, a grown man, sees an act of sexual violence upon a child, and . . . what? That's too scary to confront? And at NO point since 2002 did McQueary ever think the police should've been notified? Or any of those officials?

Is sexual violence so removed from the consciences of male athletes and coaches that when it does happen, there's no tool available in their system to dismantle the situation? But something tells me that rape and sport culture, especially football, are not strangers. What are we teaching young men? In college culture, if a woman is raped, she was either asking for it or lying. If it's a child, walk away.

If there's one thing I know about college football, coming from a Buckeye fan who married into a family who schedules weddings around college football games, there's no such thing as doing the minimum. Staff and athletes have mantras of honor, excellence, and going beyond, teamwork, brotherhood, achievement. Strength. No pain. Give it your all.

But when in the face of sexual violence, when the opportunity to save a young child comes, Mike McQueary walked away and made a call for help. The problem is, McQueary LEFT. He left. And the call of help was to help himself deal with what he saw and figure out what to do while that boy was left alone with a monster.

So, Mike McQueary, even if you never broke any law, even if everyone says you tried to do the right thing, even if Penn State somehow redeems itself in many many years from now, even if Spanier, Paterno, and others find ways to save face, there is one person that matters in this story and there's no way to hide from your memory. For all the years of studying routes and back-up plans, defense and offense, for all the lifetimes spent studying plays, recovering fumbles, and coming back from adversity, you have to live with this basic truth for the rest of your life: you left that boy to deal with his nightmare alone.

Instructions

1. Read the excerpt from the grand jury presentment (pp. 111–113) for details and criticisms of Coach McQueary's actions and omissions during and following the alleged assault.
2. Based on Lisa Factora-Borchers' blog article, the grand jury presentment excerpt, and your text, write an essay arguing what, if any, ethical duty Michael McQueary had to act in behalf of the boy. Assuming he had a duty to intervene, just what should the intervention have included?

POSSESSION AS A CRIMINAL ACT

legal fiction, pretending something is a fact when it's not, if there's a "good" reason for the pretense

Let's start this section by making clear that possession is not action; it's a passive condition (Dubber and Kelman 2009, 252). It's only by means of a **legal fiction** (pretending something is a fact when it's not, if there's a "good" reason for pretending) that the principle of *actus reus* includes possession.

LO 9

According to Professor Markus Dubber (2001):

> Possession offenses have not attracted much attention. Yet, they are everywhere in American criminal law, on the books and in action. They fill our statute books, our arrest statistics, and eventually, our prisons. By last count, New York law recognized no fewer than 153 possession offenses; one in every five prison or jail sentences handed out by New York courts in 1998 was imposed for a possession offense. That same year, possession offenses accounted for over 100,000 arrests in New York State, while drug offenses alone resulted in over 1.2 million nationwide. (834–35)

In his criticism of the expansion of possession crimes, Professor Dubber (2001, 856-57) lists thirty-eight (Table 3.2), and, he adds, "The list could go on and on." According to Dubber, "millions of people commit one of its variants every day. . . . Operating below the radars of policy pundits and academic commentators, as well as under the Constitution, possession does the crime war's dirty work."

TABLE 3.2

Criminal Possession Statutes
1. Air pistols and rifles
2. Weapons (including dangerous weapons, instruments, appliances, or substances)
3. Ammunition
4. Anti-security items
5. Body vests
6. Burglary tools
7. Computer-related material
8. Counterfeit trademarks
9. Drug paraphernalia
10. Drug precursors
11. Drugs
12. Eavesdropping devices
13. Embossing machines (to forge credit cards)
14. Firearms
15. Fireworks
16. Forged instruments
17. Forgery devices
18. Gambling devices
19. Gambling records
20. Graffiti instruments

(continues)

TABLE 3.2

Criminal Possession Statutes (*Continued*)
21. Instruments of crime
22. Noxious materials
23. Obscene material
24. Obscene sexual performances by a child
25. "Premises which [one] knows are being used for prostitution purposes"
26. Prison contraband
27. Public benefit cards
28. Slugs
29. Spearfishing equipment
30. Stolen property
31. Taximeter accelerating devices
32. Tear gas
33. Toy guns
34. Unauthorized recordings of a performance
35. Undersized catfish (in Louisiana)
36. Usurious loan records
37. Vehicle identification numbers
38. Vehicle titles without complete assignment

Source: Dubber 2001, 856–57.

actual possession, physical control of banned items on my person, for example, marijuana in my pocket

constructive possession, banned items not on my person but in places I control, for example, in my car or apartment

The most common of the many criminal possession crimes include possession of weapons, illegal drugs, and drug paraphernalia. The "good reason" for pretending possession is an act is the powerful pull of the idea that "an ounce of prevention is worth a pound of cure." Better to nip the bud of possession before it grows into an act of doing drugs or shooting someone. Also, most people get possession by their voluntary acts—for example, buying marijuana and putting it in their pocket. So their active acquisition brings about passive. But not always. Maybe a student who got a bad grade "planted" marijuana in my briefcase when I wasn't looking. Or, maybe you put your roommate's ecstasy in your pocket to take it to the police station and turn it in.

LO 10

There are two kinds of possession: actual and constructive. **Actual possession** means items "on me," such as marijuana in my pocket. **Constructive possession** means items not on my person but in places I control, for example, my car or apartment (ALI 1985, I:2, 24).

knowing possession, items possessors are aware is either on their person or in places they control

mere possession, items you possess but you don't know what they are

Possession, whether actual or constructive, can be either "knowing" or "mere." **Knowing possession** means possessors are aware of what they possess. So, if you buy crystal meth and know it's crystal meth, you have knowing possession. (Knowing doesn't mean you have to know it's a crime to possess crystal meth, only that you know it's crystal meth.) **Mere possession** means you don't know what you possess. So if you agree to carry your friend's briefcase that you don't know is filled with stolen money, you've got mere possession of the money.

What kind of possession, if any, do you think celebrity Paris Hilton had in this story?

> When police officers found a plastic "bindle" containing 0.8 grams of cocaine in her purse, Hilton told the officer "that the purse wasn't hers, that she had borrowed it from a friend." She admitted she owned $1,300 in cash, several credit cards, a package of Zig-Zag rolling papers and a broken tablet of the prescription asthma medication Albuterol that were also in the purse during her arrest at the Wynn Las Vegas resort. But, not the cocaine. She said she'd never seen it, but by looking at it, "she thought it was gum." (Ritter 2010)

"Whether Paris Hilton owned the purse she was carrying that contained cocaine is irrelevant, Las Vegas police say. What is important is she had possession of it with narcotics inside, they say" (Winton 2010).

All but two states (North Dakota and Washington) require knowing possession. Also, almost all the cases in the court reports are constructive possession cases, and they're almost all drug and/or weapons cases.

CASE

***In* Miller v. State *(1999)*,** *James Luther Miller was convicted by a jury of possession of cocaine and marijuana. He was sentenced to thirty years in prison on the cocaine possession conviction and one year in the county jail for the marijuana conviction. He appealed.*

Did he possess illegal drugs?

Miller v. State

6 S.W.3d 812 (Ark.App. 1999)

HISTORY

James Luther Miller (defendant-appellant) was convicted by a jury of possession of cocaine and marijuana and sentenced to thirty years' incarceration on the cocaine-possession conviction. He was sentenced to one year's imprisonment in the county jail on the marijuana-possession conviction and ordered to pay a $1000 fine. Miller appealed. The Court of Appeals affirmed the marijuana conviction and reversed and dismissed the cocaine conviction.

NEAL, J.

FACTS

At trial, Arkansas State Police Officer Tim Land testified that on February 23, 1997, he came into contact with James Luther Miller, who was a passenger in a vehicle driven by Michael Alexander. Officer Land became suspicious of the vehicle because it approached him from the rear and would not pass his vehicle although he slowed to thirty miles per hour.

Land pulled his car into the median, and as the car passed he noticed that it did not have a license plate. He stopped the vehicle, and as he approached the vehicle, he smelled the very strong odor of burned marijuana emanating from the vehicle. Land had the driver exit the vehicle, and after noting the odor of burned marijuana and alcohol on his person, administered field sobriety tests, which Alexander failed. Land called for assistance, and Alexander was transported to the county jail for a breathalyzer. According to Land, there were four occupants in the vehicle: Alexander, who was the driver; James Giles, who was sitting in the right front seat; Damon Albert, who was sitting in the rear seat behind the driver; and James Miller (the appellant), who was seated on the right rear seat.

Trooper Land recovered three rolling papers from three of the vehicle's occupants, but could not recall which three occupants possessed the papers. He also stated that he found three rocks of crack cocaine and marijuana in the pouch located on the back of the driver's seat, directly in front of Damon Albert.

The driver of the vehicle, Michael Alexander, testified that on the date in question he asked Miller if he wanted to ride to Hope, Arkansas, with him. He picked up Giles and Albert and took them to a residence in Hope, where they purchased crack cocaine. According to Alexander, Miller did not know that Giles and Albert were purchasing crack, and he did not know about the marijuana until it was smoked.

(continues)

(continued)
However, Alexander later testified that all of the vehicle's occupants knew that the marijuana was in the vehicle because the marijuana was in the car before the group traveled to Hope.

OPINION

. . . It is not necessary for the State to prove literal physical possession of drugs in order to prove possession. Possession of drugs can be proved by constructive possession. Constructive possession can be implied when the drugs are in the joint control of the accused and another.

However, joint occupancy of a vehicle, standing alone, is not sufficient to establish possession or joint possession. There must be some additional factor linking the accused to the drugs. Other factors to be considered in cases involving automobiles occupied by more than one person are:

1. whether the contraband is in plain view,
2. whether the contraband is found within the accused's personal effects,
3. whether it is found on the same side of the car seat as the accused was sitting or in near proximity to it,
4. whether the accused is the owner of the automobile, or exercised dominion and control over it; and
5. whether the accused acted suspiciously before or during the arrest.

. . . We believe the evidence is sufficient to conclude that the jury had substantial evidence from which it could find that appellant constructively possessed marijuana. By way of analogy, we note that had the officer observed the marijuana in plain view inside of the vehicle, the evidence would be sufficient to compel the conclusion that Miller constructively possessed the marijuana. Here, although the marijuana was not in plain view, we believe that the fact that the police officer smelled marijuana upon approaching the vehicle tends to establish that Miller had knowledge of the presence of the marijuana. It is the knowledge of the existence of the contraband that provides substantial evidence of constructive possession.

Whether the evidence is sufficient to support the conviction of possession of cocaine presents a more difficult question. . . . Our case law makes it quite clear that drugs must be found on the same side of the vehicle as the accused, or in close proximity to the accused. . . . Miller was a rear-seat passenger in his friend's car when the vehicle was stopped by Trooper Land. The contraband found was not in plain view, was not under appellant's exclusive control, and was not found near the seat in which appellant was seated. There was no testimony that appellant acted suspiciously, and, there was no evidence of any contraband found on appellant's person. There was, however, testimony that appellant did not know that there was cocaine in the car until after the police searched the vehicle.

Based upon the evidence presented, we hold that the State did not present sufficient evidence of any factor, other than occupancy, to establish Miller's constructive possession of the cocaine. Miller's conviction for possession of cocaine is reversed and dismissed. His conviction for possession of marijuana is affirmed.

DISSENT

LINKERHART, J.

. . . I would reverse and dismiss Miller's conviction for possession of marijuana. . . . The majority does not set forth any factor linking the appellant to the marijuana. Rather, the majority concludes, "We believe the fact that the police officer smelled marijuana upon approaching the vehicle tends to establish that appellant had knowledge of the presence of marijuana." Certainly, this does not establish that the appellant exercised care, control, or management of the contraband. And most certainly, "mere presence, acquiescence, silence, or knowledge that a crime is being committed, in the absence of a legal duty to act," is not sufficient to establish criminal liability. . . . One can easily imagine a "parade of horribles" in which a person who is merely present will stand convicted for merely knowing about the presence of a controlled substance. Insofar as we abide under a just system of laws, this decision cannot stand.

DISSENT

BIRD, J.

I believe that there was sufficient evidence upon which a jury could find that Miller was guilty of the crimes of possession of marijuana and cocaine on the basis that he constructively possessed both of those substances.

. . . The contraband was found in the pouch on the back of the driver's seat. Although the contraband was not on the same side of the car as Miller, it was certainly in close proximity to the other side of the back seat where he was seated. . . . Miller was seated in the right rear passenger seat and the contraband, located in the pouch on the back of the driver's seat . . . [was] accessible to him. . . .

Finally, to me, it is contradictory to hold, as the majority does, that, because the police officer smelled the aroma of marijuana smoke coming from the car, Miller is guilty of possession of marijuana, but not guilty of possession of cocaine that was located in exactly the same place in the car as the marijuana. . . . The mere smell of marijuana smoke coming from a vehicle is [not] sufficient to convict a joint occupant of the vehicle of possession of marijuana found in the vehicle. In order to be convicted, the State must prove that the joint occupant was in close proximity to the contraband or that such possession was established by virtue of the existence of one of the other linking factors. In this case, if Miller was close enough in proximity to the marijuana that the officer smelled to be found guilty of its possession, I fail to see how the majority can say that there was not sufficient evidence to sustain the jury's verdict that he was guilty of possession of cocaine that was located in exactly the same place as the marijuana. . . .

QUESTIONS

1. Identify the two elements of constructive possession discussed by the court.
2. List the five factors the court identifies that can prove possession in joint occupancy cases.
3. Match the facts of the case to the five factors you listed in (2).
4. Assume you're the prosecutor. Argue that Miller actually and constructively possessed the cocaine and marijuana. Back up your arguments with facts in the case.
5. Assume you're the defense attorney. Argue that Miller didn't physically or constructively possess the cocaine or marijuana.

EXPLORING FURTHER

Possession

Did she possess alcohol?

Kastl v. State, 796 S.W.2d 848 (Ark. 1990)

HISTORY

Tracy Kastl, a juvenile, was found to be delinquent, convicted of being a minor in possession of alcohol, and her driver's license was suspended for one year. She appealed. The Arizona Supreme Court reversed and dismissed the case.

PRICE, J.

FACTS

Tracy Kastl was one of five passengers in a vehicle that was parked in a parking lot in Waldron, Arkansas. Officers Johnny Smith and Ronnie Eisenhower of the Waldron City Police spotted beer cans beside the vehicle. They searched the vehicle with a flashlight and discovered a six pack of Coors Light beer lying on a "flat" in the hatch compartment of the vehicle behind Kastl. Randy Crowell, one of the passengers, admitted to purchasing the beer and claimed ownership.

The officers testified that Kastl did not have in her hand or lap any alcoholic beverage. The state contended that Kastl had "constructive possession" of the alcohol because it was in the vehicle in which she was an occupant. . . . The problem with joint occupancy arises because of the rule that when joint occupancy is the only evidence the State has, there must be some additional link between the accused and the contraband. . . . Tracy Kastl was clearly not in actual possession of the beer in this case.

The following was presented by the state to prove constructive possession of the beer by the appellant:

(1) beer cans were found lying between the vehicle in question and another parked vehicle;
(2) a six-pack of Coors Light beer was found lying inside the vehicle in the hatch area behind Kastl, and according to Officer Eisenhower, all she would have had to have done was "just turn around and reached and grabbed it" [the beer]; and
(3) Kastl had a smell of intoxicating alcohol about her person.

The state's evidence that there were beer cans beside the vehicle, that beer was found in the immediate proximity of Kastl in the vehicle, and that there was the smell of beer on her person are not sufficient evidence of constructive possession. The state has not proven the additional evidence necessary to link the appellant to possession of the beer.

Reversed and dismissed.

(continues)

(continued)

DISSENT

GLAZE, J., JOINED BY HAYS AND NEWBERN, JJ.

I believe substantial evidence exists to support Kastl's conviction. . . . The state need not prove Kastl had actual possession of the contraband; constructive possession is sufficient. . . . The state can sufficiently link an accused to contraband found in an automobile jointly occupied by more than one person by showing additional facts and circumstances, indicating the accused's knowledge and control. One such circumstance is when the contraband is found on the same side of the car as the accused was sitting or in his or her immediate proximity. Here, it is undisputed that Tracy was seated in the immediate proximity of a six pack of beer. However, there are even more facts to show Tracy's knowledge and control of the beer or contraband seized in this case.

. . . The evidence shows:

- Officers Smith and Eisenhower drove on to the lot where the car, in which Tracy was a passenger, was parked. There was a beer can by the car and one on the lot. The officers had been on the lot earlier and no beer cans were on it.
- Five people were in the car, two young men in the front and Tracy and two young men in the rear seat. A six pack of beer was seen immediately behind the rear seat and the beer was within arm's reach of Tracy.
- Several of the subjects were seen with open beer cans between their legs, although Tracy was not one of them.
- Both officers smelled the odor of intoxicating beverage about Tracy's person.

The foregoing evidence speaks for itself. The trial judge could have reasonably inferred that Tracy had been drinking and that Tracy was within arm's reach of the six pack of beer found in the car. Some of the others in the car had open beer cans in their possession, and it is fair to infer occupants of the car had discarded two beer cans onto the lot—one of the cans was located immediately next to the car.

From this evidence, the trial judge, as fact finder, could have reasonably believed Tracy had knowledge and control of the beer located in the car. In fact, to have found and decided otherwise would, in my estimation, have ignored the obvious. The trial judge's decision should clearly stand.

SUMMARY

LO 1 Criminal liability is criminal conduct that qualifies for criminal punishment. The following questions must be answered to determine whether criminal conduct qualifies for criminal punishment: (1) Is there criminal conduct? (2) Is the conduct justified? (3) Is the conduct excused?

The voluntary act is the first principle of criminal liability because there must be an act for a crime to have occurred. Mere thoughts can never be crimes (in the United States). All crimes include, at a minimum, a criminal act (*actus reus*). Most serious crimes also require criminal intent.

LO 2 A conduct crime is a crime requiring a (1) criminal act triggered by (2) criminal intent (3) with concurrence. A bad result crime, or result crime, is a crime that includes five elements: (1) a voluntary act, (2) a mental element, (3) circumstantial elements [concurrence along with others], (4) causation, and (5) criminal harm.

LO 3 There might be criminal conduct without criminal liability; however, there is never criminal liability without criminal conduct. Criminal conduct can qualify for criminal punishment only after it proceeds through the analytical steps (questions) in LO 1.

The importance of the voluntary act requirement is that the law punishes people only for their act(s). However, not *all* the acts need to be voluntary to satisfy the requirement; conduct has to include only one voluntary act. LO 4

A voluntary act is a *willed* action or movement. LO 5

Status can arise in two ways: (1) it can result from a prior voluntary act, or (2) it can result from no act at all, such as sex, age, sexual orientation, race, and ethnicity. LO 6

The general principle of the *actus reus* includes a voluntary act. The Constitution bans pure status as a basis for criminal liability. Yet the U.S. Supreme Court hasn't felt compelled to expand their interpretation of criminal liability and responsibility beyond that into what has traditionally been the decisions of the courts. LO 7

Failures to act, or criminal omissions, consist of two types: (1) the failure to report and (2) the failure to intervene to prevent injuries and death to persons or the damage and destruction of property. Omissions are criminal omissions only if defendants had a legal duty, not just a moral duty, to act. LO 8

Possession isn't an act; it's a passive condition. Most people charged with possession have acquired possession by the voluntary act of acquisition. LO 9

There are different types of possession according to the law: actual, constructive, knowing, and mere. LO 10

KEY TERMS

criminal liability, p. 93
elements of a crime, p. 94
actus reus, p. 94
mens rea, p. 94
conduct crimes, p. 94
criminal acts, p. 95
concurrence, p. 95
attendant circumstances element, p. 96
bad result crimes (result crimes), p. 96
manifest criminality, p. 97
one-voluntary-act-is-enough rule, p. 98
automatism, p. 100
fault-based defenses, p. 100
affirmative defenses of excuse, p. 100
status, p. 104
criminal omissions, p. 106
failure to report, p. 106
failure to intervene, p. 106
legal duty, p. 106
"Good Samaritan" doctrine, p. 106
American bystander rule, p. 107
legal fiction, p. 115
actual possession, p. 116
constructive possession, p. 116
knowing possession, p. 116
mere possession, p. 116

LEARNING OBJECTIVES

1. To understand and appreciate that most serious crimes require criminal intent and a criminal act.
2. To understand the difference between criminal intent and motive.
3. To understand the difference between general and specific intent.
4. To understand and appreciate the differences in culpability among the Model Penal Code's (MPC) four mental states: purposely, knowingly, recklessly, and negligently.
5. To understand that criminal liability, sometimes, is imposed without fault (also known as strict liability).
6. To know the definition of concurrence and why it's important in criminal liability considerations.
7. To understand that the element of causation applies only to "bad result" crimes and to be able to differentiate factual cause from legal cause.
8. To understand that ignorance of facts and law can create a reasonable doubt that the prosecution has proved the element of criminal intent.

A Botetourt County school bus is overturned on Zion Hill Road on Wednesday, May 23, 2012 in Fincastle, Virginia. The bus was carrying 39 middle school and high school students, 13 of whom suffered minor injuries. The driver was charged with reckless driving after the vehicle ran off the road and overturned.

AP Images/The Roanoke Times, Rebecca Barnett

4 THE GENERAL PRINCIPLES OF CRIMINAL LIABILITY

Mens Rea, Concurrence, Causation, Ignorance, and Mistake

CHAPTER OUTLINE

Did He Intend to Give Them AIDS?

Calvin Stark tested positive for HIV, received extensive counseling about his infection, and was taught about "safe sex," the risk of spreading the infection, and the necessity of informing his partners before engaging in sexual activity with them. He disregarded the advice and engaged in unprotected sexual activity multiple times with each of three different women. He told the first victim he was HIV positive *after* the second time they had intercourse. He told the second victim he was HIV positive after they'd had sexual intercourse six times. The third victim and Stark had sexual intercourse "almost every night for a month. It was almost nonstop with him," the victim testified. Stark told her he was HIV after she broke up with him.

Count Three. The victim and Stark had sexual relations throughout their brief relationship. It was "almost nonstop with him," "almost every night" during August 1989. Stark never wore a condom and never informed the victim he was HIV positive. When pressed, Stark denied rumors about his HIV status. The victim broke off the relationship because of Stark's drinking, after which Stark told her that he carried HIV and explained that if he had told her, she would not have had anything to do with him.

(*State v. Stark* 1992)

LO 1

"I didn't mean to" captures a basic idea about criminal liability: a criminal act (*actus reus*) is necessary, but it's not enough for criminal liability—at least not liability for the most serious crimes. They include a mental element (*mens rea*) in addition to the criminal act. Why? Because it's fair and just to punish only people we can blame. We call this **culpability** or **blameworthiness**. Justice Holmes (1963, 4) put it this way: "Even a dog distinguishes between being stumbled over and being kicked."

culpability or **blameworthiness,** the idea that it's fair and just to punish only people we can blame

Mens rea translated, in the singular, means "evil state of mind." In fact, as you'll learn in this chapter, there are several states of mind that can qualify as the mental element. The majority of states and the federal government apply a framework that began with the English common law (Chapter 1), which included general intent, specific intent, and strict liability. A substantial minority of states adopt the Model Penal Code (MPC) structure that consists of four states of mind, ranked according to the degree of their blameworthiness: purposely, knowingly, recklessly, and negligently. This book follows mainly (but not exclusively) the MPC structure. Because of the ranking by degree of blameworthiness, the MPC drafters preferred to call these mental states *levels of culpability*.

In addition to the mental state(s), we add two more elements essential to criminal liability: concurrence and causation. *Concurrence* refers to two connections: (1) In crimes of criminal conduct, criminal intent has to trigger the criminal act; (2) In result crimes, criminal conduct has to cause the bad result.

The element of causation consists of two parts; the prosecution has to prove both beyond a reasonable doubt. **Cause in fact** (also called "factual cause" or "**but for causation**") consists of the objective determination that the defendant's act triggered a chain of events that ended as the harmful result, such as the death in a homicide. Cause in fact is necessary but not enough to satisfy the causation requirement; that requires legal cause. **Legal cause** consists of the subjective judgment that it's fair and just to blame the defendant for the bad result.

cause in fact (also called "factual cause" or "**but for causation**"), the objective determination that the defendant's act triggered a chain of events that ended as the harmful result, such as the death in a homicide

legal cause, the subjective judgment that it's fair and just to blame the defendant for the bad result

Last, we examine how ignorance and mistakes can create a reasonable doubt that the prosecution has proved criminal intent. Proving *mens rea*, and in result crimes, causation, isn't always enough to prove criminal liability. (Recall from Chapter 3 that *result crimes* include causing a criminal harm in addition to the conduct.) Sometimes, mistakes negate the *mens rea*. Let's turn first to the principle of *mens rea*, then to concurrence and causation, and finally to mistakes that negate *mens rea*.

MENS REA

Mens rea, Latin for guilty mind, the mental element (also called "criminal intent," "evil mind," "mental attitude," or "state of mind") is an ancient idea. For hundreds of years, books have repeated with unbroken cadence that "An act doesn't make the actor guilty, unless his mind is guilty" (*Actus non facit reum nisi mens sit rea*) (Sayre 1932, 974).

mens rea, Latin for guilty mind, the mental element (also called "criminal intent," "evil mind," "mental attitude," or "state of mind") in crime

According to the great medieval jurist Bracton, writing in 1256:

> He who kills without intent to kill should be acquitted, because a crime is not committed unless the intent to injure intervenes; and the desire and purpose distinguish evildoing. (quoted in Sayre 1932, 985)

Six hundred years later, the distinguished U.S. criminal law scholar Joel Bishop echoed Bracton: "There can be no crime, large or small, without an evil mind" (quoted in Sayre 1932, 974). And, in a 2001 case where *mens rea* was an issue, senior U.S. District Court Judge and scholar Jack Weinstein called the "*actus non facit* . . . maxim the criminal law's 'mantra'" and noted that "Western civilized nations have long looked to the wrongdoer's mind to determine both the propriety and the grading of punishment" (*U.S. v. Cordoba-Hincapie* 1993, 489).

THE COMPLEXITY OF *MENS REA*

Mens rea isn't just ancient; it's also complex. "No problem of criminal law . . . has proved more baffling through the centuries than the determination of the precise mental element necessary to convict of any crime" (Sayre 1932, 974). Several reasons account for this bafflement. First, whatever it means, *mens rea* is difficult to discover and then prove in court. Second, courts and legislatures have used so many vague and incomplete definitions of the mental element.

According to the "Commentary on *mens rea*" accompanying the Alabama Criminal Code:

> It would be impossible to review, much less reconcile and make clear and uniform, the myriad of Alabama statutes and cases that have employed or discussed some term of mental culpability. Such mental terms and concepts, while necessarily difficult to articulate, sometimes have been vaguely or only partly defined, or otherwise seem imprecise or inconclusive, unclear or ambiguous, even confusing or contradictory, or over refined with technical, obscure and often subtle, if not dubious, distinctions. (*Burnett v. State* 1999, 575)

Table 4.1 includes a partial list of terms in the Alabama Criminal Code before it was reformed along the lines of the MPC. After listing 17, the summary ends in a sigh of resignation—"and scores of others" (*Burnett v. State* 1999, 575).

Third, *mens rea* consists of several mental attitudes that range across a broad spectrum, stretching all the way from purposely committing a crime you're totally aware

TABLE 4.1

Mental Attitudes Used in the Alabama Code
"Intentionally"
"Willfully"
"Purposely"
"Designedly"
"Knowingly"
"Deliberately"
"Maliciously"
"With premeditation"
"Recklessly"
"Negligently"
"With culpable negligence"
"With gross negligence"
"With criminal negligence"
"Without due caution"
"Wickedly"
"Unlawfully"
"Wrongfully"

Burnett v. State 1999, 575.

is criminal (stealing an iPod from an Apple store) to merely creating risks of criminal conduct or causing criminal harms—risks you're not the slightest bit aware you're creating (driving someone else's car with an open beer bottle you don't even know is in the car). We'll discuss these mental attitudes later in the chapter and in Chapters 9 through 13. For now, it's very important that you understand that intent in criminal law goes way beyond the dictionary definition of "intent," which refers to acting on purpose or deliberately.

Fourth, a different mental attitude might apply to each of the elements of a crime. So it's possible for one mental attitude to apply to *actus reus*, another to causation, another to the harm defined in the statute, and still another to attendant circumstance elements (ALI 1985, I:2, 229–33).

As you learn about the *mens rea*, you'll probably be confused by the multiple mental attitudes it includes; by the complexity and uncertainty surrounding the definitions of the multiple attitudes it encompasses; and by the practical problems of matching the attitudes to elements of the offense and then proving each one beyond a reasonable doubt. Maybe you can take some comfort in knowing that courts don't always get the definitions of mental states right, either. (Neither do I, and I've been thinking, talking, and writing about them since 1958!)

LO 2

We need to note one more complexity in *mens rea*: the relationship between mental attitude and motive. A **motive** is something that causes a person to act. Experts disagree over the difference between motive and intent. Probably for this reason, they clarify the difference with an example: if a man murders his wife for her money—his intent was to kill; his motive was to get her money.

motive, something that causes a person to act

It's often said that motive is irrelevant to criminal liability; good motive is no defense to criminal conduct, and a bad motive can't make legal conduct criminal. So if a wife poisons her husband because he's suffering from the unbearable pain of a terminal bone cancer, she's still guilty of murder. And if she wants him dead because she hates him and accidentally shoots him while they're deer hunting, she's not guilty even though she wanted him dead and she's glad he's out of the way.

Unfortunately, the relationship between motive and criminal liability is not so simple. The truth is that sometimes motive is relevant, and sometimes it's not. Greed, hate, and jealously are always relevant to proving the intent to kill. Compassion may well affect discretionary decisions, such as police decisions to arrest, prosecutors to charge, and judges to sentence, say, mercy killers.

Juries have sometimes refused to convict mercy killers of first-degree murder even though the intent to kill was clearly there (Chapter 9). The murder case of Robert Latimer is a good example of this. Latimer could no longer stand the constant pain his twelve-year-old daughter, Tracy, was suffering because of her severe and incurable cerebral palsy. She wore diapers, weighed only 38 pounds, and couldn't walk, talk, or feed herself. So he put Tracy into the cab of his pickup truck on the family farm and pumped exhaust into the cab of the truck. He told the police that he stood by, ready to stop if Tracy started to cry, but that she simply went quietly "to sleep. My priority was to put her out of her pain."

He pleaded not guilty to first-degree murder, but the jury found him guilty of second-degree murder. Despite the verdict of guilty on the lesser charge, many people in the town agreed with an eighteen-year-old high school student who said Latimer "did what he had to do for his daughter's sake. And that's the way a lot of people in town are feeling" (Farnsworth 1994, A6).

Motive is also important in some defenses. For example, it's a defense to the crime of escaping from prison if a prisoner breaks out to save her life from a rapidly spreading fire (the defense of necessity, Chapter 5). Finally, motive is sometimes an element of a crime itself. For example, one of the attendant circumstances of burglary accompanying the act of breaking and entering someone else's property is "the purpose of committing a crime" once inside (Chapter 11).

Let's look more closely at proving the *mens rea*, defining it, and classifying it, and the difficulties and complexities in doing all of these.

PROVING "STATE OF MIND"

You can't see a state of mind. Not even the finest instruments of modern technology can find or measure your attitude (Hall 1960, 106). Electroencephalograms can record brain waves, and x-rays can photograph brain tissue, but Chief Justice Brian's words are as true today as they were when he wrote them in 1477: "The thought of man is not triable, for the devil himself knoweth not the thought of man" (Williams 1961, 1). Three hundred years later, Sir William Blackstone put it simply: "A tribunal can't punish what it can't know" (Blackstone 1769, 21).

Confessions are the only direct evidence of mental attitude. Unfortunately, defendants rarely confess their true intentions, so proof of their state of mind usually depends on indirect (circumstantial) evidence. Acts and attendant circumstances are the overwhelming kind of circumstantial evidence. In everyday experience, we rely on what people do to tell us what they intend. For example, if I break into a stranger's house at night, it's reasonable to infer I'm up to no good. So by observing directly what I do, you can indirectly determine what I intend.

CRIMINAL INTENT

The long list of terms used to define the mental element(s) in the pre-reformed Alabama Criminal Code (Table 4.1, p. 125) can be reduced to two kinds of fault that satisfy the mental element in criminal liability. One is **subjective fault**, or fault that requires a "bad mind" in the actor. For example, suppose in your state, it's a crime to "receive property you know is stolen." You buy an iPod from another student who you know stole it. The bad state of mind is "knowingly," which is more culpable than "recklessly" and less culpable than "purposely."

subjective fault, fault that requires a "bad mind" in the actor

Subjective fault frequently is linked with immorality. You can see this connection in expressions in cases and statutes, such as "depravity of will," "diabolic malignity," "abandoned heart," "bad heart," "heart regardless of social duty and fatally bent on mischief," "wicked heart," "mind grievously depraved," or "mischievous vindictive spirit" (Dubber 2002, 50–51). Although these terms were typical of old laws and opinions, they're still in use in non-MPC jurisdictions, as you'll see in some of the case excerpts throughout the book.

The second kind of fault is **objective fault**, which requires no purposeful or conscious bad mind in the actor. For example, suppose it's a crime to "receive property you have reason to believe is stolen." You buy a new iPod in its original package for $10 that you honestly, but naively, don't know is stolen. You should know it was stolen; a reasonable person would know it was stolen, and in fact it was stolen. So, even though you had no "bad" mind, you're held accountable because you didn't live up to the norm of the average person.

objective fault, requires no purposeful or conscious bad mind in the actor

The third kind of criminal liability isn't on the Alabama list: criminal liability without either subjective or objective fault (called **strict liability**). Suppose a statute reads, "whoever receives stolen property" commits a crime. You buy an iPad for $45 that looks used, but you honestly and reasonably believe it wasn't stolen. It doesn't matter; under this statute, you're liable without either subjective or objective fault.

strict liability, liability without either subjective or objective fault

It's easy enough to define and give examples of these three types of liability. It's also easy to rank them according to the degree of their culpability. Subjective "bad mind" fault is most blameworthy. Objective unreasonable risk creation is less blameworthy; some maintain it shouldn't even qualify as a criminal state of mind. No-fault liability requires the least culpability; it holds people accountable for their actions without regard to fault.

We'll have more to say about mental fault and no fault shortly (and also in the remaining chapters of the book). But now, we have to examine two terms (used by many courts and some statutes) that are the source of uncertainty over what criminal intent means: general intent and specific intent (LaFave 2003b, 1:352–55).

LO 3

GENERAL AND SPECIFIC INTENT

general intent, the intent to commit the criminal act as defined in a statute

General intent is used most commonly in the cases to mean the intent to commit the criminal act as defined in a statute. In that sense, general intent is general because it states the minimum requirement of all crimes—namely, that they have to include an intentional or voluntary act, omission, or possession (Chapter 3).

It would be easy and obvious if all courts defined general intent as the intent to commit the criminal act. But they don't, and that causes confusion. For example, some courts define general intent as a "synonym for *mens rea*," so it includes all levels of both subjective and objective fault.

Another definition is the intent to commit a crime at an undetermined time and place with no specific victim in mind. For example, Clifford Hobbs threw a bag of burglar's tools out of his car during a high-speed chase by Des Moines police. He was found guilty of "possession of burglary tools" (*State v. Hobbs* 1961, 239). Hobbs argued that at the time the police apprehended him, he "had no intention of breaking into any place" and appealed his conviction (239). The Iowa Supreme Court disagreed:

> Evidence of the general intent or purpose for which the accused kept and used the tools is enough, not of present specific intent. It is sufficient to show that defendant had a general intent to use tools or implements for a burglarious purpose, and the intention as to any particular time or place of using the same is not material. (240)

specific intent, subjective fault; it refers to criminal intent in addition to the criminal act

Some courts limit **specific intent** to subjective fault—namely, where there's a "bad" mind or will that triggers the act (LaFave 2003b, 1:353–55). It's captured in these adjectives found in most ordinary dictionaries: "deliberate," "calculated," "conscious," "intended," "planned," "meant," "studied," "knowing," "willful," "purposeful," "purposive," "done on purpose," "premeditated," "preplanned," "preconceived." We'll have occasion, later in this and the remaining chapters, to define, apply, and grade the degree of blameworthiness of most of these variations of subjective fault.

general intent "plus," where "general intent" refers to the intent to commit the *actus reus* of the crime, and "plus" refers to some "special mental element" in addition to the intent to commit the criminal act

The most common definition of specific intent is what we'll call **general intent "plus,"** where "general intent" refers to the intent to commit the *actus reus* of the crime, and "plus" refers to some "special mental element" in addition to the intent to commit the criminal act (LaFave 2003b, 1:354). For example, household burglary is a specific intent crime, because in addition to the intent to commit the household burglary *actus reus*—namely, breaking into and entering someone else's house—there's the special mental element, the intent to commit a crime once inside the house (Chapter 11). Similarly, theft is a specific intent crime, because it requires the intent to commit the acts of taking and carrying away someone else's property plus the intent to deprive the owner of it permanently (Chapter 11). Sexual assault is not a specific intent crime, because it requires only the intent to commit whatever acts of sexual contact or penetration are included in the *actus reus* element of the law.

Harris v. State (1999), our next case excerpt, adopted and applied the general intent plus definition. The Maryland Court of Appeals held that carjacking is a general intent crime, because it required only that Timothy Harris intend to commit the act of carjacking and not the further intent to deprive the owner of the car's possession. The case is important not only for helping you to understand and apply the concepts of general and special intent but also to illustrate the practical importance of the distinction. The defense of voluntary intoxication (Chapter 8) is available only in specific intent crimes. Because the court ruled that carjacking is a general intent crime, Harris couldn't use the defense that he was too drunk to form the intent to commit the crime of carjacking.

CASE

In* Harris v. State *(1999)*, *the court adopted and applied the "general intent plus" definition.

Did he specifically intend to carjack his friend's car?

Harris v. State

728 A.2d 180 (Md.App. 1999)

HISTORY

Timothy Harris (the defendant/appellant) was indicted by the Grand Jury for Prince George's County with the crimes of carjacking in violation of Art. 27, § 348A, unlawful taking of a motor vehicle in violation of Art. 27, § 342A, and second-degree assault in violation of Art. 27, § 12A. He was convicted in the Circuit Court, Prince George's County, of carjacking. Defendant appealed. The Court of Appeals held that carjacking is not a specific intent crime and affirmed the trial court's conviction.

BELL, C.J., AND ELDRIDGE, RODOWSKY, CHASANOW, RAKER, WILNER, AND CATHELL, JJ.

FACTS

On November 26, 1996, Timothy Harris, Jack Tipton, and several other friends were playing cards and drinking alcohol at a friend's house. Tipton offered to drive Harris home. Tipton testified that Harris became angry when Tipton refused to go to the District of Columbia, and that Harris forcibly removed Tipton from the car and drove away. Tipton reported the car as stolen. At trial, Harris's defense was voluntary intoxication. He testified that he had consumed alcohol and smoked marijuana throughout the evening, and that he "blacked out" after leaving the get-together.

OPINION

Maryland's carjacking statute, Art. 27, § 348A reads in pertinent part:

> (b) *Elements of the offense.* An individual commits the offense of carjacking when the individual obtains unauthorized possession or control of a motor vehicle from another individual in actual possession by force or violence, or by putting that individual in fear through intimidation or threat of force or violence.
>
> (c) *Penalty—In general.* An individual convicted of carjacking . . . is guilty of a felony and shall be sentenced to imprisonment for not more than 30 years.
>
> (d) *Same—Additional to other offenses.* The sentence imposed under this section may be imposed separate from and consecutive to a sentence for any other offense arising from the conduct underlying the offenses of carjacking or armed carjacking.
>
> (e) *Defenses.* It is not a defense to the offense of carjacking or armed carjacking that the defendant did not intend to permanently deprive the owner of the motor vehicle.

Generally, there are two aspects of every crime—the *actus reus* or guilty act and the *mens rea* or the culpable mental state accompanying the forbidden act. Maryland continues to observe the distinction between general and specific intent crimes. The distinction is particularly significant when a defendant claims that his voluntary intoxication prevents him from forming the requisite intent to commit a crime. [See Chapter 8.] It has long been the law in Maryland

(continues)

(continued)

that while voluntary intoxication is a defense to a specific intent crime, it is not a defense to a general intent crime. . . . [The part of the opinion dealing with Harris' defense of intoxication is omitted from this case excerpt.]

A specific intent is not simply the intent to do the immediate act but embraces the requirement that the mind be conscious of a more remote purpose or design which shall eventuate from the doing of the immediate act. Though assault implies only the general intent to strike the blow, assault with intent to murder, rob, rape, or maim requires a fully formed and conscious purpose that those further consequences shall flow from the doing of the immediate act. To break and enter requires a mere general intent but to commit burglary requires the additional specific intent of committing a felony after the entry has been made. A trespassory taking requires a mere general intent but larceny (or robbery) requires the specific or deliberate purpose of depriving the owner permanently of the stolen goods.

It is clear that the broad aim of the statute was to enhance the penalties applicable to individuals who use force or threat of force or intimidation to obtain possession or control of a motor vehicle and to make it easier for prosecutors to obtain convictions for carjacking. By looking at the statute as a whole, including the enhanced penalties applicable to carjackers over and above those penalties for the underlying conduct, as well as the explicit rejection of the specific intent to permanently deprive, it is clear that the Legislature did not intend to require a specific intent to achieve some additional consequence beyond the immediate act of taking the vehicle.

Finally, we find no support in the nature of carjacking itself to indicate that it is a specific intent crime. Carjacking requires the general intent to commit the act of obtaining unauthorized possession or control of a motor vehicle from another individual in actual possession by force or violence, or by putting that individual in fear through intimidation or threat of force or violence. The temporary deprivation of the property is substantially certain to result, regardless of the desire of the actor. The General Assembly gave no indication that "the mind [of the perpetrator] be conscious of a more remote purpose or design which shall eventuate from the doing of the immediate act." The Legislature's clear intent was that, without any additional deliberate and conscious purpose or design of accomplishing a very specific and more remote result, the offense is committed. Simply stated, the *mens rea* . . . is implicit in the intentional doing of the act.

We hold that the intent element of carjacking is satisfied by proof that the defendant possessed the general criminal intent to commit the act, i.e., general intent to obtain unauthorized possession or control from a person in actual possession by force, intimidation, or threat of force.

Affirmed. Costs to be paid by the appellant.

QUESTIONS

1. How does the court define "general intent"?
2. How does the court define "specific intent"?
3. Summarize the court's arguments that support its conclusion that Maryland's carjacking statute is a general intent crime.
4. Do you agree that the legislature's intent is clear that carjacking consists of the general intent to commit the act and not the intent to deprive Tipton of possession even for a brief period of time? Explain your answer.
5. Which is the better policy: making carjacking a general or specific intent crime? Defend your answer.

LO 4

THE MODEL PENAL CODE (MPC) LEVELS OF CULPABILITY

The multiple mental states, confusing terms, and varied meanings of criminal intent lay behind the Model Penal Code's (MPC) provisions to make sense out of the confusing state of the law regarding criminal intent. According to Ronald L. Gainer (1988), former deputy attorney general of the United States:

> The Code's provisions concerning culpable mental states introduced both reason and structure to a previously amorphous area of American law. For centuries, the

> approach to mental components of crimes had been a quagmire of legal refuse, obscured by a thin surface of general terminology denoting wrongfulness. The archaic verbiage suggesting evil and wickedness was replaced by the drafters with concepts of purpose, knowledge, recklessness, and negligence, and the concepts were structured to apply separately to actions, circumstances in which actions took place, and results. (575)

The MPC's culpability provisions were arrived at only after enormous effort and heated debate among the leading legal minds of judges, prosecutors, defense attorneys, and professors. As we look at the MPC's four mental states, we'll discuss how they're ranked according to their degree of culpability and how they're constructed to apply to the elements of act, mental state, attendant circumstances, and causation in "bad" result crimes. From most to least blameworthy, the MPC's four mental states are:

1. Purposely
2. Knowingly
3. Recklessly
4. Negligently

The MPC specifies that all crimes requiring a mental element (most minor crimes and a few felonies don't) have to include one of these degrees of culpability. (Recklessness is the default degree of culpability where codes fail to identify a level of culpability.) The following section from the MPC defines the degrees of culpability:

> *MPC § 2.02. General Requirements of Culpability.*
>
> 1. *Minimum Requirements of Culpability.* . . . [A] person is not guilty of an offense unless he acted purposely, knowingly, recklessly or negligently . . . with respect to each material element of the offense.
> 2. *Kinds of Culpability Defined*
>   a. **Purposely.** A person acts purposely with respect to a material element of an offense when:
>   i. if the element involves the nature of his conduct or a result thereof, it is his conscious object to engage in conduct of that nature or to cause such a result;
>   ii. [omitted]
>   b. **Knowingly.** A person acts knowingly with respect to a material element of an offense when:
>   i. if the element involves the nature of his conduct or the attendant circumstances, he is aware that his conduct is of that nature or that such circumstances exist; and
>   ii. if the element involves a result of his conduct, he is aware that it is practically certain that his conduct will cause such a result.
>   c. **Recklessly.** A person acts recklessly with respect to a material element of an offense when he consciously disregards a substantial and unjustifiable risk that the material element exists or will result from his conduct. The risk must be of such a nature and degree, that considering the nature and purpose of the actor's conduct and the circumstances known to him, its disregard involves a gross standard of conduct that a law-abiding person would observe in the actor's situation.

purposely, the mental attitude that a person acts purposely with respect to a material element of an offense when, if the element involves the nature of his conduct or a result thereof, it is his conscious object to engage in conduct of that nature or to cause such a result

knowingly, the mental attitude that a person acts knowingly with respect to a material element of an offense when: (1) if the element involves the nature of his conduct or the attendant circumstances, he is aware that his conduct is of that nature or that such circumstances exist; and (2) if the element involves a result of his conduct, he is aware that it is practically certain that his conduct will cause such a result

LO 3

recklessly, the mental attitude that a person acts recklessly with respect to a material element of an offense when he consciously disregards a substantial and unjustifiable risk that the material element exists or will result from his conduct. The risk must be of such a nature and degree, that considering the nature and purpose of the actor's conduct and the circumstances known to him, its disregard involves a gross standard of conduct that a law-abiding person would observe in the actor's situation

negligently, the mental attitude that a person acts negligently with respect to a material element of an offense when he should be aware of a substantial and unjustifiable risk that the material element exists or will result from his conduct. The risk must be of such a nature and degree that the actor's failure to perceive it, considering the nature and purpose of his conduct and the circumstances known to him, involves a gross deviation from the standard of care that a reasonable person would observe in the actor's situation

d. **Negligently.** A person acts negligently with respect to a material element of an offense when he should be aware of a substantial and unjustifiable risk that the material element exists or will result from his conduct. The risk must be of such a nature and degree that the actor's failure to perceive it, considering the nature and purpose of his conduct and the circumstances known to him, involves a gross deviation from the standard of care that a reasonable person would observe in the actor's situation. (ALI 1985, 1:2, 229)

Let's examine each level of culpability in more detail.

Purposely

Purposely, the most blameworthy mental state, means what we mean by the everyday expression, "You did it on purpose." In the words of MPC, "purpose" means having the "conscious object" to commit crimes. For example, in the criminal conduct crime, common law burglary, the burglar has to break into and enter a house for the very purpose (with the conscious object) of committing a crime after the burglar gets inside. In the bad result crime of murder, the murderer's purpose (conscious object) has to be to cause the victim's death.

CASE

***In* State v. Stark *(1992)**, the Washington State Court of Appeals affirmed Calvin Stark's conviction because he purposely exposed his sexual partners to HIV.*

Did he expose his victims to HIV on purpose?

State v. Stark

832 P.2d 109 (Wash.App. 1992)

HISTORY

Calvin Stark was convicted in the Superior Court, Clallam County, Washington, of two counts of second-degree assault for intentionally exposing his sexual partners to the human immunodeficiency virus (HIV), and he appealed. The Washington Court of Appeals affirmed, and remanded the case for resentencing.

PETRICH, CJ.

FACTS

On March 25, 1988, Calvin Stark tested positive for HIV, which was confirmed by further tests on June 25 and on June 30, 1988. From June 30, 1988, to October 3, 1989, the staff of the Clallam County Health Department had five meetings with Stark during which Stark went through extensive counseling about his infection. He was taught about "safe sex," the risk of spreading the infection, and the necessity of informing his partners before engaging in sexual activity with them.

On October 3, 1989, Dr. Locke, the Clallam County Health Officer, after learning that Stark had disregarded this advice and was engaging in unprotected sexual activity, issued a cease and desist order as authorized by a Washington State statute. Stark did not cease and desist, and, consequently, on March 1, 1990, Dr. Locke went to the county prosecutor's office. . . . The prosecutor . . . had Dr. Locke complete a police report. The state then charged Stark with three counts of assault in the second degree under RCW 9A.36.021(1)(e), which provides:

> A person is guilty of assault in the second degree if he or she . . . with intent to inflict bodily harm, exposes or transmits human immunodeficiency virus. . . .

Each count involved a different victim.

Count One. The victim and Stark engaged in sexual intercourse on October 27 and October

29, 1989. On both occasions, Stark withdrew his penis from the victim prior to ejaculation. The victim, who could not become pregnant because she had previously had her fallopian tubes tied, asked Stark on the second occasion why he withdrew. He then told her that he was HIV positive.

Count Two. The victim and Stark had sexual relations on at least six occasions between October 1989 and February 1990. Stark wore a condom on two or three occasions, but on the others, he ejaculated outside of her body. On each occasion, they had vaginal intercourse. On one occasion Stark tried to force her to have anal intercourse. They also engaged in oral sex. When she told Stark that she had heard rumors that he was HIV positive, he admitted that he was and then gave the victim an AZT pill "to slow down the process of the AIDS."

Count Three. The victim and Stark had sexual relations throughout their brief relationship. It was "almost nonstop with him," "almost every night" during August 1989. Stark never wore a condom and never informed the victim he was HIV positive. When pressed, Stark denied rumors about his HIV status. The victim broke off the relationship because of Stark's drinking, after which Stark told her that he carried HIV and explained that if he had told her, she would not have had anything to do with him.

At the jury trial, the victim in count one testified to her contacts with Stark and the jury received Dr. Locke's deposition testimony regarding the Health Department's contacts with Stark. Stark did not testify. In the *bench trial* [trial without a jury], Dr. Locke testified. There the state also presented the testimony of one of Stark's neighborhood friends. She testified that one night Stark came to her apartment after drinking and told her and her daughter that he was HIV positive. When she asked him if he knew that he had to protect himself and everybody else, he replied, "I don't care. If I'm going to die, everybody's going to die." The jury found Stark guilty on count one.

A second trial judge found Stark guilty of the second and third counts at a bench trial. On count one, Stark was given an exceptional sentence of 120 months based on his future danger to the community. The standard range for that offense was 13 to 17 months. On counts two and three, Stark was given the low end of the standard range, 43 months each, to be served concurrently, but consecutively to count one.

OPINION

Stark contends that there is insufficient evidence to prove he "exposed" anyone to HIV or that he acted with intent to inflict bodily harm. Since Stark is undisputedly HIV positive, he necessarily exposed his sexual partners to the virus by engaging in unprotected sexual intercourse. The testimony of the three victims supports this conclusion.

The testimony supporting the element of intent to inflict bodily harm includes Dr. Locke's statements detailing his counseling sessions with Stark. With regard to the first victim, we know that Stark knew he was HIV positive, that he had been counseled to use "safe sex" methods, and that it had been explained to Stark that coitus interruptus will not prevent the spread of the virus. While there is evidence to support Stark's position, all the evidence viewed in a light most favorable to the State supports a finding of intent beyond a reasonable doubt. The existence of noncriminal explanations does not preclude a finding that a defendant intended to harm his sexual partners.

With regard to the later victims, we have, in addition to this same evidence, Stark's neighbor's testimony that Stark, when confronted about his sexual practices, said, "I don't care. If I'm going to die, everybody's going to die." We also have the testimony of the victim in count two that Stark attempted to have anal intercourse with her and did have oral sex, both methods the counselors told Stark he needed to avoid.

We affirm the convictions.

QUESTIONS

1. Identify all of the facts relevant to determining Stark's mental attitude regarding each of the elements in the assault statute.
2. Using the common law definition of "specific intent" and the Model Penal Code definitions of "purposely," "knowingly," "recklessly," and "negligently" and relying on the relevant facts, identify Stark's intention with respect to his acts.
3. Is motive important in this case? Should it be?

Which court's decision established the most ethical public policy regarding the control of HIV?

The Trial Court

Dwight Ralph Smallwood was convicted of assault with intent to murder, reckless endangerment, and attempted murder. The trial court sentenced Smallwood to concurrent sentences of life imprisonment for attempted rape, twenty years' imprisonment for robbery with a deadly weapon, thirty years' imprisonment for assault with intent to murder, and five years' imprisonment for reckless endangerment. The court also imposed a concurrent thirty-year sentence for each of the three counts of attempted second-degree murder. The conviction was based on evidence that Smallwood knew he had Human Immunodeficiency Virus (HIV) when he raped three women.

The Court of Appeals

Smallwood appealed to Maryland's highest court, the Court of Appeals. The court held that the evidence that Smallwood knew he had Human Immunodeficiency Virus (HIV) when he raped three women was insufficient to prove that he had the intent to kill. According to the court,

> We have no trouble concluding that Smallwood intentionally exposed his victims to the risk of HIV-infection. The problem before us, however, is whether knowingly exposing someone to a risk of HIV-infection is by itself sufficient to infer that Smallwood possessed an intent to kill. . . .
>
> The State in this case would allow the trier of fact to infer an intent to kill based solely upon the fact that Smallwood exposed his victims to the risk that they might contract HIV. Without evidence showing that such a result is sufficiently probable to support this inference, we conclude that Smallwood's convictions for attempted murder and assault with intent to murder must be reversed.

Instructions

1. Gotohttp://mdcourts.gov/opinions/cosa/1995/1678s94.pdf and read the full opinion of the Court of Special Appeals of Maryland (Maryland's intermediate appeals court).
2. Then, go to http://mdcourts.gov/opinions/coa/1996/122a95.pdf and read the Court of Appeals (Maryland's supreme court) full opinion in the case.
3. Write a paragraph for each opinion, summarizing their arguments regarding the facts required to prove the intent to kill by spreading HIV.
4. Did Smallwood intend to kill his victims, or to spread the virus? Does your answer depend at all on your position as to which interpretation of the law supports the most ethical public policy? Write a page backing up your answers.

Source: *Smallwood v. State*, 680 A.2d 512 (Md. 1996).

Knowingly

In the mental state of "knowing," the watchword is "awareness" (Dubber 2002, 65). In conduct crimes, awareness is clear—I'm aware I'm taking an iPhone 4S; therefore I'm taking it knowingly. It's a little different in bad result crimes. Here, the MPC says it's enough that I'm aware that it's "practically certain" that my conduct will cause the bad result.

It's important for you to understand that knowledge is not the same as purpose or conscious objective. So a surgeon who removes a cancerous uterus to save a pregnant woman's life knowingly kills the fetus in her womb, but killing the fetus wasn't the purpose (conscious object) of the removal. Rather, the death of the fetus is an unavoidable side effect of removing the cancerous uterus.

Similarly, treason, the only crime defined in the U.S. Constitution, requires that traitors provide aid and comfort to enemies, not just knowingly but for the purpose of overthrowing the government. Actors may provide aid and comfort to enemies of the United States knowing their actions are practically certain to contribute to overthrowing the government. But that isn't enough; they have to provide them for the purpose of overthrowing the U.S. government. If their conscious object was to get rich, then they haven't committed treason (*Haupt v. U.S.* 1947; Chapter 13 in your book).

The purpose requirement in treason led to the enactment of other statutes to fill the void—for example, making it a crime to provide secrets to the enemy, an offense that requires only that defendants purposely provide such secrets. We'll explore these crimes in Chapter 13.

CASE

In* State v. Jantzi *(1982)*, *the Oregon Court of Appeals concluded that Pete Jantzi didn't knowingly assault Rex Anderson. You'll see just how complicated the application of "knowingly" to the facts of specific cases can get.

Did he "knowingly" assault with a knife?

State v. Jantzi

641 P.2d 62 (Or.App. 1982)

HISTORY

Pete Jantzi was convicted in the Circuit Court, Klamath County, of assault in the second degree, and he appealed. The Court of Appeals held that the defendant knew he had a dangerous weapon and that a confrontation was going to occur, but that he did not intend to stab the victim. Thus, the defendant acted "recklessly," not "knowingly," and should be convicted of assault in the third degree rather than assault in the second degree. Affirmed as modified; remanded for resentencing.

GILLETTE, J.

FACTS

Pete Jantzi (Defendant) testified and the trial court judge believed that he was asked to accompany Diane Anderson, who shared a house with the defendant and several other people, to the home of her estranged husband, Rex. While Diane was in the house talking with Rex, the defendant was using the blade of his knife to let the air out of the tires on Rex's van. Another person put sugar in the gas tank of the van.

While the Andersons were arguing, Diane apparently threatened damage to Rex's van and indicated that someone might be tampering with the van at that moment. Rex's roommate ran out of the house and saw two men beside the van. He shouted and began to run toward the men. Rex ran from the house and began to chase the defendant, who ran down a bicycle path. The defendant, still holding his open knife, jumped into the bushes beside the path and landed in the weeds. He crouched there, hoping that Rex would not see him and would pass by. Rex, however, jumped on top of the defendant and grabbed his shirt. They rolled over and Rex was stabbed in the abdomen by the defendant's knife. The defendant could not remember making a thrusting or swinging motion with the knife; he did not intend to stab Rex.

OPINION

The indictment charged that defendant "did unlawfully and knowingly cause physical injury to Rex Anderson by means of a deadly weapon, to-wit: knife, by stabbing the said Rex Anderson with said knife." ORS 163.175 provides that:

> (1) A person commits the crime of assault in the second degree if he:
>
> (2) Intentionally or knowingly causes physical injury to another by means of a deadly or dangerous weapon; . . .

"Knowingly" is defined in ORS 161.085(8):

> "Knowingly" or "with knowledge" when used with respect to conduct or to a circumstance described by a statute defining an offense means that a person acts with an awareness that [his] conduct is of a nature so described or that a circumstance so described exists.

(continues)

(continued)

[According to the commentary to the New York Criminal Code that the Oregon Criminal Code was based on:]

> Under the formulations of the Model Penal Code (§ 2.02(2bii)) and the Illinois Criminal Code (§ 4–5(b)), "knowingly" is, in one phase, almost synonymous with "intentionally" in that a person achieves a given result "knowingly" when he "is practically certain" that his conduct will cause that result. This distinction between "knowingly" and "intentionally" in that context appears highly technical or semantic, and the New York Revised Penal Law does not employ the word "knowingly" in defining result offenses. Murder of the common law variety, for example, is committed intentionally or not at all. (Commentary § 15.05, New York Revised Penal Law)

[The trial court continued:]

> Basically, the facts of this case are: that Defendant was letting air out of the tires and he has an open knife. He was aware of what his knife is like. He is aware that it is a dangerous weapon. He runs up the bicycle path. He has a very firm grip on the knife, by his own admission, and he knows the knife is dangerous. It is not necessary for the state to prove that he thrust it or anything else. Quite frankly, this could have all been avoided if he had gotten rid of the knife, so he 'knowingly caused physical injury to Rex Anderson.' And, therefore, I find him guilty of that particular charge.

Although the trial judge found the defendant guilty of "knowingly" causing physical injury to Anderson, what he described in his findings is recklessness. The court found that defendant knew he had a dangerous weapon and that a confrontation was going to occur. The court believed that the defendant did not intend to stab Anderson. The court's conclusion seems to be based on the reasoning that because the defendant knew it was possible that an injury would occur, he acted "knowingly." However, a person who "is aware of and consciously disregards a substantial and unjustifiable risk" that an injury will occur acts "recklessly," not "knowingly."

We have authority, pursuant to . . . the Oregon Constitution, to enter the judgment that should have been entered in the court below. Assault in the third degree is a lesser included offense of the crime of assault in the second degree charged in the accusatory instrument in this case. We modify defendant's conviction to a conviction for the crime of assault in the third degree.

Conviction affirmed as modified; remanded for resentencing.

QUESTIONS

1. List all of the facts relevant to determining Pete Jantzi's state of mind.
2. State the Oregon statute's mental element for assault.
3. State how, and explain why, Oregon modified the MPC definition of "knowingly."
4. In your opinion, did Jantzi knowingly assault Rex Anderson? Back up your answer with the facts of the case and the trial and appellate court's opinions.

Recklessly

"Awareness" is the watchword for acting recklessly, just as it is for acting knowingly. But there's a critical difference; in acting "recklessly," it's awareness of the risk of causing a criminal result, whereas in acting "knowingly," it's awareness of causing the result itself. Notice that recklessness doesn't apply to conduct crimes for the obvious reason that you have to be aware you're committing a voluntary act (Chapter 3).

Reckless people know they're creating risks of harm but they don't intend, or at least they don't expect, to cause harm itself. Recklessness (conscious risk creation) isn't as blameworthy as acting purposely or knowingly because reckless defendants don't act for the very purpose of doing harm; they don't even act knowing harm is practically certain to follow. But reckless defendants do know they're creating a *risk* of harm.

Criminal recklessness requires more than awareness of ordinary risks; it requires awareness of "substantial and unjustifiable risks." The MPC proposes that fact finders determine recklessness according to a two-pronged test:

1. Was the defendant aware of how substantial and unjustifiable the risks that they disregarded were? Under this prong, notice that even a substantial risk isn't by itself reckless. For example, a doctor who performs life-saving surgery has created a substantial risk. But the risk is justifiable because the doctor took it to save the life of the patient. This prong doesn't answer the important questions of how substantial and how unjustifiable the risk has to be to amount to recklessness. So the second prong gives guidance to juries.
2. Does the defendant's disregard of risk amount to so "gross a deviation from the standard" that a law-abiding person would observe in that situation? This prong requires juries to make the judgment whether the risk is substantial and unjustifiable enough to deserve condemnation in the form of criminal liability.

This test has both a subjective and an objective component. The first prong of the test is subjective; it focuses on a defendant's actual awareness. The second prong is objective; it measures conduct according to how it deviates from what reasonable people do.

It should be clear to you by now that actual harm isn't the conscious object of reckless wrongdoers. In fact, most reckless actors probably hope they don't hurt anyone. Or, at most, they don't care if they hurt anyone. But the heart of their culpability is that even with full knowledge of the risks, they act anyway. For example, in one case, a large drug company knew that a medication it sold to control high blood pressure had caused severe liver damage and even death in some patients; it sold the drug anyway. The company's officers, who made the decision to sell the drug, didn't want to hurt anyone (in fact, they hoped no one would die or suffer liver damage). They sought only profit for the company, but they were prepared to risk the deaths of their customers to make a profit (Shenon 1985, A1).

Negligently

Like acting recklessly, acting negligently is about creating risks. But acting recklessly refers to *consciously* creating risks; acting negligently refers to *unconsciously* (unreasonably) creating risks. Here's an example of a negligent wrongdoer: "Okay, so you didn't mean to hurt him, and you didn't even know the odds were very high you could hurt him, but you *should* have known the odds were very high, and you did hurt him." The test for negligence is totally objective—namely, that the actors should have known, even though in fact they didn't know, they were creating risks. Put another way, a reasonable person would've known she was creating the risk.

For example, a reasonable person would know that driving 50 miles an hour down a crowded street creates a risk of harm. The driver who *should* know what a reasonable person *would* know, but doesn't, is negligent. The driver who knows it but drives too fast anyway is reckless. Negligent defendants, like reckless defendants, have to create "substantial and unjustifiable risks"—risks that grossly deviate from the ordinary standards of behavior.

CASE

In **Koppersmith v. State** *(1999), the Alabama Court of Appeals wrestled with the difficult task of drawing the line between recklessness and negligence.*

Did he kill his wife recklessly or negligently?

Koppersmith v. State

742 So.2d 206 (Ala.App. 1999)

HISTORY

Gregory Koppersmith, the appellant, was charged with the murder of his wife, Cynthia ("Cindy") Michel Koppersmith. He was convicted of reckless manslaughter, a violation of § 13A-6-3(a)(1), Ala. Code 1975, and the trial court sentenced him to 20 years in prison. The Alabama Court of Appeals reversed and remanded.

BASCHAB, J.

FACTS

Gregory Koppersmith (appellant) and his wife were arguing in the yard outside of their residence. Cindy tried to enter the house to end the argument, but Greg prevented her from going inside. A physical confrontation ensued, and Cindy fell off of a porch into the yard. She died as a result of a skull fracture to the back of her head.

In a statement he made to law enforcement officials after the incident, the appellant gave the following summary of the events leading up to Cindy's death. He and Cindy had been arguing and were on a porch outside of their residence. Cindy had wanted to go inside the house, but he had wanted to resolve the argument first. As she tried to go inside, he stepped in front of her and pushed her back. Cindy punched at him, and he grabbed her.

When Cindy tried to go inside again, he wrapped his arms around her from behind to stop her. Cindy bit him on the arm, and he "slung" her to the ground. He then jumped down and straddled her, stating that he "had her by the head" and indicating that he moved her head up and down, as if slamming it into the ground. When Cindy stopped struggling, he rolled her over and found a brick covered with blood under her head. The appellant stated that, although Cindy fell near a flowerbed, he did not know there were bricks in the grass.

At trial, Greg testified that Cindy had tried to go into the house two or three times, but he had stopped her from doing so. During that time, she punched at him and he pushed her away from him. At one point, he put his arms around her from behind to restrain her, and she turned her head and bit him. When she bit him, he pulled her by her sweater and she tripped. He then "slung" her off of him, and she tripped and fell three to four feet to the ground. He jumped off of the porch and straddled her, grabbing her by the shoulders and telling her to calm down. When he realized she was not moving, he lifted her head and noticed blood all over his hands.

Greg testified that, when he grabbed Cindy from behind, he did not intend to harm her. He also testified that, when he "slung" her away from him off of the porch, he was not trying to hurt her and did not intend to throw her onto a brick. Rather, he stated that he simply reacted after she bit his arm. He also testified that he did not know there were bricks in the yard, that he had not attempted to throw her in a particular direction, and that he was not aware of any risk or harm his actions might cause.

Greg further testified that, when he grabbed and shook her after she fell, he did not intend to harm her, he did not know there was a brick under her head, and he did not intend to hit her head on a brick or anything else. Instead, he testified that he was trying to get her to calm down.

The medical examiner, Dr. Gregory Wanger, testified that the pattern on the injury to the victim's skull matched the pattern on one of the bricks found at the scene. He stated that, based on the position of the skull fracture and the bruising to the victim's brain, the victim's head was moving when it sustained the injury. He testified that her injuries could have been caused by her falling off of the porch and hitting her head on a brick or from her head being slammed into a brick.

The indictment in this case alleged that the appellant "did, with the intent to cause the death of Cynthia Michel Koppersmith, cause the death of Cynthia Michel Koppersmith, by striking her head against a brick, in violation of § 13A-6-2 of the Code of Alabama (C.R.11)." Koppersmith requested that the trial court instruct the jury on criminally negligent homicide as a lesser included offense of murder. However, the trial court denied that request, and it instructed the jury only on the offense of reckless manslaughter.

OPINION

Section 13A-6-3(a), Ala.Code 1975, provides that a person commits the crime of manslaughter if he recklessly causes the death of another person. A person acts recklessly with respect to a result or to a circumstance described by a statute defining an offense when he is aware of and consciously disregards a substantial and unjustifiable risk that the result will occur or that the circumstance exists. The risk must be of such nature and degree that disregard thereof constitutes a gross deviation from the standard of conduct that a reasonable person would observe in the situation.

"A person commits the crime of criminally negligent homicide if he causes the death of another person by criminal negligence" § 13A-6-4(a), Ala. Code 1975. A person acts with criminal negligence with respect to a result or to a circumstance which is defined by statute as an offense when he fails to perceive a substantial and unjustifiable risk that the result will occur or that the circumstance exists. The risk must be of such nature and degree that the failure to perceive it constitutes a gross deviation from the standard of care that a reasonable person would observe in the situation. A court or jury may consider statutes or ordinances regulating the defendant's conduct as bearing upon the question of criminal negligence.

The only difference between manslaughter under Section 13A-6-3(a)(1) and criminally negligent homicide is the difference between recklessness and criminal negligence. The reckless offender is aware of the risk and "consciously disregards" it. On the other hand, the criminally negligent offender is not aware of the risk created ("fails to perceive") and, therefore, cannot be guilty of consciously disregarding it. The difference between the terms "recklessly" and "negligently" is one of kind, rather than degree. Each actor creates a risk or harm. The reckless actor is aware of the risk and disregards it; the negligent actor is not aware of the risk but should have been aware of it.

Thus, we must determine whether there was any evidence before the jury from which it could have concluded that the appellant did not perceive that his wife might die as a result of his actions. We conclude that there was evidence from which the jury could have reasonably believed that his conduct that caused her to fall was unintentional and that he was not aware he was creating a risk to his wife. He testified that, after she bit him, his reaction—which caused her to fall to the ground—was simply reflexive.

He also testified that he did not know there were bricks in the yard. Even in his statement to the police in which he said he was slamming her head against the ground, Koppersmith said he did not know at that time that there was a brick under her head.

Finally, he stated that he did not intend to throw her onto a brick or harm her in any way when he "slung" her, and that he did not intend to hit her head on a brick or otherwise harm her when he grabbed and shook her after she had fallen.

Because there was a reasonable theory from the evidence that would have supported giving a jury instruction on criminally negligent homicide, the trial court erred in refusing to instruct the jury on criminally negligent homicide. Thus, we must reverse the trial court's judgment and remand this case for a new trial.

REVERSED AND REMANDED.

QUESTIONS

1. List all of the facts relevant to determining Koppersmith's mental state with respect both to his acts and the results of his actions.
2. In your opinion, was Koppersmith reckless or negligent? Support your answer with relevant facts.
3. Is it possible to argue that Koppersmith knowingly or even purposely killed his wife? What facts, if any, support these two states of mind?

LIABILITY WITHOUT FAULT (STRICT LIABILITY)

LO 5

You've learned that criminal liability depends on at least some degree of blameworthiness when we're talking about serious crimes like the cases in the previous culpability sections. But there are enormous numbers of minor crimes where there's liability without either subjective or objective fault (Chapter 12). We call this liability without fault *strict liability*, meaning it's based on voluntary action alone. Let's be blunt: strict liability makes accidental injuries a crime. In strict liability cases, the prosecution has to prove only that defendants committed a voluntary criminal act that caused harm.

The U.S. Supreme Court has upheld the power of legislatures to create strict liability offenses to protect the "public health and safety," as long as they make clear they're imposing liability without fault (Chapter 3).

Supporters of strict liability make two main arguments. First, there's a strong public interest in protecting public health and safety. Strict liability arose during the industrial revolution when manufacturing, mining, and commerce exposed large numbers of the public to death, mutilation, and disease from poisonous fumes, unsafe railroads, workplaces, and adulterated foods, and other products. Second, the penalty for strict liability offenses is almost always mild (fines, not jail time).

Critics say it's too easy to expand strict liability beyond offenses that seriously endanger the public. They're always wary of making exceptions to blameworthiness, which is central to the *mens rea* principle. It does no good (and probably a lot of harm) to punish people who haven't harmed others purposely, knowingly, recklessly, or at least negligently. At the end of the day, the critics maintain, a criminal law without blameworthiness will lose its force as a stern moral code.

CASE

In **State v. Loge** ***(2000)****, the court decided that Minnesota's legislature had created a strict liability open bottle offense.*

Did the "open bottle law" create a strict liability offense?

State v. Loge

608 N.W.2d 152 (Minn. 2000)

HISTORY

Steven Mark Loge (Appellant) was cited for a violation of Minn. Stat. § 169.122, subd. 3 (1998), which makes it unlawful for the driver of a motor vehicle, when the owner is not present, "to keep or allow to be kept in a motor vehicle when such vehicle is upon the public highway any bottle or receptacle containing intoxicating liquors or 3.2 percent malt liquors which has been opened." Violation of the statute is a misdemeanor. Loge was convicted in the District Court, Freeborn County, and he appealed. The Court of Appeals affirmed, and Loge appealed to the Minnesota Supreme Court. The Supreme Court affirmed.

GILBERT, J.

FACTS

On September 2, 1997, Steven Loge borrowed his father's pickup truck to go to his evening job. Driving alone on his way home from work, he was stopped by two Albert Lea City police officers on County Road 18 at approximately 8:15 P.M. because he appeared to be speeding. Loge got out of his truck and stood by the driver's side door. While one officer was talking with Loge, the second officer, who was standing by the passenger side of the truck, observed a bottle, which he believed to be a beer bottle, sticking partially out of a brown paper bag underneath the passenger's side of the seat. He retrieved that bottle, which was open and had foam on the inside. He searched the rest of the truck and found one full, unopened can of beer and one empty beer can. After the second officer found the beer bottle, the first officer asked Loge if he had been drinking.

Loge stated that he had two beers while working and was on his way home. Loge passed all standard field sobriety tests. The officers gave Loge a citation for a violation of the open bottle statute.

At the trial Loge testified that the bottle was not his, that he did not know it was in the truck and had said that to one of the officers. The trial court found that one of the police officers "observed the neck of the bottle, which was wrapped in a brown paper sack, under the pickup's seat of the truck being operated by defendant." The trial court held that subdivision 3 creates "absolute liability" on a driver/owner to "inspect and determine whether there are any containers" in the motor vehicle in violation of the open bottle law and found Loge guilty. Loge was sentenced to five days in jail, execution stayed, placed on probation for one year, and fined $150 plus costs of $32.50.

Loge appealed the verdict. The Court of Appeals affirmed the decision of the trial court. The Court of Appeals held that proof of knowledge that the bottle was in the truck is not required to sustain a conviction. Loge's petition for further review was granted. The Attorney General then assumed responsibility for this case and filed a respondent's brief in which the Attorney General argues, contrary to the previous position of the state, that there is no knowledge requirement under subdivision 3.

OPINION

Loge is seeking reversal of his conviction because, he argues, the trial court and court of appeals erroneously interpreted subdivision 3 of the open bottle statute not to require proof of knowledge. Minnesota Statute § 169.122 reads in part:

> *Subdivision 1.* No person shall drink or consume intoxicating liquors or 3.2 percent malt liquors in any motor vehicle when such vehicle is upon a public highway.
>
> *Subdivision 2.* No person shall have in possession while in a private motor vehicle upon a public highway, any bottle or receptacle containing intoxicating liquor or 3.2 percent malt liquor which has been opened, or the seal broken, or the contents of which have been partially removed. This subdivision does not apply to a bottle or receptacle that is in the trunk of the vehicle if it is equipped with a trunk, or that is in another area of the vehicle not normally occupied by the driver and passengers if the vehicle is not equipped with a trunk.
>
> *Subdivision 3.* It shall be unlawful for the owner of any private motor vehicle or the driver, if the owner be not then present in the motor vehicle, to keep or allow to be kept in a motor vehicle when such vehicle is upon the public highway any bottle or receptacle containing intoxicating liquors or 3.2 percent malt liquors which has been opened, or the seal broken, or the contents of which have been partially removed except when such bottle or receptacle shall be kept in the trunk of the motor vehicle when such vehicle is equipped with a trunk, or kept in some other area of the vehicle not normally occupied by the driver or passengers, if the motor vehicle is not equipped with a trunk. A utility compartment or glove compartment shall be deemed to be within the area occupied by the driver and passengers.

An analysis of a statute must begin with a careful and close examination of the statutory language to ascertain and effectuate legislative intent. If the meaning of the statute is clear and free from all ambiguity, the letter of the law shall not be disregarded under the pretext of pursuing the spirit.

Minn.Stat. § 169.122, subd. 3 establishes liability for a driver when that driver "*keeps or allows to be kept*" [emphasis added] any open bottle containing intoxicating liquor within the area normally occupied by the driver and passengers. These two alternate concepts are separated by the disjunctive "or" not "and." Unlike the use of the word "and," "or" signifies the distinction between two factual situations. We have long held that in the absence of some ambiguity surrounding the legislature's use of the word "or," we will read it in the disjunctive and require that only one of the possible factual situations be present in order for the statute to be satisfied. Accordingly, we limit our opinion to the words "to keep."

In delineating the elements of the crime, we have also held that the legislature is entitled to consider what it deems "expedient and best suited to the prevention of crime and disorder." If knowledge was a necessary element of the open container offense, there would be a substantial, if not insurmountable, difficulty of proof. It is therefore reasonable to conclude that the legislature, weighing the significant danger to the public, decided that proof of knowledge under subdivision 3 was not required.

The legislature has made knowledge distinctions within its traffic statutes that also guide our interpretation. For example, with respect to marijuana in a motor vehicle, the Minnesota legislature has used language similar to the language found in section 169.122, subdivision 3 ("keep or allow to be kept") but added a knowledge requirement. An owner, or if the owner is not present, the driver, is guilty of a misdemeanor if he "*knowingly keeps or allows to be kept*" [emphasis added] marijuana in a motor vehicle. Minn.Stat. § 152.027, subd. 3 (1998). If the legislature had intended Section 169.122 to have a knowledge requirement, it could have added the word "knowingly," as the legislature did in Section 152.027.

Lastly, Loge argues that an interpretation excluding knowledge as an element could lead to absurd results. While it is true that the legislature does not intend a result that is absurd or unreasonable, we do not believe such a result exists here. Loge's conviction resulted from an officer standing outside the truck observing

(continues)

(continued)

the open container of beer sticking partially out of a brown bag underneath the seat on the passenger side of the truck Loge was driving. By simply taking control of the truck, Loge took control and charge of the contents of the truck, including the open bottle, even if he did not know the open bottle was in the truck.

AFFIRMED.

DISSENT

ANDERSON, J.

I respectfully dissent. In its effort to reach a correct policy decision, the majority disregards our proper role as interpreters of the law. In doing so, the majority has preempted the legislature's function and assumed the mantle of policymaker.

I agree that under certain circumstances the legislature may provide that criminal liability attach without requiring any showing of intent or knowledge on the part of the person charged. Further, in the context of open containers of alcohol in motor vehicles, there is a credible argument that it is good public policy given the social and economic costs that result from the combination of alcohol and motor vehicles. But, all of that said, the majority's analysis simply does not demonstrate the requisite clear statement of legislative intent necessary to create criminal liability in the absence of a showing of knowledge or intent.

We have stated that when the legislature intends to make an act unlawful and to impose criminal sanctions without any requirement of intent or knowledge, it must do so clearly. Historically, our substantive criminal law is based upon a theory of punishing the vicious will. It postulates a free agent confronted with a choice between doing right and doing wrong and choosing freely to do wrong. § 169.122, subd. 3, simply lacks the requisite clarity to support the imposition of criminal liability without any showing of intent or knowledge.

The majority cannot avoid the implications of the term "allow" because it is convenient to do so. In other contexts, we have held that the inclusion of words like "permit" (a synonym of "allow") clearly indicates a legislative intent to require some level of knowledge or intent.

Under the majority's holding, we now will impose criminal liability on a person, not simply for an act that the person does not know is criminal, but also for an act the person does not even know he is committing. While the district court and the majority seem to assume that everyone who drives a motor vehicle knows that he or she is obligated to search the entire passenger compartment of the vehicle before driving on the state's roads, the law imposes no such requirement.

Most drivers would be surprised to discover that after anyone else used their vehicle—children, friends, spouse—they are criminally liable for any open containers of alcohol that are present, regardless of whether they know the containers are there. This also means that any prudent operator of a motor vehicle must also carefully check any case of packaged alcohol before transport and ensure that each container's seal is not broken. See Minn. Stat. § 169.122 (defining an open bottle as a container that is open, has the contents partially removed, or has the seal broken). Under the majority's interpretation, all of these situations would render the driver criminally liable under Minn. Stat. § 169.122. Without a more clear statement by the legislature that this is the law, I cannot agree with such an outcome.

QUESTIONS

1. What words, if any, in the statute indicate a *mens rea* requirement?
2. What *mens rea*, if any, do the words in the statute require?
3. Summarize the arguments that the majority of the court give to support this as a strict liability offense.
4. What arguments did the dissent give in response to the majority's arguments?
5. Do you agree with the majority or the dissent? Defend your answer.

LO 6

CONCURRENCE

principle of concurrence, some mental fault has to trigger the criminal act in conduct crimes and the cause in result crimes

The **principle of concurrence** means that some mental fault has to trigger the criminal act in conduct crimes and the cause in result crimes. So all crimes, except strict liability offenses, are subject to the concurrence requirement. In practice, concurrence is an element in all crimes where the mental attitude was formed with purpose, knowledge, recklessness, or negligence. Suppose you and your friend agree to meet at her house on a cold winter night. She's late because her car won't start. So she texts, "break front door lock, go in 2 keep warm." But once you're inside, you decide to steal her Blu-ray HDVR. Have you committed breaking and entering?

No, because in crimes of criminal conduct, the principle of concurrence requires that a criminal intent (*mens rea*) triggers a criminal act (*actus reus*). You decided to steal her HDVR after you broke into and entered her house. Breaking and entering requires that the intent to commit the *actus reus* of breaking and entering set in the motion the act of breaking and entering your friend's house. That's how concurrence applies to *breaking and entering*, a crime of criminal conduct.

Now, let's look at an example of concurrence in murder, a result crime. Shafeah hates her sister Nazirah and plans to kill her by running over her with her Jeep Grand Cherokee. Coincidentally, just as Shafeah is headed toward Nazirah in her Cherokee, a complete stranger in an Audi TT appears out of nowhere and accidentally runs over and kills Nazirah. Shafeah gets out of her Grand Cherokee, runs over to Nazirah's dead body, and gleefully dances around it. Although definitely a creepy thing to do, Shafeah's not a murderer because her criminal conduct (driving her Cherokee with the intent to kill Nazirah) didn't cause Nazirah's death. Concurrence here means the criminal conduct has to produce the criminal harm; the harm can't be a coincidence (Hall 1960, 185–90; Chapter 11).

We'll say no more about concurrence, either here or in the remaining chapters. Not because it's not important. Quite the contrary, it's critical to criminal liability. But it's never an issue, at least not in real cases—not in the thousands of appellate court cases I've read over the years. And from what lawyers and trial judges I've known tell me, it's never an issue in the cases they try and decide. So for your purposes, know what it is, know it's a critical element, and that's enough.

CAUSATION

LO 7

Causation is about holding an actor criminally accountable for the results of her conduct. Causation applies only to result crimes, the most prominent being criminal homicide (Chapter 9). But there are others, such as causing bodily harm in assault, damage to property in malicious mischief, and destruction of property in arson. Like all elements of crime, prosecutors have to prove causation beyond a reasonable doubt. Proving causation requires proving two kinds of cause:

causation, holding an actor criminally accountable for the results of her conduct

1. Factual cause (also called "but for" cause or "cause in fact") of death, other bodily harm, and damage to and destruction of property
2. Legal cause (also called "proximate" cause) of death, other bodily harm, and damage to and destruction of property

FACTUAL CAUSE

Factual cause (also called "but for" cause or "cause in fact") is an empirical question of fact that asks whether an actor's conduct triggered a series of events that ended in causing death or other bodily harm; damage to property; or destruction of property.

factual cause, also called "but for" cause or "cause in fact"; if it weren't for an actor's conduct, the result wouldn't have occurred

In the cases and statutes, factual cause usually goes by the name "but for" cause or "cause in fact" (or if you want to be fancy and use its Latin name, *sine qua non* cause). "But for" cause means, if it weren't for an actor's conduct, the result wouldn't have occurred. Put another way, an actor's conduct triggered a chain of events that, sooner or later, ended in death or injury to a person or damage to and/or destruction of property. For example, I push a huge smooth round rock down a hill with a crowd at the bottom because I want to watch the crowd panic and scatter. The people see the rock and, to my delight, they scatter. Unfortunately, the rock hits and kills two people who couldn't get out of its path. My push is the cause in fact (the "but for") that kills the two people at the bottom. If I hadn't pushed the rock, they'd be alive. The MPC, Section 2.03(1), puts it this way: "Conduct is the cause of a result when it is an antecedent but for which the result in question would not have occurred."

Factual cause is an objective, empirical question of fact; that's why we call it factual cause. Proving factual cause in almost all real cases is as easy as the no-brainer example of pushing the rock. Proving "but for" cause is necessary, but it's not enough to satisfy the causation requirement. To be sufficient, the prosecution has to prove legal (also called "proximate" cause), too.

LEGAL ("PROXIMATE") CAUSE

legal ("proximate") cause, a subjective question that asks, "Is it fair to blame the defendant for the harm triggered by a chain of events her action(s) set in motion?"

Legal ("proximate") cause is a subjective question of fairness that appeals to the jury's sense of justice. It asks, "Is it fair to blame the defendant for the harm triggered by a chain of events her action(s) set in motion?" If the harm is accidental enough or far enough removed from the defendant's triggering act, there's a reasonable doubt about the justice of blaming the defendant, and there's no proximate cause.

Take our rock-pushing example. Change the facts: On the way down the hill, the rock runs into a tree and lodges there. A year later, a mild earthquake shakes the rock free and it finishes its roll by killing the victims at the bottom. Now, the no-brainer isn't a no-brainer anymore. Why? Because something else, facts in addition to my pushing, contributed to the deaths. We call this "something else" an **intervening cause,** an event that comes between the initial act in a sequence and the end result.

intervening cause, an event that comes between the initial act in a sequence and the end result

Now, we've got our proximate cause problem: Is it fair to punish me for something that's not entirely my fault? As with factual cause, most legal (proximate) cause cases don't create problems, but the ones that do are serious crimes involving death, mutilation, injury, and property destruction and damage.

How do we (and the jury or judge in nonjury cases) determine whether it's fair to attribute the cause of a result to a defendant's conduct? The common law, criminal codes, and the MPC have used various and highly intricate, elaborate devices to help fact finders decide the proximate cause question. For our purposes, they're not too helpful. The best way to understand how fact finders and judges answer the fairness question is to look at how they decided it was fair to impute the bad result to actors' conduct in some real cases.

CASE

In **People v. Armitage** ***(1987)****, the court decided that it was fair to attribute Peter Maskovich's death to his drinking buddy David Armitage's reckless boat driving. In other words, Armitage's conduct was the proximate cause of his friend's death.*

Is it just to blame the defendant for his drinking buddy's death?

People v. Armitage

239 Cal.Rptr. 515 (Cal.App. 1987)

HISTORY

David James Armitage (the defendant) was originally charged with one count of involuntary manslaughter (Pen. Code, § 192, subd. (b)), as well as felony drunk boating (Harb. & Nav.Code, § 655, subd. (c)). Pursuant to a bargain the People dismissed the involuntary manslaughter charge and agreed that if found guilty the defendant would not be sentenced to more than the middle base term (two years) for the felony drunk boating charge. Armitage was convicted in the Superior Court, Yolo County, of felony drunk boating causing death. The defendant appealed. The Court of Appeal, Third District, affirmed.

SPARKS, J.

FACTS

At the time of the defendant's crime, Harbors and Navigation Code, section 655, subdivision (c) provided:

> No person shall operate any boat or vessel or manipulate any water skis, aquaplane, or similar device while under the influence of intoxicating liquor, any drug, or under the combined influence of intoxicating liquor and any drug, and while so operating, do any act forbidden by law, or neglect any duty imposed by law, in the use of the boat, vessel, water skis, aquaplane, or similar device, which act or neglect proximately causes death or serious bodily injury to any person other than himself.

On the evening of May 18, 1985, the defendant and his friend, Peter Maskovich, were drinking in a bar in the riverside community of Freeport. They were observed leaving the bar around midnight. In the early morning hours, the defendant and Maskovich wound up racing defendant's boat on the Sacramento River while both of them were intoxicated. An autopsy revealed that at the time of his death Maskovich had a blood alcohol level of .25 percent. A blood sample taken from the defendant at approximately 7:00 A.M. revealed a blood alcohol level at that time of .14 percent. The defendant does not dispute that he was intoxicated at the time of the accident. The boat did not contain any personal flotation devices.

At about 3:00 A.M. Gary Bingham, who lived in a house boat in a speed zone (five miles per hour, no wake), was disturbed by a large wake. He went out to yell at the boaters and observed a small aluminum boat with two persons in it at the bend in the river. The boaters had the motor wide open, were zig-zagging, and had no running lights on at the time.

About the same time, Rodney and Susan Logan were fishing on the river near the Freeport Bridge when they observed an aluminum boat with two men in it coming up the river without running lights. The occupants were using loud and vulgar language and were operating the boat very fast and erratically.

James Snook lives near the Sacramento River in Clarksburg. Sometime around 3:00 A.M. the defendant came to his door. The defendant was soaking wet and appeared quite intoxicated. He reported that he had flipped his boat over in the river and had lost his buddy. He said that at first he and his buddy had been hanging on to the overturned boat, but that his buddy swam for shore and he did not know whether he had made it. As it turned out, Maskovich did not make it; he drowned in the river.

Mr. Snook notified the authorities of the accident. Deputy Beddingfield arrived and spent some time with the defendant in attempting to locate the scene of the accident and the victim. Eventually, Deputy Beddingfield took the defendant to the sheriff's boat shed to meet with officers who normally work on the river. At the shed they were met by Deputy Snyder.

Deputy Snyder attempted to question the defendant about the accident and the defendant stated that he had been operating the boat at a high rate of speed and zigzagging until it capsized. The defendant also stated that he told the victim to hang on to the boat but his friend ignored his warning and started swimming for the shore. As he talked to the defendant, the officer formed the opinion that the defendant was intoxicated.

OPINION

The evidence establishes that at about 3 A.M., and while he was drunk, defendant operated his boat without lights at a very high rate of speed in an erratic and zig-zagging manner until he capsized it. This evidence supports the finding that defendant not only operated his boat while intoxicated, but that he operated his boat at an unsafe speed and in a reckless or negligent manner so as to endanger the life, limb or property of other persons (Har. & Nav.Code, § 655, subd. (a); 14 Cal.Admin.Code, § 6615). In doing so defendant did an act forbidden by law, or neglected a duty imposed by law, in the operation of his boat. This evidence supports defendant's conviction.

Defendant contends his actions were not the proximate cause of the death of the victim. In order to be guilty of felony drunk boating the defendant's act or omission must be the proximate cause of the ensuing injury or death. Defendant asserts that after his boat flipped over he and the victim were holding on to it and the victim, against his advice, decided to abandon the boat and try to swim to shore. According to defendant the victim's fatally reckless decision should exonerate him from criminal responsibility for his death.

(continues)

(continued)

We reject defendant's contention. The question whether defendant's acts or omissions criminally caused the victim's death is to be determined according to the ordinary principles governing proximate causation. Proximate cause of a death has traditionally been defined in criminal cases as "a cause which, in natural and continuous sequence, produces the death, and without which the death would not have occurred."

Defendant claims that the victim's attempt to swim ashore, whether characterized as an intervening or a superseding cause, constituted a break in the natural and continuous sequence arising from the unlawful operation of the boat. The claim cannot hold water. It has long been the rule in criminal prosecutions that the contributory negligence of the victim is not a defense. In order to exonerate a defendant the victim's conduct must not only be a cause of his injury, it must be a superseding cause. A defendant may be criminally liable for a result directly caused by his act even if there is another contributing cause. If an intervening cause is a normal and reasonably foreseeable result of defendant's original act the intervening act is "dependent" and not a superseding cause, and will not relieve defendant of liability. An obvious illustration of a dependent cause is the victim's attempt to escape from a deadly attack or other danger in which he is placed by the defendant's wrongful act. Thus, it is only an unforeseeable intervening cause, an extraordinary and abnormal occurrence, which rises to the level of an exonerating, superseding cause.

Consequently, in criminal law a victim's predictable effort to escape a peril created by defendant is not considered a superseding cause (see the definition in the margin on p. 148) of the ensuing injury or death. As leading commentators have explained it, an unreflective act in response to a peril created by defendant will not break a causal connection. In such a case, the actor has a choice, but his act is nonetheless unconsidered. "When defendant's conduct causes panic an act done under the influence of panic or extreme fear will not negate causal connection unless the reaction is wholly abnormal" (Hart & Honore 1985, p. 149.) This rule is encapsulated in a standard jury instruction: "It is not a defense to a criminal charge that the deceased or some other person was guilty of negligence, which was a contributory cause of the death involved in the case" (CALJIC No. 8.56 (1979 Revision).

Here defendant, through his misconduct, placed the intoxicated victim in the middle of a dangerous river in the early morning hours clinging to an overturned boat. The fact that the panic-stricken victim recklessly abandoned the boat and tried to swim ashore was not a wholly abnormal reaction to the perceived peril of drowning. Just as "detached reflection cannot be demanded in the presence of an uplifted knife" (*Brown v. United States,* 1921), neither can caution be required of a drowning man. Having placed the inebriated victim in peril, defendant cannot obtain exoneration by claiming the victim should have reacted differently or more prudently. In sum, the evidence establishes that defendant's acts and omissions were the proximate cause of the victim's death.

The judgment is affirmed.

QUESTIONS

1. List all of the facts and circumstances relevant to deciding whether Armitage's actions were the "but for" cause of Peter Maskovich's death.
2. List all of the facts and circumstances relevant to deciding whether Armitage's actions were the proximate cause of Peter Maskovich's death.
3. According to the court, why were Maskovich's actions not a superseding cause of his own death?

EXPLORING FURTHER

Causation

1. Were his actions in the drag race the legal cause of death?

Velazquez v. State, 561 So.2d 347 (Fla.App. 1990)

FACTS

At about 2:30 A.M., Isaac Alejandro Velazquez met the deceased Adalberto Alvarez at a Hardee's restaurant in Hialeah, Florida. The two had never previously met, but in the course of their conversation agreed to "drag race" each other with their automobiles. They accordingly left the restaurant and proceeded to set up a quarter-mile drag race course on a nearby public road that ran perpendicular to a canal alongside the Palmetto Expressway in Hialeah; a guardrail and a visible stop sign stood between the end of this road and the canal.

The two men began their drag race at the end of this road and proceeded away from the canal in a westerly direction for a quarter mile. Upon completing the course without incident, the deceased

Alvarez suddenly turned his automobile 180 degrees around and proceeded east toward the starting line and the canal; Velazquez did the same and followed. Alvarez led and attained an estimated speed of 123 miles per hour; he was not wearing a seat belt and subsequent investigation revealed that he had a blood alcohol level between .11 and .12.

Velazquez, who had not been drinking, trailed Alvarez the entire distance back to the starting line and attained an estimated speed of 98 miles per hour. As both drivers approached the end of the road, they applied their brakes, but neither could stop. Alvarez, who was about a car length ahead of Velazquez, crashed through the guardrail first and was propelled over the entire canal, landing on its far bank; he was thrown from his car upon impact, was pinned under his vehicle when it landed on him, and died instantly from the resulting injuries.

Velazquez also crashed through the guardrail but landed in the canal where he was able to escape from his vehicle and swim to safety uninjured. Velazquez was charged with vehicular homicide.

Were his actions in participating in the drag race the legal (proximate) cause of Alvarez's death?

DECISION

No, according to the Appeals Court:

> In unusual cases like this one, whether certain conduct is deemed the legal cause of a certain result is ultimately a policy question. The question of legal causation thus blends into the question of whether we are willing to hold a defendant responsible for a prohibited result. Or, stated differently, the issue is not causation; it is responsibility. In my opinion, policy considerations are against imposing responsibility for the death of a participant in a race on the surviving racer when his sole contribution to the death is the participation in the activity mutually agreed upon.

2. Who legally caused his death?

People v. Kibbe, 362 N.Y.S.2d 848 (1974)

FACTS proximate cause

Barry Kibbe and a companion, Roy Krall, met George Stafford in a bar on a cold winter night. They noticed Stafford had a lot of money and was drunk. When Stafford asked them for a ride, they agreed, having already decided to rob him. The three men entered Kibbe's automobile and began the trip toward Canandaigua. Krall drove the car while Kibbe demanded that Stafford turn over any money he had. In the course of an exchange, Kibbe slapped Stafford several times, took his money, then compelled him to lower his trousers and to take off his shoes to be certain that Stafford had given up all his money. When they were satisfied that Stafford had no more money on his person, the defendants forced him to exit the Kibbe vehicle.

As he was thrust from the car, Stafford fell onto the shoulder of the rural two-lane highway on which they had been traveling. His trousers were still down around his ankles, his shirt was rolled up toward his chest, he was shoeless, and he had also been stripped of any outer clothing. Before the defendants pulled away, Kibbe placed Stafford's shoes and jacket on the shoulder of the highway. Although Stafford's eyeglasses were in Kibbe's vehicle, the defendants, either through inadvertence or perhaps by specific design, did not give them to him before they drove away.

Michael W. Blake, a college student, was driving at a reasonable speed when he saw Stafford in the middle of the road with his hands in the air. Blake could not stop in time to avoid striking Stafford and killing him.

Did Kibbe and his companion or Blake legally cause Stafford's death?

DECISION

Kibbe and his companion legally caused Stafford's death:

> To be a sufficiently direct cause of death so as to warrant the imposition of a criminal penalty, it will suffice if it can be said beyond a reasonable doubt, as indeed it can be here said, that the ultimate harm is something which should have been foreseen as being reasonably related to the acts of the accused. We conclude that Kibbe and his companion's activities were a sufficiently proximate cause of the death of George Stafford so as to warrant

(continues)

(continued)

the imposition of criminal sanctions. In engaging in what may properly be described as a despicable course of action, Kibbe and Krall left a helplessly intoxicated man without his eyeglasses in a position from which, because of these attending circumstances, he could not extricate himself and whose condition was such that he could not even protect himself from the elements.

Under the conditions surrounding Blake's operation of his truck (i.e., the fact that he had his low beams on as the two cars approached; that there was no artificial lighting on the highway; and that there was insufficient time in which to react to Stafford's presence in his lane), we do not think it may be said that any intervening wrongful act occurred to relieve the defendants from the directly foreseeable consequences of their actions.

superseding cause, an intervening act or force that the law considers sufficient to override the cause for which the original wrongdoer was responsible

IGNORANCE AND MISTAKE

> The rather simple rule that an honest mistake of fact or law is a defense when it negates a required mental element of the crime would appear to be fairly easy to apply to a variety of cases. One merely identifies the mental state or states, and then inquires whether that mental state can exist in light of the defendant's ignorance or mistake of fact or law. (LaFave 2003a, 283–304)

LO 8

mistake, a defense to criminal liability whenever the mistake prevents the formation of any fault-based mental attitude—namely, purposely, knowingly, recklessly, or negligently

failure-of-proof defense, mistake defenses in which defendants usually present enough evidence to raise a reasonable doubt that the prosecution has proved the *mens rea* required for criminal liability

Mistake is a defense whenever the mistake prevents the formation of any fault-based mental attitude—namely, purposely, knowingly, recklessly, or negligently. There's a debate over whether to call mistakes a defense (*General v. State*, 2002). On one side are those who say what the defendant did was wrong, but her mistake excused her; they call mistake a defense of excuse (Chapter 6).

The other side says that the mistake prevented the formation of a culpable state of mind; they say there's no crime at all because the mental element is missing. It's impossible to have a defense to conduct that's not criminal conduct in the first place. They're not really defenses, in the sense that they either justify or excuse criminal liability. Instead, mistakes raise a reasonable doubt that the required mental element for criminal conduct is present.

Mistakes in this sense are sometimes called a failure-of-proof defense because defendants usually present enough evidence to raise a reasonable doubt that the prosecution has proved that they formed the *mens rea* required for criminal liability. We'll see examples of defenses that can be called either defenses of excuse or failures of proof of mental attitude in Chapter 6. We won't get into the details of why, or whether to, treat mistakes as a defense of excuse or as a failure of proof here. But note that the debate isn't just an academic mental exercise; it has important procedural and other consequences (LaFave 2003a, 282–83).

To simplify matters for you, we'll follow the MPC's approach, which is that mistake matters when it prevents the formation of a mental attitude required by a criminal statute. To decide whether a mistake negates the mental element, we need to know what mental element the statute requires. Suppose it's a crime in your state for a bartender to sell alcoholic beverages to anyone under twenty-one for the purpose of supplying a minor with an alcoholic beverage. You're a bartender; you believe the customer you just sold to is twenty-one because she showed you a driver's license with a birth date more than twenty-two years prior to today's date. In fact, she's eighteen. Your mistake negates the mental element of purpose.

Suppose the statute says "recklessly supplies anyone under twenty-one." You look at another customer's license; the date looks altered, but you're not sure. You say, "This date looks like it's been changed, but what the hell, I feel like living dangerously tonight" and sell her an orange blossom martini. She's nineteen. You're guilty, because you created a "substantial and unjustifiable risk" that she was under twenty-one.

One final and important point about mistake; it doesn't work with strict liability crimes. Why? There's no mental element in strict liability offenses. In other words, the trail of mistake doesn't have to (in fact, it can't) lead to fault. To follow through with the bartender example, suppose the statute makes it a crime "to sell any alcoholic beverage to a person under twenty-one." There's no mental element to negate, so it doesn't matter whether you sold it purposely, knowingly, recklessly, or negligently.

CASE

State v. Sexton *(1999)* *adopted the MPC failure-of-proof approach to mistake, holding that Ronald Sexton's alleged mistaken belief that the gun he fired at his friend "related to whether the state failed to prove recklessness beyond a reasonable doubt."*

Did he shoot his friend by mistake?

State v. Sexton

733 A.2d 1125 (N.J. 1999)

HISTORY

Ronald Sexton (defendant) was convicted in the Superior Court, Law Division, Essex County, of reckless manslaughter as a lesser-included offense of murder and unlawful possession of a handgun without a permit. He appealed. The Superior Court, Appellate Division, reversed. The state's petition for certification was granted. The Supreme Court, O'Hern, J., held that defendant's alleged mistaken belief that the gun he fired at victim was not loaded related to whether state failed to prove essential element beyond reasonable doubt. Affirmed and remanded.

O'HERN, J. FOR A UNANIMOUS COURT

FACTS

On May 10, 1993, Shakirah Jones (then 17), friend of Ronald Sexton (then 15), the defendant, and the victim (then 17), Alquadir Matthews, overheard the two young men having what she described as a "typical argument." The two young men walked from a sidewalk into a vacant lot. Jones saw defendant with a gun in his hand, but she did not see defendant shoot Matthews.

Jones heard Matthews tell defendant, "There are no bullets in that gun," and then walk away. Defendant called Matthews back and said, "You think there are no bullets in this gun?" Matthews replied, "Yeah." Jones heard the gun go off. A single bullet killed Matthews.

A ballistics expert testified that there was a spring missing from the gun's magazine, which prevented the other bullets from going into the chamber after the first bullet was discharged. In this condition, the gun would have to be loaded manually by feeding the live cartridge into the chamber prior to firing. The expert later clarified that if the magazine had been removed after one round had been inserted into the chamber, it would be impossible to see whether the gun was loaded without pulling the slide that covered the chamber to the rear. The expert agreed that, for someone unfamiliar with guns, once the magazine was removed, it was "probably a possible assumption" that the gun was unloaded.

Defendant's version was that when the two young men were in the lot, Matthews showed defendant a gun and "told me the gun was empty." Defendant "asked him was he sure," and "he said yes." When Matthews asked if defendant would like to see the gun, defendant said "yes." Defendant "took the gun and was looking at it and it just went off." He never unloaded the gun or checked to see if there were any bullets in the gun. He had never before owned or shot a gun.

A grand jury indicted defendant for purposeful or knowing murder, possession of a handgun without a permit, and possession of a handgun for an

(continues)

(continued)

unlawful purpose. At the close of the state's case, defendant moved to dismiss the murder charge because the victim had told him that the gun was not loaded. The court denied the motion.

The court charged murder and the lesser-included offenses of aggravated manslaughter and reckless manslaughter.

OPINION

The MPC (Model Penal Code) provides that, "Ignorance or mistake as to a matter of fact or law is a defense if: the ignorance or mistake negatives the purpose, knowledge, belief, recklessness or negligence required to establish a material element of the offense. Whether a mistake would negate a required element of the offense depended on the nature of the mistake and the state of mind that the offense required. This led commentators to observe:

> Technically, such provisions [for a mistake defense] are unnecessary. They simply confirm what is stated elsewhere: "No person may be convicted of an offense unless each element of such offense is proven beyond a reasonable doubt." If the defendant's ignorance or mistake makes proof of a required culpability element impossible, the prosecution will necessarily fail in its proof of the offense.

Correctly understood, there is no difference between a positive and negative statement on the issue—what is required for liability versus what will provide a defense to liability. What is required in order to establish liability for manslaughter is recklessness (as defined by the code) about whether death will result from the conduct. A faultless or merely careless mistake may negate that reckless state of mind and provide a defense.

How can we explain these concepts to a jury? We believe that the better way to explain the concepts is to explain what is required for liability to be established. Something along the following lines will help to convey to the jury the concepts relevant to a reckless manslaughter charge:

> In this case, ladies and gentlemen of the jury, the defendant contends that he mistakenly believed that the gun was not loaded. If you find that the State has not proven beyond a reasonable doubt that the defendant was reckless in forming his belief that the gun was not loaded, defendant should be acquitted of the offense of manslaughter. On the other hand, if you find that the State has proven beyond a reasonable doubt that the defendant was reckless in forming the belief that the gun was not loaded, and consciously disregarded a substantial and unjustifiable risk that a killing would result from his conduct, then you should convict him of manslaughter.

To sum up, evidence of an actor's mistaken belief relates to whether the state has failed to prove an essential element of the charged offense beyond a reasonable doubt. As a practical matter, lawyers and judges will undoubtedly continue to consider a mistake of fact as a defense. Despite the complexities perceived by scholars, the limited number of appeals on this subject suggests to us that juries have very little difficulty in applying the concepts involved.

To require the State to disprove beyond a reasonable doubt defendant's reasonable mistake of fact introduces an unnecessary and perhaps unhelpful degree of complexity into the fairly straightforward inquiry of whether defendant consciously disregarded a substantial and unjustifiable risk that death would result from his conduct and that the risk was of such a nature and degree that, considering the nature and purpose of the actor's conduct and the circumstances known to him, its disregard involved a gross deviation from the standard of conduct that a reasonable person would observe in the actor's situation.

The judgment of the Appellate Division is affirmed. The matter is remanded to the Law Division for further proceedings in accordance with this opinion.

QUESTIONS

1. List all the facts and circumstances relevant to deciding whether Ronald Sexton shot Alquadir Matthews by mistake.
2. How does the court recommend the failure-of-proof mistake to juries?
3. Does the court's recommendation help you understand this concept of mistake? Does it help you to understand how it works in court proceedings? Explain your answers.

SUMMARY

LO 1 — A criminal act (*actus reus*) is necessary, but it's not enough for criminal liability for most serious crimes. They include a mental element (*mens rea*). It's only fair and just to punish people we can blame. We call this culpability, or blameworthiness.

LO 2 — Criminal intent, or *mens rea,* is the mental state that accompanies a forbidden act. This differs from motive, which is something that causes a person to act. Motive isn't a required element of a crime.

LO 3 — General intent consists of the intent to commit the criminal act. Specific intent consists of the intent to commit the act plus some other element.

LO 4 — The Model Penal Code (MPC) breaks down *mens rea* into four mental states, which the drafters of the code preferred to call levels of culpability—namely, purposely, knowingly, recklessly, and negligently.

LO 5 — Liability without fault, or strict liability, exists when there's a crime, minor by design, without either subjective (purpose, knowledge) or objective (recklessness, negligence) legal fault.

LO 6 — Concurrence means that some mental fault has to trigger the criminal act in conduct crimes and the cause in result crimes.

LO 7 — The element of causation applies only to "bad result" crimes. Like all elements of crime, prosecutors have to prove causation beyond a reasonable doubt. Proving causation requires proving two kinds of cause: (1) factual ("but for") cause or (2) legal (proximate) cause.

LO 8 — Ignorance of facts and law can create a reasonable doubt that the prosecution has proved the element of criminal intent. Mistake is a defense whenever the mistake prevents the formation of criminal intent.

KEY TERMS

culpability, p. 124
blameworthiness, p. 124
cause in fact, *also called* but for causation, p. 124
legal cause, p. 124
mens rea, p. 124
motive, p. 126
subjective fault, p. 127
objective fault, p. 127
strict liability, p. 127
general intent, p. 128
specific intent, p. 128
general intent "plus," p. 128
purposely, p. 131
knowingly, p. 131
recklessly, p. 131
negligently, p. 132
principle of concurrence, p. 142
causation, p. 143
factual cause, p. 143
legal ("proximate") cause, p. 144
intervening cause, p. 144
proximate cause of a death, p. 146
superseding cause, p. 148
mistake, p. 148
failure-of-proof defense, p. 148

LEARNING OBJECTIVES

1. To understand that defendants aren't criminally liable if their actions were justified under the circumstances.
2. To know that defendants aren't criminally liable if they weren't responsible for their actions.
3. To understand how the affirmative defenses operate in justified and excused conduct.
4. To appreciate that self-defense limits the use of deadly force to those who reasonably believe they're faced with the choice to kill or be killed right now.
5. To know and understand the differences among the four elements of self-defense.
6. To understand the retreat rule and appreciate its historic transformation.
7. To appreciate how the historic transformation of the retreat rule led to the stand-your-ground rule.
8. To understand that there's no duty to retreat from your own home to avoid using deadly force.
9. To appreciate how the new "castle doctrine" laws are transforming the law of self-defense.
10. To know that the choice-of-evils defense, choosing to commit a lesser crime to avoid an imminent threat of harm from a greater crime, is justified.
11. To understand that the defense of consent represents the high value placed on individual autonomy in a free society.

George Zimmerman, right, stands next to a Seminole County Deputy during a court hearing in Sanford, Florida. Zimmerman has been charged with second-degree murder in the shooting death of 17-year-old Trayvon Martin.

AP Images/Gary W. Green, Orlando Sentinel, Pool

5 DEFENSES TO CRIMINAL LIABILITY

Justifications

CHAPTER OUTLINE

"When Seconds Count, the Police Are Only Minutes Away"

Police officers were rushing to a home on Millbrook Court in Amherst, New York, which David W. Park had entered early in the morning on March 28, 2010. The officers "were about two minutes away when the frightened homeowner shot and killed Park, an award-winning Albany teacher."

At about 1 A.M., David D'Amico, 33, heard a noise and went downstairs, turning on a light and checking the first floor of the house. Finding nothing unusual, he went back upstairs to the bedroom where he had been sleeping with his wife. As he arrived upstairs, he heard more noises downstairs, which prompted him to get his shotgun and tell his wife to call 911, according to Erie County District Attorney Frank A. Sedita III. D'Amico's wife called 911 to report an intruder.

The intruder was David Park, 31, who for unknown reasons, left the party next door that he was attending, and entered the D'Amico home through an unlocked rear door at about 1 A.M. D'Amico was at the top of the stairway when he saw Park at the bottom—about 12 feet away. D'Amico repeatedly yelled out to Park that he should leave the home immediately and warned him that he had a gun. When Park refused to leave, D'Amico fired a single shot of buckshot that hit Park in the chest. D'Amico told police he believed Park was about to walk up the stairs. After a police investigation, a grand jury found "no cause for criminal charges" against David D'Amico.

(Herbeck and Gryta 2010)

LO 1

criminal conduct, a criminal act triggered by criminal intent

Proving **criminal conduct** (a criminal act triggered by criminal intent) is necessary to hold individuals accountable for the crimes they commit. But criminal *conduct* alone isn't enough to establish criminal *liability*. Recall that it's only the first of three requirements. First, we have to answer the question asked in Chapters 3 and 4, "Was there criminal conduct?" If there wasn't, the inquiry is over, and the defendant is free. If there was, we have to answer the question of this chapter, "Was the criminal conduct justified?" If it was, the inquiry ends, and the defendant goes free. If it wasn't justified, we have to go on to answer the third question (asked in Chapter 6), "Was the unjustified conduct excused?" If it wasn't, the defendant is criminally accountable for her criminal conduct. If it was, the defendant might, or might not, go free.

LO 2

justification defenses, defendants admit they were responsible for their acts but claim that, under the circumstances, what they did was right (justified)

excuse defenses, defendants admit what they did was wrong but claim that, under the circumstances, they weren't responsible for what they did

The principles of justification comprise several traditional defenses to criminal liability; we'll discuss several in this chapter. In the **justification defenses,** defendants admit they were responsible for their acts but claim that, *under the circumstances*, what they did was right (justified). The classic justification is self-defense: kill or be killed. "I killed her. I'm responsible for killing her, but, under the circumstances, it was right to kill her." So, even if the government proves all the elements in the crime beyond a reasonable doubt, the defendant walks because she's not blameworthy.

In the **excuse defenses,** defendants admit what they did was wrong but claim that, under the circumstances, they weren't *responsible* for what they did (see Chapter 6). The classic excuse is insanity. "What I did was wrong, but I was too insane to know or control what I did. So, under the circumstances, I'm not responsible for what I did."

In addition to the traditional defenses of self and home, this chapter also examines, and asks you to think about, "the epochal transformation" in self-defense and the defense of homes represented by the new "castle doctrine" statutes (Suk 2008, 237). More than forty states have either passed or proposed statutes that expand the right to use deadly force to protect self and home in two ways:

1. "They permit a home resident to kill an intruder, by presuming rather than requiring proof of reasonable fear of death or serious bodily harm."
2. "They reject a general duty to retreat from attack, even when retreat is possible, not only in the home, but also in public space." (238)

LO 3

PROVING DEFENSES

failure-of-proof defenses, the defendant only has to raise a reasonable doubt about the prosecution's proof of just one element in the crime

affirmative defenses, defendants have to "start matters off by putting in some evidence in support" of their justification or excuse defenses

Before we examine the defenses themselves, and the dramatic changes taking place in the law of self-defense, we need to clarify how to prove them. First, we have to distinguish between two kinds of defenses: *failure-of-proof* and *affirmative defenses.*

Recall that the prosecution has to prove every element of a crime beyond a reasonable doubt. In **failure-of-proof defenses**, the defendant only has to raise a reasonable doubt about the prosecution's proof of one element in the crime; it can be any element or elements. For example, in *King v. Cogdon* (Chapter 3), the defense cast a reasonable doubt on Mrs. Cogdon's act of killing her daughter Pattie by showing that she swung the ax during the involuntary act of sleepwalking.

Recall that a voluntary act is required for criminal liability. The defenses of justification and excuse are **affirmative defenses**, which operate like this: Defendants have to "start matters off by putting in some evidence in support" of their justification or excuse. (Review Chapter 1 on "The Presumption of Innocence" and "The Burden of Proof," p. 30.)

LO 4

perfect defenses, defenses in which defendants are acquitted if they're successful

Most affirmative defenses are **perfect defenses;** this means that if they're successful, defendants are acquitted. There's one major exception. Defendants who successfully plead the excuse of insanity don't "walk"—at least not right away. Special hearings are held to determine if these defendants are still insane. Most hearings decide they are, and so they're sent to maximum-security hospitals to be confined there until they regain their sanity. In most serious crimes, that's never (Chapter 6).

Evidence that doesn't amount to a perfect defense might amount to an **imperfect defense**; that is, defendants are guilty of lesser offenses. For example, in *Swann v. U.S.* (1994), Ted Swann and Steve Crawford got into an argument while shooting baskets. Crawford's ball hit Swann in the stomach, where someone had recently stabbed him. Crawford ordered Swann off the court. When Swann instead walked past him, ignoring the order, Crawford said, "You think you stabbed up now, just watch." Then, placing his hands to his side, Crawford appeared to be reaching for his back pocket. Swann, who had seen a bulge in Crawford's pocket, thought that he was reaching for a gun to kill him. Swann pulled his own gun from his waistband and shot Crawford twice in the head (929).

imperfect defense, when a defendant fails in the full defense but is found guilty of a lesser offense

The court ruled that Swann was entitled to a jury instruction on imperfect defense that would reduce the murder charge to manslaughter, because there was enough evidence for a jury to conclude that

> Swann's belief that he was in imminent danger and that he had to use deadly force to repel that danger was in fact actually and honestly held but was in one or both respects objectively unreasonable. (930)

Even when the evidence doesn't add up to an imperfect defense, it might still show **mitigating circumstances** that convince judges or juries that defendants don't deserve the maximum penalty for the crime they're convicted of. For example, words, however insulting, can't reduce murder to manslaughter in most states, but they might mitigate a death sentence to life in prison without parole. So when a Black man killed a White man in a rage brought on by the White man's relentless taunting, "nigger, nigger," the killing was still murder but the taunting mitigated the death penalty to life without parole (Chapter 9).

mitigating circumstances, circumstances that convince fact finders (judges or juries) that defendants don't deserve the maximum penalty for the crime they're convicted of

Now, let's look at five justification defenses: self-defense, the defense of others, the defense of home and property, the choice-of-evils defense, and consent.

SELF-DEFENSE

LO 4

If you use force to protect yourself, your home or property, or the people you care about, you've violated the rule of law, which our legal system is deeply committed to (Chapter 1). According to the rule of law, the government has a monopoly on the use of force; so when you use force, you're "taking the law into your own hands." With that great monopoly on force goes the equally great responsibility of protecting individuals who are banned from using force themselves.

Sometimes, the government isn't, or can't be, there to protect you when you need it. So necessity—the heart of self-defense—allows "self-help" to kick in. Self-defense is a grudging concession to necessity. It's only good before the law when three circumstances come together:

1. The necessity is great.
2. It exists "right now."
3. It's for prevention only.

Preemptive strikes aren't allowed; you can't use force to prevent an attack that's going to take place tomorrow, or even this afternoon. Retaliation isn't allowed either; you can't use it to "pay back" an attack that took place last year or even this morning. In short, preemptive strikes come too soon and retaliation too late; they both fail the necessity test. Individuals have to rely on conventional means to prevent future attacks, and only the state can punish past attacks (Fletcher 1988, 18–19).

Let's examine the elements of self-defense. Then, we'll look at if and when claims of self-defense are justifiable when it's possible to retreat to escape harm.

THE ELEMENTS OF SELF-DEFENSE

When can we ignore the government's monopoly on force and take the law into our own hands to defend ourselves? With common law, anyone who was subjected to an unprovoked attack could protect themselves by force from attacks that were going to happen right now. However, today, to justify the use of deadly force, the defender has to honestly and reasonably believe that she's faced with the choice of "kill, or be killed, right now!"

LO 5

Self-defense consists of four elements:

1. **UNPROVOKED ATTACK.** The defender didn't start or provoke the attack.
2. **NECESSITY.** Defenders can use deadly force only if they reasonably believe it's necessary to repel an imminent deadly attack—namely, one that's going to happen right now.
3. **PROPORTIONALITY.** Defenders can use deadly force only if the use of nondeadly force isn't enough to repel the attack. Excessive force isn't allowed.
4. **REASONABLE BELIEF.** The defender has to reasonably believe that it's necessary to use deadly force to repel the imminent deadly attack.

UNPR

Unprovoked Attack

Self-defense is available only against unprovoked attacks. So self-defense isn't available to an initial aggressor; someone who provokes an attack can't then use force to defend herself against the attack she provoked. With one exception: according to the withdrawal exception, if attackers completely withdraw from attacks they provoke, they can defend themselves against an attack by their initial victims.

initial aggressor, someone who provokes an attack and can't then use force to defend herself against the attack she provoked

withdrawal exception, if initial aggressors completely withdraw from attacks they provoke, they can defend themselves against an attack by their initial victims

In a classic old case *State v. Good* (1917, 1006), a son threatened to shoot his father with a shotgun. The father went to a neighbor's, borrowed the neighbor's shotgun, and came back. The son told him to "stop." When the father shot, the son turned and ran and the father pursued him. The son then turned and shot his father, killing him. The trial court failed to instruct the jury on the withdrawal exception. The Supreme Court of Missouri reversed because the trial judge's instruction ignored and excluded the defendant's right of self-defense.

Although he might have brought on the difficulty with the intent to kill his father, still:

- If he was attempting to withdraw from the difficulty, and
- Was fleeing from his father in good faith for the purpose of such withdrawal, and
- If his father, knowing that the defendant was endeavoring to withdraw from such conflict,
- Pursued the defendant and sought to kill him, or
- Do him some great bodily harm,
- Then the defendant's right of self-defense is revived. (1007)

Necessity, Proportionality, and Reasonable Belief

Necessity refers to an imminent danger of attack. Simply put, it means, "The time for defense is right now!" When is "right now"? The majority view is "right now" means "right now." That's what the court concluded in *Sydnor v. State* (2001). Roosevelt Sydnor was sitting with some friends on the front steps of 907 North Chester Street, in Baltimore, when Anthony Jackson came up and asked if he had any "weed" to sell. When Sydnor said no, Jackson, "eyeing a gold chain" Sydnor was wearing, pulled a gun and told him to "give it up." Jackson hit Sydnor on the head with the gun and, while threatening to kill him, took $30. He was about to take the gold chain, but Sydnor, with his friends' help, wrestled the gun away from Jackson.

necessity, a defense that argues an imminent danger of attack was prevented

imminent danger of attack, the danger is "right now"!

As Jackson fled, Sydnor fired five shots at him, hitting him four times—once in the front of his thigh, once in the forearm, and twice in his back. One of the back wounds indicated that the gun was fired from close range. Jackson collapsed and died in the street (669).

Sydnor was convicted of voluntary manslaughter. The Maryland Court of Appeals held that self-defense wasn't available to him as a defense:

> [D]eadly force must be confined to repulsion of the robber at the moment that the robber exerts force or exhibits a threat of force but that, once the imminent threat of death or serious bodily harm dissipates, a lethal response is no longer warranted. (672)

What if the danger of a deadly attack won't go away "at the moment" of the crime but will inevitably and eventually come back? Is *inevitable* harm the same as *imminent* harm? Let's look at what the court said about what happened to Xi Van Ha (*Xi Van Ha v. State* 1995).

Late in the evening, Buu Van Truong, a Vietnamese fisherman working in Alaska, attacked another fisherman Xi Van Ha with a hammer and threatened to kill Ha. At 1:30 P.M. the next day, Ha shot Buu in the back, killing him instantly. On appeal from a murder conviction, the Alaska Supreme Court affirmed the conviction. Here's why. According to the court:

> There was sufficient evidence that a reasonable person in Ha's position would have feared death or serious physical injury from Buu. Buu had threatened Ha with death. Buu was a violent man who nursed grudges and who was likely to carry out his threat someday. Moreover, the evidence suggested that Buu came from a violent, criminal clan, and that Buu's relatives might very well help Buu carry out the threat—or might carry it out themselves if Buu was unable.
>
> In sum, Ha produced evidence to justify the remarks his attorney made during the defense opening statement: "A threat from Buu that he would kill you was as good, had as much weight, as a kiss on the cheek by a Mafia godfather. That's how deadly Buu's threats were. From knowing Buu, Ha knew that there was no escape. Buu comes from a family of thugs who have a reputation for violence and extortion. Ha knew that he would have to deal with the family, or with Buu himself. Today, tomorrow, they would stalk him down."
>
> However, "inevitable" harm is not the same as "imminent" harm. Even though Ha may have reasonably feared that Buu (or one of Buu's relatives) would someday kill him, a reasonable fear of future harm does not authorize a person to hunt down and kill an enemy. (191)

Here's how U.S. Circuit Court Judge Frank Easterbrook, known for his pithy comments, put his position argument against inevitable danger: "'later' and 'imminent' are opposites" (*U.S. v. Haynes* 1998, 1090).

CASE

In* U.S. v. Haynes *(1998), the U.S. Seventh Circuit Court of Appeals held that a prisoner who was attacked wasn't in imminent danger.

Can a sneak attack be self-defense?

U.S. v. Haynes

143 F.3d 1089 (C.A.7 Wis. 1998)

HISTORY

Charles E. HAYNES (Defendant-Appellant) entered a conditional plea of guilty in the United States District Court for the Western District of Wisconsin, to assault. Haynes appealed. The Court of Appeals affirmed.

EASTERBROOK J.

FACTS

Nelson Flores-Pedroso was playing dominoes after lunch in the cafeteria of the federal prison in Oxford, Wisconsin, when Charles Haynes emerged from the kitchen and poured scalding oil on his head. Severely burned over 18% of his body,

(continues)

(continued)
Flores-Pedroso is disfigured for life. Haynes pleaded guilty to assault, and was sentenced to 33 months' imprisonment (consecutive to the 10-year term he was serving for a drug offense). The guilty plea reserved the right to argue on appeal that the district judge erred in foreclosing Haynes from arguing to the jury that the attack was justified as a measure of self-defense.

Self-defense? How can a sneak attack be self-defense? Haynes made an offer of proof that Flores-Pedroso was a bully who had a reputation for coercing smaller inmates (such as Haynes) to provide favors of all kinds—food, commissary items, and sex. About a month before the incident in the cafeteria, Flores-Pedroso began pressuring Haynes to use Haynes' position as a food preparer in the kitchen to do favors for him. Haynes refused, and in response Flores-Pedroso threatened to make Haynes his "bitch" (homosexual plaything).

For the next month staredowns and jostling occurred, while Flores-Pedroso kept up a stream of threats. One time Flores-Pedroso cornered Haynes in a bathroom, and Haynes thought that rape was imminent, but another inmate entered and Flores-Pedroso left.

A day before Haynes poured the oil, Flores-Pedroso picked up Haynes and slammed him to the ground within sight of a guard, who did nothing. On the day of the oil incident, Flores-Pedroso told Haynes that as soon as food service was closed for the afternoon he would "finish what he started." Haynes contends that he believed that he would be attacked as soon as he left the cafeteria, and that he struck first in order to protect himself.

OPINION

Under the law of the jungle a good offense may be the best defense. But although prisons are nasty places, they are not jungles—and it is the law of the United States rather than Hobbes' state of nature that regulates inmates' conduct. Haynes concedes that he never reported Flores-Pedroso to the guards or sought protection—protection a prison is constitutionally obliged to provide.

Haynes asserted in his offer of proof:

> He could not go to "the police"—a term used to describe the guards. If the guards elected to take him out of population, he would be forced to stay in administrative segregation which meant twenty-four hour per day lock-up. If his protective custody status resulted in a transfer, all the inmates of the receiving institution would know that he was in protective custody, for being victimized by another inmate and by being a "snitch," which would result in further victimization and perhaps invite an assault by not just one inmate, but several. If Haynes went to the guards and they did not believe him and left him in population, things would only get worse. He would certainly be attacked, not only by [Flores-] Pedroso, but by others who labeled him a "snitch." Haynes did not believe he could go to the guards and help himself in any appreciable way.

In other words, Haynes did not fancy the prospect of administrative segregation, feared the consequences of appearing to be an informer, and decided that it was better to take matters into his own hands. What his claim of self-defense comes down to is the proposition that an inmate is entitled to attack and maim a prison bully even if there is ample time to report the threats and obtain protection from the guards.

The district court ruled that Haynes would not be allowed to argue self-defense or inform the jury about Flores-Pedroso's threats. The evidence and line of defense Haynes wanted to pursue, as the district court saw things, was just a request for jury nullification—a plea to jurors to let the Davids of federal prisons smite the Goliaths, to give the predators a taste of their own medicine, without legal consequences. The judge ruled that an inmate must use available, lawful options to avoid violence, even if they find those options unpalatable. Haynes asks us to hold that the existence of lawful alternatives is irrelevant to a claim of self-defense.

All doubts about the role of lawful alternatives to one side, it is hard to see how Haynes' offer of proof conforms to the normal understanding of self-defense: a use of force necessary to defend against an imminent use of unlawful force. Haynes was not faced with an imminent use of force by Flores-Pedroso. There was a threat of action later that afternoon, but Flores-Pedroso had made unfulfilled threats before, and anyway "later" and "imminent" are opposites.

A judge may, and generally should, block the introduction of evidence supporting a proposed defense unless all of its elements can be established. But we need not dwell on timing, because we agree with the district judge's reason: absence of lawful alternatives is an element of all lesser-evil defenses [see "Choice of Evils," on p. 180], of which self-defense is one. When A threatens B, and B hits A, the defense receives the name "self-defense." When A threatens C, and B hits A, the name is "defense of another."

But in all of these cases, the defense fails if the use of force was unjustified. This is the idea behind the "imminence" requirement (if the threat is not imminent, a retreat or similar step avoids injury) as well as the requirement that the object of the threat prefer a lawful response to an unlawful one.

Prisons collect violent persons who have little respect for the law, which makes them hard to control without the use of devices such as segregation that are unpleasant in their own right. If prisoners could decide for themselves when to seek protection from the guards and when to settle matters by violence, prisons would be impossible to regulate. The guards might as well throw the inmates together, withdraw to the perimeter, and let them kill one another, after the fashion of *Escape From New York*.

Perhaps Haynes was hoping that a jury would have this view of the right way to manage prisons. But it is not the view reflected in the United States Code or the United States Constitution. A prisoner who requests protection from the guards without success (or who lacks time to do so) may defend himself with force proportioned to the threat. But Haynes, who listened to Flores-Pedroso's menaces for a month without seeking help, had no conceivable justification for a preemptive strike. The district judge correctly barred Haynes from making his proposed defense.

Affirmed.

QUESTIONS

1. List the facts and circumstances relevant to deciding whether Charles Haynes was entitled to the defense of self-defense.
2. State the court's definition of "imminent" danger.
3. Summarize the court's arguments for ruling against imminent danger.

What kinds of attacks justify the use of deadly force? The best-known cases involve individuals who need to kill to save their own lives, but self-defense is broader than that. It also includes killing someone who's about to kill a member of your family—or any innocent person for that matter.

Necessity doesn't limit you to killing someone who's going to *kill* either. You can also kill an attacker whom you reasonably believe is right now going to hurt you or someone else badly enough to send you or them to the hospital for the treatment of serious injury. This is what serious (sometimes called "grievous") bodily injury means in most self-defense statutes.

Some self-defense statutes go even further. They allow you to kill someone you reasonably believe is about to commit a serious felony against you that doesn't threaten either your life or serious bodily injury. These felonies usually include rape, sodomy, kidnapping, and armed robbery. But the list also almost always includes home burglary and, sometimes, even personal property (discussed in "Defense of Home and Property" later).

What kind of belief does self-defense require? Is it enough that you *honestly* believe the imminence of the danger, the need for force, and the amount of force used? No. Almost all statutes require that your belief also be reasonable; that is, a reasonable person in the same situation would have believed that the attack was imminent and that the need for force and the amount of force used were necessary to repel an attack.

CASE

In **People v. Goetz** *(1986), the 1980s' sensational "New York Subway Vigilante Case," the New York Court of Appeals examined these elements as applied to the defense against the armed robbery provision in New York's self-defense statute (Fletcher 1988, 18–27).*

Did he shoot in self-defense?

People v. Goetz

497 N.E.2d 41 (N.Y. 1986)

HISTORY

Bernhard Goetz (defendant) was indicted for criminal possession of a weapon, attempted murder, assault, and reckless endangerment. The Supreme Court, Trial Term, New York County, dismissed the indictment and the People appealed. The Supreme Court, Appellate Division affirmed, and the People appealed. The Court of Appeals reversed and dismissed, and reinstated all the counts of the indictment.

WACHTLER, CJ.

FACTS

On Saturday afternoon, December 22, 1984, Troy Canty, Darryl Cabey, James Ramseur, and Barry Allen boarded an IRT express subway train in the Bronx and headed south toward lower Manhattan. The four youths rode together in the rear portion of the seventh car of the train. Two of the four, Ramseur and Cabey, had screwdrivers inside their coats, which they said were to be used to break into the coin boxes of video machines.

Bernhard Goetz boarded this subway train at 14th Street in Manhattan and sat down on a bench toward the rear section of the same car occupied by the four youths. Goetz was carrying an unlicensed .38-caliber pistol loaded with five rounds of ammunition in a waistband holster. The train left the 14th Street station and headed toward Chambers Street.

Canty approached Goetz, possibly with Allen beside him, and stated, "Give me five dollars." Neither Canty nor any of the other youths displayed a weapon. Goetz responded by standing up, pulling out his handgun, and firing four shots in rapid succession. The first shot hit Canty in the chest; the second struck Allen in the back; the third went through Ramseur's arm and into his left side; the fourth was fired at Cabey, who apparently was then standing in the corner of the car, but missed, deflecting instead off of a wall of the conductor's cab.

After Goetz briefly surveyed the scene around him, he fired another shot at Cabey, who then was sitting on the end bench of the car. The bullet entered the rear of Cabey's side and severed his spinal cord.

All but two of the other passengers fled the car when, or immediately after, the shots were fired. The conductor, who had been in the next car, heard the shots and instructed the motorman to radio for emergency assistance. The conductor then went into the car where the shooting occurred and saw Goetz sitting on a bench, the injured youths lying on the floor or slumped against a seat, and two women who had apparently taken cover, also lying on the floor.

Goetz told the conductor that the four youths had tried to rob him. While the conductor was aiding the youths, Goetz headed toward the front of the car. The train had stopped just before the Chambers Street station and Goetz went between two of the cars, jumped onto the tracks, and fled.

Police and ambulance crews arrived at the scene shortly thereafter. Ramseur and Canty, initially listed in critical condition, have fully recovered. Cabey remains paralyzed and has suffered some degree of brain damage.

On December 31, 1984, Goetz surrendered to police in Concord, New Hampshire, identifying himself as the gunman being sought for the subway shootings in New York nine days earlier.

Later that day, after receiving *Miranda* warnings, he made two lengthy statements, both of which were tape recorded with his permission. In the statements, which are substantially similar, Goetz admitted that he had been illegally carrying a handgun in New York City for three years. He stated that he had first purchased a gun in 1981 after he had been injured in a mugging. Goetz also revealed that twice between 1981 and 1984 he had successfully warded off assailants simply by displaying the pistol.

According to Goetz's statement, the first contact he had with the four youths came when Canty, sitting or lying on the bench across from him, asked, "How are you?" to which he replied, "Fine." Shortly thereafter, Canty, followed by one of the other youths, walked over to the defendant and stood to his left, while the other two youths remained to his right, in the corner of the subway car.

Canty then said, "Give me five dollars." Goetz stated that he knew from the smile on Canty's face that they wanted to "play with me." Although he was certain that none of the youths had a gun, he had a fear, based on prior experiences, of being "maimed."

Goetz then established "a pattern of fire," deciding specifically to fire from left to right. His stated intention at that point was to "murder, to hurt them, to make them suffer as much as possible." When Canty again requested money, Goetz stood up, drew his weapon, and began firing, aiming for the center of the body of each of the four.

Goetz recalled that the first two he shot "tried to run through the crowd but they had nowhere to run." Goetz then turned to his right to "go after the other two." One of these two "tried to run through the wall of the train, but . . . he had nowhere to go." The other youth (Cabey) "tried pretending that he wasn't with [the others]," by standing still, holding on to one of the subway hand straps, and not looking at Goetz. Goetz nonetheless fired his fourth shot at him.

He then ran back to the first two youths to make sure they had been "taken care of." Seeing that they had both been shot, he spun back to check on the latter two. Goetz noticed that the youth who had been standing still was now sitting on a bench and seemed unhurt. As Goetz told the police, "I said, 'you seem to be all right, here's another,'" and he then fired the shot which severed Cabey's spinal cord. Goetz added that "If I was a little more under self-control . . . I would have put the barrel against his forehead and fired." He also admitted that "If I had had more [bullets], I would have shot them again, and again, and again."

After waiving extradition, Goetz was brought back to New York and arraigned on a felony complaint charging him with attempted murder and criminal possession of a weapon. The matter was presented to a grand jury in January 1985, with the prosecutor seeking an indictment for attempted murder, assault, reckless endangerment, and criminal possession of a weapon. Neither the defendant nor any of the wounded youths testified before this grand jury.

On January 25, 1985, the grand jury indicted Goetz on one count of criminal possession of a weapon in the third degree (Penal Law § 265.02) for possessing the gun used in the subway shootings, and two counts of criminal possession of a weapon in the fourth degree (Penal Law § 265.01) for possessing two other guns in his apartment building. It dismissed, however, the attempted murder and other charges stemming from the shootings themselves.

Several weeks after the grand jury's action, the People, asserting that they had newly available evidence, moved for an order authorizing them to resubmit the dismissed charges to a second grand jury. Supreme Court, Criminal Term, after conducting an *in camera* [in the judge's chambers] inquiry, granted the motion. Presentation of the case to the second Grand Jury began on March 14, 1985. Two of the four youths, Canty and Ramseur, testified. Among the other witnesses were four passengers from the seventh car of the subway who had seen some portions of the incident.

Goetz again chose not to testify, though the tapes of his two statements were played for the grand jurors, as had been done with the first grand jury.

On March 27, 1985, the second grand jury filed a ten-count indictment, containing four charges of attempted murder (Penal Law §§ 110.00, 125.25 [1]), four charges of assault in the first degree (Penal Law § 120.10[1]), one charge of reckless endangerment in the first degree (Penal Law § 120.25), and one charge of criminal possession of a weapon in the second degree (Penal Law § 265.03 [possession of a loaded firearm with intent to use it unlawfully against another]). Goetz was arraigned on this indictment on March 28, 1985, and it was consolidated with the earlier three-count indictment.

On October 14, 1985, Goetz moved to dismiss the charges contained in the second indictment, alleging, among other things, that the prosecutor's instructions to that grand jury on the defense of justification were erroneous and prejudicial to the defendant so as to render its proceedings defective.

On November 25, 1985, while the motion to dismiss was pending before Criminal Term, a column appeared in the *New York Daily News* containing an interview which the columnist had conducted with Darryl Cabey the previous day in Cabey's hospital room. The columnist claimed that Cabey had told him in this interview that the other three youths had all approached Goetz with the intention of robbing him.

The day after the column was published, a New York City police officer informed the prosecutor that

(continues)

(continued)

he had been one of the first police officers to enter the subway car after the shootings and that Canty had said to him, "We were going to rob [Goetz]." The prosecutor immediately disclosed this information to the Court and to defense counsel, adding that this was the first time his office had been told of this alleged statement and that none of the police reports filed on the incident contained any such information.

In an order dated January 21, 1986, the Court, after inspection of the grand jury minutes held that the prosecutor, in a supplemental charge elaborating upon the justification defense, had erroneously introduced an objective element into this defense by instructing the grand jurors to consider whether Goetz's conduct was that of a "reasonable man in [Goetz's] situation."

The Court concluded that the statutory test for whether the use of deadly force is justified to protect a person should be wholly subjective, focusing entirely on the defendant's state of mind when he used such force. It concluded that dismissal was required for this error because the justification issue was at the heart of the case. [We disagree.]

OPINION

Penal Law article 35 recognizes the defense of justification, which "permits the use of force under certain circumstances." One such set of circumstances pertains to the use of force in defense of a person, encompassing both self-defense and defense of a third person (Penal Law § 35.15). Penal Law § 35.15(1) sets forth the general principles governing all such uses of force:

> A person may use physical force upon another person when and to the extent he reasonably believes such to be necessary to defend himself or a third person from what he *reasonably* [emphasis added] believes to be the use or imminent use of unlawful physical force by such other person.

Section 35.15(2) sets forth further limitations on these general principles with respect to the use of "deadly physical force":

> A person may not use deadly physical force upon another person under circumstances specified in subdivision one unless
>
> a. He reasonably *believes* [emphasis added] that such other person is using or about to use deadly physical force or
>
> b. He reasonably believes that such other person is committing or attempting to commit a kidnapping, forcible rape, forcible sodomy or robbery.

Section 35.15(2)(a) further provides, however, that even under these circumstances a person ordinarily must retreat if he knows that he can with complete safety to himself and others avoid the necessity of using deadly physical force by retreating.

Thus, consistent with most justification provisions, Penal Law § 35.15 permits the use of deadly physical force only where requirements as to triggering conditions and the necessity of a particular response are met. As to the triggering conditions, the statute requires that the actor "reasonably believes" that another person either is using or about to use deadly physical force or is committing or attempting to commit one of certain enumerated felonies, including robbery.

As to the need for the use of deadly physical force as a response, the statute requires that the actor "reasonably believes" that such force is necessary to avert the perceived threat. While the portion of section 35.15(2)(b) pertaining to the use of deadly physical force to avert a felony such as robbery does not contain a separate "retreat" requirement, it is clear from reading subdivisions (1) and (2) of section 35.15 together, as the statute requires, that the general "necessity" requirement in subdivision (1) applies to all uses of force under section 35.15, including the use of deadly physical force under subdivision (2)(b).

Because the evidence before the second Grand Jury included statements by Goetz that he acted to protect himself from being maimed or to avert a robbery, the prosecutor correctly chose to charge the justification defense in section 35.15 to the Grand Jury. The prosecutor properly instructed the grand jurors to consider whether the use of deadly physical force was justified to prevent either serious physical injury or a robbery, and, in doing so, to separately analyze the defense with respect to each of the charges. He elaborated upon the prerequisites for the use of deadly physical force essentially by reading or paraphrasing the language in Penal Law § 35.15. The defense does not contend that he committed any error in this portion of the charge.

When the prosecutor had completed his charge, one of the grand jurors asked for clarification of the term "reasonably believes." The prosecutor responded by instructing the grand jurors that they were to consider the circumstances of the incident and determine "whether the defendant's conduct was that of a reasonable man in the defendant's situation." It is this response by the prosecutor—and specifically his use of "a reasonable man"—which is the basis for the dismissal of the charges by the lower courts. As expressed repeatedly in the Appellate Division's plurality opinion, because section 35.15 uses the term "he reasonably believes," the appropriate test, according to that court, is whether a defendant's beliefs and reactions were "reasonable to him."

Under that reading of the statute, a jury which believed a defendant's testimony that he felt that his own actions were warranted and were reasonable would have to acquit him, regardless of what anyone else in defendant's situation might have concluded. Such an interpretation defies the ordinary meaning and significance of the term "reasonably" in a statute, and misconstrues the clear intent of the Legislature, in enacting section 35.15, to retain an objective element as part of any provision authorizing the use of deadly physical force.

Penal statutes in New York have long codified the right recognized at common law to use deadly physical force, under appropriate circumstances, in self-defense. These provisions have never required that an actor's belief as to the intention of another person to inflict serious injury be *correct* in order for the use of deadly force to be justified, but they have uniformly required that the belief comport with an *objective notion of reasonableness* [emphasis added]. . . .

The plurality below agreed with defendant's argument that the change in the statutory language from "reasonable ground," used prior to 1965, to "he reasonably believes" in Penal Law § 35.15 evinced a legislative intent to conform to the subjective standard.

We cannot lightly impute to the Legislature an intent to fundamentally alter the principles of justification to allow the perpetrator of a serious crime to go free simply because that person believed his actions were reasonable and necessary to prevent some perceived harm. To completely exonerate such an individual, no matter how aberrational or bizarre his thought patterns, would allow citizens to set their own standards for the permissible use of force. It would also allow a legally competent defendant suffering from delusions to kill or perform acts of violence with impunity, contrary to fundamental principles of justice and criminal law.

We can only conclude that the Legislature retained a reasonableness requirement to avoid giving a license for such actions. Statutes or rules of law requiring a person to act "reasonably" or to have a "reasonable belief" uniformly prescribe conduct meeting an objective standard measured with reference to how "a reasonable person" could have acted.

Goetz argues that the introduction of an objective element will preclude a jury from considering factors such as the prior experiences of a given actor and thus require it to make a determination of "reasonableness" without regard to the actual circumstances of a particular incident. This argument, however, falsely presupposes that an objective standard means that the background and other relevant characteristics of a particular actor must be ignored. To the contrary, we have frequently noted that a determination of reasonableness must be based on the "circumstances" facing a defendant or his "situation." Such terms encompass more than the physical movements of the potential assailant.

As just discussed, these terms include any relevant knowledge the defendant had about that person. They also necessarily bring in the physical attributes of all persons involved, including the defendant. Furthermore, the defendant's circumstances encompass any prior experiences he had which could provide a reasonable basis for a belief that another person's intentions were to injure or rob him or that the use of deadly force was necessary under the circumstances.

Accordingly, a jury should be instructed to consider this type of evidence in weighing the defendant's actions. The jury must first determine whether the defendant had the requisite beliefs under section 35.15, that is, whether he believed deadly force was necessary to avert the imminent use of deadly force or the commission of one of the felonies enumerated therein. If the People do not prove beyond a reasonable doubt that he did not have such beliefs, then the jury must also consider whether these beliefs were reasonable. The jury would have to determine, in light of all the "circumstances," as explicated above, if a reasonable person could have had these beliefs.

(continues)

(continued)

The prosecutor's instruction to the second Grand Jury that it had to determine whether, under the circumstances, Goetz's conduct was that of a reasonable man in his situation was thus essentially an accurate charge.

The order of the Appellate Division should be REVERSED, and the dismissed counts of the indictment reinstated.

QUESTIONS

1. Consider the following:
   a. New York tried Goetz for attempted murder and assault. The jury acquitted him of both charges. The jury said Goetz "was justified in shooting the four men with the silver-plated .38-caliber revolver he purchased in Florida." They did convict him of illegal possession of a firearm, for which the court sentenced Goetz to one year in jail.
   b. Following the sentencing, Goetz told the court: "This case is really more about the deterioration of society than it is about me. . . . I believe society needs to be protected from criminals."
   c. Criminal law professor George Fletcher followed the trial closely. After the acquittal, he commented:

      > The facts of the Goetz case were relatively clear, but the primary fight was over the moral interpretation of the facts. . . . I am not in the slightest bit convinced that the four young men were about to mug Goetz. If he had said, "Listen buddy, I wish I had $5, but I don't," and walked to the other side of the car the chances are 60–40 nothing would have happened. Street-wise kids like that are more attuned to the costs of their behavior than Goetz was. (quoted in Roberts 1989)

      If Professor Fletcher is right, was Goetz justified in shooting?
2. Under what circumstances can people use deadly force, according to the New York statutes cited in the opinion?
3. Do you agree with those circumstances?
4. Would you add more? Remove some? Which ones? Why?
5. Were Goetz's shots a preemptive strike? Retaliation? Necessary for self-protection? Explain.

LO 6

Retreat

What if you can avoid an attack by escaping? Do you have to retreat? Or can you stand your ground and fight back? According to Richard Maxwell Brown (1991), the leading modern authority on American violence, "As far back as the thirteenth century, English common law dealt harshly with the act of homicide" (3). The burden was on defendants to prove their innocence, and no one could prove innocence unless he (all homicides were committed by men) proved he'd "retreated to the wall." The English common law "retreat to the wall" survived in a minority of American states:

> But one of the most important transformations in American legal and social history occurred in the nineteenth century when the nation as a whole repudiated the English common-law tradition in favor of an American theme of no duty to retreat: that one was legally justified in standing one's ground to kill in self-defense.
>
> Recognized at the time as a crucial change in the "American mind," it was a combination of Eastern legal authorities and Western judges who wrought the legal transformation from an English law that, as they saw it, upheld cowardice to an American law suited to the bravery of the "true man." The centuries-long English legal severity against homicide was replaced in our country by a proud new tolerance for killing in situations where it might have been avoided by obeying a legal duty to retreat. (5)

Who was this "true man"? According to Jeannie Suk (2008), various social meanings contributed to the definition. A true man was honest; he made decisions based on what he believed to be true, and he shouldn't have to flee from attack because he'd done nothing wrong to provoke or deserve the attack. The "true" man also did whatever he had to do to provide for his wife and children; he was the source of strength for his vulnerable dependents. The true man's duty to his family extended to his country:

> True men were patriots and protectors of the nation who would fight if necessary . . . to safeguard the legal rights fundamental to freedom. They had a sense of civic responsibility tied to the duty to ensure the rule of law and leadership of the nation. (Suk 2008, 245)

LO 6, LO 7

stand-your-ground rule, if you didn't start a fight, you can stand your ground and kill to defend yourself without retreating from any place you have a right to be

retreat rule, you have to retreat from an attack if you reasonably believe (1) that you're in danger of death or serious bodily harm *and* (2) that backing off won't unreasonably put you in danger of death or serious bodily harm

Relying on these meanings, judges and legislators generalized the right to self-defense into the majority stand-your-ground rule; namely, if he didn't start the fight, he could stand his ground and kill to "defend himself without retreating from any place he had a right to be" (245).

The minority rule, the retreat rule, says you have to retreat, if you reasonably believe

1. that you're in danger of death or serious bodily harm and
2. that backing off won't unreasonably put you in danger of death or serious bodily harm.

LO 8

castle exception, when you're attacked in your home, you can stand your ground and use deadly force to fend off an unprovoked attack, but only if you reasonably believe the attack threatens death or serious bodily injury

States that require retreat have carved out an exception to the retreat doctrine. According to this castle exception, when you're attacked in your home, you can stand your ground and use deadly force to fend off an unprovoked attack, but only if you reasonably believe the attack threatens death or serious bodily injury (*State v. Kennamore* 1980, 858).

Later on in this chapter, we'll explore the explosion of new statutes that vastly expand ordinary people's power to defend themselves in their homes and in public places. But now, let's look at how the elements of self-defense apply to domestic violence, especially battered women.

DOMESTIC VIOLENCE

What if two men live in the same "castle"? Can they both stand their ground? It was these cases of cohabitants that gave birth to the rules governing domestic violence. One of the most famous and most often-cited cohabitant cases, the World War I era *People v. Tomlins* (1914), involved a man who killed his 22-year-old son, who had attacked him in their cottage. Then Judge Cardozo (later a U.S. Supreme Court Associate Justice), wrote:

> It is not now and never has been the law that a man assailed in his own dwelling is bound to retreat. If assailed there, he may stand his ground and resist the attack. He is under no duty to take to the fields and the highways, a fugitive from his own home. More than 200 years ago it was said by Lord Chief Justice Hale (1 Hale's Pleas of the Crown, 486):
>
> > In case a man "is assailed in his own house, he need not flee as far as he can, as in other cases of self-defense for he hath the protection of his house to excuse him from flying, as that would be to give up the protection of his house to his adversary by flight."

cohabitant exception, in the exception jurisdictions that follow the retreat rule, people who live in the same home don't have to retreat

The Connecticut Supreme Court relied on family violence to back up its creation of the cohabitant exception to the Connecticut retreat rule, even though it involved male roommates (*State v. Shaw* 1981). James Shaw Jr. rented one of two bedrooms in Wilson's owner-occupied house. They got into an argument, which escalated into a fist-fight. (Each claimed that the other started the fight.) Wilson went to his bedroom and grabbed his .30-30 Winchester rifle, intending to order Shaw to leave. Shaw went to his bedroom and got his .22 revolver. Weapons in hand, they both entered the kitchen from their bedrooms. Shaw fired five or six shots hitting Wilson three times (562).

The timing of the case coincided with the growing public recognition that domestic violence was a "serious and widespread crime." The feminist movement had convincingly argued that women were victims of violence at home. Law enforcement was beginning to treat domestic violence as a crime and not a private family matter (Suk 2008, 250). According to the court:

> In the great majority of homicides the killer and the victim are relatives or close acquaintances. We cannot conclude that the Connecticut legislature intended to sanction the reenactment of the climactic scene from "High Noon" in the familial kitchens of this state. (*State v. Shaw* 1981, 566)

By the late 1990s, the recognition that battered women cases fit the "real man" protecting his castle paradigm had definitely influenced the law of self-defense. Courts in several castle doctrine states have adopted rules that allow women to "stand their ground and kill their batterers." All of these courts supported their decisions with a "sympathetic understanding of the dynamics of domestic violence and its victims" (Suk 2008, 252).

CASE

In* State v. Stewart *(1988), the Supreme Court of Kansas ruled that Peggy Stewart, a battered woman, wasn't justified in killing her husband while he was asleep in their home.

Was she justified in shooting her cohabitant husband while he was asleep?

State v. Stewart

763 P.2d 572 (Kans. 1988)

HISTORY

Peggy Stewart (Defendant) was charged with murder in the first degree of her husband. The Butler District Court entered verdict of not guilty. The prosecution filed a special appeal (called an "appeal on a question reserved"). The reserved question was: In future cases does the statutory justification for the use of deadly force in self-defense provided by K.S.A. 21–3211 justify a homicide committed by a battered wife where there is no evidence of a deadly threat or imminent danger contemporaneous with the killing?

The Supreme Court ruled that, in future cases, the statutory justification for use of deadly force in self-defense doesn't justify a homicide committed by a battered wife where there was no evidence of deadly threat or imminent danger contemporaneous with the killing. Appeal sustained. (Notice that this is not an appeal from the jury's verdict of acquittal. That's not legally possible because the state can't appeal a jury's acquittal. So Peggy Stewart's acquittal stands. The rule only applies to future cases.)

LOCKETT, J.

FACTS

Following an annulment from her first husband and two subsequent divorces in which she was the petitioner, Peggy Stewart married Mike Stewart in 1974. Evidence at trial disclosed a long history of abuse by Mike against Peggy and her two daughters from one of her prior marriages. Laura, one of Peggy's daughters, testified that early in the marriage Mike hit and kicked Peggy, and that after the first year of the marriage Peggy exhibited signs of severe psychological problems. Subsequently, Peggy was hospitalized and diagnosed as having symptoms of paranoid schizophrenia; she responded to treatment and was soon released. It appeared to Laura, however, that Mike was encouraging Peggy to take more than her prescribed dosage of medication.

In 1977, two social workers informed Peggy that they had received reports that Mike was taking indecent liberties with her daughters. Because the social workers did not want Mike to be left alone with the girls, Peggy quit her job. In 1978, Mike began to taunt Peggy by stating that Carla, her 12-year-old daughter, was "more of a wife" to him than Peggy.

Later, Carla was placed in a detention center, and Mike forbade Peggy and Laura to visit her. When Mike finally allowed Carla to return home in the middle of summer, he forced her to sleep in an un-air conditioned room with the windows nailed shut, to wear a heavy flannel nightgown, and to cover herself with heavy blankets. Mike would then wake Carla at 5:30 A.M. and force her to do all the housework. Peggy and Laura were not allowed to help Carla or speak to her.

When Peggy confronted Mike and demanded that the situation cease, Mike responded by holding a shotgun to Peggy's head and threatening to kill her. Mike once kicked Peggy so violently in the chest and ribs that she required hospitalization. Finally, when Mike ordered Peggy to kill and bury Carla, she filed for divorce. Peggy's attorney in the divorce action testified in the murder trial that Peggy was afraid for both her and her children's lives.

One night, in a fit of anger, Mike threw Carla out of the house. Carla, who was not yet in her teens, was forced out of the home with no money, no coat, and no place to go. When the family heard that Carla was in Colorado, Mike refused to allow Peggy to contact or even talk about Carla.

Mike's intimidation of Peggy continued to escalate. One morning, Laura found her mother hiding on the school bus, terrified and begging the driver to take her to a neighbor's home. That Christmas, Mike threw the turkey dinner to the floor, chased Peggy outside, grabbed her by the hair, rubbed her face in the dirt, and then kicked and beat her.

After Laura moved away, Peggy's life became even more isolated. Once, when Peggy was working at a cafe, Mike came in and ran all the customers off with a gun because he wanted Peggy to go home and have sex with him right that minute. He abused both drugs and alcohol, and amused himself by terrifying Peggy, once waking her from a sound sleep by beating her with a baseball bat. He shot one of Peggy's pet cats, and then held the gun against her head and threatened to pull the trigger. Peggy told friends that Mike would hold a shotgun to her head and threaten to blow it off, and indicated that one day he would probably do it.

In May 1986, Peggy left Mike and ran away to Laura's home in Oklahoma. It was the first time Peggy had left Mike without telling him. Because Peggy was suicidal, Laura had her admitted to a hospital. There, she was diagnosed as having toxic psychosis as a result of an overdose of her medication. On May 30, 1986, Mike called to say he was coming to get her. Peggy agreed to return to Kansas. Peggy told a nurse she felt like she wanted to shoot her husband. At trial, she testified that she decided to return with Mike because she was not able to get the medical help she needed in Oklahoma.

When Mike arrived at the hospital, he told the staff that he "needed his housekeeper." The hospital released Peggy to Mike's care, and he immediately drove her back to Kansas. Mike told Peggy that all her problems were in her head and he would be the one to tell her what was good for her, not the doctors. Peggy testified that Mike threatened to kill her if she ever ran away again. As soon as they arrived at the house, Mike forced Peggy into the house and forced her to have oral sex several times.

The next morning, Peggy discovered a loaded .357 magnum. She testified she was afraid of the gun. She hid the gun under the mattress of the bed in a spare room. Later that morning, as she cleaned house, Mike kept making remarks that she should not bother because she would not be there long, or that she should not bother with her things because she could not take them with her. She testified she was afraid Mike was going to kill her.

Mike's parents visited Mike and Peggy that afternoon. Mike's father testified that Peggy and Mike were affectionate with each other during the visit. Later, after Mike's parents had left, Mike forced Peggy to perform oral sex. After watching television, Mike and Peggy went to bed at 8:00 P.M. As Mike slept, Peggy thought about suicide and heard voices in her head repeating over and over, "kill or be killed." At this time, there were two vehicles in the driveway and Peggy had access to the car keys. About 10:00 P.M., Peggy went to the spare bedroom and removed the gun from under the mattress, walked back to the bedroom, and killed her husband while he slept. She then ran to the home of a neighbor, who called the police.

When the police questioned Peggy regarding the events leading up to the shooting, Peggy stated that things had not gone quite right that day, and that when she got the chance she hid the gun under the mattress. She stated that she shot Mike to "get this

(continues)

(continued)

over with, this misery and this torment." When asked why she got the gun out, Peggy stated to the police:

> I'm not sure exactly what led up to it and my head started playing games with me and I got to thinking about things and I said I didn't want to be by myself again. I got the gun out because there had been remarks made about me being out there alone. It was as if Mike was going to do something again like had been done before. He had gotten me down here from McPherson one time and he went and told them that I had done something and he had me put out of the house and was taking everything I had. And it was like he was going to pull the same thing over again.

Two expert witnesses testified during the trial. The expert for the defense, psychologist Marilyn Hutchinson, diagnosed Peggy as suffering from "battered woman syndrome," or post-traumatic stress syndrome. The State's expert, psychiatrist Herbert Modlin, neither subscribed to a belief in the battered woman syndrome nor to a theory of learned helplessness as an explanation for why women do not leave an abusive relationship. Dr. Modlin testified that abuse such as repeated forced oral sex would not be trauma sufficient to trigger a post-traumatic stress disorder.

At defense counsel's request, the trial judge gave an instruction on self-defense to the jury. The jury found Peggy not guilty.

OPINION

The first issue is whether we have jurisdiction to hear this appeal. We will not entertain an appeal by the prosecution merely to determine whether the trial court committed error. The appeal by the prosecution must raise a question of statewide interest, the answer to which is essential to the just administration of criminal law. The question reserved is whether the trial judge erred in instructing on self-defense when there was no imminent threat to the defendant and no evidence of any argument or altercation between the defendant and the victim contemporaneous with the killing. We find this question and the related question of the extent to which evidence of the battered woman syndrome will be allowed to expand the statutory justification for the use of deadly force in self-defense are questions of statewide importance.

K.S.A. 21–3211 provides:

> A person is justified in the use of force against an aggressor when and to the extent it appears to him and he reasonably believes that such conduct is necessary to defend himself or another against such aggressor's imminent use of unlawful force."

The traditional concept of self-defense has posited one-time conflicts between persons of somewhat equal size and strength. When the defendant claiming self-defense is a victim of long-term domestic violence, such as a battered spouse, such traditional concepts may not apply. Because of the prior history of abuse, and the difference in strength and size between the abused and the abuser, the accused in such cases may choose to defend during a momentary lull in the abuse, rather than during a conflict. However, in order to warrant the giving of a self-defense instruction, the facts of the case must still show that the spouse was in imminent danger close to the time of the killing.

Where self-defense is asserted, evidence of the deceased's long-term cruelty and violence towards the defendant is admissible. In cases involving battered spouses, expert evidence of the battered woman syndrome is relevant to a determination of the reasonableness of the defendant's perception of danger. However, no jurisdictions have held that the existence of the battered woman syndrome in and of itself operates as a defense to murder.

In order to instruct a jury on self-defense, there must be some showing of an imminent threat or a confrontational circumstance involving an overt act by an aggressor. There is no exception to this requirement where the defendant has suffered long-term domestic abuse and the victim is the abuser. In such cases, the issue is not whether the defendant believes homicide is the solution to past or future problems with the batterer, but rather whether circumstances surrounding the killing were sufficient to create a reasonable belief in the defendant that the use of deadly force was necessary.

Here, there is an absence of imminent danger to defendant: Peggy told a nurse at the Oklahoma hospital of her desire to kill Mike. She later voluntarily agreed to return home with Mike when he telephoned her. She stated that after leaving the hospital Mike threatened to kill her if she left him again. Peggy showed no inclination to leave. In fact, immediately after the shooting, Peggy told the police that she was upset because she thought Mike would leave her. Prior to the shooting, Peggy hid the loaded gun. The cars were in the driveway and Peggy had access to the car keys. After being abused, Peggy went to bed with Mike at 8 P.M. Peggy lay there for two hours, then retrieved the gun from where she had hidden it and shot Mike while he slept.

Under these facts, the giving of the self-defense instruction was erroneous. Under such circumstances, a battered woman cannot reasonably fear imminent life-threatening danger from her sleeping spouse. We note that other courts have held that the sole fact that the victim was asleep does not preclude a self-defense instruction. In *State v. Norman,* 366 S.E.2d 586 (1988), cited by defendant, the defendant's evidence disclosed a long history of abuse. The North Carolina Court of Appeals held it was reversible error to fail to instruct on self-defense. The court found that, although decedent was napping at the time defendant shot him, defendant's unlawful act was closely related in time to an assault and threat of death by decedent against defendant and that the decedent's nap was "but a momentary hiatus in a continuous reign of terror."

There is no doubt that the North Carolina court determined that the sleeping husband was an evil man who deserved the justice he received from his battered wife. Here, similar comparable and compelling facts exist. But, as one court has stated: "To permit capital punishment to be imposed upon the subjective conclusion of the [abused] individual that prior acts and conduct of the deceased justified the killing would amount to a leap into the abyss of anarchy." *Jahnke v. State,* 682 P.2d 991, 997 (Wyo.1984).

Finally, our legislature has not provided for capital punishment for even the most heinous crimes. We must, therefore, hold that when a battered woman kills her sleeping spouse when there is no imminent danger, the killing is not reasonably necessary and a self-defense instruction may not be given. To hold otherwise in this case would in effect allow the execution of the abuser for past or future acts and conduct.

Our test for self-defense is a two-pronged one. We first use a subjective standard to determine whether the defendant sincerely and honestly believed it necessary to kill in order to defend. We then use an objective standard to determine whether defendant's belief was reasonable—specifically, whether a reasonable person in defendant's circumstances would have perceived self-defense as necessary. In *State v. Hundley,* we stated that, in cases involving battered spouses, "[t]he objective test is how a reasonably prudent battered wife would perceive [the aggressor's] demeanor." *Hundley* makes clear that it was error for the trial court to instruct the jury to employ solely a subjective test in determining the reasonableness of defendant's actions. The appeal is sustained.

DISSENT

HERD, J.

Psychologist Marilyn Hutchinson qualified as an expert on the battered woman syndrome and analyzed the uncontroverted facts for the jury. She concluded appellee was a victim of the syndrome and reasonably believed she was in imminent danger. In *State v. Hodges* (1986), we held it appropriate to permit expert testimony on the battered woman syndrome to prove the reasonableness of the defendant's belief she was in imminent danger.

Dr. Hutchinson explained to the jury at appellee's trial the "cycle of violence" which induces a state of "learned helplessness" and keeps a battered woman in the relationship. She testified appellee was caught in such a cycle. The cycle begins with an initial building of tension and violence, culminates in an explosion, and ends with a "honeymoon." The woman becomes conditioned to trying to make it through one more violent explosion with its battering in order to be rewarded by the "honeymoon phase," with its expressions of remorse and eternal love and the standard promise of "never again."

After all promises are broken time after time and she is beaten again and again, the battered woman falls into a state of learned helplessness where she gives up trying to extract herself from the cycle of violence. She learns fighting back only delays the honeymoon and escalates the violence. If she tries to leave the relationship, she is located and returned and the violence increases. She is a captive. She begins to believe her husband is omnipotent, and resistance will be futile at best.

It is a jury question to determine if the battered woman who kills her husband as he sleeps fears he will find and kill her if she leaves, as is usually claimed. Under such circumstances the battered woman is not under actual physical attack when she kills but such attack is imminent, and as a result she

(continues)

(continued)

believes her life is in imminent danger. She may kill during the tension-building stage when the abuse is apparently not as severe as it sometimes has been, but nevertheless has escalated so that she is afraid the acute stage to come will be fatal to her. She only acts on such fear if she has some survival instinct remaining after the husband-induced "learned helplessness."

Dr. Hutchinson testified the typical batterer has a dichotomous personality, in which he only shows his violent side to his wife or his family. A batterer's major characteristic is the need to blame all frustration on someone else. In a typical battering relationship, she said, the husband and wife are in traditional sex roles, the wife has low self-esteem, and the husband abuses drugs or alcohol. The husband believes the wife is his property and what he does to her is no one's business. There is usually a sense of isolation, with the woman not allowed to speak with friends or children. Overlying the violence is the intimation of death, often created by threats with weapons.

The majority claims permitting a jury to consider self-defense under these facts would permit anarchy. This underestimates the jury's ability to recognize an invalid claim of self-defense. The majority bases its opinion on its conclusion Stewart was not in imminent danger, usurping the right of the jury to make that determination of fact. The majority believes a person could not be in imminent danger from an aggressor merely because the aggressor dropped off to sleep. This is a fallacious conclusion. For instance, picture a hostage situation where the armed guard inadvertently drops off to sleep and the hostage grabs his gun and shoots him. The majority opinion would preclude the use of self-defense in such a case. I would deny this appeal.

QUESTIONS

1. List all the facts and circumstances relevant to deciding whether Peggy Stewart was in "imminent" danger.
2. Summarize the court majority's arguments against imminent danger. Summarize the dissent's arguments for imminent danger.
3. Consider the following comments:
   a. Retaliation, as opposed to defense, is a common problem in cases arising from wife battering and domestic violence. The injured wife waits for the first possibility of striking against a distracted or unarmed husband. The man may even be asleep when the wife finally reacts.
   b. Retaliation is the standard case of "taking the law into your own hands." There is no way, under the law, to justify killing a wife batterer or a rapist in retaliation or revenge, however much sympathy there may be for the wife wreaking retaliation. Private citizens cannot act as judge and jury toward each other. They have no authority to pass judgment and to punish each other for past wrongs (Fletcher 1988, 21–22).
   c. "The right to use force in the defense of one's person, family, habitation, lands, or goods is one of the unalienable rights of man. As it is a right not granted by any human code, no human code can take it away. It was recognized by the Roman law, declared by that law to be a natural right, and part of the law of nations. It is no doubt recognized by the code of every civilized State" (Thompson 1880, 546).
   d. "A man is not born to run away. The law must consider human nature and make some allowance for the fighting instinct at critical moments. In Texas it is well settled, as you might imagine, that a man is not born to run away" (DeWolfe Howe 1953, I:331).

   Are any of the statements relevant to battered woman domestic violence cases? Do you agree with the statements? Explain your answer.
4. In your opinion, did Peggy Stewart kill Mike Stewart in self-defense? As a preemptive strike? Or as retaliation? Defend your answer.

THE DEFENSE OF OTHERS

The law must consider human nature and make some allowance. Historically, self-defense meant protecting yourself and the members of your immediate family. Although several states still require a special relationship, the trend is in the opposite direction. Many states have abandoned the special relationship requirement altogether, replacing it with the defense of anyone who needs immediate protection from attack.

Several states that retain the requirement have expanded it to include lovers and friends. The "others" must have the right to defend themselves before someone else can claim the defense. This is important in cases involving abortion rights protestors. In *State v. Aguillard* (1990, 674), protestors argued they had the right to prevent abortions by violating the law because they were defending the right of unborn children to live. In rejecting the defense of others, the court said:

> The "defense of others" specifically limits the use of force or violence in protection of others to situations where the person attacked would have been justified in using such force or violence to protect himself. In view of *Roe v. Wade* and the provisions of the Louisiana abortion statute, defense of others as justification for the defendants' otherwise criminal conduct is not available in these cases. Since abortion is legal in Louisiana, the defendants had no legal right to protect the unborn by means not even available to the unborn themselves. (676)

THE DEFENSE OF HOME AND PROPERTY

The right to use force in the defense of one's person, family, habitation, lands, or goods is one of the natural and unalienable rights of man. As it is a right not granted by any human code, no human code can take it away. It was recognized by the Roman law; it was declared by that law to be a natural right and a part of the law of nations. It is no doubt recognized by the code of every civilized State (Thompson 1880, 546).

The right to use force to defend your home is rooted deeply in the common law idea that "a man's home is his castle." As early as 1604, Sir Edward Coke, the great common law judge, in his report of *Semayne's Case*, wrote:

> The house of everyone is to him his castle and fortress, as well for his defense against injury and violence, as for his repose; and although the life of a man is a thing precious and favored in law . . . if thieves come to a man's house to rob him, or murder, and the owner or his servants kill any of the thieves in defense of himself and his house, it is not felony and he shall lose nothing. (*State v. Mitcheson* 1977, 1122)

The most impassioned statement of the supreme value placed on the sanctity of homes came from the Earl of Chatham during a debate in the British Parliament in 1764:

> The poorest man may in his cottage bid defiance to all the forces of the Crown. It may be frail; its roof may shake; the wind may blow through it; the storm may enter; the rain may enter; but the King of England may not enter; all his force dares not cross the threshold of the ruined tenement. (quoted in Hall 1991, 2:4)

Don't let the Earl of Chatham's moving words lure you into thinking you can automatically kill an intruder to defend the sanctity of your home. Sir William Blackstone (1769), in his eighteenth-century *Commentaries* (the best-known—and often the only known—law book to American lawyers at that time), argues that the right is broad but limited. He writes:

> If any person attempts to break open a house in the nighttime and shall be killed in such attempt, the slayer shall be acquitted and discharged. This reaches not to the breaking open of any house in the daytime, unless it carries with it an attempt of robbery. (180)

You can see that the defense was limited to nighttime invasions, except for breaking into homes to commit daytime robberies. Most modern statutes limit the use of deadly force to cases where it's reasonable to believe intruders intend to commit crimes of violence (like homicide, assault, rape, and robbery) against occupants.

curtilage, the area immediately surrounding the home

Statutes vary as to the area that the use of deadly force covers. Most require entry into the home itself. This doesn't include the curtilage, the area immediately surrounding the home. Many require entry into an occupied home. This means you can't set some automatic device to shoot whoever trips the switch when you're not home.

Homes are special places; they're not in the same category as our "stuff." Can you use force to protect your "stuff"? Not deadly force. But you can use the amount of nondeadly force you *reasonably* believe is necessary to prevent someone from taking your stuff. You also can run after and take back what someone has just taken from you.

But, as with all the justifications based on necessity, you can't use force if there's time to call the police. For example, O. J. Simpson and his friends burst into a Las Vegas hotel room, with guns drawn and O. J. demanding, "I want my stuff! I want my stuff!" At his trial later for armed robbery and burglary, his argument that he was justified didn't work. He had time to call the police (ABC News, 2007).

LO 9

THE NEW "CASTLE LAWS": "RIGHT TO DEFEND" OR "LICENSE TO KILL"?

Self-defense is undergoing an epochal transformation. Since 2005, more than forty states have passed or proposed new "Castle Doctrine" legislation intended to expand the right to use deadly force in self-defense (see Figure 5.1) (Suk 2008, 237).

The first castle doctrine passed the Florida legislature in October 2005, unanimously in the state senate and by a hefty majority, 94–20, in the state house of representatives. The Florida Personal Protection Law (2009) became the model for most of the new castle laws. It includes the following provisions:

FIGURE 5.1 CASTLE DOCTRINE MAP UPDATE FOR JANUARY 2009

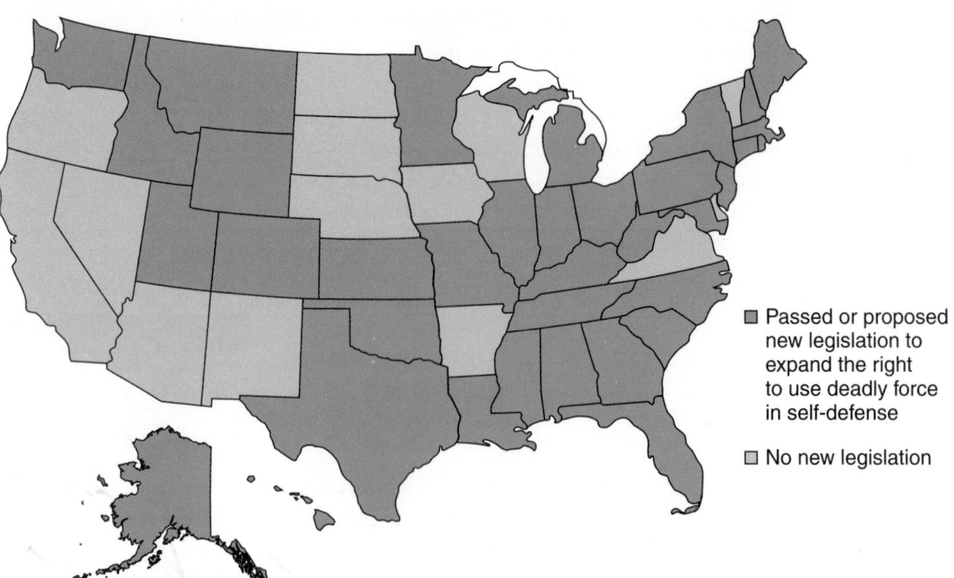

Source: "Tekel," University of Oregon law student blog, http://tekel.wordpress.com/2009/01/24/castle-doctrine-map-update-for-January-2009/.

Section 776.012.

A person is justified in using . . . deadly force and does not have a duty to retreat if:

(1) He or she reasonably believes that such force is necessary to prevent imminent death or great bodily harm to himself or herself or another or to prevent the imminent commission of a forcible felony; or

(2) Under those circumstances permitted pursuant to Section 776.013.

Section 776.013.

(1) A person is presumed to have held a reasonable fear of imminent peril of death or great bodily harm to himself or herself or another when using defensive force that is intended or likely to cause death or great bodily harm to another if:

  (a) The person against whom the defensive force was used was in the process of unlawfully and forcefully entering, or had unlawfully and forcibly entered, a dwelling, residence, or occupied vehicle, or if that person had removed or was attempting to remove another against that person's will from the dwelling, residence, or occupied vehicle; and

  (b) The person who uses defensive force knew or had reason to believe that an unlawful and forcible entry or unlawful and forcible act was occurring or had occurred. . . .

(3) A person who is not engaged in an unlawful activity and who is attacked in any other place where he or she has a right to be has no duty to retreat and has the right to stand his or her ground and meet force with force, including deadly force if he or she reasonably believes it is necessary to do so to prevent death or great bodily harm to himself or herself or another or to prevent the commission of a forcible felony.

(4) A person who unlawfully and by force enters or attempts to enter a person's dwelling, residence, or occupied vehicle is presumed to be doing so with the intent to commit an unlawful act involving force or violence.

(5) As used in this section, the term:

  (a) "Dwelling" means a building or conveyance of any kind, including any attached porch, whether the building or conveyance is temporary or permanent, mobile or immobile, which has a roof over it, including a tent, and is designed to be occupied by people lodging therein at night.

  (b) "Residence" means a dwelling in which a person resides either temporarily or permanently or is visiting as an invited guest.

  (c) "Vehicle" means a conveyance of any kind, whether or not motorized, which is designed to transport people or property.

Section 776.032.

(1) A person who uses force as permitted in Sections 776.012 and 776.013 is justified in using such force and is immune from criminal prosecution and civil action for the use of such force, unless the person against whom force was used is a law enforcement officer who was acting in the performance of his or her official duties, and the officer identified himself or herself in accordance with any applicable law, or the person using force knew or reasonably should have known that the person was a law enforcement officer. As used in this subsection, the term "criminal prosecution" includes arresting, detaining in custody, and charging or prosecuting the defendant.

(2) A law enforcement agency may use standard procedures for investigating the use of force as described in subsection (1), but the agency may not arrest the person for using force unless it determines that there is probable cause that the force that was used was unlawful.

TABLE 5.1

Summary of Florida Castle Law Changes
1. Abolished the duty to retreat rule
2. Replaced the common law "reasonable person" requirement, which placed the burden on defendants to prove the reasonableness of their actions with a presumption of reasonableness or fear. The presumption shifts the burden of proof to prosecutors, forcing them to disprove reasonableness. Proving this negative, always a very difficult burden, makes the reasonableness presumption almost unrebuttable.
3. Extended the right to use deadly force outside the home to "any place you have a right to be"
4. Broadened the legitimate circumstances where deadly force applies, including threats to property and threats that aren't imminent
5. Created blanket criminal and civil immunity for anyone using force permitted by the law (This immunity is broader than law enforcement officers' immunity.) (Jansen and Nugent-Borakove 2008, 5–6)

(3) The court shall award reasonable attorney's fees, court costs, compensation for loss of income, and all expenses incurred by the defendant in defense of any civil action brought by a plaintiff if the court finds that the defendant is immune from prosecution as provided in subsection (1).

Table 5.1 summarizes the changes created by the Florida Castle Law.

LO 10

"Right to Defend" or "License to Kill"?

Opponents and supporters of the castle laws see them in fundamentally different ways. Supporters claim them as the public reasserting fundamental rights. Marion Hammer, the first woman president of the National Rifle Association, says the castle law codifies the "right of the people to use any manner of force to protect their home and its inhabitants." She contends this right goes back to the 1400s, and that Florida prosecutors and courts took away that right by requiring that "law-abiding citizens who are attacked by criminals" have to retreat:

> When they take away your basic rights and freedoms, every once in a while you have to take them back. No law abiding citizen should be forced to retreat from an attacker in their homes or any place they have a legal right to be. Under the existing law [before the castle law was enacted] you had a duty to try to run and maybe get chased down, and beat to death. Now, if you have a knife, firearm or pepper spray, you can use force to protect yourself. (Kleindienst 2005)

Don't confuse the U.S. Supreme Court cases *District of Columbia v. Heller* (2008) and *McDonald v. City of Chicago* (2010), discussed in Chapter 2, with the castle laws. *Heller* and *McDonald* both dealt with the Second Amendment guaranteed right to *have* a gun; the castle laws authorize individuals to *use* the guns they have the right to have.

Gun control advocates say the laws "are ushering in a violent new era where civilians may have more freedom to use deadly force than even the police." They're not a "right to defend"; they're a "license to kill" (Rather 2009). The Brady Campaign to Prevent Gun Violence, established by Jim Brady and his wife Sarah, sees the laws entirely differently. Brady was badly wounded and paralyzed during John Hinckley's attempt to assassinate President Reagan (Chapter 6). According to Peter Hamm, communications director for the campaign:

> The biggest myth in Florida is that this is about protecting people who use legitimate self-defense. This law sends a message to people who are potentially dangerous and have an itchy trigger finger that as long as they can make a reasonable case they were

> in fear, they can use deadly force against somebody. It's a particular risk faced by travelers coming to Florida for a vacation because they have no idea it's going to be the law of the land. If they get into a road-rage argument, the other person may feel he has the right to use deadly force. (Kleindienst 2005)

Why the Spread of Castle Laws Now?

There's no empirical research to help explain why so many states have adopted the "new castle laws." There was no similar reaction in the 1980s when Colorado's "make-my-day" law, enacted in 1985, expanded traditional self-defense to resemble in most respects the new laws. But there's plenty of speculation as to why these laws have proliferated now. Two commonly mentioned reasons are Americans' heightened consciousness and concern about their security since 9/11 and the lack of enough police officers to protect the public.

Florida and Mississippi are examples:

- During the series of hurricanes that battered Florida in 2005, "In a lot of these devastated areas, law enforcement would tell communities, 'You're on your own, we can't get to you.' So we needed to be sure that when people protected themselves, their families and their property, that they weren't gonna be prosecuted by some criminal-coddling prosecutor" (Rather 2009).
- With the cuts in law enforcement officers in Jackson, Mississippi, Police Chief McMillin "says he's waging a battle of attrition with a force that's nearly 200 officers short of the 600 the city needs." So he says it's no wonder that civilians are taking up the fight and using tools like the castle doctrine to help protect themselves:

> People are sick and tired of being victims. They're tired of being robbed. They're tired of their houses being broken into. They think that they have to take matters into their own hands if they're gonna be safe. (Rather 2009)

Cliff Cargill, a firearms instructor certified by the National Rifle Association, says business has been booming with Jackson's crime on the rise and the new laws on the books. "If I'm in my home, my place of business or my vehicle, I don't have to justify my existence in my surroundings. If somebody breaks into my house to rob and/or do me harm, then I should be presumed innocent by anybody that comes to investigate that situation." Cargill says, "Packing heat is not paranoia, but common sense." There's an old saying, 'When seconds count, the police are only minutes away.' Well in the meantime, the clock's running. What's that intruder doing to you?" That's especially true in Jackson, where locals say the police are badly out-gunned (Rather 2009).

LAW ENFORCEMENT CONCERNS

In March 2007, the American Prosecutors Research Institute (APRI) held a symposium consisting of prosecution, law enforcement, government, public health, and academic experts from twelve states. The purpose? Discuss the possible unintended negative consequences for public safety created by the new castle laws. The main concerns included officers' use of force; operations and training requirements; increased investigation burdens; law enforcement attitudes and their impact on officer performance; and doubts that the castle laws deter crime (Jansen and Nugent-Barakove 2008, 8–9). Let's look briefly at each of these concerns.

Officers' Use of Force

Police officers are held to a higher standard than individuals when they use deadly force; officers aren't protected by the blanket immunity granted to citizens under the castle laws. Close scrutiny of officers can lead to internal discipline as well as civil and criminal liability. This imbalance between citizen and police power to use deadly force "has created a dangerous situation for law enforcement." Take officer safety during "no-knock" searches as one important example. Officers have to get a judge's approval to enter homes without warrants by demonstrating that it would be dangerous to knock and announce their presence. Individuals inside aren't held to similar restraints; under the new laws' presumption of reasonableness of danger provision, they can shoot officers (Jansen and Nugent-Barakove 2008, 8–9).

Operations and Training Requirements

Law enforcement officials attending the symposium noted that it's impossible to train officers effectively on the new laws. This is especially true of the presumption of reasonableness. Because the courts' interpretation of the new standard is only in its infancy, law enforcement officers may find it difficult—if not impossible—to determine whether the new law is being invoked properly. Officer training would have to be continually updated to help define when and where the castle expansion might apply (Jansen and Nugent-Barakove 2008, 9).

Increased Investigative Burdens

Before the castle laws, officers responding to "public places" crime scenes involving deadly force had to investigate only whether the danger was imminent and whether there was a duty to retreat. Now, they have to anticipate self-defense claims in far more cases. So both prosecutors and police officers have to gather evidence *and*

> demonstrate beyond a reasonable doubt that there was not a self-defense claim that would excuse or justify the use of deadly force, ideally before charges are brought. Proving a negative is very difficult when the evidence is in the hands of the defendant. . . . As a result . . . police chiefs, sheriffs, and prosecutors have officers and line prosecutors investigating each shooting or assault as a potential claim under the Castle Doctrine. The increased investigative time needed to prove or disprove self-defense claims are a major concern for already overworked and understaffed law enforcement.

The Effect of Law Enforcement Attitudes on Performance

The castle laws have also generated practical concerns about law enforcement attitudes and their effect on officer performance. For example, officers might feel like the dead "victims" deserved what they got, especially if both parties are criminals. So they don't carry out the more intensive investigation the castle laws require.

Because a large number of assaults occur outside the home, the expansion of no-retreat laws to areas outside the home will logically increase the number of defendants invoking the castle expansion. This will further burden police officers' time. Police officers may become apathetic to hearing such self-defense claims every time they respond to a crime scene, which will only benefit those who deny liability because of the presumption of fear.

Doubts That the Castle Laws Will Deter Crime

Symposium experts saw one possible positive effect of the castle laws—that they'll deter crime. But they believe that the deterrent effect depends on:

1. Whether the expansion of citizens' right to use deadly force is publicized widely so that citizens will know they've got the right
2. Whether would-be criminals appreciate that citizens are armed and might shoot, stab, or otherwise kill or seriously injure them

According to the symposium members, the possible negative consequence of the castle doctrine is that it raises questions about whether it's good public policy. People might feel safer because they have a right to defend themselves. Or they might feel less safe because they don't know who might be carrying a weapon, misinterpret behavior as threatening, and shoot them. Also, people may opt to carry weapons because they feel less safe, and people who already carried weapons might respond to threats by using force more readily.

With little to no empirical research at present to answer these important questions, the symposium advised that

> It would be prudent for states considering expansions to their self-defense laws to wait until there is better evidence that the unintended negative consequences of these laws do not outweigh the possible positive impacts. (13)

CASES UNDER NEW CASTLE LAWS

Let's look at some of the cases illustrating how citizens are using the new laws and how police, prosecutors, and courts are responding to citizens' actions under the laws (see Table 5.2).

TABLE 5.2

Expansion of New "Castle Laws"

STATE	YEAR	NAME	FACTS	DISPOSITION
Florida	2006	Jennifer Galas, 23	Prostitute shot and killed 72-year-old client with his gun	Not charged
Florida	2006	Robert Lee Smiley, 56	Taxi driver shot and killed drunk passenger outside cab after altercation	Charged with first-degree murder; trial jury deadlocked 9–3
Mississippi	2008	Sarbrinder Pannu, 31	Convenience store clerk followed shoplifter outside store and shot him twice	Charged with murder and acquitted
Mississippi	2008	Unidentified clerk in gas mart	Terrence Prior, 23, wearing a clown mask, shot after bursting through the door of a gas mart waving a gun, demanding money from the register; clerk followed him out the door, shot, and killed him outside the station; store had been robbed three times in recent weeks by a masked man	Not charged
Texas	2007	Joe Horn, 62	Retired computer consultant shot two men in the back and killed two men from his front porch, as they were leaving his neighbor's house with money and jewelry	Grand jury refused to indict
Arizona	2004	Harold Fish, 59	Retired teacher on a hike fatally shot Grant Kuenzli, 43, claiming the man and his dogs charged at him	Convicted and sentenced to ten years in prison before Arizona passed a castle law to protect people like Fish

Two Shootings in Florida

1. **JACQUELINE GALAS.** A New Port Richey prostitute, Jacqueline Galas, 23, said that a longtime client, Frank Labiento, 72, threatened to kill her and then kill himself last month. A suicide note he had left and other evidence supported her contention. The law came into play when Ms. Galas grabbed Mr. Labiento's gun and chose not to flee but to kill him. "Before that law," Mr. Halkitis said, "before you could use deadly force, you had to retreat. Under the new law, you don't have to do that." The decision not to charge Ms. Galas was straightforward, Mr. Halkitis said. "It would have been a more difficult situation with the old law," he said, "much more difficult." (Liptak 2006)
2. **ROBERT LEE SMILEY JR.** In November 2004, before the new law was enacted, Robert Lee Smiley Jr., then 56, a cabdriver in West Palm Beach, killed a drunken passenger in an altercation after dropping him off. Mr. Smiley killed Jimmie Morningstar, 43. A sports bar had paid Mr. Smiley $10 to drive Mr. Morningstar home in the early morning of November 6, 2004. Mr. Morningstar was apparently reluctant to leave the cab once it reached its destination, and Mr. Smiley used a stun gun to hasten his exit. Once outside the cab, Mr. Morningstar flashed a knife, Mr. Smiley testified at his first trial, though one was never found. Mr. Smiley, who had gotten out of his cab, reacted by shooting at his passenger's feet and then into his body, killing him.

   Cliff Morningstar, the dead man's uncle, said he was baffled by the killing. "He had a radio," Mr. Morningstar said of Mr. Smiley. "He could have gotten in his car and left. He could have shot him in his knee." Carey Haughwout, the public defender who represents Mr. Smiley, conceded that no knife was found. "However," Ms. Haughwout said, "there is evidence to support that the victim came at Smiley after Smiley fired two warning shots, and that he did have something in his hand."

   Smiley was charged and tried for murder. The jury deadlocked 9–3 in favor of convicting him. According to Henry Munnilal, the jury foreman, a 62-year-old accountant, "Mr. Smiley had a lot of chances to retreat and to avoid an escalation. He could have just gotten in his cab and left. The thing could have been avoided, and a man's life would have been saved." Mr. Smiley tried to invoke the new law, which does away with the duty to retreat and would almost certainly have meant his acquittal, but an appeals court refused to apply it retroactively.

   In April 2006, a Florida appeals court indicated that the new law, had it applied to Mr. Smiley's case, would have affected its outcome. "Prior to the legislative enactment, a person was required to 'retreat to the wall' before using his or her right of self-defense by exercising deadly force," Judge Martha C. Warner wrote. The new law, Judge Warner said, abolished that duty. (Liptak 2006)

Two Robberies in Mississippi

1. **SARBRINDER PANNU**

Rather: It was just after ten on a hot Mississippi night in August 2008 at a gas mart on the outskirts of Jackson. A man in a black SUV pulled into the lot, walked inside, grabbed a case of beer from the cooler, and walked right out the door. Without paying. A single case of beer wasn't going to break the bank, but according to the property owner, Mr. Surinder Singh, who operates several sister stores nearby, the man was just the latest of a seemingly endless stream of thieves.

Surinder Singh, owner of the BP station property: They come, they take stuff. . . . By the time we call the police they are already gone. And they know that. So when . . . when the police come, they say, "Well, call us if they come back."

Rather: But the clerk manning the counter that night wasn't willing to wait for anyone to come back. According to police, he ran outside with a .357 magnum, aimed at the man in the black SUV, and fired three shots.

Singh: Somebody got to stop him. The police cannot be there 24 hours. The only person who was there to stop him was the clerk. And he stopped him, whatever means he could.

Rather: Thirty-six-year-old James Hawthorne Jr. was pronounced dead at the hospital. (Rather 2009)

2. UNIDENTIFIED GAS MART CLERK

Rather: Just a few nights later, there was another shooting at a gas mart a few miles away; police say a man in a clown mask burst through the door waving a gun, demanding money from the register. It was the third time in recent weeks the store was robbed by a man in a clown mask, as captured on this surveillance video. But when the masked man ran out with the cash, this time the clerk didn't let him get away.

Reporter, WJTV Live Broadcast: The clerk went after him and shot him outside the store. . . .

Rather: Ten rounds, according to the police report. Twenty-three-year-old Terrence Prior was pronounced dead at the hospital. (Rather 2009)

Do the New Castle Laws protect the right to defend or provide a license to kill?

Marion Hammer, executive director of Unified Sportsmen of Florida, representative of the National Rife Association in Florida:

> When you are prosecuting law-abiding people for defending themselves against criminals, it's wrong and it has to be fixed. And the castle doctrine laws fixed that.

Gregory Hicks, Warren City attorney:

> I believe in protecting one's property. I believe in the fact that your home is your castle. But I don't believe you have the right to use that kind of deadly force on a prank. I'm sorry, that's not the way an ordered society acts.

Dan Rather, from "Dan Rather Reports":

> To shoot or not to shoot? For even the most seasoned police officer, it's the ultimate dilemma. A split-second choice that could prevent a violent crime or be a fatal mistake. But it's no longer just police who are deciding whether or not to pull the trigger. There's a new breed of laws that's expanding the rights of civilians to use deadly force. They are called the "castle doctrine" laws, and since 2005, they've been passed or proposed in more than 35 states.
>
> The new laws are not about the right to bear arms, but the right to use them. The National Rifle Association says the castle doctrine is restoring a tradition of self-defense that dates back to medieval England, when a man's home was considered his castle. But others say these laws are ushering in a violent new era where civilians may have more freedom to use deadly force than even the police.

Source: Rather 2009.

Instructions

Write a one-page essay stating what you believe best balances the right to defend yourself while protecting the lives of innocent people. Explain how your position represents the most ethical public policy regarding the right to bear arms. Back up your answer with "The New 'Castle Laws'" sections from your text.

LO 10

"CHOICE OF EVILS" (THE GENERAL DEFENSE OF NECESSITY)

The core of the choice-of-evils defense is the necessity to prevent imminent danger; in that respect, it's like all the defenses we've discussed up to now. The justifications based on the necessity of defending yourself, other people, and your home aren't controversial. Why? Because we see the attackers of ourselves, our families, and our homes as evil and the defenders as good. However, in the general choice-of-evils defense, the line between good and evil isn't always drawn as clearly as it is in self-defense and the defense of home.

LO 10

The choice-of-evils defense, also called the general defense of necessity, justifies the choice to commit a lesser crime to avoid the harm of a greater crime. The defense enjoys a long history in the law of Europe and the Americas.

choice-of-evils defense, also called the **general defense of necessity,** it justifies the choice to commit a lesser crime to avoid the harm of a greater crime

And throughout that history, the defense has generated heated controversy. Bracton, the great thirteenth-century jurist of English and Roman law, declared that what "is not otherwise lawful, necessity makes lawful." Other distinguished English commentators, such as Sir Francis Bacon, Sir Edward Coke, and Sir Matthew Hale in the sixteenth and seventeenth centuries, agreed with Bracton. The influential seventeenth-century English judge Hobart expressed the argument this way: "All laws admit certain cases of just excuse, when they are offended in letter, and where the offender is under necessity, either of compulsion or inconvenience."

On the other side of the debate, the distinguished nineteenth-century English historian of criminal law Judge Sir James F. Stephen believed that the defense of necessity was so vague that judges could interpret it to mean anything they wanted. In the mid-1950s, the distinguished professor of criminal law Glanville Williams (1961) wrote: "It is just possible to imagine cases in which the expediency of breaking the law is so overwhelmingly great that people may be justified in breaking it, but these cases cannot be defined beforehand" (724–25).

Early cases record occasional instances of defendants who successfully pleaded the necessity defense. In 1500, a prisoner successfully pleaded necessity to a charge of prison break; he was trying to escape a fire that burned down the jail. The most common example in the older cases is destroying houses to stop fires from spreading. In 1912, a man was acquitted on the defense of necessity when he burned a strip of the owner's heather to prevent a fire from spreading to his house (Hall 1960, 425).

The most famous case of imminent necessity is *The Queen v. Dudley and Stephens* (1884). Dudley and Stephens, two adults with families, and Brooks, an eighteen-year-old man without any family responsibilities, were lost in a lifeboat on the high seas. They had no food or water except for two cans of turnips and a turtle they caught in the sea on the fourth day. After twenty days (the last eight without food), perhaps a thousand miles from land and with virtually no hope of rescue, Dudley and Stephens—after failing to get Brooks to cast lots—told him that, if no rescue vessel appeared by the next day, they were going to kill him for food. They explained to Brooks that his life was the most expendable because they each had family responsibilities and he didn't.

The following day, no vessel appeared. After saying a prayer for him, Dudley and Stephens killed Brooks, who was too weak to resist. They survived on his flesh and blood for four days, when they were finally rescued. Dudley and Stephens were prosecuted, convicted, and sentenced to death for murder. They appealed, pleading the defense of necessity.

Lord Coleridge, in this famous passage, rejected the defense of necessity:

> The temptation to act here was not what the law ever called necessity. Nor is this to be regretted. Though law and morality are not the same, and many things may be immoral which are not necessarily illegal, yet the absolute divorce of law from morality would be of fatal consequence; and such divorce would follow if the temptation to murder in this case were to be held by law an absolute defense of it. It is not so.

> To preserve one's life is generally speaking a duty, but it may be the plainest and the highest duty to sacrifice it. War is full of instances in which it is a man's duty not to live, but to die. The duty, in case of shipwreck, of a captain to his crew, of the crew to the passengers, of soldiers to women and children; these duties impose on men the moral necessity, not of the preservation, but of the sacrifice of their lives for others. It is not correct, therefore, to say that there is any absolute or unqualified necessity to preserve one's own life.
>
> It is not needful to point out the awful danger of admitting the principle contended for.
>
> Who is to be the judge of this sort of necessity? By what measure of the comparative value of lives to be measured? Is it to be strength, or intellect, or what? It is plain that the principle leaves to him who is to profit by it to determine the necessity which will justify him in deliberately taking another's life to save his own.
>
> In this case, the weakest, the youngest, the most unresisting, was chosen. Was it more necessary to kill him than one of the grown men? The answer must be "No"—
> "So spake the Fiend, and with necessity, The tyrant's plea, executed his devilish deeds."
> It is not suggested that in this particular case, the deeds were "devilish," but it is quite plain that such a principle once admitted might be made the legal cloak for unbridled passion and atrocious crime.

Lord Coleridge sentenced them to death, but expressed his hope that Queen Victoria would pardon them. The queen didn't pardon them, but she almost did—she commuted their death penalty to six months in prison.

The choice-of-evils defense consists of proving that the defendant made the right choice, the only choice—namely, the necessity of choosing now to do a lesser evil to avoid a greater evil. The Model Penal Code choice-of-evils provision contains three elements laid out in three steps:

1. Identify the evils.
2. Rank the evils.
3. Choose based on the reasonable belief that the greater evil is imminent; namely, it's going to happen right now. (ALI 1985, 1:2, 8–22)

Simply put, the choice-of-evils defense justifies choosing to commit a lesser crime to avoid the harm of a greater crime. The choice of the greater evil has to be both imminent and necessary. Those who choose to do the lesser evil have to believe reasonably that their only choice is to cause the lesser evil to avoid the imminent greater evil.

The Model Penal Code (ALI 1985, 1:2, 8) lists all of the following "right" choices:

1. Destroying property to prevent spreading fire
2. Violating a speed limit to get a dying person to a hospital
3. Throwing cargo overboard to save a sinking vessel and its crew
4. Dispensing drugs without a prescription in an emergency
5. Breaking into and entering a mountain cabin to avoid freezing to death

The right choices are life, safety, and health over property. Why? Because according to the American Law Institute, the values of life, safety, and health always trump property interests (ALI 1985, 12).

The MPC doesn't leave the ranking of evils to individuals; it charges legislatures or judges and juries at trial with the task. Once an individual has made the "right" choice, she's either acquitted or it's considered a mitigating circumstance that can lessen the punishment. Courts rarely uphold choice-of-evils claims by defendants.

CASE

In* Toops v. State *(1994), *the court ruled that Terry Toops was entitled to a jury instruction on the defense of necessity in a drunk-driving case.*

Was driving drunk a lesser evil than a car out of control?

Toops v. State

643 N.E.2d 387 (Ind.App. 1994)

HISTORY

Terry Toops (Defendant) was convicted in the Cass Superior Court of operating a vehicle while intoxicated, operating a vehicle with 10% or more alcohol in the blood, operating a vehicle while intoxicated with a prior offense of operating a vehicle while intoxicated, and operating a vehicle with 10% or more alcohol in the blood with a prior offense of operating a vehicle while intoxicated. Toops appealed. The Court of Appeals reversed and remanded.

RUCKER, J.

FACTS

In the late evening hours of October 30, 1992, Terry Toops, Warren Cripe, and Ed Raisor were at Toops's home in Logansport, Indiana, drinking beer. Around 3:00 A.M. the following morning the trio decided to drive to a store in town. Because he was intoxicated, Toops agreed to allow Cripe to drive Toops's car. Toops sat in the front passenger seat and Raisor sat in the rear. Toops began to feel ill during the drive and stuck his head out the window for fresh air. In the meantime, Sheriff's Deputy Michael Day and Town Marshall Gary Layer were on routine patrol when they observed a person later identified as Toops hanging out the car window. The officers decided to investigate and made a u-turn to follow the car. Cripe saw the patrol car turn around and panicked because he was a minor and had been drinking. He let go of the steering wheel and jumped into the back seat of the car. The car began to careen out of control, leaving its lane, veering into the northbound lane of traffic, then veering back into the southbound lane. Toops finally slid into the driver's seat and brought the car under control.

The officers overtook the car and noted that Toops, whom they had originally seen hanging out of the car window, was now seated behind the steering wheel. The officers also noted that Cripe and Raisor were seated in the back seat of the car. At the officers' request, Toops submitted to a breath test that revealed a BAC of .21%. As a result Toops was arrested and charged with various alcohol related traffic offenses. He was also charged with Criminal Recklessness, Operating a Vehicle Without a Seat Belt, and Driving Left of Center, all of which the State dismissed prior to trial. After a trial by jury Toops was convicted on all remaining counts.

At the close of evidence Toops tendered the proposed jury instruction:

> The Defendant in this case has raised the defense of "Necessity" to excuse his assuming the controls of the vehicle at a time when he was intoxicated. "Necessity" involves a choice between two admitted evils where other options are unavailable. "Necessity" justifies illegal conduct if that conduct was the sole reasonable alternative available to Defendant given the circumstances of the case.
>
> In this case, the Defendant, Terry Toops, has admitted that he assumed control of the vehicle at a time when he was intoxicated. If you find that the Defendant's illegal conduct was justified by the circumstances, then you should find the Defendant "Not Guilty."

The trial court refused to give the instruction indicating "I cannot find that necessity is a recognized defense in the State of Indiana."

OPINION

The origins of the necessity defense are lost in antiquity. At least one writer advances the notion that it may be traced to the Bible itself, the analogy being the destruction of property to save human lives: "Then the mariners were afraid, and cried every man unto his god, and cast forth the wares that were in the ship into the sea, to lighten it of them."

The defense of necessity arose in the common law to excuse criminal conduct when a defendant was confronted with two evils and chose to engage in the prohibited conduct because it represented the lesser of the two evils. The underlying rationale is that to impose punishment upon a person who acted reasonably to avoid the greater harm serves neither to rehabilitate that person nor to deter others presented with a similar situation.

One of the leading decisions in this country recognizing the defense of necessity in a criminal law context is found in the landmark case of *United States v. Holmes,* 26 Fed.Cas. 360 (No. 15,383) (C.C.E.D.Pa.1842). In that case a ship sank at sea forcing the survivors to crowd into a leaking lifeboat. The crew decided to throw sixteen passengers overboard to prevent the boat from sinking. Holmes, a crew member who participated in tossing passengers into the sea, was convicted of manslaughter and sentenced to six months' imprisonment. On appeal Holmes argued that his conduct was justified given the choices confronting him. Although rejecting Holmes's argument because the method of determining who was to live or die was not fair, the court nonetheless accepted the principle that committing a harm, even the taking of human life, could sometimes be justified because it avoided the loss of even more lives, which was a greater harm.

The common law defense of necessity has evolved over the years and is often referred to as the "choice of evils" defense. The central element involves the emergency nature of the situation. Under the force of extreme circumstances, conduct that would otherwise constitute a crime is justifiable and not criminal because of the greater harm which the illegal act seeks to prevent. Neither this court nor our supreme court has had occasion to discuss the parameters or the applicability of the common law necessity defense in a criminal context. However, our supreme court has recognized the existence of the defense. In any event, contrary to the State's argument, to say that the common law defense of necessity is not a recognized defense in the State of Indiana is incorrect.

While there are no common law crimes in this State, the same is not true for common law defenses. The law in this jurisdiction is well settled that a defendant in a criminal case is entitled to have the jury instructed on any theory or defense which has some foundation in the evidence. There is no question that the evidence presented in this case raised a jury question as to whether Toops's control of the car while intoxicated, an illegal act, was necessary to prevent a greater harm, namely: an automobile collision potentially resulting in personal injury or property damage. Because the trial judge has a statutory duty to state to the jury "all matters of law which are necessary for their information in giving their verdict" the failure to give any instruction on the necessity defense in this case was error.

However, having determined error does not mean that we endorse the wording of Toops's proposed instruction. The instruction represents an incomplete statement of the law. That incompleteness is understandable however because no Indiana case has specifically set forth the elements of the necessity defense. In that regard we agree with the California court's holding in *People v. Pena* (1983), 197 Cal. Rptr. 264, 271, that the following requirements have traditionally been held to be prerequisites in establishing a necessity defense:

(1) the act charged as criminal must have been done to prevent a significant evil;

(2) there must have been no adequate alternative to the commission of the act;

(3) the harm caused by the act must not be disproportionate to the harm avoided;

(4) the accused must entertain a good-faith belief that his act was necessary to prevent greater harm;

(5) such belief must be objectively reasonable under all the circumstances; and

(6) the accused must not have substantially contributed to the creation of the emergency.

In the event of retrial on remand the foregoing elements should be incorporated into any tendered instruction on the defense of necessity.

Reversed and remanded.

QUESTIONS

1. List all the facts and circumstances relevant to deciding whether Terry Toops was justified in driving while he was drunk.
2. State the elements of the defense as the court identifies them. How do they compare with the elements stated in the text?
3. In your opinion, was Toops entitled to the necessity defense? Defend your answer with case and opinion details and the text section on the defense.

(continues)

(continued)

EXPLORING FURTHER

Choice of Evils

Was burglary the lesser evil?

State v. Celli, 263 N.W.2d 145 (S.D. 1978)

FACTS

On a cold winter day, William Celli and his friend, Glynis Brooks, left Deadwood, South Dakota, hoping to hitchhike to Newcastle, Wyoming, to look for work. The weather turned colder, they were afraid of frostbite, and there was no place of business open for them to get warm. Their feet were so stiff from the cold that it was difficult for them to walk.

They broke the lock on the front door and entered the only structure around, a cabin. Celli immediately crawled into a bed to warm up, and Brooks tried to light a fire in the fireplace. They rummaged through drawers to look for matches, which they finally located, and started a fire. Finally, Celli came out of the bedroom, took off his wet moccasins, socks, and coat; placed them near the fire; and sat down to warm himself. After warming up somewhat they checked the kitchen for edible food. That morning, they had shared a can of beans but had not eaten since. All they found was dry macaroni, which they could not cook because there was no water.

A neighbor noticed the smoke from the fireplace and called the police. When the police entered the cabin, Celli and Brooks were warming themselves in front of the fireplace. The police searched them but turned up nothing belonging to the cabin owners.

Did Celli and his friend choose the lesser of two evils?

DECISION

The trial court convicted Celli and Brooks of fourth-degree burglary. The appellate court reversed on other grounds, so, unfortunately for us, the court never got to the issue of the defense of necessity.

LO 11

CONSENT

defense of consent, the justification that competent adults voluntarily consented to crimes against themselves and knew what they were consenting to

Consent has nothing to do with necessity. Nevertheless, it can be a justification. The defense of consent is based on the idea that competent adults voluntarily consented to crimes against themselves and knew what they were consenting to. The heart of the defense of consent is the high value placed on individual autonomy in a free society. If mentally competent adults want to be crime victims, so the argument for the justification of consent goes, no paternalistic government should get in their way.

Consent may make sense in the larger context of individual freedom and responsibility, but the criminal law is hostile to consent as a justification for committing crimes. For all the noise about choice, you know already that except for the voluntary act requirement (discussed in Chapter 3), there are many examples of crimes where the freedom to choose one course of action instead of another is either a total fiction or very limited. We've seen some major examples in the chapters so far. There's the void-for-vagueness doctrine discussed in Chapter 2. Other examples were the mental state of negligence and the absence of mental fault in strict liability discussed in Chapter 4.

Individuals can take their own lives and inflict injuries on themselves, but in most states they can't authorize others to kill them or beat them. Let's look at how confined choice is in the defense of consent and examine some of the reasons. Here's an example from the Alabama Criminal Code:

Alabama Criminal Code (1977) Section 13a-2-7

(a) *In general.* The consent of the victim to conduct charged to constitute an offense or to the result thereof is a defense if such consent negatives a required element of the offense or precludes the infliction of the harm or evil sought to be prevented by the law defining the offense.

(b) *Consent to bodily harm.* When conduct is charged to constitute an offense because it causes or threatens bodily harm, consent to such conduct or to the infliction of such harm is a defense only if:

(1) The bodily harm consented to or threatened by the conduct consented to is not serious; or

(2) The conduct and the harm are reasonably foreseeable hazards of joint participation in a lawful athletic contest or competitive sport.

(c) *Ineffective consent.* Unless otherwise provided by this Criminal Code or by the law defining the offense, assent does not constitute consent if:

(1) It is given by a person who is legally incompetent to authorize the conduct; or

(2) It is given by a person who by reason of immaturity, mental disease or defect, or intoxication is manifestly unable and known by the actor to be unable to make a reasonable judgment as to the nature or harmfulness of the conduct; or

(3) It is given by a person whose consent is sought to be prevented by the law defining the offense; or

(4) It is induced by force, duress or deception.

In most states, the law recognizes only four situations where consent justifies otherwise criminal conduct:

1. No serious injury results from the consensual crime.
2. The injury happens during a sporting event.
3. The conduct benefits the consenting person, such as when a patient consents to surgery.
4. The consent is to sexual conduct. (Fletcher 1978, 770)

Fitting into one of these four exceptions is necessary, but it's not enough to entitle defendants to the defense. They also have to prove that the consent was voluntary, knowing, and authorized. **Voluntary consent** means consent was the product of free will, not of force, threat of force, promise, or trickery. Forgiveness after the commission of a crime doesn't qualify as voluntary consent. **Knowing consent** means the person consenting understands what she's consenting to; she's not too young or insane to understand. **Authorized consent** means the person consenting has the authority to give consent; I can't give consent for someone else for whom I'm not legally responsible.

voluntary consent, consent was the product of free will, not of force, threat of force, promise, or trickery

knowing consent, the person consenting understands what she's consenting to; she's not too young or insane to understand

authorized consent, the person consenting has the authority to give consent

CASE

In* State v. Shelley *(1997), *the court dealt with the sporting event exception.*

Did he consent to the attack?

State v. Shelley

929 P.2d 489 (Wash.App. 1997)

HISTORY

Jason Shelley was convicted in the Superior Court, King County, of second-degree assault, arising out of an incident in which Shelley intentionally punched another basketball player during a game. Shelley appealed. The Court of Appeals affirmed the conviction.

GROSSE, J.

FACTS

On March 31, 1993, Jason Shelley and Mario Gonzalez played "pickup" basketball on opposing teams at the University of Washington Intramural Activities Building (the IMA). Pickup games are not refereed by

(continues)

(continued)

an official; rather, the players take responsibility for calling their own fouls.

During the course of three games, Gonzalez fouled Shelley several times. Gonzalez had a reputation for playing overly aggressive defense at the IMA. Toward the end of the evening, after trying to hit the ball away from Shelley, he scratched Shelley's face and drew blood. After getting scratched, Shelley briefly left the game and then returned.

Shelley and Gonzalez have differing versions of what occurred after Shelley returned to the game. According to Gonzalez, while he was waiting for play in the game to return to Gonzalez's side of the court, Shelley suddenly hit him. Gonzalez did not see Shelley punch him. According to Shelley's version of events, when Shelley rejoined the game, he was running down the court and he saw Gonzalez make "a move towards me as if he was maybe going to prevent me from getting the ball." The move was with his hand up "across my vision." Angry, he "just reacted" and swung. He said he hit him because he was afraid of being hurt, like the previous scratch. He testified that Gonzalez continually beat him up during the game by fouling him hard.

A week after the incident, a school police detective interviewed Shelley and prepared a statement for Shelley to sign based on the interview. Shelley reported to the police that Gonzalez had been "continually slapping and scratching him" during the game. Shelley "had been getting mad" at Gonzalez, and the scratch on Shelley's face was the "final straw."

As the two were running down the court side by side, "I swung my right hand around and hit him with my fist on the right side of his face." Shelley asserted that he also told the detective that Gonzalez waved a hand at him just before Shelley threw the punch and that he told the detective that he was afraid of being injured.

Gonzalez required emergency surgery to repair his jaw. Broken in three places, it was wired shut for six weeks. His treating physician believed that a "significant" blow caused the damage.

During the course of the trial, defense counsel told the court he intended to propose a jury instruction that: "A person legally consents to conduct that causes or threatens bodily harm if the conduct and the harm are reasonably foreseeable hazards of joint participation in a lawful, athletic contest or competitive sport."

Although the trial court agreed that there were risks involved in sports, it stated that "the risk of being intentionally punched by another player is one that I don't think we ever do assume." The court noted, "In basketball you consent to a certain amount of rough contact. If they were both going for a rebound and Mr. Shelley's elbow or even his fist hit Mr. Gonzalez as they were both jumping for the rebound and Mr. Gonzalez's jaw was fractured in exactly the same way then you would have an issue."

Reasoning that "our laws are intended to uphold the public peace and regulate behavior of individuals," the court ruled "that as a matter of law, consent cannot be a defense to an assault." The court indicated that Shelley could not claim consent because his conduct "exceeded" what is considered within the rules of that particular sport:

> Consent is a contact that is contemplated within the rules of the game and that is incidental to the furtherance of the goals of that particular game. If you can show me any rule book for basketball at any level that says an intentional punch to the face in some way is a part of the game, then I would take another look at your argument. I don't believe any such rule book exists.

Later, Shelley proposed jury instructions on the subject of consent:

> An act is not an assault, if it is done with the consent of the person alleged to be assaulted. It is a defense to a charge of second degree assault occurring in the course of an athletic contest if the conduct and the harm are reasonably foreseeable hazards of joint participation in a lawful athletic contest or competitive sport.

The trial court rejected these, and Shelley excerpted. The trial court did instruct the jury about self-defense.

OPINION

First, we hold that consent is a defense to an assault occurring during an athletic contest. This is consistent with the law of assault as it has developed in Washington. A person is guilty of second-degree assault if he or she "intentionally assaults another and thereby recklessly inflicts substantial bodily harm."

One common law definition of assault recognized in Washington is "an unlawful touching with criminal intent." At the common law, a touching is unlawful when the person touched did not give consent to it, and it was either harmful or offensive. As our Supreme Court stated in *State v. Simmons*, "Where there is consent, there is no assault." The State argues that because *Simmons* was a sexual assault case, the defense of consent should be limited to that realm. We decline to apply the defense so narrowly.

Logically, consent must be an issue in sporting events because a person participates in a game knowing that it will involve potentially offensive contact and with this consent the "touchings" involved are not "unlawful." The rationale that courts offer in limiting consent as a defense is that society has an interest in punishing assaults as breaches of the public peace and order, so that an individual cannot consent to a wrong that is committed against the public peace.

Urging us to reject the defense of consent because an assault violates the public peace, the State argues that this principle precludes Shelley from being entitled to argue the consent defense on the facts of his case. If consent cannot be a defense to assault, then most athletic contests would need to be banned because many involve "invasions of one's physical integrity." Because society has chosen to foster sports competitions, players necessarily must be able to consent to physical contact and other players must be able to rely on that consent when playing the game. This is the view adopted by the drafters of the Model Penal Code:

> There are, however, situations in which consent to bodily injury should be recognized as a defense to crime. There is the obvious case of participation in an athletic contest or competitive sport, where the nature of the enterprise often involves risk of serious injury. Here, the social judgment that permits the contest to flourish necessarily involves the companion judgment that reasonably foreseeable hazards can be consented to by virtue of participation.

The more difficult question is the proper standard by which to judge whether a person consented to the particular conduct at issue. The State argues that when the conduct in question is not within the rules of a given sport, a victim cannot be deemed to have consented to this act. The trial court apparently agreed with this approach.

Although we recognize that there is authority supporting this approach, we reject a reliance on the rules of the games as too limiting. Rollin M. Perkins in *Criminal Law* explains:

> The test is not necessarily whether the blow exceeds the conduct allowed by the rules of the game. Certain excesses and inconveniences are to be expected beyond the formal rules of the game. It may be ordinary and expected conduct for minor assaults to occur. However, intentional excesses beyond those reasonably contemplated in the sport are not justified.

Instead, we adopt the approach of the Model Penal Code which provides:

> (2) *Consent to Bodily Injury*. When conduct is charged to constitute an offense because it causes or threatens bodily injury, consent to such conduct or to the infliction of such injury is a defense if:
>
> (b) the conduct and the injury are reasonably foreseeable hazards of joint participation in a lawful athletic contest or competitive sport or other concerted activity not forbidden by law.

The State argues the law does not allow "the victim to 'consent' to a broken jaw simply by participating in an unrefereed, informal basketball game." This argument presupposes that the harm suffered dictates whether the defense is available or not. This is not the correct inquiry. The correct inquiry is whether the conduct of defendant constituted foreseeable behavior in the play of the game.

Additionally, the injury must have occurred as a byproduct of the game itself. In *State v. Floyd*, a fight broke out during a basketball game and the defendant, who was on the sidelines, punched and severely injured several opposing team members. The defense did not apply because the statute "contemplated a person who commits acts during the course of play." There is a "continuum, or sliding scale, grounded in the circumstances under which voluntary participants engage in sport which governs the type of incidents in which an individual volunteers (i.e., consents) to participate."

The New York courts provide another example. In a football game, while tackling the defendant, the victim hit the defendant. After the play was over and all of the players got off the defendant, the defendant

(continues)

(continued)

punched the victim in the eye. . . . Initially it may be assumed that the very first punch thrown in the course of the tackle was consented to by defendant. The act of tackling an opponent in the course of a football game may often involve "contact" that could easily be interpreted to be a "punch." Defendant's response after the pileup to complainant's initial act of "aggression" cannot be mistaken. This was not a consented to act. *People v. Freer*, 381 N.Y.S.2d 976, 978 (1976).

The State may argue that the defendant's conduct exceeded behavior foreseeable in the game. Although in "all sports players consent to many risks, hazards and blows," there is "a limit to the magnitude and dangerousness of a blow to which another is deemed to consent." This limit, like the foreseeability of the risks, is determined by presenting evidence to the jury about the nature of the game, the participants' expectations, the location where the game has been played, as well as the rules of the game.

Here, taking Shelley's version of the events as true, the magnitude and dangerousness of Shelley's actions were beyond the limit. There is no question that Shelley lashed out at Gonzalez with sufficient force to land a substantial blow to the jaw, and there is no question but that Shelley intended to hit Gonzalez. There is nothing in the game of basketball, or even rugby or hockey, that would permit consent as a defense to such conduct. Shelley admitted to an assault and was not precluded from arguing that the assault justified self-defense; but justification and consent are not the same inquiry.

We AFFIRM.

QUESTIONS

1. According to the court, why can participants in a sporting event consent to conduct that would otherwise be a crime?
2. Why should they be allowed to consent to such conduct when in other situations (such as those enumerated in the Exploring Further cases that follow) they can't consent?
3. Should individuals be allowed to knowingly and voluntarily consent to the commission of crimes against themselves? Why or why not?
4. Why was Shelley not allowed the defense of consent in this case?
5. Do you agree with the court's decision? Relying on the relevant facts in the case, defend your answer.

EXPLORING FURTHER

Consent

1. Is shooting BB guns a sport?

State v. Hiott, 987 P.2d 135 (Wash.App. 1999)

FACTS

Richard Hiott and his friend Jose were playing a game of shooting at each other with BB guns. During the game, Jose was hit in the eye and lost his eye as a result. Richard was charged with third-degree assault. His defense was consent. Was he entitled to the defense?

DECISION

No, said the Washington Court of Appeals;

> Hiott argues that the game they were playing "is within the limits of games for which society permits consent." Hiott compares the boys' shooting of BB guns at each other to dodgeball, football, rugby, hockey, boxing, wrestling, "ultimate fighting," fencing, and "paintball." We disagree.
>
> The games Hiott uses for comparison, although capable of producing injuries, have been generally accepted by society as lawful athletic contests, competitive sports, or concerted activities not forbidden by law. And these games carry with them generally accepted rules, at least some of which are intended to prevent or minimize injuries. In addition, such games commonly prescribe the use of protective devices or clothing to prevent injuries.
>
> Shooting BB guns at each other is not a generally accepted game or athletic contest; the activity has no generally accepted rules; and the activity is not characterized by the common use of protective devices or clothing.
>
> Moreover, consent is not a valid defense if the activity consented to is against public policy. Thus, a child cannot consent to hazing, a gang member cannot consent to an initiation beating, and an individual cannot consent to being shot with a pistol. Assaults are breaches of the public peace. And we consider shooting at another person with a BB gun a breach of the public peace and, therefore, against public policy.

2. Can she consent to being assaulted?

State v. Brown, 364 A.2d 27 (N.J. 1976)

FACTS

Mrs. Brown was an alcoholic. On the day of the alleged crime she had been drinking, apparently to her husband Reginald Brown's displeasure. Acting according to the terms of an agreement between the defendant Reginald Brown and his wife, he punished her by beating her severely with his hands and other objects.

Brown was charged with atrocious assault and battery. He argued he wasn't guilty of atrocious assault and battery because he and Mrs. Brown, the victim, had an understanding to the effect that if she consumed any alcoholic beverages (and/or became intoxicated), he would punish her by physically assaulting her. The trial court refused the defense of consent.

Was Mr. Brown justified because of Mrs. Brown's consent?

DECISION

No, said the New Jersey Appellate Court:

> The laws are simply and unequivocally clear that the defense of consent cannot be available to a defendant charged with any type of physical assault that causes appreciable injury. If the law were otherwise, it would not be conducive to a peaceful, orderly and healthy society.
>
> This court concludes that, as a matter of law, no one has the right to beat another even though that person may ask for it. Assault and battery cannot be consented to by a victim, for the State makes it unlawful and is not a party to any such agreement between the victim and perpetrator. To allow an otherwise criminal act to go unpunished because of the victim's consent would not only threaten the security of our society but also might tend to detract from the force of the moral principles underlying the criminal law.
>
> Thus, for the reasons given, the State has an interest in protecting those persons who invite, consent to and permit others to assault and batter them. Not to enforce these laws which are geared to protect such people would seriously threaten the dignity, peace, health and security of our society.

3. Can he consent to being shot?

State v. Fransua, 510 P.2d 106 (N.Mex.App. 1973)

FACTS

Daniel Fransua and the victim were in a bar in Albuquerque. Fransua had been drinking heavily that day and the previous day. Sometime around 3:00 P.M., after an argument, Fransua told the victim he'd shoot him if he had a gun. The victim got up, walked out of the bar, went to his car, took out a loaded pistol, and went back in the bar. He came up to Fransua, laid the pistol on the bar, and said, "There's the gun. If you want to shoot me, go ahead." Fransua picked up the pistol, put the barrel next to the victim's head, and pulled the trigger, wounding him seriously.

Was the victim's consent a justification that meant Fransua wasn't guilty of aggravated battery?

DECISION

No, said the New Mexico Court of Appeals:

> It is generally conceded that a state enacts criminal statutes making certain violent acts crimes for at least two reasons: One reason is to protect the persons of its citizens; the second, however, is to prevent a breach of the public peace. While we entertain little sympathy for either the victim's absurd actions or the defendant's equally unjustified act of pulling the trigger, we will not permit the defense of consent to be raised in such cases.
>
> Whether or not the victims of crimes have so little regard for their own safety as to request injury, the public has a stronger and overriding interest in preventing and prohibiting acts such as these. We hold that consent is not a defense to the crime of aggravated battery, irrespective of whether the victim invites the act and consents to the battery.

SUMMARY

LO 1, LO 2

Defendants who plead justification admit they're responsible for committing crimes but contend they're right under the circumstances. If a defendant pleads excuse, she admits she's wrong but contends that, under the circumstances, she's not responsible.

LO 2

There's no criminal liability if someone is not responsible for an illegal act.

LO 3

Most justifications and excuses are affirmative defenses, in which defendants have to start by presenting some evidence in support of their argument of defense.

LO 4

To justify the use of deadly force in self-defense, the defender has to honestly and reasonably believe that she's faced with the choice of "kill or be killed, right now." When you use force to protect yourself, your home or property, or the people you care about, you're "taking the law into your own hands." Sometimes, the government isn't, or can't be, there to protect you when you need it. So necessity is the heart of the defense of self-defense.

LO 5

The four elements of self-defense are (1) unprovoked attack, (2) necessity, (3) proportionality, and (4) reasonable belief.

LO 6, LO 7

The English common law put the burden on defendants to prove they "retreated to the wall" before acting in self-defense. The American majority "stand-your-ground rule" is based on the idea that a "man" shouldn't have to flee from attack because he's done nothing wrong to provoke or deserve the attack. The rule gives him the right to protect his family and country, stand his ground, and kill to "defend himself without retreating from any place he has a right to be."

LO 7

The law of self-defense is undergoing major transformation. Current views that people may defend themselves wherever they have a "right to be" paved the way for many new statutes. These "stand-your-ground" rules have replaced retreat rules in most states. Retreat rules require people under attack to retreat if possible rather than defend themselves against attackers.

LO 8

There's no duty to retreat from your own home to avoid using deadly force. The minority of states that adopt the retreat rule carve out a major exception to it. Known as the "castle exception," it allows defendants to stand their ground and use deadly force to fend off an unprovoked attack.

LO 9

The new "castle doctrine" statutes vastly expand ordinary people's power to defend themselves in their homes, in public places, or anywhere else they have a legal right to be.

LO 10

At the heart of the choice-of-evils defense is the necessity to prevent imminent danger as is true of most other defenses. The difference is this defense justifies choosing to commit a lesser crime to avoid the harm of a greater crime.

LO 11

If mentally competent adults want to be crime victims, the justification of consent says that no paternalistic government should get in their way. The consent has to be voluntary, knowing, and authorized.

KEY TERMS

criminal conduct, p. 154
justification defenses, p. 154
excuse defenses, p. 154
failure-of-proof defenses, p. 154
affirmative defenses, p. 154
perfect defenses, p. 154
imperfect defense, p. 155
mitigating circumstances, p. 155
initial aggressor, p. 156
withdrawal exception, p. 156
necessity, p. 156
imminent danger of attack, p. 156
stand-your-ground rule, p. 165
retreat rule, p. 165
castle exception, p. 165
cohabitant exception, p. 165
curtilage, p. 172
choice-of-evils defense (general defense of necessity), p. 180
defense of consent, p. 184
voluntary consent, p. 185
knowing consent, p. 185
authorized consent, p. 185

LEARNING OBJECTIVES

1. To understand that defendants who plead an excuse defense admit what they did was wrong but argue that, under the circumstances, they weren't responsible for their actions.

2. To know that the defense of insanity excuses criminal liability when it seriously damages defendants' capacity to control their acts and/or to reason and understand the wrongfulness of their conduct.

3. To understand that insanity isn't the same as mental disease or defect.

4. To appreciate that very few defendants plead the insanity defense, and those who do rarely succeed.

5. To understand how the right-wrong test focuses on defect in reason or cognition.

6. To understand how the irresistible impulse test focuses on defect in self-control or will.

7. To understand how the product-of-mental-illness test focuses on criminal acts resulting from mental diseases.

8. To understand how the substantial capacity test focuses on reason and self-control.

9. To know why current trends favor shifting the burden of proof for insanity to defendants.

10. To understand the difference between diminished capacity and diminished responsibility and appreciate how they apply only to homicide.

11. To understand the different processes regarding how the law handles age and that juvenile court judges can use their discretion to transfer a juvenile to adult criminal court.

12. To understand how it's sometimes okay to excuse people who harm innocent people to save themselves.

13. To know the four elements of duress.

14. To understand that voluntary intoxication is no excuse for committing a crime; involuntary intoxication is.

15. To understand that entrapment is used in all societies even though it violates a basic purpose of government in free societies—to prevent crime, not to encourage it.

16. To understand why, despite criticism of them, syndrome excuses should be taken seriously.

Lorena Bobbitt, flanked by her attorneys James Lowe, left, and Lisa Kemler, meets reporters outside the court in Manassas, Virginia, on Monday, February 28, 1994. A judge ordered her release from a mental hospital five weeks after her acquittal by reason of insanity for cutting off her husband's penis.

DEFENSES TO CRIMINAL LIABILITY 6

Excuses

CHAPTER OUTLINE

Did He Know It Was "Wrong" to Kill His Father?

On Sunday, April 23, 2000, Darren Odell attended Easter dinner at his great aunt's house. While his father was seated at the dining room table, Odell retrieved a 9mm Beretta handgun from his truck. When he returned, Odell waited until some of the guests cleared the dining room area. While two guests remained seated beside his father, Odell fired three bullets into his father's chest, which resulted in fatal wounds. Immediately following the shooting, Odell fled the crime scene but returned shortly thereafter and peacefully surrendered himself to police. Odell admitted that he shot his father, but claims he was not guilty because of his mental illness.

(*State v. Odell* 2004)

LO 1

In Chapter 5, you learned that defendants who plead defenses of justification accept responsibility for their actions but claim that, under the circumstances (necessity and consent), what they did was justified. In this chapter, you'll learn about defendants who plead excuse. They admit what they did was wrong but claim that, under the circumstances, they weren't responsible for what they did. The best-known excuse is insanity, but you'll learn about others in this chapter, too.

Excuses operate according to two legal schemes. In the first scheme, they're affirmative defenses akin to justifications (Table 6.1, step 2) in determining criminal liability. They're presented *after* the prosecution has proved its case beyond a reasonable doubt (Table 6.1, step 1) and the defendant hasn't proved that her conduct was justified (Table 6.1, step 2). Now (step 3), she claims she's excused. Legally, she's pleading an affirmative defense. As an affirmative

TABLE 6.1

Three Analytical Steps of Criminal Liability
1. Was there criminal conduct? (Chapters 3 and 4)
2. If there was criminal conduct, was it justified? (Chapter 5)
3. If it wasn't justified, was it excused? (That's where we are now.)

defense, defendants have to carry some of the burden of proving they have an excuse that will relieve them of criminal responsibility. We'll examine this later on in the "The Burden of Proof" section.

failure-of-proof scheme, defendants raise a reasonable doubt that the prosecution has proven the mental element of the crime, so they don't have to justify or excuse their conduct because it's not criminal conduct

Chronologically, the second scheme, the **failure-of-proof scheme**, comes during step 1, proving criminal conduct. At this stage, defendants have no burden to prove their conduct was *not* criminal, but they can raise a reasonable doubt about the prosecution's case that their conduct *is* criminal. Defendants can present evidence that creates a reasonable doubt about their capacity to form the intent required by the crime they're charged with committing. If they're successful, they negate the mental element. In other words, the prosecutor hasn't proved criminal conduct beyond a reasonable doubt.

So these "failure of proof" defenses aren't really defenses. Defenses justify or excuse criminal conduct. Logically, you can't (and legally you don't have to) justify or excuse what's not criminal. We'll discuss only one failure-of-proof defense—diminished responsibility.

In this chapter, we'll look at the affirmative defenses of excuse: insanity, diminished capacity, age, duress, intoxication, entrapment, and syndrome defenses.

LO 2

THE INSANITY DEFENSE

Thanks to CNN, in 1994, the whole world knew that Lorena Bobbitt walked out of a mental hospital shortly after she successfully pleaded "not guilty by reason of insanity" for cutting off her husband's penis with a kitchen knife. By contrast, no one knew that John Smith, who drove a Greyhound bus out of the New York City Port Authority bus terminal in 1980, crashed it, and was acquitted "by reason of insanity," might still be locked up in the Manhattan Psychiatric Center on Ward's Island in New York City.

For a brief moment in 1994, CNN made "Lorena Bobbitt" a household name throughout the world. By contrast, no one but the lawyers, doctors, and hospital staff probably knows of John Smith or where he is. But empirical evidence demonstrates that Smith's case is hands down the more typical insanity defense case; Bobbitt's is extremely rare (Perlin 1989–90; Sherman 1994, 24). The **affirmative defense of insanity** (hereafter called the **"insanity defense"**) legally excuses a person from criminal liability because of a mental disease or defect of the kinds we'll discuss in this chapter.

affirmative defense of insanity (also **"insanity defense"**), the legal excuse that defendants aren't responsible for their criminal conduct because it was caused by a mental disease or defect

In this section, we'll look at the history of the insanity defense, the myths and reality surrounding it, and the tests used to determine legal insanity.

THE HISTORY OF THE INSANITY DEFENSE

In about 350 BC, when the Greek philosopher Plato was old, he recommended in *Laws*, that "if anyone be insane, let him not be seen openly in the town, but let his kinfolk watch over him as best they may, under a penalty of a fine" (Walker 1985, 26). By 1350, the English kings were granting pardons to insane criminals, leaving them in the care of guardians to protect them from harming themselves and the neighborhood from their potential wrongdoing. For example, in one case Professor Nigel Walker found, the jury's verdict said that the madman killed his daughter but not "feloniously or with malice aforethought" (27).

A number of high-profile cases, involving attacks on the monarchs or people in their service, led to various tests of insanity. Most focused on impaired reason (mental diseases or defects that impaired the ability to know "good from evil" and later "right from wrong"). In *Rex v. Arnold* (1724), the delusional Edward Arnold attempted to assassinate one of King George III's courtiers. The judge instructed the jury that to succeed in a plea of insanity, Arnold had to prove that he was "a man that is totally deprived of his understanding and memory, and does not know what he is doing, no more than an infant, than a brute, or a wild beast" (765).

Another high-profile case, *Regina v. McNaughtan* (1843), had far and away the most influence on English and U.S. insanity defense law. From 1843, when it was decided, to present U.S. law, with few exceptions and interruptions, it remains the law in the majority of the states and the federal government.

Like almost all the high-profile insanity defense cases, it involved an attack on a powerful political figure. The intended victim was the English Prime Minister, Sir Robert Peel. The attacker was the young Scottish Chartist, Daniel McNaughtan. Chartism was a mid-Victorian activist reform movement with strong support in Scotland. It was feared and hated by middle and upper classes who viewed Chartists as dangerous radicals and terrorists fomenting class warfare.

McNaughtan was afraid, too. According to his lawyer, he was suffering from the "fierce and fearful delusion" that Sir Robert and his Tory party were his enemies. On January 20, 1843, mistaking Peel's private secretary Edward Drummond for the prime minister, McNaughtan fatally shot Drummond in the back. He was instantly apprehended, locked up in Newgate prison, and put on trial on March 4. He was backed by an enormously competent team of four trial lawyers, nine prominent medical experts, and eight lay witnesses from Glasgow (Moran 1985, 37–38).

Both the defense and the Crown agreed that McNaughtan "was sane on all matters except politics"; the case boiled down to what was a valid defense of insanity. The defense argued that suffering from partial insanity should qualify for the defense. Specifically, McNaughtan acted out of a delusion, and any act during that delusion excused him. The Crown argued that the insane are criminally responsible unless "they're totally incapable of knowing right from wrong" (38). (Wild beasts?)

The Crown decided not to rebut the medical testimony claiming that McNaughtan suffered from insane delusions that caused his act of shooting Drummond. At this point, Chief Justice Nicholas Tindal stopped the trial abruptly. The chief justice was impressed with the impartial medical testimony from two medical experts, impartial because neither side paid for their services. The Crown was probably also impressed—in his closing statement to the jury, he withdrew the case. Tindal essentially gave the jury a directed verdict: "If you find the prisoner not guilty . . . on the ground of insanity . . . proper care will be taken of him" (39).

After deliberating "less than two minutes, the jury declared, 'We find the defendant not guilty, on the ground of insanity'" (Hermann and Sor 1983, 510). The verdict caused great consternation. The public feared that madmen could kill without fear of punishment. This poem written shortly after captures the public reaction brilliantly:

> Ye people of England: exult and be glad,
> For you're now at the will of the merciless mad.
>
> Why say you that but three authorities reign—
> Crown, Commons, and Lords! You omit the insane!
>
> They're a privileged class, whom no statute controls,
> And their murderous charter exists in their souls.

Do they wish to spill blood—they have only to play
A few pranks—get asylumed a month and a day

Then heigh! to escape from the mad-doctor's keys,
And to pistol or stab whomsoever they please.

(Thomas Campbell 1843; quoted in Hermann and Sor 1983, 500)

Queen Victoria displayed her own consternation when she pressed the prime minister to get Parliament to *force* the judges to "follow the law" (39–40).

> We have seen the trials of Oxford [who almost assassinated the queen] and McNaughtan conducted by the ablest lawyers of the day and they allow and advise the jury to pronounce the verdict of not guilty on account of insanity, whilst everybody is morally convinced that both malefactors were perfectly conscious and aware of what they did! Could not the legislature lay down the [right-wrong] rule that the Lord Chancellor does in his paper, and why could the judges not be bound to interpret the law in this and no other sense in their charges to the Juries? (Herman and Sor 1983, 510)

The queen's consternation reflected the growing public anger expressed in the poem. The muddled state of the insanity defense prompted the House of Lords to ask the common law judges to attend one of their sessions and advise them on exactly what the law of insanity was. This would enable them to pass adequate legislation to codify the insanity defense. On June 19, just five months after Daniel McNaughtan shot Edward Drummond, the judges obliged. *The McNaughtan rules*, which codified the insanity defense, comprise the elements of the right-wrong test that remain the law in most states and the federal government today. (See "Right-Wrong Test" later.)

Before we turn to the right-wrong and other insanity tests, we need to note that these high-profile insanity defense trials were attacks on royal and legislative power during times of war and domestic unrest. In other words, they were clearly the product of their times. Medical and legal arguments were mere props in morality plays, of good and evil, right and wrong, social peace and chaos. Professor Moran (1985), the acclaimed authority on the insanity defense and McNaughtan's case writes:

> Formal legal doctrine and actual courtroom decisions are often shaped by the same social forces that influence all other human endeavors. The view that the insanity defense is a legal loophole through which the guilty defendant often escapes punishment seems too narrow, for it can also be a powerful mechanism by which the court retains the authority to confine a defendant who is otherwise beyond the reach of the criminal law. James Hadfield, although he was acquitted spent the last 41 years of his life in confinement. And Daniel McNaughtan spent his last 22 years in confinement following his acquittal by reason of insanity. (42)

LO 2, LO 3

THE INSANITY DEFENSE: MYTHS AND REALITY

The public badly misunderstands "insanity," the defense of insanity, and how the defense actually works today—just as they have throughout its history (see Table 6.2). Let's clear up some misunderstandings and then look at some of the myths and the realities about the defense of insanity.

First, insanity doesn't mean "mental disease or mental defect." Mental disease (also called "mental illness") and mental defect are medical terms; insanity is a legal term.

TABLE 6.2

Popular Myths and Empirical Realities about the Insanity Defense

MYTH	REALITY
The insanity defense is overused.	All empirical analyses are consistent: "the public, legal profession and—specifically—legislators 'dramatically' and 'grossly' overestimate both the frequency and the success rate of the insanity plea" (Perlin 1997). Less than one percent (0.87%) of defendants plead insanity, and a mere 23.55 percent of those who do plead, succeed (Valdes 2005, 1723).
The use of the insanity defense is limited to murder cases.	In one jurisdiction where the data have been closely studied, slightly fewer than one-third of the successful insanity pleas entered over an eight-year period were reached in cases involving a victim's death. Further, individuals who plead insanity in murder cases are no more successful at being found "Not Guilty by Reason of Insanity" (NGRI) than persons charged with other crimes (Perlin 1997).
There's no risk to the defendant who pleads insanity.	Defendants who asserted an insanity defense at trial and who were ultimately found guilty of their charges served significantly longer sentences than defendants tried on similar charges who didn't assert the insanity defense (Perlin 1997).
NGRI acquittees are quickly released from custody.	Of all the individuals found NGRI over an eight-year period in one jurisdiction, only 15 percent had been released from all restraints; 35 percent remained in institutional custody; and 47 percent were under partial court restraint following conditional release (Perlin 1997).
NGRI acquittees spend much less time in custody than do defendants convicted of the same offenses.	NGRI acquittees actually spend almost double the amount of time that defendants convicted of similar charges spend in prison settings and often face a lifetime of post-release judicial oversight (Perlin 1997).
Criminal defendants who plead insanity are usually faking.	Of 141 individuals found NGRI in one jurisdiction over an eight-year period, there was no dispute that 115 were schizophrenic (including 38 of the 46 cases involving a victim's death), and in only 3 cases was the diagnostician unable to specify the nature of the patient's mental illness (Perlin 1997).
Criminal defense attorneys employ the insanity defense plea solely to "beat the rap."	First, the level of representation afforded to mentally disabled defendants is frequently substandard. Second, the few studies that have been done paint an entirely different picture: lawyers may enter an insanity plea to obtain immediate mental health treatment for their client, as a plea-bargaining device to ensure that their client ultimately receives mandatory mental health care, and to avoid malpractice litigation. Third, the best available research suggests that jury biases exist relatively independent of lawyer functioning and are generally "not induced by attorneys" (Perlin 1997).

Sources: Perlin 1997, 648–55; Valdes 2005, 1722–25.

But—and here's one source of confusion and misunderstanding—mental disease and mental defect are *part* of the definition of insanity. What psychiatry calls "mental disease" or "mental defect" might, or might not, be insanity. Mental disease and mental defect are legal insanity *only* when the disease or defect affects a person's reason. In a few states, they're legal insanity when they affect a person's will (willpower)—namely, the power to control your actions.

insanity, the legal term that refers to a mental disease or defect that impairs the reason and/or will

LO 4

Another source of confusion, and a dominant myth, is that the consequences resulting from the "not guilty by reason of insanity" verdict are too lenient or nonexistent. It's widely believed that not guilty by reason of insanity means that defendants go home. Where do they get this idea? From a few high-profile cases, such as those of Lorena Bobbitt and John Hinckley. The world watched as television cameras caught Hinckley stepping out of a crowd, pulling out a revolver, shooting, wounding, and almost killing President Reagan. Hinckley also shot and permanently disabled James Brady, the president's press secretary. Months later, the world watched as Hinckley was found not guilty by reason of insanity. What the world doesn't see on camera or hear any talk about is that Hinckley remains tightly secured in St. Elizabeth's Hospital. Similarly, you know—but very few do—that Daniel McNaughtan also never went free, and neither did most of the other high-profile defendants who attacked powerful people.

LO 4

Contrary to widespread belief, few defendants plead the insanity defense (only a few thousand a year in the United States). The few who do plead insanity hardly ever succeed.

civil commitment, a noncriminal (civil) proceeding, in which courts have the power to decide if defendants who were insane when they committed their crimes are still insane

The few who "succeed" don't go free. In a noncriminal (civil) proceeding, called **civil commitment**, courts have to decide if defendants who were insane when they committed their crimes are still insane. If they are—and courts almost always decide they are—they're locked up in maximum-security prisons called "hospitals." And like John Smith, but unlike Lorena Bobbitt, they stay there for a long time—until they're no longer "mentally ill and dangerous"—often for the rest of their lives.

The case of John Hinckley is an excellent example. Hinckley shot and almost killed President Reagan in an attempt to assassinate him to impress the actress Jodie Foster. (Hinckley was obsessed with Foster, whom he'd never met.) Hinckley was found not guilty by reason of insanity. The public was outraged, believing that Hinckley "walked" for attempting to assassinate the president. (Hinckley still isn't free.)

CASE

U.S. v. Hinckley ***(2009)*** *details the difficulties proposals for even brief furloughs for Hinckley face and the stringent conditions still attached them, nearly thirty years after a jury found him "not guilty by reason of insanity."*

Should his furlough releases be expanded?

U.S. v. Hinckley

625 F.Supp.2d 3 (D.C. 2009)

HISTORY

St. Elizabeth's Hospital submitted a proposal for the conditional release of John Hinckley, a patient committed to the hospital following a jury finding of not guilty, by reason of insanity, of attempted assassination of the president of the United States.

FRIEDMAN, J.

FACTS

This is the latest in a series of proposals submitted by the Hospital to this Court over the years. On each occasion, the Hospital has sought to enlarge the scope and/or the duration of Mr. Hinckley's activities beyond the grounds of the Hospital, and the government has opposed the Hospital's proposals in whole or in part. . . . [First, the Court allowed local day visits by Mr. Hinckley with his parents outside of the confines of St. Elizabeth's Hospital without the supervision of Hospital personnel; then local overnight visits with his parents; then, three overnights at his parents' home; then four; then six.] Lastly, at the conclusion of the most recent evidentiary hearing, the Court permitted Mr. Hinckley "to continue with visits to [his] mother's home outside the Washington, D.C. area for six nights in duration, until further order of this Court[.]" These periodic visits have continued to this day and each, according to the Hospital's written reports to the Court, has been therapeutic, without incident and, by all measures, successful.

The Hospital's current (e) Letter is premised on the notion that Mr. Hinckley is ready for a next phase in which (1) Mr. Hinckley is permitted to utilize more absences from the Hospital, increased freedom, and additional privileges to begin integrating himself into his mother's community, and (2) the Hospital evaluates this process to determine whether Mr. Hinckley is ready to be released from the Hospital to live independently in his mother's community. "The ultimate goal of this phase is to determine if Mr. Hinckley is ready to be released from the Hospital to live independently in his parents' community." The Court views this as a "transitional stage" in which Mr. Hinckley would be expected to focus on "social and potential vocational" integration into his mother's community.

I. The Parties' Arguments

The Hospital and Mr. Hinckley . . . contend that by compiling "a perfect . . . record of success on conditional release" thus far, Mr. Hinckley has demonstrated his readiness for an increase in conditional release privileges; that Mr. Hinckley would benefit therapeutically from an increase in conditional release privileges; and that the terms under which the Hospital proposes to expand Mr. Hinckley's conditional release privileges adequately guard against the (remote) possibility that Mr. Hinckley may decompensate and become dangerous.

The government argues that the Hospital underestimates the risk that Mr. Hinckley's mental illness may cause him to become dangerous to himself or to others. The government argues that during the preceding year "we have seen a further development of several behaviors that have been universally recognized as risk factors for further violence." Much of the government's argument on this score focuses on Mr. Hinckley's relationships with women. In the government's view, "Mr. Hinckley's [mental] illness [still] prevents him from realistically appreciating his relationships with women; this puts him at an increased risk for violence due to depression or due to a request to act out to demonstrate his love for a woman." Thus, according to the government, it is worrisome that over the course of the preceding year

> [Mr. Hinckley] maintain[ed] near simultaneous sexual relationships with ["Ms. M," who suffers from bipolar disorder, and "Ms. G," who is in a long-term relationship with another man]. While he was maintaining these two relationships, he rekindled his relationship with [former girlfriend Leslie DeVeau in June 2007]. Then, in November 2007, he met a fourth woman [through Ms. G], [named "Ms. B"]. It is unclear whether his relationship with her has become romantic, but they meet and converse regularly. . . . The Hospital has asked Mr. Hinckley to keep a written log of his interactions with women "[b]ecause of the significant increase in his interactions with women."

At the evidentiary hearing, there was also testimony to the effect that Mr. Hinckley had recently struck up a friendship with a "Ms. K." That friendship apparently continues to this day.

The government finds troubling not only the number of Mr. Hinckley's relationships but also certain decisions he has made and certain actions he has taken in the context of those relationships. For example, the government argues that Mr. Hinckley demonstrated poor judgment when he attempted to invite Ms. G to a "neighborhood block party" during one of his conditional releases, despite the objections of some of his family members. Ultimately, the treatment team did not permit Mr. Hinckley to invite Ms. G to the party. Relatedly, the government believes that Mr. Hinckley has demonstrated poor judgment (and perhaps a willingness to deceive) by being less than candid with his treaters about several matters, especially his relationships with women.

The government also argues that Mr. Hinckley has demonstrated a troubling lack of initiative during his home visits, and that this indicates that Mr. Hinckley is neither prepared for nor "committed to the difficult work of transitioning to his mother's hometown." Mr. Hinckley "will go to great lengths

(continues)

(continued)

to contact women, play and record his music, and arrange for art lessons," but that he lacks initiative when it comes to less appealing tasks. In the government's view, the primary evidence of Mr. Hinckley's lack of initiative is (1) Mr. Hinckley's failure, in general, to pursue as vigorously as possible volunteer positions in his mother's hometown; (2) Mr. Hinckley's failure, specifically, to keep an appointment to discuss a volunteer position with a particular volunteer organization in his mother's hometown; and (3) Mr. Hinckley's reluctance to end inappropriate or counterproductive relationships with women, even when advised to do so by family members or treaters.

Finally, the government argues that "there is evidence that Mr. Hinckley continues to maintain inappropriate thoughts of violence." In support of this argument, the government observes that Mr. Hinckley "recently recorded a music CD ROM which included a song he wrote prior to the assassination attempt that is entitled 'The Ballad of the Outlaw,' a song reflecting suicide and lawlessness."

A. Witnesses for the Hospital and Mr. Hinckley

Mr. Hinckley's siblings testified that Mr. Hinckley has been conscientious about observing the terms of his conditional release while in their mother's hometown, and that they have observed no signs of decompensation or dangerousness during any of the visits in which they participated. In addition, both siblings testified that during the visits Mr. Hinckley fully participated in family activities (including visiting Mr. Hinckley's ailing father in an assisted living facility); communicated openly and candidly about his relationships; demonstrated empathy and compassion for all of his family members; and did not seek any media attention.

Both acknowledged, however, that during his visits to his mother's hometown Mr. Hinckley could have tried harder to pursue volunteer opportunities, and that in their view his failure to do so indicated some "immaturity."

Neither of Mr. Hinckley's siblings witnessed any evidence of decompensation or dangerousness as a result of Mr. Hinckley's relationships with women, though both conceded that Mr. Hinckley has not always exercised sound judgment in pursuing or maintaining these relationships.

Dr. Montalbano was permitted to offer expert testimony on behalf of the Hospital. Dr. Montalbano testified "to a reasonable degree of psychological certainty that Mr. Hinckley would not pose a danger to self or others due to mental illness under" the Hospital's proposal.

Mr. Hyde, Mr. Hinckley's music therapist at the Hospital, testified that Mr. Hinckley frequently "turns to [writing and recording songs] as a coping mechanism." He also testified that music therapy allows Mr. Hinckley to "access topics that have been historically difficult for [him] to discuss." In Mr. Hyde's view, Mr. Hinckley's music and his behavior in music therapy indicate that he has a strong fix on reality and a sense of hope about his future. Notably, Mr. Hyde firmly rejects the government's argument that Mr. Hinckley's decision to record "The Ballad of the Outlaw" indicates that Mr. Hinckley harbors inappropriate thoughts of violence. Rather, Mr. Hyde believes that this decision "show[ed] an effort on his part to look at how he was prior to his instant offense and how that set of emotions, set of events . . . brought him to the place where he is today," and therefore indicates insight and openness.

B. Witnesses for the Government

Dr. Phillips was "not as willing to join the chorus that heralds Mr. Hinckley's openness and candor concerning his relationships with women. . . . Simply put, I believe Mr. Hinckley tells us only what he wants us to know."

Most importantly, in Dr. Phillips . . . view, the Hospital's proposal . . . does not adequately guard against the risk that Mr. Hinckley may . . . become dangerous to himself or others.

Second, Dr. Phillips testified that the Hospital's proposal does not include "adequate work and social structures . . . [to] manage the risks posed by Mr. Hinckley's clinical conditions[.]" Specifically, Dr. Phillips was troubled . . . that, at the time of the hearing, there seemed to be much "uncertainty and confusion" about Mr. Hinckley's volunteer opportunities in his mother's hometown.

OPINION

All of the relevant psychological evidence—including the testimony at the evidentiary hearing, evaluations conducted by the parties' experts and the tests administered by Dr. Montalbano—indicates that

Mr. Hinckley remains mentally ill. Furthermore, Mr. Hinckley failed to pursue volunteer opportunities in his mother's hometown with the utmost vigor. (To be fair, it should be noted that since the evidentiary hearing Mr. Hinckley has been diligent about staying in contact with the two organizations that have offered him volunteer positions, thereby ensuring the continued availability of those positions.)

In the government's view, these indications of ongoing mental illness require the Court to deny the Hospital's current proposal and adopt the government's more conservative proposal. The Court disagrees. . . . The statutory regime under which the Court conducts these proceedings and evaluates the Hospital's (e) Letter does not require Mr. Hinckley to recover completely in order to proceed to the next level of conditional release. Nor would such a requirement be feasible or desirable as a practical matter. Thus, the ultimate question is not whether Mr. Hinckley remains mentally ill—though of course that is an important issue.

The ultimate question is whether a preponderance of the evidence supports the proposition that Mr. Hinckley will not, in the reasonable future, be a danger to himself or to others under the proposed conditions of release and/or other reasonable conditions of release imposed by the Court. After careful consideration, the Court answers that ultimate question in the affirmative. The evidence suggesting that Mr. Hinckley will *not* become dangerous under the Hospital's proposal—including his uncontested record of abiding by the terms of this Court's orders; his uncontested empathy and compassion for his family members over the last year; his increased (if still imperfect) openness with his treaters; his ability generally to cope with the fluctuations in his romantic relationships without decompensating; and his demonstrated ability to cope with major, life-altering stressors, such as the loss of a father—far outweighs the evidence suggesting that he *will* become dangerous under the Hospital's proposal.

The Court therefore concludes that Mr. Hinckley will not in the reasonable future be a danger to himself or to others under the conditions of release proposed by the Hospital. The Court further concludes that even if Mr. Hinckley were to decompensate during the course of the extended releases proposed by the Hospital—an event the Court regards as highly unlikely—his decompensation would not occur suddenly but would occur gradually over weeks or months and would be detected easily by his family members and the mental health professionals responsible for monitoring him.

C. Duration of Releases

The government adamantly opposes extending the duration of Mr. Hinckley's conditional releases as proposed by the Hospital. The government opposes longer conditional releases. According to the government, longer releases are not necessary to allow Mr. Hinckley to begin engaging in more community type activities. Second, the government argues that Mr. Hinckley's conduct during the year preceding the hearing point to the need for *more* Hospital-based treatment and monitoring. . . .

. . . The Court does not agree with the government that longer releases should be rejected. In the Hospital's view, longer and more frequent conditional releases will not only allow Mr. Hinckley to engage in new activities, but will also provide substantial therapeutic benefits to Mr. Hinckley without increasing the risk that he will decompensate and become dangerous.

While the government's concerns about reducing Mr. Hinckley's interactions with his Hospital-based treaters are legitimate, the Court concludes that they are not an adequate reason to reject the moderate extension of conditional releases proposed by the Hospital.

D. Volunteer Work

It is now clear that there are two volunteer opportunities for Mr. Hinckley in his mother's hometown, both of which the Hospital considers appropriate. It is also clear that Mr. Hinckley is enthusiastic about both positions. Thus, the Court will permit Mr. Hinckley to begin volunteering at whichever one of these two organizations the Hospital deems most appropriate. But, before Mr. Hinckley begins any volunteer position, it must be approved by Mr. Hinckley's treatment team and the Hospital's review board. The Hospital must also notify the Court and counsel for the government at least two weeks in advance of Mr. Hinckley beginning any volunteer. The Hospital's notification must include enough detail to permit the

(continues)

(continued)
Court to evaluate the appropriateness of the volunteer position in question.

Second, Mr. Hinckley shall not be permitted to enjoy the expanded social privileges contemplated by the Hospital's (e) Letter until he has successfully completed volunteer work on three overnight visits. Third, and relatedly, Mr. Hinckley shall not be permitted to enjoy those expanded social privileges in the future unless he continues to maintain and participate in a Hospital-approved volunteer position.

Finally, as an added precaution, Mr. Hinckley will be required to carry a GPS-enabled cell phone "so that he can contact the treatment team and be contacted and also so that his movements can be measured to assure he has adhered to the itineraries and requirements set by the treatment team" any time he ventures beyond the Hospital grounds and is not accompanied by Hospital personnel, his mother or his siblings. Accordingly, it is hereby

ORDERED that, on or before July 1, 2009, the Hospital shall submit to the Court a proposed Order setting forth the proposed terms of Mr. Hinckley's conditions of release consistent with this Opinion. The Hospital shall circulate the proposed Order to counsel for both parties for their comments (consistent with this Opinion) before submitting it to the Court.

SO ORDERED.

QUESTIONS

1. Summarize the arguments for and against St. Elizabeth's proposal for John Hinckley's furloughs.
2. Summarize Judge Friedman's reasons for attaching additional conditions to Hinckley's furloughs.
3. In your opinion, were the conditions Judge Friedman attached to the furlough "fair"? Back up your answer with details from the case.
4. Has your opinion of the insanity defense changed after reading the excerpt? Explain your answer.

THE TESTS OF INSANITY

It might be used only rarely, but the insanity defense stands for two important moral ideals—familiar to you by now: (1) it's only right to blame people who are responsible, and (2) if we can't blame them, it's wrong to punish them. Four tests determine whether people with mental disease or defects aren't responsible enough to blame and punish. In other words, they're excused from criminal liability:

1. **RIGHT-WRONG TEST (THE MCNAUGHTAN RULE).** The oldest rule, it's used in twenty-eight states and the federal courts (*Clark v. Arizona* 2006, slip opinion, majority 9).
2. **IRRESISTIBLE IMPULSE TEST.** Only a few jurisdictions use this rule (LaFave 2003b, 389).
3. **PRODUCT TEST (DURHAM RULE).** It's followed only in New Hampshire.
4. **SUBSTANTIAL CAPACITY TEST (THE MPC TEST).** This was the majority rule until John Hinckley attempted to murder President Reagan in 1981. It's still the rule in fourteen jurisdictions (*Clark v. Arizona* 2006, slip opinion, majority, 10) but not in federal courts, where it was abolished in 1984 and replaced with the right-wrong test.

reason, psychologists call it "*cognition*"; the capacity to tell right from wrong

will, psychologists call it "volition," most of us call it "willpower"; in the insanity tests, it refers to defendants' power to control their actions

All four tests look at defendants' mental capacity, but they differ in what they're looking for. The right-wrong test focuses exclusively on reason—psychologists call it "*cognition*"—that is, on the capacity to tell right from wrong. The other tests focus on reason *and/or* will. Will—psychologists call it "volition"—it's what most of us call "willpower"; in the insanity tests, it refers to defendants' power to control their actions.

The Right-Wrong Test (McNaughtan Rule)

LO 5

Boiled down to their essence, there are two elements to the right-wrong test (the *McNaughtan* rule) created in *McNaughtan*:

1. The defendant suffered a defect of reason caused by a disease of the mind.
2. Consequently, at the time of the act she did not know
   a. the nature and quality of the act (she didn't know what she was doing) *or*
   b. that the act was wrong.

right-wrong test (also called the ***McNaughtan* rule**), the defendant suffered a defect of reason caused by a disease of the mind, and, consequently, at the time of the act didn't know what she was doing or that the act was wrong

***McNaughtan* rule**, the right-wrong test

mental disease, most courts define it as psychosis, mostly paranoia and schizophrenia

mental defect, refers to mental retardation or brain damage severe enough to make it impossible to know what you're doing, or if you know, you don't know that it's wrong

Although the right-wrong test was adopted quickly and has been followed almost exclusively in the United States for over a century, it has always had strong critics among both lawyers and psychiatrists. According to both, cognition is only part of the human psyche and can't alone determine human behavior (Hermann and Sor 1983, 512).

There's also lots of back and forth in the courts about just what words in the test, such as "disease," "defect," "know," and "wrong," mean. Statutes rarely give the courts much guidance, leaving them to "legislate" judicially on the matter. Most courts say that mental disease means psychosis, mostly paranoia and schizophrenia. It doesn't include personality disorders, such as psychopathic and sociopathic personalities that lead to criminal or antisocial conduct. Mental defect refers to mental retardation or brain damage severe enough to make it impossible to know what you're doing, or if you know, you don't know that it's wrong.

In most states, "know" means cognition, which means "intellectual awareness." Some states require more—that defendants understand or "appreciate" (grasp the true significance of) their actions (Freud's "There's knowing, and there's *knowing*"). Most courts don't define the term, leaving juries to define it by applying it to the facts of specific cases as they see fit. The "nature and quality of the act" means you don't know what you're doing (ALI 1985 1:2, 174–76). (To use an old law school example, "If a man believes he's squeezing lemons when in fact he's strangling his wife," he doesn't know the "nature and quality of his act.")

Deciding what "wrong" means has created problems. Some states require that defendants didn't know their conduct was *legally* wrong; others say it means *morally* wrong. In *People v. Schmidt* (1915), Schmidt confessed to killing Anna Aumuller by slitting her throat. He pleaded insanity, telling physicians who examined him that

> he had heard the voice of God calling upon him to kill the woman as a sacrifice and atonement. He confessed to a life of unspeakable excesses and hideous crimes, broken, he said, by spells of religious ecstasy and exaltation. In one of these moments, believing himself, he tells us, in the visible presence of God, he committed this fearful crime. (325)

The trial judge instructed the jury that Schmidt had to know that slitting Aumuller's throat was a crime. The New York Court of Appeals disagreed: "We are unable to accept the view that the word 'wrong' . . . is to receive such a narrow construction." The Court of Appeals recommended this as a suitable jury instruction:

> Knowledge of the nature and quality of the act has reference to its physical nature and quality, and that knowledge that it is wrong refers to its moral side; that to know that the act is wrong, the defendant must know that it is "contrary to law, and contrary to the accepted standards of morality, and then he added . . . that it must be known to be contrary to the laws of God and man." (336)

CASE

In* State v. Odell *(2004), the Minnesota Supreme Court upheld Odell's murder conviction against the challenge that he didn't know the "nature and wrongfulness" of killing his father.

Did he know "the nature and wrongfulness" of his acts?

State v. Odell

676 N.W.2d 646 (Minn. 2004)

HISTORY

Darren Paul Odell (Phipps) was indicted on one count of first-degree murder under Minn.Stat. § 609.185(a)(1) (2002) as a result of the shooting death of his father, Dennis Raymond Odell. At trial, Odell pleaded not guilty and not guilty by reason of mental illness under Minn.Stat. § 611.026 (2002), commonly referred to as the *M'Naghten* [*sic*] rule, which has long been part of Minnesota law. [The statute provides:]

> *11.026 CRIMINAL RESPONSIBILITY OF MENTALLY ILL OR DEFICIENT.*
>
> No person shall . . . be excused from criminal liability except upon proof that at the time of committing the alleged criminal act the person was laboring under such a defect of reason . . . as not to know the nature of the act, or that it was wrong.

A defendant who pleads not guilty by reason of mental illness is afforded a **bifurcated** [two-stage] trial (see definition on p. 207). The first phase of the trial determines whether the state has met its burden of proof as to the defendant's guilt. If the defendant is found guilty, the second phase determines whether the defendant has sustained the burden of establishing the mental illness defense.

Odell waived his right to a jury trial and at the conclusion of the guilt phase of the trial, the court found that Odell acted with premeditation and intent to kill his father. This finding was not appealed. After the mental illness phase, the trial court found that Odell failed to sustain his burden in proving a mental illness defense and sentenced him to life in prison. On direct appeal, Odell contests the trial court's ruling with respect to the *M'Naghten* rule.

GILBERT, J.

FACTS

On Sunday, April 23, 2000, Odell attended Easter dinner at his great aunt's house. While his father was seated at the dining room table, Odell retrieved a 9mm Beretta handgun from his truck. When he returned, Odell waited until some of the guests cleared the dining room area. While two guests remained seated beside his father, Odell fired three bullets into his father's chest, which resulted in fatal wounds. Immediately following the shooting, Odell fled the crime scene, but returned shortly thereafter and peacefully surrendered himself to police. On appeal, Odell admits to shooting his father, but challenges the trial court's decision as to his mental illness.

At trial, extensive evidence relevant to Odell's mental state was introduced. In phase two of the trial, the court found the following doctors, who evaluated Odell, qualified to render expert witness testimony: Dr. James H. Gilbertson was called to testify for the defense, Dr. Dallas D. Erdmann was appointed by the court, and Drs. Michael G. Farnsworth and Kristine Kienlen were called to testify for the state.

On May 1, 2001, Drs. Erdmann and Farnsworth examined Odell to determine whether he was competent to proceed to trial. Both doctors concluded that as a result of Odell's mental illness, he was incapable of understanding the proceedings or participating in his defense. Thereafter, Odell was committed to the Minnesota Security Hospital in St. Peter, Minnesota for treatment. In the fall of 2002, Odell was found competent to proceed to trial.

After initial interviews with Odell, all four doctors agreed that Odell did not qualify for the *M'Naghten* defense. Although Drs. Gilbertson and Erdmann diagnosed Odell as suffering from schizophrenia at the time of the murder, both believed Odell understood the nature and wrongfulness of shooting his father, yet elected to engage in the criminal behavior regardless of the consequences. Drs. Farnsworth and Kienlen agreed that Odell was suffering from a mental illness at the time of the shooting and concluded, as Drs. Gilbertson and Erdmann did, that Odell did not satisfy the *M'Naghten* rule, that is, Odell understood the nature and wrongfulness of his acts.

Following the first set of mental evaluations, Odell's sister, while cleaning Odell's house, found a popcorn tin containing several post-it notes and other writings apparently authored by Odell.

The contents of the notes and writings contained bizarre references to celebrities Reba McIntyre and Elvis Presley, and numerology, but did not reference Odell's relationship with or animus toward his father. Subsequently, counsel stipulated to and the trial court granted Odell's request to be reexamined.

Based on a review of the post-it notes, updated medical reports, and a second interview with Odell, Drs. Gilbertson and Erdmann revised their opinions and concluded that Odell did not know it was morally wrong to kill his father. Therefore, Drs. Gilbertson and Erdmann believed Odell met the requirements of the *M'Naghten* rule. However, Dr. Farnsworth did not waver from his original conclusion that, at the time of the offense, Odell knew the nature and wrongfulness of the act and did not have the *M'Naghten* defense available to him. Dr. Kienlen did not prepare a second report, but testified at trial that after reviewing the post-it notes, medical records, and a videotape of Dr. Farnsworth's second interview with Odell, she saw no reason to deviate from her initial opinion that Odell did not have the *M'Naghten* defense available to him.

OPINION

The *M'Naghten* rule requires that in order to be excused from criminal liability by reason of insanity, a defendant must show that he either did not know the nature of his act or that the act was wrong. A defendant must prove mental illness at the time of the crime by a preponderance of the evidence.

The narrow question before this court is whether the evidence presented at trial was sufficient to prove, by a preponderance of the evidence, that Odell did not understand the wrongfulness of his acts on April 23, 2000. The parties do not dispute that Odell suffered from a mental illness at the time of the offense. Further, it is undisputed that Odell knew that he was shooting his father and that such a shooting would result in his father's death. Therefore, Odell concedes that he knew the nature of his actions.

On appeal, this Court conducts a rigorous review of the record to determine whether the evidence, direct and circumstantial, viewed most favorably to support a finding of guilt, was sufficient to permit the trial court to reach its conclusion. When reviewing a defendant's challenge to sufficiency of evidence, this court cannot retry facts, but must assume the fact-finder—here, the trial court—believed the state's witnesses and disbelieved any contradictory evidence. This court has held that the issue of legal mental illness is a question for the finder of fact to resolve. Broad deference is granted to the fact-finder in determining the appropriate weight to assign expert psychiatric testimony.

In the trial court's extensive findings of fact and verdict, it carefully considered the evidence presented by all four experts and determined the believability and weight to be given to each expert's testimony. Accordingly, the court decided to give greater weight to the opinions of Drs. Farnsworth and Kienlen because their reports were more consistent with Odell's behavior and belief system.

The court could not reconcile the opinions of Drs. Gilbertson and Erdmann with several facts of the case; namely, that on April 23, 2000, immediately before and after the murder, Odell was able to communicate and interact with others normally. Further, the court questioned some of the underpinnings of Dr. Erdmann's revised analysis and found that in his first and second opinions Dr. Erdmann had relied on similar facts to support divergent conclusions. Finally, the court concluded that Odell had proved by a preponderance of the evidence that, at the time of the murder, he was suffering from a severe mental illness, but that Odell had failed to prove that because of his mental illness he did not understand the nature of his act or that the act constituting the offense was wrong.

Upon a rigorous review of the record, noting the broad deference granted to the fact-finder in determining the appropriate weight to assign expert psychiatric testimony and viewing the evidence most favorably to support a finding of guilt, we hold that sufficient evidence existed to support the trial court's conviction of Odell.

Affirmed.

QUESTIONS

1. State the elements in Minnesota's version of the right-wrong test.
2. List all the facts relevant to each element of the test.
3. Summarize the court's arguments for its decision.
4. In your opinion, was Darren Odell entitled to the defense of insanity, according to the Minnesota

(continues)

(continued)

statute? Back up your answer with facts and arguments in the case excerpt.

5. Now, read the more detailed version of the case that appeared in *City Pages* (Hawkins 2003). Assume Hawkins's version to be true:

> Darren Odell had just about finished Easter dinner when he killed his father. There had been ham, of course, and potatoes, and some kind of salad with whipped cream in it, he later told detectives. Just before 6:00 P.M., while his relatives were eating dessert, Odell left the dining room to get the gun he had hidden in his pickup, and more ice for his Pepsi. "I like Pepsi with ice just because it's watered down a little bit," he explained afterward. "I watch my health and that now. I usually don't drink a can of pop straight."
>
> It was Sunday, April 23, 2000, and Darren had been thinking about killing his father for more than two years. Several times he'd brought the gun to family gatherings at his great-aunt's house in Blaine. But the time never seemed right. Sometimes there were too many people in the way who might get injured; sometimes his three-year-old niece was present, and he didn't want to upset her.
>
> Dennis Odell had arrived at the Easter gathering with a card for Darren signed "Love, Dad." Darren later said he knew his father was trying hard to do something nice, but he didn't believe the words on the card. "His eyes were kind of teary," Darren commented later. "He knew he wasn't handling it right, not making things better."
>
> After he got his gun, Darren retrieved a few cubes of ice from his aunt's freezer and poured the rest of his Pepsi into his glass, which was resting on the kitchen table. Instead of picking up the drink, though, he walked to the dining room and fired four [*sic*] shots into his father's chest.
>
> Darren walked back into the kitchen, turned and looked at the people still seated at the dinner table, and left the house. He drove away, but ended up just circling the block. When the police came, he lay down in the driveway, told the officers where to find his gun, and suggested they take the spare magazine of ammunition out of his back pocket.
>
> He was equally cooperative at the police station, although he seemed to think that the interrogation was a formality. "It feels like a ton of bricks off me," he explained to the detectives. "I can go back out there now and just leave, live a normal life again, without having to deal with my dad and all. Do you think I'll have to go to trial for this? I just would like to go home and really not deal with anything anymore. Just start over."
>
> Odell did not get to go home that day. It quickly became clear that he was so severely mentally ill he couldn't even stand trial. He was sent to a state psychiatric hospital, where he was kept on heavy medication for the next two and a half years. At first, the doctors who evaluated his mental health were convinced that he knew right from wrong and should eventually be tried. . . .
>
> As Odell flitted in and out of sanity, and as the new evidence regarding the strength of his delusions was uncovered, a small army of psychiatrists and psychologists examined and re-examined him. In the end, all would agree that Odell suffered from chronic paranoid schizophrenia and that he killed his father because he believed the two were locked in a contest for survival. But they wouldn't be able to agree whether Odell was legally insane. . . .
>
> Darren Odell may well have known that his actions would be seen as wrong. On one hand, he took a number of steps to make sure that no one else would be hurt during the shooting, and that his niece wouldn't have to see the killing. He even bought a silencer to spare everyone's ears. He practiced regularly at a target range. After he shot his father, he waited for the police. . . .
>
> In May 1998 Darren bought a gun, a 9mm Beretta, and took up target practice. From the start, he said, he was concerned about causing injury to anyone but his father. He used earplugs and bought a silencer. He would head right home after visiting the shooting range so that there would be no chance the weapon might be stolen and used.

Several times over the years he loaded the gun and took it to his aunt's house for family get-togethers. But there were always too many people milling around, he later said, too many children he didn't want to see the shooting.

That Easter, when Darren realized he had a clear shot at Dennis from his aunt's kitchen doorway and the kids were outside, he paced back and forth in the kitchen trying to decide whether the moment had really arrived. Eventually, he concluded that it had. He aimed carefully because he wanted his father to die as quickly as possible. "I hit him point-blank, in the heart I believe," Darren Odell told police. "I know it was a painful death, but I thought it could have been more painful if he was hit in the head or if he suffered a long time.

"It's difficult for me to talk about, 'cause I love my dad so, so much when I was growin' up and that," he continued. "Inside I feel terrible. But I suffered enough emotionally and physically and I sure wasn't gonna have my dad put me back down into, you know, into a place or mental institution or something again for anything." . . .

Odell was to find himself back in a psychiatric ward within a couple of weeks, however. Separate experts had been retained by the prosecution, defense, and court. . . . The experts . . . concluded that Odell knew that shooting his father was wrong, and that he did not meet the legal definition of insanity. . . .

Did Hawkins's version of the facts in the case change your mind? Explain your answer.

The Irresistible Impulse Test

LO 6

Just because you know something is wrong—even if you fully *appreciate* its wrongfulness—doesn't mean you can stop yourself from doing it. (I used to be fat. I knew and fully appreciated the "wrongfulness" of overeating. I can remember so many times knowing those french fries were really bad for me, but I just couldn't stop myself from shoving them in.) Critics who faulted the narrow cognitive bent of the right-wrong test recommended bringing will, or volition, into the picture (it *was* an equal part of the picture during the Middle Ages). According to the **irresistible impulse test,** we can't blame or deter people who because of a mental disease or defect know that what they're doing is "wrong" but can't bring their actions into line with their knowledge of right and wrong.

Only a few jurisdictions have supplemented the right-wrong test with a test that takes volition into account. According to the test, even if defendants know what they're doing, and know it's wrong, they can qualify for a verdict of not guilty by reason of insanity if they suffer from a mental disease that damages their volition (willpower).

In 1877, the court in *Parsons v. State* spelled out the application of the right-wrong test with its irresistible impulse supplement:

1. At the time of the crime, was the defendant afflicted with "a disease of the mind"?
2. If so, did the defendant know right from wrong with respect to the act charged? If not, the law excuses the defendant.
3. If the defendant did have such knowledge, the law will still excuse him if two conditions concur:
    a. If the mental disease caused the defendant to so far lose the power to choose between right and wrong and to avoid doing the alleged act that the disease destroyed his free will and
    b. If the mental disease was the sole cause of the act

bifurcated (two-stage) trial, a two-phase trial, in which the first phase determines whether the state has met its burden of proof and, if so, the second phase determines whether the defendant has sustained the burden of establishing a mental illness defense

irresistible impulse test, we can't blame or deter people who because of a mental disease or defect know that what they're doing is "wrong" but can't bring their actions into line with their knowledge of right and wrong

Georgia's Criminal Code (2006, Title 16, Section 16-3-3) provides:

> A person shall not be found guilty of a crime when, at the time of the act, . . . because of mental disease, injury, or congenital deficiency, [he] acted as he did because of a delusional compulsion as to such act which overmastered his will to resist committing the crime.

Some critics say the irresistible impulse supplement doesn't go far enough. First, they argue that it should include not just *sudden* impulses but also conduct "characterized by brooding and reflection." Others claim that the irresistible requirement requires that defendants lack total control over their actions. Still others maintain that it's impossible to distinguish between irresistible impulses and those that are simply *unresisted*. In other words, it allows too much room for fakers.

Other critics reject volition utterly. They argue that allowing people who lack self-control to escape punishment cripples both retribution and deterrence. They point to the high-profile case of John Hinckley Jr., acquitted because the jury found him insane when, in 1981, he attempted to assassinate President Ronald Reagan to get actress Jodie Foster's attention.

After the "river of fury" that followed Hinckley's trial (Perlin 1989–90, 637), the federal government and several states abolished the irresistible impulse defense on the ground that juries can't distinguish between irresistible impulses beyond the power to control and those that aren't. The federal statute (U.S. Code 2003) abolishing the irresistible impulse test in federal cases provides as follows:

> It is an affirmative defense to a prosecution under any Federal statute that, at the time of the commission of the acts constituting the offense, the defendant, as a result of a severe mental disease or defect, was unable to appreciate the nature and quality or the wrongfulness of his acts. Mental disease or defect does not otherwise constitute a defense.

LO 7

*The Product of Mental Illness Test (*Durham *Rule)*

As the science of psychiatry and psychology advanced, the right-wrong test generated increasing criticism. One line of criticism began in the 1950s, when many social reformers thought that Freudian psychology could cure individual and social "diseases." *Durham v. U.S.* (1954) reflects the influence of that psychology. According to the Court:

> The science of psychiatry now recognizes that a man is an integrated personality and that reason, which is only one element in that personality, is not the sole determinant of his conduct. The right-wrong test, which considers knowledge or reason alone, is therefore an inadequate guide to mental responsibility for criminal behavior. (871)

product-of-mental-illness test, also known as the ***Durham*** **rule,** acts that are the "products" of mental disease or defect excuse criminal liability

Durham **rule,** the product-of-mental-illness test; acts that are the "products" of mental disease or defect excuse criminal liability

Based on these insights, the U.S. Circuit Court for the District of Columbia replaced the right-wrong test with the product-of-mental-illness test, also known as the *Durham* rule. According to this "new" test (New Hampshire adopted it in 1871), acts that are the "products" of mental disease or defect excuse criminal liability. So, with this test, the court stretched the concept of insanity beyond the purely intellectual knowledge examined by the right-wrong test into deeper areas of cognition and will.

Disillusionment with Freudian psychology, a major shift in public opinion from rehabilitation to punishment, and the anger and disgust following the verdict in John

Hinckley's trial for attempting to kill President Reagan prompted the U.S. Congress to replace the product test with the right-wrong test. That legislation did away with the product test in the District of Columbia, where *Durham* was decided. Only two states, New Hampshire and Maine, ever adopted the product test. Maine abandoned the test. That leaves the product test in effect only in New Hampshire, where it was created in 1871.

The Substantial Capacity Test (Model Penal Code Test)

LO 8

The substantial capacity test, adopted in the MPC, is supposed to remove the objections to the right-wrong test, its irresistible impulse supplement, and the psychiatric-oriented *Durham* rule. It emphasizes both of the qualities in insanity that should determine culpability: reason and will (Schoop 1988).

substantial capacity test (the MPC test), MPC test designed to remove the objections to the right-wrong test, its irresistible impulse supplement, and the *Durham* rule

The MPC test changes the *McNaughtan* right-wrong/irresistible impulse supplement tests in several ways. First, as the name of the test indicates, defendants need not lack total mental capacity; the test adds the word "substantial capacity" to remove the possibility of requiring "total lack of reason (the "wild beast") cognition test. And it removes the possibility that "irresistible" in "irresistible impulse" means total lack of knowledge and control. So people who can tell right from wrong only modestly and/or who have only a feeble will to resist are insane.

Most substantial capacity test states follow the MPC's definition of "substantial capacity":

> A person is not responsible for criminal conduct if at the time of such conduct as a result of mental disease or defect he lacks substantial capacity either to appreciate the criminality [wrongfulness] of his conduct or to conform his conduct to the requirements of law. (ALI 1985 [3], 163)

Second, the use of "appreciate" instead of "know" makes clear that intellectual awareness by itself isn't enough to create culpability; emotional (affective) components of understanding are required. The phrase "conform his conduct" removes the requirement of a "sudden" lack of control. In other words, the code provision eliminates the suggestion that losing control means losing it on the spur of the moment, as the "impulse" in "irresistible impulse test" can be read to mean. The MPC's definition of "mental disease or defect" excludes psychopathic personalities, habitual criminals, and antisocial personalities from the defense (Hermann and Sor 1983, 522).

Third, the word "wrong" was changed twice, first to "criminality" and then finally to "wrongfulness." The drafters took the position that the insanity defense deals with an impaired "moral sense," stemming from a broader application of the guilty mind (*mens rea*), rather than a strict criminal mind. Supporters of the MPC test believe that the simpler, plain language will help jurors to avoid feeling forced to rely on experts so they can "reason to its own conclusions about the criminal responsibility of the defendant based on whether he was insane at the time the crime was committed" (522–23).

The MPC test has its critics. Some claim that "substantial impairment" is "vague" and that it allows too many defendants to escape criminal responsibility. But the strongest criticism is that it "continues the faults of the *McNaughten* [*sic*] rules and the irresistible impulse tests by providing separate knowledge and control tests; in doing so, this test seems to rest on a bifurcated rather than an integrated view of the human personality" (524).

LO 9

THE BURDEN OF PROOF

The defense of insanity not only poses definition problems but also gives rise to difficulties in who has the burden to prove insanity, however it's defined. States vary as to who has to prove insanity and how convincingly they have to do so. The Hinckley trial made these questions the subject of heated debate and considerable legislative reform in the 1980s.

Federal law required the government to prove Hinckley's sanity beyond a reasonable doubt. So if Hinckley's lawyers could raise a doubt in jurors' minds about his sanity, the jury had to acquit him. That means that even though the jury thought Hinckley was sane, if they weren't convinced beyond a reasonable doubt that he was, they had to acquit him.

And that's just what happened: the jury did believe Hinckley was sane but had their doubts, so they acquitted him. In 1984, the federal Comprehensive Crime Control Act (Federal Criminal Code and Rules 1988, § 17[b]) shifted the burden of proof from the government having to prove sanity beyond a reasonable doubt to defendants having to prove they were insane by clear and convincing evidence.

Most states don't follow the federal standard; they call insanity an affirmative defense. As an affirmative defense, sanity and, therefore, responsibility are presumed. The practical reason for the presumption saves the government the time and effort to prove sanity in the vast number of cases where insanity isn't an issue. In that sense, it's like concurrence: it's necessary but practically never an issue (*Clark v. Arizona* 2006).

To overcome the sanity presumption, the defense has the burden to offer some evidence of insanity. If they do, the burden shifts to the government to prove sanity. States differ as to how heavy the government's burden to prove sanity is. Some states require proof beyond a reasonable doubt; some require clear and convincing evidence; and some require a preponderance of the evidence. There's a trend in favor of shifting the burden to defendants and making that burden heavier. This is both because Hinckley's trial generated antagonism toward the insanity defense and because of growing hostility toward rules that the public believes coddle criminals (ALI 1985 [3], 226; Perlin 1989–90).

LO 10

THE DEFENSE OF DIMINISHED CAPACITY

diminished capacity, an attempt to prove that the defendant, incapable of the requisite intent of the crime charged, is innocent of that crime but may well be guilty of a lesser one

diminished responsibility, the defendant argues, "What I did was wrong, but under the circumstances I'm *less* responsible"

"Diminished capacity" is an unfortunate term. First, it's not an affirmative defense in the sense that it excuses criminal conduct. It's a failure-of-proof defense (discussed at the beginning of the chapter), "a rule of evidence that allows the defense to introduce evidence to negate . . . specific intent" in a very narrow set of cases—premeditation in first-degree murder. "It is an attempt to prove that the defendant, incapable of the requisite intent of the crime charged, is innocent of that crime but may well be guilty of a lesser one" (*State v. Phipps* 1994, 143)—second-degree murder instead of first-degree murder.

Second, diminished capacity isn't the same as diminished responsibility, with which it's often confused. Diminished responsibility is a defense of excuse; it's a variation on the defendant's argument, "What I did was wrong, but under the circumstances I'm not responsible." In diminished responsibility, the defendant argues, "What I did was wrong, but under the circumstances I'm *less* responsible." According to *State v. Phipps* (1994; excerpted later in "The Syndrome Defenses"):

> A defendant pleading diminished responsibility does not seek relief from punishment by justification or excuse, but seeks to be punished for a lesser offense which he generally admits committing. In contrast, diminished capacity focuses on a defendant's

> capacity to commit a specific intent crime, and, if established, does not excuse punishment, but results in punishment instead for the general intent crime defendant was capable of committing. Evidence to demonstrate such a lack of specific intent is not equivalent to evidence to establish diminished responsibility. (144)

Most states reject both types of diminished capacity. California is one example. The legislature abolished diminished capacity, mostly because of public hostility to it:

> The defense of diminished capacity is hereby abolished. In a criminal action . . . evidence concerning an accused person's . . . mental illness, disease, or defect shall not be admissible to show or negate capacity to form the particular purpose, intent, motive, malice aforethought, knowledge, or other mental state required for the commission of the crime charged. . . . (California Penal Code 2003, § 25)

The statute didn't eliminate diminished capacity altogether. It provided that "diminished capacity or a mental disorder may be considered by the court [but] only at the time of sentencing."

In practice, diminished capacity and diminished responsibility apply only to homicide. Most of the cases involve reducing first- to second-degree murder. In a very few cases, defendants are allowed to introduce evidence to reduce murder to manslaughter. In other words, diminished capacity and diminished responsibility are very rare issues in criminal law (LaFave 2003a, 453). How often do defendants succeed in reducing their liability when they're allowed to introduce "diminishment" evidence? Unfortunately, we don't know.

THE EXCUSE OF AGE

LO 11

The common law divided children into three categories for the purpose of deciding their capacity to commit crimes:

1. **UNDER 7.** Children had no criminal capacity.
2. **AGES 7–14.** Children were presumed to have no criminal capacity, but the presumption could be overcome.
3. **OVER 14.** Children had the same capacity as adults.

Today, statutes determine when young people can be convicted of crimes. These statutes come in several varieties, and they vary as to the age of capacity to commit crimes. One type of statute identifies a specific age, usually 14, but sometimes as young as 10 and as old as 18. These statutes usually provide that children under the specified age are subject to juvenile delinquency proceedings, even very young children. Another type of statute grants exclusive jurisdiction to juvenile courts up to a certain age but makes exceptions for a list of serious crimes. A third type of statute simply states that juvenile court jurisdiction isn't exclusive (LaFave 2003a, 487).

All states have established juvenile justice systems to handle juvenile delinquency. One kind of delinquency, and the one we're concerned with here, is conduct that violates the criminal law. Most juvenile court statutes place no lower age limit on delinquency; they all place an upper age limit, almost always 18. Don't misunderstand this to mean that all juvenile cases will be handled in juvenile court. Every state has a statute that provides for the transfer of juveniles to adult criminal court. The technical term for this transfer is "**waiver to adult criminal court**," meaning the juvenile court gives up its jurisdiction over the case and turns it over to the adult criminal court.

waiver to adult criminal court, meaning the juvenile court gives up its jurisdiction over the case and turns it over to the adult criminal court

The shift from the philosophy of rehabilitation to retribution has led to more juveniles at younger ages being tried as adults (Table 6.3).

TABLE 6.3

Juveniles Tried as Adults
• In New York, two fifteen-year-old private school students stand accused of savagely slashing to death a forty-four-year-old real estate agent and dumping his body in the lake at midnight in Central Park.
• In New Jersey, a fifteen-year-old awaits trial for the murder, sexual assault, and robbery of an eleven-year-old who had been going door to door collecting for his school's PTA fundraiser.
• In Mississippi, a sixteen-year-old slit the throat of his own mother before going to Pearl High School to hunt down the girl who had just broken up with him—killing her, killing another girl, and wounding seven of his high school classmates.
• In Arizona, three teenagers (out of a believed ten), ages thirteen, fourteen, and sixteen, face prosecution for the eighteen-hour abduction and gang rape of a fourteen-year-old.
• In California, three Satan-worshipping high school students, ages fifteen, sixteen, and seventeen, stand charged with drugging, raping, torturing, and murdering a fifteen-year-old, reportedly in hopes that a virgin sacrifice would earn them "a ticket to hell." (Gordon 1999, 193–94)

judicial waiver, when juvenile court judges use their discretion to transfer a juvenile to adult criminal court

Waivers to adult court come in three varieties: judicial, prosecutorial, and legislative. By far, the most common is **judicial waiver**; that's when a juvenile court judge uses her discretion to transfer a juvenile to adult criminal court. Most states have adopted the criteria for making the waiver decision approved by the U.S. Supreme Court (*Kent v. United States* 1966) for the District of Columbia. These include:

- The seriousness of the offense
- Whether the offense was committed in an aggressive, violent, premeditated, willful manner
- Whether the offense was against a person
- The amount of evidence against the juvenile
- The sophistication and maturity of the juvenile
- The prior record of the juvenile
- The threat the juvenile poses to public safety (LaFave 2003a, 490)

CASE

In **State v. K.R.L.** *(1992), the Washington State Supreme Court rejected the state's argument that an eight-year-old boy had the capacity to form the intent to commit burglary.*

Was he too young to commit burglary?

State v. K.R.L.

840 P.2d 210 (Wash.App. 1992)

HISTORY

K.R.L., an eight-year-old boy, was convicted of residential burglary by the Superior Court, Clallam County, and he appealed. The Court of Appeals reversed.

ALEXANDER, J.

FACTS

In July 1990, K.R.L., who was then 8 years and 2 months old, was playing with a friend behind a business building in Sequim. Catherine Alder, who lived near the business, heard the boys playing and she instructed them to leave because she believed the area was dangerous. Alder said that K.R.L.'s response was belligerent, the child indicating that he would leave "in a minute." Losing patience with the boys, Alder said "no, not in a minute, now, get out of there now." The boys then ran off. Three days later, during daylight hours, K.R.L. entered Alder's home without her permission. He proceeded to pull a live goldfish from her fishbowl, chopped it into several pieces with a steak knife, and "smeared it all over the counter." He then went into Alder's bathroom and clamped a "plugged in" hair curling iron onto a towel.

Upon discovering what had taken place, Alder called the Sequim police on the telephone and reported the incident.

A Sequim police officer contacted K.R.L.'s mother and told her that he suspected that K.R.L. was the perpetrator of the offense against Alder. K.R.L.'s mother confronted the child with the accusation and he admitted to her that he had entered the house. She then took K.R.L. to the Sequim Police Department where the child was advised of his constitutional rights by a Sequim police officer.

This took place in the presence of K.R.L.'s mother, who indicated that she did not believe "he really understood." K.R.L. told the police officer that he knew it was wrong to enter Alder's home. The statement given by K.R.L. to the officer was not offered by the State to prove guilt. Initially, the State took the position that K.R.L. fully understood those rights and that he had made a free and voluntary waiver of rights. Defense counsel objected to the admission of the statements and eventually the State withdrew its offer of the evidence, concluding that the evidence was cumulative in that K.R.L.'s admissions were already in evidence through the testimony of his mother. K.R.L. was charged in Clallam County Juvenile Court with residential burglary, a class B felony. Residential burglary is defined in RCW 9A.52.025 as:

> A person is guilty of residential burglary if, with intent to commit a crime against a person or property therein, the person enters or remains unlawfully in a dwelling....

At trial, considerable testimony was devoted to the issue of whether K.R.L. possessed sufficient capacity to commit that crime. The juvenile court judge heard testimony in that regard from K.R.L.'s mother, Catherine Alder, two school officials, a Sequim policeman who had dealt with K.R.L. on two prior occasions as well as the incident leading to the charge, one of K.R.L.'s neighbors, and the neighbor's son. K.R.L.'s mother, the neighbor, the neighbor's son, and the police officer testified to an incident that had occurred several months before the alleged residential burglary.

This incident was referred to by the police officer as the "Easter Candy Episode." Their testimony revealed that K.R.L. had taken some Easter candy from a neighbor's house without permission. As a consequence, the Sequim police were called to investigate. K.R.L. responded to a question by the investigating officer, saying to him that he "knew it was wrong and he wouldn't like it if somebody took his candy."

The same officer testified to another incident involving K.R.L. This was described as the "Joyriding Incident," and it occurred prior to the "Easter Candy Episode." It involved K.R.L. riding the bicycles of two neighbor children without having their permission to do so. K.R.L. told the police officer that he "knew it was wrong" to ride the bicycles.

The assistant principal of K.R.L.'s elementary school testified about K.R.L.'s development. He said that K.R.L. was of "very normal" intelligence. K.R.L.'s first grade teacher said that K.R.L. had "some difficulty" in school. He said that he would put K.R.L. in the "lower age academically."

K.R.L.'s mother testified at some length about her son and, in particular, about the admissions he made to her regarding his entry into Alder's home. Speaking of that incident, she said that he admitted to her that what he did was wrong "after I beat him with a belt, black and blue." She also said that her son told her "that the Devil was making him do bad things."

The juvenile court rejected the argument of K.R.L.'s counsel that the State had not presented sufficient evidence to show that K.R.L. was capable of committing a crime. It found him guilty, saying:

> From my experience in my eight, nine years on the bench, it's my belief that the so-called juvenile criminal system is a paper tiger and it's not going to be much of a threat to Mr. [K.R.L.], so I don't think that for that reason there is a whole lot to protect him from.

OPINION

There is only one issue—did the trial court err in concluding that K.R.L. had the capacity to commit the crime of residential burglary? RCW 9A.04.050

(continues)

(continued)
speaks to the capability of children to commit crimes and, in pertinent part, provides:

> Children under the age of eight years are incapable of committing crime. Children of eight and under twelve years of age are presumed to be incapable of committing crime, but this presumption may be removed by proof that they have sufficient capacity to understand the act or neglect, and to know that it was wrong.

This statute applies in juvenile proceedings. Because K.R.L. was 8 years old at the time he is alleged to have committed residential burglary, he was presumed incapable of committing that offense. The burden was, therefore, on the State to overcome that presumption and that burden could only be removed by evidence that was "clear and convincing." Thus, on review we must determine if there is evidence from which a rational trier of fact could find capacity by clear and convincing evidence.

There are no reported cases in Washington dealing with the capacity of 8-year-old children to commit crimes. That is not too surprising in light of the fact that up to age 8, children are deemed incapable of committing crimes.

The State emphasizes that K.R.L. appeared to appreciate that what he did at Alder's home and on prior occasions was wrong. When K.R.L. was being beaten "black and blue" by his mother, he undoubtedly came to the realization that what he had done was wrong. We are certain that this conditioned the child, after the fact, to know that what he did was wrong. That is a far different thing than one appreciating the quality of his or her acts at the time the act is being committed.

In arguing that it met its burden, the State placed great reliance on the fact that K.R.L. had exhibited bad conduct several months before during the so-called "Easter Candy" and "Joyriding" incidents. Again, we do not know much about these incidents, but it seems clear that neither of them involved serious misconduct and they shed little light on whether this child understood the elements of the act of burglary or knew that it was wrong.

Here, we have a child of very tender years—only two months over 8 years. While the State made a valiant effort to show prior bad acts on the part of the child, an objective observer would have to conclude that these were examples of behavior not uncommon to many young children.

Furthermore, there was no expert testimony in this case from a psychologist or other expert who told the court anything about the ability of K.R.L. to know and appreciate the gravity of his conduct. Although two school officials testified, one of them said K.R.L. was of an age lower than 8, "academically." In short, there is simply not enough here so that we can say that in light of the State's significant burden, there is sufficient evidence to support a finding of capacity.

REVERSED.

QUESTIONS

1. Was the trial judge or the Supreme Court of Washington right in the ruling on the capacity of K.R.L. to form criminal intent? Back up your answer with facts from the case.
2. Did K.R.L. know what he was doing intellectually yet not sufficiently appreciate what he was doing? What facts support this conclusion?
3. Should it matter whether he appreciated what he did as long as he knew what he did was wrong? Explain your answer.

EXPLORING FURTHER

The Excuse of Age

1. Was he too old to be responsible?

FACTS

A prosecutor was faced with the question of whether the other end of the age spectrum, old age, should affect the capacity to commit crimes:

> You have this married couple, married for over 50 years, living in a retirement home. The guy sends his wife out for bagels and while the wife can still get around she forgets and brings back onion rolls. Not a capital offense, right?
>
> Anyway, the guy goes berserk and he axes his wife; he kills the poor woman with a Boy Scout–type axe! What do we do now? Set a

high bail? Prosecute? Get a conviction and send the fellow to prison? You tell me! We did nothing. The media dropped it quickly and, I hope, that's it. (Cohen 1985, 9)

DECISION

The prosecutor declined to prosecute.

2. Can age aggravate an offense?

People v. Muñoz, 200 N.Y.S.2d 957 (1961)

Youth doesn't always excuse criminal conduct; it can also make the consequences worse. For example, 17-year-old Miguel Muñoz was convicted of possessing a switch-blade under a New York City ordinance that prohibited youths under 21 from carrying such knives. Had Muñoz been over 21, what he did wouldn't have been a crime.

ETHICAL DILEMMA

Is it ethical policy to try an eight-year-old for murder?

St. Johns Boy, 8, Suspected of Double Murder

Dad, 2nd Man Found Shot to Death; Charges Planned

Nov. 8, 2008, 12:00 AM An eight-year-old boy faces double-murder charges in the shooting death of his father and another man while residents in the bucolic community of St. Johns try to make sense of the chilling crime. "This is precedent-setting. We're going to charge an eight-year-old with two counts of homicide," Police Chief Roy Melnick said. "We haven't had anything like this in Apache County in my 23 years as a prosecutor," County Attorney Criss Candelaria said. "We need to figure out what was going on in this boy's head."

The child's father, 29, and a boarder, Tim Romans, 39, were found dead at the family residence about 5 P.M. Wednesday, shortly after neighbors reported the sound of gunfire. The *Arizona Republic* is withholding the father's and child's names to avoid identifying a juvenile. Melnick said police discovered one of the bodies outside the front door, the other in an upstairs room.

Instructions

Write a one-page essay answering the question: Is it ethical public policy to charge an eight-year-old with first-degree murder. Back up your answer with the information you got from the "The Excuse of Age" section (p. 211).

Source: Wagner, Dennis. 2008 (November 8). *Arizona Republic.*

THE DEFENSE OF DURESS

LO 12

"Sometimes people are forced to do what they do," writes Professor Hyman Gross (1978). What if what they're forced to do is a crime? Should they be excused? The defense of duress is about answering these questions. According to Professor Gross, "It seems that the compulsion ought to count in their favor. After all, we say, such a person wasn't free to do otherwise—he couldn't help himself" (276).

defense of duress, when defendants use the excuse that they were forced to do what they did

On the other hand, he continues:

> There are times . . . when we ought to stand firm and run the risk of harm to ourselves instead of taking a way out that means harm to others. In such a situation we must expect to pay the price if we cause harm when we prefer ourselves, for then the harm is our fault even though we did not mean it and deeply regret it. (276)

Let's take a closer look at duress and its elements.

THE PROBLEM WITH THE DEFENSE OF DURESS

Professor Gross's comments strike at the heart of the problem of duress: it's hard to blame someone who's forced to commit a crime, but should we excuse people who harm innocent people to save themselves? The positions taken by three of the last two centuries' great authorities on criminal law show how different the answers can be. At one extreme is the great historian of the criminal law and judge, Sir James Stephen (1883, 108), who maintained that duress is never an excuse for crime. (Stephen did say, however, that duress should mitigate the punishment.) At the other extreme is Professor Glanville Williams (1961, 755). Author of a highly respected treatise on criminal law, he says the law should excuse individuals if they're so "in thrall[ed] to some power" the law can't control their choice. Professor Jerome Hall (1960, 448), author of yet another distinguished treatise, took the middle position that duress shouldn't excuse the most serious crimes, but it should be an excuse when the choice is "Commit a minor crime or die—*now*!"

LO 13

THE ELEMENTS OF THE DEFENSE OF DURESS

There are four elements in the defense of duress:

1. *Nature of the threat.* Death threats are required in some states. Threats of "serious bodily injury" qualify in several. Others don't specify what threats qualify.
2. *Immediacy of the threats.* In some states, the harm has to be "instant." In others, "imminent" harm is required. In Louisiana, duress is an excuse only if the defendant reasonably believed the person making the threats would "immediately carry out the threats if the crime were not committed."
3. *Crimes the defense applies to.* In the majority of states, duress isn't a defense to murder. In other states, it's a defense to all crimes. Some states are silent on the point.
4. *Level of belief regarding the threat.* Most states require a reasonable belief the threat is real. Others demand the threat actually be real. Some say nothing on the point.

Figure 6.1 provides excerpts from the duress statutes in three states.

DURESS STATUTES

New York Penal Code, § 40.00

In any prosecution for an offense, it is an affirmative defense that the defendant engaged in the proscribed conduct because he was coerced to do so by the use or threatened imminent use of unlawful physical force upon him or a third person, which force or threatened force a person of reasonable firmness in his situation would have been unable to resist.

Alabama Penal Code, Section 13A-3-30 (a)

It is a defense to prosecution that the actor engaged in the proscribed conduct because he was compelled to do so by the threat of imminent death or serious physical injury to himself or another. . . .

(d) The defense provided by this section is unavailable in a prosecution for:
  (1) murder; or
  (2) any killing of another under aggravated circumstances.

Minnesota Criminal Code, § 609.08 (3)

When any crime is committed or participated in by two or more persons, any one of whom participates only under compulsion by another engaged therein, who by threats creates a reasonable apprehension in the mind of such participator that in case of refusal that participator is liable to instant death, such threats and apprehension constitute duress which will excuse such participator from criminal liability.

FIGURE 6.1

THE DEFENSE OF INTOXICATION

LO 14

Johnny James went quietly to his death by lethal injection . . . inside the Texas prison system's Huntsville Unit. His crimes were disgusting. He abducted two women, forced them to have sex with each other, raped them, and then shot them both in the head. One died, but the other lived to identify him at trial. The Texas courts turned a deaf ear to James's plea that he was too drunk to know what he was doing when he abducted, raped, and shot his victims.

According to Professor George Fletcher (1978), the defense of intoxication is "buffeted between two conflicting principles":

1. **ACCOUNTABILITY.** Those who get drunk should take the consequences of their actions. Someone who gets drunk is liable for the violent consequences.
2. **CULPABILITY.** Criminal liability and punishment depend on blameworthiness (846).

The common law approach focused on the first principle:

> As to artificial, voluntarily contracted madness, by drunkenness or intoxication, which, depriving men of their reason, puts them in a temporary frenzy; our law looks upon this as an aggravation of the offense, rather than as an excuse for any criminal misbehavior. (Blackstone 1769, 25–26)

The Johnny James case is only one dramatic example that the common law principle is alive and well today. John Gibeaut (1997), who wrote about the *James* case in the article "Sobering Thoughts," notes the contemporary emphasis on accountability in the subtitle: "Legislatures and courts increasingly are just saying no to intoxication as a defense or mitigating factor." Section 13-03 of the Arizona Criminal Code (2003) is a typical accountability statute:

> Temporary intoxication resulting from the voluntary ingestion, consumption, inhalation or injection of alcohol, an illegal substance under chapter 34 of this title or other psychoactive substances or the abuse of prescribed medications does not constitute insanity and is not a defense for any criminal act or requisite state of mind.

Between November 1996 and May 1997, at least ten states introduced bills similar to the Arizona statute. According to a member of the Prosecution Function Committee of the American Bar Association's Criminal Justice Section, "The fight goes back to the ancient struggle over just how much free will one has" (Gibeaut 1997, 57).

What we have said so far applies only to *voluntary* intoxication. **Involuntary intoxication** is an excuse to criminal liability in all states. Involuntary intoxication includes cases in which defendants don't know they're taking intoxicants or know but are forced to take them. In *People v. Penman* (1915), a man took what his friend told him were "breath perfumer" pills; in fact, they were cocaine tablets. While under their influence, he killed someone. The court allowed the defense of intoxication.

involuntary intoxication, an excuse to criminal liability in all states; it includes cases in which defendants don't know they're taking intoxicants or know but are forced to take them

Involuntary intoxication applies only under extreme conditions. According to one authority (Hall 1960), "A person would need to be bound hand and foot and the liquor literally poured down his throat, or . . . would have to be threatened with immediate serious injury" (540). In another case, *Burrows v. State* (1931), where the defendant claimed involuntary intoxication, an eighteen-year-old man was traveling with an older man across the desert. The older man insisted that the young man drink some whiskey with him. When he said no, the older man got abusive. Afraid that the older man would throw him out of the car in the middle of the desert without any money, he drank the whiskey, got drunk, and killed the older man. The court rejected his defense of involuntary intoxication, because the older man had not compelled the youth "to drink against his will and consent."

The reason the law excuses involuntary intoxication and not voluntary intoxication is that we can blame voluntarily intoxicated persons and hold them accountable for their actions. Why? They chose to put themselves in a state where they either didn't know or couldn't control what they were doing. We can't blame involuntarily intoxicated persons for their actions. Why not? Because people forced or tricked into an intoxicated state didn't choose to put themselves out of control. (Review Chapter 3, p. 104, on voluntarily induced involuntary conditions that qualify as *actus reus*.)

Alcohol isn't the only intoxicant covered by the defense of intoxication. In most states, it includes all "substances" that disturb mental and physical capacities. In *State v. Hall* (1974), Hall's friend gave him a pill, telling him it was only a "little sunshine" to make him feel "groovy." In fact, the pill contained LSD (lysergic acid diethylamide). A car picked up Hall while he was hitchhiking. The drug caused Hall to hallucinate that the driver was a rabid dog, and, under this sad delusion, Hall shot and killed the driver. The court said that criminal responsibility recognizes no difference between alcohol and other intoxicants.

LO 15

THE DEFENSE OF ENTRAPMENT

Ancient tyrants and modern dictators alike have relied on secret agents as a law enforcement tool. From the days of Henry VIII to the era of Hitler and Stalin, to Slobodan Milosevic, Saddam Hussein, and Moammar Gadhafi, the world's police states have relied on persuading people to commit crimes, so they could catch and then crush their opponents.

But government persuasion isn't only a dictator's tool. All societies rely on it, even though it violates a basic purpose of government in free societies. The great Victorian British Prime Minister William Gladstone was referring to this purpose when he advised government to make it *easy* to do right and *difficult* to do wrong. Persuading people to commit crimes also flies in the face of the entreaty of the Lord's Prayer to "lead us not into temptation, but deliver us from evil" (Carlson 1987).

entrapment, excuse that argues government agents got people to commit crimes they wouldn't otherwise commit

For a long time, U.S. courts rejected the idea that **entrapment** (government agents getting people to commit crimes they wouldn't otherwise commit) excused criminal liability. In *Board of Commissioners v. Backus* (1864), the New York Supreme Court explained why:

> Even if inducements to commit crime could be assumed to exist in this case, the allegation of the defendant would be but the repetition of the pleas as ancient as the world, and first interposed in Paradise: "The serpent beguiled me and I did eat." That defense was overruled by the great Lawgiver, and whatever estimate we may form, or whatever judgment pass upon the character or conduct of the tempter, this plea has never since availed to shield crime or give indemnity to the culprit, and it is safe to say that under any code of civilized, not to say Christian ethics, it never will. (42)

The court in *People v. Mills* (1904) summed up the acceptance of entrapment this way:

> We are asked to protect the defendant, not because he is innocent, but because a zealous public officer exceeded his powers and held out a bait. The courts do not look to see who held out the bait, but to see who took it. (791)

The earlier attitude was based on indifference to government encouragement to commit crimes. After all, "once the crime is committed, why should it matter what particular incentives were involved and who offered them?" However, attitudes have shifted from indifference to both a "limited sympathy" toward entrapped defendants and a growing intolerance of government inducements to entrap otherwise law-abiding people (Marcus 1986).

The practice of entrapment arose because of the difficulty in enforcing laws against consensual crimes, such as drug offenses, pornography, official wrongdoing, and prostitution. There's no constitutional right not to be entrapped. Entrapment is an affirmative defense created by statutes; that is, defendants have to show some evidence they were entrapped. If they do this, the burden shifts to the prosecution to prove defendants weren't entrapped. The jury—or the judge in trials without juries—decides whether officers in fact entrapped defendants. The courts have adopted two types of tests for entrapment; one is subjective and the other objective.

THE SUBJECTIVE TEST OF ENTRAPMENT

The majority of state and all federal courts have adopted a **subjective test of entrapment.** The subjective test of entrapment focuses on the predisposition of defendants to commit crimes. According to the test, the defense has to prove the government pressured the defendants to commit crimes they wouldn't have committed without the pressure.

subjective test of entrapment, asks whether the intent to commit the crime originated with the defendant

The crucial question in the subjective test is: "Where did the criminal intent originate?" If it originated with the defendant, then the government didn't entrap the defendant. If it originated with the government, then the government did entrap the defendant. For example, in a leading U.S. Supreme Court entrapment case, *Sherman v. U.S.* (1958), Kalchinian, a government informant and undercover agent, met Sherman in a drug treatment center. He struck up a friendship with Sherman and eventually asked Sherman to get him some heroin. Sherman (a heroin addict) refused. Following weeks of persistent begging and pleading, Sherman finally gave in and got Kalchinian some heroin. The police arrested Sherman. The U.S. Supreme Court found that the intent originated with the government. According to the Court, Sherman was hardly predisposed to commit a drug offense given that he was seriously committed to a drug treatment program to cure his addiction.

After defendants present some evidence that the government persuaded them to commit crimes they wouldn't have committed otherwise, the government can prove disposition to commit the crimes in one of the following ways:

- Defendants' prior convictions for similar offenses
- Defendants' willingness to commit similar offenses
- Defendants' display of criminal expertise in carrying out the offense
- Defendants' readiness to commit the crime

Consensual crimes, especially drug offenses, are the usual target of law enforcement inducement tactics, but some police departments have also used them to combat street muggings.

CASE

In **Oliver v. State** ***(1985) and*** **DePasquale v. State** ***(1988),*** *the Nevada Supreme Court dealt with two street mugging decoy cases operating in an area of Las Vegas with a high population of "street people."*

Were they entrapped?

Oliver v. State

703 P.2d 869 (Nev. 1985)

HISTORY

Ernest Oliver was convicted of larceny from the person in the Eighth Judicial District Court and sentenced to ten years in prison. He appealed. The Supreme Court reversed.

GUNDERSON, J.

FACTS

On the night of Oliver's arrest, three policemen undertook to conduct a "decoy operation" near the intersection of Main and Ogden in Las Vegas. That corner is in a downtown area frequented by substantial numbers of persons commonly characterized as "street people," "vagrants," and "derelicts." It appears Oliver, a black man, is one of these.

(continues)

(continued)

Disguised as a vagrant in an old Marine Corps jacket, the decoy officer slumped against a palm tree, pretending to be intoxicated and asleep. His associates concealed themselves nearby. The decoy prominently displayed a ten-dollar bill, positioning it to protrude from the left breast pocket of his jacket. This was done, the decoy later testified, "to provide an opportunity for a dishonest person to prove himself." Oliver, who had the misfortune to come walking down the street, saw the decoy and evidently felt moved to assist him. Shaking and nudging the decoy with his foot, Oliver attempted to warn the decoy that the police would arrest him if he did not move on. The decoy did not respond, and Oliver stepped away. Up to this point, Oliver had shown no predisposition whatever to commit any criminal act.

Then, Oliver saw the ten-dollar bill protruding from the decoy's pocket. He reached down and took it. "Thanks, Home Boy," he said. Thereupon, he was arrested by the decoy and the two other officers. Following the trial, a jury convicted Oliver of larceny from the person, and he has been sentenced to ten years' imprisonment.

OPINION

Oliver's counsel contends he was entrapped into committing the offense in question. We agree. Government agents or officers may not employ extraordinary temptations or inducements. They may not manufacture crime.

We have repeatedly endorsed the following concept: Entrapment is the seduction or improper inducement to commit a crime for the purpose of instituting a criminal prosecution, but if a person in good faith and for the purpose of detecting or discovering a crime or offense furnishes the opportunity for the commission thereof by one who has the requisite criminal intent, it is not entrapment.

Thus, because we discern several facts which we believe combined to create an extraordinary temptation, which was inappropriate to apprehending merely those bent on criminal activity, we feel constrained to reverse Oliver's conviction. We note, first of all, that the decoy portrayed himself as completely susceptible and vulnerable. He did not respond when Oliver attempted to wake him, urging him to avoid arrest by moving to another location. Moreover, the decoy displayed his ten-dollar bill in a manner calculated to tempt any needy person in the area, whether immediately disposed to crime or not.

In the case of Oliver, the police succeeded in tempting a man who apparently did not approach the decoy with larceny in mind, but rather to help him. Even after being lured into petty theft by the decoy's open display of currency and apparent helplessness, Oliver did not go on to search the decoy's pockets or to remove his wallet.

He appealed and the Nevada Supreme Court affirmed.

De Pasquale v. State

757 P.2d 367 (Nev. 1988)

YOUNG, J.

FACTS

In *DePasquale*, four officers on the LVMPD's S.C.A.T. Unit (Street Crime Attack Team) were performing a decoy operation near the intersection of Fremont Street and Casino Center Blvd. in Las Vegas on April 30, 1983, at 11:45 P.M. Officer Debbie Gautwier was the decoy, and Officers Shalhoob, Young, and Harkness were assigned to "backup." Officer Gautwier was dressed in plain clothes and was carrying a tan shoulder bag draped over her left shoulder.

Within one of the side, zippered pockets of the bag, she had placed a $5 bill and $1 bill wrapped with a simulated $100 bill. The money, including the numbers of the simulated $100 bill, were exposed so as to be visible to persons near by; however, the zipper was pulled tight against the money so as to require a concentrated effort to remove it.

Officer Young, also in plain clothes, was standing approximately six to seven feet away from Officer Gautwier (the decoy), near the entrance of the Horseshoe Club, when Randall DeBelloy approached Officer Gautwier from behind and asked if he could borrow a pen. Officer Gautwier stated that she did not have a pen, and DeBelloy retreated eight to ten feet. Within a few seconds he approached a second time, asking for a piece of paper. Again the response was "no." During these approaches Officer Young observed DeBelloy reach around Officer Gautwier toward the exposed cash.

DeBelloy again retreated eight to ten feet from Officer Gautwier. He then motioned with his hand to two men who were another eight to ten feet away, and the trio huddled together for 15 to 30 seconds. As DeBelloy talked with the two men, he looked up and over in the direction of Officer Gautwier. Vincent DePasquale was one of the two men who joined DeBelloy in this huddle.

While this trio was conversing, Officer Gautwier had been waiting for the walk signal at the intersection. When the light changed, she crossed Fremont Street and proceeded southbound on the west sidewalk of Casino Center Blvd. DePasquale and DeBelloy followed her, 15 to 20 feet behind. After crossing the street, Officer Gautwier looked back briefly and saw DeBelloy following her. DePasquale was four to seven feet behind DeBelloy and to his right.

As they walked in this formation, DePasquale yelled out, "Wait lady, can I talk to you for a minute." As Officer Gautwier turned to her right in response—seeing DePasquale whom she identified in court—DeBelloy took a few quick steps to her left side, took the money with his right hand, and ran.

DeBelloy was arrested, with the marked money in his possession, by Officers Harkness and Shalhoob. DePasquale was arrested by Officers Gautwier and Young. Both were charged with larceny from the person and convicted by a jury.

OPINION

DePasquale argues that he was entrapped, that the district court erred in its instruction to the jury on the law of entrapment, that the evidence fails to support the verdict, and that the sentence of ten years is disproportionate and, therefore, cruel and unusual.

Upon these facts, the decoy simply provided the opportunity to commit a crime to anyone who succumbed to the lure of the bait. Entrapment encompasses two elements:

1. an opportunity to commit a crime is presented by the state
2. to a person not predisposed to commit the act.

Thus, this subjective approach focuses upon the defendant's predisposition to commit the crime. In the present case, the cash, although exposed, was zipped tightly to the edge of a zippered pocket, not hanging temptingly from the pocket of an unconscious derelict. Admittedly, the money was exposed; however, that attraction alone fails to cast a pall over the defendant's predisposition. The exposed valuables (money) were presented in a realistic situation, an alert and well-dressed woman walking on the open sidewalks in the casino area.

The fact that the money was exposed simply presented a generally identified social predator with a logical target. These facts suggest that DePasquale was predisposed to commit this crime. Furthermore, the fact that DePasquale had no contact with the decoy but rather succumbed to the apparent temptation of his co-defendant to systematically stalk their target evidences his predisposition.

Lastly, DePasquale complains that his sentence was disproportionate to the crime and, therefore, cruel and unusual punishment. A sentence is unconstitutional if it is so disproportionate to the crime for which it is inflicted that it shocks the conscience and offends fundamental notions of human dignity. While the punishment authorized in Nevada is strict, it is not cruel and unusual.

Accordingly, we AFFIRM the judgment of conviction.

QUESTIONS

1. State the test for entrapment according to Nevada law.
2. What facts led the Court to conclude that Oliver was entrapped but DePasquale wasn't?

THE OBJECTIVE TEST OF ENTRAPMENT

A minority of courts follows an **objective test of entrapment**. The objective test focuses not on the predisposition of defendants but instead on the actions that government agents take to induce individuals to commit crimes. According to the objective test, if the intent originates with the government and their actions would tempt an "ordinarily law-abiding" person to commit the crime, the court should dismiss the case even if the defendant was predisposed to commit the crime. This test is a prophylactic rule aimed to deter "unsavory police methods" (ALI 1985 1:2, 406–7).

objective test of entrapment, if the intent originates with the government and their actions would tempt an "ordinarily law-abiding" person to commit the crime, the court should dismiss the case

LO 16

THE SYNDROME DEFENSES

syndrome, a group of symptoms or signs typical of a disease, disturbance, or condition

Since the 1970s, a range of syndromes, describing affected mental states, has led to novel defenses in criminal law. Webster defines a **syndrome** as "a group of symptoms or signs typical of a disease, disturbance, or condition." Law professor and famous defense attorney Alan Dershowitz (1994) has written a book about these novel defenses. Its title, *The Abuse Excuse and Other Cop-Outs, Sob Stories, and Evasions of Responsibility*, makes clear his opinion of them.

Dershowitz's book includes discussions of the policeman's love, fear, chronic brain, and holocaust syndromes. He worries these excuses are "quickly becoming a license to kill and maim" (3). His is probably a needless worry because defendants rarely plead these excuses, and, except for a few notorious cases picked up by television, the newspapers, and more on the web, defendants rarely succeed when they do plead syndromes and other "abuse excuses."

premenstrual syndrome (PMS), excuse that PMS led to the defendant committing the criminal acts

Some syndromes are (and should be) taken seriously as excuses. For example, some women have claimed the battered woman syndrome to justify killing spouses in self-defense, even though they weren't in imminent danger (Chapter 7). Occasionally, women also have used the **premenstrual syndrome (PMS)** to excuse their crimes. In a New York case, Shirley Santos called the police, telling them, "My little girl is sick." The medical team in the hospital emergency room diagnosed the welts on her little girl's legs and the blood in her urine as the results of child abuse. The police arrested Santos, who explained, "I don't remember what happened. . . . I would never hurt my baby. . . . I just got my period" (Press and Clausen 1982, 111).

At a preliminary hearing, Santos asserted PMS as a complete defense to assault and endangering the welfare of a child, both felonies. She admitted beating her child but argued that she had blacked out because of PMS; hence, she couldn't have formed the intent to assault or endanger her child's welfare. After lengthy plea bargaining, the prosecutor dropped the felony charges, and Santos pleaded guilty to the misdemeanor of harassment. She received no sentence, not even probation or a fine, even though her daughter spent two weeks in the hospital from the injuries. The plea bargaining prevented a legal test of the PMS defense in this case. Nevertheless, the judge's leniency suggests that PMS affected the outcome informally.

There are three obstacles to proving the PMS defense (Carney and Williams 1983):

1. Defendants have to prove that PMS is a disease; little medical research exists to prove that it is.
2. The defendant has to suffer from PMS; rarely do medical records document the condition.
3. PMS has to cause the mental impairment that excuses the conduct; too much skepticism still surrounds PMS to expect ready acceptance that it excuses criminal conduct.

post-traumatic stress disorder (PTSD) defense, excuse that argues the defendant wasn't responsible because of PTSD

The Vietnam War led to an awareness of another syndrome defense, the **post-traumatic stress disorder (PTSD) defense.** Many of the war's combat soldiers suffered emotional and mental casualties that were often more lasting and serious than their physical wounds. PTSD is another defense that can be treated either as a failure to prove the mental element, so there's no criminal conduct at all, or as an affirmative excuse defense. ("What I did was wrong, but I'm not responsible because my PTSD made me do it.")

CASE

In* State v. Phipps *(1994), *the Tennessee Court of Criminal Appeals ruled that a first Gulf War veteran's PTSD could negate premeditation and purpose to kill.*

Is post-traumatic stress disorder an excuse?

State v. Phipps

883 S.W.2d 138 (Tenn.App. 1994)

HISTORY

David Phipps, the defendant, was convicted of first-degree murder of his wife's boyfriend following a trial in the Circuit Court, Henry County. The defendant appealed. The Court of Criminal Appeals reversed and remanded for new trial.

WHITE, J.

FACTS

In the fall of 1990, David Phipps, a career soldier, was sent to Saudi Arabia as part of the forces in Desert Shield and Desert Storm. His military occupational specialty was that of a nuclear-chemical/biological-chemical warfare coordinator with an emphasis on decontamination. He was responsible for providing appropriate chemical measures and countermeasures and served in a front line unit that was one of the first to enter Iraq. Phipps received a bronze star for his exemplary service in Desert Storm.

Within a month of Phipps's return to the States, his wife informed him that she had been living with Michael Presson while he was overseas and that she wanted a divorce. She then moved her possessions out of their home. Marcie Phipps continued to communicate with Phipps, visited him occasionally to discuss financial matters, shared meals, and had sexual relations with him. Phipps accompanied her to a trial in which she was a plaintiff. Phipps implored her to move back home, but she refused. Approximately a week after his wife left him, Phipps attempted suicide.

At approximately 4:45 A.M. on June 1, 1990, several of the victim's neighbors were awakened by the sounds of a struggle. The neighbors heard cries for help, grunting, and moaning. In the dark, one neighbor saw "something" being dragged across the yard to a vehicle. In response to a disturbance call at 4:51 A.M., Officer Damon Lowe, a Henry County deputy sheriff, went to the scene. He found a white Oldsmobile Cutlass parked in the driveway and a white male, Phipps, sitting on the driver's side. The keys were in the ignition. The victim, who was still alive, was lying on the back seat of the car. He appeared to have been brutally and savagely beaten.

When the deputy found Phipps in the car, his pants, shirt, and shoes were covered with blood, he was sweating profusely, and he appeared to be very exhausted. He was wearing a knife in a sheath. At first, Phipps said that as he was driving down the road he saw a fight and had stopped to take the injured man to the emergency room. A few minutes later, he told the officer that he thought the man's name was David Presson and that his wife had been living with Presson.

Phipps did not deny beating Presson to death. He testified that he went to the house to wait for his wife to return from work in the hope that he could convince her to leave Presson and come back to him. However, at some point, he approached the house carrying the knapsack. According to Phipps, Presson was watching television. Phipps knocked on the screen door and entered. Presson jumped up, threw a glass at Phipps, and ran out a side door.

Presson went to his car and Phipps thought he was going to leave. However, Presson returned to the house with a stick in his hand. Presson told Phipps that Marcie was no longer his and to leave. According to Phipps, Presson threatened him with the stick. Phipps grabbed the stick and a struggle ensued. Although Phipps said that he had no clear memory of the events that followed, he had no doubt that he struck many blows to the body and head of Presson. He remembered moving the body and being in the car with the body.

On cross-examination, Richard Hixson testified that two weeks before the murder, he, Phipps, and a third party had discussed a murder in which the body was hidden in the woods and burned.

Four experts testified as to Phipps's mental state. Dr. Samuel Craddock and Dr. Jackson B. White testified for the state and Dr. William D. Kenner and Dr. Patricia Auble testified for Phipps. All four experts agreed that David Phipps was competent to stand trial and that he was not legally insane at the time of the murder. However, all four experts also agreed

(continues)

(continued)

that Phipps was suffering from major depression and post-traumatic stress disorder.

Phipps testified to his experiences during Operation Desert Storm, which included his killing a young Iraqi soldier outside the camp and the suicide of an officer. Soldiers who served with the defendant testified to the constant tension created by being on the front line and the anxiety caused by Iraqi Scud attacks. They also recounted two incidents in which Phipps had behaved in an unusual manner. In addition to failing to report to his superiors the incident with the young Iraqi, Phipps threw his gun into the sand when ordered to remain in Iraq after the rest of his unit moved out. Witnesses viewed those actions as totally out of character for Phipps, who was considered an outstanding soldier with an exemplary military record.

Dr. Craddock testified that Phipps's depression was "of a sufficient level to significantly affect his thinking, reasoning, judgment, and emotional well-being," and that the "components of his post-traumatic stress disorder may have lessened his threshold or made him more sensitive to defending himself and protecting himself and increased the likelihood of him over-reacting to a real or perceived threat." Dr. White, the other state expert, agreed that Phipps's anxiety was sufficient to significantly affect his thinking and reasoning.

Dr. Kenner, testifying for the defense, stated that while the defendant was not insane, he was unable to make a calculated decision to murder someone. While Dr. Auble, a psychologist, expressed no opinion on Phipps's ability to formulate intent, she agreed with the other three experts that Phipps was suffering from major depression, severe anxiety, and post-traumatic stress disorder.

All experts expressed the opinion that Phipps was truthful and that he was not dissembling or faking any symptoms.

OPINION

At trial, Phipps did not deny committing the murder, nor did he plead insanity. His theory of defense was that at the time of the killing he could not and did not formulate the specific intent required to commit first-degree murder.

After giving instructions on the elements of first-degree murder, including premeditation and deliberation, second-degree murder, and voluntary manslaughter, [the court] issued the following instruction:

> The defendant contends that he was suffering from mental conditions known as post traumatic stress disorder, and major depression at the time of the commission of the criminal offense giving rise to this case. I charge you that post traumatic stress disorder and major depression are not defenses to a criminal charge. Insanity may be a defense, however, the defendant makes no claim that he was insane at the time of the killing giving rise to this case.

The essence of Phipps's defense was that at the time of the killing he lacked the requisite mental state for first-degree murder. In support of that defense he offered expert and lay testimony which, without contradiction, indicated that he was suffering from post-traumatic stress syndrome and major depression. The court instructed the jury that the evidence offered did not constitute a defense and refused to instruct the jury, as Phipps requested, that the evidence could be considered on the issue of proof of requisite mental state.

Phipps contends that the jury instruction given by the trial court which stated that post-traumatic stress syndrome and major depression were not defenses to a criminal offense in effect precluded the jury from considering the expert testimony relating to his mental state on the element of intent. We agree.

Although the trial court correctly instructed the jury on the elements of first-degree murder, second-degree murder, and voluntary manslaughter, the comment on the nonexistence of the "defense" of post-traumatic stress disorder did not clearly reflect the state of the law in Tennessee. Moreover, it suggested that the evidence was impertinent. As such it served to exclude from jury consideration defendant's theory of the case.

Phipps did not rely on an insanity defense or on any affirmative defense. The cornerstone of Phipps's case was that he did not have the requisite intent to commit first-degree murder. Virtually all of his testimony was directed toward negating the specific intent element of first-degree murder. While those schooled in the law may be able to discern the difference between considering expert testimony on defendant's mental condition as a complete defense to the charge and considering it to determine whether the requisite mental state has been proved, that subtlety would be lost on most jurors absent clear instructions.

DISSENT

CORNELIUS, SJ.

In my opinion the direct evidence overwhelmingly established a most brutal and atrocious homicide. The evidence points unerringly to this having been an intentional, deliberately premeditated killing of another human being.

QUESTIONS

1. State the exact rule the court adopted regarding post-traumatic stress disorder.
2. Summarize the court's arguments for admitting evidence of post-traumatic stress disorder.
3. List all the evidence supporting the claim that David Phipps suffered from post-traumatic stress disorder.
4. Assume you're the prosecutor, and argue Phipps had the specific intent to kill his wife's boyfriend.
5. Assume you're the defense attorney, and argue Phipps didn't have the specific intent to kill his wife's boyfriend.
6. Now, assume you're a juror. Would you vote to convict or acquit? Defend your answer.

SUMMARY

LO 1

Defendants who plead an excuse defense admit what they did was wrong but argue that, under the circumstances, they weren't responsible for their actions. Defenses can be viewed according to two theories. In affirmative defenses of excuse, defendants have to carry some of the burden of proving they have an excuse that will relieve them of criminal responsibility. In failure-of-proof schemes, defendants don't have any burden to prove their conduct wasn't criminal, but they can raise a reasonable doubt about the prosecution's case.

LO 2

The defense of insanity excuses criminal liability when it seriously damages defendants' capacity to control their acts and/or their capacity to reason and understand the wrongfulness of their conduct.

LO 3

Insanity is a legal term; it's not the same as mental disease or mental defect.

LO 4

Insanity might be used only rarely, but the insanity defense stands for the important proposition that we can only blame people who are responsible. There are four "tests" used to determine insanity.

LO 5

The right-wrong test (the *McNaughtan* rule) focuses on defect in reason or cognition.

LO 6

The irresistible impulse test focuses on defect in self-control or will.

LO 7

The product-of-mental-illness test (*Durham* rule) focuses on criminal acts resulting from mental disease.

LO 8

The substantial capacity test (the MPC test) focuses on both reason and self-control.

LO 9

Current trends favor shifting the burden of proof for insanity to defendants and making that burden heavier.

LO 10

Diminished capacity is the attempt to prove the defendant is guilty of a lesser crime by negating specific intent.

LO 11 The common law divided children into three categories for the purpose of deciding their capacity to commit crimes: (1) under 7, children had no criminal capacity; (2) 7–14, children were presumed to have no criminal capacity, but the presumption could be overcome; (3) over 14, children had the same capacity as adults.

Today, statutes focus on when young people can be convicted of crimes. These statutes come in several varieties, and they vary as to the age of capacity to commit crimes. Every state has a statute that provides for the transfer (waiver) of juveniles to adult criminal court. There are three types of waivers: judicial, prosecutorial, and legislative.

LO 12 The heart of the problem of duress is that it's hard to blame someone who's forced to commit a crime, but excusing people who harm innocent people to save themselves causes debate. The elements of duress vary from state to state.

LO 13 The duress defense consists of four elements: the (1) nature of the threat, (2) immediacy of the threats, (3) crimes the defense applies to, and (4) level of belief regarding the threat.

LO 14 The defense of voluntary intoxication is buffeted between two conflicting principles: (1) accountability: those who get drunk and commit a crime should take the consequences of their actions, and (2) culpability: criminal liability and punishment depend on blameworthiness. Involuntary intoxication, on the other hand, is an excuse to criminal liability in all states.

LO 15 For a long time, U.S. courts rejected the idea that entrapment excused criminal liability, based on the idea that once the crime is committed it didn't matter what particular incentives were involved and who offered them. However, attitudes have shifted from indifference to both a limited sympathy toward entrapped defendants and a growing intolerance of government inducements to entrap otherwise law-abiding people.

LO 16 Since the 1970s, a range of syndromes has led to novel defenses in criminal law. Though there's criticism because of a few notorious cases, some syndromes are taken seriously as excuses. Defendants rarely plead these excuses, and they rarely succeed when they do plead syndromes.

KEY TERMS

failure-of-proof scheme, p. 194
affirmative defense of insanity (insanity defense), p. 194
insanity, p. 197
civil commitment, p. 198
reason, p. 202
will, p. 202
right-wrong test (*McNaughtan* rule), p. 203
McNaughtan rule, p. 203
mental disease, p. 203
mental defect, p. 203
bifurcated (two-stage) trial, p. 204
irresistible impulse test, p. 207
product-of-mental-illness test, p. 208
Durham rule, p. 208
substantial capacity test (the MPC test), p. 209
diminished capacity, p. 210
diminished responsibility, p. 210
waiver to adult criminal court, p. 211
judicial waiver, p. 212
defense of duress, p. 215
involuntary intoxication, p. 217
entrapment, p. 218
subjective test of entrapment, p. 219
objective test of entrapment, p. 221
syndrome, p. 222
premenstrual syndrome (PMS), p. 222
post-traumatic stress disorder (PTSD) defense, p. 222

LEARNING OBJECTIVES

1. To understand the different parties to crime and appreciate the difference between complicity and vicarious liability.
2. To appreciate that participants before and during the commission of crimes are guilty of the crime itself.
3. To understand that participants after the commission of crimes are guilty of a separate, less serious offense.
4. To understand the difference between accomplice liability and conspiracy.
5. To know that mere presence or inaction isn't enough to establish accomplice *actus reus*; the defendant had to take some positive act to aid the commission of the offense.
6. To appreciate that courts are divided over whether knowledge is sufficient to prove accomplice *mens rea*.
7. To understand that the core idea of accessory liability is that it's not as blameworthy to help someone else escape prosecution and punishment as it is to participate in the crime itself.
8. To know the definition of vicarious liability.
9. To understand that vicarious liability can apply either to enterprises (mainly business) or to individuals.
10. To know that vicarious liability has to be created by statute.

Four trains passing in Little Falls, New York. The New York Central & Hudson River Railroad Company, commonly known as the New York Central, was convicted of and fined $180,000 for paying "kickbacks" to the American Sugar Refining Company for shipments of sugar from New York City to the city of Detroit, Michigan. In this case, the U.S. Supreme Court established the rule that corporations can commit crimes.

7 PARTIES TO CRIME AND VICARIOUS LIABILITY

CHAPTER OUTLINE

Was He an Accessory?

On the evening of August 26, in Shreveport, Tony Duke gave Brian Chism a ride in his automobile. Brian Chism was impersonating a female, and Duke was apparently unaware of Chism's disguise. After a brief visit at a friend's house, the two stopped to pick up some beer at the residence of Chism's grandmother. Chism's one-legged uncle, Ira Lloyd, joined them, and the three continued on their way, drinking as Duke drove the automobile. When Duke expressed a desire to have sexual relations with Chism, Lloyd announced that he wanted to find his ex-wife Gloria for the same purpose. Shortly after midnight, the trio arrived at the St. Vincent Avenue Church of Christ and persuaded Gloria Lloyd to come outside. As Ira Lloyd stood outside the car attempting to persuade Gloria to come with them, Chism and Duke hugged and kissed on the front seat as Duke sat behind the steering wheel.

Gloria and Ira Lloyd got into an argument, and Ira stabbed Gloria with a knife several times in the stomach and once in the neck. Gloria's shouts attracted the attention of two neighbors, who unsuccessfully tried to prevent Ira from pushing Gloria into the front seat of the car alongside Chism and Duke. Ira Lloyd climbed into the front seat also, and Duke drove off. One of the bystanders testified that she could not be sure but she thought she saw Brian's foot on the accelerator as the car left.

Lloyd ordered Duke to drive to Willow Point, near Cross Lake. When they arrived, Chism and Duke, under Lloyd's direction, removed Gloria from the vehicle and placed her on some high grass on the side of the roadway, near a wood line. Ira was unable to help the two because his wooden leg had come off. Afterward, as Lloyd requested, the two drove off, leaving Gloria with him. There

(continues)

(continued)

was no evidence that Chism or Duke protested, resisted, or attempted to avoid the actions which Lloyd ordered them to take. Although Lloyd was armed with a knife, there was no evidence that he threatened either of his companions with harm.

Duke proceeded to drop Chism off at a friend's house, where he changed to male clothing. He placed the bloodstained women's clothes in a trash bin. Afterward, Chism went with his mother to the police station at 1:15 A.M. He gave the police a complete statement, and took the officers to the place where Gloria had been left with Ira Lloyd. The police found Gloria's body in some tall grass several feet from that spot. An autopsy indicated that stab wounds had caused her death. Chism's discarded clothing disappeared before the police arrived at the trash bin.

(*State v. Chism* 1983)

complicity, establishes when you can be criminally liable for someone else's conduct; applies criminal liability to accomplices and accessories

vicarious liability, establishes when a party can be criminally liable because of a relationship; transfers the criminal conduct of one party to another because of their relationship

The principle of *actus reus* stands on the fundamental idea that we punish people for what they do, not for who they are. The principle of *mens rea* stands on the fundamental idea that we can only punish people we can blame. This chapter affirms another basic idea of our criminal law: that one person can be liable for someone else's crimes. This liability arises in two ways:

1. When an actor is liable for someone else's conduct (*complicity*)
2. When the relationship between two parties makes one party criminally liable for another party's conduct (*vicarious liability*)

In this chapter, we'll look more closely at parties to crimes; participation before, during, and after the commission of a crime; and vicarious liability.

LO 1

PARTIES TO CRIME

"Two heads are better than one." "The whole is greater than the sum of its parts." These popular sayings express the positive side of teamwork, an ordinary phenomenon under ordinary circumstances. When, under extraordinary circumstances, teamwork turns malicious, then benign "teamwork" can become "complicity" in criminal law. A group of young men playing football generates no criminal liability; a gang rape—teamwork turned malicious—is aggravated rape. **Complicity** establishes when you can be criminally liable for someone else's conduct. It applies criminal liability to accomplices and accessories because they participate in crimes.

agency theory, accomplice liability theory that assumes we're autonomous agents with the freedom to choose our actions and become accountable for someone else's actions when we voluntarily "join in and identify with those actions"

forfeited personal identity theory, the idea that when you choose to participate in crime, you forfeit your right to be treated as an individual; "your acts are my acts"

Vicarious liability establishes when a party can be criminally liable because of a relationship. Vicarious liability transfers the criminal conduct of one party to another because of their relationship. By far the most common relationships are business relationships, such as employer–employee, corporation–manager, buyer–seller, producer–consumer, and service provider–recipient. But vicarious liability can also arise in other situations, such as making the owner of a car liable for the driver's traffic violations and holding parents liable for their children's crimes.

Why should you be held to account for someone else's crimes? Two theories explain why. First, the **agency theory** of accomplice liability assumes that we're autonomous agents with the freedom to choose our actions. We become accountable for someone else's actions when we voluntarily "join in and identify with those actions" (Kadish 1985, 355). Underlying the second theory, **forfeited personal identity theory,** is the idea that when you choose to participate in crime, you forfeit your right to be treated as an individual. In effect, you say, "Your acts are my acts" (Dressler 2009, 467).

At common law, there were four parties to crime:

1. **Principals in the first degree** persons who actually commit the crime
2. **Principals in the second degree** persons present when the crime is committed and who help commit it (lookouts and getaway drivers)
3. **Accessories before the fact** persons not present when the crimes are committed but who help before the crime is committed (for example, someone who provided a weapon used in a murder)
4. **Accessories after the fact** persons who help after the crime is committed (harboring a fugitive)

These distinctions used to be important because of the common law rule that the government couldn't try accomplices until principals in the first degree were convicted. This ban applied even if there was absolute proof of guilt. Why? Probably, because all felonies were capital offenses. But as the number of capital crimes shrank, so did the need for the complicated law of principals and accessories.

Today, there are two parties to criminal complicity:

1. **Accomplices** participants before and during the commission of crimes
2. **Accessories** participants after crimes are committed

principals in the first degree, persons who actually commit the crime

principals in the second degree, persons present when the crime is committed and who help commit it (lookouts and getaway drivers)

accessories before the fact, persons not present when the crimes are committed but who help before the crime is committed (for example, someone who provided a weapon used in a murder)

accessories after the fact, persons who help after the crime is committed (harboring a fugitive)

PARTICIPATION BEFORE AND DURING THE COMMISSION OF A CRIME

LO 2

All participants before and during the commission of a crime (accomplices) are prosecuted for the crime itself (for example, accomplices to murder are prosecuted as murderers). So participation before and during a crime (**accomplice liability**) is a very serious business, because the punishment for being an accomplice is the same as for the person who actually committed the crime.

LO 3

Participation after crimes are committed (**accessory liability**) is prosecuted as a separate, minor offense (accessory to murder). Accessories are punished for misdemeanors, a much less serious offense because accessories are considered obstructors of justice, not felons.

LO 4

We need to clear up a problem before we get further into accomplice liability. Accomplices are often confused with co-conspirators (Chapter 8), because both accomplice and conspiracy cases have more than one participant, but they're two completely different crimes. **Conspiracy** is an agreement to commit some other crime. A conspiracy to commit murder is not murder; it's the lesser offense of *agreeing* to commit murder (Chapter 8). Participating in a murder is the crime of murder itself. For example, two people agree to commit a murder. At this point, they've committed conspiracy to murder. Now they go to a gun shop, buy a gun, and drive together to the victim's house. One acts as a lookout while the other shoots the victim, who dies instantly. They drive away together. They're both murderers. They've committed two separate crimes—the less serious crime of conspiracy to commit murder and the crime of murder.

The rule that the crime of conspiracy and the crime the conspirators agree to commit are separate offenses is called the ***Pinkerton* rule**. The name comes from a leading U.S. Supreme Court case, *Pinkerton v. U.S.* (1946). The two Pinkerton brothers conspired to evade taxes. They were found guilty of both conspiracy to evade taxes and tax evasion itself. According to Justice Douglas, who wrote the opinion for the Court: "It has been long and consistently recognized by the Court that the commission of the offense and a conspiracy to commit it are separate and distinct offenses" (643).

accomplices, participants before and during the commission of crimes

accessories, participants after crimes are committed

accomplice liability, liability that attaches for participation before and during a crime

accessory liability, liability that attaches for participation after crimes are committed

conspiracy, an agreement to commit some other crime

***Pinkerton* rule,** the crime of conspiracy and the crime the conspirators agree to commit are separate offenses

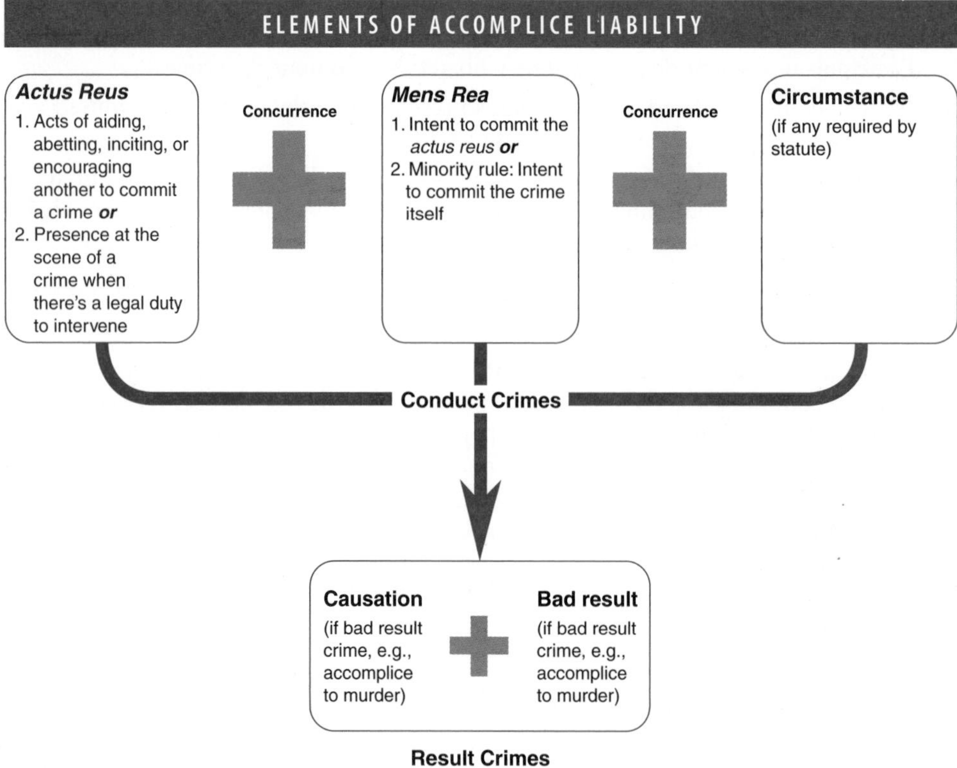

LO 5

ACCOMPLICE *ACTUS REUS*

accomplice *actus reus*, defendant took "some positive act in aid of the commission of the offense"

You'll usually see words borrowed from the old common law of principals and accessories to define accomplice *actus reus* in modern accomplice statutes. The words "aid," "abet," "assist," "counsel," "procure," "hire," or "induce" are widespread. The meaning of these words boils down to one core idea: The actor took "some positive act in aid of the commission of the offense." How much aid is enough? It's not always easy to decide, but here are a few acts that definitely qualify:

- Providing guns, supplies, or other instruments of crime
- Serving as a lookout
- Driving a getaway car
- Sending the victim to the principal
- Preventing warnings from getting to the victim (ALI 1953, 43)

mere presence rule, a person's presence at the scene of a crime doesn't by itself satisfy the *actus reus* requirement of accomplice liability

Words can also qualify as accomplice *actus reus* if they encourage and approve the commission of the crime. Mere presence at the scene of a crime isn't accomplice *actus reus*. According to the mere presence rule, even presence at the scene of a crime followed by flight isn't enough action.

For example, in *Bailey v. U.S.* (1969), Bailey spent most of the afternoon shooting craps with another man. Then, when a man carrying cash walked by, Bailey's craps partner pulled a gun and robbed the man with the cash. Both Bailey and his craps partner fled the scene. Bailey was caught; his partner never was. The court held that although flight from the scene of a crime can be taken into account, it's not enough to prove accomplice *actus reus*.

According to the court:

> We no longer hold tenable the notion that "the wicked flee when no man pursueth, but the righteous are as bold as a lion." The proposition that "one flees shortly after a

> criminal act is committed or when he is accused of something does so because he feels some guilt concerning the act" is not absolute as a legal doctrine "since it is a matter of common knowledge that men who are entirely innocent do sometimes fly from the scene of a crime through fear of being apprehended as guilty parties or from an unwillingness to appear as witnesses." (1114)

There's one major exception to the mere presence rule: when defendants have a legal duty to act, presence alone is enough to satisfy the *actus reus* requirement. In *State v. Walden* (1982), George Hoskins beat Aleen Walden's one-year-old son Lamont "repeatedly over an extended period of time," with a leather belt, until he was bloody. Walden "looked on the entire time the beating took place but did not say anything or do anything to stop the 'Bishop' [Hoskins] from beating Lamont or to otherwise deter such conduct" (783).

A jury found Walden guilty as an accomplice to assault. On appeal, the court said that

> the trial court properly allowed the jury to consider a verdict of guilty of assault upon a theory of aiding and abetting, solely on the ground that the defendant was present when her child was brutally beaten. A person who so aids or abets under another in the commission of a crime is equally guilty with that other person as a principal. (787)

One final point about accomplice *actus reus*: actions taken *after* crimes are committed aren't themselves accomplice *actus reus*, but juries can use participation after the crime to prove defendants participated before or during the commission of the crime. In the grisly murder case, *State v. Ulvinen* (1981), the Minnesota Supreme Court dealt with these issues in connection with Helen Ulvinen's participation in her son David's murder of his wife, Carol:

1. Words of encouragement before and during the commission of the crime
2. Accomplices not present when the crime was committed
3. Inferring participation before and during the commission of the crime from actions to help after the commission of the crime

CASE

In **State v. Ulvinen** ***(1981)****, the Minnesota Supreme Court reversed Helen Ulvinen's conviction as her son David's accomplice to the grisly murder and dismemberment of his wife Carol.*

Did she murder her daughter-in-law?

State v. Ulvinen

313 N.W.2d 425 (Minn. 1981)

HISTORY

Helen Ulvinen was convicted of first-degree murder pursuant to Minn. Stat. § 609.05, subd. 1 (1980), which imposes criminal liability on one who "intentionally aids, advises, hires, counsels, or conspires with or otherwise procures" another to commit a crime. The Minnesota Supreme Court reversed.

OTIS, J.

FACTS

Carol Hoffman, Helen Ulvinen's daughter-in-law, was murdered late on the evening of August 10 or the very early morning of August 11 by her husband, David Hoffman. She and David had spent an amicable evening together playing with their children, and when they went to bed David wanted to make love to his wife.

When she refused him he lost his temper and began choking her. While he was choking her, he began to believe he was "doing the right thing" and that to get "the evil out of her" he had to dismember her body.

After his wife was dead, David called down to the basement to wake his mother, asking her to come upstairs to sit on the living room couch. From there she would be able to see the kitchen, bathroom, and

(continues)

(continued)
bedroom doors and could stop the older child if she awoke and tried to use the bathroom.

Mrs. Ulvinen didn't respond at first but after being called once, possibly twice more, she came upstairs to lie on the couch. In the meantime, David had moved the body to the bathtub. Mrs. Ulvinen was aware that while she was in the living room her son was dismembering the body but she turned her head away so that she could not see.

After dismembering the body and putting it in bags, Hoffman cleaned the bathroom, took the body to Weaver Lake, and disposed of it. On returning home, he told his mother to wash the cloth covers from the bathroom toilet and tank, which she did. David fabricated a story about Carol leaving the house the previous night after an argument, and Helen agreed to corroborate it. David phoned the police with a missing person report, and during the ensuing searches and interviews with the police, he and his mother continued to tell the fabricated story.

On August 19, 1980, David confessed to the police that he had murdered his wife. In his statement, he indicated that not only had his mother helped him cover up the crime but she had known of his intent to kill his wife that night. After hearing Hoffman's statement the police arrested Mrs. Ulvinen and questioned her with respect to her part in the cover up [*sic*]. Police typed up a two-page statement, which she read and signed. The following day a detective questioned her further regarding events surrounding the crime, including her knowledge that it was planned.

Mrs. Ulvinen's relationship with her daughter-in-law had been a strained one. She moved in with the Hoffmans on July 26, two weeks earlier to act as a live-in babysitter for their two children. Carol was unhappy about having her move in and told friends that she hated Helen, but she told both David and his mother that they could try the arrangement to see how it worked.

On the morning of the murder, Helen told her son that she was going to move out of the Hoffman residence because "Carol had been so nasty to me." In his statement to the police, David reported the conversation that morning as follows:

> Sunday morning I went downstairs and my mom was in the bedroom reading the newspaper and she had tears in her eyes, and she said in a very frustrated voice, "I've got to find another house." She said, "Carol don't want me here," and she said, "I probably shouldn't have moved in here." And I said then, "Don't let what Carol said hurt you. It's going to take a little more period of readjustment for her." Then, "I told mom that I've got to do it tonight so that there can be peace in this house."

Q: What did you tell your mom that you were going to have to do that night?

A: I told my mom I was going to have to put her to sleep.

Q: Dave, will you tell us exactly what you told your mother that morning, to the best of your recollection?

A: I said I'm going to have to choke her tonight, and I'll have to dispose of her body so that it will never be found. That's the best of my knowledge.

Q: What did your mother say when you told her that?

A: She just—she looked at me with very sad eyes and just started to weep. I think she said something like "it will be for the best." David spent the day fishing with a friend of his. When he got home that afternoon he had another conversation with his mother. She told him at that time about a phone conversation Carol had had in which she discussed taking the children and leaving home. David told the police that during the conversation with his mother that afternoon he told her, "Mom, tonight's got to be the night."

Q: When you told your mother, "Tonight's got to be the night," did your mother understand that you were going to kill Carol later that evening?

A: She thought I was just kidding her about doing it. She didn't think I could.

Q: Why didn't your mother think that you could do it?

A: Because for some time I had been telling her I was going to take Carol scuba diving and make it look like an accident.

Q: And she said?

A: And she always said, "Oh, you're just kidding me."

Q: But your mother knew you were going to do it that night?

A: I think my mother sensed that I was really going to do it that night.

Q: Why do you think your mother sensed you were really going to do it that night?

A: Because when I came home and she told me what had happened at the house, and I told her, "Tonight's got to be the night," I think she said, again I'm not certain, that "it would be the best for the kids."

OPINION

In this state, presence, companionship, and conduct before and after the offense are circumstances from which a person's participation in the criminal intent may be inferred. The evidence is undisputed that Ulvinen was asleep when her son choked his wife. She took no active part in the dismembering of the body but came upstairs to intercept the children, should they awake, and prevent them from going into the bathroom.

She cooperated with her son by cleaning some items from the bathroom and corroborating David's story to prevent anyone from finding out about the murder. She is insulated by statute from guilt as an accomplice after-the-fact for such conduct because of her relation as a parent of the offender. (See Minn. Stat. § 609.495, subd. 2 (1980).)

The jury might well have considered Ulvinen's conduct in sitting by while her son dismembered his wife so shocking that it deserved punishment. Nonetheless, these subsequent actions do not succeed in transforming her behavior prior to the crime to active instigation and encouragement. Minn.Stat. § 609.05, subd. 1 (1980) implies a high level of activity on the part of an aider and abettor in the form of conduct that encourages another to act. Use of terms such as "aids," "advises," and "conspires" requires something more of a person than mere inaction to impose liability as a principal.

The evidence presented to the jury at best supports a finding that Ulvinen passively acquiesced in her son's plan to kill his wife. The jury might have believed that David told his mother of his intent to kill his wife that night and that she neither actively discouraged him nor told anyone in time to prevent the murder. Her response that "it would be the best for the kids" or "it will be the best" was not, however, active encouragement or instigation. There is no evidence that her remark had any influence on her son's decision to kill his wife.

Minn.Stat. § 609.05, subd. 1 (1980) imposes liability for actions which affect the principal, encouraging him to take a course of action which he might not otherwise have taken. The state has not proved beyond a reasonable doubt that appellant was guilty of anything but passive approval.

However morally reprehensible it may be to fail to warn someone of their impending death, our statutes do not make such an omission a criminal offense. We note that mere knowledge of a contemplated crime or failure to disclose such information without evidence of any further involvement in the crime does not make that person liable as a party to the crime under any state's statutes.

David told many people besides appellant of his intent to kill his wife but no one took him seriously. He told a co-worker, approximately three times a week, that he was going to murder his wife, and confided two different plans for doing so. Another co-worker heard him tell his plan to cut Carol's air hose while she was scuba diving, making her death look accidental, but did not believe him. Two or three weeks before the murder, David told a friend of his that he and Carol were having problems and he expected Carol "to have an accident sometime." None of these people has a duty imposed by law to warn the victim of impending danger, whatever their moral obligation may be.

Her conviction must be reversed.

QUESTIONS

1. List all the facts (including words) surrounding Mrs. Ulvinen's behavior before or during the murder that might make her an accomplice.
2. List all the facts after the murder that a jury could infer proved Mrs. Ulvinen participated before or during the murder itself.
3. According to the court, why isn't Mrs. Ulvinen guilty of murder?
4. Do you agree with the court that however morally reprehensible her behavior, she, nonetheless, wasn't an accomplice? Defend your answer.

LO 6

ACCOMPLICE *MENS REA*

My friend Steve: Lend me your gun.
Me: What for?
Steve: So I can rob the grocery store.
Me: OK, but only if you give me half the take.

My intent is clear in this scenario (as it is in most complicity cases): my purpose in lending Steve my gun is to help him rob the grocery store, and I definitely want the robbery to succeed. So we can say my mental attitude is "purposely"; I'm acting for the very purposes of (1) helping Steve and (2) committing a robbery. Cases like this scenario don't give courts much trouble. Others do—like knowingly helping someone who is going to commit a crime but not for the very purpose of benefiting from the criminal venture (Figure 7.1).

Early court decisions ruled that knowingly helping someone was enough to prove the mental element required for accomplice liability. For example, in *Backun v. United States* (1940), Max Backun sold silver to Zucker, silver that he knew was stolen. But Backun didn't sell the silver for the purpose of sharing any profits with Zucker. Still, according to the court, knowingly selling the stolen property was good enough:

> Guilt depends, not on having a stake in the outcome of crime but on aiding and assisting the perpetrators; and those who make a profit by furnishing to criminals, whether by sale or otherwise, the means to carry on their nefarious undertakings, aid them just as truly as if they were actual partners with them, having a stake in the fruits of their enterprise. (637)

In another famous federal case, *U.S. v. Peoni* (1938, 401), decided by the well-known and enormously respected Judge Learned Hand, the outcome was the opposite. Joseph Peoni sold counterfeit money to Dorsey in the Bronx. Dorsey was caught trying to pass the fake money in Brooklyn. Peoni was indicted as an accomplice to Dorsey. At the trial, the prosecution relied on the words "aids, abets, counsels, commands, induces, or procures" in the U.S. Criminal Code's accomplice statute. The prosecution argued that Peoni knew Dorsey possessed counterfeit money and that knowledge was enough to convict him. The jury convicted Peoni, but, on appeal, Judge Hand didn't buy the prosecution's argument. According to Judge Hand, if someone were suing Peoni for damages, knowledge would be good enough, but, this was a criminal case, where all the words in the statute

> demand that he in some sort associate himself with the venture, that he participate in it as in something that he wishes to bring about, that he seek by his action to make it

FIGURE 7.1

ACCOMPLICE *MENS REA*

Examples of knowingly but not purposely helping someone:

- I lease an apartment to someone I know is going to use it for prostitution.
- A gun dealer sells me a gun she knows I'm going to use to shoot someone.
- A telephone company provides service to a customer it knows is going to use it for illegal gambling.
- A farmer leases 200 acres of farmland to a renter he knows is going to grow marijuana for sale. (ALI 1985 I:2, 316)

> succeed. All the words used—even the most colorless, "abet"—carry an implication of purposive attitude towards it. (402)

U.S. v. Peoni is cited over and over again as defining the *mens rea* of accomplice liability. If only it were that clear, but it's not. In a 2002 survey of only federal court cases, Assistant U.S. Attorney Baruch Weiss (2002) cited "a few examples" illustrating the confusion. Here are some answers to the question, Is simple knowledge enough?

1. Yes, said the Supreme Court in 1870
2. No, said Judge Learned Hand in 1938
3. Yes, implied the Supreme Court in 1947
4. No, said the Supreme Court in 1949
5. Yes, if it's accompanied by an act that substantially facilitates the commission of the underlying offense, said the Supreme Court in 1961
6. Usually, said the Second Circuit in 1962
7. Only if knowledge is enough for the underlying offense, said the Second Circuit in another case in 1962
8. Sometimes, said the Seventh Circuit in 1985
9. Always, implied the Seventh Circuit in 1995
10. No, said the Second Circuit in 1995 and the Seventh Circuit in 1998 (1351–52)

Further confusion arises because both recklessness and negligence can satisfy the *mens rea* requirement. For example, if participants can predict that aiding and abetting one crime might reasonably lead to another crime, they're guilty of both.

PARTICIPATION AFTER THE COMMISSION OF A CRIME

LO 7

At common law, accessories after the fact were punished like accomplices; they were treated as if they'd committed the crime itself. So if you gave a burglar a place to hide after he'd committed burglary, you were guilty of burglary, too. But accessories aren't really burglars; they don't come on the scene until the burglary is over. That's why they used to be called "accessories *after* the fact." And (so the thinking goes), it's not as bad to help someone who's already committed a crime as it is to help her commit the crime in the first place.

LO 3, LO 7

accessory, accessory after the fact; usually a misdemeanor

Modern statutes have reduced the punishment to fit this less serious offense. Accessory after the fact (now called simply, "accessory") is a separate offense, usually a misdemeanor. Sometimes, it's even got a different name, such as "obstructing justice," "interfering with prosecution," and "aiding in escape."

Most accessory-after-the-fact statutes have four elements, which includes one *actus reus*, two *mens rea*, and one circumstance element:

1. The accessory personally aided the person who committed the crime (the *actus reus* element).
2. The accessory knew the felony was committed (*mens rea* element).
3. The accessory aided the person who committed the crime for the purpose of hindering the prosecution of that person (*mens rea* element).
4. Someone besides the accessory actually committed a felony (the circumstance element).

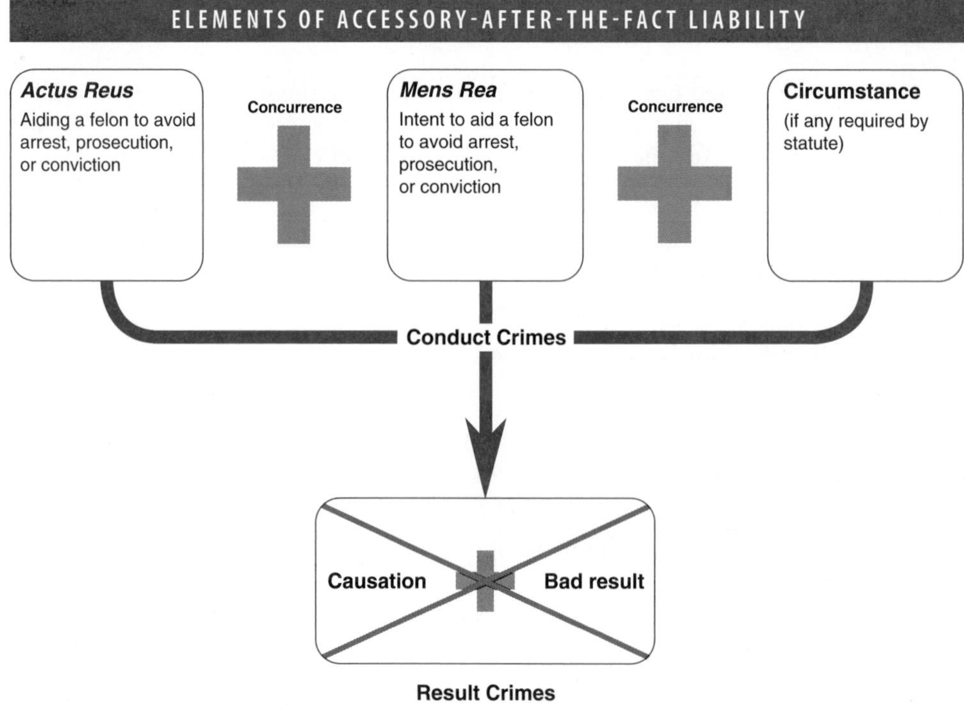

CASE

In* State v. Chism *(1983)*, *a bizarre case, the Supreme Court of Louisiana dealt with Louisiana's accessory-after-the-fact statute.

Was he an accessory after the fact?

State v. Chism

436 So.2d 464 (La. 1983)

HISTORY

Brian Chism (the defendant) was convicted before the First Judicial District Court, Caddo Parish, of being an accessory after the fact, and was sentenced to three years in Parish Prison, with two and one-half years suspended, and the defendant appealed. The Louisiana Supreme Court affirmed the conviction, vacated the sentence, and remanded the case for resentencing.

DENNIS, J.

FACTS

On the evening of August 26, 1981, in Shreveport, Tony Duke gave Brian Chism a ride in his automobile. Brian Chism was impersonating a female, and Duke was apparently unaware of Chism's disguise. After a brief visit at a friend's house, the two stopped to pick up some beer at the residence of Chism's grandmother.

Chism's one-legged uncle, Ira Lloyd, joined them, and the three continued on their way, drinking as Duke drove the automobile. When Duke expressed a desire to have sexual relations with Chism, Lloyd announced that he wanted to find his ex-wife Gloria for the same purpose. Shortly after midnight, the trio arrived at the St. Vincent Avenue Church of Christ and persuaded Gloria Lloyd to come outside. As Ira Lloyd stood outside the car attempting to persuade Gloria to come with them, Chism and Duke hugged and kissed on the front seat as Duke sat behind the steering wheel.

Gloria and Ira Lloyd got into an argument, and Ira stabbed Gloria with a knife several times in the stomach and once in the neck. Gloria's shouts attracted the attention of two neighbors, who unsuccessfully tried to prevent Ira from pushing Gloria into the front seat of the car alongside Chism and Duke. Ira Lloyd climbed into the front seat also, and

Duke drove off. One of the bystanders testified that she could not be sure but she thought she saw Brian's foot on the accelerator as the car left.

Lloyd ordered Duke to drive to Willow Point, near Cross Lake. When they arrived, Chism and Duke, under Lloyd's direction, removed Gloria from the vehicle and placed her on some high grass on the side of the roadway, near a wood line. Ira was unable to help the two because his wooden leg had come off. Afterward, as Lloyd requested, the two drove off, leaving Gloria with him.

There was no evidence that Chism or Duke protested, resisted, or attempted to avoid the actions which Lloyd ordered them to take. Although Lloyd was armed with a knife, there was no evidence that he threatened either of his companions with harm.

Duke proceeded to drop Chism off at a friend's house, where he changed to male clothing. He placed the bloodstained women's clothes in a trash bin. Afterward, Chism went with his mother to the police station at 1:15 A.M. He gave the police a complete statement, and took the officers to the place where Gloria had been left with Ira Lloyd. The police found Gloria's body in some tall grass several feet from that spot.

An autopsy indicated that stab wounds had caused her death. Chism's discarded clothing disappeared before the police arrived at the trash bin.

OPINION

According to Louisiana statute 14:25:

> An accessory after the fact is any person who, after the commission of a felony, shall harbor, conceal, or aid the offender, knowing or having reasonable ground to believe that he has committed the felony, and with the intent that he may avoid or escape from arrest, trial, conviction, or punishment. . . .
>
> Whoever becomes an accessory after the fact shall be fined not more than five hundred dollars, or imprisoned, with or without hard labor, for not more than five years, or both; provided that in no case shall his punishment be greater than one-half of the maximum provided by law for a principal offender.

Chism appealed from his conviction and sentence and argues that the evidence was not sufficient to support the judgment. Consequently, in reviewing the defendant's assigned error, we must determine whether, after viewing the evidence in the light most favorable to the prosecution, any rational trier of fact could have found beyond a reasonable doubt that:

1. a completed felony had been committed by Ira Lloyd before Brian Chism rendered him the assistance described below; and
2. Chism knew or had reasonable grounds to know of the commission of the felony by Lloyd; and
3. Chism gave aid to Lloyd personally under circumstances that indicate either that he actively desired that the felon avoid or escape arrest, trial conviction, or punishment or that he believed that one of these consequences was substantially certain to result from his assistance.

There was clearly enough evidence to justify the finding that a felony had been completed before any assistance was rendered to Lloyd by the defendant. The record vividly demonstrates that Lloyd fatally stabbed his ex-wife before she was transported to Willow Point and left in the high grass near a wood line. Thus, Lloyd committed the felonies of attempted murder, aggravated battery, and simple kidnapping, before Chism aided him in any way. A person cannot be convicted as an accessory after the fact to a murder because of aid given after the murderer's acts but before the victim's death, but under these circumstances the aider may be found to be an accessory after the fact to the felonious assault.

The evidence overwhelmingly indicates that Chism had reasonable grounds to believe that Lloyd had committed a felony before any assistance was rendered. In his confessions and his testimony Chism indicates that the victim was bleeding profusely when Lloyd pushed her into the vehicle, that she was limp and moaned as they drove to Willow Point, and that he knew Lloyd had inflicted her wounds with a knife.

The Louisiana offense of accessory after the fact deviates somewhat from the original common law offense in that it does not require that the defendant actually know that a completed felony has occurred. Rather, it incorporates an objective standard by requiring only that the defendant render aid "knowing or having reasonable grounds to believe" that a felony has been committed.

The closest question presented is whether any reasonable trier of fact could have found beyond a

(continues)

(continued)

reasonable doubt that Chism assisted Lloyd under circumstances that indicate that either Chism actively desired that Lloyd would avoid or escape arrest, trial, conviction, or punishment, or that Chism believed that one of these consequences was substantially certain to result from his assistance.

In this case we conclude that a trier of fact reasonably could have found that Chism acted with at least a general intent to help Lloyd avoid arrest because:

1. Chism did not protest or attempt to leave the car when his uncle, Lloyd, shoved the mortally wounded victim inside;
2. he did not attempt to persuade Duke, his would-be lover, to exit out the driver's side of the car and flee from his uncle, whom he knew to be one-legged and armed only with a knife;
3. he did not take any of these actions at any point during the considerable ride to Willow Point;
4. at their destination, he docilely complied with Lloyd's directions to remove the victim from the car and leave Lloyd with her, despite the fact that Lloyd made no threats and that his wooden leg had become detached;
5. after leaving Lloyd with the dying victim, he made no immediate effort to report the victim's whereabouts or to obtain emergency medical treatment for her;
6. before going home or reporting the victim's dire condition he went to a friend's house, changed clothing and discarded his own in a trash bin from which the police were unable to recover them as evidence;
7. he went home without reporting the victim's condition or location;
8. and he went to the police station to report the crime only after arriving home and discussing the matter with his mother.

Chism asserted that he helped to remove the victim from the car and to carry her to the edge of the bushes because he feared that his uncle would use the knife on him. However, fear as a motivation to help his uncle is inconsistent with some of Chism's actions after he left his uncle. Consequently, we conclude that despite Chism's testimony, the trier of fact could have reasonably found that he acted voluntarily and not out of fear when he aided Lloyd and that he did so under circumstances indicating that he believed that it was substantially certain to follow from his assistance that Lloyd would avoid arrest, trial, conviction, or punishment.

For the foregoing reasons, it is also clear that the judge's verdict was warranted. There is evidence in this record from which a reasonable trier of fact could find a defendant guilty beyond a reasonable doubt. Therefore, we affirm the defendant's conviction.

We note, however, that the sentence imposed by the trial judge is illegal. The judge imposed a sentence of three years. He suspended two and one-half years of the term. The trial judge has no authority to suspend part of a sentence in a felony case. The correct sentence would have been a suspension of all three years of the term, with a six-month term as a condition of two years probation. We therefore vacate the defendant's sentence and remand the case for resentencing.

Conviction AFFIRMED; sentence vacated; REMANDED.

DISSENT

DIXON, CJ.

I respectfully dissent from what appears to be a finding of guilt by association. The majority lists five instances of inaction, or failure to act, by defendant:

1. did not protest or leave the car;
2. did not attempt to persuade Duke to leave the car;
3. did neither (1) nor (2) on ride to Willow Point; . . .
4. made no immediate effort to report crime or get aid for the victim; . . .
5. failed to report victim's condition or location after changing clothes.

The three instances of defendant's action relied on by the majority for conviction were stated to be:

1. complying with Lloyd's direction to remove the victim from the car and leave the victim and Lloyd at Willow Point;
2. changing clothes and discarding bloody garments; and . . .
3. discussing the matter with defendant's mother before going to the police station to report the crime.

None of these actions or failures to act tended to prove defendant's intent, specifically or generally, to aid defendant avoid arrest, trial, conviction or punishment.

QUESTIONS

1. Identify the elements of accessory after the fact according to the Louisiana statute.
2. List all the facts stated by the court, and then match them to each of the elements of the statute.
3. Summarize the court's conclusions regarding the evidence of each of the elements.
4. Do you agree with the court that Chism is guilty of being an accessory after the fact? Back up your answer with facts in the case.
5. Summarize the reasons the dissent couldn't go along with the majority. Do you agree with the dissent? Defend your answer.

VICARIOUS LIABILITY

LO 8, LO 9

Recall that *vicarious liability* is liability that is imposed for someone else's acts. It transfers the *actus reus* and the *mens rea* from one person to another person—or from one or more persons to an enterprise—because of their *relationship*.

Most vicarious liability involves business relationships, such as employer–employee, manager–corporation, buyer–seller, producer–consumer, and service provider–recipient. But it can also apply to other enterprises, such as the college fraternity (*Zeta Chi* case excerpt, p. 245), and relationships between individuals, such as making the owner of a car liable for the driver's traffic violations and holding parents liable for their children's crimes.

Let's look first at the vicarious criminal liability of corporations based on their relationships with those employed by the corporation.

CORPORATE LIABILITY

LO 9

> Did you ever expect a corporation to have a conscience when it has no soul to be damned, and no body to be kicked?
>
> Lord Chancellor Edward Thurlow (Weismann 2009)

> Since a corporation acts by its officers and agents, their purposes, motives, and intent are just as much those of the corporation as are the things done. If, for example, the invisible, intangible essence or air which we term a corporation can level mountains, fill up valleys, lay down iron tracks, and run railroad cars on them, it can intend to do it, and can act therein as well viciously as virtuously.
>
> *New York Central & Hudson River Railroad Company v. U.S.* (1909)

Let's turn now to discussions of the history of corporate liability and the effects of making a corporation an "artificial being" who can commit crimes and be held responsible for those committed by employees.

History

Criminologist Edwin Sutherland introduced us to the "white collar criminal" and "white collar crime" in 1939, but as the introductory quotations demonstrate, concern about corporate crime is centuries old. The history of corporations began with the charters the English monarchs granted as a privilege exchanged for money. In other words, they were government entities. The industrial revolution dramatically changed the nature of corporations from government entities controlled by government to private business operated by internal management.

LO 10

Corporate criminal law began as, and still is, the creature of federal law, stemming from the "contracts" and "commerce" clauses in the U.S. Constitution. The contracts clause (Article 1, Section 10, paragraph 1) provides: "No State shall . . . pass any . . . law impairing the Obligation of Contracts. . . ." The interstate commerce clause (Article I, Section 8) provides: "The Congress shall have power to . . . regulate Commerce with foreign Nations, and among the several States, and with the Indian Tribes." As corporate business increasingly affected interstate commerce in the late nineteenth century, Congress stepped in to legislate, and U.S. attorneys to prosecute, corporate crime.

During most of the twentieth century, the belief that self-regulation is the best model to make sure that corporations are meeting their obligations to shareholders and the public prevailed. That belief continues today.

Speaking to the Hartford Bond Club in 1938, then chairman of the Securities and Exchange Commission (SEC), and later Supreme Court Justice, William O. Douglas told the audience:

> Self-discipline is always more welcome than discipline imposed from above. From the broad public viewpoint, such regulation can be far more effective . . . and persuasive and subtle in its conditioning over business practices and business morality. By and large, the government can operate satisfactorily only by proscription. That leaves untouched large areas of conduct and activity; some of it susceptible of government regulation but in fact too minute for satisfactory control, some of it lying beyond the periphery of the law in ethics and morality. Into these large areas, self-regulation is by far the preferable course from all viewpoints. (Seligman 2004, 1361–62)

Earlier the same year, Douglas told a congressional committee that if self-regulation of the stock market was to succeed, the Securities and Exchange Commission had to play an important, but residual, role. In Douglas's typical blunt words:

> Government would keep the shotgun, so to speak, behind the door, loaded, well-oiled, cleaned, ready to use, but with hope that it would never have to be used. (1361)

According to Professor Joel Seligman (2004), the leading expert on the history of the SEC, after seventy years, "stock market self-regulation remains a work in progress" (1348). The same can be said for all corporate regulation (Weismann 2009, 2). The weaknesses of self-regulation are well-recognized, as this list in 1973 demonstrates:

- Lack of enthusiasm for regulation by the regulated group
- Temptation to use a corporate façade of regulation as a "shield to ward off meaningful regulation"
- Businesspeople's "tendency to use collective action to advance their interests through the imposition of purely anticompetitive restraints as opposed to those justified by regulatory needs"
- Resistance to regulatory changes because of the economic interest in preserving the current status (Seligman 2004, 1347)

Writing after the subprime crisis, the collapse of the financial corporate giants, and the ensuing recession in 2008, former white-collar-crime defense attorney and then prosecutor Professor Miriam Weismann (2009) sums up the history and current state of corporate regulation:

> Corporate regulation is, therefore, dependent for the most part on self-restraint and ethical corporate governance within the regulatory environment mandated by

> Congress. The role of the regulators and law enforcement is proscriptive in nature as opposed to proactive. This means that the government is not in a meaningful position to prevent misconduct. Instead, its role is largely reactive, punishing and/or prosecuting once the misconduct is uncovered. (2)

Let's look now at the legal and policy bases for vicarious corporate criminal liability—namely, the doctrine of *respondeat superior* ("let the master answer").

Respondeat Superior *("Let the Master Answer")*

LO 9

We begin with a legal fiction created by the U.S. Supreme Court in *Trustees of Dartmouth College v. Woodward* (1918). According to the Court, "A corporation is an artificial being, invisible, intangible." So a corporation can sue, be sued, and enter into contracts. And, most important for us—corporations can commit crimes. The Supreme Court decided that in *New York Central & Hudson River Railroad Company v. U.S.* (1909).

The New York Central and Hudson River Railroad Company was convicted and fined $180,000 for paying "kickbacks" to the American Sugar Refining Company for shipments of sugar from New York City to the city of Detroit, Michigan. The railroad fixed the shipping rate for sugar at 23 cents per 100 pounds from New York City to Detroit. The railroad's general traffic manager and assistant traffic manager entered into an unlawful agreement with the shippers—the American Sugar Refining Company of New York and the American Sugar Refining Company of New Jersey—and the consignees of the sugar, W. H. Edgar & Son, of Detroit. Pursuant to the agreement, the shippers paid the full rate, and the railroad "kicked back" to the shippers 5 cents for each 100 pounds.

The purpose of the kickback was to "prevent them from resorting to transportation by the water route between New York and Detroit, thereby depriving the roads interested of the business, and to assist Edgar & Son in meeting the severe competition with other shippers and dealers" (490–91).

The railroad attacked the constitutional validity of certain features of the Elkins Act, the law the railroad was convicted under. According to the act:

> Anything done or omitted to be done by a corporation common carrier subject to the act to regulate commerce, and the acts amendatory thereof, which, if done or omitted to be done by any director or officer thereof, or any receiver, trustee, lessee, agent, or person acting for or employed by such corporation, would constitute a misdemeanor under said acts, or under this act, shall also be held to be a misdemeanor committed by such corporation; and, upon conviction thereof, it shall be subject to like penalties as are prescribed in said acts, or by this act, with reference to such persons, except as such penalties are herein changed.
>
> In construing and enforcing the provisions of this section, the act, omission, or failure of any officer, agent, or other person acting for or employed by any common carrier, acting within the scope of his employment, shall, in every case, be also deemed to be the act, omission, or failure of such carrier, as well as that of the person. (491–92)

The railroad argued that

> these provisions of the law are unconstitutional because Congress has no authority to impute to a corporation the commission of criminal offenses, or to subject a corporation to a criminal prosecution by reason of the things charged. The argument is that to thus punish the corporation is in reality to punish the innocent stockholders, and to deprive them of their property without opportunity to be heard, consequently without due process of law. (492)

respondeat superior, a doctrine in tort law that makes a master liable for the wrong of a servant; in modern terms an employer may be liable for the wrong of an employee

The Court rejected the argument and relied on the doctrine of *respondeat superior* ("let the master answer"), borrowed from tort (noncriminal wrongs) law.

According to *respondeat superior*, corporate employees' acts are imputed to the corporation.

> The general freight traffic manager and the assistant freight traffic manager were authorized to establish rates at which freight should be carried over the line of the New York Central & Hudson River Company, and were authorized to unite with other companies in the establishing, filing, and publishing of through rates, including the through rate or rates between New York and Detroit referred to in the indictment. Thus, the subject-matter of making and fixing rates was within the scope of the authority and employment of the agents of the company, whose acts in this connection are sought to be charged upon the company.
>
> Thus clothed with authority, the agents were bound to respect the regulation of interstate commerce enacted by Congress, requiring the filing and publication of rates and punishing departures therefrom. Applying the principle governing civil liability, we go only a step farther in holding that the act of the agent, while exercising the authority delegated to him to make rates for transportation, may be controlled, in the interest of public policy, by imputing his act to his employer and imposing penalties upon the corporation for which he is acting. (494)

The Court's rationale for extending vicarious liability by the doctrine of *respondeat superior* was the "history of the times":

> It is a part of the public history of the times that statutes against rebates could not be effectually enforced so long as individuals only were subject to punishment for violation of the law, when the giving of rebates or concessions inured to the benefit of the corporations of which the individuals were but the instruments. This situation . . . was no doubt influential in bringing about the enactment of the Elkins law, making corporations criminally liable. (495)
>
> . . .
>
> While the law should have regard to the rights of all, and to those of corporations no less than to those of individuals, it cannot shut its eyes to the fact that the great majority of business transactions in modern times are conducted through these bodies, and particularly that interstate commerce is almost entirely in their hands, and to give them immunity from all punishment because of the old and exploded doctrine that a corporation cannot commit a crime would virtually take away the only means of effectually controlling the subject-matter and correcting the abuses aimed at.
>
> . . . It would be a distinct step backward to hold that Congress cannot control those who are conducting this interstate commerce by holding them responsible for the intent and purposes of the agents to whom they have delegated the power to act in the premises. (495–96)

Those were the "good old days," when the typical corporate crime case involved "slush funds," fraudulent billing schemes, and tax cheats. Corporate crime was an "inside job," and the corporate criminals hid misconduct from their accountants and lawyers. Now, there's a whole new kind of corporate crime and criminal. Corporate "watchdogs" (law firms, accounting firms, auditors, investment advisors, banks, and even regulators) who were supposed to "bark" when the public interest was threatened were silent; even worse, they were part of the "runaway organizational corporate behavior that injected chaos into America's capital markets" (Weismann 2009, xvii–xviii).

U.S. v. Arthur Andersen, LLP (2004) is the story of how Arthur Andersen, one of the largest accounting and consulting firms in the world, was brought down as a member of the "supporting cast" in the "rubble" of Enron Corporation. (Andersen was Enron's auditor. It audited Enron's publicly filed financial statements and provided internal audit and consulting services to it.) Enron switched its business from operating natural gas pipelines to an energy conglomerate, coupled with "aggressive accounting practices and rapid growth" (*Arthur Andersen LLP v. U.S.* 2005, 2).

Enron's financial performance began to decline in 2000. In August, an Enron senior accountant warned Kenneth Lay, CEO, that Enron "could implode in a wave of accounting scandals." An SEC investigation soon loomed. Before the SEC investigation formally began, Enron began to destroy documents pursuant to its documents "retention" policy. On October 16, SEC notified Enron that it had opened an investigation in August and requested certain information and documents. On October 19, Enron forwarded a copy to Andersen (3–4).

On the same day Enron sent an e-mail to Andersen's internal team of accounting experts and attached a copy of its documents retention policy to Andersen. On October 23, after a conference call with Kenneth Lay, Enron CEO, David Duncan, head of Andersen's internal team of accounting experts, instructed everyone to "make sure to follow the document policy." Substantial destruction of paper and electronic documents followed. On October 26, a senior Andersen partner warned in an e-mail that "the problems are just beginning and we will be in the cross hairs. The marketplace is going to keep the pressure on this and is going to force SEC to be tough" (4).

Throughout this period, Andersen continued to destroy documents. In March 2002, Andersen was indicted. "The indictment alleged that, between October 10 and November 9, 2001, Andersen 'did knowingly, intentionally and corruptly persuade . . . Andersen's employees, with intent to cause them to withhold documents from, and alter documents for use in, 'official proceedings, namely: regulatory and criminal proceedings and investigations'" (3–4).

The case went to trial, and the jury convicted Andersen. The U.S. Circuit Court affirmed. The U.S. Supreme Court overturned the verdict (4–5). But Arthur Andersen has all but disappeared. It has shrunk from a worldwide firm of enormous prestige and reputation to a small Chicago firm devoted mostly to handling the scores of civil suits against it arising out of the Enron debacle.

Not all corporate vicarious criminal liability arises out of giant businesses and their giant "watchdogs" in finance. Even college fraternities that incorporate may find themselves in criminal court.

CASE

In* State v. Zeta Chi Fraternity *(1997), *Zeta Chi was charged with and convicted of recklessly selling alcohol to minors and knowingly permitting prostitution.*

Did the fraternity sell alcohol to a minor and allow prostitution?

State v. Zeta Chi Fraternity

686 A.2d. 530 (N.H. 1997)

HISTORY

Zeta Chi (Defendant), a college fraternity, was convicted, following trial in the Superior Court, Strafford County, of selling alcohol to a person under the age of 21, and of prostitution. Defendant appealed. The Supreme Court affirmed the convictions.

HORTON, J.

FACTS

Zeta Chi, a New Hampshire corporation and fraternity at the University of New Hampshire in Durham, held a "rush" at its fraternity house to attract new members. In order to encourage people to attend the rush, Zeta Chi hired two female strippers to perform at the event. Fraternity brothers encouraged guests to give the strippers dollar bills so that they would continue to perform. The brothers also told guests

(continues)

(continued)

that the more money the strippers were given, the more that they would do. One of the members of the fraternity was providing change for larger bills. As part of the performance, the dancers lay on a mattress brought out by members of the fraternity and simulated oral sex on each other. At one point, a guest gave five dollars to one of the strippers who sat on the guest's lap. When a brother moved the dancer along, the guest complained that he had given five dollars. The stripper took the guest to the mattress and pushed his head into her crotch. Two witnesses testified at trial that they saw guests being led to the mattress after they gave money, at which point the guests then performed oral sex on the dancer.

In addition, Andrew Strachan, a nineteen-year-old guest at the fraternity party, testified that at some point during the evening he learned that beer was available from a soda machine. He made his way to an apartment in another part of the fraternity house where the machine was located, waited in line with three or four other people, and purchased three to five cans of beer. Strachan also testified that he noticed someone making change for the machine. The fraternity's secretary testified that the fraternity members voted not to provide alcohol at the rush and that they moved the vending machine that contained beer to a separate apartment in another part of the fraternity house for the rush. He also testified, however, that the fraternity had control over the vending machine and its proceeds and that only fraternity members would have an interest in making change for the machine.

OPINION

I. Sufficiency of Evidence

A. Illegal Sale of Alcohol

Zeta Chi argues that the State failed to prove that it caused alcohol to be sold to Strachan. See RSA 179:5:

I. No licensee, salesperson, direct shipper, common carrier, delivery agent, nor any other person, shall sell or give away or cause or allow or procure to be sold, delivered or given away any liquor or beverage to a person under the age of 21 or to an intoxicated individual.

II. No licensee, manager or person in charge of a licensed premises shall allow or permit any individual, who is under the age of 21, to possess or consume any liquor or beverage on the licensed premises.

Zeta Chi asserts that because the fraternity voted not to provide beer at the rush and the soda machine was moved from the main area in the fraternity house to a separate apartment at the back of the house, Zeta Chi did not have control over the machine, and, therefore, could not have caused the sale of alcohol from the machine. Essentially, Zeta Chi is arguing that the individuals responsible for making the beer available for sale to Strachan were not acting on behalf of the corporation or within the scope of their authority.

We begin by noting that the only defendant in this case is a corporate entity. A corporation is a jural person, but not a person in fact. It is an artificial creature, acting only through agents. . . . A corporation may be held criminally liable for criminal acts performed on its behalf by agents or employees acting within the scope of their authority or employment. The criminal conduct need not have been performed, authorized, ratified, adopted or tolerated by the corporation's directors, officers or other high managerial agents in order to be chargeable to the corporation.

In fact, a corporation can be convicted for actions of its agents even if it expressly instructed the agents not to engage in the criminal conduct. The agents, however, must have been acting within the scope of their actual or apparent authority. Express authority exists when the principal explicitly manifests its authorization for the agent to act. Implied authority is the reasonable incident or construction of the terms of express authority or results from acquiescence by the principal in a course of dealing by the agent. Apparent authority, on the other hand, exists where the principal so conducts itself as to cause a third party to reasonably believe that the agent is authorized to act.

It is the rare case in which the corporate leadership explicitly authorizes its agents to engage in criminal conduct. Of necessity, the proof of authority to so act must rest on all the circumstances and conduct in a given situation and the reasonable inferences to be drawn therefrom.

Evidence at trial indicates that Zeta Chi had control over the apartment in which the vending machine was located, even though it had voted to make the apartment separate from the fraternity house. More importantly, however, witnesses testified that Zeta

Chi had control over the soda machine; that only Zeta Chi had an interest in the proceeds from the machine; that only fraternity members had keys to the apartment in which the machine was located; that someone was making change for the machine; and that no one would have an interest in making change except a member of the fraternity. We believe that from these facts the jury could reasonably have found that an agent of Zeta Chi sold beer from the vending machine and that this agent was acting on behalf of the corporation and within the scope of his authority.

Zeta Chi next argues that the evidence was insufficient for the jury to find that Zeta Chi acted recklessly, the *mens rea* charged in the indictment. Because Zeta Chi is a corporation, its mental state depends on the knowledge of its agents. The corporation is considered to have acquired the collective knowledge of its employees and is held responsible for their failure to act accordingly.

A person acts recklessly with respect to a material element of an offense when he is aware of and consciously disregards a substantial and unjustifiable risk that the material element exists or will result from his conduct. The risk must be of such a nature and degree that, considering the circumstances known to him, its disregard constitutes a gross deviation from the conduct that a law-abiding person would observe in the situation.

In this case, the jury could reasonably have found that Zeta Chi acted recklessly from the facts that about 150 guests, many of them under the age of twenty-one, were at the rush party that had been widely publicized on campus; that it was Zeta Chi's vending machine; that only fraternity members had keys to the apartment in which the machine was located; that party guests gained access to the machine; that someone was making change; and that a number of people were waiting in line to use the machine.

B. Prostitution

Zeta Chi contends that the State failed to prove that it knowingly allowed the prostitution and that if prostitution occurred, the individuals who allowed it were not acting within the scope of their authority.

We will first address the issue of agency. As noted above, in the context of corporate criminal liability, the corporation acts through its agents and those agents must be acting within the scope of either their actual or apparent authority in order for the corporation to be liable for their actions. Zeta Chi asserts that because the members of the fraternity announced that guests were not allowed to touch the dancers and that, if the dancer stayed too long with one guest, members of the fraternity would move her along, this indicated the lack of actual or apparent authority.

Whether an agent has acted within his actual or apparent authority . . . is a question for the trier of fact. Apparent authority can result when the principal fails to disapprove of the agent's act or course of action so as to lead the public to believe that his agent possesses authority to act . . . in the name of the principal. In this case, there was testimony that the guests were told that if they paid more money the dancers would do more; that on more than one occasion guests were led to the mattress that was brought into the room by the brothers to perform oral sex in exchange for money; and that at least one guest performed oral sex on the dancer for "quite a while." From these facts the jury could reasonably have found that members of the fraternity acted within the scope of their authority and on behalf of the corporation in allowing oral sex to be performed in exchange for money.

Zeta Chi argues that the State failed to prove the requisite *mens rea* with regard to the prostitution charge, that is, that Zeta Chi knowingly permitted oral sex to occur at the party. "A person acts knowingly with respect to conduct or to a circumstance that is a material element of an offense when he is aware that his conduct is of such nature or that such circumstances exist." Zeta Chi argues that the material element to which the "knowingly" *mens rea* applies is permission. Zeta Chi contends that there was no opportunity for Zeta Chi to manifest its lack of permission before the oral sex occurred because the dancer's actions were unexpected.

Based on the facts of this case, Zeta Chi's argument is without merit. As noted above, because Zeta Chi is a corporation, and a corporation acts through its agents, the knowledge obtained by the agents of the corporation acting within the scope of their agency is imputed to the corporation. There was testimony that several guests performed oral sex on the dancer and that on at least one occasion it occurred for several minutes. Moreover, the fraternity

(continues)

(continued)

president testified that he "was very well in control" of the party. Therefore, even if the first act caught members of the fraternity by surprise, the jury could reasonably have inferred that Zeta Chi knowingly permitted oral sex to occur from Zeta Chi's failure to prevent the subsequent conduct. A corporation is not insulated from criminal liability merely because it published instructions and policies which are violated by its employee; the corporation must place the acts outside the scope of an employee's employment by adequately enforcing its rules.

Convictions affirmed.

QUESTIONS

1. State the elements of vicarious liability according to New Hampshire law.
2. List all the facts relevant to deciding whether Zeta Chi, through its officers, was acting within its authority in each of the crimes.
3. Summarize the court's arguments upholding the trial court's conviction in each of the offenses.
4. In your opinion, was Zeta Chi guilty of selling alcohol to a minor? Of prostitution? Back up your answer with facts and arguments from the court's opinion.

LO 9

INDIVIDUAL VICARIOUS LIABILITY

Vicarious liability cases that attract the most attention involve large national corporations like Enron and their derivatives, like Arthur Andersen LLC, in trials that are tried in federal courts. But *Zeta Chi* shows us that not all vicarious liability involves federal cases against huge corporations. Individuals are vicariously liable for their agents' actions in state cases; most don't attract our attention. Most common are cases of employees' crimes, committed within the scope of their employment but without the approval or knowledge of their employers.

LO 10

Because state individual vicarious liability, like federal corporate vicarious criminal liability, depends on statutes, the issue in most vicarious liability cases is interpreting whether the statute actually imposes vicarious liability.

CASE

In* State v. Tomaino *(1999), the Ohio Court of Appeals interpreted the Ohio "disseminating harmful matter to juveniles" statute not to include vicarious liability.

Was the owner liable for the clerk renting "pornos" to a minor?

State v. Tomaino

733 N.E.2d 1191 (Ohio App. 1999)

HISTORY

Peter Tomaino, the owner of an adult video store, was convicted in the Court of Common Pleas, Butler County, of disseminating matter harmful to juveniles. He appealed. The Court of Appeals reversed and remanded.

WALSH, J.

FACTS

Peter Tomaino, the appellant, owns VIP Video, a video sales and rental store in Millville, Ohio. VIP Video's inventory includes only sexually oriented videotapes and materials. On October 13, 1997, Carl Frybarger, age 37, and his son Mark, age 17, decided that Mark should attempt to rent a video from VIP. Mark entered the store, selected a video, and presented it to the clerk along with his father's driver's license and credit card.

The purchase was completed and the Frybargers contacted the Butler County Sheriff's Department. After interviewing Mark and his father, Sergeant Greg Blankenship, supervisor of the Drug and Vice Unit, determined that Mark should again attempt to purchase videos at VIP Video with marked money while wearing a radio transmitter wire.

On October 14, 1997, Mark again entered the store. A different clerk was on duty. Following Blankenship's instructions, Mark selected four videos and approached the clerk. He told her that he had been in the store the previous day and that he was 37. Mark told the clerk that he had used a credit card on that occasion and that he was using cash this time and thus did not have his identification with him. The clerk accepted the cash ($100) and did not require any identification or proof of Mark's age. It is this video transaction that constitutes the basis of the indictment.

The clerk, Billie Doan, was then informed by Blankenship that she had sold the videos to a juvenile and that she would be arrested. Doan said that she needed to call the appellant and made several unsuccessful attempts to contact the appellant at different locations.

The grand jury indicted appellant Tomaino and Doan on two counts. Count One charged the defendants with recklessly disseminating obscene material to juveniles and Count Two charged the defendants with disseminating matter that was harmful to juveniles.

OPINION

Appellant was convicted of disseminating matter harmful to juveniles. R.C. 2907.31 provides in relevant part:

> No person, with knowledge of its character or content, shall recklessly do any of the following: Sell, deliver, furnish, disseminate, provide, exhibit, rent, present to a juvenile any material or performance that is obscene or harmful to juveniles.

Ohio has no common law offenses. Criminal liability is rigidly and precisely limited to those situations that the General Assembly has specifically delineated by statute. In R.C. 2901.21, the legislature has further provided that a person is not guilty of an offense unless both of the following apply:

1. His liability is based on conduct which includes either a voluntary act, or an omission to perform an act or duty which he is capable of performing;
2. He has the requisite degree of culpability for each element as to which a culpable mental state is specified by the section defining the offense.

Vicarious liability for another's criminal conduct or failure to prevent another's criminal conduct can be delineated by statute; it cannot be created by the courts. Statutes defining offenses are to be strictly construed against the state and liberally construed in favor of the accused. The elements of a crime must be gathered wholly from the statute.

Liability based on ownership or operation of a business may be specifically imposed by statute. For instance, the owner of premises used for gambling—even if he is not present while gambling occurs—can be criminally liable under the statute prohibiting operating a gambling house. Such premises-oriented liability is specifically imposed by the statute, which provides in part that "no person being the owner of premises shall recklessly permit such premises to be used or occupied for gambling" (R.C. 2915.03).

It is undisputed that the clerk furnished the video to the minor and that appellant was not present. Because we find that a plain reading of the disseminating matter harmful to juveniles statute requires personal action by a defendant and does not by its terms impose vicarious or premises-oriented liability, the jury was not correctly instructed in this case.

Judgment reversed and cause remanded.

QUESTIONS

1. State the elements of the Ohio statute relevant to Peter Tomaino's liability for Billie Doan's acts.
2. Summarize the events that led to Tomaino's prosecution.
3. Summarize the Ohio Court of Appeals' reasons for rejecting vicarious liability under the Ohio statute referred to in (1).
4. In your opinion, should Peter Tomaino be liable for Billie Doan's acts? Back up your answer with facts from the case and the arguments from the state, Tomaino, and the court.

LO 9, LO 10

Virtually all vicarious liability statutes involve the employer–employee relationship. But not all do, as we saw in *State v. Zeta Chi*. Also, in some states and municipalities, registered vehicle owners are liable for some traffic violations involving their vehicles, regardless of who violated the law. So if you let your friend drive your car to go shopping, and he didn't feed the parking meter, you're liable for paying the fine.

Another nonbusiness relationship subject to individual vicarious criminal liability is parents' criminal liability for their kids' crimes. For example, in 1995, Salt Lake City enacted an ordinance that made it a crime for parents to fail to "supervise and control their children." By 1997, seventeen states and cities had adopted one of these parental responsibility laws.

The idea of holding parents responsible for their children's crimes is nothing new. Contributing to the delinquency of a minor is an old offense. Contributing to the delinquency of minors statutes mandate that the acts of minor children were done at the direction or with the consent of their parents. So, in one case, a father was found guilty for "allowing his child to violate a curfew ordinance," and, in another, a mother was convicted for "knowingly" permitting her children "to go at large in violation of a valid quarantine order."

One disturbing case involved the Detroit suburb of St. Clair Shores, which has an ordinance making it a crime to fail to "exercise reasonable control" to prevent children from committing delinquent acts. Alex Provenzino, 16, committed a string of seven burglaries. The local police ordered his parents to "take control" of Alex. When his father tried to discipline him, Alex "punched his father." When he tried to restrain him, Alex escaped by pressing his fingers into his father's eyes. When Alex tried to attack him with a golf club, his father called the police. The parents were charged with, but acquitted of, both vicariously committing the seven burglaries and failing to supervise their son (Siegel 1996, A1).

parental responsibility statutes, based on parents' acts and omissions; differ from vicarious liability statutes, which are based on the parent–child relationship

Traditional parental responsibility statutes aren't the same as vicarious liability. Parental responsibility statutes are based on parents' acts and omissions; vicarious liability statutes are based on the parent–child relationship. Vicarious liability statutes grew out of public fear, frustration, and anger over juvenile violence and parents' failure to control their kids. However, there are only a few cases in the appellate courts based on these vicarious liability statutes that make the crimes of kids the crimes of their parent solely on the basis of the parent–child relationship (DiFonzo 2001). One of these rare cases is now more than thirty years old.

CASE

In* State v. Akers *(1979)*, *the New Hampshire Supreme Court dealt with a state statute making parents liable for their children's illegal snowmobile driving.

Are the parents guilty of illegal snowmobiling?

State v. Akers

400 A.2d 38 (N.H. 1979)

HISTORY

Parent defendants were found guilty of violating a snowmobile statute which makes parents vicariously liable for the acts of their children simply because they occupy the status of parents. The parents waived all right to an appeal *de novo* ("new trial") to superior court. The parents objected to the constitutionality of the parental responsibility statute. The New Hampshire Supreme Court sustained the objections.

GRIMES, J.

FACTS

The defendants are fathers whose minor sons were found guilty of driving snowmobiles in violation of RSA 269-C:6—a II (operating on public way) and III (reasonable speed) (Supp.1977). RSA 269-C:24 IV, which pertains to the operation and licensing of

Off Highway Recreational Vehicles (OHRV) and provides that "the parents or guardians or persons assuming responsibility will be responsible for any damage incurred or for any violations of this chapter by any person under the age of 18." Following a verdict of guilty for violating RSA 269-C:24 IV the two defendants waived all right to an appeal de novo to the superior court and all questions of law were reserved and transferred by the District Court to the New Hampshire Supreme Court.

OPINION

The defendants argue that (1) RSA 269-C:24 IV, the statute under which they were convicted, was not intended by the legislature to impose criminal responsibility, and (2) if in fact the legislative intention was to impose criminal responsibility, then the statute would violate N.H.Const. pt. 1, art. 15 and U.S.Const. amend. XIV, § 1.

The language of RSA 269-C:24 IV, "Parents will be responsible for any violations of this chapter by any person under the age of 18," clearly indicates the legislature's intention to hold the parents criminally responsible for the OHRV violations of their minor children. It is a general principle of this State's Criminal Code that "a person is not guilty of an offense unless his criminal liability is based on conduct that includes a voluntary act or the voluntary omission to perform an act of which he is physically capable." RSA 269-C:24 IV seeks to impose criminal liability on parents for the acts of their children without basing liability on any voluntary act or omission on the part of the parent. Because the statute makes no reference at all to parental conduct or acts it seeks to impose criminal responsibility solely because of their parental status contrary to the provisions of RSA 626:1.

The legislature has not specified any voluntary acts or omissions for which parents are sought to be made criminally responsible and it is not a judicial function to supply them. It is fundamental to the rule of law and due process that acts or omissions which are to be the basis of criminal liability must be specified in advance and not ex post facto. N.H.Const. pt. 1, art. 23.

It is argued that liability may be imposed on parents under the provisions of RSA 626:8 II(b), which authorizes imposing criminal liability for conduct of another when "he is made accountable for the conduct of such other person by the law defining the offense." This provision comes from the Model Penal Code § 2.04(2)(b). The illustrations of this type of liability in the comments to the Code all relate to situations involving employees and agents, and no suggestion is made that it was intended to authorize imposing vicarious criminal liability on one merely because of his status as a parent.

Without passing upon the validity of statutes that might seek to impose vicarious criminal liability on the part of an employer for acts of his employees, we have no hesitancy in holding that any attempt to impose such liability on parents simply because they occupy the status of parents, without more, offends the due process clause of our State constitution.

Parenthood lies at the very foundation of our civilization. The continuance of the human race is entirely dependent upon it. It was firmly entrenched in the Judeo-Christian ethic when "in the beginning" man was commanded to "be fruitful and multiply" (Genesis I). Considering the nature of parenthood, we are convinced that the status of parenthood cannot be made a crime. This, however, is the effect of RSA 269-C:24 IV. Even if the parent has been as careful as anyone could be, even if the parent has forbidden the conduct, and even if the parent is justifiably unaware of the activities of the child, criminal liability is still imposed under the wording of the present statute.

There is no other basis for criminal responsibility other than the fact that a person is the parent of one who violates the law. One hundred and twenty seven years ago the justices of this court in giving their opinions regarding a proposed law that would have imposed vicarious criminal liability on an employer for acts of his employee stated, "(b)ut this does not seem to be in accordance with the spirit of our Constitution . . ." Because the net effect of the statute is to punish parenthood, the result is forbidden by substantive due process requirements of N.H.Const. pt. 1, art. 15.

Exceptions sustained.

DISSENT

BOIS, J.

The majority read RSA 269-C:24 IV in isolation. They conveniently ignore RSA 626:8 (Criminal Liability for Conduct of Another), which provides

(continues)

(continued)

in subsection II that "(a) person is legally accountable for the conduct of another person when: (b) he is made accountable for the conduct of such other person by the law defining the offense." RSA 269-C:24 IV is such a law. Imposing criminal liability based on status for certain violations of a *mala prohibitum* nature does not offend constitutional requirements.

Even if I were to accept the majority's conclusion that the vicarious imposition of criminal liability on parents of children who have committed an OHRV [Off Highway Recreational Vehicles] violation under RSA ch. 269-C is constitutionally impermissible, I would still uphold the validity of RSA 269-C:24 IV. A closer reading of this State's Criminal Code belies the majority's reasoning that RSA 269-C:24 IV holds parents of minor offenders criminally responsible for their children's offenses solely on the basis of their parental status. RSA 626:1 I, enunciating the fundamental principle of the Criminal Code, states that all criminal liability must be based on a "voluntary act" or "voluntary omission."

When RSA 269-C:24 IV is read in conjunction with RSA 626:1 I, a parental conviction can result only when the State shows beyond a reasonable doubt that a minor child has committed a violation under a provision of chapter 269-C, and that his parent voluntarily performed or omitted to perform an act such as participating in the minor's conduct, or entrusting, or negligently allowing his minor child to operate an OHRV.

When RSA 269-C:24 IV is construed to require a voluntary act or voluntary omission in accordance with RSA 626:1 I, there are no due process infirmities, either under N.H.Const. pt. 1, art. 15 or U.S. Const. amend. XIV, § 1. Culpable intent is not required to impose criminal penalties for minor infractions. "It is well settled in this jurisdiction that the Legislature may declare criminal a certain act or omission to act without requiring it to be done with intent." When the legislature imposes criminal responsibility without requiring intent, we will override it only when such imposition violates concepts of fundamental fairness.

In the present case, there is a demonstrable public interest to assure the safe operation of OHRVs, and the minor penalties imposed upon violators of RSA 269-C:24 IV are insubstantial. In such circumstances, we will not second guess the wisdom of the legislature.

Public welfare offenses requiring no criminal intent have also been held consistent with the due process requirements of U.S. Const. amend. XIV, § 1. "There is wide latitude in the lawmakers to declare an offense and to exclude elements of knowledge and diligence from its definition. . . . In vindicating its public policy a State in punishing particular acts may provide that "he shall do them at his peril."

QUESTIONS

1. Exactly what does the New Hampshire statute prohibit?
2. Summarize all of the arguments of the majority and dissenting opinions. Which side do you agree with? Defend your answer.
3. Apart from the legal and constitutional arguments, do you think it's good public policy to make parents criminally liable for their children's crimes? Defend your answer.

ETHICAL DILEMMA

Is it wise public policy to make parents guilty for their children's crimes?

Susan and Anthony Provenzino of St. Clair Shores, Michigan, knew their 16-year-old son, Alex, was troubled. His first arrest occurred in May 1995, and in the year that followed, he continued his delinquent behavior by committing burglary, drinking alcohol, and using and selling marijuana. Alex was difficult at home as well, verbally abusing his parents and once attacking his father with a golf club. Although the Provenzinos were disturbed by Alex's behavior, they supported his release from juvenile custody during the fall of 1995, fearing he would be mistreated in the youth facility where he was detained—a facility where juveniles charged with more violent crimes were housed.

It is unlikely that the Provenzinos expected to be the first parents tried and convicted of violating a two-year-old St. Clair Shores ordinance that places an affirmative responsibility on parents to "exercise reasonable control over their children." On May 5, 1996, however, after a jury deliberated only 15 minutes, the Provenzinos were convicted of violating the parental accountability ordinance. They were each fined $100 and ordered to pay an additional $1,000 in court fees.

Instructions

1. Go to the Office of Juvenile Justice and Delinquency Prevention's essay, "Parental Responsibility Laws," at http://www.ojjdp.gov/pubs/reform/ch2_d.html.
2. Read the section on parents' responsibility for their children's crimes.
3. Compile a list of the various responses—criminal, civil, and private—to parental responsibility for their children's crimes.
4. Write a one-page essay explaining which of the alternatives is the wisest ethical public policy.

SUMMARY

LO 1 Although both complicity and vicarious liability involve more than one party, they differ critically. Complicity establishes when you can be criminally liable for someone else's conduct. Vicarious liability establishes when a party can be criminally liable because of a relationship. Today, there are two parties to criminal complicity: (1) accomplices, participants before and during the commission of crimes, and (2) accessories, participants after crimes are committed.

LO 2 Participants before and during the commission of crimes are guilty of the crime itself.

LO 3 Accessory to a crime (after-the-fact assistance) is a separate offense, usually a misdemeanor.

LO 4 Accomplice liability and conspiracy differ. Conspirators agree to commit a separate crime; this differs from actually committing the crime. It's a separate, less serious crime.

LO 5 Accomplice *actus reus* boils down to one core idea: the actor took "some positive act in aid of the commission of the offense." Being present when a crime is committed isn't enough to satisfy the *actus reus* requirement of accomplice liability. Failing to act to stop the crime also fails to meet the requirement unless there was a duty to act.

LO 6 Courts remain divided over the question of whether knowledge is enough to establish accomplice *mens rea*.

LO 7 Accessory liability isn't as blameworthy as participation in the crime itself.

LO 8 Vicarious liability transfers the *actus reus* and the *mens rea* of one person to another person—or from one or more persons to an enterprise—because of their relationship.

LO 9 Most vicarious liability involves business relationships, such as employer–employee, manager–corporation, buyer–seller, producer–consumer, and service provider–recipient. Sometimes, individuals are vicariously liable for their agents' actions.

LO 10 Virtually all vicarious liability statutes involve the employer–employee relationship. Vicarious liability has to be created by statute.

KEY TERMS

complicity, p. 230
vicarious liability, p. 230
agency theory, p. 230
forfeited personal identity theory, p. 230
principals in the first degree, p. 231
principals in the second degree, p. 231
accessories before the fact, p. 231
accessories after the fact, p. 231
accomplices, p. 231
accessories, p. 231
accomplice liability, p. 231
accessory liability, p. 231
conspiracy, p. 231
Pinkerton rule, p. 231
accomplice *actus reus*, p. 232
mere presence rule, p. 232
accessory, p. 237
respondeat superior, p. 244
parental responsibility statutes, p. 250

LEARNING OBJECTIVES

1. To understand that inchoate offenses punish people for crimes they've started to commit but haven't finished committing.
2. To appreciate the dilemma inchoate offenses present to free societies and know the three different ways inchoate offenses are resolved.
3. To understand that liability for criminal attempt offenses is based on two rationales: preventing dangerous conduct and neutralizing dangerous people.
4. To know the *mens rea* of inchoate crimes is always the purpose or specific intent to commit a specific crime.
5. To understand that the *actus reus* of attempt is an act that goes beyond mere preparation but not far enough to complete the crime.
6. To understand that legal impossibility is a defense to attempt liability and that factual impossibility is not.
7. To understand that voluntary and complete abandonment of an attempt in progress is a defense to attempt liability in about half the states.
8. To understand that punishing conspiracy and solicitation to commit a crime is based on nipping in the bud the special danger of group criminality.
9. To know the different types of conspiracies.
10. To understand the Racketeer Influenced and Corrupt Organizations (RICO) Act and how it works against organized crime.
11. To understand that punishing solicitation is based on the same idea as punishing conspiracy: to stop such crimes from happening before they start, anticipating the dangers of group criminality.

Galina Vouk is led in handcuffs from FBI headquarters in New York. Vouk is one of 73 people across the country charged by federal prosecutors in a scheme to cheat Medicare out of $163 million, the largest fraud by one criminal enterprise in the program's history, U.S. authorities said.

AP Images/ Louis Lanzano

8 INCHOATE CRIMES

CHAPTER OUTLINE

Did He Attempt to Rape?

Jodean Randen, a housewife, was walking home across a fairly well-traveled railroad bridge in Eau Claire, Wisconsin. She is a slight woman whose normal weight is 95 to 100 pounds. As she approached the opposite side of the bridge, she passed a man who was walking in the opposite direction. The man turned and followed her, grabbed her arm, and demanded her purse. She surrendered her purse and at the command of the man began walking away as fast as she could. Upon discovering that the purse was empty, he caught up with her again, grabbed her arm, and told her that if she did not scream he would not hurt her. He then led her—willingly, she testified, so as to avoid being hurt by him—to the end of the bridge. While walking he shoved her head down and warned her not to look up or do anything and he would not hurt her.

On the other side of the bridge along the railroad tracks there is a coal shack. As they approached the coal shack he grabbed her, put one hand over her mouth, and an arm around her shoulder and told her not to scream or he would kill her. At this time Mrs. Randen thought he had a knife in his hand. He then forced her into the shack and up against the wall. As she struggled for her breath he said, "You know what else I want," unzipped his pants and started pulling up her

(continues)

(continued)

skirt. She finally succeeded in removing his hand from her mouth, and after reassuring him that she would not scream, told him she was pregnant and pleaded with him to desist or he would hurt her baby.

He then felt her stomach and took her over to the door of the shack, where in the better light he was able to ascertain that, under her coat, she was wearing maternity clothes. He thereafter let her alone and left after warning her not to scream or call the police, or he would kill her.

(*LeBarron v. State* 1966)

criminal attempts, trying but failing to commit crimes

criminal conspiracy, making an agreement to commit a crime

criminal solicitation, trying to get someone else to commit a crime

We all know that a man who chases his wife around a restaurant parking lot and shoots her in the head and kills her with a loaded gun in his hand when she trips and falls commits murder. However, what if the man does the same thing, but the gun isn't loaded? Is that a crime? That's what this chapter is about—criminal liability for:

1. Trying to commit crimes but failing to complete them, **criminal attempts**
2. Making agreements to commit crimes, **criminal conspiracy**
3. Trying to get someone else to commit a crime, **criminal solicitation**

LO 1

inchoate offenses, from the Latin "to begin"; crimes that satisfy the *mens rea* of purpose or specific intent and the *actus reus* of taking *some* steps toward accomplishing the criminal purpose—but not enough steps to complete the intended crime

We call these three crimes **inchoate offenses**. The word "inchoate" comes from Latin and means "to begin." Each inchoate offense has some of its own elements, but they all share two elements: the *mens rea* of purpose or specific intent (Chapter 4) and the *actus reus* of taking some steps toward accomplishing the criminal purpose—but not enough steps to complete the intended crime.

Just to keep your bearings about where you are in the "big picture" of criminal law—and in your book—the inchoate offenses stand partly in the general and partly in the special part. Unlike the principles in the general part, they're specific crimes, such as attempted robbery. But, like the general part, they apply to many crimes, such as in the mental attitude of specific intent or purpose and the voluntary acts that fall short of completing the intended crime. That's why the Model Penal Code calls them "offenses of general application" (Dubber 2002, 142).

LO 2

Incomplete criminal conduct poses a dilemma: whether to punish someone who's done no harm or to set free someone who's determined to commit a crime. The doctrine of inchoate crimes asks the question: How far should criminal law go to prevent crime by punishing people who haven't accomplished their criminal purpose?

Creating criminal liability for uncompleted crimes flies in the face of the notion that free societies punish people for what they've done, not for what they might do. On the other hand, the doctrine of inchoate crimes reflects the widely held belief that "an ounce of prevention is worth a pound of cure." The law of inchoate crimes resolves the dilemma by three means:

1. Requiring a specific intent or purpose to commit the crime or cause a harm
2. Requiring some action to carry out the purpose
3. Punishing inchoate crimes less severely than completed crimes (ALI 1985, 3:293–98; Perkins and Boyce 1982, 611–58)

ATTEMPT

Failure is an unwelcome part of everyday life that we'd like to avoid. But in criminal law, we want those who wish others ill to fail. We're relieved when a would-be murderer shoots and misses the target, and we're happy when a store detective interrupts an aspiring thief just about to steal a Blu-ray disc of the latest Academy Award winner from a bin in Wal-Mart.

In this section, we'll look at how the history of attempt law has evolved over more than two thousand years; the rationales for attempt law; the elements of criminal attempt; and how failures to complete crimes due to either impossibility or voluntary abandonment are treated within the law.

THE HISTORY OF ATTEMPT LAW

> One who has a purpose and intention to slay another and only wounds him should be regarded as a murderer.
>
> (Plato, *Laws*, 360 BC)

> For what harm did the attempt cause, since the injury took no effect?
>
> (Henry of Bracton, about 1300, in Bracton 1968–77, 3:21)

These quotes, almost a thousand years apart, underscore how long philosophers and judges have struggled with how the criminal law should respond to criminal attempts. Until the 1500s, the English common law sided with Bracton; in attempts, "a miss was as good as a mile" (Hall 1960, 560). A few cases of attempted murder in the 1300s adopted Plato's view according to the maxim, "The intent shall be taken for the deed." One was a servant who cut his master's throat and ran off with his goods; the other was a man who attacked his lover's husband, leaving him for dead (561). But according to the great scholar of medieval English law, Maitland, "The adoption of this perilous saying was but a momentary aberration" provoked by excessive leniency in these "murderous assaults that which did not cause death" (560).

Modern attempt law began in 1500s England out of frustration with this "excessive leniency" in a violent society where tempers were short and hot, and everyone was armed. The famous royal court (a special court of the monarch not bound by common law rules) that met in the Star Chamber started punishing a wide range of potential harms, hoping to nip violence in the bud. Typical cases included lying in wait, threats, challenges, and even words that "tended to challenge." Surviving records are full of efforts to punish budding violence that too often erupted into serious injury and death (Elton 1972, 170–71).

In the early 1600s, stressing the need to prevent the serious harms spawned by dueling, Francis Bacon maintained that "all the acts of preparation should be punished" (Samaha 1974; 1981, 189).

By the late 1700s, the English common law courts had created a full-fledged law of attempt. In the great case of *Rex v. Scofield* (1784), a servant put a lighted candle in his master's house, intending to burn the house down. The house didn't burn, but the servant was punished anyway. According to the court, "The intent may make an act, innocent in itself, criminal; nor is the completion of an act, criminal in itself, necessary to constitute criminality."

By the 1800s, common law attempt was well-defined:

> All attempts whatever to commit indictable offenses, whether felonies or misdemeanors are misdemeanors, unless by some special statutory enactment they are subjected to special punishment. (Stephen 1883, 2:224)

Some jurisdictions still follow the common law of attempt. In 1979, a Maryland judge confidently wrote that "the common law is still alive and well in Maryland" and that the common law of attempt "still prospers on these shores" (*Gray v. State* 1979, 854). As of June 2012, no cases in Maryland had disputed this claim.

LO 3

THE RATIONALES FOR ATTEMPT LAW

dangerous act rationale, looks at how close defendants came to completing their crimes

dangerous person rationale, concentrates on how fully defendants have developed their intent to commit their crime

Why do we punish people who haven't hurt anyone? There are two old and firmly entrenched rationales. One focuses on dangerous acts (*actus reus*), the other on dangerous persons (*mens rea*). The **dangerous act rationale** looks at how close defendants came to completing their crimes. The **dangerous person rationale** concentrates on how fully defendants have developed their intent to commit their crime.

Both rationales measure dangerousness according to actions, but they do so for different reasons. The dangerous act rationale aims to prevent harm from dangerous conduct, so its concern is how close to completion the crime was. The dangerous person rationale aims to neutralize dangerous people, so it looks at how developed the defendant's criminal purpose was (Brodie 1995, 237–38).

THE ELEMENTS OF ATTEMPT LAW

The crime of attempt consists of two elements:

1. Intent or purpose to commit a specific crime and
2. An act, or acts, to carry out the intent

See the Elements of Attempt Liability illustration of these requirements.

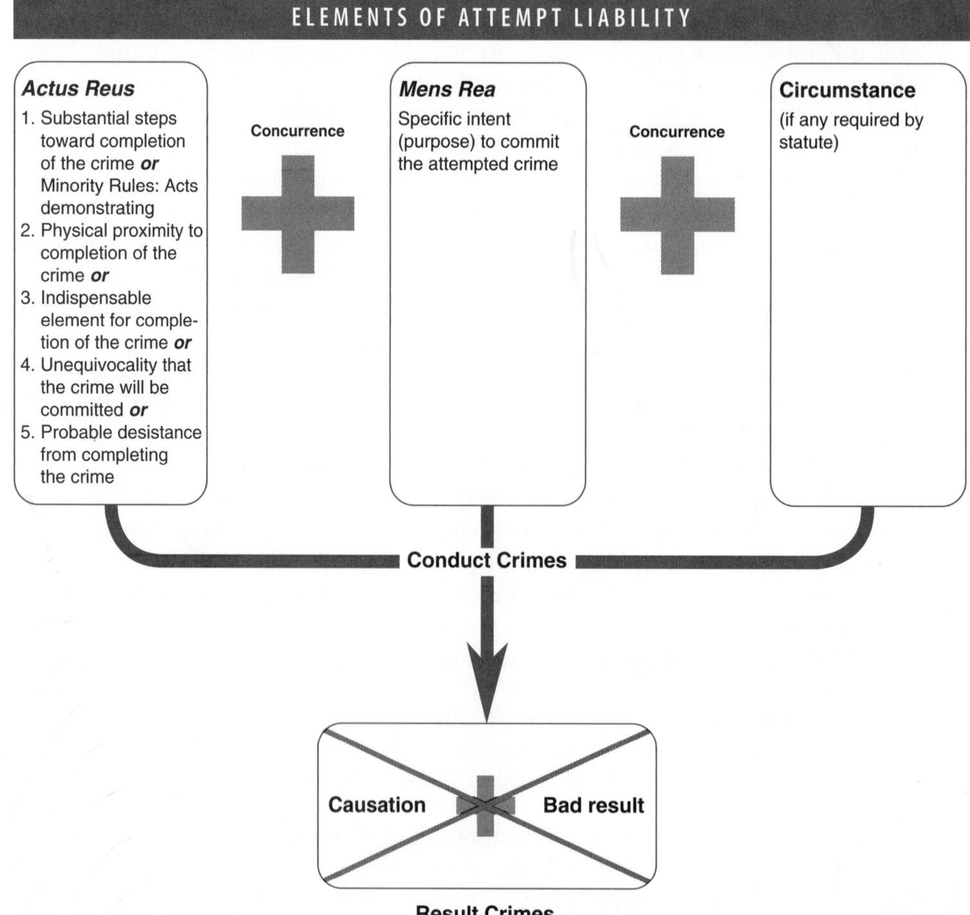

There are two types of attempt statutes, general attempt and specific intent. A **general attempt statute** is a single statute that applies to the attempt to commit any crime in the state's criminal code. Alabama's attempt statute is a typical general attempt statute: "A person is guilty of an attempt to commit a crime if, with the intent to commit a specific offense, he does any overt act towards the commission of such offense" (Alabama Criminal Code 1975). **Specific attempt statutes** define attempts in terms of specific crimes in the criminal code, such as attempted murder, attempted robbery, and attempted rape in separate statutes. These are crimes in which a specific intent was involved.

Let's look at each of the two elements the prosecution has to prove beyond a reasonable doubt in criminal attempt cases, attempt *mens rea* and *actus reus*.

general attempt statute, a single statute that applies to the attempt to commit any crime in the state's criminal code

specific attempt statutes, separate statutes that define attempts in terms of specific crimes in the criminal code, such as attempted murder, attempted robbery, and attempted rape—crimes that involved a specific intent

Attempt *Mens Rea*

LO 4

You can't "blunder into an attempt," because attempt is a crime of purpose (Sayre 1928, 841). "Attempt" means to try, and you can't try to do what you don't specifically intend to do. As one authority put it, "An attempt without intent is unthinkable; it cannot be" (Enker 1977, 847). So, when it comes to **attempt *mens rea***, you don't have to worry about the difficult task of figuring out whether it was knowing, reckless, negligent, or strict liability.

attempt *mens rea*, the specific intent to commit a crime

CASE

***In* People v. Kimball *(1981)*,** *the Michigan Court of Appeals examined, and rejected, James Kimball's claim that he didn't intend to rob the Alpine Party Store—he was only joking.*

Did he intend to rob the store?

People v. Kimball

311 N.W.2d 343 (Mich.App.1981)

HISTORY

James Kimball, the defendant, was charged with and convicted of attempted unarmed robbery, at a bench trial conducted in early August 1979. He was sentenced to a prison term of from three to five years and appeals by leave granted. Reversed and remanded.

MAHER, J.

There is really very little dispute as to what happened on May 21, 1979, at the Alpine Party Store near Suttons Bay, Michigan. Instead, the dispute at trial centered on whether what took place amounted to a criminal offense or merely a bad joke.

FACTS

James Kimball, the defendant, went to the home of a friend, Sandra Storey, where he proceeded to consume a large amount of vodka mixed with orange juice. The defendant was still suffering from insect stings acquired the previous day so he also took a pill called "Eskaleth 300," containing 300 milligrams of Lithium, which Storey had given him.

After about an hour, the pair each mixed a half-gallon container of their favorite drinks (vodka and orange juice, in the defendant's case), and set off down the road in Storey's '74 MGB roadster. At approximately 8:15 or 8:30 in the evening, the defendant (who was driving) pulled into the parking lot of the Alpine Party Store. Although he apparently did not tell Storey why he pulled in, the defendant testified that the reason for the stop was to buy a pack of cigarettes.

Concerning events inside the store, testimony was presented by Susan Stanchfield, the clerk and sole employee present at the time. She testified that the defendant came in and began talking to and whistling at the Doberman Pinscher guard dog on duty at the time. She gave him a "dirty look," because she didn't want him playing with the dog. The defendant then approached the cash register, where Stanchfield was stationed, and demanded money.

Stanchfield testified that she thought the defendant was joking, and told him so, until he demanded money again in a "firmer tone."

(continues)

(continued)

> *Stanchfield*: "By his tone I knew he meant business; that he wanted the money."
> *Prosecution*: "You felt he was serious?"
> *Stanchfield*: "I knew he was serious."

Stanchfield then began fumbling with the one dollar bills until the defendant directed her to the "big bills." Stanchfield testified that as she was separating the checks from the twenty dollar bills the defendant said, "I won't do it to you; you're good looking and I won't do it to you this time, but if you're here next time, it won't matter."

A woman then came in (Storey), who put a hand on the defendant's shoulder and another on his stomach and directed him out of the store. Stanchfield testified that she called after the defendant, saying that she would not call the police if he would "swear never to show your face around here again." To this the defendant is alleged to have responded, "You could only get me on attempted anyway." Stanchfield then directed a customer to get the license plate number on the defendant's car while she phoned the owner of the store.

The defendant also testified concerning events inside the store. He stated that the first thing he noticed when he walked in the door was the Doberman Pinscher. When he whistled the dog came to him and started licking his hand. The defendant testified that while he was petting the dog Stanchfield said, "Watch out for the dog; he's trained to protect the premises."

> *Defendant*: Well, as soon as she told me that the dog was a watchdog and a guarddog [*sic*], I just walked up in front of the cash register and said to Sue (Stanchfield), I said, "I want your money."
>
> I was really loaded and it just seemed to me like it was kind of a cliché because of the fact that they've got this big bad watchdog there that's supposed to watch the place and there I was just petting it, and it was kind of an open door to carry it a little further and say hey, I want all your money because this dog isn't going to protect you. It just kind of happened all at once.
>
> She said, I can't quote it, but something to the effect that if this is just a joke, it's a bad joke, and I said, "Just give me your big bills."
>
> Then she started fumbling in the drawer, and before she pulled any money out of the drawer I don't know whether she went to the ones or the twenties I said as soon as she went toward the drawer to actually give me the money, I said, "Hey, I'm just kidding," and something to the effect that "you're too good looking to take your money."
>
> And she said, "Well, if you leave right now and don't ever come back, I won't call the police," and I said, "Okay, okay," and I started to back up. And Sandy (Storey) I mean I don't know if I was stumbling back or stepping back, but I know she grabbed me, my arm, and said, "Let's go," and we turned around and left, and that was it.

Both Stanchfield and the defendant testified that there were other people in the store during the time that the defendant was in the store, but the testimony of these people revealed that they did not hear what was said between Stanchfield and the defendant.

Storey testified that she remained in the car while the defendant went into the store but that after waiting a reasonable time she went inside to see what was happening. As she approached the defendant she heard Stanchfield say, "Just promise you will never do that again and I won't take your license number." She then took defendant's arm, turned around, gave Stanchfield an "apologetic smile," and took the defendant back to the car.

Once in the car, the defendant told Storey what had happened in the store, saying "But I told her (Stanchfield) I was only kidding." The defendant and Storey then drove to a shopping center where the defendant was subsequently arrested.

OPINION

The general attempt statute, under which defendant was prosecuted, provides in part as follows:

> Any person who shall attempt to commit an offense prohibited by law, and in such attempt shall do any act towards the commission of such offense, but shall fail in the perpetration, or shall be intercepted or prevented in the execution of the same, when no express provision is made by law for the punishment of such attempt, shall be punished. (M.C.L. § 750.92; M.S.A. § 28.287)

The elements of an attempt are:

1. the specific intent to commit the crime attempted and
2. an overt act going beyond mere preparation towards the commission of the crime.

Considering the second element first, it is clear that in the instant case defendant committed sufficient overt acts. As the trial court noted, there was evidence on every element of an unarmed robbery except for the actual taking of money. From the evidence presented, including the evidence of defendant's intoxication, the question of whether defendant undertook these acts with the specific intent to commit an unarmed robbery is a much closer question. After hearing all the evidence, however, the trial court found that defendant possessed the requisite intent and we do not believe that finding was clearly erroneous.

REVERSED AND REMANDED. [The court reversed and remanded because the trial court didn't allow the defendant to prove that he voluntarily abandoned his attempt to rob the store. Abandonment is discussed later in the chapter.]

QUESTIONS

1. Summarize Susan Stanchfield's version and then James Kimball's version of what happened in the Alpine Party Store.
2. If you were a juror, which version would you believe? Explain your answer.
3. List all the facts relevant to deciding whether Kimball specifically intended to rob the store.
4. Did Kimball specifically intend to rob the store? Back up your answer with the relevant facts and portions of the opinion.

Attempt *Actus Reus*

You're sitting in your apartment, planning in detail when, how, and where you're going to kill your boyfriend and your best friend because they cheated on you with each other. You decide to do it tonight with your roommate's gun. You get up, go to her room, get the gun, pick up your car keys, and go to your car. Then, the enormity of what you're going to do hits you. You say to yourself, "What's wrong with me? What am I doing? I can't kill them." You go back and turn on the TV.

LO 5

I don't believe anyone would think you committed attempted murder. Why? First, because, as we learned in Chapters 3 and 4, we don't punish people for their bare intentions. Justice Oliver Wendell Holmes (1963) in a famous passage wrote, "There is no law against a man's intending to commit a murder the day after tomorrow" (54). Of course, there's no more than bare intention in our example. You got the gun, picked up your car keys, and went to your car. But we have a deeply entrenched rule that preparing to carry out your intention to commit a crime doesn't qualify as an attempt to commit a crime. Attempt *actus reus* requires that you take steps toward completing the crime.

attempt *actus reus*, taking some steps toward completing a crime

What if you went into your room, took the gun, loaded it, got your car keys, got in your car, and drove to your boyfriend's apartment. When he answered the door, you took out the gun, and pulled the trigger, but your hands were shaking so much you missed? I believe everybody would think you attempted to murder your boyfriend. Why? Because you did everything you could to kill him. This version of the example represents the strictest rule of attempt *actus reus* called the last act rule—namely, that someone has committed all but the last act necessary to complete the crime.

last act rule, attempt *actus reus* requires all but the last act needed to complete the crime

Most real cases aren't so easy. They fall somewhere between mere intent and "all but the last act" necessary to complete the crime. The toughest question in attempt law may be, "How close to completing a crime is close enough to satisfy the criminal act requirement of attempt?" The general answer is somewhere on a continuum between preparation and the last act. This general answer is so general that it's useless as a guide for deciding (and for us, understanding) real cases. So courts and attempt statutes have established proximity tests that help to decide when defendants' acts have taken them further than just getting ready to attempt and brought them close enough to completing crimes to qualify as attempt *actus reus.*

proximity tests, help courts decide when defendants' acts have taken them further than just getting ready to attempt and brought them close enough to completing crimes to qualify as attempt *actus reus*

LO 5

dangerous proximity tests, focus on dangerous conduct; they look at what remains for actors to do before they hurt society by completing the crime

dangerous person tests, look at what actors have already done to demonstrate that they're a danger to society, not just in this crime but, more important, in crimes they might commit in the future if they're not dealt with now

The tests reflect the focus of the two theories of attempt: dangerous conduct and dangerous people. **Dangerous proximity tests** focus on dangerous conduct; they look at what remains for actors to do before they hurt society by completing the crime. (*Proximity* here means the act closest to the act necessary to complete the crime.) **Dangerous person tests** look at what actors have already done to demonstrate that they're a danger to society, not just in this crime but, more important, in crimes they might commit in the future if they're not dealt with now.

As we examine the main tests of dangerous conduct (*actus reus*) and dangerous persons (*mens rea*), keep in mind that the approaches of the tests aren't mutually exclusive. As you work your way through the tests, don't look at them as conflicting definitions of the one single "true" test. Instead, think of them as a variety of approaches available to describe more definitely the acts that are enough to fall within the spectrum between the end of preparation yet short of the completed crime and/or that demonstrate a clear mental determination to commit the crime.

According to the Florida Court of Appeals, "It does not appear that Florida has ever expressly adopted one of the approaches." It went on to note that "adopting one approach to the exclusion of the others may not be advisable" (*State v. Hudson* 1999, 1000). Why isn't it advisable? So courts can use the tests as flexible instruments that best fit the countless variations in facts among individual cases. Now, let's look at the tests.

The proximity tests ask, "Were the defendant's acts close enough to the intended crime to count as the criminal act in the attempt?" Before we can answer that, we have to answer the question, "How close is close enough?" We'll look at six tests that try to answer this question:

1. The all but the last act test
2. The dangerous proximity to success test
3. The indispensable element test
4. The unequivocality test
5. The probable desistance test
6. The substantial steps test

all but the last act, a strict test for whether "all but the last act" undertaken by the defendant, which does meet the proximity test, satisfies the attempt *actus reus* of the crime

THE ALL BUT THE LAST ACT No cases or statutes have limited attempt *actus reus* to the last act. Of course, "**all but the last act**" satisfies the proximity test. The problem with this strict test is that it excludes dangerous conduct that falls short of the last proximate act that should be included. For example, the first dose of poison in a case of intended killing by small doses of poison wouldn't satisfy the last proximate act test for attempted murder *actus reus*. But the first dose should qualify as the *actus reus* (LaFave 2003a, 590). According to widely cited and quoted criminal law Professor Joshua Dressler (2009), "Today, there is general agreement that an attempt occurs *at least* by the time of the last act, but no jurisdiction *requires* it" (398; emphasis in the original).

dangerous proximity to success test (also called the **physical proximity test**), asks whether defendants have come "dangerously close" to completing the crime

Some courts have adopted broader proximity tests to help judges decide whether the facts that juries have found the prosecution has proven beyond a reasonable doubt are enough. That is, they help to decide whether the defendant's acts fall within the spectrum between preparation (which clearly doesn't satisfy the proximity test) and the last proximate act, which clearly does. Let's look at two of these broader proximity tests: the dangerous proximity to success and indispensable element tests.

LO 5

THE "DANGEROUS PROXIMITY TO SUCCESS" TEST The **dangerous proximity to success test** (also called the **physical proximity test**) asks whether defendants have come "dangerously close" to completing the crime. In Justice Holmes's words, "There must be a dangerous proximity to success" (*Hyde v. U.S.* 1912, 388).

This test focuses on what actors still have to do to carry out their purpose to commit crimes, not on what they've done already to commit them. For example, if you plan to rob a bank messenger, and you're driving around checking out places where you think she might be, but you haven't found her yet, have you attempted to rob her? No, according to the court that decided the famous case of *People v. Rizzo* (1927):

> These defendants had planned to commit a crime, and were looking around the city for an opportunity to commit it, but the opportunity fortunately never came. Men would not be guilty of attempt at burglary if they planned to break into a building while they were hunting about the streets for the building not knowing where it was. Neither would a man be guilty of an attempt to commit murder if he armed himself and started out to find the person he intended to kill but could not find him. So here these defendants were not guilty of an attempt to commit robbery . . . when they had not found or reached the presence of the person they intended to rob. (888)

LO 5

indispensable element test, asks whether defendants have reached a point where they've gotten control of everything they need to complete the crime

THE "INDISPENSABLE ELEMENT" TEST The **indispensable element test** asks whether defendants have reached a point where they've gotten control of everything they need to complete the crime. For example, a drug dealer can't attempt to sell Ecstasy until she gets some Ecstasy, even if she has a customer right there, ready, and waiting to buy it. Once she's got the Ecstasy, she's close (proximate) enough to completing the crime to satisfy the attempt criminal act requirement.

Now, let's turn to two dangerous person tests that look at what defendants have already done, not at what they still have to do: the unequivocality and substantial steps tests.

LO 5

unequivocality test, also called the ***res ipsaloquiter* test** ("the act speaks for itself"), examines whether an ordinary person who saw the defendant's acts without knowing her intent would believe she was determined to commit the intended crime

THE "UNEQUIVOCALITY" TEST The **unequivocality test**, also called the ***res ipsaloquiter* test** ("the act speaks for itself"), examines whether an ordinary person who saw the defendant's acts without knowing his intent would believe he was determined to commit the intended crime. Notice, it's the *intended* crime, not any crime. Here's a frequently used example to describe the test:

> It is as though a cinematograph film, which had so far depicted the accused person's act without stating what was his intention, had been suddenly stopped, and the audience were asked to say to what end those acts were directed. If there is only one reasonable answer to this question then the accused has done what amounts to an "attempt" to attain that end. (Turner 1934, 238)

Walter Lee Stewart passed the "stop the film test" in *State v. Stewart* (1988, 50). Here's the story:

> Scott Kodanko was waiting for a bus on a Saturday afternoon after leaving work. He was alone in a three-sided plexiglas bus shelter open to the street in downtown Milwaukee. Two men, Mr. Moore and Walter Lee Stewart, the defendant, entered the bus shelter while a third man, Mr. Levy, remained outside.
>
> Moore and the defendant stood one to two feet from Kodanko. Kodanko was in a corner of the shelter, his exit to the street blocked by the two men. Moore asked Kodanko if he wanted to buy some cigarettes. Kodanko responded that he did not. Moore then said, "Give us some change." When Kodanko refused, the defendant said "Give us some change, man." The defendant repeated this demand in an increasingly loud voice three to four times. Kodanko still refused to give the two men change.

> The defendant then reached into his coat with his right hand at about the waist level, whereupon Moore stated something to the effect of "put that gun away." At that point Levy, who had been waiting outside the bus shelter, entered and said to the defendant and Moore "Come on, let's go." Levy showed Kodanko some money, stating, "I don't want your money, I got lots of money." (45–46)

According to the Court:

> If the defendant had been filmed in this case and the film stopped just before Levy entered the bus stop and the three men departed, we conclude that a trier of fact could find beyond a reasonable doubt that the defendant's acts were directed toward robbery. The film would show the defendant demanding money and appearing to reach for a gun. This evidence is sufficient to prove that the defendant had taken sufficient steps for his conduct to constitute an attempted robbery. (50)

The distinguished Professor Glanville Williams (1961) criticizes the unequivocality test because in ambiguous cases, it "would acquit many undoubted criminals." For example:

probable desistance test, determines if defendants have gone far enough toward completing the crime that it's unlikely they'll turn back

> D goes up to a haystack, fills his pipe, and lights a match. The act of lighting a match, even to a suspicious-minded person, is ambiguous. It may indicate only that D is going to light his pipe; but, perhaps on the other hand, the pipe is only a 'blind' and D is really bent on setting fire to the stack. We do not know. Therefore, on the equivocality test, the act is not proximate. (630)

LO 5

The "probable desistance" test The **probable desistance test**, another dangerous person test, focuses on how far defendants have gone, not on what's left for them to do to complete the crime. The test determines if defendants have gone far enough toward completing the crime that it's unlikely they'll turn back.

LO 5

The Model Penal Code (MPC) "substantial steps" test The Model Penal Code's **substantial steps test** (also called the "MPC test") was designed to accomplish three important goals:

MPC substantial steps test, test that requires that attempters take enough steps toward completing the crime to prove that they're determined to commit it

1. Replace (or at least drastically reform) the proximity and unequivocality tests with a clearer and easier to understand and apply test
2. Draw more sharply (and push back further toward preparation) the line between preparation and beginning to attempt the crime
3. Base the law of attempt firmly on the theory of neutralizing dangerous persons, not just on preventing dangerous conduct

In line with these goals, the MPC's substantial steps test for attempt *actus reus* includes two elements:

1. "Substantial steps" toward completing the crime
2. Steps that "strongly corroborate the actor's criminal purpose"

In other words, the code requires that attempters take enough steps toward completing the crime not to show that a crime is about to occur but to prove that the attempters are determined to commit it.

To sharpen the line between preparation and attempt, push it back closer to preparation, and make clear the commitment to neutralizing dangerous people, the code lists seven acts (most of which would qualify as mere preparation in traditional attempt statutes) that can amount to "substantial steps" if they strongly corroborate the actor's criminal purpose to commit the intended crime:

1. Lying in wait, searching for, or following the contemplated victim of the crime
2. Enticing, or seeking to entice, the contemplated victim of the crime to go to the place contemplated for its commission
3. Reconnoitering [or "casing"] the place contemplated for the commission of the crime
4. Unlawful entry of a structure, vehicle, or enclosure in which it is contemplated that the crime will be committed
5. Possession of materials to be employed in the commission of the crime that are specially designed for such unlawful use or that can serve no lawful purpose of the actor under the circumstances
6. Possession, collection, or fabrication of materials to be employed in the commission of the crime, at or near the place contemplated for its commission, if such possession, collection, or fabrication serves no lawful purpose of the actor under the circumstances
7. Soliciting an innocent agent to engage in conduct constituting an element of the crime (ALI 1985, 3:296)

The "vast majority" of current criminal codes have adopted the MPC "substantial steps" language, but most have not included the MPC seven facts that push attempt back into what traditionally and still are considered acts of preparation, not of attempt (LaFave 2003a, 594). It's probably as true now as it was in 1967 that:

> Much ink has been spilt in an attempt to arrive at a satisfactory standard for telling where preparations [*sic*] ends and attempt begins, but the tests adopted in the various jurisdictions fall somewhere between the two extremes represented respectively by the old common law guide and the one suggested by the Model Penal Code of the American Law Institute. (*Mims v. U.S.* 1967, 148)

CASE

In* Mims v. U.S. *(1967), the U.S. Fifth Circuit Court of Appeals sent the case back to the trial court to determine whether George Lee Mims Sr. attempted or only prepared to rob the Madeira Beach Bank.

Did he attempt to rob the bank?

George Lee Mims, Sr. v. U.S.

375 F.2d 135 (5th Cir. 1967)

HISTORY

George Lee Mims, Sr. was prosecuted for an attempt to enter the Madeira Beach Bank with intent to rob it by force and violence and by intimidation. The United States District Court for the Middle District of Florida entered a judgment of conviction, and Mims appealed. The Court of Appeals reversed and sent the case back for retrial.

BREWSTER, J.

FACTS

George Lee Mims, Sr. (Appellant) was a middle-aged mechanic who had been employed at the municipal garage in Treasure Island, Florida, near Madeira Beach, for several years prior to the incidents here involved. His wife died in March, 1962, leaving him with two children by their marriage. One of them was George Lee Mims, Jr., 13 years of age, and the other was a daughter several years older. Within less

(continues)

(continued)

than 60 days after the death of his wife, he and a married woman with two children had agreed to marry each other if she could persuade her husband to get a divorce. There was some delay about the divorce, and she moved into appellant's house with her children in the middle of June, and continued to live there with him without benefit of clergy until they married shortly before the trial in the following year.

The additions to the appellant's household brought on financial difficulties, even though he was moonlighting on a filling station job three evenings a week and was handling a little repair work on his friends' personal cars on some weekends. He was also having some serious problems with his children. The nature of them was not disclosed. He apparently tried to solve his problems by drinking, and during June and July he frequently drank to excess. Some calls to the Madeira Beach Bank prior to June for the purpose of repairing adding machines had given him access to and familiarity with the area of the bank where the money was kept and he began to consider robbing it. In early June, he implicated Willie Joe Henderson, a 22 year old Negro with an eleventh grade education who worked under him at the garage. He also involved his son, George Lee Mims, Jr., Dennis O'Connor, a 15 year old boy who had run away from home and moved into appellant's house, and Stephen O'Connor, 14 years old.

Guns and ammunition were procured, so that at the time of the two trips to the bank each participant was armed with a loaded pistol, a shotgun or a rifle. For disguises, they had coveralls, sailor hats and face masks. Appellant explained to his companions that the advantage of the coveralls was that they could be put on over street clothes and taken off quickly. By virtue of knowledge gained while working on the adding machines in the bank, the appellant gave each of his companions a definite assignment to do while in the bank. He had also concluded that the fewest customers would be in the bank around closing time, so he planned to enter it just before it closed its doors to the public for the day.

The first trip to the bank for the purpose of robbing it was Saturday, July 7th. At that time Thomas Napper was not involved. All the other participants met at the garage where appellant and Henderson worked at a time when it was closed for business that day. They put on their coveralls and disguises, got into a car and drove to the bank, intending to reach there about five minutes before closing time. However, they miscalculated the time, and got there a few minutes after it had closed. When they arrived and saw the situation, they left without making any attempt to go into the bank.

The next visit to the bank was on Wednesday, July 11th. On the previous day, the appellant rented from the King Car Rentals Service in Treasure Island a Ford Galaxie [*sic*] bearing Florida license plates for use in going to and from the bank. Before going to the bank he put some stolen out-of-state license plates over the Florida plates. He also rented an apartment with a private garage in an area that could be reached quickly after leaving the bank. The rented car was put in the garage at the apartment on July 10th and left there until it was used for transportation to the bank. The plan was that the participants could come to the apartment in their own cars, put on their disguises there, go to the bank in the rented car, rob the bank and return to the apartment before police began to watch the cars on the streets, shed their disguises, hide the get away car, guns and disguises in the apartment and garage, and then leave in their regular clothes in small groups in the other cars.

Willie Joe Henderson brought his cousin, Thomas Napper, to the apartment and had him included in the group that was to rob the bank. The appellant was under the influence of whiskey when he appeared that day, and brought two bottles of whiskey with him. When all the parties had put on their disguises and were ready to go, appellant suggested to them that a drink of whiskey would settle their nerves. Some of them took a drink. They drove to the bank parking lot in the rented car, and sent Henderson around to see if the bank was still open. It was, but he was getting reluctant to go through with the robbery and went back and told them the bank was closed. They knew that he had been wavering, and began to doubt his statement after a few minutes; so all of them went around to the bank entrance with intention to go in and commit the robbery, if the bank was still open.

The proof indicates that they had no more intention of forcing their way in if the bank was closed, than they had when they went to the bank on the preceding Saturday. By the time they got to the entrance, the bank had actually closed for the day. A Mrs. Barkiewicz was at the door shaking it to attract the attention of one of the bank employees to get him to let her in to correct an error in a deposit she had made a few minutes before closing time. One of the boys placed the muzzle of his pistol at the side of her head, and another one told her that they were going to rob the bank. She thought it was a prank. When she replied that it was too late, as the bank had already closed, one of appellant's party said, "Let's get out of here" and they ran back to their car and fled.

OPINION

The court instructed the jury that they need not spend any time debating as to whether or not an attempt was made to rob the bank, as the evidence showed such attempt as a matter of law. Counsel for the appellant did not object to that instruction, even though he had indicated in his opening statement at the beginning of the trial that the charge would be contested . . . on the ground "that there was never a valid attempt, an actual attempt to commit the crime as alleged . . .". The instruction was so peremptory in nature that the error must be noticed without an objection having been made.

The appellant was entitled to have the question of whether there was an attempt to enter the bank for the purpose of robbing it submitted to the jury under appropriate instructions covering, among other things, for determining whether the conduct of the participants had gone beyond the intent and preparation stage and had reached the point where an overt act had been committed directly tending to effect the commission of the substantive offense.

Much ink has been spilt in an attempt to arrive at a satisfactory standard for telling where preparations ends and attempt begins, but the tests adopted in the various jurisdictions fall somewhere between the two extremes represented respectively by the old common law guide and the one suggested by the Model Penal Code of the American Law Institute. The question has not been decided by this Court; but, in the event of another trial, help can be obtained from the few federal cases on it.

The *Buffum* case states a test that has been frequently approved:

> Preparation alone is not enough, there must be some appreciable fragment of the crime committed, it must be in such progress that it will be consummated unless interrupted by circumstances independent of the will of the attempter, and the act must not be equivocal in nature.

The *Gregg* case approves that test laid down by Cardozo, Jr., . . . [that] the act must "carry the project forward within dangerous proximity to the criminal end to be attained."

The *Coplon* case quoted with approval the following from the opinion of Holmes, J., in the *Peaslee* case,

> Preparation is not an attempt. But some preparations may amount to an attempt. It is a question of degree. If the preparation comes very near to the accomplishment of the act, the intent to complete it renders the crime so probable that the act will be a misdemeanor, although there is still the need of a further exertion of the will to complete the crime.

In discussing the same question in the *Kennedy* case, Holmes, J., said: "Every question of proximity must be determined by its own circumstances, and analogy is too imperfect to give much help."

The conviction . . . is reversed and remanded.

QUESTIONS

1. List all of the facts and circumstances relevant to deciding whether George Lee Mims Sr. attempted to rob the bank.
2. Assume you're the prosecutor. On the facts and circumstances available from the excerpt, argue that the case went far enough beyond preparation to satisfy the *actus reus* element.
3. Now, assume you're the defense attorney. On the facts and circumstances available from the excerpt, argue that the case went no further than preparation.
4. Now, you be the judge. Write an opinion deciding the case, relying on your answers to 2 and 3.

EXPLORING FURTHER

Attempt Actus Reus

1. Did they get "very near" to robbing the clerk?

People v. Rizzo, 158 N.E. 888 (N.Y.App. 1927)

FACTS

Charles Rizzo, Anthony J. Dorio, Thomas Milo, and John Thomasello were driving through New York City looking for a payroll clerk they intended to rob.

(continues)

(continued)

While they were still looking for their victim, the police apprehended and arrested them. They were tried and convicted of attempted robbery. Rizzo appealed. Did their acts add up to attempt *actus reus*?

DECISION

The trial court said yes. The New York Court of Appeals (New York's highest court) reversed:

> The Penal Law, § 2, prescribes that:
>
> An act, done with intent to commit a crime, and tending but failing to effect its commission, is "an attempt to commit that crime." The word "tending" is very indefinite. It is perfectly evident that there will arise differences of opinion as to whether an act in a given case is one tending to commit a crime. "Tending" means to exert activity in a particular direction. Any act in preparation to commit a crime may be said to have a tendency toward its accomplishment. The procuring of the automobile, searching the streets looking for the desired victim, were in reality acts tending toward the commission of the proposed crime.
>
> The law, however, had recognized that many acts in the way of preparation are too remote to constitute the crime of attempt. The line has been drawn between those acts which are remote and those which are proximate and near to the consummation. The law must be practical, and therefore considers those acts only as tending to the commission of the crime which are so near to its accomplishment that in all reasonable probability the crime itself would have been committed, but for timely interference. The cases which have been before the courts express this idea in different language, but the idea remains the same. The act or acts must come or advance very near to the accomplishment of the intended crime.

2. Was it "preparation" or "all but the last act"?

Commonwealth v. Peaslee, 59 N.E. 55 (Mass. 1901)

FACTS

Lincoln Peaslee had made and arranged combustibles in a building he owned so they were ready to be lighted and, if lighted, would have set fire to the building and its contents. He got within a quarter of a mile of the building, but his would-be accomplice refused to light the fire. Did Peaslee attempt to commit arson?

DECISION

No, said the court:

> A mere collection and preparation of materials in a room, for the purpose of setting fire to them, unaccompanied by any present intent to set the fire, would be too remote and not all but "the last act" necessary to complete the crime.

LO 6

DEFENSES TO ATTEMPT LIABILITY: LEGAL IMPOSSIBILITY AND VOLUNTARY ABANDONMENT

Remember that "attempts are cases of failure" (Fletcher 1978, 131). Failure can be due to several causes: police officers might show up; victims might resist and escape; a passerby might appear. These are all circumstances beyond the attempter's control, and they're not defenses to a charge of attempt. We'll look at two that can be—legally impossible attempts and abandoned attempts. Both of these are affirmative defenses. (Recall that defendants have to prove affirmative defenses, in most states by a preponderance of the evidence—Chapter 1, p. 31.)

Legal Impossibility

To avoid paying customs, a man sneaks an antique book past customs, not knowing that there's an exception in the law for antique books. Has he attempted to evade customs laws? No. A woman stabs her batterer husband repeatedly, thinking he's asleep.

In fact, he had died of a heart attack two hours before she stabbed him. Has she committed attempted murder? No.

The first scenario is an example of **legal impossibility**. A legal impossibility occurs when actors intend to commit crimes, and do everything they can to carry out their criminal intent, but the criminal law doesn't ban what they did. So even though he wanted to evade customs laws, and did all he could to commit the crime of tax evasion, it's legally impossible to commit a crime that doesn't exist. If the law were different, he'd be guilty; but it isn't, so legal impossibility is a defense to criminal liability.

legal impossibility, occurs when actors intend to commit crimes, and do everything they can to carry out their criminal intent, but the criminal law doesn't ban what they did

Stabbing an already dead victim is an example of **factual impossibility**. A factual impossibility occurs when actors intend to commit a crime and try to but it's physically impossible due to some fact or circumstance unknown to them. The woman intended to murder her battering husband. She did all she could to commit it by stabbing him; if the facts had been different—that is, if her victim had been alive—she would have murdered him.

factual impossibility, occurs when actors intend to commit a crime and try to but it's physically impossible because some fact or circumstance unknown to them interrupts or prevents the completion of the crime

Legal impossibility requires a different law to make the conduct criminal; factual impossibility requires different facts to complete the crime. In most jurisdictions, legal impossibility is a defense to criminal attempt; factual impossibility isn't. The main reason for the difference is that to convict someone for conduct that the law doesn't prohibit, no matter what the actor's intentions, violates the principle of legality—no crime without a law, no punishment without a crime (Chapter 1). Factual impossibility, on the other hand, would allow chance to determine criminal liability. A person who's determined to commit a crime, and who does enough to succeed in that determination, shouldn't escape responsibility and punishment because of a stroke of good luck.

CASE

In **State v. Damms** *(1960), the Wisconsin Supreme Court affirmed Ralph Damms's conviction for attempting to murder his wife because his unloaded gun was considered a "stroke of luck."*

Was the unloaded gun a "stroke of luck"?

State v. Damms

100 N.W.2d 592 (Wis. 1960)

HISTORY

The defendant, Ralph Damms, was charged by *information* [a criminal charge by the prosecutor without a grand jury] with the offense of attempt to commit murder in the first degree. The jury found the defendant guilty as charged, and the defendant was sentenced to imprisonment in the state prison at Waupun for a term of not more than ten years. Damms appealed to the Wisconsin Supreme Court. The Supreme Court affirmed the conviction.

CURRIE, J.

FACTS

The alleged crime occurred on April 6, 1959, near Menomonee Falls in Waukesha County. Prior to that date Marjory Damms, wife of the defendant, had instituted an action for divorce against him and the parties lived apart. She was 39 years old and he 33 years of age. Marjory Damms was also estranged from her mother, Mrs. Laura Grant.

That morning, a little before eight o'clock, Damms drove his automobile to the vicinity in Milwaukee where he knew Mrs. Damms would take the bus to go to work. He saw her walking along the sidewalk, stopped, and induced her to enter the car by falsely stating that Mrs. Grant was ill and dying. They drove to Mrs. Grant's home. Mrs. Damms then discovered that her mother was up and about and not seriously ill. Nevertheless, the two Damms remained there nearly two hours conversing and drinking coffee. Apparently, it was the intention of Damms to induce a reconciliation between mother and daughter,

(continues)

(continued)

hoping it would result in one between himself and his wife, but not much progress was achieved in such direction.

At the conclusion of the conversation, Mrs. Damms expressed the wish to phone for a taxicab to take her to work. Damms insisted on her getting into his car, and said he would drive her to work. They again entered his car, but instead of driving south toward her place of employment, he drove in the opposite direction. Some conversation was had in which he stated that it was possible for a person to die quickly and not be able to make amends for anything done in the past, and he referred to the possibility of "judgment day" occurring suddenly.

Mrs. Damms' testimony as to what then took place is as follows: "When he was telling me about this being judgment day, he pulled a cardboard box from under the seat of the car and brought it up to the seat and opened it up and took a gun out of a paper bag. He aimed it at my side and he said, 'This is to show you I'm not kidding.' I tried to quiet him down. He said he wasn't fooling. I said if it was just a matter of my saying to my mother that everything was all right, we could go back and I would tell her that."

They did return to Mrs. Grant's home and Mrs. Damms went inside and Damms stayed outside. In a few minutes he went inside and asked Mrs. Damms to leave with him. Mrs. Grant requested that they leave quietly so as not to attract the attention of the neighbors. They again got into the car, and this time drove out on Highway 41 toward Menomonee Falls. Damms stated to Mrs. Damms that he was taking her "up north" for a few days, the apparent purpose of which was to effect a reconciliation between them.

As they approached a roadside restaurant, he asked her if she would like something to eat. She replied that she wasn't hungry but would drink some coffee. Damms then drove the car off the highway beside the restaurant and parked it with the front facing, and in close proximity to, the restaurant wall.

Damms then asked Mrs. Damms how much money she had with her and she said "a couple of dollars." He then requested to see her checkbook and she refused to give it to him. A quarrel ensued between them. Mrs. Damms opened the car door and started to run around the restaurant building screaming, "Help!" Damms pursued her with the pistol in his hand.

Mrs. Damms' cries for help attracted the attention of the persons inside the restaurant, including two officers of the state traffic patrol who were eating their lunch. One officer rushed out of the front door and the other the rear door. In the meantime, Mrs. Damms had run nearly around three sides of the building. In seeking to avoid colliding with a child, who was in her path, she turned, slipped, and fell. Damms crouched down, held the pistol at her head, and pulled the trigger, but nothing happened. He then exclaimed, "It won't fire. It won't fire."

Damms testified that at the time he pulled the trigger the gun was pointing down at the ground and not at Mrs. Damms' head. However, the two traffic patrol officers both testified that Damms had the gun pointed directly at her head when he pulled the trigger. The officers placed Damms under arrest. They found that the pistol was unloaded. The clip holding the cartridges, which is inserted in the butt of the gun to load it, was later found in the cardboard box in Damms' car together with a box of cartridges.

That afternoon, Damms was questioned by a deputy sheriff at the Waukesha county jail, and a clerk in the sheriff's office typed out the questions and Damms' answers as they were given. Damms later read over such typed statement of questions and answers, but refused to sign it. In such statement Damms stated that he thought the gun was loaded at the time of the alleged attempt to murder. Both the deputy sheriff and the undersheriff testified that Damms had stated to them that he thought the gun was loaded. To the contrary, though, Damms testified at the trial that he knew at the time of the alleged attempt that the pistol was not loaded.

OPINION

The two questions raised on this appeal are:

1. Did the fact that it was impossible for the accused to have committed the act of murder because the gun was unloaded preclude his conviction of the offense of attempt to commit murder?
2. Assuming that the foregoing question is answered in the negative, does the evidence establish the guilt of the accused beyond a reasonable doubt?

Sec. 939.32(2), Stats., provides as follows:

> An attempt to commit a crime requires that the actor have an intent to perform acts and attain a result which, if accomplished, would constitute such crime and that he does acts toward the commission of the crime which demonstrate unequivocally, under all the circumstances, that he formed that intent and would *commit* the crime *except for the intervention of another person or some other extraneous factor.* [emphasis added, see definition on p. 276]

The issue with respect to the first of the aforestated two questions boils down to whether the impossibility of accomplishment due to the gun being unloaded falls within the statutory words "except for the intervention of some other extraneous factor." We conclude that it does.

An article in 1956 Wisconsin Law Review, by Assistant Attorney General Platz, points out that "attempt" [in the Wisconsin statute] is more intelligible fashion than using such tests as "beyond mere preparation," the place at which the actor may repent and withdraw, or "dangerous proximity to success." Quoting the author:

> Emphasis upon the dangerous propensities of the actor as shown by his conduct, rather than upon how close he came to succeeding, is more appropriate to the purposes of the criminal law to protect society and reform offenders or render them temporarily harmless.

Sound public policy would seem to support the majority view that impossibility not apparent to the actor should not absolve him from the offense of attempt to commit the crime he intended. An unequivocal act accompanied by intent should be sufficient to constitute a criminal attempt. Insofar as the actor knows, he has done everything necessary to insure the commission of the crime intended, and he should not escape punishment because of the fortuitous circumstance that by reason of some fact unknown to him it was impossible to effectuate the intended result.

It is our considered judgment that the fact that the gun was unloaded when Damms pointed it at his wife's head and pulled the trigger did not absolve him of the offense charged, if he actually thought at the time that it was loaded.

We do not believe that the further contention raised in behalf of the accused, that the evidence does not establish his guilt of the crime charged beyond a reasonable doubt, requires extensive consideration on our part.

The jury undoubtedly believed the testimony of the deputy sheriff and undersheriff that Damms told them on the day of the act that he thought the gun was loaded. This is also substantiated by the written statement constituting a transcript of his answers given in his interrogation at the county jail on the same day.

The gun itself, which is an exhibit in the record, is the strongest piece of evidence in favor of Damms' present contention that he at all times knew the gun was unloaded. Practically the entire bottom end of the butt of the pistol is open. Such opening is caused by the absence of the clip into which the cartridges must be inserted in order to load the pistol. This readily demonstrates to anyone looking at the gun that it could not be loaded. Because the unloaded gun with this large opening in the butt was an exhibit which went to the jury room, we must assume that the jury examined the gun and duly considered it in arriving at their verdict.

We are not prepared to hold that the jury could not come to the reasonable conclusion that, because of Damms' condition of excitement when he grabbed the gun and pursued his wife, he so grasped it as not to see the opening in the end of the butt which would have unmistakably informed him that the gun was unloaded. Having so concluded, they could rightfully disregard Damms' testimony given at the trial that he knew the pistol was unloaded.

Judgment affirmed.

DISSENT

DIETERICH, J.

I disagree with the majority opinion in respect to their interpretations and conclusions of sec. 939.32(2), Stats.

The issue raised on this appeal: Could the defendant be convicted of murder, under sec. 939.32(2), Stats., when it was impossible for the defendant to have caused the death of anyone because the gun or pistol involved was unloaded?

(continues)

(continued)

Sec. 939.32(2), Stats., provides:

> An attempt to commit a crime requires that the actor have an intent to perform acts and attain a result which, if accomplished, would constitute such crime and that he does acts toward the commission of the crime which demonstrate unequivocally, under all the circumstances, that he formed that intent and would commit the crime except for the intervention of another person or some other *extraneous factor.* [emphasis added]

In view of the statute, the question arising under sec. 939.32(2), is whether the impossibility of accomplishment due to the pistol being unloaded falls within the statutory words "except for the intervention of . . . or some other extraneous factor." It does not.

In interpreting the statute we must look to the ordinary meaning of words. Webster's New International Dictionary defines "extraneous" as not belonging to or dependent upon a thing, originated or coming from without. The plain distinct meaning of the statute is: A person must form an intent to commit a particular crime and this intent must be coupled with sufficient preparation on his part and with overt acts from which it can be determined clearly, surely and absolutely the crime would be committed except for the intervention of some independent thing or something originating or coming from someone or something over which the actor has no control.

As an example, if the defendant actor had formed an intent to kill someone, had in his possession a loaded pistol, pulled the trigger while his intended victim was within range and the pistol did not fire because the bullet or cartridge in the chamber was defective or because someone unknown to the actor had removed the cartridges or bullets or because of any other thing happening which happening or thing was beyond the control of the actor, the actor could be guilty under sec. 339.32(2), Stats.

But when as in the present case (as disclosed by the testimony) the defendant had never loaded the pistol, although having ample opportunity to do so, then he had never completed performance of the act essential to kill someone, through the means of pulling the trigger of the pistol. This act, of loading the pistol, or using a loaded pistol, was dependent on the defendant himself. It was in no way an extraneous factor since by definition an extraneous factor is one which originates or comes from without.

Under the majority opinion the interpretations of the statute are if a person points an unloaded gun (pistol) at someone, knowing it to be unloaded and pulls the trigger, he can be found guilty of an attempt to commit murder. This type of reasoning I cannot agree with.

He could be guilty of some offense, but not attempt to commit murder. If a person uses a pistol as a bludgeon and had struck someone, but was prevented from killing his victim because he (the actor) suffered a heart attack at that moment, the illness would be an extraneous factor within the statute and the actor could be found guilty of attempt to commit murder, provided the necessary intent was proved.

In this case, there is no doubt that the pistol was not loaded. The defendant testified that it had never been loaded or fired. The following steps must be taken before the weapon would be capable of killing:

1. To load pistol requires pulling of slide operating around barrel toward holder or operator of pistol.
2. After pulling slide to rear, safety latch is pushed into place by operator of pistol to hold pistol in position for loading.
3. A spring lock is located at one side of opening of magazine located at the bottom grip or butt of gun.
4. This spring is pulled back and the clip is inserted into magazine or bottom of pistol and closes the bottom of the grip or butt of the pistol.
5. The recoil or release of the safety latch on the slide loads the chamber of the pistol and it is now ready to fire or be used as a pistol.

The law judges intent objectively. It is impossible to peer into a man's mind particularly long after the act has been committed. Viewing objectively the physical salient facts, it was the defendant who put the gun, clip and cartridges under the car seat. It was he, same defendant, who took the pistol out of the box without taking clip or cartridges. It is plain he told the truth—he knew the gun would not fire;

nobody else knew that so well. In fact his exclamation was "It won't fire. It won't fire."

The real intent showed up objectively in those calm moments while driving around the county with his wife for two hours, making two visits with her at her mother's home, and drinking coffee at the home. He could have loaded the pistol while staying on the outside at his mother-in-law's home on his second trip, if he intended to use the pistol to kill, but he did not do this required act.

The majority states:

> The gun itself, which is an exhibit in the record, is the strongest piece of evidence in favor of Damms' present contention that he at all times knew the gun was unloaded. Practically the entire bottom end of the butt of the pistol is open. This readily demonstrates to anyone looking at the gun that it could not be loaded.

They are so correct. The defendant had the pistol in his hand several times before chasing his wife at the restaurant and it was his pistol. He, no doubt, had examined this pistol at various times during his period of ownership—unless he was devoid of all sense of touch and feeling in his hands and fingers it would be impossible for him not to be aware or know that the pistol was unloaded. He could feel the hole in the bottom of the butt, and this on at least two separate occasions for he handled the pistol by taking it out of the box and showing it to his wife before he took her back to her mother's home the second time, and prior to chasing her at the restaurant.

Objective evidence here raises reasonable doubt of intent to attempt murder. It negatives [*sic*] intent to kill. The defendant would have loaded the pistol had he intended to kill or murder or used it as a bludgeon. The Assistant Attorney General contends and states in his brief:

> In the instant case, the failure of the attempt was due to lack of bullets in the gun but a loaded magazine was in the car. If defendant had not been prevented by the intervention of the two police officers, or possibly someone else, or conceivably by the flight of his wife from the scene, he could have returned to the car, loaded the gun, and killed her. Under all the circumstances the jury were justified in concluding that that is what he would have done, but for the intervention.

If that conclusion is correct, and juries are allowed to convict persons based on speculation of what might have been done, we will have seriously and maybe permanently, curtailed the basic rights of our citizenry to be tried only on the basis of proven facts. I cannot agree with his contention or conclusion.

The total inadequacy of the means (in this case the unloaded gun or pistol) in the manner intended to commit the overt act of murder, precludes a finding of guilty of the crime charged under sec. 939.32(2), Stats.

QUESTIONS

1. List all the facts relevant to deciding whether Ralph Damms intended to murder Marjory Damms.
2. List all the facts relevant to deciding whether Damms had taken enough steps to attempt to murder Marjory Damms according to the Wisconsin statute.
3. Summarize the majority's arguments that the unloaded gun was an extraneous factor, a stroke of luck Damms shouldn't benefit from.
4. Summarize the dissent's arguments that the unloaded gun wasn't an extraneous factor but an impossibility that prevents Damms from attempting to murder Marjory Damms.
5. In your opinion, is the majority or dissent right? Explain your answer in terms of what effect impossibility should have on liability for criminal attempt.
6. Should it matter why the gun was unloaded? Explain your answer.
7. What if Damms knew the gun was unloaded? Should he still be guilty of attempted murder? Explain your answer.
8. Is the Wisconsin rule punishing attempts that are about half the actions needed to complete the crime a good idea?
9. Some states punish attempts at the same level as completed crimes because people bent on committing crimes shouldn't benefit at all from a stroke of luck. Do you agree? Defend your answer with arguments from the case excerpt and the text.

Voluntary Abandonment

LO 7

extraneous factor, a "stroke of luck"—namely, a circumstance beyond the attempter's control that prevents the completion of the crime

voluntary abandonment defense (also called **voluntary renunciation defense**), defendants who voluntarily and completely renounce their criminal purpose can avoid criminal liability

We know from the last section that those bent on committing crimes who've taken steps to carry out their criminal plans can't escape criminal liability just because an outside force or person interrupted them. But what about people who clearly intend to commit crimes, take enough steps to carry out their intent, and then change their mind and voluntarily abandon the scheme? Should the law benefit those who themselves are the force that intercepts the crimes they wanted to commit and are marching toward completing? The answer depends on which jurisdiction they're in.

According to the voluntary abandonment defense (also called voluntary renunciation defense), defendants who voluntarily and completely renounce their criminal purpose can avoid criminal liability.

Michigan has a typical voluntary abandonment statute:

> It is an affirmative defense . . . that, under circumstances manifesting a voluntary and complete renunciation of his criminal purpose, the actor avoided the commission of the offense attempted by abandoning his criminal effort.

A renunciation is not "voluntary and complete" within the meaning of this chapter if it is motivated in whole or in part by either of the following:

1. A circumstance which increases the probability of detection or apprehension of the defendant or another participant in the criminal operation or which makes more difficult the consummation of the crime.
2. A decision to postpone the criminal conduct until another time or to substitute another victim or another but similar objective. (*People v. Kimball*, 346–48)

According to the Model Penal Code, voluntary abandonment means:

> A change in the actor's purpose not influenced by outside circumstances, what may be termed repentance or change of heart. Lack of resolution or timidity may suffice. A reappraisal by the actor of the criminal sanctions hanging over his conduct would presumably be a motivation of the voluntary type as long as the actor's fear of the law is not related to a particular threat of apprehension or detection. (ALI 1985, 3:356)

Supporters of the voluntary abandonment defense favor it for two reasons. First, those who voluntarily renounce their criminal attempts in progress (especially during the first acts following preparation) aren't the dangerous people the law of attempt is designed to punish; they probably weren't even bent on committing the crime in the first place. Second, at the very end of the progress to completing the crime, it prevents what we most want—the harm the completed crime is about to inflict on victims.

This defense encourages would-be criminals to give up their criminal designs by the promise of escaping punishment. Opponents say the defense encourages bad people to take the first steps to commit crimes because they know they can escape punishment (Moriarity 1989, 1).

The drafters of the Model Penal Code claim that the "prevailing view" favors the voluntary abandonment defense. But Professor LaFave (2003a) notes that the

> American cases cited in support of allowing voluntary desistance for the most part contain such statements *in dictum* [comments not part of the law of the case] or in concurring or dissenting opinions. Cases in which the defendant's claim of voluntary withdrawal was plausible enough to make failure to instruct on the defense reversible error are extremely rare. (608)

Nevertheless, he concludes that, "On balance" arguments in favor of the defense are "more persuasive than the arguments against the defense" (608).

The arguments supporting the defense include:

1. Complete and voluntary renunciation of criminal purpose shows the defendant isn't dangerous.
2. Those "who have crossed the threshold of attempt will still be encouraged to desist and thereby escape punishment."

The counterargument is that the defense may "embolden" those who are thinking about committing a crime to take the first steps toward committing the crime when they know they can withdraw without negative consequences (609).

CASE

In* Le Barron v. State *(1966), *the court rejected David Le Barron's defense that he voluntarily abandoned his plan to rape Jodean Randen.*

Did he voluntarily abandon his attempt to rape?

Le Barron v. State

145 N.W.2d 79 (Wis. 1966)

HISTORY

David Le Barron was convicted of attempted rape and sentenced to not more than 15 years in prison. He appealed. The Wisconsin Supreme Court affirmed the conviction.

CURRIE, J.

FACTS

On March 3, 1965, at 6:55 P.M., the complaining witness, Jodean Randen, a housewife, was walking home across a fairly well-traveled railroad bridge in Eau Claire, Wisconsin. She is a slight woman whose normal weight is 95 to 100 pounds. As she approached the opposite side of the bridge, she passed a man who was walking in the opposite direction.

The man turned and followed her, grabbed her arm, and demanded her purse. She surrendered her purse and at the command of the man began walking away as fast as she could. Upon discovering that the purse was empty, he caught up with her again, grabbed her arm, and told her that if she did not scream he would not hurt her.

He then led her—willingly, she testified, so as to avoid being hurt by him—to the end of the bridge. While walking he shoved her head down and warned her not to look up or do anything and he would not hurt her.

On the other side of the bridge along the railroad tracks there is a coal shack. As they approached the coal shack he grabbed her, put one hand over her mouth, and an arm around her shoulder and told her not to scream or he would kill her. At this time Mrs. Randen thought he had a knife in his hand.

He then forced her into the shack and up against the wall. As she struggled for her breath he said, "You know what else I want," unzipped his pants and started pulling up her skirt. She finally succeeded in removing his hand from her mouth, and after reassuring him that she would not scream, told him she was pregnant and pleaded with him to desist or he would hurt her baby.

He then felt her stomach and took her over to the door of the shack, where in the better light he was able to ascertain that, under her coat, she was wearing maternity clothes. He thereafter let her alone and left after warning her not to scream or call the police, or he would kill her.

OPINION

The material portions of the controlling statutes provide:

> § 944.01(1), Stats. Any male who has sexual intercourse with a female he knows is not his wife, by force and against her will, may be imprisoned not more than 30 years.

> § 939.32(2), Stats. An attempt to commit a crime requires that the actor have an intent to perform acts and attain a result which, if

(continues)

(continued)

> accomplished, would constitute such crime and that he does acts toward the commission of the crime which demonstrate unequivocally, under all the circumstances, that he formed that intent and would commit the crime except for the intervention of another person or some other extraneous factor.

The two statutory requirements of intent and overt acts which must concur in order to have attempt to rape are as follows:

1. The male must have the intent to act so as to have intercourse with the female by overcoming or preventing her utmost resistance by physical violence, or overcoming her will to resist by the use of threats of imminent physical violence likely to cause great bodily harm;
2. the male must act toward the commission of the rape by overt acts which demonstrate unequivocally, under all the circumstances, that he formed the intent to rape and would have committed the rape except for the intervention of another person or some other extraneous factor.

The thrust of defendant's argument, that the evidence was not sufficient to convict him of the crime of attempted rape, is two-fold: first, defendant desisted from his endeavor to have sexual intercourse with complainant before he had an opportunity to form an intent to accomplish such intercourse by force and against her will; and, second, the factor which caused him to desist, viz., the pregnancy of complainant, was intrinsic and not an "extraneous factor" within the meaning of sec. 939.32(2), Stats.

It is difficult to consider the factor of intent apart from that of overt acts since the sole evidence of intent in attempted rape cases is almost always confined to the overt acts of the accused, and intent must be inferred therefrom. In fact, the express wording of sec. 939.32(2), Stats. recognizes that this is so.

We consider defendant's overt acts, which support a reasonable inference that he intended to have sexual intercourse with complainant by force and against her will, to be these:

1. He threatened complainant that he would kill her if she refused to cooperate with him;
2. he forced complainant into the shack and against the wall; and
3. he stated, "You know what else I want," unzipped his pants, and started pulling up her skirt.

The jury had the right to assume that defendant had the requisite physical strength and weapon (the supposed knife) to carry out the threat over any resistance of complainant.

We conclude that a jury could infer beyond a reasonable doubt from these overt acts of defendant that he intended to have sexual intercourse with defendant by force and against her will. The fact that he desisted from his attempt to have sexual intercourse as a result of the plea of complainant that she was pregnant would permit of the opposite inference. However, such desistance did not compel the drawing of such inference nor compel, as a matter of law, the raising of a reasonable doubt to a finding that defendant had previously intended to carry through with having intercourse by force and against complainant's will.

The argument that the pregnancy which caused defendant's desistance does not qualify as an "extraneous factor" is in conflict with our holding in *State v. Damms*. [See case excerpt under "Legal Impossibility."]

AFFIRMED.

QUESTIONS

1. List all the facts relevant to deciding whether Le Barron had the intent to rape Jodean Randen.
2. At what point, if any, did his acts cross the line from preparation to the *actus reus* of attempt under Wisconsin law?
3. Describe the details surrounding Le Barron's decision to abandon the attempted rape of Randen.
4. Why did Le Barron abandon his attempt to rape Randen? Because he believed it was morally wrong to rape a pregnant woman? Or did the pregnancy simply repel him sexually? Does it matter? Explain your answer.
5. Is Le Barron equally dangerous, whichever reason led to interrupting the rape? Explain.
6. The court said a jury could have concluded Randen's pregnancy was either an extraneous factor he couldn't benefit from or an intrinsic factor that caused Le Barron to renounce voluntarily his intention to rape. If you were a juror, how would you have voted on whether the pregnancy was an extraneous or an intrinsic factor?

"Should both women be treated equally?"

In the heat of an argument, a woman grabs a gun and fires at her spouse, trying to kill him. She misses. Realizing the horror of what she has tried to do, she throws down the gun and embraces her husband. Another woman, also arguing with her spouse, grabs a gun and shoots at him. She, too, misses on the first shot. She fires again and again, a total of four times. Three of the bullets strike her husband and cause serious injury, but he is eventually able to run away from her and escape to safety.

Instructions

Write a one-page essay explaining why you believe the defense of abandonment as an ethical public policy should apply to the first woman, who shot at her husband, but not to the second woman. Be sure to include the rationales for abandonment from this section to support your answer.

CONSPIRACY

> The mere agreement to murder a man fifty miles away could not possibly constitute an attempt, but might easily be indictable as a conspiracy.
>
> (*Hyde v. U.S.* 1912, 388)

> The core of conspiracy is an agreement to commit a crime. It's this agreement that gives rise to criminal liability, by transforming a lonely criminal thought hatched in the mind of a single, powerless individual into an agreement with another person. I reveal myself as one of those persons who suffer from an abnormal disposition to engage in criminal conduct, by distinguishing myself from those untold millions who harbor criminal thoughts, but never share them with others, never mind act on them in any way. But my decision to seek out likeminded proto criminals, and to join hands with them in the pursuit of a common criminal goal is symptomatic of my extraordinary dangerousness. By combining forces with another similarly dangerous person, I multiply my already considerable dangerousness through the magic of cooperation.
>
> (Dubber 2002, 163)

LO 8

Conspiracy, the crime of agreeing with one or more people to commit a crime, is further removed from actually committing a crime than attempts to commit crimes. In fact, there are two public policy justifications for attaching criminal liability to actions further away from completion than attempts:

conspiracy, the crime of agreeing with one or more people to commit a crime

1. Conspiracy works hand in hand with attempts to nip criminal purpose in the bud.
2. Conspiracy strikes at the special danger of group criminal activity. (ALI 1985, 3:377–78)

See the Elements of Conspiracy illustration, which identifies the components of conspiracy, on the next page.

In this section, we'll look at what's necessary to prove the *actus reus* and *mens rea* of conspiracy, how the law treats the parties to conspiracies, how large-scale conspiracies differ, and how the law limits the definition of the criminal objective of a conspiracy.

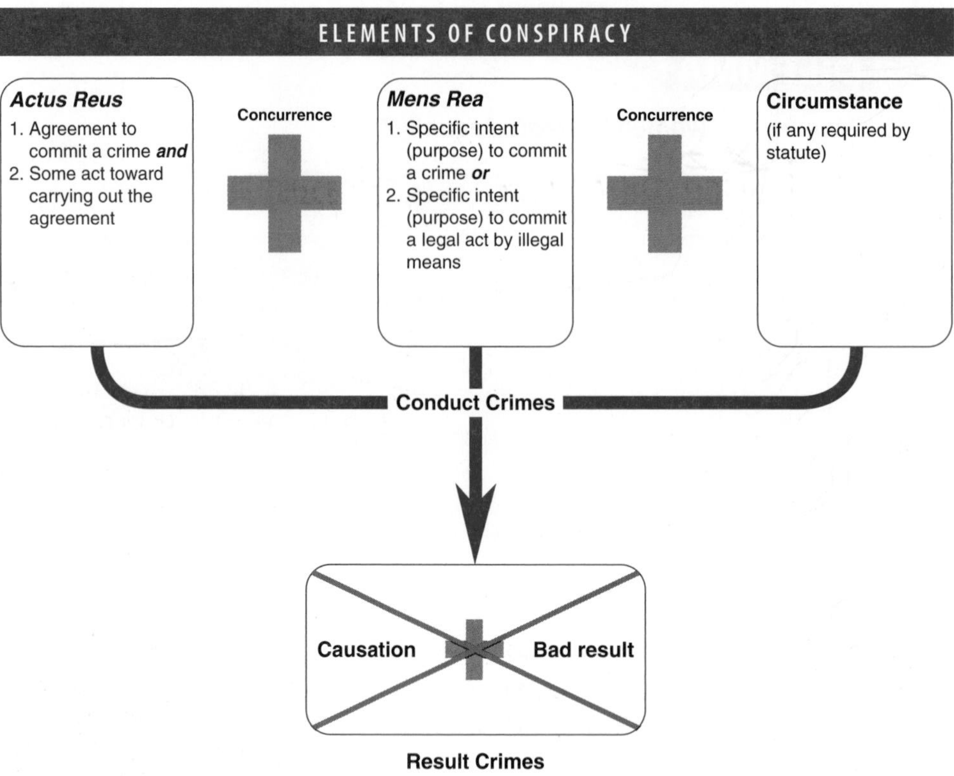

CONSPIRACY *ACTUS REUS*

conspiracy *actus reus*, consists of two parts: (1) an agreement to commit a crime and (2) an overt act in furtherance of the agreement

Conspiracy *actus reus* consists of two parts: (1) an agreement to commit a crime (in all states) and (2) an overt act in furtherance of the agreement (in about half the states). Let's look at each part.

The Agreement

The heart of the crime of conspiracy is the act of agreement between two or more people to commit a crime. The agreement doesn't have to be a signed written contract. It's "not necessary to establish that the defendant and his coconspirators signed papers, shook hands, or uttered the words 'we have an agreement'" (*State v. Vargas* 2003, 208–9). Facts and circumstances that point to an unspoken understanding between the conspirators are good enough to prove the conspirators agreed to commit a crime. This rule makes sense because conspirators rarely put their agreements in writing.

The rule might make sense, but it encourages vague definitions of "agreement" that can lead to injustice. In one famous trial during the Vietnam War, the government tried the well-known baby doctor turned war protestor, Dr. Benjamin Spock, for conspiracy to avoid the draft law. Videotapes showed several hundred spectators clapping while Dr. Spock urged young men to resist the draft. Spurred on by antagonism to antiwar protestors, the prosecutor in the case made the ridiculous assertion that any person seen clapping on the videotape was a co-conspirator. According to the prosecutor, these people were aiding Spock, and that made them parties to a conspiracy to violate the draft law (Mitford 1969, 70–71).

The Overt Act

In about half the states, the agreement itself satisfies the *actus reus* of conspiracy. The other half and the federal courts require the act of agreeing to commit a crime plus another act to further the agreement; the second act is called the **overt act requirement**.

overt act requirement, the requirement of an act that furthers the agreement in conspiracy

Why the requirement of an "overt act"? To verify the firmness of the agreement. The overt act doesn't have to amount to much. In the words of the American Law Institute's commentator (1985, [3] 387), it may "be of very small significance." And according to the U.S. Supreme Court Justice Oliver Wendell Holmes (*Hyde v. U.S.* 1912):

> If the overt act is required, it does not matter how remote the act may be from accomplishing the [criminal] purpose, if done to effect it; that is, I suppose, in furtherance of it in any degree. (388)

The U.S. Ninth Circuit Court of Appeals found the agreement plus an overt act missing in a charge that Cody Garcia, a member of the "Bloods" gang, conspired to assault three rival "Crips" with a deadly weapon and that there was no evidence Garcia fired.

CASE

In* U.S. v. Garcia *(1998), *the U.S. Ninth Circuit Court of Appeals found the agreement plus an overt act missing in a charge that Cody Garcia, a member of the "Bloods" gang, conspired to assault three rival "Crips" with a deadly weapon and that there was no evidence Garcia fired.*

Did he "agree" to assault three Crips members with a deadly weapon?

U.S. v. Garcia

151 F.3d 1243 (9th Cir. 1998)

HISTORY

Leon Garcia, also known as Cody Garcia, the defendant, was convicted in the U.S. District Court for the District of Arizona of conspiracy to assault with a dangerous weapon and was sentenced to 60 months in prison. The defendant appealed. The Court of Appeals reversed and remanded.

REINHARDT, J.

FACTS

One evening, a confrontation broke out between rival gangs at a party on the Pasqua Yaqui Indian reservation. The resultant gunfire injured four young people, including appellant Cody Garcia. Two young men involved in the shooting, Garcia and Noah Humo, were charged with conspiracy to assault three named individuals with dangerous weapons. A jury acquitted Humo but convicted Garcia.

The party at which the shootings occurred was held in territory controlled by the Crips gang. The participants were apparently mainly young Native Americans. Although many of the attendees were associated with the Crips, some members of the Bloods gang were also present. Cody Garcia arrived at the party in a truck driven by his uncle, waving a red bandanna (the Bloods claim the color red and the Crips the color blue) out the truck window and calling out his gang affiliation: "ESPB Blood!" Upon arrival, Garcia began "talking smack" to (insulting) several Crips members. Prosecution witnesses testified that Garcia's actions suggested that he was looking for trouble and issuing a challenge to fight to the Crips at the party.

Meanwhile, Garcia's fellow Bloods member Julio Baltazar was also "talking smack" to Crips members, and Blood Noah Humo bumped shoulders with one Crips member and called another by a derogatory Spanish term. Neither Baltazar nor Humo had arrived with Garcia, nor is there any indication that they had met before the party to discuss plans or that they were seen talking together during the party.

At some point, shooting broke out. Witnesses saw both Bloods and Crips, including Garcia and Humo, shooting at one another. Baltazar was seen waving a knife or trying to stab a Crip. The testimony at trial does not shed light on what took place immediately prior to the shooting, other than the fact that one witness heard Garcia ask, "Who has the gun?" There is some indication that members of the two gangs may have "squared off" before the shooting

(continues)

(continued)
began. No testimony establishes whether the shooting followed a provocation or verbal or physical confrontation.

Four individuals were injured by the gunfire: the defendant, Stacy Romero, Gabriel Valenzuela, and Gilbert Baumea. Stacy Romero who at the time was 12 years old was the cousin both of Garcia's co-defendant Humo and his fellow Blood, Baltazar. No evidence presented at trial established that any of the injured persons was shot by Garcia, and he was charged only with conspiracy. The government charged both Garcia and Humo with conspiracy to assault Romero, Valenzuela, and Baumea with dangerous weapons under 18 U.S.C. §§ 371, 113(a)(3) and 1153.

OPINION

In order to prove a conspiracy, the government must present sufficient evidence to demonstrate both an overt act and an agreement to engage in the specific criminal activity charged in the indictment. While an implicit agreement may be inferred from circumstantial evidence, proof that an individual engaged in illegal acts with others is not sufficient to demonstrate the existence of a conspiracy. Both the existence of and the individual's connection to the conspiracy must be proven beyond a reasonable doubt. Even though a defendant's connection to the conspiracy may be slight, the connection must nonetheless be proven beyond a reasonable doubt.

The government claims that it can establish the agreement to assault in two ways: first, that the concerted provocative and violent acts by Garcia, Humo and Baltazar are sufficient to show the existence of a prior agreement; and second, that by agreeing to become a member of the gang, Garcia implicitly agreed to support his fellow gang members in violent confrontations.

However, no inference of the existence of any agreement could reasonably be drawn from the actions of Garcia and other Bloods members on the night of the shooting. An inference of an agreement is permissible only when the nature of the acts would logically require coordination and planning.

The government presented no witnesses who could explain the series of events immediately preceding the shooting, so there is nothing to suggest that the violence began in accordance with some prearrangement. The facts establish only that perceived insults escalated tensions between members of rival gangs and that an ongoing gang-related dispute erupted into shooting. Testimony presented at trial suggests more chaos than concert. Such evidence does not establish that parties to a conspiracy worked together understandingly, with a single design for the accomplishment of a common purpose.

Given that this circumstantial evidence fails to suggest the existence of an agreement, we are left only with gang membership as proof that Garcia conspired with fellow Bloods to shoot the three named individuals. The government points to expert testimony at the trial by a local gang unit detective, who stated that generally gang members have a "basic agreement" to back one another up in fights, an agreement which requires no advance planning or coordination. This testimony, which at most establishes one of the characteristics of gangs but not a specific objective of a particular gang—let alone a specific agreement on the part of its members to accomplish an illegal objective—is insufficient to provide proof of a conspiracy to commit assault or other illegal acts.

Recent authority in this circuit establishes that "membership in a gang cannot serve as proof of intent, or of the facilitation, advice, aid, promotion, encouragement or instigation needed to establish aiding and abetting." In overturning the state conviction of a gang member that rested on the theory that the defendant aided and abetted a murder by "fanning the fires of gang warfare," . . . *Mitchell v. Prunty*, 107 F.3d. 1337, expressed concern that allowing a conviction on this basis would "smack of guilt by association." The same concern is implicated when a conspiracy conviction is based on evidence that an individual is affiliated with a gang which has a general rivalry with other gangs, and that this rivalry sometimes escalates into violent confrontations.

Acts of provocation such as "talking smack" or bumping into rival gang members certainly does not prove a high level of planning or coordination. Rather, it may be fairly typical behavior in a situation in which individuals who belong to rival gangs attend the same events. At most, it indicates that members of a particular gang may be looking for trouble, or ready to fight. It does not demonstrate a coordinated effort with a specific illegal objective in mind.

Conspiracy requires proof of both an intention and agreement to accomplish a specific illegal objective. The fact that gang members attend a function armed with weapons may prove that they are prepared for violence, but without other evidence it does not establish that they have made plans to initiate it. And the fact that more than one member of the Bloods was shooting at rival gang members also does not prove a prearrangement—the Crips, too, were able to pull out their guns almost immediately, suggesting that readiness for a gunfight requires no prior agreement. Such readiness may be a sad commentary on the state of mind of many of the nation's youth, but it is not indicative of a criminal conspiracy.

Finally, allowing a general agreement among gang members to back each other up to serve as sufficient evidence of a conspiracy would mean that any time more than one gang member was involved in a fight it would constitute an act in furtherance of the conspiracy and all gang members could be held criminally responsible—whether they participated in or had knowledge of the particular criminal act, and whether or not they were present when the act occurred. Indeed, were we to accept fighting the enemy as an illegal objective, all gang members would probably be subject to felony prosecutions sooner rather than later, even though they had never personally committed an improper act. This is contrary to fundamental principles of our justice system. There can be no conviction for guilt by association.

Because of these concerns, evidence of gang membership cannot itself prove that an individual has entered a criminal agreement to attack members of rival gangs. Moreover, here the conspiracy allegation was even more specific: the state charged Garcia with conspiracy to assault three specific individuals—Romero, Baumea and Valenzuela—with deadly weapons. Even if the testimony presented by the state had sufficed to establish a general conspiracy to assault Crips, it certainly did not even hint at a conspiracy to assault the three individuals listed in the indictment. Of course, a more general indictment would not have solved the state's problems in this case. In some cases, when evidence establishes that a particular gang has a specific illegal objective such as selling drugs, evidence of gang membership may help to link gang members to that objective. However, a general practice of supporting one another in fights, which is one of the ordinary characteristics of gangs, does not constitute the type of illegal objective that can form the predicate for a conspiracy charge.

Because the government introduced no evidence from which a jury could reasonably have found the existence of an agreement to engage in any unlawful conduct, the evidence of conspiracy was insufficient as a matter of law. A contrary result would allow courts to assume an ongoing conspiracy, universal among gangs and gang members, to commit any number of violent acts, rendering gang members automatically guilty of conspiracy for any improper conduct by any member. We therefore reverse Garcia's conviction and remand to the district court to order his immediate release. As a result of this decision, Garcia is not subject to retrial. He has already served over a year in prison.

REVERSED AND REMANDED.

QUESTIONS

1. State the two parts of the element of agreement in conspiracy, according to the court of appeals.
2. Summarize the government's evidence and arguments that support the conclusion that Garcia was part of an agreement to assault Romero, Valenzuela, and Baumea with dangerous weapons.
3. Summarize the reasons the court rejected the government's arguments and ordered that Garcia should go free.
4. In your opinion, was there an agreement to assault Romero, Valenzuela, and Baumea with dangerous weapons? Back up your answer with relevant facts and arguments from the case excerpt.
5. According to the court, what "fundamental principle of our justice system" would the government's definition of "agreement" violate? Do you agree? Explain your answer.

CONSPIRACY *MENS REA*

conspiracy *mens rea*, the mental element in conspiracy, frequently identified as specific intent by authorities, but it's not defined clearly in statutes and it's defined inconsistently by courts

criminal objective, the criminal goal of an agreement to commit a crime

Conspiracy *mens rea*, the mental element in conspiracy, wasn't defined clearly at common law, and most modern legislatures haven't made it any clearer. This leaves the courts to define it. The courts in turn have taken imprecise, widely divergent, and inconsistent approaches to the *mens rea* problem. According to former Supreme Court Justice Robert Jackson, "The modern crime of conspiracy is so vague that it almost defies definition" (*Krulewitch v. U.S.* 1949, 445–46).

Authorities frequently call conspiracy a specific-intent crime. But what does that mean? Does it mean that conspiracy involves intent to enter an agreement to commit a crime? Or does conspiracy also have to include an intent to attain a specific criminal objective? A **criminal objective** is the criminal goal of an agreement to commit a crime.

For example, if two men agree to burn down a building, they intend to commit arson. But if they don't intend to hurt anyone and someone dies, did they also conspire to commit murder? Not if the conspiracy *mens rea* means the specific intent to achieve a particular criminal objective.

This example demonstrates an important distinction between, on one hand, the intent to make agreements and, on the other hand, the intent to achieve a criminal objective. If the objective is to commit a specific crime, it has to satisfy that crime's *mens rea.* So conspiring to take another's property isn't conspiring to commit larceny unless the conspirators intended to deprive the owner of possession permanently (Chapter 11).

Courts further complicate conspiracy *mens rea* by not clarifying whether it requires purpose. Consider cases involving suppliers of goods and services, such as doctors who order drugs from pharmaceutical companies that they then use or sell illegally. At what point do the suppliers become co-conspirators, even though they haven't agreed specifically to supply drugs for illegal distribution?

Do prosecutors have to prove the suppliers agreed specifically to further the buyers' criminal purposes? Most courts say yes, even though that kind of proof is difficult to obtain, because as we've already seen, conspirators aren't foolish enough to put proof of their crimes in writing. So purpose has to be inferred from circumstances surrounding the agreement, such as quantities of sales, the continuity of the supplier–recipient relationship, the seller's initiative, a failure to keep records, and the relationship's clandestine nature. Some argue that knowing, or conscious, wrongdoing ought to satisfy the conspiracy *mens rea* (*Direct Sales Co. v. U.S.* 1943).

PARTIES TO CONSPIRACY

unilateral approach to conspiracy parties, the rule that not all conspirators have to agree with—or even know—the other conspirators

The traditional definition of "conspiracy" includes the attendant circumstance element that agreements involve "two or more parties agreeing or combining to commit a crime" (ALI 1985, 3:398). Most modern statutes have replaced this traditional definition with a **unilateral approach to conspiracy parties** that doesn't require that all conspirators agree—or even know—the other conspirators. For example, if one of two conspirators secretly has no intention to go through with the agreement, the other conspirator is still a party.

When there's more than one party, failure to convict one party doesn't prevent conviction of other parties to the conspiracy. Typically, statutes are similar to the Illinois Criminal Code (Illinois Criminal Law and Procedure 1988), which provides:

> It shall not be a defense to conspiracy that the person or persons with whom the accused is alleged to have conspired:
>
> 1. Has not been prosecuted or convicted, or
> 2. Has been convicted of a different offense, or

3. Is not amenable to justice, or
4. Has been acquitted, or
5. Lacked the capacity to commit an offense. (chap. 38, § 8-4)

LARGE-SCALE CONSPIRACIES

LO 9

The relationship of parties to conspiracies can get intricate, particularly when they involve large operations. Most of these large-scale conspiracies fall into two major patterns: "wheel" and "chain" conspiracies. In wheel conspiracies, one or more defendants participate in every transaction. These participants make up the hub of the wheel conspiracy. Others participate in only one transaction; they are the spokes in the wheel. In chain conspiracies, participants at one end of the chain may know nothing of those at the other end, but every participant handles the same commodity at different points, such as manufacture, distribution, and sale.

wheel conspiracies, one or more defendants participate in every transaction (the hub of the wheel) and others participate in only one transaction (the spokes in the wheel)

chain conspiracies, participants at one end of the chain may know nothing of those at the other end, but every participant handles the same commodity at different points, such as manufacture, distribution, and sale

Chain conspiracies often involve the distribution of some commodity, such as illegal drugs. In one famous old case still relevant today, *U.S. v. Bruno* (1939), smugglers brought narcotics into New York, middlemen purchased the narcotics, and two groups of "retailers" (one operating in New York and the other in Louisiana) bought narcotics from the middlemen.

THE CRIMINAL OBJECTIVE OF THE CONSPIRACY

criminal objective of the conspiracy, the object of conspiracy agreements has to be to commit crimes

Conspiracy is an agreement but an agreement to do what? In the old days, the criminal objective of the conspiracy was defined to cover a broad spectrum. The objective could be as narrow as an agreement to commit a felony or as broad as agreements to

- commit "any crime."
- do "anything unlawful."
- commit "any act injurious to the public health, or for the perversion of or obstruction of justice, or due administration of the laws" (ALI 1985, 3:395).
- do even "lawful things by unlawful means."

In most modern statutes, the criminal objective of the conspiracy is almost always limited to agreements to commit crimes.

The vague definitions of the elements in conspiracy offer considerable opportunity for prosecutorial and judicial discretion. At times, this discretion borders on abuse, leading to charges that conspiracy law is unjust. First, a general criticism is that conspiracy law punishes conduct too far remote from the actual crime. Second, labor organizations, civil liberties groups, and large corporations charge that conspiracy is a weapon against their legitimate interests of, respectively, collective bargaining and strikes, dissent from accepted points of view and public policies, and profit making.

Critics say that when prosecutors don't have enough evidence to convict for the crime itself, they turn, as their last hope, to conspiracy. Conspiracy's vague definitions greatly enhance the chance for a guilty verdict. Not often mentioned, but extremely important, is that intense media attention to conspiracy trials can lead to abuse. This happened in the conspiracy trials of Dr. Benjamin Spock, the Chicago Eight, and others involving radical politics during the 1960s.

It also occurred in the Watergate conspiracy trials involving President Nixon's associates during the 1970s, in the alleged conspiracies surrounding the sale of arms to Iran for hostages and the subsequent alleged diversion of funds during the 1980s, and in the alleged conspiracy of Osama bin Laden's chauffer and the various alleged conspiracies of officials in the White House during the early 2000s. Several states have made efforts to overcome these criticisms by defining conspiracy elements more narrowly. The definitions of "agreement or combination" (two or more parties combining to commit crimes) are no longer as vague as they once were.

The Model Penal Code has adopted the overt act requirement (acts in furtherance of the act of agreement), and about half the states are following that lead. Those states have refined *mens rea* to include only purposeful conduct—that is, a specific intent to carry out the objective of the agreement or combination. Knowledge, recklessness, and negligence are increasingly attacked as insufficient culpability for an offense as remote from completion as conspiracy. Furthermore, most recent legislation restricts conspiratorial objectives to criminal ends. Phrases such as "unlawful objects," "lawful objects by unlawful means," and "objectives harmful to public health, morals, trade, and commerce" are increasingly regarded as too broad and, therefore, unacceptable.

LO 10

THE RACKETEER INFLUENCED AND CORRUPT ORGANIZATIONS ACT (RICO)

Despite these efforts to restrict the reach of conspiracy, the **Racketeer Influenced and Corrupt Organizations Act (RICO)** demonstrates the continued vitality of conspiracy law. RICO reflects the need for effective means to meet the threat of **racketeering** posed by organized crime. It imposes enhanced penalties for "all types of organized criminal behavior, that is, enterprise criminality—from simple political to sophisticated white collar schemes to traditional Mafia-type endeavors" (Blakely and Gettings 1980, 1013–14). Racketeering originally referred to the extortion of money or advantage by threat or force. Today, the meaning has expanded to encompass a pattern of illegal activity (such as extortion and murder) carried out in the furtherance of an enterprise owned or controlled by those engaged in the activity.

The clumsy title Racketeer Influenced Corrupt Organization Act (universally called by its acronym RICO) refers to a controversial federal statute that originated under President Lyndon Johnson in 1968 and was signed into law by President Richard Nixon in 1970. RICO created several new crimes, reinstated property forfeiture as punishment for crime, and introduced a new civil action that allows RICO victims to sue RICO offenders (Lynch 2002, 1343).

RICO grew out of fear that organized crime was infiltrating legitimate businesses, a problem widely publicized after President Johnson's Crime Commission highlighted the problem in 1967. The original idea was to make it a crime to invest money gotten by crime in legitimate businesses. But RICO as enacted created a series of crimes that went far beyond organized crime's investing their ill-gotten money to infiltrate legitimate businesses. RICO's broadest and most often prosecuted crime consists of three elements:

1. conducting the affairs of *any* "**enterprise**" (defined as "just about any form of human endeavor")
2. by means of a "**pattern of racketeering activity**" (defined as committing two or more of a huge list of related crimes)
3. that do or threaten to continue for a period of time. (Lynch 2002, 1343)

Notice that RICO crimes aren't like the crimes governed by the principles of criminal liability we covered in Chapter 3 (criminal conduct) and Chapter 4 (criminal conduct that causes a harmful result). In fact, it's not clear that RICO involves any conduct at all. Judge Lynch has called RICO crimes "the crime of being a criminal" (Lynch 1987, 661). Probably more accurately, RICO is akin to accomplice and vicarious criminal liability (Chapter 7) and to conspiracy. But it's broader; it depends on "abstract relationships: the "enterprise"' is a structure of relationships among individuals, and the "pattern of racketeering" is a form of relationship among crimes.

Racketeer Influenced and Corrupt Organizations Act (RICO), imposes enhanced penalties for "all types of organized criminal behavior, that is, enterprise criminality—from simple political to sophisticated white collar schemes to traditional Mafia-type endeavors"

racketeering, original meaning was the extortion of money or advantage by threat or force; now the meaning has expanded to include a pattern of illegal activity (such as extortion and murder) carried out in the furtherance of an enterprise owned or controlled by those engaged in the activity

enterprise, just about any form of human endeavor

pattern of racketeering activity, committing two or more of a huge list of related crimes

RICO's broad definitions make it a crime for anyone with a "significant role in operating a business, government office, labor union, social or political organization, or informal grouping" to commit a series of crimes (two is enough) either to further the organization's or informal group's goals or simply by using its resources.

RICO raises the question: Why create crimes out of conduct and relationships that are already criminal? Let's look at three types of RICO cases that may help to answer that question and give you a better understanding of how the U.S. government uses RICO: organized crime, white-collar crime, and government corruption.

PROSECUTING ORGANIZED CRIME

RICO's most dramatic success story is its use in organized crime cases. Its success is due to the relational nature of RICO that we noted earlier. Almost all murder, rape, robbery, and other "traditional" trials focus on a single defendant who's committed a single crime. The rules are established to keep each crime and each defendant separate from one another. It's the opposite in RICO prosecutions.

The operation of an enterprise—say a "criminal gang"—through a pattern of racketeering (at least two separate crimes) is defined in RICO as a single crime. RICO trials look and feel different. Here's how:

1. Evidence that the defendant associates with disreputable people isn't prejudicial like it is in a traditional trial; it's essential to the government's proof of the "enterprise" element.
2. Multiple crimes, even crimes very different in nature, are relevant to prove the pattern element.
3. Mass trials of large numbers of defendants charged with the same RICO enterprise are expected. (Lynch 1990, 786–91)

Why prosecute organized crime under RICO? One reason is that organized crime operates in more than one state, which under ordinary law would require a separate prosecution for each individual crime. RICO's "pattern" element allows these crimes to be tried as only one case. There are other procedural advantages for prosecutors that we won't get into here. The pattern element has facilitated trying large numbers of organized crime defendants like the Mafia in a single trial. Critics have attacked these "mega trials" for several reasons, including:

1. They weaken defendants' protections against wrongful convictions by complicating the jury's job of finding the facts.
2. They drag out trials, making it more expensive for defendants.
3. They foster unfair "spillover" of inferences of guilt in other crimes and to other defendants where the evidence is weak. (Lynch 2002, 1344)

PROSECUTING WHITE-COLLAR CRIME

RICO's broad definition has also made RICO an "attractive tool for prosecutors in serious white-collar criminal cases." These prosecutions have their critics too. Most RICO white-collar crime prosecutions rely on federal mail and wire fraud statutes. These laws ban the use of the mail and interstate electronic communications to aid a "scheme to defraud." And, they're "almost infinitely adaptable to cover a wide range of financial and business misconduct." But, they, as well as securities law violations, also count as the predicate offenses ("pattern offenses") that trigger RICO prosecution. Every use of the mails, for example, counts as a separate crime. So mailing two letters to further a scheme to defraud a single victim is two crimes—and RICO's pattern element is satisfied.

United States v. Porcelli (1989) is a good example of how this works. The defendant owned a chain of gas stations. He regularly understated his New York sales tax. (This wasn't even a crime at the time in New York.) Federal prosecutors charged him with RICO violations because he committed mail fraud by mailing in his phony sales tax returns. The penalty—forfeiture of his business, worth many times more than the $5 million in unpaid taxes.

Destruction of someone's business, not to mention, reputation—both of which white-collar criminals value highly—is a severe penalty. It's often enough to intimidate them into pleading guilty. But is it worse than what "street criminals" face? Judge Lynch (1990) has his doubts:

> Try telling an accused street seller of drugs about the excessive leverage RICO gives the U.S. Attorney to "force" guilty pleas from rich and powerful financial institutions, after he has been detained pretrial in lieu of bail in an overcrowded jail, offered a guilty plea with a sentence of time served, and confronted with the reality that if he goes to trial he not only risks a much longer sentence, but faces certain confinement until the overcrowded court reaches his case.
>
> RICO gives wealthy white-collar defendants, who have the resources to fight the system that most defendants lack, a taste of the realities of plea bargaining justice as it is experienced every day by less well-healed defendants. (784–85)

PROSECUTING GOVERNMENT CORRUPTION

Government corruption cases make up the largest number of RICO cases under RICO Section 1962(c). Government employees are charged in these cases with conducting the affairs of a government agency through a pattern of bribery, corruption, and mail fraud. Notice that these cases—the most numerous—have nothing to do with organized crime, for example, the Mafia.

Many of these cases involve state and local government officials' corruption in their own state, county, or city. Why? Not because there's more state- and local-level corruption or that state and local corruption is more serious. It's because there's no federal statute making state and local government corruption a *federal* crime. But RICO fills this gap, allowing federal prosecutors to prosecute state and local officials—with much more severe penalties and without the hesitation local prosecutors might feel about prosecuting fellow officials (777–78).

Critics aren't pleased with this federal "meddling" in local political affairs. There's also a problem of fairness. Under RICO, "racketeering" doesn't have to involve serious offenses. For example, taking small bribes is a misdemeanor in all localities. But taking two small bribes satisfies the "pattern" element of RICO and triggers its severe criminal sentence and civil forfeiture provisions. RICO permits prosecutors to decide to seek harsher penalties without proving any aggravating circumstances (Lynch 1990, 779–80).

PUNISHING RICO OFFENDERS

RICO authorizes high maximum fines ($250,000 for *each* violation) and long maximum prison sentences (imprisonment for 25 years and life if one of the predicate crimes is murder). In addition, RICO imposes a mandatory penalty of forfeiture to the U.S. government of not only any money and property derived from the crime but any interest the defendant holds in the enterprise or any property of any kind that "provides a source of influence over the enterprise." Forfeiture aims not only to punish the offender but to "deny continuing power over an enterprise to anyone who has corrupted it to criminal ends" (Lynch 2002, 344).

CASE

***In* Alexander v. U.S. *(1993)*,** *Ferris Alexander found out just how harsh forfeiture can be after he was convicted of selling pornography, sentenced to six years in prison; fined $100,000; ordered to pay the cost of prosecution, incarceration, and supervised release; and ordered to forfeit his interest in ten pieces of commercial real estate and thirty-one current or former businesses.*

Was the forfeiture an excessive fine?

Alexander v. U.S.

510 U.S. 909 (1993)

HISTORY

Ferris Alexander, Sr. (Defendant, now Petitioner) was convicted in the United States District Court for the District of Minnesota, of tax offenses, obscenity offenses, and Racketeer Influenced and Corrupt Organizations Act (RICO) violations, and he appealed. The Eighth Circuit Court of Appeals affirmed. Certiorari was granted. The Supreme Court remanded. The U.S. District Court, Minnesota reaffirmed after remand. The U.S. Seventh Circuit Court of Appeals affirmed.

REHNQUIST, CJ., JOINED BY WHITE, O'CONNOR, SCALIA, AND THOMAS, JJ.

After a full criminal trial, petitioner Ferris J. Alexander, owner of more than a dozen stores and theaters dealing in sexually explicit materials, was convicted on 17 obscenity counts and 3 counts of violating the Racketeer Influenced and Corrupt Organizations Act (RICO). The obscenity convictions, based on the jury's findings that four magazines and three videotapes sold at several of petitioner's stores were obscene, served as the predicates for his three RICO convictions.

In addition to imposing a prison term and fine, the District Court ordered petitioner to forfeit, pursuant to 18 U.S.C. § 1963 (1988 ed. and Supp. III), certain assets that were directly related to his racketeering activity as punishment for his RICO violations. Petitioner argues that this forfeiture violated the First and Eighth Amendments to the Constitution. We reject petitioner's claims under the First Amendment but remand for reconsideration of his Eighth Amendment challenge.

FACTS

Ferris Alexander was in the so-called "adult entertainment" business for more than 30 years, selling pornographic magazines and sexual paraphernalia, showing sexually explicit movies, and eventually selling and renting videotapes of a similar nature. He received shipments of these materials at a warehouse in Minneapolis, Minnesota, where they were wrapped in plastic, priced, and boxed. He then sold his products through some 13 retail stores in several different Minnesota cities, generating millions of dollars in annual revenues. In 1989, federal authorities filed a 41–count indictment against petitioner and others, alleging operation of a racketeering enterprise in violation of RICO. The indictment charged 34 obscenity counts and 3 RICO counts, the racketeering counts being predicated on the obscenity charges. The indictment also charged numerous counts of tax evasion and related offenses that are not relevant to the questions before us.

Following a 4–month jury trial in the United States District Court for the District of Minnesota, petitioner was convicted of 17 substantive obscenity offenses: 12 counts of transporting obscene material in interstate commerce for the purpose of sale or distribution, in violation of 18 U.S.C. § 1465; and 5 counts of engaging in the business of selling obscene material, in violation of 18 U.S.C. § 1466 (1988 ed. and Supp. III). He also was convicted of 3 RICO offenses that were predicated on the obscenity convictions: one count of receiving and using income derived from a pattern of racketeering activity, in violation of 18 U.S.C. § 1962(a); one count of conducting a RICO enterprise, in violation of § 1962(c); and one count of conspiring to conduct a RICO enterprise, in violation of § 1962(d). As a basis for the obscenity and RICO convictions, the jury determined that four magazines and three videotapes were obscene. Multiple copies of these magazines and videos, which graphically depicted a variety of "hard core" sexual acts, were distributed throughout petitioner's adult entertainment empire.

Petitioner was sentenced to a total of six years in prison, fined $100,000, and ordered to pay the cost of prosecution, incarceration, and supervised release. In addition to these punishments, the District Court reconvened the same jury and conducted a forfeiture

(continues)

(continued)

proceeding pursuant to § 1963(a)(2). At this proceeding, the Government sought forfeiture of the businesses and real estate that represented petitioner's interest in the racketeering enterprise, § 1963(a)(2)(A), the property that afforded petitioner influence over that enterprise, § 1963(a)(2)(D), and the assets and proceeds petitioner had obtained from his racketeering offenses, §§ 1963(a)(1), (3).

The jury found that petitioner had an interest in 10 pieces of commercial real estate and 31 current or former businesses, all of which had been used to conduct his racketeering enterprise. Sitting without the jury, the District Court then found that petitioner had acquired a variety of assets as a result of his racketeering activities. The court ultimately ordered petitioner to forfeit his wholesale and retail businesses (including all the assets of those businesses) and almost $9 million in moneys acquired through racketeering activity. Not wishing to go into the business of selling pornographic materials—regardless of whether they were legally obscene—the Government decided that it would be better to destroy the forfeited expressive materials than sell them to members of the public.

OPINION

Petitioner also argues that the forfeiture order in this case—considered atop his 6-year prison term and $100,000 fine—is disproportionate to the gravity of his offenses and therefore violates the Eighth Amendment, either as a "cruel and unusual punishment" or as an "excessive fine." The Court of Appeals, though, failed to distinguish between these two components of petitioner's Eighth Amendment challenge. Instead, the court lumped the two together, disposing of them both with the general statement that the Eighth Amendment does not require any proportionality review of a sentence less than life imprisonment without the possibility of parole. But that statement has relevance only to the Eighth Amendment's prohibition against cruel and unusual punishments. Unlike the Cruel and Unusual Punishments Clause, which is concerned with matters such as the duration or conditions of confinement, "[t]he Excessive Fines Clause limits the government's power to extract payments, whether in cash or in kind, as punishment for some offense." The criminal forfeiture at issue here is clearly a form of monetary punishment no different, for Eighth Amendment purposes, from a traditional "fine." Accordingly, the forfeiture in this case should be analyzed under the Excessive Fines Clause.

Petitioner contends that forfeiture of his entire business was an "excessive" penalty for the Government to exact "[o]n the basis of a few materials the jury ultimately decided were obscene." It is somewhat misleading, we think, to characterize the racketeering crimes for which petitioner was convicted as involving just a few materials ultimately found to be obscene. Petitioner was convicted of creating and managing what the District Court described as "an enormous racketeering enterprise." It is in the light of the extensive criminal activities which petitioner apparently conducted through this racketeering enterprise over a substantial period of time that the question whether the forfeiture was "excessive" must be considered. We think it preferable that this question be addressed by the Court of Appeals in the first instance.

For these reasons, we hold that the Court of Appeals should have considered whether they resulted in an "excessive" penalty within the meaning of the Eighth Amendment's Excessive Fines Clause. Accordingly, we vacate the judgment of the Court of Appeals and remand the case for further proceedings consistent with this opinion.

It is so ordered.

QUESTIONS

1. List all of the specific items in the forfeiture.
2. Summarize Ferris Alexander Sr.'s arguments that the forfeiture was an excessive fine.
3. Summarize the U.S. Supreme Court's arguments supporting the forfeiture.
4. Do you think the forfeiture was excessive?

LO 11

SOLICITATION

Suppose I want to murder my wife, but I'm afraid to do it. If I ask a friend to kill her and she does, we're both murderers. If she tries to kill her and fails because her gun isn't loaded, then we've committed attempted murder. If she agrees to kill her and buys the gun but doesn't follow through, we've committed conspiracy to commit murder.

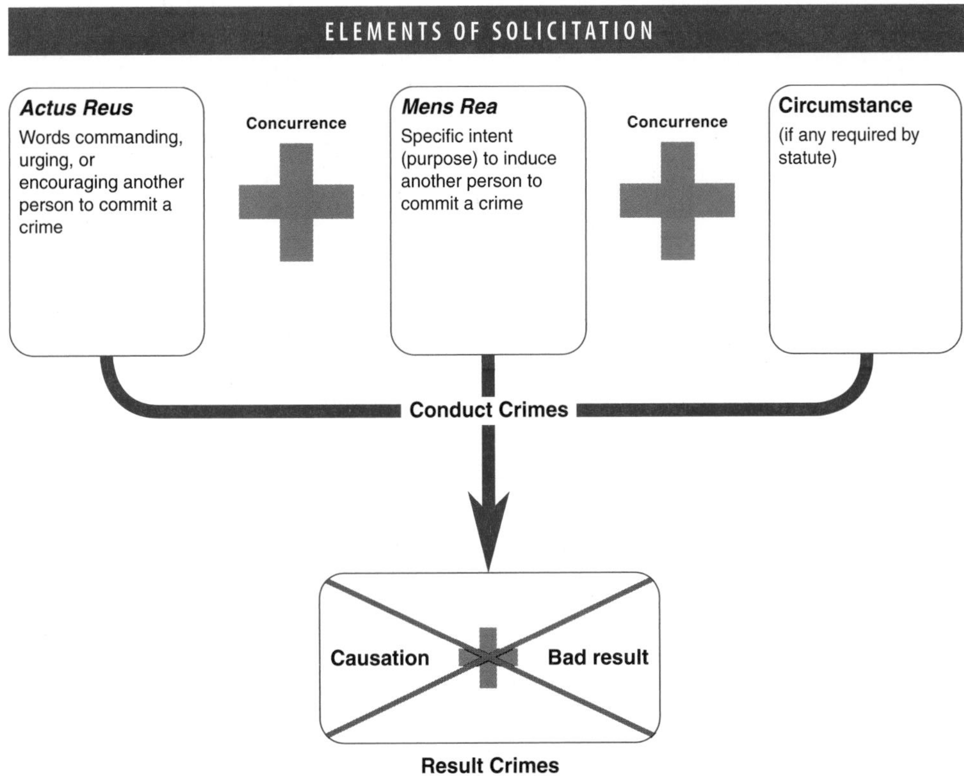

But what if I try to get my friend to kill my wife by offering her $5,000, and she turns me down? That's a crime, too—**solicitation**, the crime of trying to get someone else to commit a crime. The crime is complete the instant the solicitor communicates the solicitation to the other person. Against the objection that to punish the bare act of solicitation was punishing the "intent to commit evil," which isn't a crime, the Connecticut Supreme Court wrote, "The solicitation is an act; and God forbid that it should not be considered as an offense (Michael and Wechsler 1940, 607).

solicitation, the crime of trying to get someone else to commit a crime.

There's disagreement about whether trying to get someone else to commit a crime, even though they don't comply, is dangerous enough to be a crime. Those in the "not dangerous enough" group make two arguments to support their position. First, solicitation isn't dangerous enough *conduct* because an independent moral agent (the person solicited) stands between solicitors and their criminal objectives. Second, solicitors aren't dangerous enough *people*. They prove it by turning to someone else to do what they're too timid to do themselves.

LO 8

Those in the "dangerous enough" group have their own arguments. First, they say solicitation is just another form of the danger created by group participation in crime (Chapter 7), only more removed from the completed crime than conspiracy—kind of like an attempted conspiracy. Second, solicitors are intelligent, artful masters at manipulating others to do their dirty work.

Let's look at the elements of solicitation—the *actus reus*, *mens rea*, and the attendant circumstance of the criminal objective of the solicitation. (See the Elements of Solicitation illustration.)

SOLICITATION *ACTUS REUS*

solicitation *actus reus*, acts that include some kind of inducement to commit the solicited crime

The criminal act in criminal solicitation consists of words, but the law only imprecisely tells us what words qualify as **solicitation *actus reus***. Courts agree that statements that merely favor committing a crime aren't enough to qualify as criminal acts. So someone who says, "I think it'd be great if someone killed that terrorist" hasn't solicited murder.

There has to be some kind of inducement to commit a crime. The typical words we see in the statutes and court opinions are like the ones we saw in accomplice liability (Chapter 7): "advises," "commands," "counsels," "encourages," "entices," "entreats," "importunes," "incites," "induces," "instigates," "procures," "requests," "solicits," or "urges." In other words, the criminal act in solicitation consists of the effort to get another to commit a crime, whether or not the solicitation ever ripens into a completed crime (LaFave 2003a, 573–74).

Does the solicitor have to address the words to precise individuals? Not necessarily. Soliciting "audiences" *can* be precise enough. One speaker was convicted for urging his audience to commit murder and robbery. But, in another case, a New York court dismissed solicitation charges against Robert Quentin and John Garcia. The pamphlet they distributed was "a general solicitation (however reprehensible) to a large indefinable group to commit a crime" (*People v. Quentin* 1968, 448). The pamphlet contained these paragraphs:

> America is carnivorous. She eats the world for desert. Behind slick pictures of pretty-suburban-middle-churchgoing-family lie hamburgers seasoned with napalm, race crimes too brutal to recall, cultures plundered, and triviality elevated into a way of life. The rich are rich because they are thieves, the poor because they are victims, and the future will condemn those who accept the present as reality.
>
> Break down the family, church, nation, city, economy. Subversiveness saves us. Our professors are spies; let us close the schools and flow into the streets. Grow hair long and become too freaky to fit into the machine culture.
>
> What's needed is a generation of people who are freaky, crazy, irrational, sexy, angry, irreligious, childish and mad: people who burn draft cards, burn high school and college degrees: people who say: "To hell with your goals"; people who lure the youth with music, pot and acid: people who re-define reality, who re-define the normal; * * * The white youth of America have more in common with Indians plundered, than they do with their own parents. Burn their house down, and you will be free. (445)

This was followed by a paragraph entitled "How to make a fire bomb, and a recipe for Tryptamine, a psychedelic agent." The recipe ends with the statements:

> Tetrahydrofurane is a very powerful reducing agent; wear safety glasses, add very cautiously, and perform this step with ventilation, away from flames (H[2] is evolved). The yield is about 40 grams of DMT, in tetrahydrofurane solution. This cannot be drunk or injected, but may be smoked by sprinkling on mint or cannabis leaves and letting the solution evaporate. It's evaporated when it starts smelling like DMT instead of tetrahydrofurane. (445)

SOLICITATION *MENS REA*

solicitation *mens rea*, requires words that convey that their purpose is to get someone to commit a specific crime

Solicitation is a specific-intent crime; that is, it's a crime of purpose. The solicitation *mens rea* requires words that convey that their purpose is to get someone to commit a specific crime. If I urge my friend who works in an expensive jewelry shop to take a gold chain for me, I've solicited her to steal the chain. If, on the other hand, I ask another friend who works in a clothing shop to get a coat for me to use for the evening, and I plan to return the coat the next morning before anyone knows it's missing, I haven't solicited her to steal the coat because I don't intend to steal the coat, only to use it for the night (Chapter 11).

CASE

In **State v. Schleifer** ***(1923),*** *the Connecticut Supreme Court ruled that the labor leader Ernest Schleifer was talking to every individual in the large audience gathered to hear him when he called for violence against the railroad management and its property.*

Did he solicit his audience to destroy their employers' homes and businesses?

State v. Schleifer

121 A. 805 (Conn. 1923)

HISTORY

Ernest Schleifer was charged in an information with solicitation to commit crimes. The trial court granted Schleifer's motion to dismiss the charge. The State appealed the dismissal. The Connecticut Supreme Court of Errors reversed.

WHEELER, CJ.

Ernest Schleifer by oral address to [a large crowd, spoke] in language in substance as follows:

> You will never win the strike with soft methods. You young men ought to go out on the bridge. Don't use eggs; use coal or indelible ink. Break foremen's windows at their homes. Watch the scabs when they come from work, lay for them, especially on pay day. Take them in a dark alley and hit them with a lead pipe. That is the softest thing you can use.
>
> Reimburse yourselves for what we have sacrificed for five months. Don't forget to bump off a few now and then, so Mr. Pearson will know that you are not getting cold feet. You car men know how to take a brake shoe off. Take the brake shoe and put it under something that will put the cars off the irons. A little sand or emery in the journal boxes will help greatly.
>
> Don't be satisfied with trimming the engines. Put some of the cars on the bum. Also, if convenient, put something in between the frames and rods of engines on sidings. Get busy, young fellows, and trim these scabs. Things are running too smooth on the New Haven Road, but let me hear from you while I am here. Go ahead and rip things, and don't let the injunction stop you from trimming these scabs. Don't forget to tie them up with derailments. You boys ought to cut them all up.

To this information, Schleifer filed a motion to quash, which the trial court sustained upon the grounds as stated in part therein, viz.:

> (2) That the information fails to set forth any offense or crime. . . .
>
> (8) That the information merely charges the defendant with having uttered certain words set forth in said information, and such utterances do not constitute a crime by virtue of any statute of this state, or at common law.
>
> (9) That the information merely states that the defendant entertained certain intentions, as evidenced by certain expressions made by him, and such intentions do not either at common law or by virtue of any statute constitute crime.

In his memorandum on the motion to quash the court held that in the common-law crime of solicitation "the inducement or invitation must have been directed to one individual soliciting the accomplishment of some particular act which, if complied with, would result in the commission of some specific offense." The trial court further held:

> While it cannot be seriously denied that the public utterance in a promiscuous assembly of such entreaties and exhortations as are charged in this information is highly prejudicial to the public peace, and ought to be seriously penalized, it is a situation that should be met by appropriate legislation. I do not feel warranted in view of all the authorities in undertaking to extend the present limitations of the common law crime of solicitation so as to include the acts of the accused now under consideration.

The accused supports his motion to quash and the ruling of the trial court thereon by maintaining that solicitation alone is not a crime under the common law, and has never been treated as such except in cases where the solicitation was in fact the crime of an attempt. It is necessary that we meet this proposition directly.

(continues)

(continued)

If the law be as counsel for the accused claim, we might well say, as Lord Kenyon, the Chief Justice of the court of King's Bench, said in *King v. Higgins*:

> The offense imputed to this defendant is of the most serious kind, no less than that for his own wicked gains he solicited and incited a servant to rob his master; and can it be a question in a country professing to have laws subservient to justice and morality whether this be an offense?

The crimes which the state charges the accused intended by his oral address to urge his hearers to commit were felonies or aggravator crimes akin to felonies, to wit, murder, robbery, aggravated assault with deadly or dangerous weapons, assault with intent to murder, and assault with intent to rob. The language alleged to have been used by this accused does advise, incite, and urge those to whom it was directed to the commission of these crimes, as well as the crime of breach of the peace.

It would be difficult to conceive of an evil minded and desperate criminal urging a more dangerous and dastardly course of action. It invited and commanded not alone deeds of violence towards the railroad employees who remained on their jobs and the members of their households, but also the most serious injury and in all probability death to the innocent travelers upon the railroad and to the crew hands.

The immediate question for us to decide is whether our law is remediless to punish the individual who, with wanton disregard of life and property, incites and commands not one, but many, to the commission of gravest crimes. We determined in 1828 in *State v. Avery*, that the solicitation to another, by letter, to commit adultery was a high crime and misdemeanor nearly allied and equal in guilt to felony, and that an information charging this offense was sufficient under our common law. It was urged that such a solicitation was not a crime because it was no more than an intent to commit evil. We disposed of the claim in these words:

> But it is argued, that a mere intent to commit evil is not indictable, without an act done; but is there not an act done, when it is charged, that the defendant solicited another to commit adultery? The solicitation is an act; and God forbid, that it should not be considered as an offense.

The trial court criticizes the information because it does not charge that any particular person was solicited to the commission of any particular crime in any specified place, and the state assigns this among its other alleged errors. It was not necessary to make such an allegation. The solicitation was directed to each one present in the assemblage. It would not have been more direct or more compulsive if each one in the assemblage had been called by name by the accused.

The law of criminal pleading is settled upon this point. [According to Lord Chief Justice Coleridge:]

> The argument has been well put that an orator who makes a speech to 2,000 people does not address it to any one individual amongst those 2,000; it is addressed to the whole number. It is endeavoring to persuade the whole number or large portions of that number, and if a particular individual amongst that number addressed by the orator is persuaded, or listens to it and is encouraged, it is plain that the words of this statute are complied with; because according to well-known principles of law, the person who addresses those words to a number of persons, must be taken to address them to the persons who he knows hear them, who he knows will understand them in a particular way, do understand them in that particular way, and do act upon them.

Aside from the conclusion which we think should have been "and may act upon them," instead of "and do act upon them," we coincide with this statement. To the argument in behalf of the accused that the existence of statutes to punish solicitation to crime as an independent offense shows that there was no such common-law offense, hence the statutory offense was created, it is enough to say that these statutes are as a rule declaratory of the common law, as has been quite frequently pointed out, or they have been adopted for the purpose of adding to or taking from the penalty under the common law.

The [argument] . . . that the information merely states that the defendant entertained certain intentions may be answered briefly. The mere intention, unexpressed, of the accused does not, and is not claimed to, subject the accused to criminal punishment. But when the intention be expressed in the form of a solicitation, or incitement, or a command to another to commit a crime, and that crime a felony or a high crime and misdemeanor akin to felony, it is a crime under our common law.

Our consideration of the case has led to the approval of a rule somewhat broader than that of some of these authorities, but one which the consideration of this case has shown as to be necessary for the public safety. Suppose the accused had carefully incited and commanded his hearers to the commission of crimes against the public peace and safety which were neither felonies nor aggravated crimes; he could not under the rule of these authorities be informed against, for he would have committed no crime. Yet who can doubt that his inflamed hearers, if they acted upon his words, would not distinguish between the high and aggravated crime and the lesser crime of his specific advice and command, and that their beginning of a breach of the public peace and safety, and of the destruction of property, would inevitably lead to consequences of serious harm alike to the individual and to the state?

The judgment is set aside, and the cause remanded, to be proceeded with according to law. The other Judges concurred.

QUESTIONS

1. List the facts and circumstances relevant to deciding whether Ernest Schleifer is guilty of criminal solicitation.
2. Summarize the arguments of the trial court and the prosecution in favor of criminal solicitation.
3. Summarize the arguments of the defendant and the Connecticut Supreme Court against criminal solicitation.
4. Which side do you agree with? Back up your answer with specific facts and circumstances and the arguments in the case and the text.

SOLICITATION CRIMINAL OBJECTIVE

Some statutes restrict the circumstance element of the **criminal objective of the solicitation** to committing felonies—in some cases, to committing violent felonies. In other jurisdictions, it's a crime to solicit another to commit any crime, whether it's a felony, misdemeanor, or violation. Furthermore, solicitation doesn't have to include an inducement to commit a criminal act at all. For example, suppose a robber urges a friend to borrow money and lend it to him for a plane ticket to escape from the jurisdiction. The robber has solicited escape or aiding and abetting a robbery. Although borrowing money isn't a crime, and lending money to a robber isn't by itself a crime, both escape and aiding and abetting robbers are crimes. Someone who urges another to commit those crimes has committed the crime of solicitation.

criminal objective of the solicitation, circumstance element that the objective of the solicitation is law breaking; the seriousness varies from any violation to violent felony

SUMMARY

LO 1

Each inchoate offense has some of its own elements, but they all share two elements: the *mens rea* of purpose or specific intent and the *actus reus* of taking some steps toward accomplishing the criminal purpose—but not enough steps to complete the intended crime.

LO 2

Incomplete criminal conduct poses a dilemma: whether to punish someone who's done no harm or to set free someone who's determined to commit a crime.

LO 3

Liability for criminal attempt offenses is based on two old and firmly entrenched rationales. One focuses on dangerous acts (*actus reus*), the other on dangerous persons (*mens rea*).

LO 4

The *mens rea* of inchoate crimes is always purpose, the intent to commit a specific crime

LO 5 Attempt *actus reus* is based on two theories of attempt: the social harm from dangerous conduct and the social harm from dangerous people.

LO 6 A legal impossibility occurs when actors intend to commit crimes and do everything they can to carry out their criminal intent, but the criminal law doesn't ban what they did. A factual impossibility occurs when actors intend to commit a crime and try to but some fact or circumstance—an extraneous factor—interrupts them to prevent the completion of the crime.

LO 7 A little more than half the states and the U.S. government accept the affirmative defense of voluntary abandonment to attempt liability. According to the Model Penal Code, voluntary abandonment means a change in the actor's purpose not influenced by outside circumstances, what may be termed "repentance" or "change of heart."

LO 8 Conspiracy, the crime of agreeing with one or more people to commit a crime, is further removed from actually committing a crime than attempts to commit crimes. In fact, one can become guilty of conspiracy long before his act has come so dangerously near to completion as to make him criminally liable for the attempted crime. The law punishes conspirators to nip in the bud the dangers posed by group criminality.

LO 9 There are two types of large-scale conspiracies: wheel and chain. Wheel conspiracies involve parties differently, with some participating in every transaction and others participating only in one. Chain conspiracies involve parties equally, with each participant handling the same commodity at different points through the process of manufacture, distribution, and sale.

LO 10 RICO (Racketeer Influenced and Corrupt Organizations Act) makes criminal enterprise or illicit activity that is run like a business illegal. It applies harsh penalties to those engaged in such activity.

LO 11 Solicitation is the crime of trying to get someone else to commit a crime. The *actus reus* of solicitation requires words that actually try to get someone to commit a crime. Solicitation *mens rea* requires purpose or specific intent to get someone to commit a crime. Solicitation is punished similarly to conspiracy, with the notion that nipping this activity in the bud helps to prevent the dangers of group criminality.

KEY TERMS

criminal attempts, p. 258
criminal conspiracy, p. 258
criminal solicitation, p. 258
inchoate offenses, p. 258
dangerous act rationale, p. 260
dangerous person rationale, p. 260
general attempt statute, p. 261
specific attempt statutes, p. 261
attempt *mens rea*, p. 261
attempt *actus reus*, p. 263
last act rule, p. 263
proximity tests, p. 263
dangerous proximity tests, p. 264
dangerous person tests, p. 264
all but the last act test, p. 264
dangerous proximity to success test/physical proximity test, p. 264
indispensable element test, p. 265
unequivocality test/*res ipsaloquiter* test ("the act speaks for itself"), p. 265
probable desistance test, p. 266
MPC substantial steps test, p. 266

legal impossibility, p. 271
factual impossibility, p. 271
extraneous factor, p. 273
voluntary abandonment defense (voluntary renunciation defense), p. 276
conspiracy, p. 279
conspiracy *actus reus*, p. 280
overt act requirement, p. 281
conspiracy *mens rea*, p. 284
criminal objective, p. 284
unilateral approach to conspiracy parties, p. 284
wheel conspiracies, p. 285
chain conspiracies, p. 285
criminal objective of the conspiracy, p. 285
Racketeer Influenced and Corrupt Organizations Act (RICO), p. 286
racketeering, p. 286
enterprise, p. 286
pattern of racketeering activity, p. 286
solicitation, p. 291
solicitation *actus reus*, p. 291
solicitation *mens rea*, p. 292
criminal objective of the solicitation, p. 295

LEARNING OBJECTIVES

1. To understand that criminal homicide is different from all other crimes because of the finality of its result: the death of the victim.
2. To appreciate that most of the law regarding criminal homicide is about grading the seriousness of the offense. Grading murder into first and second degree is important because only first-degree murder qualifies for the death penalty.
3. To appreciate that the meaning of "person" is integral to homicide law and understand how that presents problems at both ends of the life cycle.
4. To understand how degrees of murder developed throughout history and their relation to capital punishment.
5. To know the elements of murder.
6. To learn the degrees of murder that exist in the United States today.
7. To know the definition, history, and current use of felony murder as a charge.
8. To understand that most criminal homicide statutes can be applied to corporations, but prosecutions are rare.
9. To understand that the heart of voluntary manslaughter is an intentional, sudden killing triggered by an adequate provocation.
10. To know that provocation isn't an excuse for criminal homicide; it only reduces the seriousness of the crime and the punishment to allow for human frailty.
11. To know that the central elements in involuntary manslaughter are its *actus reus* (voluntary act or omission) and its *mens rea* (unintentional killing), causing the criminal harm of death.
12. To understand that criminal negligence homicide statutes cover a wide field, from the most common, unintentional deaths caused by operating vehicles and firearms to practicing medicine illegally, handling explosives, delivering dangerous drugs, allowing vicious animals to run free, failing to care for a sick child, and not providing fire exits in businesses.

Three suspects in the assault of University of Wyoming student Matthew Shepard wait to be arraigned Friday, October 9, 1998, in Laramie, Wyoming. From left are Russell Henderson, 21; Aaron McKinney, 22; and Chastity Pasley, 20. Another suspect, Kristin Price, was freed on bail. Shepard, a gay student, was beaten, burned, and tied to a fence like a scarecrow.

AP Images/Ed Andrieski

CRIMES AGAINST PERSONS I 9

Murder and Manslaughter

CHAPTER OUTLINE

Is Doctor-Assisted Suicide Murder?

Just hours before they died, Sherry Miller, Marjorie Wantz, and their family members met with Kevorkian at the home of Miller's parents on October 22, 1991. Miller, 43, had advanced multiple sclerosis and had approached Kevorkian a year earlier. She kept pursuing him and told her story several times on television. Marjorie Wantz, 58, also had sought Kevorkian's help for years. Although not terminally ill, she suffered excruciating pain after many surgeries to remove benign vaginal tumors. She had tried to kill herself several times. Psychiatrists said she was depressed and suicidal and some felt her pain was psychosomatic. (Later, when the medical examiner conducted her autopsy he found no physical cause for her pain.) The day after this interview, they committed suicide in a rustic cabin. Wantz used a machine Kevorkian invented, which injected a fatal substance; Miller inhaled carbon monoxide because her veins were too weak for a needle.

(*Frontline* 1996)

LO 1

"Death is different," the U.S. Supreme Court said about capital punishment. Killing is different, too—it's the most serious of all crimes. In 1769, Blackstone, the great eighteenth-century commentator on the criminal law, introduced his chapter on homicide with words that are pretty close to describing the crimes you'll be learning about in this chapter:

> Of crimes injurious to persons, the most important is the offence of taking away that life, which is the immediate gift of the great creator; and which therefore no man can be entitled to deprive another of. The subject therefore of the present chapter will be, the offense of homicide or destroying the life of man, in its several stages of guilt, arising from the particular circumstances of mitigation or aggravation. (4:177)

Of course, raping, assaulting, and kidnapping harm people, too; but however awful they may be, they leave their victims alive (Chapter 10). Crimes against homes and property (Chapter 11) and crimes against public order and morals (Chapter 12) also hurt their victims and society, but these are injuries to worldly things. According to the distinguished professor of criminal law George P. Fletcher (1978):

> Killing another human being is not only a worldly deprivation; in the Western conception of homicide, killing is an assault on the sacred, natural order. In the Biblical view, the person who slays another was thought to acquire control over the blood—the life force—of the victim. The only way that this life force could be returned to God, the origin of all life, was to execute the slayer himself. In this conception of crime and punishment, capital execution for homicide served to expiate the desecration of the natural order. (235–36)

CRIMINAL HOMICIDE IN CONTEXT

To put criminal homicide in the context of the crimes you'll be studying throughout the rest of the book, they're rare events. In 2010, there were 14,748 murders reported to the FBI compared with 1,246,248 total violent felonies. The total number of all crimes in the FBI index of serious crimes (homicide, forcible rape, robbery, aggravated assault, burglary, theft, motor vehicle theft, and arson) was 12,961,116 (FBI 2011). Figure 9.1 breaks down the 2010 totals from the FBI's index of serious crimes.

FIGURE 9.1 THE FBI'S INDEX OF SERIOUS CRIMES IN THE UNITED STATES (2010)

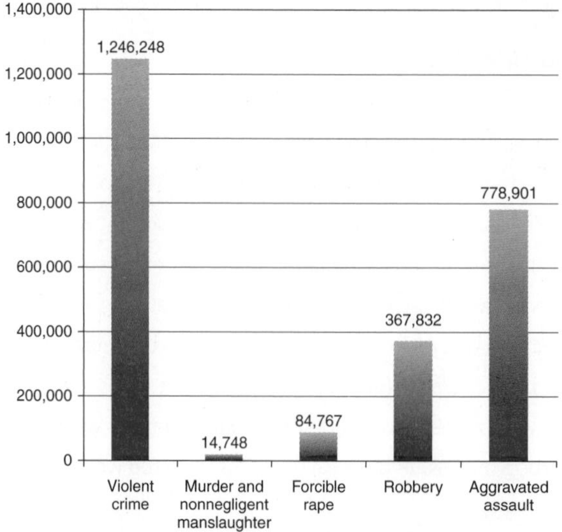

Source: FBI Uniform Crime Report 2011 (Sept.), Table 1.

These numbers aren't meant to diminish the seriousness of killing another person—an act that stands alone in its awfulness. But there are more reasons than raw numbers why we study criminal homicide. Much of what you've learned in the earlier chapters grew out of the law of criminal homicide. This is especially true of the mental element, or *mens rea*, and the justification of self-defense. But there's more: the three-step analysis of criminal liability—(1) criminal conduct, (2) without justification, or (3) excuse—grew out of the great work on the law of criminal homicide written by the principal drafter of the Model Penal Code (MPC), Professor Herbert Wechsler at Columbia Law School (Michael and Wechsler 1937; Dubber and Kelman 2005, 846).

LO 2

Most of the law of homicide is devoted to answering questions like: Is this murder first or second degree? Is that killing murder or manslaughter? Is this manslaughter voluntary or involuntary? Students ask: "Does it really matter?" Certainly not to the victim—who's already and always dead! But it does make a big practical difference. Why? Because the punishment for criminal homicide depends on the degree of murder or the type of manslaughter committed.

Three elements of criminal homicide—*actus reus, mens rea,* and special mitigating and aggravating circumstances—are used to define the kinds and grade the seriousness of the criminal homicides you'll learn about in this chapter. Defining what kind of criminal homicide a particular killing is and grading its seriousness will make you think about deep philosophical questions regarding crime and punishment. This is good and proper.

But there's more than a philosophical question here. There's the practical question of the kind and amount of punishment to inflict on people who kill other people. Should we kill them? Lock them up for the rest of their lives? Lock them up for a certain number of years? Fine them? All of these are provided for in the state and federal criminal codes. And they vary not only from one criminal homicide to another but also from state to state, sometimes drastically. For the most striking example, first-degree murder is the only crime you can die for, and, in non–death penalty states, it's the only crime for which you can get life in prison without a chance of parole.

As you read the chapter, keep in focus both the moral or ethical dimension and the practical dimension of criminal homicide and their importance in shaping the definition, grading, and punishment of how and why one person kills another.

In this chapter, we'll examine the history of the law of criminal homicide and the elements of murder and manslaughter—namely, the (1) *actus reus,* (2) the *mens rea,* and (3) the circumstance elements—and how they affect the punishment of the various degrees of murder and voluntary manslaughter. Then, we'll turn to the lesser offenses of involuntary manslaughter and criminal negligence homicide. But before we do, let's examine the important preliminary question: What does "person" or "human being" mean in criminal homicide law?

THE MEANING OF "PERSON" OR "HUMAN BEING"

LO 3

Killing another "person" is central to criminal homicide liability because it defines who's a victim. "Person" seems like a simple concept to understand. However, it raises deep philosophical questions and hot controversy. We won't get deeply into the broad controversy, except as a preliminary matter to understanding the elements of criminal homicide. The definition of "person" for purposes of criminal homicide presents problems at both ends of the life cycle—when life begins and when it ends. When life begins tells us when a potential victim becomes a real victim; when life ends tells us when a real victim is no longer a victim.

LO 3

WHEN DOES LIFE BEGIN?

> The person killed must be a reasonable creature in being. . . . at the time of the killing. . . . To kill a child in it's mother's womb, is now no murder, but a great felony. But if the child be born alive, and dies by reason of the potion or bruises it received in the womb, it is murder in such as administered or gave them.
>
> (Blackstone 1769, 198)

born-alive rule, the rule that to be a person, and therefore a homicide victim, a baby had to be "born alive" and capable of breathing and maintaining a heartbeat on its own

Throughout most of its history, homicide law has followed the **born-alive rule.** The opening quote from Blackstone's *Commentaries on the Laws of England* (1769) stated the rule in its common law form. To be a person, and therefore a homicide victim, a baby had to be "born alive" and capable of breathing and maintaining a heartbeat on its own. Eighteen states still follow the "born alive" rule (Smith 2000, 1848).

Some courts in states that follow the born-alive rule have interpreted their statutes to include deaths caused by prenatal injuries if the fetus dies *after* it's born alive. (Notice that Blackstone says that was the law in 1769.) For example, in *State v. Cotton* (2000), Lawrence Cotton accidentally shot his girlfriend, L.W., in the back of the head. L.W. was eight and a half months pregnant at the time. Although L.W. died shortly after arriving at the hospital, her daughter was delivered alive. But the fatal injury to L.W. had so decreased the baby's blood supply that the infant died the following day (920). Cotton was convicted on two counts of reckless homicide, one for L.W. and one for the infant. Cotton argued that the cause of death, his accidental shot that killed his girlfriend, occurred before the fetus was born. The Arizona Court of Appeals rejected Cotton's argument:

> That the shooting in this case occurred while the infant was in utero does not preclude her post-birth status as a "person" for purposes of Arizona's homicide statutes. While the homicide statutes require that the victim be a "person," they do not limit the nature or timing of the injury that causes the death of the "person." Because the infant here was undeniably a "person" at the time of her death a day after the shooting, it is irrelevant that the injuries that led to her death were inflicted while she was still in utero. (922–23)

Twenty-four states make it a crime to kill a fetus (Smith 2000, 1851). They do so by three means:

1. States revise existing homicide statutes to include fetuses as homicide victims.
2. States create new fetal homicide statutes aimed exclusively at fetuses.
3. States create statutes that punish attacks on pregnant women that cause death to the fetuses they're carrying.

The California legislature added just three words ("or a fetus") to its existing murder statute in order to overturn *Keeler v. Superior Court* (1970). (Recall that in *Keeler*, discussed in Chapter 1, the California Supreme Court refused to push back the definition of "person" to include fetuses before the birth process. Keeler was convicted of manslaughter for causing the death of his wife's unborn fetus by kicking her in the stomach.) Before *Keeler*, the statute read, "Murder is the unlawful killing of a human being with malice aforethought." Now it reads "Murder is the unlawful killing of a human being, *or a fetus*, with malice aforethought" (emphasis added) (California Penal Code 2006, § 187(a)).

feticide, killing a fetus

Other state legislatures have left their homicide statutes intact and created the new crime of **feticide,** specifically directed at the killing of fetuses. These special feticide statutes vary as to when in the gestational development of the fetus criminal liability attaches. Some say it's at viability; some say at "quickening"; some specify the number of weeks; and some say criminal liability attaches at "conception" or "fertilization" (Smith 2000, 1851; LaFave 2003a, 729).

Table 9.1 shows the breakdown of states and the stage of development their statutes adopt. I've arranged them from the latest to the earliest stage of development; the first is the narrowest definition of life for the purpose of the law of criminal homicide, and the last is the broadest definition.

WHEN DOES LIFE END?

LO 3

It used to be easy to define "death": when the heart and breathing stop. Not anymore. Determining when life ends has become increasingly complex as organ transplants and sophisticated artificial life support mechanisms make it possible to maintain vital life signs. Still, to kill a dying person, to accelerate a person's death, or to kill a "worthless" person is clearly homicide under current law. In *State v. Fiero* (1979, 77–78) a doctor who removed a vital organ too soon committed criminal homicide. And anyone who kills another by purposely disconnecting a respirator has also committed criminal homicide.

The concept of brain death has complicated the simple definition as to when the heart and breathing stop. This complication has implications not just for medicine and morals but also for criminal law. If artificial supports alone maintain breathing and the heartbeat while brain waves remain minimal or flat, brain death has occurred. The Uniform Brain Death Act provides that an individual who has suffered irreversible

TABLE 9.1

Stage of Fetal Development in Feticide Statutes

STAGE OF DEVELOPMENT	DEFINITION	STATES
Born alive	Fully outside the mother, with an "independent circulation"	(18 states) Alabama, Alaska, Colorado, Connecticut, Hawaii, Idaho, Kentucky, Maryland, Maine, Montana, Nebraska, New Jersey, New York, North Carolina, Oregon, Texas, Vermont, West Virginia
Viability	End of the second trimester when the fetus can live outside the womb; usually at 28 weeks of pregnancy	(6 states) Indiana, Massachusetts, Michigan, Oklahoma, South Carolina, Tennessee
Quickening	When the mother first feels the fetus moving in the womb (i.e., quickening), usually between the 16th and 18th week of pregnancy	(5 states) Florida, Mississippi, Nevada, Rhode Island, Washington
12 weeks		Arkansas
7 to 8 weeks		California
Fertilization/conception		(7 states) Illinois, Louisiana, Minnesota, Missouri, North Dakota, Pennsylvania, Wisconsin
No stage of development designated		(3 states) Arizona, South Dakota, and Utah

Source: Constructed from Smith (2000).

cessation of all brain functions, including those of the brain stem, is dead (ALI 1985, 2:1, 10–11).

More difficult cases involve individuals with enough brain functions to sustain breathing and a heartbeat but nothing more, such as patients in a deep coma. They may breathe and their hearts may beat on their own, but are they alive according to the criminal law? Troubling cases arise in which patients in a deep coma have been described by medical specialists as "vegetables" but regain consciousness and live for a considerable time afterward, such as the Minneapolis police officer who was shot and written off for dead after more than a year in a deep coma. He regained consciousness and lived for several more years.

MURDER

The common law divided homicides into two kinds, and so do modern criminal codes, the MPC, and this chapter. The two kinds are:

murder, killing a person with "malice aforethought"

manslaughter, killing a person without malice aforethought

1. **MURDER.** Killing a person with "malice aforethought," which we'll define and discuss in this section
2. **MANSLAUGHTER.** Killing a person without malice aforethought, which we'll discuss in the "Manslaughter" section

According to Blackstone, writing in 1769, malice aforethought was the "grand criterion, which now distinguishes murder from other killing" (188–89). (See the Elements of Common Law Murder illustration.) These two divisions were in turn divided into several kinds of murder and manslaughter, and, eventually, some special kinds of homicide, such as vehicular homicide (which we'll discuss later in the chapter), were added.

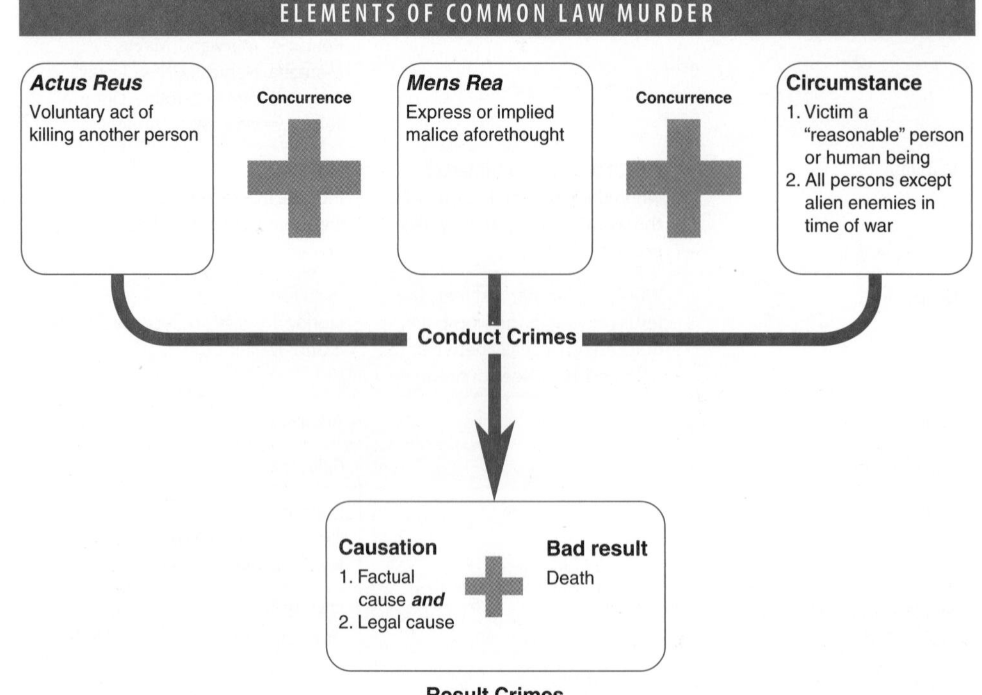

A long history of criminal homicides preceded the publication of Blackstone's classic work in 1769; we'll look at a little bit of it in this section. We'll also examine the elements of murder, the kinds and degrees of murder, first-degree murder, second-degree murder, and corporation murder.

THE HISTORY OF MURDER LAW

LO 4

Our modern law of criminal homicide took centuries to develop. Over several centuries, the English common law judges had developed two broad kinds of homicide, criminal and noncriminal. By the 1550s, the common law judges, with the help of a growing number of statutes, had further divided criminal homicide into murder and manslaughter and noncriminal homicide into justifiable and excusable homicide (Chapters 5 and 6).

By 1700, the English common and statute laws of homicide and the American colonies' law recognized three kinds of homicide:

1. **JUSTIFIABLE HOMICIDE.** Killing in self-defense (Chapter 5), capital punishment, and law enforcement use of deadly force
2. **EXCUSABLE HOMICIDE.** Killings done by someone "not of sound memory and discretion" (insane and immature) (Chapter 6)
3. **CRIMINAL HOMICIDE.** All homicides that are neither justified nor excused

justifiable homicide, killing in self-defense

excusable homicide, killings done by someone "not of sound memory and discretion"

criminal homicide, all homicides that are neither justified nor excused

We'll examine manslaughter later in the chapter. For now, let's concentrate on murder. In the early 1600s, Sir Edward Coke wrote that common law murder occurred when a person "of sound memory and discretion, unlawfully killeth any reasonable creature in being and under the king's peace, with malice aforethought, either express or implied" (Blackstone 1769, 4:195, quoting from Coke 1628, 3:47).

Here's how Blackstone defined the elements of common law murder in 1769:

1. *Sound memory and discretion* excused "lunatics and infants" from criminal liability.
2. *"Unlawfully"* meant killing without justification (Chapter 5) or excuse (Chapter 6).
3. *Killeth* included causing death by "poisoning, striking, starving, drowning, and a thousand other forms of death, by which human nature may be overcome" (196).
4. *Reasonable creature in being* was someone already born alive and breathing at the time of the killing (198).
5. *Under the king's peace* meant "to kill an alien, a Jew, or an outlaw, who are all under the king's protection, is as much murder as to kill the most regular Englishman; except he be an alien enemy in time of war" (198).
6. *With malice aforethought, express or implied.*

Let's take a closer look at the mental element—killing with malice aforethought. At first, "malice" meant with specific intent or killing on purpose—and probably with some amount of spite, hate, or bad will. "Aforethought" meant the acts were planned in advance of the killing. The English homicide statutes in the 1550s defined "murder" as killing someone intentionally by "poison" or "lying in wait," classic examples of acts planned in advance. So the only kind of murder was intentional, premeditated killing—in other words, killing with malice aforethought.

malice aforethought, originally the mental state of intentional killing, with some amount of spite, hate, or bad will, planned in advance of the killing

After that, the judges invented new kinds of murder. First, they added intentional (malicious) killings that weren't premeditated. These included sudden killings during the heat of passion, "unreasonably" provoked by the victim's conduct. We'll discuss "unreasonably" provoked when we get to voluntary manslaughter, but it's enough for now to think of it this way: if a reasonable person would have cooled off between the provocation and the killing, the killing was murder, even though it wasn't premeditated. For example, suppose Pete, a student in my Criminal Law class, doesn't like being touched by men. As he's leaving class, Nick comes up, puts his arm around Pete, and says, "Boring class, huh?" Very offended, Pete pulls away, saying "Back off, jerk." Nick responds with, "Oh, come on, I'm just being friendly" and approaches Pete again. Pete pulls out his gun and shoots Nick; Nick dies. Pete was "unreasonably" provoked.

Next, the judges added unintended killings if they occurred during the commission of felonies. For example, an arsonist set fire to a house when she believed no one was at home. Unfortunately, someone was at home, and he burned to death. She didn't intend to kill him, and because she didn't intend to kill him, obviously she couldn't have planned to kill him before she set fire to the house.

depraved heart murder, extremely reckless killings

Then came **depraved heart murder**, defined as extremely reckless killings. Recall here the definition of "recklessly" (Chapter 4): knowingly creating a substantial and unjustifiable risk. In the case of a depraved heart murder, the risk is of death. For example, a roofer on a tall building, without bothering to look, throws a heavy board onto a busy street below; the board kills three people. He didn't intend to kill them, but he knew he was creating a high risk that the board would kill someone, and he threw it anyway. These are extremely reckless killings, or depraved heart murders.

intent to cause serious bodily injury murder, no intent to kill is required when a victim dies following acts triggered by the intent to inflict serious bodily injury short of death

The judges took one last step away from the premeditated, intentional killing requirement. They created **intent to cause serious bodily injury murder**. No intent to kill was required when a victim died following acts triggered by the intent to inflict serious bodily injury short of death. Suppose a parent has a seventeen-year-old son who regularly drinks heavily, cuts school, and steals to buy alcohol; he's just generally out of control. Talking to him, grounding him, taking away his car, sending him to counseling—nothing works. So his father, angry and frustrated, decides to "beat him within an inch of his life." He does, and his son dies. He commits an intent to cause serious bodily injury murder.

"*Serious bodily injury*" has a technical meaning. Some states define it by statute. Here's Tennessee's (Tennessee Criminal Code 2005, 39-11-106(a)(34)) definition, which is similar to other states' definitions: "**Serious bodily injury**" means bodily injury that involves:

serious bodily injury, bodily injury that involves a substantial risk of death; protracted unconsciousness; extreme physical pain; protracted or obvious disfigurement; or protracted loss or substantial impairment of a function of a bodily member, organ or mental faculty

1. A substantial risk of death;
2. Protracted unconsciousness;
3. Extreme physical pain;
4. Protracted or obvious disfigurement; or
5. Protracted loss or substantial impairment of a function of a bodily member, organ or mental faculty.

Throughout the centuries when judges were expanding the definition of "murder" to include these very different kinds of killings, they continued to call them all by the same name—"killing another with malice aforethought." But they added the critical phrase "express or implied." "**Express" malice aforethought** was reserved for killings that fit the original meaning of "murder"—intentional killings planned in advance.

"express" malice aforethought, killings that fit the original meaning of "murder"—intentional killings planned in advance

According to Blackstone (1769):

> Express malice is when one, with a sedate deliberate mind and formed design, doth kill another, which formed design is evidenced by external circumstances discovering that inward intention; as lying in wait, antecedent menaces, former grudges, and concerted schemes to do him some bodily harm. (199)

"Implied" malice aforethought referred to the four additional kinds of murder we just discussed:

"implied" malice aforethought, intentional killings without premeditation or reasonable provocation; unintentional killings during the commission of felonies; depraved heart killings; and intent to inflict grievous bodily harm killings

1. Intentional killings without premeditation or reasonable provocation
2. Unintentional killings during the commission of felonies
3. Depraved heart killings
4. Intent to inflict grievous bodily harm killings

THE ELEMENTS OF MURDER

LO 5

Murder is a result crime. (Recall from Chapter 3 that result crimes consist of criminal conduct that causes a criminal harm.) Therefore, proving murder requires proof beyond a reasonable doubt of these elements:

1. Murder *actus reus*, the act of killing
2. Murder *mens rea*, intentional, knowing, or extremely reckless killing
3. Causation, the act caused
4. Death
5. Attendant circumstances, if there are any

See the Elements of Murder illustration of these requirements.

Before we go any further, it's important to keep in mind throughout the following discussion that the required criminal acts, mental attitudes, tests of causation, and attendant circumstances vary from state to state. So if you're interested in finding out what the elements of murder (or any of the specific kinds of homicide, or for that matter, any of the crimes in the rest of the book) are in your state, you can find them

ELEMENTS OF MURDER

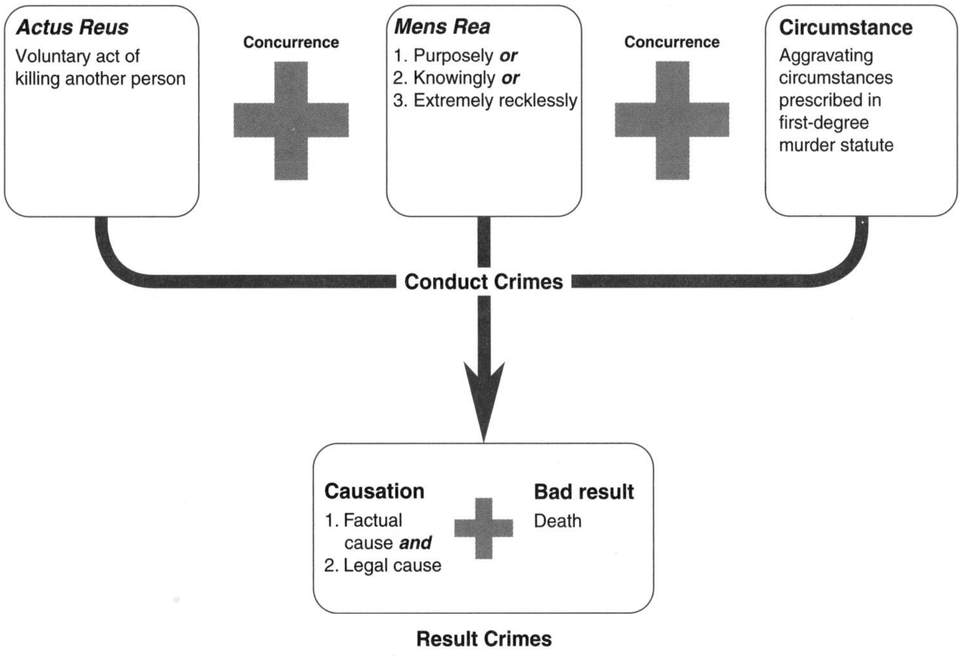

Actus Reus
Voluntary act of killing another person

Concurrence

Mens Rea
1. Purposely ***or***
2. Knowingly ***or***
3. Extremely recklessly

Concurrence

Circumstance
Aggravating circumstances prescribed in first-degree murder statute

Conduct Crimes

Causation
1. Factual cause ***and***
2. Legal cause

Bad result
Death

Result Crimes

online free. (One of the several links to your state's code is http://www.law.cornell.edu/topics/state_statutes2.html#criminal_code. They're also available on apps for tablets and smartphones.)

Now, let's turn to the elements of murder. We won't discuss causation here because Chapter 4 and the "Doctor-Assisted Suicide" sections later in this chapter cover all you need to know about it. As for the result, the death of a person, we said all that was necessary in the "The Meaning of 'Person' or 'Human Being'" section earlier. Finally, we'll leave the discussion of the circumstance element to the places in the text where there's a circumstance element. We'll focus on how the general principles of *actus reus* and *mens rea* apply to the criminal act and mental attitude elements of criminal homicide.

Murder Actus Reus

murder *actus reus*, the act of killing by poisoning, striking, starving, drowning, and a thousand other forms by which human nature can be overcome

"Killing" or "causing death" is the heart of **murder *actus reus***, and it's easy to define. We can't improve on Blackstone's (1769) words: "The killing may be by poisoning, striking, starving, drowning, and a thousand other forms by which human nature can be overcome" (196). It can also result from failures to act—such as a husband who stands by and watches his blind wife, whom he hates, walk off the edge of a cliff. It can result from words—such as a wife who sneaks up behind her husband, whom she hates, who is standing at the edge of the Grand Canyon and yells, "Boo!" causing him to fall over the edge.

Notice that *how* the murderer kills someone doesn't matter in most cases. But it can be a circumstance element in first-degree murder or an aggravating circumstance in death penalty cases. Even though there were no degrees of murder at the time, Blackstone (1769) teaches us that it's murder if a victim dies after "one beats another in a cruel and unusual manner":

> As when a park keeper tied a boy, that was stealing wood, to a horse's tail and dragged him along the park; when a master corrected his servant with an iron bar; and a school master stamped on his scholar's belly, so that each of the sufferers died. These were justly held to be murders because, the correction being excessive and such as could not proceed but from a bad heart, it was equivalent to an act of slaughter. (199–200)

Murder Mens Rea

murder *mens rea*, can include purposeful, knowing, or reckless killing

Murder *mens rea* can include every state of mind included in the concept of malice aforethought (discussed in the last section). In the language of the Model Penal Code (discussed in Chapter 4), purpose, knowledge, and recklessness can qualify as the mental element in murder. We'll have more to say about the mental element in each of the degrees of murder, which we'll turn to now.

LO 6

THE KINDS AND DEGREES OF MURDER

The English judges never *formally* divided murder into degrees. All murders were capital offenses. But the judges had enormous discretion to free all convicted felons by means of "benefit of clergy," a practice that began with a rule that allowed priests to be tried only in ecclesiastical courts. To get transferred from the common law to the ecclesiastical courts, priests had to prove they were clerics by reading a passage from the Bible. At first, this was a reliable test because only clerics could read. Eventually, "reading the book" became a pure formality, for two reasons. First, the passage in the "book" convicted felons had to "read" was always the same few words; and second, literacy increased well beyond the clergy.

The judges manipulated the formality to mitigate *informally* the harshness of the common law, which mandated that all felons, from cold-blooded murderers to petty thieves, should hang. By the reign of Henry VIII (1509–37), successful pleas of clergy were so widely granted by the judges that Parliament enacted a form of mandatory sentencing to curb judicial discretion; it banned the plea in all cases of premeditated murder (Samaha 1974). The list of "nonclergyable" offenses would grow in the centuries that followed.

Dividing murder into degrees expanded the idea that not all felons—in this case, not all murderers—should be executed. In the new United States, degrees of murder were created by legislatures, not judges. Pennsylvania was the first state to depart from the common law, enacting a statute in 1794 that divided murder into first and second degrees. The Pennsylvania statute provided that

> all murder, which shall be perpetrated by means of poison, lying in wait, or by any other kind of willful, deliberate or premeditated killing, or which shall be committed in the perpetration, or attempt to perpetrate any arson, rape, robbery or burglary shall be deemed murder in the first degree; and all other kinds of murder shall be deemed murder in the second degree. (Pennsylvania Laws 1794, chap. 257, §§ 1–2)

So under the statute, premeditated intent to kill murders and some felony murders were capital offenses, just as they were under the old common law. And they still are. All other murders (depraved heart and intent to cause serious bodily injury) were second-degree murders, just as they were under the old law. *Sometimes*, they still are. The Model Penal Code doesn't use the term "degrees," but, since its publication in 1960, state criminal codes have increasingly used the MPC's scheme of dividing murder according to mental attitude—purposely, knowingly, and extremely recklessly.

Most states quickly followed Pennsylvania's example. Behind this quick adoption of the statutes was the first of numerous waves of opposition to the death penalty throughout U.S. history. Three results followed, results that influenced the criminal law you're studying in this book profoundly:

1. The gradual peeling away of layers of criminal homicides that were thought not to deserve the death penalty
2. The emergence of more detailed grading schemes, placing various types of criminal homicide along the spectrum of available criminal punishments
3. The development of various justifications and excuses making certain homicides noncriminal (Low 1990, 335)

Today, most states divide homicide into two degrees, and a few divide it into three degrees. We'll look at first-degree and second-degree murder.

FIRST-DEGREE MURDER

Almost all states that divide murder into degrees establish two kinds of **first-degree murder**: (1) premeditated, deliberate intent to kill murders and (2) felony murders. First-degree murder is the only crime today in which the death penalty can be imposed (Chapter 2). Because of a series of U.S. Supreme Court cases, death penalty cases are complicated proceedings. So we need to look at first-degree murder and the death penalty before we go further.

first-degree murder, consists of (1) premeditated, deliberate intent to kill murders and (2) felony murders; the only crime today in which the death penalty can be imposed

The Death Penalty and First-Degree Murder

The death penalty is discretionary in all states that authorize it. To guide judges' and juries' decisions whether to execute or sentence to life in prison a person convicted of first-degree murder, the U.S. Supreme Court, in a series of decisions since the 1970s, has completely revised the procedures for imposing capital punishment. The matter is highly complicated, and the Court's cases haven't always made it clear just what's required, but here's a list of the main practices the Constitution bans, requires, and allows:

1. *Mandatory death sentences* are banned. States can't require the death penalty in *all* first-degree murders.
2. *Unguided discretionary death penalty* decisions are banned. Judges and juries can't impose the death penalty without a list of specific criteria for and against the death penalty to guide their decision.
3. *Mitigating factors* are required. States can't limit the range of mitigating factors that might favor life imprisonment instead of death.
4. *Additional aggravating factors* are allowed. Jurors and/or judges are allowed to consider factors in favor of death not specifically included in statutory lists of aggravating factors.

Most states have adopted the MPC's two recommended procedures—bifurcation and the criteria for guiding the decision to impose the death sentence in capital cases. (We define "capital cases" as death penalty cases in death penalty states and "mandatory life sentence without parole" cases in non–death penalty states.)

capital cases, death penalty cases in death penalty states and "mandatory life sentence without parole" cases in non–death penalty states

bifurcation procedure, the requirement that the death penalty decision be made in two phases: a trial to determine guilt and a second separate proceeding, after a finding of guilt, to consider the aggravating factors for, and mitigating factors against, capital punishment

The bifurcation procedure mandates that the death penalty decision be made in two phases: a trial to determine guilt and a second separate proceeding, after a finding of guilt, to consider the aggravating factors for, and mitigating factors against, capital punishment. At the penalty phase, prosecutors get the opportunity to present evidence not presented at the trial phase, and defendants can offer evidence in mitigation.

The criteria for decision in death penalty cases must be limited by the criteria established and announced *before* the decision to sentence the defendant to death. Juries, or judges where state law authorizes judges to decide, have to consider aggravating and mitigating factors before making their decision. They can't actually impose the death penalty unless they find "one of the aggravated circumstances and further find that there are no mitigating circumstances sufficiently substantial to call for leniency" (ALI 1985, Art. 210.6).

The list of aggravating circumstances includes:

1. The murder was committed by a convict under sentence of imprisonment.
2. The defendant was previously convicted of another murder or of a felony involving the use or threat of violence to the person.
3. At the time the murder was committed, the defendant also committed another murder.
4. The defendant knowingly created a great risk of death to many persons.
5. The murder was committed while the defendant was engaged or was an accomplice in the commission, or an attempt to commit, or flight after committing or attempting to commit, robbery, rape, or deviant sexual intercourse by force or threat of force, arson, burglary, or kidnapping.
6. The murder was committed for the purpose of avoiding or preventing a lawful arrest or effecting an escape from lawful custody.
7. The murder was committed for pecuniary gain.
8. The murder was especially heinous, atrocious, or cruel, manifesting exceptional depravity.

The list of mitigating factors includes:

1. The defendant has no significant history of criminal activity.
2. The murder was committed while the defendant was under the influence of extreme mental or emotional disturbance.
3. The victim was a participant in the defendant's homicidal conduct or consented to the homicidal act.
4. The murder was committed under circumstances that the defendant believed to provide a moral justification or extenuation for his conduct.
5. The defendant was an accomplice in a murder committed by another person and his participation in the homicidal act was relatively minor.
6. The defendant acted under duress or under the domination of another person.
7. At the time of the murder, the capacity of the defendant to appreciate the criminality [wrongfulness] of his conduct or to conform his conduct to the requirements of law was impaired as a result of mental disease or defect or intoxication.
8. The defendant was a young age at the time of the crime.

First-Degree Murder Mens Rea

"All murder which is perpetrated by . . . willful, deliberate, and premeditated killing . . . is murder of the first degree" (California Penal Code 2006, ß 189). This is the broad, even vague, definition of "first-degree murder" often found in criminal codes.

Let's look at these terms. "Willful" means the intent to kill. "If an intention to kill exists, it is willful," a judge instructed the jury in a Pennsylvania murder trial just after the Civil War (*Commonwealth v. Drum* 1868, 6). The same isn't true of "deliberate" and "premeditated." They're frequently issues in the cases, and the courts define them differently, sometimes radically so.

Most courts say that "premeditated" and "deliberate" mean something more than the intent to kill. In other words, they refine the mental attitude of the MPC's "purposely" and "knowingly" and the common law's "specific intent." Judges understand that the purpose of the refinement is to distinguish between murders so awful that they deserve the harshest punishment the law allows from murders that don't deserve the worst punishment.

But just what the refinement consists of varies greatly, and there's often disagreement, sometimes among judges on the same court, not just on the definitions but whether they apply to the facts of the case they're deciding. Unfortunately, some courts blur the line between intentional killings and the more refined deliberate, premeditated intentional killings. The result is that there's no meaningful difference between first- and second-degree murder. This is serious business, not just theoretically but practically, too, because it could mean, literally, the difference between life and death.

Professor Wayne LaFave (2003a) teaches us (and many judges too!) that it's "not easy to give a meaningful definition of the words 'premeditate' and 'deliberate'" (766). He tries to help us with this example:

> . . . For premeditation the killer asks himself the question, "Shall I kill him?" The intent to kill aspect of the crime is found in the answer, "Yes I shall." The deliberation part of the crime requires a thought like, "Wait, what about the consequences? Well, I'll do it anyway." (766)

And then he adds,

> Perhaps the best that can be said of "deliberation" is that it requires a cool mind that is capable of reflection, and of "premeditation" that it requires that one with the cool mind did in fact reflect, at least for a short period of time, before killing. (766–67)

Blackstone (1769) called "willful, premeditated, deliberate killings" the "grand criterion" of murder because they reflect "the dictate of a wicked, depraved, and malignant heart" (199). Modern court opinions display a far broader spectrum of definitions. At one extreme are those that fit the definitions of the original "grand criterion"—killings planned in advance and then committed in "cold blood" that we've just reviewed.

A good example is *People v. Anderson* (1968):

> We have repeatedly pointed out that the legislative classification of murder into two degrees would be meaningless if "deliberation" and "premeditation" were construed as requiring no more reflection than may be involved in the mere formation of a specific intent to kill. A verdict of murder in the first degree (on a theory of a willful, deliberate, and premeditated killing) is proper only if the slayer killed as a result of careful thought and weighing of considerations; as a deliberate judgment or plan; carried on coolly and steadily. (948)

States that adopt this *specific-intent-plus-real-premeditation-deliberation* definition rely on three categories of evidence to prove murders really were premeditated and deliberate:

CATEGORY 1. Facts about how and what defendant did prior to the actual killing which show that the defendant was engaged in activity directed toward, and explicable as intended to result in, the killing—what may be characterized as planning activity;

CATEGORY 2. Facts about the defendant's prior relationship and/or conduct with the victim from which the jury could reasonably infer a "motive" to kill the victim, which inference of motive, together with facts of type (1) or (3), would in turn support an inference that the killing was the result of "a pre-existing reflection and careful thought and weighing of considerations rather than mere unconsidered or rash impulse hastily";

CATEGORY 3. Facts about the nature of the killing from which the jury could infer that the manner of killing was so particular and exacting that the defendant must have intentionally killed according to a preconceived design to take his victim's life in a particular way for a reason which the jury can reasonably infer from facts of type (1) or (2). (949)

Table 9.2 highlights cases that demonstrate each of the three categories.

TABLE 9.2 Proving Premeditated, Deliberate Intent

CATEGORY 1	CATEGORY 2	CATEGORY 3
• *U.S. v. Blue Thunder* (1979): brought the murder weapon, a knife, to the murder scene • *People v. Kemp* (1961): entered the house through a bedroom window • *U.S. v. Downs* (1995): arranged to meet the victim at home when no one would be home	• *State v. Crawford* (1996): prior threats to kill the victim • *State v. Thomas* (1999): starving the child to death would conceal a prior killing • *State v. Hamlet* (1984): victim had bragged about knocking out the defendant in a prior fight	• *U.S. v. Treas-Wilson* (1993): precise and fatal injury; 4-inch incision severing • *People v. Steele* (2002): stabbed victim eight times in the chest • *State v. Taylor* (2002): eight blows to the head with a heavy object

At the other extreme are courts that define "willful, premeditated, deliberate" killing as the equivalent of the specific intent to kill. A good example is *Macias v. State* (1929):

> There need be no appreciable space of time between the intention to kill and the act of killing. They may be as instantaneous as successive thoughts of the mind. It is only necessary that the act of killing be preceded by a concurrence of will, deliberation, and premeditation on the part of the slayer, and, if such is the case, the killing is murder in the first degree. (715)

There's considerable criticism in court decisions and among commentators that this *equivalent of specific intent* definition renders the difference between first- and second-degree murder meaningless. That's serious because it means there's no real difference between capital murder that can lead to execution in death penalty states or to life in prison without the chance of parole in non–death penalty states.

CASE

In* State v. Snowden *(1957), *Ray Snowden picked up Cora Dean in a bar. They danced, drank, fought, and Snowden stabbed Dean to death. He was convicted of first degree, premeditated murder. His appeal is the subject of our next case excerpt.*

Did he premeditatedly and deliberately murder?

State v. Snowden

313 P.2d 706 (Idaho 1957)

HISTORY

Raymond Alien Snowden, Defendant, pleaded guilty to murder in the first degree. The District Court, 3rd Judicial District, Ada County, entered judgment and the sentence of death, and Snowden appealed. The Supreme Court, held that where it appeared that upon being struck by Cora Lucyle Dean, Snowden deliberately opened up his pocket knife, cut the woman's throat, and then hacked and cut until he killed her, and expended himself, imposition of the death sentence was not an abuse of discretion by the trial court. Affirmed.

McQUADE, J.

FACTS

The victim, Cora Lucyle Dean, was stabbed to death September 22, 1956, in Garden City, Idaho. Defendant Snowden had been playing pool and drinking in a Boise pool room early in the evening. With a companion, one Carrier, he visited a club near Boise, then went to nearby Garden City. There the two men visited a number of bars, and defendant had several drinks. Their last stop was the HiHo Club.

Witnesses related that while Snowden was in the HiHo Club he met and talked to Cora Lucyle Dean. He said he hadn't been acquainted with Mrs. Dean prior to that time, but he had "seen her in a couple of the joints up town." He danced with Mrs. Dean while at the HiHo Club. Upon departing from the tavern, the two left together.

In statements to police officers, that were admitted in evidence, Snowden said after they left the club Mrs. Dean wanted him to find a cab and take her back to Boise, and he refused because he didn't feel he should pay her fare. After some words, he related, "she got mad at me so I got pretty hot and I don't know whether I back handed her there or not. And, we got calmed down and decided to walk across to the gas station and call a cab.

They crossed the street, and began arguing again. Snowden said, "She swung and at the same time she kneed me again. I blew my top." Snowden said he pushed Dean over beside a pickup truck which was standing near a business building. There he pulled his knife—a pocket knife with a two-inch blade—and cut her throat.

The body, which was found the next morning, was viciously and sadistically cut and mutilated. An autopsy surgeon testified the voice box had been cut, and that this would have prevented the victim from making any intelligible outcry. There were other

(continues)

(continued)

wounds inflicted while she was still alive—one in her neck, one in her abdomen, two in the face, and two on the back of the neck. The second neck wound severed the spinal cord and caused death. There were other wounds all over her body, and her clothing had been cut away. The nipple of the right breast was missing.

There was no evidence of a sexual attack on the victim; however, some of the lacerations were around the breasts and vagina of the deceased. A blood test showed Mrs. Dean was intoxicated at the time of her death.

Snowden took Dean's wallet. He hailed a passing motorist and rode back to Boise with him. There he went to a bowling alley and changed clothes. He dropped his knife into a sewer, and threw the wallet away. Then he went to his hotel and cleaned up again. He put the clothes he had worn that evening into a trash barrel.

After hearing the testimony of police officers and other witnesses, the trial court determined the killing was murder in the first degree and there were no circumstances in mitigation of the offense or of the punishment to be inflicted. Snowden was sentenced to death.

OPINION

By statute, murder is defined as the unlawful killing of a human being with malice aforethought. I.C. § 18-4001. In the present case Snowden killed a human being, and his actions indicate malice aforethought. *There was no considerable provocation shown, and the circumstances attending the killing show an abandoned and malignant heart* [emphasis added]. The rule is malice is implied for any deliberate and cruel act against another, however sudden, which shows an abandoned and malignant heart, and the facts show there was malice in the acts of the defendant at the time of the killing.

Snowden's principal argument pertaining to malice aforethought is that he did not have sufficient time to develop a desire to take the life of the deceased, but rather his action was instantaneous and a normal reaction to the physical injury which she had dealt him. Inasmuch as Snowden took the life of Cora Lucyle Dean, and did so with malice aforethought, it necessarily must follow that he is guilty of murder.

Degrees of murder are defined by statute as follows:

> All murder which is perpetrated by means of poison, or lying in wait, torture, or by any other kind of willful, deliberate and premeditated killing, or which is committed in the perpetration of, or attempt to perpetrate arson, rape, robbery, burglary, kidnapping or mayhem, is murder of the first degree. All other kinds of murder are of the second degree. I.C. § 18-4003.

[The trial court] found . . . that Snowden's acts in taking the life of Cora Dean were willful, deliberate, and premeditated. I.C. § 18-4003 requires first degree homicide to be perpetrated by any kind of willful, deliberate, and premeditated killing. . . . The test to determine if the killing was willful, deliberate, and premeditated has been set out in *State v. Shuff*:

> The unlawful killing must be accompanied with a deliberate and clear intent to take life, in order to constitute murder of the first degree. The intent to kill must be the result of deliberate premeditation. It must be formed upon the pre-existing reflection, and not upon a sudden heat of passion sufficient to preclude the idea of deliberation.

The court further stated in this case while approving an instruction:

> . . . Any unlawful killing of a human being, with malice aforethought, is murder; but if nothing further characterizes the offense it is murder of the second degree. To constitute the higher offense there must be superadded, to the general definition above given, willfulness, deliberation, and premeditation. By willfulness is meant that it was of purpose, with the intent that, by the given act, the life of the party should be taken. It must be deliberate and premeditated.
>
> By this it is not meant that the killing must have been conceived or intended for any particular length of time. It is sufficient if it was done with reflection and conceived beforehand. And in this view, as I have said before, the deliberate purpose to kill and the killing may follow each other as rapidly as successive impulses or thoughts of the mind.

In the present case, the trial court had no other alternative than to find the defendant guilty of willful, deliberate, and premeditated killing with malice aforethought in view of the defendant's acts in deliberately opening up a pocket knife, next cutting the victim's throat, and then hacking and cutting until he had killed Cora Lucyle Dean and expended himself. The full purpose and design of defendant's conduct was to take the life of the deceased.

[Snowden also contended that the trial court erred in its] . . . imposition of the penalty of death. Punishment for murder is set out in I.C. § 18-4004:

> Every person guilty of murder in the first degree shall suffer death or be punished by imprisonment in the state prison for life, and the jury may decide which punishment shall be inflicted.

It was stated in *State v. Powell*, 227 P.2d 582, 585:

> Upon a plea of guilty, the trial judge is clothed by the statute with the power and duty of fixing the punishment. It is within his sound discretion to determine whether the punishment shall be life imprisonment or death. Unless such discretion is abused, it will not be disturbed by this court.

The trial court could have imposed life imprisonment, or, as in the instant case, sentenced the defendant to death. It is abuse of discretion we are dealing with, and in particular the alleged abuse of discretion in prescribing the punishment for murder in the first degree as committed by the defendant. To choose between the punishments of life imprisonment and death there must be some distinction between one homicide and another. This case exemplifies an abandoned and malignant heart and sadistic mind, bent upon taking human life. It is our considered conclusion, from all the facts and circumstances, the imposition of the death sentence was not an abuse of discretion by the trial court.

The judgment is affirmed.

QUESTIONS

1. How does the court define the terms "willful," "deliberate," and "premeditated"?
2. Sort and arrange the facts of the case according to the definitions of the three terms in (1).
3. In your opinion, did Ray Snowden commit first-degree murder?
4. Assuming Snowden is guilty of first-degree murder, should he be sentenced to death? Consider the lists of aggravating and mitigating circumstances in the "The Death Penalty" section (pp. 309–310). Which items on the list might apply to him? Explain your answer, based on the facts in the case.

The Deadly Weapon Doctrine

However the statutes define and judges interpret the intent to kill requirement, how do prosecutors prove that the defendant acted with the required intent? Rarely will defendants announce to witnesses, "See this slime bag who slept with the love of my life? Well, it's pay back time. Watch me pay him back with the bullets in this gun in my hand." In fact, most will do it secretly, and silently, so there won't be witnesses. So prosecutors have to make their case by the circumstantial evidence they gather to present in court.

The deadly weapon doctrine is one of these circumstances. According to the deadly weapon doctrine, "one who intentionally uses a deadly weapon on another human being and thereby kills him presumably intends to kill him" (LaFave 2003, 734). The doctrine was hinted at as early as 1675, in a case reported by Sir Matthew Hale. A was sitting and drinking in an alehouse. B, a woman, called him a "son of a whore." He picked up a broomstick and threw it at her; it hit her and she died. Was the killing murder or manslaughter? The judges rejected the argument that her words were adequate provocation to reduce murder to manslaughter (see "Adequate Provocation," p. 332).

deadly weapon doctrine, one who intentionally uses a deadly weapon on another human being and thereby kills him presumably intends to kill him

But the judges had a problem with malice aforethought because of the broomstick. If it was a "striking with such an instrument as necessarily would have caused death, as stabbing with a sword, or pistoling," it would definitely not be manslaughter; they could imply malice from the yet unformed deadly weapon doctrine. But whether "this striking, that was so improbable to cause death," could be the basis for malice aforethought, they couldn't agree. So they recommended that the king pardon him, which he did (Oberer 1962, 1572, n. 38).

The doctrine grew out of widely accepted proposition in both civil and criminal cases that individuals are presumed to intend the natural and probable consequences of their acts. Here's an example of the deadly weapon presumption: Suppose that, if without a word, and with no one in sight, Hannah loads her Ruger .357 revolver, carefully aims it at Zack, and pulls the trigger to get him for giving her a bad grade, and the bullet hits him in the head and kills him. It's logical to conclude that Hannah intended to kill Zack. Hence, the deadly weapon presumption.

Be careful not to conclude that the presumption is mandatory. In fact, in homicide, it's more a permissible inference than a mandatory presumption. In Professor LaFave's (2003) words, "The conclusion *may* be drawn, rather than *must* be drawn, in the absence of counter proof" that because the killer intentionally used a deadly weapon, the killer intended to kill the victim (734–35). In other words, the use of a deadly weapon that kills isn't automatically murder. The shooter still has a chance to convince a jury (or a judge in a trial without a jury) that although she shot intentionally she didn't intend to kill, as where she intended to scare or inflict a minor wound (735).

Let's return to the question raised by the broomstick in Lord Hale's report of the alehouse killing: What's a deadly weapon? "One which, from the manner used, is calculated or likely to produce death or serious bodily injury" (*Wilson v. State* 1909, 1015).

Not everyone agrees that premeditated, deliberate killings—even if they're truly planned and committed in cold blood—are the worst kind of murders. According to the nineteenth-century English judge and criminal law reformer James F. Stephen (1883):

> As much cruelty, as much indifference to the life of others, a disposition at least as dangerous to society, probably even more dangerous, is shown by sudden as by premeditated murders. The following cases appear to me to set this in a clear light. A man, passing along the road, sees a boy sitting on a bridge over a deep river and, out of mere wanton barbarity, pushes him into it and so drowns him. A man makes advances to a girl who repels him. He deliberately but instantly cuts her throat. A man civilly asked to pay a just debt pretends to get the money, loads a rifle and blows out his creditor's brains. In none of these cases is there premeditation unless the word is used in a sense as unnatural as "aforethought" in "malice aforethought," but each represents even more diabolical cruelty and ferocity than that which is involved in murders premeditated in the natural sense of the word. (94)

Could an especially brutal *actus reus* be one of these other kinds of first-degree murder? Let's look for the answer in first-degree murder *actus reus*.

First-Degree Murder Actus Reus

As you've already learned, how a murderer kills doesn't matter, at least not most of the time. As Blackstone taught us in 1769: "The killing may be by poisoning, striking, starving, drowning, and a thousand other forms by which human nature can be overcome." But first-degree murder *actus reus* can be critical when it comes to deciding whether to sentence a person convicted of first-degree murder to death, to prison for life without parole in states without the death penalty, or to a lesser penalty. Killing by means of "heinous, atrocious, or cruel" acts, meaning especially brutal murders or torture murders intended to cause lingering death, appears on the list of aggravating factors that qualifies a murderer for the death penalty.

CASE

In* Duest v. State *(1985), the Florida Supreme Court applied the state's "heinous, atrocious, or cruel" aggravating circumstance provision to approve the death penalty for Lloyd Duest, who was convicted of first-degree murder in a "gay bashing" killing during a robbery.

Was the murder heinous, atrocious, or cruel?

Duest v. State

462 So.2d 446 (Fla. 1985)

HISTORY

Lloyd Duest (the defendant) was convicted in the Circuit Court, Broward County, Patricia W. Cocalis, J., of first-degree murder, for which the sentence of death was imposed, and the defendant appealed. The Supreme Court, Adkins, J., held that evidence was sufficient to support the conviction; and evidence was sufficient to support the findings on challenged aggravating circumstances.

ADKINS, J. BOYD, CJ., and OVERTON, ALDERMAN, McDONALD, EHRLICH and SHAW, JJ., concur.

FACTS

On February 15, 1982, the defendant was seen by witnesses carrying a knife in the waistband of his pants. Subsequently, he told a witness that he was going to a gay bar to "roll a fag." The defendant was later seen at a predominantly gay bar with John Pope, the victim. The two of them then left the bar in Pope's gold Camaro. Several hours later, Pope's roommate returned home and found the house unlocked, the lights on, the stereo on loud, and blood on the bed. The sheriff was contacted. Upon arrival, the deputy sheriff found Pope on the bathroom floor in a pool of blood with multiple stab wounds. The defendant was found and arrested on April 18, 1982.

OPINION

Defendant contends that there was insufficient evidence of premeditated murder to convict him as charged in the indictment. Premeditation, like other factual circumstances, may be established by circumstantial evidence. Such circumstantial evidence must not only be consistent with the defendant's guilt, but must also be inconsistent with any reasonable hypothesis of innocence.

The record reflects that defendant had stated he gets his money by "rolling gay guys" and that he intended to do the same on the day that the victim was murdered. Defendant was seen with the victim at a gay bar immediately prior to the murder and was seen leaving the bar with the victim in the victim's car. Shortly thereafter, defendant was seen driving the victim's car alone. At that time, witnesses saw blood stains on the sleeve of his jogging suit. The victim's stolen jewelry case was also seen in the car, which was being driven by defendant after the murder. Moreover, on the day of the murder, defendant had in his possession a seven-inch knife. The cause of death in this case was multiple stab wounds. We find that there was sufficient circumstantial evidence to sustain defendant's conviction of premeditated murder.

Defendant objects to the trial court's findings with respect to the aggravating and mitigating circumstances. The trial court found the following aggravating circumstances:

1. the defendant had been previously convicted of armed robbery and assault with intent to commit murder, section 921.141(5)(b);
2. the capital felony was committed while the defendant was engaged in the commission of a robbery, section 921.141(5)(d);
3. the capital felony was committed for pecuniary gain, section 921.141(5)(f);
4. the capital felony was especially heinous, atrocious, or cruel, section 921.141(5)(h);
5. the capital felony was a homicide which was committed in a cold, calculated, and premeditated manner without any pretense of moral or legal justification, section 921.141(5)(i).

The trial court considered circumstances 2 and 3 as one circumstance because of overlapping facts and legal definitions. Therefore, four aggravating circumstances were applicable. As to mitigating circumstances, none were applied to this case.

Defendant only challenges two of the aggravating circumstances. He asserts that the murder was not particularly heinous, atrocious or cruel. We disagree with the defendant. The evidence presented at trial

(continues)

(continued)
shows that the victim received eleven stab wounds, some of which were inflicted in the bedroom and some inflicted in the bathroom. The medical examiner's testimony revealed that the victim lived some few minutes before dying.

This case is similar to *Morgan v. State*, 415 So. 2d 6 (Fla.1982), where the evidence showed that the death was caused by one or more of ten stab wounds. In that case, this Court approved the finding that the homicide was especially heinous, atrocious, or cruel. Under the totality of the circumstances and applying our previous decisions to the facts of the instant case, we find that trial court properly applied this aggravating circumstance.

Defendant also challenges the finding that the homicide was committed in a cold, calculated, and premeditated manner. In finding that this aggravating circumstance applied, the trial court found:

> Evidence adduced at trial indicated that defendant informed witness Demezio some two days prior to the murder that he brings homosexuals back to their apartments, beats them up, and takes their money or jewelry. Defendant on the day of the murder went to his temporary residence with the victim, went into the closet where Demezio kept a dagger and left the residence with John Pope, Jr., the victim. The dagger was later discovered missing, and John Pope, Jr. was later discovered at his home, dead. His car and jewelry box were missing.

We find that the evidence supports the finding that the homicide was committed in a cold, calculated, and premeditated manner. In the instant case, even if we were to find that one or two of the aggravating circumstances found by the trial judge, was inapplicable, it would still be appropriate to maintain the death penalty.

For the reasons expressed, we affirm the defendant's conviction and the imposition of the death sentence.

It is so ordered.

QUESTIONS

1. How does the court define "heinous, atrocious, or cruel"?
2. List the facts in the case that are relevant to deciding whether this was a "heinous, atrocious, or cruel" murder.
3. Summarize the arguments in favor of and against classifying this as a "heinous, cruel, and atrocious" murder.

EXPLORING FURTHER

First-Degree Murder *Actus Reus*

Was beating him to death with a baseball bat atrocious first-degree murder?

Commonwealth v. Golston, 249, 366 N.E.2d 744 (Mass. 1977)

FACTS

About 2:00 p.m. on Sunday, August 24, 1975, a white man about 34 years old came out of a store and walked toward his car. Siegfried Golston, a 19-year-old African American man, tiptoed up behind the victim and hit him on the head with a baseball bat. A witness testified to the sound made by Golston's blow to the victim's head: "Just like you hit a wet, you know, like a bat hit a wet baseball; that's how it sounded." Golston then went into a building, changed his clothes, and crossed the street to the store, where he worked. When asked why he had hit the man, Golston replied, "For kicks." The victim later died. Was this "atrocious murder," a form of first-degree murder that qualified Golston for the death penalty?

DECISION

According to the Court, it was:

> There was evidence of great and unusual violence in the blow, which caused a four-inch cut on the side of the skull. There was also evidence that after he was struck the victim fell to the street, and that five minutes later he tried to get up, staggered to his feet and fell again to the ground. He was breathing very hard and a neighbor wiped vomit from his nose and mouth. Later, according to the testimony, the defendant said he did it, "For kicks." There is no requirement that the defendant know that his act was extremely atrocious or cruel, and no requirement of deliberate premeditation. A murder may be committed with extreme atrocity or cruelty even though death results from a single blow. Indifference to the victim's pain, as well as actual knowledge of it and taking pleasure in it, is cruelty; and extreme cruelty is only a higher degree of cruelty.

SECOND-DEGREE MURDER

As you learned earlier in the chapter, the reason for creating first- and second-degree murders, beginning with Pennsylvania in 1794, was to separate murders that deserved the death penalty from those that didn't. The goal was to *limit* capital punishment without *eliminating* it. Second-degree murders included intentional murders that weren't premeditated or deliberate. But not all second-degree murders required intentional killing. These are "implied malice" murders, created by the common law judges, which still exist in common law states and by statute today. They include felony murders, intent to inflict serious bodily injury murders, and depraved heart murders.

second-degree murders, murders that aren't first-degree murders, including intentional murders that weren't premeditated or deliberate, felony murders, intent to inflict serious bodily injury murders, and depraved heart murders

Sometimes, second-degree murder is treated as a default murder category, meaning it includes all murders that aren't first-degree murders. Some state statutes make this default definition explicit. Michigan's statute (Michigan Criminal Code 2006, § 750.317) is a good example. After defining first-degree murder, the Michigan second-degree murder section provides:

> All other kinds of murder shall be murder of the second degree, and shall be punished by imprisonment in the state prison for life, or any term of years, in the discretion of the court trying the same.

CASE

In* People v. Thomas *(1978), *the Michigan Court of Appeals interpreted Michigan's second-degree murder statute to include Daniel Thomas' conduct.*

Did he commit second-degree murder?

People v. Thomas

272 N.W.2d 157 (Mich.App. 1978)

HISTORY

Charged with second-degree murder, M.C.L. § 750.317; M.S.A. § 28.549, Daniel Lindley Thomas (the defendant) was convicted by a jury of involuntary manslaughter, M.C.L. § 750.321; M.S.A. § 28.553. Thereafter, sentenced to a prison term of 5 to 15 years, the defendant appeals as of right. The Court of Appeals affirmed.

HOLBROOK, J.

FACTS

The victim, a 19-year-old male "catatonic schizophrenic," was at the time of his death a resident of Oak Haven, a religious practical training school. When it appeared he was not properly responding to ordinary treatment, Daniel Thomas (the defendant), the work coordinator at Oak Haven, obtained permission from the victim's parents to discipline him if such seemed necessary. Thereafter Thomas, together with another supervisor at Oak Haven, took decedent to the edge of the campus, whereupon decedent's pants were taken down, following which he was spanked with a rubber hose. Such disciplinary session lasted approximately 15 to 30 minutes. During a portion thereof the decedent's hands were tied behind his back for failure to cooperate.

Following the disciplinary session, Thomas testified that the young man improved for a while but then commenced to backslide. Thomas received permission from the decedent's parents to subject him to further discipline. On September 30, 1976, Thomas again took the decedent to the approximate same location, removed his pants, bound his hands behind him with a rope looped over a tree limb, and proceeded to beat him with a doubled-over rubber hose.

This beating lasted approximately 45 minutes to an hour. While the evidence conflicted, it appears that the victim was struck between 30 to 100 times. The beating resulted in severe bruises ranging from the victim's waist to his feet. The decedent's roommate testified that the decedent had open bleeding sores on his thighs. On the date of death, which was nine days after the beating, the decedent's legs were immobile. At no time did Thomas obtain medical attention for the victim.

Thomas admitted he had exercised poor judgment, after seeing the bruises, in continuing the

(continues)

(continued)

discipline. He further testified that in the two days following the discipline, the decedent seemed to be suffering from the flu, but by Sunday was up and walking and was in apparent good health until one week following the beating, when the decedent became sick with nausea and an upset stomach. These symptoms continued for two days, when the decedent died.

As a result of the autopsy, one Dr. Clark testified that the bruises were the result of a trauma and that the decedent was in a state of continuous traumatization because he was trying to walk on his injured legs. Dr. Clark testified that the decedent's legs were swollen to possibly twice their normal size. He further testified that the actual cause of death was acute pulmonary edema, resulting from the aspiration of stomach contents. The aspiration caused a laryngeal spasm, causing the decedent to suffocate on his own vomit. Although pulmonary edema was the direct cause of death, Dr. Clark testified that said condition usually had some underlying cause and that, while there were literally hundreds of potential underlying causes, it was his opinion that in the instant case the underlying cause was the trauma to the decedent's legs. In explaining how the trauma ultimately led to the pulmonary edema, Dr. Clark testified that the trauma to the legs produced "crush syndrome" or "blast trauma," also known as "tubular necrosis."

"Crush syndrome" is a condition caused when a part of the body has been compressed for a long period of time and then released. In such cases, there is a tremendous amount of tissue damage to the body part that has been crushed. When the compression is relieved, the tissues begin to return to their normal position, but due to the compression, gaps appear between the layers of tissues, and these areas fill up with blood and other body fluids, causing swelling. In the present case, Dr. Clark estimated that about 10 to 15 percent of the decedent's entire body fluids were contained in the legs, adding an additional ten pounds in weight to the normal weight of the legs and swelling them to twice their normal size. This extra blood and body fluid decreased the amount of blood available for circulation in the rest of the body and would cause the person to become weak, faint, and pass out if he attempted to sit up or do other activities. The decedent was sitting up when he died. It was Dr. Clark's opinion that the causal connection between the trauma and death was more than medically probable and that it was "medically likely." He further testified he could say with a reasonable degree of medical certainty that the trauma to the legs was the cause of death.

Agatha Thrash, a pathologist called by the defense, offered testimony to refute that of Dr. Clark, although she did admit that pulmonary edema could have been the final cause of death and that Dr. Clark was correct in finding acute tubular necrosis. She concluded that death was probably caused by "encephalomyocarditas," which is an acute swelling of the brain and heart.

OPINION

Appellant (Thomas) claims that the prosecution failed to establish the malice element of second-degree murder. We disagree. Malice or intent to kill may be inferred from the acts of the defendant. The intent to kill may be implied where the actor actually intends to inflict great bodily harm or the natural tendency of his behavior is to cause death or great bodily harm. In the instant case defendant's savage and brutal beating of the decedent is amply sufficient to establish malice. He clearly intended to beat the victim and the natural tendency of defendant's behavior was to cause great bodily harm.

Next Thomas claims that the trial court erred by allowing evidence of the first beating to be admitted. We hold such to have been properly admitted as a like act tending to show defendant's motive, intent, the absence of mistake or accident on defendant's part.

Affirmed.

QUESTIONS

1. List all the facts relevant to proving Daniel Thomas's mental attitude.
2. According to the court, what's the mental element required for second-degree murder?
3. In your opinion, is Thomas guilty of murder? If so, what degree—first or second degree? Explain your answer.
4. If he's not guilty, should he be guilty of some lesser degree of criminal homicide? Give a preliminary answer now; then, when we get to manslaughter, you can give a more informed answer.

Intent to inflict serious bodily injury murders, like the one in *People v. Thomas*, are often called depraved heart murders and treated as a subset of second-degree murders. Let's turn to two varieties of second-degree murder, depraved heart and felony murder.

Depraved Heart Murder

Depraved heart murders are unintentional but extremely reckless murders. Recall that the reckless mental attitude consists of consciously creating a substantial risk of criminal harm, in this case death. (There are also reckless manslaughters, which are difficult to distinguish from depraved heart murders. You'll encounter some in the "Manslaughter" section.) For now, let's put the difference crudely: reckless manslaughter is killing very recklessly, and reckless murder (depraved heart murder) is killing very, very, very recklessly.

Some states have specific depraved heart second-degree murder statutes. California's provision reads, "Malice is implied, when the circumstances attending the killing show an abandoned and malignant heart" (quoted in *People v. Protopappas* 1988, 922).

Felony Murder

LO 7

> If A meaning to steal a deer in the park of B, shooteth at the deer, and by the glance of the arrow killeth a boy that is hidden in a bush, this is murder, for that the act was unlawful, although A had no intent to hurt the boy, nor knew not of him. But, if B the owner of the park has shot at his own deer, and without any ill intent had killed the boy by the glance of his arrow, this had been homicide by misadventure [mistake], and no felony. (Kadish, Schulhofer, and Steiker 2007, 436 quoting from Coke 1644)

From this hypothetical in Sir Edward Coke's *Third Institute*, the great seventeenth-century English judge and commentator on the laws of England, the modern U.S. **felony murder rule** derives. According to the doctrine, unintentional deaths that occur during the commission of another felony are murders. The court in *People v. Stamp* (1969) stated the doctrine in an armed robbery case where the owner of the business being robbed died of a heart attack during the robbery:

felony murder rule, unintentional deaths that occur during the commission of some felonies are murders

> A felon is held strictly liable for all killings committed by him or his accomplices in the course of the felony. As long as the homicide is the direct causal result of the robbery, the felony-murder rule applies whether or not the death was a natural or probable consequence of the robbery. (603)

In other words, felony murder is a "sweeping doctrine holding felons strictly liable for any death resulting from any felony" (Binder 2004, 60), with a long history stretching back more than three hundred years. In this sweeping rule, all the prosecution has to do is prove two elements: (1) the commission of the predicate or underlying felony, such as the robbery in *Stamp*, and (2) a death during the commission of the other felony. (See the Elements of Felony Murder illustration on the next page.)

Criminal law teachers, scholars, lawyers, and courts have accepted—but hotly criticized—the sweeping rule known as the default felony murder rule. Thanks to Professor Guyora Binder's (2004) painstaking research, we now know that despite Lord Coke's rule that accidental deaths resulting from unlawful acts were murders, "English common law had no felony murder rule at the time of the American Revolution." And, if Lord Coke was stating a general rule of law, it was "emphatically rejected by English courts and commentators" (201).

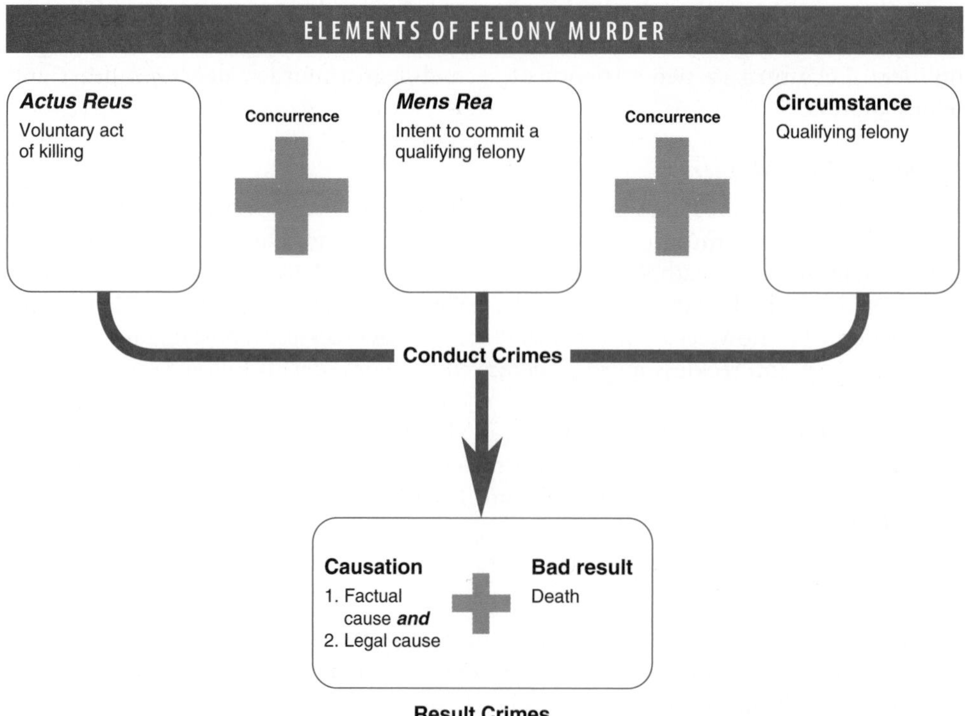

In the United States, less strict felony murder statutes were common during the nineteenth century. In the "great bulk" of state statutes, and the "great bulk" of court cases, "felony murder liability was predicated on the dangerous felonies of robbery, burglary, rape, arson, or murder." In Professor Binder's report of his analysis of the cases:

> Apart from one case predicated on a bungled suicide and four cases predicated on putatively consensual abortions, none of the known felony murders punished in nineteenth-century America could plausibly be described as accidental. In almost all of these cases, death resulted from the deliberate infliction of violence. In a few cases defendants knowingly imposed a great risk of death on their victims in pursuit of their criminal ends. In short, the felony murder rules put into practice in nineteenth-century America had requirements of culpability built into the requisite felonies. (202)

The same holds true today in most jurisdictions (Binder 2000, 770). The law varies widely, due mainly to efforts to limit the rule in one of the following ways:

1. Limits the crimes the rule applies to
2. Strict interpretation of the cause of death
3. Limit on the time period that commission of the predicate crime includes
4. Underlying crime has to be independent of the death (LaFave 2003, 744)

Let's look at each.

Crimes the rule applies to Many states limit the rule to felonies committed, or *attempted*, that are inherently dangerous to human life. Others limit the rules to a short list of the common law felonies, including rape, sodomy, robbery, burglary, arson, mayhem, and larceny. Still others include only felonies *malum in se* (Chapter 1).

Statutes take two approaches to the "inherently dangerous to human life" limit. Under one approach, followed by a minority of the states, the question is whether the facts and circumstances of the particular case create a foreseeable danger to human life. For example, although false imprisonment (detention without victim's consent) isn't inherently dangerous, death was considered foreseeable in *State v. Harrison* (1977).

Frank Harrison and his friend Emmett Cunejo were driving in their car with guns and ammunition to go prairie dog hunting. They stopped to pick up Susan Brown walking along the road. They picked her up and kept her in the car against her will. Cunejo fired the gun, pulled the trigger thinking the gun was unloaded. It was loaded, and the bullets hit Brown in the head, killing her instantly. He was charged and convicted of felony murder, the predicate felony being false imprisonment. In upholding the conviction, the court wrote that to qualify for felony murder the false imprisonment "must be inherently dangerous or committed under circumstances that are inherently dangerous." It was up to the jury to decide whether those circumstances were inherently dangerous (1324).

The other approach limits the rule to inherently dangerous predicate crimes. Under this approach the elements of the crime in the abstract determine whether the rule applies. So when a chiropractor convinced an eight-year-old girl's Christian Science parents that he could cure her eye cancer without surgery and she died, he was acquitted because the underlying felony—grand theft—wasn't inherently dangerous.

CASE

In* People v. Phillips *(1966), our felony murder case excerpt, the California Court of Appeals decided that grand theft isn't an inherently dangerous felony.

Is grand theft an underlying felony for felony murder?

People v. Phillips

414 P.2d 353 (Cal.App. 1966)

HISTORY

Marvin Phillips, Defendant, was convicted in the Superior Court, Los Angeles County, of second-degree murder in connection with the death from cancer of one of his patients. He appealed. The California Supreme Court reversed.

TOBRINER, J.

We reverse solely on the ground that the trial court erred in giving a felony murder instruction.

Linda Epping died on December 29, 1961, at the age of eight, from a rare and fast-growing form of eye cancer. Linda's mother first observed a swelling over the girl's left eye in June of that year. The doctor whom she consulted recommended that Linda be taken to Dr. Straatsma, an ophthalmologist at the UCLA Medical Center. On July 10th Dr. Straatsma first saw Linda; on July 17th the girl, suffering great pain, was admitted to the center. Dr. Straatsma performed an exploratory operation and the resulting biopsy established the nature of the child's affliction.

Dr. Straatsma advised Linda's parents that her only hope for survival lay in immediate surgical removal of the affected eye. The Eppings were loath to permit such surgery, but on the morning of July 21st Mr. Epping called the hospital and gave his oral consent. The Eppings arrived at the hospital that afternoon to consult with the surgeon. While waiting they encountered a Mrs. Eaton who told them that Phillips had cured her son of a brain tumor without surgery.

Mrs. Epping called Phillips at his office. According to the Eppings, Phillips repeatedly assured them that he could cure Linda without surgery. They testified that Phillips urged them to take Linda out of the hospital, claiming that the hospital was "an experimental place," that the doctors there would use Linda as "a human guinea pig" and would relieve the Eppings of their money as well.

(continues)

(continued)

The Eppings testified that in reliance upon Phillips's statements they took Linda out of the hospital and placed her under Phillips's care. They stated that if Phillips had not represented to them that he could cure the child without surgery and that the UCLA doctors were only interested in experimentation, they would have proceeded with the scheduled operation. The prosecution introduced medical testimony which tended to prove that if Linda had undergone surgery on July 21st her life would have been prolonged or she would have been completely cured.

Phillips treated Linda from July 22 to August 12, 1961. He charged an advance fee of $500 for three months' care as well as a sum exceeding $200 for pills and medicines. On August 13th Linda's condition had not improved; the Eppings dismissed Phillips.

Later the Eppings sought to cure Linda by means of a Mexican herbal drug known as yerba mansa and, about the 1st of September, they placed her under the care of the Christian Science movement. They did not take her back to the hospital for treatment.

Phillips testified that he knew that he could not cure cancer, that he did not represent to the Eppings that he could do so, that he urged them to return Linda to the hospital and that he agreed to treat her only when it became clear that the Eppings would never consent to surgery. He further testified that in administering treatment he sought to build up Linda's general health and so prolong her life. He insisted that he had never purported to "treat" cancer as such, but only to give "supportive" care to the body as a whole. He variously described his purpose as being "to build up her resistance," "assisting the body to overcome its own deficiencies" and "supporting the body defenses."

OPINION

As we have noted, the trial court gave an instruction on felony murder; we point out that, although Phillips could, of course, be prosecuted for grand theft, such a crime, not an inherently dangerous felony, does not support an instruction on felony murder. The giving of that instruction caused Phillips prejudice and compels reversal. Initially, however, we dispose of Phillips's argument that the prosecution failed to establish such causal relationship between Phillips's conduct and the death as is requisite to his criminal responsibility.

Legal Cause

We cannot accept Phillips's contention that his conduct did not proximately cause Linda's death. Phillips's argument rests upon either of two unsupportable propositions: (1) that the testimony failed as a matter of law to establish a causal relationship between the absence of surgery on July 21st and any shortening of Linda's life; (2) that the conduct of Linda's parents subsequent to Phillips's dismissal constituted an "independent intervening force" between the misrepresentation and Linda's death.

The fact that Phillips represented that he could cure Linda without surgery and that such representation caused the Eppings to remove Linda from the hospital finds ample substantiation in the record. The medical evidence likewise supports the jury's conclusion that the cancellation of the operation had the effect of shortening the child's life. Dr. Straatsma testified with "reasonable medical certainty" that the performance of the operation on July 21st would have extended Linda's life by a minimum of two months. He also gave his opinion that surgery on that date could have effected a complete cure.

The showing that the length of Linda's life had thus been limited sufficed for this aspect of the prosecution's case; no burden rested upon the prosecution to prove that the operation would have cured the disease. Murder is never more than the shortening of life; if Phillips's culpable act has significantly decreased the span of a human life, the law will not hear him say that his victim would thereafter have died in any event. The jury could properly have found that Phllips's conduct proximately caused Linda's death.

The Instruction on Second-Degree Felony Murder

Phillips challenges the propriety of the trial court's instructions to the jury. . . .

> (3) If the killing is done in the perpetration or attempt to perpetrate a felony such as Grand Theft. If a death occurs in the perpetration of a course of conduct amounting to Grand Theft, which course of conduct is a proximate cause of the unlawful killing of a human being, such course of conduct constitutes murder in the second degree, even though the death was not intended.

The third part of this instruction rests upon the felony murder rule and reflects the prosecution's theory that Phillips's conduct amounted to grand theft by false pretenses in violation of Penal Code section 484. The felony murder instruction given here was erroneous in that such a charge can properly be grounded only upon a felony "inherently dangerous to life," and grand theft is not such a crime. . . .

Despite Phillips's contention that the Penal Code does not expressly set forth any provision for second-degree felony murder and that, therefore, we should not follow any such doctrine here, the concept lies imbedded in our law. We have held, however, that only such felonies as are in themselves "inherently dangerous to human life" can support the application of the felony murder rule. We have ruled that in assessing such peril to human life inherent in any given felony we look to the elements of the felony in the abstract, not the particular "facts" of the case.

No case to our knowledge in any jurisdiction has held that because death results from a course of conduct involving a felonious perpetration of a fraud, the felony murder doctrine can be invoked. The felony murder instruction should not, then, have been given.

The judgment is reversed.

QUESTIONS

1. List all the facts and circumstances relevant to decide whether Dr. Phillips was guilty of felony murder.
2. Summarize the court's arguments for concluding that Dr. Phillips's conduct caused the victim's death.
3. Summarize the court's arguments for adopting the "inherently dangerous felony" rule.
4. Summarize the court's arguments supporting its conclusion that the "inherently dangerous" rule doesn't apply to the facts and circumstances in this case.
5. Do you agree with the court's decision? Support your answer.

Figure 9.2 cites cases that have been held inherently dangerous to life and those held not to be inherently dangerous to life.

FIGURE 9.2

INHERENTLY DANGEROUS TO LIFE IN THE ABSTRACT FELONIES

Felonies that have been held inherently dangerous to life include:

- Shooting at an inhabited dwelling (*People v. Hansen*, 885 P.2d 1022 [1994])
- Poisoning with intent to injure (*People v. Mattison*, 481 P.2d 193 [1971])
- Arson of a motor vehicle (*People v. Nichols*, 474 P.2d 6733 [1970])
- Grossly negligent discharge of a firearm (*People v. Clem*, 78 Cal.App.4th 346 [2000])
- Manufacturing methamphetamine (*People v. James*, 62 Cal.App.4th 244 [1998])
- Kidnapping (*People v. Greenberger*, 58 Cal.App.4th 298, 377, 68 Cal.Rptr.2d 61 [1997]); (*People v. Pearch*, 229 Cal.App.3d 1282, 1299, 280 Cal.Rptr. 584 [1991])
- Reckless or malicious possession of a destructive device (*People v. Morse*, 2 Cal.App.4th 620 [1992])

Felonies that have been held *not* inherently dangerous to life in the abstract include:

- Practicing medicine without a license under conditions creating a risk of great bodily harm, serious physical or mental illness, or death (*People v. Burroughs*, 678 P.2d 894 [1984])
- False imprisonment by violence, menace, fraud, or deceit (*People v. Henderson*, 560 P.2d 1180 [1977])
- Possession of a concealable firearm by a convicted felon (*People v. Satchell*, 489 P.2d 1361 [1971])
- Possession of a sawed-off shotgun (*People v. Satchell*, 489 P.2d 1361 [1971])
- Escape (*People v. Lopez*, 489 P.2d 1372 [1971])
- Grand theft (*People v. Phillips*, 414 P.2d 353 [1966])
- Conspiracy to possess methedrine (*People v. Williams*, 406 P.2d 647 [1965])
- Extortion (*People v. Smith*, 62 Cal.App.4th 1233 [1998])
- Furnishing phencyclidine (*People v. Taylor*, 6 Cal.App.4th 1084 [1992])
- Child endangerment or abuse (*People v. Lee*, 234 Cal.App.3d 1214 [1991])

How do we justify substituting the *mens rea* of lesser offenses for the *mens rea* of murder? The lesser offense accompanying the felony has its own punishment. How does that lesser offense add to the "criminality of the killing (as by making an otherwise noncriminal [accidental] killing criminal), or to the grade of the criminal killing (as by making murder what otherwise would be manslaughter)"? (Kadish, Schulhofer, and Steiker 2007, 439).

Three reasons say supporters of the felony murder rule:

1. It encourages felons to "exercise maximum care during felonies.
2. It "prompts potential felons to refrain from committing felonies in the first place."
3. "It warns prospective felons that they will not be able to hide behind false claims of accident or mere negligence." (Tomkovicz 1994,1454)

The problem, says Professor Tomkovicz, is that the rule rests on "unproven and highly questionable assumptions." Why? Because the number of killings during felonies is "relatively low." Adding a "small risk" of punishment for these few killings is "probably not a major influence on" these would-be killers' behavior. And a "good number" of those whom the rule somehow affects "probably" wouldn't have killed anyway (1456).

Tomkovicz concedes that "it would be difficult, if not impossible to prove" that the rule doesn't save considerable numbers of lives every year:

> Nonetheless, nonetheless, in a world in which the evidence is uncertain (or nonexistent) and in which it seems unlikely that felons actually hear the rules deterrent message in the ways that courts presume that they do, common sense would suggest putting the burden of proof upon those who contend that deterrent gains are sufficient to outweigh the infringement of our fundamental philosophy of fault and punishment. (1456–57)

Professor George Fletcher (1981) criticizes the "unrefined ways of thinking about criminal responsibility" that underlie the rule: "That someone who engages in a felony lowers the threshold of moral responsibility for the resulting death. If there is a principle behind this way of thinking, it is that a wrongdoer must run the risk that things will turn out worse than she expects" (426). This thinking "violates a basic principle of just punishment. Punishment must be proportional to wrongdoing."

> When the felony-murder rule converts an accidental death into first-degree murder, then punishment is rendered disproportionate to the wrong for which the offender is personally responsible. The principle that the wrongdoer must run the risk explicitly obscures the question of actual responsibility for the harmful result. (427–28).

The attacks on the justice of the rule and the lack of empirical research demonstrating that the rule deters dangerous felons and reduces the number of deaths during the commission of felonies probably explain why four states—Ohio, Hawaii, Michigan, and Kentucky—have abolished felony murder—and why most others have restricted felony murder to deaths that were foreseeable during the commission of the underlying felony.

LO 8

CORPORATION MURDER

Can corporations commit murder? Yes, according to a few prosecutors who've prosecuted corporations for murder (Cullen, Maakestad, and Cavender 1987). Probably the most publicized corporate murder case involved the deaths of three young women who were killed on an Indiana highway in 1978 when their Ford Pinto exploded after being struck from behind by another vehicle.

The explosion followed several other similar incidents involving Pintos that led to grisly deaths. Published evidence revealed that Ford might have known that the Pinto gas tanks weren't safe but took the risk that they wouldn't explode and injure or kill anyone. Following the three young women's deaths, the state of Indiana indicted Ford Motor Company for reckless homicide, charging that Ford had recklessly authorized, approved, designed, and manufactured the Pinto and allowed the car to remain in use with defectively designed fuel tanks. These tanks, the indictment charged, killed the three young women in Indiana. For a number of reasons not related directly to whether corporations can commit murder, the case was later dismissed.

In another case that drew wide public attention during the 1980s, Autumn Hills Convalescent Centers, a corporation that operated nursing homes, went on trial for charges that it had murdered an eighty-seven-year-old woman by neglect. David Marks, a Texas assistant attorney general, said, "From the first day until her last breath, she was unattended to and allowed to lie day and night in her own urine and waste."

The case attracted attention because of allegations that as many as sixty elderly people had died from substandard care at the Autumn Hills nursing home near Galveston, Texas. The indictment charged that the company had failed to provide nutrients, fluids, and incontinent care for the woman, Mrs. Breed, and neglected to turn and reposition her regularly to combat bedsores. One prosecution witness testified that Mrs. Breed's bed was wet constantly and the staff seldom cleaned her. The corporation defended against the charges, claiming that Mrs. Breed had died from colon cancer, not improper care (Reinhold 1985, 17).

Most state criminal codes apply to corporate criminal homicide in the same way that they apply to other crimes committed for the corporation's benefit. Specifically, both corporations and high corporate officers acting within the scope of their authority and for the benefit of a corporation can commit murder. In practice, however, prosecutors rarely charge corporations or their officers with criminal homicide, and convictions rarely follow.

The reluctance to prosecute corporations for murder, or for any homicide requiring the intent to kill or inflict serious bodily injury, is due largely to the hesitation to view corporations as persons. Although, theoretically, the law clearly makes that possible, in practice, prosecutors and courts have drawn the line at involuntary manslaughter, a crime whose *mens rea* is negligence and occasionally recklessness.

As for corporate executives, the reluctance to prosecute stems from vicarious liability and the questions it raises about culpability (see Chapter 4). It has been difficult to attribute deaths linked with corporate benefit to corporate officers who were in charge generally but didn't order or authorize a killing, didn't know about it, or even didn't want it to happen.

Only in outrageous cases that receive widespread public attention, such as the Pinto and nursing home cases, do prosecutors risk acquittal by trying corporations and their officers for criminal homicide. In these cases, prosecutors aren't hoping to win the case in traditional terms, meaning to secure convictions. Business law professor William J. Maakestad says, "At this point, success of this type of corporate criminal prosecution is defined by establishing the legitimacy of the case. If you can get the case to trial, you have really achieved success" (Lewin 1985, D2). Of course, you can't send a corporation to jail, but you can punish its officers as representatives of the corporation. Don't confuse this with punishing corporate officers for official criminal behavior. Here, they go to jail for their individual criminal conduct—and for the corporation's.

CASE

In **People v. O'Neil** *(1990), our next case excerpt, a jury convicted corporate and individual officers of murder, but the appellate court reversed their convictions.*

Did they "murder" their employee?

People v. O'Neil

550 N.E.2d 1090 (Ill.App. 1990)

HISTORY

Following a joint *bench trial* [trial by a judge without a jury], Steven O'Neil, Charles Kirschbaum, and Daniel Rodriguez, agents of Film Recovery Systems, Inc. (Film Recovery), were convicted of the murder of Stefan Golab, a Film Recovery employee, from cyanide poisoning stemming from conditions in Film Recovery's plant in Elk Grove Village, Illinois. Corporate defendants Film Recovery and its sister corporation Metallic Marketing Systems, Inc. (Metallic Marketing), were convicted of involuntary manslaughter in the same death.

O'Neil, Kirschbaum, and Rodriguez each received sentences of 25 years' imprisonment for murder. O'Neil and Kirschbaum were also each fined $10,000 with respect to the murder convictions. Corporate defendants Film Recovery and Metallic Marketing were each fined $10,000 with respect to the convictions for involuntary manslaughter.

The defendants appealed, and the Appellate Court reversed the convictions.

LORENZ, J.

FACTS

In 1982, Film Recovery occupied premises at 1855 and 1875 Greenleaf Avenue in Elk Grove Village. Film Recovery was there engaged in the business of extracting, for resale, silver from used X-ray and photographic film. Metallic Marketing operated out of the same premises on Greenleaf Avenue and owned 50 percent of the stock of Film Recovery. The recovery process was performed at Film Recovery's plant located at the 1855 address and involved "chipping" the film product and soaking the granulated pieces in large open bubbling vats containing a solution of water and sodium cyanide. The cyanide solution caused silver contained in the film to be released. A continuous flow system pumped the silver-laden solution into polyurethane tanks, which contained electrically charged stainless steel plates to which the separated silver adhered. The plates were removed from the tanks to another room where the accumulated silver was scraped off. The remaining solution was pumped out of the tanks and the granulated film, devoid of silver, shoveled out.

On the morning of February 10, 1983, shortly after he disconnected a pump on one of the tanks and began to stir the contents of the tank with a rake, Stefan Golab became dizzy and faint. He left the production area to go rest in the lunchroom area of the plant. Plant workers present on that day testified that Golab's body had trembled and he had foamed at the mouth. Golab eventually lost consciousness and was taken outside of the plant. Paramedics summoned to the plant were unable to revive him. Golab was pronounced dead upon arrival at Alexian Brothers Hospital.

The Cook County medical examiner performed an autopsy on Golab the following day. Although the medical examiner initially indicated that Golab could have died from cardiac arrest, he reserved final determination of death pending examination of results of toxicological laboratory tests on Golab's blood and other body specimens. After receiving the toxicological report, the medical examiner determined that Golab died from acute cyanide poisoning through the inhalation of cyanide fumes in the plant air.

The defendants were subsequently indicted by a Cook County grand jury. The grand jury charged defendants O'Neil, Kirschbaum, Rodriguez, Pett, and Mackay with murder, stating that, as individuals and as officers and high managerial agents of Film Recovery, they had, on February 10, 1983, knowingly created a strong probability of Golab's death.

The indictment stated the individual defendants failed to disclose to Golab that he was working with substances containing cyanide and failed to advise him about, train him to anticipate, and provide adequate equipment to protect him from, attendant dangers involved.

The grand jury charged Film Recovery and Metallic Marketing with involuntary manslaughter stating that, through the reckless acts of their officers, directors, agents, and others, all acting within the scope of their employment, the corporate entities had, on February 10, 1983, unintentionally killed

Golab. Finally, the grand jury charged both individual and corporate defendants with reckless conduct as to 20 other Film Recovery employees based on the same conduct alleged in the murder indictment, but expanding the time of that conduct to "on or about March 1982 through March 1983."

Proceedings commenced in the circuit court in January 1985 and continued through the conclusion of trial in June of that year. In the course of the 24-day trial, evidence from 59 witnesses was presented, either directly or through stipulation of the parties. That testimony is contained in over 2,300 pages of trial transcript. The parties also presented numerous exhibits including photographs, corporate documents, and correspondence, as well as physical evidence.

On June 14, 1985, the trial judge pronounced his judgment of the defendants' guilt. The trial judge found that "the mind and mental state of a corporation is the mind and mental state of the directors, officers and high managerial personnel because they act on behalf of the corporation for both the benefit of the corporation and for themselves." Further, "If the corporation's officers, directors and high managerial personnel act within the scope of their corporate responsibilities and employment for their benefit and for the benefit of the profits of the corporation, the corporation must be held liable for what occurred in the work place." The defendants filed timely notices of appeal, the matters were consolidated for review, and arguments were had before this court in July 1987. . . .

OPINION

The Criminal Code of 1961 defines murder as follows:

> A person who kills an individual without lawful justification commits murder if, in performing the acts which cause the death: He knows that such acts create a strong probability of death or great bodily harm to that individual. (Ill.Rev.Stat.1981, ch. 38, par.9-1(a)(2).)

Involuntary manslaughter is defined as:

> A person who unintentionally kills an individual without lawful justification commits involuntary manslaughter if his acts whether lawful or unlawful which cause the death are such as are likely to cause death or great bodily harm to some individual, and he performs them recklessly. (Ill.Rev.Stat.1981, ch. 38, par. 9-3(a).)

Reckless conduct is defined as:

> A person who causes bodily harm to or endangers the bodily safety of an individual by any means, commits reckless conduct if he performs recklessly the acts which cause the harm or endanger safety, whether they otherwise are lawful or unlawful. (Ill.Rev.Stat.1981, ch. 38, par. 12-5(a).)

In Illinois, a corporation is criminally responsible for offenses "authorized, requested, commanded, or performed by the board of directors or by a high managerial agent acting within the scope of his employment." A high managerial agent is defined as "an officer of the corporation, or any other agent who has a position of comparable authority for the formulation of corporate policy or the supervision of subordinate employees in a managerial capacity" (Ill. Rev.Stat. 1981, ch. 38, par. 5-4(c)(2)). Thus, a corporation is criminally responsible whenever any of its high managerial agents possess the requisite mental state and is responsible for a criminal offense while acting within the scope of his employment.

Evidence at trial indicated Golab died after inhaling poisonous cyanide fumes while working in a plant operated by Film Recovery and its sister corporation Metallic Marketing where such fumes resulted from a process employed to remove silver from used X-ray and photographic film. The record contains substantial evidence regarding the nature of working conditions inside the plant. Testimony established that air inside the plant was foul smelling and made breathing difficult and painful. Plant workers experienced dizziness, nausea, headaches, and bouts of vomiting.

There is evidence that plant workers were not informed they were working with cyanide. Nor were they informed of the presence of, or danger of breathing, cyanide gas. Ventilation in the plant was poor. Plant workers were given neither safety instruction nor adequate protective clothing.

Finally, testimony established that defendants O'Neil, Kirschbaum, and Rodriguez were responsible for operating the plant under those conditions. For purposes of our disposition, we find further elaboration on the evidence unnecessary.

(continues)

(continued)

Moreover, although we have determined evidence in the record is not so insufficient as to bar retrial, our determination of the sufficiency of the evidence should not be in any way interpreted as a finding as to defendants' guilt that would be binding on the court on retrial.

Reversed and remanded.

QUESTIONS

1. List all the evidence for and against the corporations' and the individuals' liability for murder and involuntary manslaughter.
2. Why did the court reverse and remand the case?
3. On remand, would you find the defendants guilty of murder? Explain your answer.
4. Do you agree that it's inconsistent to find that the corporation had one state of mind and the individuals another?
5. Consider the following remarks made after the convictions in the original trial (Greenhouse 1985, 1):
   a. Following the conviction in the original trial, then attorney Richard M. Daley said the verdicts meant that employers who knowingly expose their workers to dangerous conditions leading to injury or even death can be held criminally responsible for the results of their actions.
   b. Ralph Nader, consumer advocate lawyer, said, "The public is pretty upset with dangerously defective products, bribery, toxic waste, and job hazards. The polls all show it. The verdict today will encourage other prosecutors and judges to take more seriously the need to have the criminal law catch up with corporate crime."
   c. Professor John Coffee, Columbia Law School, said, "When you threaten the principal adequately, he will monitor the behavior of his agent."
   d. A California deputy district attorney put it more bluntly: "A person facing a jail sentence is the best deterrent against wrongdoing."
   e. Joseph E. Hadley Jr., a corporate lawyer who specializes in health and safety issues, said the decision would not send shockwaves through the corporate community: "I don't think corporate America should be viewed as in the ballpark with these folks. This was a highly unusual situation, but now people see that where the egregious situation occurs, there could be a criminal remedy."
   f. Robert Stephenson, a lawyer defending another corporation, said, "I don't believe these statutes [murder and aggravated battery] were ever meant to be used in this way."
   g. Utah's governor, Scott M. Matheson, refused to extradite Michael T. McKay, a former Film Recovery vice president then living in Utah, because he was an "exemplary citizen who should not be subjected to the sensational charges in Illinois."

Which of the statements best describes what you think is proper policy regarding prosecutions of corporate executives for murder? Defend your answer.

LO 9

MANSLAUGHTER

> Manslaughter arises from the sudden heat of the passions, murder from the wickedness of the heart.
>
> (Blackstone 1769, 190)

manslaughter, an ancient common law crime created by judges, not by legislators, consisting of two crimes: voluntarily or involuntarily killing another person

Manslaughter, like murder, is an ancient common law crime created by judges, not by legislators. Manslaughter was originally one crime. Later, it became two crimes—voluntary manslaughter (intentional killing) and involuntary manslaughter (unintentional killing). Eventually, involuntary manslaughter developed, and is still developing, into various and often inconsistent and confusing types. We'll get into this later in the chapter (LaFave 2003, 793–94).

But let's start with the eighteenth-century division. According to eighteenth-century commentator Blackstone (1769):

> Manslaughter is . . . the unlawful killing of another, which may be either voluntarily upon a sudden heat, or involuntarily . . . where one had no intent to do another any personal mischief. (191–92)

Blackstone's definition is more than three centuries old, but it goes straight to *mens rea*—the heart of manslaughter, as it is in most murder classifications: "Was it intentional (voluntary) or unintentional (involuntary)?

VOLUNTARY MANSLAUGHTER

LO 9

> If upon a sudden quarrel two persons fight, and one of them kills the other, this is [voluntary] manslaughter. And, so it is, if they upon such an occasion go out and fight in a field, for this is one continued act of passion and the law pays that regard to human frailty, as not to put a hasty and a deliberate act upon the same footing with regard to guilt. So also a man be greatly provoked, as by pulling his nose, or other great indignity, and immediately kills the aggressor, though this is not excusable, since there is no absolute necessity for doing so to preserve himself, yet neither is it murder for there is no previous malice.
>
> (Blackstone 1769, 191)

voluntary manslaughter, suddenly and intentionally killing another person in the heat of anger following adequate provocation; elements include murder *actus reus, mens rea*, causation, and death

Blackstone's description of voluntary manslaughter in the late 1700s is an excellent way to begin our discussion of today's voluntary manslaughter. **Voluntary manslaughter** is about letting your anger get the best of you in the worst possible way—killing another person. The law of voluntary manslaughter (as in all criminal homicides) requires proof of the *actus reus, mens rea*, causation, and death. One additional element has to be proved: the circumstance element of *adequate provocation* (discussed next). (See the Elements of Voluntary Manslaughter illustration.)

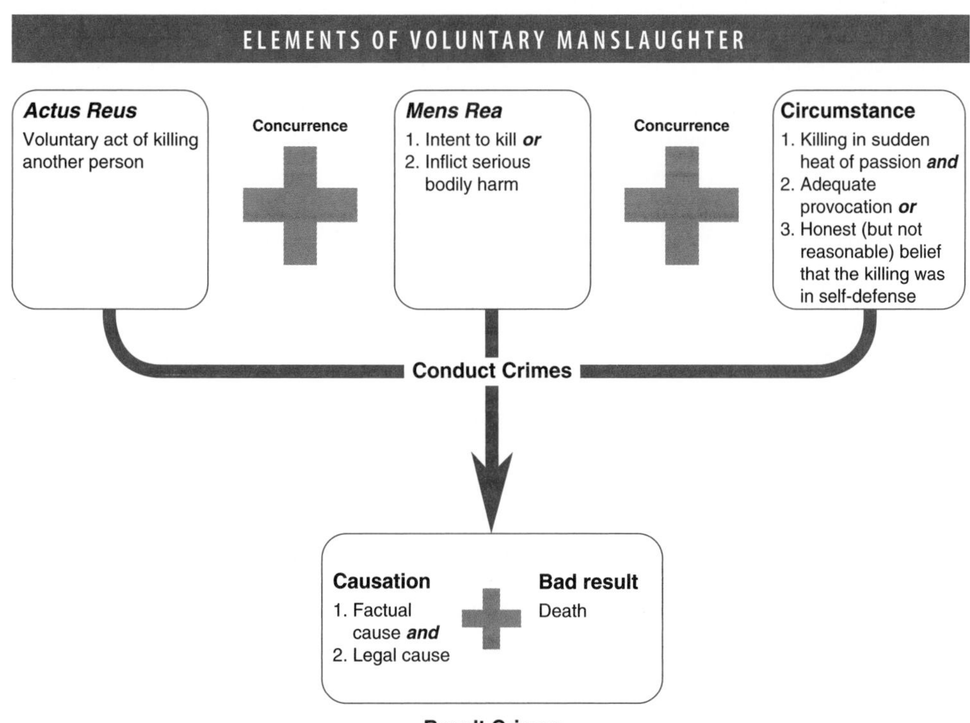

Criminal law aims to bridle passions and build self-control, but it also recognizes the frailty of human nature. The law of voluntary manslaughter takes into account both the seriousness of this felony and the reality of human frailty. So although a sudden intentional killing in anger is a very serious felony, it's not the most serious; that's reserved for murder. Let's be clear that the law of voluntary manslaughter doesn't reward individuals who give in to their rages by letting them walk; it punishes them severely, but it punishes them less than they'd get for murder. Why? Because it recognizes the effect that adequate provocation can have. But what is adequate provocation, the circumstance element of voluntary manslaughter?

LO 10

Adequate Provocation

Voluntary manslaughter has one element not present in murder, and one we haven't discussed—namely, the circumstance element of adequate provocation. In voluntary manslaughter, adequate provocation is the trigger that sets off the sudden killing of another person.

Not everyone who is provoked to fly into a rage and suddenly kills has committed voluntary manslaughter instead of murder. The law requires *adequate* provocation. Adequate provocation has three elements:

adequate provocation, the requirement that the provocation for killing in anger has to be something the law recognizes, the defendant himself had to be provoked, and that a reasonable person would have been provoked

1. It has to be a provocation that the law recognizes.
2. The defendant himself has to be provoked (subjective provocation)
3. The provocation has to be one that would provoke a reasonable person under the circumstances in this case (objective provocation).

The Maryland Court of Appeals put it this way in *Dennis v. State* (1995):

> For a provocation to be "adequate," it must be "calculated to inflame the passion of a reasonable person and tend to cause *that person* to act for the moment from passion rather than reason." [emphasis added]

The Maryland Court describes one aspect of "adequacy." There is another,

> which flows from the requirement that the passion be that of a reasonable person; the provocation must be one the law is prepared to recognize as minimally sufficient, in proper circumstances, to overcome the restraint normally expected from reasonable persons. There are many "slings and arrows of outrageous fortune" that people either must tolerate or find an alternative way, other than homicide, to redress. (695)

The thinking is that *reasonable* persons, however great the provocation, would never kill someone except in self-defense (Chapter 5). That's why voluntary manslaughter isn't *justifiable* homicide; it's only a lesser version of intentional murder.

Who is this "reasonable person" whose provocation we're supposed to compare the defendant's to? "Reasonable" sounds odd here. Throughout the law, reasonable person refers to "the public embodiment of rational behavior." When you think of rational behavior, the picture of a provoked killer probably doesn't come immediately to your mind's eye, does it? It's "more accurate . . . to describe . . . the [reasonable person] . . . as an 'ordinary' person . . . who sometimes, unfortunately, acts out of uncontrolled emotion rather than reason" (Dressler 2009, 538). English and U.S. courts have described the reasonable person variously, in phrases like a person of "average disposition, i.e. not exceptionally belligerent; sober at the time of provocation; and of normal mental capacity" (539).

The common law (and most laws today) recognized four adequate provocations:

1. **MUTUAL COMBAT (FIGHTING).** Only serious fights qualify as adequate provocation; scuffles don't. Some batteries—but not all offensive touching (see Chapter 10)—are adequate provocation. Being pistol whipped on the head, being struck hard in the face by fists, or enduring "staggering" body blows qualify. Being slapped or shoved doesn't.
2. **ASSAULT AND BATTERY.** (Chapter 10). Assault without body contact is sometimes adequate provocation. In *Beasley v. State* (1886), a man shot at Beasley and missed him. Beasley was so enraged he shot his attacker in the back as the assailant ran away. The court ruled the shot in the back wasn't justified as self-defense, but the initial incident was provocative enough to reduce murder to manslaughter.

   Insulting gestures by themselves aren't adequate provocation, but if they indicate an intent to attack with deadly force, they are. So "flipping someone the bird" isn't adequate provocation, but waving a gun around in a threatening manner can be.
3. **TRESPASS.** (Chapter 11). Trespassing is adequate provocation only if the trespassers invade a home and threaten someone with death.
4. **ADULTERY.** Almost everywhere spouses who catch their spouse in an act of adultery are reasonably provoked. In most states, the law extends to spouses who reasonably believe their spouses are committing adultery, even though they don't see it happening, or it's not true.

"Sudden Heat of Passion" with No "Cooling Off" Period

Voluntary manslaughter requires killing in the "sudden heat of passion" with no "cooling off" period (Perkins and Boyce 1982, 95–96). Whether the actual time between the provocation and the killing—seconds, hours, or even days—qualifies as the "sudden heat of passion" depends upon the facts of the individual case. Courts apply an objective test of cooling-off time; namely, would a reasonable person under the same circumstances have had time to cool off? If defendants have a reasonable time for their murderous rages to subside, the law views their killings as murders even if they take place immediately following the provocations.

objective test of cooling-off time, requires that a reasonable person under the same circumstances would have had time to cool off

The court applied the objective test in a famous old case, *State v. Flory* (1929). E. T. Ostrum (age sixty-five to seventy) stayed with his daughter Daisy Flory (age twenty-one) and her husband Charles Flory (age twenty-two), at their farm in Montana, while Flory left to go trapping. (Flory was a farmer in summer and a trapper in winter). When Flory returned just before Christmas, Ostrum went back to his own farm in Campbell County, Wyoming, about fifty miles from Charles and Daisy's farm. After Ostrum left, Daisy told Charles that her father had raped her. Charles left their farm with his gun, which he always carried with him, and walked all day, staying over night at a Mr. Hudsonpillar's house. The next morning he walked the rest of the way, arriving at his father-in-law's at about 11 A.M. They exchanged angry words, and Flory shot Ostrum, who was unarmed. According to Charles, "I was mad on the way over [from Mr. Hudsonpillar's] but not any madder than anyone else under the circumstances" (460).

A jury convicted Charles of second-degree murder. He appealed. The appeals court ruled that although the incest and rape couldn't justify the killing, they could be used to reduce Charles Flory's crime to voluntary manslaughter because a jury could find that Flory's passion hadn't reasonably cooled. The court said that the heinous combination of incest and rape was more than enough to keep a reasonable person in a murderous rage for at least several days (464).

Causation

To prove voluntary manslaughter, the prosecution has to prove that the provocation caused the passion and the killing. Suppose Sonny intends to kill his wife Carly because she lied to him. He goes to her bedroom, finds her in bed with his worst enemy, and shoots her to death. Is it voluntary manslaughter or murder? It's murder, because Carly's lie, not her adultery, provoked Sonny to kill her.

Let's look more closely at causation, or triggers, the law considers adequate provocation. Is provocation by words enough? How about provocation by spouses and other intimates? Should nonviolent advances by a gay person or "gay panic" by the killer be viewed as adequate provocation? We'll examine each of these questions next.

"words can never provoke" rule, the rule that words are never adequate provocation to reduce murder to manslaughter

PROVOCATION BY WORDS It's often said that words are never adequate provocation. That was true when the **"words can never provoke" rule** was created in the days of the common law. It's still the rule in most states but not everywhere. For example, the Minnesota Criminal Code provides:

> *§609.20 Manslaughter in the First Degree*
>
> Whoever does any of the following is guilty of manslaughter in the first degree and may be sentenced to imprisonment for not more than 15 years or to payment of a fine of not more than $30,000, or both: intentionally causes the death of another person in the heat of passion provoked by such words or acts of another as would provoke a person of ordinary self-control under like circumstances, provided that the crying of a child does not constitute provocation.

"last-straw" rule (also called the **"long smoldering"** or **"slow burn" rule**), adequate provocation defined as "a smoldering resentment or pent-up rage resulting from earlier insults or humiliating events culminating in a triggering event that, by itself, might be insufficient to provoke the deadly act"

extreme mental or emotional disturbance manslaughter, a homicide committed under the influence of extreme mental or emotional disturbance for which there is reasonable explanation or excuse. The reasonableness of such explanation or excuse shall be determined from the viewpoint of the person in the actor's situation under the circumstances as he believes them to be

There are more signs besides the Minnesota provision that the bright-line rule "words can never provoke" isn't as bright as it used to be. Some courts have adopted a more flexible approach that "words can sometimes amount to adequate provocation" (LaFave 2003a, 780–81). California and Pennsylvania courts have adopted the **"last-straw" rule** (also called the **"long smoldering"** or **"slow burn" rule**) of adequate provocation. It's defined as "a smoldering resentment or pent-up rage resulting from earlier insults or humiliating events culminating in a triggering event that, by itself, might be insufficient to provoke the deadly act" (*Dennis v. State* 1995, 689).

Probably the most significant development is the adoption by several states of the Model Penal Code (MPC) **extreme mental or emotional disturbance manslaughter** provision:

> *Section 210.3 Manslaughter*
>
> Criminal homicide constitutes manslaughter when:
>
> (a) it is committed recklessly; or
>
> (b) a homicide which would otherwise be murder is committed under the influence of extreme mental or emotional disturbance for which there is reasonable explanation or excuse. The reasonableness of such explanation or excuse shall be determined from the viewpoint of the person in the actor's situation under the circumstances as he believes them to be. (ALI 1985, Model Penal Code)

Other states (probably most) continue to follow the words-can-never-provoke rule. Maryland is one. In *Dennis v. State* (1995), for example, the Maryland Court of Appeals rejected the last-straw rule. John Patrick Dennis married his high school sweetheart Robin when she became pregnant with their child. According to Dennis, he worked hard to support his family, but they ran into money problems because of Robin's illegal drug use and spending habits. Robin moved out of their house and in with her boyfriend, Dantz. After learning that Robin and Dantz did drugs in front of their son, Dennis became really agitated. He went to confront them at Dantz's. When he got there, he saw Robin and Dantz through the window; they were hugging and maybe getting "sexual." Dennis claims to have blacked out at that point. Robin called the police, screaming that Dantz was dead (690).

Dennis was convicted of voluntary manslaughter. The trial court rejected his claim that he was adequately provoked. He appealed. The Court of Appeals affirmed, rejecting the last-straw rule, and held that "rejected taunts and verbal assaults" aren't "adequate provocation, even when taking on their humiliating and enraging character from antecedent events" (689).

Provocation by intimates According to the common law **paramour rule**, a husband who caught his wife in the act of adultery had adequate provocation to kill. (Some state statutes went even further than the common law rule; they called paramour killings justifiable homicide.) In the early days, the rule was only available to husbands. Today, it applies to both. Many cases have held that it's voluntary manslaughter for a spouse to kill the adulterous spouse, the paramour, or both, if the killing took place in the first heat of passion following the sight of the adultery.

paramour rule, the common law rule that a husband who caught his wife in the act of adultery had adequate provocation to kill

Many voluntary manslaughter cases in states that have adopted these reforms don't involve "sordid affairs and bedside confrontations." According to Professor Victoria Nourse (1997), significant numbers of cases in her empirical study of states who've adopted the MPC extreme mental or emotional disturbance manslaughter provision (quoted earlier)

> involved no sexual infidelity whatsoever, but only the desire of the killer's victim to leave a miserable relationship. Reform has permitted juries to return a manslaughter verdict in cases where the defendant claims passion because the victim left, moved the furniture out, planned a divorce, or sought a protective order.
>
> Even infidelity has been transformed under reform's gaze into something quite different from the sexual betrayal we might expect—it is the infidelity of a fiancé who danced with another, of a girlfriend who decided to date someone else, and of the divorcee found pursuing a new relationship months after the final decree. (1332–33)

CASE

Commonwealth v. Schnopps *(1983),* *our next case excerpt, involved dancing, an affair, and a spouse who wanted to leave. The court wasn't "reform" minded; it rejected the spouse's arguments of adequate provocation and upheld his conviction for first-degree murder.*

Did he commit first-degree murder?

Commonwealth v. Schnopps

459 N.E.2d 98 (Mass. 1983)

HISTORY

George Schnopps, the defendant, was convicted before the Superior Court, Berkshire County, Massachusetts, of first-degree murder of his estranged wife and of unlawfully carrying a firearm. At a retrial, the defendant, Schnopps, again was convicted of first-degree murder, and he appealed again. The Massachusetts Supreme Judicial Court affirmed.

ABRAMS, J.

FACTS

On October 13, 1979, George Schnopps fatally shot his wife of 14 years. The victim and Schnopps began having marital problems approximately six months earlier when Schnopps became suspicious that his wife was seeing another man. Schnopps and his wife argued during this period over his suspicion that she had a relationship with a particular man, whom Schnopps regarded as a "bum." On a few occasions

(continues)

(continued)
Schnopps threatened to harm his wife with scissors, with a knife, with a shotgun, and with a plastic pistol.

A few days prior to the slaying, Schnopps threatened to make his wife suffer as "she had never suffered before." However, there is no evidence that Schnopps physically harmed the victim prior to October 13.

On October 12, 1979, while at work, Schnopps asked a coworker to buy him a gun. He told the coworker he had been receiving threatening telephone calls. After work, Schnopps and the coworker went to Pownal, Vermont, where the coworker purchased a .22-caliber pistol and a box of ammunition for the defendant. Schnopps purchased a starter pistol to scare the caller if there was an attempted break-in. Schnopps stated he wanted to protect himself and his son, who had moved back with him.

Schnopps and his coworker had some drinks at a Vermont bar. The coworker instructed Schnopps in the use of the .22-caliber pistol. Schnopps paid his coworker for the gun and the ammunition. While at the bar Schnopps told the coworker that he was "mad enough to kill." The coworker asked Schnopps "if he was going to get in any trouble with the gun." Schnopps replied that "a bullet was too good for her, he would choke her to death." Schnopps testified that his wife had left him three weeks prior to the slaying. He claims that he first became aware of problems in his 14-year marriage at a point about six months before the slaying. According to Schnopps, on that occasion he took his wife to a club to dance, and she spent the evening dancing with a coworker.

On arriving home, Schnopps and his wife argued over her conduct. She told him that she no longer loved him and that she wanted a divorce. Schnopps became very upset. He admitted that he took out his shotgun during the course of this argument, but he denied that he intended to use it.

During the next few months, Schnopps argued frequently with his wife. Schnopps accused her of seeing another man, but she steadfastly denied the accusations. On more than one occasion Schnopps threatened his wife with physical harm. He testified he never intended to hurt his wife but only wanted to scare her so that she would end the relationship with her coworker.

One day in September 1979, Schnopps became aware that the suspected boyfriend used a "signal" in telephoning Schnopps' wife. Schnopps used the signal, and his wife answered the phone with "Hi, Lover." She hung up immediately when she recognized Schnopps' voice. That afternoon she did not return home. Later that evening, she informed Schnopps by telephone that she had moved to her mother's house and that she had the children with her. On that day she moved to her mother's home and took their three children with her. (The children were two daughters, age thirteen and age four, and a son, age eleven.)

On October 6, the son returned to his father's home. She told Schnopps she would not return to their home. Thereafter she "froze me out" and would not talk to him. During this period, Schnopps spoke with a lawyer about a divorce and was told that he had a good chance of getting custody of the children due to his wife's "desertion and adultery."

On the day of the slaying, Schnopps told a neighbor he was going to call his wife and have her come down to pick up some things. He said he was thinking of letting his wife have the apartment. This was the first time Schnopps indicated he might leave the apartment. He asked the neighbor to keep the youngest child with her if his wife brought her so he could talk with his wife.

Schnopps told his wife that he wanted his children at home and that he wanted the family to remain intact. Schnopps cried during the conversation, and begged his wife to let the children live with him and to keep their family together.

His wife replied, "No, I am going to court, you are going to give me all the furniture, you are going to have to get the Hell out of here, you won't have nothing." Then, pointing to her crotch, she said, "You will never touch this again, because I have got something bigger and better for it."

Schnopps said that these words "cracked" him. He explained that everything went "around" in his head, that he saw "stars." He went "toward the guns in the dining room." He asked his wife, "Why don't you try" (to salvage the marriage). He told her, "I have nothing more to live for," but she replied, "Never, I am never coming back to you."

The victim jumped up to leave and Schnopps shot her. He was seated at that time. He told her she would never love anyone else. After shooting the victim, Schnopps said, "I want to go with you," and he shot himself.

Shortly before 3:00 P.M., Schnopps called a neighbor and said he had shot his wife and also had tried to kill himself. Schnopps told the first person to arrive at his apartment that he shot his wife "because of what she had done to him."

Neighbors notified the police of the slaying. On their arrival, Schnopps asked an officer to check to see if his wife had died. The officer told him that she had, and he replied, "Good." A police officer took Schnopps to a hospital for treatment of his wounds. The officer had known Schnopps for 29 years. Schnopps said to the officer that he would not hurt a fly. The officer advised Schnopps not to say anything until he spoke with a lawyer.

Schnopps then said, "The devil made me do it." The officer repeated his warning at least three times. Schnopps said that he "loved his wife and his children." He added, "Just between you and I, I did it because she was cheating on me." The victim died of three gunshot wounds to the heart and lungs. Ballistic evidence indicated that the gun was fired within two to four feet of the victim. The evidence also indicated that one shot had been fired while the victim was on the floor.

The defense offered evidence from friends and coworkers who noticed a deterioration in Schnopps' physical and emotional health after the victim had left Schnopps. Schnopps wept at work and at home; he did not eat or sleep well; he was distracted and agitated. On two occasions, he was taken home early by supervisors because of emotional upset and agitation. He was drinking.

Schnopps was diagnosed at a local hospital as suffering from a "severe anxiety state." He was given Valium. Schnopps claimed he was receiving threatening telephone calls. Schnopps and the Commonwealth each offered expert testimony on the issue of criminal responsibility.

Schnopps' expert claimed Schnopps was suffering from a "major affective disorder, a major depression," a "psychotic condition," at the time of the slaying. The expert was of the opinion Schnopps was not criminally responsible.

The Commonwealth's expert claimed that Schnopps' depression was a grief reaction, a reaction generally associated with death. The expert was of the opinion Schnopps was grieving over the breakup of his marriage, but that he was criminally responsible.

The judge instructed the jurors on every possible verdict available on the evidence. The jurors were told they could return a verdict of murder in the first degree on the ground of deliberately premeditated malice aforethought; murder in the second degree; manslaughter; not guilty by reason of insanity; or not guilty.

OPINION

On appeal, Schnopps does not now quarrel with that range of possible verdicts nor with the instruction which the trial court gave to the jury. Nor does Schnopps now dispute that there may be some view of some of the evidence which might support the verdict returned in this matter.

Rather, Schnopps claims that his case is "not of the nature that judges and juries, in weighing evidence, ordinarily equate with murder in the first degree." Schnopps therefore concludes that this is an appropriate case in which to exercise our power under G.L. c. 278, § 33E. We do not agree.

Pursuant to G.L. c. 278, § 33E, we consider whether the verdict of murder in the first degree was against the weight of the evidence, considered in a large or nontechnical sense. Our power under § 33E is to be used with restraint.

Moreover, "We do not sit as a second jury to pass anew on the question of Schnopps's guilt." Schnopps argues that the evidence as a whole demonstrates that his wife was the emotional aggressor, and that her conduct shattered him and destroyed him as a husband and a father. Schnopps points to the fact that he was not a hoodlum or gangster, that he had no prior criminal record, and that he had a "good relationship" with his wife prior to the last six months of their marriage. Schnopps concludes these factors should be sufficient to entitle him to a new trial or the entry of a verdict of a lesser degree of guilt.

The Commonwealth argues that the evidence is more than ample to sustain the verdict. The Commonwealth points out that at the time of the killing there was not a good relationship between the parties; that Schnopps had threatened to harm his wife physically on several occasions; and that he had threatened to kill his wife. Schnopps obtained a gun and ammunition the day before the killing.

Schnopps arranged to have his younger child cared for by a neighbor when his wife came to see him. The jury could have found that Schnopps lured his wife to the apartment by suggesting that he might leave and let her live in it with the children. The evidence permits a finding that the killing

(continues)

(continued)
occurred within a few minutes of the victim's arrival at Schnopps's apartment and before she had time to take off her jacket.

From the facts, the jury could infer that Schnopps had planned to kill his wife on October 13, and that the killing was not the spontaneous result of the quarrel but was the result of a deliberately premeditated plan to murder his wife almost as soon as she arrived.

Ballistic evidence indicated that as the victim was lying on the floor, a third bullet was fired into her. From the number of wounds, the type of weapon used, as well as the effort made to procure the weapon, the jurors could find that Schnopps had "a conscious and fixed purpose to kill continuing for a length of time."

If conflicting inferences are possible, "it is for the jury to determine where the truth lies." There was ample evidence which suggested the jurors' conclusion that Schnopps acted with deliberately premeditated malice aforethought.

On appeal, Schnopps complains that the prosecutor's summation, which stressed that premeditated murder requires "a thought and an act," could have confused the jurors by suggesting that if "at any time earlier Schnopps merely thought about killing that person," that was sufficient to constitute deliberately "premeditated malice aforethought."

We do not read the prosecutor's argument as suggesting that conclusion. The prosecutor focused on the Commonwealth's evidence of deliberately premeditated malice aforethought throughout his argument. There was no error.

In any event, the argument, read as a whole, does not create a "substantial likelihood of a miscarriage of justice." Schnopps's domestic difficulties were fully explored before the jury. The jurors rejected Schnopps's claim that his domestic difficulties were an adequate ground to return a verdict of a lesser degree of guilt. The degree of guilt, of course, is a jury determination. The evidence supports a conclusion that Schnopps, angered by his wife's conduct, shot her with deliberately premeditated malice aforethought.

The jurors were in the best position to determine whether the domestic difficulties were so egregious as to require a verdict of a lesser degree of guilt. We conclude, on review of the record as a whole, that there is no reason for us to order a new trial or direct the entry of a lesser verdict.

Judgment affirmed.

QUESTIONS

1. If you were a juror, could you in good conscience say that Schnopps was adequately provoked? Explain your answer, relying on the facts in the case, the court's opinion, and the text prior to the excerpt.
2. If so, was it the adultery that provoked him or the provocative words his wife used to describe her adulterous relationship?
3. Do you think the prohibition against provocative words makes sense?
4. If you were writing a voluntary manslaughter law, state the elements of the offense as you believe they should be.

Provocation by Nonviolent Homosexual Advance (NHA)

Mike, an honors student at the local junior college, plays quarterback on the football team. Good-looking and well-liked by his classmates, Mike prides himself on being an All-American guy. One day, Mike takes a hard fall on his shoulder during football training. After practice, Mike decides to relax in the school's sauna where he finds his friend and fellow teammate Gary. Gary asks him about his shoulder. Mike tells him that it's pretty sore. Gary, who is openly gay, asks if Mike wants him to massage his shoulder. Mike says that would be great.

Mike, clad only in a short white towel, lies face down on a nearby bench. Gary starts to massage Mike's shoulders and back. Mike tries to muffle a groan of pleasure. The massage feels good, almost too good. Mike starts to feel uneasy. What if another teammate comes in and sees Gary touching his body? What if this teammate tells others that he is gay? What if Gary tries to make a pass at him?

As these thoughts are racing through his mind, Mike feels Gary's hands move down to his legs, then up his thighs, underneath the small white towel. Gary starts to rub Mike's buttocks. Mike jumps up and yells, "You pervert! What the f— do you think you're doing!" Mike starts punching and kicking until Gary falls to the ground. Even though Gary is not fighting back, Mike continues to beat and stomp on him until he stops moving. Gary dies the next day. (Lee 2003, 1–2)

Most men and women—gay and straight—would justifiably get angry if someone touched their genitals without their consent. According to Professor Joshua Dressler (1995), most NHA cases that find their way into the appellate courts demonstrate that "unwanted sexual advance is a basis for justifiable indignation" (754). Professor Dressler offers the following general statements about NHA cases:

1. Indignation in response to a violation of one's sexual privacy or autonomy is justifiable.
2. Anger, one possible manifestation of such indignation, is justifiable or excusable.
3. Any resulting killing is wholly unjustifiable. (So self-defense doesn't apply—you can't kill in response to an unwanted sexual advance.)
4. But, if the invasion of privacy is significant, ordinary, fallible human beings might become so upset that their out-of-control reaction deserves mitigated punishment (754).

Although he was referring to cases involving *homosexual strangers*, the points in Professor Dressler's list should apply to all acquaintance nonviolent advances—homosexual *and* heterosexual. In other words, "there's a partial excuse in many sexual-advance cases." And this "partial excuse" for the "impassioned killing" spawned by an unwanted sexual advance *might* reduce the killing from murder to manslaughter (754–55).

"GAY PANIC" Mike might take a different road to getting a murder prosecution reduced to voluntary manslaughter—"gay panic." The gay panic claim is based on "the theory that a person with latent homosexual tendencies will have an extreme and uncontrollably violent reaction when confronted with a homosexual proposition" (1542). Mike might succeed if he can prove that (1) he's a latent homosexual and (2) this "condition" (sometimes labeled a psychological disorder) caused him to react violently to homosexual sexual advances (Note 1989). Gay panic is sometimes considered one form of the excuse of diminished capacity (which we discussed in Chapter 6). Here we treat it as an adequate provocation.

gay panic, based on "the theory that a person with latent homosexual tendencies will have an extreme and uncontrollably violent reaction when confronted with a homosexual proposition"

CASE

In **Commonwealth v. Carr** *(1990), Stephen Roy Carr argued that his mother's lesbian relationship when he was a boy, along with the sexual abuse against him while he was in prison, was behind his homicidal rage set off when he saw Claudia Brenner and Rebecca Wight having sex.*

Did seeing the lesbian lovemaking cause a "gay panic"?

Commonwealth v. Carr

580 A.2d 1362 (Penn.Supp. 1990)

HISTORY

Stephen Roy Carr (Defendant) was convicted of murder in the first degree before the Court of Common Pleas of Adams County, Criminal Division, and he was sentenced to life imprisonment. He appealed. The Superior Court affirmed.

WIEAND, J.

On May 13, 1988, Claudia Brenner and Rebecca Wight were hiking along the Appalachian Trail in Adams County, when they found an appropriate campsite and stopped for the night. There, they were resting and engaging in lesbian lovemaking when Claudia Brenner was shot in the right arm. After a short pause, additional shots were fired, as a result of which Brenner was struck four additional times in and about her face, neck and head. Rebecca Wight ran for cover behind a tree and was shot in the head and back. Brenner attempted to help Wight, who was unable to walk, but was unable to rouse her. Brenner

(continues)

(continued)
thereupon went for help, but by the time help arrived, Wight was dead. Suspicion subsequently focused on Stephen Roy Carr. He was arrested and taken into custody on a fugitive warrant from the State of Florida. He was subsequently tried without a jury and found guilty of murder in the first degree.

OPINION

Carr defended at trial on grounds that he had shot Brenner and Wight in the heat of passion caused by the serious provocation of their nude homosexual lovemaking. In support of this defense and to show the existence of passion, Carr offered to show a history of constant rejection by women, including his mother who may have been involved in a lesbian relationship, sexual abuse while in prison in Florida, inability to hold a job, and retreat to the mountains to avoid further rejection. This was relevant, he contended, to show that he was impassioned when provoked by the "show" put on by the women, including their nakedness, their hugging and kissing and their oral sex. The trial court refused to allow evidence of Carr's psychosexual history, finding it irrelevant.

The crime of voluntary manslaughter is defined by the Pennsylvania Crimes Code as follows:

> A person who kills an individual without lawful justification commits voluntary manslaughter if at the time of the killing he is acting under a sudden and intense passion resulting from serious provocation. . . .

The passion which will reduce an unlawful killing to voluntary manslaughter must be caused by legally adequate provocation. The test for determining the existence of legally adequate provocation is an objective test. In making the objective determination as to what constitutes sufficient provocation reliance may be placed upon the cumulative impact of a series of related events. The ultimate test for adequate provocation remains whether a reasonable man, confronted with this series of events, became impassioned to the extent that his mind was "incapable of cool reflection."

If and when sufficient provocation is found, then the focus of inquiry shifts to the defendant's response to that provocation. If sufficient provocation exists, the fact finder must also determine whether the defendant actually acted in the heat of passion when he committed the homicide and thus whether the provocation led directly to the killing or whether there was sufficient "cooling" period so that a reasonable man would have regained his capacity to reflect.

The sight of naked women engaged in lesbian lovemaking is not adequate provocation to reduce an unlawful killing from murder to voluntary manslaughter. It is not an event which is sufficient to cause a reasonable person to become so impassioned as to be incapable of cool reflection. Whatever a person's views about homosexuality, the law does not condone or excuse the killing of homosexuals any more than it condones the killing of heterosexuals. Similarly, it does not recognize homosexual activity between two persons as legal provocation sufficient to reduce an unlawful killing of one or both of the actors by a third person from murder to voluntary manslaughter.

A trial court must make an initial determination whether sufficient evidence has been presented of serious provocation. In the instant case, the judge was both court and jury. Carr was permitted to show the nature of the activities in which his victims were engaged when he came upon them in the woods. In a provocation defense, the actions of the victim establishing provocation are relevant. Those are the victim's actions on the [day] in question because the provocation must lead *directly* to the killing. After it had been determined that these activities were inadequate to provoke a heat of passion response, however, Carr's rejection by women and his mother's sexual preference were irrelevant. Carr's history of misfortunes is not events which are in any way related to the events which he claims provoked him on May 13, 1988. An accused cannot, by recalling some past injury or insult, establish a foundation for a manslaughter verdict. The trial court did not err when it excluded evidence of appellant's psychosexual history.

The judgment of sentence is affirmed.

QUESTIONS

1. List all of the relevant facts and circumstances that provoked Stephen Roy Carter to kill Rebecca Wight.
2. Summarize the reason why Carter claims he committed voluntary manslaughter.
3. State the court's definition of provocation.
4. Summarize the court's reasons for rejecting Carter's claim.
5. In your opinion, was Carter guilty of murder or voluntary manslaughter? Back up your answer with details and arguments from the excerpt.

The Emotion-Act Distinction

All of us can empathize with Mike's *emotions* when Gary made his unwanted advances. Who wouldn't feel indignant, violated, outraged? In other words, any *reasonable* person (I mean here any ordinary person) *could* feel similarly. *But* what about Mike's acts in response to Gary's advances? Would a reasonable person stomp Gary to death? Proponents of the emotion-act distinction make the sensible claim that we should separate the reasonableness of lethal action from the emotions that led to the killing (Lee 2003, 261). Why? Because, according to Professor Cynthia Lee (2003), there's a "big difference between reasonable emotions (fear, anger, outrage) and reasonable action. Even if a particular *emotion* is reasonable under the circumstances, this does not mean that acting on that emotion by using deadly force is also reasonable" (261).

emotion-act distinction, separating the emotions that led to a killing from the question of whether it was reasonable

Just because the distinction makes sense doesn't mean the law recognizes it. Professor Lee examined model jury instructions to determine whether states required act reasonableness, meaning "a finding that a reasonable person in the defendant's shoes would have responded as violently as the defendant did" (262). Only two states followed this approach.

act reasonableness, meaning "a finding that a reasonable person in the defendant's shoes would have responded as violently as the defendant did"

Most states adopt an emotional reasonableness approach, meaning a finding that "the defendant's *emotional* outrage or *passion* was reasonable." A few states require both act and emotional reasonableness (262-63). Professor Lee recommends implementation of the act-emotion distinction in voluntary manslaughter law (268; Figure 9.3).

emotional reasonableness, a finding that "the defendant's *emotional* outrage or *passion* was reasonable

INVOLUNTARY MANSLAUGHTER

LO 11

> The second branch, or involuntary manslaughter . . . is where a person does an act lawful in itself, but in an unlawful manner and without due caution and circumspection: as when a workman flings down a stone or piece of timber into the street and kills a man. . . .
>
> (Blackstone 1769, 192)

The central elements in involuntary manslaughter are its *actus reus* (killing by a voluntary act or omission) and its *mens rea* (an *un*intentional killing). Of course, as in all crimes of criminal conduct causing criminal harm, involuntary manslaughter also includes the elements of causation and resulting harm (death here). We won't repeat our discussion of causation from Chapter 4 here. (See the Elements of Involuntary Manslaughter illustration on the next page.)

involuntary manslaughter, an unintentional killing (*mens rea*) by a voluntary act or omission (*actus reus*)

FIGURE 9.3

SAMPLE PROVOCATION JURY INSTRUCTION

Voluntary manslaughter. An individual who kills in response to legally adequate provocation is guilty of voluntary manslaughter rather than murder. Legally adequate provocation is defined as provocation which would provoke the reasonable person in the defendant's shoes into a state of uncontrolled passion. Before you may return a verdict of voluntary manslaughter, you must be satisfied that the following three requirements are met:

Actual heat of passion. The defendant was actually provoked into a heat of passion.

Emotional reasonableness. The defendant's emotions were reasonable. A defendant's emotions may be considered reasonable if the reasonable (i.e., ordinary) person in the defendant's shoes would have been provoked into a heat of passion.

Act reasonableness. The defendant's acts were also normatively reasonable. A defendant's acts may be considered normatively reasonable if the defendant's response bears a reasonable relationship to the provoking act or incident.

Source: Lee 2003, 268.

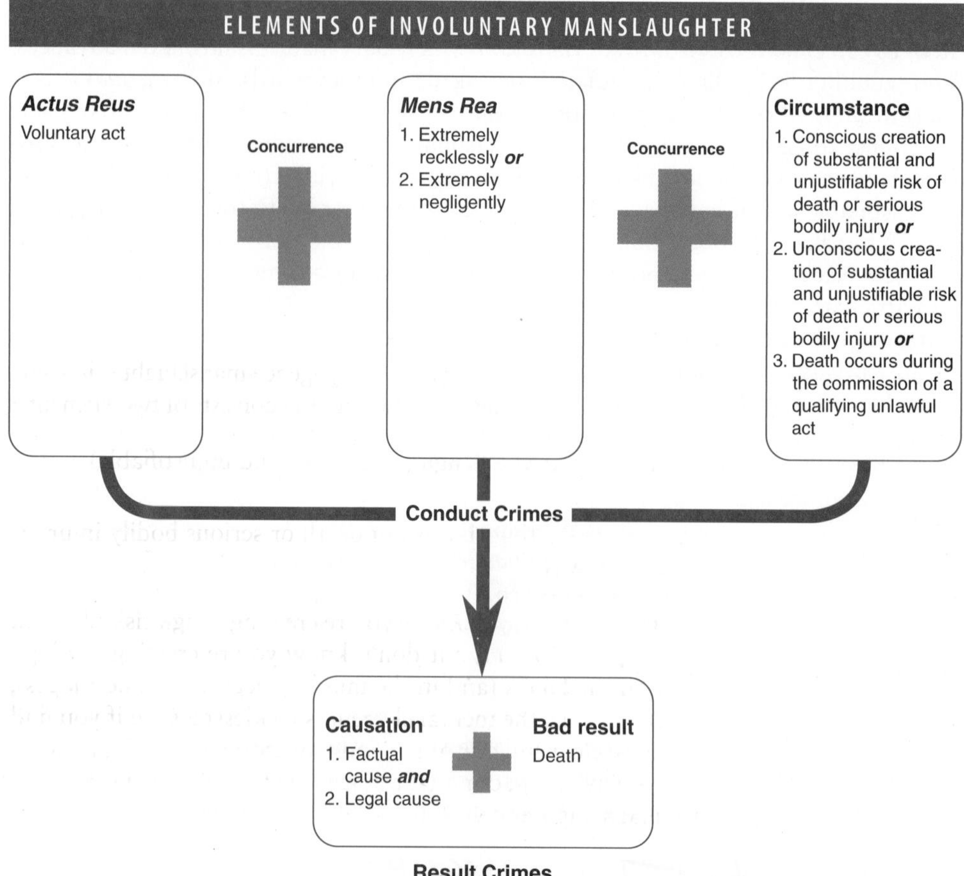

All states have punished involuntary manslaughter from their earliest days, but they didn't define it, and if they did, they did so vaguely. For example, most statutes used terms like "culpable negligence," "criminal negligence," or "gross negligence" but left in doubt the meaning of the terms. Most comprehensive modern criminal codes have

FIGURE 9.4

MODEL PENAL CODE HOMICIDE SECTIONS

Article 210. Criminal Homicide,

§ 210.1

(1) A person is guilty of criminal homicide if he purposely, knowingly, recklessly or negligently causes the death of another human being.
(2) Criminal homicide is murder, manslaughter or negligent homicide.

§ 210.3. Manslaughter.

(1) Criminal homicide constitutes manslaughter when:
    (a) it is committed recklessly; or
    (b) a homicide which would otherwise be murder is committed under the influence of extreme mental or emotional disturbance for which there is reasonable explanation or excuse. The reasonableness of such explanation or excuse shall be determined from the viewpoint of a person in the actor's situation under the circumstances as he believes them to be.
(2) Manslaughter is a felony of the second degree.

§ 210.4. Negligent Homicide.

(1) Criminal homicide constitutes negligent homicide when it is committed negligently.
(2) Negligent homicide is a felony of the third degree.

adopted at least some of the Model Penal Code (MPC) homicide sections in Figure 9.4 (LaFave 2003, 794–95).

LO 12

Most state codes have not adopted the MPC general criminal reckless and negligence provisions. Instead, they've created criminal liability for deaths caused by a variety of circumstances, including deaths from failures to furnish medical care for helpless, sick, or injured persons they have a duty to care for; permitting overcrowded conditions; failure to provide adequate fire exits in public entertainment places; delivery of dangerous drugs; and conducting dangerous blasting operations. But two—operating motor vehicles and handling firearms—"lead the list" (LaFave 2003, 796–97).

Criminal Negligence Manslaughter

Involuntary manslaughter goes by the name of criminal negligence manslaughter in some statutes and cases. In practice, **criminal negligence manslaughter** consists of two elements:

criminal negligence manslaughter, death caused by a person who is aware that her acts create a substantial and unjustifiable risk of death or serious bodily injury, but acts anyway

1. *Actus reus* The defendant's acts create a high (substantial and unjustifiable) risk of death or serious bodily injury.
2. *Mens rea* The defendant is aware that the risk of death or serious bodily injury is high but commits the acts anyway.

Recall that when you're acting recklessly, you *know* you're creating a high risk of harm; when you're acting negligently, you *should*, but don't, know you're creating the high risk. There's often confusion in the labels (and in the minds of legislators and judges), but the reality is that most of the time, the mental element is recklessness. So if you find it difficult to keep the difference clear in your mind, you have company in high places. When there's a doubt about the meaning, criminal negligence probably means criminal recklessness in involuntary manslaughter cases.

CASE

***In* State v. Mays *(2000)*,** *19-year-old Nicholas Mays killed Michael Boumer, in a grocery store parking, when Mays "messed with" him by "nudging" Boumer with his car.*

Did he commit aggravated vehicular homicide?

State v. Mays

743 N.E.2d 447 (OhioApp. 2000)

HISTORY

Upon convictions entered pursuant to guilty pleas, Nicholas Mays, the defendant, was sentenced by the Hamilton County Court of Common Pleas to five years' incarceration for aggravated vehicular homicide. He appealed. The Ohio Court of Appeals affirmed in part, and reversed and remanded in part.

DOAN, J.

FACTS

On August 19, 1999, 19-year-old Mays was operating an automobile in which his cousin was a passenger. At approximately 1:45 A.M., they saw a pedestrian, later identified as Michael Boumer, in a grocery store parking lot. According to Mays, Boumer appeared to be intoxicated. (Investigating officers confirmed that Boumer had consumed some alcohol. However, the record also indicates that Boumer was mentally handicapped.) The two young men decided that they would "mess with" Boumer by appearing to offer him a ride. Mays intended to nudge Boumer with the vehicle and then drive away.

Mays did drive the vehicle in the direction of Boumer, but instead of merely nudging him, he inadvertently ran over him, causing him fatal injuries. Upon seeing that Boumer was injured, Mays drove to another location and called for emergency aid. He then went to a car wash, where he cleaned the vehicle to remove evidence of the fatal collision.

On the day after the incident, Mays took a planned trip to Florida, during which his mother convinced him that he should report his involvement in the crime. Mays did so, returning to Cincinnati and giving a full confession to the police.

(continues)

(continued)

OPINION

The Ohio Revised Code vehicular homicide statute (Section 2903.06) reads in part:

(A) No person, while operating or participating in the operation of a motor vehicle, motorcycle, snowmobile, locomotive, watercraft, or aircraft, shall cause the death of another or the unlawful termination of another's pregnancy in any of the following ways:

. . .

(2) Recklessly;

(3) Negligently;

(1) Whoever violates division (A) (2) of this section is guilty of aggravated vehicular homicide and shall be punished as provided in divisions (B)(1) (b) of this section.

. . .

(b) Except as otherwise provided in this division, aggravated vehicular homicide committed in violation of division (A)(2) of this section is a felony of the third degree. In addition to any other sanctions imposed, the court shall suspend the offender's driver's license, commercial driver's license, temporary instruction permit, probationary license, or nonresident operating privilege for a definite period of three years to life.

(2) Whoever violates division (A)(3) of this section is guilty of vehicular homicide. Except as otherwise provided in this division, vehicular homicide is a misdemeanor of the first degree.

Mays first argues that the court erred in imposing terms of incarceration greater than the minimum. To impose a prison term more than the minimum for the offender's first prison term, the court must find that the minimum sentence would demean the seriousness of the offense or not adequately protect the public from future crime. Here, the trial court found both to be applicable.

We hold that the trial court's finding with respect to the seriousness of the offenses is supported by the record. Mays conceded that his intention was to "mess with" a person whom he perceived to be impaired in some way, and in doing so, he deprived the thirty-nine-year-old victim of his life. Mays did not immediately seek help for Boumer, but instead thought first of his own interest in evading detection for the crime. His concealment of the crime was compounded when he washed the car and left the jurisdiction. Under these circumstances, the trial court reasonably concluded that the minimum term would demean the seriousness of the offenses. Because the trial court's finding with respect to the seriousness of the offenses was proper, we need not address Mays's argument concerning the adequate protection of the public.

In his second argument, Mays claims that the trial court erred in imposing the maximum sentence for aggravated vehicular homicide. Before imposing the maximum term of incarceration for an offense, the court must find that the offender has committed the worst form of the offense, poses the greatest likelihood of recidivism, or is of a certain class of repeat offenders. In the case at bar, the court found that Mays had committed the worst form of aggravated vehicular homicide. We disagree.

In past cases, this court has grappled with the somewhat vague concept of what constitutes the "worst form" of an offense. And while the concept is difficult to define in concrete terms, we hold that Mays's conduct in the case at bar did not constitute the worst form of aggravated vehicular homicide. Though the evidence certainly indicates that Mays exercised extremely poor judgment in carrying out his wish to "mess with" Boumer, there is no indication that he harbored any malice toward the victim.

Instead, the record indicates that Mays's conduct started as a reckless, poorly conceived prank and ended in tragedy. And while we in no way wish to minimize the loss of a human life or to condone Mays's actions, this is not the type of conduct for which the legislature has reserved the maximum sentence. Furthermore, although he admittedly thought of his own interests before seeking help for Boumer, Mays did take steps to ensure that emergency personnel were notified promptly. His actions therefore did not reflect an utter lack of concern for Boumer or otherwise demonstrate a perversity of character that would justify the imposition of the maximum sentence. Further, there is no indication that the victim suffered for a prolonged period of time before he died or suffered to a greater degree than any other victim of a vehicular homicide.

Finally, Mays surrendered to authorities and confessed to the crimes. Under these circumstances, we cannot say that Mays committed the worst form of the offense within the meaning of R.C. 2929.14(C). We therefore hold that the trial court erred in imposing the maximum term for that offense.

Mays next argues that the trial court erred in imposing consecutive sentences. To impose consecutive terms of imprisonment, the court must find that consecutive sentences are necessary to protect the public from future crime and that consecutive sentences are not disproportionate to the offender's conduct and to the danger the offender poses to the public.

The trial court must also find one of the following:

1. that the offenses occurred while the offender was under community control;
2. that the harm caused was great or unusual; or
3. that the offender's criminal history requires consecutive sentences.

Of the latter factors, the court in the instant case found that the harm caused was unusual or great.

We agree with Mays that the trial court's findings with respect to consecutive sentences are not supported by the record. Concerning the protection of the public from future crime, Mays's criminal record included no adult convictions and only one juvenile delinquency adjudication. Thus, there is little indication that Mays is likely to recidivate.

Also, the trial court revoked Mays's operator's license, thereby reducing the likelihood that future vehicular offenses would occur.

Further, as to the finding that consecutive terms were not disproportionate to Mays's conduct and to the danger that he posed to the public, we have already noted that Mays's conduct, while reckless and ill-conceived, was not the product of malice.

Given the revocation of Mays's license, his confession, and his demonstrated remorse, the conduct also appears not likely to be repeated. The investigating officers and the author of the presentence-investigation report indicated that Mays was genuinely remorseful.

Finally, the harm caused by the offense, while senseless and tragic, was not greater than the harm caused in every other aggravated-vehicular-homicide case. Under these circumstances, we hold that the trial court erred in imposing consecutive sentences.

Having held that the trial court erred in imposing the maximum sentence for the aggravated vehicular homicide and in otherwise imposing consecutive sentences, we hereby reverse those parts of the trial court's judgment and remand the cause for resentencing in accordance with law.

Judgment affirmed in part, reversed in part and cause remanded.

DISSENT

HILDEBRANDT, PJ.

Mays senselessly took the life of the victim because he wished to "mess with" him. The wantonness of that conduct alone could have justified the trial court in imposing the maximum sentence. However, Mays compounded his misconduct by leaving the scene of the collision, thereby making it clear that he valued his own interest in evading detection above the life of Boumer. The majority concedes as much, yet persists in holding that Mays did not commit the worst form of the offense. His eventual call for emergency aid and his subsequent remorse for his actions did not erase the fact that his conduct was egregious and deserving of the greatest punishment.

For many of the same reasons, I believe that the imposition of consecutive sentences was proper. The utter lack of regard for human life that Mays exhibited by using his automobile to "mess with" a person whom he believed to be impaired provided ample support for the trial court's conclusion that consecutive sentences were necessary to prevent future crimes and to protect the public. Moreover, the fact that death is caused in all aggravated-vehicular-homicide cases should not prevent a finding that the harm caused in the instant case was great or unusual.

Mays's taking of a life in such a wanton manner justified the court in finding that the harm done was great or unusual. . . . In my view, nine years of incarceration is not excessive when weighed against the taking of a human life under these circumstances. I therefore respectfully dissent in part.

QUESTIONS

1. How does the Ohio statute define "vehicular homicide"?
2. Relying on the evidence in the case and referring to the Ohio provision, explain why Nicholas Mays was guilty of aggravated vehicular homicide.
3. How would you define "vehicular homicide"? Defend your definition.
4. Do you agree with the majority opinion's reasons for reversing the sentence? Or do the dissent and the trial court have the better arguments? Back up your answer.

Unlawful Act Manslaughter

In 1260, long before the common law judges created a division between murder and manslaughter, the great jurist Bracton wrote that unintended deaths that occur during unlawful acts are criminal homicides. In today's statutes and court opinions, they're called **unlawful act manslaughter** or **misdemeanor manslaughter.**

unlawful act manslaughter or **misdemeanor manslaughter,** unintended deaths occurring during the commission of nonhomicide offenses

Sometime after the judges created the offense of manslaughter, unlawful act manslaughters became a form of involuntary manslaughter. In modern times, statutes have restricted unlawful act manslaughter because the penalty is considered too harsh. In fact, there's a trend to abolish unlawful act manslaughter, leaving criminal negligence manslaughter as the only kind of involuntary manslaughter.

Unlawful acts taken literally could include everything, including felonies, misdemeanors, and even traffic violations, city ordinances, administrative crimes, and even noncriminal wrongs, such as civil trespass and other torts (Chapter 1). Misdemeanors are certainly included among these possibly unlawful acts; that's why the unlawful act manslaughter is often called "misdemeanor manslaughter." The most common misdemeanors that come up in the cases are speeding and drunk driving, and battery (Chapter 10), mostly hitting someone who dies from the blow.

This is what happened in *People v. Datema* (1995). Greg and Pamela Datema were sitting around in their living room with friends talking, smoking pot, and drinking. The conversation turned to their previous romances. Pam and Greg started arguing about the people they'd slept with. Pam claimed she'd had sex with some of her paramours in front of their sons. Greg slapped her in the face—once. Pam slumped back; the other three thought she'd passed out. After 10 minutes, they got worried. When they shook her and she didn't wake up, they called for an ambulance. Pam never regained consciousness.

The medical examiner found that Pam Datema had a blood-alcohol level between 0.03 and 0.05 percent. He stated that death was caused by a tear in an artery in the head that occurred as a result of Greg's slap:

> Most people, when slapped, reflexively stiffen their necks and avoid serious injury. Occasionally, however, when a person is intoxicated, the reflexes do not react quickly enough, and a blow could result in a tearing. Generally, a higher blood-alcohol level is necessary, but the ingested marijuana, which was not able to be tested, was undoubtedly a contributing factor. (274)

As mentioned earlier, there's a trend toward abolishing unlawful act manslaughter; about half of the states have already done so (LaFave 2003a, 801). Where it still exists, the states have placed limits on it. Most states limit the underlying offense to *mala in se* offenses. (Recall that *mala in se* offenses are ones that are inherently evil—for example, the battery in *People v. Datema* and the "nudge" in *State v. Mays.*)

***malum prohibitum* crime,** death has to be a foreseeable consequence of the unlawful act; the act is unlawful only because it's prohibited by a specific statute or ordinance

To count as a **malum prohibitum crime,** death has to be a foreseeable consequence of the unlawful act. Recall from Chapter 1 that a *malum prohibitum* crime is a crime only because a specific statute or ordinance prohibits it. In *Todd v. State* (1992), Todd ran off with the church collection plate. A congregation member jumped in his car and pursued the thief. He suffered a heart attack, hit a tree, and died of cardiac arrest. The court held this wasn't a case of unlawful act manslaughter because death isn't a foreseeable risk in petty theft.

LO 3

DOCTOR-ASSISTED SUICIDE

> Whoever no longer wishes to live shall state his reasons to the Senate [ancient Greek government], and after having received permission shall abandon life. If your existence is hateful to you, die; if you are overwhelmed by fate, drink the hemlock.

> If you are bowed with grief, abandon life. Let the unhappy man recount his misfortune, let the magistrate supply him with the remedy, and his wretchedness will come to an end.
>
> (Libanius, ancient Greek philosopher, quoted in Messinger 1993, 183)

> It would seem unlawful to kill any living thing. For the Apostle says (Romans 13:2): "They that resist the ordinance of God purchase to themselves damnation." Now Divine providence has ordained that all living things should be preserved, according to Psalm 146:8–9, "Who maketh grass to grow on the mountains . . . Who giveth to beasts their food." Therefore it seems unlawful to take the life of any living thing.
>
> (St. Thomas Aquinas, *Summa Theologica* 1265–68)

> The sick they see to with great affection, and let nothing at all pass concerning either physic or good diet whereby they may be restored again to their health. Them that be sick of incurable diseases they comfort with sitting by them, with talking with them, and to be short, with all manner of helps that may be.
>
> But if the disease be not only incurable, but also full of continual pain and anguish; then the priests and the magistrates exhort the man, seeing his is not able to do any duty of life, and by outliving his own death is noisome and irksome to others and grievous to himself, that he will determine with himself no longer to cherish that pestilent and painful disease.
>
> And seeing his life is to him but a torment, that he will not be unwilling to die, but rather take a good hope to him, and either dispatch himself out of that painful life, as out of a prison, or a rack of torment, or else suffer himself willingly to be rid of it by others. And in so doing they tell him he shall do so wisely, seeing by his death he shall lose no commodity, but end his pain. But they cause none such to die against his will, nor they use no less diligence and attendance about him, believing this to be an honorable death.
>
> (Sir Thomas More, *Utopia* 1516)

> Medical jurisprudence is subordinate to medical ethics which expresses the moral order willed by God. Medical jurisprudence cannot, therefore, in any circumstances permit a doctor or patient to carry out euthanasia directly, nor may a doctor ever perform it upon himself or anyone else.
>
> (Pope Pius XII 1956)

These samples from history, philosophy, religion, and law make clear that the subject of helping others die has confronted societies throughout history with "the troubling dilemma of defining the meaning of death and the value of life" (Messinger 1993, 175). In our time, we call helping others die (assisted suicide) "**euthanasia**." The *Oxford English Dictionary*'s (2009) eloquent definition: "a gentle and easy death" or "the means of bringing about a gentle and easy death" hides the deep, emotional, and irreconcilable division over helping others die.

euthanasia, helping another person to die

In our look at doctor-assisted suicide, we'll discuss the kinds of euthanasia in our society, arguments against and for doctor-assisted suicide, where criminal law stands on the issue, and the public's opinion of doctor-assisted suicide.

THE KINDS OF EUTHANASIA

Euthanasia exists in several forms. It can be passive (failing to take any extraordinary measures to keep someone alive) or active (deliberate acts to cause death). It can be voluntary, whereby a dying person can make a rational request and be examined to guarantee the validity of the request, or involuntary. Involuntary euthanasia can be beneficent (a family and court decision with good intentions) or malevolent (purposeful disregard of legal process or by co-opting the legal process) (Messinger 1993, 180–81). We'll concentrate on active voluntary euthanasia through doctor-assisted suicide.

ARGUMENTS AGAINST DOCTOR-ASSISTED SUICIDE

There are two primary arguments against doctor-assisted suicide: First, it's intrinsically immoral and wrong; second, unacceptable consequences will follow from it ("the slippery slope" argument) (Messinger 1993, 215). Let's look at each.

The Intrinsically Immoral and Wrong Argument

The intrinsically immoral and wrong argument stems from the Judeo-Christian heritage's asserting the immorality of bringing about "premature" death. The Sixth Commandment, "Thou shalt not kill," leaves no doubt where the Judeo-Christian God stands on the issue. Humans are banned from killing in all circumstances. Why? The sanctity of human life and the merits of suffering. Either obey the divine will or take the consequences. In other words, divine will trumps human suffering, no matter how extreme that suffering is (Messinger 1993, 214–15).

The "Slippery Slope" Argument

According to the "slippery slope" argument, honest mistakes and malevolent motives can happen, and we can't control them. The potential for wrong diagnoses and the threat of nonmercy killings are too great to justify any exceptions to a total ban on doctor-assisted suicides. In addition, society's interest, not just the individual's, are at stake. When it runs amok, it can wreak great havoc, such as the Nazi atrocities, opponents point out (Messinger 1993, 215).

Mary Senender (1988), of the Anti-Euthanasia Task Force, makes this argument for the impact on society:

> If you want to commit suicide, you can do that. It's not illegal. If you want to hang yourself with a velvet cord from the rafters of your garage—I'm not recommending it and I wish you wouldn't—you *can* do that. If you want to blow your brains out with a diamond-studded pistol—I hope you won't, for your sake and for your family's—you can *do* that. If you want to save up pills and poison yourself—I'd try to talk you out of it—you *could* do it. But what you're asking for—what proponents of euthanasia are demanding—is *my approval* and *acceptance* of your actions. What's more you expect—and proponents of "aid dying" demand—someone *else* to help.
>
> When you ask for social and legal approval of killing, you're asking ME to participate in YOUR death, to share a communal responsibility and burden. And guilt. And blame. And I *won't do it*! Now, you're meddling with MY choices and MY conscience. Don't expect me to be silent when those issues of public policy are debated; I have my rights too.

ARGUMENTS IN FAVOR OF DOCTOR-ASSISTED SUICIDE

> Darkling I listen; and for many a time
> I have been half in love with easeful Death,
> Call'd him soft names in many a mused rhyme,

To take into the air my quiet breath;
Now more than ever seems it rich to die,
To cease upon the midnight with no pain . . .

(John Keats, "Ode to a Nightingale," 1819)

Supporters say that the argument for doctor-assisted suicide isn't so much an argument *for* euthanasia. It's an argument *against* "insufferable and unending pain; in a word, it's about compassion" (Messinger 1993, 223). But they don't stop with compassion. They maintain that there's a constitutional right to assisted suicide.

According to proponents of the right to doctor-assisted suicide, the "right" is closely linked to the principle of personal autonomy embodied in the Court-created and controversial right to privacy (Chapter 2).

Resting the right to assisted suicide on the shaky controversial right to privacy has led proponents to look elsewhere and rely on a "**presumption of bodily integrity.**" This argument relies on the English philosopher John Stuart Mill's statement that a state can't exercise power over individual members of society except to prevent harm to others (Messinger 1993, 236). While the right to privacy is controversial, the right to bodily integrity is difficult to raise technically because of the judicial restrictions on "creating" law and rights (Chapters 1 and 2).

presumption of bodily integrity, a state can't exercise power over individual members of society except to prevent harm to others

Others have argued that the "liberty interest" guaranteed in the due process clauses of the Fifth and Fourteenth Amendments to the U.S. Constitution includes the right to die and to seek assistance in exercising the right. But the U.S. Supreme Court upheld Washington State's ban on assisting another to commit suicide because recognizing a right to doctor-assisted suicide would require the reversal of "centuries of legal doctrine and practice" (*Washington v. Glucksberg* 1997, 723).

Washington v. Glucksberg leaves to state legislatures the decision to criminalize doctor-assisted suicide. In a decisive Washington State ballot initiative on election day in 2008, three out of five Washington State voters approved an initiative to decriminalize doctor-assisted suicide. Washington used as its model Oregon's Death with Dignity Act, which allows individuals to get a doctor to help them commit suicide (Figure 9.5). The Oregon act was upheld by the U.S. Supreme Court in *Gonzalez v. Oregon* (2005).

DOCTOR-ASSISTED SUICIDE AND THE CRIMINAL LAW

To justify doctor-assisted suicide runs up against the subject of this chapter—criminal homicide. The law of criminal homicide makes it difficult to distinguish doctor-assisted suicide from first-degree murder. Proponents argue that murder is condemned because it both violates a person's interest in continuing to live and is a destructive force in society. Neither of these is present in doctor-assisted suicide. The disruption to society has already taken place by the loss of a productive member of society. And violation of the right to live is obviously lacking—the person has decided she doesn't want to live (Messinger 1993, 237–38).

It should be clear that the for and against positions on doctor-assisted suicide are irreconcilable because they reflect opposing strongly held beliefs about the meaning of life. Professor Thane Josef Messinger (1993) wrote words still applicable today:

> People view "life" as either sacrosanct, in which case any infinitesimally minute portion always has positive value, or as relative, in which case life can become negative at some variable point in the future, the only question being when. (224)

FIGURE 9.5

OREGON DEATH WITH DIGNITY ACT

Written Request for Medication to End One's Life in a Humane and Dignified Manner
127.805 s.2.01. Who may initiate a written request for medication.

(1) An adult who is capable, is a resident of Oregon, and has been determined by the attending physician and consulting physician to be suffering from a terminal disease, and who has voluntarily expressed his or her wish to die, may make a written request for medication for the purpose of ending his or her life in a humane and dignified manner in accordance with ORS 127.800 to 127.897.

(2) No person shall qualify under the provisions of ORS 127.800 to 127.897 solely because of age or disability. [1995 c.3 s.2.01; 1999 c.423 s.2]

127.897 s.6.01. Form of the request.

A request for a medication as authorized by ORS 127.800 to 127.897 shall be in substantially the following form:

Request for Medication to End My Life in a Humane and Dignified Manner

I, ______________________________, am an adult of sound mind.

I am suffering from ______________________________, which my attending physician has determined is a terminal disease and which has been medically confirmed by a consulting physician.

I have been fully informed of my diagnosis, prognosis, the nature of medication to be prescribed and potential associated risks, the expected result, and the feasible alternatives, including comfort care, hospice care and pain control.

I request that my attending physician prescribe medication that will end my life in a humane and dignified manner.

Initial one:

_____ I have informed my family of my decision and taken their opinions into consideration.

_____ I have decided not to inform my family of my decision.

_____ I have no family to inform of my decision.

I understand that I have the right to rescind this request at any time.

I understand the full import of this request and I expect to die when I take the medication to be prescribed. I further understand that although most deaths occur within three hours, my death may take longer and my physician has counseled me about this possibility.

I make this request voluntarily and without reservation, and I accept full moral responsibility for my actions.

Signed: ______________________________

Dated: ____________________

Declaration of Witness

We declare that the person signing this request:

(a) Is personally known to us or has provided proof of identity;
(b) Signed this request in our presence;
(c) Appears to be of sound mind and not under duress, fraud or undue influence;
(d) Is not a patient for whom either of us is attending physician.

______________________________ Witness 1/Date

______________________________ Witness 2/Date

(continues)

NOTE: One witness shall not be a relative (by blood, marriage or adoption) of the person signing this request, shall not be entitled to any portion of the person's estate upon death and shall not own, operate or be employed at a health care facility where the person is a patient or resident. If the patient is an inpatient at a health care facility, one of the witnesses shall be an individual designated by the facility.

FIGURE 9.5 *(Continued)*

PUBLIC OPINION AND DOCTOR-ASSISTED SUICIDE

The public, like the criminal law, is divided on the question of doctor-assisted suicide. The key finding of the 2007 Gallup annual Values and Beliefs poll reflects this division. Even so, 56 percent of respondents answered "should" and 38 percent answered "should not" to the question: "When a person has a disease that cannot be cured and is living in severe pain, do you think doctors should or should not be allowed by law to assist the patient to commit suicide if the patient requests it?" (Carroll 2007).

Should doctor-assisted suicide be considered murder?

Just hours before they died, Sherry Miller, Marjorie Wantz, and their family members met with Kevorkian at the home of Sherry Miller's parents on October 22, 1991. Miller, 43, had advanced multiple sclerosis and had approached Kevorkian a year earlier. She kept pursuing him and told her story several times on television. Marjorie Wantz, 58, also had sought Kevorkian's help for years. Although not terminally ill, she suffered excruciating pain after many surgeries to remove benign vaginal tumors. She had tried to kill herself several times. Psychiatrists said she was depressed and suicidal and some felt her pain was psychosomatic. (Later, when the medical examiner conducted her autopsy he found no physical cause for her pain.) The day after this interview, they committed suicide in a rustic cabin. Wantz used a machine Kevorkian invented, which injected a fatal substance; Miller inhaled carbon monoxide because her veins were too weak for a needle.

He called the machine the Thanatron—"death machine" in Greek. It was devised so that the patient could pull the trigger. It started with an intravenous drip of saline solution. Then the patient would press a button starting a device that stopped the saline solution and started releasing a drug of thiopental with a 60-second timer. This would put the patient into a deep coma. Finally, the timer's click would begin a lethal dose of potassium chloride, which, in minutes, would stop the heart. The patient would die of a heart attack while asleep.

The Thanatron was made from odd bits and pieces of household tools and toy parts, magnets, and electrical switches. It had an electric clock motor with a pulley axle, and a chain and two coils acting as electric bar magnets. Kevorkian showed it off, including an appearance on *The Donahue Show*. He called it "dignified, humane, and painless, and the patient can do it in the comfort of their own home at any time they want."

Everyone who has known Jack Kevorkian first talks about his brain. "He could tell you any major league baseball player's batting average," his boyhood chum Richard Dakesian told me, his voice tinged with awe. "He probably could have graduated from high school when he was 13 or 14. He's the smartest man I ever knew. I think he was born ahead of his time."

Instructions

1. Consult the *Frontline* website "The Kevorkian Verdict" at http://www.pbs.org/wgbh/pages/frontline/kevorkian/tindex.html.
2. Write an essay answering the question, "Is it ethical public policy to make doctor-assisted suicide criminal homicide?" Support your answer with points made in the section on "Doctor-Assisted Suicide," and the *Frontline* website content.

Source: *Frontline.* 1996 (May 14). "The Kevorkian Verdict." http://www.pbs.org/wgbh/pages/frontline/kevorkian/interviews/.

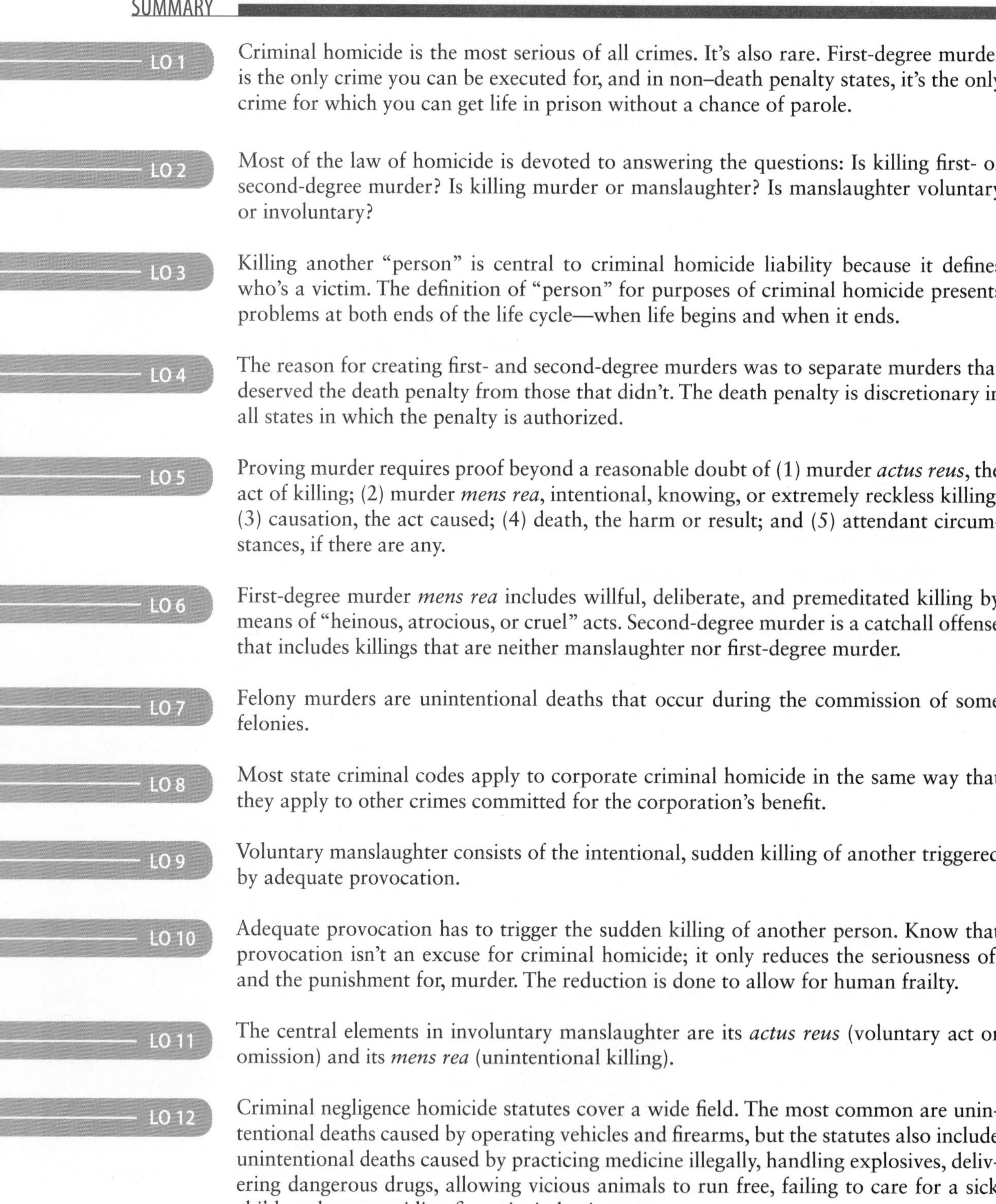

SUMMARY

LO 1 Criminal homicide is the most serious of all crimes. It's also rare. First-degree murder is the only crime you can be executed for, and in non–death penalty states, it's the only crime for which you can get life in prison without a chance of parole.

LO 2 Most of the law of homicide is devoted to answering the questions: Is killing first- or second-degree murder? Is killing murder or manslaughter? Is manslaughter voluntary or involuntary?

LO 3 Killing another "person" is central to criminal homicide liability because it defines who's a victim. The definition of "person" for purposes of criminal homicide presents problems at both ends of the life cycle—when life begins and when it ends.

LO 4 The reason for creating first- and second-degree murders was to separate murders that deserved the death penalty from those that didn't. The death penalty is discretionary in all states in which the penalty is authorized.

LO 5 Proving murder requires proof beyond a reasonable doubt of (1) murder *actus reus*, the act of killing; (2) murder *mens rea*, intentional, knowing, or extremely reckless killing; (3) causation, the act caused; (4) death, the harm or result; and (5) attendant circumstances, if there are any.

LO 6 First-degree murder *mens rea* includes willful, deliberate, and premeditated killing by means of "heinous, atrocious, or cruel" acts. Second-degree murder is a catchall offense that includes killings that are neither manslaughter nor first-degree murder.

LO 7 Felony murders are unintentional deaths that occur during the commission of some felonies.

LO 8 Most state criminal codes apply to corporate criminal homicide in the same way that they apply to other crimes committed for the corporation's benefit.

LO 9 Voluntary manslaughter consists of the intentional, sudden killing of another triggered by adequate provocation.

LO 10 Adequate provocation has to trigger the sudden killing of another person. Know that provocation isn't an excuse for criminal homicide; it only reduces the seriousness of, and the punishment for, murder. The reduction is done to allow for human frailty.

LO 11 The central elements in involuntary manslaughter are its *actus reus* (voluntary act or omission) and its *mens rea* (unintentional killing).

LO 12 Criminal negligence homicide statutes cover a wide field. The most common are unintentional deaths caused by operating vehicles and firearms, but the statutes also include unintentional deaths caused by practicing medicine illegally, handling explosives, delivering dangerous drugs, allowing vicious animals to run free, failing to care for a sick child, and not providing fire exits in businesses.

KEY TERMS

born-alive rule, p. 302
feticide, p. 302
murder, p. 304
manslaughter, p. 304
justifiable homicide, p. 305
excusable homicide, p. 305
criminal homicide, p. 305
malice aforethought, p. 305
depraved heart murder, p. 306
intent to cause serious bodily injury murder, p. 306
serious bodily injury, p. 306
express malice aforethought, p. 306
implied malice aforethought, p. 307
murder *actus reus*, p. 308
murder *mens rea*, p. 308
first-degree murder, p. 309
capital cases, p. 310
bifurcation procedure, p. 310
deadly weapon doctrine, p. 315
second-degree murder, p. 319
felony murder rule, p. 321
manslaughter, p. 330
voluntary manslaughter, p. 331
adequate provocation (voluntary manslaughter), p. 332
objective test of cooling-off time (voluntary manslaughter), p. 333
"words can never provoke" rule, p. 334
last-straw rule/long smoldering or slow burn rule, p. 334
extreme mental or emotional disturbance manslaughter, p. 334
paramour rule, p. 335
gay panic, p. 339
emotion-act distinction, p. 341
act reasonableness, p. 341
emotional reasonableness, p. 341
involuntary manslaughter, p. 341
criminal negligence manslaughter, p. 343
unlawful act manslaughter (misdemeanor manslaughter), p. 346
malum prohibitum crime, p. 346
euthanasia, p. 347
presumption of bodily integrity, p. 349

LEARNING OBJECTIVES

1. To appreciate that voluntary and knowing consensual sexual behavior between two adults is legal, healthy, and desired.
2. To know that crimes against persons boil down to four types: taking a life, unwanted sexual invasions, bodily injury, and personal restraint.
3. To understand that the vast majority of rape victims are raped by individuals they know.
4. To know that the requirements of common law rape have been dramatically altered in modern rape statutes.
5. To know that during the 1970s and 1980s, sexual assault reform changed the face of criminal sexual assault law.
6. To know and understand the elements of modern rape law.
7. To understand that force beyond the degree required to complete sexual penetration or contact isn't always required to satisfy the force requirement in rape.
8. To understand that rape can be accomplished with no extrinsic force—or threat of force—if fraud of fact or fraud of inducement is used by the perpetrator.
9. To know that rape is a general-intent crime.
10. To remember that statutory rape is a strict liability crime in most states.
11. To know that sex offenses are graded based on several criteria.
12. To know that assault and battery are two separate crimes.
13. To appreciate that since the early 1970s, domestic violence crimes have been transformed from a private concern to a criminal justice problem.
14. To remember that stalking, although an ancient practice, is a new crime that's based on causing fear.
15. To know that kidnapping and false imprisonment violate the right of locomotion.

Ty Oliver McDowell waits for the start of his preliminary hearing in Circuit Court in Casper, Wyoming. McDowell was accused of violently raping a Casper woman after responding to a fake Craigslist ad for a rough sexual fantasy.

AP Images/Casper Star-Tribune, Dan Cepeda, File

CRIMES AGAINST PERSONS II 10

Sex Offenses, Bodily Injury, and Personal Restraint

CHAPTER OUTLINE

Did He Seduce or Rape Her?

Martin Evans, a bachelor about 37 years old, aptly described in the testimony as "glib," met an incoming plane at LaGuardia Airport, from which disembarked Lucy Elizabeth Peterson of Charlotte, North Carolina, a 20-year-old petite, attractive second-year student at Wellesley College, an unworldly girl, evidently unacquainted with New York City and the sophisticated city ways, a girl who proved to be incredibly gullible, trusting and naive.

Evans struck up a conversation with her, posing as a psychologist doing a magazine article and using a name that was not his, inducing Miss Peterson to answer questions for an interview. Evans and a girl named Bridget took Miss Peterson to Maxwell's Plum, a singles bar, which Evans explained was for the purpose of conducting a sociological experiment in which he would observe her reactions and the reactions of males towards her in the setting of a singles bar.

After several hours there, in which Miss Peterson evidently was still under the belief that her stopping for a drink at Maxwell's Plum was part of this psychological and sociological experiment, she was persuaded to accompany Evans . . . and induced to come up to an apartment on the 14th floor. In the apartment the psychological interviewing continued, Evans having explained to Miss Peterson that he was searching for the missing link between the "girl-woman" and the "woman-girl."

(continues)

(continued)

She had been there for one to two hours when the defendant made his move and pulled her on to the opened sofa bed in the living room of that apartment and attempted to disrobe her. She resisted that, and she claims that as articles of clothing were attempted to be removed she would pull them back on and ultimately she was able to ward off these advances and to get herself dressed again.

(*People v. Evans* 1975)

LO 1

Rape is second only to murder in being regarded by law and society as the most serious crime. This isn't just true today. From colonial times, rape was punishable by death in several states, until 1977, when the U.S. Supreme Court declared it was cruel and unusual punishment (Chapter 2; *Coker v. Georgia* 1977). Rape is a serious crime even if victims suffer no physical injury, not even minor cuts and bruises. That's because rape violates intimacy and autonomy in a way that physical injuries can't. Even less-invasive sexually generated touching, such as pinching buttocks or fondling breasts, is treated as a serious felony.

Rape and other sexual assaults are different from all other felonies in one very important respect. Under other circumstances, some of the behaviors connected with them aren't just legal, they're healthy and wanted. One of the most critical problems in sex offenses is distinguishing between flirting and seduction and sexual assault. In prosecuting the grave crimes against individual autonomy and violence involved in these offenses, we don't want to inhibit the healthy pursuit of consensual, desirable, healthy, legal sexual activity.

LO 2

In addition to the elements of rape and other sexual assaults, you'll learn about the elements of two other kinds of crimes against persons—nonsexual assaults and bodily injury (battery; its close relative, assault; and stalking)—particularly as they relate to domestic violence—and criminal restraints on liberty (kidnapping and false imprisonment). Most of these crimes can be result crimes, in which case, they include elements of causing a result as well as an act, state of mind, and attendant circumstance elements. As we did in homicide, we'll leave discussion of the elements of causation and result to what you've already learned in the "Causation" section of Chapter 4. Here, we'll concentrate on the act or omission, the state of mind, and frequently the attendant circumstance elements.

LO 3

SEX OFFENSES

Originally, the criminal law recognized only two sex offenses—rape and sodomy. Common law rape was strictly limited to intentional, forced, nonconsensual, heterosexual vaginal penetration. It was aimed at the traditional view of rape: a male stranger leaps from the shadows at night and sexually attacks a defenseless woman. Legally, men couldn't rape their wives. Common law sodomy meant anal intercourse between two males.

Modern court opinions have relaxed the strict definition of "rape." And criminal sexual conduct statutes enacted in the 1970s and the 1980s (discussed later) have expanded the definition of "sex offenses" to embrace a wide range of nonconsensual penetrations and contacts, even if they fall far short of violent. Statutes and cases refer to "sex offenses" as either "sexual assault" or "criminal sexual conduct." In the text, we'll use the terms sex offense, sexual assault, and criminal sexual conduct interchangeably.

aggravated rape, rape by strangers or individuals with weapons who physically injure their victims

These reforms in sex offense law were brought about because a dirty secret was "outed": the vast majority of rape victims are raped by men they know. In this chapter, we'll distinguish between two kinds of rape: (1) aggravated rape—rape by strangers or individuals with weapons who physically injure their victims—and (2) **unarmed acquaintance rape**—nonconsensual sex between "dates, lovers, neighbors, co-workers, employers, and so on" (Bryden 2000, 318).

unarmed acquaintance rape, nonconsensual sex between individuals who are known to one another

The criminal justice system deals fairly well with aggravated rapes, but it has failed miserably when it comes to unarmed acquaintance rapes. Why? Several reasons, including:

- Victims aren't likely to report unarmed acquaintance rapists, or they don't recognize them as rapes.
- When victims do report them, the police are less likely to believe the victims than they are the victims of aggravated rape.
- Prosecutors are less likely to charge unarmed acquaintance rapists.
- Juries are less likely to convict unarmed acquaintance rapists.
- Unarmed acquaintance rapists are likely to escape punishment if their victims don't follow the rules of middle-class morality.

According to Professor David P. Bryden's excellent article "Redefining Rape" (2000):

> An acquaintance rapist is most likely to escape justice if his victim violated traditional norms of female morality and prudence: for example, by engaging in casual sex, drinking heavily, or hitchhiking. When the victim is a norm-violating woman, people often blame her rather than the rapist. (318)

The criminal justice system's poor performance in dealing with unarmed acquaintance rapes is a serious problem, but it's made worse by the social reality that the overwhelming number of rapes are acquaintance rapes. In one survey of women who didn't report rapes to the police, more than 80 percent of the women said they were raped by men they knew (Williams 1984). In three separate surveys of college women, one in five reported being "physically forced" to have sexual intercourse by her date (Foreman 1986, 27).

Figure 10.1 shows the results of the Bureau of Justice Statistics (2011) victim survey on rape and other sexual assaults. (These are for the year 2010, the latest numbers available when this book went to press.) The survey found 75 percent of rape victims knew their assailant.

Another aspect of the social reality of rape is the substantial number of rapes committed against men (McMullen 1990). It's almost impossible to get details about male rape victims. The FBI's Uniform Crime Reports, the most widely cited statistics of crimes reported to the police, don't break down the numbers of rape victims by sex. The National Crime Victim Survey, the most thorough government victimization survey, reported that

RELATIONSHIP OF RAPE VICTIM TO RAPIST

FIGURE 10.1

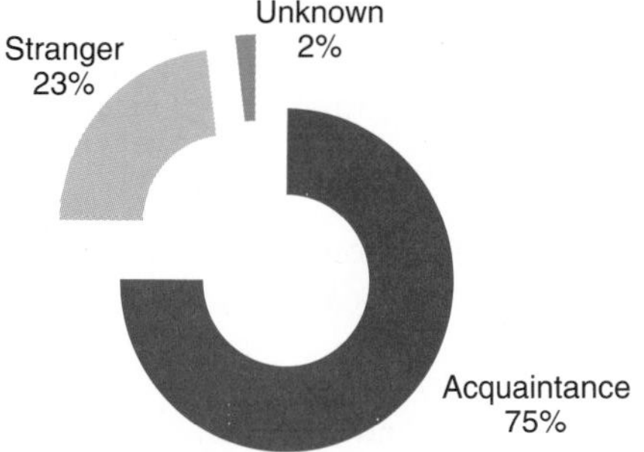

Source: U.S. Department of Justice. Bureau of Justice Statistics. 2011 (Sept. 15).

in 2010, 78% of male rape/sexual assault victims knew their assailant. The survey notes warned "Interpret with Caution!" because of the small numbers of respondents. (About 15,000 men contrasted with 169,000 females responded in 2010; statistically, 169,000 is a small number for a population of about 200 million women in the United States.)

To learn more about how the law treats rape, in this section we'll study the history of rape law; statutes defining criminal sexual conduct; the elements of modern rape law; statutory rape; and how the law grades the seriousness of sex offenses and the penalties it prescribes for them.

LO 4

THE HISTORY OF RAPE LAW

common law rape, intentional forced heterosexual vaginal penetration by a man of a woman who isn't his wife

As early as the year 800, rape was a capital offense in Anglo-Saxon England. In 1769, William Blackstone, the leading eighteenth-century authority on the common law in both England and the colonies, defined "**common law rape**" as the "carnal knowledge of a woman [sexual intercourse] forcibly and against her will" (210).

This definition boiled down to four elements:

1. Sexual intercourse by force or a threat of severe bodily harm (*actus reus*)
2. Intentional vaginal intercourse (*mens rea*)
3. Intercourse between a man and a woman who wasn't his wife (attendant circumstance)
4. Intercourse without the woman's consent (attendant circumstance)

The common law required proof beyond a reasonable doubt of all four elements because, as Sir Matthew Hale (1847), the highly regarded seventeenth-century chief justice and legal scholar of the criminal law, noted:

> It is true that rape is a most detestable crime, and therefore ought severely and impartially to be punished; but it must be remembered, that it is an accusation easy to be made, hard to be proved, and harder to be defended by the party accused, though innocent. (634)

And Blackstone (1769), the Americans' favorite authority, added:

> The heinousness of the offence many times transporting the judge and jury with so much indignation, that they are overhastily carried to the conviction of the person accused thereof, by the confident testimony of sometimes false and malicious witnesses. (215)

In common law trials, rape victims were allowed to testify against accused rapists; it was up to the jury to decide whether to believe them. But the victim's credibility depended on three conditions, always difficult (and often impossible) to satisfy:

1. Her chastity
2. Whether she promptly reported the rape
3. Whether other witnesses corroborated the rape

Blackstone (1769) talked tough enough when he asserted that even prostitutes could be of good fame, but he mostly took it back when he added this warning about victim witnesses:

> If the ravished be of evil fame, and stand unsupported by others; if she concealed the injury for any considerable time after she had opportunity to complain; if the place

> where the fact was alleged to be committed, was where it was possible she might have been heard, and she made no outcry; these and the like circumstances carry a strong, but not conclusive, presumption that her testimony is false or feigned. (213–14)

CRIMINAL SEXUAL CONDUCT STATUTES

LO 5

The 1970s and 1980s were a time of major reform of sex offense laws. First, states changed rape prosecution procedures that had been in effect since the 1600s. Many states abolished the corroboration rule that required the prosecution to back up rape victims' testimony with that of other witnesses (rarely possible to obtain). Also, most states passed rape shield statutes, which banned the prosecution from introducing evidence of victims' past sexual conduct. Many states also relaxed the prompt-reporting rule that banned prosecution unless women promptly reported rapes.

corroboration rule, an element in rape that the prosecution had to prove rape by the testimony of witnesses other than the victim

rape shield statutes, statutes that prohibit introducing evidence of victims' past conduct

prompt-reporting rule, requires that rape victims report the rape soon after it occurs

marital rape exception, provided that legally husbands couldn't rape their wives

States also expanded the definition of "rape." For example, all but a few states did away with the marital rape exception, the old common law rule that husbands couldn't rape their wives. Sexual assault statutes have also shifted the emphasis away from victim consent to perpetrator unwanted advances. For example, the Pennsylvania Superior Court, in *Commonwealth v. Mlinarich* (1985), ruled that the common law emphasis on lack of consent had "worked to the unfair disadvantage of the woman who, when threatened with violence, chose quite rationally to submit to her assailant's advances rather than risk death or serious bodily injury."

The MPC (ALI 1985 2:279–81) rape provision eliminated consent as an element in rape because of its "disproportionate emphasis upon objective manifestations by the woman." But Code's drafters also recognized that the relationship between force and consent is complex. Unlike the acts in all other criminal assaults, consenting victims may want the physical act in rape—sexual intercourse:

> This unique feature of the offense requires drawing a line between forcible rape on the one hand and reluctant submission on the other, between true aggression and desired intimacy. The difficulty in drawing this line is compounded by the fact that there will often be no witness to the event other than the participants and that their perceptions may change over time. The trial may turn as much on an assessment of the motives of the victim as of the actor. (281)

CASE

People v. Evans ***(1975)*** *presents the question of "whether the sexual conquest by a predatory male of a resisting female constitutes rape or seduction."*

Was it rape or seduction?

People v. Evans

379 N.Y.S.2d 912 (1975)

HISTORY

Martin Evans (Defendant) was charged with first-degree rape. The Supreme Court, New York County, in a bench trial, the judge acquitted Evans of rape in the first degree. But he found him guilty of the lesser included offense of criminal trespass in the second degree and escape in the second degree.

GREENFIELD, J.

FACTS

Martin Evans, Also Known as Martin Sage (Defendant), a bachelor of approximately 37 years of age, aptly described in the testimony as "glib," on July 15, 1974 met an incoming plane at LaGuardia Airport, from which disembarked Lucy Elizabeth Peterson of Charlotte, North Carolina, a 20-year-old petite,

(continues)

(continued)
attractive second-year student at Wellesley College, an unworldly girl, evidently unacquainted with New York City and the sophisticated city ways, a girl who proved to be, as indicated by the testimony, incredibly gullible, trusting and naive.

Evans struck up a conversation with her, posing as a psychologist doing a magazine article and using a name that was not his, inducing Miss Peterson to answer questions for an interview. Evans invited Miss Peterson to accompany him by automobile to Manhattan, her destination being Grand Central Station. They were accompanied in the automobile by other persons, some of whom were introduced by Evans as colleagues on a professional basis. But it appears that a funny thing happened on the way to the station. There were numerous detours before Beth Peterson ever found her way to Grand Central Station. First, they were taken to an apartment on the East Side.

Then Evans and a girl named Bridget took Miss Peterson to an establishment called Maxwell's Plum, which Evans explained was for the purpose of conducting a sociological experiment in which he would observe her reactions and the reactions of males towards her in the setting of a singles bar. After several hours there, in which Miss Peterson evidently was still under the belief that her stopping for a drink at Maxwell's Plum was part of this psychological and sociological experiment, she was persuaded to accompany Evans to the West Side, upon his explanation that he was there going to pick up his automobile and drive her to Grand Central Station.

Instead of going to the automobile, she was induced to come up to an apartment on the 14th floor, which Evans explained was used as one of his five offices or apartments throughout the city; and Miss Peterson, still believing that Evans was in fact what he purported to be, went up and accompanied him there. That apartment, Apartment 14-D, at 1 Lincoln Plaza, was in truth and in fact the apartment of one Heinz Patzak, who ran the Austrian National Tourist Bureau and who at that time was in Austria. Mr. Patzak has testified that he never had given approval or permission for the defendant to enter, use or occupy that apartment.

Miss Peterson came to the apartment and her questions as to the existence of photographs of children, a crib, stuffed animals and toys, were readily explained away by Evans as being connected with his treatment of patients as a psychologist, the explanation of the crib and the toys being that these were used for the purposes of primal therapy to enable his patients to associate with their childhood years more readily. In the apartment the psychological interviewing continued, the defendant having explained to Miss Peterson that he was searching for the missing link between the "girl-woman" and the "woman-girl." Miss Peterson, who was then working in a psychiatric branch of New York Hospital, Cornell Medical School, in White Plains, and who had some training in psychology, believed that all of this legitimately related to a psychological research project, which the defendant was conducting.

During the course of the interview in the apartment Evans probed Miss Peterson's life and she had, during the course of their conversation together, made a revelation of her prior intimacies and her feelings, and her experiences with respect to various people. In the apartment she was asked to participate in an adjective word game, applying five adjectives to certain designated persons, including herself and the defendant.

She had been there for one to two hours when Evans made his move and pulled her on to the opened sofa bed in the living room of that apartment and attempted to disrobe her. She resisted that, and she claims that as articles of clothing were attempted to be removed she would pull them back on and ultimately she was able to ward off these advances and to get herself dressed again. At that point, Evans's tactics, according to her testimony, appeared to have changed.

First, he informed her of his disappointment that she had failed the test, that this was all part of his psychological experiment, that, in fact, this was a way in which he was trying to reach her innermost consciousness, one of the ways in which that could be done. Then, after expressing disappointment in the failure of this psychological experiment, he took steps to cause doubt and fear to arise in the mind of Miss Peterson. He said, "Look where you are. You are in the apartment of a strange man. How do you know that I am really who I say I am? How do you know that I am really a psychologist?" Then, he went on and said, "I could kill you. I could rape you. I could hurt you physically."

Miss Peterson testified that at that point she became extremely frightened, that she realized, indeed, how vulnerable she was. Evans did not strike her, did not beat her, he exhibited no weapons at the time, but he made the statement, "I could kill you; I could rape you."

Then there was yelling and screaming, further to intimidate Evans, and then an abrupt switch in which Evans attempted to play on the sympathy of Miss Peterson by telling her a story about his lost love, how Miss Peterson had reminded him of her, and the hurt that he had sustained when she had driven her car off a cliff. Obviously, Miss Peterson's sympathy was engaged, and at that time acting instinctively, she took a step forward and reached out for him and put her hand on his shoulders, and then he grabbed her and said, "You're mine, you are mine." There followed an act of sexual intercourse, an act of oral-genital contact; a half-hour later a second act of sexual intercourse, and then, before she left, about seven o'clock that morning, an additional act.

During these various sexual acts Miss Peterson, in fact, offered little resistance. She said that she was pinned down by Evans's body weight, but in some manner all her clothing was removed, all his clothing was removed, and the acts took place. There was no torn clothing, there were no scratches, and there were no bruises. Finally, at approximately 7:00 A.M. Miss Peterson dressed and left the apartment. She says that Evans acknowledged to her that he was aware that it had been against her will, but he nevertheless gave her three telephone numbers. Miss Peterson then returned to White Plains, where later that day she recited some of the events to a fellow worker, and then to a roommate. Ultimately she reported the facts to the New York City Police and to the Westchester County Sheriff's office. After he had been apprehended and arrested Evans escaped from the police car. Detective Kelleher chased him in and around the streets and up 15 flights of a building, where he ultimately located Evans on a water tower. The explanation given to Detective Magnusson was that he was looking for a lawyer.

OPINION

There are some factors which point toward guilt and some towards innocence. Factors indicating guilt are the assumption of the false identity by the defendant, his not giving his true name, his denial to the police when first confronted of what his name was, and his denial of any knowledge of Miss Peterson, which denials he ultimately retracted. Then, of course, there is the evidence about flight, which is always evidence that can be considered as evincing some consciousness of guilt.

On the other hand, there are some factors pointing to innocence, and a lack of criminal culpability on his part. The fact that Miss Peterson had no bruises or scratches, no torn clothing, that she had been allowed to proceed from the apartment without any further threats or concealment as to location. The fact that she was given phone numbers by the defendant which made it relatively easy to trace his location and whereabouts; the fact that he attempted to call her on several occasions after she had left the apartment. From all this, the court concludes that the defendant inveigled Miss Peterson, deceived her, put her on, and took advantage of her.

It is clear from the evidence that Beth Peterson was intimidated; that she was confused; that she had been drowned in a torrent of words and perhaps was terrified. But it is likewise clear from the evidence that the defendant did not resort to actual physical force. There was no act of violence, no struggle, no outcry, and no attempt to restrain or confine the person . . . which constitute the usual . . . and essential evidence of rape. The restraint which was imposed upon Miss Peterson was a restraint imposed by his body weight, which would be the normal situation in which any sexual contact would be achieved.

Miss Peterson manifested little or no resistance. She indicated at some point she kicked. I asked her what she was doing with her arms and hands at the time. The answers indicated that it was not very much. Now, that can be understandable. A woman is not obligated to resist to the uttermost under all circumstances, when her will to resist has been paralyzed by fear and by threats. That is why the law recognizes the existence of a threat as being the equivalent of the use of actual force. So the question here is not so much the use of force, but whether threats uttered by the defendant had paralyzed her capacity to resist and had, in fact, undermined her will. Now, what was it the defendant said? He said, "Look where you are. You are in the apartment of a strange man. How do you know that I really am who I say I am? How do you know that I am really a psychologist? I could kill you. I could rape you. I could hurt you physically."

Those words, as uttered, are susceptible to two possible and diverse interpretations. The first would be in essence that—you had better do what I say, for you are helpless and I have the power to use ultimate force should you resist. That clearly would be a threat which would induce fear and

(continues)

(continued)

overcome resistance. The second possible meaning of those words is, in effect, that—you are a foolish girl. You are in the apartment of a strange man. You put yourself in the hands of a stranger, and you are vulnerable and defenseless. The possibility would exist of physical harm to you were you being confronted by someone other than the person who uttered this statement.

Of course, it is entirely possible that Miss Peterson, who heard the statements, construed that as a threat, even though it may not have been intended as such by the person who uttered those words. The question arises as to which is the controlling state of mind—that of a person who hears the words and interprets them as a threat, or the state of mind of the person who utters such words.

It appears to the court that the controlling state of mind must be that of the speaker. She, the hearer, may, in fact, take the words as a threat and be terrified by them. But this being a criminal trial, the criminal intent of the defendant must be shown beyond a reasonable doubt. It is his intent when he acts, his intent when he speaks, which must therefore be controlling. And so, if he utters words which are taken as a threat by the person who hears them, but are not intended as a threat by the person who utters them, there would be no basis for finding the necessary criminal intent to establish culpability under the law.

The words which were uttered both as to what the defendant could do, "I could kill you. I could rape you." and subsequent words that he was going to do to the complainant what his lost love had done to him—the court finds are ambiguous. They were not accompanied by violence. They were not accompanied by a demonstration of the intention to carry out the threats. There was no beating. There was no weapon displayed. There was a statement as to a possibility, a statement of vulnerability. The court finds it cannot conclude that there was the utterance of a threat of such a nature as to enable the court to find the defendant guilty of the crime of rape in the first degree beyond a reasonable doubt. Since the court, therefore, can find neither forcible compulsion nor threat beyond a reasonable doubt, the defendant is found not guilty on the charges of rape, sodomy and unlawful imprisonment.

Now, acquittal on these charges does not imply that the court condones the conduct of the defendant. The testimony in the case reveals that the defendant was a predator, and that naive and gullible girls like Beth Peterson were his natural prey. He posed. He lied. He pretended and he deceived. He used confidences which were innocently bestowed as leverage to affect his will. He used psychological techniques to achieve vulnerability and sympathy, and the erosion of resistance.

A young and inexperienced girl like Beth Peterson was then unable to withstand the practiced onslaught of the defendant. The defendant apparently got his kicks through the exercise of these techniques. He apparently spurned the readily available women, the acquiescent women, like Bridget, who was living in the same apartment. To him, the game was worth more than the prize. He boasted to the police that this was a game he played with girls' heads. The court finds his conduct, if not criminal, to be reprehensible. It was conquest by con job. Truly, therefore, this defendant may be called "The Abominable Snowman."

So bachelors, and other men on the make, fear not. It is still not illegal to feed a girl a line, to continue the attempt, not to take no for a final answer. It is not criminal conduct for a male to make promises that will not be kept, to indulge in exaggeration and hyperbole, or to assure any trusting female that, as in the ancient fairy tale, the ugly frog is really the handsome prince. Every man is free, under the law, to be a gentleman or a cad. But take heed. Violence, force and threats are totally out of bounds. Their employment will transform a heel into a criminal.

[Note. Although the court acquitted Evans of rape, it found him guilty on two lesser offenses: trespass on Heinz Patzak's apartment and escape from the arresting police officers' squad car.]

QUESTIONS

1. List the facts and circumstances the judge found pointed toward Evans's guilt.
2. According to the judge, whose words should we look at to determine whether Evans threatened Lucy Peterson? Explain his reasons for the answer.
3. In your opinion, did Martin Evans rape or seduce Lucy Peterson? Back up your answer with the facts and circumstances in the case and the relevant text.

LO 5

The most far-reaching reforms in the definition of "rape" are the sexual assault statutes of the 1970s and the 1980s, which consolidated the sex offenses into one comprehensive statute. They expanded the definition of "rape" and other sex offenses to include all sexual penetrations: vaginal, anal, and oral. Then, they created less serious crimes of sexual contacts—such as offensive touching of breasts and buttocks. (See "Grading the Degrees of Rape" later on p. 376 for details.) Finally, they made sex offenses sex-neutral; men can sexually assault men or women, and women can sexually assault women or men (Minnesota Criminal Code 2005, § 341).

Despite these advances in rape law, keep in mind Professor David Bryden's (2000) assessment of the reality of current sexual assault law:

> Most legislatures and courts still define rape narrowly. In acquaintance rape cases, in most states, nonconsensual sex is not rape unless the perpetrator employs force or a threat of force, or the victim is unconscious, badly drunk, underage, or otherwise incapacitated. Even if the victim verbally declines sex, the encounter is not rape in most states unless the man employs "force." Sex obtained by nonviolent threats ("you'll lose your job," etc.), or by deception, usually is not a crime. (321)

THE ELEMENTS OF MODERN RAPE LAW

LO 6

Most traditional rape statutes, and the newer criminal sexual assault laws, define "rape" as intentional sexual penetration by force without consent. There are many variations in the statutes, but in most jurisdictions, rape today boils down to three elements:

1. *ACTUS REUS.* Sexual penetration by force or threat of force
2. *MENS REA.* Intentional sexual penetration
3. CIRCUMSTANCE. Nonconsent by the victim

(See the Elements of Rape illustration.) Let's look at each of these elements.

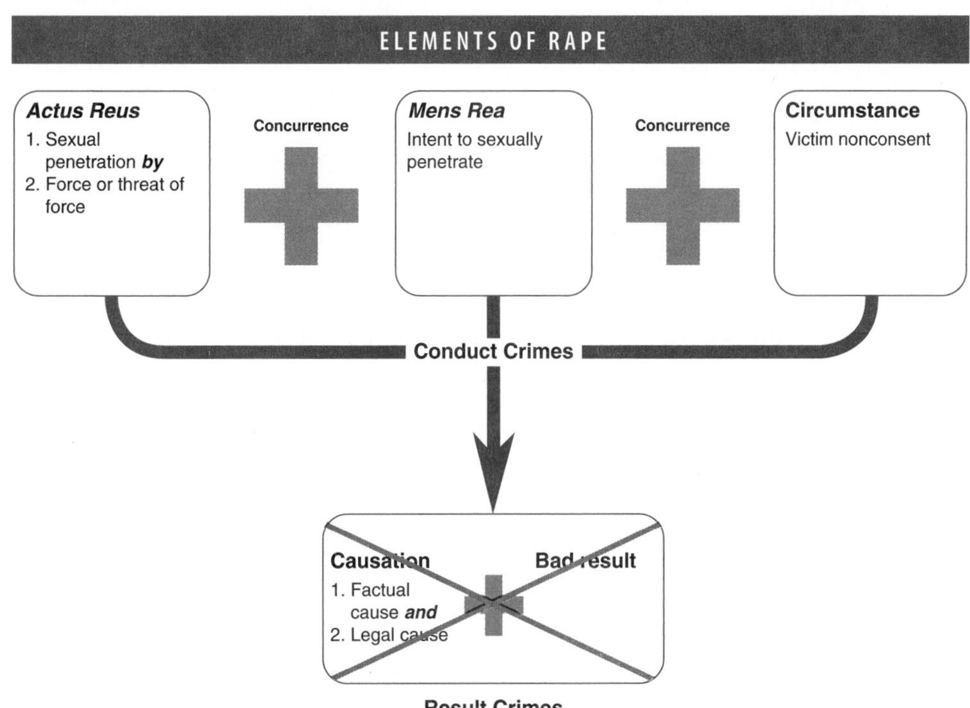

LO 7

Rape Actus Reus: *The Force and Resistance Rule*

force and resistance rule, provided that victims had to prove to the courts that they didn't consent to rape by demonstrating that they resisted the force of the rapist

Rape is a crime of violence; its *actus reus* is sexual intercourse by force. For most of its history, rape *actus reus* was governed by the force and resistance rule. The "force" part of the rule wasn't satisfied if victims consented to sexual intercourse. In practice, the prosecution didn't have to prove that victims consented; victims had to prove they didn't consent. This is where the "resistance" part of the rule comes in. Victims had to prove they didn't consent by proving they resisted the force of the accused rapist.

According to an early frequently cited case, *Reynolds v. State* (1889):

> Voluntary submission by the woman, while she has power to resist, no matter how reluctantly yielded, removes from the act an essential element of the crime of rape if the carnal knowledge was with the consent of the woman, no matter how tardily given, or how much force had theretofore been employed, it is not rape. (904)

Proof of nonconsent by resistance is peculiar to the law of rape. In no other crime where lack of consent is an element of the crime does the law treat passive acceptance as consent. Robbery requires taking someone's property by force or threat of force, but it's outrageous even to think that the element of force puts the burden on victims to prove they resisted. Entering an unlocked apartment house without consent to commit a crime is burglary, but it would be absurd to demand that residents prove they didn't consent to the entry. The same is true of theft. According to Lani Anne Remick (1993):

> A common defense to a charge of auto theft is that the car's owner consented to the defendant's use of the vehicle. A mere showing that the owner never gave the defendant permission to take the car is enough to defeat this defense; no showing that the owner actually told the defendant not to take the car is necessary.
>
> In rape law, however, the "default" position is consent. Proof of the absence of affirmative indications by the victim is not enough to defeat a consent defense; instead, the prosecution must show that the alleged victim indicated to the defendant through her overt actions and/or words that she did not wish to participate in sexual activity with him.
>
> Thus, "the law presumes that one will not give away that which is his to a robber, but makes no similar presumption as to the conduct of women and rapists." In fact, quite the opposite is true: in the context of sexual activity the law presumes consent. For example, proving both that a woman did not verbally consent and that her actions consist of lying still and not moving does not raise a presumption of nonconsent but of consent. Only through evidence of some sort of overt behavior such as a verbal "no" or an attempt to push away the defendant can the prosecution meet its burden of proving nonconsent. (1111)

Factors that have influenced courts' view of nonconsent include the amount of resistance the victim offered, the threat of force, and the danger to the victim if she resisted. We'll look at each of these and exceptions to the force and resistance rule.

utmost resistance standard, requirement that rape victims had to use all the physical strength they had to prevent penetration

THE AMOUNT OF RESISTANCE STANDARD The amount of resistance required to prove lack of consent has changed over time. From the 1800s until the 1950s, the utmost resistance standard prevailed. According to the standard, to show they didn't consent, victims had to resist with all the physical power they possessed. In *Brown v. State* (1906), a 16-year-old virgin testified that her neighbor grabbed her, tripped her to the ground, and forced himself on her:

> I tried as hard as I could to get away. I was trying all the time to get away just as hard as I could. I was trying to get up; I pulled at the grass; I screamed as hard as I could, and he told me to shut up, and I didn't, and then he held his hand on my mouth until I was almost strangled. (538)

The jury convicted the neighbor of rape, but, on appeal, the Wisconsin Supreme Court reversed, deciding the victim hadn't resisted enough:

> Not only must there be entire absence of mental consent or assent, but there must be the most vehement exercise of every physical means or faculty within the woman's power to resist the penetration of her person, and this must be shown to persist until the offense is consummated. (538)

The Nebraska Supreme Court's language was even tougher in *Casico v. State* (1947):

> The general rule is that a mentally competent woman must in good faith resist to the utmost with the most vehement exercise of every physical means or faculty naturally within her power to prevent carnal knowledge, and she must persist in such resistance as long as she has the power to do so until the offense is consummated. (900)

reasonable resistance rule, provides that the amount of force required to repel rapists shows nonconsent in rape prosecutions

In the 1950s, most courts softened the utmost resistance definition to the **reasonable resistance rule**, the rule followed in almost all states today. According to the rule, the amount of resistance depends on the totality of circumstances in each case. For example, in *Jones v. State* (1984), Marvin Jones ran N.M. off the road while she was on the way to a fast-food store with her daughters. Jones opened the door, grabbed her arm, choked her, and forced her toward his car.

Fearing for her life, N.M. got into the car with her daughters. Jones drove to a secluded spot, threatened her, and forced her to commit oral sodomy. Then, he took her out on the road and raped her. At his first-degree rape and oral sodomy trial, Jones argued that N.M. consented. He was convicted and sentenced to fifty years in prison. He appealed, arguing there wasn't enough evidence that N.M. submitted because of "the threat of immediate and great bodily harm." The Oklahoma Court of Criminal Appeals affirmed his conviction and sentence:

> In Oklahoma, a woman threatened with rape is not required to resist to the uttermost; instead, she is not required to do more than her age, strength, and the surrounding circumstances make reasonable. In light of the facts of this case, as recited above, we find that there was more than ample evidence to establish that the prosecutrix submitted due to the threats of great bodily harm. (757)

Many new rape and sexual assault statutes have dropped the resistance requirement entirely—at least in formal law. This has had little or no effect in practice in stranger rape cases because it's pretty clear that these rapists use force against victims they don't know. Unarmed acquaintance rapes are a different matter; evidence of reasonable resistance is often critical. In practical terms, force means resistance. This is because acquaintance rapists don't use force unless victims resist their advances. In other words, force and resistance are two sides of the same coin; if force is an element, then so is resistance (Bryden 2000, 356).

Jones v. State (1992) illustrates this close, often inseparable connection between force and reasonable resistance in acquaintance rape. The victim, twenty-six-year-old C.L., lived in the same home with Jones, Jones's wife and child, and C.L.'s foster mother. One night, when Jones had been drinking, he came into C.L.'s bedroom and asked her to have sex with him. She said "no" and asked him why he didn't have intercourse with his wife.

He asked her again to have intercourse; she refused again "because it wouldn't be fair to his wife and child." He asked her a third time and C.L. testified that she "just let him have it, you know." She was lying on her side, and he turned her over and had sexual intercourse with her. She testified he told her not to tell anyone, particularly not to tell his wife.

She said she didn't give him permission to have sexual intercourse with her. She didn't yell out or cry for help because she was afraid. She testified on cross-examination that she was afraid of Jones, his wife, and her own foster mother; that it was difficult to tell her foster mother; that Jones didn't have a weapon; and that she didn't think to hit him (242).

The trial court convicted Jones of rape under Indiana's rape statute, which defined a "rapist" as someone who "knowingly or intentionally has sexual intercourse with a member of the opposite sex when the other person is compelled by force or imminent threat of force. . . ." The Indiana Supreme Court reversed the conviction:

> There was no evidence that Jones used any force or threats to encourage C.L. to engage in sexual intercourse. He asked her three times, and on the third time she "just let him have it." There was no evidence of any previous threats or force against C.L. from which the trier of fact could infer a fear of force or threats on this occasion. The circumstances do not lead to an inference of constructive or implied force. C.L. stated she was afraid to yell for help, but there was no evidence she was afraid because Jones had forced her to do anything or threatened her. There are reasons a person might be afraid to attract attention other than fear of forced activity. (243)

The court didn't mention the word "resistance." It didn't have to; the implication was clear that resistance was an implied requirement. Otherwise, how could the court have concluded that this was a consensual case? You might think of it this way: If Jones had been a stranger, is there any doubt that this would be rape?

extrinsic force, in rape cases, requires some force in addition to the amount needed to accomplish the penetration

intrinsic force, in rape, requires only the amount of force necessary to accomplish the penetration

Courts today have adopted either of two definitions of "force":

1. **EXTRINSIC FORCE** Requires some act of force in addition to the muscular movements needed to accomplish penetration. The amount of force required varies according to the circumstances of particular cases.
2. **INTRINSIC FORCE** Requires only the amount of physical effort necessary to accomplish penetration.

We'll use the next two case excerpts to show you how important the facts in each case are in applying the extrinsic and intrinsic force requirements to acquaintance rape.

CASE

In* Commonwealth v. Berkowitz *(1994), the Pennsylvania Supreme Court applied the extrinsic force standard.

Did he have sexual intercourse by force?

Commonwealth v. Berkowitz

609 A.2d 1338 (Penn.Sup. 1992)
641 A.2d 1161 (Penn. 1994)

HISTORY

Robert Berkowitz, the defendant, was convicted in the Court of Common Pleas, Monroe County, of rape and indecent assault and he appealed. The Superior Court, Philadelphia, reversed the rape conviction. The Pennsylvania Supreme Court affirmed the Superior Court's reversal of the conviction.

PER CURIAM [by the whole court]

FACTS

609 A.2d 1338 (Penn.Sup. 1992)

In the spring of 1988, Robert Berkowitz and the victim were both college sophomores at East Stroudsburg State University, ages 20 and 19 years old, respectively. They had mutual friends and acquaintances. On April 19 of that year, the victim went to Berkowitz's dormitory room. What transpired in that dorm room between Berkowitz and the victim thereafter is the subject of the instant appeal.

During a one-day jury trial held on September 14, 1988, the victim gave the following account during direct examination by the Commonwealth. At roughly 2:00 on the afternoon of April 19, 1988, after attending two morning classes, the victim returned to her dormitory room. There, she drank a martini to "loosen up a little bit" before going to meet her boyfriend, with whom she had argued the night before. Roughly 10 minutes later she walked to her boyfriend's dormitory lounge to meet him. He had not yet arrived.

Having nothing else to do while she waited for her boyfriend, the victim walked up to Berkowitz's room to look for Earl Hassel, Berkowitz's roommate. She knocked on the door several times but received no answer. She therefore wrote a note to Mr. Hassel, which read, "Hi Earl, I'm drunk. That's not why I came to see you. I haven't seen you in a while. I'll talk to you later, [Victim's name]." She did so, although she had not felt any intoxicating effects from the martini, "for a laugh."

After the victim had knocked again, she tried the knob on Berkowitz's door. Finding it open, she walked in. She saw someone lying on the bed with a pillow over his head, whom she thought to be Earl Hassel. After lifting the pillow from his head, she realized it was Berkowitz. She asked him which dresser was his roommate's. He told her, and the victim left the note.

Before the victim could leave Berkowitz's room, however, he asked her to stay and "hang out for a while." She complied because she "had time to kill" and because she didn't really know Berkowitz and wanted to give him "a fair chance." Berkowitz asked her to give him a back rub but she declined, explaining that she did not "trust" him. He then asked her to have a seat on his bed. Instead, she found a seat on the floor, and conversed for a while about a mutual friend.

On cross-examination, the victim testified that during this conversation she had explained she was having problems with her boyfriend. No physical contact between the two had, to this point, taken place.

Thereafter, however, Berkowitz moved off the bed and down on the floor, and "kind of pushed [the victim] back with his body. It wasn't a shove, it was just kind of a leaning-type of thing." Next Berkowitz "straddled" and started kissing the victim. The victim responded by saying, "Look, I gotta go. I'm going to meet [my boyfriend]." Then Berkowitz lifted up her shirt and bra and began fondling her. The victim then said "no."

After roughly 30 seconds of kissing and fondling, Berkowitz "undid his pants and he kind of moved his body up a little bit." The victim was still saying "no" but "really couldn't move because Berkowitz was shifting her body so he was over me." Berkowitz then tried to put his penis in her mouth. The victim did not physically resist, but rather continued to verbally protest, saying "No, I gotta go, let me go," in a "scolding" manner.

Ten or 15 more seconds passed before the two rose to their feet. Berkowitz disregarded the victim's continual complaints that she "had to go," and instead walked two feet away to the door and locked it so that no one from the outside could enter. The victim testified that she realized at the time that the lock was not of a type that could lock people inside the room.

Then, in the victim's words, "He put me down on the bed. It was kind of like—he didn't throw me on the bed. It's hard to explain. It was kind of like a push but no. . . ." She did not bounce off the bed. "It wasn't slow like a romantic kind of thing, but it wasn't a fast shove either. It was kind of in the middle."

Once the victim was on the bed, Berkowitz began "straddling" her again while he undid the knot in her sweatpants. He then removed her sweatpants and underwear from one of her legs. The victim did not physically resist in any way while on the bed because Berkowitz was on top of her, and she "couldn't like go anywhere." She did not scream out at anytime because "it was like a dream was happening or something."

Berkowitz then used one of his hands to "guide" his penis into her vagina. At that point, after Berkowitz was inside her, the victim began saying "no, no to him softly in a moaning kind of way because it was just so scary." After about 30 seconds, Berkowitz pulled out his penis and ejaculated onto the victim's stomach.

(continues)

(continued)

Immediately thereafter, Berkowitz got off the victim and said, "Wow, I guess we just got carried away." To this the victim retorted, "No, we didn't get carried away, you got carried away." The victim then quickly dressed, grabbed her school books, and raced downstairs to her boyfriend who was by then waiting for her in the lounge. Once there, the victim began crying. Her boyfriend and she went up to his dorm room where, after watching the victim clean off Berkowitz's semen from her stomach, he called the police.

Defense counsel's cross-examination elicited more details regarding the contact between Berkowitz and the victim before the incident in question. The victim testified that roughly two weeks prior to the incident, she had attended a school seminar entitled, "Does 'no' sometimes mean 'yes'?" Among other things, the lecturer at this seminar had discussed the average length and circumference of human penises. After the seminar, the victim and several of her friends had discussed the subject matter of the seminar over a speaker-telephone with Berkowitz and his roommate, Earl Hassel. The victim testified that during that telephone conversation, she had asked Berkowitz the size of his penis. According to the victim, Berkowitz responded by suggesting that the victim "come over and find out." She declined.

When questioned further regarding her communications with Berkowitz prior to the April 19, 1988, incident, the victim testified that on two other occasions, she had stopped by Berkowitz's room while intoxicated. During one of those times, she had laid down on his bed. When asked whether she had asked Berkowitz again at that time what his penis size was, the victim testified that she did not remember.

Berkowitz took the stand in his own defense and offered an account of the incident and the events leading up to it which differed only as to the consent involved. According to Berkowitz, the victim had begun communication with him after the school seminar by asking him of the size of his penis and of whether he would show it to her. Berkowitz had suspected that the victim wanted to pursue a sexual relationship with him because she had stopped by his room twice after the phone call while intoxicated, lying down on his bed with her legs spread and again asking to see his penis. He believed that his suspicions were confirmed when she initiated the April 19, 1988, encounter by stopping by his room (again after drinking) and waking him up.

Berkowitz testified that, on the day in question, he did initiate the first physical contact, but added that the victim warmly responded to his advances by passionately returning his kisses. He conceded that she was continually "whispering no's," but claimed that she did so while "amorously . . . passionately" moaning. In effect, he took such protests to be thinly veiled acts of encouragement. When asked why he locked the door, he explained that "that's not something you want somebody to just walk in on you doing."

According to Berkowitz, the two then lay down on the bed, the victim helped him take her clothing off, and he entered her. He agreed that the victim continued to say "no" while on the bed, but carefully qualified his agreement, explaining that the statements were "moaned passionately." According to Berkowitz, when he saw a "blank look on her face," he immediately withdrew and asked "is anything wrong, is something the matter, is anything wrong." He ejaculated on her stomach thereafter because he could no longer "control" himself. Berkowitz testified that after this, the victim "saw that it was over and then she made her move. She gets right off the bed . . . she just swings her legs over and then she puts her clothes back on." Then, in wholly corroborating an aspect of the victim's account, he testified that he remarked, "Well, I guess we got carried away," to which she rebuked, "No, we didn't get carried, you got carried away."

OPINION

641 A.2d 1161 (Penn. 1994)

CAPPY, J.

The crime of rape is defined as follows:

§ 3121. RAPE

> A person commits a felony of the first degree when he engages in sexual intercourse with another person not one's spouse:
>
> 1. by forcible compulsion;
> 2. by threat of forcible compulsion that would prevent resistance by a person of reasonable resolution;

3. who is unconscious; or
4. who is so mentally deranged or deficient that such person is incapable of consent.

The victim of a rape need not resist.

> The force necessary to support a conviction of rape need only be such as to establish lack of consent and to induce the victim to submit without additional resistance. The degree of force required to constitute rape is relative and depends on the facts and particular circumstance of the case.

In regard to the critical issue of forcible compulsion, the complainant's testimony is devoid of any statement which clearly or adequately describes the use of force or the threat of force against her. In response to defense counsel's question, "Is it possible that [when Appellee lifted your bra and shirt] you took no physical action to discourage him," the complainant replied, "It's possible." When asked, "Is it possible that Berkowitz was not making any physical contact with you aside from attempting to untie the knot in the drawstrings of complainant's sweatpants," she answered, "It's possible." She testified that "He put me down on the bed. It was kind of like—He didn't throw me on the bed. It's hard to explain. It was kind of like a push but not—I can't explain what I'm trying to say."

She concluded that "it wasn't much" in reference to whether she bounced on the bed, and further detailed that their movement to the bed "wasn't slow like a romantic kind of thing, but it wasn't a fast shove either. It was kind of in the middle." She agreed that Appellee's hands were not restraining her in any manner during the actual penetration, and that the weight of his body on top of her was the only force applied.

She testified that at no time did Berkowitz verbally threaten her. The complainant did testify that she sought to leave the room, and said "no" throughout the encounter. As to the complainant's desire to leave the room, the record clearly demonstrates that the door could be unlocked easily from the inside, that she was aware of this fact, but that she never attempted to go to the door or unlock it. As to the complainant's testimony that she stated "no" throughout the encounter with Berkowitz, we point out that, while such an allegation of fact would be relevant to the issue of consent, it is not relevant to the issue of force. Where there is a lack of consent, but no showing of either physical force, a threat of physical force, or psychological coercion, the "forcible compulsion" requirement under 18 Pa.C.S. § 3121 is not met.

The degree of physical force, threat of physical force, or psychological coercion required under 18 Pa.C.S. § 3121 must be sufficient to prevent resistance by a person of reasonable resolution, but the "peculiar situation" of the victim and other subjective factors should be considered by the court in determining "resistance," "assent," and "consent."

Reviewed in light of the above described standard, the complainant's testimony simply fails to establish that the Appellee forcibly compelled her to engage in sexual intercourse as required under 18 Pa.C.S. § 3121. Thus, even if all of the complainant's testimony was believed, the jury, as a matter of law, could not have found Appellee guilty of rape. Accordingly, we hold that the Superior Court did not err in reversing Appellee's conviction of rape.

Accordingly, the order of the Superior Court reversing the rape conviction is affirmed.

QUESTIONS

1. Explain how the court came to the conclusion that the Pennsylvania rape statute required extrinsic force.
2. List all the facts relevant to deciding whether Robert Berkowitz's actions satisfy the extrinsic force requirement.
3. Assume you're the prosecutor, and argue that Robert Berkowitz did use extrinsic force to achieve sexual penetration.
4. Now, assume you're the prosecutor, and argue that Robert Berkowitz didn't use extrinsic force to achieve sexual penetration.

Now, let's look at how the New Jersey Supreme Court applied the intrinsic force standard in *State in the Interest of M.T.S.* (1992).

CASE

In **State in the Interest of M.T.S.** ***(1992),*** *the New Jersey Supreme Court applied the intrinsic force standard to rule in the case of a juvenile.*

Did he have sexual intercourse by force?

State in the Interest of M.T.S.

609 A.2d 1266 (N.J. 1992)

HISTORY

The trial court determined that M.T.S., a juvenile, was delinquent for committing a sexual assault. The Appellate Division reversed. The New Jersey Supreme Court granted the state's petition for certification to review the law regarding the element of force in rape, and reversed.

HANDLER, J.

FACTS

On Monday, May 21, 1990, 15-year-old C.G. was living with her mother, her three siblings, and several other people, including M.T.S. and his girlfriend. A total of 10 people resided in the three-bedroom town home at the time of the incident. M.T.S., then age 17, was temporarily residing at the home with the permission of C.G.'s mother; he slept downstairs on a couch. C.G. had her own room on the second floor.

At approximately 11:30 P.M. on May 21, C.G. went upstairs to sleep after having watched television with her mother, M.T.S., and his girlfriend. When C.G. went to bed, she was wearing underpants, a bra, shorts, and a shirt. At trial, C.G. and M.T S. offered very different accounts concerning the nature of their relationship and the events that occurred after C.G. had gone upstairs. The trial court did not credit fully either teenager's testimony.

C.G. stated that earlier in the day, M.T.S. had told her three or four times that he "was going to make a surprise visit up in her bedroom." She said that she had not taken M.T.S. seriously and considered his comments a joke because he frequently teased her. She testified that M.T.S. had attempted to kiss her on numerous other occasions and at least once had attempted to put his hands inside of her pants, but that she had rejected all of his previous advances.

C.G. testified that on May 22, at approximately 1:30 A.M., she awoke to use the bathroom. As she was getting out of bed, she said, she saw M.T.S., fully clothed, standing in her doorway. According to C.G., M.T.S. then said that "he was going to tease [her] a little bit." C.G. testified that she "didn't think anything of it"; she walked past him, used the bathroom, and then returned to bed, falling into a "heavy" sleep within 15 minutes.

The next event C.G. claimed to recall of that morning was waking up with M.T.S. on top of her, her underpants and shorts removed. She said "his penis was into her vagina." As soon as C.G. realized what had happened, she said, she immediately slapped M.T.S. once in the face, then "told him to get off [her], and get out." She did not scream or cry out. She testified that M.T.S. complied in less than one minute after being struck; according to C.G., "He jumped right off of [her]." She said she did not know how long M.T.S. had been inside of her before she awoke.

C.G. said that after M.T.S. left the room, she "fell asleep crying" because "she couldn't believe that he did what he did to her." She explained that she did not immediately tell her mother or anyone else in the house of the events of that morning because she was "scared and in shock." According to C.G., M.T.S. engaged in intercourse with her "without [her] wanting it or telling him to come up [to her bedroom]." By her own account, C.G. was not otherwise harmed by M.T.S.

At about 7:00 A.M., C.G. went downstairs and told her mother about her encounter with M.T.S. earlier in the morning and said that they would have to "get [him] out of the house." While M.T.S. was out on an errand, C.G.'s mother gathered his clothes and put them outside in his car; when he returned, he was told that "[he] better not even get near the house." C.G. and her mother then filed a complaint with the police.

According to M.T.S., he and C.G. had been good friends for a long time, and their relationship "kept leading on to more and more." He had been living at C.G.'s home for about five days before the incident occurred; he testified that during the three days preceding the incident they had been "kissing and necking" and had discussed having sexual intercourse. The first time M.T.S. kissed C.G., he said, she "didn't want him to, but she did after that." He said C.G. repeatedly had encouraged him to "make a surprise visit up in her room." M.T.S. testified that at exactly 1:15 A.M. on May 22, he entered C.G.'s bedroom as she was walking to the bathroom.

He said C.G. soon returned from the bathroom, and the two began "kissing and all," eventually moving to the bed. Once they were in bed, he said, they undressed each other and continued to kiss and touch for about five minutes. M.T.S. and C.G. proceeded to engage in sexual intercourse.

According to M.T.S., who was on top of C.G., he "stuck it in" and "did it [thrust] three times, and then the fourth time he stuck it in," that's when she "pulled him off" of her. M.T.S. said that as C.G. pushed him off, she said "stop, get off," and he "hopped off right away." According to M.T.S., after about one minute, he asked C.G. what was wrong; she replied with a backhand to his face. He recalled asking C.G. what was wrong a second time, and her replying, "How can you take advantage of me or something like that."

M.T.S. said that he proceeded to get dressed and told C.G. to calm down, but that she then told him to get away from her and began to cry. Before leaving the room, he told C.G., "I'm leaving. I'm going with my real girlfriend; don't talk to me. I don't want nothing to do with you or anything; stay out of my life; don't tell anybody about this, it would just screw everything up." He then walked downstairs and went to sleep.

On May 23, 1990, M.T.S. was charged with conduct that if engaged in by an adult would constitute second-degree sexual assault of the victim, contrary to N.J.S.A. 2C:142c(1).

Following a two-day trial on the sexual assault charge, M.T.S. was adjudicated delinquent. After reviewing the testimony, the Court concluded that the victim had consented to a session of kissing and heavy petting with M.T.S. The trial court did not find that C.G. had been sleeping at the time of penetration, but nevertheless found that she had not consented to the actual sexual act. Accordingly, the Court concluded that the State had proven second-degree sexual assault beyond a reasonable doubt.

On appeal, following the imposition of suspended sentences on the sexual assault and the other remaining charges, the Appellate Division determined that the absence of force beyond that involved in the act of sexual penetration precluded a finding of second-degree sexual assault. It therefore reversed the juvenile's adjudication of delinquency for that offense.

OPINION

Under New Jersey law a person who commits an act of sexual penetration using physical force or coercion is guilty of second-degree sexual assault. The sexual assault statute does not define the words "physical force." The question posed by this appeal is whether the element of "physical force" is met simply by an act of nonconsensual penetration involving no more force than necessary to accomplish that result.

That issue is presented in the context of what is often referred to as "acquaintance rape." The record in the case discloses that the juvenile, a seventeen-year-old boy, engaged in consensual kissing and heavy petting with a fifteen-year-old girl and thereafter engaged in actual sexual penetration of the girl to which she had not consented.

Pre-reform rape law in New Jersey, with its insistence on resistance by the victim, greatly minimized the importance of the forcible and assaultive aspect of the defendant's conduct. Rape prosecutions turned then not so much on the forcible or assaultive character of the defendant's actions as on the nature of the victim's response. That the law put the rape victim on trial was clear.

The New Jersey Code of Criminal Justice reformed the law of rape in 1978. The Code does not refer to force in relation to "overcoming the will" of the victim, or to the "physical overpowering" of the victim, or the "submission" of the victim. It does not require the demonstrated nonconsent of the victim.

In reforming the rape laws, the Legislature placed primary emphasis on the assaultive nature of the crime, altering its constituent elements so that they focus exclusively on the forceful or assaultive conduct of the defendant.

We conclude, therefore, that any act of sexual penetration engaged in by the defendant without the affirmative and freely given permission of the victim

(continues)

(continued)

to the specific act of penetration constitutes the offense of sexual assault.

Today the law of sexual assault is indispensable to the system of legal rules that assures each of us the right to decide who may touch our bodies, when, and under what circumstances. The decision to engage in sexual relations with another person is one of the most private and intimate decisions a person can make. Each person has the right not only to decide whether to engage in sexual contact with another, but also to control the circumstances and character of that contact.

Notwithstanding the stereotype of rape as a violent attack by a stranger, the vast majority of sexual assaults are perpetrated by someone known to the victim. Contrary to common myths, perpetrators generally do not use guns or knives and victims generally do not suffer external bruises or cuts. Although this more realistic and accurate view of rape only recently has achieved widespread public circulation, it was a central concern of the proponents of reform in the 1970s.

We acknowledge that cases such as this are inherently fact sensitive and depend on the reasoned judgment and common sense of judges and juries. The trial court concluded that the victim had not expressed consent to the act of intercourse, either through her words or actions. We conclude that the record provides reasonable support for the trial court's disposition.

Accordingly, we reverse the judgment of the Appellate Division and reinstate the disposition of juvenile delinquency for the commission of second-degree sexual assault.

QUESTIONS

1. List all of the evidence relevant to determining whether M.T.S.'s actions satisfied the intrinsic force element of the New Jersey sexual assault statute.
2. Summarize the reasons the court gives for adopting the intrinsic force standard.
3. Taking into account the evidence, decision, and reasoning of *Commonwealth v. Berkowitz*, which do you think is the better approach to the force requirement—intrinsic or extrinsic force? Defend your answer.
4. Should legislatures or courts decide whether to adopt the intrinsic or extrinsic force standard? Defend your answer.

LO 7

The threat of force The actual use of force isn't required to satisfy the force requirement. The threat of force is enough. To satisfy the threat-of-force requirement, the prosecution has to prove the victim experienced two kinds of fear:

subjective fear, means that the victim honestly feared imminent and serious bodily harm

objective fear, means that the fear was reasonable under the circumstances

1. **SUBJECTIVE FEAR** The victim honestly feared imminent and serious bodily harm.
2. **OBJECTIVE FEAR** The fear was reasonable under the circumstances.

Brandishing a weapon satisfies the requirement. So do verbal threats—such as threats to kill, seriously injure, or kidnap. But the threat doesn't have to include showing weapons or using specifically threatening words. Courts can consider all of the following in deciding whether the victim's fear was reasonable (Edwards 1996, 260–61):

- The respective ages of the perpetrator and the victim
- The physical sizes of the perpetrator and the victim
- The mental condition of the perpetrator and the victim
- The physical setting of the assault
- Whether the perpetrator had a position of authority, domination, or custodial control over the victim

Resistance and danger to the victim Some empirical research from the late 1970s and early 1980s reported that resistance "may threaten rape victims' lives" (Schwartz 1983, 577). Fifty-five percent of rapists in one widely publicized study reported "getting more violent, sometimes losing control" when their victims resisted (579). Another study, funded by the U.S. Department of Justice, found that 66 percent of victims who resisted were injured compared to 34 percent who didn't (580).

Studies from the 1990s have uncovered shortcomings in these earlier findings. For one thing, stranger rapes were overrepresented because it's easier to study convicted rapists, who are overwhelmingly violent stranger rapists. As you've already learned, acquaintance rapists far outnumber stranger rapists.

Let's add some details about acquaintance rape that can help you to understand the effect of victim resistance. First, victims usually resist unwanted advances because they're not afraid that men they know will hurt them. Second, and important, they're right: resistance usually succeeds.

According to Patricia Dooze and her colleagues, "Most rapes are attempted but not completed and the woman succeeds in escaping with little or no injury" (Bryden 2000, 366, n. 196). As to injuries, the National Victim Center's report, "Rape in America," reported that 4 percent of acquaintance rape victims reported serious injuries, 24 percent reported minor injuries, and 70 percent reported no injuries (Bryden 2000, 367, n. 198).

Finally, the most sophisticated empirical studies of the 1990s found that it's not initial victim resistance that provokes rapists to injure their victims. It's the other way around; initial rapist violence provokes victim resistance (Bryden 2000, 367).

LO 8

Exceptions to the force and resistance rule The law has never required physical resistance in all cases. No resistance is required if victims were incapacitated at the time of the assault by intoxication, mental deficiency, or insanity.

Also, deception (fraud) can substitute for force. These cases often involve doctors who trick their patients into having sexual intercourse. These cases fall into two categories, fraud in the fact and fraud in the inducement. **Fraud in the fact** consists of tricking the victim into believing the act she consented to wasn't sexual intercourse.

fraud in the fact, in rape, occurs when the rapist fraudulently convinces his victim that the act consented to was something other than sexual intercourse

This type of intercourse is rape. In a famous old case still cited, *Moran v. People* (1872), Dr. Moran told a patient he needed to insert an instrument into her vagina for treatment. She consented. In fact, the doctor was engaging in intercourse. The court rejected the argument that his victim consented, and the appeals court upheld the doctor's rape conviction.

Intercourse obtained by **fraud in the inducement** isn't rape. The fraud is in the benefits promised for consenting to sex, not in the act. For example, "Dr. Feelgood" in the 1980s had sexual assault charges against him dropped, but he didn't benefit from his victims' consent, because his fraud was in the benefits he promised his victims, not in the act of intercourse. Daniel Boro, posing as "Dr. Feelgood," tricked several women into believing he could cure their fatal blood disease by having sexual intercourse with him. He convinced them that they had two choices: they could undergo an extremely painful and expensive surgery or have intercourse with a donor (Boro, of course) who'd been injected with a special serum. The court ruled the women consented even though Boro used fraud to induce them to have intercourse with them (*Boro v. Superior Court* 1985).

fraud in the inducement, in rape, occurs when the fraud is in the benefits promised, not in the act

Finally, sexual intercourse with a minor who consented is rape because the law doesn't recognize the consent of minors. You'll learn more about statutory rape later in the chapter.

LO 9

Rape Mens Rea

Rape is a general-intent crime. Recall from Chapter 4 that one common meaning of "general intent" is that defendants intended to commit the act defined in the crime—in the case of rape, the act is forcible sexual penetration. This, of course, doesn't mean there can't be a different state of mind regarding circumstance elements, specifically nonconsent. These circumstance elements center around mistakes—mistakes about age in the cases involving underage victims or mistakes about the consent to sexual penetration by competent adult victims.

It's impossible to purposely, or even knowingly, make a mistake. That leaves three possibilities: reckless mistakes, negligent mistakes, or no-fault mistakes (strict liability). The states are divided as to which mental element to require.

At one extreme are states that adopt strict liability. An example of strict liability regarding consent is *Commonwealth v. Fischer* (1998). Kurt Fischer and another Lafayette College freshman gave "grossly divergent" stories regarding their encounter in Fischer's dorm room. The victim testified that when they went to his room, Fischer locked the door, pushed her onto the bed, straddled her, held her wrists above her head, and forced his penis into her mouth. She struggled through the whole encounter, warned him that "someone would find out," told him she had to be at a class, and didn't want to have sex with him. Fischer ignored all this, forced his hands inside a hole in her jeans, pushed his penis through the hole, removed it, and ejaculated on her face, hair, and sweater (1112–13).

Fischer testified that when they got to his room, the victim told him it would have to be a "quick one." Fischer admitted he held the victim's arms above her head, straddled her, and put his penis in her mouth, and said, "I know you want my dick in your mouth." When she replied, "no," Fischer said, "no means yes." After Fischer insisted again that she "wanted it," and she replied, "No, I honestly don't," he stopped trying. Then they just lay on the bed fondling and kissing each other (1113).

The jury found Fischer guilty of involuntary deviate sexual intercourse and aggravated indecent assault; he was sentenced to five years in prison. On appeal, Fischer argued that he honestly, but mistakenly, believed the victim consented. The Pennsylvania Superior Court expressed approval of an honest and reasonable mistake rule—that is, a negligence mental element—because of changing sexual habits, particularly on college campuses (1114).

honest and reasonable mistake rule, a negligence mental element in rape cases in which the defendant argues that he honestly, but mistakenly, believed the victim consented to sex

Nevertheless, the court ruled, it didn't have the authority to replace the state's strict liability rule with a negligence rule on its own. Quoting from a rape case involving two Temple University students, the court said the reasonable and honest mistake of fact rule regarding consent

> is not now and has never been the law of Pennsylvania. When one individual uses force or the threat of force to have sexual relations with a person not his spouse and without the person's consent he has committed the crime of rape. *If the element of the defendant's belief as to the victim's state of mind is to be established as a defense to the crime of rape then it should be done by the legislature which has the power to define crimes and defenses. We refuse to create such a defense.* (1114) [emphasis in original]

Several states have adopted the negligence standard that the court in *Commonwealth v. Fischer* referred to favorably. A frequently cited example is *People v. Mayberry* (1975). Booker T. Mayberry and "Miss B." gave conflicting stories of what happened. Miss B. testified that Mayberry repeatedly hit her and threatened to hurt her if she didn't come to his apartment for sex. Mayberry testified that she came voluntarily to his apartment where she willingly engaged in sexual intercourse with him.

The trial court refused Mayberry's request that the judge instruct the jury as to mistake of fact regarding Mayberry's belief that Miss B. consented to the intercourse. The California Supreme Court reversed the conviction. Although the statute said nothing about the mental attitude required for consent, the court read into the statute the requirement that Mayberry's mistake as to Miss B.'s consent had to be negligent:

> The severe penalty imposed for rape and the serious loss of reputation following conviction make it extremely unlikely that the legislature intended to exclude the element of wrongful intent. If a defendant entertains a reasonable and bona fide belief that a prosecutrix voluntarily consented to accompany him and to engage in sexual intercourse, it is apparent he does not possess the wrongful intent that is a prerequisite to a conviction of rape by means of force or threat. (1345)

A few courts have adopted a recklessness requirement, requiring that the defendant has to be aware that there's a risk the victim hasn't consented to sexual intercourse. The most famous example of requiring recklessness is the controversial English case, *Regina v. Morgan* (1975), which the court, with great understatement, called "somewhat bizarre." The case generated enormous attention and equally severe criticism, not just in the United Kingdom but in the United States.

William Morgan, an officer in the Royal Air Force (RAF), was out drinking with Robert McDonald, Robert McClarty, and Michael Parker, three other RAF men, much younger and junior in rank to Morgan. The four men weren't just drinking; they were looking for women. When they couldn't find any women to have sex with, Officer Morgan suggested that they go back to his house and have sex with his wife, Daphne. The younger men were complete strangers to Mrs. Morgan and at first didn't take their superior's suggestion seriously. But they realized Morgan was serious when he told them stories about Mrs. Morgan's "sexual aberrations" and then gave them condoms to wear.

Morgan told the men to expect his wife to resist but not to take her resistance seriously, "since it was a mere pretense whereby she stimulated her own sexual excitement." The men went to Morgan's house; Mrs. Morgan did resist. All four men overcame her resistance, and each had sexual intercourse with Mrs. Morgan while the others watched.

Daphne Morgan's account of what happened was that

> she was awakened from sleep in a single bed in a room which she shared with one of her children. Her husband and the other men in part dragged and in part carried her out on to a landing and thence into another room which contained a double bed. She struggled and screamed and shouted to her son to call the police, but one of the men put a hand over her mouth. Once on the double bed the defendants had intercourse with her in turn, finishing with her husband. During intercourse with the other three she was continuously being held, and this, coupled with her fear of further violence, restricted the scope of her struggles, but she repeatedly called out to her husband to tell the men to stop.

McDonald, McClarty, and Parker were charged with and convicted of rape. Officer Morgan was charged with and convicted of aiding and abetting the rapes by the younger men. (The marital rape exception prevented charging Morgan with rape.) They appealed. Their case eventually reached England's highest court, the House of Lords, where they argued that their convictions should be overturned because they believed Mrs. Morgan consented to the rape.

There was long and detailed argument about mistake and consent. It centered on whether a negligent mistake regarding Daphne Morgan's consent was enough to satisfy the *mens rea* requirement or whether recklessness was required. After more than fifty pages of analysis, the Lords decided on recklessness and reversed the convictions. Lord Hailsham put it succinctly:

> In rape the prohibited act is intercourse without the consent of the victim and the mental element lies in the intention to commit the act willy-nilly or not caring whether the victim consents or not. A failure to prove this element involves an acquittal,

> because an essential ingredient is lacking and it matters not that it is lacking because of a belief not based on reasonable ground.

Critics argue that rape is too serious a charge and the penalties are too severe to allow convictions based on a negligent or even a reckless mistake. They demand that defendants have to know their victims didn't consent before they can be subjected to the stigma of such a heinous crime and such severe punishment.

Law professor Susan Estrich (1987), a rape law scholar and herself a rape victim, disagrees:

> If inaccuracy or indifference to consent is "the best that this man can do" because he lacks the capacity to act reasonably, then it might well be unjust and ineffective to punish him for it. More common is the case of the man who could have done better but did not; heard her refusal or saw her tears, but decided to ignore them.
>
> The man who has the inherent capacity to act reasonably but fails to has, through that failure, made a blameworthy choice for which he can justly be punished. The law has long punished unreasonable action which leads to the loss of human life as manslaughter—a lesser crime than murder, but a crime nonetheless. The injury of sexual violation is sufficiently great, the need to provide that additional incentive pressing enough, to justify negligence liability for rape as for killing. (97–98)

LO 10

STATUTORY RAPE

statutory rape, to have carnal knowledge of a person under the age of consent whether or not accomplished by force

defense of reasonable mistake of age, a defense to statutory rape in California and Alaska if the defendant reasonably believed his victim was at or over the age of consent

Statutory rape means having sex with minors. Statutory rapists don't have to use force; the victim's immaturity substitutes for force. Furthermore, nonconsent isn't an element, nor is consent a defense, because minors can't legally consent to sex. In other words, statutory rape is a strict liability crime in most states.

A few states, such as California and Alaska, however, do permit the **defense of reasonable mistake of age**. In those states, the defense applies if a man reasonably believes his victim is over the age of consent. In other words, negligence is the required *mens rea* regarding the circumstance element of age.

GRADING THE DEGREES OF RAPE

Most statutes divide rape into two degrees: simple (second-degree) rape and aggravated (first-degree) rape. *Aggravated rape* involves at least one of the following circumstances:

LO 11

- The victim suffers serious bodily injury.
- A stranger commits the rape.
- The rape occurs in connection with another crime.
- The rapist is armed.
- The rapist has accomplices.
- The victim is a minor and the rapist is several years older.

simple rape, also known as second-degree rape, it's rape committed without aggravated circumstances

All other rapes are "**simple" rapes**, for which the penalties are less severe.

The criminal sexual conduct statutes comprise a broad range of criminal sexual penetrations and contacts that grades penetrations more seriously than contacts but also takes into account the aggravating circumstances just listed.

The reforms adopted in the criminal sexual conduct statutes (see "Criminal Sexual Conduct Statutes" on p. 359) grade the seriousness of sexual assault according to several criteria:

1. Penetrations are more serious than contacts.
2. Forcible penetrations and contacts are more serious than simple nonconsensual penetrations and contacts.

FIGURE 10.2

MICHIGAN CRIMINAL SEXUAL CONDUCT STATUTE

First degree This consists of "sexual penetration," defined as sexual intercourse, cunnilingus, fellatio, anal intercourse, "or any other intrusion, however slight, of any part of a person's body or of any object into the genital or anal openings of another person's body." In addition one of the following must have occurred:

1. The defendant must have been armed with a weapon.
2. Force or coercion was used, and the defendant was aided by another person.
3. Force or coercion was used, and personal injury to the victim was caused.

Second degree This consists of "sexual contact," defined as the intentional touching of the victim's or actor's personal parts or the intentional touching of the clothing covering the immediate area of the victim's intimate parts for purposes of sexual arousal or gratification.

"Intimate parts" is defined as including the primary genital area, groin, inner thigh, buttock, or breast. In addition, one of the circumstances required for first-degree criminal sexual conduct must have existed.

Third degree This consists of sexual penetration accomplished by force or coercion.

Fourth degree This consists of sexual contact accomplished by force or coercion.

3. Physical injury to the victim aggravates the offense.
4. Rapes involving more than one rapist, "gang rapes," are more serious than those involving a single rapist.

One of the earliest and best known of the new sexual assault laws is Michigan's statute, which incorporated language defining unwanted sexual conduct in 1974 (Michigan Criminal Code 2005, § 750.520; see Figure 10.2).

BODILY INJURY AND THREATS OF BODILY INJURY CRIMES

LO 12

Assault and battery, although combined in many modern statutes, are two separate crimes. A **battery** is an unwanted and unjustified offensive touching. Body contact is central to the crime of battery. An **assault** is either an attempted or a threatened battery, depending on how the statute defines it. The essential difference between assault and battery is that assault requires no physical contact; an assault is complete before the offender touches the victim. **Stalking** involves intentionally scaring another person by following, tormenting, or harassing him or her.

battery, unwanted and unjustified offensive touching

assault, an attempt to commit battery or intentionally putting another in fear

stalking, intentionally scaring another person by following, tormenting, or harassing

In this section, we'll look at the bodily injury crime of battery and the threats of bodily injury crimes of assault and stalking.

BATTERY

The battery *actus reus* is unlawful touching, but not every offensive physical contact is unlawful. Spanking children is offensive, at least to the children, but it's not battery. Why? Because the law recognizes it as the lawful act of disciplining children. Unlawful touching includes a broad spectrum of acts but usually means any unjustified touching without consent. Some courts have even included spitting in the face of someone you want to insult (*State v. Humphries* 1978).

Statutes don't always spell out the battery *mens rea*. At common law, battery was an *intentionally* inflicted injury. Modern courts and statutes extend battery *mens rea* to reckless and negligent contacts. The MPC (ALI 1953, no. 11) defines "battery *mens rea*" as "purposely, recklessly, or negligently causing bodily injury," or "negligently causing bodily injury . . . with a deadly weapon."

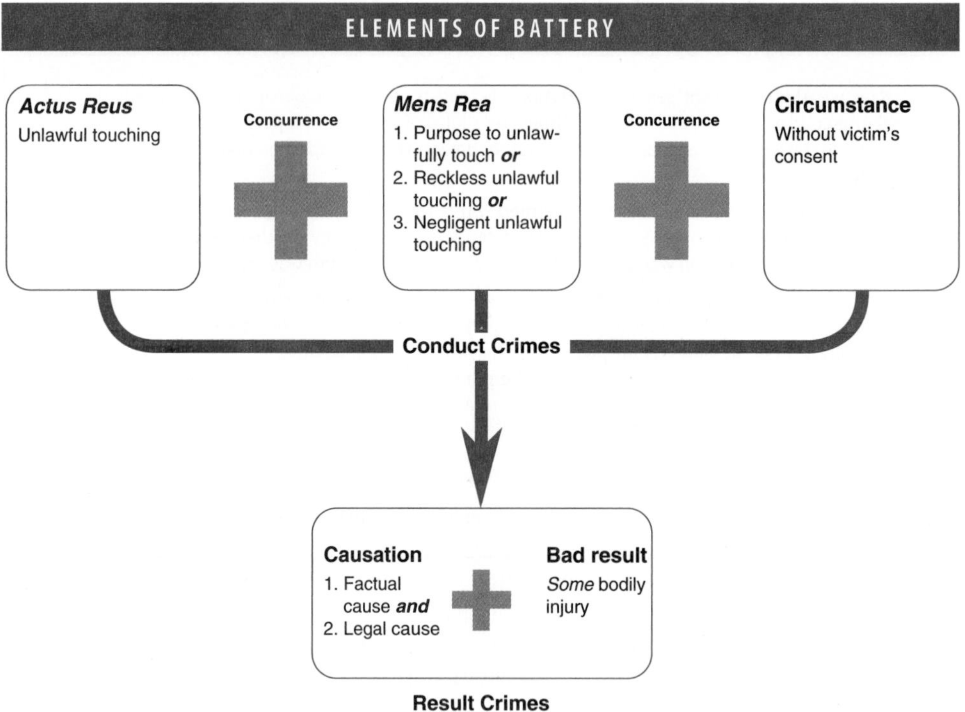

Some state statutes call this expanded offense by a different name. Louisiana (Louisiana Statutes Annotated 1974, 17-A, 14.39), for example, provides that "inflicting any injury upon the person of another by criminal negligence" is "negligent injuring." (See the Elements of Battery illustration.)

Battery requires *some* injury. Batteries that cause minor physical injury or emotional injury are misdemeanors in most states. Batteries that cause serious bodily injury are felonies. Some code provisions are directed at injuries caused by special circumstances. For example, injuries caused by pit bulls prompted the Minnesota legislature (Minnesota Statutes Annotated 1989, § 609.26) to enact the following provision:

> Section 609.26. A person who causes great or substantial bodily harm to another by negligently or intentionally permitting any dog to run uncontrolled off the owner's premises, or negligently failing to keep it properly confined is guilty of a petty misdemeanor. . . .
>
> Subd. 3. If proven by a preponderance of the evidence, it shall be an affirmative defense to liability under this section that the victim provoked the dog to cause the victim's bodily harm.

Injuries and deaths resulting from drug abuse led the same legislature to enact this provision:

> 609.228 Whoever proximately causes great bodily harm by, directly or indirectly, unlawfully selling, giving away, bartering, delivering, exchanging, distributing, or administering a controlled substance . . . may be sentenced to imprisonment for not more than ten years or to payment of a fine of not more than $20,000, or both.

The MPC grades bodily harm offenses as follows:

§ 211.1 2.

Bodily injury is a felony when such injury is inflicted purposely or knowingly with a deadly weapon; or

a. serious bodily injury is inflicted purposely, or knowingly or recklessly under circumstances manifesting extreme indifference to the value of human life.
b. except as provided in paragraph (2), bodily injury is a misdemeanor, unless it was caused in a fight or scuffle entered into by mutual consent, in which case it is a petty misdemeanor.

ASSAULT

Assaults are either attempted batteries or threatened batteries, depending on the state. (Notice both kinds are complete crimes without touching the victim.) **Attempted battery assault** consists of having the specific intent to commit a battery and taking substantial steps toward carrying it out without actually completing the attempt. Threatened battery assault, sometimes called the crime of "**intentional scaring**," requires only that actors intend to frighten their victims, thus expanding assault beyond attempted battery. Threatened battery doesn't require actually having the intent to injure their victims physically; the intent to frighten victims into believing the actor will hurt them is enough. (See the Elements of Assault illustration.)

attempted battery assault, consists of having the specific intent to commit battery and taking substantial steps toward carrying it out without actually completing the attempt

intentional scaring, threatened battery assault (sometimes called "intentional scaring") requires only that actors intend to frighten their victims, thus expanding assault beyond attempted battery

Victims' awareness is critical to proving threatened battery assault. Specifically, victims' fear of an immediate battery has to be reasonable. Words alone aren't assaults; threatening gestures have to accompany them. But this requirement isn't always fair. For example, what if an assailant approaches from behind a victim, saying, "Don't move, or I'll shoot!" These words obviously are reasonable grounds to fear imminent injury, but they aren't assault because they are, after all, only words.

ELEMENTS OF ASSAULT

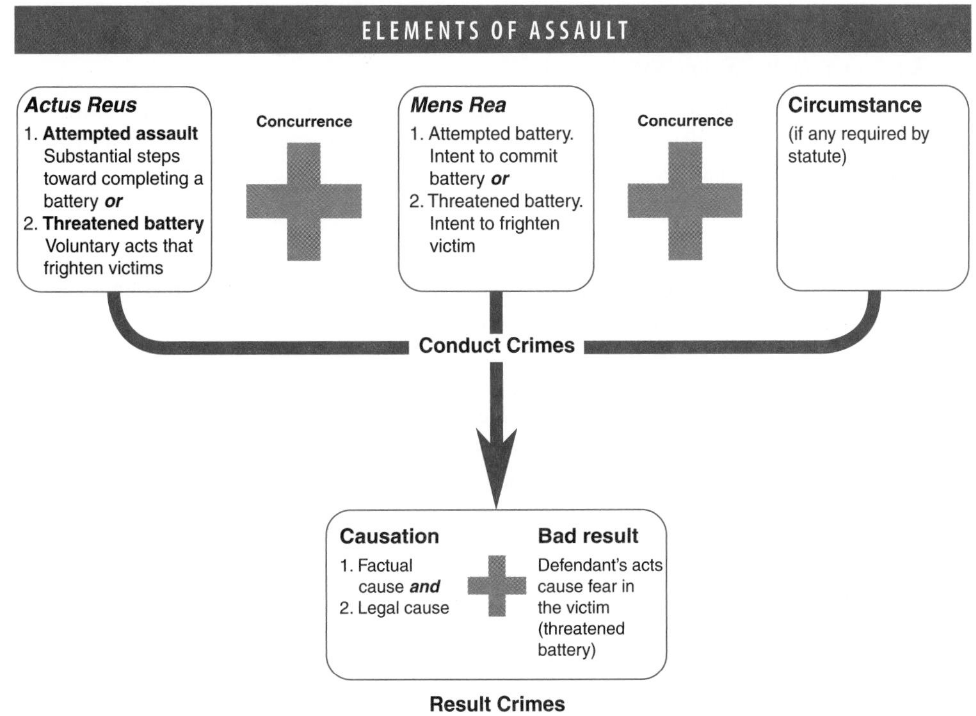

conditional threats, threats based upon the existence of certain conditions that don't presently exist aren't enough to satisfy the *mens rea* of assault because they're not immediate

Conditional threats, threats based upon the existence of specified conditions that don't yet exist, aren't enough either because they're not immediate. The conditional threat "I'd punch you out if you weren't a kid" isn't immediate because it depends on the victim's age. In a few jurisdictions, a present ability to carry out the threat has to exist. But in most, even a person who approaches a victim with a gun she knows is unloaded, points the gun at the victim, and pulls the trigger (intending only to frighten her victim) has committed threatened battery (Encyclopedia of Crime and Justice 1983, 1:89).

Attempted and threatened battery assaults are aimed at separate harms. Attempted battery assault deals with an incomplete physical injury. Threatened battery assault is directed at a present psychological or emotional harm—namely, putting a victim in fear. So in attempted battery assault, a victim's awareness doesn't matter; in threatened battery assault, it's indispensable.

The MPC deals with threatened and attempted battery assaults as follows:

§ 211.1 Simple Assault

A person is guilty of assault if he:

a. attempts to cause . . . bodily injury to another; or
b. attempts by physical menace to put another in fear of imminent serious bodily harm.

Simple assault is a misdemeanor unless committed in a fight or scuffle entered into by mutual consent, in which case the assault is a petty misdemeanor (ALI 1985).

Historically, all assaults were misdemeanors. However, modern statutes have created several aggravated or felonious assaults. Most common are assaults with the intent to commit violent felonies (murder, rape, and robbery, for example), assaults with deadly weapons (such as guns and knives), and assaults on police officers.

The MPC includes a comprehensive assault and battery statute that integrates, rationalizes, and grades assault and battery. It takes into account *actus reus*, *mens rea*, circumstance elements, and intended harm. Note the careful attention paid to these elements:

§ 211.2

A person is guilty of aggravated assault if he:

a. attempts to cause serious bodily injury to another, or causes such injury purposely, knowingly or recklessly under circumstances manifesting extreme indifference to the value of human life; or
b. attempts to cause or purposely or knowingly causes bodily injury to another with a deadly weapon.

Aggravated assault under paragraph (a) is a felony of the second degree; aggravated assault under paragraph (b) is a felony of the third degree.

§ 211.3

A person commits a misdemeanor if he recklessly engages in conduct which places or may place another person in danger of death or serious bodily injury. Recklessness and danger shall be presumed where a person knowingly points a firearm at or in the direction of another, whether or not the actor believed the firearm to be loaded. (ALI 1985)

LO 13

DOMESTIC VIOLENCE CRIMES

Since the early 1970s, violence in the family has been transformed from a private concern to a criminal justice problem. Violence in intimate relationships is extensive and isn't limited to one socioeconomic group, one society, or one period of time. Every type and form of family and intimate relationship has the potential of being violent (Gelles 2002, 671).

Numerous case excerpts in earlier chapters show how pervasive domestic violence is in the cases in this book: Chapter 4 (*mens rea* of purposely, knowingly, recklessly, and negligently); Chapter 5 (justifications, domestic violence, and self-defense; domestic violence and consent); Chapter 6 (excuse of post-traumatic stress syndrome); Chapter 7 (accomplice to murder, mother and son; vicarious liability of parents for their children's crimes); Chapter 8 (attempted murder, husband and wife); Chapter 9 (voluntary manslaughter, husband and wife). We'll see it again in Chapter 11 (burglary and identity theft).

The Ohio Domestic Violence statute (Figure 10.3) is an example of how the law of assault and battery affects the definition and application of domestic violence. Study the provisions of the Ohio statute before you read the case excerpt following it.

OHIO DOMESTIC VIOLENCE ACT

2919.25 Domestic Violence.

A. No person shall knowingly cause or attempt to cause physical harm to a family or household member.
B. No person shall recklessly cause serious physical harm to a family or household member.
C. No person, by threat of force, shall knowingly cause a family or household member to believe that the offender will cause imminent physical harm to the family or household member.
D. (1) Whoever violates this section is guilty of domestic violence, and the court shall sentence the offender as provided in divisions (D)(2) to (6) of this section.
   (2) A violation of division (C) of this section is a misdemeanor of the fourth degree, and a violation of division (A) or (B) of this section is a misdemeanor of the first degree (up to 6 months in jail and/or up to $1,000 fine).
   (3) If the offender previously has pleaded guilty to or been convicted of domestic violence, or any offense of violence if the victim of the offense was a family or household member at the time of the commission of the offense, a violation of division (A) or (B) of this section is a felony of the fourth degree (6–18 months incarceration and/or a fine up to $5,000), and a violation of division (C) of this section is a misdemeanor of the second degree.
   (4) If the offender previously has pleaded guilty to or been convicted of two or more offenses of domestic violence, or any offense of violence if the victim of the offense was a family or household member at the time of the commission of the offense, a violation of division (A) or (B) of this section is a felony of the third degree (1–5 years in prison and/or a fine up to $10,000), and a violation of division (C) of this section is a misdemeanor of the first degree.

[(E) is irrelevant for our discussion.]

F. As used in this section and sections 2919.251 and 2919.26 of the Revised Code:
   (1) "Family or household member" means any of the following:
      (a) Any of the following who is residing or has resided with the offender:
         i. A spouse, a person living as a spouse, or a former spouse of the offender;
         ii. A parent or a child of the offender, or another person related by consanguinity or affinity to the offender;
         iii. A parent or a child of a spouse, person living as a spouse, or former spouse of the offender, or another person related by consanguinity or affinity to a spouse, person living as a spouse, or former spouse of the offender.
      (b) The natural parent of any child of whom the offender is the other natural parent or is the putative other natural parent.
   (2) "Person living as a spouse" means a person who is living or has lived with the offender in a common law marital relationship, who otherwise is cohabiting with the offender, or who otherwise has cohabited with the offender within five years prior to the date of the alleged commission of the act in question.

Effective Date: 11-09-2003; 2008 HB280 04-07-2009

FELONY PUNISHMENTS

DEGREE	PRISON TIME	MAXIMUM FINE
1st	3–10 years	$20,000
2nd	2–8 years	$15,000
3rd	1–5 years	$10,000
4th	6–18 months	$5,000
5th	6–12 months	$2,500

(continues)

FIGURE 10.3

MISDEMEANOR PUNISHMENTS

DEGREE	MAXIMUM JAIL TIME	MAXIMUM FINE
1st	6 months	$1,000
2nd	90 days	$750
3rd	60 days	$500
4th	30 days	$250
5th	No jail	$150

Source: Reynard 2008.

FIGURE 10.3 *(Continued)*

CASE

In* Hamilton v. Cameron *(1997), the Ohio Court of Appeals overturned a trial court's guilty verdict because the state failed to prove the elements of domestic violence.

Was he guilty of domestic violence?

Hamilton v. Cameron

700 N.E.2d 336 (OhioApp.3d 1997)

HISTORY

Bobby J. Cameron (the defendant) was found guilty in the Municipal Court, Hamilton County, of committing domestic violence. The Municipal Court judge sentenced Cameron for a violation of "R.C. 2919.25." Cameron was fined $50 plus court costs, and Cameron's shotguns were confiscated. The defendant appealed. The Court of Appeals, Walsh, J., held that the defendant did not commit domestic violence by telling his wife "I'd probably have to blow your head off to get you to shut up," and reversed the Municipal Judge's decision.

WALSH, J.

Cameron and his wife, Darlene Cameron ("Darlene"), had an argument on February 22, 1996. Darlene wanted to discuss matters involving their 12-year-old son. Darlene testified that Cameron did not want to discuss the matters at the time and that she continued to "push the issue." During the argument, Cameron claims that he said, "I'd probably have to blow your head off to get you to shut up." Darlene testified, "He was telling me to shut up. He said something about blowing my head off that would necessitate, be necessary in order for that to occur, to get me to shut up." Deputy Michael Jacobs testified that Darlene told him that Cameron said that he was going to blow her head off.

After the argument had finished, Darlene went into another room of the house and called her mother because she was "still upset and angry." Darlene told her mother about the argument with Cameron. After the call, Darlene's mother called Darlene's sister, and then Darlene's sister called the police and reported that Cameron had threatened to shoot Darlene.

Officers arrived at Cameron's home approximately 45 minutes after the argument and found no disturbance at the home. The officers found Cameron in the living room working on a computer with their 12-year-old son, and Darlene in the back bedroom watching their 6-year-old son play Nintendo. The officers noticed a shotgun on a gun rack in the home and asked if Cameron had any more weapons. Cameron told the officers that there was another shotgun in the closet. Both of the shotguns were loaded.

A complaint was filed against Cameron, which was signed by Darlene. The complaint states that Cameron violated R.C. 2919.25(A)(B) by threatening "to shoot his wife, Darlene, with a shotgun. Two shotguns were loaded and in reach of the couple's children." On the back of the complaint was a written statement that reads: "Mr. Cameron did threaten

(continues)

to shoot his wife, Darlene, with a shotgun. Two shotguns were loaded and available and in reach of couple's children." During Cameron's trial, Darlene testified as to why she signed the complaint against Cameron.

> *Q*. Did you then subsequently come down [to the police station] and sign a complaint?
>
> *A*. After the fact, [Cameron] and I [were] talking together, we were told someone had to go. There was I guess [a] new law because I had read it in the journal. But like, if they are called on a domestic violence call, someone gets arrested. We were told that someone had to go and I heard my husband say in the living room, "No, I don't want to sign a complaint against my wife." So, I know one officer came in and asked [Officer] Jacobs will she sign a complaint, and he said yes. I said nothing.
>
> *Q*. And you subsequently ended up signing it?
>
> *A*. I did, but I didn't know I had the choice between doing it and not doing it.
>
> *Q*. Did your complaint say that he threatened to shoot you with a loaded shotgun on February 22, 1996, at 9:30 P.M.?
>
> *A*. Yes it does.
>
> *Q*. That is your signature on the bottom of that correct?
>
> *A*. That is my signature.
>
> *Q*. You read that both the front and back where you signed that complaint twice with the same allegations?
>
> *A*. Actually, I didn't read it. It was prepared. I believe that was the desk sergeant at the police station next door. My children and I waited in the lobby for over an hour and a half. We were very tired, very thirsty. Very upset, everyone. The kids, because of their tiredness. They were very testy. And when I [was] finally call[ed] in to sign it, I can recall the person who presented it to me saying that he just wrote down what was in the report. I just signed it. I just wanted to go home. I knew [what] I was there for and I just signed it. I didn't read it.

Darlene also testified that she signed a restraining order against Cameron because "I was just thinking separation, distance at my control. If that's what it took, then I wanted time to think. I just wanted time." Darlene testified that at the time she was not in fear of Cameron and that he never made a movement toward the shotgun on the gun rack.

Darlene did not testify that she believed that Cameron intended to carry out the threat of shooting her, or that she believed that she was in imminent physical harm. No evidence was presented of prior acts by Cameron showing that he had harmed or had threatened to harm Darlene before the incident. Cameron claims that he did not make the statement intending to threaten Darlene.

OPINION

Cameron presents one assignment of error: "The trial court erred to the prejudice of Cameron in finding Cameron guilty of domestic violence when an essential element of the crime is lacking."

The judgment entry states that Cameron violated "R.C. 2919.25." R.C. 2919.25 reads as follows:

> A. No person shall knowingly cause or attempt to cause physical harm to a family or household member.
>
> B. No person shall recklessly cause serious physical harm to a family or household member.
>
> C. No person, by threat of force, shall knowingly cause a family or household member to believe that the offender will cause imminent physical harm to the family or household member.

The elements of the crime of domestic violence (R.C. 2919.25[A]) are that a charged defendant must have "knowingly caused, or attempted to cause, physical harm to a family or household member." Physical harm is defined as "any injury, illness, or other physiological impairment, regardless of its gravity or duration" R.C. 2901.01(C). After reviewing the record, we cannot find any evidence that Cameron caused physical harm to Darlene, or even an allegation by Darlene that she had been physically harmed.

A violation of R.C. 2919.25(A) can also be demonstrated by a showing that Cameron attempted to commit physical harm. The evidence in the record shows that the only act Cameron committed was the statement "I'd probably have to blow your head off to get you to shut up." No evidence was presented

(continues)

(continued)

to show that Cameron knowingly attempted to carry out the threat. Accordingly, we hold that the trial court erred in finding Cameron had committed domestic violence by violating R.C. 2919.25(A) or (B). R.C. 2919.25(B) substitutes the culpable mental state of "recklessly" for "intentionally" as described in paragraph (A). The analysis of the harm element is the same.

Although the complaint does not state that Cameron had violated R.C. 2919.25(C), the language of the complaint does state one of the elements of R.C. 2919.25(C) by stating that Cameron "threatened to shoot his wife." However, in order to show that a person violated R.C. 2919.25(C), it must be shown by the prosecution that "the victim believed the offender would cause her imminent physical harm at the time the incident took place." The state of mind of the victim is an essential element of this crime. While it is true that victims may change their testimony to protect a spouse, there must be some evidence either that a victim stated, or that from other evidence it could be inferred, that the victim thought that the accused would cause imminent physical harm.

Under the facts of this case, we find no violation of R.C. 2919.25(C). The record shows that Darlene did not call the police and that she remained in the house. Further, when the police arrived, Darlene was watching the six-year-old play Nintendo, and the twelve-year-old was with Cameron. The only evidence presented is that Cameron uttered a statement which could at best be described as a conditional threat, and that the means to carry out the threat were available to Cameron. No evidence was presented that Cameron ever made a motion toward a shotgun, or that he took any other action or made any other statement in furtherance of the threat which would cause the victim to believe she would suffer imminent physical harm. The victim in fact stated that she did not believe the threat.

Further, R.C. 2919.25(C) is not a lesser offense of R.C. 2919.25(A) or (B) because R.C. 2919.25(A) or (B) can be violated without the victim believing that the offender "will cause imminent physical harm." Because R.C. 2919.25(C) is not a lesser offense of R.C. 2919.25(A) or (B), the complaint against Cameron cannot be amended to show a violation of R.C. 2919.25(C) because it would change the identity of the crime, and would be a violation of Crim.R. 7(D). Id. at 628, 656 N.E.2d at 373–374. The court's order is hereby vacated.

Accordingly, the judgment of the trial court is reversed. All fines paid and/or property confiscated is to be returned to Cameron. Judgment is entered for Cameron.

Judgment reversed.

DISSENT

POWELL, J.

I must respectfully dissent. The record in this case shows simply that the defendant threatened to blow his wife's head off to get her to shut up; that the threat worked and the victim "shut up"; that the victim called her family, who in turn called the police; that the police arrived at the victim's home forty-five minutes later and found the victim in the bedroom with her child, still "visibly shaken"; that the officers found loaded firearms in the room with the defendant; that defendant acknowledged making the statement; and that the victim signed the complaint and the restraining order so she would have time to think.

Applying the standard advanced by the Ohio Supreme Court, I feel that there is ample evidence upon which the trial court could rely to find the essential elements of the crime proven beyond a reasonable doubt. The trial court judge is the fact finder, not this court. The trial judge clearly did not believe the victim's testimony that would protect her spouse, but rather chose to believe the disinterested police officer's testimony as to the victim's state when they found her still "visibly shaken" forty-five minutes later. This evidence is sufficient for the fact finder to infer that the victim thought that the accused would cause her imminent physical harm.

QUESTIONS

1. State the elements of the offense of domestic violence that Bobby J. Cameron was convicted of.
2. List the facts relevant to deciding whether Cameron is guilty of domestic violence.
3. Summarize the arguments of the majority opinion reversing the guilty verdict.
4. Summarize the dissent's argument in favor of upholding the trial court's judgment.
5. Which opinion do you think is "right"? Defend your answer.

Is criminal law the best response to promote ethical domestic violence public policy?

On the night of June 23, 1993, John Wayne Bobbitt arrived at the couple's Manassas, Virginia, apartment highly intoxicated after a night of partying and, according to testimony by Lorena Bobbitt in a 1994 court hearing, raped his wife. (John was tried and acquitted for this alleged spousal rape in 1994; he was prosecuted by the same district attorney who prosecuted Lorena for allegedly attacking John.) Afterward, Lorena Bobbitt got out of bed and went to the kitchen for a drink of water. According to an article in the *National Women's Studies Association Journal,* in the kitchen she noticed a carving knife on the counter and "memories of past domestic abuses raced through her head." Grabbing the knife, Lorena Bobbitt entered the bedroom where John was asleep, and she proceeded to cut off more than half of his penis.

After assaulting her husband, Lorena left the apartment with the severed penis. After driving a short while, she rolled down the car window and threw the penis into a field. Realizing the severity of the incident, she stopped and called 911. After an exhaustive search, the penis was located, packed in ice, and brought to the hospital where John was located. The two-and-a-half-inch penis was reattached by Dr. David Berman during a nine-and-a-half-hour operation.

Lorena was taken into custody. During the trial, the couple revealed details of their volatile relationship and the events leading up to the assault. Lorena stated that John sexually, physically, and emotionally abused her during their marriage. She also stated that John flaunted his infidelities and forced her to have an abortion. Several witnesses provided testimony supporting Lorena's claims. Lorena's defense attorneys maintained that John's constant abuse caused Lorena to eventually "snap" as she was suffering from clinical depression and a possible bout of post-traumatic stress disorder due to the abuse.

John denied the allegations of abuse. However, when he was cross-examined, his statements often conflicted with known facts, severely weakening the prosecution's case. After seven hours of deliberation, the jury found Lorena "not guilty" due to insanity causing an irresistible impulse to sexually wound her husband. As a result, she could not be held liable for her actions. Under state law, the judge ordered Lorena to undergo a 45-day evaluation period at a mental hospital, after which she would be released.

Instructions

1. Watch "Lorena Bobbitt, 15 Years Later," and read the selections concerning the response to domestic violence that best promotes the best ethical public policy.
2. Based on the video and readings, write an essay that (a) lists and briefly describes the criminal and noncriminal responses described and discussed on the video and in the articles and (b) takes a position on which one most effectively promotes the best ethical public policy.

Source: *"Lorena Bobbitt, 15 Years Later."* CBS News. 2008.

STALKING CRIMES

LO 14

Stalking is an ancient practice but only a modern crime; it involves intentionally scaring another person by following, tormenting, or harassing him or her. Statutes criminalizing stalking "intended to fill gaps in the law by criminalizing conduct that fell short of assault or battery . . . by insuring that victims did not have to be injured or threatened with death before stopping a stalker's harassment" (*Curry v. State* 2002).

Statutes making stalking a crime began in California, after actress Rebecca Schaeffer was murdered at her Los Angeles apartment by an obsessed fan who stalked her for two years. Within a five-week period, four other women in Orange County were murdered by their stalkers—after they got restraining orders against them! (Bradfield 1998, 243–44). California enacted its path-breaking antistalking statute in 1990.

Other states quickly followed California's example; today, every state and the U.S. government have stalking statutes. The laws reflect widespread concern over the "stalking phenomenon" (LaFave 2003a, 828–29). Although many victims are celebrities like Rebecca Schaeffer, the vast majority are "ordinary" people, most of them women. Nearly 1.5 million people are stalked every year. Seventy-five to eighty percent involve men stalking women. Stalking has major negative effects on its victim, including depression, substance abuse, phobias, anxiety, obsessive-compulsive behaviors, and dissociative disorders (829). We'll look more closely at antistalking statutes, stalking *actus reus* and *mens rea*, the bad result in stalking, and cyberstalking.

Antistalking Statutes

Antistalking statutes vary enormously from state to state and the U.S. statute. Let's begin with the National Criminal Justice Association's model stalking law. It was commissioned by the U.S. Department of Justice's National Institute of Justice. Many states have adopted parts of it:

> *Section 1*
>
> For purposes of this code:
>
> a) "Course of conduct" means repeatedly maintaining a visual or physical proximity to a person or repeatedly conveying verbal or written threats or threats implied by conduct or a combination thereof directed at or toward a person;
>
> b) "Repeatedly" means on two or more occasions; and
>
> c) "Immediate family" means a spouse, parent, child, sibling, or any other person who regularly resides in the household or who within the past six months regularly resided in the household.
>
> *Section 2*
>
> Any person who
>
> a) Purposely engages in a course of conduct directed at a specific person that would cause a reasonable person to fear bodily injury to himself or herself or a member of his or her immediate family or to fear the death of himself or herself or a member of his or her immediate family; and
>
> b) Has knowledge or should have knowledge that the specific person will be placed in reasonable fear of bodily injury to himself or herself or a member of his or her immediate family or to fear the death of himself or herself or his or her immediate family; and
>
> c) Whose acts induce fear in the specific person of bodily injury to himself or herself or a member of his or her immediate family or induce fear in the specific individual of the death of himself or herself or a member of his or her immediate family; is guilty of stalking.

Stalking Actus Reus

Despite great diversity from state to state, the stalking statutes all share some common requirements when it comes to the criminal act of stalking. First, as in the model code, all fifty states require that the act happen more than once (LaFave 2003a, 831). Some codes use the word "repeatedly"; others, as in the model code, say there has to be a "course of conduct."

As to the kind of conduct that has to be repeated, all states require some variation of the model code's "maintaining a visual or physical proximity." These acts include following, pursuing, spying, and/or harassing. About half the states require some kind of threat, including the model code's "verbal or written threats or threats implied by conduct," "threat," "terroristic threat," or "credible threat" (LaFave 2003a, 832).

Other statutes list very specific acts, including one or more of the following: interfering with the victim; approaching or confronting the victim; appearing at the victim's job or home; placing objects on the victim's property; causing damage to the victim's pet; calling the victim on the phone, or sending letters or e-mail to the victim (832).

Stalking Mens Rea

Stalking is a result crime. All statutes require a specific intent to commit the acts discussed in the *actus reus* section. They also require some mental attitude causing the bad result, but the exact mental attitude varies considerably among the states (836).

Slightly more than half the states require some level of subjective fault; recall that "subjective fault" refers to purpose, knowledge, or recklessness. Most of these states require that the actor's purpose was to cause the bad result. A few of these subjective fault states require either that stalkers know their acts will cause the bad result or that they act recklessly; that is, they know their acts create a substantial and unjustifiable risk of causing the bad result (837).

About one-third of the states require only objective fault—namely, negligence. In other words, the requirement is objective reasonableness: actors don't know their acts are creating a substantial and unjustifiable risk of causing the bad result, but they should know. The remaining states require no mental attitude; they provide for strict liability. The only requirement is a voluntary act (837).

Stalking Bad Result

The bad result in stalking is placing stalkers' victims in fear. States take four different approaches to the fear caused. Most states adopt a subjective and objective fear test. The model code is a good example. The defendant's acts "induce fear in the specific person"; this is subjective fear. It also requires objective fear; that is, the defendant's acts "would cause a reasonable person to fear." The second is the subjective fear only test: the victim was actually afraid. The third is the objective fear only test; a reasonable person would be afraid. The fourth is the intent to instill fear test. Here, the actor's intent to instill fear is enough, whether the acts actually caused fear or would have caused fear in a reasonable person (LaFave 2003a, 835–36). See the Elements of Stalking illustration.

Cyberstalking

The Internet is a "fertile ground for stalking" (Merschman 2001, 275). This "dark side of the Web" provides cyberstalkers with cheap and powerful tools for instilling fear in their victims—mostly e-mail but also chat rooms and bulletin boards. Cyberstalking is defined as "the use of the Internet, e-mail or other electronic communications devices to stalk another person through threatening behavior" (Mishler 2000, 117). In 1999, the Los Angeles and Manhattan District Attorneys reported that 20 percent of its stalking victims were cyberstalked (Attorney General 1999).

cyberstalking, the use of the Internet, email, or other electronic communication devices to stalk another person through threatening behavior

Cyberstalking reaches victims in their homes, where they feel safest; what's worse, stalkers can stalk from the comfort of their homes. "Make no mistake: this kind of stalking can be as frightening and as real as being followed and watched in your neighborhood or in your home" (Mishler 2000, 117).

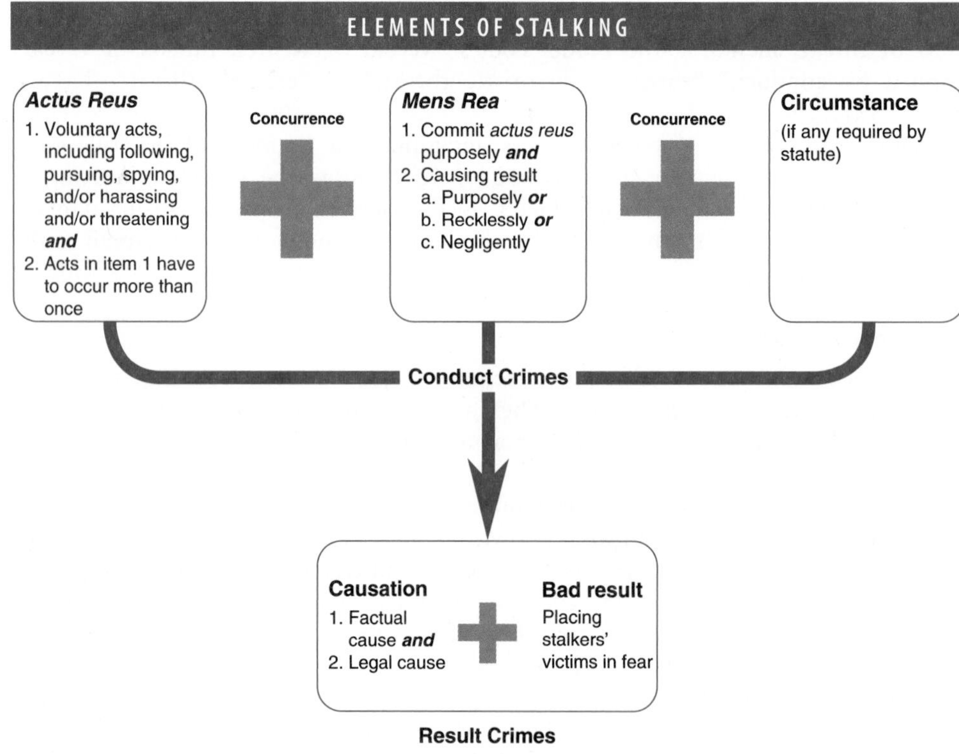

CASE

In* State v. Hoying *(2005)*, *Ted Hoying, insisted his endless e-mails didn't cause his coworker Kelly Criswell either physical or mental harm. The court applied the elements of stalking to Hoying's e-mail cyberstalking setting.

Did he cyberstalk her?

State v. Hoying

WL 678989 (OhioApp. 2005)

HISTORY

Ted Hoying, the defendant, was convicted by a jury in the Court of Common Pleas, of menacing by stalking and intimidation of a victim. He was sentenced to a total of six and one-half years in prison. The defendant appealed. The Ohio Court of Appeals affirmed.

BROGAN, J.

FACTS

Ted Hoying met the victim, Kelly Criswell, when they both worked at a local restaurant. In June 2002, Hoying asked Criswell for a date and became quite angry when she declined. When Hoying persisted in contacting Ms. Criswell after she left her employment with the restaurant, Ms. Criswell obtained a civil protection order against Hoying in February 2003. Subsequently, between August 15, 2003, and September 7, 2003, Hoying sent 105 e-mails to Ms. Criswell in violation of the protection order.

In the first e-mail, which is dated August 15, 2003, Hoying acknowledged that he could get in trouble for writing. He then asked Ms. Criswell to remove the civil protection order. Ms. Criswell did not reply to any of Hoying's e-mails, which became increasingly agitated.

(continues)

The first threatening e-mail is dated August 16. This e-mail states, "Maybe I still have your picture and I will post it on the Net. Fair is fair. Ted." Subsequently, Hoying wrote, "Why don't you tell the authorities I shot three boxes of shells at clay birds yesterday? I'm going to do that the rest of my life at least once a week. I don't give a rat's ass what number eight says on that civil protection order. Ted." That e-mail is also dated August 16, 2003.

In another e-mail dated August 16, 2003, Hoying threatened to come to Ms. Criswell's place of employment unless she met with him. The same day, in another e-mail message, Hoying indicated that he would persist in sending e-mails until Ms. Criswell agreed to talk to him.

In an e-mail dated August 17, 2003, Hoying made a significant threat to Ms. Criswell. Specifically, he said:

> Kelly, set me free. I'm no longer a man. I'm shackled like a beast. What is a man if he is not free? Let me take away your freedom and you feel the sting. Also, it's not pleasant. Set me free. Ted H.

In another e-mail written on the same day, Hoying again threatened to go to Ms. Criswell's place of employment. He reiterated that threat in another e-mail, which was also written on August 17, 2003.

As a result of receiving these e-mails, Ms. Criswell filed charges in Xenia Municipal Court, alleging that Hoying had violated the civil protection order. Hoying acknowledged receiving the charge in an e-mail dated August 28, 2003. In that e-mail, Hoying said, "Kelly, why did you do that at Xenia? All I wanted was for things to be normal. I thought you could be nice." The same day, Hoying threatened to file criminal charges against Ms. Criswell's boyfriend, whom Hoying thought was named "Grinstead."

Subsequently, on August 30, 2003, Hoying sent Ms. Criswell another message. In that e-mail, Hoying threatened that "If the stuff in Xenia is not handled then some things are going to happen." The next day, Hoying sent a message, which said:

> Ms. Criswell, tell your old man to get rid of the Xenia stuff or the hammer is going to fall heavy on him. It will take three years to get all of this stuff straightened out. If not, remember you are going to be subpoenaed for the thefts since you supplied some of the info, so you might as well say good bye to your job. I've been nice to you. I don't deserve to be paid back like this. I don't want to hurt you, but if you choose their side then that is that. This is such high school shit. I'm not coming to court anyway. I have an important doctor's appointment. My life is just as important as yours. If it is not handled and they come for me, they better bring an army. Ted.

As a result of the e-mails, Ms. Criswell changed her address, changed her license plate, changed employment, and eventually moved away. (Ms. Criswell's current living arrangement was not revealed in court, for her protection.) Ms. Criswell also testified that she could possibly need psychiatric or psychological assistance in the future because of everything Hoying had done.

OPINION

Hoying claims that his conviction for menacing by stalking was based on insufficient evidence. As support for this contention, Hoying notes that he did not cause physical harm to Ms. Criswell and she did not seek professional help for mental distress. He also notes a lack of evidence that he was aware that Ms. Criswell believed he would cause her physical harm or mental distress.

The essential elements of menacing by stalking are found in R.C. 2903.211, which provides, in pertinent part, that:

> A. No person by engaging in a pattern of conduct shall knowingly cause another person to believe that the offender will cause physical harm to the other person or cause mental distress to the other person. . . .
>
> B. Whoever violates this section is guilty of menacing by stalking.
>
> (2). Menacing by stalking is a felony of the fourth degree if any of the following applies:
>
> (g) At the time of the commission of the offense, the offender was the subject of a protection order issued under section 2903.213 or 2903.214 of the Revised Code, regardless of whether the person to be protected under the order is the victim of the offense or another person.

(continues)

(continues)

After reviewing the evidence, we agree with the State that a reasonable jury could have inferred from the content of the e-mails that Hoying knew Ms. Criswell would consider the messages to be a threat to her physical safety or to that of her father. A reasonable jury could also have found that the messages would cause Ms. Criswell mental distress. The fact that Ms. Criswell previously sought a civil protection order was some evidence that she was afraid of the defendant, and the e-mails were sent after the protection order was issued to the defendant. Ms. Criswell also testified that she was "scared to death" of Hoying and that he had caused her much mental distress.

As an additional matter, Hoying's conduct in court did not help his case, as he interrupted Ms. Criswell's testimony several times with inappropriate comments, including calling her a liar. In one outburst, Hoying made what could be interpreted as a threat, stating, "She'd better start telling the truth and quit lying, that's for sure."

Hoying did not present any evidence to counteract the victim's testimony, or to prove that she was lying. Accordingly, any rational trier of fact had more than an ample basis for finding Hoying guilty of menacing by stalking.

Hoyer also challenges the trial court's action in sentencing Hoying to the maximum term for the conviction of menacing by stalking, which is a fourth-degree felony, at least under the circumstances of this case. See R.C. 2903.211(B)(2)(g). Although community control sanctions are available for fourth-degree felonies, Hoying admits that they are not guaranteed. Hoying further concedes that he probably forfeited the ability to obtain community control by his conduct during trial and the sentencing hearing, and by his refusal to participate in the presentence investigation process. Having reviewed the record, we fully agree with that statement.

Nonetheless, Hoying contends that he should not have received the maximum sentence for menacing by stalking because the record does not support a finding that he poses the greatest likelihood of recidivism. We disagree.

Under R.C. 2929.14(A)(4), the potential term for a fourth-degree felony is six to eighteen months. R.C. 2929.14(C) additionally states that: Except as provided in division (G) of this section or in Chapter 2925. of the Revised Code, the court imposing a sentence upon an offender for a felony may impose the longest prison term authorized for the offense pursuant to division (A) of this section only upon offenders who committed the worst forms of the offense, upon offenders who pose the greatest likelihood of committing future crimes, upon certain major drug offenders under division (D)(3) of this section, and upon certain repeat violent offenders in accordance with division (D)(2) of this section.

When a trial court imposes maximum sentences, it must state its findings and reasoning at the sentencing hearing. Also, when a trial court states its reasons for imposing a maximum sentence, it must connect those reasons to the finding which the reason supports. The court cannot merely pronounce causes that objectively may be its reasons. The court must also identify which of those causes are the particular reasons for each of the statutory findings that the court made.

In the present case, the trial court complied with the requirement of making findings at the sentencing hearing. The court also adequately connected its reasons for imposing a maximum sentence to the finding that the reason supported. At the sentencing hearing, the court stated that it found that Hoying had the greatest likelihood to re-offend, and that Hoying had committed the worst form of the offense.

Before reciting the court's specific reasons for these findings, we should note that the very night the jury verdict was issued, Hoying attempted to contact the victim. According to the State, Hoying attempted to contact Ms. Criswell five times. Hoying denied making five attempts, but did admit that he tried to contact the victim after the verdict to ask for help with his appeal. In view of the nature of the crime (menacing by stalking) and the jury verdict of "guilty," an attempt to contact the victim of the crime shows either a disconnection from reality or an obstinate refusal to submit to the authority of the law.

Hoying also refused to cooperate in any way with the presentence investigation. In addition, Hoying disrupted the sentencing process, showering foul language and abuse on the victim, her family, and even the court, to the point that Hoying eventually had to be removed from the courtroom. Ultimately, in discussing the length of the sentence, the trial court specifically connected the following reasons to its findings, by stating that:

> when the victim in this case testified, the Defendant's conduct as to her testimony was absolutely parallel to the conduct of the crime in which he was charged, beginning with his sense of enjoyment of the presence of the victim as she testified, and as her testimony became less beneficial to the Defendant, he proceeded to become more aggravated and agitated, writing notes, ultimately basically yelling at the victim during the course of that testimony, clearly, giving an indication as to his attitude and conduct toward the victim in this matter which brought this case forward in the first place.

For that reason, the Court finds that the shortest prison term would not protect the public from future crimes, and the court has the greatest fear for Kelly Criswell, which the record will reflect, has moved from the immediate area and has taken extraordinary steps to prevent her location from being identified by this Defendant.

The Court notes for the record that testimony in this case and the information subsequently received indicates that the particular victim in this case had no relationship whatsoever with the Defendant, can't even suggest there ever was a scintilla of a relationship, yet the Defendant's attitude toward her is just a classic stalking attitude, and the harm caused to her is so significant that it is necessary to take extreme measures so the Court can protect her, as well as others from future crime.

The Court clearly feels the Defendant's conduct as demonstrated at his arrest, at his arraignment, during the conduct of this matter, the trial, and the sentencing here demonstrates an attitude on his part of failure to comply with authority, the failure to respect the integrity of other individuals, and quite candidly, makes this Defendant a very dangerous individual.

The shortest prison term will demean the seriousness of the Defendant's conduct.

The Court further finds based upon the facts stated herein and the information provided, which will be made a part of the record in this matter, that the Defendant's conduct has, to a great degree, established the worst form of the offense. I do not discount Counsel's statement that a first time offender is one in which there is an indication from the legislature that the least restrictive setting should apply; however, this Court can say unequivocally, in all the time that I've been on the Bench, I've never seen a Defendant that I'm more sure of is a serious threat to society and to the public.

The Court also finds the Defendant clearly poses the greatest likelihood to commit future crimes in this matter, and as such, the Court makes reference particularly to the competency report prepared earlier this year where the Defendant indicated in his evaluation, quote, I know I'm not crazy. I knew what I was doing when I contacted her knowing I was violating the order, end quote.

We find that the above discussion by the trial court fully complies with requirements for imposing maximum sentences. We also agree with the trial court that a maximum sentence was warranted. The record in this case is quite troubling, since it portrays an individual who either has no remorse for his actions, or refuses to admit he needs mental health treatment. Even though Hoying was found competent to stand trial, that does not mean that he is free of mental health problems that should be addressed, hopefully while he is in the prison system.

The judgment of the trial court is affirmed.

QUESTIONS

1. State the elements of stalking according to the Ohio stalking statute.
2. List all the facts relevant to deciding whether the prosecution proved each of the elements.
3. Assume you're the prosecutor. Relying on the facts of the case and the reasoning of the trial and the appellate court, argue that Hoying was guilty of stalking.
4. Assume you're Hoying's attorney. Relying on the facts of the case and Hoying's arguments, argue that Hoying wasn't guilty of stalking.
5. In your opinion, do the facts support a guilty verdict? Was the six-and-one-half-year sentence too harsh? Explain your answers.

LO 15

PERSONAL RESTRAINT CRIMES

right of locomotion, the right to come and go without restraint

One of the greatest things about living in a free society is the right to control our freedom of movement, even though we may not appreciate it until it's taken away from us. In the eighteenth century, they called it the right of locomotion—the right to come and go as we please, to stay if we don't want to move, and to move if we don't want to stay.

I'm reminded of how precious this right is every time we get several inches of snow (which can be pretty often here in Minnesota). My house has a long driveway that needs plowing before I can get out. As much as I love my house, I feel trapped if the snowplow doesn't get there within an hour. This is a silly example, but it underscores the issues of the two crimes against personal liberty we'll look at in this section: kidnapping and false imprisonment.

KIDNAPPING

kidnapping, the taking and carrying away of another person with the intent to deprive the other person of personal liberty

Kidnapping is an ancient result crime that originally involved holding the king's relatives for ransom. Of course, it was considered a serious offense because it interfered with the personal liberty of members of royal families. Kidnapping is taking and carrying away another person with the intent to deprive that person of personal liberty.

At common law, kidnapping consisted of six elements:

1. seizing,
2. carrying away (asportation of), and
3. confining,
4. by force, threat of force, fraud, or deception,
5. another person,
6. with the intent to deprive the other person of his or her liberty.

See the Elements of Kidnapping illustration on the next page.

In the 1900s, kidnapping came to be considered a very serious felony in the United States—even a capital offense in some states. The seriousness had nothing to do with royalty but a lot to do with events during the first half of the twentieth century.

During Prohibition (1919 to 1933), kidnapping was prevalent in the organized crime world. One gang member might abduct a rival, "take him for a ride," and kill him. Much more frequently, rivals were captured and held hostage for ransom. Before long, kidnapping spread to include the spouses and children of law-abiding wealthy and prominent citizens. The most famous case was *State v. Hauptmann* (1935), involving the prosecution of the man charged with and convicted of the ransom kidnap and murder of Charles Lindbergh's son. The famous and beloved aviator captured Americans' hearts and imaginations when he flew solo across the Atlantic Ocean.

Kidnapping was a misdemeanor in New Jersey in 1932 when the crime occurred. But the tremendous sympathy that Lindbergh's popular hero status generated, and the public outrage toward what was perceived as a rampant increase in random kidnappings of America's "pillars of wealth and virtue," led legislatures to enact harsh new kidnapping statutes. These statutes remain largely in force today, even though they were passed in an emotional overreaction to a few notorious cases.

In 1974, another widely publicized case breathed new life into these harsh statutes when Patricia Hearst, heiress to newspaper tycoon William Randolph Hearst, was kidnapped. The case met with public outrage, not only because of sympathy for the prominent Hearst family but also because of shock at the psychological and physical dimensions of the crime. The kidnappers were self-styled revolutionaries calling themselves the Symbionese Liberation Army (SLA). One of the SLA's first demands was that

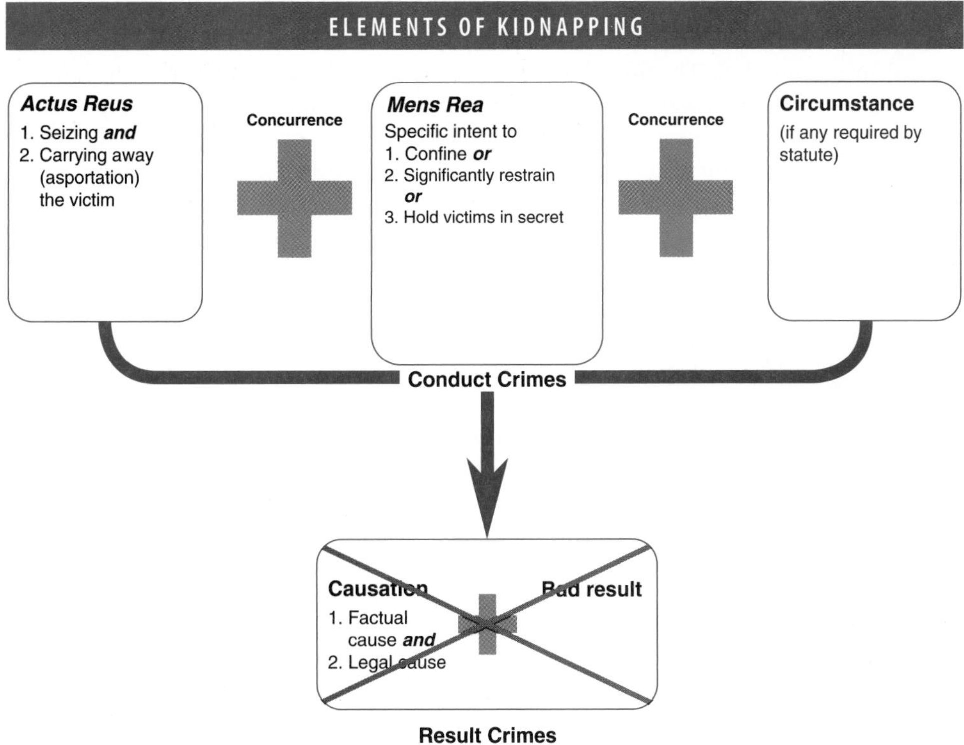

Hearst's father, Randolph, distribute $1 million in food to the poor of California. Later on, much to her parents' and the public's horror, Patricia Hearst was accused of converting to the SLA and was later convicted of participating in bank robberies to raise money for the "revolution."

All this took place during a time when radicalism and violence were very much feared and when the Vietnam War protest and airline hijackings for terrorist political purposes were very much on the public's mind. The public saw Patty Hearst's capture and her family's deep trauma not just as one family's suffering but a threat to destroy American society.

The Hearst case focused attention on how monstrous kidnapping can be. It drew together in one story capture, detention, terror, violence, and political radicalism. The details were trumpeted every day in newspapers and on radio and television. Hope that existing harsh and sweeping kidnapping legislation would be reassessed calmly vanished in this inflamed, emotional atmosphere.

President Nixon expressed his hope—a hope that many others shared—that the Supreme Court wouldn't declare capital punishment for kidnapping unconstitutional. California governor Ronald Reagan reflected the deep public outrage against kidnapping when he wished aloud that the kidnappers' demand for a free food program would set off a botulism epidemic among the poor.

Let's look at the *actus reus* and *mens rea* elements of kidnapping and at how the law grades the seriousness of acts of kidnapping.

Kidnapping Actus Reus

The heart of kidnapping *actus reus* consists of seizing and carrying away (asportation of) the victim. Since at least the eighteenth century, carrying a victim into a foreign country where no friends or family could give her aid and comfort, and the law couldn't offer protection, added a terrifying dimension to kidnapping.

In those early days, the victim had to be carried at least as far as another country and usually across its border. Modern interpretations have made the asportation requirement meaningless. The notorious case of *People v. Chessman* (1951) is the best example. Caryl Chessman was a serial rapist who, in one instance, forced a young woman to leave her car and get into his, which was only 22 feet away. The Court held that the mere fact of moving the victim, not how far she was moved, satisfied the asportation requirement. So moving his victim 22 feet was enough to convict and sentence Chessman to the gas chamber.

CASE

In* People v. Allen *(1997), the California Supreme Court ruled that it's not the number of feet the carjacker moved the victims but the "quality and character" of his movement that matters in asportation.

Did he move her a "substantial" distance?

People v. Allen

64 Cal.Rptr.2d 497 (1997)

HISTORY

Tyrone Allen was convicted in the Superior Court, City and County of San Francisco, of the kidnapping of a person under the age of 14. He appealed. The Court of Appeal affirmed.

RUVOLO, J.

FACTS

On August 7, 1995, May SunYoung and her family lived at 2951 Treat Street in San Francisco. That morning, Ms. SunYoung was on her way to take her seven-year-old daughter, Kirstie, to summer camp and stopped her automobile briefly in the driveway to close her garage door manually as she was backing out onto the street.

As Ms. SunYoung closed her garage door, a man approached her from behind and said, "Excuse me, can you do me a favor?" While turning around she saw Tyrone Allen getting into her vehicle, whose engine was still running. He then locked the car doors. Kirstie was still in the vehicle with her seatbelt on and began crying. Because the driver's side window was rolled down about seven inches, Ms. SunYoung put her arms through the window and struggled with Allen in an attempt to reach the ignition key and turn off the engine.

Allen then released the parking brake, put the vehicle in reverse, and backed out of the driveway with Kirstie inside and Ms. SunYoung running alongside the vehicle still attempting to reach the ignition key. The vehicle backed across Treat Street, which was a two-lane road with two parking lanes, until it hit the opposite curb and came to a stop. Allen estimated the vehicle movement was 30 to 40 feet. While Allen now claims this estimate to be "speculation," both sides at different times suggested that the distance moved was approximately five car lengths, or 50 feet.

Allen exited the vehicle, threw the car keys onto the ground, shoved Ms. SunYoung against a fence, and ran down the street carrying her purse, which had been left in the vehicle. Shortly thereafter, a neighbor on Treat Street several blocks away saw a man run by. In response to the neighbor's attempts to stop the man, the fleeing suspect stated, "Stay back, I got a gun." After a brief struggle, the man ran off but was later apprehended by San Francisco police officers and identified as Allen.

The jury instruction given regarding the simple kidnapping count was CALJIC No. 9.52, which sets forth the elements of kidnapping of a person under 14 years of age as follows:

> Every person who unlawfully and with physical force or by any other means of instilling fear moves any other person under 14 years of age without her consent for a substantial distance, that is, a distance more than slight or trivial, is guilty of the crime of kidnapping. . . . (Pen. Code, § 208, subd. (b); all further statutory references are to the Penal Code unless otherwise indicated.)

OPINION

The only element of the crime for which Allen asserts there was insufficient evidence and inadequate jury instructions is asportation. For "simple" kidnapping, that is, a kidnapping not elevated to a statutory form of "aggravated" kidnapping, the movement needed must be "substantial," or a distance that is more than "trivial, slight, or insignificant."

Allen argues that his conviction for simple kidnapping must be reversed because the minimum distance requirement for asportation is not met. He asserts the movement of Ms. SunYoung's vehicle 30–50 feet down her driveway and across Treat Street with Kirstie inside as a matter of law cannot be "substantial," or a distance that is more than "trivial, slight, or insignificant."

Allen is correct that under most cases decided pre-1981 which have examined only the actual distance involved, the movement here would not meet the legal test of substantiality. Those cases which have considered the quality and character of the movement in addition to its absolute distance have weighed the purpose for the movement, whether it posed an increased risk of harm to the victim, and the context of the environment in which the movement occurred.

Purposes for movement found to be relevant have been those undertaken to facilitate the commission of a further crime, to aid in flight, or to prevent detection. We believe these factors are appropriate considerations.

"Substantiality" implies something more than only measured distance. While "slight" is consistent with a quantitative analysis, the term "trivial" is a qualitative term suggestive of the conclusion that more is envisioned in determining whether a kidnapping occurs than simply how far the victim is moved. The legal requirement for asportation is satisfied by a finding of either.

In so holding, we conclude that while in absolute footage the distance moved here may have been empirically short, it was of a character sufficient to justify a finding of "substantiality" by the jury. The movement, in part, was plainly made to prevent Ms. SunYoung from regaining possession of her vehicle and to facilitate Allen's flight from the area with Kirstie. In addition to evasion of capture, the vehicle was moved from a position of relative safety onto a thoroughfare. The boundary crossed was significant because it placed Kirstie at greater risk of injury.

We confirm these factors, coupled with the distance traveled, are sufficient to satisfy the "substantial movement" requirement for the crime of simple kidnapping. . . .

AFFIRMED.

DISSENT

KLINE, J.

Movement as short a distance as that shown here—30 to 40 feet—has never been held to satisfy the asportation requirement of kidnapping. Indeed, considerably greater distances have often been held insufficient. As the majority opinion points out, movement of 90 feet, nearly three times the distance the victim in this case was moved, was held insufficient. The shortest distance this court has ever held to be "substantial" for this purpose was a full city block.

I agree that by moving the child in the vehicle across the street Allen committed a crime other than carjacking and the various other offenses of which he was properly convicted; that crime was not kidnapping, however, but false imprisonment (Pen.Code, § 236), which does not require any movement.

Because the asportation in this case was trivial within the meaning of the applicable case law, I would reverse the judgment of conviction of simple kidnapping for lack of evidentiary support. I agree that in all other respects the judgment should be affirmed.

QUESTIONS

1. What test did the court establish to determine how far defendants have to move victims to satisfy the asportation element of kidnapping *actus reus*?
2. What reasons does the majority give to support its definition of "asportation"?
3. How does the dissent's definition of "asportation" differ from that of the majority's?
4. What reasons does the dissent give for its definition?
5. Do you agree with the majority or the dissent's definition of "asportation"? Defend your answer.

Kidnapping Mens Rea

Kidnapping *mens rea* is stated usually as the specific intent to confine, significantly restrain, or hold victims in secret. The Wisconsin statute, for example, defines a "kidnapper" as one who "seizes or confines another without his consent and with intent to cause him to be secretly confined." Whatever the exact wording of the statutes, the heart of the kidnapping mental attitude remains to "isolate the victim from the prospect of release or friendly intervention" (Wisconsin Criminal Code 2006, ß 940.31).

Grading Kidnapping Seriousness

Kidnapping is usually divided into two degrees: simple and aggravated. The most common aggravating circumstances include kidnapping for the purpose of:

- Sexual invasions
- Obtaining a hostage
- Obtaining ransom
- Robbing the victim
- Murdering the victim
- Blackmailing
- Terrorizing the victim
- Achieving political aims

The penalty for aggravated kidnapping is usually life imprisonment and, until recently, occasionally even death.

FALSE IMPRISONMENT

false imprisonment, depriving others of their personal liberty without the asportation requirement

False imprisonment is a lesser form of personal restraint than kidnapping, but the heart of the crime remains depriving others of their personal liberty. It's a lesser offense because there's no asportation requirement; the deprivation of liberty is brief; and the detention is less stressful. "False imprisonment" was succinctly defined as compelling a person "to remain where he does not wish to remain" (*McKendree v. Christy* 1961, 381).

Most forcible detentions or confinements, however brief, satisfy the *actus reus* of false imprisonment. This doesn't include restraints authorized by law—for example, when parents restrict their children's activities or victims detain their victimizers.

The Model Penal Code (MPC) requires the restraint to "interfere substantially with the victim's liberty," but, in most state statutes, any interference with another person's liberty is enough. For example, here's the way the Florida statute defines the *actus reus* of false imprisonment:

> False imprisonment means forcibly, by threat, or secretly confining, abducting, imprisoning, or restraining another person without lawful authority and against her or his will. (Florida Criminal Code 2006)

Although physical force often accomplishes the detention, it doesn't have to; threatened force is enough. So the threat "If you don't come with me, I'll drag you along" is enough. Even nonthreatening words can qualify, such as when a police officer who has no right to do so orders someone on the street into a squad car, asserting, "You're under arrest."

False imprisonment is a specific-intent crime. According to a typical statute: False imprisonment consists of intentionally confining or restraining another person without his consent (New Mexico Criminal Code 2006). The motive for the detention doesn't matter. For example, if police officers make unlawful arrests, they can be prosecuted for false imprisonment even if they believed the arrests were lawful.

SUMMARY

LO 1 Rape and other sexual assaults are different from all other felonies in that in other circumstances, some of the behaviors connected with them are legal, healthy, and desired.

LO 2 Crimes against persons boil down to four types: taking a life; unwanted sexual invasions; bodily injury; and personal restraint.

LO 3 The vast majority of rape victims are raped by individuals they know. The law treats differently two kinds of rape: (1) aggravated rape—that is, rape by strangers or men with weapons who physically injure their victim; (2) unarmed acquaintance rape—nonconsensual sex between people who know each other.

LO 4 Common law definitions of rape were altered dramatically in modern-day rape law. Many states abolished the corroboration rule that required witnesses to back up rape victims' testimony. Most also passed rape shield statutes to protect victims' privacy. They banned prosecutors from introducing evidence of victims' past sexual conduct. The prompt-reporting rule was also relaxed, allowing rape crimes to be prosecuted even if the victim did not report it right away. Statutes also recognize rape by husbands as a crime.

LO 5 Modern court opinions have relaxed the strict definitions of "rape." Sexual assault, or criminal sexual conduct, statutes enacted in the 1970s and the 1980s have expanded the definition of "sex offenses" to embrace a wide range of nonconsensual penetrations and contacts, even if they fall far short of violent contact.

LO 6 The elements of modern rape law include the *actus reus* of sexual penetration for force or threat, the *mens rea* of intent to penetrate, and nonconsent by the victim.

LO 7 Courts today have adopted either of two definitions of "force": (1) extrinsic force and (2) intrinsic force. Extrinsic force requires force additional to that required for penetration; intrinsic force only requires the force to accomplish penetration.

LO 8 Rape can be accomplished without any extrinsic force if fraud of fact or of inducement is used by the perpetrator. Fraud of fact is fraudulently convincing the victim that she's agreeing to something other than sexual intercourse. Fraud of inducement is the use of fraud to gain consent to sexual intercourse.

LO 9 Rape is a general-intent crime: defendants intended to commit the act of forcible sexual penetration.

LO 10 Statutory rape is a strict liability crime in most states. Statutory rapists don't have to use force; the victim's immaturity takes the place of force. Minors can't legally consent to sexual conduct. Only Alaska and California allow for mistake of age as a defense.

LO 11 The seriousness of sex offenses under the reform laws of the 1970s and 1980s is graded according to several criteria, including (1) penetrations and contacts; (2) forcible and nonconsensual; (3) physical injury to the victim or not; and (4) "gang rapes" and single rapist rapes. Most traditional rape statutes, and the newer criminal sexual assault laws, define "rape" as intentional sexual penetration by force without consent.

LO 12 The essential difference between assault and battery is that assault requires no physical contact; an assault is complete before the offender touches the victim.

LO 13 Since the early 1970s, domestic violence crimes have been transformed from a private concern to a criminal justice problem. Violence in intimate relationships is extensive and isn't limited to one socioeconomic group, one society, or one period of time.

LO 14 Stalking involves intentionally scaring another person by following, tormenting, or harassing him or her. Victims need not be injured or threatened. Cyberstalking is the use of the Internet, e-mail, or other electronic communications devices to stalk another person through threatening behavior.

LO 15 Kidnapping is an ancient result crime that consisted of holding the monarch's relatives for ransom. False imprisonment is a lesser form of personal restraint than kidnapping, but the heart of the crime remains depriving others of their personal liberty.

KEY TERMS

aggravated rape, p. 356
unarmed acquaintance rape, p. 357
common law rape, p. 358
corroboration rule, p. 359
rape shield statutes, p. 359
prompt-reporting rule, p. 359
marital rape exception, p. 359
force and resistance rule, p. 364
utmost resistance standard, p. 364
reasonable resistance rule, p. 365
extrinsic force, p. 366
intrinsic force, p. 366
subjective fear, p. 372
objective fear, p. 372
fraud in the fact, p. 373
fraud in the inducement, p. 373
honest and reasonable mistake rule, p. 374
statutory rape, p. 376
defense of reasonable mistake of age, p. 376
simple rape, p. 376
battery, p. 377
assault, p. 377
stalking, p. 377
attempted battery assault, p. 379
intentional scaring, p. 379
conditional threats, p. 380
cyberstalking, p. 387
right of locomotion, p. 392
kidnapping, p. 392
false imprisonment, p. 396

LEARNING OBJECTIVES

1. To know that crimes against other people's property consist of taking, damaging or destroying, and invading property.
2. To understand that the crime of theft grew out of the general social concern with violent crimes against persons.
3. To know the different "taking" crimes—larceny, embezzlement, false pretenses, white-collar crime, robbery, and receiving stolen property.
4. To know how consolidated theft statutes combined the laws of larceny, embezzlement, and false pretenses into one offense called "theft."
5. To know that the federal mail fraud statute defines false pretenses much more broadly than common law crimes of fraudulently taking other people's property.
6. To appreciate that the heart of robbery is the use of actual or threatened force to obtain someone else's property right now.
7. To know that it's illegal to receive stolen property, but only if you intend to keep it permanently.
8. To know that "destroying or damaging" property crimes include both the felony of arson and the misdemeanor criminal mischief.
9. To know the elements of criminal mischief.
10. To appreciate that the heart of both burglary and criminal trespass is invading other people's property, not taking, destroying, or damaging it.
11. To understand that criminal trespass used to be limited to unauthorized invasions of physical property, but now it includes unauthorized access to electronic information systems.
12. To know and appreciate that there are more than twice as many victims of identity theft in the United States than burglary, vehicle theft, and robbery combined.
13. To appreciate that intellectual property theft causes annual losses of billions of dollars each year, and the amount appears to be increasing greatly.

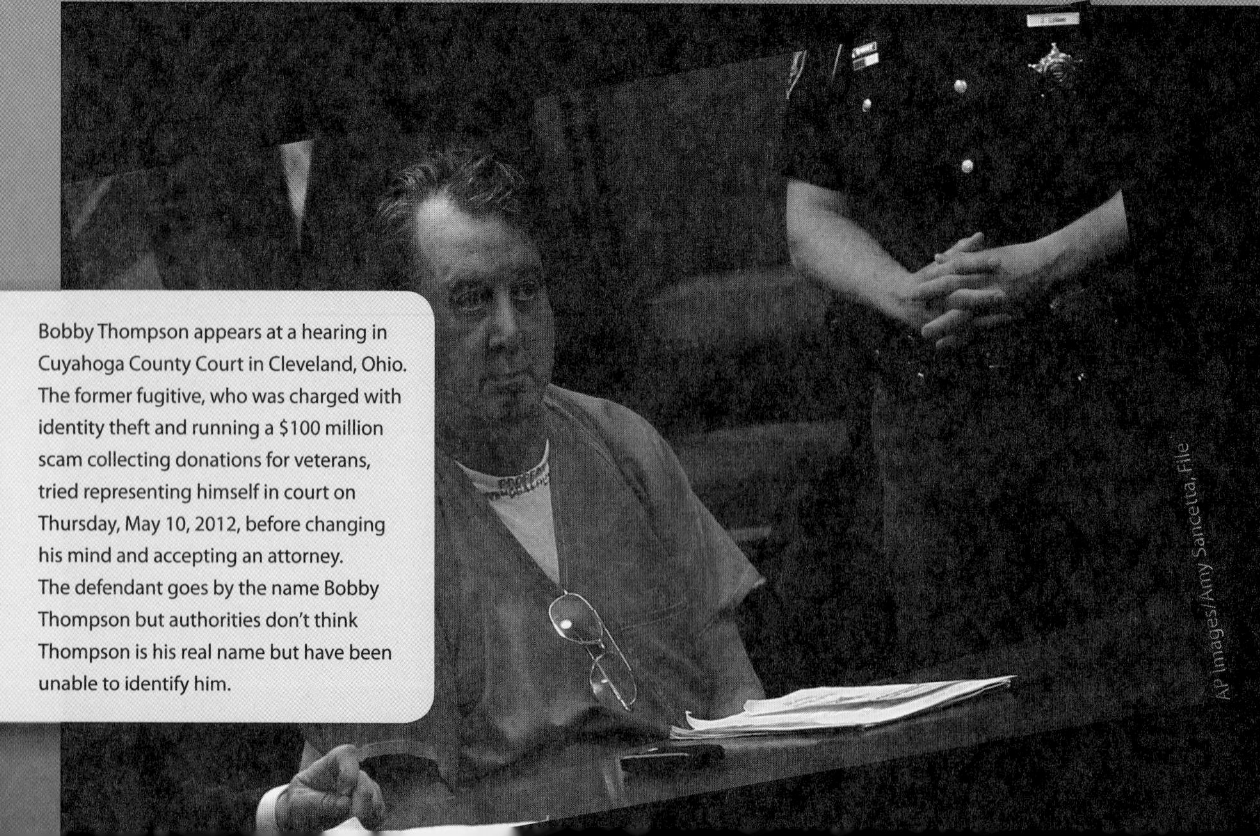

Bobby Thompson appears at a hearing in Cuyahoga County Court in Cleveland, Ohio. The former fugitive, who was charged with identity theft and running a $100 million scam collecting donations for veterans, tried representing himself in court on Thursday, May 10, 2012, before changing his mind and accepting an attorney. The defendant goes by the name Bobby Thompson but authorities don't think Thompson is his real name but have been unable to identify him.

AP Images/Amy Sancetta, File

11 CRIMES AGAINST PROPERTY

CHAPTER OUTLINE

Did He Commit Credit Card Fraud?

Thomas E. Maze moved to Louisville, Kentucky, and there shared an apartment with Charles L. Meredith. In the spring of that year Maze's fancy lightly turned to thoughts of the sunny Southland, and he thereupon took Meredith's BankAmericard and his 1968 automobile and headed for Southern California. By presenting the BankAmericard and signing Meredith's name, Maze obtained food and lodging at motels located in California, Florida, and Louisiana. Each of these establishments transmitted to the Citizens Fidelity Bank & Trust Co. in Louisville, which had issued the BankAmericard to Meredith, the invoices representing goods and services furnished to Maze. Meredith, meanwhile, on the day after Maze's departure from Louisville, notified the Louisville bank that his credit card had been stolen.

(*U.S. v. Maze* 1974)

LO 1

There are many specific crimes against property—too many to list, let alone discuss here. To simplify, we'll look at three categories of crimes against property and a few representative crimes within each. The three categories are:

1. Taking other people's property
2. Damaging or destroying other people's property
3. Invading other people's property

First, we'll look at four crimes that consist of taking someone else's property:

1. *Theft* Sneaking away with an iPod left unattended in the library
2. *Fraud* Abuse of trust: Bernard Madoff's Ponzi scheme that took billions of dollars from investors who trusted him with their fortunes; Navy Commander Charles E. Coughlin who was charged with and convicted of fraudulently trying to collect over $150,000 from the 9-11 victims' funds
3. *Robbery* Sticking a gun in someone's side and demanding the $100 she just withdrew from an ATM machine
4. *Receiving stolen property* Buying a new notebook computer for $75 that you know is stolen

Second, we'll look at two crimes involving destroying and damaging someone else's property:

1. *Arson* Setting a house on fire
2. *Criminal mischief* Damaging someone else's property (such as driving your car up on an obnoxious neighbor's new sod and spinning the wheels)

Third, we'll look at two criminal invasions of someone else's property:

1. *Burglary* Unlawfully entering someone else's house with the intent to steal a TV inside
2. *Criminal trespass* Entering your neighbor's yard where a "no trespassing" sign is posted

cybercrime, crimes aimed at the valuable information contained in computers and wireless devices, especially computer databases accessible through the Internet

The examples provided represent the *traditional* ways to take, destroy or damage, and invade other people's property. **Cybercrime**, defined as crimes committed through the Internet or some other wireless network, is a serious and rapidly growing new problem. There are four types of cybercrimes (Yang and Hoffstadt 2006, 203–204):

1. *Crimes against information brokers* Data collectors (credit reporting agencies) and data aggregators (LexisNexis)
2. *Crimes against manufacturers and distributors of digital media* Movie, recording, and software companies
3. *Crimes against online product and service sales* Businesses that offer their products and services for sale on the Internet
4. *Crimes against business computer systems* Internal computer systems connected to the Internet, used to conduct daily business affairs, and house companies' asset data, including their trade secrets

We often call cybercrimes "new crimes." But they're really new ways (admittedly sometimes very complex and sophisticated ways) to commit the three ancient kinds of property crimes: taking it, damaging or destroying it, and invading it. According to *The Electronic Frontier* (2000):

Advances in technology—the advent of the automobile and the telephone for instance—have always given wrongdoers new means for engaging in unlawful conduct. The internet is no different: it is simply a new medium through which traditional crimes can now be committed.

HISTORY OF CRIMINALLY TAKING OTHER PEOPLE'S PROPERTY

LO 2

The long history of criminal taking began as part of the social concern with violent crimes against the person (Chapters 9 and 10). That concern led to the creation of the common law felony of **robbery**—taking property by force or the threat of force—which is a violent crime against persons and their property.

robbery, taking property by force or the threat of force—a violent crime against persons and their property

Criminal law next expanded to include taking property without consent, even if the thief used no force. The first nonconsensual, nonviolent taking felony was **larceny**, the ancient crime of stealing. Larceny consisted (and still consists) of (1) taking and (2) carrying away (3) someone else's property without their consent and, most of the time, without their knowledge, (4) with the intent to permanently deprive victims of possession.

LO 3

larceny, taking and carrying away a person's property without the use of force and with the intent to permanently deprive the owner of possession

Larceny was born as the common law tool to protect the Anglo-Saxons' most valuable possession—livestock—from dishonest or untrustworthy thieves (LaFave and Scott 1986, chap. 8; Perkins and Boyce 1982, chap. 4).

Larceny didn't protect the property of those who voluntarily handed it over to a caretaker—for example, a carrier who delivered property to someone else or a bank that held depositors' money. Larceny required that thieves "take and carry away" the property. Caretakers did neither; what they did was "convert" property that was lawfully in their possession to their own use. In criminal law, **conversion** means "wrongfully possessing or disposing of someone else's property as if it were yours."

conversion, wrongfully possessing or disposing of someone else's property as if it were yours

As society advanced, the failure of larceny to protect adequately against conversion by caretakers created a growing gap in the criminal law. This was especially true in a society with exploding quantities and kinds of valuable and easily *portable* possessions. These possessions included both **tangible property** (personal property items like jewelry) and **intangible property** (stocks, bonds, and promissory notes)—namely, paper worth nothing by itself but which was proof of (it represented) something of value.

tangible property, personal property, not real estate

intangible property, property worth nothing by itself but is proof of something of value (such as stock options, bonds, notes, trademarks, licenses, and patents)

As society became more complex, caretakers' converting property that owners voluntarily handed over to them grew into an enormous problem. Legislatures responded to this problem of unlawful conversion of property by creating the felony of **embezzlement**.

The earliest embezzlement statutes were directed at occupations handling other people's money, such as bank clerks. Eventually, statutes reached broadly to include all kinds of breaches of trust. According to the MPC reporter (ALI 1985, 2:223.1):

embezzlement, the crime of lawfully gaining possession of someone else's property and later converting it to one's own use

> A few American legislatures enacted fraudulent-conversion statutes penalizing misappropriation by anyone who received or had in his possession or control the property of another, or property which someone else "is entitled to receive and have." Indeed, some modern embezzlement statutes go so far as to penalize breach of faith without regard to whether anything is misappropriated. Thus, the fiduciary who makes forbidden investments, the official who deposits public funds in an unauthorized depository, the financial advisor who betrays his client into paying more for a property than fair market value, may be designated an embezzler. (129)

Embezzlement was the first of what we call the **abuse-of-trust crimes**. Most of these eventually became what we now call **white-collar crimes**—crimes growing out of opportunities to get someone else's property that was entrusted to the perpetrators because of their occupation (see White-Collar Crime, p. 407).

abuse-of-trust crimes, crimes growing out of opportunities to get someone else's property that was entrusted to the perpetrators because of their occupation, now known as white-collar crimes

white-collar crimes, crimes growing out of opportunities to get someone else's property that was entrusted to the perpetrators because of their occupation

Although the term at first referred only to crimes committed by business executives, it now includes property crimes that grow out of opportunities created by any lawful occupation (for example, if I take the MacBook Air the university provided to help me teach my classes, and I use it, instead, to promote the sales of the book you're reading, I'd be a "white-collar criminal"). Statutes and courts are still creating new crimes to combat the same old evil of satisfying the excessive desire to get other people's property by the new methods, such as stealing their identities from computers and the Internet.

So robbery applied to those who took or threatened to take someone else's property by force; larceny applied to those who sneaked away with someone else's property; and embezzlement applied to those who kept permanently someone else's property they had only a temporary right to possess. But what about crafty scam artists who tricked owners into giving up possession or ownership? The deceivers hadn't "taken" the property, because the owners willingly gave it to them. They hadn't converted it either, because they didn't have even a temporary right to possess it.

fraud, a general term that means getting property by deception

common law fraud, obtaining another's property by "simple deception"

obtaining property by false pretenses, in modern law, often called "theft by deceit"; making false representations concerning past or present facts with the intent to defraud another

They got it by **fraud**, a general term that means getting property by deception. Influenced by the doctrine of *caveat emptor* ("Let the buyer beware"), **common law fraud**, obtaining another's property by "simple deception," wasn't a crime. The English common law court, in *Regina v. Jones* (1703), put it succinctly: "Making a fool of another is not a crime" (330). It was, however, a common law misdemeanor to cheat, which in criminal law was limited to using false weights and other "tokens" to cheat the general public.

In 1753, the English Parliament enacted a statute that expanded cheating to include a new misdemeanor, which was defined as obtaining "'money, goods, wares or merchandizes by false pretenses with intent to cheat or defraud" (Kadish, Schulhofer, and Steiker 2007, 956). This statute became the prototype for the modern felony of **obtaining property by false pretenses**, which filled the gap left by larceny and embezzlement when it came to fraudulently getting *ownership* (not just possession) of other people's property.

In false pretenses *actus reus*, "deceiving" (defrauding) replaces "taking" in larceny and "converting" in embezzlement. Deception requires a lie, such as promising you that if you give me $100 I'll get you an iPad, a promise I know I can't keep or don't intend even to try to keep.

theft, intentionally getting control of someone else's property, includes larceny, embezzlement, and false pretense crimes

So, with history and law to help us, we'll start our study of crimes related to misappropriating someone else's property. These include the ancient "taking" felony of larceny and its modern descendant, theft; white-collar crimes, focusing on federal mail fraud and Ponzi schemes; taking property by force (robbery); and receiving property someone else has stolen.

LO 4

LARCENY AND THEFT

The logic of social and economic history lies behind the separation of the three ways to get other people's property into separate crimes. But the distinctions still make sense. As we saw earlier, when society changed, embezzlement supplemented larceny, and then theft by deceit (false pretenses) supplemented both larceny and embezzlement to fight the new ways of unlawfully taking other people's money.

consolidated theft statutes, eliminate needlessly separating theft into distinct offenses according to their *actus reus*; comprises crimes of taking and carrying away, converting, or swindling to gain possession of someone else's property

Most states have consolidated the old crimes of larceny, embezzlement, and false pretenses into one offense called **theft**. They accept the social reality that all these ancient crimes were aimed at the same evil—intentionally getting control of someone else's property.

Consolidated theft statutes eliminate needlessly separating theft into distinct offenses according to their *actus reus*. Thus, modern theft statute *actus reus* comprises "taking and carrying away," "converting," or "swindling" to obtain possession of

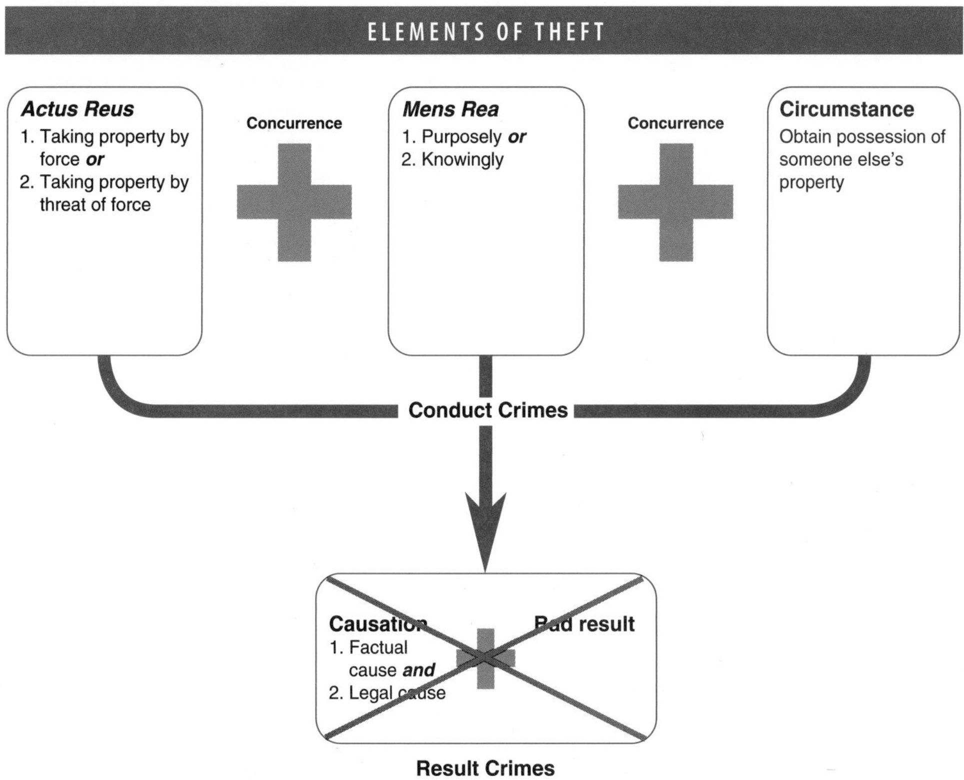

someone else's property. The *mens rea* in modern theft statutes remains as it always was—acquiring someone else's property "purposely" or "knowingly" in MPC language, or "intentionally" in non-MPC states, for the purpose of permanently depriving the owner of her possession.

CASE

In* People v. Gasparik *(1981), *New York's highest court, the New York Court of Appeals, upheld the convictions of three defendants for shoplifting, by adapting ancient larceny to fit modern shoplifting.*

Did he "steal" the leather jacket?

People v. Gasparik

420 N.E.2d 40 (1981)

HISTORY

Stefan Gasparik was convicted of petit larceny, and he appealed. The Supreme Court, First Judicial Department, and the Supreme Court, Second Judicial Department, affirmed, and he appealed. The Court of Appeals, Cooke, CJ, affirmed.

COOKE, CJ.

This case presents a recurring question in this era of the self-service store that has never been resolved by this Court: may a person be convicted of larceny for shoplifting if the person is caught with goods while still inside the store? For reasons outlined below, it is concluded that a larceny conviction may be sustained, in certain situations, even though the shoplifter was apprehended before leaving the store.

(continues)

(continued)

FACTS

I

Stefan Gasparik, the defendant, was in a department store trying on a leather jacket. Two store detectives observed him tear off the price tag and remove a "sensormatic" device designed to set off an alarm if the jacket were carried through a detection machine. There was at least one such machine at the exit of each floor. The defendant placed the tag and the device in the pocket of another jacket on the merchandise rack. He took his own jacket, which he had been carrying with him, and placed it on a table. Leaving his own jacket, the defendant put on the leather jacket and walked through the store, still on the same floor, bypassing several cash registers.

When he headed for the exit from that floor, in the direction of the main floor, he was apprehended by security personnel. At trial, Gasparik denied removing the price tag and the sensormatic device from the jacket, and testified that he was looking for a cashier without a long line when he was stopped. The Court, sitting without a jury, convicted the defendant of petit larceny. Appellate Term affirmed.

OPINION

The primary issue is whether the evidence, viewed in the light most favorable to the prosecution, was sufficient to establish the elements of larceny as defined by the Penal Law. Larceny at common law was defined as a trespassory taking and carrying away of the property of another with intent to steal it. Gradually, the courts began to expand the reach of the offense, initially by subtle alterations in the common-law concept of possession. As the reach of larceny expanded, the intent element of the crime became of increasing importance, while the requirement of a trespassory taking became less significant.

Modern penal statutes generally have incorporated these developments under a unified definition of larceny (MPC: theft is appropriation of property of another, which includes unauthorized exercise of control). Case law, too, now tends to focus upon the actor's intent and the exercise of dominion and control over the property.

Also required is some movement when property other than an automobile is involved. As a practical matter, in shoplifting cases the same evidence which proves the taking will usually involve movement. The movement, or asportation requirement, has traditionally been satisfied by a slight moving of the property. This accords with the purpose of the asportation element which is to show that the thief had indeed gained possession and control of the property.

It is this element that forms the core of the controversy in this case. The defendant argues that the crime is not established unless there is evidence that the customer departed the shop without paying for the merchandise. Although this court has not addressed the issue, case law from other jurisdictions seems unanimous in holding that a shoplifter need not leave the store to be guilty of larceny. This is because a shopper may treat merchandise in a manner inconsistent with the owner's continued rights—and in a manner not in accord with that of prospective purchaser—without actually walking out of the store. Indeed, depending upon the circumstances of each case, a variety of conduct may be sufficient to allow the trier of fact to find a taking.

It would be well-nigh impossible, and unwise, to attempt to delineate all the situations which would establish a taking. But it is possible to identify some of the factors used in determining whether the evidence is sufficient to be submitted to the fact finder.

In many cases, it will be particularly relevant that defendant concealed the goods under clothing or in a container. Such conduct is not generally expected in a self-service store and may in a proper case be deemed an exercise of dominion and control inconsistent with the store's continued rights. Other furtive or unusual behavior on the part of the defendant should also be weighed. Thus, if the defendant surveys the area while secreting the merchandise or abandoned his or her own property in exchange for the concealed goods, this may evince larcenous rather than innocent behavior. Relevant too is the customer's proximity to or movement toward one of the store's exits. Certainly it is highly probative of guilt that the customer was in possession of secreted goods just a few short steps from the door or moving in that direction. Finally, possession of a known shoplifting device actually used to conceal merchandise, such as a specially designed outer garment or false bottomed carrying case, would be all but decisive.

Of course, in a particular case, any one or any combination of these factors may take on special significance. And there may be other considerations, not now identified, which should be examined. So long as it bears upon the principal issue—whether the shopper exercised control wholly inconsistent with the owner's continued rights—any attending circumstance is relevant and may be taken into account.

Under these principles, there was ample evidence in each case to raise a factual question as to the defendants' guilt.

Gasparik removed the price tag and sensor device from a jacket, abandoned his own garment, put the jacket on, and ultimately headed for the main floor of the store. Removal of the price tag and sensor device, and careful concealment of those items, is highly unusual and suspicious conduct for a shopper. Coupled with defendant's abandonment of his own coat and his attempt to leave the floor, those factors were sufficient to make out a prima facie case of a taking.

In sum, in view of the modern definition of the crime of larceny, and its purpose of protecting individual property rights, a taking of property in the self-service store context can be established by evidence that a customer exercised control over merchandise wholly inconsistent with the store's continued rights. Quite simply, a customer who crosses the line between the limited right he or she has to deal with merchandise and the store owner's rights may be subject to prosecution for larceny. Such a rule should foster the legitimate interests and continued operation of self-service shops, a convenience which most members of the society enjoy.

Affirmed.

QUESTIONS

1. State the elements of larceny.
2. Summarize the court's arguments to support the proof of each of the elements of larceny.
3. Did the court stretch the original meaning of the elements? Explain.
4. Is the decision good public policy? Explain.
5. Should the court, or the legislature, change the meaning of the elements of larceny to fit modern conditions? Explain your answer.

WHITE-COLLAR CRIME

> This paper . . . is a comparison of crime in the upper or white-collar class, composed of respectable or at least respected business and professional men, and crime in the lower classes, composed of persons of low socioeconomic status. . . . The criminal statistics show unequivocally that crime, *as popularly conceived and officially measured*, has a high incidence in the lower class and a low incidence in the upper class. Less than two percent of the persons committed to prisons in a year belong to the upper class. These statistics refer to criminals handled by police, the criminal and juvenile courts, and the prisons, and to such crimes as murder, assault, burglary, larceny, sex offenses, and drunkenness. . . .
>
> (Edwin Sutherland 1940, 1)

The quote is taken from criminologist Edwin Sutherland's Presidential Address to the American Sociological Association in 1940, "White-Collar Criminality." He was referring to two kinds of business and professional crime:

1. "*fraud and swindling*." (for example, misrepresentation in corporate financial statements and tax fraud);
2. "*double cross*." corporation director, acting on insider information buys land the corporation needs, and sells it at a "fantastic profit" to his corporation. (3)

Sutherland wrote that they're what the racketeer "Al Capone called 'the legitimate rackets' " (3).

Sutherland called attention to a large and growing variety of criminal behavior that criminologists had ignored. And, although his language sounds out of date, and may even grate on the ears of the politically correct, "his instinct was right, even in the context of a basic criminal law context. Whatever white collar crime may be, exactly, it is important to recognize that crimes are committed on a regular basis, by those who qualify as white collar workers, including among others—lawyers" (Dubber and Kelman 2009, 917).

But this is a criminal law book, not a book about white-collar criminals. So we'll focus on Sutherland's fraud and swindling crimes against property. And we'll home in on mail fraud and Ponzi schemes.

LO 5

Federal Mail Fraud

federal mail fraud, includes "schemes to defraud or for obtaining money or property" using the U.S. mail

Federal mail fraud includes "schemes to defraud or for obtaining money or property" (U.S. Code Title 18, Section 1341). Notice that the statute doesn't require actual deprivation. It applies to anyone who "having devised, or intending to devise any scheme . . . to defraud," uses the mail "for the purpose of executing such scheme or attempting to do so" (Dubber and Kelman 2005, 953). According to authors Markus Dubber and Mark Kelman:

> For over a generation, the mail and wire fraud statutes have provided federal prosecutors with a residual catch-all that was available when nothing else in their arsenal seemed likely to work. . . . At first glance, [the federal mail fraud statute] may seem only intended to protect the integrity of a federally administered service, the post office. Yet, its key phrase, "scheme . . . to defraud" . . . has long served instead as a charter of authority for courts to decide retroactively what forms of unfair or questionable conduct in commercial, public and even private life should be deemed criminal. In so doing, this phrase has provided more expansive interpretations from prosecutors and judges than probably any other phrase in criminal law. (957)

CASE

In* U.S. v. Maze *(1974), the U.S. government relied on the mail fraud statute to prosecute Thomas Maze for stealing his roommate's BankAmericard and using it to pay his bills for a cross-national road trip to California in his roommate's car—which he also stole.

Did he commit federal mail fraud?

U.S. v. Maze

414 U.S. 395, 94 S.Ct. 645 (1974)

HISTORY

Thomas Maze, Defendant, was convicted in the United States District Court for the Western District of Kentucky at Louisville on four counts of mail fraud. The Court of Appeals reversed. The Supreme Court affirmed.

REHNQUIST, J.

FACTS

Thomas E. Maze moved to Louisville, Kentucky, and there shared an apartment with Charles L. Meredith. In the spring of that year Maze's fancy lightly turned to thoughts of the sunny Southland, and he thereupon took Meredith's BankAmericard and his 1968 automobile and headed for Southern California. By presenting the BankAmericard and signing Meredith's name, Maze obtained food and lodging at motels located in California, Florida, and Louisiana. Each of these establishments transmitted to the Citizens Fidelity Bank & Trust Co. in Louisville, which had issued the BankAmericard to Meredith, the invoices representing goods and services furnished to Maze. Meredith, meanwhile, on the day after Maze's departure from Louisville, notified the Louisville bank that his credit card had been stolen.

Upon Maze's return to Louisville he was indicted on four counts of violation of the federal mail fraud statute (18 U.S.C. §1341).

The mail fraud counts of the indictment charged that Maze had devised a scheme to defraud the Louisville bank, Charles L. Meredith, and several merchants in different States by unlawfully obtaining possession of the BankAmericard issued by the Louisville bank to Meredith, and using the card to obtain goods and services. The indictment charged that Maze had obtained goods and services at four specified motels by presenting Meredith's BankAmericard for payment and representing himself to be Meredith, and that Maze knew that each merchant would cause the sales slips of the purchases to be delivered by mail to the Louisville bank which would in turn mail them to Meredith for payment. The indictment also charged that the delay in this mailing would enable Maze to continue purchasing goods and services for an appreciable period of time.

Maze was tried by a jury in the United States District Court for the Western District of Kentucky. At trial, representatives of the four motels identified the sales invoices from the transactions on Meredith's BankAmericard which were forwarded to the Louisville bank by their motels. An official of the Louisville bank testified that all of the sales invoices for those transactions were received by the bank in due course through the mail, and that this was the customary method by which invoices representing BankAmericard purchases were transmitted to the Louisville bank. The jury found Maze guilty as charged on all counts, and he appealed the judgment of conviction to the Court of Appeals for the Sixth Circuit. That court reversed the judgment as to the mail fraud statute. Because of an apparent conflict among the courts of appeals as to the circumstances under which the fraudulent use of a credit card may violate the mail fraud statute, we granted the Government's petition for certiorari. For the reasons stated below, we affirm the judgment of the Court of Appeals.

OPINION

The applicable parts of the mail fraud statute provide as follows:

> Whoever, having devised or intending to devise any scheme or artifice to defraud, or for obtaining money or property by means of false or fraudulent pretenses, representations, or promises . . . for the purpose of executing such scheme or artifice or attempting so to do . . . knowingly causes to be delivered by mail according to the direction thereon, or at the place at which it is directed to be delivered by the person to whom it is addressed, any (matter or thing whatever to be sent or delivered by the Postal Service) shall be fined not more than $1,000 or imprisoned not more than five years, or both. 18 U.S.C. § 1341.

We assume, as did the Court of Appeals, that the evidence would support a finding by the jury that Maze "caused" the mailings of the invoices he signed from the out-of-state motels to the Louisville bank. But the more difficult question is whether these mailings were sufficiently closely related to Maze's scheme to bring his conduct within the statute.

Under the statute, the mailing must be for the purpose of executing the scheme, as the statute requires, but it is not necessary that the scheme contemplate the use of the mails as an essential element. (*Pereira v. United States*). The Government relies on *Pereira*, supra, and *United States v. Sampson*, 371 U.S. 75, 83 S.Ct. 173, 9 L.Ed.2d 136 (1962), to support its position, while Maze relies on *Kann v. United States*, supra, and *Parr v. United States*, 363 U.S. 370, 80 S.Ct. 1171, 4 L.Ed.2d 1277 (1960).

In *Kann*, corporate officers and directors were accused of having set up a dummy corporation through which to divert profits of their own corporation to their own use. As a part of the scheme, the defendants were accused of having fraudulently obtained checks payable to them which were cashed or deposited at a bank and then mailed for collection to the drawee bank. This Court held that the fraud was completed at the point at which defendants cashed the checks.

The Government, however, relying on *United States v. Sampson*, argues that essential to the success of any fraudulent credit-card scheme is the "delay" caused by use of the mails "which aids the perpetrator . . . in the continuation of a fraudulent credit card scheme and the postponement of its detection." In *Sampson*, various employees of a nationwide corporation were charged with a scheme to defraud businessmen by obtaining advance fees on the promise

(continues)

(continued)
that the defendants would either help the businessmen to obtain loans or to sell their businesses.

Even after the checks representing the fees had been deposited to the accounts of the defendants, however, the plan called for the mailing of the accepted application together with a form letter assuring the victims that the services for which they had contracted would be performed. The Court found that *Kann* did not preclude the application of the mail fraud statute to "a deliberate, planned use of the mails after the victims' money had been obtained."

We do not believe that *Sampson* sustains the Government's position. The subsequent mailings there were designed to lull the victims into a false sense of security, postpone their ultimate complaint to the authorities, and therefore make the apprehension of the defendants less likely than if no mailings had taken place. But the successful completion of the mailings from the motel owners here to the Louisville bank increased the probability that Maze would be detected and apprehended. There was undoubtedly delay in transmitting invoices to the Louisville bank, as there is in the physical transmission of any business correspondence between cities separated by large distances. Mail service as a means of transmitting such correspondence from one city to another is designed to overcome the effect of the distance which separates the places. But it is the distance, and not the mail service, which causes the time lag in the physical transmission of such correspondence. (Since we are admonished that we may not as judges ignore what we know as men, we do not wish to be understood as suggesting that delays in mail service are solely attributable to the distance involved. If the Postal Service appears on occasion to be something less than a 20th century version of the wingfooted Mercury, the fact remains that the invoices were mailed to and were ultimately received by the Louisville bank.)

Congress could have drafted the mail fraud statute so as to require only that the mails be in fact used as a result of the fraudulent scheme. But it did not do this; instead, it required that the use of the mails be "for the purpose of executing such scheme or artifice. . . ." Since the mailings in this case were not for that purpose, the judgment of the Court of Appeals is

Affirmed.

DISSENT

BURGER, CJ., JOINED BY WHITE, J.

Section 1341 of Title 18 U.S.C. has traditionally been used against fraudulent activity as a first line of defense. When a "new" fraud develops—as constantly happens—the mail fraud statute becomes a stopgap device to deal on a temporary basis with the new phenomenon, until particularized legislation can be developed and passed to deal directly with the evil.

The criminal mail fraud statute must remain strong to be able to cope with the new varieties of fraud that the ever-inventive American "con artist" is sure to develop. Abuses in franchising and the growing scandals from pyramid sales schemes are but some of the threats to the financial security of our citizenry that the Federal Government must be ever alert to combat.

MR. JUSTICE WHITE, WITH WHOM THE CHIEF JUSTICE, MR. JUSTICE BRENNAN, AND MR. JUSTICE BLACKMUN CONCUR, DISSENTING.

Until today the acts charged in the indictment in this case—knowingly causing four separate sales invoices to be mailed by merchants to the bank that had issued the stolen BankAmericard in furtherance of a scheme to defraud the bank by using the credit card without authorization and by falsely securing credit—would have been a criminal offense punishable as mail fraud under 18 U.S.C. § 1341. But no more. By misreading this Court's prior decisions and giving an unambiguous federal criminal statute an unrealistic reading, the majority places beyond the reach of the statute a fraudulent scheme that by law is not consummated until after the mails have been used, that utilizes the mails as a central, necessary instrumentality in its perpetration, and that demands federal investigatory and prosecutorial resources if it is to be effectively checked. Because I cannot subscribe to the majority's reasoning or the result it reaches, I dissent.

The majority's decision has ramifications far beyond the mere reversal of a lone criminal conviction. In this era of the "cashless" society, Americans are increasingly resorting to the use of credit cards in their day-to-day consumer purchases. Today well over 300 million credit cards are in circulation, and annual charges exceed $60 billion. In 1969 alone, 1.5 million credit cards were lost or stolen, resulting in fraud losses exceeding $100 million. Current estimates of annual credit card fraud losses are put as high as $200 million. Under the result reached by the majority, only those credit card frauds exceeding $5,000 covered by 15 U.S.C. 1644 will be subject to federal criminal jurisdiction.

Yet this burgeoning criminal activity, as evidenced by the very facts of this case, does not recognize artificial state boundaries. In the future, nationwide credit card fraud schemes will have to be prosecuted in each individual State in which a fraudulent transaction transpired. Here, for example, Maze must now be charged and tried in California, Louisiana, and Florida. This result, never intended by Congress, may precipitate a widespread inability to apprehend and/or prosecute those who would hijack the credit card system.

I dissent.

QUESTIONS

1. State the elements of the federal mail fraud statute relevant to deciding whether Thomas Maze was guilty of mail fraud.
2. List the facts relevant to deciding whether Thomas Maze violated the statute.
3. Summarize the arguments for the majority's opinion reversing Maze's conviction.
4. Summarize the dissent's arguments in favor of upholding Maze's conviction.
5. Which position do you favor? Defend your answer.
6. Is the dissent's worry over the social problem the Mail Fraud Act is aimed at misplaced? Is it still a problem?

The federal mail fraud statute played an essential role in the government's case against Thomas Maze.

Ponzi Schemes

The "great recession" that began in 2007 hurt legitimate industries—automobiles, real estate, and banking. We're all aware of these casualties. What you probably *don't* know is that the downturn also hurt an old form of false pretenses—Ponzi schemes (named after a con artist who ripped off millions from gullible victims in 1920). In Ponzi schemes, schemers tell investors they're buying assets such as real estate, stocks and bonds, or consumer products. In fact, they're buying nothing. Instead, Ponzi schemers use the money to pay earlier investors. Eventually, the money dries up and everything collapses.

Ponzi scheme, a fraudulent investment operation that pays returns to investors from their own money or money paid by subsequent investors rather from any actual profit earned

During this recession, Ponzi schemes have collapsed at record rates. The FBI has about five hundred open Ponzi investigations nationwide, up from three hundred in 2006.

Why the increase in Ponzi schemes? In order to answer that question, we need to put *increase* in perspective. Traditionally, Ponzis were small scams spread by "word of mouth, direct mail and advertisements in magazines" (Wilber 2009). The Internet and modern communications dramatically changed that. These technology advances, and the economic boom of the 1990s and early 2000s, enabled Ponzi schemers to lure institutional investors into handing over billions of dollars, and small ones into using their home equity loans to cash in on the bonanza.

Enter the "Great Recession of 2009." Ponzi scheme investors demanded their money back. When they couldn't get it, they reported the schemers to federal agents. Also, wary *potential* investors in increasing numbers, reported investment opportunities that seemed too good to be true. This seriously wounded the Ponzis. But, Professor William K. Black, former executive director of the Institute for Fraud Prevention, believes that when good times return, so will Ponzis. "The crooks know that potential investors, some desperate for a quick return, will not always be so wary." (quoted in Wilber 2009)

In 2009, Bernie Madoff pleaded guilty to eleven felony charges stemming from running a massive Ponzi scheme for years. Madoff defrauded his victims of more than $65 billion. The government entered a $170 billion legal judgment against him, and he was sentenced to 150 years in prison for his crimes. See Figure 11.1 for an excerpt of the forfeiture of assets order issued after his conviction. The order called for the "forfeiture of all property, real and personal, that . . . is derived from proceeds traceable to the commission of the said offenses."

Civil Liability

In our emphasis on the centuries-old *criminal* response to protect property from swindlers, we can't overlook that thefts, frauds, and swindles are also civil wrongs. "The history of larceny and fraud is also the history of supplementing civil actions with criminal punishment." What was once a tort is now also a crime (Dubber and Kelman 2005, 919).

The case of Navy Commander Charles E. Coughlin is an excellent example of a case pursued simultaneously on both tracks. A jury found Coughlin guilty of filing a false claim with the September 11th Victim Compensation Fund and stealing $151,000 from the government. Coughlin collected money for a neck injury that he said he suffered during the 9-11 attacks. In fact, the injury had occurred three years before the attack. He was sentenced to 41 months in federal prison. The civil suit, in which the U.S. government hopes to recoup the money Commander Coughlin was convicted of taking, was ongoing as of this writing.

ETHICAL DILEMMA

Should he forfeit his property even if a jury didn't convict him?

The U.S. military granted Navy commander Charles E. Coughlin a Purple Heart and the government awarded him $331,000 for neck and other injuries he claimed to have suffered when American Airlines Flight 77 crashed into the Pentagon on September 11, 2001. Now government lawyers have concluded that Coughlin lied about his injuries—and they are seeking to seize his $1 million house in Severna Park, his Mercedes-Benz, and his minivan. The U.S. attorney's office has filed a civil suit alleging that the now-retired commander falsely claimed he suffered "a partial permanent disability" after falling debris struck him on the head at the Pentagon, where 184 people were killed.

Instructions

Write a one-page essay answering the question, "Is it ethical for the government to continue its civil action to seize Coughlin's house and car, even though he's serving his time in prison for his fraud?" To answer the question, consider the sections on "Crimes and Noncriminal Wrongs," and "What's the Appropriate Punishment for Criminal Behavior?" in Chapter 1.

MADOFF FORFEITURE ORDER

FIGURE 11.1

UNITED STATES DISTRICT COURT
SOUTHERN DISTRICT OF NEW YORK
- x

UNITED STATES OF AMERICA :

SECOND FINAL ORDER
OF FORFEITURE
(1st Pub. Group–Selected Assets;
2nd Pub. Group)

- v. -

BERNARD L. MADOFF, : 09 Cr. 213 (DC)

Defendant. :

- x

USDC SDNY
DOCUMENT
ELECTRONICALLY FILED
DOC #: ________
DATE FILED: 09/22/10

BACKGROUND

The Criminal Proceedings

WHEREAS, on or about June 26, 2009, the Court entered a Preliminary Order of Forfeiture (Final as to the Defendant) (the "Preliminary Order") as to BERNARD L. MADOFF, the defendant ("MADOFF" or the "defendant"), which is incorporated herein by reference as if set out in full;

WHEREAS, on June 29, 2009, the Court sentenced the defendant to, *inter alia*, 150 years' imprisonment and criminal forfeiture in accordance with the terms of the Preliminary Order;

WHEREAS, in the Preliminary Order, the Court imposed an aggregate money judgment upon the defendant in the amount of $170.799 billion ($170 billion as to the First Forfeiture Allegation and $799 million as to the Second Forfeiture Allegation), and ordered the defendant to forfeit all of his right, title and interest in any and all property and other interests belonging to, owed to or controlled in whole or in part by the defendant, and all property traceable to such property, including, but not limited to, all right, title and interest of the defendant in the property listed in Exhibit A to the Preliminary Order (the "Specific Property");

WHEREAS, pursuant to 21 U.S.C. § 853(n)(7), the United States is therefore entitled to have clear title to the Subject Property and to warrant good title to any subsequent purchaser or transferee.

NOW, THEREFORE, on the application of Preet Bharara, United States Attorney for the Southern District of New York, Barbara A. Ward and Matthew L. Schwartz, Assistant United States Attorneys, of counsel,

(continues)

FIGURE 11.1 (continued)

MADOFF FORFEITURE ORDER

IT IS ORDERED, ADJUDGED AND DECREED THAT:

1. All right, title and interest in the Subject Property is hereby forfeited to the United States of America for disposition according to law.

2. All right, title and interest in any and all interest and/or income ("Interest") accrued on the Subject Property (or the proceeds of its sale, where applicable) while on deposit in the Seized Assets Deposit Account is hereby forfeited to the United States of America for disposition according to law. The United States Marshals Service shall calculate such Interest, accruing from the dates of deposit in the Seized Assets Deposit Account, and transfer any and all such Interest to the Department of Justice Assets Forfeiture Fund along with the forfeited property, in anticipation of remission proceedings for the benefit of victims to be conducted by the Department of Justice pursuant to 21 U.S.C. § 853(i) and 28 C.F.R. Part 9.

3. The net proceeds from the sale of the Subject Property, together with Interest (as defined in the next preceding paragraph), shall be applied to the Money Judgments imposed upon the defendant, in partial satisfaction thereof.

4. Nothing in this Order shall affect any property subject to the Preliminary Order of Forfeiture other than the Subject Property, or any petition asserting an interest in any such property.

5. The Court retains jurisdiction to take additional action, enter further orders, and amend this and any future orders as necessary to implement and enforce this Order.

6. The Clerk of the Court shall forward certified copies of this Order to Assistant United States Attorney Barbara A. Ward, One St. Andrew's Plaza, New York, New York, 10007.

Dated: New York, New York
September 22, 2010

DENNY CHIN
United States ~~District~~ Circuit Judge,
Sitting by Designation

Source: Second Final Order of Forfeiture in *United States v. Madoff*. Some material has been deleted. http://www.justice.gov/usao/nys/madoff/20100922madoffsecondfofecf.pdf.

ROBBERY

LO 6

Now that you've seen the ancient crime of larceny brought up to date by modern fraud, let's turn to robbery, the other ancient property crime brought up to date in modern statutes and case law. *Robbery* consists of hurting, or threatening to hurt, someone right now if they don't give up their property.

Robbery is really two crimes, theft and assault (Chapter 10). But the criminal law has never treated it that way, because robbery is considered more serious than the sum of these two parts. The MPC reporter explains why:

> The violent petty thief operating in the streets and alleys of big cities—the "mugger"—is one of the main sources of insecurity and concern in the population at large. There is a special element of terror in this kind of depredation. The ordinary citizen does not feel particularly threatened by the surreptitious larceny, embezzlement, or fraud. But there is understandable abhorrence of the robber who accosts on the streets and who menaces his victims with actual or threatened violence against which there is a general sense of helplessness. In proportion as the ordinary person fears and detests such behavior, the offender exhibits himself as seriously deviated from community norms, thus justifying more serious sanctions. In addition, the robber may be distinguished from the stealthy thief by the hardihood that enables him to carry out his purpose in the presence of his victim and over his opposition—obstacles that might deter ordinary sneak thieves and that justify the feeling of special danger evoked by the robber. (98)

As a victim of more than one mugging on Chicago streets, I can vouch for the fear, anger, and sense of violation that goes along with losing something valuable, like the watch my mother gave me as a high school graduation present. But it's more than the value of what I lost that that signifies. It's the personal violation that accompanied fear and humiliation, even when the threat isn't real. During the second mugging, I gave up my money because the mugger showed me his "weapon" bulging in his coat pocket. After I handed over the money, he pulled the "weapon" out of his pocket—a comb—and ran his thumb down the teeth, sneering, "Hey man, you should be more careful in the future," snickering as he swaggered away.

Let's look at the elements of robbery: its *actus reus*, *mens rea*, and required attendant circumstances. (See the Elements of Robbery illustration on the next page.)

Robbery Actus Reus *(Criminal Act)*

An act of force, or threat of force, is the essence of the robbery criminal act—the robbery *actus reus*. Any amount of force beyond the amount needed to take and carry away someone else's property is enough. Picking a pocket isn't robbery because "picking pockets" is defined as requiring only enough force to remove the contents of the pocket. But even slightly mishandling the victim, like a push, turns the pickpocket into a robber. Robbery doesn't even require the use of actual force; threatened force (a drawn gun or knife) is enough.

robbery *actus reus*, an act or threat of force beyond the amount needed to take and carry away someone else's property

Does a "shove" satisfy the force requirement in robbery? The victim in *State v. Curley* (1997) was walking out of a mall with her daughter when Erwin Curley, who was drunk at the time, grabbed her purse and ran away. According to the victim,

> I had my purse on my left side . . . and I felt kind of a shove of my left shoulder where I had my purse strap with my thumb through it and I kind of leaned—was pushed—toward my daughter, and this person came and just grabbed the strap of my purse and continued to run. (1105)

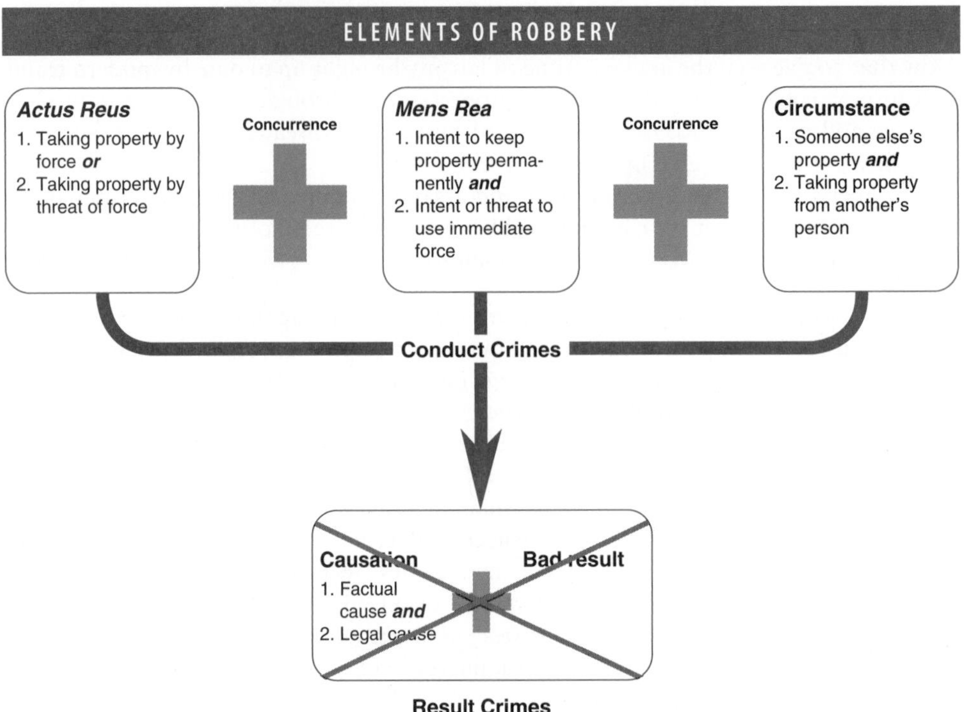

On appeal after he was convicted of robbery, Curley argued that the jury could have found that "shoving of the victim was part of his drunkenness, and then the purse was taken without force sufficient to constitute robbery." The New Mexico Court of appeals agreed:

> There is not sufficient force to constitute robbery when the thief snatches property from the owner's grasp so suddenly that the owner cannot offer any resistance to the taking. On the other hand, when the owner, aware of an impending snatching, resists it, or when, the thief's first attempt being ineffective to separate the owner from his property, a struggle for the property is necessary before the thief can get possession thereof, there is enough force to make the taking robbery.
>
> Taking the owner's property by stealthily picking his pocket is not taking by force and so is not robbery; but if the pickpocket or his confederate jostles the owner, or if the owner, catching the pickpocket in the act, struggles unsuccessfully to keep possession, the pickpocket's crime becomes robbery. To remove an article of value, attached to the owner's person or clothing, by a sudden snatching or by stealth is not robbery unless the article in question (e.g., an earring, pin or watch) is so attached to the person or his clothes as to require some force to effect its removal. (1105, quoting LaFave 2003, 1002–1003)

robbery *mens rea*, the intent to take another person's property and keep it permanently with the additional intent to use immediate force, or the threat of immediate force, to get it

Robbery Mens Rea *(Intent)*

Robbery *mens rea* is the same as theft *mens rea* (the intent to take another person's property and keep it permanently) but with the additional intent to use immediate force, or the threat of immediate force, to get it. So it's not robbery to take an iPod away from someone if you honestly, but mistakenly, believe it's yours. Of course, it's still a crime (battery if you use force or assault if you threaten to use it); it's just not robbery (LaFave and Scott 1986, 778–79).

The Degrees of Robbery

Most states have divided robbery into degrees, based on three circumstances:

1. Whether robbers are armed
2. Whether the robber acted alone or with accomplices
3. The kind and degree of injury robbers inflict on their victims

New York's Penal Code (2003, § 160.00) is typical. First-degree robbers (§ 160.15) carry deadly weapons (or "play weapons" that look real) and seriously injure their victims. Second-degree robbers (§ 160.10) have accomplices or display play weapons and inflict some injury on their victims. Third-degree robbers (§ 160.05) are unarmed, and they inflict no injury on their victims.

RECEIVING STOLEN PROPERTY

LO 7

It's not only a crime to take someone else's property by theft, it's also a crime to "receive" property that someone else has stolen. Called "receiving stolen property," the purpose of making it a crime is to prevent and to punish individuals who benefit from someone else's theft, even though they didn't have anything to do with the original theft.

receiving stolen property, benefiting from the theft of someone else's property without having participated in the wrongful acquisition in the first place

Although "receiving" is primarily directed at fences (professionals who sell stolen property for profit), it also targets people who know, or should know, they're buying stolen stuff because the prices are too low.

fences, receivers of stolen goods or places where stolen goods are bought

Receiving Stolen Property Actus Reus

Receiving stolen property *actus reus* is the act of receiving the property. Receiving requires that the receiver control the property, at least briefly. But the receiver doesn't have to possess the property physically. So if I buy a stolen set of Bose mini speakers from a fence for a friend, and the fence hands them over directly to my friend, I've received the stolen speakers, even though I've never seen or touched them. If my friend gives the speakers to her friend, her friend also has received them. Also, anyone who temporarily hides stolen goods for someone else has received the stolen goods.

receiving stolen property *actus reus*, the act of receiving and controlling at least temporarily (but not necessarily possessing) the property

Receiving Stolen Property Mens Rea

Receiving stolen property *mens rea* varies. In some states, receivers have to *know* the goods are stolen. In others, *believing* the goods are stolen is enough. In all jurisdictions, knowledge may be inferred from surrounding circumstances, such as receiving goods from a known thief or buying goods at a fraction of their real value (for example, buying a new top-of-the-line 3DTV for $75). Some jurisdictions require only that receivers were reckless or negligent about whether the property was stolen. Recklessness and negligence as to whether the property was stolen are often directed at likely fences, usually junk dealers and pawn shop operators. (See the Elements of Receiving Stolen Property illustration on the next page.)

receiving stolen property *mens rea*, depending on the jurisdiction, knowing or believing that received goods are stolen

Receivers have to intend to keep the property permanently. This excludes police officers who knowingly accept stolen property and secretly place it in the hands of suspected fences to catch them. They haven't received stolen property because they don't intend to keep it, only to use it as bait.

Texas is one state that requires that receivers know that the property they control is stolen. The state has to prove actual knowledge beyond a reasonable doubt, but the prosecution can use circumstantial evidence to meet its burden.

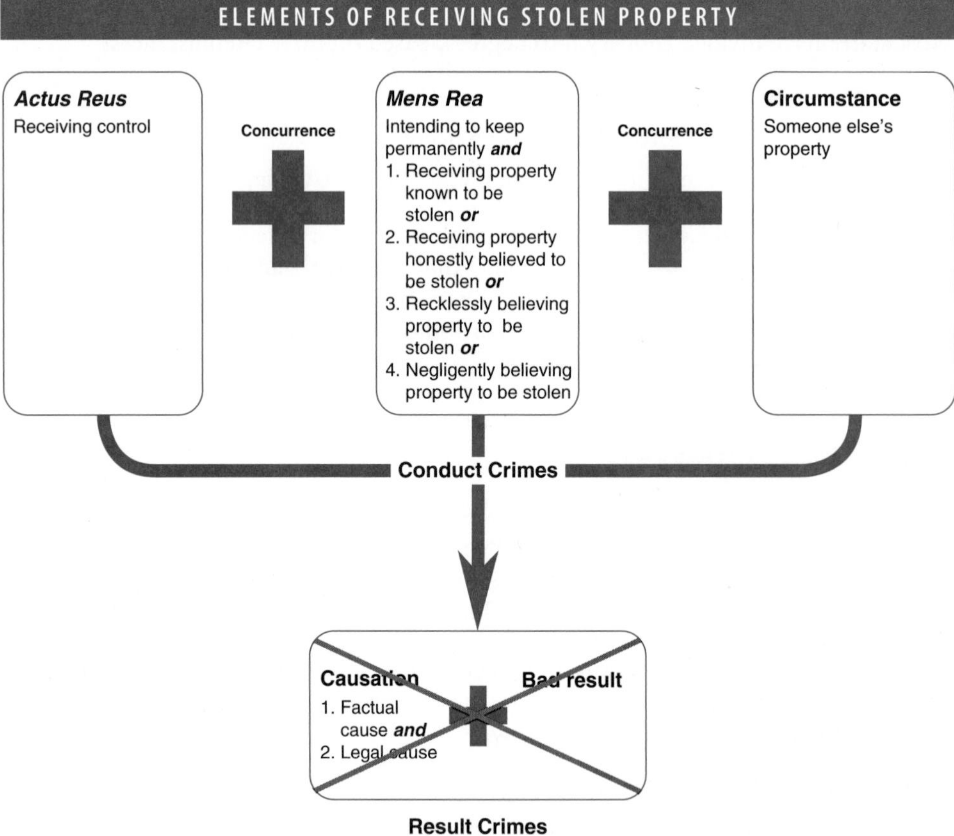

CASE

In* Sonnier v. State *(1992), a Texas trial court convicted Olga Sonnier of receiving stolen property and sentenced her to fifteen years in prison for knowingly pawning four stolen P.V. amplifier speakers for $275 that were worth $1,400.

Did she know the speakers were stolen?

Sonnier v. State

849 S.W.2d 828 (Tex.App. 1992)

HISTORY

Olga Lee Sonnier, the defendant, was convicted after a bench trial in the 230th District Court, Harris County, of theft. She was sentenced to 15 years confinement, and she appealed. The Court of Appeals reversed and judgment of acquittal was ordered.

MIRABAL, J.

FACTS

On November 2, 1989, John L. Clough, the complainant, discovered several items missing from his establishment, the Houstonian Club. Among the items missing were four amplifier speakers, known as "P.V." or "Peavey" speakers. The speakers are the type that are connected to an amplifier system when bands play at the club. When the four speakers are stacked and connected, they stand about four feet tall and three feet wide. The speakers were valued at $1,400 when purchased, and could not be replaced for less than $2,000.

The complainant last saw the speakers on the night of November 1, 1989. He did not know the appellant, she was not his employee, and he did not give anyone permission to take the speakers from his club. An employee, Gaylord or "Ricky" Burton, worked for him a couple of months, but vanished at the same time the speakers did. Burton was supposed to be at the club on the morning the speakers disappeared.

The complainant reported the theft to the police. He told them he believed Burton had stolen the speakers. One of the complainant's employees had seen Burton take the speakers the morning of November 2, 1989. The speakers were found in a pawn shop. The complainant identified the speakers by their serial numbers.

Two employees of the pawn shop said two men came into the shop on November 2, 1989, and tried to pawn the speakers. The men had no identification, and the employees could not accept the speakers without some identification. The men came back later with the appellant (Olga Sonnier), who had a driver's license, and she pawned the four speakers for $225.

The police, after an investigation, were unable to locate Burton, but did locate the appellant because her name, address, and signature were on the pawn tickets. The appellant was charged with theft. A pawn shop employee positively identified the appellant as the woman who pawned the speakers. The appellant called two witnesses, an employee of the pawn shop, Anthony Smith, and Sergeant Graves of the Houston Police Department. The appellant did not testify.

Smith testified two men tried to pawn the speakers. When he would not accept the speakers without some identification, the men left, but came back later with the appellant. She presented a driver's license and pawned the speakers. Sergeant Graves testified that the appellant phoned him and said she pawned the speakers for some friends who did not have a driver's license.

OPINION

Sonnier asserts that the evidence is insufficient to show she had actual knowledge that the speakers were stolen. The essential elements of theft by receiving are:

1. that a theft occurred by another person;
2. the defendant received the stolen property; and
3. when the defendant received the stolen property she knew it was stolen.

TEXAS CRIMINAL CODE
SEC. 31.03. THEFT

1. A person commits an offense if he unlawfully appropriates property with intent to deprive the owner of property.
2. Appropriation of property is unlawful
   a. if it is without the owner's effective consent;
   b. the property is stolen and the actor appropriates the property knowing it was stolen by another. . . .

Under the statute and the indictment, the State had the burden to prove beyond a reasonable doubt that appellant had actual subjective knowledge that the speakers were stolen. The evidence, viewed in the light most favorable to the prosecution, shows:

1. On the same day the speakers were stolen, two men brought them to a pawn shop to hock them.
2. When the pawn shop refused to accept the speakers because neither man would offer identification, the two men left, and then returned with appellant.
3. Appellant pawned the four speakers for the two men. She used her driver's license, giving her correct name and address. She received $225 for the four speakers, about $56 for each, while they were worth at least $350 each.

The State emphasized in the trial court, and on appeal, that the sheer value of the speakers is enough for the trial court to find appellant knew they were stolen. The State argues that selling stolen property for less than market value is some evidence that the seller knew the property was stolen.

However, here the speakers were pawned, not sold, and the evidence does not indicate that the pawn shop paid an unusually low amount to pawn the speakers. Further, the evidence does not show that appellant, or any reasonable person of common experience, would likely even know the market value of the speakers.

We cannot say that the circumstances in this case exclude every other reasonable hypothesis except the hypothesis that appellant knew the speakers were stolen when she pawned them. We find, under the circumstances, appellant just as reasonably could have been doing a favor for her friends or acquaintances when she accompanied them to the pawn shop and used her own ID so the speakers could be pawned. We sustain appellant's point of error one.

Sonnier asserts the evidence was also insufficient to support her conviction under the "straight theft" paragraph of the indictment which alleged appellant.

(continues)

(continued)

1. unlawfully appropriated the speakers by acquiring them and otherwise exercising control over them,
2. with the intent to deprive the owner of the property,
3. without the effective consent of the owner. Tex. Penal Code Ann. § 31.03(a), (b)(1). . . .

The evidence before the trial court placed appellant in possession of the speakers on the day they were stolen. The unexplained possession of stolen property may be sufficient to sustain a conviction for theft. To warrant such an inference of guilt from the circumstances of possession alone, the possession must be personal, recent, unexplained, and must involve a distinct and conscious assertion of a right to the property by the defendant.

When the party in possession gives a reasonable explanation for having the recently stolen property, the State must prove the explanation is false. Whether the explanation is reasonable and true is a question of fact. The fact finder is not bound to accept a defendant's explanation for possession of recently stolen property. A trial judge, sitting without a jury, is authorized to accept or reject any or all of the evidence.

Sonnier was in possession of the speakers when she pledged them at the pawn shop. This was a distinct and conscious assertion of a right to the property. She pawned the speakers on the day they were stolen, a "recent" possession. The explanation for appellant's possession of the speakers came from the State's witnesses, as well as appellant's. The evidence is uncontradicted that two men possessed the speakers and tried to pawn them. It was only when the two men were not allowed to pawn the speakers that they left, and then returned to the same pawn shop accompanied by appellant.

The explanation for Sonnier's possession or control over the speakers is clear and uncontested—the two men requested her help in getting the speakers pawned. There is no evidence of what the two men told Sonnier in order to get her help. We find nothing in the record to contradict the hypothesis that Sonnier may have believed the speakers belonged to one of the two men. There is not one shred of evidence placing Sonnier at the complainant's club at the time the speakers were removed; the evidence, instead, points only to complainant's prior employee, Burton, as the likely thief.

In addition to the inference of guilt raised by possession of recently stolen property, the evidence when viewed as a whole must still be sufficient under normal standards of appellate review, and if the evidence supports a reasonable hypothesis other than the guilt of Sonnier, a finding of guilt beyond a reasonable doubt is not a rational finding.

When viewed in its totality, we find the evidence in this case does not support a guilty verdict.

We reverse the judgment and order a judgment of acquittal.

QUESTIONS

1. State the elements of theft without consent of the owner and the elements of receiving stolen property in the Texas theft statute.
2. List all the facts relevant to deciding each of the elements of theft without consent and receiving stolen property.
3. Assume you're the prosecutor. Argue that Olga Sonnier is guilty of theft without consent and receiving stolen property. Back up your answer with the facts you listed in (2).
4. Assume you're the defense counsel. Argue that Olga Sonnier should be acquitted of theft without consent and receiving stolen property. Back up your answer with the facts you listed in (2).

Let's turn now to the second category of property crimes: damaging and destroying other people's property, which includes the specific crimes of arson and criminal mischief.

LO 8

DAMAGING AND DESTROYING OTHER PEOPLE'S PROPERTY

In this section, we'll discuss two crimes of destroying property: arson (damaging or destroying buildings by burning) and criminal mischief (damaging or destroying personal property).

ARSON

In the 1700s, "arson" was defined as "the malicious and willful burning of the house or outhouses of another." Blackstone (1769) called it an "offense of very great malignity, and much more serious than simple theft." According to Blackstone, here's why:

arson, damaging or destroying structures by burning

criminal mischief, damaging or destroying personal property

> Because, first, it is an offence against that right, of habitation, which is acquired by the law of nature as well as the laws of society. Next, because of the terror and confusion that necessarily attends it. And, lastly, because in simple theft the thing stolen only changes its master, but still remains in essence for the benefit of the public, whereas by burning the very substance is absolutely destroyed. (220)

Arson has grown far beyond its origins in burning houses to include burning almost any kind of building, vessel, or vehicle. Also, the property burned doesn't have to be someone else's. Today, arson is a crime against possession and occupancy, not just against ownership. So even where owners aren't in possession of, or don't occupy, their own property, arson can still be committed against it. For example, if I lease my house and become its landlord, and I set fire to it to collect insurance on it, I've committed arson because I transferred occupancy to my tenant.

One thing hasn't changed; arson is still a very serious crime against property and persons. Arson kills hundreds and injures thousands of people every year. It damages and destroys more than a billion dollars worth of property and costs millions in lost taxes and jobs. It has also significantly increased insurance rates. Most states prescribe harsh penalties for arson. For example, in Texas and Alabama, arson is punishable by life imprisonment.

Let's look further at the *actus reus*, *mens rea*, and degrees of arson.

Actus Reus: *Burning*

At common law, burning had its obvious meaning—setting a building on fire. However, just setting the fire wasn't enough; the fire had to reach the structure and burn it. But burning didn't mean burning to the ground. Once the building caught on fire, the arson was complete, however slight the actual burning was.

burning, setting a building on fire

Modern statutes have adopted the common law rule, and the cases pour great effort into deciding whether the smoke from the fire only blackened or discolored buildings, whether the fire scorched them, or whether the fire burned only the outside wall or the wood under it. The MPC (ALI 1985, 2:2, 3) tries to clear up many of the technical questions in common law arson by providing that "burning" means "starting a fire," even if the fire never touches the structure it was meant to burn. The drafters justify this expansion of common law burning on the ground that there's no meaningful difference between a fire that has already started but hasn't reached the structure and a fire that's reached the structure but hasn't done any real damage to it. Burning also includes explosions, even though the phrase "set on fire" doesn't usually mean "to explode." (See the Elements of Arson illustration on the next page.)

In *Williams v. State* (1992), when Tonyia Williams, one of the guests at a New Year's Eve party, started a fire, "the only physical damage caused by fire was smoke throughout the house and soot and smoke damage to one of the walls in the basement" (963). Indiana's arson statute defined "arson" as: "A person who, by means of fire or explosive, knowingly or intentionally damages: (1) a dwelling of another person without his consent" (964). Williams argued that the "soot and smoke damage to the wall of the basement do not constitute 'damages' within the meaning of the arson statute." She argued that arson "requires proof of burning or charring as was the case at common law" (964).

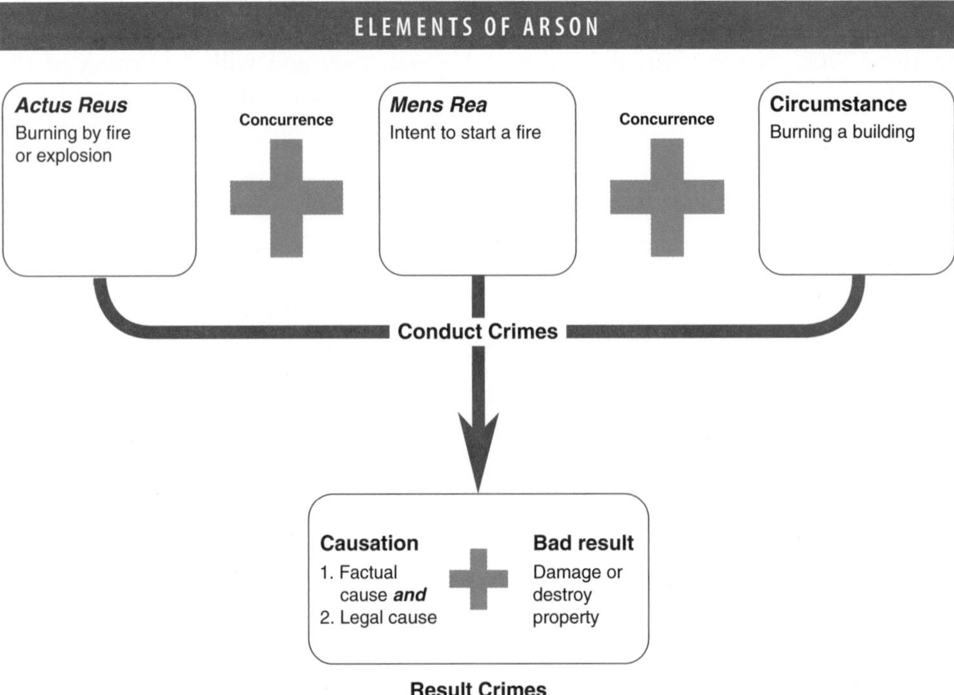

The state argued that

> damages in our present statute is not tied to the common law definition of the word "burning" and should therefore be construed in its plain and ordinary sense. Any damage, even smoke damage, would therefore be enough to satisfy the requirements of the statute. (964)

Williams was convicted, and she appealed. According to the Indiana Appeals Court:

> Traditionally the common law rigidly required an actual burning. The fire must have been actually communicated to the object to such an extent as to have taken effect upon it. In general, any charring of the wood of a building, so that the fiber of the wood was destroyed, was enough to constitute a sufficient burning to complete the crime of arson.

However, merely singeing, smoking, scorching, or discoloring by heat weren't considered enough to support a conviction (964). The Indiana Appeals Court agreed with the state: "We find that the smoke damage and the soot on the basement wall were enough to support a conviction for arson" (965).

Arson Mens Rea

arson *mens rea*, common law *mens rea* requires a malicious and willful intent to burn or set fire to buildings; general-intent *mens rea* requires only the intent to start a fire

Most statutes follow the common law **arson *mens rea*** requirement that arsonists have to "maliciously and willfully" burn or set fire to buildings. Some courts call arson *mens rea* general intent. According to the general-intent definition, purpose refers to the act in arson (burning or setting fire to buildings), not to the resulting harm (damaging or destroying them). So a prisoner who burned a hole in his cell to escape was guilty of arson because he purposely started the fire. So was a sailor who lit a match to find his way into a dark hold in a ship to steal rum. The criminal intent in arson is general—an intent to start a fire, even if there is no intent to burn a specific structure.

The Degrees of Arson

Typically, there are two degrees of arson. Most serious, first-degree arson, is burning homes or other occupied structures (such as schools, offices, and churches) where there's danger to human life. Second-degree arson includes burning unoccupied structures, vehicles, and boats.

first-degree arson, burning homes or other occupied structures (such as schools, offices, and churches) where there's danger to human life

second-degree arson, includes burning unoccupied structures, vehicles, and boats

The MPC divides arson into two degrees, based on defendants' blameworthiness. The most blameworthy are defendants who intend to destroy buildings, not merely set fire to or burn them; these are first-degree arsonists. Second-degree arsonists set buildings on fire for other purposes. For example, if I burn a wall with an acetylene torch because I want to steal valuable fixtures attached to the wall, I'm guilty of second-degree arson for "recklessly" exposing the building to destruction even though I meant only to steal fixtures.

Statutes don't grade arson according to motive, but it probably ought to play some part, if not in formal degrees, then in sentencing. Why? Because arsonists act for a variety of motives. Some are so consumed by rage they burn down their enemies' homes. Then there are the pyromaniacs, whose psychotic compulsion drives them to set buildings on fire for thrills. And there are the rational, but equally deadly, arsonists who burn down their own buildings or destroy their own property to collect insurance. Finally, and most deadly and difficult to catch, the professional torch commits arson for hire.

CRIMINAL MISCHIEF

LO 9

Arson under the common law was, and still is, the serious felony of intentionally burning occupied buildings. Criminal mischief descends from another common law crime, the misdemeanor called "malicious mischief." Malicious mischief consisted of destroying or damaging tangible property ("anything of value" that you can see, weigh, measure, or feel).

malicious mischief, common law crime of intentionally damaging or destroying another's tangible property

The modern counterpart of malicious mischief (the MPC calls it "criminal" mischief) includes three types of harm to tangible property:

1. Destruction or damage by fire, explosives, or other "dangerous acts" (the original malicious mischief)
2. Tampering with tangible property so as to endanger property
3. Deception or threat that causes someone to suffer money loss

All three forms of damage and destruction usually are defined as felonies but less serious felonies than the more serious felony arson. (See the Elements of Criminal Mischief illustration on the next page.)

Criminal Mischief Actus Reus

Criminal mischief *actus reus* mirrors the three types of criminal mischief. In destruction or damage criminal mischief, the *actus reus* is burning, exploding, flooding, or committing some other dangerous act. Tampering is any act that creates a danger to property, even if it doesn't actually cause any damage to the property. So a cross burning on the lawn of an interracial couple's house wasn't "tampering" with the property, because the burning cross by itself created no damage and it didn't pose a threat of damage to the property (*Commonwealth v. Kozak* 1993).

criminal mischief *actus reus*, in destruction or damage criminal mischief, the *actus reus* is burning, exploding, flooding, or committing some other dangerous act; in tampering, it's any act that threatens or endangers property; in deception or threat, it's causing harm through deception or threats

Deception or threat *actus reus* usually consists of "expensive practical jokes," such as "sending a false telegram notifying the victim that his mother is dying so that he spends several hundred dollars on a vain trip" or "misinforming a neighboring farmer that local tests of a particular seed variety have been highly successful, so that he wastes money and a year's work planting that seed" (ALI 1985, 2:2, 49).

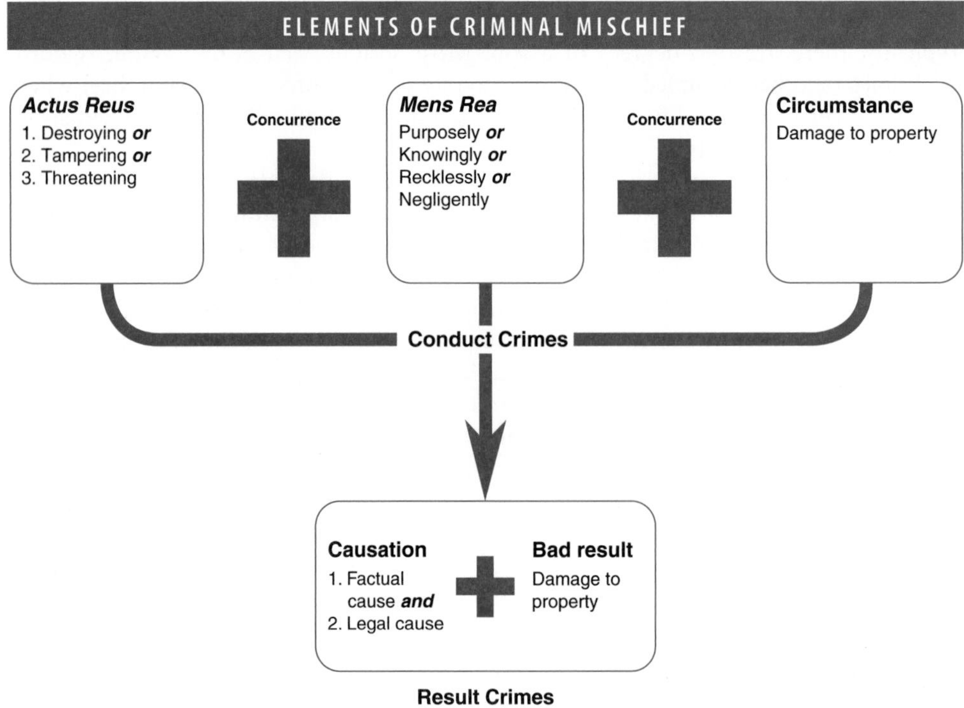

Criminal Mischief Mens Rea

Generalizations about criminal mischief *mens rea* are impossible because the statutes are all over the place, including whether they contain all the mental states we've encountered throughout the book (purposely, knowingly, recklessly, and negligently). So you need to check the malicious (or criminal) mischief statute of an individual state to find out how it defines the element of criminal intent.

We'll quote the MPC's provision because its *actus reus* and *mens rea* requirements make sense, and they're comprehensive.

§ 220.3. Criminal Mischief

1. *Offense Defined.* A person is guilty of criminal mischief if he
    a. damages tangible property of another purposely, recklessly, or by negligence in the employment of fire, explosives, or other dangerous means; or
    b. purposely or recklessly tampers with tangible property of another so as to endanger person or property; or
    c. purposely or recklessly causes another to suffer pecuniary loss by deception or threat.
2. *Grading.* Criminal mischief is a felony of the third degree if the actor purposely causes pecuniary loss in excess of $5,000, or a substantial interruption or impairment of public communication, transportation, supply of water, gas or power, or other public service. It is a misdemeanor if the actor purposely causes pecuniary loss in excess of $100, or a petty misdemeanor if he purposely or recklessly causes pecuniary loss in excess of $25. Otherwise criminal mischief is a violation.

CASE

In **Commonwealth v. Mitchell** *(1993), the Pennsylvania Superior Court affirmed Duane Mitchell's conviction for criminal mischief by painting "nigger," "KKK," and other racial slurs on Betty Jo and James Johnson's house.*

Was he guilty of malicious mischief?

Commonwealth v. Mitchell

WL 773785 (Penn.Com.Pl. 1993)

HISTORY

Following a nonjury trial, held on December 22, 1992, Duane Mitchell (the defendant) was convicted of the criminal mischief . . . graded as a misdemeanor of the third degree. The defendant filed timely post-trial motions, which were denied, and the defendant was sentenced to pay a fine of $150. The defendant filed post-trial motions, which were denied. The Superior Court affirmed the trial court's denial of the motions.

CRONIN, J.

FACTS

Following a report to the Upper Darby Police Department on Sunday, June 21, 1992, at 9:49 P.M., Lieutenant Michael Kenney and Officer Mark Manley of the Upper Darby Police Department proceeded to 7142 Stockley Road, Upper Darby, Pennsylvania. Upon arriving at the above location, both officers observed the following: painted on the front walk the word "nigger," the letters "KKK," and a cross painted under three dark marks; on each of the steps leading to the house was spray painted the word "nigger"; the front screen door had a painted cross with three marks above it; the patio was painted with the word "nigger" and a cross with three dark marks; the front walk had the word "nigger" and a cross with three dark marks; the front walk had the words "nigger get out" painted on it; the rear wall had painted the words "nigger get out or else" and a cross with the letters "KKK"; and the rear door had the words "KKK Jungle Fever Death" and a cross painted on it.

The owners of 7142 Stockley Road, Upper Darby, Pennsylvania, are James and Betty Jo Johnson, who had made settlement on the property on June 15, 1992, but had not occupied the home with their seven-year-old daughter, Zena. The Johnsons are an interracial couple, James Johnson being Afro-American and Betty Jo Johnson being Caucasian. The Johnsons had not given the defendant or any other person permission to spray paint on their property.

On June 25, 1992, the defendant, Duane Mitchell, was taken into custody by the Upper Darby Police Department. The defendant voluntarily waived, in writing, his right to counsel and his right to remain silent and freely gave a statement to the police. The defendant told the Upper Darby Police that he, the defendant, alone spray painted the above-mentioned words and symbols on the Johnson property located at 7142 Stockley Road, Upper Darby, Pennsylvania; at the time that he did the spray painting, he had been drinking.

Following a nonjury trial, held on December 22, 1992, the defendant was convicted of the summary offense of criminal mischief and the offense of ethnic intimidation, graded as a misdemeanor of the third degree in accordance with 18 Pa.C.S. § 2710(B). The defendant filed timely post-trial motions, which were denied by the order of trial court dated May 17, 1993.

OPINION

Criminal mischief is defined at 18 Pa.C.S. § 3304 as follows:

§ 3304. CRIMINAL MISCHIEF

1. Offense Defined—A person is guilty of criminal mischief if he:
   a. damages the tangible property of another intentionally, recklessly, or by negligence in the employment of fire, explosives, or other dangerous means listed in section 3302(A) of this title (relating to causing or risking catastrophe);
   b. intentionally or recklessly tampers with tangible property of another so as to endanger person or property; or
   c. intentionally or recklessly causes another to suffer pecuniary loss by deception or threat. 18 Pa.C.S. § 3304(A),

(continues)

(continued)

The defendant argues that the evidence was insufficient to prove that tangible property was damaged in the employment of fire, explosion, or other dangerous means. 1 Pa.C.S. § 1903 states that "(A) Words and phrases shall be construed according to rules of grammar and according to their common usage; . . ." Section 1 of 18 Pa.C.S. § 3304 makes a person guilty of the crime of criminal mischief if that person either intentionally damages the tangible property of another; recklessly damages the tangible property of another; or negligently damages the tangible personal property of another in the employment of fire, explosives or other dangerous means listed in section 3302(A) of title 18.

In this case it is abundantly clear that the defendant spray painted the phrases and words mentioned herein on the Johnsons' home located at 7142 Stockley Road, Upper Darby, Pennsylvania and that the defendant did so without the permission of the Johnsons. Sufficient evidence exists to support a verdict if the evidence, when viewed in a light most favorable to the verdict winner along with all reasonable inferences drawn therefrom, allows a fact finder to find that all elements of a crime have been established beyond a reasonable doubt.

The evidence was sufficient to prove beyond a reasonable doubt that the defendant intentionally damaged the tangible property of the Johnsons.

A court must interpret a statute to ascertain the intent of the legislature. It is clear from the use of the conjunctive "or" in Section 1 of 18 Pa.C.S. § 3304 that the legislature intended to punish either the intentional or the reckless or the negligent damaging of the tangible property of another person. The intentional spray painting of graffiti on the walls of a building is factually sufficient to support a conviction for criminal mischief.

It is equally clear that the commission of any of the other acts specified in either Section 1 or Section 2 or Section 3 of 18 Pa.C.S. § 3304 is sufficient to support a conviction for criminal mischief since the conjunctive "or" is used between Sections 2 and 3 of 18 Pa.C.S. § 3304 and the conjunctive "or" is to be given the same meaning and legislative intent as "or" is given with the states of mind (intent, reckless or negligent) in Section 1 of 18 Pa.C.S. § 3304. See 1 Pa.C.S. § 1903(A), 1 Pa.C.S. § 1921(A)(B). For the foregoing reasons the defendant's post-trial motions were denied.

QUESTIONS

1. State the elements of *actus reus* and *mens rea* as the Pennsylvania criminal mischief statute defines them.
2. List the facts relevant to each of the elements.
3. Assume you're Duane Mitchell's lawyer and argue that the facts don't prove the elements beyond a reasonable doubt.
4. Assume you're the state's prosecutor and argue that the facts prove the elements beyond a reasonable doubt.

LO 10

INVADING OTHER PEOPLE'S PROPERTY: BURGLARY AND CRIMINAL TRESPASS

The heart of burglary and criminal trespass is invading others' property, not taking, receiving, destroying, or damaging it. Invasion itself is the harm. So the two main crimes of invading someone else's property—their home, or other occupied structure (burglary) or invading other property (criminal trespass)—are crimes of criminal conduct (see Chapter 3); they don't require causing a bad result. So they're crimes even if no property is taken, damaged, or destroyed during the invasion.

BURGLARY

> Burglary, or nighttime housebreaking, has always been looked upon as a very heinous offense, not only because of the abundant terror that it naturally carries with it, but also as it is a forcible invasion and disturbance of that right of habitation, which every individual might acquire in a state of nature. And the law of England has so particular and tender regard to the immunity of a man's house, that it styles it a castle and will never suffer it to be violated. (Blackstone 1769, 223)

Blackstone's definition of burglary written just before the American Revolution emphasizes the special nature of homes. Why are they special? For many people, their homes are their most valuable if not their only material asset. But homes are more than property that's worth money. The novelist Sinclair Lewis (1922) described this difference between homes as things with money value and homes as special places ("castles") that can't be measured by money alone:

> The Babbitts' house was five years old. It had the best of taste, the best of inexpensive rugs, a simple and laudable architecture, and the latest conveniences. Throughout, electricity took the place of candles and slatternly hearth-fires. Along the bedroom baseboard were three plugs for electric lamps, concealed by little brass doors. In the halls were plugs for the vacuum cleaner, and in the living-room plugs for the piano lamp, for the electric fan. The trim dining-room (with its admirable oak buffet, its leaded-glass cupboard, its creamy plaster walls, its modest scene of a salmon expiring upon a pile of oysters) had plugs which supplied the electric percolator and the electric toaster.
>
> In fact there was but one thing wrong with the Babbitt house: It was not a *home*. (chap. 2; emphasis added)

Lewis means that a house is the material thing worth money, but a home is the haven of refuge where we seek security and privacy from the outside world.

Burglary is breaking and entering a building with intent to commit a crime inside the building. The elements of common law burglary from which our modern law of burglary descends included:

burglary, breaking and entering a building or structure with intent to commit a crime inside the building

1. Breaking and entering (*actus reus*)
2. The dwelling of another (circumstance element)
3. In the nighttime (circumstance element)
4. With the intent to commit a felony inside (*mens rea*)

Modern burglary has outgrown its common law origin of protecting only homes. Now, you can "burglarize" all kinds of structures, even vehicles, at any time of the day or night. Definitions such as "any structure" or "any building" are common in many statutes. One writer (Note 1951, 411) who surveyed the subject concluded that any structure with "four walls and a roof" was included.

Here's California's list of "structures" you can burglarize:

> Every person who enters any house, room, apartment, tenement, shop, warehouse, store, mill, barn, stable, outhouse or other building, tent, vessel, floating home, locked or sealed cargo container, whether or not mounted on a vehicle, trailer coach, any house car, inhabited camper, vehicle, when the doors are locked, aircraft, or mine or any underground portion thereof. (California Penal Code 2003, § 459)

Let's look at the elements needed to prove burglary and then the degrees of burglary. (See the Elements of Burglary illustration on the next page.)

breaking (in burglary), part of the *actus reus* of common law burglary, requiring an unlawful, frequently destructive, entry into someone else's building

Burglary Actus Reus

Until the 1900s, burglary *actus reus* consisted of two actions—breaking and entering. In the early days of the common law, breaking meant making a violent entry, usually knocking down doors and smashing windows.

By 1900, the common law element of breaking had become a mere technicality, and most statutes today have eliminated it entirely, leaving entering as the only element. Entering, like breaking, has a broad meaning. The entering of burglary *actus reus* refers to coming or going into the building or structure.

entering (in burglary), part of the *actus reus* of burglary, meaning to come or go into the building or structure

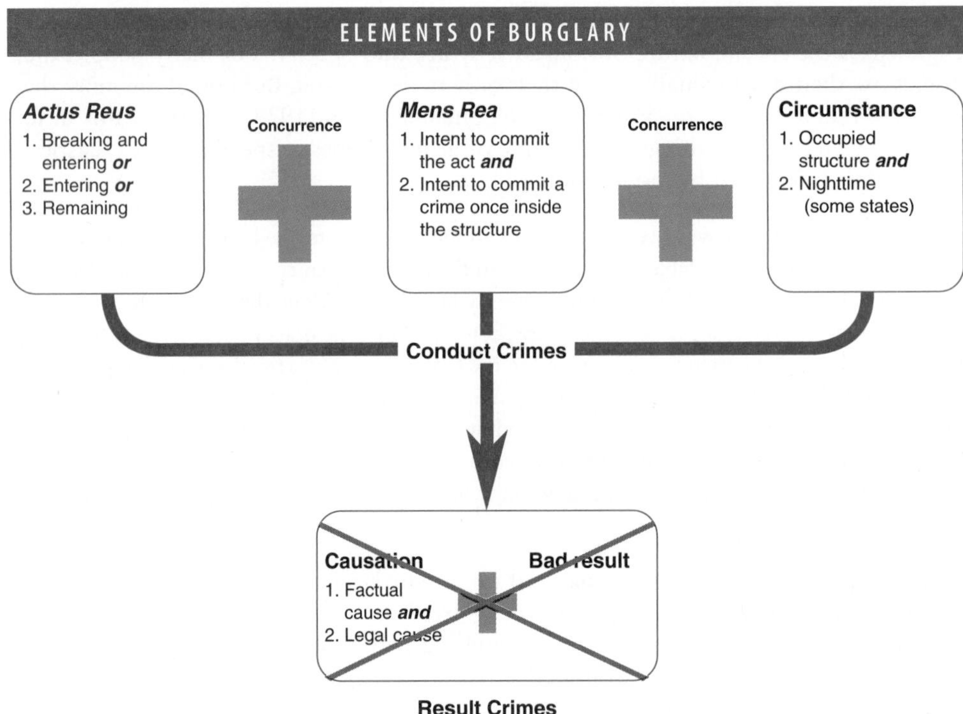

Even as early as 1650, partial entry was enough to satisfy burglary. One court (*Rex v. Bailey* 1818) ruled that a burglar "entered" a house because his finger was inside the windowsill when he was caught. Today, some statutes have completely removed the entering element by providing that "remaining" in a structure lawfully entered is enough. So it's burglary to go into a store during business hours and hide in a restroom until the store closes with the intent to steal.

Some states don't even require burglars to get inside at all; it's enough if they *try* to enter. In *State v. Myrick* (1982), a man who got a door ajar but never set foot inside was convicted because the state's burglary statute didn't require entering or remaining. To some criminal law reformers, substituting "remaining" for "breaking and entering" badly distorts burglary's core idea—nighttime invasions into homes.

surreptitious remaining element, the entering of a structure lawfully with the intent to remain and commit a crime inside

The MPC and several states take a middle ground between the old common law requirement of actual entry and eliminating entering completely. They've adopted a **surreptitious remaining element**, which means the burglar entered lawfully (for example, going into a bank during business hours and waiting inside until after the bank closed).

Circumstance Elements

occupied structure, "any structure, vehicle, or place adapted for overnight accommodations of persons, or for carrying on business therein, whether or not a person is actually present"

dwelling of another, anyplace where other people live

The MPC's (ALI 1985, 2:2, 60) definition limits burglary to occupied structures, because they're the "intrusions that are typically the most alarming and dangerous." According to the code, "**occupied structure**" means "any structure, vehicle, or place adapted for overnight accommodations of persons, or for carrying on business therein, whether or not a person is actually present" (72). Most states take occupancy into account either as an element or as part of grading burglary as "aggravated burglary."

Another circumstance element of common law burglary was that burglars had to break and enter the **dwelling "of another"**—that is, anyplace where other people live. Modern law has expanded the common law definition from the victim's home to include homes that burglars own; for example, landlords can burglarize their tenants' apartments.

CASE

In* Jewell v. State *(1996), *the Indiana Court of Appeals affirmed Barry Jewell's conviction for burglarizing his own house.*

Did he burglarize his own home?

Jewell v. State

672 N.E.2d 417 (Ind.App. 1996)

HISTORY

Barry L. Jewell, after a jury trial, was convicted of burglary with a deadly weapon resulting in serious bodily injury, a class A felony, and battery resulting in serious bodily injury, a class C felony. Jewell was sentenced to an aggregate term of 48 years imprisonment. After a retrial Jewell appealed. The Indiana Court of Appeals affirmed.

ROBERTSON, J.

FACTS

In 1989, Bridget Fisher, who later married Jewell and changed her name to Bridget Jewell, purchased a home on contract in her maiden name from her relatives. Bridget and Jewell lived in the house together on and off before and after they married in 1990. Jewell helped fix the house up, and therefore, had some "sweat equity" in the house.

Jewell and Bridget experienced marital difficulties and dissolution proceedings were initiated. Jewell moved out of the house and Bridget changed the locks so that Jewell could not reenter. At a preliminary hearing in the dissolution proceedings, Bridget's attorney informed Jewell that Bridget wanted a divorce and wanted Jewell to stop coming by the house. Jewell moved into a friend's house, agreeing to pay him $100 per month in rent and to split the utility expenses.

Bridget resumed a romantic relationship with her former boyfriend, Chris Jones. Jewell told a friend that he wanted to get Jones in a dark place, hit him over the head with a two-by-four and cut his "dick" off. Jewell confronted Jones at his place of employment and threatened to kill him if he were to continue to see Bridget.

Jewell was observed on numerous occasions watching Bridget's house. Jewell used a shortwave radio to intercept and listen to the phone conversations on Bridget's cordless phone.

At approximately 4:00 A.M. on the morning of June 13, 1991, Jewell gained entry to Bridget's house through the kitchen window after having removed a window screen.

Bridget and Jones were inside sleeping. Jewell struck Jones over the head with a two by four until he was unconscious, amputated Jones' penis with a knife, and fed the severed penis to the dog. Jones' severed penis was never found and he underwent reconstructive surgery. His physicians fashioned him a new penis made from tissue and bone taken from his leg. Jones experienced complications and the result was not entirely satisfactory.

OPINION

Jewell attacks the sufficiency of evidence supporting his conviction of Burglary, which is defined as: A person who breaks and enters the building or structure of another person, with intent to commit a felony in it, commits burglary. (Ind. Code 354321.) Jewell argues he was improperly convicted of breaking into his own house.

The burglary statute's requirement that the dwelling be that "of another person" is satisfied if the evidence demonstrates that the entry was unauthorized. In the present case, Bridget had purchased the house in her own name before the marriage. When she and Jewell experienced marital difficulties, Jewell moved out and Bridget changed the locks to prevent Jewell from reentering the house. Bridget alone controlled access to the house. Jewell entered the house at 4:00 A.M. through the kitchen window after having removed the screen.

The evidence supports the conclusion that the entry was unauthorized; and, therefore, we find no error.

Judgment AFFIRMED.

QUESTIONS

1. List all of the facts relevant to determining whether Barry Jewell burglarized his own home.
2. How does the state of Indiana define the "dwelling of another" element?
3. How did the court arrive at the conclusion that Barry Jewell burglarized his own home?
4. What's the reason for the "unauthorized entry" requirement?
5. Do you agree with it? Defend your answer.

At common law, another circumstance element was "in the nighttime." Why? Nighttime intrusions frighten victims more than daytime intrusions. At least eighteen states retain the nighttime requirement. Some make it a circumstance element; others treat it as an aggravating circumstance. The rest have eliminated the nighttime requirement entirely.

Burglary Mens Rea

Burglary is a specific-intent crime. The prosecution has to prove two *mens rea* elements:

1. The intent to commit the *actus reus* (breaking, entering, or remaining)
2. The intent to commit a crime once inside the structure broken into, entered, or remained in

The intended crime doesn't have to be serious. Intent to steal is usually good enough, but some states go further to include "any crime," "any misdemeanor," or even "any public offense" (Note 1951, 420).

Keep in mind another important point: it isn't necessary to complete or even attempt (Chapter 8) to commit the intended crime. Suppose I sneak into my rich former student Patrick's luxurious condo in Kona, Hawaii, while he's out making more money, intending to steal one of his three wireless notebook computers he doesn't need or use. Right after I get inside the front door, and not even close to where the notebooks are, my conscience gets the better of me. I say to myself, "I can't do this, even if Pat does have three notebook computers," and I slink back out the front door. I still committed burglary, because the burglary was complete the moment I was inside with the intent to steal one of the notebooks.

The Degrees of Burglary

Because burglary is defined so broadly, many states divide it into several degrees. Alabama's burglary statute is typical:

§ 13A-7-5. Burglary in the First Degree

(a) A person commits the crime of burglary in the first degree if he knowingly and unlawfully enters or remains unlawfully in a dwelling with intent to commit a crime therein, and, if, in effecting entry or while in dwelling or in immediate flight therefrom, he or another participant in the crime:

 (1) Is armed with explosives or a deadly weapon; or

 (2) Causes physical injury to any person who is not a participant in the crime; or

 (3) Uses or threatens the immediate use of a dangerous instrument.

Sentence: 10 years to life

§ 13A-7-6. Burglary in the Second Degree

(a) A person commits the crime of burglary in the second degree if he knowingly enters or remains unlawfully in a building with intent to commit theft or a felony therein and, if in effecting entry or while in the building or in immediate flight therefrom, he or another participant in the crime:

 (1) Is armed with explosives or a deadly weapon; or

 (2) Causes physical injury to any person who is not a participant in the crime; or

 (3) Uses or threatens the immediate use of a dangerous instrument.

(b) In the alternative to subsection (a) of this section, a person commits the crime of burglary in the second degree if he unlawfully enters a lawfully occupied dwelling-house with intent to commit a theft or a felony therein.

Sentence: 2–20 years

§ 13A-7-7. Burglary in the Third Degree

(a) A person commits the crime of burglary in the third degree if he knowingly enters or remains unlawfully in a building with intent to commit a crime therein.

Sentence: 1–10 years

Despite efforts to grade burglary according to seriousness, the broad scope of the offense invites injustices. This is true in large part because burglary punishes the invasion and not the underlying crime—namely, the crime the burglar entered to commit. In many cases, the penalty for burglary is a lot harsher than the penalty for the intended crime. The difference between a five-year sentence and a twenty-year sentence sometimes depends upon the largely philosophical question of whether a thief forms the intent to steal before or after entering a building.

CRIMINAL TRESPASS

LO 10, LO 11

criminal trespass (in property crime), the unwanted, unauthorized invading of another person's property

Criminal trespass is the crime of invading another person's property without authorization. It's a broader but less serious crime than burglary. It's broader because it's not limited to invasions of occupied buildings, and the trespasser doesn't have to intend to commit a crime in addition to the trespass. The heart of criminal trespass is *unwanted presence*. The ancient misdemeanor called "trespass" referred to unwanted presence on (invasion of) another person's land. Not all unwanted presence was (or is) criminal trespass; only *unauthorized* presence qualifies. So, of course, law enforcement officers investigating a crime or gas company employees reading the meter, no matter how unwanted they are, aren't trespassers because they're authorized to be there.

Trespass used to be limited to unauthorized invasions of physical property. At first, only entry onto land was included; then entering and remaining on land and in buildings were added; and since the explosion of computers and the Internet, unauthorized access to electronic information systems has been included.

Let's look at the elements and degrees of criminal trespass and at the special trespassing offense of computer trespass. (See the Elements of Criminal Trespass illustration on the next page.)

The Elements of Criminal Trespass

The *actus reus* of criminal trespass is the unauthorized entering of or remaining on the premises of another person (ALI 1985, 2:2, 87). The *mens rea* varies. Here are three variations:

1. The defendant knowingly enters or remains without authority or by invitation, license, privilege, or legality (most states).
2. The defendant has the specific intent to enter or remain without authority for some unlawful purpose (a few states).
3. The defendant bears strict liability for entering or remaining (Missouri, enters "unlawfully") (88).

The Degrees of Criminal Trespass

The MPC created three degrees of criminal trespass:

1. Misdemeanor entering or remaining in an occupied dwelling at night
2. Petty misdemeanor entering or remaining in any occupied building or structure
3. Violation entering or remaining in anyplace where a "no trespass" notice is given (warning to person, "no trespassing" sign, or fence)

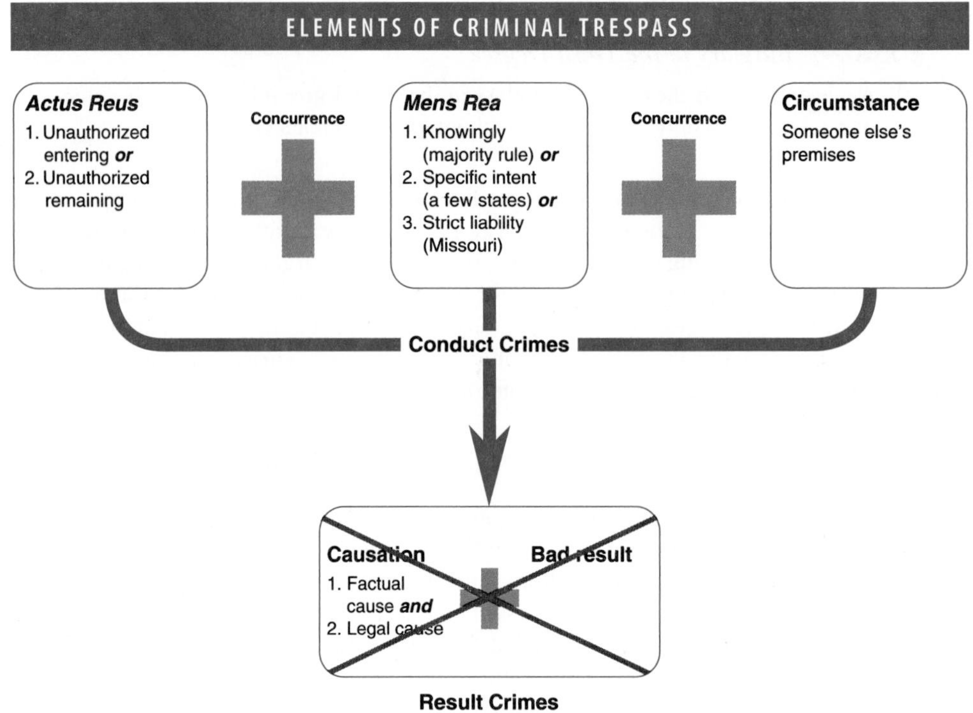

CYBERCRIMES

> Whenever you visit a website, buy a book, shop for groceries, conduct a Google search, buy a magazine, or vote in an election, a person or software program is likely watching—and making note of your activities. A surprising amount of information about you is stored in private databases, and that information is not just collecting digital dust. These data are being used by the company that collected them, and are often aggregated with other information about you and then sold. And, sometimes, it's stolen.
>
> (Roethlisberger 2011, 1793–94)

We may be "digital people" living in an "Information Age," but data collection isn't new. When mass markets were replacing the relationships between small shop owners and customers who knew each other personally, advertising was aimed at customers most likely to buy their products. The General Motors sales department tried out this new "targeted marketing" in the 1920s. Ford owners became the target. GM learned that first-time Ford owners still owned their Fords after two years. So GM targeted these Ford owners and sent them a brochure on GM cars. Then, they sent out questionnaires asking for input on GM cars. They thought this would be a good marketing device—showing that here's a big corporation that cared enough to listen to ordinary people. It worked (Solove 2006, 16–17).

Today, computers, "smart phones," "tablets," and the Internet have exponentially enhanced the capacity to exploit information about individuals and about ideas. "Life is built upon computerized data bases" (V. Johnson 2005, 255) that can be used for good and for ill. Personal information about our health, our finances, and our likes and dislikes helps doctors, banks, and merchants help us. But it also helps identity thieves take our money and wreck our lives (V. Johnson 2005, 256–57) and, in extreme cases, even kill us and the people we love (see the *Remsburg v. Docusearch, Inc.* (2003) case excerpt later in this section).

Ideas and their practical application, intellectual property, can be the most valuable property of any individual, business, or society. Whether this intellectual property is the copyright of a popular song, the patent on a breakthrough drug, a trade secret to an innovative product, or a trademark to a valuable brand, it's a source of wealth, jobs, and social and economic strength and stability (U.S. Department of Justice 2006, 13).

intellectual property, ideas and their practical application owned by an individual, a business, or a society

But these strengths, enhanced by computers and the Internet, bring with them enhanced vulnerabilities to cybercrime. *Cybercrime* means any crime that uses computers and other smart devices and the Internet. Cybercrimes subsume the three types of property crime you've learned about in the previous sections: taking property (identity theft, downloading illegal music files); invading property (posting confidential business and personal information); and damaging property (spreading computer viruses or posting confidential business information), We'll focus here on cybercrimes aimed at the valuable information contained in computers and wireless devices, especially computer databases accessible through the Internet (Yang and Hoffstadt 2006, 201; also *U.S. v. Ancheta*, case excerpt later in this section).

Let's look at two cybercrimes that computers and wireless devices can use the Internet to facilitate their commission: identity theft and intellectual property theft.

IDENTITY THEFT

LO 12

Identity theft is stealing another person's identity for the purpose of getting something of value. Except for ordinary theft, identity theft claims more than twice as many victims in the United States as all other crimes of taking other people's property combined (Figure 11.2). This isn't surprising, given the enormous range of personal information contained in business, nonprofit organization, and government electronic databases. These organizations collect, update, and use "masses of computerized information" about anyone who "voluntarily or involuntarily" deals with their institutions (see Table 11.1).

identity theft, the most frequently committed crime in the United States, it's stealing another person's identity for the purpose of getting something of value

The consequences of wrongful access to personal information can be devastating, and they go beyond the money victims lose to identify thieves. The more than nine

FIGURE 11.2

PROPERTY VICTIMIZATION, 2010

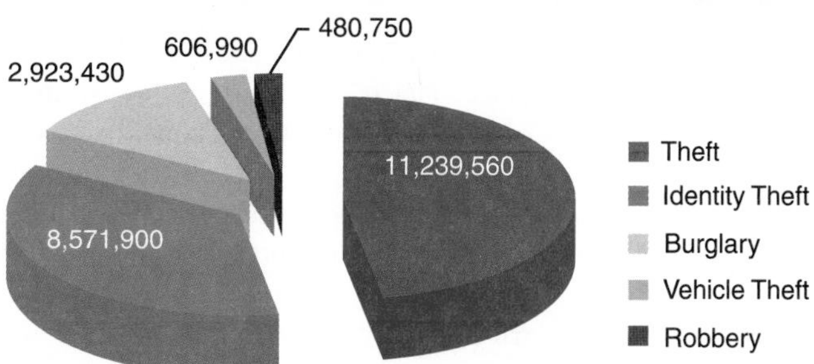

Sources: U.S. Department of Justice. Bureau of Justice Statistics. *Criminal Victimization, 2010* (November 2011); *Identity Theft Reported by Households, 2005–2010* (September 2011).

TABLE 11.1 Types of Information Collected by Government, Business, and Nonprofit Organizations

TYPES	EXAMPLES OF THE INFORMATION COLLECTED
Names	First, middle, and last names
Relationships	Family members and employers
Contact information	Phone, physical addresses, e-mail addresses, websites
Personal information	Birthday, medical information, physical description, educational records
Official identifiers	Social security, driver's license, passport numbers
Financial records	Bank, credit card, frequent fliers, and investment accounts

Source: V. Johnson 2005 (256).

million annual identity theft victims spend an average of six hundred hours over two to four years and $1,400 to clear their names (V. Johnson 2005, 257, n. 7). Victims may also lose job opportunities; be refused loans, education, housing, or cars; and be arrested for crimes they didn't commit. In extreme cases, victims are blackmailed (a former chemistry graduate student found a security flaw in a commercial website and demanded ransom from the company to keep his mouth shut; Rustad 2001, 63); stalked (Chapter 10, case excerpt, *State v. Hoying*); or even murdered (later in this section, case excerpt *Remsburg v. Docusearch, Inc.*).

The motivations for stealing other people's identity vary. They may be jilted lovers (*Remsburg v. Docusearch, Inc.*); "bored juveniles, disgruntled employees, corporate spies, or organized crime networks" (Rustad 2001, 65); or just your "run-of-the-mill" thieves (V. Johnson 2005, 257).

Whatever their reasons for stealing identities, identity thieves are extremely hard to catch. When they *are* caught, they're hard to convict (McMahon 2004). That has led some victims to turn to suing the providers of victims' identity. That's the route Helen Remsburg took. Liam Youens got Remsburg's twenty-year-old daughter Amy's Social Security number, home address, and her job location from Docusearch, Inc. It cost him $204. A week later, Youens went to Amy's workplace. As she was leaving work, he shot her and then himself to death.

CASE

In* Remsburg v. Docusearch, Inc. *(2003), *Amy Lynn Boyer's mother sued Docusearch Inc., which had provided information that led her daughter's stalker, Liam Youens, to her workplace, where he shot her as she was leaving work and then shot and killed himself.*

Is she entitled to damages from the identity information providers?

Remsburg v. Docusearch, Inc.

816 A.2d 1001 (N.H. 2003)

HISTORY

After her daughter was fatally shot at her workplace, Helen Remsburg, administrator of the estate of her daughter, Amy Lynn Boyer, sued in the U.S. District Court for the District of New Hampshire, defendants Docusearch, Inc., Wing and a Prayer, Inc., Daniel Cohn, Kenneth Zeiss, and Michele Gambino for wrongful death; invasion of privacy through intrusion upon seclusion; invasion of privacy through commercial appropriation of private information; violation of the federal Fair Credit Reporting Act, 15

U.S.C. §§ 1681a et seq.; and violation of the New Hampshire Consumer Protection Act, N.H.Rev.Stat. Ann. 358-A:1 et seq.

The defendants Docusearch, Inc., Wing and a Prayer, Inc., Daniel Cohn, and Kenneth Zeiss filed motions for *summary judgment.* [The facts don't amount to a case against the defendant and should be dismissed without further proceedings.]

The material facts supporting the motions are undisputed. Because the "motions raised important questions of New Hampshire law that should be resolved by the New Hampshire Supreme Court rather than a federal court," the U.S. District Court judge sent the following questions to the N.H. Supreme Court.

1. Investigation service had duty to exercise reasonable care in disclosing personal information about daughter to client;
2. Daughter's work address was not something secret, secluded, or private, and thus disclosure of that address could not support claim for invasion of privacy by intrusion upon seclusion;
3. New Hampshire recognizes cause of action for invasion of privacy by appropriation of individual's name or likeness;
4. Mother did not have a cause of action for appropriation; and
5. Investigation service, which obtained daughter's work address through a pretextual phone call, was subject to liability for damages under the Consumer Protection Act.

DALIANIS, J.

Docusearch, Inc. and Wing and a Prayer, Inc. (WAAP) jointly own and operate an Internet-based investigation and information service known as Docusearch.com. Daniel Cohn and Kenneth Zeiss each own 50 percent of each company's stock. Cohn serves as president of both companies and Zeiss serves as a director of WAAP. Cohn is licensed as a private investigator by both the State of Florida and Palm Beach County, Florida.

FACTS

On July 29, 1999, New Hampshire resident Liam Youens contacted Docusearch through its Internet website and requested the date of birth for Amy Lynn Boyer, another New Hampshire resident. Youens provided Docusearch his name, New Hampshire address, and a contact telephone number. He paid the $20 fee by credit card. Zeiss placed a telephone call to Youens in New Hampshire on the same day. Zeiss cannot recall the reason for the phone call, but speculates that it was to verify the order. The next day, July 30, 1999, Docusearch provided Youens with the birth dates for several Amy Boyers, but none was for the Amy Boyer sought by Youens.

In response, Youens e-mailed Docusearch inquiring whether it would be possible to get better results using Boyer's home address, which he provided. Youens gave Docusearch a different contact phone number.

Later that same day, Youens again contacted Docusearch and placed an order for Boyer's Social Security number (SSN), paying the $45 fee by credit card. On August 2, 1999, Docusearch obtained Boyer's Social Security number from a credit reporting agency as a part of a "credit header" and provided it to Youens. A "credit header" is typically provided at the top of a credit report and includes a person's name, address, and Social Security number.

The next day, Youens placed an order with Docusearch for Boyer's employment information, paying the $109 fee by credit card and giving Docusearch the same phone number he had provided originally. Docusearch phone records indicate that Zeiss placed a phone call to Youens on August 6, 1999. The phone number used was the one Youens had provided with his follow-up inquiry regarding Boyer's birth date. The phone call lasted for less than one minute, and no record exists concerning its topic or whether Zeiss was able to speak with Youens.

On August 20, 1999, having received no response to his latest request, Youens placed a second request for Boyer's employment information, again paying the $109 fee by credit card. On September 1, 1999, Docusearch refunded Youens' first payment of $109 because its efforts to fulfill his first request for Boyer's employment information had failed.

With his second request for Boyer's employment information pending, Youens placed yet another order for information with Docusearch on September 6, 1999. This time, he requested a "locate by Social Security number" search for Boyer. Youens paid the $30 fee by credit card, and received the results of the search—Boyer's home address—on September 7, 1999.

On September 8, 1999, Docusearch informed Youens of Boyer's employment address. Docusearch

(continues)

(continued)

acquired this address through a subcontractor, Michele Gambino, who had obtained the information by placing a "pretext" telephone call to Boyer in New Hampshire. Gambino lied about who she was and the purpose of her call in order to convince Boyer to reveal her employment information. Gambino had no contact with Youens, nor did she know why Youens was requesting the information.

On October 15, 1999, Youens drove to Boyer's workplace and fatally shot her as she left work. Youens then shot and killed himself. A subsequent police investigation revealed that Youens kept firearms and ammunition in his bedroom, and maintained a website containing references to stalking and killing Boyer as well as other information and statements related to violence and killing.

OPINION

Question 1

All persons have a duty to exercise reasonable care not to subject others to an unreasonable risk of harm.

A private citizen has no general duty to protect others from the criminal attacks of third parties. This rule is grounded in the fundamental unfairness of holding private citizens responsible for the unanticipated criminal acts of third parties, because under all ordinary and normal circumstances, in the absence of any reason to expect the contrary, the actor may reasonably proceed upon the assumption that others will obey the law.

In certain limited circumstances, however, we have recognized that there are exceptions to the general rule where a duty to exercise reasonable care will arise. We have held that such a duty may arise because:

1. a special relationship exists;
2. special circumstances exist; or
3. the duty has been voluntarily assumed.

The special circumstances exception includes situations where there is an especial temptation and opportunity for criminal misconduct brought about by the defendant.

Identity theft, i.e., the use of one person's identity by another, is an increasingly common risk associated with the disclosure of personal information, such as a SSN. A person's SSN has attained the status of a quasi-universal personal identification number. At the same time, however, a person's privacy interest in his or her SSN is recognized by state and federal statutes, including RSA 260:14, IV-a (Supp. 2002), which prohibits the release of SSNs contained within drivers' license records. Armed with one's SSN, an unscrupulous individual could obtain a person's welfare benefits or Social Security benefits, order new checks at a new address on that person's checking account, obtain credit cards, or even obtain the person's paycheck.

The consequences of identity theft can be severe. The best estimates place the number of victims in excess of 100,000 per year and the dollar loss in excess of $2 billion per year. LoPucki, Human Identification Theory and the Identity Theft Problem, 80 Tex. L.Rev. 89, 89 (2001). [See Figure 11.2, Property Victimization, 2010, for much higher numbers in 2010.]

Victims of identity theft risk the destruction of their good credit histories. This often destroys a victim's ability to obtain credit from any source and may, in some cases, render the victim unemployable or even cause the victim to be incarcerated.

The threats posed by identity theft lead us to conclude that the risk of criminal misconduct is sufficiently foreseeable so that an investigator has a duty to exercise reasonable care in disclosing a third person's personal information to a client. And we so hold. This is especially true when, as in this case, the investigator does not know the client or the client's purpose in seeking the information.

Questions 2 and 3

A tort action based upon an intrusion upon seclusion must relate to something secret, secluded or private pertaining to the plaintiff. In addressing whether a person's SSN is something secret, secluded or private, we must determine whether a person has a reasonable expectation of privacy in the number. SSNs are used to identify people to track Social Security benefits, as well as when taxes and credit applications are filed. In fact, "the widespread use of SSNs as universal identifiers in the public and private sectors is one of the most serious manifestations of privacy concerns in the Nation. Thus, while a SSN must be disclosed in certain circumstances, a person may reasonably expect that the number will remain private.

We next address whether a person has a cause of action for intrusion upon seclusion where an investigator obtains the person's work address by using a pretextual phone call. We must first establish whether a work address is something secret, secluded or private about the plaintiff.

In most cases, a person works in a public place. On the public street, or in any other public place, a person has no legal right to be alone. A person's employment, where he lives, and where he works are exposures which we all must suffer. We have no reasonable expectation of privacy as to our identity or as to where we live or work. Our commuting to and from where we live and work is not done clandestinely and each place provides a facet of our total identity.

Question 4

One who appropriates to his own use or benefit the name or likeness of another is subject to liability to the other for invasion of his privacy. New Hampshire recognizes the tort of invasion of privacy by appropriation of an individual's name or likeness. The interest protected by the rule is the interest of the individual in the exclusive use of his own identity, in so far as it is represented by his name or likeness, and in so far as the use may be of benefit to him or to others.

An investigator who sells personal information sells the information for the value of the information itself, not to take advantage of the person's reputation or prestige. The investigator does not capitalize upon the goodwill value associated with the information but rather upon the client's willingness to pay for the information. In other words, the benefit derived from the sale in no way relates to the social or commercial standing of the person whose information is sold. Thus, a person whose personal information is sold does not have a cause of action for appropriation against the investigator who sold the information.

Question 5

The last issue relates to the construction of the Consumer Protection Act, RSA chapter 358-A. We begin by considering the plain meaning of the words of the statute. RSA 358-A:2 (1995) states, in pertinent part:

> It shall be unlawful for any person to use any unfair or deceptive act or practice in the conduct of any trade or commerce within this state. Such unfair or deceptive act or practice shall include, but is not limited to, the following:
>
> III. Causing likelihood of confusion or of misunderstanding as to affiliation, connection or association with another.

Pretext phone calling has been described as the use of deception and trickery to obtain a person's private information for resale to others. The target of the phone call is deceived into believing that the caller is affiliated with a reliable entity who has a legitimate purpose in requesting the information. RSA 358-A:2, III explicitly prohibits this conduct. The pretext clearly creates a misunderstanding as to the investigator's affiliation.

The defendant argues that an investigator who makes a pretextual phone call to obtain information for sale does not conduct any "trade" or "commerce" with the person deceived by the phone call. The Consumer Protection Act defines "trade" and "commerce" as including "the advertising, offering for sale, sale, or distribution of any services and any property."

There is no language in the Act that would restrict the definition of "trade" and "commerce" to that affecting the party deceived by the prohibited conduct. In fact, the Act explicitly includes "trade or commerce directly or *indirectly* affecting the people of this state" (emphasis added). Here, the investigator used the pretext phone call to complete the sale of information to a client. Thus, the investigator's pretextual phone call occurred in the conduct of trade or commerce within the State.

We conclude that an investigator who obtains a person's work address by means of pretextual phone calling, and then sells the information, may be liable for damages under RSA chapter 358-A to the person deceived.

Remanded.

QUESTIONS

1. State the five questions the U.S. District Court asked the New Hampshire Supreme Court to answer.
2. Summarize the court's answers and the reasons for its answers.
3. If you were a juror, would you vote to award Helen Remsburg damages? How much? Back up your answer with the rich facts supplied by the court.
4. About a year after the New Hampshire Supreme Court decided the case, the Remsburgs settled

(continues)

(continued)

for $85,000. They wanted their day in court but grew frustrated with the court system. According to Amy's stepfather, "This has never been about money. . . . We needed to get our lives back and focus on putting this behind us."

And, it was some consolation that even without the trial, the case attracted enough attention that information brokers like Docusearch will "now think twice about selling private information." (Ramer 2004)

Describe your reaction to the case after reading the excerpt and the final outcome.

INTELLECTUAL PROPERTY THEFT

> The Congress shall have power to promote the progress of science and useful arts, by securing for limited times to authors and inventors the exclusive right to their respective writings and discoveries. (U.S. Constitution, Article I, Section 8)

The importance of intellectual property wasn't lost on our nation's founders. They wrote it into the Constitution. We recognize it today in the copyright laws that protect against unauthorized copying and distribution of books, films, music compositions, sound recordings, and software programs. Other laws protect intellectual property from infringement on trademarks, trade secrets, and patents and thefts, damage, and destruction of intellectual property.

LO 13

Intellectual property definitely needs protection. First, intellectual property theft costs at least $250 billion every year (U.S. Department of Justice 2006, 13). The cost may be a lot higher because businesses don't report these thefts, fearing it will hurt business. Second, intellectual property thefts go undetected because of the difficulty of catching cybercriminals (Rustad 2001, 65). Third, cybercriminals are smart, skilled, and highly motivated, not just by money but by the darker and dangerous side of our nature—revenge, hate, ideology, and the powerful, seductive, addictive thrill of hacking.

Hackers on the borderless Internet have obtained unauthorized access into computer systems to rob banks, infringe copyrights, commit fraud, distribute child pornography, and plan terrorist attacks (Rustad 2001, 63–64).

A whole new vocabulary has grown to describe the ways hackers commit cybercrimes. In addition to viruses and wiretapping, methods known even to functional computer illiterates like me, here's a list of some others compiled by Professor Michael Rustad (2001, 64):

- *Spoofing* When an attacker compromises routing packets to direct a file or transmission to a different location
- *Piggybacking* Programs that hackers use to piggyback onto other programs to enter computer systems
- *Data diddling* The practice by employees and other knowledgeable insiders of altering or manipulating data, credit limits, or other financial information
- *Salami attack* A series of minor computer crimes—slices of a larger crime—that are difficult to detect. (For example, a hacker finds a way to get into a bank's computers. He quietly skims off a penny or so from each account. Once he has $200,000, he quits.)
- *E-mail flood attack* When so much e-mail is sent to a target that the transfer agent is overwhelmed, causing other communication programs to destabilize and crash the system
- *Password sniffing* Using password sniffing programs to monitor and record the name and password of network users as they log in and impersonating the authorized users to access restricted documents

- *Worm* Uses a network to send copies of itself to other systems and it does so without any intervention. In general, worms harm the network and consume bandwidth, whereas viruses infect or corrupt files on a targeted computer. Viruses generally do not affect network performance, because their malicious activities are mostly confined within the target computer itself.

Twenty-year-old cyberthief Jeanson Ancheta, in *U.S. v. Ancheta* (2006), got caught and pleaded guilty to multiple counts of cybercrime fraud and damaging computers protected by the "Fraud and Related Activity in Connection with Computers" (U.S. Code 2006, Title 18, Part I, Chapter 47 §1030(a)(5)(A)(i), 1030(a)(5)(B)(i), and 1030(b)). Ancheta worked in an Internet café in Downey, California. According to his aunt, he had modest ambitions—to join the military reserves—but he lived a luxurious lifestyle as an Internet café employee. He was often seen driving his BMW and spending more than $600 a week on new clothes and car parts.

The explanation was the profits he made from the results of a worm he authored. The worm allowed him to infect as many computers on the Internet as he could with off-the-shelf remote access Trojans (RATs) (Vamosi 2006). Ancheta pleaded guilty to multiple counts of cybercrime fraud; he received fifty-seven months in prison—the longest prison cybercrime theft sentence to date—and had to forfeit his BMW.

Ancheta pleaded guilty to the federal cybercrime of "Fraud and Related Activity in Connection with Computers." That statute defines the crime as follows:

> Whoever knowingly causes [or attempts to cause] the transmission of a program, information, code, or command, and as a result of such conduct, intentionally causes damage without authorization, to a protected computer . . . [affecting]1 or more persons during any 1-year period . . . [and] affecting 1 or more other protected computers aggregating at least $5,000 in value . . .

The punishment under the statute is a fine and/or imprisonment for up to twenty years.

CASE

***In* U.S. v. Ancheta *(2006),* twenty-year-old cyberthief Jeanson Ancheta got caught and pleaded guilty to multiple counts of computer fraud.**

Did he commit computer fraud?

U.S. v. Ancheta

(C.D. Cal. 2006)

AQUILINA, J.

Concluding the first prosecution of its kind in the United States, a well known member of the "botmaster underground" was sentenced this afternoon to nearly five years in prison for profiting from his use of "botnets"—armies of compromised computers—that he used to launch destructive attacks, to send huge quantities of spam across the Internet, and to receive surreptitious installations of adware.

Jeanson James Ancheta, 21, of Downey, California, was sentenced to 57 months in federal prison by U.S. District Judge R. Gary Klausner in Los Angeles. During the sentencing hearing, Judge Klausner characterized Ancheta's crimes as "extensive, serious and sophisticated." The prison term is the longest known sentence for a defendant who spread computer viruses.

Ancheta pleaded guilty in January to conspiring to violate the Computer Fraud Abuse Act, conspiring to violate the CAN-SPAM Act, causing damage to computers used by the federal government in national defense, and accessing protected computers without authorization to commit fraud. When he pleaded guilty, Ancheta admitted using computer servers he controlled to transmit malicious code over the Internet to scan for and exploit vulnerable computers. Ancheta caused thousands of compromised computers to be

(continues)

(continued)

directed to an Internet Relay Chat channel, where they were instructed to scan for other computers vulnerable to similar infection, and to remain "zombies" vulnerable to further unauthorized accesses.

Ancheta further admitted that, in more than 30 separate transactions, he earned approximately $3,000 by selling access to his botnets. The botnets were sold to other computer users, who used the machines to launch distributed denial of service (DDOS) attacks and to send unsolicited commercial e-mail, or spam. Ancheta acknowledged specifically discussing with the purchasers the nature and extent of the DDOS attacks or proxy spamming they were interested in conducting. Ancheta suggested the number of bots or proxies they would need to accomplish the specified acts, tested the botnets with them to ensure that the DDOS attacks or proxy spamming were successfully carried out, and advised them on how to properly maintain, update, and strengthen their purchased armies.

In relation to the computer fraud scheme, Ancheta admitted generating for himself and an unindicted co-conspirator more than $107,000 in advertising affiliate proceeds by downloading adware to more than 400,000 infected computers that he controlled. By varying the download times and rates of the adware installations, as well as by redirecting the compromised computers between various servers equipped to install different types of modified adware, Ancheta avoided detection by the advertising affiliate companies who paid him for every install. Ancheta further admitted using the advertising affiliate proceeds he earned to pay for, among other things, the multiple servers he used to conduct his illegal activity.

Following the prison term, Ancheta will serve three years on supervised release. During that time, his access to computers and the Internet will be limited, and he will be required to pay approximately $15,000 in restitution to the Weapons Division of the U.S. Naval Air Warfare Center in China Lake and the Defense Information Systems Agency, whose national defense networks were intentionally damaged by Ancheta's malicious code. The proceeds of Ancheta's illegal activity—including more than $60,000 in cash, a BMW automobile, and computer equipment—have been forfeited to the government.

Addressing the defendant at the conclusion of the sentencing hearing, Judge Klausner said: "Your worst enemy is your own intellectual arrogance that somehow the world cannot touch you on this." This case was investigated by the Los Angeles Field Office of the Federal Bureau of Investigation, which received assistance from the Southwest Field Office of the Naval Criminal Investigative Service and the Western Field Office of the Defense Criminal Investigative Service.

QUESTIONS

1. State the *actus reus*, *mens rea*, attendance circumstance(s), and "bad result" elements of the federal "Fraud and Related Activity in Connection with Computers" statute.
2. List the relevant facts Ancheta admitted, and match them up with the elements you stated in (1).
3. What purposes of punishment do the forfeiture and sentence reflect? Recall the purposes of punishment laid out in Chapter 1: punishment requires (a) condemnation and hard treatment; (b) retribution; (c) a means of prevention (general and special deterrence, incapacitation, and rehabilitation); and (d) restitution. Back up your answer using these purposes of punishment requirements.
4. Was the sentence fair? Too harsh? Too lenient? Explain your answer.

SUMMARY

LO 1 There are three categories of crimes against property: (1) taking other people's property (theft, fraud, robbery, and receiving stolen property); (2) damaging or destroying other people's property (arson, criminal mischief); and (3) invading other people's property (burglary, criminal trespass).

LO 2 The crime of theft grew out of the general social concern with violent crime against persons.

The different "taking" property crimes are larceny, embezzlement, false pretenses, white-collar crimes, robbery, and receiving stolen property. The history of larceny and fraud is also the history of supplementing civil actions with criminal punishment. Common law false pretenses *mens rea* requires the purpose or specific intent to obtain property by deceit and lies. The concern with violent crimes against the person led to the creation of the common law felony of robbery, which involves the use of force or the threat of the use of force. LO 3

Consolidated theft statutes are a modern approach to certain "taking" crimes (larceny, embezzlement, and false pretenses). These statutes eliminate the artificial need to separate theft into distinct offenses according to the *actus reus*. Under modern theft statutes, *actus reus* includes taking and carrying away, converting, or swindling to obtain possession of someone else's property. LO 4

The federal mail fraud statute defines "false pretenses" (fraud) much more broadly than common law fraud. It includes "schemes to defraud or for obtaining money or property." LO 5

The core of robbery is theft accomplished under circumstances intended to terrorize the victim by actual injury or the threat of immediate injury to the victim. The use of force, or the threat of force, is the essence of the robbery criminal act. Most states have divided robbery into degrees. LO 6

Receiving stolen property requires that the receiver control the property, at least briefly. In some states, receivers of stolen property have to know the goods are stolen; in others, believing the goods are stolen is enough. LO 7

Arson is a felony and an example of a "damaging or destroying" property crime. Arson includes burning almost any kind of building, vessel, or vehicle; it's a very serious crime against property and persons. Criminal mischief is another example of a "damaging or destroying" property crime and is a misdemeanor. LO 8

There are three kinds of criminal mischief: (1) destruction or damage criminal mischief, (2) tampering, and (3) deception or threat. Criminal mischief *actus reus* mirrors the three types: in destruction or damage criminal mischief, the *actus reus* is burning, exploding, flooding, or committing some other dangerous act; in tampering, it's any act that creates a danger to property, even if it doesn't actually cause any damage to the property; in deception or threat, it's causing harm through deception or threats. The *mens rea* varies, but generally it looks at whether the person purposely, knowingly, or negligently caused damage to or pecuniary loss of property. LO 9

The heart of burglary is invading others' property. Burglary is a specific-intent crime and an example of an invasion type of property crime. LO 10

Criminal trespass is a broader but less serious invasion type of property crime than burglary. The heart of criminal trespass is unwanted presence. Besides traditional ways to take, destroy or damage, and invade other people's property, cybercrime—crimes committed through the Internet or some other computer network—is a serious and rapidly growing new problem. Computers and the Internet have greatly enhanced the capacity to exploit information about individuals and steal ideas. LO 11

LO 12 More people are victims of identity theft than burglary, vehicle theft, and robbery combined in the United States. Only ordinary theft claims more victims than identity theft. The consequences of wrongful access to personal information can be devastating.

LO 13 Intellectual property definitely needs protection, even more today than before the widespread use of computers and the Internet.

KEY TERMS

cybercrime, p. 402
robbery, p. 403
larceny, p. 403
conversion, p. 403
tangible property, p. 403
intangible property, p. 403
embezzlement, p. 403
abuse-of-trust crimes, p. 403
white-collar crimes, p. 403
fraud, p. 404
common law fraud, p. 404
obtaining property by false pretenses, p. 404
theft, p. 404
consolidated theft statutes, p. 404
federal mail fraud statute, p. 408
Ponzi schemes, p. 411
robbery *actus reus*, p. 415
robbery *mens rea*, p. 416
receiving stolen property, p. 417
fences, p. 417
receiving stolen property *actus reus*, p. 417
receiving stolen property *mens rea*, p. 417
arson, p. 420
criminal mischief, p. 421
burning (in arson), p. 421
arson *mens rea*, p. 422
first-degree arson, p. 423
second-degree arson, p. 423
malicious mischief, p. 423
criminal mischief *actus reus*, p. 423
burglary, p. 427
breaking (in burglary), p. 427
entering (in burglary), p. 427
surreptitious remaining element (in burglary), p. 428
occupied structure, p. 428
dwelling of another, p. 428
criminal trespass, p. 431
intellectual property, p. 433
identity theft, p. 433

LEARNING OBJECTIVES

1. To know and understand how our present "quality of life" offenses aimed at controlling "bad manners" in public grew out of the ancient offense of disorderly conduct.
2. To understand and appreciate that efforts to control bad manners in public create a tension between order and liberty in constitutional democracies.
3. To know the definition of disorderly conduct and its individual and group forms.
4. To know and understand why the "broken windows" theory claims that "quality of life" crimes are linked to serious crime.
5. To understand that most people are more worried about bad public manners than they are about serious crimes.
6. To appreciate that a consensus among all classes, races, and communities that bad public behavior of "street peoples" and "street gangs" should be controlled has shaped the content of the criminal law.
7. To know the difference between vagrancy and loitering and to understand the history of laws that address these crimes.
8. To know the definition of panhandling and understand how laws to restrict it have led to claims that they violate the First Amendment ban on free speech.
9. To understand that fear of gangs has led state and city governments to enact criminal laws that allow them to obtain civil gang injunctions that regulate gang behavior.
10. To appreciate that the empirical evidence on the effectiveness of civil gang injunctions in controlling gang behavior is mixed.
11. To know that "victimless crimes" against public decency (the ancient "crimes against public morals") generate heated disagreement and debate between those who believe that criminal law should enforce morality and those who believe the nonviolent behavior of competent adults is none of the law's business. An example of such a crime is prostitution.

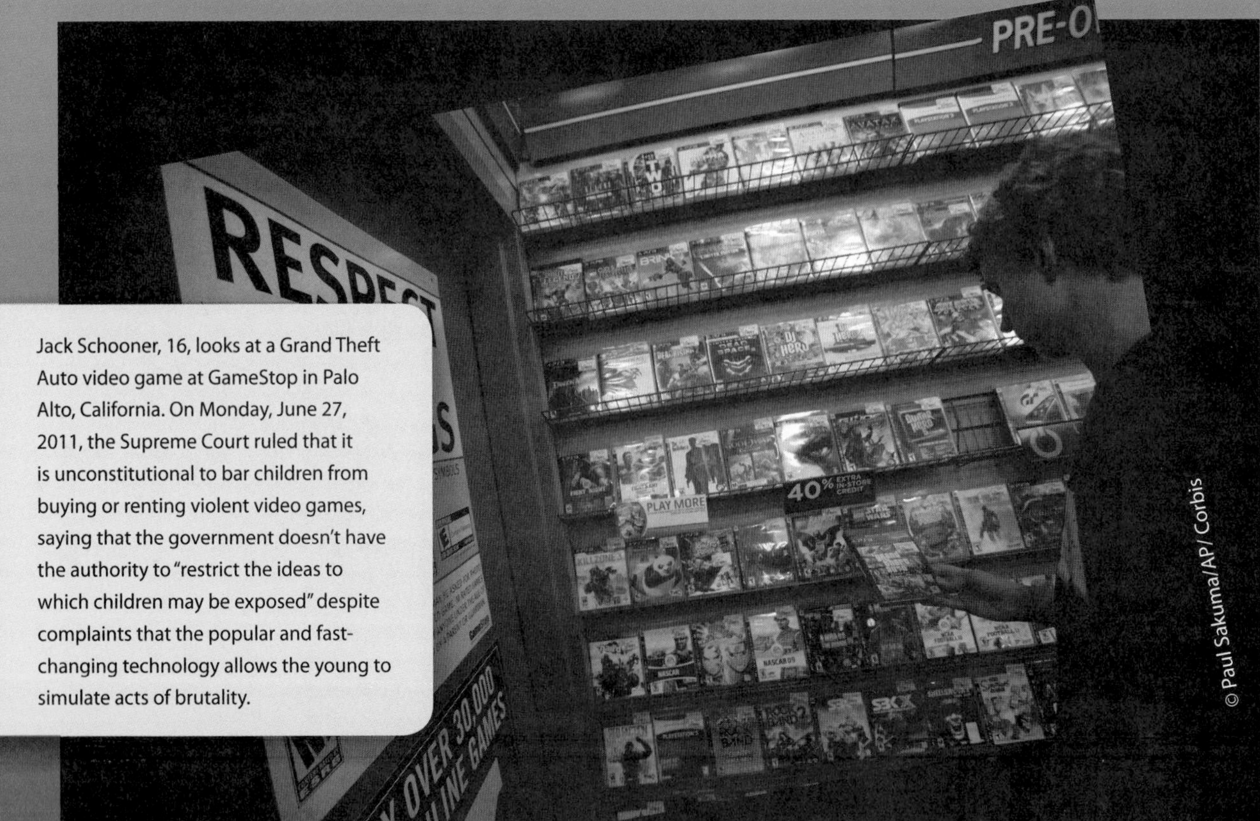

Jack Schooner, 16, looks at a Grand Theft Auto video game at GameStop in Palo Alto, California. On Monday, June 27, 2011, the Supreme Court ruled that it is unconstitutional to bar children from buying or renting violent video games, saying that the government doesn't have the authority to "restrict the ideas to which children may be exposed" despite complaints that the popular and fast-changing technology allows the young to simulate acts of brutality.

© Paul Sakuma/AP/Corbis

CRIMES AGAINST PUBLIC ORDER AND MORALS 12

CHAPTER OUTLINE

Will Banning Video Games in Arcades Reduce Youth Violence?

A St. Louis, Missouri, ordinance requires owners and managers of arcades to place video games which they know to be harmful to minors separate and apart from other video games, and designate such areas as "Restricted-17." The Ordinance makes it unlawful to knowingly sell or rent a video game, which is harmful to a minor, unless that minor is accompanied by a parent or guardian who consents to the purchase or sale.

The Ordinance also makes it unlawful to knowingly admit a minor to a "Restricted-17" area, and to knowingly permit the free play of a video game which is harmful to minors on premises on which video games are sold or rented.

Interactive Digital Software Association, and other companies or associations of companies that create, publish, distribute, sell, rent, and/or make available to the public, video games, including both computer and arcade games, and related software (Plaintiffs) sued St. Louis County, the County Executive of St. Louis County, and the Chief of Police of St. Louis County (Defendants), alleging that the ordinance violated their First Amendment right to "free expression."

The video game industry and the technology employed in creating video games have changed drastically in the last few decades. There are a variety of different types of video games,

(continues)

(continued)

including, but not limited to, adventure games, puzzle games, sports games, racing games, simulator games, hunting games, teenage and adult educational games, role-playing games, and shooting games.

Plaintiffs provided the affidavit of Douglas Lowenstein, President of the Interactive Digital Software Association. Mr. Lowenstein attempted to explain the process of creating video games and included some examples; however, the Court did not get to view the final product of these games. St. Louis County did provide a videotape depicting four different games: "The Resident of Evil Creek," "Mortal Combat," "DOOM," and "Fear Effect."

(*Interactive Digital Software Association v. St. Louis County*, 200 Fed.Supp.2d 1126 [E.D.Mo. 2002])

> The last species of offenses which especially affect the commonwealth are . . . the due regulation and domestic order of the kingdom. The individuals of the state, like members of a well-governed family, are bound to conform their general behavior to the rules of propriety, good neighborhood, and good manners; and to be decent, industrious, and inoffensive. This head of offenses must therefore be very miscellaneous, as it comprises all such crimes as especially affect public society. (Blackstone 1769, 162)

Blackstone's eighteenth-century introduction to his chapter on crimes related to the "regulation and domestic order of the kingdom" is a good way to introduce you to the subject of this chapter, crimes against public order and morals. These crimes cover two vast areas of criminal law that involve mostly very minor crimes: disorderly conduct and "quality of life" crimes. Nonetheless, they affect many more people than the crimes against persons and their property we've already discussed (Chapters 9–11, Table 12.1) and the crimes against the state we'll discuss in Chapter 13.

LO 1, LO 2

Throughout most of our history, "bad manners" crimes have been called **crimes against public order**. Today, we call them "quality of life" crimes. The list of quality-of-life offenses is long, including public drinking and drunkenness; begging and aggressive panhandling; threatening behavior and harassment; blocking streets and public places; graffiti and vandalism; street prostitution; public urination and defecation; unlicensed vending; and even "squeegeeing"—washing the windshields of stopped cars and demanding money for the "service."

crimes against public order, formerly called "bad manners" crimes; today called "quality of life" crimes, they include public drinking, aggressive panhandling, harassment, graffiti and vandalism, and street prostitution

Significant numbers of people across the spectrums of age, sex, race, ethnicity, and class believe strongly that "bad manners" in public places create disorder and threaten the quality of life of ordinary people (Skogan 1990). Others believe just as strongly that making bad manners a crime denies individuals their liberty without due process of law (Fifth and Fourteenth Amendments to the U.S. Constitution; Chapter 2).

LO 2

Constitutional democracy can't survive without *order* and *liberty*, but there's a natural tension between them because they're fundamental values in conflict. The U.S. Supreme Court has recognized the need to balance order and liberty by holding repeatedly that "ordered liberty" is a fundamental requirement of our constitutional system (Chapter 2). In this chapter, **"order"** refers to acting according to ordinary people's standard of "good manners." **"Liberty"** refers to the right of individuals to come and go as they please without government interference.

order, refers to acting according to ordinary people's standard of "good manners"

liberty, refers to the right of individuals to come and go as they please without government interference

In this chapter, we'll look first at *disorderly conduct* crimes—the misdemeanor of individual disorderly conduct and the group disorderly conduct felony of riot. Next, we'll examine in depth the application of disorderly conduct laws to what are now called *"quality of life" crimes*. These are crimes of "bad manners" in public.

Then, in our look at quality-of-life crimes surrounding gang activity, we'll examine the facts and myths about youth gang activity enforcement tactics. Specifically, we'll learn what the

TABLE 12.1

Estimated Number of Arrests, 2010

OFFENSES	ESTIMATED NUMBER
Disorderly conduct, drunkenness, gambling, prostitution, curfew/loitering, vagrancy, vandalism, liquor law	2,140,872
Drug abuse violations	1,638,846
Driving under the influence	1,412,223
Other assaults	1,292,449
Larceny-theft	1,271,410
Aggravated assault	408,488
Burglary	289,769
Fraud	187,887
Weapons; carrying, possessing, etc.	159,020
Robbery	112,300
Offenses against the family and children	111,062
Stolen property; buying, receiving, possessing	94,802
Forgery and counterfeiting	78,101
Sex offenses (except forcible rape and prostitution)	72,628
Motor vehicle theft	71,487
Forcible rape	20,088
Embezzlement	16,616
Arson	11,296
Murder and nonnegligent manslaughter	11,201
Total	**13,120,947**

Source: FBI Uniform Crime Report 2011 (Sept.), *Crime in the United States 2010*, Table 29.

empirical research on the effectiveness of the noncriminal preventive response—namely, the civil gang injunction (CGI)—tells us.

We'll also examine the ban on violent video games and the empirical research that led a U.S. district court (*Interactive Digital Software Association v. St. Louis County* 2002) to find that

> exposure of children to graphic and lifelike violence contained in some video games has been correlated to violent behavior, and in fact the perpetrators of recent school shootings in Columbine, Colorado; Jonesboro, Arkansas; and Paducah, Kentucky were reported to be avid fans of such games. (1129)

Finally, we'll examine separately another type of quality-of-life crime: "victimless crimes." These crimes involve willing participants or participants who don't see themselves as victims. We begin with a look at disorderly conduct in our society.

DISORDERLY CONDUCT

Disorderly conduct crimes are offenses against public order and morals. Except for riot, they are minor crimes that legislators, judges, and scholars didn't pay much attention to until the 1950s when the Model Penal Code (MPC) was adopted by the American Law

disorderly conduct crimes, offenses against public order and morals

Institute (ALI). Why the lack of attention? The punishment was minor (small fines or a few days in jail); most defendants were poor; and convictions were rarely appealed. But disorderly conduct offenses are an important part of the criminal justice system for three reasons: they "affect large numbers of defendants, involve a great proportion of public activity, and powerfully influence the view of public justice held by millions of people" (ALI 1985, Part II, Vol. 3, Art. 250, 251, 309).

We'll divide our discussion of these crimes into two sections: the minor offenses included in individual disorderly conduct statutes (e.g., fighting in public) and the felony of riot (group disorderly conduct).

LO 2, LO 3

INDIVIDUAL DISORDERLY CONDUCT

actual disorderly conduct, breach-of-the-peace misdemeanor that includes fighting in public and making unreasonable noise

constructive disorderly conduct, conduct that "tends to provoke or excite others to break the peace"

Disorderly conduct statutes grew out of the ancient common law crime known as "breach of the peace" (see Chapter 2, "Free Speech" section). It included both the misdemeanors of actual disorderly conduct (e.g., fighting in public, making unreasonable noise) and constructive disorderly conduct, which was conduct that "tends to provoke or excite others to break it [the peace]" (Blackstone 1769, 148).

Wisconsin's "disorderly conduct" statute, for example, follows Blackstone:

> Whoever, in a public or private place, engages in violent, abusive, indecent, profane, boisterous, unreasonably loud or otherwise disorderly conduct under circumstances in which the conduct tends to cause or provoke a disturbance is guilty of a Class B misdemeanor. (Wisconsin Criminal Code 2003, § 947.01)

The problem with Wisconsin's statute, and those of most states with similar statutes, is twofold. First, they're too vague to give individuals and law enforcement officers notice of what the law prohibits (see Chapter 2, "Void-for-Vagueness Doctrine" section). Second, neither requires *mens rea* (Chapter 4). The MPC (ALI 1985, Part II, Vol. 3, 324–25) addresses both of these problems in Section 250.2:

> *§ 250.2. DISORDERLY CONDUCT*
>
> (1) Offense Defined. A person is guilty of disorderly conduct if, with purpose to cause public inconvenience, annoyance or alarm, or recklessly creating a risk thereof, he:
>
> (a) engages in fighting or threatening, or in violent or tumultuous behavior; or
>
> (b) makes unreasonable noise or offensively coarse utterance, gesture or display, or addresses abusive language to any person present; or
>
> (c) creates a hazardous or physically offensive condition by any act which serves no legitimate purpose of the actor.
>
> "Public" means affecting or likely to affect persons in a place to which the public or a substantial group has access; among the places included are highways, transport facilities, schools, prisons, apartment houses, places of business or amusement, or any neighborhood.
>
> (2) Grading. An offense under this section is a petty misdemeanor if the actor's purpose is to cause substantial harm or serious inconvenience, or if he persists in disorderly conduct after reasonable warning or request to desist. Otherwise disorderly conduct is a violation.

Notice that Section 250.2(1) requires a mental attitude of subjective fault (Chapter 4)—knowledge or recklessness. So conscious risk creation is the minimum level of culpability; negligence isn't good enough (see Chapter 4, "The Model Penal Code (MPC) Levels of Culpability" section).

Next, notice that the MPC limits conduct that qualifies as disorderly conduct *actus reus* to three actions:

1. Fighting in public
2. Making "unreasonable noise" or using "abusive language" (see Chapter 2, "Free Speech" section)
3. Creating a "hazardous or physically offensive condition," such as strewing garbage, setting off "stink bombs," or turning off lights in crowded public places

In practice, the most common use of disorderly conduct statutes is the ban on fighting in public. Fighting can cause two harms: (1) disturbing community peace and quiet and (2) disturbing or endangering innocent bystanders. The MPC also includes several "special" sections devoted to other specifically defined acts of disorderly conduct (Table 12.2). The majority of states have adopted the *actus reus* and the *mens rea* provisions of the MPC.

group disorderly conduct, consisted of three misdemeanors at common law: unlawful assembly, rout, and riot

GROUP DISORDERLY CONDUCT (RIOT)

unlawful assembly, the ancient crime of three or more persons gathering together to commit an unlawful act

Group disorderly conduct consisted of three misdemeanors at the common law: unlawful assembly, rout, and riot. All three were aimed at preventing "the ultimate evil of open disorder and breach of the public peace" (ALI 1985, 3:313). Unlawful assembly was committed when a group of at least three persons joined for the purpose of committing

TABLE 12.2

Model Penal Code Special Disorderly Conduct Sections

OFFENSE	ELEMENT	DESCRIPTION
False public alarms (250.3)	*Mens rea*	Knowingly
	Actus reus	Initiating or circulating a report or warning of a bombing or a catastrophe
	Harm	Likely to cause evacuation or public inconvenience or alarm
Public drunkenness (250.5)	*Actus reus*	Appearing in a public place "manifestly under the influence of alcohol, narcotics, or other drug, not therapeutically administered"
	Harm	To the degree it may "endanger himself or other persons or property, or annoy persons in his vicinity"
Loitering or prowling (250.6)	*Actus reus*	Loitering or prowling
	Circumstances	"In a place, at a time, or in a manner not usual for law-abiding individuals"
	Harm	Warrant "alarm for the safety of persons or property in the vicinity"
Obstructing highways or other public passages (250.7)	*Mens rea*	Purposely or recklessly
	Actus reus	Obstructs highway or public passage (except if exercising lawful First Amendment rights) (Chapter 2)
Disrupting meetings and processions (250.8)	*Mens rea*	Purposely
	Actus reus	Prevent or disrupt a lawful meeting, procession, or gathering either physically or by words, gestures, or displays designed to "outrage the sensibilities of the group"

an unlawful act. If the three or more took action toward achieving their purpose, they committed **rout**. If the group actually committed an unlawful violent act, or performed a lawful act in a "violent or tumultuous manner," they committed **riot**.

rout, common law misdemeanor that occurred when three or more people joined and moved toward the commission of a riot

riot, common law misdemeanor that occurred when three or more persons committed an unlawful violent act, or performed a lawful act in a "violent or tumultuous manner"; felony consisting of twelve or more persons who stayed together unlawfully, riotously, and tumultuously for one hour after being warned to disperse by the reading of a proclamation

Riot didn't require the group to plan their unlawful violent act before they got together; it was enough that once together they came up with the riotous plan of violence. The Riot Act of 1714 turned the common law misdemeanor of riot into a felony. The felony consisted of twelve or more persons who "being unlawfully, riotously, and tumultuously assembled together" stayed together for one hour after being warned to disperse by the reading of a proclamation. (Now you know the original meaning of "reading the riot act.") Here's the version from Queen Victoria's reign:

> Our sovereign lady the Queen chargeth and commandeth all persons being assembled immediately to disperse themselves and peaceably to depart to their habitations or to their lawful business, upon the pains contained in the Act made in the first year of King George for preventing tumults and riotous assemblies. God Save the Queen. (ALI 1985, 3:314, n. 8)

Riot is still a felony. Why? First, it provides harsher penalties for disorderly conduct when group behavior gets "especially alarming or dangerous." Second, it allows punishment for individuals in a disorderly crowd who disobey police orders to disperse (ALI 1985, 3:316–17). Every state has some form of riot act; many have adopted the MPC provision:

RIOT §250.1(1) (1) RIOT

A person is guilty of riot, a felony of the third degree, if he participates with [two] or more others in a course of disorderly conduct:

(a) with purpose to commit or facilitate the commission of a felony or misdemeanor;

(b) with purpose to prevent or coerce official action; or

(c) when the actor or any other participant to the knowledge of the actor uses or plans to use a firearm or other deadly weapon.

LO 4

"QUALITY OF LIFE" CRIMES

"quality of life" crimes, "bad manners" crimes that threaten to disrupt public order

broken-windows theory, first espoused by James Q. Wilson and George L. Kelling, the theory that minor offenses or disorderly conduct can lead to a rise in serious crime

"Quality of life" crimes are "bad manners" crimes that threaten to disrupt public order. In the 1980s, two prominent scholars sensed a deep public yearning for recovering what they called a lost sense of public "good manners," especially in our largest cities. Professors James Q. Wilson and George L. Kelling (1982) suggested that what were labeled "petty crimes" weren't just "bothering" law-abiding people and creating a yearning for a more polite past; they were connected to serious crime. They called this connection between disorderly conduct and serious crime the **broken-windows theory**.

According to Kelling, research conducted since the article was written in 1982 has demonstrated "a direct link between disorder and crime." But in 1996, Wilson described the broken-windows theory more cautiously. In the foreword to a book written by Kelling and Catherine M. Coles, *Fixing Broken Windows* (1996), Wilson wrote:

> We used the image of broken windows to explain how neighborhoods might decay into disorder and even crime if no one attends faithfully to their maintenance. If a factory or office window is broken, passersby observing it will conclude that no one cares or no one is in charge. In time, a few will begin throwing rocks to break more windows. Soon all the windows will be broken, and now passersby will think that, not only is no one in charge of the building no one is in charge of the street on which it

> faces. Only the young, the criminal, or the foolhardy have any business on an unprotected avenue, and so more and more citizens will abandon the street to those they assume prowl it. Small disorders lead to larger and larger ones, and perhaps even to crime. (xiv)

Professor Wesley G. Skogan (1990), the author of some of the research on which Kelling relies, characterized his and others' research more cautiously than Kelling:

> Our concern with common crime is limited to whether disorder is a cause of it. . . . Neighborhood levels of disorder are closely related to crime rates, to fear of crime, and the belief that serious crime is a neighborhood problem. This relationship could reflect the fact that the link between crime and disorder is a *causal* one, or that both are dependent on some third set of factors (such as poverty or neighborhood instability). (10) (emphasis added)

Despite the caution, Skogan still concluded that the data "support the proposition that disorder needs to be taken seriously in research on neighborhood crime and that, both directly and through crime, it plays an important role in neighborhood decline" (75).

Professor Bernard Harcourt (2001), at the University of Chicago Law School, replicated Skogan's research and found a weak-to-no causal link between disorder and serious crime (8–9). The best recent research strongly suggests that disorder and serious crime have common causes, but they don't cause each other, at least not directly (Sampson and Raudenbush 1999, 637–38).

LO 5

Most of the national debate over crime, criminal law books (this one included), and criminal justice courses concentrate on the serious crimes we've analyzed in Chapters 9 through 11. But there's a disconnect between this national focus on one side and local concern on the other. Mayors and local residents do worry about murder, rape, burglary, and theft, but they also care a lot about order on their streets, in their parks, and in other public places.

In one extensive survey of a representative sample of high- and low-crime neighborhoods in major cities, public drinking, followed closely by loitering youths, topped the list of worries among all classes, races, and ethnic groups, among both men and women. Survey participants also listed begging, street harassment, noisy neighbors, vandalism, street prostitution, and illegal vending (Skogan 1990, 2).

Prosecutor Karen Hayter found this out when she created Kalamazoo, Michigan's Neighborhood Prosecutor Program. When Hayter "asked residents what crimes worried them the most, she thought it would be the big ones: murder, assault, breaking and entering," but that's not what she was told. Instead, said Hayter, "Loud noise, littering, loitering, curfew violations, junk autos, rundown houses—those are considered quality-of-life crimes, and they're very important to residents in an area" (National Public Radio 2003).

LO 6

Any examination of criminal law has to recognize quality-of-life crimes as part of early twenty-first-century life. Since the 1980s, state statutes and city ordinances have reinvigorated and molded the old crimes against public order and morals to fit the public's demand that criminal justice preserve, protect, and even restore the quality of life in their communities. The courts have assumed the burden of balancing the social interest in public order against the social interest in individual liberty and privacy (Skogan 1990, 21).

Let's examine how states and localities have shaped traditional public order and morals laws to control the behavior of some "street people" (the homeless, youth gangs, and sex workers) and the quality-of-life crimes commonly associated with them: vagrancy, loitering, panhandling, and gang activity. We'll also examine recent concerns with violent video games and the new statutes that criminalize giving unrestricted access to them by minors. Prostitution is a quality-of-life crime, but we'll discuss it and important issues it raises about equal treatment before the law later in our discussion of "victimless crimes."

LO 7

VAGRANCY AND LOITERING

vagrancy, the ancient crime of poor people wandering with no visible means of support

loitering, the crime of remaining in one place with no apparent purpose

For at least six hundred years, it's been a crime for poor people to roam without visible means of support (vagrancy) or to stand around with no apparent purpose (loitering). The Articles of Confederation specifically denied to paupers the freedom to travel from state to state. In 1837, in *Mayor of New York v. Miln*, the U.S. Supreme Court approved the efforts by the state of New York to exclude paupers arriving by ship. According to the Court, it's as necessary for a state to provide precautionary measures against the moral pestilence of paupers, vagabonds, and possibly convicts as it is to guard against physical pestilence, which may arise from unsound and infectious articles. Every state in the union had and enforced vagrancy and loitering statutes that wrote the Court's view into law (Simon 1992, 631).

Vagrancy

Laws targeting poor people's behavior, and the attitudes behind these laws, began to change during the Great Depression of the 1930s. In 1941, the U.S. Supreme Court struck down a vagrancy statute that prohibited the importation of paupers into California. In response to the argument that the regulation of paupers enjoyed a long history, the Court dismissed the earlier decisions as out of date. According to the Court, "We do not think that it will now be seriously contended that because a person is without employment and without funds he constitutes a 'moral pestilence.'" In a concurring opinion, Justice Robert Jackson encouraged the Court to "say now, in no uncertain terms, that a mere property status, without more, cannot be used by a state to test, qualify, or limit his rights as a citizen of the United States" (*Edwards v. California* 1941, 184).

During the 1960s and 1970s, courts began to strike down vagrancy laws because they unfairly discriminated against the poor. The following excerpt from an opinion written by Chief Justice Thompson of the Nevada Supreme Court in *Parker v. Municipal Judge* (1967) reflects this trend:

> It is simply not a crime to be unemployed, without funds, and in a public place. To punish the unfortunate for this circumstance debases society. The comment of [U.S. Associate Supreme Court] Justice Douglas is relevant: "How can we hold our heads high and still confuse with crime the need for welfare or the need for work?"

In *Papichristou v. City of Jacksonville* (1972), the U.S. Supreme Court struck down the Jacksonville, Florida, vagrancy ordinance, which was nearly identical to virtually every other vagrancy law in the country. Writing for a unanimous Court, Justice Douglas declared the ordinance void for vagueness, because it both failed to give adequate notice to individuals and it encouraged arbitrary law enforcement (Chapter 2). The Court warned that criminal statutes aimed at the poor

> teach that the scales of justice are so tipped that even-handed administration of the law is not possible. The rule of law, evenly applied to minorities as well as majorities, to the poor as well as the rich, is the great mucilage that holds society together. (169)

Loitering

In *Kolender v. Lawson* (1983), the U.S. Supreme Court tightened the constitutional restrictions on loitering statutes. The counterpart to vagrancy, which means to *roam* with no visible means of support, loitering means to "*remain* in one place with no apparent purpose." In *Kolender*, the Court struck down a California statute that combined ancient vagrancy and loitering into a new crime defined as "wandering the streets and failing to produce credible identification" when a police officer asked for it. As it did with the vagrancy statute in *Papachristou*, the Court ruled that the statute was void for vagueness.

According to Harry Simon (1992), staff attorney for the Legal Aid Society in Santa Ana, California:

> With the Supreme Court's decisions in *Papachristou* and *Kolender*, loitering and vagrancy laws ceased to be effective tools to punish and control the displaced poor. While judicial attitudes on vagrancy and loitering laws had changed, local officials perceived the invalidation of these laws as a dangerous assault on their authority to enforce social order. (645)

According to Robert C. Ellickson (1996), professor of Property and Urban Law at the Yale Law School:

> Many judges at the time seemed blind to the fact that their constitutional rulings might adversely affect the quality of urban life and the viability of city centers. It is one thing to protect unpopular persons from wrongful confinement; it is another to imply that these persons have no duty to behave themselves in public places. In addition, federal constitutional rulings are one of the most centralized and inflexible forms of lawmaking. In a diverse and dynamic nation committed to separation of powers and federalism, there is much to be said for giving state and local legislative bodies substantial leeway to tailor street codes to city conditions, and for giving state judges ample scope to interpret the relevant provisions of state constitutions. (1213–14)

At the same time these decisions were easing up on control over the behavior of poor people in public, other events were creating a rapidly—and, to many, a frightening—growth of an underclass. Mental institutions were in the midst of major deinstitutionalization of the mentally ill; family breakdowns and breakups were increasing steeply; crack cocaine was becoming more available on the streets; hard economic times were upon us; and budgets for social programs were tightening.

By the late 1980s, this rising underclass and its public presence and behavior led many city dwellers to conclude that things had gone too far. Liberal columnist Ellen Goodman, in "Swarms of Beggars Cause 'Compassion Fatigue,'" captured this attitude when she wrote, "Today at least, this tourist, walking from one block to another, one cup to another, one city to another, wants to join in a citizens' chorus: 'Enough's enough'" (Simon 1992, 1218).

Municipal codes reflected this growing intolerance of street people's behavior. By the late 1990s, Juliette Smith (1996) found that "at least thirty-nine American cities had initiated or continued policies that criminalize activities associated with homelessness" (29).

Enforcing the laws regulating the behavior of homeless and other street people generates controversy because these laws seem to target the poorest and weakest members of the community to provide for the comfort and convenience of better-off residents. But James Q. Wilson defends these laws, noting that the special competence of courts lies in defining and applying rights; courts typically hear the cases of "an individual beggar, sleeper, or solicitor." Such an individual rarely poses a threat to anyone, "and so the claims of communal order often seem, in the particular case, to be suspect or overdrawn."

On the other hand, according to George Kelling and Catherine Coles (1996):

> But the effects on a community of many such individuals taking advantage of the rights granted to an individual (or often, as the Court sees it, an abstract

> depersonalized individual) are qualitatively different from the effects of a single person. A public space—a bus stop, a market square, a subway entrance—is more than the sum of its parts; it is a complex pattern of interactions that can become dramatically more threatening as the scale and frequency of those interactions increase. As the number of unconventional individuals increases arithmetically, the number of worrisome behaviors increases geometrically. (Kelling and Coles 1996, xiv)

San Francisco is one of many cities whose officials enforced the quality-of-life laws against the "bad public manners" of street people, but it's also a city where a few individuals turned to the courts to fight for the constitutional rights of homeless people. In *Joyce v. City and County of San Francisco* (1994), U.S. District Judge Lowell Jensen heard a motion to grant a **preliminary injunction** (a temporary court order to do or to stop doing something) to stop the city of San Francisco from continuing its Matrix Program. The program was designed to preserve the quality of life on San Francisco streets and other public places. Be aware that granting a preliminary injunction isn't a decision that the plaintiff is right; it only means the plaintiff has presented enough evidence to justify a temporary freeze to give the Court time to decide whether to rule in the plaintiff's favor.

preliminary injunction, a temporary court order to do or to stop doing something

CASE

In* Joyce v. City and County of San Francisco *(1994), *U.S. District Judge Lowell Jensen heard a motion to grant a preliminary injunction to stop the city of San Francisco from continuing its Matrix Program.*

Did the program violate the rights of homeless people?

Joyce v. City and County of San Francisco

846 F. Supp. 843 (N.D.Cal. 1994)

HISTORY

Bobby Joe Joyce, Timothy E. Smith, Thomas O'Halloran, and Jim Tullah, homeless persons, brought an action against the city seeking a preliminary injunction against the Matrix Program that targeted violation of certain ordinances (quality of life offenses) and thus allegedly penalized homeless persons for engaging in life-sustaining activities. U.S. District Judge Lowell Jensen denied the plaintiffs' motion for a preliminary injunction.

JENSEN, J.

FACTS

Plaintiffs to this action seek preliminary injunctive relief, an order to stop enforcing the ordinances, on behalf of themselves and a class of homeless individuals alleged to be adversely affected by the City and County of San Francisco's (the "City's") "Matrix Program." Institution of the Matrix Program followed the issuance of a report in April 1992 by the San Francisco Mayor's Office of Economic Planning and Development, which attributed to homelessness a $173 million drain on sales in the City.

In August of 1993, the City announced commencement of the Matrix Program, and the San Francisco Police Department began stringently enforcing a number of criminal laws. The City describes the program as "initiated to address citizen complaints about a broad range of offenses occurring on the streets and in parks and neighborhoods. [The Matrix Program is] a directed effort to end street crimes of all kinds."

The program addresses quality of life offenses including public drinking and inebriation, obstruction of sidewalks, lodging, camping or sleeping in public parks, littering, public urination and defecation, aggressive panhandling, dumping of refuse, graffiti, vandalism, street prostitution, and street sales of narcotics, among others.

A four-page intradepartmental memorandum addressed to the Police Department's Southern Station Personnel condemned quality of life violations, the "type of behavior [which] tends to make San Francisco a less desirable place in which to live, work or visit," and directed the vigorous enforcement of 18 specified code sections, including prohibitions against trespassing, public inebriation, urinating or defecating in public, removal and possession of shopping carts, solicitation on or near a highway, erection of tents or structures in parks, obstruction and aggressive panhandling.

The memorandum directed all station personnel, "When not otherwise engaged, pay special attention and enforce observed 'Quality of Life' violations. . . ." In a police department bulletin entitled "Update on Matrix Quality of Life Program," Deputy Chief Thomas Petrini referred to the intended nondiscriminatory policy of the program's enforcement measures:

> All persons have the right to use the public streets and places so long as they are not engaged in specific criminal activity. Factors such as race, sex, sexual preference, age, dress, unusual or disheveled or impoverished appearance do not alone justify enforcement action. Nor can generalized complaints by residents or merchants or others justify detention of any person absent such individualized suspicion.

The memorandum stated that the "rights of the homeless must be preserved" and included as an attachment a department bulletin on "Rights of the Homeless," which stated that:

> All members of the Department are obligated to treat all persons equally, regardless of their economic or living conditions. The homeless enjoy the same legal and individual rights afforded to others. Members shall at all times respect these rights.

The police department has, during the pendency of the Matrix Program, conducted continuing education for officers regarding nondiscriminatory enforcement of the program.

The plaintiffs, pointing to the discretion inherent in policing the law enforcement measures of the Matrix Program, allege certain actions taken by police to be "calculated to punish the homeless." As a general practice, the program is depicted by plaintiffs as "targeting hundreds of homeless persons who are guilty of nothing more than sitting on a park bench or on the ground with their possessions, or lying or sleeping on the ground covered by or on top of a blanket or cardboard carton."

The City contests the depiction of Matrix as a singularly focused, punitive effort designed to move "an untidy problem out of sight and out of mind." The City emphasizes its history as one of the largest public providers of assistance to the homeless in the State, asserting that "individuals on general assistance in San Francisco are eligible for larger monthly grants than are available almost anywhere else in California."

By its own estimate, the City will spend $46.4 million for services to the homeless for 1993–94. Of that amount, over $8 million is specifically earmarked to provide housing, and is spent primarily on emergency shelter beds for adults, families, battered women, and youths. An additional $12 million in general assistance grants is provided to those describing themselves as homeless, and free health care is provided by the City to the homeless at a cost of approximately $3 million.

Since its implementation, the Matrix Program has resulted in the issuance of over 3,000 citations to homeless persons.

OPINION

The Court is called upon to decide whether to grant a preliminary injunction. Such relief constitutes an extraordinary use of the Court's powers, and is to be granted sparingly and with the ultimate aim of preserving the status quo pending trial on the merits. The decision whether to grant preliminary injunctive relief is largely left to its discretion. However, this discretion has been circumscribed by the presence or not of various factors, notably, the likelihood that the moving party will prevail on the merits and the likelihood of harm to the parties from granting or denying the injunctive relief.

The injunction sought by plaintiffs at this juncture of the litigation must be denied for each of two independent reasons. First, the proposed injunction lacks the necessary specificity to be enforceable, and would give rise to enforcement problems sufficiently inherent as to be incurable by modification of the proposal. Second, those legal theories upon which plaintiffs rely are not plainly applicable to the grievances sought to be vindicated, with the effect that the Court cannot find at this time that, upon conducting the required balance of harm and merit, plaintiffs have established a sufficient probability of success on the merits to warrant injunctive relief.

(continues)

(continued)

Equal Protection Clause

[Denial of equal protection requires proof that] governmental action [was] undertaken with an intent to discriminate against a particular individual or class of individuals. Such intent may be evinced by statutory language, or in instances where an impact which cannot be explained on a neutral ground unmasks an invidious discrimination. Under the latter approach, a neutral law found to have a disproportionately adverse effect upon a minority classification will be deemed unconstitutional only if that impact can be traced to a discriminatory purpose.

In the present case, plaintiffs have not at this time demonstrated a likelihood of success on the merits of the equal protection claim, since the City's action has not been taken with an evinced intent to discriminate against an identifiable group. Various directives issued within the Police Department mandate the nondiscriminatory enforcement of Matrix. Further, the Police Department has, during the pendency of the Matrix Program, conducted continuing education for officers regarding nondiscriminatory enforcement of the Program. It has not been proven at this time that Matrix was implemented with the aim of discriminating against the homeless. That enforcement of Matrix will, de facto, fall predominantly on the homeless does not in itself effect an equal protection clause violation.

Even were plaintiffs able at this time to prove an intent to discriminate against the homeless, the challenged sections of the Program might nonetheless survive constitutional scrutiny. Only in cases where the challenged action is aimed at a suspect classification, such as race or gender, or premised upon the exercise of a fundamental right, will the governmental action be subjected to a heightened scrutiny.

Counsel for plaintiff proposed at the hearing that this Court should be the first to recognize as a fundamental right the "right to sleep." This is an invitation the Court, in its exercise of judicial restraint, must decline. The discovery of a right to sleep concomitantly requires prohibition of the government's interference with that right. This endeavor, aside from creating a jurisprudential morass, would involve this unelected branch of government in a legislative role for which it is neither fit, nor easily divested once established.

Due Process of Law

Plaintiffs contend the Matrix Program has been enforced in violation of the due process clause of the United States Constitution. Plaintiffs specifically argue that due process has been violated by employing punitive policing measures against the homeless for sleeping in public parks. Plaintiffs claim that San Francisco Park Code section 3.12 has been applied by police in an unconstitutional manner. That section provides,

> No person shall construct or maintain any building, structure, tent or any other thing in any park that may be used for housing accommodations or camping, except by permission from the Recreation and Park Commission.

Plaintiffs contend the Police Department has impermissibly construed this provision to justify citing, arresting, threatening and "moving along" those "persons guilty of nothing more than sitting on park benches with their personal possessions or lying on or under blankets on the ground." Plaintiffs have submitted declarations of various homeless persons supporting the asserted application of the San Francisco Park Code section. It appears, if plaintiffs have accurately depicted the manner in which the section is enforced, that the section may have been applied to conduct not covered by the section and may have been enforced unconstitutionally.

CONCLUSION

In common with many communities across the country, the City is faced with a homeless population of tragic dimension. Today, plaintiffs have brought that societal problem before the Court, seeking a legal judgment on the efforts adopted by the City in response to this problem. The role of the Court is limited structurally by the fact that it may exercise only judicial power, and technically by the fact that plaintiffs seek extraordinary pretrial relief.

The Court does not find that plaintiffs have made a showing at this time that constitutional barriers exist which preclude that effort. Accordingly, the Court's judgment at this stage of the litigation is to permit the City to continue enforcing those aspects of the Matrix Program now challenged by plaintiffs.

Accordingly, plaintiffs' motion for a preliminary injunction is DENIED.

IT IS SO ORDERED.

QUESTIONS

1. Describe the main elements of the Matrix Program.
2. Why did San Francisco adopt the Matrix Program?
3. What are the plaintiffs' objections to the Matrix Program?
4. Assume you're the attorney for San Francisco and argue that the Court should deny the injunction.
5. Assume you're the attorney for the homeless people and argue that the Court should issue the injunction.
6. If you could, what terms would you include in an injunction in this case?

PANHANDLING

According to Robert Tier (1993), general counsel for the American Alliance for Rights and Responsibilities:

> Many City Councils have been convinced to adopt new and innovative controls on antisocial behavior to maintain minimal standards of public conduct and to keep public spaces safe and attractive. . . . One of the most common examples of these efforts are ordinances aimed at aggressive begging. (286)

LO 8

These "new and innovative controls" rely on ancient laws against begging, or panhandling. **Panhandling** consists of stopping people on the street to ask them for food or money. Keep in mind that these antibegging ordinances don't apply to organized charities. So although it's a crime for a private beggar to panhandle for money, it's legal for the Salvation Army to ring their bells to get contributions.

panhandling, stopping people on the street to ask them for food or money

Why the distinction? Supporters of the distinction say the rights revolution has simply gone too far. It's reached the point, they say, where the rights of a minority of offensive individuals trump the quality of life of the whole community. Associate Supreme Court Justice Clarence Thomas (1996) commenting on "how judicial interpretations of the First Amendment and of 'unenumerated' constitutional rights have affected the ability of urban communities to deal with crime, disorder, and incivility on their public streets," told the Federalist Society:

> Vagrancy, loitering, and panhandling laws were challenged [during the rights revolution] because the poor and minorities could be victims of discrimination under the guise of broad discretion to ensure public safety. Moreover, as a consequence of the modern tendency to challenge society's authority to dictate social norms, the legal system began to prefer the ideal of self-expression without much attention to self-discipline or self-control.
>
> What resulted was a culture that declined to curb the excesses of self-indulgence—vagrants and others who regularly roamed the streets had rights that could not be circumscribed by the community's sense of decency or decorum. (269)

"Hey, buddy, can you spare some change?" is clearly speech. And, of course, the First Amendment guarantees individuals freedom of speech. But recall that free speech doesn't mean you can say anything you want anywhere at anytime (Chapter 2). The U.S. Supreme Court has "rejected the notion that a city is powerless to protect its citizens from unwanted exposure to certain methods of expression which may legitimately be deemed a public nuisance" (Scheidegger 1993, 7).

The Court has established a number of tests to determine whether ordinances violate the First Amendment guarantee of free speech. One is to look at the place where the speech takes place. In traditional public forums—streets, sidewalks, and parks—where people have since ancient times expressed their views, the freedom to solicit is virtually unrestricted. In designated public forums—places the government chooses to make available to the public—the government has more leeway to regulate solicitation. In nonpublic forums—airports, bus stations, railroad stations, subways, and shopping malls—the government has broad power to restrict and even prohibit solicitation (Scheidegger 1993, 7–9).

The First Amendment free speech clause also permits time, place, and manner regulations. According to the U.S. Supreme Court (*R.A.V. v. City of St. Paul* 1992; Chapter 2), to be constitutional, restrictions have to satisfy three elements of a time, place, and manner test:

time, place, and manner test, to be constitutional, restrictions on free speech can't be based on the content of the speech, serve a significant government interest, and leave open other channels of expression

1. They're not based on the content of the speech.
2. They serve a significant government interest—for example, maintaining the free flow of pedestrian traffic.
3. They leave open other channels of expression.

The first element in the test bars the use of the regulation to suppress any message about social conditions that panhandlers are trying to convey. The second element is hotly contested. Advocates for panhandlers argue that the regulation of panhandling is really a government policy of removing "unsightly" poor people from public view. Others maintain that the "purpose is to permit people to use the streets, sidewalks, and public transportation free from the borderline robbery and pervasive fraud which characterizes so much of today's panhandling" (Scheidegger 1993, 10–11). The third element requires the regulation to allow panhandlers to beg in other ways. So a panhandling ordinance that prohibits "aggressive panhandling" leaves panhandlers free to beg peaceably. So do bans on fraudulent panhandling or panhandling in subways. Panhandlers can beg honestly on streets and in parks (10–11).

In addition to forum and time, place, and manner restrictions, the First Amendment gives the government considerable leeway to regulate nonverbal expression (expressive conduct; Chapter 2). This would allow direct efforts to stop panhandlers from approaching people or blocking the sidewalk to beg or receiving the money they solicited.

Finally, the First Amendment grants commercial speech (advertising and other means of "asking for" money) less protection than other types of speech. Because begging relies

Criminalizing being poor: Is it ethical public policy?

It's too bad so many people are falling into poverty at a time when it's almost illegal to be poor. You won't be arrested for shopping in a Dollar Store, but if you are truly, deeply, in-the-streets poor, you're well advised not to engage in any of the biological necessities of life—like sitting, sleeping, lying down, or loitering. City officials boast that there is nothing discriminatory about the ordinances that afflict the destitute, most of which go back to the dawn of gentrification in the '80s and '90s. "If you're lying on a sidewalk, whether you're homeless or a millionaire, you're in violation of the ordinance," a city attorney in St. Petersburg, Florida, said in June, echoing Anatole France's immortal observation that "the law, in its majestic equality, forbids the rich as well as the poor to sleep under bridges."

Instructions

1. Read "Is It Now a Crime to Be Poor?" by *New York Times* columnist Barbara Ehrenreich.
2. Assume you're a policy advisor to the mayor of your town or city. Write a one-page position paper on the "right" response to the "problem" of using the streets for the "biological necessities of life."

Source: Ehrenreich, Barbara. 2009 (August 9). "Is It Now a Crime to Be Poor?" *The New York Times.*

on talking listeners into handing over their money, panhandling is commercial speech. Jimmy Gresham, a homeless person, took that argument to the U.S. District Court and asked for an injunction against the enforcement of the Indianapolis ban on aggressive panhandling. The District Court rejected his commercial speech argument and denied his request for the injunction. The U.S. Court of Appeals for the Seventh Circuit affirmed the District Court's decision in *Gresham v. Peterson* (2000).

GANG ACTIVITY

LO 9

"Bands of loitering youth" seriously threaten their quality of life, say many city residents (Skogan 1990, 23). Gangs can include everything from casual groups of kids who are just hanging out drinking a little bit all the way to "organized fighting squads" who terrorize neighborhoods. The casual groups do little more than "bother" residents. According to one observer, "They are neighborhood kids, and they sometimes make a nuisance of themselves. Actually they stand there because they have no place to go" (23). Gangs composed of older, rowdier members are more threatening.

According to a resident in a neighborhood with one of these gangs:

> Sometimes I walk out of my house and start to try to walk down the street, and a gang will cross the street and try to scare me and my mother. A gang used to sit and drink beer and smoke pot in front of our stairs. My mom used to come out and tell them to get off; they would, and then when she would go into the house they'd come back, sit down, and look at us. Actually we're afraid to walk around in the neighborhood after it gets dark. I stay right in front of the house where my mom can see me. (24)

Let's look at some criminal law and civil law efforts to control gang activities and then review the latest research on the effectiveness of these efforts.

Criminal Law Responses to Gang Activity

LO 9

A number of state and city governments have passed criminal laws to regulate gang behavior. In some places, it's a crime to participate in a gang. Some statutes and ordinances have stiffened the penalties for crimes committed by gang members. Others make it a crime to encourage minors to participate in gangs. Some have applied organized crime statutes to gangs. A few have punished parents for their children's gang activities. Cities have also passed ordinances banning gang members from certain public places, particularly city parks.

In 1992, Chicago was facing a skyrocketing increase in crime rates that many outspoken people blamed on street gangs. But unlike the sweeping antiloitering injunction approved in California, the Chicago City Council passed a modern version of the ancient loitering ordinances (discussed in the "Loitering" section). Chicago's ordinance gave its police the power to order groups of loiterers (people who "remain in one place with no apparent purpose") to disperse or face arrest if officers reasonably believed that one of the loiterers was a gang member (Poulos 1995, 379–81).

No one was surprised when the ordinance set off an angry debate. Mayor Richard Daley Jr. expressed one view: "In some areas of the city, street gangs are terrorizing residents and laying claim to whole communities." Bobbie Crawford, a waitress, expressed another view: "When kids reach a certain age they hang around on street corners. I sure wouldn't like my children taken to a police station for hanging around." And Joan Suglich, mother of six, asked, "What if somebody asks his boys to walk him home so gang members don't jump him. Are police going to arrest them?"

Nor was anyone surprised when the debate ended up in the U.S. Supreme Court. In *City of Chicago v. Morales* (1999), a divided Court decided that the ordinance was void for vagueness. Several justices, but not a majority, also argued that the ordinance violated the right to come and go as you please without unreasonable government interference.

CASE

In **City of Chicago v. Morales** *(1999), a divided Supreme Court decided that the ordinance that gave the police the power to order groups of loiterers to disperse or face arrest was void for vagueness.*

Was the loitering ordinance void for vagueness?

City of Chicago v. Morales

527 U.S. 41 (1999)

HISTORY

Jesus Morales and other defendants in several separate cases were charged in the Circuit Court of Cook County with violating the Chicago anti-gang ordinance. Morales and the defendants in one case moved to dismiss the actions against them. The Circuit Court, Cook County, granted the motion. The city appealed. The Illinois Appellate Court affirmed.

The defendants in a second case were charged with violating the ordinance. The Circuit Court dismissed the charges. The Appellate Court affirmed. The city petitioned for leave to appeal, which the Appellate Court granted.

In a third case, the defendants were charged, in the Circuit Court, with violating the ordinance, were convicted, and were sentenced to jail terms. The defendants appealed. The Appellate Court reversed. The city petitioned for leave to appeal.

After granting the petitions to appeal in all three cases, and consolidating the cases for one hearing, the Supreme Court of Illinois affirmed.

The U.S. Supreme Court granted certiorari and affirmed the judgment of the Illinois Supreme Court.

STEVENS, J.

FACTS

In 1992, the Chicago City Council enacted the Gang Congregation Ordinance, which prohibits "criminal street gang members" from "loitering" with one another or with other persons in any public place. The ordinance creates a criminal offense punishable by a fine of up to $500, imprisonment for not more than six months, and a requirement to perform up to 120 hours of community service. Commission of the offense involves four elements.

First, the police officer must reasonably believe that at least one of the two or more persons present in a "public place" is a "criminal street gang member." Second, the persons must be "loitering," which the ordinance defines as "remain[ing] in any one place with no apparent purpose." Third, the officer must then order "all" of the persons to disperse and remove themselves "from the area." Fourth, a person must disobey the officer's order. If any person, whether a gang member or not, disobeys the officer's order, that person is guilty of violating the ordinance.

Two months after the ordinance was adopted, the Chicago Police Department promulgated General Order 92-4 to provide guidelines to govern its enforcement. That order purported to establish limitations on the enforcement discretion of police officers "to ensure that the antigang loitering ordinance is not enforced in an arbitrary or discriminatory way."

The limitations confine the authority to arrest gang members who violate the ordinance to sworn "members of the Gang Crime Section" and certain other designated officers and establish detailed criteria for defining street gangs and membership in such gangs.

In addition, the order directs district commanders to "designate areas in which the presence of gang members has a demonstrable effect on the activities of law abiding persons in the surrounding community," and provides that the ordinance "will be enforced only within the designated areas." The city, however, does not release the locations of these "designated areas" to the public.

During the three years of its enforcement, the police issued over 89,000 dispersal orders and arrested over 42,000 people for violating the ordinance. In the ensuing enforcement proceedings, two trial judges upheld the constitutionality of the ordinance, but 11 others ruled that it was invalid.

The city believes that the ordinance resulted in a significant decline in gang-related homicides. It notes that in 1995, the last year the ordinance was enforced, the gang-related homicide rate fell by 26 percent. In 1996, after the ordinance had been held invalid, the gang-related homicide rate rose 11 percent. However, gang-related homicides fell by 19 percent in 1997, over a year after the suspension of the ordinance.

Given the myriad factors that influence levels of violence, it is difficult to evaluate the probative value of this statistical evidence, or to reach any firm conclusion about the ordinance's efficacy.

OPINION

The basic factual predicate for the city's ordinance is not in dispute. The very presence of a large collection of obviously brazen, insistent, and lawless gang members and hangers-on on the public ways intimidates residents, who become afraid even to leave their homes and go about their business. That, in turn, imperils community residents' sense of safety and security, detracts from property values, and can ultimately destabilize entire neighborhoods.

We have no doubt that a law that directly prohibited such intimidating conduct . . . [as described in the facts] would be constitutional, but this ordinance broadly covers a significant amount of additional activity. Uncertainty about the scope of that additional coverage provides the basis for respondents' claim that the ordinance is too vague.

The freedom to loiter for innocent purposes is part of the "liberty" protected by the Due Process Clause of the Fourteenth Amendment. We have expressly identified this "right to remove from one place to another according to inclination" as "an attribute of personal liberty" protected by the Constitution. Indeed, it is apparent that an individual's decision to remain in a public place of his choice is as much a part of his liberty as the freedom of movement inside frontiers that is "a part of our heritage" or the right to move "to whatsoever place one's own inclination may direct" identified in Blackstone's Commentaries.

Vagueness may invalidate a criminal law for either of two independent reasons. First, it may fail to provide the kind of notice that will enable ordinary people to understand what conduct it prohibits; second, it may authorize and even encourage arbitrary and discriminatory enforcement.

A law fails to meet the requirements of the Due Process Clause if it is so vague and standardless that it leaves the public uncertain as to the conduct it prohibits. It is difficult to imagine how any citizen of the city of Chicago standing in a public place with a group of people would know if he or she had an "apparent purpose." If she were talking to another person, would she have an apparent purpose? If she were frequently checking her watch and looking expectantly down the street, would she have an apparent purpose?

Since the city cannot conceivably have meant to criminalize each instance a citizen stands in public with a gang member, the vagueness that dooms this ordinance is not the product of uncertainty about the normal meaning of "loitering," but rather about what loitering is covered by the ordinance and what is not.

The Illinois Supreme Court emphasized the law's failure to distinguish between innocent conduct and conduct threatening harm. Its decision followed the precedent set by a number of state courts that have upheld ordinances that criminalize loitering combined with some other overt act or evidence of criminal intent (ordinance criminalizing loitering with purpose to engage in drug-related activities; ordinance criminalizing loitering for the purpose of engaging in or soliciting lewd act).

The city's principal response to this concern about adequate notice is that loiterers are not subject to sanction until after they have failed to comply with an officer's order to disperse. "Whatever problem is created by a law that criminalizes conduct people normally believe to be innocent is solved when persons receive actual notice from a police order of what they are expected to do."

We find this response unpersuasive for at least two reasons. First, the purpose of the fair notice requirement is to enable the ordinary citizen to conform his or her conduct to the law. No one may be required at peril of life, liberty or property to speculate as to the meaning of penal statutes. Such an order cannot retroactively give adequate warning of the boundary between the permissible and the impermissible applications of the law.

Second, the terms of the dispersal order compound the inadequacy of the notice afforded by the ordinance. It provides that the officer "shall order all such persons to disperse and remove themselves from the area." This vague phrasing raises a host of questions. After such an order issues, how long must the loiterers remain apart? How far must they move? If each loiterer walks around the block and they meet again at the same location, are they subject to arrest or merely to being ordered to disperse again? As we do here, we have found vagueness in a criminal statute exacerbated by the use of the standards of "neighborhood" and "locality." . . . Both terms are elastic and, dependent upon circumstances, may be equally satisfied by areas measured by rods or by miles.

(continues)

(continued)

The Constitution does not permit a legislature to set a net large enough to catch all possible offenders, and leave it to the courts to step inside and say who could be rightfully detained, and who should be set at large. This ordinance is therefore vague "not in the sense that it requires a person to conform his conduct to an imprecise but comprehensible normative standard, but rather in the sense that no standard of conduct is specified at all."

The broad sweep of the ordinance also violates the requirement that a legislature establish minimal guidelines to govern law enforcement. There are no such guidelines in the ordinance. In any public place in the city of Chicago, persons who stand or sit in the company of a gang member may be ordered to disperse unless their purpose is apparent.

The mandatory language in the enactment directs the police to issue an order without first making any inquiry about their possible purposes. It matters not whether the reason that a gang member and his father, for example, might loiter near Wrigley Field is to rob an unsuspecting fan or just to get a glimpse of Sammy Sosa leaving the ballpark; in either event, if their purpose is not apparent to a nearby police officer, she may—indeed, she "shall"—order them to disperse. Recognizing that the ordinance does reach a substantial amount of innocent conduct, we turn, then, to its language to determine if it "necessarily entrusts lawmaking to the moment-to-moment judgment of the policeman on his beat."

The principal source of the vast discretion conferred on the police in this case is the definition of loitering as "to remain in any one place with no apparent purpose." [That definition] provides absolute discretion to police officers to determine what activities constitute loitering.

It is true that the requirement that the officer reasonably believes that a group of loiterers contains a gang member does place a limit on the authority to order dispersal. That limitation would no doubt be sufficient if the ordinance only applied to loitering that had an apparently harmful purpose or effect, or possibly if it only applied to loitering by persons reasonably believed to be criminal gang members. Not all of the respondents in this case, for example, are gang members.

The city admits that it was unable to prove that Morales is a gang member but justifies his arrest and conviction by the fact that Morales admitted "that he knew he was with criminal street gang members." But this ordinance requires no harmful purpose and applies to non-gang members as well as suspected gang members. It applies to everyone in the city who may remain in one place with one suspected gang member as long as their purpose is not apparent to an officer observing them. Friends, relatives, teachers, counselors, or even total strangers might unwittingly engage in forbidden loitering if they happen to engage in idle conversation with a gang member.

In our judgment, the Illinois Supreme Court correctly concluded that the ordinance does not provide sufficiently specific limits on the enforcement discretion of the police "to meet constitutional standards for definiteness and clarity."

We recognize the serious and difficult problems testified to by the citizens of Chicago that led to the enactment of this ordinance. We are mindful that the preservation of liberty depends in part on the maintenance of social order. However, in this instance the city has enacted an ordinance that affords too much discretion to the police and too little notice to citizens who wish to use the public streets.

Accordingly, the judgment of the Supreme Court of Illinois is AFFIRMED.

DISSENT

THOMAS, J. JOINED BY
REHNQUIST, CJ. AND SCALIA, J.

The duly elected members of the Chicago City Council enacted the ordinance at issue as part of a larger effort to prevent gangs from establishing dominion over the public streets. By invalidating Chicago's ordinance, I fear that the Court has unnecessarily sentenced law-abiding citizens to lives of terror and misery. The ordinance is not vague. Any fool would know that a particular category of conduct would be within its reach. Nor does it violate the Due Process Clause. The asserted "freedom to loiter for innocent purposes" is in no way "deeply rooted in this Nation's history and tradition."

The human costs exacted by criminal street gangs are inestimable. In many of our Nation's cities, gangs have "virtually overtaken certain neighborhoods, contributing to the economic and social decline of these areas and causing fear and lifestyle changes among law-abiding residents."

Ordinary citizens like Ms. D'Ivory Gordon explained that she struggled just to walk to work:

> When I walk out my door, these guys are out there. They watch you. They know where you live. They know what time you leave, what time you come home. I am afraid of them. I have even come to the point now that I carry a meat cleaver to work with me. I don't want to hurt anyone, and I don't want to be hurt. We need to clean these corners up. Clean these communities up and take it back from them.

Eighty-eight-year-old Susan Mary Jackson echoed her sentiments, testifying:

> We used to have a nice neighborhood. We don't have it anymore. I am scared to go out in the daytime, you can't pass because they are standing. I am afraid to go to the store. I don't go to the store because I am afraid. At my age if they look at me real hard, I be ready to holler.

Another long-time resident testified:

> I have never had the terror that I feel everyday when I walk down the streets of Chicago. I have had my windows broken out. I have had guns pulled on me. I have been threatened. I get intimidated on a daily basis, and it's come to the point where I say, well, do I go out today? Do I put my ax in my briefcase? Do I walk around dressed like a bum so I am not looking rich or got any money or anything like that?

Today, the Court focuses extensively on the "rights" of gang members and their companions. It can safely do so—the people who will have to live with the consequences of today's opinion do not live in our neighborhoods. Rather, the people who will suffer from our lofty pronouncements are people like Ms. Susan Mary Jackson; people who have seen their neighborhoods literally destroyed by gangs and violence and drugs.

They are good, decent people who must struggle to overcome their desperate situation, against all odds, in order to raise their families, earn a living, and remain good citizens. As one resident described, "There is only about maybe 1 or 2 percent of the people in the city causing these problems maybe, but it's keeping 98 percent of us in our houses and off the streets and afraid to shop."

By focusing exclusively on the imagined "rights" of the 2 percent, the Court today has denied our most vulnerable citizens the very thing that Justice STEVENS elevates above all else—the "freedom of movement." And that is a shame.

QUESTIONS

1. List the four elements in the Chicago antigang ordinance.
2. List the specific arguments the majority gave to support its conclusion that the ordinance was vague.
3. Explain specifically all of the reasons why the dissenting judges disagreed.
4. Would "any fool" know what conduct this ordinance prohibited? Defend your answer.
5. Did the majority properly balance the interest in community order with the individual liberty? Explain your answer.
6. If the majority didn't properly strike the balance, how would you do it differently? Explain your answer.

Civil Law Responses to Gang Activity

LO 10

In addition to criminal penalties, cities have also turned to civil remedies to control gang activity. For example, in the ancient civil remedy, the injunction to abate public nuisances (which is still used), city attorneys ask courts to declare gang activities and gang members public nuisances. They ask the courts to issue **public nuisance injunctions**, which are court orders to eliminate the particular nuisance.

public nuisance injunctions, court orders to eliminate the particular nuisance

According to the California Supreme Court, in *People ex rel. Gallo v. Acuna* (1997), a public nuisance may be any act

> which alternatively is injurious to health or is indecent, or offensive to the senses; the result of the act must interfere with the comfortable enjoyment of life or property; and those affected by the act may be an entire neighborhood or a considerable number of people.

The city attorney of Santa Clara in *Acuna* asked for an injunction ordering gang members to stop doing all of the following:

1. Standing, sitting, walking, driving, gathering or appearing anywhere in public view with any other defendant herein, or with any other known "VST" (VarrioSureno Town or VarrioSureno Locos) member;
2. Drinking alcoholic beverages in public excepting consumption on properly licensed premises or using drugs;
3. Possessing any weapons including but not limited to knives, dirks, daggers, clubs, nunchukas, BB guns, concealed or loaded firearms, and any other illegal weapons as defined in the California Penal Code, and any object capable of inflicting serious bodily injury including but not limited to the following: metal pipes or rods, glass bottles, rocks, bricks, chains, tire irons, screwdrivers, hammers, crowbars, bumper jacks, spikes, razor blades, razors, sling shots, marbles, ball bearings;
4. Engaging in fighting in the public streets, alleys, and/or public and private property;
5. Using or possessing marker pens, spray paint cans, nails, razor blades, screwdrivers, or other sharp objects capable of defacing private or public property;
6. Spray painting or otherwise applying graffiti on any public or private property, including but not limited to the street, alley, residences, block walls, vehicles and/or any other real or personal property;
7. Trespassing on or encouraging others to trespass on any private property;
8. Blocking free ingress and egress to the public sidewalks or street, or any driveways leading or appurtenant thereto in "Rocksprings";
9. Approaching vehicles, engaging in conversation, or otherwise communicating with the occupants of any vehicle or doing anything to obstruct or delay the free flow of vehicular or pedestrian traffic;
10. Discharging any firearms;
11. In any manner confronting, intimidating, annoying, harassing, threatening, challenging, provoking, assaulting and/or battering any residents or patrons, or visitors to "Rocksprings," or any other persons who are known to have complained about gang activities, including any persons who have provided information in support of this Complaint and requests for Temporary Restraining Order, Preliminary Injunction and Permanent Injunction;
12. Causing, encouraging, or participating in the use, possession and/or sale of narcotics;
13. Owning, possessing or driving a vehicle found to have any contraband, narcotics, or illegal or deadly weapons;
14. Using or possessing pagers or beepers in any public space;
15. Possessing channel lock pliers, picks, wire cutters, dent pullers, sling shots, marbles, steel shot, spark plugs, rocks, screwdrivers, "slim jims" and other devices capable of being used to break into locked vehicles;
16. Demanding entry into another person's residence at any time of the day or night;
17. Sheltering, concealing or permitting another person to enter into a residence not their own when said person appears to be running, hiding, or otherwise evading a law enforcement officer;
18. Signaling to or acting as a lookout for other persons to warn of the approach of police officers and soliciting, encouraging, employing or offering payment to others to do the same;

19. Climbing any tree, wall, or fence, or passing through any wall or fence by using tunnels or other holes in such structures;
20. Littering in any public place or place open to public view;
21. Urinating or defecating in any public place or place open to public view;
22. Using words, phrases, physical gestures, or symbols commonly known as hand signs or engaging in other forms of communication which describe or refer to the gang known as "VST" or "VSL" as described in this Complaint or any of the accompanying pleadings or declarations;
23. Wearing clothing which bears the name or letters of the gang known as "VST" or "VSL";
24. Making, causing, or encouraging others to make loud noise of any kind, including but not limited to yelling and loud music at any time of the day or night.

The California trial court issued the injunction, and the California Supreme Court upheld the injunction against challenges that it both violated freedom of association and was void for vagueness. Injunctions, like crimes that outlaw gang activities, call for balancing community and individual rights. The community interest in the quality of life requires peace, quiet, order, and a sense of security. At the same time, even members of street gangs have the right to associate, express themselves, travel freely, and be free from vague laws (see Chapter 2, "The Void-for-Vagueness Doctrine" section).

Review of Empirical Research on Gangs and Gang Activity

LO 10

Youth crime in the United States remains near the lowest levels seen in the past three decades, yet public concern and media coverage of gang activity has skyrocketed since 2000. Fear has spread from neighborhoods with long-standing gang problems to communities with historically low levels of crime, and some policy makers have declared the arrival of a national gang "crisis." Yet many questions remain unanswered. How can communities and policy makers differentiate between perceived threats and actual challenges presented by gangs? Which communities are most affected by gangs, and what is the nature of that impact? How much of the crime that plagues poor urban neighborhoods is attributable to gangs? And what approaches work to promote public safety?

The Justice Policy Institute (Greene and Pranis 2007) conducted an extensive review of research on gangs "because we believe that the costs of uninformed policy making—including thousands of lives lost to violence or imprisonment—are simply too high" (5). They point out that the news is full of stories that hammer home a cycle, repeated in city after city: crime goes up in [you name the city]; law enforcement cracks down on gang activity; and crime goes down (7). But a review of the investigations of gang enforcement efforts in seventeen jurisdictions since the 1980s tells a different story. Findings from the investigations include:

- Lack of correspondence between the problem, typically lethal and/or serious violence, and a law-enforcement response that targets low-level, nonviolent misbehavior
- Resistance on the part of key agency personnel to collaboration or implementation of the strategy as designed
- Evidence that the intervention had no effect or a negative effect on crime and violence
- A tendency for any reductions in violent crime to evaporate quickly, often before the end of the intervention
- Poorly designed evaluations that make it impossible to draw any conclusions about the effects of an intervention

- Failure of replication efforts to achieve results comparable to those of pilot programs
- Severe imbalance of power and resources between law enforcement and community partners that hampers the implementation of balanced gang control initiatives (7)

civil gang injunctions (CGI), noncriminal lawsuits brought by cities seeking restraining orders to bar gang members from gang activities

In this section, we'll focus on the latest available research on the effectiveness of civil injunctions to control gangs. Civil gang injunctions (CGI) are a growing gang suppression strategy. They're noncriminal lawsuits brought by cities seeking restraining orders to bar gang members from gang activities, which can include interacting with one another, entering specific sections of the city, and wearing gang colors.

Sociologists Cheryl Maxson, Karen Hennigan, and David Sloane (2005) conducted the first scientific assessment of CGIs in San Bernardino, California. They surveyed residents in five neighborhoods about their perceptions and experience of crime, gang activity, and neighborhood quality eighteen months before and six months after the injunction was issued. They found positive evidence of short-term effects in the disordered, primary injunction area, including less gang presence, fewer reports of gang intimidation, and less fear of confrontation with gang members, but no significant changes in intermediate or long-term outcomes except for less fear of crime (577).

Professor Jeffrey Grogger (2002) also evaluated the effectiveness of CGIs. Grogger developed an extensive database of neighborhood-level reported crime counts from four police jurisdictions within Los Angeles County. He constructed two different comparison samples of neighborhoods not covered by injunctions to control for underlying trends that could cause an overstatement of the CGIs' effects. The analysis indicates that, in the first year after the injunctions are imposed, they lead the level of violent crime to decrease by 5 to 10 percent (69).

Saint Paul, Minnesota, is an excellent example of the cycle of news coverage, the findings from the investigations reported in the Gang Wars report (Grogger 2002), and the adoption of the city's CGI (next case excerpt).

CASE

City of Saint Paul v. East Side Boys and Selby Siders (2009) *involves the 2009 civil gang injunctions in the city of Saint Paul, Minnesota.*

Should members of the gang be banned from attending the Rondo Days celebration?

City of Saint Paul v. East Side Boys and Selby Siders

(City of Saint Paul 2009*)

HISTORY

On June 30, 2009, Saint Paul, Minnesota, initiated two CGI lawsuits against the East Side Boys and the Selby Siders, two local gangs with a long history of violent criminal conduct, including a recent murder and numerous recent confrontations involving gunfire.

FACTS

"As we have clearly stated, criminal gangs are not welcome in our community. The public has a right to be free from criminal gang violence and intimidation, and as the home of some of the most prominent community festivals in the country like Rondo Days, we are doing everything we can to protect our community from gang activity. Saint Paul is a safe city, and these injunctions are an innovative tool to send a clear message to gangs that we will not tolerate any violence in our community," Mayor Chris Coleman said.

*This case excerpt is based on information from the Saint Paul, Minnesota, website.

"These civil injunctions have proven to be worthwhile tools, as they specifically focus on those gangs who have repeatedly demonstrated purpose and action that tears at the safety and fabric of the community events like Rondo," Saint Paul Police Chief John Harrington said. "In addition to the benefits of enforceability, these injunctions speak to Saint Paul's historical standards of community safety."

The civil legal actions are intended to help prevent criminal gang activity from occurring during the Rondo Days festival on July 18. [The Rondo Days Festival is an annual celebration to remember the African-American neighborhood of Rondo, which was split by the construction of Interstate 94 in the mid-1960s.] City Attorney John Choi said the two civil actions are a part of an important law enforcement strategy to proactively disrupt criminal gang activity in Saint Paul's neighborhoods. "We had great public safety results because of the civil gang injunction against the Sureño 13 earlier this year, and we have every expectation that this proactive effort will work again with the Selby Siders and East Side Boys," Choi said.

The Civil Gang Injunction Statute (Minn. Stat. §§ 617.91–617.97) authorizes a city attorney, county attorney or the attorney general to commence a civil action against criminal gangs to enjoin criminal gang activity. The civil lawsuit filed by Choi seeks injunctive relief pursuant to the Civil Gang Injunction Statute that was developed by the Community Prosecution Unit of the Saint Paul City Attorney's Office and passed by the Minnesota Legislature in 2007. In May, the Ramsey County District Court issued Minnesota's first civil gang injunction against a criminal gang in *City of Saint Paul v. Sureño 13* (Ramsey County District Court Case Number 62-CV-09–3113). The use of civil gang injunctions has been upheld by the California Supreme Court and Appellate Courts in Texas.

Among other things, the City of Saint Paul is seeking a court order prohibiting the known leaders of the East Side Boys and Selby Siders from associating with known gang members anywhere near the Rondo Days Festival.

. . . "From our city attorney's office to our police department to our Second Shift initiative, much of what we do in Saint Paul is about public safety and improving the lives of our residents," Mayor Coleman said. "The civil lawsuits filed demonstrate the proactive approach Saint Paul is taking to prevent gangs from taking root in Saint Paul."

QUESTIONS

1. Assume you're an aide to the city. Would you recommend that the city go forward with the injunction?
2. Relying on the information in your text, what specifically would you want the mayor, police chief, city attorney, and the public to know about CGIs?

VIOLENT VIDEO GAMES

LO 2

On Tuesday, April 20, 1999, students Eric Harris and Dylan Klebold, two students at Columbine High School near Littleton, Colorado, murdered twelve students and one teacher, wounded twenty-four others, and then committed suicide. A number of municipal ordinances banning violent video games from arcades followed, because, it was contended, playing the games can cause violent behavior in youths who watch them. For example, the preamble to the Indianapolis video game ordinance reads:

> [E]xposure of children to graphic and lifelike violence contained in some video games has been correlated to violent behavior, and in fact the perpetrators of recent school shootings in Columbine, Colorado; Jonesboro, Arkansas; and Paducah, Kentucky were reported to be avid fans of such games. (*Interactive Digital Software Association v. St. Louis County* 2002, 1129)

The ban on violent video games echoes the ancient common law crime known as "breach of the peace," which included both actual disorderly conduct and conduct that "tends to provoke or excite others to break it [the peace]" (p. 448, Blackstone 1769, 148). More, it reflects the *broken windows theory* that minor disorder leads to serious crimes (p. 450).

CASE

In **Interactive Digital Software Association** *(2002), digital software companies brought suit against St. Louis County, the County Executive of St. Louis County, and the Chief of Police of St. Louis County alleging that the county's anti–violent video game ordinance violated their right of free expression.*

Can counties ban juveniles from playing violent video games in arcades?

Interactive Digital Software Association v. St. Louis County

200 Fed.Supp.2d 1126 (E.D.Mo., 2002)

HISTORY

Interactive Digital Software Association, and other companies or associations of companies that create, publish, distribute, sell, rent, and/or make available to the public, video games, including both computer and arcade games, and related software. They brought suit against St. Louis County, the County Executive of St. Louis County, and the Chief of Police of St. Louis County alleging that St. Louis County Ordinance No. 20,193 (Oct. 26, 2000), . . . infringes upon constitutionally protected rights of free expression. The Ordinance . . . makes it unlawful for someone to knowingly sell, rent, make available, or permit the "free play" of violent video games to minors without a parent or guardian's consent. The U.S. District Court, Eastern Division, of Missouri denied the plaintiff's motion for summary judgment.

LIMBAUGH, Senior District Judge.

FACTS

Prior to the passage of the Ordinance, the St. Louis County Council's Justice, Health and Welfare Committee held two hearings on the Ordinance, on October 12, 2000, and October 19, 2000. There was testimony at the hearings by Dr. Craig Anderson, a psychology professor at Iowa State University, and Dr. Margaret Dolan, the Principal of McNair Elementary School in University City, Missouri. In his testimony, Dr. Anderson referred to studies which found that violent video games caused psychological damage to children. . . . Representatives from the video game industry also testified before the Committee hearings. . . . Most of the industry's representatives stated that . . . their only problem with the Ordinance is that they believe it violates the First Amendment.

The Ordinance starts out with a six paragraph Preamble indicating why the ordinance was being enacted and what compelling interests the County has in enacting this legislation. The Preamble is as follows:

> WHEREAS, exposure of children to graphic and lifelike violence contained in some video games has been correlated to violent behavior, and in fact the perpetrators of recent school shootings in Columbine, Colorado; Jonesboro, Arkansas; and Paducah, Kentucky were reported to be avid fans of such games; and
>
> WHEREAS, numerous medical studies have cited a link between prolonged playing of violent video games and violent, antisocial and otherwise harmful behavioral patterns, and the American Medical Association suggests that exposure to violence, such as in these video games, causes children to imitate violent behavior, glorify violent heroes, become desensitized to violence and learn that violence is rewarded; and
>
> WHEREAS, violence by and between children has become a severe threat to the physical and emotional health of children; and
>
> WHEREAS, disruptive behavior by children who regularly watch or play violent video games has become a problem in schools and inhibits educators' ability to educate their students; and
>
> WHEREAS, St. Louis County as a political subdivision of the State of Missouri has a compelling interest in protecting the physical and emotional health of children; and
>
> WHEREAS, parents and guardians should have the power to control the types of games their children play and to control their exposure to violent and sexual materials. (Plaintiffs do not challenge the provisions of the Ordinance insofar as they are applied solely to sexual content. Therefore, the Court will not address those portions of the Ordinance.)

The Ordinance requires owners and managers of arcades to place video games which they know to be harmful to minors separate and apart from other video games, and designate such areas as "Restricted–17." The Ordinance makes it unlawful to knowingly sell or rent a video game, which is harmful to a minor, unless that minor is accompanied by a parent or guardian who consents to the purchase or sale.

The Ordinance also makes it unlawful to knowingly admit a minor to a "Restricted–17" area, and to knowingly permit the free play of a video game which is harmful to minors on premises which video games are sold or rented.

"Harmful to minors" is defined in the Ordinance to mean a video game that "predominantly appeals to minors' morbid interest in violence," "is patently offensive to prevailing standards in the adult community as a whole with respect to what is suitable material for minors, lacks serious literary, artistic, political or scientific value as a whole for minors, and contains . . . graphic violence." The term "graphic violence" is defined in the Ordinance as the "visual depiction or representation of realistic serious injury to a human or human-like being where such serious injury includes amputation, decapitation, dismemberment, bloodshed, mutilation, maiming or disfiguration."

. . .

The video game industry and the technology employed in creating video games has changed drastically in the last few decades. There are a variety of different types of video games, including, but not limited to, adventure games, puzzle games, sports games, racing games, simulator games, hunting games, teenage and adult educational games, role-playing games, and shooting games. Plaintiffs provided the affidavit of Douglas Lowenstein, President of the Interactive Digital Software Association in support of its motion. Mr. Lowenstein attempted to explain the process of creating video games and included some examples, however, the Court did not get to view the final product of these games. St. Louis County did provide a videotape depicting four different games: "The Resident of Evil Creek," "Mortal Combat," "DOOM," and "Fear Effect."

OPINION

. . .

The Court must first decide whether video games even constitute speech so as to receive at least some protection from the First Amendment. If video games do fall within the category of protected speech, the Court must then determine what standard of scrutiny to apply to the regulations. The next step in the Court's analysis is to apply the proper standard of scrutiny to the facts of this case. Finally, the Court must review whether the Ordinance is vague and overbroad.

I. Are Video Games a Form of Speech?

. . .

In order to find speech, there must exist both an intent to convey a particularized message and a great likelihood that this message will be understood.

. . .

In the early 1980s, courts began facing the issue of whether video games were forms of expression entitled to First Amendment protection. Courts almost unanimously held that video games lacked the expressive element necessary to trigger the First Amendment. [According to one court,] a video game, like a pinball game, a game of chess, or a game of baseball, is pure entertainment with no informational element. Some of the games "talk" to the participant, play music, or have written instructions, but that alone does not provide the missing element of "information." . . . Video games "contain so little in the way of particularized form of expression" that they cannot be "fairly characterized as a form of speech protected by the First Amendment."

. . .

This Court reviewed four different video games, and found no conveyance of ideas, expression, or anything else that could possibly amount to speech. . . . The Court fails to see how video games express ideas, impressions, feelings, or information unrelated to the game itself. The Court also finds that "violent" video games do not have any more expressive elements than other video games just because they are deemed to be violent. In other words, "violence" does not automatically create expression. Just as a baseball game is not a form of expression, neither is a hockey game. If within that hockey game, two players get in a fight, or someone gets sliced with a hockey stick and blood flies, the game does not suddenly become a form of expression. Another applicable analogy is boxing, where the main objective is to punch and knock out the opponent. However, boxing is still just a sport, not speech. In the same light, video games do not become a form of expression just because they contain violence.

(continues)

(continued)

II. Standard of Scrutiny If Video Games Are Speech

. . .

The Court finds that, assuming the video games are a form of expression protected by the First Amendment, the regulations in the Ordinance are content-based. Video games that show graphic violence are treated differently than other video games, and therefore the regulations are based on the content of the games. . . . Therefore, the Court finds that strict scrutiny would apply if the Ordinance did in fact regulate speech. The government would have to show a compelling interest in regulating these types of games and show that the regulations are narrowly tailored to advance that interest.

III. Applying Strict Scrutiny to the Ordinance If It Does Restrict Speech

The Ordinance survives strict scrutiny if the regulations on video games serve a compelling governmental interest, and if those restrictions are carefully tailored to achieve the stated interests. The County has two stated interests: 1) to protect the physical and emotional health of the children in St. Louis County, and 2) to assist parents to be the guardians of their children's well-being.

The well-being of its children is a subject within the County's constitutional power to regulate. "Constitutional interpretation has consistently recognized that the parents' claim to authority in their own household to direct the rearing of their children is basic in the structure of our society." It is essential that the custody, care and nurture of the child reside first in the parents, and parents who have this "primary responsibility for children's well-being are entitled to the support of laws designed to aid discharge of that responsibility."

Government also has an independent interest in the well-being of its youth. The knowledge that parental control cannot always be provided and "society's transcendent interest in protecting the welfare of children justify reasonable regulation of the sale of material to them." Accordingly, the County's stated interests are legitimate in the abstract. The remaining issue is whether the County can conclude, as it has, that exposure to these video games are harmful to the children's well-being.

The County relied on testimony from Dr. Anderson and Dr. Dolan, as well as the studies referred to by these witnesses, in concluding that video games are physically and emotionally harmful to children. Dr. Anderson testified regarding a study in which he and Dr. Brad Bushman had just completed concerning the playing of violent video games. He told the Council that they found that playing violent video games for as short of a time as 10 to 15 minutes does in fact lead to aggressive behavior in the immediate situation. He discussed these effects and how aggressive behavior occurs. He also found that pro-social behavior decreases after exposure to violent video games. He also indicated that children have more aggressive thoughts and frequently more aggressive behavior after playing violent video games.

Dr. Anderson testified that there are a number of studies on the effect of watching violent movies and violent TV shows. The conclusions of these studies are that there is a causal connection between viewing violent movies and TV programs and violent acts. Dr. Anderson indicated that there is a distinction between the passive viewing of violent movies and TV programs and these interactive video games. He explained that with video games players are acting out acts of violence and depending on the skill of the player the acts of violence per minute increases. Players are told to identify with the aggressor and the player controls the action of the character. In addition, unlike TV or movies, video games are addictive in nature. Dr. Anderson found in his study that violent video games provide a complete learning environment for aggression, with simultaneous exposure to modeling, reinforcement, and rehearsal of behaviors.

At the hearing, Dr. Anderson referred to a Lt. Colonel Dave Grossman who has written books on the subject of violent video games and his publications suggest that these violent video games are killing simulators. According to Grossman, the United States Army and Marines use the same techniques that violent video games depend on to train recruits to kill. The Army actually uses a video game—"Doom"—to train soldiers. Dr. Anderson indicated that with movies and TV children may learn violence as a response but with video games they learn how to carry out these acts.

. . .

Society in general believes that continued exposure to violence can be harmful to children. The motion picture industry accepts this theory, which is why extremely violent movies are rated-R. Children under seventeen are prohibited from seeing rated-R movies at the theaters unless accompanied by an adult, and movie rental stores will not rent rated-R movies to minors without parental consent.

The Court also finds that the statute is narrowly drawn to regulate only that expression which is necessary to address the government's compelling interests. . . . The Ordinance does not prohibit video game "creators" from making any video games, however, the Ordinance does limit the number of people video game makers can reach with their video games. Nonviolent video games can be purchased and played by everyone. According to plaintiffs, that is the majority of the games. Violent video games can be purchased and played by all those over seventeen, which according to plaintiffs are the majority of the purchasers. Violent video games can also be purchased and played by those under the age of seventeen if the parents have given their consent. So in practice, the video game industry is only restricted in conveying their violent "message" to those under seventeen years of age whose parents do not want their children viewing and/or playing that particular type of game.

The Ordinance makes it as easy as possible for parents to give their consent. The parents can physically be present to give their permission. They can also give pre-approval of the purchase or rental if the vendor has established an electronic or manual system for pre-approval. At the arcades, parents can appear with the minor and give permission for the minor to be stamped or otherwise marked to signify that the minor has permission on that date, or the parent can give pre-approval of the minor's presence in Restricted–17 areas if the arcade has established an electronic or manual system for pre-approval. The Court finds that the regulations in the Ordinance are narrowly drawn to only serve those stated governmental interests.

. . . The Court finds, based on the evidence in the record, that plaintiffs failed to show that St. Louis County Ordinance No. 20,193 (Oct. 26, 2000), is unconstitutional and that they are entitled to judgment as a matter of law. Therefore, plaintiffs' summary judgment motion is denied.

QUESTIONS

1. List exactly what the ordinance prohibits.
2. Identify the County's interests in banning minors from playing violent video games.
3. Summarize the court's reasons for upholding the ordinance's constitutionality.
4. Summarize the findings of the empirical evidence linking violent behavior to violent video games.
5. Do you agree that violent video games can lead to horrors like that at Columbine? Before you answer, consider Judge Richard Posner's (2001, 578) assessment of the same empirical findings in a case involving an Indianapolis ordinance almost identical to St. Louis County's:

> The City [Indianapolis] appeals to social science to establish that games such as "The House of the Dead" and "Ultimate Mortal Kombat 3," games culturally isomorphic with [identical to] (and often derivative from) movies aimed at the same under 18 crowd, are dangerous to public safety. The social science evidence on which the City relies consists primarily of the pair of psychological studies . . . which are reported in Craig A. Anderson & Karen E. Dill, "Personality Processes and Individual Differences—Video Games and Aggressive Thoughts, Feelings, and Behavior in the Laboratory and in Life," 78 *J. Personality & Soc. Psych.* 772 (2000).
>
> Those studies do not support the ordinance. . . . The studies do not find that video games have ever caused anyone to commit a violent act, as opposed to feeling aggressive, or have caused the average level of violence to increase anywhere. And they do not suggest that it is the *interactive* character of the games, as opposed to the violence of the images in them, that is the cause of the aggressive feelings.
>
> The studies thus are not evidence that violent video games are any more harmful to the consumer or to the public safety than violent movies or other violent, but passive, entertainments. It is highly unlikely that they are more harmful, because "passive" entertainment aspires to be interactive too and often succeeds. When Dirty Harry or some other avenging hero kills off a string of villains, the audience is expected to identify with him, to revel in his success, to feel their own finger on the trigger. It is conceivable that pushing a button or manipulating a toggle stick engenders an even deeper surge of aggressive joy, but of that there is no evidence at all.

Does Judge Posner have a point? Explain your answer.

"VICTIMLESS CRIMES"

victimless crimes, crimes involving willing adult participants who don't see themselves as victims

"Victimless crimes" are crimes involving willing participants. Let's be clear about how we're going to use this term in this section. First, it applies only to consenting adults, not minors. Second, it refers to crimes committed by adults who don't see themselves as victims of their behavior. Referring to many crimes in which the perpetrators don't see themselves as victimized as "victimless crimes" is controversial; Table 12.3 lists some of these crimes.

LO 11

We've already covered the crimes associated with illegal drugs in a constitutional democracy (Chapters 2 and 3, *Robinson v. California* and *Powell v. Texas*, respectively). And we've discussed the application of the principles of *actus reus* and *mens rea* to drug crimes (Chapters 3 and 4). Let's look at the controversy surrounding the issue and then focus on **prostitution**, engaging in sex in exchange for money or its equivalent.

prostitution, engaging in sex in exchange for money or its equivalent

First, a little history: In medieval days, when the Church was more powerful than kings and queens, ecclesiastical courts had total power to try and punish crimes against "family and morals," including all nonviolent sexual behavior and marital relations breaches. As monarchs grew stronger, royal courts eventually gained control over most of these offenses. Once the monarch's courts took them over, they became the crimes against public morals, most of which would be on the list of anyone who subscribes to the idea of victimless crimes (Morris and Hawkins 1970, chap. 1).

Controversy makes it tough to balance public good and individual privacy in these cases. There's broad agreement that the crimes against persons and property you read about in Chapters 9 through 11 deserve punishment. However, no such agreement exists when it comes to whether those listed in Table 12.3 should be crimes. In fact, there's a deep rift between those who believe criminal law should enforce morals to "purify" society and those who believe just as deeply that consenting adults' nonviolent sexual conduct is none of the criminal law's business (Morris and Hawkins 1970).

Perhaps no issue in criminal policy has caused more acrimonious debate over a longer time than that of the role law should play in enforcing public morals. Two English Victorian scholars, the philosopher John Stuart Mill and the historian Sir James F. Stephen, started the debate. Their two major positions were summed up in the widely known and debated Wolfenden Report, an English document recommending the decriminalization of private sexual conduct of two types, between adult consenting male homosexuals and between adult sex workers and their customers.

TABLE 12.3

"Victimless Crimes"
Substance abuse (Chapters 2 and 3)
Internet censorship
Loitering
Prostitution
Sodomy (*Lawrence v. Texas*, Chapter 2)
Seat-belt law violations
Helmet law violations
Violating bans on bungee jumping
Assisted suicide

Here's the summary of the majority of the commission's position:

> There remains one additional argument which we believe to be decisive, namely, the importance which society and the law ought to give to individual freedom of choice and action in matters of private morality. Unless a deliberate attempt is to be made by society, acting through the agency of the law, to equate the sphere of crime with that of sin, there must remain a realm of private morality and immorality which is, in brief and crude terms, not the law's business. To say this is not to condone or encourage private immorality. On the contrary, to emphasize the personal private nature of moral or immoral conduct is to emphasize the personal and private responsibility of the individual for his own actions, and that is a responsibility which a mature agent can properly be expected to carry for himself without the threat of punishment from the law. (Wolfendon Report 1957, 20–21)

And here's English jurist Sir Patrick Devlin's rebuttal to the majority position:

> Society is entitled by means of its laws to protect itself from dangers. . . . There is disintegration when no common morality is observed and history shows that the loosening of moral bonds is often the first state of disintegration, so that society is justified in taking the same steps to preserve its moral code as it does to preserve its government and other essential institutions. The suppression of vice is as much the law's business as the suppression of subversive activities; it is no more possible to define a sphere of private morality than it is to define one of private subversive activity. (Wolfendon Report 1957, 48)

For most of U.S. history, prostitution was discussed solely within the framework of victimless crimes—whether it's the law's business to interfere with adults' rights to buy and sell sex. In previous editions, we did the same. But prostitution is so much more than that, so we'll discuss it in the larger context that it deserves. That larger context is the unequal treatment of men and women in the United States in the twenty-first century. Let's turn to that discussion now.

PROSTITUTION

> The law's desire to punish bad girls has often been moderated by its wish to save nice boys from harm, inconvenience or embarrassment.
>
> (Lefler 1999, 13)

Prostitution involves at least two people—the prostitute who provides the sexual service and the client ("john," or "trick" or patron) who buys the service. Frequently, there's also a third party—the promoter (pimp) who controls, finds johns, and takes a cut of the earnings. We'll concentrate in this section on the double standard in law and social reality for prostitutes and johns. Vice squad officers accost prostitutes on the street, or act as decoys to catch them offering sex for money, and arrest them. The same officers allow their clients to remain anonymous and leave. (That's where the name "john" originated.) In this section, we'll examine the history of this ancient crime; the double standard today; and two remedies for the double standard—equal protection lawsuits and local government programs that target johns.

The History of Prostitution Laws

From colonial times, prostitution was the common law crime of "selling one's body for money." In the 1800s, states passed statutes that made prostitution a crime. By 1900, there were anti-prostitution statutes in every state (Kandel 1992, 341). (That remains true today, except for seven counties in Nevada.) The criminal law moved from a "hands off" approach to enforcing these laws during most of the 1800s to an aggressive "swift and harsh" punishment response by 1900. The aggressive response went beyond targeting women for actually "selling one's body for money." Police officers arrested women who were on the street after dark on the assumption that "any woman on the street at that time intended to solicit money for sex" (Kandel 1992, 341).

Inside the courtroom, the harsh treatment continued; judges sentenced women based on their sexual history, not on the elements of prostitution—selling sex for money. But, while women were hauled into court to answer charges, no johns were in sight to answer for buying sex, let alone having to answer for their sexual history. "Thus, men satisfied their sexual desires with no consequences while women alone paid the price" (Lefler 1999, 14).

Why did the double standard persist throughout so much of U.S. history? Most scholars point to two beliefs with deep roots in Victorian culture and society:

1. "While males were viewed as reformable, even though they committed an immoral sexual act," women were "lost causes, incapable of redemption." (Lefler 1999, 4)
2. Men can't control their sex drive, but women don't even have a sex drive. So the justice system didn't punish the men, treating prostitutes as necessary. (Of course, they were necessary *evils*.) (14–15)

The Double Standard Today

The solution to the double standard required two major changes. First, legislatures had to enact statutes to provide for punishing the prostitute *and* the john. These laws are necessary, but they're not enough to reach true equal treatment without a second change—namely, that law enforcement, prosecutors, and courts have to enforce the statutes equally against prostitutes and johns.

At present, there are three types of prostitution statutes—those that

1. punish the prostitute but not the john.
2. punish both but punish the prostitute more severely.
3. punish both the prostitute and the john equally.

A few states retain the double standard in its traditional form (number 1). Those that punish both but punish the prostitute more (number 2) follow the MPC § 251.2 (ALI 1985). Johns can never go to jail, only be fined, no matter how many times they're arrested. Prostitutes can do time for multiple offenses. MPC reporters justify the difference on the ground that because prostitutes receive money, their involvement in the crime is greater and, therefore, they deserve harsher punishment. Courts often agree with the reporters' double standard rationale. Many state statutes now follow 3; they provide for full equality of punishment for both prostitutes and johns.

Let's turn our attention from the law on the books to the law in action—namely, the equality of *enforcement*, where the available statistics show that the double standard is far from dead. The FBI collects numbers of arrests for "Prostitution and Commercialized Vice," which it defines as:

> The unlawful promotion of or participation in sexual activities for profit, including attempts. To solicit customers or transport persons for prostitution purposes; to own, manage, or operate a dwelling or other establishment for the purpose of providing a place where prostitution is performed; or to otherwise assist or promote prostitution.

In 2010, the FBI reported 10,844 prostitution arrests nationwide. Figure 12.1 depicts the percentages of those arrests by sex.

MALE–FEMALE PROSTITUTION ARRESTS, 2010

FIGURE 12.1

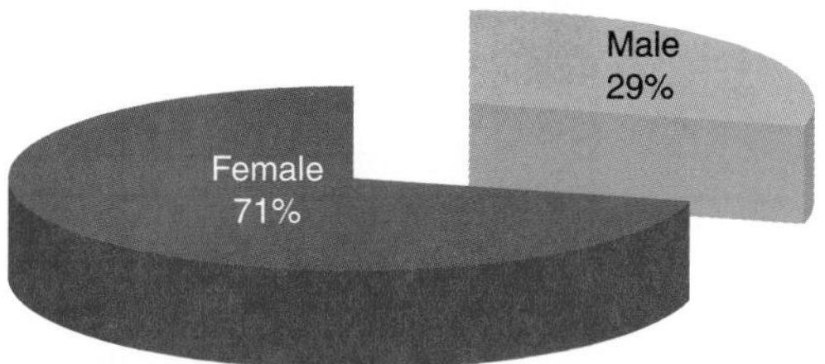

Source: FBI Uniform Crime Report 2011 (Sept.), *Crime in the United States, 2010,* Table 33.

Look at this gap between men and women with some caution. We don't know how many men are johns because we don't know how many men are pimps and prostitutes. And we don't know how many women are madams (e.g., Heidi Fleiss). Furthermore, and more important, we don't know how many prostitution arrests are hidden in the "disorderly conduct" numbers (see FBI UCR 2011, Table 33) because of officer discretion and department policy to arrest prostitutes (but not johns) for disorderly conduct (Kandel 1992, 332). Still, on balance, it's safe to assume that the number of johns is likely less, and the number of prostitutes even greater, than the chart depicts.

What accounts for this persistent double standard, whatever the size of the gender gap? One explanation is that police decoys arrest prostitutes; therefore, there are no johns to arrest (Lefler 1999, 20). Another is that by arresting prostitutes, they're catching the "profiteer." But one lawyer wondered, if that's true why don't they go after the pimps? They're the ones who "exploit women for profit" (21).

Court Remedies for the Double Standard

Some individual judges have acted to fight discriminatory enforcement. For example, former Boston Municipal Court Judge Sarah Hunt, who heard prostitution cases daily, refused to hear cases against prostitutes unless officers had arrested the john, too (Kandel 1992, 340). Some prostitutes argue that the no-johns-to-arrest problem created by decoys denies them equal protection of the law. It's extraordinarily difficult to succeed in equal protection challenges (as you learned in Chapter 2, p. 47).

CASE

In* Commonwealth v. An Unnamed Defendant *(1986), *the Massachusetts Appeals Court upheld the dismissal of prostitution and nightwalking charges because the police only arrested prostitutes, not johns.*

Is it constitutional to arrest only prostitutes and not johns?

Commonwealth v. An Unnamed Defendant

492 N.E.2d 1184 (Mass.App. 1986)

HISTORY

The defendant was charged and convicted in a bench trial in the Brockton District Court, and sentenced to two concurrent one-month terms in the house of correction. She appealed. The Superior Court, Plymouth, dismissed charges of prostitution and nightwalking. The Commonwealth appealed. The Appeals Court affirmed the Superior Court's dismissal of the complaints.

CUTTER, J.

The first complaint charged (see G.L. c. 272, § 53A) that the defendant on February 4, 1985, in Brockton, "did unlawfully solicit or receive compensation for soliciting for a prostitute." A second complaint charged (G.L. c. 272, § 53) that on

(continues)

(continued)
February 21, 1985, also in Brockton, the defendant was "a common nightwalker, habitually walking in the streets in the night-time for the purpose of prostitution." This is an appeal by the Commonwealth from the dismissal of the two complaints because of discriminatory enforcement of the applicable statutes.

> General Laws c. 272, § 53A, reads: "Any person who engages, agrees to engage, or offers to engage in sexual conduct with another person in return for a fee, or any person who pays, agrees to pay or offers to pay another person to engage in sexual conduct, or to agree to engage in sexual conduct with another natural person may be punished by imprisonment in a jail or house of correction for not more than one year, or by a fine of not more than five hundred dollars, or by both such fine and imprisonment."

> General Laws c. 272, § 53 reads: "Common night walkers, common street walkers, both male and female, common railers and brawlers, persons who with offensive and disorderly acts or language accost or annoy persons of the opposite sex, lewd, wanton and lascivious persons in speech or behavior . . . and persons guilty of indecent exposure may be punished by imprisonment in a jail or house of correction for not more than six months, or by a fine of not more than two hundred dollars, or by both such fine and imprisonment."

There she filed a motion to dismiss the complaints alleging discriminatory enforcement of the statutes. This motion was accompanied by an affidavit of the defendant and also by an affidavit of the defendant's counsel. The defendant's affidavit asserted that, when she was arrested, no male person was arrested with her on either charge, and that "the practice of the Brockton police department is to arrest female prostitutes and to decline to arrest male customers and male prostitutes." Attached to that the defendant on February 4, 1985, in Brockton, "did unlawfully solicit or receive compensation for soliciting for a prostitute." A second complaint charged (G.L. c. 272, § 53) that on February 21, 1985, also in Brockton, the defendant was "a common nightwalker, habitually walking in the streets in the night-time for the purpose of prostitution." The defendant was convicted of both charges at a bench trial in the Brockton District Court and sentenced to two concurrent one-month terms in a house of correction. She appealed to the jury session of the District Court.

Attached to her affidavit were four pages of lists of arrests by the Brockton police for prostitution, for soliciting prostitution, and for being a common nightwalker, showing the results set out in the margin, for a period of about one year. The arrests by Brockton police for prostitution and related offenses June 6, 1984, to May 10, 1985, were compiled (by a process described in the affidavit of the defendant's attorney) from police department computer records. These records, in summary, showed the following arrests:

The records also showed seventeen arrests for open and gross behavior—mostly for offenses such as indecent exposure. Only one of these arrests was of a female. There were no arrests for adultery or fornication and one arrest of a male for "unnatural acts."

A district court judge (not the judge who had presided at the defendant's bench trials) held an evidentiary hearing on June 14, 1985. No opposing affidavits, filed in behalf of the prosecution, appear in the record. One Brockton police detective, called by the defendant, testified about the department's typical methods of surveillance of female suspects on certain streets in Brockton. [The transcript of the hearing furnished to this court was faint and illegible.

	PROSTITUTION	SOLICIT PROSTITUTION	COMMON NIGHTWALKER
Female	36	23	104
Male	1	2	2
Total	37	25	106

In the future, counsel should expect such transcripts to be rejected by the clerk. The panel expresses thanks to defense appellate counsel for attaching to her brief a readable copy of this transcript.] These methods involve observation of (a) males in motor vehicles being waved at by females on the street, (b) the female entering the vehicle and driving off with the male, and (c) both returning after an interval, and then (d) a repetition of the process with a different male. The detective testified that, in such circumstances, "ordinarily" the police do not arrest the driver of the vehicle, or "radio ahead to another unit" to make an arrest. In cases where the vehicle is followed, and a "sexual act is [found] going on," only the female is arrested. This defendant, when the detective arrested her on February 4, 1985, was performing fellatio on the male then in the vehicle. The male was not arrested.

Defense counsel in an attempt further to show discrimination inquired about a later arrest of another alleged female nightwalker. Upon objection the judge praised the "candid and forthright" testimony of the detective, and said that the officer has "indicated that they're searching for female nightwalkers." In answer to an inquiry by the judge whether it was department policy not to arrest the male on prostitution related charges, the detective replied, "There hasn't been a male arrested . . . since we've been working on the prostitution area."

As to the offense of being a nightwalker charged as taking place on February 21, 1985, the detective testified that they saw "several males leaving with" the defendant "at different times." Not one of these males was arrested. On one occasion they "did radio ahead that the car in which . . . [the defendant] was a passenger was to be stopped." This was done. The male operator of the vehicle was not arrested.

On cross-examination, the prosecutor received one answer that when the detective made an arrest on "a soliciting charge and there's a male present . . . it's . . . general policy that you don't arrest the male." The detective stated the basic reason for the policy was that complaints from area citizens related "mainly [to] the girls," and that the women arrested are known to the police, whereas the males are not "familiar" to the police. Defense counsel's offer to put on another officer to corroborate the first detective's testimony was not accepted. The judge directed the discussion to whether there was a difference in the effect of the assertions of discrimination (based upon the sex of the participants) between (a) the charge of soliciting, and (b) the charge of being a nightwalker.

In *Commonwealth v. King,* 372 N.E.2d 196 (1977), decided prior to the enactment of § 53A in 1983, the Supreme Judicial Court dealt under the earlier statutory law with somewhat the same situation now presented. The opinion stated that the term "prostitution" did not "include the conduct of persons who hire . . . another to engage in sexual activity." It, on that account, did not accept the contention (by the female defendants in the cases then considered) that § 53 as thus defined "unconstitutionally criminalizes female conduct but not male conduct" in violation of art. 106 of the Amendments to the Constitution of the Commonwealth, the Equal Rights Amendment (ERA), adopted in 1976. The decision stated "that § 53 was designed to attack merely one phase of a problem." As to discriminatory enforcement, the *King* opinion said that the defendants' contention "fails because they [the female prostitute defendants] presented no evidence to show that their customers were not arrested and prosecuted" and, particularly "when there is no statutory provision for the prosecution of the customers."

The author of the *King* opinion (in a separate opinion) pointed out (that he would broaden the opinion to assert "that unlawful discrimination in enforcement can be proved by a showing that the police department or prosecutor's office followed an unjustifiable policy of prosecuting prostitutes and not their customers," which could be treated as sex-based on "a showing that most prostitutes are women and most customers are males." Later in the separate opinion it was said, "If a police custom exists of invariably, and regardless of the circumstances, sending the male customer on his way while at the same time escorting the accused female prostitute into the police car or patrol wagon, this in my view departs from the purpose of the equal rights amendment, and may not even conform to the expressed legislative intention to control prostitution through the processes of the criminal law."

After the *King* case, was decided, the views expressed in the separate opinion in that case were given support by the 1983 statute, now found in c. 272, § 53A. The broad form of § 53A provided the

(continues)

(continued)

statutory criminalization of acts of the prostitute's customers which was thought to be absent in the *King* case.

We are of the opinion that the judge correctly concluded that the proof made before him warranted dismissal of the complaints because they were the product of an arbitrary or unequal application of impartial laws. Because we presume that criminal prosecutions are undertaken in good faith, without intent to discriminate, the defendant bears the initial burden of demonstrating selective enforcement. To meet this burden, the defendant must present evidence which raises at least a reasonable inference of impermissible discrimination. . . . The defendant must show

(1) that a broader class of persons than those prosecuted has violated the law

(2) that failure to prosecute was either consistent or deliberate . . . and

(3) that the decision not to prosecute was based on an impermissible classification such as race, religion, or *sex*. (emphasis supplied)

We think each of the three mentioned requisites of the defendant's proof was satisfied by the material before the trial judge. We hold that once a defendant has raised a reasonable inference of selective prosecution, the Commonwealth must rebut that inference or suffer dismissal of the underlying complaint. At that point, and where it appears that the government is in ready possession of the facts, it is not unreasonable to require the government to come forward with evidence and to make its records and evidence available. This the prosecution did not do in the present case and thus nothing was before the judge (or now is before us even by affidavit) which controverts the essentially uncontradicted proof of police practices on which the judge relied.

Order dismissing complaints affirmed.

QUESTIONS

1. State the elements of the two crimes the prostitute was charged with and convicted of in the trial court.
2. Summarize the facts about how the johns were treated differently from prostitutes and why they were treated differently.
3. Summarize the arguments the defendant made and the evidence she submitted to support her argument that she was discriminated against in the enforcement of the statutes.
4. Summarize the court's reasons for ruling that the defendant was denied equal protection of the laws in this case.
5. Summarize the arguments made to support the decision in *Commonwealth v. King* (1997), which the court discussed.
6. Do you believe she was denied equal protection of the laws? Back up your answer with points in the case and from your text.

LOCAL GOVERNMENT PROGRAMS TARGETING JOHNS

Some local governments have created new programs directed at johns. They differ from the traditional policy of incarcerating only prostitutes. They may deter johns, but are programs directed only at johns discriminatory and, therefore, no better than the double standard that punishes only prostitutes? Think about that in connection with three john-focused policies: car forfeiture, driver's license revocation, and publishing the names of arrested johns in local newspapers and online.

Car Forfeiture

Men who police arrest for paying to have sex in their cars have their cars impounded automatically. Some statutes require the return of the cars if johns pay heavy fines. Others go further and sell the impounded cars. There's no empirical data to tell us whether these laws reduce the amount of prostitution. But, even if they do deter prostitution-related activities, they're not enough to solve the problem. They only apply to johns arrested in their cars. Also, the johns don't always own the cars they're driving. In addition, some courts have ruled that seizing johns' cars before they're convicted denies them the right to due process. Cities such as Oakland, California, have solved this problem by providing for an immediate civil forfeiture hearing (Lefler 1999, 28–29).

Driver's License Revocation

This proposal allows police officers to revoke johns' driver's licenses if they're caught in their cars having sex with a prostitute. Minnesota has adopted a variation on this type of law, placing a notation on the driver's license of any john convicted of prostitution-related crimes committed in his car. Section 609.324 of the Minnesota Criminal Code, Penalties for Patrons, Subdivision 5, "Use of motor vehicle to patronize prostitutes; driving record notation," provides that, "When a court sentences a person convicted of violating this section while acting as a patron, the court shall determine whether the person used a motor vehicle during the commission of the offense and whether the person has previously been convicted of violating this section."

If the court finds that the person used a motor vehicle during the commission of the offense, it shall forward its finding along with an indication of whether the person has previously been convicted of a prostitution offense to the commissioner of public safety who shall record the finding on the person's driving record. If the person has previously been convicted of a violation of this section, the finding becomes public data (Minnesota Criminal Code 2011, §609.324).

Revocation, like forfeiture, is only a partial solution. It targets only johns who commit the offense while they're in their cars. Critics such as Julie Lefler (1992) recommend that states should pass statutes that mandate revocation for all johns, whether cars are involved or not. "This would provide police with another weapon in their arsenal to deter johns from these offenses." Lefler concedes that it won't affect johns who don't have licenses. She also points out that revoking johns' driver's licenses who weren't arrested in their cars might be unconstitutional. She argues, however, that

> having a driver's license is a privilege rather than a right. If prostitutes can be forced to give up their entire freedom by being incarcerated for their offense, it is more than fair that johns in turn be forced to give up a mere privilege as a consequence of their crimes. (Lefler 1992, 30)

Publishing Names in Various Media

"No one entering La Mesa, Calif., can miss the billboards that announce 'Attention johns: We take pictures.' La Mesa Mayor Art Madrid says the signs—and the promise to print those pictures in local papers—have reduced prostitution. 'If we have no johns, we'll have no hookers,' he says" (Larrabee 1995, A3). According to attorney Courtney Guyton Persons (1996), the secrecy of anonymous sex "has been slapped on billboards as communities, desperate to disinfect their crime-ridden streets, expose solicitors' secret sins to sunlight" (1526–27):

> Critics question its effectiveness and its cost. They point to a New Jersey paper that listed a young engineer who had just lost his wife and three children. When he saw his name in the paper, he killed himself (1527). City attorneys and defense lawyers worry about its constitutionality. Newspapers worry about getting sued. Editorials call it inhumane and disproportionate. But law enforcement "insists that nothing else has worked, and community groups figure it's worth a try." (1527)

Persons is wary of the wisdom of choosing the policy of shaming johns:

> Unlike other types of penalties, shame punishments are explicitly designed to make a public spectacle of the offender's conviction and punishment, and to trigger a negative, downward change in the offender's self-concept. Colonial society's sense of community and common faith may once have imbued shame penalties with some power to reinforce normative consensus. Today, however, in a climate of increasing normative fragmentation, that function seems unlikely. Instead, shame punishments may sacrifice individuals' dignity with little discernible impact on prostitution. Whatever their meaning, shame punishments' qualitative distinction from other sanctions raises humaneness concerns that form a possible cost of selecting shaming. (1570)

SUMMARY

LO 1 Crimes against public order and morals are areas of criminal law that involve mostly very minor crimes but, nonetheless, affect many more people than the crimes against persons and their property.

LO 2 "Quality of life" crimes refer to the laws that are meant to control "bad manners" in public places. They underscore the tension between liberty and order in a constitutional democracy.

LO 3 Disorderly conduct crimes are crimes against public order and morals. They take two main forms: individual or group disorderly conduct. Historically, group disorderly conduct consisted of three misdemeanors at the common law: unlawful assembly, rout, and riot. In unlawful assembly three or more people gathered to commit an unlawful act. In rout, three or more people moved in the direction of commission of a riot. In riot, three or more people committed disorderly conduct.

LO 4 The "broken windows" theory states there's a link between minor quality-of-life offenses and more serious crimes. The empirical findings as to whether there's a link are mixed.

LO 5 Most people are more worried about bad public manners than they are about serious crimes. These results have been found in a number of studies conducted in the United States.

LO 6 There's wide consensus within high- and low-crime neighborhoods in major cities that public drinking, followed closely by loitering youths, tops the worries among all classes, races, and ethnic groups, among both men and women.

LO 7 For at least six hundred years, it's been a crime for poor people to roam without visible means of support (vagrancy) or to stand around with no apparent purpose (loitering).

LO 8 New and innovative controls against aggressive begging by street people rely on ancient laws against begging, or panhandling. States can control the time, place, and manner of panhandling but not the content of panhandling.

LO 9 "Bands of loitering youth" seriously threaten the quality of life in communities. A number of state and city governments have passed criminal laws to regulate gang behavior. Antigang ordinances meet due process and liberty requirements if they define "loitering" more specifically than just hanging out with no apparent purpose.

Cities have sought civil gang injunctions (CGIs) to control gang behavior, but the evidence is mixed as to the effectiveness of CGIs. LO 10

The term "victimless crime" applies to (1) consenting adults, not minors and (2) to crimes committed by adults who don't see themselves as victims of their behavior. An example is prostitution. Prostitution is an ancient business, prospering in all cultures at all times no matter the condemnation of religion and morals. LO 11

KEY TERMS

crimes against public order, p. 446
order, p. 446
liberty, p. 446
disorderly conduct crimes, p. 447
actual disorderly conduct, p. 448
constructive disorderly conduct, p. 448
group disorderly conduct, p. 449
unlawful assembly, p. 449
rout, p. 450
riot, p. 450
"quality of life" crimes, p. 450
broken-windows theory, p. 450
vagrancy, p. 452
loitering, p. 452
preliminary injunction, p. 454
panhandling, p. 457
time, place, and manner test, p. 458
public nuisance injunctions, p. 463
civil gang injunctions (CGI), p. 466
"victimless crimes," p. 472
prostitution, p. 472

LEARNING OBJECTIVES

1. To understand how defining and applying crimes against the state reflects the enduring idea of balancing security and freedom during wartime emergencies.
2. To know that treason is the only crime defined in the Constitution; that it's a fundamental weapon against present allegiance and support to foreign enemies; and that it's very difficult to prove because of its history.
3. To know the definition of three ancient crimes of disloyalty: sedition, sabotage, and espionage.
4. To appreciate that crimes against potential terrorist attacks are subject to the limits placed on traditional criminal law.
5. To know that the most commonly prosecuted crimes against the state since September 11, 2001, have involved alleged terrorists or terrorist organizations.
6. To appreciate that "providing material support or resources" is open to constitutional challenges.

Former CIA officer John Kiriakou, left, and his attorney, John Hundley, leave federal court in Alexandria, Virginia, on Monday, January 23, 2012. In the latest criminal case in the Obama administration's effort to punish leakers, Kiriakou, who helped track down and capture a top terror suspect, was charged with disclosing classified secrets about his teammates to the media.

AP Images/Jacquelyn Martin

CRIMES AGAINST THE STATE 13

CHAPTER OUTLINE

Did he provide material support to a terrorist organization?

Ralph Fertig, a lifelong pacifist and human activist, and the Humanitarian Law Project—all United States citizens or associations—seek an injunction and declaration providing that, without violating the statute, they can

(1) "train members of the Kurdistan Workers' Party (PKK), a designated terrorist organization, on how to use humanitarian and international law to peacefully resolve disputes" to achieve their goal of establishing an independent Kurdish state in southeastern Turkey;

(2) "engage in political advocacy on behalf of Kurds who live in Turkey";

(3) "teach PKK members how to petition various representative bodies such as the United Nations for relief"; and

(4) "engage in political advocacy on behalf of the designated terrorist organization, Liberation Tigers of Tamil Eelam (LTTE) who live in Sri Lanka." Their goal is to create an independent Tamil state in Sri Lanka.

(*Holder v. Humanitarian Law Project* 2010)

You don't have to wait until the fuse is being lit. If that were the standard, a lot of bombs would go off and a lot of people would lose their lives.

(Michael Chertoff, U.S. Department of Homeland Security, in Anderson 2003)

> If you cast too wide a net and you don't use appropriate discretion to limit these prosecutions, you risk ensnaring innocent people and you demean the entire process of prosecuting terror.
>
> (Neal Sonnett, National Association of Criminal Defense Lawyers, in Anderson 2003)

LO 1

In these different views, you can see the tension between two core values in our constitutional democracy—the need for safety and security and the desire for privacy and liberty. This chapter is about how we apply the enduring principles of criminal law (Chapters 1–4) to protect the core values of security and freedom in a time of testing by threats from individuals and groups who are prepared to kill innocent Americans both in the United States and around the world. Grave as the threat may be today, we should remember that our Constitution, too, was adopted during a time of threats to our nation's security.

We'll examine the history and modern law of treason, the other ancient crimes of disloyalty (sedition, sabotage, and espionage), and how the specific crimes against domestic and international terrorism enacted after the Oklahoma City bombing in 1993 were strengthened after the attacks on the World Trade Center and the Pentagon on September 11, 2001.

LO 2

TREASON

treason, the crime of levying war against the United States or of giving aid and comfort to its enemies

Treason is the only crime defined in the U.S. Constitution. This is how Article III, Section 3, defines this most heinous of all crimes against the state:

> Treason against the United States shall consist only in levying War against them, or, in adhering to their Enemies, giving them Aid and Comfort. No Person shall be convicted of Treason unless on the Testimony of two Witnesses to the same overt Act, or on Confession in open Court.

There's also a treason statute (Treason Act 2006) that includes the constitutional definition and adds this penalty provision:

> Whoever, owing allegiance to the United States, levies war against them or adheres to their enemies, giving them aid and comfort within the United States or elsewhere, is guilty of treason and shall suffer death, or shall be imprisoned not less than five years and fined under this title but not less than $10,000; and shall be incapable of holding any office under the United States. (Title 18, § 2381)

Let's look at how treason laws were viewed both before and after the Revolution.

LO 1, LO 2

TREASON LAWS AND THE AMERICAN REVOLUTION

The revolutionaries who wrote the U.S. Constitution knew that the new government they were about to create couldn't survive without the active support (or at least the passive submission) of most of the people. They also realized that it was going to be some time before this new republican form of government took hold among the people.

The people's allegiance would be especially important to the newborn nation's survival in the early years following the Revolution, a time of gigantic threats from enemies inside and outside the new country. From within, Benedict Arnold's betrayal of General Washington was fresh in their minds, and English royalists among them remained loyal to King George III. From without, hostile old countries had designs on the new country's territory. To the north in Canada, England was hovering, smarting from the loss of the American colonies and looking for payback. Spain to the south had just taken back Florida and claimed the whole Mississippi Valley. And the colonists had only recently thrown France out of the Ohio Valley. These unfriendly nations formed alliances with Native American nations by taking advantage of deep injustices the colonists continued to inflict on the tribes.

These threats led the authors of the Constitution to take a tough stand against individuals who broke their allegiance in the face of these dangers. But there was a flip side to their tough stand. Many of the drafters' ancestors had fled to the colonies for the very purpose of escaping persecution for heresy and prosecution for treason. More to the point, they were traitors themselves under English law. English treason consisted either of levying war against the king or giving aid and comfort to the king's enemies. They'd done plenty of both. They'd levied war against the King of England by fighting the Revolutionary War, and they'd given aid and comfort to England's bitterest enemy, France.

Everything they did to further the interests of the colonies was done under threat of prosecution for treason. English prosecutions for treason weren't pretty. Thomas Jefferson referred to the English law of treason as a "deadly weapon in the hands of tyrannical kings" and "weak and wicked Ministers which had drawn the blood of the best and honestest men in the kingdom" (Jefferson 1853, 1:215). Treason prosecutions were probably on Benjamin Franklin's mind when he quipped at the signing of the Declaration of Independence, "We must all hang together, or most assuredly we shall all hang separately" (Lederer 1988, 27).

What were they worried about? The existing law in England defined *treason* as "**adherence to the enemy.**" *Adherence* here means breaking allegiance to your own country by forming an "attachment to the enemy." Criminalizing attachment—joining the enemy's military forces—wasn't an issue; everybody agreed that was treason. But what about "giving aid and comfort to the enemy"? With this loose phrase, "attachment" could lead to attacks on thoughts and feelings. Suppose "disloyalty" took the forms of sympathy for our enemies or even apathy toward our own cause. Were they treason, too? (They were in England.) And would zealous patriotism, so needed in troubled times, tempt the government to bend the rules in its attempt to protect the country? (It did in England.)

adherence to the enemy, the definition of treason under English common law, meaning breaking allegiance to your own country by forming an "attachment to the enemy"

The worries that treason law would be abused boiled down to two concerns:

1. That peaceful opposition to the government, not just rebellion, would be repressed.
2. That innocent people might be convicted of treason because of perjury, passion, and/or insufficient evidence. The authors of the Constitution were determined that disloyal feelings or opinions and the passions of the time wouldn't be a part of the law of treason.

So as much as they recognized the need for allegiance to the new government, their fear of abusive prosecutions for treason led them to adopt "every limitation that the practice of governments had evolved or that politico-legal philosophy to that time had advanced" (*Cramer v. U.S.* 1945, 23–24). By the time the Constitution was adopted, the new government and current thinking among the governing class came to limit treason to two disloyal behaviors: (1) levying war against your own country and (2) giving aid and comfort to the enemy.

The authors of the Constitution adopted these two acts and then, for more protection, added three more limits to the reach of treason:

1. They banned legislatures and courts from creating new treasons.
2. They required two witnesses to at least one overt (unconcealed) act of treason or a confession in open court.
3. They wrote these limits into the body of the U.S. Constitution, where it would be very tough to tamper with them because of the intentionally cumbersome constitutional amendment process.

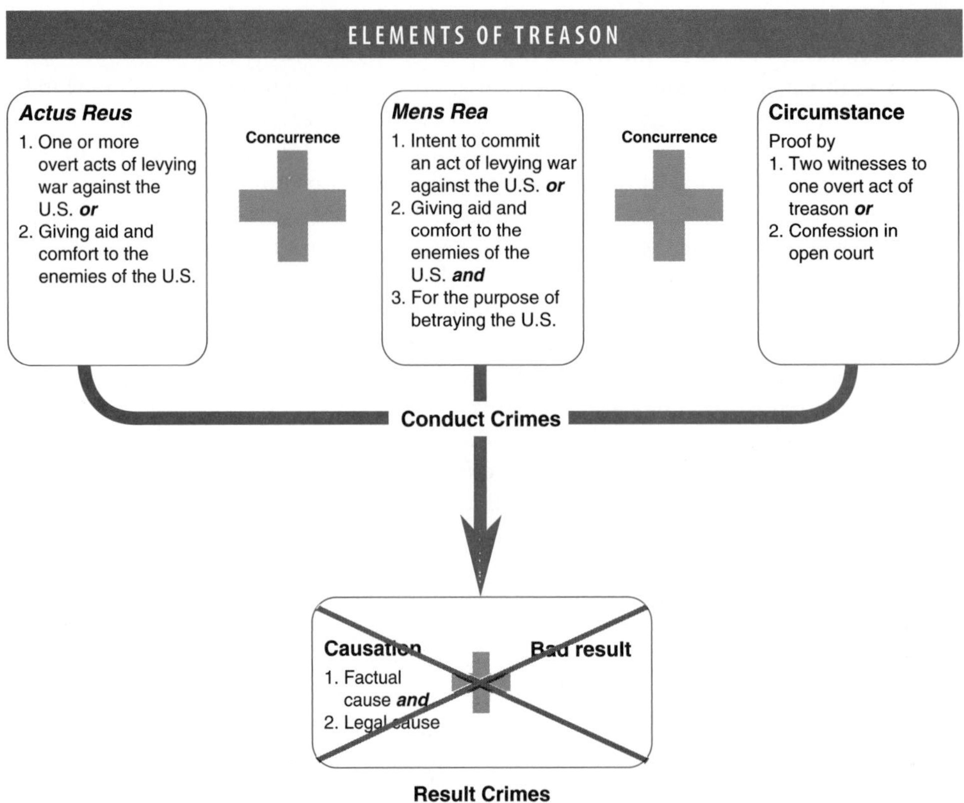

treason *actus reus*, consists of either levying war against the United States or giving aid and comfort to the enemies of the United States

treason *mens rea*, consists of intentionally giving aid and comfort for the very purpose of betraying the United States

proof of treason requires either two witnesses to the *actus reus* or confession in open court

Treason consists of three elements. First, treason *actus reus* consists of either levying war against the United States or giving aid and comfort to the enemies of the United States. Second, treason *mens rea* consists of intentionally giving aid and comfort for the very purpose of betraying the United States. Third, proof of treason requires either two witnesses to the *actus reus* or confession in open court. (See the Elements of Treason illustration.)

Associate U.S. Supreme Court Justice Robert Jackson stated the elements of treason in this straightforward language in one of the very few treason cases in U.S. history, *Cramer v. U.S.* (1945):

> The crime of treason consists of two elements: adherence to the enemy; and rendering him aid and comfort. A citizen intellectually or emotionally may favor the enemy and harbor sympathies or convictions disloyal to this country's policy or interest, but so long as he commits no act of aid and comfort to the enemy, there is no treason. On the other hand, a citizen may take actions, which do aid and comfort the enemy—making a speech critical of the government or opposing its measures, profiteering, striking in defense plants or essential work, and the hundred other things which impair our cohesion and diminish our strength—but if there is no adherence to the enemy in this, if there is no intent to betray, there is no treason. (29)

TREASON LAW SINCE THE ADOPTION OF THE U.S. CONSTITUTION

Distrust of treason prosecutions didn't end with the adoption of the Constitution. Throughout U.S. history, the government has prosecuted only a handful of people for treason, and presidents have pardoned or at least mitigated death sentences of most of those few who've been found guilty. The only exception was President Eisenhower's refusal to stop the execution of Ethel Rosenberg, convicted of conspiring to give atomic bomb secrets to the Soviet Union. She and her husband, Julius, were executed in 1951. There's still plenty of controversy surrounding the Rosenbergs' executions (Meerpol 2003).

In 1945, six years before the Rosenbergs' executions, the U.S. Supreme Court dealt with disloyalty—giving aid and comfort to Nazi Germany for the purpose of betraying the United States—and proving it, in *Cramer v. U.S.* (1945). This case was part of the fallout from the darkest days of World War II.

Early in June 1942, when the war was going badly for the Allies, German submarines were able to get close enough to the East Coast of the United States to allow eight Germans to get ashore, four on Long Island and four in Florida. They managed to bring along several crates of dynamite and lots of cash. The plan was to blow up bridges, factories, and maybe a department store owned by Jews. The object of the plot was, first, to sabotage the war effort by destroying strategic places. Second, they planned to demoralize the American public by terror—namely, by the brazen act of coming right onto U.S. soil and blowing up our places of defense and business.

The would-be saboteurs never committed sabotage. Within days of their landing, they turned themselves in to the FBI. The reason they went to the FBI isn't clear. They may have had a change of heart, or feared getting caught, or perhaps they never were really saboteurs at all but Germans disillusioned with Hitler, hoping to escape to the United States (Nazi Saboteur Case 1942, "Transcript of Military Commission"). Whatever the reason, the eight saboteurs were immediately tried by a secret military commission and convicted. Six were quickly executed; two were sentenced to life in prison.

Shortly before the saboteur hopefuls were caught, Anthony Cramer got together with two of them, Werner Thiel and Edward Kerling, at the Lexington Inn in New York City. Later that day, Cramer had dinner with Werner Thiel at Thompson's Cafeteria in New York City.

In 1943, Cramer was arrested and charged with treason based on his meetings with the by-then executed Thiel and Kerling. At Cramer's treason trial, two FBI agents testified they had witnessed his meetings with Thiel and Kerling and that the three ate, drank, and "engaged long and earnestly in conversation."

The government claimed these acts amounted to "giving aid and comfort to the enemy" and that the FBI agents' testimony satisfied the constitutional requirement of two witnesses. The trial judge and jury agreed; Cramer was convicted (*Cramer v. U.S.*, 1945). However, the U.S. Supreme Court, by a vote of 5–4, disagreed and reversed Cramer's conviction. According to Justice Jackson, writing for the majority, two witnesses to the dinner wasn't good enough to prove treason:

> The whole purpose of the constitutional [two witness] provision is to make sure that a treason conviction shall rest on direct proof of two witnesses and not even a little on imagination.
>
> And without the use of some imagination it is difficult to perceive any advantage which this meeting afforded to Thiel and Kerling as enemies or how it strengthened Germany or weakened the United States in any way whatever. It may be true that the saboteurs were cultivating Cramer as a potential "source of information and an avenue for contact." But there is no proof either by two witnesses or by even one witness or by any circumstance that Cramer gave them information. . . .
>
> Meeting with Cramer in public drinking places to tipple and trifle was no part of the saboteurs' mission and did not advance it. It may well have been a digression which jeopardized its success. (38)

LO 3

SEDITION, SABOTAGE, AND ESPIONAGE

The lesson of *Cramer v. U.S.* is clear: It's very hard to convict someone of treason—and as you've already learned, that's just what the authors intended. But treason isn't the only crime aimed at combating disloyalty and keeping the allegiance of our citizens. Let's look at three of these crimes, which are very much like ancient crimes with the same names—sedition, sabotage, and espionage. Then, we'll examine some specific antiterrorist laws that borrowed from these three ancient crimes.

SEDITION

For centuries, it's been a crime against the state not just to commit treason but to "stir up" others to overthrow the government by violence. Advocating the violent overthrow of the government was called **sedition**. The "stirring up" could be done by speeches (**seditious speech**), writings (**seditious libel**), or agreement (**seditious conspiracy**).

sedition, the crime of advocating the violent overthrow of the government

seditious speech, advocating the overthrow of the government in speeches

seditious libel, advocating the overthrow of the government in writings

seditious conspiracy, conspiring to the violent overthrow of the government

In 1798, during the French Revolution and impending war with France, the U.S. Congress enacted the country's first sedition act. Banning a lot more than stirring up the violent overthrow of the government, it made it a crime to

> unlawfully combine or conspire together with intent to oppose any measure or measures of the government of the United States, or to impede the operation of any law of the United States, or to intimidate or prevent any [official] from undertaking, performing, or executing his duty. (Urofsky and Finkelman 2002a, I:141)

The Sedition Act also made it a crime to

> write, print, utter, or publish any false, scandalous and malicious writing or writings with intent to "defame" the U.S. Government or excite the hatred of the good people [against the U.S. Government]. (142)

The U.S. Code (Seditious Conspiracy 2006) definition of "seditious conspiracy" sticks to conspiracies that advocate violence. It provides:

> If two or more persons in any State or Territory, or in any place subject to the jurisdiction of the United States, conspire to overthrow, put down, or to destroy by force the Government of the United States, or to levy war against them, or to oppose by force the authority thereof, or by force to prevent, hinder, or delay the execution of any law of the United States, or by force to seize, take, or possess any property of the United States contrary to the authority thereof, they shall each be fined under this title or imprisoned not more than twenty years, or both. (Title 18, § 2384)

Smith Act of 1940, Congress made it a crime to conspire to teach or advocate overthrowing the government by force or to be a member of a group that advocated the violent overthrow of the government

In the **Smith Act of 1940**, Congress made it a crime to conspire to teach or advocate overthrowing the government by force or to be a member of a group that advocated the violent overthrow of the government. In 1948, a federal grand jury indicted twelve national leaders of the U.S. Communist Party. After an often-explosive trial that lasted nine months, the leaders were convicted in 1949 (Urofsky and Finkelman 2002b, II:758–59). In *Dennis v. U.S.* (1951), the U.S. Supreme Court upheld the convictions of the Communist Party leaders against a challenge that the Smith Act violated the First Amendment's ban on laws that "abridge" free speech and association.

sabotage, the crime of damaging or destroying property for the purpose of hindering preparations for war and national defense during national emergencies

SABOTAGE

Sabotage is the crime of damaging or destroying property for the purpose of interfering with and hindering preparations for war and defense during national emergencies.

Here's how the U.S. Code (Sabotage Act 2012) defines the criminal sabotage of war and defense materials, buildings, and utilities:

> Whoever, when the United States is at war or in times of national emergency, with intent to injure, interfere with, or obstruct the United States or any associate nation in preparing for or carrying on the war or defense activities, or, with reason to believe that his act may injure, interfere with, or obstruct the United States or any associate nation in preparing for or carrying on the war or defense activities, willfully injures, destroys, contaminates or infects, or attempts to so injure, destroy, contaminate or infect any war material, war premises, or war utilities, shall be fined under this title or imprisoned not more than thirty years, or both.

Sabotage *actus reus* consists of injuring, destroying, contaminating or infecting (or attempting to) any war material, war premises, or war utilities. (See the Elements of Sabotage illustration on the next page.)

Other sections of Chapter 105 apply to similar acts against forts, harbors, and sea areas (§ 2152); production of defective war (§ 2154) or national defense (§ 2155) material, premises, and utilities; and destruction of national defense materials, premises, and utilities. Utilities include this copious list:

> railroads, railways, electric lines, roads of whatever description, any railroad or railway fixture, canal, lock, dam, wharf, pier, dock, bridge, building, structure, engine, machine, mechanical contrivance, car, vehicle, boat, aircraft, airfields, air lanes, and fixtures or appurtenances thereof, or any other means of transportation whatsoever, whereon or whereby such war material or any troops of the United States, or of any associate nation, are being or may be transported either within the limits of the United States or upon the high seas or elsewhere; and all air-conditioning systems, dams, reservoirs, aqueducts, water and gas mains and pipes, structures and buildings, whereby or in connection with which air, water or gas is being furnished, or may be furnished, to any war premises or to the Armed Forces of the United States, or any associate nation, and all electric light and power, steam or pneumatic power, telephone and telegraph plants, poles, wires, and fixtures, and wireless stations, and the buildings connected with the maintenance and operation thereof used to supply air, water, light, heat, power, or facilities of communication to any war premises or to the Armed Forces of the United States, or any associate nation. (§ 2151)

The sabotage *mens rea*, or levels of culpability, varies in the statute. Most often, it's "willfully," sometimes "with intent to," and at least once "with reason to believe." Whatever the exact words, it's probably closest to the highest levels of culpability—purposely and/or knowingly (Chapter 4).

As if these provisions in the sabotage chapter in the code aren't copious and gnarled enough, sabotage appears if not by name, in substance in other code provisions. Take the case of Douglas James Duchak, indicted by a federal grand jury for "Fraud and Related Activity in Connection with Computers" (Duchak Indictment 2010; U.S. Code 18, §1030 2012; U.S. Attorney's Office, Denver 2011). Duchak worked for the U.S. Transportation Security Administration (TSA) as a data analyst in their Colorado Springs facility.

The TSA is responsible for safeguarding the land, air, and sea transportation network of the United States. The TSA safeguards this network by using electronic databases that contain information regarding "persons who may pose a threat to our nation's security based on information sent to TSA, and using those databases to vet persons who seek access to U.S. air space." (You may recognize this process as the source for the widely discussed, and hotly debated, "no fly lists" that the TSA generates.) Colorado

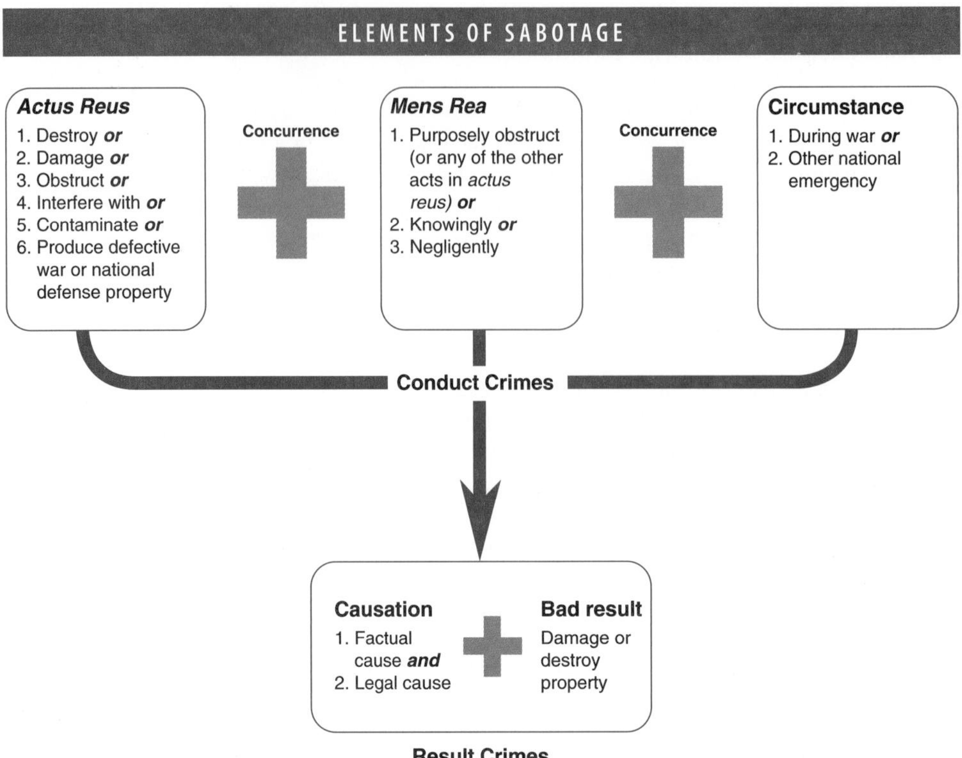

Springs, Colorado, maintains a facility that houses computer networks and databases that carry out the TSA's screening mission (U.S. Attorney's Office, Denver 2011).

From 2004 until August 2009, Duchak was responsible for receiving information from government databases and preparing it for uploading to the TSA's vetting database. On August 12, 2009, the government contractor told Duchak that another employee was going to take over his responsibilities and that Duchak would be doing something else. Duchak trained the new employee on how to upload the information. Then, on October 15, the contractor told Duchak that his position was being eliminated and that his employment would be terminated on October 30. On October 22, Duchak accessed a sensitive database, deleting instructional code from the program. On October 23, he created and transmitted a new code that would disrupt the TSA's security screening function (U.S. Attorney's Office, Denver 2011).

The TSA stopped operation until they could determine the source and scope of the problem. They told Duchak not to come back to work; they had concluded that he "attempted to intentionally cause damage to TSA's vetting databases." According to the Colorado U.S. Attorney John Walsh, if Duchak had completed his attempt:

> he would have caused damage affecting a computer used by the U.S. Government in furtherance of national security. The TSA databases are critical to protecting the traveling public. Thanks to the hard work of TSA and the FBI and Department of Homeland Security, a man was stopped from attempting to corrupt these databases. (U.S. Attorney's Office, Denver 2011)

Duchak was indicted on March 9, 2010. The indictment included two counts of "Attempted Intentional Damage to Protected Computer" (Fraud and Related Activity in Connection with Computers 2012; Table 13.1). The first count was for removing the existing code from the computer program, on October 22, 2009, and the second was for adding the new destructive code on October 23.

TABLE 13.1

Attempted Intentional Damage to Protected Computer
§1030. Fraud and related activity in connection with computers
(a) Whoever—
(5)(A) knowingly causes the transmission of a program, information, code, or command, and as a result of such conduct, intentionally causes damage without authorization, to a protected computer;
(b) Whoever conspires to commit or attempts to commit an offense under subsection (a) of this section shall be punished as provided in subsection (c) of this section.
(c) The punishment for an offense under subsection (a) or (b) of this section is—
(4)(B) a fine, imprisonment for not more than 10 years, or both.

Source: *Fraud and Related Activity in Connection with Computers, U.S. Code* 18 (2012), § 1030.

On October 19, 2009, Duchak pleaded guilty to both counts. On January 11, 2011, U.S. District Judge David M. Ebel, pursuant to a plea agreement, sentenced Duchak to twenty-four months in prison; three years of supervised release after prison; and ordered him to pay $60,587.07 in restitution to the TSA. (As of this writing, Duchak is serving his time at the Federal Bureau of Prisons Community Corrections Center in Pittsburgh, Pennsylvania; his scheduled release date is September 15, 2012.)

ESPIONAGE

espionage, the crime of spying for the enemy

Espionage is the crime of spying for the enemy. The U.S. Code (Espionage and Censorship Act 2006) separates espionage into two crimes: (1) espionage during peace and (2) espionage during war.

espionage during peace, turning or attempting to turn over information about national defense to any foreign country with "intent or with reason to believe" the information is "to be used" to either hurt the United States or help any foreign country

The code defines "**espionage during peace**" as turning or attempting to turn over information about national defense to any foreign country with "intent or with reason to believe" the information is "to be used" to either hurt the United States or help any foreign country. The penalty is any term of imprisonment up to life or, if someone died as a result of the espionage, death (§ 794[a]).

espionage during war, consists of collecting, recording, publishing, or communicating (or attempting to do any of these) "any information" about troop movements, ships, aircraft, or war materials and any other information "which might be useful to the enemy"

The crime of **espionage during war** consists of collecting, recording, publishing, or communicating (or attempting to do any of these) "any information" about troop movements, ships, aircraft, or war materials and any other information "which might be useful to the enemy." The penalty is death or any term of imprisonment up to life (§794[b]). (See the Elements of Espionage illustration on the next page.)

The History of the Espionage Act

> I am one of those who believe that when my country is at war, engaged in deadly strife with an enemy, as a matter of policy, we ought to surrender our individual views and get behind the government if we can possibly do so. In such times we ought to reconcile ourselves to our government's successful conduct of the war. But while that is my belief, it is also my contention, grounded in the deepest principles of free government, that if a man thinks a war is unjust or improvident, or that it is being carried on in a corrupt manner, it is his absolute right to say so. Indeed, if it is a question of the method of carrying on the war and he believes it is unwise or unjust, it is his duty to say so. (Spartacus Educational Website 2012, "Espionage Act")

Senator William Borah, speaking in 1923, was referring to the hundreds of individuals still locked up for violating the Espionage Act of 1917. This isn't the place for a detailed history of those times, but here are a few highlights we should note. By 1915, President

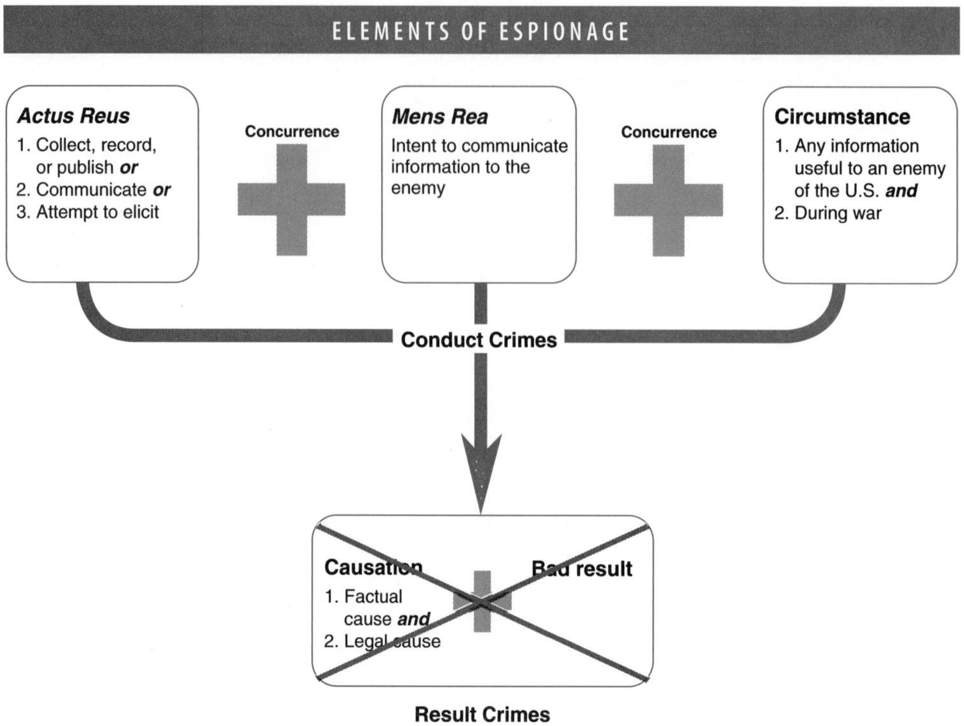

Woodrow Wilson was moving the government from neutrality toward Great Britain's side in World War I. Moving the country wasn't so easy. At the same time, there were significant opponents to U.S. involvement in the war. There were the pacifists opposed to all wars; the socialists who opposed "profiteering" wars; and the "hyphenated" U.S. Americans, especially the vocal German-Americans supporting Germany.

President Wilson was greatly concerned about pro-Germany sentiment and played on the general public's anxiety about "strangers in the land," especially those who supported the Kaiser. In his Third Annual Message to Congress on December 7, 1915, President Wilson played to this anxiety when he delivered these lines:

> There are citizens of the United States, I blush to admit, born under other flags but welcomed by our generous naturalization laws to full freedom and opportunity of America, who have poured the poison of disloyalty into the very arteries of our national life; who have sought to bring the authority and good name of our Government into contempt, to destroy our industries wherever they thought it effective for their vindictive purposes to strike at them, and to debase our politics to the uses of foreign intrigue. . . . A little while ago such a thing would have seemed incredible. But the ugly and incredible thing has actually come about and we are without adequate federal laws to deal with it. I urge you to enact such laws at the earliest possible moment and feel that in doing so I am urging you to do nothing less than save the honor and self-respect of the nation. Such creatures of passion, disloyalty, and anarchy must be crushed out. (Wilson 1915)

The Espionage Act became law just after the United States entered World War I. Most of it, like the provisions that made espionage and sabotage crimes, was noncontroversial. It was Section 3, amended in 1918 to become the Sedition Act of 1918, that generated over two thousand cases, in which the government obtained over one thousand convictions. The amended Section 3 provided:

> Whoever, when the United States is at war, shall willfully utter, print, write, or publish any disloyal, profane, scurrilous, or abusive language about the form of government of the United States, or the Constitution of the United States, or the military or naval forces of the United States, or the flag or the uniform of the Army or Navy of the United States, or any language intended to bring the form of government, or the Constitution or the military or naval forces or the flag of the United States into contempt, scorn, contumely, or disrepute or shall willfully display the flag of any foreign enemy, or shall willfully urge, incite, or advocate any curtailment of production in this country of any thing or things necessary to the prosecution of the war and whoever shall advocate, teach, or defend, or suggest the doing of any of the acts or things in this section enumerated and whoever shall by word or act support or favor the cause of any country with which the United States is at war or by word or act oppose the cause of the United States shall be punished by a fine of not more than $10,000 or imprisonment of not more than twenty years, or both. (Sedition Act 1918, § 3)

The broad sweep of Section 3 became apparent within a month of U.S. entry into the war, when the film *The Spirit of '76* premiered in May. The U.S. government seized the film, arrested the producer, German immigrant Robert Goldstein, and tried and convicted him under Section 3 of the Espionage Act. The judge sentenced him to ten years in prison (*U.S. v. Motion Picture Film, "The Spirit of '76"* 1917). Here's how U.S. District Court Judge of the Southern District of California Benjamin Franklin Bledsoe described the film and explained the reasons for his decision.

> [The film depicts] some of the more important phases of the American War for Independence, and special scenes, like Paul Revere's Ride, the signing of the Declaration of Independence, and the like, are given particular mention and prominence. In addition—and these are the parts of the film inveighed against—scenes purporting to illustrate the Wyoming Valley Massacre are shown. A British soldier is pictured impaling on a bayonet a baby lying in its cradle and then whirling it around his head so impaled. Other unspeakable atrocities committed by British soldiers, including the shooting of harmless women, the dragging off, sometimes by the hair of the head, of young American girls, etc., are exhibited. . . . (946–47)
>
> Assuming that [the film company] and their associates are going to suffer some considerable loss, this court at this time is in no mood to weigh the financial losses of a few individuals as against possible detriment to the United States of America. If it be that some will have to suffer loss, yet it is only a financial loss, and, at worst, will be only a fractional part of the loss that others are going to have to suffer—some even of their lives—because of the war in which we are now engaged.
>
> History is history, and fact is fact. There is no doubt about that. At the present time, however, the United States is confronted with what I conceive to be the greatest emergency we have ever been confronted with at any time in our history. . . . We are engaged in a war in which Great Britain is an ally of the United States. . . . This is no time for . . . sowing dissension among our people, and of creating animosity or want of confidence between us and our allies, because so to do weakens our efforts, weakens the chance of our success, impairs our solidarity, and renders less useful the lives we are giving, to the end that this war may soon be over and peace may soon become a thing substantial and permanent with us. I am in no mood, either . . . to consider the suggestion that the film be returned, and so much of it be permitted to be exhibited as has not met with special objection. (947–48)

> It is a fair inference from the circumstances . . . the language used in characterizing its scenes of atrocity as being "reprehensible" and as evidencing "malice," that the disposition and purpose of the whole play . . . is to incite hatred of England and England's soldiers. And it is not at all necessary that it should be shown to have such effect; it is enough if it is calculated reasonably so to excite or inflame the passions of our people, or some of them, as that they will be deterred from giving that full measure of co-operation, sympathy, assistance, and sacrifice which is due to Great Britain, simply because of the fact that Great Britain, as an ally of ours, is working with us to fight the battle which we think strikes at our very existence as a nation. (948)

By far, the largest sedition trials were the three International Workers of the World (IWW) trials in Chicago, Sacramento, and Wichita. Of these, Chicago's was surely the most sensational. But they all started on September 5, 1917, when U.S. Justice Department agents simultaneously raided 48 IWW local halls across the country and seized five tons of documents. Based partly on these documents, a federal grand jury in Chicago indicted 101 IWW leaders—"principal organizers, speakers, editors, and executives of the IWW" (Taft 1962, 76). (Forty-six members were tried and convicted in Sacramento and 26 in Wichita.)

In the Chicago trial, each defendant was charged with conspiring with thousands of others to obstruct the war effort by sabotage and by speaking and writing against the war and the draft (Taft 1962, 57). The Chicago U.S. attorney opened the trial with the words, "It is the IWW that is on trial here" (Renshaw 1968, 67). All 101 IWW leaders were convicted; William ("Big Bill") Haywood, the IWW Secretary Treasurer, and 14 other defendants were fined $30,000 each; 33 got ten years; 35 got five years; and the rest under five (Renshaw, 68).

In *U.S. v. Nagler* (1918), Louis Nagler was tried for sedition based on uttering these words "in the presence of numerous people," in Madison, Wisconsin:

> I am through contributing to your private grafts. There is too much graft in these subscriptions. No; I do not believe in the work of the Y.M.C.A. or the Red Cross, for I think they are nothing but a bunch of grafters. No, sir. I can prove it. I won't give you a cent. The Y.M.C.A., the Y.W.C.A., and the Red Cross is a bunch of grafters. Not over 10 or 15 per cent of the money collected goes to the soldiers or is used for the purpose for which it is collected. Who is the government? Who is running this war? A bunch of capitalists composed of the steel trust and munition makers. (218)

In *Stokes V. U.S.* (1920), Rosa Pastor Stokes was convicted and sentenced to ten years in prison for writing a letter to the *Kansas City Star*, a newspaper with "large circulation in Kansas City and the surrounding country." Here's the letter she wrote:

> A headline in this evening's issue of the Star reads: "Mrs. Stokes for Government and Against War at the Same Time." I am not for the government. In the interview that follows I am quoted as having said, "I believe the Government of the United States should have the unqualified support of every citizen in its war aims." I made no such statement, and I believe no such thing. No government which is for the profiteers can also be for the people, and I am for the people, while the government is for the profiteers. I expect my working class point of view to receive no sympathy from your paper, but I do expect that the traditional courtesy of publication by the newspapers of a signed statement of correction, which even our most Bourbon papers grant, will be extended to this statement by yours. (20)

By the middle of the 1920s, large-scale sedition prosecutions under the Espionage Act largely disappeared. But they didn't die. This is especially true during times like

World War II, the Cold War, the Vietnam War, and now in Iraq and Afghanistan, when U.S. troops are engaged in combat and dangerous peacekeeping operations abroad. The Espionage Act then aims mainly at U.S. government employees who leak information they're sworn to keep secret because it's related to national security.

The U.S. government has occasionally prosecuted these employees. To cite one sensational example, in 1971, at the height of the Vietnam War, the government charged the whistleblowers Pentagon military analyst Daniel Ellsberg and Anthony Russo under the Espionage Act for leaking the Pentagon Papers to *The New York Times*. Up to that point, it was the largest leak in U.S. history. The case ended in a mistrial. The government also failed in its attempt to block *The New York Times* from publishing the documents.

The Espionage Act Today

Now, the Espionage Act is back. Since 2009, the U.S. government has charged six U.S. government employees under the act. Let's look at each.

1. *Bradley Manning.* Private Manning was arrested in May 2010 as part of the fallout from the largest leak in U.S. history—the documents given to "WikiLeaks," the website that proclaims it's dedicated to making secret information public. (Critics say it's devoted to attacking the U.S. government). Private Manning, a U.S. Army intelligence analyst, is charged with turning over to WikiLeaks more than 260,000 diplomatic cables, more than 90,000 intelligence reports on the war in Afghanistan, and one video of a military helicopter shooting journalists in Baghdad. Depending on your point of view, Private Manning is either a "premeditated traitor" or an "accidental hero" (Liebelson 2012). The Manning trial in military court is scheduled to begin on September 21, 2012.
2. *Thomas Drake.* Drake, a former senior executive in the National Security Agency (NSA), was charged in 2010 under the Espionage Act with retaining top-secret national defense documents for the purpose of unauthorized disclosure. To Drake's defenders, he was a whistleblower who was a key witness in a Defense Department Inspector General audit that found that the NSA spent $1.2 billion on an ineffective private contract when it could've done the work in-house for $3 million! The case ended when Drake pleaded guilty to a misdemeanor in exchange for dropping the Espionage Act charges (Liebelson 2012).
3. *Shamai Leibowitz.* Leibowitz, a duel U.S.-Israeli citizen, worked as a contract Hebrew translator for the FBI. In the Obama administration's first prosecution for leaking to the media, Leibowitz was convicted in 2010 under the Espionage Act and sentenced to twenty months for leaking transcripts caught on FBI wiretaps of the Israeli Embassy in Washington, DC. Leibowitz released the transcripts because he was concerned about Israel's "aggressive efforts to influence public opinion, and fears that Israel might strike nuclear facilities in Iran, a move he saw as potentially disastrous" (Shane 2011).
4. *Stephen Jin-Woo Kim.* Kim, a former contractor for the State Department, was indicted in August 2010, for leaking information about North Korea to Fox News. He pleaded not guilty, and his lawyer has denounced the charges, claiming that the leak is an example of "the type of government-media exchanges that happen hundreds a times a day in Washington" (Liebelson 2012).
5. *Jeffrey Sterling.* On January 6, 2011, Jeffrey Sterling became the fifth Espionage Act defendant during the Obama administration. Sterling, a former CIA agent, was indicted for disclosing unauthorized national defense information to *New York Times* reporter James Risen for Risen's 2006 book, *State of War: The Secret History of the CIA* (Savage 2010). Specifically, prosecutors believe Sterling revealed

information about a "botched U.S. effort to thwart Iran's nuclear weapons program" (Liebelson 2012.) Sterling pleaded "not guilty." As I write (May 24, 2012), Sterling's case is on hold while the U.S. Fourth Circuit Court of Appeals decides whether James Risen can be forced to testify in Sterling's case.

6. *John Kiriakou.* On January 12, 2012, the government charged former CIA officer John Kiriakou with disclosing to journalists the identity of a CIA analyst who worked on the 2002 operation that located, captured, and interrogated Abu Zubaydah. Zubaydah was purported to be second or third in the Al Qaeda hierarchy on September 11, 2001, and to have been involved in every major terrorist operation carried out by Al Qaeda. Kiriakou was a member of the team that captured and interrogated Zubaydah. On January 23, 2012, after appearing in federal court in Alexandria, Virginia, he was released on $250,000 bond (Savage 2012).

The espionage cases, especially the U.S. government employee whistleblowing/leaks cases, have drawn lots of (probably disproportionate) attention in the national press and in the world of blogs and tweets. And yes, even in the book you're reading. Notice that we've covered 100 percent of the U.S. government's leak cases—a total of six. We'll turn now to the specific antiterrorist crimes.

LO 4

ANTITERRORIST CRIMES

"Congress has given prosecutors a formidable arsenal of criminal statutes to deploy in criminal prosecutions" (Zabel and Benjamin 2009, 13). They include the specific terrorism crimes in the U.S. Code in Chapter 113B, §§2331–2339 (Table 13.2), which we'll discuss, as well as the traditional crimes of murder (Chapter 9), financial fraud (Chapter 11), false statements, banned firearms training and possession (Chapter 3), and general conspiracy (Chapter 8).

terrorism, the use of violence or intimidation in the pursuit of political aims

Before we discuss the crimes, let's establish what we mean by **terrorism** in this book: the use of violence or intimidation to achieve political or ideological aims. The U.S. Code (Terrorism Act 2012) breaks down terrorism into international terrorism crimes and domestic terrorism crimes (Table 13.2).

THE USA PATRIOT ACT

USA Patriot Act, passed by Congress after the September 11, 2001, attacks, creating some new (and enhancing the penalties for existing) crimes of domestic and international terrorism

The specific antiterrorist crimes are included in U.S. Code, Chapter 113B, *Terrorism* (Title 18, Part I), under the sections frequently referred to as the **USA Patriot Act** (2001), an acronym for the **U**niting and **S**trengthening **A**merica by **P**roviding **A**ppropriate **T**ools **R**equired to **I**ntercept and **O**bstruct **T**errorism Act.

These sections include the following crimes:

1. Use of certain weapons of mass destruction (§ 2332a)
2. Acts of terrorism transcending national boundaries (§ 2332b)
3. Harboring or concealing terrorists (§ 2339)
4. Providing material support to terrorists (§ 2339A)
5. Providing material support or resources to designated foreign terrorist organizations (§ 2339B)
6. Providing financial support for terrorism (§2339C)
7. Receiving training from a foreign terrorist organization (§2339D)

See the Elements of Material Support to Terrorists and the Elements of Material Support to Terrorist Organizations illustrations.

TABLE 13.2

Definitions of International and Domestic Terrorism in the U.S. Code

§2331. Definitions

As used in this chapter—

(1) the term "international terrorism" means activities that—

(A) involve violent acts or acts dangerous to human life that are a violation of the criminal laws of the United States or of any State, or that would be a criminal violation if committed within the jurisdiction of the United States or of any State;

(B) appear to be intended—

(i) to intimidate or coerce a civilian population;

(ii) to influence the policy of a government by intimidation or coercion; or

(iii) to affect the conduct of a government by mass destruction, assassination, or kidnapping; and

(C) occur primarily outside the territorial jurisdiction of the United States, or transcend national boundaries in terms of the means by which they are accomplished, the persons they appear intended to intimidate or coerce, or the locale in which their perpetrators operate or seek asylum;

(5) the term "domestic terrorism" means activities that—

(A) involve acts dangerous to human life that are a violation of the criminal laws of the United States or of any State;

(B) appear to be intended—

(i) to intimidate or coerce a civilian population;

(ii) to influence the policy of a government by intimidation or coercion; or

(iii) to affect the conduct of a government by mass destruction, assassination, or kidnapping; and

(C) occur primarily within the territorial jurisdiction of the United States.

ELEMENTS OF MATERIAL SUPPORT TO TERRORISTS

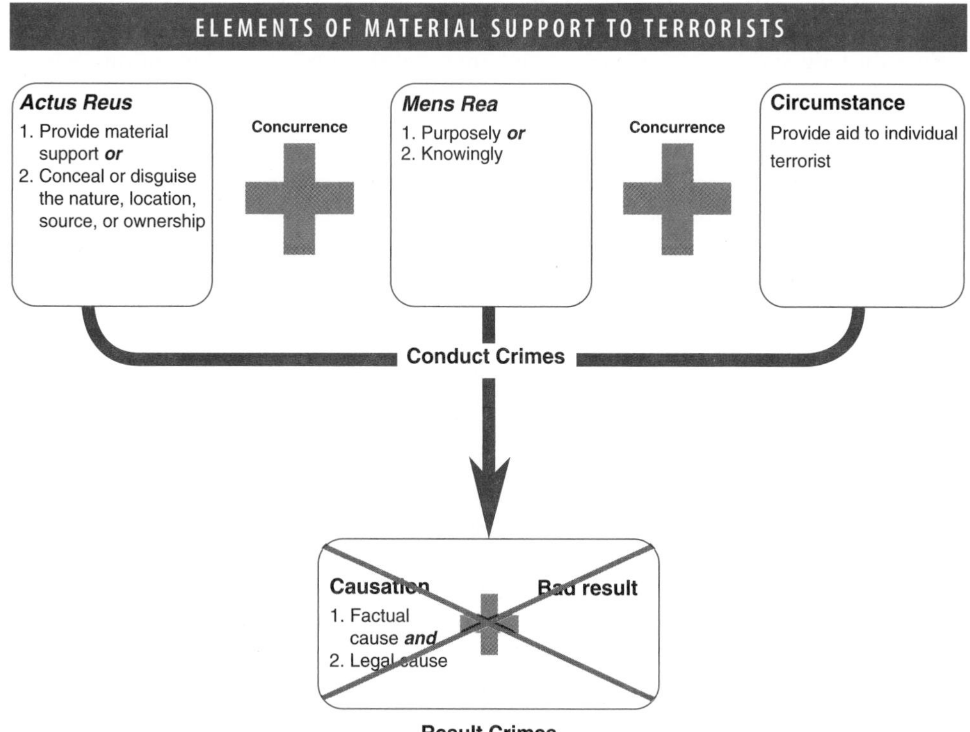

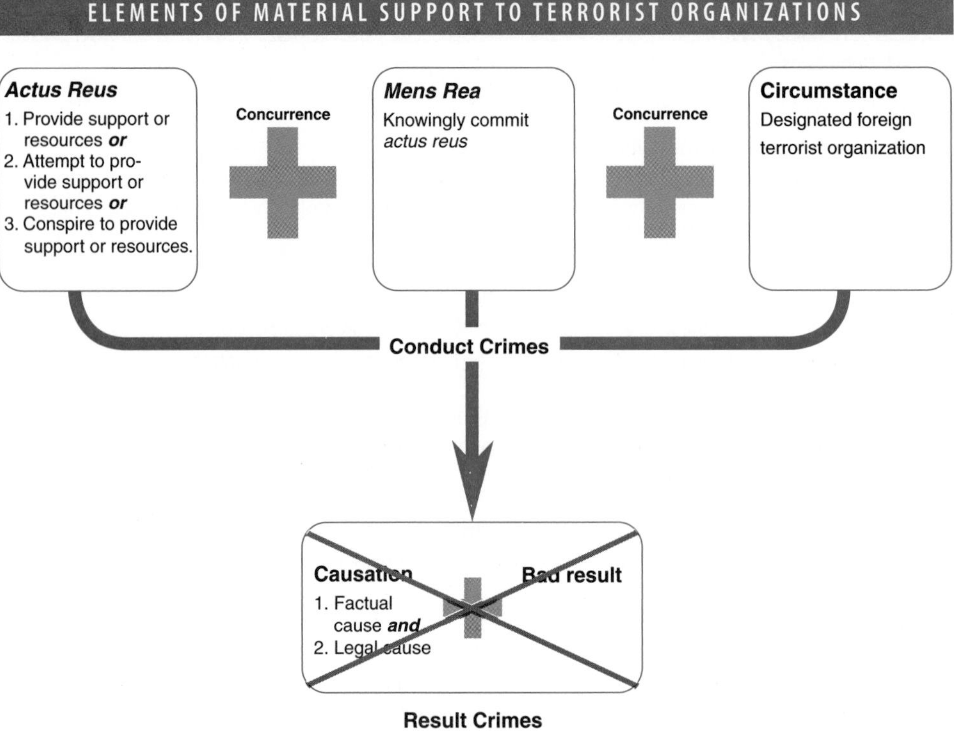

LO 5

THE TOP TERRORIST PLOT CASES

As of September 2010, the U.S. government had prosecuted about one thousand terrorist cases since September 11, 2001 (Center on Law and Security TTRC 2010, 6). The Center on Law and Security collected and analyzed the available information about a subset of those cases—the top fifty alleged terrorist plots (Table 13.3 and Figure 13.1). The center is

> an independent, nonpartisan institute committed to promoting an informed understanding of the most pressing legal, security, and foreign policy issues of the post-911 era and of the 21st century, bringing together practitioners, scholars, journalists, law enforcement officials, military officers, and lawyers ensures a multilayered perspective on these issues. (Center on Law and Security TTRC 2011)

The top plots include only defendants whose actions were inspired by jihadist ideas—namely, "defendants who were formally or informally associated with an Islamist terror group—whether one with a global jihadist ideology (Al Qaeda) or a local Islamist movement (Hamas). It also includes defendants unaffiliated with any terrorist group who aspired to such affiliation or who subscribed to a global jihadist ideology" (Center on Law and Security TTRC 2011, 7). But it excludes terrorist cases *not* inspired by jihadist ideas, such as far right (militias) or far left (environmentalist extremists) ideologues. Why the limit? According to Zabel and Benjamin (2009), they limited their collection of terrorism cases since 9/11 "in light of the legal, intelligence, and security concerns that are thought to make al Qaeda and similar groups a *special* threat to our national security" (emphasis added) (5).

FIGURE 13.1

HOMEGROWN TERRORIST DEFENDANTS BORN IN THE UNITED STATES, 2001–2010

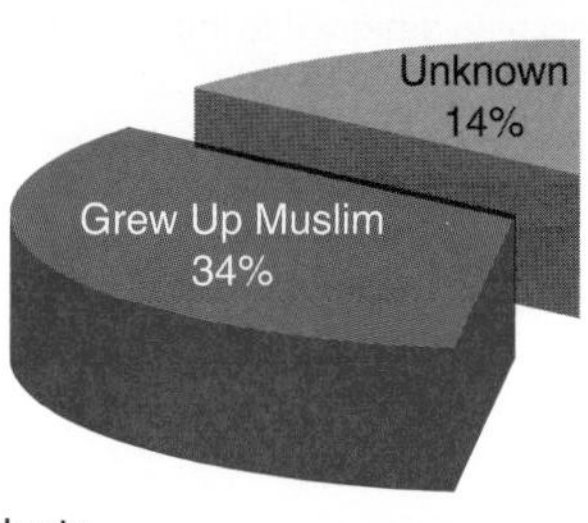

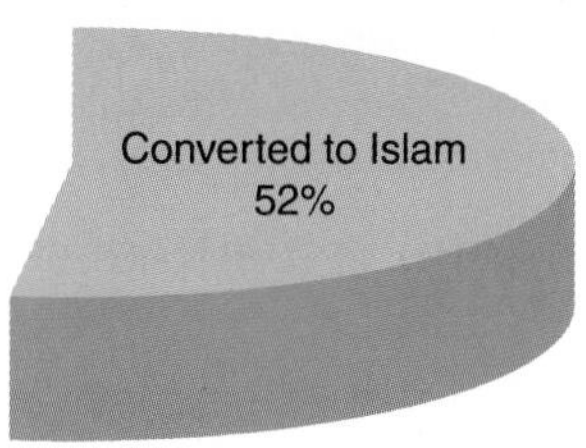

73 defendants

Source: Center on Law and Security TTRC 2010, p. 16.

"HOMEGROWN" TERRORISTS

Is the United States creating its own terrorists? Yes, according to the Law and Security Center. Eighty-one percent (127) of the defendants in the top fifty plot cases were legal residents of the United States. Seventy-three (57%) were born in the United States; the rest had lived in the United States for at least ten years and several as long as twenty years, long enough to become familiar with U.S. culture and habits (Center on Law and Security TTRC 2010, 3). Figure 13.1 provides a breakdown of the religious background of the defendants born in the United States.

Homegrown terrorist defendants have been among high-profile cases ever since 2011, but the number seemed to spike in 2010, partly because of lengthy investigations. But also, some defendants spent years trying to become terrorists before they were arrested. Take Tarek Mehanna and his co-defendant Ahmed Abousamra, who began plotting to join a terrorist training in 2002; they were indicted in 2009. And Daniel Boyd first traveled to join the mujahideen [translated, "those who engage in jihad"] in Afghanistan in 1989, but he wasn't indicted until 2009 for a conspiracy that was hatched in 2006 (Center on Law and Security TTRC 2010, 14).

TABLE 13.3

Statutes Charged in Top 50 Terrorist Plots, 2001–2010

1. Providing material support to terrorists

U.S. Code, Title 18, Chapter 113B, Terrorism, § 2339A

(a) Offense.—Whoever provides material support or resources or conceals or disguises the nature, location, source, or ownership of material support or resources, knowing or intending that they are to be used in preparation for, or in carrying out, a violation of [a long list of federal statutes] or in preparation for, or in carrying out, the concealment of an escape from the commission of any such violation, or attempts or conspires to do such an act, shall be fined under this title, imprisoned not more than15 years, or both, and, if the death of any person results, shall be imprisoned for any term of years or for life.

(b) Definitions.—As used in this section—

(1) the term "material support or resources" means any property, tangible or intangible, or service, including currency or monetary instruments or financial securities, financial services, lodging, training, expert advice or assistance, safehouses, false documentation or identification, communications equipment, facilities, weapons, lethal substances, explosives, personnel (1 or more individuals who may be or include oneself), and transportation, except medicine or religious materials;

(continues)

TABLE 13.3 **Statutes Charged in Top 50 Terrorist Plots, 2001–2010 (*Continued*)**

(2) the term "training" means instruction or teaching designed to impart a specific skill, as opposed to general knowledge; and

(3) the term "expert advice or assistance" means advice or assistance derived from scientific, technical or other specialized knowledge.

2. Providing material support or resources to designated foreign terrorist organizations

U.S. Code, Title 18, Chapter 113B, Terrorism, § 2339B

(1) Unlawful conduct.—Whoever knowingly provides material support or resources to a foreign terrorist organization, or attempts or conspires to do so, shall be fined under this title or imprisoned not more than 15 years, or both, and, if the death of any person results, shall be imprisoned for any term of years or for life.

(2) Financial institutions.—any financial institution that becomes aware that it has possession of, or control over, any funds in which a foreign terrorist organization, or its agent, has an interest, shall—

(A) retain possession of, or maintain control over, such funds; and

(B) report to the Secretary the existence of such funds in accordance with regulations issued by the Secretary.

3. Use of weapons of mass destruction

U.S. Code, Title 18, Chapter 113B, Terrorism, § 2332a

(a) A person who, without lawful authority, uses, threatens, or attempts or conspires to use, a weapon of mass destruction—

(1) against a national of the United States while such national is outside of the United States;

(2) against any person or property within the United States, and

(A) the mail or any facility of interstate or foreign commerce is used in furtherance of the offense;

(B) such property is used in interstate or foreign commerce or in an activity that affects interstate or foreign commerce;

(C) any perpetrator travels in or causes another to travel in interstate or foreign commerce in furtherance of the offense; or

(D) the offense, or the results of the offense, affect interstate or foreign commerce, or, in the case of a threat, attempt, or conspiracy, would have affected interstate or foreign commerce;

(3) against any property that is owned, leased or used by the United States or by any department or agency of the United States, whether the property is within or outside of the United States; or

(4) against any property within the United States that is owned, leased, or used by a foreign government, shall be imprisoned for any term of years or for life, and if death results, shall be punished by death or imprisoned for any term of years or for life.

(b) Offense by National of the United States Outside of the United States.—Any national of the United States who, without lawful authority, uses, or threatens, attempts, or conspires to use, a weapon of mass destruction outside of the United States shall be imprisoned for any term of years or for life, and if death results, shall be punished by death, or by imprisonment for any term of years or for life.

(c) Definitions.—For purposes of this section—

(1) the term "national of the United States" has the meaning given in section 101(a)(22) of the Immigration and Nationality Act (8 U.S.C. 1101(a)(22));

(2) the term "weapon of mass destruction" means—

(A) any destructive device as defined in section 921 of this title;

TABLE 13.3

Statutes Charged in Top 50 Terrorist Plots, 2001–2010 (*Continued*)

[§921.] (3) The term "firearm" means (A) any weapon (including a starter gun) which will or is designed to or may readily be converted to expel a projectile by the action of an explosive; (B) the frame or receiver of any such weapon; (C) any firearm muffler or firearm silencer; or (D) any destructive device. Such term does not include an antique firearm.

(4) The term "destructive device" means—
- (A) any explosive, incendiary, or poison gas—
  - (i) bomb,
  - (ii) grenade,
  - (iii) rocket having a propellant charge of more than four ounces,
  - (iv) missile having an explosive or incendiary charge of more than one-quarter ounce,
  - (v) mine, or
  - (vi) device similar to any of the devices described in the preceding clauses;
- (B) any type of weapon (other than a shotgun or a shotgun shell which the Attorney General finds is generally recognized as particularly suitable for sporting purposes) by whatever name known which will, or which may be readily converted to, expel a projectile by the action of an explosive or other propellant, and which has any barrel with a bore of more than one-half inch in diameter; and
- (C) any combination of parts either designed or intended for use in converting any device into any destructive device described in subparagraph (A) or (B) and from which a destructive device may be readily assembled.]

(B) any weapon that is designed or intended to cause death or serious bodily injury through the release, dissemination, or impact of toxic or poisonous chemicals, or their precursors;

(C) any weapon involving a biological agent, toxin, or vector (as those terms are defined in section 178 of this title); or

(D) any weapon that is designed to release radiation or radioactivity at a level dangerous to human life . . .

4. Prohibitions against the financing of terrorism

U.S. Code, Title 18, Chapter 133B, Terrorism, § 2339C

(a) Offenses.—
- (1) In general.—Whoever, in a circumstance described in subsection (b), by any means, directly or indirectly, unlawfully and willfully provides or collects funds with the intention that such funds be used, or with the knowledge that such funds are to be used, in full or in part, in order to carry out—
  - (A) an act which constitutes an offense within the scope of a treaty specified in subsection (e)(7), as implemented by the United States, or
  - (B) any other act intended to cause death or serious bodily injury to a civilian, or to any other person not taking an active part in the hostilities in a situation of armed conflict, when the purpose of such act, by its nature or context, is to intimidate a population, or to compel a government or an international organization to do or to abstain from doing any act,
- (2) Attempts and conspiracies.—Whoever attempts or conspires to commit an offense under paragraph (1) shall be punished as prescribed in subsection (d)(1).
- (3) Relationship to predicate act.—For an act to constitute an offense set forth in this subsection, it shall not be necessary that the funds were actually used to carry out a predicate act.

. . .

(d) Penalties.—Whoever violates subsection (a) shall be fined under this title, imprisoned for not more than 20 years, or both.

(continues)

TABLE 13.3 Statutes Charged in Top 50 Terrorist Plots, 2001–2010 (*Continued*)

5. Receiving military-type training from a foreign terrorist organization

U.S. Code, Title 18, Chapter 113B, Terrorism, § 2339D

(a) Offense.—Whoever knowingly receives military-type training from or on behalf of any organization designated as a foreign terrorist organization shall be fined under this title or imprisoned for ten years, or both. To violate this subsection, a person must have knowledge that the organization is a designated terrorist organization, that the organization has engaged or engages in terrorist activity, or that the organization has engaged or engages in terrorism.

LO 6

MATERIAL SUPPORT TO TERRORISTS AND TERRORIST ORGANIZATIONS

"material support" offenses, the federal crime of providing "training," "expert advice or assistance," "service," and "personnel to terrorists or terrorist organizations

As Figure 13.2 makes clear, the predominant number of cases are "material support" offenses (in fact, the statute reads support *and* resources) to terrorists and terrorist organizations. A number of lower courts have decided challenges to the constitutionality of the "material support" sections—namely, the First Amendment rights of free speech and assembly and the Fifth and Fourteenth Amendments' denial of due process (vagueness). (See Chapter 2 for discussion of the application of these constitutional limits on criminal law generally.) They have reached conflicting results. Then, in 2010, the U.S. Supreme Court decided that as applied to the facts of the case in *Holder v. Humanitarian Law Project* that the "material support" for terrorist organization was neither constitutionally vague nor did it violate First Amendment speech and assembly rights.

FIGURE 13.2 TOP 50 PLOT PROSECUTIONS, 2001–2010

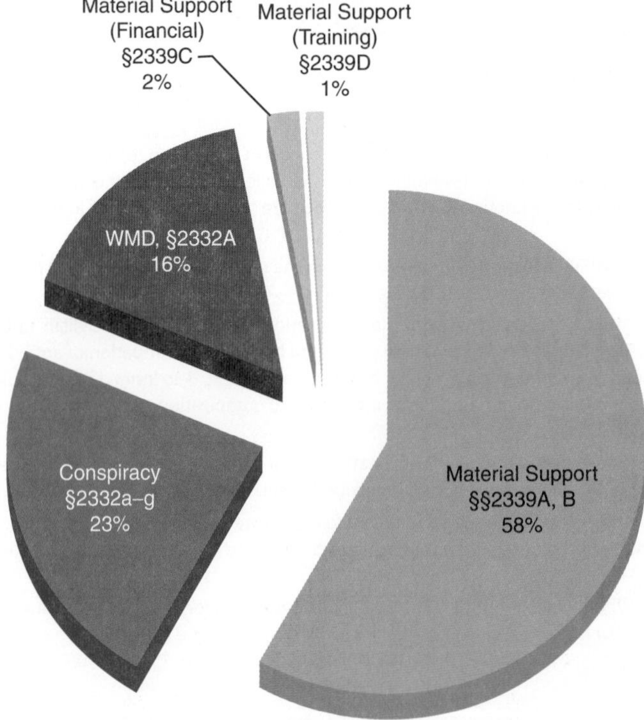

Source: Center on Law and Security TTRC 2010, pp. 11–12.

CASE

In **Holder v. Humanitarian Law Project** *(2010), the U.S. Supreme Court, in a 5–4 decision, rejected the claim that the material support and resources provisions in the USA Patriot Act runs afoul of the First Amendment ban on all laws infringing on the rights of free speech and assembly. Further, the provisions aren't void for vagueness.*

Did they provide "material support" to terrorist organizations?

Holder, Attorney General, et al. v. Humanitarian Law Project et al.

Humanitarian Law Project et al. v. Holder, Attorney General, et al.

130 S.Ct 2705 (2010)

HISTORY

Lead plaintiff, retired Judge and long-time pacifist and human rights activist, Ralph Fertig, and the other plaintiff, Humanitarian Law Project (HLP), sought an injunction to prohibit enforcement of a criminal ban on providing material support to two terrorist organizations. The U.S. District Court for the Central District of California (2001) issued the injunction. A three-judge panel of the Ninth Circuit U.S. Court of Appeals affirmed. The full court, on rehearing en banc, vacated its panel decision, and remanded to the District Court. On remand, the District Court, granted plaintiffs partial relief on vagueness grounds but not on First Amendment free speech and assembly. The Court of Appeals, affirmed. The U.S. Supreme Court granted certiorari, and affirmed.

ROBERTS, CJ., JOINED BY STEVENS, SCALIA, KENNEDY, THOMAS, AND ALITO, JJ.

FACTS

This litigation concerns 18 U.S.C. § 2339B, which makes it a federal crime to "knowingly provide material support or resources to a foreign terrorist organization." [See Table 13.3.] In 1997, the Secretary of State designated as terrorist organizations the Kurdistan Workers' Party (PKK) and the Liberation Tigers of Tamil Eelam (LTTE). The PKK is an organization founded in 1974 with the aim of establishing an independent Kurdish state in southeastern Turkey. The LTTE is an organization founded in 1976 for the purpose of creating an independent Tamil state in Sri Lanka.

In 1998, plaintiffs filed suit in federal court challenging the constitutionality of the material-support statute, § 2339B. . . . Plaintiffs claimed that the material-support statute . . . violated their freedom of speech and freedom of association under the First Amendment. . . . We . . . consider whether the material-support statute, as applied to plaintiffs, violates the freedom of speech guaranteed by the First Amendment.

. . .

OPINION

Everyone agrees that the Government's interest in combating terrorism is an urgent objective of the highest order. Plaintiffs' complaint is that the ban on material support, applied to what they wish to do, is not "necessary to further that interest." The objective of combating terrorism does not justify prohibiting their speech, plaintiffs argue, because their support will advance only the legitimate activities of the designated terrorist organizations, not their terrorism.

Whether foreign terrorist organizations meaningfully segregate support of their legitimate activities from support of terrorism is an empirical question. When it enacted § 2339B in 1996, Congress made specific findings regarding the serious threat posed by international terrorism. One of those findings explicitly rejects plaintiffs' contention that their support would not further the terrorist activities of the PKK and LTTE: "Foreign organizations that engage in terrorist activity are so tainted by their criminal conduct that *any contribution to such an organization* facilitates that conduct" (emphasis added).

. . .

The PKK and the LTTE are deadly groups. "The PKK's insurgency has claimed more than 22,000 lives." The LTTE has engaged in extensive suicide bombings and political assassinations, including killings of the Sri Lankan President, Security Minister, and Deputy Defense Minister. "On January 31, 1996, the LTTE exploded a truck bomb filled with an estimated 1,000 pounds of explosives at the Central Bank in Colombo, killing 100 people and injuring more than 1,400. This

(continues)

(continued)

bombing was the most deadly terrorist incident in the world in 1996. It is not difficult to conclude as Congress did that the "taint" of such violent activities is so great that working in coordination with or at the command of the PKK and LTTE serves to legitimize and further their terrorist means.

Material support meant to "promote peaceable, lawful conduct," can further terrorism by foreign groups in multiple ways. Such support frees up other resources within the organization that may be put to violent ends. It also importantly helps lend legitimacy to foreign terrorist groups—legitimacy that makes it easier for those groups to persist, to recruit members, and to raise funds—all of which facilitate more terrorist attacks. . . .

Money is fungible, and when foreign terrorist organizations that have a dual structure raise funds, they highlight the civilian and humanitarian ends to which such moneys could be put. But there is reason to believe that foreign terrorist organizations do not maintain legitimate *financial* firewalls between those funds raised for civil, nonviolent activities, and those ultimately used to support violent, terrorist operations. . . . There is evidence that the PKK and the LTTE, in particular, have not respected the line between humanitarian and violent activities. Providing foreign terrorist groups with material support in any form also furthers terrorism by straining the United States' relationships with its allies and undermining cooperative efforts between nations to prevent terrorist attacks. . . . The material-support statute furthers this international effort by prohibiting aid for foreign terrorist groups that harm the United States' partners abroad.

. . .

In analyzing whether it is possible in practice to distinguish material support for a foreign terrorist group's violent activities and its nonviolent activities, we do not rely exclusively on our own inferences drawn from the record evidence. We have before us an affidavit stating the Executive Branch's conclusion on that question. The State Department informs us that "the experience and analysis of the U.S. government agencies charged with combating terrorism strongly support" Congress's finding that all contributions to foreign terrorist organizations further their terrorism. . . .

That evaluation of the facts by the Executive, like Congress's assessment, is entitled to deference. This litigation implicates sensitive and weighty interests of national security and foreign affairs. . . . Neither the Members of this Court nor most federal judges begin the day with briefings that may describe new and serious threats to our Nation and its people. It is vital in this context not to substitute . . . our own evaluation of evidence for a reasonable evaluation by the Legislative Branch. . . .

The Government's authority and expertise in these matters do not automatically trump the Court's own obligation to secure the protection that the Constitution grants to individuals. But when it comes to collecting evidence and drawing factual inferences in this area, the lack of competence on the part of the courts is marked, and respect for the Government's conclusions is appropriate.

One reason for that respect is that national security and foreign policy concerns arise in connection with efforts to confront evolving threats in an area where information can be difficult to obtain and the impact of certain conduct difficult to assess. . . . The material-support statute is, on its face, a preventive measure—it criminalizes not terrorist attacks themselves, but aid that makes the attacks more likely to occur. The Government, when seeking to prevent imminent harms in the context of international affairs and national security, is not required to conclusively link all the pieces in the puzzle before we grant weight to its empirical conclusions.

. . .

We also find it significant that Congress has been conscious of its own responsibility to consider how its actions may implicate constitutional concerns. First, § 2339B only applies to designated foreign terrorist organizations. . . . Second, . . . Congress added clarity to the statute by providing narrowing definitions of the terms "training," "personnel," and "expert advice or assistance," as well as an explanation of the knowledge required to violate § 2339B. Third, in effectuating its stated intent not to abridge First Amendment rights, see § 2339B(i), Congress has also displayed a careful balancing of interests in creating limited exceptions to the ban on material support. The definition of material support, for example, excludes medicine and religious materials. See § 2339A(b)(1). . . . Finally, and most importantly, Congress has avoided any restriction on independent advocacy, or indeed any activities not directed to, coordinated with, or controlled by foreign terrorist groups.

. . . Given the sensitive interests in national security and foreign affairs at stake, the political branches have adequately substantiated their determination that, to serve the Government's interest in preventing terrorism, it was necessary to prohibit providing material support in the form of training, expert advice, personnel, and services to foreign terrorist groups, even if the supporters meant to promote only the groups' nonviolent ends.

We turn to the particular speech plaintiffs propose to undertake. First, plaintiffs propose to "train members of [the] PKK on how to use humanitarian and international law to peacefully resolve disputes." Congress can, consistent with the First Amendment, prohibit this direct training. It is wholly foreseeable that the PKK could use the "specific skills" that plaintiffs propose to impart, § 2339A(b)(2), as part of a broader strategy to promote terrorism. . . . This possibility is real, not remote.

Second, plaintiffs propose to "teach PKK members how to petition various representative bodies such as the United Nations for relief." The Government acts within First Amendment strictures in banning this proposed speech because it teaches the organization how to acquire "relief," which . . . could readily include monetary aid. . . . Congress logically concluded that money a terrorist group such as the PKK obtains using the techniques plaintiffs propose to teach could be redirected to funding the group's violent activities.

Finally, plaintiffs propose to "engage in political advocacy on behalf of Kurds who live in Turkey," and "engage in political advocacy on behalf of Tamils who live in Sri Lanka." . . . Plaintiffs do not specify their expected level of coordination with the PKK or LTTE or suggest what exactly their "advocacy" would consist of. Plaintiffs' proposals are phrased at such a high level of generality that they cannot prevail in this preenforcement challenge [which requires more exact description of the advocacy].

. . .

All this is not to say that any future applications of the material-support statute to speech or advocacy will survive First Amendment scrutiny. . . . We simply hold that, in prohibiting the particular forms of support that plaintiffs seek to provide to foreign terrorist groups, § 2339B does not violate the freedom of speech.

Plaintiffs' final claim is that the material-support statute violates their freedom of association under the First Amendment. Plaintiffs argue that the statute criminalizes the mere fact of their associating with the PKK and the LTTE. The statute does not penalize mere association with a foreign terrorist organization. The statute does not prohibit being a member of one of the designated groups or vigorously promoting and supporting the political goals of the group. . . . What [§ 2339B] prohibits is the act of giving material support. Plaintiffs want to do the latter. . . .

. . .

The Preamble to the Constitution proclaims that the people of the United States ordained and established that charter of government in part to "provide for the common defence." As Madison explained, "security against foreign danger is . . . an avowed and essential object of the American Union." We hold that, in regulating the particular forms of support that plaintiffs seek to provide to foreign terrorist organizations, Congress has pursued that objective consistent with the limitations of the First and Fifth Amendments.

The judgment of the United States Court of Appeals for the Ninth Circuit is affirmed [on the First Amendment issue]. . . . and the cases are remanded for further proceedings consistent with this opinion.

It is so ordered.

DISSENT

BREYER, J., JOINED GINSBURG AND SOTOMAYOR, JJ.

The plaintiffs, all United States citizens or associations, seek an injunction and declaration providing that, without violating the statute, they can (1) "train members of [the] PKK on how to use humanitarian and international law to peacefully resolve disputes"; (2) "engage in political advocacy on behalf of Kurds who live in Turkey"; (3) "teach PKK members how to petition various representative bodies such as the United Nations for relief"; and (4) "engage in political advocacy on behalf of Tamils who live in Sri Lanka." All these activities are of a kind that the First Amendment ordinarily protects.

In my view, the Government has not made the strong showing necessary to justify under the First Amendment the criminal prosecution of those who engage in these activities. All the activities involve the communication and advocacy of political ideas

(continues)

(continued)

and lawful means of achieving political ends. Even the subjects the plaintiffs wish to teach—using international law to resolve disputes peacefully or petitioning the United Nations, for instance—concern political speech. . . . That this speech and association for political purposes is the *kind* of activity to which the First Amendment ordinarily offers its strongest protection is elementary. If the First Amendment has any force, it prohibits Congress from fining or jailing citizens, or associations of citizens, for simply engaging in political speech.

Although in the Court's view the statute applies only where the PKK helps to coordinate a defendant's activities, the simple fact of "coordination" alone cannot readily remove protection that the First Amendment would otherwise grant. That amendment, after all, also protects the freedom of association. The right of peaceable assembly is a right cognate to those of free speech and free presses and equally fundamental. . . . Moreover, the Court has previously held that a person who associates with a group that uses unlawful means to achieve its ends does not thereby necessarily forfeit the First Amendment's protection for freedom of association. . . . Not even the serious and deadly problem of international terrorism can require *automatic* forfeiture of First Amendment rights. . . . Not even the war power removes constitutional limitations safeguarding essential liberties. . . .

. . .

I doubt that the statute . . . can survive any reasonably applicable First Amendment standard. The Government does identify a compelling countervailing interest, namely, the interest in protecting the security of the United States and its nationals from the threats that foreign terrorist organizations pose by denying those organizations financial and other fungible resources. I do not dispute the importance of this interest. But I do dispute whether the interest can justify the statute's criminal prohibition.

. . .

I would read the statute as criminalizing First–Amendment–protected pure speech and association only when the defendant knows or intends that those activities will assist the organization's unlawful terrorist actions. Under this reading, the Government would have to show, at a minimum, that such defendants provided support that they knew was significantly likely to help the organization pursue its unlawful terrorist aims.

A person acts with the requisite knowledge if he is aware of (or willfully blinds himself to) a significant likelihood that his or her conduct will materially support the organization's terrorist ends. . . . On the other hand, knowledge or intent that this assistance (aimed at lawful activities) could or would help further terrorism simply by helping to legitimate the organization is not sufficient.

This reading of the statute protects those who engage in pure speech and association ordinarily protected by the First Amendment. But it does not protect that activity where a defendant purposefully intends it to help terrorism or where a defendant knows (or willfully blinds himself to the fact) that the activity is significantly likely to assist terrorism. Where the activity fits into these categories of purposefully or knowingly supporting terrorist ends, the act of providing material support to a known terrorist organization bears a close enough relation to terrorist acts that, in my view, it likely can be prohibited notwithstanding any First Amendment interest. At the same time, this reading does not require the Government to undertake the difficult task of proving which, as between peaceful and nonpeaceful purposes, a defendant specifically preferred; knowledge is enough.

. . .

In sum, these cases require us to consider how to apply the First Amendment where national security interests are at stake. When deciding such cases, courts are aware and must respect the fact that the Constitution entrusts to the Executive and Legislative Branches the power to provide for the national defense, and that it grants particular authority to the President in matters of foreign affairs. Nonetheless, this Court has also made clear that authority and expertise in these matters do not automatically trump the Court's own obligation to secure the protection that the Constitution grants to individuals. *Hamdi v. Rumsfeld,* 542 U.S. 507 (2004) ("We have long since made clear that a state of war is not a blank check . . . when it comes to the rights of th[is] Nation's citizens"). In these cases, I believe the Court has failed to examine the Government's justifications with sufficient care. It has failed to insist upon specific evidence, rather than general assertion. It has failed to require tailoring of means to fit compelling ends. And ultimately it deprives the individuals before us of the protection that the First Amendment demands.

That is why, with respect, I dissent.

QUESTIONS

1. List the activities Judge Fertig and the HLP wish to pursue.
2. Summarize the majority's arguments supporting their conclusion that the "providing material support and resources to terrorist organizations" provisions don't run afoul of the First Amendment ban on laws abridging the rights to free speech and peaceable assembly.
3. Summarize the dissent's argument that the "material support and resources" provisions *do* violate First Amendment rights of free speech and peaceable assembly.
4. Which do you agree with, the majority or the dissent? Defend your answer.
5. Judge Ralph Fertig, the lead plaintiff, a longtime pacifist and human rights advocate, says:

> he wants no part of terrorism or violence, but rather the right to advocate for the rights of the Kurdish minority in Turkey. He is troubled that the Kurds can be punished for speaking their own language and displaying their national colors. And he believes the 1st Amendment protects his right to counsel Kurdish leaders away from violence and to take their cause to the United Nations. (Savage 2010)

In his words, "I am opposed to violence. It seems crazy to me that I could go to jail for trying to persuade people to engage in nonviolence" (Savage 2010). What do you say to Judge Fertig?

Which of the following actions is it ethical to ban as "material support and resources" to terrorists?

1. Former President Jimmy Carter, while he monitored elections in Lebanon, met with leaders of all the parties, including designated terrorist organization Hezbollah to advise them on fair election procedures.
2. A reporter published an interview with a terrorist fighter.
3. A social media platform included accounts claiming to be from the Somalian designated terrorist group al Shabab.
4. The *New York Times* and *Washington Post* published an op-ed from representatives of the designated terrorist organization.

Instructions

1. Read the following:
   a. "The Roberts Court's free speech problem" (2010), by David Cole.
   b. http://www.nybooks.com/blogs/nyrblog/2010/jun/28/roberts-courts-free-speech-problem/.
   c. "Can the U.S. government close social media accounts?" (2011) by Glenn Greenwald. http://www.salon.com/2011/12/20/the_u_s_government_targets_twitter_terrorism/.
2. Even if the incidents described in the links don't violate the First Amendment, or other provisions in the Constitution, what would be the ethical thing to do regarding their publication?

SUMMARY

LO 1 The revolutionaries who wrote the U.S. Constitution knew that the new government they were about to create couldn't survive without the active support of most of the people. The people's allegiance would be especially important to the newborn nation's survival in the early years following the Revolution, a time of great threats from enemies inside (traitor, spies, and other disloyal individuals) and outside (England, Spain, France, and Native American nations) the new country.

LO 2 Treason is the only crime defined in the U.S. Constitution. The authors of the Constitution had mixed feelings about treason because, in the eyes of the English government, they were traitors and their own ancestors had fled from religious persecution and prosecution for treason. They had two worries: (1) that peaceful opposition to the government, not just rebellion, would be repressed and (2) that innocent people might be convicted of treason because of perjury, passion, and/or insufficient evidence.

Treason is very difficult to prove, and throughout U.S. history, the government has prosecuted only a handful of people for treason. Furthermore, presidents have pardoned or at least mitigated death sentences of most of those few who have been found guilty.

LO 3 Other ancient crimes of disloyalty still exist today, specifically sedition, sabotage, and espionage. Sedition is the crime of advocating the violent overthrow of the government. Sabotage is the crime of damaging or destroying property for the purpose of hindering preparations for war and national defense during national emergences. Espionage is the crime of spying for the enemy. All of the definitions of these crimes have evolved to accommodate changes in society and technology.

LO 4 A number of sections of the U.S. Code make available crimes related to terrorists and terrorist organizations for prosecuting offenders. The most comprehensive law developed to fight terror is the USA Patriot Act, passed by Congress soon after the terrorist attacks on the United States on September 11, 2001.

LO 5 Not surprisingly, the most commonly prosecuted crime against the state since September 11, 2001, involves alleged terrorists or terrorist organizations.

LO 6 The most-argued issues in material support cases include: (1) Due process—"Is the term 'material support' void for vagueness?" and the (2) First Amendment—"Does providing material support violate the right to free speech and association?" We see in our ongoing current events the same struggle that the drafters of the Constitution witnessed and addressed: the "push-and-pull" between our cherished individual liberties versus the role of government to protect and preserve its people and the country in which they live.

KEY TERMS

treason, p. 484
adherence to the enemy, p. 485
treason *actus reus*, p. 486
treason *mens rea*, p. 486
proof of treason, p. 486
sedition, p. 488
seditious speech, p. 488
seditious libel, p. 488
seditious conspiracy, p. 488
Smith Act of 1940, p. 488
sabotage, p. 488
espionage, p. 491
espionage during peace, p. 491
espionage during war, p. 491
terrorism, p. 496
USA Patriot Act, p. 496
material support offenses, p. 502

APPENDIX

Selected Amendments of the Constitution of the United States: The Bill of Rights and Amendment XIV

Amendment I Congress shall make no law respecting an establishment of religion, or prohibiting the free exercise thereof; or abridging the freedom of speech, or of the press; or the right of the people peaceably to assemble, and to petition the Government for a redress of grievances.

Amendment II A well regulated Militia, being necessary to the security of a free State, the right of the people to keep and bear Arms, shall not be infringed.

Amendment III No Soldier shall, in time of peace be quartered in any house, without the consent of the Owner, nor in time of war, but in a manner to be prescribed by law.

Amendment IV The right of the people to be secure in their persons, houses, papers, and effects, against unreasonable searches and seizures, shall not be violated, and no Warrants shall issue, but upon probable cause, supported by Oath or affirmation, and particularly describing the place to be searched, and the persons or things to be seized.

Amendment V No person shall be held to answer for a capital, or otherwise infamous crime, unless on a presentment or indictment of a Grand Jury, except in cases arising in the land or naval forces, or in the Militia, when in actual service in time of War or public danger; nor shall any person be subject for the same offence to be twice put in jeopardy of life or limb; nor shall be compelled in any criminal case to be a witness against himself, nor be deprived of life, liberty, or property, without due process of law; nor shall private property be taken for public use, without just compensation.

Amendment VI In all criminal prosecutions, the accused shall enjoy the right to a speedy and public trial, by an impartial jury of the State and district wherein the crime shall have been committed, which district shall have been previously ascertained by law, and to be informed of the nature and cause of the accusation; to be confronted with the witnesses against him; to have compulsory process for obtaining witnesses in his favor, and to have the Assistance of Counsel for his defence.

Amendment VII In Suits at common law, where the value in controversy shall exceed twenty dollars, the right of trial by jury shall be preserved, and no fact tried by a jury, shall be otherwise re-examined in any Court of the United States, than according to the rules of the common law.

Amendment VIII Excessive bail shall not be required, nor excessive fines imposed, nor cruel and unusual punishments inflicted.

Amendment IX The enumeration in the Constitution, of certain rights, shall not be construed to deny or disparage others retained by the people.

Amendment X

The powers not delegated to the United States by the Constitution, nor prohibited by it to the States, are reserved to the States respectively, or to the people.

Amendment XIV

Passed by Congress June 13, 1866. Ratified July 9, 1868.

Section 1 All persons born or naturalized in the United States, and subject to the jurisdiction thereof, are citizens of the United States and of the State wherein they reside. No State shall make or enforce any law which shall abridge the privileges or immunities of citizens of the United States; nor shall any State deprive any person of life, liberty, or property, without due process of law; nor deny to any person within its jurisdiction the equal protection of the laws.

Section 2 Representatives shall be apportioned among the several States according to their respective numbers, counting the whole number of persons in each State, excluding Indians not taxed. But when the right to vote at any election for the choice of electors for President and Vice President of the United States, Representatives in Congress, the Executive and Judicial officers of a State, or the members of the Legislature thereof, is denied to any of the male inhabitants of such State, being twenty-one years of age, and citizens of the United States, or in any way abridged, except for participation in rebellion, or other crime, the basis of representation therein shall be reduced in the proportion which the number of such male citizens shall bear to the whole number of male citizens twenty-one years of age in such State.

Section 3 No person shall be a Senator or Representative in Congress, or elector of President and Vice-President, or hold any office, civil or military, under the United States, or under any State, who having previously taken an oath, as a member of Congress, or as an officer of the United States, or as a member of any State legislature, or as an executive or judicial officer of any State, to support the Constitution of the United States, shall have engaged in insurrection or rebellion against the same, or given aid or comfort to the enemies thereof. But Congress may by a vote of two thirds of each House, remove such disability.

Section 4 The validity of the public debt of the United States, authorized by law, including debts incurred for payment of pensions and bounties for services in suppressing insurrection or rebellion, shall not be questioned. But neither the United States nor any State shall assume or pay any debt or obligation incurred in aid of insurrection or rebellion against the United States, or any claim for the loss or emancipation of any slave; but all such debts, obligations and claims shall be held illegal and void.

Section 5 The Congress shall have power to enforce, by appropriate legislation, the provisions of this article.

GLOSSARY

abuse-of-discretion standard failure to exercise sound, reasonable, and legal decision making; an appellate court's standard for reviewing a decision that is asserted to be grossly unsound, unreasonable, illegal, or unsupported by the evidence

abuse-of-trust crimes crimes growing out of opportunities to get someone else's property that was entrusted to the perpetrators because of their occupation, now known as *white-collar crimes*

accessories participants after crimes are committed; also known as *accessory after the fact*

accessories after the fact persons who help after the crime is committed (harboring a fugitive)

accessories before the fact persons not present when the crimes are committed but who help before the crime is committed (for example, someone who provided a weapon used in a murder)

accessory liability liability that attaches for participation after crimes are committed

accomplice participant before and during the commission of crimes

accomplice *actus reus* defendant took "some positive act in aid of the commission of the offense"

accomplice liability liability that attaches for participation before and during a crime

act reasonableness meaning "a finding that a reasonable person in the defendant's shoes would have responded as violently as the defendant did"

actual disorderly conduct breach-of-the-peace misdemeanor that includes fighting in public and making unreasonable noise

actual possession physical control of banned items on my person, for example, marijuana in my pocket

actus reus the requirement that all crimes have to include a voluntary criminal act, which is the physical element and the first principle of criminal liability

adequate provocation (voluntary manslaughter) the requirement that the provocation for killing in anger has to be something the law recognizes, the defendant himself had to be provoked, and that a reasonable person would have been provoked

adherence to the enemy the definition of treason under English common law, meaning breaking allegiance to your own country by forming an "attachment to the enemy"

administrative crimes violations of federal and state agency rules that make up a controversial but rapidly growing source of criminal law

affirmative defense of insanity (insanity defense) the legal excuse that defendants aren't responsible for their criminal conduct because it was caused by a mental disease or defect

affirmative defenses defendants have to "start matters off by putting in some evidence in support" of their justification or excuse defenses; defenses of excuse for criminal liability, which take place after the prosecution has proved the defendant's criminal conduct

agency theory accomplice liability theory that assumes we're autonomous agents with the freedom to choose our actions and become accountable for someone else's actions when we voluntarily "join in and identify with those actions"

aggravated rape rape by strangers or individuals with weapons who physically injure their victims

all but the last act test a strict test for whether "all but the last act" undertaken by the defendant, which does meet the proximity test, satisfies the attempt *actus reus* of the crime

American bystander rule there's no legal duty to rescue or summon help for someone who's in danger, even if the bystander risks nothing by helping

appellate courts in most states and the federal government, the two levels of appeals courts: an intermediate court of appeals and a supreme court

***Apprendi* rule** other than the fact of prior conviction, any fact that *increases* the penalty for a crime beyond the prescribed statutory maximum must be submitted to a jury and proved beyond a reasonable doubt

arson damaging or destroying structures by burning

arson *mens rea* common law *mens rea* requires a malicious and willful intent to burn or set fire to buildings; general-intent *mens rea* requires only the intent to start a fire

assault an attempt to commit battery or intentionally putting another in fear

attempt *actus reus* taking some steps toward completing a crime

attempted battery assault consists of having the specific intent to commit battery and taking substantial steps toward carrying it out without actually completing the attempt

attempt *mens rea* the specific intent to commit a crime

attendant circumstances element a "circumstance" connected to an act, an intent, and/or a bad result

authorized consent the person consenting has the authority to give consent

automatism unconscious bodily movements

bad result crimes (result crimes) crimes that include five elements: (1) a voluntary act, (2) the mental element, (3) circumstantial elements, (4) causation, and (5) criminal harm

barbaric punishments punishments considered no longer acceptable to civilized society

battery unwanted and unjustified offensive touching

bench trial cases in which the accused give up their right to a jury trial and are tried by judges who decide whether prosecutors have proved their guilt

bifurcated (two-stage) trial a two-phase trial, in which the first phase determines whether the state has met its burden of proof and, if so, the second phase determines whether the defendant has sustained the burden of establishing a mental illness defense

bifurcation procedure the requirement that the death penalty decision be made in two phases: a trial to determine guilt and a second separate proceeding, after a finding of guilt, to consider the aggravating factors for, and mitigating factors against, capital punishment

blameworthiness see *culpability*

born-alive rule the rule that to be a person, and therefore a homicide victim, a baby had to be "born alive" and capable of breathing and maintaining a heartbeat on its own

breaking (in burglary) part of the *actus reus* of common law burglary, requiring an unlawful, frequently destructive, entry into someone else's building

broken-windows theory first espoused by James Q. Wilson and George L. Kelling, the theory that minor offenses or disorderly conduct can lead to a rise in serious crime

burden of persuasion defendants have to prove their justification or excuse defenses by a preponderance of the evidence

burden of production to make defendants responsible for presenting evidence in their own justification or excuse defense

burden of proof to have to prove beyond a reasonable doubt "every fact necessary to constitute the crime charged"

burglary breaking and entering a building or structure with intent to commit a crime inside the building

burning (in arson) setting a building on fire

but for causation see *cause in fact*

"but for" cause see *factual cause*

capital cases death penalty cases in death penalty states and "mandatory life sentence without parole" cases in non–death penalty states

case citation the numbers, letters, and punctuation that tell you where to locate the full case report; they follow the title of a case in the excerpts or in the bibliography at the end of the book

castle exception when you're attacked in your home, you can stand your ground and use deadly force to fend off an unprovoked attack but only if you reasonably believe the attack threatens death or serious bodily injury

causation holding an actor criminally accountable for the results of her conduct

cause in fact the objective determination that the defendant's act triggered a chain of events that ended as the harmful result, such as the death in a homicide

chain conspiracies participants at one end of the chain may know nothing of those at the other end, but every participant handles the same commodity at different points, such as manufacture, distribution, and sale

choice-of-evils defense (also called the **general defense of necessity**) justifies the choice to commit a lesser crime to avoid the harm of a greater crime

civil commitment a noncriminal (civil) proceeding, in which courts have the power to decide if defendants who were insane when they committed their crimes are still insane

civil gang injunctions (CGI) noncriminal lawsuits brought by cities seeking restraining orders to bar gang members from gang activities

codified written definitions of crimes and punishment enacted by legislatures and published

cohabitant exception in the exception jurisdictions that follow the retreat rule, people who live in the same home don't have to retreat

common law judge-made law, the original source of law, in which judge's court opinions formed the law

common law crimes crimes created before legislatures existed and when social order depended on obedience to unwritten rules (the *lex non scripta*) based on community customs and traditions that over the centuries became incorporated into court decisions

common law fraud obtaining another's property by "simple deception"

common law rape intentional forced heterosexual vaginal penetration by a man of a woman who isn't his wife

complicity establishes when you can be criminally liable for someone else's conduct; applies criminal liability to accomplices and accessories

concurrence the principle of criminal liability that requires that a criminal intent has to trigger the criminal act

concurring opinion agrees with the conclusions of either the majority or the dissenting opinion but provides different reasons for reaching the conclusion

conditional threats threats based upon the existence of certain conditions that don't presently exist aren't enough to satisfy the *mens rea* of assault because they're not immediate

conduct crimes crimes requiring a criminal act triggered by criminal intent

consolidated theft statutes eliminate needlessly separating theft into distinct offenses according to their *actus reus*; comprises crimes of taking and carrying away, converting, or swindling to gain possession of someone else's property

conspiracy the crime of agreeing with one or more people to commit a crime

conspiracy *actus reus* consists of two parts: (1) an agreement to commit a crime and (2) an overt act in furtherance of the agreement

conspiracy *mens rea* the mental element in conspiracy, frequently identified as specific intent by authorities, but it's not defined clearly in statutes and it's defined inconsistently by courts

constitutional democracy the majority can't make a crime out of conduct protected by the fundamental rights in the U.S. Constitution

constitutional right to privacy a right that bans "all governmental invasions of the sanctity of a man's home and the privacies of life"

constructive disorderly conduct conduct that "tends to provoke or excite others to break the peace

constructive possession banned items not on my person but in places I control, for example, in my car or apartment

conversion wrongfully possessing or disposing of someone else's property as if it were yours

corpus delicti Latin for "body of the crime," it refers to the body of the victim in homicides and to the elements of the crime in other offenses

corroboration rule an element in rape that the prosecution had to prove rape by the testimony of witnesses other than the victim

court's holding the legal rule the court has decided to apply to the facts of the cases

court's reasoning the reasons the court gives to support its holding

crimes against public order formerly called "bad manners" crimes; today called *"quality of life" crimes*, they include public drinking, aggressive panhandling, harassment, graffiti and vandalism, and street prostitution

criminal acts *actus reus*, voluntary bodily movements

criminal attempts trying but failing to commit crimes

criminal conduct voluntary criminal acts triggered by criminal intent

criminal conspiracy making an agreement to commit a crime

criminal homicide all homicides that are neither justified nor excused

criminal liability conduct that unjustifiably and inexcusably inflicts or threatens substantial harm to individual or public interests

criminal mischief damaging or destroying personal property

criminal mischief *actus reus* in destruction or damage criminal mischief, the *actus reus* is burning, exploding, flooding, or committing some other dangerous act; in tampering, it's any act that threatens or endangers property; in deception or threat, it's causing harm through deception or threats

criminal negligence manslaughter see *involuntary manslaughter*

criminal objective the criminal goal of an agreement to commit a crime

criminal objective of the conspiracy the object of conspiracy agreements has to be to commit crimes

criminal objective of the solicitation circumstance element that the objective of the solicitation is law breaking; the seriousness varies from any violation to violent felony

criminal omissions the failure to act when there's a legal duty to act

criminal punishment penalties that meet four criteria: (1) inflict pain or other unpleasant consequences; (2) prescribe a punishment in the same law that defines the crime; (3) administered intentionally; (4) administered by the state

criminal solicitation trying to get someone else to commit a crime

criminal trespass the unwanted, unauthorized invading of another person's property

cruel and unusual punishment "barbaric" punishments and punishments that are disproportionate to the crime committed

culpability blameworthiness, the idea that it's fair and just to punish only people we can blame; only someone who intends to harm her victim deserves punishment; accidents don't qualify

curtilage the area immediately surrounding the home

cybercrime crimes aimed at the valuable information contained in computers and wireless devices, especially computer databases accessible through the Internet

cyberstalking the use of the Internet, e-mail, or other electronic communication devices to stalk another person through threatening behavior

dangerous act rationale looks at how close defendants came to completing their crimes

dangerous person rationale concentrates on how fully defendants have developed their intent to commit their crime

dangerous person tests look at what actors have already done to demonstrate that they're a danger to society, not just in this crime but, more important, in crimes they might commit in the future if they're not dealt with now

dangerous proximity tests focus on dangerous conduct; they look at what remains for actors to do before they hurt society by completing the crime

dangerous proximity to success test/physical proximity test (also called the **physical proximity test**) asks whether defendants have come "dangerously close" to completing the crime

deadly weapon doctrine one who intentionally uses a deadly weapon on another human being and thereby kills him presumably intends to kill him

defense of consent the justification that competent adults voluntarily consented to crimes against themselves and knew what they were consenting to

defense of duress when defendants use the excuse that they were forced to do what they did

defense of reasonable mistake of age a defense to statutory rape in California and Alaska if the defendant reasonably believed his victim was at or over the age of consent

depraved heart murder extremely reckless killings

determinism forces beyond offenders' control cause them to commit crimes

deterrence theory rational human beings won't commit crimes if they know that the pain of punishment outweighs the pleasure gained from committing crimes

diminished capacity an attempt to prove that the defendant, incapable of the requisite intent of the crime charged, is innocent of that crime but may well be guilty of a lesser one

diminished responsibility the defendant argues, "What I did was wrong, but under the circumstances I'm *less* responsible"

disorderly conduct crimes offenses against public order and morals

***Durham* rule** the product-of-mental-illness test; acts that are the "products" of mental disease or defect excuse criminal liability

dwelling of another anyplace where other people live

elements of a crime to convict, the prosecution must prove beyond a reasonable doubt (1) a criminal act (in all crimes), (2) criminal intent (in some crimes), (3) concurrence (in all crimes), (4) attendant circumstances (in some crimes), and (5) that criminal conduct caused a criminal harm (in bad result crimes only)

embezzlement the crime of lawfully gaining possession of someone else's property and later converting it to one's own use

emotion-act distinction separating the emotions that led to a killing from the question of whether it was reasonable

emotional reasonableness a finding that "the defendant's *emotional* outrage or *passion* was reasonable

entering (in burglary) part of the *actus reus* of burglary, meaning to come or go into the building or structure

enterprise just about any form of human endeavor

entrapment excuse that argues government agents got people to commit crimes they wouldn't otherwise commit

equal protection of the laws a constitutional command that criminal laws can treat groups of people and types of conduct differently only if the different treatment is reasonable

espionage the crime of spying for the enemy

espionage during peace turning or attempting to turn over information about national defense to any foreign country with "intent or with reason to believe" the information is "to be used" to either hurt the United States or help any foreign country

espionage during war consists of collecting, recording, publishing, or communicating (or attempting to do any of these) "any information" about troop movements, ships, aircraft, or war materials and any other information "which might be useful to the enemy"

euthanasia helping another person to die

excusable homicide killings done by someone "not of sound memory and discretion"

excuse defenses defendants admit what they did was wrong but claim that, under the circumstances, they weren't responsible for what they did

ex post facto law a retroactive law that does one of three things: (1) criminalizes an act that wasn't a crime when it was committed, (2) increases the punishment for a crime after the crime was committed, or (3) takes away a defense that was available to a defendant when the crime was committed

expressive conduct (in First Amendment) nonverbal actions that communicate ideas and feelings

express malice aforethought killings that fit the original meaning of "murder"—intentional killings planned in advance

extraneous factor a "stroke of luck"—namely, a circumstance beyond the attempter's control that prevents the completion of the crime

extreme mental or emotional disturbance manslaughter a homicide committed under the influence of extreme mental or emotional disturbance for which there is reasonable explanation or excuse. The reasonableness of such explanation or excuse shall be determined from the viewpoint of the person in the actor's situation under the circumstances as he believes them to be

extrinsic force in rape cases, requires some force in addition to the amount needed to accomplish the penetration

factual cause also called "but for" cause or "cause in fact"; if it weren't for an actor's conduct, the result wouldn't have occurred

factual impossibility occurs when actors intend to commit a crime and try to but it's physically impossible because some fact or circumstance unknown to them interrupts or prevents the completion of the crime

failure-of-proof defense mistake defenses in which defendants usually present enough evidence to raise a reasonable doubt that the prosecution has proved the *mens rea* required for criminal liability; the defendant only has to raise a reasonable doubt about the prosecution's proof of just one element in the crime

failure-of-proof scheme defendants raise a reasonable doubt that the prosecution has proven the mental element of the crime, so they don't have to justify or excuse their conduct because it's not criminal conduct

failure to intervene actively preventing or interrupting injuries and death to persons or damage and destruction of property

failure to report not reporting something the law requires you to report

fair notice (in void-for-vagueness doctrine) in ex post facto laws, it isn't whether the defendant knows there's a law against the act but whether an ordinary, reasonable person would know that the act is a crime

false imprisonment depriving others of their personal liberty without the asportation requirement

fault-based defenses defenses based on creating a reasonable doubt about the prosecution's proof of a voluntary act

federal mail fraud statute includes "schemes to defraud or for obtaining money or property" using the U.S. mail

federal system fifty-two criminal codes, one for each of the fifty states, one for the District of Columbia, and one for the U.S. criminal code

felonies crimes punishable by death or confinement in the state's prison for one year to life without parole

felony murder rule unintentional deaths that occur during the commission of some felonies are murders

fences receivers of stolen goods or a place where stolen goods are bought

feticide killing a fetus

first-degree arson burning homes or other occupied structures (such as schools, offices, and churches) where there's danger to human life

first-degree murder consists of premeditated, deliberate intent to kill murders and (2) felony murders; the only crime today in which the death penalty can be imposed

fixed (determinate) sentences a legislative sentencing scheme that "fixes" or determines sentence length according to the seriousness of the crime; sentence depends on the criminal harm suffered by the victim, not the rehabilitation of the offender

Florida Personal Protection Law the model for most of the new castle laws; a person is justified in using deadly force and doesn't have a duty to retreat if he reasonably believes that the force is necessary to prevent imminent death or great bodily harm to himself or the imminent commission of a forcible felony

force and resistance rule provided that victims had to prove to the courts that they didn't consent to rape by demonstrating that they resisted the force of the rapist

forfeited personal identity theory the idea that when you choose to participate in crime, you forfeit your right to be treated as an individual; "your acts are my acts"

fraud a general term that means getting property by deception

fraud in the fact in rape, occurs when the rapist fraudulently convinces his victim that the act consented to was something other than sexual intercourse

fraud in the inducement in rape, occurs when the fraud is in the benefits promised, not in the act

fundamental right to privacy a right that requires the government to prove that a compelling interest justifies invading it

gay panic based on "the theory that a person with latent homosexual tendencies will have an extreme and uncontrollably violent reaction when confronted with a homosexual proposition"

general attempt statute a single statute that applies to the attempt to commit any crime in the state's criminal code

general deterrence aims, by the threat of punishment, to prevent the general population who haven't committed crimes from doing so

general intent the intent to commit the criminal act as defined in a statute

general intent "plus" where "general intent" refers to the intent to commit the *actus reus* of the crime and "plus" refers to some "special mental element" in addition to the intent to commit the criminal act

general part of criminal law principles that apply to more than one crime

"Good Samaritan" doctrine imposes a legal duty to help or call for help for imperiled strangers

group disorderly conduct consisted of three misdemeanors at common law: unlawful assembly, rout, and riot

guilty verdict *legally*, not necessarily *factually*, guilty; it means the government proved its case beyond a reasonable doubt

hedonism the natural law that human beings seek pleasure and avoid pain

honest and reasonable mistake rule a negligence mental element in rape cases in which the defendant argues that he honestly, but mistakenly, believed the victim consented to sex

identity theft the most frequently committed crime in the United States, it's stealing another person's identity for the purpose of getting something of value

imminent danger of attack the danger is "right now!"

imperfect defense when a defendant fails in the full defense but is found guilty of a lesser offense

implied malice aforethought intentional killings without premeditation or reasonable provocation; unintentional killings during the commission of felonies; depraved heart killings; and intent to inflict grievous bodily harm killings

incapacitation prevents convicted criminals from committing future crimes by locking them up, or more rarely, by altering them surgically or executing them

inchoate offenses from the Latin "to begin"; crimes that satisfy the *mens rea* of purpose or specific intent and the *actus reus* of taking *some* steps toward accomplishing the criminal purpose—but not enough steps to complete the intended crime

indeterminate sentencing laws prison release depends on the rehabilitation of individual prisoners

indispensable element test asks whether defendants have reached a point where they've gotten control of everything they need to complete the crime

informal discretionary decision making the invisible day-to-day process, in which law enforcement professionals make judgments based on unwritten rules, their training, and their experience

initial aggressor someone who provokes an attack and can't then use force to defend herself against the attack she provoked

insanity the legal term that refers to a mental disease or defect that impairs the reason and/or will

intangible property property worth nothing by itself but is proof of something of value (such as stock options, bonds, notes, trademarks, licenses, and patents)

intellectual property ideas and their practical application owned by an individual, a business, or a society

intentional scaring threatened battery assault (sometimes called "intentional scaring") requires only that actors intend to frighten their victims, thus expanding assault beyond attempted

intent to cause serious bodily injury murder no intent to kill is required when a victim dies following acts triggered by the intent to inflict serious bodily injury short of death

intermediate scrutiny the law is constitutional law as long as it is *substantially* related to an important government interest, such as protecting the First Amendment right to the free exercise of religion

intervening cause an event that comes between the initial act in a sequence and the end result

intrinsic force in rape, requires only the amount of force necessary to accomplish the penetration

involuntary intoxication an excuse to criminal liability in all states; it includes cases in which defendants don't know they're taking intoxicants or know but are forced to take them

involuntary manslaughter an unintentional killing (*mens rea*) by a voluntary act or omission (*actus reus*)

irresistible impulse test we can't blame or deter people who because of a mental disease or defect know that what they're doing is "wrong" but can't bring their actions into line with their knowledge of right and wrong

judgment the court's judgment (sometimes called the court's "decision") is how the court disposes of the case

judicial waiver when juvenile court judges use their discretion to transfer a juvenile to adult criminal court

justice depends on culpability, only those who deserve punishment can justly receive it

justifiable homicide killing in self-defense

justification defenses defendants admit they were responsible for their acts but claim that, under the circumstances, what they did was right (justified)

kidnapping the taking and carrying away of another person with the intent to deprive the other person of personal liberty

knowing consent the person consenting understands what she's consenting to; she's not too young or insane to understand

knowingly the mental attitude that a person acts knowingly with respect to a material element of an offense when (1) if the element involves the nature of his conduct or the attendant circumstances, he is aware that his conduct is of that nature or that such circumstances exist; and (2) if the element involves a result of his conduct, he is aware that it is practically certain that his conduct will cause such a result

knowing possession items possessors are aware is either on their person or in places they control

larceny taking and carrying away a person's property without the use of force and with the intent to permanently deprive the owner of possession

last act rule attempt *actus reus* requires all but the last act needed to complete the crime

last-straw rule/long smoldering or slow burn rule (also called the **"long smoldering"** or **"slow burn"** rule) adequate provocation defined as "a smoldering resentment or pent-up rage resulting from earlier insults or humiliating events culminating in a triggering event that, by itself, might be insufficient to provoke the deadly act"

legal ("proximate") cause a subjective question that asks, "Is it fair to blame the defendant for the harm triggered by a chain of events her action(s) set in motion?"

legal duty a duty created by a statute, contract, or special relationship, and enforceable by law

legal fiction pretending something is a fact when it's not if there's a "good" reason for the pretense

legal impossibility occurs when actors intend to commit crimes, and do everything they can to carry out their criminal intent, but the criminal law doesn't ban what they did

liberty refers to the right of individuals to come and go as they please without government interference

loitering the crime of remaining in one place with no apparent purpose

majority opinion the law of the case; the opinion of the majority of the justices on the court who participated in the case

***mala in se* crimes** offenses that require some level of criminal intent

***mala prohibita* crimes** crimes only because a specific statute or ordinance prohibits them

malice aforethought originally the mental state of intentional killing, with some amount of spite, hate, or bad will, planned in advance of the killing

malicious mischief common law crime of intentionally damaging or destroying another's tangible property

***malum prohibitum* crime** death has to be a foreseeable consequence of the unlawful act; the act is unlawful only because it's prohibited by a specific statute or ordinance; also see *mala prohibitum crimes*

mandatory minimum sentences statutes that require judges to impose a nondiscretionary minimum amount of prison time that all offenders have to serve

manifest criminality the requirement that mental attitudes have to turn into deeds for a "crime" to be committed

manslaughter killing a person without malice aforethought; an ancient common law crime created by judges, not by legislators, consisting of two crimes: voluntarily or involuntarily killing another person

marital rape exception provided that legally husbands couldn't rape their wives

material support offenses the federal crime of providing "training," "expert advice or assistance," "service," and "personnel to terrorists or terrorist organizations

***McNaughtan* rule** see *right-wrong test*

medical model of criminal law crime is a "disease," and criminals are "sick" and need "treatment" and "cure

mens rea criminal intent, the mental element in crime; Latin for guilty mind (also called "criminal intent," "evil mind," "mental attitude," or "state of mind") in crime

mental defect refers to mental retardation or brain damage severe enough to make it impossible to know what you're doing, or if you know, you don't know that it's wrong

mental disease most courts define it as psychosis, mostly paranoia and schizophrenia

mere possession items you possess but you don't know what they are

mere presence rule a person's presence at the scene of a crime doesn't by itself satisfy the *actus reus* requirement of accomplice liability

misdemeanors offenses punishable by fine and/or confinement in the local jail for up to one year

mistake a defense to criminal liability whenever the mistake prevents the formation of any fault-based mental attitude—namely, purposely, knowingly, recklessly, or negligently

mitigating circumstances circumstances that convince fact finders (judges or juries) that defendants don't deserve the maximum penalty for the crime they're convicted of

Model Penal Code (MPC) proposed criminal code drafted by the American Law Institute and used to reform criminal codes

motive something that causes a person to act

MPC's analysis of criminal liability analysis of statutes and cases to determine what behavior deserves criminal punishment and its definition of criminal liability: "conduct that unjustifiably and inexcusably inflicts or threatens substantial harm to individual or public interests"

MPC substantial steps test test that requires that attempters take enough steps toward completing the crime to prove that they're determined to commit it

murder killing a person with "malice aforethought"

murder *actus reus* the act of killing by poisoning, striking, starving, drowning, and a thousand other forms by which human nature can be overcome

murder *mens rea* can include purposeful, knowing, or reckless killing

necessity a defense that argues an imminent danger of attack was prevented

negligently the mental attitude that a person acts negligently with respect to a material element of an offense when he should be aware of a substantial and unjustifiable risk that the material element exists or will result from his conduct. The risk must be of such a nature and degree that the actor's failure to perceive it, considering the nature and purpose of his conduct and the circumstances known to him, involves a gross deviation from the standard of care that a reasonable person would observe in the actor's situation

not guilty verdict doesn't mean "innocent"; it means that the government didn't prove its case beyond a reasonable doubt

objective fault requires no purposeful or conscious bad mind in the actor

objective fear means that the fear was reasonable under the circumstances

objective test of cooling-off time (voluntary manslaughter) requires that a reasonable person under the same circumstances would have had time to cool off

objective test of entrapment if the intent originates with the government and their actions would tempt an "ordinarily law-abiding" person to commit the crime, the court should dismiss the case

obtaining property by false pretenses in modern law, often called "theft by deceit"; making false representations concerning past or present facts with the intent to defraud another

occupied structure "any structure, vehicle, or place adapted for overnight accommodations of persons, or for carrying on business therein, whether or not a person is actually present"

one-voluntary-act-is-enough conduct that includes a voluntary act satisfies the voluntary act requirement

opinion "the point of the story"; the court backs up its judgment by explaining how and why it applied the law (general principles and the elements of crimes) to the facts of the case

order refers to acting according to ordinary people's standard of "good manners"

overt act requirement the requirement of an act that furthers the agreement in conspiracy

panhandling stopping people on the street to ask them for food or money

paramour rule the common law rule that a husband who caught his wife in the act of adultery had adequate provocation to kill

parental responsibility statutes based on parents' acts and omissions; differ from vicarious liability statutes, which are based on the parent–child relationship

pattern of racketeering activity committing two or more of a huge list of related crimes

perfect defenses defenses in which defendants are acquitted if they're successful

***Pinkerton* rule** the crime of conspiracy and the crime the conspirators agree to commit are separate offenses

plurality opinion an opinion that represents the reasoning of the greatest number (but less than a majority) of justices

Ponzi schemes a fraudulent investment operation that pays returns to investors from their own money or money paid by subsequent investors rather from any actual profit earned

post-traumatic stress disorder (PTSD) defense excuse that argues the defendant wasn't responsible because of PTSD

preliminary injunction a temporary court order to do or to stop doing something

premenstrual syndrome (PMS) excuse that PMS led to the defendant committing the criminal acts

preponderance of the evidence more than 50 percent of the evidence proves justification or excuse

presumption of bodily integrity a state can't exercise power over individual members of society except to prevent harm to others

presumption of innocence which means that the prosecution has the burden of proof when it comes to proving the criminal act and intent

prevention punishment is only a means to a greater good, usually the prevention or at least the reduction of future crime

principals in the first degree persons who actually commit the crime

principals in the second degree persons present when the crime is committed and who help commit it (lookouts and getaway drivers)

principle of concurrence some mental fault has to trigger the criminal act in conduct crimes and the cause in result crimes

principle of legality no one can be convicted of, or punished for, a crime unless the law defined the crime and prescribed the punishment before the person engaged in the behavior that was defined as a crime

principle of proportionality the punishment has to fit the crime

principle of utility permits only the minimum amount of pain necessary to prevent the crime

probable desistance test determines if defendants have gone far enough toward completing the crime that it's unlikely they'll turn back

product-of-mental-illness test also known as the ***Durham* rule**; acts that are the "products" of mental disease or defect excuse criminal liability

prompt-reporting rule requires that rape victims report the rape soon after it occurs

proof beyond a reasonable doubt the highest standard of proof known to the law, it doesn't mean proof beyond all doubt or to the level of absolute certainty

proof of treason requires either two witnesses to the *actus reus* or confession in open court

prostitution engaging in sex in exchange for money or its equivalent

proximate cause of a death a cause where an act is directly connected with the resulting injury, with no intervening force operating

proximity tests help courts decide when defendants' acts have taken them further than just getting ready to attempt and brought them close enough to completing crimes to qualify as attempt *actus reus*

public nuisance injunctions court orders to eliminate the particular nuisance

punishment intentionally inflicting pain or other unpleasant consequences on another person

purposely the mental attitude that a person acts purposely with respect to a material element of an offense when, if the element involves the nature of his conduct or a result thereof, it is his conscious object to engage in conduct of that nature or to cause such a result

"quality of life" crimes "bad manners" crimes that threaten to disrupt public order

Racketeer Influenced and Corrupt Organizations Act (RICO) imposes enhanced penalties for "all types of organized criminal behavior, that is, enterprise criminality—from simple political to sophisticated white collar schemes to traditional Mafia-type endeavors"

racketeering originally meaning was the extortion of money or advantage by threat or force; now the meaning has expanded to include a pattern of illegal activity (such as extortion and murder) carried out in the furtherance of an enterprise owned or controlled by those engaged in the activity

rape shield statutes statutes that prohibit introducing evidence of victims' past conduct

rates of imprisonment measured by the numbers of prisoners per 100,000 people in the general population

rationalism the natural law that individuals can act to maximize pleasure and minimize pain, permitting human beings to apply natural laws *mechanistically* (according to rules) instead of having to rely on the discretionary judgment of individual decision makers

reason psychologists call it "*cognition*"; the capacity to tell right from wrong

reasonable doubt consists of "the proof that prevents one from being convinced of the defendant's guilt or the belief that there is a real possibility that the defendant is not guilty"

reasonable resistance rule provides that the amount of force required to repel rapists shows nonconsent in rape prosecutions

receiving stolen property benefiting from the theft of someone else's property without having participated in the wrongful acquisition in the first place

receiving stolen property *actus reus* the act of receiving and controlling at least temporarily (but not necessarily possessing) the property

receiving stolen property *mens rea* depending on the jurisdiction, knowing or believing that received goods are stolen

recklessly the mental attitude that a person acts recklessly with respect to a material element of an offense when he consciously disregards a substantial and unjustifiable risk that the material element exists or will result from his conduct. The risk must be of such a nature and degree, that considering the nature and purpose of the actor's conduct and the circumstances known to him, its disregard involves a gross standard of conduct that a law-abiding person would observe in the actor's situation

rehabilitation aims to prevent future crimes by changing individual offenders so they'll want to play by the rules and won't commit any more crimes in the future

respondeat superior a doctrine in tort law that makes a master liable for the wrong of a servant; in modern terms an employer may be liable for the wrong of an employee

retreat rule you have to retreat from an attack if you reasonably believe (1) that you're in danger of death or serious bodily harm *and* (2) that backing off won't unreasonably put you in danger of death or serious bodily harm

retribution inflicting on offenders physical and psychological pain ("hard treatment") so that they can pay for their crimes

right of locomotion the right to come and go without restraint

right-wrong test (also called the ***McNaughtan* rule**) the defendant suffered a defect of reason caused by a disease of the mind, and, consequently, at the time of the act didn't know what she was doing or that the act was wrong

riot common law misdemeanor that occurred when three or more persons committed an unlawful violent act, or performed a lawful act in a "violent or tumultuous manner"; felony consisting of twelve or more persons who stayed together unlawfully, riotously, and tumultuously for one hour after being warned to disperse by the reading of a proclamation

robbery taking property by force or the threat of force—a violent crime against persons and their property

robbery *actus reus* an act or threat of force beyond the amount needed to take and carry away someone else's property

robbery *mens rea* the intent to take another person's property and keep it permanently with the additional intent to use immediate force, or the threat of immediate force, to get it

rout common law misdemeanor that occurred when three or more people joined and moved toward the commission of a riot

rule of law the idea that government power should be defined and limited by laws

sabotage the crime of damaging or destroying property for the purpose of hindering preparations for war and national defense during national emergencies

Second Amendment "the right of law-abiding, responsible citizens to use arms in defense of hearth and home"

second-degree arson includes burning unoccupied structures, vehicles, and boats

second-degree murder murders that aren't first-degree murders, including intentional murders that weren't premeditated or deliberate, felony murders, intent to inflict serious bodily injury murders, and depraved heart murders

sedition the crime of advocating the violent overthrow of the government

seditious conspiracy conspiring to the violent overthrow of the government

seditious libel advocating the overthrow of the government in writings

seditious speech advocating the overthrow of the government in speeches

sentencing guidelines a commission establishes a narrow range of penalties, and judges choose a specific sentence within that range; guideline sentence depends on a combination of the seriousness of the crime and the prior criminal record of the offender

serious bodily injury bodily injury that involves a substantial risk of death; protracted unconsciousness; extreme physical pain; protracted or obvious disfigurement; or protracted loss or substantial impairment of a function of a bodily member, organ, or mental faculty

simple rape second-degree rape; rape without aggravated circumstances

Smith Act of 1940 Congress made it a crime to conspire to teach or advocate overthrowing the government by force or to be a member of a group that advocated the violent overthrow of the government

solicitation the crime of trying to get someone else to commit a crime

solicitation *actus reus* acts that include some kind of inducement to commit the solicited crime

solicitation *mens rea* requires words that convey that their purpose is to get someone to commit a specific crime

special deterrence aims, by punishing already convicted offenders, to prevent them from committing any more crimes in the future

special part of criminal law defines specific crimes and arranges them into groups according to subject matter

specific attempt statutes separate statutes that define attempts in terms of specific crimes in the criminal code, such as attempted murder, attempted robbery, and attempted rape—crimes that involved a specific intent

specific intent subjective fault; it refers to criminal intent in addition to the criminal act

stalking intentionally scaring another person by following, tormenting, or harassing

stand-your-ground rule if you didn't start a fight, you can stand your ground and kill to defend yourself without retreating from any place you have a right to be

status the character or condition of a person or thing

statutory rape to have carnal knowledge of a person under the age of consent whether or not accomplished by force

strict liability liability without either subjective or objective fault

subjective fault fault that requires a "bad mind" in the actor

subjective fear means that the victim honestly feared imminent and serious bodily harm

subjective test of entrapment asks whether the intent to commit the crime originated with the defendant

substantial capacity test (the MPC test) MPC test designed to remove the objections to the *right-wrong test*, its irresistible impulse supplement, and the *Durham* rule

superseding cause an intervening act or force that the law considers sufficient to override the cause for which the original wrongdoer was responsible

surreptitious remaining element (in burglary) the entering of a structure lawfully with the intent to remain and commit a crime inside

syndrome a group of symptoms or signs typical of a disease, disturbance, or condition

tangible property personal property, not real estate

terrorism the use of violence or intimidation in the pursuit of political aims

theft intentionally getting control of someone else's property, includes larceny, embezzlement, and false pretense crimes

three-strikes laws laws intended to make sure that offenders who are convicted of a third felony get locked up for a very long time (sometimes for life)

time, place, and manner test to be constitutional, restrictions on free speech have to not be based on the content of the speech; serve a significant government interest, and leave open other channels of expression

torts private wrongs for which you can sue the party who wronged you and recover money

treason the crime of levying war against the United States or of giving aid and comfort to its enemies

treason *actus reus* consists of either levying war against the United States or giving aid and comfort to the enemies of the United States

treason *mens rea* consists of intentionally giving aid and comfort for the very purpose of betraying the United States

trial courts where the cases for the state and the defense are presented; their witnesses and the physical evidence are introduced; and the fact finders (juries in jury trials or judges in nonjury bench trials) decide what the "true" story is and whether the evidence all adds up to proof of guilt beyond a reasonable doubt

unarmed acquaintance rape nonconsensual sex between individuals who are known to one another

unequivocality test/res ipsaloquiter test ("the act speaks for itself") examines whether an ordinary person who saw the defendant's acts without knowing her intent would believe she was determined to commit the intended crime

unilateral approach to conspiracy parties the rule that not all conspirators have to agree with—or even know—the other conspirators

unlawful act manslaughter (also called misdemeanor manslaughter) unintended deaths occurring during the commission of nonhomicide offenses

unlawful assembly the ancient crime of three or more persons gathering together to commit an unlawful act

USA Patriot Act passed by Congress after the September 11, 2001, attacks, creating some new (and enhancing the penalties for existing) crimes of domestic and international terrorism

utmost resistance standard requirement that rape victims had to use all the physical strength they had to prevent penetration

vagrancy the ancient crime of poor people wandering with no visible means of support

vicarious liability establishes when a party can be criminally liable because of a relationship; transfers the criminal conduct of one party to another because of their relationship

"victimless crimes" crimes involving willing adult participants who don't see themselves as victims

void-for-overbreadth doctrine protects speech guaranteed by the First Amendment by invalidating laws written so broadly that the fear of prosecution creates a "chilling effect" that discourages people from exercising that freedom

void-for-vagueness doctrine the principle that statutes violate due process if they don't define a crime and its punishment clearly enough for ordinary people to know what is lawful

voluntary abandonment defense (also called **voluntary renunciation defense**) defendants who voluntarily and completely renounce their criminal purpose can avoid criminal liability

voluntary consent consent was the product of free will, not of force, threat of force, promise, or trickery

voluntary manslaughter suddenly and intentionally killing another person in the heat of anger following adequate provocation; elements include murder *actus reus*, *mens rea*, causation, and death

waiver to adult criminal court the juvenile court gives up its jurisdiction over the case and turns it over to the adult criminal court

wheel conspiracies one or more defendants participate in every transaction (the hub of the wheel) and others participate in only one transaction (the spokes in the wheel)

white-collar crimes crimes growing out of opportunities to get someone else's property that was entrusted to the perpetrators because of their occupation

will psychologists call it "volition," most of us call it "willpower"; in the insanity tests, it refers to defendants' power to control their actions

withdrawal exception if initial aggressors completely withdraw from attacks they provoke, they can defend themselves against an attack by their initial victims

"words can never provoke" rule the rule that words are never adequate provocation to reduce murder to manslaughter

BIBLIOGRAPHY

ABC News. 2007. "Memorabilia Dealer and Former Friend Said Simpson Was in the Room during Robbery." *Good Morning America*, September 17. Accessed March 14, 2012. http://abcnews.go.com/GMA/story?id=3611324&page=1#.T2Cpwsw3_Gc.

Ainsworth, Bill. 2004. "Poll Finds Broad Support for Limits on 3-Strikes Laws." *San Diego Union*, June 10.

Alabama Criminal Code. 1975. Accessed July 24, 2012. http://alisondb.legislature.state.al.us/acas/CodeOfAlabama/1975/13297.htm.

Alexander v. U.S. 1993. 510 U.S. 909.

Allen, Francis A. 1993. *The Habits of Legality: Criminal Justice and the Rule of Law*. New York: Oxford University Press.

American Amusement Machine Association v. Kendrick. 2001. 244 F.3d 572, 577–79 (7th Cir.).

American Law Institute (ALI). 1953. *Model Penal Code Tentative Draft No. 1*. Philadelphia: ALI.

———. 1985. *Model Penal Code and Commentaries*. Philadelphia: ALI.

———. 2007. *Model Penal Code: Sentencing, Tentative Draft No. 1*. Philadelphia: ALI.

Andenæs, Johannes. 1983. "Deterrence." In *Encyclopedia of Crime and Justice*, edited by Sanford H. Kadish. New York: Free Press.

Anderson, Craig, A., and Karen E. Dill. 2000. "Video Games and Aggressive Thoughts, Feelings, and Behavior in the Laboratory and in Life." *Journal of Personality and Social Psychology* 78(4):772–90.

Anderson, Curt. 2003. "'Material Support' Charge under Legal Eye." Associated Press, August 13. Accessed July 20, 2012. http://www.apnewsarchive.com/2003/-Material-Support-Charge-Under-Legal-Eye/id-04da349c6f1955afbbbde9eab9bbb2b4.

Apprendi v. New Jersey. 2000. 530 U.S. 466.

Aquinas, St. Thomas. [1265–68] 2012. *Summa Theologica*. 2nd ed. Edited and translated by the Dominican Friars. Los Angeles: Viewforth Press.

Arizona Criminal Code. 2003. Effect of Alcohol or Drug Use. Accessed July 24, 2012. http://www.azleg.state.az.us/ars/13/00503.htm.

Arthur Andersen LLP v. U.S. 2005. 544 U.S. 696.

Atkins v. Virginia. 2002. 536 U.S. 304.

Attorney General. 1999. *1999 Report on Cyberstalking: A New Challenge for Law Enforcement and Industry*. Washington, DC: U.S. Department of Justice.

Bachun v. U.S. 1940. 112 F.2d 635 (4th Cir.).

Bailey v. U.S. 1969. 416 F.2d 1110 (D.C. Cir.).

Barnes v. Glen Theatre, Inc., et al. 1991. 501 U.S. 560.

Batey, Robert. 1997. "Vagueness and the Construction of Criminal Statutes—Balancing Act." *Virginia Journal of Social Policy and Law* 5:1.

Beazell v. Ohio. 1925. 269 U.S. 167.

Benekos, Peter, and Alido Merlo. 1995. "Three Strikes and You're Out!: The Political Sentencing Game." *Federal Probation*, March.

Bering, Jesse. 2011. "Sex, Sleep, and the Law." *Scientific American*, May 20. Accessed July 20, 2012. http://blogs.scientificamerican.com/bering-in-mind/2011/05/20/sex-sleep-and-the-law-when-nocturnal-genitals-pose-a-moral-dilemma/.

Binder, Guyora. 2000. "Meaning and Motive in the Law of Homicide." *Buffalo Criminal Law Review* 3:755–74.

———. 2004. "The Origins of American Felony Murder Rules." *Stanford Law Review* 57:59–208.

Black, Henry Campbell. 1983. *Black's Law Dictionary*. 5th ed. St. Paul, Minn.: Thomson West.

———. 2004. *Black's Law Dictionary*. 8th ed. Edited by Bryan A. Garner. St. Paul, Minn.: Thomson West.

Blackstone, Sir William. 1769. *Commentaries on the Laws of England, IV*. Oxford: Clarendon Press.

Blakely v. Washington. 2004. 542 U.S. 296.

Blakely, Richard, and Mark Gettings. 1980. "Racketeer Influenced and Corrupt Organizations (RICO): Basic Concepts—Criminal and Civil Remedies." *Temple Law Quarterly* 53.

Board of Commissioners v. Backus. 1864. 29 How. Pr. 33.

Bond, Julian P., ed. 1950. *Papers of Thomas Jefferson*. Vol. 2, *January 1777 to June 1779*. Princeton, N.J.: Princeton University Press.

Boro v. Superior Court. 1985. 210 Cal.Rptr.122 (Cal.App.).

Bowers v. Hardwick. 1986. 478 U.S. 186.

Bracton, Henry of. 1968. *On the Laws and Customs of England*. Translated by Samuel E. Thorne. Cambridge: Harvard University Press.

———. 1968–77. *On the Laws and Customs of England*. Translated by Samuel E. Thorne. Cambridge: Harvard University Press.

Bradfield, Jennifer L. 1998. "Anti-Stalking Laws: Do They Adequately Protect Stalking Victims?" *Harvard Women's Law Journal* 21:229, 249.

Brodie, Kyle S. 1995. "The Obviously Impossible Attempt: A Proposed Revision to the Model Penal Code. *Northern Illinois University Law Review* 15:237.

Brown v. State. 1906. 106 N.W. 536 (Wis.).

Brown v. United States. 1921. 256 U.S. 335.

Bryden, David P. 2000. "Redefining Rape." *Buffalo Criminal Law Review* 3:318.

Buck v. Bell. 1927. 274 U.S. 200.

Burnett v. State. 1999. 807 So.2d 573 (Ala.App.).

Burrows v. State. 1931. 297 P. 1029.

California Penal Code. 2003. Accessed July 20, 2012. http://www.leginfo.ca.gov/.html/pen_table_of_contents.html.

______. 2006. Accessed July 20, 2012. http://www.leginfo.ca.gov/cgi-bin/calawquery?codesection=pen&codebody=&hits=20.

______. 2006. Sections 187–99. Accessed July 20, 2012. http://www.leginfo.ca.gov/cgi-bin/displaycode?section=pen&group=00001-01000&file=187-199.

Campbell v. State. 1982. 444 A.2d 1034.

Campbell, Thomas. 1843. Quoted in Donald H. J. Hermann and Yvonne S. Sor, "Convicting or Confining? Alternative Directions in Insanity Law Reform: Guilty But Mentally Ill Versus New Rules for Release of Insanity Acquittees." *Brigham Young Law Review* 1983:499, 508.

Carey v. Population Services International. 1977. 431 U.S. 678.

Carlson, Jonathan C. 1987. "The Act Requirement and the Foundations of the Entrapment Defense." *Virginia Law Review* 73:1011.

Carney, Robert Mark, and Brian D. Williams. 1983. "Premenstrual Syndrome: A Criminal Defense." *Notre Dame Law Review* 59:263–69.

Carroll, Joseph. 2007. "Public Divided over Moral Acceptability of Doctor-Assisted Suicide." Gallup News Service, May 31. Accessed July 20, 2012. http://www.gallup.com/poll/27727/public-divided-over-moral-acceptability-doctorassisted-suicide.aspx.

Casico v. State. 1947. 25 N.W.2d 897 (Neb.).

CBS News. 2008. "Lorena Bobbitt, 15 Years Later." *Early Show*, June 25. http://www.cbsnews.com/stories/2008/06/25/earlyshow/leisure/celebspot/main4207517.shtml.

Chambers v. Florida. 1940. 309 U.S. 227.

Chaplinsky v. New Hampshire. 1942. 315 U.S. 568.

Chicago v. Roman. 1998. 705 N.E.2d 81 (Ill.).

City of Chicago v. Morales. 1999. 527 U.S. 41.

City of Saint Paul. 2009. "Mayor Coleman Announces Civil Gang Injunction Lawsuit against the East Side Boys, Selby Siders." Saint Paul Minnesota Website, July 1. Accessed July 8, 2012. http://stpaul.gov/civicalerts.aspx?aid=529&arc=1060&preview=yes.

Clark v. Arizona. 2006. 548 U.S. 735.

Coffee, John C., Jr. 1992. "Paradigms Lost: The Blurring of the Criminal and Civil Law Models—and What Can Be Done about It." *Yale Law Journal* 101:1875.

Cohen, Fred. 1985. "Old Age Defense." *Criminal Law Bulletin* 21.

Coke, Sir Edward. 1628. *Institutes of the Laws of England*. London: Flesher, Haviland, and Young.

______. 1644. *Third Part of the Institutes of the Laws of England: Concerning High Treason, and Other Pleas of the Crown, and Criminal Causes*. London: Flesher.

Coker v. Georgia. 1977. 433 U.S. 584.

Cole, David. 2010. "The Roberts Court's Free Speech Problem." *New York Review of Books*, June 28. http://www.nybooks.com/blogs/nyrblog/2010/jun/28/roberts-courts-free-speech-problem/.

Commonwealth v. An Unnamed Defendant. 1986. 492 N.E.2d 1184 (Mass.App.).

Commonwealth v. Berkowitz. 1992. 609 A.2d 1338 (Pa. Super.).

______. 1994. 641 A.2d 1161 (Pa.).

Commonwealth v. Carr. 1990. 580 A.2d 1362 (Pa.Supp.).

Commonwealth v. Drum. 1868. WL 7210 (Pa.).

Commonwealth v. Fischer. 1998. 721 A.2d 1111 (Pa.Super.).

Commonwealth v. Golston. 1977. 249, 366 N.E.2d 744 (Mass.).

Commonwealth v. King. 1977. 372 N.E.2d 196 (Mass.).

Commonwealth v. Kozak. 1993. WL 768932 (Pa.Com.Pl.).

Commonwealth v. Mitchell. 1993. WL 773785 (Pa.Com.Pl.).

Commonwealth v. Mlinarich. 1985. 542 A.2d 1335 (Pa.).

Commonwealth v. Peaslee. 1901. 59 N.E. 55 (Mass.).

Commonwealth v. Pestinakas. 1992. 617 A.2d 1339.

Commonwealth v. Rhodes. 1996. 920 S.W.2d 531 (Ky.App.).

Commonwealth v. Schnopps. 1983. 459 N.E.2d 98 (Mass.).

Cook, Philip J., Jens Ludwig, and Adam Samaha. 2009. "Gun Control after *Heller*: Threats and Side Shows from a Social Welfare Perspective." *UCLA Law Review* 56:1041–93.

Corrado, Michael. 1994. "Is There an Act Requirement in the Criminal Law?" *University of Pennsylvania Law Review* 142:1529.

Cramer v. U.S. 1945. 325 U.S. 1.

Cullen, Francis T., William J. Maakestad, and Gray Cavender. 1987. *Corporate Crime under Attack: The Ford Pinto Case and Beyond*. Cincinnati: Anderson.

Curry v. State. 2002. 811 So.2d 736 (Fla.App.).

Darby, Joe. 2003. "Penalty for Rape May Not Stand: Louisiana Law May Be Unconstitutional." *New Orleans Times-Picayune*, August 28.

D.C. Gun Laws. 2009. § 7-2502.01. http://dcguncase.com/blog/dc-gun-laws/.

Dennis v. State. 1995. 105 Md.App. 687.

Dennis v. U.S. 1951. 341 U.S. 494.

De Pasquale v. State. 1988. 757 P.2d 367 (Nev.).

Dershowitz, Alan. 1994. *The Abuse Excuse and Other Cop-Outs, Sob Stories, and Evasions of Responsibility*. Boston: Little, Brown.

Diamond, John L. 1996. "The Myth of Morality and Fault in Criminal Law." *American Criminal Law* 34.

DiFonzo, James. 2001. "Parental Responsibility for Juvenile Crime." *Oregon Law Review* 80:1.

DiGiacinto v. Rector and Visitors of George Mason University. 2011. 704 S.E.2d 365 (Va.).

Direct Sales Co. v. U.S. 1943. 319 U.S. 703.

District of Columbia v. Heller. 2008. 554 U.S. 570.

Dressler, Joshua. 1995. "When 'Heterosexual Men' Men Kill 'Homosexual' Men: Sexual Advances, Provocation Law,

Sexual Advances, and the 'Reasonable Man' Standard." *Journal of Criminal Law & Criminology* 85(3):726–63.

———. 2001. *Understanding Criminal Law*. 3rd ed. Danvers, Mass.: LexisNexis.

———. 2009. *Understanding Criminal Law*. 5th ed. Newark, N.J.: Matthew Bender & Company, Inc.

———, and Alan C. Michaels. 2006. *Understanding Criminal Procedure*. Vol. II: *Adjudication*. Newark, N.J.: Matthew Bender & Company, Inc.

Dubber, Markus D. 2001. "Policing Possession: The War on Crime and the End of Criminal Law." *Journal of Criminal Law and Criminology* 91:829.

———. 2002. *Criminal Law: Model Penal Code*. New York: Foundation Press.

———, and Mark G. Kelman. 2005. *American Criminal Law*. New York: Foundation Press.

———. 2009. *Criminal Law*. 2nd ed. Eagan, Minn.: West.

Duchak Indictment. 2010. U.S. District Court District of Colorado. Accessed May 22, 2012. http://extras.mnginteractive.com/live/media/site36/2010/0310/20100310_013757_douglas_duchak_indictment.pdf.

Duest v. State. 1985. 462 So.2d 446 (Fla.).

Durham v. U.S. 1954. 214 F.2d 862 (D.C. Cir.).

Edwards v. California. 1941. 314 U.S. 162.

Edwards, Daphne. 1996. "Acquaintance Rape and the 'Force' Element: When 'No' Is Not Enough." *Golden Gate Law Review* 26:241.

Ehrenreich, Barbara. 2009. "Is It Now a Crime to Be Poor?" *New York Times*, August 9. http://www.nytimes.com/2009/08/09/opinion/09ehrenreich.html?page wanted=all.

Ehrlich, Isaac. 1975. "The Deterrent Effect of Capital Punishment: A Question of Life and Death." *American Economic Review* LXV(3):414.

Eisenstadt v. Baird. 1972. 405 U.S. 438.

"Electronic Frontier: The Challenge of Unlawful Conduct Involving the Use of the Internet." 2000. Executive Summary. http://www.politechbot.com/docs/unlawful conduct.html.

Ellickson, Robert C. 1996. "Controlling Chronic Misconduct in City Spaces: Of Panhandlers, Skid Rows, and Public-Space Zoning." *Yale Law Journal* 105.

Elton, Geoffrey R. 1972. *The Tudor Constitution*. Cambridge, UK: Cambridge University Press.

Enker, Arnold. 1977. "*Mens Rea* in Criminal Attempt." *American Bar Foundation Research Journal* 845–79.

Epilepsy Therapy Project. 2011a. "Driving and the Law." Epilepsy.com. Accessed November 21, 2011. http://www.epilepsy.com/epilepsy/rights_driving.

———. 2011b. "Auras." Epilepsy.com. Accessed November 21, 2011. http://www.epilepsy.com/epilepsy/auras.

Espionage Act. 1917. "Primary Documents—U.S. Espionage Act, 15 June 1917." FirstWorldWar.com. Accessed May 23, 2012. http://www.firstworldwar.com/source/espionageact.htm.

Espionage and Censorship Act. 2006. *U.S. Code*. "Gathering or Delivering Defense Information to Aid Foreign Government." Title 18, Part I, Chapter 37, § 794.

Estrich, Susan. 1987. *Real Rape*. Cambridge, Mass.: Harvard University Press.

Ewing v. California. 2003. 538 U.S. 11.

Factora-Borchers, Lisa. 2011. "Penn State Sexual Abuse Scandal: How Not to Walk Like Mike McQueary." *My Ecdysis* (blog). Accessed November 23, 2011. http://www.myecdysis.com/2011/11/penn-state-sexual-abuse-scandal-how-not-to-walk-like-mike-mcqueary/.

Fagundes, David. 2001. "Notes: What We Talk about When We Talk about Persons: The Language of a Legal Fiction." *Harvard Law Review* 114:1745–68.

Farnsworth, Clyde. 1994. "Mercy Killing in Canada Stirs Calls for Changes in Law." *New York Times*, November 21.

Farrand, Max, ed. 1929. Introduction to *The Laws and Liberties of Massachusetts*. Cambridge, Mass.: Harvard University Press.

FBI. 2005. *Crime in the U.S.* Washington, DC: Department of Justice. Accessed July 23, 2012. http://www2.fbi.gov/ucr/cius_04/offenses_reported/property_crime/index.html.

———. 2011. "Violent Crime." *Crime in the United States, 2010*. Washington, DC: U.S. Department of Justice (September). Accessed December 14, 2011. http://www.fbi.gov/about-us/cjis/ucr/crime-in-the-u.s/2010/crime-in-the-u.s.-2010/violent-crime/violent-crime.

FBI Uniform Crime Report. 2011. *Crime in the United States, 1991–2010*. Washington, DC: U.S. Department of Justice (September). Table 1. Accessed December 14, 2011. http://www.fbi.gov/about-us/cjis/ucr/crime-in-the-u.s/2010/crime-in-the-u.s.-2010/tables/10tbl01.xls.

———. 2011. *Crime in the United States, 2010*. Washington, DC: U.S. Department of Justice (September). Table 29. Accessed December 14, 2011. http://www.fbi.gov/about-us/cjis/ucr/crime-in-the-u.s/2010/crime-in-the-u.s.-2010/tables/10tbl29.xls.

———. 2011. *Crime in the United States, 2010*. Washington, DC: U.S. Department of Justice (September). Table 33. Accessed December 14, 2011. http://www.fbi.gov/about-us/cjis/ucr/crime-in-the-u.s/2010/crime-in-the-u.s.-2010/tables/10tbl33.xls.

Federal Criminal Code and Rules. 1988. St. Paul, Minn.: West.

Feeley, Malcolm M. 1983. *Court Reform on Trial*. New York: Basic Books.

Finkel, Norman J., and Sharon F. Handel. 1989. "How Jurors Construe 'Insanity.'" *Law and Human Behavior* 13:41–59.

Finkel, Norman J., and W. Gerrod Parrott. 2006. *Emotions and Culpability: How the Law Is at Odds with Psychology, Jurors, and It Sells*. Washington, DC. American Psychological Association.

Fletcher, George. 1978. *Rethinking Criminal Law*. Boston: Little, Brown.

———. 1981. "Reflections on Felony Murder," *Southwestern University Law Review* 12:413–29.

———. 1988. *A Crime of Self-Defense: Bernhard Goetz and the Law on Trial*. New York: Free Press.

Florida Criminal Code. 2006. § 787.02. Accessed July 22, 2012. http://archive.flsenate.gov/statutes/index.cfm?StatuteYear=2006&AppMode=Display_Results&Mode=Search%2520Statutes&Submenu=2&Tab=statutes&Search_String=787.02.

Florida Personal Protection Law. 2009. Accessed July 24, 2012. http://www.jacksonvillelawyerhelp.com/2012/07/florida-statute-776-012-use-of-force-in-defense-of-person/; http://www.jacksonvillelawyerhelp.com/2012/07/florida-statute-776-013-home-protection-use-of-deadly-force/

Foreman, Judy. 1986. "Most Rape Victims Know Assailant, Don't Report to Police, Police Report Says." *Boston Globe*, April 16.

Fox, Everett. 1995. *The Five Books of Moses*. New York: Schocken Books.

Fraud and Related Activity in Connection with Computers. 2012. *U.S. Code*. Title 18, Part I, Chapter 47, § 1030. http://uscodebeta.house.gov/view.xhtml?req=granuleid:USC-title18-section1030&num=0.

Fries, Jacob H. 2001. "4,000 Cars Seized in Effort to Halt Drunk Driving." *New York Times*, July 3.

Frontline. 1996. "The Kevorkian Verdict." Public Broadcasting Service. May 14. Accessed June 14, 2012. http://www.pbs.org/wgbh/pages/frontline/kevorkian/interviews/.

Gainer, Ronald L. 1988. "The Culpability Provisions of the Model Penal Code." *Rutgers Law Journal* 19(Spring): 575–91.

Gall v. U.S. 2007. 552 U.S. 38.

Garner, Bryan A., ed. 2004. *Black's Law Dictionary*. Eagan, Minn.: West.

Garvey, Stephen P. 1998. "Can Shaming Punishments Educate?" *University of Chicago Law Review* 65:4. Accessed October 31, 2011. http://papers.ssrn.com/sol3/papers.cfm?abstract_id=137063.

Gaylin, Willard. 1982. *The Killing of Bonnie Garland*. New York: Simon and Schuster.

Gelles, Richard J. 2002. "Family Abuse and Crime." *Encyclopedia of Crime and Justice*. Eagan, Minn.: Thomson Learning.

General v. State. 2002. 789 A.2d 102 (Md.).

GeorgiaCarry.Org, Inc. v. Georgia. 2011. 764 F.Supp.2d 1306 (M.D.Ga.).

Georgia Criminal Code. 2006. Title 17, Chapter 3, Section 3. Accessed July 23, 2012. http://law.justia.com/codes/georgia/2006/16/16-3-3.html.

Gibeaut, John. 1997. "Sobering Thoughts." *American Bar Association Journal* 83.

Gitlow v. New York. 1925. 268 U.S. 652.

Glionna, John. 2009. "South Korean Cameras Zero in on Crime." *Los Angeles Times*, February 17. Accessed October 13, 2011. http://seattletimes.nwsource.com/html/nationworld/2008751061_korea17.html.

Gonzalez v. Oregon. 2005. 546 U.S. 243.

Gordon, Brenda. 1999. "A Criminal's Justice or a Child's Justice? Trends in the Waiver of Juvenile Court Jurisdiction and the Flaws in the Arizona Response." *Arizona Law Review* 41:193.

Graham v. Texas. 2010. 560 U.S. ___ (Slip opinion).

Grayned v. City of Rockford. 1972. 408 U.S. 104.

Gray v. State. 1979. 403 A.2d 853.

Greene, Judith, and Kevin Pranis. 2007. *Gang Wars*. Washington, DC: Justice Policy Institute.

Greenhouse, Linda. 2003. "Justices Deny Appeal in Execution of Juveniles." *New York Times*, January 27.

Greenhouse, Steven. 1985. "Three Executives Convicted of Murder for Unsafe Workplace Conditions." *New York Times*, June 15.

Greenwald, Glenn. 2011. "Can the U.S. Government Close Social Media Accounts?" *Salon* (blog), December 20. Accessed May 29, 2012. http://www.salon.com/2011/12/20/the_u_s_government _targets_twitter_terrorism/.

Gresham v. Peterson. 2000. 225 F.3d 899 (7th Cir.).

Griswold v. Connecticut. 1965. 381 U.S. 479.

Grogger, Jeffrey. 2002. "The Effects of Civil Gang Injunctions on Reported Violent Crime: Evidence from Los Angeles County." *Journal of Law and Economics* VLV:69–90.

Gross, Hyman. 1978. *A Theory of Criminal Justice*. New York: Oxford University Press.

Hale, Sir Matthew. 1847. *The History of the Pleas of the Crown*. Philadelphia: R. H. Small.

Hall, Jerome. 1960. *The General Principles of Criminal Law*. 2nd ed. Indianapolis: Bobbs-Merrill.

Hall, John Wesley, Jr. 1991. *Search and Seizure*. 2nd ed. Deerfield, Ill.: Clark Boardman Callaghan.

Hamilton v. Cameron. 1997. 700 N.E.2d 336 (OhioApp.3d).

Harcourt, Bernard E. 2001. *Illusions of Order*. Cambridge, Mass.: Harvard University Press.

______. 2005. "Carceral Imaginations." *Carceral Notebooks* 1:3–19.

Harris v. State. 1999. 728 A.2d 180 (Md.App.).

Hart, Henry M., Jr. 1958. "The Aims of the Criminal Law." *Law and Contemporary Problems* 23:401.

______, and Albert M. Sacks. 1994. *The Legal Process: Basic Problems in the Making and Application of Law*. Edited by William N. Eskridge Jr. and Philip P. Frickey. New York: Foundation Press.

Hart, Herbert L. A., and Tony Honoré. 1995. *Causation in the Law*. 2nd ed. New York: Oxford University Press.

Haupt v. U.S. 1947. 330 U.S. 631.

Ha v. State. 1995. 892 P.2d 184, 194–95 (AlaskaApp.).

Hawkins, Beth. 2003. "The Sad, Strange Case of Darren Odell and the Sorry State of Our Insanity Laws." City Pages, May 7. Accessed July 20, 2012. http://www.citypages.com/2003-05-07/news/crazy/.

Herbeck, Dan, and Matt Gryta. 2010. "Grand Jury Clears Man in Killing of Intruder." *Buffalo News*, May 12. Accessed March 5, 2012. http://www.buffalonews.com/city/article47096.ece.

Hermann, Donald H. J., and Yvonne S. Sor. 1983. "Convicting or Confining? Alternative Directions in Insanity Law Reform: Guilty But Mentally Ill Versus

New Rules for Release of Insanity Acquittees." *Brigham Young Law Review* (1983):499, 508.

Holder v. Humanitarian Law Project. 2010. 130 S.Ct. 2705.

Holder, Eric. 2010. Press Release. "Eric Holder on the Times Square Investigation." May 4. Washington, DC: U.S. Department of Justice. http://www.justice.gov/opa/pr/2010/May/10-ag-517.html.

Holmes, Oliver Wendell. 1963. *The Common Law*. Boston: Little, Brown.

Horton v. City of Oakland. 2000. 98 Cal.Rptr.2d 371.

Howe, Mark DeWolfe, ed. 1953. *Holmes-Laski Letters*. Cambridge, Mass: Harvard University Press.

Hughes v. State. 1994. 888 P.2d 730 (Okla.).

Humanitarian Law Project v. Holder. 2010. 130 S.Ct. 2705.

Human Rights Watch. 2002. "World Report. U.S. Death Penalty." Accessed July 23, 2012. http://www.hrw.org/wr2k2/us.html#Death%20Penalty.

Hyde v. U.S. 1912. 225 U.S. 347.

Illinois Criminal Law and Procedure. 1988. St. Paul, Minn.: West.

In re Kemmler. 1890. 136 U.S. 436.

In re Medley. 1890. 134 U.S. 160.

In re Winship. 1970. 397 U.S. 358.

Interactive Digital Software Association v. St. Louis County. 2002. 200 Fed. Supp.2d 1126 (E.D.Mo.).

Jahnke v. State. 1984. 682 P.2d 991, 997 (Wyo.).

Jansen, Steven A., and M. Elaine Nugent-Borakove. 2008. *Expansions to the Castle Doctrine: Implications for Policy and Practice*. Alexandria, Va.: National District Attorney's Association. Accessed July 20, 2012. http://www.ndaa.org/pdf/Castle%20%Doctrine.pdf.

Jefferson, Thomas. 1853. *The Writings of Thomas Jefferson*. Edited by Albert Ellery Bergh. Washington, DC: GPO.

Jewell v. State. 1996. 672 N.E.2d 417 (Ind.App.).

Johnson, Andrew, and Emily Dugan. 2009. "Wealthy Quiet, Unassuming: The Christmas Day Bomb Suspect." *Independent*, December 27. Accessed May 26, 2012. http://www.independent.co.uk/news/world/americas/wealthy-quiet-unassuming-the-christmas-day-bomb-suspect-1851090.html.

Johnson, Vincent R. 2005. "Cybersecurity, Identity Theft, and the Limits of Tort Liability." *South Carolina Law Review* 57:255.

Jones v. State. 1984. 682 P.2d 757 (Okla.Crim.App.).

Jones v. State. 1992. 589 N.E.2d 241 (Ind.).

Joyce v. City and County of San Francisco. 1994. 846 F.Supp. 843 (N.D.Cal.).

Kadish, Sanford H. 1985. "Complicity, Cause, and Blame: A Study in the Interpretation of Doctrine." *California Law Review* 73:323–410.

______, ed. 1983. *Encyclopedia of Crime and Justice*. Vol. 1. New York: Free Press.

Kadish, Sanford, Stephen Schulhofer, and Carol Steiker. 2007. *Criminal Law and Its Processes*. 8th ed. New York: Aspen Publishers.

Kahan, Dan M. 1994. "Lenity and Federal Common Law Crimes." *Supreme Court Review* 345.

______. 1996. "What Do Alternative Sanctions Mean? *University of Chicago Law Review* 63:591.

______. 1997. "Some Realism about Retroactive Criminal Lawmaking." *Roger Williams University Law Review* 3:95–117.

Kandel, Minouche. 1992. "Whores in Court: Judicial Processing of Prostitutes in Boston Municipal Court in 1990." *Yale Journal of Law and Feminism* 4:329–52.

Kastl v. State. 1990. 796 S.W.2d 848 (Ark.).

Keats, John. 1819. "Ode to a Nightingale." Accessed July 20, 2012. http://www.bartleby.com/101/624.html.

Keeler v. Superior Court. 1970. 470 P.2d 617 (Cal.).

Kelling, George L., and Catherine M. Coles. 1996. *Fixing Broken Windows*. New York: Free Press.

Kennedy v. Louisiana. 2008. 554 U.S. 407.

Kent v. United States. 1966. 383 U.S. 541.

King v. Cogdon. 1951. Taken from Norval Morris, "Somnambulistic Homicide: Ghosts, Spiders, and North Koreans," *Res Judicata* 5.

Kleindienst, Linda. 2005. "Gun Foes to Warn Tourists on Law; Beginning Saturday, Floridians Can Use Deadly Force in Self-Defense." *Orlando Sentinel*, September 26.

Kolender v. Lawson. 1983. 461 U.S. 352.

Koppersmith v. State. 1999. 742 So.2d 206 (Ala.App.).

Krulewitch v. U.S. 1949. 336 U.S. 440.

LaFave, Wayne R. 2003a. *Criminal Law*. 4th ed. St. Paul, Minn.: Thomson West.

______. 2003b. *Substantive Criminal Law*. 2nd ed. Vol. 1. St. Paul, Minn.: Thomson West.

______, and Austen Scott. 1986. *Criminal Law*. 2nd ed. St. Paul, Minn.: West.

Lanzetta v. New Jersey. 1939. 306 U.S. 451.

Larrabee, John. 1995. "Fighting Crime with a Dose of Shame; in Some Communities, Old-Fashioned Public Humiliation Has Returned." *USA Today*, June 19.

Lawrence v. Texas. 2003. 539 U.S. 558.

Le Barron v. State. 1966. 145 N.W.2d 79 (Wis.).

Lederer, Richard. 1988. *Get Thee to a Punnery*. New York: Bantam Doubleday.

Lee, Cynthia. 2003. *Murder and the Reasonable Man: Passion and Fear in the Criminal Courtroom*. New York. New York University Press.

Lefler, Julie. 1999. "Shining the Spotlight on Johns: Moving toward Equal Treatment of Male Customers and Female Prostitutes." *Hastings Women Law Journal* 10:11–35.

Legal Community against Violence. 2011. "Post-*Heller* Litigation Summary." *Law Center to Prevent Gun Violence*. July 2, 2012. Accessed July 22, 2012. http://smartgunlaws.org/post-heller-litigation-summary/.

Lewis, C. S. 1953. "The Humanitarian Theory of Punishment." *Res Judicata* 6:224.

Lewis, Sinclair. 1922. *Babbitt*. New York: Harcourt Brace.

Liebelson, Dana. 2012. "Six Americans Obama and Holder Charged under the Espionage Act." *Project on Government Oversight (POGO)*, January 27.

Accessed May 25, 2012. http://pogoblog.typepad.com/pogo/2012/01/six-americans-obama-and-holder-charged-under-the-espionage-act-and-one-bonus-whistleblower.html.

Liptak, Adam. 2003. "Louisiana Sentence Renews Debate on the Death Penalty." *New York Times*, August 28.

______. 2006. "15 States Expand Right to Shoot in Self-Defense." *New York Times*, August 7.

______. 2008. "American Exception: Inmate Count in U.S. Dwarfs Other Nations'." *New York Times*, April 23. Accessed July 211, 2012. http://www.nytimes.com/2008/04/23/us/23prison.html?_r=1&scp=6&sq=Adam+Liptak&st=nyt.

Loewy, Arnold. 1987. *Criminal Law.* St. Paul, Minn.: West.

Logan, Wayne A. 2001. "The Shadow Criminal Law of Municipal Governance." *Ohio State Law Journal* 62:1409.

Louisiana Statutes Annotated. 1974. Rev. Stat. Title 17-A.

Low, Peter. 1990. *Criminal Law.* St. Paul, Minn.: West.

Lynch, Gerard E. 1987. "The Crime of Being a Criminal." *Columbia Law Review* 87:661–764; 920–84.

______. 1990. "A Conceptual, Practical, and Political Guide to RICO Reform." *Vanderbilt Law Review* 43:769–803.

______. 2002. "RICO (Racketeer Influenced and Corrupt Organizations) Act." *Encyclopedia of Crime and Justice.* 2nd ed. Vol. 3. New York: Gale Group. Thomson Learning.

Macias v. State. 1929. 283 P. 711.

Madison, James. [1787] 1961. "The Federalist No. 51." In *The Federalist*, edited by Jacob E. Cooke. Middletown, Conn.: Wesleyan University Press.

Marcus, Paul. 1986. "The Development of Entrapment Law." *Wayne Law Review* 33:5.

Martinson, Robert. 1974. "What Works? Questions and Answers about Prison Reform." *Public Interest* 35: 22–54.

Maxson, Cheryl, Karen Hennigan, and David Sloane. 2005. "'It's Getting Crazy Out There': Can a Civil Gang Injunction Change a Community?" *Criminology and Public Policy* 4(3):577–606.

Mayer, Andre, and Michael Wheeler. 1982. *The Crocodile Man: A Case of Brain Chemistry and Criminal Violence.* Boston: Houghton-Mifflin.

Mayor of New York v. Miln. 1837. 36 U.S. (11 Pet.) 102.

McDonald v. City of Chicago. 2010. 130 S.Ct. 3020.

McKendree v. Christy. 1961. 172 N.E.2d 380.

McMahon, R. Bradley. 2004. "After Billions Spent to Comply with HIPPA and GBA Provisions, Why Is Identity Theft the Most Prevalent Crime in America?" *Villanova Law Review* 49:625.

McMullen, Richie. 1990. *Male Rape: Breaking the Silence on the Last Taboo.* London: Gay Men's Press.

McNally v. U.S. 1987. 483 U.S. 350.

Meerpol, Robert. 2003. *An Execution in the Family: One Son's Journey.* New York: St. Martin's Press.

Merschman, Joseph. 2001. "The Dark Side of the Web: Cyberstalking and the Need for Contemporary Legislation." *Harvard Women's Law Journal* 24:255.

Messinger, Thane Josef. 1993. "A Gentle and Easy Death: From Ancient Greece to beyond Cruzan toward a Reasoned Legal Response to the Societal Dilemma of Euthanasia." *Denver University Law Review* 71: 175–251.

Michael, Jerome, and Herbert Wechsler. 1937. "A Rationale of the Law of Homicide." *Columbia Law Review* 701, 1261.

______. 1940. *Criminal Law and Its Administration.* Chicago: Foundation Press.

Michael M. v. Superior Court of Sonoma County. 1981. 450 U.S. 464.

Michigan Criminal Code. 2005. *Rape.* § 750.520. http://www.legislature.mi.gov/(S(gp0glz552tmoxh45i5emeu45))/mileg.aspx?page=getObject&objectName=mcl-328-1931-LXXVI.

______. 2006. *Second-Degree Murder*; *Penalty.* § 750.317. http://www.legislature.mi.gov/(S(chfhmr55ac4mdwzs-scw41s55))/mileg.aspx?page=getobject&objectname=mcl-750–17&queryid=15730297&highlight=317.

Miller v. State. 1999. 6 S.W.3d 812 (Ark.App.).

Mims v. U.S. 1967. 375 F.2d 135 (5th Cir.).

Minnesota Criminal Code. 2005. *Definitions.* § 609.341. http://www.revisor.leg.state.mn.us/stats/609/341.html.

______. 2011. *Patrons; Prostitutes; Housing Individuals Engaged in Prostitution; Penalties.* § 609.324. https://www.revisor.mn.gov/statutes/?id=609.324.

Minnesota Statutes Annotated. 1989. Cumulative Supplement.

Mishaga v. Monken, Director of Illinois State Police. 2010. 753 F.Supp.2d 750 (C.D. Ill.).

Mishler, Joanna Lee. 2000. "Cyberstalking: Can Communication via the Internet Constitute a Credible Threat, and Should an Internet Service Provider Be Liable If It Does?" *Santa Clara Computer and High Technology Law Journal* 17(December): 115.

Mitford, Jessica. 1969. *The Trial of Dr. Spock*. New York: Knopf.

M'Naghten's Case. 1843. 8 Eng.Rep. 718.

Model Penal Code and Commentaries. 1985. Philadelphia: American Law Institute (ALI).

Moran v. People. 1872. 25 Mich. 356.

Moran, Richard. 1985. "The Modern Foundation for the Insanity Defense: The Cases of James Hadfield (1800) and Daniel McNaughtan (1843)." *Annals of the American Academy of Political and Social Science* 477(January): 31–42.

More, Sir Thomas. 1516. *Utopia*. London: Reeves & Turner.

Morgan v. State. 1982. 415 So.2d 6 (Fla.).

Moriarty, Daniel G. 1989. "Extending the Defense of Renunciation." *Temple Law Review* 62.

Morris, Herbert. 1976. *On Guilt and Innocence*. Los Angeles: University of California Press.

Morris Norval. 1951. "Somnambulistic Homicide: Ghosts, Spiders, and North Koreans." *Res Judicata* 5.

______. 1974. *The Future of Imprisonment.* Chicago: University of Chicago Press.

———, and Gordon Hawkins. 1970. *An Honest Politician's Guide to Crime Control.* Chicago: University of Chicago Press.

National Public Radio. 2003. Morning Edition, September 18.

Nazi Saboteur Case. 1942. Transcript of Military Commission (copy owned by author). Washington, DC: National Archives.

New Mexico Criminal Code. 2006. *False Imprisonment.* § 30-4-3. http://law.justia.com/codes/new-mexico/2006/nmrc/jd_30-4-3-c297.html.

New York Central & Hudson River Railroad Company v. United States. 1909. 212 U.S. 481.

New York Penal Code. 2003. http://public.leginfo.state.ny.us/menugetf.cgi?COMMONQUERY=LAWS.

Note. 1951. "Statutory Burglary: The Magic of Four Walls and a Roof." *University of Pennsylvania Law Review* 100:411.

Note. 1989. "Developments—Sexual-Orientation and the Law." *Harvard Law Review* 102:1508.

Nourse, Victoria. 1997. "Passion's Progress: Modern Law Reform and the Provocation Defense." *Yale Law Journal* 106:1331.

Novak, William J. 1996. *The People's Welfare: Law and Regulation in Nineteenth-Century America.* Chapel Hill: University of North Carolina Press.

Oberer, Walter E. 1962. "The Deadly Weapon Doctrine—Common Law Origin." *Harvard Law Review* 75:1565.

Oliver v. State. 1985. 703 P.2d 869 (Nev.).

Olmstead v. U.S. 1928. 277 U.S. 438.

Oxford English Dictionary. 2009. Edited by John Simpson. New York: Oxford University Press.

Packer, Herbert L. 1968. *The Limits of the Criminal Sanction.* Stanford, Calif.: Stanford University Press.

Papichristou v. City of Jacksonville. 1972. 405 U.S. 156.

Parker v. Municipal Judge. 1967. 427 P.2d 642 (Nev.).

Parr v. United States. 1960. 363 U.S. 370, 80 S.Ct. 1171, 4 L.Ed.2d 1277.

Parsons v. State. 1877. 2 So. 854 (Ala.).

Pennsylvania Laws. 1794. chap. 257, §§ 1–2.

Penry v. Lynaugh. 1989. 492 U.S. 302.

People ex rel. Gallo v. Acuna. 1997. 929 P.2d 596.

People v. Allen. 1997. 64 Cal.Rptr.2d 497.

People v. Anderson. 1968. 447 P.2d 942.

People v. Armitage. 1987. 239 Cal.Rptr.515 (Cal.App.).

People v. Burroughs. 1984. 668 P.2d 894.

People v. Chessman. 1951. 238 P.2d 1001 (Cal.).

People v. Clem. 2000. 78 Cal.App. 4th 346.

People v. Datema. 1995. 533 N.W.2d 272 (Mich.).

People v. Decima. 1956. 138 N.E.2d 799 (N.Y.).

People v. Evans. 1975. 379 N.Y.S.2d 912.

People v. Freer. 1976. 381 N.Y.S.2d 976, 978.

People v. Gasparik. 1981. 420 N.E.2d 40.

People v. Goetz. 1986. 497 N.E.2d 41 (N.Y.).

People v. Greenberger. 1997. 58 Cal.App.4th 298, 377; 68 Cal.Rptr.2d 61.

People v. Hansen. 1994. 885 P.2d 1022.

People v. Henderson. 1977. 560 P.2d 1180.

People v. James. 1998. 62 Cal.App.4th 244.

People v. Kemp. 1961. 359 P.2d 913 (Cal.).

People v. Kibbe. 1974. 362 N.Y.S.2d 848.

People v. Kimball. 1981. 311 N.W.2d 343 (Mich.App.).

People v. Lee. 1991. 234 Cal.App.3d 1214.

People v. Lopez. 1971. 489 P.2d 1372.

People v. Mattison. 1971. 481 P.2d 193.

People v. Mayberry. 1975. 542 P.2d 1337 (Cal.).

People v. Mills. 1904. 70 N.E. 786.

People v. Morse. 1992. 2 Cal.App.4th 620.

People v. Muñoz. 1960. 200 N.Y.S.2d 957.

People v. Nichols. 1970. 474 P.2d 6733.

People v. Oliver. 1989. 258 Cal.Rptr.138.

People v. O'Neil. 1990. 550 N.E.2d 1090 (Ill.App.).

People v. Pena. 1983. 197 Cal.Rptr. 264, 271.

People v. Penman. 1915. 110 N.E. 894.

People v. Phillips. 1966. 414 P.2d 353 (Cal.App.).

People v. Protopappas. 1988. 201 Cal.App.3d 152 (Cal.App.).

People v. Quentin. 1968. 296 N.Y.S.2d 443.

People v. Pearch. 1991. 229 Cal.App.3d 1282, 1299; 280 Cal.Rptr. 584.

People v. Rizzo. 1927. 158 N.E. 888 (N.Y.App.).

People v. Rokicki. 1999. 718 N.E.2d 333 (Ill.App.).

People v. Satchell. 1971. 489 P.2d 1361.

People v. Schmidt. 1915. 216 N.Y. 324.

People v. Smith. 1998. 62 Cal.App.4th 1233.

People v. Stamp. 1969. 2 Cal.App.3d 203.

People v. Steele. 2002. 47 P.3d 225. (Cal.).

People v. Taylor. 1992. 6 Cal.App.4th 1084.

People v. Thomas. 1978. 272 N.W.2d 157 (Mich.App.).

People v. Tomlins. 1914. 213 N.Y. 240, 107 N.E. 496.

People v. Williams. 1965. 205 N.E.2d 749 (Ill.App.).

Perkins, Rollin M., and Ronald N. Boyce. 1982. *Criminal Law.* 3rd ed. Mineola, N.Y.: Foundation Press.

Perlin, Michael. 1987. "Unpacking the Myths: The Symbolism Mythology and Insanity Defense Jurisprudence." *Case Western Reserve Law Review* 40:599.

———. 1989–90. "Mythology of Insanity Defense Jurisprudence." *Case Western Reserve University* 40:599–731.

Persons, Courtney Guyton. 1996. "Sex in the Sunlight: The Effectiveness, Efficiency, and the Constitutionality and Advisability of Publishing Names and Pictures of Prostitutes' Patrons." *Vanderbilt Law Review* 49:1525–75.

Pinkerton v. U.S. 1946. 328 U.S. 640.

Planned Parenthood v. Casey. 1991. 505 U.S. 833.

Plato. 1975. *Laws.* Translated by Trevor J. Saunders. Middlesex, England: Penguin Books.

Platt, Anthony, and Bernard L. Diamond. 1966. "The Origins of the 'Right and Wrong' Test of Criminal Responsibility and Its Subsequent Development in the United States." *California Law Review* 54:1227–60.

Pope Pius XII. 1956. "Discourse to Those Taking Part in the Second Naples World Congress on Fertility and Human Sterility." *AAS* 48(May 19): 470.

Posner, Judge Richard. 2001. *American Amusement Machine Association v. Kendrick*. 244 F.3d 572, 577–79 (7th Cir.).

"Post-*Heller* Litigation Summary." *Law Center to Prevent Gun Violence*. July 2, 2012. Accessed July 22, 2012. http://smartgunlaws.org/post-heller-litigation-summary/.

Poulos, Peter W. 1995. "Chicago's Ban on Gang Loitering: Making Sense Out of Vagueness and Overbreadth in Loitering Laws." *California Law Review* 83:379.

Powell v. Texas. 1968. 392 U.S. 514.

Press, Ann, and Peggy Clausen. 1982. "Not Guilty Because of PMS?" *Newsweek*, November 8.

Preyer, Kathryn. 1983. "Crime, the Criminal Law, and Reform in Post-Revolutionary Virginia." *Law and History Review* 1.

Price, Michael, Robert Rubenstein, and David Price. 2011. "Material Support." *Anthropology Today* 28(1):3–5.

Queen v. Dudley and Stephens. 1884. 14 Q. B. 273.

Rather, Dan. 2009. "Dan Rather Reports, 'The Castle Doctrine.'" *Dan Rather Reports*, September 9. Episode 405. http://www.axs.tv/ui/inc/show_transcripts.php?ami=A5849&t=Dan_Rather_Reports&en=405.

R.A.V. v. City of St. Paul. 1992. 505 U.S. 377, 112 S.Ct. 2538.

Regina v. Jones. 1703. 91 Eng. Rep. 330.

Regina v. McNaughtan. 1843. 8 Eng. Rep. 718.

Regina v. Morgan. 1975. 2. W.L.R. 923 (H.L.).

Regina v. Oxford. 1840. 173 *English Reports* 941.

Reinhold, Robert. 1985. "Trial Opens in Death at Texas Nursing Home." *New York Times*, October 1.

Remick, Lani Anne. 1993. "Read Her Lips: An Argument for a Verbal Consent Standard in Rape." *University of Pennsylvania Law Review* 141:1103.

Remsburg v. Docusearch, Inc. 2003. 816 A.2d 1001 (N.H.).

Renshaw, Patrick. 1968. "The IWW and the Red Scare 1917–24." *Journal of Contemporary History* 3:63–72.

Rex v. Arnold. 1724. *Howell's State Trials* 16:695.

Rex v. Bailey. 1818. *Crown Cases Reserved*.

Rex v. Scofield. 1784. Cald. 397.

Reynard. Jeff. 2008. "Criminal Sentencing in Ohio." JDRLaw.com. Accessed February 9, 2012. http://www.jdrlaw.com/ohiocriminalattorney/criminal-sentencing-in-ohio.html.

Reynolds v. State. 1889. 42 N.W. 903.

Rimer, Sara, and Raymond Bonner. 2000. "Whether to Kill Those Who Killed as Youths." *New York Times*, August 22.

Ritter, Ken. 2010. "Las Vegas Police: Paris Hilton Denied Purse with Cocaine Was Hers." Associated Press, August 30. Accessed February 20, 2012. http://www.usatoday.com/life/people/2010–08–30-hilton_N.htm.

Robinson v. California. 1962. 370 U.S. 660.

Robinson, Paul, and Markus Dubber. 2004. "An Introduction to the Model Penal Code of the American Law Institute." Social Science Research Network. Accessed July 22, 2012. http://papers.ssrn.com/sol3/papers.cfm?abstract_id=661165.

Robinson, Paul. 2008. *Distributive Principles of Criminal Law: Who Should Be Punished How Much?* Accessed August 7, 2012. http://www.law.upenn.edu/fac/.../DP_full_SNT_rev_4_1_08_phr.pdf

Roethlisberger, Nic. 2011. "Someone Is Watching: The Need for Enhanced Data Protection." *Hastings Law Journal* 62:1793–1838.

Roe v. Wade. 1973. 410 U.S. 113.

Roper v. Simmons. 2005. 543 U.S. 551.

Rosenberg, Ben. 2002. "The Growth of Federal Criminal Common Law." *American Journal of Criminal Law* 29:193.

Rothman, David J. 1980. *Conscience and Convenience*. Boston: Little, Brown.

Rustad, Michael L. 2001. "Private Enforcement of Cybercrime on the Electronic Frontier." *Southern California Interdisciplinary Law Journal* 11:63.

Sabotage Act. 2012. *U.S. Code*. Title 18, § 2153. http://www4.law.cornell.edu/uscode/html/uscode18/usc_sup_01_18_10_I_20_105.html.

Samaha, Joel. 1974. *Law and Order in Historical Perspective*. New York: Academic Press.

______. 1978. "Hanging for Felony." *Historical Journal* 21.

______. 1981. "The Recognizance in Elizabethan Law Enforcement." *American Journal of Legal History* 25.

Sampson, Robert J., and Stephen W. Raudenbush. 1999. "Deterrent Effect of the Police on Crime." *American Journal of Sociology* 105:163–89.

Sang-Hun, Choe. 2011. "Help Wanted: Busybodies with Cameras." *New York Times*, September 28. http://www.nytimes.com/2011/09/29/world/asia/in-south-korea-where-digital-tattling-is-a-growth-industry.html?_r=1&scp=1&sq=Bang%20Jae-won&st=cse.

Savage, Charlie. 2011. "Ex-CIA Officer Named in Disclosure Indictment." *New York Times*, January 6. Accessed May 25, 2012. http://www.nytimes.com/2011/01/07/us/07indict.html.

______. 2012. "Ex-CIA Officer Charged in Information Leak." *New York Times*, January 23. Accessed May 25, 2012. http://www.nytimes.com/2012/01/24/us/ex-cia-officer-john-kiriakou-accused-in-leak.html.

Savage, David G. 2010. "Activist's Case Will Test U.S. Anti-Terrorism Law." *Los Angeles Times*, February 18. Accessed May 29, 2012. http://articles.latimes.com/2010/feb/18/nation/la-na-court-terrorism18-2010feb18.

Sayre, Francis Bowes. 1921–22. "Criminal Conspiracy." *Harvard Law Review* 35:399.

______. 1928. "Criminal Attempts." *Harvard Law Review* 41:821–59.

______. 1932. "*Mens Rea*." *Harvard Law Review* 45:974.

Scheidegger, Kent S. 1993. *A Guide to Regulating Panhandling*. Sacramento, Calif.: Criminal Justice Legal Foundation.

Schenck v. U.S. 1919. 249 U.S. 47.

Schopp, Robert F. 1988. "Returning to *M'Naghten* to Avoid Moral Mistakes: One Step Forward, or Two Steps

Backward for the Insanity Defense?" *Arizona Law Review* 30:135.

Schwartz, Richard. 1983. "Rehabilitation." *Encyclopedia of Crime and Justice*. New York: Free Press.

Secret, Mosi. 2012. "Terror Defendant Convicted in New York Subway Plot." *New York Times*, May 1. Accessed May 26, 2012. http://www.nytimes.com/2012/05/02/nyregion/terror-defendant-convicted-in-plot-to-bomb-new-york-subways.html?_r=2&hp.

Sedition Act. 1918. "Primary Documents—U.S. Espionage Act, 7 May 1918." FirstWorldWar.com. Accessed May 23, 2012. http://www.firstworldwar.com/source/espionageact1918.htm.

Seditious Conspiracy. 2011. *U.S. Code*. Title 18, Part I, Chapter 115, § 2384.

Seligman, Joel. 2004. "Cautious Evolution or Perennial Irresolution: Stock Market Self-Regulation during the First Seventy Years of the Securities and Exchange Commission." *Business Lawyer* 59:1347–87.

Senander, Mary. 1988. International Anti-Euthanasia Task Force, Death on Demand: "Don't Count Me In!" Quoted in Thane Joseph Messinger, "A Gentle and Easy Death: From Ancient Greece to beyond Cruzan: Toward a Reasoned Legal Response to the Societal Dilemma of Euthanasia," *Denver University Law Review* 71(1993): 219–20.

Shane, Scott. 2011. "Leak Offers Look at Efforts by U.S. to Spy on Israel." *New York Times*, September 5. Accessed May 25, 2012. http://www.nytimes.com/2011/09/06/us/06leak.html?pagewanted=all.

Shaw, Lemuel. 1850. *Commonwealth v. Webster*. 1850. 59 Mass. 295.

Shenon, Philip. 1985. "Dispute over Intent in Drug Cases Divided FDA and Justice Department." *New York Times*, September 19.

Shepherd, Joanna. 2002. "Fear of the First Strike: The Full Deterrent Effect of California's Two- and Three-Strikes Legislation." *Journal of Legal Studies* XXXI (January): 159.

Sherman v. U.S. 1958. 356 U.S. 369.

Sherman, Rorie. 1994. "Insanity Defense: A New Challenge." *National Law Journal* (March 28).

Siegel, Barry. 1996. "Held Accountable for Son's Burglaries." *Los Angeles Times*, May 10.

Simon, Harry. 1992. "Towns without Pity: A Constitutional and Historical Analysis of Official Efforts to Drive Homeless Persons from American Cities." *Tulane Law Review* 66.

Skogan, Wesley G. 1990. *Disorder and Decline*. New York: Free Press.

Smallwood v. State. 1996. 680 A.2d 512 (Md.).

Smith, Juliette. 1996. "Arresting the Homeless for Sleeping in Public: A Paradigm for Expanding the *Robinson* Doctrine." *Columbia Journal of Law and Social Problems* 29.

Smith, Sandra. 2000. "Fetal Homicide: Woman or Fetus as Victim? A Survey of Current State Approaches and Recommendations for Future State Application." *William & Mary Law Review* 41:1845–84.

Solem v. Helm. 1983. 463 U.S. 277.

Solove, Daniel J. 2006. *The Digital Person: Technology and Privacy in the Information Age*. New York: New York University Press.

Sonnier v. State. 1992. 849 S.W.2d 828 (Tex.App.).

Spartacus Educational. 2010. "Espionage Act." Spartacus Educational. Accessed July 13, 2012. http://www.spartacus.schoolnet.co.uk/FWWespionage.htm.

Stanford v. Kentucky. 1989. 492 U.S. 361.

Stanley v. Georgia. 1969. 394 U.S. 557.

State in the Interest of M.T.S. 1992. 609 A.2d 1266 (N.J.).

State v. Aguillard. 1990. 567 So.2d 674 (La.).

State v. Akers. 1979. 400 A.2d 38 (N.H.).

State v. Anderson. 1991. 566 N.E. 2d 1224 (Ohio).

State v. Brown. 1976. 364 A.2d 27 (N.J.).

State v. Celli. 1978. 263 N.W.2d 145 (S.D.).

State v. Chaney. 1970. 477 P.2d 441 (Alaska).

State v. Chism. 1983. 436 So.2d 464 (La.).

State v. Cotton. 2000. 5 P.3d. 918 (Ariz.App.).

State v. Crawford. 1996. 472 S.E.2d 920 (N.C.).

State v. Curley. 1997. 939 P.2d 1103 (N.Mex.App.).

State v. Damms. 1960. 100 N.W.2d 592 (Wis.).

State v. Fiero. 1979. 603 P.2d 74.

State v. Flory. 1929. 276 P. 458 (Wyo.).

State v. Fransua. 1973. 510 P.2d 106 (N.Mex.App.).

State v. Good. 1917. 195 S.W. 1006.

State v. Hall. 1974. 214 N.W.2d 205.

State v. Hamlet. 1984. 321 S.E.2d 837 (N.C.).

State v. Harrison. 1977. 564 P.2d 1321 (N.M.).

State v. Hauptmann. 1935. 180 A.2d 809 (N.J.).

State v. Hiott. 1999. 987 P.2d 135 (Wash.App.).

State v. Hobbs. 1961. 107 N.W.2d 238.

State v. Hoying. 2005. WL 678989 (OhioApp.).

State v. Hudson. 1999. 745 So. 2d. 997 (Fla.App.)

State v. Humphries. 1978. 586 P.2d. 130 (Wash.App.).

State v. Jantzi. 1982. 56, 57, 641 P.2d 62 (Ore.App.).

State v. Jerrett. 1983. 307 S.E.2d 339.

State v. Kennamore. 1980. 604 S.W.2d 856 (Tenn.).

State v. K.R.L. 1992. 840 P.2d 210 (Wash.App.).

State v. Kuntz. 2000. 995 P.2d 951 (Mont.).

State v. Loge. 2000. 608 N.W.2d 152 (Minn.).

State v. Mays. 2000. 743 N.E.2d 447 (OhioApp.).

State v. Metzger. 1982. 319 N.W.2d 459 (Neb.).

State v. Miranda. 1998. 715 A.2d 680.

State v. Mitcheson. 1977. 560 P.2d 1120 (Utah).

State v. Myrick. 1982. 291 S.E.2d 577.

State v. Ninham. 2011. 797 N.W.2d 451 (Wis.).

State v. Norman. 1988. 366 S.E.2d 586.

State v. Odell. 2004. 676 N.W.2d 646 (Minn.).

State v. Pete. 1966. 420 P.2d 338 (Alaska).

State v. Phipps. 1994. 883 S.W.2d 138 (Tenn.App.).

State v. Powell 1951. 227 P.2d 582, 585.

State v. Robinson. 2011. N.J.Sup. Unpub. (App.Div. Aug. 23).

State v. Schleifer. 1923. 432 121 A. 805 (Conn.).

State v. Sexton. 1999. 733 A.2d 1125 (N.J.).

State v. Shaw. 1981. 185 Conn. 372, 441 A.2d 561.

State v. Shelley. 1997. 929 P.2d 489 (Wash.App.).

State v. Snowden. 1957. 313 P.2d 706 (Idaho).

State v. Stark. 1992. 832 P.2d 109 (Wash.App.).

State v. Stewart. 1988. 763 P.2d 572 (Kans.).

State v. Taylor. 2002. 650 N.W.2d 190 (Minn.).

State v. Thomas. 1999. 590 N.W.2d 755 (Minn.).

State v. Tomaino. 1999. 733 N.E.2d 1191 (OhioApp.).

State v. Ulvinen. 1981. 313 N.W.2d 425 (Minn.).

State v. Vargas. 2003. 812 A.2d. 205.

State v. Walden. 1982. 293 S.E.2d 780.

State v. Zeta Chi Fraternity. 1997. 686 A.2d. 530 (N.H.).

Stephen, Sir James F. 1883. *A History of the Criminal Law of England*. London: Macmillan.

Stokes v. U.S. 1920. 564 F. 18.

Suk, Jeannie. 2008. "The True Woman: Scenes from the Law of Self-Defense." *Harvard Journal of Law and Gender* 31(Summer): 237–75.

Sutherland, Edwin. 1940. "White-Collar Criminality." *American Sociological Review* 5(1):1–12. http://www.cooley.libarts.wsu.edu/criminology/Documents/sutherland \.pdf.

Swann v. U.S. 1994. 648 A.2d 928.

Sydnor v. State. 2001. 776 A.2d 669.

"Symposium: Wrongful Convictions and Systemic Reform." 2005. *American Criminal Law Reform* 42:4.

Taft, Philip. 1962. "The Federal Trials of the IWW." *Labor History* 3(1): 57–91.

Tennessee Criminal Code. 2005. "Serious Bodily Injury." Title 39, Chapter 11, Section 106(a)(34). Accessed July 23, 2012. http://law.justia.com/codes/tennessee/2010/title-39/chapter-11/part-1/39-11-106/.

Terrorism Act. 2012. *U.S. Code*. Title 18, § 2331.

Texas v. Johnson. 1989. 491 U.S. 397.

Thomas, Clarence. 1996. "Federalist Society Symposium: The Rights Revolution." *Michigan Law and Policy Review* 1:269.

Thompson v. Oklahoma. 1988. 487 U.S. 815.

Thompson, Seymour. 1880. "Homicide in Self-Defense." *American Criminal Law Review* 14:545.

Tier, Robert. 1993. "Maintaining Safety and Civility in Public Spaces: A Constitutional Approach to Aggressive Begging." *Louisiana Law Review* 54:285.

Todd v. State. 1992. 594 So.2d 802 (Fla.App.).

Toops v. State. 1994. 643 N.E.2d 387 (Ind.App.).

Tomkowicz, James J. 1994. "The Endurance of the Felony-Murder Rule." *Washington and Lee Law Review* 51:1429–80.

Treason Act. 2006. *U.S. Code*. Title 18, § 2381.

Trop v. Dulles. 1958. 356 U.S. 86.

Trustees of Dartmouth College v. Woodward. 1918. 17 U.S. (4 Wheat.) 518.

TTRC 2010. 2010. "Terrorist Trial Report Card (TTRC): September 11, 2001–September 11, 2010." Center on Law and Security. New York: Center on Law and Security. Accessed May 28, 2012. http://www.lawandsecurity.org/Portals/0/documents/01_TTRC2010Final1.pdf.

TTRC 2011. 2011. "Terrorist Trial Report Card (TTRC): September 11, 2001–September 11, 2011." Center on Law and Security. New York: Center on Law and Security. Accessed May 26, 2012. http://www.lawandsecurity.org/Portals/0/Documents/TTRC%20Ten%20Year%20Issue.pdf.

Turley, Jonathan. 2005. "Shame on You: Enough with Humiliating Punishments." *Washington Post*, September 18. Accessed October 31, 2011. http://www.washingtonpost.com/wp-dyn/content/article/2005/09/17/AR2005091700064.html.

Turner, J. W. Cecil. 1934. *Cambridge Law Journal* 5:230–47.

Turner, Michael, Jody Sundt, Brandon Applegate, and Francis Cullen. 1995. "'Three Strikes and You're Out' Legislation: A National Assessment." *Federal Probation* (September).

Underwood, Barbara. 1977. "The Thumb on the Scales of Justice: Burdens of Persuasion in Criminal Cases." *Yale Law Journal* 86:1299–1348.

Urofsky, Melvin, and Paul Finkelman. 2002a. *Documents of American Constitutional and Legal History*. New York: Oxford University Press.

______. 2002b. *A March of Liberty*. New York: Oxford University Press.

USA Patriot Act. 2001. http://frwebgate.access.gpo.gov/cgi-bin/getdoc.cgi?dbname=107_cong_bills&docid=f:h3162enr.txt.pdf.

U.S. v. Ancheta. 2006. (C.D. Cal.).

U.S. v. Arthur Anderson, LLP. 2004. 544 U.S. 696.

U.S. v. Booker. 2005. 543 U.S. 220.

U.S. v. Blue Thunder. 1979. 604 F.2d 550 (8th Cir.).

U.S. v. Bruno. 1939. 105 F.2d 921.

U.S. v. Cordoba-Hincapie. 1993. 825 F.Supp. 485.

U.S. v. Downs. 1995. 56 F.3d 973 (8th Cir.).

U.S. v. Garcia. 1998. 151 F.3d 1243 (9th Cir.).

U.S. v. Gementara. 2004. 379 F.3d 596. Accessed October 31, 2011. http://law.justia.com/cases/federal/appellate-courts/F3/379/596/475040/.

U.S. v. Haynes. 1998. 143 F.3d 1089 (7th Cir., Wis.).

U.S. v. Hinckley. 2009. 625 F.Supp.2d 3 (D.C.).

U.S. v. Holmes. 1842. 26 Fed.Cas. 360.

U.S. v. Hudson and Goodwin. 1812. 11 U.S. 32.

U.S. v. Maze. 1974. 414 U.S. 395, 94 S.Ct. 645.

U.S. v. Mims. 1967. 375 F.2d 135 (5th Cir.).

U.S. v. Motion Picture Film, "The Spirit of '76." 1917. 252 F. 946.

U.S. v. Nagler. 1918. 252 F. 217.

U.S. v. Peoni. 1938. 100 F.2d 401 (2nd Cir.).

U.S. v. Porcelli. 1989. 865 F.2d 1352 (2nd Cir.).

U.S. v. Reese. 1875. 92 U.S. 214.

U.S. v. Sampson. 1962. 371 U.S. 75, 83 S.Ct. 173, 9 L.Ed.2d.

U.S. v. Treas-Wilson. 1993. 3 F.3d 1406 (10th Cir.).

U.S. Attorney's Office, Denver. 2011. Press Release. "Former Colorado Springs Man Sentenced to Federal Prison for Attempting to Corrupt TSA Computer Database." January 12. Accessed May 22, 2012. http://www.fbi.gov/denver/press-releases/2011/dn011211.htm.

U.S. Code. 2003. *Insanity Defense.* Title 18, Part I, Chapter 1, Section 17.

———. 2006. *Destructive Device.* Title 18, Part I, Chapter 44, Section 921. http://www4.law.cornell.edu/uscode/html/uscode18/usc_sec_18_00000921----000-.html.

———. 2006. *Fraud and Related Activity in Connection with Computers.* Title 18, Part I, Chapter 47, Section 1030. http://www4.law.cornell.edu/uscode/html/uscode18/usc_sec_18_00001030----000-.html.

———. 2006. *Sabotage.* Title 18, Part I, Chapter 105, Section 2151. http://www4.law.cornell.edu/uscode/html/uscode18/usc_sup_01_18_10_I_20_105.html.

———. 2006. *Seditious Conspiracy.* Title 18, Part I, Chapter 115, Section 2384. http://www4.law.cornell.edu/uscode/html/uscode18/usc_sec_18_00002384----000-.html.

———. 2006. *Treason.* Title 18, Part I, Chapter 115, Section 2381. http://www4.law.cornell.edu/uscode/html/uscode18/usc_sec_18_00002381----000-.html.

U.S. Code. 2008. *Frauds and Swindles.* Title 18, Part I, Chapter 63, Section 1341. http://www.law.cornell.edu/uscode/text/18/1341.

U.S. Code. 2012. Accessed May 22, 2012. http://uscodebeta.house.gov/.

U.S. Code. 2012. *Terrorism.* Title 18, Part I, Chapter 113B, Section 2331. http://www.law.cornell.edu/uscode/text/18/2331.

U.S. Criminal Code. 2012. http://143.231.180.80/browse/title18.

U.S. Department of Justice. 2006. *Progress Report of the Department of Justice's Task Force on Intellectual Property.* Washington, DC: Department of Justice. http://www.justice.gov/opa/documents/ipreport61906.pdf.

U.S. Department of Justice. Bureau of Justice Statistics. 2011. *Criminal Victimization, 2010* by Jennifer Truman, PhD. Washington, DC: GPO (September 15). http://bjs.ojp.usdoj.gov/index.cfm?ty=pbdetail&iid=2224.

———. 2011. *Identity Theft Reported by Households, 2005–2010* by Lynn Langton. Washington, DC: GPO (November). http://bjs.ojp.usdoj.gov/content/pub/pdf/itrh0510.pdf.

U.S. Sentencing Commission. 2006. *Final Report on the Impact of* United States v. Booker *on Federal Sentencing.* Washington, DC: U.S. Sentencing Commission.

Valdes, Stephen G. 2005. "Frequency and Success: An Empirical Study of Criminal Law Defenses, Federal Constitutional Evidence Claims, and Plea Negotiations." *New York University Law Review* 153:1709–1814.

Vamosi, Robert. 2006. "An American Cybervillain." CNET Reviews. Accessed July 23, 2012. http://reviews.cnet.com/4520–3513_7–6427016–1.html.

Velazquez v. State. 1990. 561 So.2d 347 (Fla.App.).

Von Hirsh, Andrew, and Andrew Ashworth. 2005. *Proportionate Sentencing.* Oxford University Press.

Wagner, Dennis. 2008. "St. Johns Boy, 8, Suspected of Double Murder." *Arizona Republic*, November 8.

Walker, Nigel. 1968. *Crime and Insanity in England.* Edinburgh: University Press.

———. 1985. "The Insanity Defense before 1800." *Annals of the American Academy of Political and Social Science* 477(January): 25–30.

Wallace, Henry Scott. 1993. "Mandatory Minimums and the Betrayal of Sentencing Reform: A Legislative Dr. Jekyll and Mr. Hyde." *Federal Probation* 57(3):9.

Walmsley. Roy. 2009. *World Prison Population List.* 8th ed. London: King's College London. Accessed October 9, 2011. http://www.kcl.ac.uk/depsta/law/news/news_details.php?id=203.

Washington v. Glucksberg. 1997. 521 U.S. 702.

Weems v. U.S. 1910. 217 U.S. 349.

Weismann, Miriam, 2009. *Crime, Incorporated.* Chicago: American Bar Association.

Weiss, Baruch. 2002. "What Were They Thinking? The Mental States of Aider and Abettor, and the Causer under Federal Law." *Fordham Law Review* 70:1341.

West's California Penal Code. 1988. § 187(a). St. Paul, Minn.: West.

West's Florida Statutes Annotated. 2005. Title XLVI, § 775.01. Accessed July 23, 2012. http://www.flsenate.gov/Statutes/index.cfm?App_mode=Display_Index&Title_Request=XLVI#TitleXLVI.

West, Heather, and William Sabol. 2009. *Prisoners in 2009.* Accessed August 7, 2012. http://www.bjs.ojp.usdoj.gov/content/pub/pdf/p09.pdf.

Williams v. State. 1992. 600 N.E.2d 962 (Ind.App.).

Williams, Glanville. 1961. *Criminal Law.* 2nd ed. London: Stevens and Sons.

Williams, Linda. 1984. "The Classic Rape: When Do Victims Report?" *Social Problems* 31:464.

Wilson, James Q. 1975. *Thinking about Crime.* New York: Basic Books.

———, and Richard Herrnstein. 1985. *Crime and Human Nature.* New York: Simon and Schuster.

———, and George L. Kelling. 1982. "Broken Windows." *Atlantic Monthly*, March.

Wilson v. State. 1909. 38 S.W.2d 1013 (Tex.Cr.App.).

Wilson, Woodrow. 1915. "Third Annual Message, December 7, 1915." Miller Center. Accessed May 23, 2012. http://millercenter.org/president/speeches/detail/3794.

Winton, Richard. 2010. "Who Owns Paris Hilton's Purse? Doesn't Matter, Las Vegas Police Say." *L.A. Times Blog*, September 23. Accessed February 20, 2012. http://latimesblogs.latimes.com/lanow/2010/09/who-owns-paris-hiltons-purse-doesnt-matter-las-vegas-police-say.html.

Wisconsin Criminal Code. 2003. § 947.01. http://folio.legis.state.wi.us/cgi-bin/om_isapi.dll?clientID=547736967&infobase=stats.nfo&jump=ch.%20947.

———. 2006. § 940.31. http://nxt.legis.state.wi.us/nxt/gateway.dll?f=templates&fn=default.htm&vid=WI:Default&d=stats&jd=ch.%20940.

Wolfenden Report. 1957. *Report of Committee on Homosexual Offenses and Prostitution*. London: Stationer's Office.

Yang, Debra Wong, and Brian M. Hoffstadt. 2006. "Countering the Cyber-Crime Threat." *American Criminal Law Review* 43:201.

Young v. State. 1985. 493 A.2d 352 (Md.).

Zabel, Richard B., and James J. Benjamin. 2009. *In Pursuit of Justice: Prosecuting Terrorism Cases in the Federal Courts. 2009 Update and Recent Developments.* Washington, DC: Human Rights First.

CASE INDEX

T

U

INDEX

Note: Page numbers in boldface denote glossary terms.